CORPORATE TAKEOVERS
MODERN EMPIRICAL
DEVELOPMENTS

VOLUME 2

BIDDING STRATEGIES, FINANCING, AND CORPORATE CONTROL

CORPORATE TAKEOVERS
MODERN EMPIRICAL
DEVELOPMENTS

VOLUME 2

BIDDING STRATEGIES, FINANCING, AND CORPORATE CONTROL

Edited by

B. ESPEN ECKBO
Tuck School of Business
Dartmouth College
Hanover, New Hampshire, USA

AMSTERDAM • BOSTON • HEIDELBERG • LONDON
NEW YORK • OXFORD • PARIS • SAN DIEGO
SAN FRANCISCO • SINGAPORE • SYDNEY • TOKYO
ELSEVIER   Academic Press is an imprint of Elsevier

Academic Press is an imprint of Elsevier
525 B Street, Suite 1900, San Diego, CA 92101-4495,USA
30Corporate Drive, Suite 400, Burlington, MA01803, USA
32 Jamestown Road, London, NW1 7BY, UK
Radarweg 29, PO Box 211, 1000 AE Amsterdam, The Netherlands

Material in the work originally appeared in *Handbook of Corporate Finance: Empirical Corporate Finance, Volume 1* (Elsevier, B.V. 2007), *Finance* (Elsevier, B.V. 1995), *Journal of Corporate Finance* (Elsevier, B.V.), *Journal of Financial Economics (Elsevier, B.V.)*, and *Journal of Financial Intermediation* (Academic Press)

Notice
No responsibility is assumed by the publisher for any injury and/or damage to persons or property as a matter of products liability, negligence or otherwise, or from any use or operation of any methods, products, instructions or ideas contained in the material herein. Because of rapid advances in the medical sciences, in particular, independent verification of diagnoses and drug dosages should be made

ISBN 13: 978-0-12-382016-7 (set)
ISBN 13: 978-0-12-381983-3 (vol. 1)
ISBN 13: 978-0-12-381982-6 (vol. 2)

For information on all Academic Press publications
visit our website at *elsevierdirect.com*

Printed and bound in USA
10 11 12   10 9 8 7 6 5 4 3 2 1

Working together to grow
libraries in developing countries
www.elsevier.com | www.bookaid.org | www.sabre.org

ELSEVIER   BOOK AID   Sabre Foundation
             International

FOREWORD

This two-volume collection presents 44 empirical articles on corporate takeovers published by Elsevier Science. The two volumes form a coherent study of interesting empirical issues, theoretical propositions, econometric methodologies, and large-sample evidence in the field. The articles—with only five exceptions—were published since the millennium, so the collection is truly modern in scope. These articles reflect the significant shift toward greater sample sizes and increased transaction detail permitted by the Securities Data Company's (SDC) Merger and Acquisition Database over the past decade. As the collection provides a comprehensive status report on the modern scientific evidence on corporate takeovers, it is my hope that it will be useful as a graduate-level text for a course on corporate takeovers and as a convenient reference for those familiar with the main material.

The sole purpose of restricting the collection to Elsevier publications is to make the collection more cost effective in a world where most journal articles may be downloaded from the Web. Not surprisingly, most of the articles were originally published in the *Journal of Financial Economics*, the primary outlet for top research on takeovers since the late 1970s. However, the collection also includes six comprehensive review articles that previously appeared as chapters in two of Elsevier's *Handbook* Series, six articles from the *Journal of Corporate Finance*, and one previously published in the *Journal of Financial Intermediation*.

The body of research reprinted here builds on classic articles from the 1980s and 1990s. Given the general accessibility of those classic pieces, and my desire to report on modern developments, the seminal works predating year 2000 are excluded unless deemed absolutely necessary for the context. Also, the Elsevier restriction excludes (of course) work published in the *Journal of Finance* and the *Review of Financial Studies*. To mitigate those shortcomings, the reader will find a comprehensive discussion of more than 500 articles in the survey "Corporate Takeovers" by Betton et al. (2008), reprinted at the beginning of Volume 1. Moreover, although the focus of this collection is on corporate takeovers, Volume 1 also includes at the end a broad survey of more than 300 empirical articles on divestitures, spin-offs, leveraged buyouts, and other highly leveraged transactions in "Corporate Restructuring: Breakups and LBOs" by Eckbo and Thorburn (2008). In sum, the collection provides detailed references to the bulk of the empirical literature on takeovers and restructurings.

To make the collection as self-contained as possible, Volume 1 also includes two surveys on how to handle econometric issues when estimating valuation effects of voluntary corporate events. These surveys discuss sampling distributions and test statistics typically used in event studies, as well as criteria for reliability, specification, and power. Moreover, self-selection is endemic to voluntary corporate events, creating a statistical wedge between the population distribution and the distribution within a selected sample. Correcting for a potential self-selection bias is particularly relevant when drawing inferences about the determinants of event-induced abnormal stock returns from multivariate regressions, a technique used by most event studies today, including those reprinted here.

The collection focuses primarily on large-scale empirical research because it is in the empirical domain that one finds the major advances in the takeover literature over the past decade. However, to prepare the reader for key theoretical propositions, the collection also includes two comprehensive theoretical surveys on auctions and strategic bidding (in Volume 2). In addition, several of the empirical articles in Volume 2 develop their own, unique theoretical foundations for the hypotheses being tested. As a result, the careful reader of this collection will be able to acquire a good understanding of both the mainstream theoretical and empirical propositions existing in the takeover literature today.

The two volumes are organized as follows: Volume 1—Takeover Activity, Valuation Estimates, and Sources of Merger Gains—focuses on classical issues such as the existence and source of merger waves, empirical estimates of takeover announcement returns and the division of takeover gains between bidders and targets, and tests for potential sources of takeover gains (primarily involving estimation of industry wealth effects of takeovers).

Volume 2—Bidding Strategies, Financing, and Corporate Control—focuses on a range of special topics, ranging from theories and evidence on strategic bidding behavior (offer premiums, toeholds, bidder competition, winner's curse adjustments, and managerial overconfidence), issues arising when bidding for targets in bankruptcy auctions, effects of deal protection devices (termination agreements, poison pills), role of large shareholder voting in promoting takeover gains, deal financing issues (such as raising the cash used to pay for the target), managerial incentive effects of takeovers, governance spillovers from cross-border mergers, and returns to merger arbitrage.

In sum, this collection represents a "smorgasbord" of interesting topics, research methodologies, and empirical evidence. Bon appétit!

B. Espen Eckbo
Tuck School of Business at Dartmouth College
Hanover, New Hampshire
January 2010

CONTENTS OF VOLUMES

VOLUME 1: TAKEOVER ACTIVITY, VALUATION ESTIMATES, AND SOURCES OF MERGER GAINS

VOLUME 2: BIDDING STRATEGIES, FINANCING, AND CORPORATE CONTROL

Part 5:   Does Large Shareholder Voting Improve Takeover Gains?

Part 6:   Raising Cash: Does Deal Financing Matter?

Part 7:   How does Takeover Affect CEO and Director Compensation?

CONTENTS OF VOLUME 2

PART 4: DO DEAL PROTECTION DEVICES AFFECT
   TAKEOVER PREMIUMS?   431

INTRODUCTION TO CORPORATE TAKEOVERS: MODERN EMPIRICAL DEVELOPMENTS

B. ESPEN ECKBO

Tuck School of Business at Dartmouth, Hanover, New Hampshire, USA

Abstract

This two-volume collection of 44 recently published articles separate the empirical takeover literature into roughly two parts. Volume I, the first part, begins with a comprehensive overview of the empirical evidence, followed by introductions to the econometrics of event studies and various techniques for dealing with corporate self-selection issues. Volume I then delves into classic issues such as the nature of aggregate merger activity (merger waves), market valuation effects of merger announcements (the stock price performance of bidder and target firms), and the nature of the sources of merger gains in the context of industrial organization (much of it involving estimating the effects of mergers on industry competitors). Volume I ends with a review of restructuring transactions other than takeovers, such as divestitures, spin-offs, leveraged buyouts and other highly leveraged transactions.

Volume II, the second part, presents a series of specific deal-related topics—and provides reviews of both theory and associated empirical evidence. It begins with surveys of principles for optimal bidding in specific auction settings, followed by a review of actual takeover premiums and their determinants. Volume II then showcases recent empirical contributions on topics such as toehold bidding and winner's curse (does overbidding exist?), bidding for distressed targets (do bankruptcy auctions cause fire-sales?), effects of deal protection devices (do termination agreements and poison pills affect takeover premiums?), large shareholder voting on takeover outcomes (does institutional activism matter?), deal financing issues (does it matter how the bidder finances any cash payment for the target), managerial compensation effects of take-overs (what's in it for the CEO), governance spillovers from cross-border mergers (are there any?) and, finally, the returns to merger arbitrage activity (market efficiency and limits to arbitrage).

1. Volume I: Takeover activity, valuation estimates, and sources of merger gains

1.1. Surveys of takeover evidence and econometrics

Volume I begins with the survey "Corporate takeovers" by Betton et al. (2008) which covers empirical research reported by more than 500 articles. The survey covers topics ranging from the impact of statutory and regulatory restrictions on the acquisition process (disclosure and target defenses), strategic bidding behavior (preemption, markup pricing, bid jumps, toeholds, payment method choice, hostility), short- and long-run abnormal stock returns (CARs) to bidder and targets (size and division of takeover gains), to the origin and competitive effects of corporate combinations (efficiency, market power, and antitrust policy).

Importantly, the Betton et al. survey provides original empirical updates on both short- and long-horizon CARs using a sample of more than 35,000 takeover contests for US public targets from the period 1980–2005 (available on the SDC database). The main conclusions are listed in the survey's Table 15, in the form of 68 summary statements. Several of these conclusions are listed below when characterizing individual reprinted articles in the collection.[1]

The immediate stock price effect of a takeover announcement provides an important window into the economics of the corporate investment decision. Long-horizon returns also serve an important purpose as a way of examining market efficiency (conditional on some assumed return generating process). In "Econometrics of event studies," Kothari and Warner (2007) review methods for isolating the valuation impact of corporate events. The survey discusses sampling distributions and test statistics typically used in event studies, as well as criteria for reliability, specification, and power for both short- and long-horizon returns.

While much is known about the statistical properties of short-horizon event studies, the survey provides a critical review of potential pitfalls of long-horizon abnormal return estimates. Serious challenges related to model specification, skewness and cross-correlation remain. As Kothari-Warner also point out, events are likely to be associated with return-variance increases, which are equivalent to abnormal returns varying across sample securities. Misspecification induced by variance increases can cause the null hypothesis to be rejected too often unless the test statistic is adjusted to reflect the variance shift. Moreover, the authors emphasize the importance of paying close attention to specification issues for nonrandom samples of corporate events.

Self-selection is endemic to voluntary corporate events such as takeovers. The survey "Self-selection models in corporate finance" by Li and Prabhala (2007) reviews the relevant econometric issues with applications to takeovers and other corporate finance events. The statistical issue raised by self-selection is the wedge between the population distribution and the distribution within a selected sample,

---

[1] With the exception of the articles on cross-border mergers in Volume II, this two-volume collection focuses primarily on takeovers of US domiciled targets.

which renders standard linear (OLS/GLS) estimators biased and inconsistent. This issue is particularly relevant when drawing inferences about the determinants of event-induced CARs from multivariate regressions, a technique used by most event studies today. Cross-sectional regressions are typically run using samples that exclude none-vent firms. The standard solution is to include a scaled estimate of the event probability—the so-called inverse Mills ratio (the expected value of the true but unobservable regression error term)—as an additional variable in the cross-sectional regression.

Testing for the significance of the inverse Mills ratio is equivalent to testing whether the sample firms use private information when they self-select to undertake the event. Conversely, if one believes that the particular event being studied is induced by or reflect private information (market overpricing of equity, arrival of new investment projects, merger opportunities, etc.), then consistent estimation of the parameters in the cross-sectional regression requires the appropriate control for self-selection. What is appropriate generally depends on the specific application and should ideally be guided by economic theory. The Li and Prabhala survey also reviews related econometric techniques—including matching (treatment effect) models, panel data with fixed effects, and Bayesian self-selection models—with specific applications.

1.2. Aggregate takeover activity

Stock exchange delistings by US firms due to merger tend to occur in distinct waves—peaks of heavy activity followed by troughs of relatively few transactions.[2] Merger activity tends to be greatest in periods of general economic expansion. This is hardly surprising as external expansion through takeovers is just one of the available corporate growth strategies. Thus, aggregate takeover activity was relatively high in the late 1960s, throughout the 1980s, and again in the late 1990s. A majority of the mergers in the 1960s were between firms operating in unrelated industries (conglomerate mergers). The merger wave of the 1980s includes a number of mergers designed either to downsize or to specialize operations. Some of these corrected excessive conglomeration, others responded to excess capacity created by the 1970s recession (following the creation of the OPEC oil cartel), while yet others responded to the important advances in information and communication technologies. The 1980s also experienced the largest number of hostile bids in US history. The subsequent spread of strong takeover defenses in the late 1980s halted the use of hostile bids, and the late 1990s saw a "friendly" merger wave, with a primary focus on mergers with global strategic partners.

A complex set of factors are at play in any given merger wave. For example, merger waves may be affected by changes in legal and regulatory regimes, such as the stricter antitrust laws enacted in the United States in the early 1950s, and the deregulations of

---

[2] See Figure 1 in Betton et al. (2008), which shows the annual frequency distribution of delistings from 1926 through 2005.

the airline industry in 1970s and of the utility industry in 1992. The perhaps most compelling theory of merger waves rests on the technological link between firms in the same industry: a merger implementing a new technological innovation may, as news of the innovation spreads, induce follow-on takeovers among industry rivals for these to remain competitive.

In fact, there is substantial evidence of industry-clustering of mergers. In "Investigating the economic role of mergers," Andrade and Stafford (2004) find that mergers play both an expansionary and a contractionary role in industry restructurings. During the 1970s and 1980s, excess capacity tended to drive industry consolidation through merger, while peak capacity utilization triggered industry expansion through nonmerger investment (internal expansion). This phenomenon appears to have reversed itself in the 1990s, as industries with strong growth prospects, high profitability, and near capacity also experienced the most intense merger activity.[3]

The fact that merger waves are correlated with economic expansions and high stock market valuations has also spurred the development of models in which merger waves result from market overvaluation and managerial timing. The idea is that bull markets may lead bidders with overvalued stock as currency to purchase the assets of undervalued (or less overvalued) targets. In Shleifer and Vishny (2003), target managements accept overpriced bidder stock as they are assumed to have a short time horizon. In Rhodes-Kropf and Viswanathan (2004), target management accepts more bids from overvalued bidders during market valuation peaks because they overestimate synergies during these periods. In both models, the bidder gets away with selling overpriced stock.[4]

In "Valuation waves and merger activity," Rhodes-Kropf et al. (2005) find that merger waves coincide with high market-to-book (M/B) ratios.[5] If one views the M/B ratio as a proxy for market overvaluation, then this finding is consistent with the basic overvaluation arguments of Rhodes-Kropf and Viswanathan (2004) and Shleifer and Vishny (2003). In "What drives merger waves?," Harford (2005) contrasts behavioral explanations for merger waves with a neoclassical argument in which the key driver of merger waves is market liquidity. That is, under the neoclassical view, market liquidity is the fundamental driver of *both* M/B ratios and merger waves.[6]

Harford constructs a measure of aggregate capital liquidity based on interest rate (default) spreads and uses this measure in a horse race with M/B ratios in predicting industry merger waves. He finds that waves are preceded by deregulatory events and

---

[3] See also Mitchell and Mulherin (1996), Mulherin and Boone (2000), and Maksimovic and Phillips (2001).

[4] The model of Shleifer and Vishny (2003) assumes agents are irrational. In Rhodes-Kropf and Viswanathan (2004), rational (Bayesian) managers end up accepting too many all-stock merger bids when the stock market booms and too few when the market is low.

[5] See also Ang and Cheng (2006) and Dong et al. (2006).

[6] For example, Shleifer and Vishny (1992) argue that merger waves tend to occur in booms because increases in cash flows simultaneously raise fundamental values and relax financial constraints, bringing market values closer to fundamental values. Harford (1999) shows that firms that have built up large cash reserves are more prone to acquire other firms.

high capital liquidity. More importantly, he shows that the capital liquidity variable eliminates the ability of M/B ratios to predict industry merger waves. He concludes that aggregate merger waves are caused by the clustering of shock-driven industry merger waves, not by attempts to time the market.

Consistent with Hartford's conclusion, Betton et al. (2008) show that despite the market boom in the second half of the 1990s, the relative proportions of all-cash, all-stock, and mixed cash-stock offers in their sample of more than 15,000 merger bids did *not* change from the first half of the decade (Figure 7, p. 323). Also, during the 1996–2000 period with peak market valuations, the sum of all-cash and mixed cash-stock bids in mergers equals the number of all-stock merger bids. In sum, although the issue requires additional research, the existing evidence does not favor a behavioral explanation for merger waves.

Betton et al. also make the following descriptions concerning takeover activity:

- When organizing all SDC control bids into contest for US targets, there were a total of 35,727 control contests over the period 1980–2005. Of these, the initial bidder proposed a merger in 28,994 cases and made a public tender offer in another 4500 cases (the balance being 2224 controlling-block trades).
- In constant 2000 dollars, the merger deal was valued at $436 million on average (median $35 million), while the deal value of the average tender offer was $480 million (median $79 million).
- SDC provides information on the payment method for about half of the cases. Of these, 26% were all-cash deals, 37% were all-stock deals, and 37% were mixed cash-stock deals. All-cash and mixed offers have similar deal sizes, slightly above all-stock deals.
- A total of 590 initial bids are classified as "hostile" and another 435 deals are "unsolicited." Hostile bids have substantially higher than average deal values.
- In approximately 30% of all deals, the initial bidder and target operate in the same four-digit SIC industry (horizontal takeover). The two most active takeover sectors are Manufacturing, and Finance/Insurance/Real Estate.
- Two-thirds of the 35,727 initial bidders are public companies, while 37% of the targets are public. In 44% of the initial bids, a public bidder is pursuing a private target (the largest single group of takeovers), with an average deal value of $114 million (median $23 million). The total number of deals involving either a public bidder or target rose sharply in the 1990s.
- Of the 35,727 initial bidders, 11% were foreign companies (primarily Canada and the United Kingdom). Deals involving foreign bidders are relatively large.

1.3. Takeover gains

Volume I contains five recent papers significantly expanding our empirical knowledge of the size and division of takeover gains to bidder and target firms. In "Firm size and the gains from acquisitions," Moeller et al. (2004) find that, in a sample of 12,023 acquisitions by public firms from 1980 to 2001, the equally weighted abnormal announcement return is 1.1%, but acquiring-firm shareholders lose $25.2 million on average upon announcement. This disparity suggests the existence of a size effect in acquisition announcement returns. The announcement return for acquiring-firm share-holders is roughly two percentage points higher for small acquirers irrespective of the form of financing and whether the acquired firm is public or private. The size effect is robust to firm and deal characteristics, and it is not reversed over time.[7]

In "Why do private acquirers pay so little compared to public acquirers?," Bargeron et al. (2008) report that public target shareholders receive a 63% (14%) higher premium when the acquirer is a public firm rather than a private equity firm (private operating firm). The premium difference holds with the usual controls for deal and target characteristics, and it is highest when acquisitions by private bidders are compared to acquisitions by public companies with low managerial ownership. There is no significant difference between premiums paid by private equity firms and public firms when the public firms have high managerial ownership. Further, the premium paid by public bidders (not private bidders) increases with target managerial and institutional ownership. The authors note that unobservable target characteristics may be responsible for why some firms only attract the attention of private bidders or are ultimately more valuable for private equity bidders, and that further research is needed to help explain the premium difference.

In "The underpricing of private targets," Cooney et al. (2009) begin by noting that while the evidence of positive announcement returns to acquirers of private targets is pervasive and robust, explanations are sparse. They examine the relation between valuation changes of private firms and the announcement returns of their public acquirers. Using a sample of acquisitions of private firms that withdraw an initial public offering (IPO), they calculate the change in firm value from the planned IPO to the acquisition and find a positive relation between this valuation revision and acquirer announcement returns. Similar to other studies, acquirer announcement returns are positive, on average. However, positive acquirer announcement returns are mainly driven by targets that are acquired for more than their prior valuation. The authors argue that this relation is consistent with pricing effects associated with target valu-ation uncertainty as well as with behavioral biases in negotiation outcomes.

In "Gains in bank mergers: Evidence from the bond markets," Pena and Unal (2004) look at the effect of bank mergers on bondholder returns. In general, if the merger is synergistic, both bondholders and shareholders gain because firm value can increase by achieving economies of scale and scope and by eliminating less-efficient management. In nonsynergistic mergers, bondholders can still gain if the merger reduces cash flow volatility and leads to a lower risk of default.

---

[7] For early evidence on a size effect in bidder returns, see Asquith and Mullins (1983) and Eckbo and Thorburn (2000). Moeller et al. (2005) also demonstrate significant losses to relatively large acquirers.

In the case of bank mergers there are at least two additional layers of complexity. First, the federal deposit insurer might consider the combined bank too big to fail (TBTF) as a result of the merger. This strategy allows all uninsured liabilities to have de facto insurance coverage and thereby maximizes the value of the implicit guarantees received from the government. Second, unlike nonfinancial firms, banks are subject to regulatory capital requirements. As a result, shareholders cannot simply increase leverage to make up for a merger that coinsures bondholders. Hence, even with no TBTF, bondholders could gain and shareholders could lose as bondholders expropriate some of the gains associated with the acquisition. The authors present evidence that the adjusted returns of merging banks bonds are positive and significant across premerger and announcement months. The cross-sectional evidence indicates that the primary determinants of merger-related bondholder gains are diversification gains, gains associated with achieving TBTF status, and, to a lesser degree, synergy gains. They make a similar conclusion after examining the acquiring banks credit spreads on new debt issues both before and after the merger. Moreover, the paper shows that a source of acquirer gains is lower cost of funds on postmerger debt issues.

In "Do tender offers create value?," Bhagat et al. (2005) note that attempts to estimate the value effects of takeovers face two challenges. The first is the truncation dilemma. Given that not all takeover bids succeed, a short event window that extends only a few days past the bid announcement date estimates only a fraction of the value effects that would be brought about by a successful transaction. A long window that extends through successful completion of the transaction can capture the markets assessment of the full effect of takeover on value. However, this comes at the cost of introducing much greater noise and return benchmark errors. Adjusting for the truncation bias involves probability-weighting the announcement-induced stock returns.[8]

The second challenge, the revelation bias, is that the bidders return on the announcement date reflects not just news about the value to be derived from combination, but also news about the stand-alone value of the bidder. To address these issues, Bhagat-et al. estimate the stock markets perception of value improvements from tender offers using both conventional CARs at the time of the initial bid and two new approaches. They find that all approaches imply substantial value improvements. Furthermore, the new methods imply estimates of shareholder value improvement that are much larger than those implied by traditional methods.[9]

Betton et al. (2008) summarize (in Table 15) some of their own large-sample evidence on bidder and target takeover gains as follows:

---

[8] See Betton and Eckbo (2000) for a first attempt to addresses this truncation bias using a structural estimation technique.

[9] To adjust for the revelation bias, Bhagat et al. extract information about value improvement from the stock returns associated with intervening events such as the announcement of a competing bid.

- The average target cumulative average CAR is positive and significant, both over the takeover preannouncement (run-up) period and the announcement period. The run-up constitutes about one-third of the total run-up plus announcement CAR. The largest target CAR occurs in all-cash offers.
- The average, value-weighted combined CAR to bidders and targets is positive and significant over both the run-up period and the announcement period.[10] For the overall sample, the sum of the combined CAR for the run-up- and announcement periods is a significant 1.79%.
- Bidder announcement period CARs average close to zero for the overall sample, with 49% of the bidders having negative CAR.[11] The combination large bidder (in the upper size quartile), payment in all-stock, and the target being a public company represent a "worst-case scenario" with average bidder announcement-period CAR of a significant −2.21%. The "best-case scenario" for the bidder is the combination of a small bidder (lower size-quartile), private target and *all-stock* as payment. This produces a significant average bidder announcement-period CAR of 6.46%.
- The major driver of negative bidder returns is not, as previously thought, the all-stock payment. Rather, the two key drivers are the target's status a public or private, and bidder size. Bidder announcement returns tend to be positive and significant when the acquirer is small and the target is a private firm, and negative for large acquirers bidding for public targets.
- Bidder size was particularly large in 1999 and 2000. These years were unusual relative to years before *and* years after. Cisco, with a (constant 2000 dollar) market capitalization of $180 billion was the dominant bidder in *both* the upper 1% and lower 1% tails of the distribution of bidder abnormal announcement returns. Removing Cisco from the sample reduces the aggregate bidder dollar wealth loss in 1999–2000 period by almost $100 billion.
- Studies of long-run CARs use either the matched-firm technique or Jensen's alpha (regression constant in an asset pricing model) to measure expected return to the merged firms in the sample. In the survey-sample of 15,298 successful takeovers completed during the period 1980–2003, long-run returns are significantly negative based on the matched-firm technique but insignificantly different from zero based on Jensen's alpha.
- The standard matched-firm procedure identifies firms that have significantly different factor loadings than the event firms—which undermines their role as "matches."
- A zero-investment portfolio strategy which is long in the merged firms and short in the matched firms fail to produce long-run CARs which are significantly different from zero, even for the sample of all-stock mergers.

[10] The average value-weighted sum of the announcement returns to *publicly traded* bidders and targets is also positive and significant. This confirms an important conclusion in the early survey by Jensen and Ruback (1983).
[11] Bidder announcement returns are subject to attenuation bias due to partial anticipation, and they reflect valuation impacts of factors beyond the value of the takeover per se (including revelations about bidder managerial quality and exogenous changes in industry conditions).

1.4. Sources of takeover gains

At the conclusion of their influential literature review, Jensen and Ruback (1983) admit that the sources of merger gains are "elusive." Volume I contains five papers attempting to shed light on the likely sources of merger gains. The first four of these use the methodology developed independently by Eckbo (1983) and Stillman (1983) and which combines traditional event studies in finance with models of industrial organization.

In "Horizontal mergers, collusion, and stockholder wealth," Eckbo (1983) develops and tests the hypothesis that horizontal mergers generate positive abnormal returns to stockholders of the bidder and target firms because they increase the probability of successful collusion among rival producers. Under the collusion hypothesis, *product market rivals* of the merging firms benefit from the merger since successful collusion limits output and raises product prices and/or lowers factor prices. Thus, a unique test of the collusion hypothesis is that events which increases the probability of a collusive merger (such as a merger proposal announcement) should cause a positive revaluation of the market value of the emerging firms' rivals, while subsequent events which decrease the probability of the collusive merger being consummated (such as a government challenge under antitrust laws) should reverse the positive effect (cause negative abnormal returns to the rivals).

Eckbo tests this proposition on a large sample of horizontal mergers in mining and manufacturing industries, including 55 mergers that were challenged by the government with violating antitrust laws (Section 7 of the Clayton Act). He also includes a control sample of vertical mergers taking place in the same industries (which by definition do not have horizontal anticompetitive effects). He finds that the antitrust law enforcement agencies (the US Department of Justice and the Federal Trade Commission) systematically select relatively profitable mergers for prosecution. More importantly, he finds that there is a small but positive (1.5%) industry wealth effect of the initial horizontal merger announcements. However, he also finds that rival firms receive a second *positive* market value boost when the government signals announce that it will seek to block the merger, which rejects the proposition that the mergers would have collusive effects.[12] Thus, Eckbo concludes against market power as representing the source of merger gains even for the cases where the antitrust authorities decided market power *was* a problem and that the mergers had to be stopped.[13]

The power of Eckbo's methodology to test the collusion hypothesis comes from having access to *both* probability-increasing (merger proposal) and probability-decreasing

---

[12] In Eckbo's sample, the government is successful in stopping the proposed merger in 80% of the cases it challenges.

[13] A horizontal merger *causes* a measurable increase in industry concentration. The classical market concentration doctrine holds that increases in concentration reliably increases the industry's market power and thus industry monopoly rents. Since the abnormal returns to industry rivals directly measures changes in industry rents, regressing the merger-induced rival abnormal returns on the change in industry concentration provides a powerful test of the market concentration doctrine. Eckbo (1985) and Eckbo (1992) perform this test and reject the doctrine.

(antitrust challenge) events for a given merger, *and* where the latter event is initiated by the antitrust authorities.[14] These test conditions are not available for merger samples more generally—where typically only the probability-increasing event (the merger proposal and/or the final merger agreement) is seen. Eckbo emphasizes strongly that finding a positive industry wealth effect of a probability-increasing event by itself is necessary but *not* sufficient to conclude in favor of the collusion hypothesis.

The reason for this ambiguity is that the net industry wealth effect of an efficient merger may be either positive or negative. On the one hand, scale-increasing efficient mergers tend to have a negative impact on the industry's equilibrium product price, which harms rival firms and by itself causes a negative industry wealth effect.[15] On the other hand, news of the merger may reveal positive information about the value of the resources controlled by the rival firms. That is, the merger may reveal increased demand for resources owned by other firms, causing a positive revaluation of these rivals. For example, the increased demand may lead to expectations of future merger activity, resulting in a positive "in-play" effect on rival firms from the announcement of the initial merger. In sum, the efficiency hypothesis does not restrict the abnormal returns to industry rivals.

Eckbo (1983) suggests that one should in principle be able to discriminate between the collusion and efficiency theories in single-event merger samples by examining the abnormal returns to the merging firms *corporate customers and suppliers of inputs.* For example, relative to the merger proposal announcement, corporate customers and suppliers should lose under the collusion hypothesis and gain under the efficiency hypothesis. Tests based on this notion are difficult since it is necessary to identify customers and suppliers who cannot switch their purchases/sales to other industries at a low cost (the customers/suppliers must to some extent be locked in).

The two papers "Sources of gains in horizontal mergers: Evidence from customers, suppliers, and rival firms" by Fee and Thomas (2004) and "Industry structure and horizontal takeovers: Analysis of wealth effects on rivals, suppliers, and corporate customers" by Shahrur (2005), follow Eckbo's original suggestion and expand the industry wealth effect estimation to upstream suppliers and downstream customers. They identify publicly traded suppliers and corporate customers using Compustat industry segment information. The major focus in both studies is the "buyer power" hypothesis, that is, the possibility that a horizontal merger increases the monopsony power of the combined firm over its input suppliers. In this case, the merger benefits the merging firms and (possibly) its industry rivals at the expense of upstream suppliers. Consumers benefit as well provided some of the increased monopsony rents are passed on downstream from the merging firms' industry. Both papers

---

[14] Several recent papers use the Eckbo-methodology to asses the likely anticompetitive effects of mergers reviewed under the competition laws of the European Union. See Section 6 in Betton et al. (2008) for a review.

[15] Rivals may minimize the negative product price impact by racing to adopt similar technological innovations as the merging firms—prompting industry merger waves.

conclude that the evidence is inconsistent with increased monopolistic collusion (they fail to identify a wealth loss to corporate customers), but consistent with improved efficiency and buying power of the merged firms.[16]

Eckbo (1983) also suggests that a positive industry wealth effect of horizontal merger announcements may simply reflect an increased probability that rival firms will become targets. Song and Walkling (2000) test this "in-play" effect on rival firms. An in-play effect follows naturally from the fact that rival firms uses similar production technologies and own some of the same (and possibly scarce) productive resources. A takeover may signal increased resource scarcity, causing a positive revaluation of every firm holding those resources. Song and Walkling increase the power to detect an in-play effect by focusing on cases where the merger announcements were particularly surprising ("dormant" industries with no merger announcement over the prior 12 months). The results of their study, as well as most of the earlier papers in this area, are consistent with the existence of a positive industry in-play (information) effect.[17]

Finally, in the paper, "Where do merger gains come from? Bank mergers from the perspective of insiders and outsiders," Houston et al. (2001) take the unusual approach of examining management estimates of projected cost savings and revenue enhancements to investigate the potential sources of takeover gains. They focus on large bank mergers as consolidation between banks removes geographic and product market entry restrictions—thus improving operating efficiency. The data on management projections allow identification of management's primary rationale for the acquisitions. The paper estimates the present value of the incremental earnings that management expects from the merger, and investigates the relation between these estimated gains and the change in the market value of the stock of the bidder and the target.

Houston et al. find that the primary source of management's expected merger-related gains is cost savings. Revenue enhancements are far less important as the paper's valuation of estimated revenue gains account for, on average, only 7% (median zero) of the total valuation gains implied by management's estimates. Moreover, under optimistic assumptions that incremental merger-related earnings are perpetual and grow at the inflation rate, the paper estimates that the average sample merger should increase the combined value of the bidder and target by 13%. Looking at the market's reaction to merger announcements, the paper finds that management's projected merger gains explain roughly 60% of the cross-sectional variation in the combined bidder and target stock returns. Interestingly, while valuation estimates of projected cost savings are positively related to the combined stock market returns of the bidder

---

[16] Fee and Thomas (2004) and Shahrur (2005) sample horizontal mergers. For a large-sample study of vertical mergers, with a focus on the potential for foreclosure following increased buying power, see Shenoy (2008). Eckbo (1983) samples both horizontal and vertical mergers but does not test for upstream buying power.

[17] Exceptions are Eckbo (1992), Akdogu (2009), and Becher et al. (2008) who find a negative industry wealth effect of multiindustry horizontal merger announcements in Canada, and in single-industry studies of the US telecommunications and utility firms, respectively.

and target, the valuation estimates of projected revenue increases are negatively related to these same stock market returns. Thus, the results suggest that cost savings represent the primary source of gains in the large majority of recent bank mergers and that managerial cost savings projections have significant capital market credibility.

1.5. Survey of other restructuring activity other than takeovers

Shocks to the corporate economic environment may give rise to severe organizational inefficiencies. For example, a vertically integrated firm may find that long-term contracts and/or spot market purchases of a key input have become more efficient. Or increased general capital market liquidity may have rendered internal capital markets a relatively costly divisional funding mechanism for conglomerates. High leverage may be optimal as financial innovations and expertise make it less expensive to manage financial distress. Financial innovations and general market liquidity may also render it optimal to securitize an entire division. The result is increased divisional managerial focus. In the survey "Corporate restructurings: Breakups and LBOs," Eckbo and Thorburn (2008b) refer to the transactions that implement these and other changes in asset composition, financial contracting, and ownership structure as "corporate restructurings."

The survey focuses on garden-variety restructuring procedures used to securitize and sell off part of the firm. It includes leveraged buyouts (LBOs) in which the entire firm is acquired by a financial buyer such as a buyout fund. The survey classifies corporate restructurings into two broad groups: breakups and highly leveraged transactions. Breakup transactions focus primarily on the separation of company assets and therefore include divestitures, spin-offs, equity carveouts, and tracking stock. Highly leveraged transactions involve a significant increase of debt in the firm's capital structure, either through a debt-financed special dividend in a leveraged recapitalization or in an LBO.

Corporate restructurings may be initiated by the firm's top-level management, by divisional managers, or by outside sponsors like buyout funds. Occasionally, the restructuring is defensive, arising in response to a control threat from the market for corporate control. Regardless of who initiates the transaction, the parties are seeking to improve operating efficiency, increase cash flow, and ultimately, enhance firm profitability. In breakup transactions, assets are transferred to higher value users, while highly leveraged transactions involve optimizing capital structure, improving managerial incentives and achieving tax efficiency.

The empirical evidence shows that the typical restructuring creates substantial value for shareholders, and there is evidence of improved operating performance. The value-drivers include elimination of costly cross-subsidizations characterizing internal capital markets, reduction in financing costs for subsidiaries through asset securitization and increased divisional transparency, improved (and more focused) investment programs, reduction in agency costs of free cash flow, implementation of executive compensation schemes with greater pay-performance sensitivity, and increased monitoring by lenders and LBO sponsors.

Buyouts after the turn of the century created value similar to LBOs of the 1980s. Recent developments include club deals (consortiums of LBO sponsors bidding together), fund-to-fund exits (LBO funds selling the portfolio firm to another LBO fund), a highly liquid (until mid-2007) leveraged loan market, and evidence of persistence in fund returns (perhaps because brand-sponsors borrow at better rates). Perhaps the greatest challenge to the restructuring literature is to achieve a modicum of integration of the analysis across transaction types. Another challenge is to produce precise estimates of the expected return from buyout investments in the presence of limited data on those portfolio companies that do not return to public status.

2. Volume II: Bidding strategies, financing, and corporate control

2.1. Surveys of bidding theory and takeover premiums

There is growing research interest in the details of the takeover process from the initial bid through the final contest outcome. Volume II begins with three survey articles covering the takeover bidding process: two surveys exposing optimal bidding theories—"Mergers and acquisitions: Strategic and informational issues" by Hirshleifer (1995) and "Auctions in corporate finance" by Dasgupta and Hansen (2007)—and the empirical review "Bidding strategies and takeover premiums" by Eckbo (2009).[1]

Figure 1 shows the six possible outcomes of an initial bid and their associated probabilities π_i ($i = 1, \ldots, 6$). It is useful to keep this contest tree structure in mind when thinking about theoretical bidding strategies. The time-line starts with the first bid—which may be an offer to negotiate a merger agreement or a tender offer directly to target shareholders.[2] The "contest" may be single-bid (first offer is accepted or rejected with no further observed bids) or multiple-bid (several bids and/or bid revisions are observed). The initial bidder may win, a rival bidder may win, or all bids may be rejected (no-bidder-wins).

The two surveys explain optimal bidding strategies given additional restrictions on the bidding environment. For example, as explained by Dasgupta and Hansen, auction models typically assume that the seller is a single decision maker credibly committed

---

[1] The latter review is also substantially contained in the discussion of strategic bidding issues found in Section 3 of Betton et al. (2008) (reprinted in Volume I of this collection).

[2] After signing a merger agreement, the target board is normally required to consider any new outside offers until target shareholders have voted to give final approval (the so-called "fiduciary out" clause). In other words, potential competition affects even signed merger agreements—thus the term "contest" to describe the takeover process also for merger proposals. In the data, the time from the initial offer to the effective takeover date averages 108 trading days (median 96) when the initial bid is a tender offer, and 71 days (median 49) for merger bids. In cases where there are more than one control bid for the target, the time from the first to the second bid averages 40 trading days (median 19).

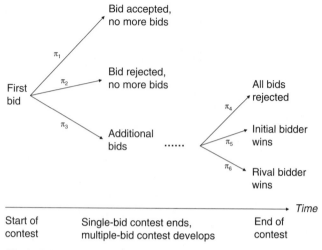

Fig. 1. Takeover contest structure, timeline, and outcome probabilities π.

to sell, and where alternative auction structures determine optimal bids and sales revenues. Hirshleifer focuses on bidding strategies when the seller consists of individual shareholders who may or may not coordinate their selling (share tendering) decisions. Lack of coordination may lead to free-rider problems (Grossman and Hart, 1980), while the existence of a large pivotal shareholder (e.g., management) may lead to issues of strategic defenses. Auction models typically imply that the probability of a successful bid (by the initial or a rival bidder) is equal to 1, while the success probability with multiple sellers and informational asymmetries among the transacting parties may be less than 1 but is assumed to be exogenously given in equilibrium.

As is apparent from the surveys, the typical theoretical settings are more restrictive than the type of contest games allowed in contest structures such as Figure 1. In particular, the "no-bidder-wins" outcome is an enigma to standard bidding theories where *some* bidder always wins.[3] In fact, despite an initial offer premium which average close to 50%,[4] the no-bidder-win outcome is surprisingly important in the data. As reviewed by Eckbo (2009), in samples exceeding 10,000 initial bids for US public targets from 1980 to 2005, the initial bidder wins the target in only two-thirds of cases. Surprisingly, the initial bidder wins *less* often when the initial bid is in the form of an invitation to negotiate a merger as opposed to a tender offer.

---

[3] Two bidding models which allow all bids to be optimally rejected by the target are Shleifer and Vishny (1986) and Giammarino and Heinkel (1986). There is also a growing auction literature assuming stochastic seller reserve prices, which allow no-bidder-wins outcomes.

[4] This premium average is measured relative to the target stock price 40 trading days prior to the initial bid.

The initial bidder is more likely to win when it has a toehold (ownership stake) in the target (Betton and Eckbo, 2000). Hostility substantially reduces the probability of winning, a rival bidder enters the contest, the rival wins the auction twice as often as the initial bidder. Moreover, the initial bidder wins less often when it is a private company, which is intuitive as it may be difficult to get shareholders of a public target to exchange their shares for nonlisted bidder shares. In sum, initiating a takeover is risky business. With the substantial resources committed to the takeover process, bidders obviously need to think strategically in order to maximize the expected value of bid initiation.

The growing empirical research on strategic bidding, some of which is reprinted in Volume II, seeks to answer a variety of questions: What determines the initial bid premium? If the initial bid is rejected, what should be the bid revision strategy (bid jump)? Do bidders fully account for the possibility of a winner's curse? Do bidders mark up the initially planned offer price in response to a run-up in the target stock price ("markup pricing")? Should the bidder acquire a toehold in the target, and is there evidence of toehold-induced (rational) overbidding in offer premiums? Do auction bids for financially distressed firms reflect a "fire-sale" discount? How does the choice of payment method affect bid premiums? How do offer premiums respond to a target defensive mechanism such as a poison pill?

Empirical tests of bidding theories are also important for the broader debate over bidder rationally and the efficiency of the market for corporate control. As discussed in Volume I, bidder CARs are typically small and often negative around takeover announcements. Roll (1986) was the first to suggest that bidder overconfidence or "hubris" may go a long way in explaining the surprisingly low bidder takeover gains. The relatively poor bidder performance remains a pervasive and puzzling phenomenon also today. Since part of the problem is one of properly estimating and interpreting bidder announcement returns, direct evidence on offer premiums and bidding behavior is of key interest in this debate.

2.2. Toeholds, winner's curse and overconfidence: do bidders behave strategically?

The substantial control premium typically observed in corporate takeovers makes a compelling case for acquiring targets hares (a toehold) in the market prior to launching a bid. Moreover, auction theory suggests that toehold bidding may yield a competitive advantage over rival bidders.[5] Nevertheless, with a sample exceeding 10,000 initial control bids for US public targets, Betton et al. (2009) show that toehold bidding has declined steadily since the early 1980s and is now surprisingly rare. At the same time, the average toehold is large when it occurs (20%), and toeholds are the norm in hostile bids.

To explain these puzzling observations, Betton et al. develop and test a two-stage takeover model where attempted merger negotiations are followed by open auction.

---

[5] If the toehold bidder loses to a rival, it gets to sell the toehold at a capital gain. If the toehold bidder wins, it needs to pay the full takeover premium on the remaining target shares only.

This formalizes the idea that merger negotiations occur in the "shadow" of an auction, and where the expected auction outcome (assuming optimal bidding behavior) affects the bargaining power of the negotiating parties. In their model, a toehold imposes a cost on target management, causing some targets to (rationally) reject merger negotiations. Optimal toeholds are therefore either zero (to avoid rejection costs) or greater than a threshold (so that toehold benefits offset rejection costs).

The toehold threshold estimate averages 9% across initial bidders, reflecting in part the bidders opportunity loss of a merger termination agreement. In the presence of market liquidity costs, a threshold of this size may well induce a broad range of bidders to select zero toehold. As predicted, the probability of toehold bidding decreases, and the toehold size increases, with the threshold estimate. The model also predicts a relatively high frequency of toehold bidding in hostile bids, as observed. Overall, these test results are consistent with rational bidder behavior with respect to the toehold decision.

In the vast majority of cases, there are no additional observed rival bids following the public announcement of the initial merger agreement. Boone and Mulherin (2007) show that the apparent lack of competition following the public announcement is somewhat deceptive as may targets invite multiple bidders to signal their interest in acquiring the target before selecting a negotiation partner. Nevertheless, given the substantial time between the signing of the merger proposal agreement, there should be ample opportunities for rival bidders to compete to break up a merger proposal which they judge to be too generous to the initial bidder.

Aktas et al. (2009) seek to determine whether acquirers in such friendly deals are truly insulated from competitive pressures. They study two countervailing influences: (1) potential but unobserved latent competition, the likelihood that rival bidders could appear, and (2) anticipated auction costs when negotiations fail. Using various proxies, they find that latent competition does increase the bid premium offered in negotiated deals, while auction costs reduce the premium as expected.

The winner's curse is a concept developed for auction settings where bidder valuations have a common component. At the extreme, every bidder has the *same* valuation for the auctioned item—a "pure" common value setting. An example would be a target where bidders are going to use the target resources simply as a financing vehicle for future investments by the bidder. Or, the change of control may allow the bidder to simply replace inefficient target management. A third example would be that the bidder is purchasing the target purely as a speculation in its future resale value. In a common-value setting, bidders receive private and noisy signals as to the true (common) value of the target. Bidding the full value of the signal would cause the bidder with the largest positive signal error to win and overpay (the "curse"). Optimal bidding takes this possibility into account by reducing the bid to the point where the expected value of the bid *conditional on winning* is nonnegative. Thus, testing for the presence of a winner's curse is equivalent to testing the hypothesis that bidders are rational (properly shave the bids).

Boone and Mulherin (2008) contrast the winner's curse hypothesis and the competitive market hypothesis as potential explanations for the observed returns to bidders in corporate takeovers. The authors posit that failing to properly adjust to the winner's curse will cause bidder returns to be inversely related to the level of competition in a given deal and to the uncertainty in the value of the target. They construct a measure of takeover competition based on the private auction process that occurs prior to the announcement of a takeover documented by Boone and Mulherin (2007). Controlling for endogeneity between bidder returns and the level of competition in takeover deals, they find that the returns to bidders are not significantly related to takeover competition. They also find that uncertainty in the value of the target does not reduce bidder returns. They infer from this that the break-even returns often observed to bidders in corporate takeovers stem not from the winner's curse but from the competitive market for targets that occurs predominantly prior to the public announcement of bids.

Malmendier and Tate (2008) ask whether CEO overconfidence helps to explain merger decisions. By definition, overconfident CEOs overestimate their ability to generate returns. As a result, they may overpay for target companies and undertake value-destroying mergers. The authors also argue that the effect of overconfidence should be strongest when the CEOs have access to internal financing (as outside financing would attract capital market monitoring in terms of the value of the deal). They test these predictions using two proxies for overconfidence: CEOs personal over-investment in their company and their press portrayal. They find that the odds of making an acquisition are 65% higher if the CEO is classified as overconfident. The effect is largest if the merger is diversifying and does not require external financing. The market reaction at merger announcement (-90 basis points) is significantly more negative than for nonoverconfident CEOs (-12 basis points). They also consider alternative interpretations including inside information, signaling, and risk tolerance. Overall, they conclude that the evidence corroborate the overconfidence explanation for mergers.

2.3. Auction bidding for bankrupt targets: do fire-sales exist?

Volume II contains four papers providing evidence on the acquisition of target firms that have filed for bankruptcy. Since bankruptcy law alters the bargaining position of the target, one expects the outcome for bidders to be different than for out-of-court acquisitions. The first two papers, Hotchkiss and Mooradian (1998) and Pulvino (1999), examine targets in Chapter 11 of the US Bankruptcy Code, where a decision to put the bankrupt firm up for sale is driven jointly by incumbent management and creditor committee votes. The final two papers, Eckbo and Thorburn (2008a, 2009), consider targets sold in the automatic auction bankruptcy system in Sweden. This code essentially eliminates the target's bargaining opportunities, and relies on bidder competition to maximize debt recovery and an efficient reallocation of the target assets.

An important research question is whether the form of a country's bankruptcy code distorts the efficient allocation of corporate resources. In particular, when introducing

Chapter 11 in 1978 lawmakers wished to give bankrupt firms ample time to restructure assets and financial claims under court protection.[6] The belief was—and still tends to be—that selling off distressed firms' assets under the time pressure of an auction will cause sales prices (and therefore debt recovery rates) to be low relative to their value in best alternative use.

Empirical evidence on this "fire-sale" hypothesis is, however, sparse. There are two issues. The first, which is addressed by the papers reprinted here, is to what extent bankruptcy auctions cause fire-sales. The second is whether the cost of a fire-sale exceeds the cost of a traditional Chapter 11 reorganization. Chapter 11 costs are significant, both because the average traditional reorganization takes close to 2 years and because personal managerial incentives may be to excessively continue economically failing firms. Over the past 10 years, we have seen a growing use of market-based mechanisms to lower the costs of Chapter 11 proceedings. These include "prepackaged" bankruptcies with a reorganization plan in place at filing, acquisition of distressed debt by "vulture" investors in order to make voting more efficient, and as studied by Hotchkiss and Mooradian (1998) voluntary sales in Chapter 11.[7]

Hotchkiss and Mooradian find that acquirers tend to be firms in the same industry as the target and to have some prior relationship with the target such as an ownership stake. Multiple bidders are not unusual indicating that the sales proceedings allow competition. They also report that the bankrupt targets in their sample on average are purchased at a 45% discount relative to prices paid for nonbankrupt targets in the same industry. However, they do not consider this as evidence of allocative inefficiency: "Although the transactions are at discount prices, the high proportion of acquirers operating in the same industry as the target, as well as the competitive bidding environment, does not support the conclusion that acquisitions in bankruptcy are sales to lower value users" (p. 243).[8] This conclusion is further supported by their finding that the postmerger cash flow performance of firms combined with bankrupt targets is better than that reported by Hotchkiss (1995) for firms emerging from Chapter 11. Hotchkiss and Mooradian also present evidence of positive and significant CARs to both bidders and bankrupt targets for the days surrounding the announcement of the acquisition.

---

[6] Chapter 11 grants the incumbent management exclusive rights within a limited time period (rolling 6 months) to propose a reorganization plan. If management fails to get creditor approval for the proposed plan, a new 6-month period may be granted, and so on.

[7] There are two ways in which a firm in Chapter 11 can sell substantially all of its assets: through a Section 363 (of the US Bankruptcy Code) sale or as part of a confirmed reorganization plan. Under a Section 363 sale, management must first obtain an offer and then notify the court, who in turn notifies creditors. The Bankruptcy Code invalidates no-shop agreements and allows creditors to retain advisors at the expense of the debtor firm to search for competing buyers. If there are several potential buyers, the court holds an auction. See Hotchkiss et al. (2008) for a broad review of empirical evidence on bankruptcy restructurings.

[8] Maksimovic and Phillips (1998) study divisional sales by firms in Chapter 11 and also conclude that buyers tend to be efficient.

Pulvino (1999) uses commercial aircraft transactions to determine whether prices obtained from asset sales are greater under US Chapter 11 reorganization than under Chapter 7 liquidation. His results indicate that prices obtained under both bankruptcy regimes are substantially lower than prices obtained by nondistressed airlines. Furthermore, there is no evidence that prices obtained by firms reorganizing under Chapter 11 are greater than those obtained by firms liquidating under Chapter 7. An analysis of aircraft sales indicates that Chapter 11 is also ineffective in limiting the number of aircraft sold at discounted prices. Pulvino's findings are interesting because they control for the industry in which the distressed sales take place. Since financial distress tends to be contagious within an industry, high-valuation industry rivals may themselves be financially constrained and unable to bid in the auction—which may be one reason for the discounted prices observed for distressed airline sales.

Eckbo and Thorburn (2008a, 2009) present the first comprehensive empirical analysis of the tendency for automatic bankruptcy auctions to induce fire-sale discounts in prices and debt recovery rates. In Sweden, filing firms are automatically turned over to a court-appointed trustee who organizes an open, cash-only auction. This mandatory auction system has an attractive simplicity. All debt claims are stayed during the auction period and the bids determine whether the firm will be continued as a going concern or liquidated piecemeal. As a result, the cross-sectional variation in auction prices is determined largely by demand-side conditions, which is ideal for the identification of fire-sale discounts.[9]

Eckbo and Thorburn (2008a) show that auction prices and debt recovery rate in *going concern sales* are unaffected by industry distress, and there is no evidence of lower prices when the buyer is an industry outsider. This conclusion holds also for cases where the buyer in the auction is a former manager/owner of the bankrupt firm (a saleback transaction), suggesting there is little scope for bypassing the discipline of the auction mechanism even if the buyer is the former target owner. The typical going concern auction attracts five interested bidders and three actual bids, which appears sufficient to counter potential fire-sale tendencies. Eckbo and Thorburn do, however, find a small (average 2%) price discount in auctions resulting in *piecemeal liquidation* of the target firm.

Eckbo and Thorburn (2009) develop the first structural test for the existence of auction overbidding, also using the context of going-concern sales of bankrupt firms in Sweden. They begin by noting that the main creditor (always a single bank) can neither bid in the auction nor refuse to sell in order to support a minimum price. Essentially, regulations try to ensure that the bank is a passive bystander to the auction process. However, Eckbo and Thorburn argue that the bank may increase its expected revenue by financing a bidder in return for a joint bid strategy. They derive the optimal coalition bid and show that it exceeds the bidder's private valuation (overbidding)

---

[9] A going-concern sale takes place by merging the assets and operations of the auctioned firm into the bidder firm, or into an empty corporate shell—much like a leveraged buyout transaction. Payment must be in cash, allowing the auction proceeds to be distributed to creditors strictly according to absolute priority.

by an amount that is increasing in the bank's ex ante debt impairment.[10] Since both the ex ante debt impairment and the final auction prices are observable quantities, the optimal coalition bid rule can be used to test for the existence of overbidding.

Eckbo and Thorburn find that bankbidder financing arrangements are common, and cross-sectional regressions show that winning bids are increasing in the bank-debt impairment as predicted. Also, while overbidding may in principle result in the coalition winning against a more efficient rival bidder, the evidence on postbankruptcy operating performance fails to support such allocative inefficiency effects. Since the fire-sale hypothesis and the overbidding hypothesis are effectively nested (flip sides of the same coin), it appears that creditor incentives help prevent fire-sales, in particular when the firm's debt is greatly impaired.

2.4. Do deal protection devices affect offer premiums?

A merger agreement is the result of negotiations between the bidder and target management teams. Merger negotiations protect the negotiating parties against opportunistic behavior. Before negotiations start, the parties sign agreements covering confidentiality, standstill, and nonsolicitation. The confidentiality agreement allows the target board to negotiate a sale of the firm without having to publicly disclose the proceedings, and it permits the target to open its books to the bidder. The standstill commits the bidder not to purchase target shares in the market during negotiations, while nonsolicitation ensures that neither the bidder nor the target tries to hire key employees away from the other firm. It is also common for the bidder to obtain tender agreements from target insiders, under which these insiders forsake the right to tender to a rival bidder.

Recent Delaware case law suggests that a merger agreement must include a "fiduciary out" clause enabling the target board to agree to a superior proposal if one is forthcoming from a third party. As a result, the target board cannot give its negotiating partner exclusionary rights to negotiate a control transfer: it must remain open to other bidders along the way. The resulting potential for bidder competition (even after the merger agreement has been signed but before the shareholder vote) has given rise to target termination agreements, starting in the mid-1980s. A termination agreement provides the bidder with a compensation in the form of a fixed fee ("breakup fee") or an option to purchase target shares at a discount ("lock-up option") should the target withdraw from the agreement.[11] As shown by the analysis in Betton et al. (2009), the

---

[10] It is instructive to think of the bankruptcy filing as creating an instant bank toehold equal to one when bank debt is impaired (100% bank ownership of the auctioned firm). As with toehold bidding in general (Betton et al., 2009), toeholds raise the bidder's reserve price above and beyond its private valuation—referred to as overbidding. Tests for auction overbidding based on creditor toeholds have the advantage that the toehold acquisition itself (i.e., the bankruptcy event) is exogenous to the creditor.

[11] The Delaware court views termination fees anywhere in the range of 2–5% of the transaction value as reasonable. Termination agreements sometimes allow a reduction in the breakup fee if the target strikes a competing deal within a 30/45 day time-frame. There are also cases where the deal includes a bidder termination agreement.

value of a target termination agreement may be substantial, and it may affect the initial bidder's optimal toehold strategy.

Does termination agreement affect offer premiums? Officer (2003) provides evidence on the effects of including a target termination fee in a merger contract. He tests the implications of the hypothesis that termination fees are used by self-interested target managers to deter competing bids and protect "sweetheart" deals with white knight bidders, presumably resulting in lower premiums for target shareholders. The alternative hypothesis is that target managers use termination fees to encourage bidder participation by ensuring that the bidder is compensated for the revelation of valuable private information released during merger negotiations.

Officer finds that merger deals with target termination fees involve significantly higher premiums and success rates than deals without such clauses. Furthermore, only weak support is found for the contention that termination fees deter competing bids. Overall, Officer's evidence suggests that termination fee use is at least not harmful, and is likely beneficial, to target shareholders.[12] It is worth noting that since deal protection devices such as termination agreements and toeholds are to some extent economic substitutes, it is important to control for the endogenous choice of bidder toeholds when considering premium effects of termination agreement (Betton et al., 2009).

A poison pill (also labeled "shareholder rights plan") is a permanent threat to dilute the value of a blockholder—typically defined as one holding 15% or more of the company's stock. The dilution takes place by allowing shareholders other than the blockholder to purchase (or exchange old for) new shares at half price. As this right is akin to a dividend, the pill may be adopted by the board anytime (including the day after receiving an unsolicited bid—a "morning after pill") and without shareholder vote. Since, to my knowledge, no bidder has yet triggered a pill, the perceived cost of triggering must be high, effectively forcing the would-be acquirer to negotiate with the target board and management. Should the target refuse to negotiate (appealing to the board's right to "just say no"), the only way around the pill appears to be to launch a proxy contest simultaneously with the offer. If the proxy contest succeeds, the bidder replaces the board with directors who are willing to rescind the pill. Board classification (staggered election of directors), however, prevents this strategy from working.

As summarized by Betton et al. (2008), the fraction of hostile bids (sum of unsolicited bids and bids where target is explicitly hostile) drops sharply after 1989, from more than 20% in the 1980s to less than 3% by the end of the 1990s. This drop coincides with the widespread adoption of poison pill plans by US publicly traded companies. Defenders of poison pills argue that a pill enhances shareholder wealth by improving the target's bargaining strength (conditional on receiving a bid). This argument suggests that poison pills should be associated with higher takeover premiums. However, the evidence in Comment and Schwert (1995) show that targets

---

[12] See also Bates and Lemmon (2003), an empirical evidence on termination agreements in a corporate governance context.

with poison pills receive offer premiums that are on average indistinguishable from offer premiums received by nonpill targets.[13]

What explains the surprising neutral impact of pills on observed offer premiums? Eckbo (2009) presents the following four alternative explanations:

H1: Poison pills do not convey bargaining power.

H2: Poison pills convey bargaining power and increases takeover premiums relative to what premiums would have been for the same target without a pill.

H3: Poison pills convey bargaining power which is used to benefit target management at the expense of target shareholders.

H4: Poison pills provide bargaining power, but "shadow" pills are as effective as adopted pills.

H1 maintains that pills are ineffective as a bargaining tool. For example, the bidder may believe that target board is not committed to trigger the pill. As pointed out by Schwert (2000), the definition of target "hostility" used in the literature probably captures plenty of targets that are ready to negotiate with or without the pill. Bidders that are able to look beyond the pill and determine whether negotiations are possible (based on observable target characteristic or on the bidder's own ability to persuade a hostile target management) may reach a final bargaining outcome that is largely indistinguishable from that observed in samples of ex ante "friendly" targets. This may also help explain why empirical evidence shows that the probability of receiving a bid (and ultimate bid success) is either unaffected or only slightly lower for targets with strong antitakeover defenses.[14]

H2–H4 maintain that pills convey bargaining power, but that a comparison of offer premiums in samples of firms with or without pills is difficult econometrically. For example, since pill adoptions are voluntary, they raise issues of endogeneity (H2). Controlling for self-selection is also difficult, however, because the marginal effect of a poison pill depends on the firm's entire governance system, including executive compensation (H3). Also, in order to isolate true premium effects of pills, empirical work relies on the existence of two samples, one representing "poison" and the other "placebo" effects (Comment and Schwert, 1995). This sampling procedure may simply be ineffective if as in H4 *all* firms effectively have ready access to the pill at any point in time (Coates, 2000).

Bates et al. (2008) find that board classification reduces the likelihood of receiving a takeover bid; however, the economic effect of bid deterrence on the value of the firm is quite small. Targets with classified boards appear to extract premiums equivalent to those of single-class boards. Moreover, shareholders of targets with a classified board realize bid returns that are equivalent to those of targets with a single class of directors, but receive a higher proportion of total bid surplus. Overall, the evidence in Bates et al.

---

[13] A similar result has been reported by studies, including Field and Karpoff (2002), Heron and Lie (2006), and Betton et al. (2009).

[14] Comment and Schwert (1995), Field and Karpoff (2002), Heron and Lie (2006).

is inconsistent with the conventional wisdom that board classification is an antitakeover device that facilitates managerial entrenchment.[15]

2.5. Large shareholder voting: does it improve takeover gains?

There is growing interest in the voting behavior of large shareholders—including managers and directors—in protecting their investment by influencing merger outcomes. Voting by large shareholders to approve mergers in which they hold shares in both the bidder and the target is a particularly interesting topic: these shareholders may effectively extract rents through the voting process.

Using a sample of 388 takeovers announced in the friendly environment of the 1990s, Moeller (2005) show that target shareholder control, proxied by low target chief executive officer share ownership, low fractions of inside directors, and the presence of large outside blockholders, is positively correlated with takeover premiums. Moeller concludes that targets with powerful CEOs receive lower takeover premiums.

Matvos and Ostrovsky (2008) show that institutional shareholders of acquiring companies on average do not lose money around public merger announcements, because they hold substantial stakes in the targets and make up for the losses from the acquirers with the gains from the targets. Depending on their holdings in the target, acquirer shareholders generally realize different returns from the same merger, some losing money, and others gaining. This conflict of interest is reflected in the mutual fund voting behavior: In mergers with negative acquirer announcement returns, cross-owners are significantly more likely to vote for the merger.

Greenwood and Schor (2009) begin by noting that recent work documents large positive abnormal returns when a hedge fund announces activist intentions regarding a publicly listed firm. They show that these returns are largely explained by the ability of activists to force target firms into a takeover. For a comprehensive sample of 13D filings by portfolio investors between 1993 and 2006, announcement returns and long-term abnormal returns are high for targets that are ultimately acquired, but not detectably different from zero for firms that remain independent. Firms targeted by activists are more likely than control firms to get acquired. Finally, activist investors' portfolios perform poorly during a period in which market wide takeover interest declined.

2.6. Does deal financing matter?

There is substantial theoretical work on the bidder's choice of payment method in takeovers. As reviewed by Eckbo (2009), the bidder's choice of payment method (cash

---

[15] Rose (2009) concludes that the presence of staggered boards have more of a detrimental impact of firm value when management is relatively entrenched. Also, Masulis et al. (2007) report that acquisition announcement-period stock returns are significantly lower for bidders with staggered boards, and suggest that board classification may reduce forced board turnover and quality.

vs. bidder shares) is potentially affected by factors such as corporate and personal taxes, information asymmetries between the bidder and the target (Eckbo et al., 1990; Fishman, 1989; Hansen, 1987; Myers and Majluf, 1984), capital structure and corporate control motives (Harris and Raviv, 1988; Jensen, 1986; Ross, 1977; Stulz, 1988), and behavioral issues (Rhodes-Kropf and Viswanathan, 2004; Shleifer and Vishny, 2003). Empirical evidence shows that offer premiums are greater for all-cash bids than for all-stock bids (Betton et al., 2009; Eckbo and Langohr, 1989; Franks et al., 1988; Huang and Walkling, 1987, and others), and that bidder announcement returns tend to be greater for all-cash bids than for all-stock bids (Asquith et al., 1987; Betton et al., 2009; Eckbo and Thorburn, 2000; Eckbo et al., 1990; Heron and Lie, 2004; Travlos, 1987, and others).

Much less work has been done examining the effects of the ways in which the bidder finances its cash payment to the target. Potential sources of the cash are retained earnings (financial slack), short-term debt (such as draw-down of a credit line), or issuances of debt or equity securities prior to the takeover. Integrating evidence on the cash financing is important in order to fully understand the deal financing choice, as the market reaction to the payment method conditions on this type of historical information. That is, while the market is aware of any prebid public security issues, the acquisition bid announcement possibly resolves uncertainty regarding the use of the issue proceeds. If this resolution is economically important, the source of financing for the cash portion of the bid will affect the market reaction to the takeover attempt. The collection reprints three empirical studies which touches on this issue. The empirical results indicate a prior-cash-financing-source component in acquisition announcement returns.

Bharadwaj and Shivdasani (2003) provide evidence on bank financing of 115 cash tender offers from the 1990s. Banks are found to extend financing in 70% of the tender offers and finance the entire tender offer in half of the takeovers. Bank financing of tender offers is more likely when internal cash reserves are low. Acquisitions that are entirely financed by banks are associated with large and significantly positive acquirer announcement returns. Announcement returns are also positively related to the fraction of the acquisition value financed by bank debt. The benefits of bank financing are found to be most pronounced for poorly performing acquirers and for acquirers facing substantial informational asymmetries. To explain these results, the authors suggest that bank debt performs an important certification and monitoring role for acquirers in tender offers.

Schlingemann (2004) reports that, after controlling for the form of payment, financing decisions during the year before a takeover play an important role in explaining the cross section of bidder gains. Bidder announcement period abnormal returns are positively and significantly related to the amount of ex ante equity financing. This relation is particularly strong for high Q firms. He further reports a negative and significant relation between bidder gains and free cash flow. This relation is particularly strong for firms classified as having poor investment opportunities. The amount of debt financing before a takeover announcement is not significantly related to bidder gains. Together, Schlingemann takes these findings as supportive of pecking-order theory of financing (Myers, 1984) and of the free cash flow hypothesis (Jensen, 1986).

Harford et al. (2009) use large investments such as acquisitions to examine firms' capital structure choices more generally. If firms have target capital structures, deviations from these targets should affect how bidders choose to finance acquisitions and how they adjust their capital structure following the acquisitions. They show that when a bidders leverage is over its target level, it is less likely to finance the acquisition with debt and more likely to finance the acquisition with equity. Also, they find a positive association between the merger-induced changes in target and actual leverage, and they show that bidders incorporate more than two-thirds of the change to the merged firms new target leverage. Following debt-financed acquisitions, managers actively move the firm back to its target leverage, reversing more than 75% of the acquisitions leverage effect within 5 years. Overall, the authors conclude that the results are consistent with a model of capital structure that includes a target level and adjustment costs.

2.7. Takeovers—what's in it for top executives?

Does the structure of CEO compensation packages affect the quality of takeover decisions? Or, as Lehn and Zhao (2006) puts it: "Are Bad Bidders Fired?" The presumption of the literature on optimal compensation is that a strong pay-performance sensitivity helps promote better acquisition decisions.[16] A key question is what package of capital gains, cash, and subsequent employment do target CEOs accept in exchange for relinquishing control. Another important issue is whether target CEOs sacrifice premiums paid to their own outside shareholders in return for a favorable "golden handshake." Walkling and Long (1984), Cotter and Zenner (1994), Wulf (2004), and Hartzell et al. (2004) all present evidence on acquisition-induced compensation of target firm CEOs. Hartzell et al. (2004) analyze a sample of 311 negotiated mergers between 1995 and 1997. They conclude from their evidence that "acquirers overtly pay certain CEOs to surrender managerial control over the firm's assets, or equivalently, that some CEOs 'purchase' executive jobs in the buyer by foregoing cash payments that they might otherwise have obtained" (p. 39). Also, they present some evidence indicating an inverse association between selling shareholder premia and unusual bonuses received by the target CEO as a reward to "step aside."[17]

There is evidence that target firms tend to underperform prior to becoming targets, that targets of hostile bids tend to show a prior history of value-decreasing acquisitions, and that CEO turnover increases after hostile bids. Moreover, Offenberg (2009) finds

---

[16] See, for example, Murphy (1999) and Aggarwal (2008) for comprehensive reviews of the literature on executive compensation and pay-performance sensitivity.

[17] As the authors recognize, since the study uses a sample of completed mergers only, it does not provide information on the sort of packages that other target CEOs turn down in attempted mergers that were not completed. Thus, the question of whether larger CEO packages come at the expense of target shareholders remains open.

evidence that CEOs of larger firm are more likely to be replaced following a series of poor acquisitions than CEOs of smaller firms. This indicates that the market for corporate control play a disciplinary role. On the other hand, with the spread of poison pill defense and subsequent decline of hostile takeovers after the 1980s, the market for corporate control may have become a "court of last resort"—with internal governance structures being the primary mechanism for disciplining poor managers.[18]

Lehn and Zhao (2006) show that managers who undertake value-reducing acquisitions in the period 1990–1998 face a significantly higher probability of being replaced than managers who make value-enhancing acquisitions, either by internal governance, takeovers, or bankruptcy. They also show that CEOs who cancel an acquisition after observing a reduction in their company's stock price face significantly lower replacement risk than their counterparts who proceed with value-reducing acquisitions. Among firms not subjected to takeover or bankruptcy, they find no association between a firm's governance characteristics and the probability that the CEO who make value-reducing acquisitions are replaced. Lehn and Zhao conclude that "corporate governance and the external market for corporate control generally work well in disciplining managers who pursue acquisitions to the detriment of their stockholders."

Several recent papers provide evidence on CEO compensation changes (other than turnover) following acquisition activity. Bliss and Rosen (2001) study bank mergers over the period 1985–1995, a period characterized by overcapacity and frequent mergers. Mergers are found to have a net positive effect on bidder firm CEO compensation, mainly via the effect of size on compensation. Compensation increases even if the merger causes the acquiring bank's stock price to decline (which is typical upon merger announcement). However, CEOs with more stock-based compensation are less likely to make an acquisition, suggesting that bank management are motivated by their compensation contracts.

Datta et al. (2001) study 1719 acquisitions over the period 1993–1998, and separate the acquirers into whether the equity-based compensation of their respective CEOs are above ("high") or below ("low") the median. While the market reaction to the merger announcements is insignificantly different from zero on average, it is significantly positive for bidder CEOs with high equity-based compensation and significantly negative when the equity-based compensation is low. Moreover, the compensation structure impacts the selection of target: high equity-based managers tend to seek out targets with relatively high M/B ratio (growth targets), whereas CEOs in the low incentive compensation group tend to acquire targets with low growth prospects. Thus, it appears that managers with high equity-based compensation are willing to take on riskier and more valuable acquisition projects that managers with low equity-based compensation.

---

[18] With data from 1979 through 1998, Kini et al. (2004) conclude that the corporate takeover market intercedes when internal control mechanisms are relatively weak of ineffective.

Grinstein and Hribar (2004) examine mergers and acquisitions (M&A) bonuses (typically all-cash) paid to CEOs of bidder firm after 327 large merger deals over the period 1993–1999. Bonuses are larger for larger deals. Other than size, measures of CEO "power" is the single most powerful variable explaining the cross-sectional variation in M&A bonuses. Much as in Bebchuk and Fried (2003), CEO power is measured as the CEO's ability to influence directors (and thereby the compensation decision). A CEO gains influence as a chairman of the board, as a member of the nominating committee, as the proportion of insiders on the board increases, and as board size increases.

Grinstein and Hribar find that the size and power variables explain much more of the variation in bonuses than variables capturing CEO skill, effort and performance. Moreover, the deal announcement-induced CAR is significantly lower (more negative) in the sample of CEOs with high power than with low power. Moeller (2005) also concludes that targets with powerful CEOs receive lower takeover premiums. However, Bauguess et al. (2009) present evidence that inside (managerial) ownership has a positive relation with target returns, whereas active-outside (nonmanaging director) ownership has a negative relation with target returns. They suggest that the latter effect reflects outsiders' willingness to share gains with the bidder.

Harford and Li (2007) also study how CEO pay and pay-performance sensitivity is affected by acquisitions. With a sample of 1508 mergers completed over the period 1993 and 2000, they show that bidding firm CEOs receive substantial rewards in the form of new stock and options grants following acquisitions. While a poorly performing acquisition reduces the value of the CEO's portfolio of stocks and options obtained prior to the acquisition, the new postacquisition grants more than compensate for this personal value-reduction. As a result, "CEO's pay and wealth are completely insensitive to poor postacquisition performance, but CEO's wealth remains sensitive to good postacquisition performance" (p. 919). Interestingly, they show that bidding firms with stronger boards retain the sensitivity of their CEO's compensation to poor postacquisition performance.

Harford and Li (2007) also document that compensation changes around major capital expenditures are much smaller and more sensitive to performance than those following acquisitions. That is, similarly to conclusions made by Andrade and Stafford (2004), external and internal expansion decisions are treated fundamentally differently by the board. This difference may be rooted in the greater degree of uncertainty and information asymmetry surrounding acquisitions, which may allow the CEO to demand (and receive) some degree of protection for the downside risk to her personal wealth.

There is some evidence on the role of board structure and director compensation in affecting the outcome of takeovers. Byrd and Hickman (1992) and Cotter et al. (1997) find that boards dominated by outsider directors increase value for their shareholders during an acquisition attempt. Harford (2003) document the effect of a takeover bid on target directors, both financially and in terms of its effect on the number of future board seats held by those directors. He finds that directors are rarely retained following a completed offer, and that target directors as a group hold fewer directorships after a takeover, suggesting that the target board seat is difficult to replace. Moreover, he shows that for outside directors, the direct financial impact of a completed merger is largely negative. In sum, failing as a monitor imposes a personal cost on outside directors.

Finally, Denis and Kruse (2000) examine the incidence of disciplinary events that reduce the control of current managers, and corporate restructuring among firms experiencing a large decline in operating performance during an active takeover period (1985–1988) and a less active period (1989–1992). They document a significant decline in the disciplinary events from the active to the less active period that is driven by a significant decline in disciplinary takeovers, those takeovers that result in a top executive change. Following the performance decline, however, there is a substantial amount of corporate restructuring, and a significant improvement in operating performance, during both the active and the less active takeover period. Denis and Kruse conclude that, although some managerial disciplinary events are related to overall takeover activity, the decline in takeover activity does not appear to result in fewer performance-enhancing restructurings following performance declines.

2.8. Cross-border mergers: positive governance spillover effects?

Rossi and Volpin (2004) study the determinants of M&A around the world by focusing on differences in laws and regulation across countries. They find that the volume of M&A activity is significantly larger in countries with better accounting standards and stronger shareholder protection. The probability of an all-cash bid decreases with the level of shareholder protection in the acquirer country. In cross-border deals, targets are typically from countries with poorer investor protection than their acquirers' countries, suggesting that cross-border transactions play a governance role by improving the degree of investor protection within target firms.

Martynova and Renneboog (2008) find that in cross-border acquisitions, the differences between the bidder and target corporate governance (measured by newly constructed indices capturing shareholder, minority shareholder, and creditor protection) have an important impact on the takeover returns. Their country-level corporate governance indices appear to capture well the changes in the quality of the national corporate governance regulations over the past 15 years. Their evidence suggests that when the bidder is from a country with a strong shareholder orientation (relative to the target), part of the total synergy value of the takeover result from the improvement in the governance of the target assets.

Martynova and Renneboog distinguish between complete takeovers, for which the corporate governance regulation of the bidder is imposed on the target (the positive spillover by law hypothesis), and partial takeovers, where improvements in the target corporate governance occur on voluntary basis (the spillover by control hypothesis). Their empirical analysis corroborates both spillover effects. In contrast, when the bidder is from a country with poorer shareholder protection, the negative spillover by law hypothesis states that the anticipated takeover gains will be lower as the poorer corporate governance regime of the bidder will be imposed on the target. The alternative bootstrapping hypothesis argues that poor governance bidders voluntarily bootstrap to the better-governance regime of the target. Martynova and Renneboog find some support for the bootstrapping effect.

Bris et al. (2008) also posit that cross-border mergers allow firms to alter the level of protection they provide to their investors, because target firms usually import the corporate governance system of the acquiring company by law. They construct measures of the change in investor protection induced by cross-border mergers in a sample of 7330 national industry years (spanning 39 industries in 41 countries in the period 1990–2001). They find that the Tobin's Q of an industry—including its unmerged firms—increases when firms within that industry are acquired by foreign firms coming from countries with better shareholder protection and better accounting standards. They present evidence that the transfer of corporate governance practices through cross-border mergers is Pareto improving. Firms that can adopt better practices willingly do so, and the market assigns more value to better protection.

2.9. Market efficiency and returns to merger arbitrage

After the announcement of a takeover bid, the target stock price adjusts upwards but typically still trades at a discount from the offer price. The difference between the offer price and the postannouncement market price is called the arbitrage spread. Merger arbitrage (or risk arbitrage) is a specialized investment strategy that tries to profit from this spread. Specifically, it is a bet on the likelihood that the proposed transaction closes. If the bid (or a rival bid) is successful and the target is acquired, the arbitrageur captures the price differential. If the takeover fails and the target remains independent, however, the target stock tends to fall back to prebid levels and the arbitrage position has to be closed at a loss. Since the position carries the transaction risk, it is not an arbitrage in the true (riskless) sense of the word. It is, however, designed to be neutral to subsequent market movements and to price fluctuations between the bidder and the target, would the deal succeed.

For a cash bid, a merger arbitrage position simply involves a long position in the target stock. When the acquisition is consummated, the target stock is exchanged for cash. With a positive arbitrage spread, the cash received at closing will exceed the initial investment in the target stock, hence generating a profit. In contrast, if the takeover fails and the target stock price falls, the speculative position has to be sold at a loss equal to the price decline in the target stock.

The arbitrage position in a stock-for-stock transaction is more complex, since target shareholders are offered acquirer stock as payment. Here, the arbitrage position consists of a long target stock and short acquirer stock in the same proportion as the exchange ratio. For example, with an offer of two acquirer shares for each target share, the arbitrage position is long one target share and short two acquirer shares. If the bid is subsequently revised, the arbitrage position must be adjusted to reflect the new exchange ratio. When the transaction closes, the arbitrageur receives in return for the target share the promised number of acquirer shares, which are used to cover the short position. The profit from a successful arbitrage position in a stock deal is the difference between the price of the short acquirer stock and the price of the target at the point in time when the position is established. If the bid fails, the arbitrageur will likely incur a loss from selling its target share holdings. The effect of closing out the short position in the acquirer is more uncertain: if the bidder stock falls, there may be an offsetting gain; and if the bidder stock appreciates, there may be additional losses.

Several empirical studies suggest that merger arbitrage strategies systematically generate excess risk-adjusted returns (Bhagat and Loewenstein, 1987; Jindra and Walkling, 2004; Larcker and Lys, 1987; Mitchell and Pulvino, 2001; Mitchell et al., 2004, and others). The literature proposes various explanations for the existence of these returns. One is that risk arbitrageurs may be compensated for carrying the risk of deal failure. Jensen (1986) points to three important roles played by merger arbitrageurs and for which they should be compensated: (i) they help value alternative offers; (ii) they provide risk-bearing services for investors who do not want the uncertainty associated with the outcome of the takeover offer; and (iii) they help resolve the free rider problems of small, diffuse shareholders who cannot organize to negotiate directly with competing bidders for the target. Moreover, transactions costs and other practical constraints may limit the possibilities to successfully implement an arbitrage strategy.

Hsieh and Walking (2005) examine the importance of merger arbitrageurs for the market for corporate control using a sample of 680 all-cash and all-stock takeover offers during the period 1992–1999. They find that arbitrage holdings increase in offers that are likely to be successful, and that these changes are positively correlated to the probability of bid success, bid premia, and arbitrage returns. They suggest that the former is evidence of the participation of passive arbitrageurs, whose accumulation of target stock does not affect the outcome of the deal, and the latter of the involvement of active arbitrageurs, who influence the outcome and the terms of the deal.

Baker and Savasoglu (2002) show that a diversified portfolio of risk arbitrage positions produces an abnormal return of 0.60.9% per month over the period from 1981 to 1996. They trace these profits to practical limits on risk arbitrage. In their model of risk arbitrage, arbitrageurs risk-bearing capacity is constrained by deal completion risk and the size of the position they hold. Consistent with this model, Baker and Savasoglu document that the returns to risk arbitrage increase in an ex ante measure of completion risk and target size. They also examine the influence of the general supply of arbitrage capital, measured by the total equity holdings of arbitrageurs, on arbitrage profits.

References

Aggarwal, R., 2008, "Executive Compensation and Incentives," In: B. E. Eckbo (Ed.), *Handbook of Corporate Finance: Empirical Corporate Finance*, Vol. 2, Chapter 17, Elsevier/North-Holland, Handbooks in Finance Series, pp. 497–538.

Akdogu, E., 2009, "Gaining a Competitive Edge Through Acquisitions: Evidence from the Telecommunications Industry," *Journal of Corporate Finance*, 15, 99–112.

Andrade, G. and E. Stafford, 2004, "Investigating the Economic Role of Mergers," *Journal of Corporate Finance*, 10, 1–36.

Ang, J. S. and Y. Cheng, 2006, "Direct Evidence on the Market-Driven Acquisition Theory," *Journal of Financial Research*, 29, 199–216.

Asquith, P. and D. W. Mullins, Jr., 1983, "The Impact of Initiating Dividend Payments on Shareholders Wealth," *Journal of Business*, 56, 77–96.

Asquith, P., R. Bruner and D. Mullins, 1987, "Merger Returns and the Form of Financing," *Proceedings of the Seminar on the Analysis of Securities Prices*, 34, 115–146.

Aktas, N., E. de Bodt and R. Roll, 2009, "Negotiations Under the Threat of an Auction," *Journal of Financial Economics*, forthcoming.

Baker, M. and S. Savasoglu, 2002, "Limited Arbitrage in Mergers and Acquisitions," *Journal of Financial Economics*, 64, 91–15.

Bargeron, L. L., F. P. Schlingemann, R. M. Stulz and C. Zutter, 2008, "Why Do Private Acquirers Pay So Little Compared to Public Acquirers?" *Journal of Financial Economics*, 89, 375–390.

Bates, T. H. and M. L. Lemmon, 2003, "Breaking Up is Hard to Do? An Analysis of Termination Fee Provisions and Merger Outcomes," *Journal of Financial Economics*, 69, 460–504.

Bates, T. W., D. A. Becher and M. L. Lemmon, 2008, "Board Classification and Managerial Entrenchment: Evidence from the Market for Corporate Control," *Journal of Financial Economics*, 87, 656–677.

Bauguess, S. W., S. B. Moeller, F. P. Schlingemenn and C. J. Zutter, 2009, "Ownership Structure and Target Returns," *Journal of Corporate Finance*, 15, 48–65.

Bebchuk, L. A. and J. M. Fried, 2003, "Executive Compensation as an Agency Problem," *Journal of Economic Perspectives*, 17, 71–92.

Becher, D. A, J. H. Mulherin and R. A. Walkling, 2008, "Industry Shocks and Merger Activity: An Analysis of U.S. Public Utilities," Working Paper, Drexel University.

Betton, S. and B. E. Eckbo, 2000, "Toeholds, Bid Jumps, and Expected Payoff in Takeovers," *Review of Financial Studies*, 13, 841–882.

Betton, S., B. E. Eckbo and K. S. Thorburn, 2008, "Corporate Takeovers," In: B. E. Eckbo (Ed.), *Handbook of Corporate Finance: Empirical Corporate Finance*, Vol. 2, Chapter 15, Elsevier/North-Holland, Handbooks in Finance Series, pp. 291–430.

Betton, S., B. E. Eckbo and K. S. Thorburn, 2009, "Merger Negotiations and the Toehold Puzzle," *Journal of Financial Economics*, 91, 158–178.

Bhagat, S., J. A. Brickley and U. Loewenstein, 1987, "The Pricing Effects of Interfirm Cash Tender Offers," *Journal of Finance*, 42 (4), 965–986.

Bhagat, S., M. Dong, D. Hirshleifer and R. Noah, 2005, "Do Tender Offers Create Value? New Methods and Evidence," *Journal of Financial Economics*, 76, 3–60.

Bharadwaj, A. and A. Shivdasani, 2003, "Valuation Effects of Bank Financing in Acquisitions," *Journal of Financial Economics*, 67, 113–148.

Bliss, R. T. and R. J. Rosen, 2001, "CEO Compensation and Bank Mergers," *Journal of Financial Economics*, 61, 107–138.

Boone, A. L. and J. H. Mulherin, 2007, "How Are Firms Sold?" *Journal of Finance*, 62, 847–875.

Boone, A. L. and J. H. Mulherin, 2008, "Do Auctions Induce a Winner's Curse? New Evidence from the Corporate Takeover Market," *Journal of Financial Economics*, 89, 1–19.

Bris, A., N. Brisley and C. Cabolis, 2008, "Adopting Better Corporate Governance: Evidence from Cross-Border Mergers," *Journal of Corporate Finance*, 14, 224–240.

Byrd, J. and K. Hickman, 1992, "Do Outside Directors Monitor Managers? Evidence from Tender Offer Bids," *Journal of Financial Economics*, 32, 195–222.

Coates, J. C., 2000, "Takeover Defenses in the Shadow of the Pill: A Critique of the Scientific Evidence," *Texas Law Review*, 79, 271–382.

Comment, R. and G. W. Schwert, 1995, "Poison or Placebo? Evidence on the Deterrent and Wealth Effects of Modern Antitakeover Measures," *Journal of Financial Economics*, 39, 3–43.

Cooney, J. W., T. Moeller and M. Stegemoller, 2009, "The Underpricing of Private Targets," *Journal of Financial Economics*, 93, 51–66.

Cotter, J and M Zenner, 1994, "How Managerial Wealth Affects the Tender Offer Process," *Journal of Financial Economics*, 35, 63–97.

Cotter, J., A. Shivdasani and M. Zenner, 1997, "Do Independent Directors Enhance Target Shareholder Wealth During Tender Offers?" *Journal of Financial Economics*, 43, 195–218.

Dasgupta, S. and R. G. Hansen, 2007, "Auctions in Corporate Finance," In: B. E. Eckbo (Ed.), *Handbook of Corporate Finance: Empirical Corporate Finance*, Vol. 1, Chapter 3, Elsevier/North-Holland, Handbooks in Finance Series, pp. 87–143.

Datta, S., M. Iskandar-Datt and K. Raman, 2001, "Executive Compensation and Corporate Acquisition Decisions," *Journal of Finance*, 56, 2299–2336.

Denis, D. J. and T. A. Kruse, 2000, "Managerial Discipline and Corporate Restructuring Following Performance Declines," *Journal of Financial Economics*, 55, 391–424.

Dong, M., D. Hisrshleifer, S. Richardson and S. H. Teoh, 2006, "Does Investor Misvaluation Drive the Takeover Market?" *Journal of Finance*, 61, 725–762.

Eckbo, B. E., 1983, "Horizontal Mergers, Collusion, and Stockholder Wealth," *Journal of Financial Economics*, 11, 241–272.

Eckbo, B. E., 1985, "Mergers and the Market Concentration Doctrine: Evidence from the Capital Market," *Journal of Business*, 58, 325–349.

Eckbo, B. E., 1992, "Mergers and the Value of Antitrust Deterrence," *Journal of Finance*, 47, 1005–1029.

Eckbo, B. E., 2009, "Bidding Strategies and Takeover Premiums: A Review," *Journal of Corporate Finance*, 15, 149–178.

Eckbo, B. E. and H. Langohr, 1989, "Information Disclosure, Method of Payment, and Takeover Premiums: Public and Private Tender Offers in France," *Journal of Financial Economics*, 24, 363–403.

Eckbo, B. E. and K. S. Thorburn, 2000, "Gains to Bidder Firms Revisited: Domestic and Foreign Acquisitions in Canada," *Journal of Financial and Quantitative Analysis*, 35, 1–25.

Eckbo, B. E. and K. S. Thorburn, 2008a, "Automatic Bankruptcy Auctions and Fire-Sales," *Journal of Financial Economics*, 89, 404–422.

Eckbo, B. E. and K. S. Thorburn, 2008b, "Corporate Restructuring: Breakups and LBOs," In: B. E. Eckbo (Ed.), *Handbook of Corporate Finance: Empirical Corporate Finance*, Vol. 2, Chapter 16, Elsevier/North-Holland, Handbooks in Finance Series, pp. 431–496.

Eckbo, B. E. and K. S. Thorburn, 2009, "Creditor Financing and Overbidding in Bankruptcy Auctions: Theory and Tests," *Journal of Corporate Finance*, 15, 10–29.

Eckbo, B. E., R. M. Giammarino and R. L. Heinkel, 1990, "Asymmetric Information and the Medium of Exchange in Takeovers: Theory and Tests," *Review of Financial Studies*, 3, 651–675.

Fee, C. E. and S. Thomas, 2004, "Sources of Gains in Horizontal Mergers: Evidence from Customers, Supplier, and Rival Firms," *Journal of Financial Economics*, 74, 423–460.

Field, L. C. and J. M. Karpoff, 2002, "Takeover Defenses at IPO Firms," *Journal of Finance*, 57, 1857–1889.

Fishman, M. J., 1989, "Preemptive Bidding and the Role of the Medium of Exchange in Acquisitions," *Journal of Finance*, 44, 41–57.

Franks, J. R., R. S. Harris and C. Mayer, 1988, "Means of Payment in Takeovers: Results for the U.K. and the U.S.," In: A. Auerbach (Ed.), *Corporate Takeovers*, NBER, University of Chicago Press, Chicago.

Giammarino, R. M. and R. L. Heinkel, 1986, "A Model of Dynamic Takeover Behavior," *Journal of Finance*, 41, 465–480.

Greenwood, R. and M. Schor, 2009, "Investor Activism and Takeovers," *Journal of Financial Economics*, 92, 362–375.

Grinstein, Y. and P. Hribar, 2004, "CEO Compensation and Incentives—Evidence from M&A Bonuses," *Journal of Financial Economics*, 73, 119–143.

Grossman, S. J. and O. D. Hart, 1980, "Takeover Bids, the Free-Rider Problem, and the Theory of the Corporation," *Bell Journal of Economics*, 11, 42–64.

Hansen, R. G., 1987, "A Theory for the Choice of Exchange Medium in the Market for Corporate Control," *Journal of Business*, 60, 75–95.

Harford, J, 1999, "Corporate Cash Reserves and Acquistions," *Journal of Finance*, 54 (6, December), 1969–1997.

Harford, J., 2003, "Takeover Bids and Target Directors' Incentives: The Impact of a Bid on Directors' Wealth and Board Seats," *Journal of Financial Economics*, 69, 51–83.

Harford, J., 2005, "What Drives Merger Waves?" *Journal of Financial Economics*, 77, 529–560.

Harford, J. and K. Li, 2007, "Decoupling CEO Wealth and Firm Performance: The Case of Acquiring CEOs," *Journal of Finance*, 62, 917–949.

Harford, J., S. Klasa and N. Walcott, 2009, "Do Firms Have Leverage Targets? Evidence from Acquisitions," *Journal of Financial Economics*, 93, 1–14.

Harris, M. and A. Raviv, 1988, "Corporate Control Contests and Capital Structure," *Journal of Financial Economics*, 20, 55–86.

Hartzell, J. C., E. Ofek and D. Yermack, 2004, "What's In It for Me? CEOs Whose Firms are Acquired," *Review of Financial Studies*, 17, 37–61.

Heron, R. A. and E. Lie, 2004, "A Comparison of the Motivations for and the Information Content of Different Types of Equity Offerings," *Journal of Business*, 77, 605–632.

Heron, R. A. and E. Lie, 2006, "On the Use of Poison Pill and Defensive Payouts by Takeover Targets," *Journal of Business*, 79, 1783–1807.

Hirshleifer, D., 1995, "Mergers and Acquisitions: Strategic and Informational Issues," In: R. A. Jarrow, V. Maksimovic and W. T. Ziemba (Eds.), *Finance, Vol. 9 of Handbooks in Operation Research and Management Science*, Chapter 26, North-Holland, pp. 839–885.

Hotchkiss, E. S., 1995, "Post-Bankruptcy Performance and Management Turnover," *Journal of Finance*, 50, 3–21.

Hotchkiss, E. S. and R. M. Mooradian, 1998, "Acquisitions as a Means of Restructuring Firms in Chapter 11," *Journal of Financial Intermediation*, 7, 240–262.

Hotchkiss, E. S., K. John, R. Mooradian and K. S. Thorburn, 2008, "Bankruptcy and the Resolution of Financial Distress," In: B. E. Eckbo (Ed.), *Handbook of Corporate Finance: Empirical Corporate Finance*, Vol. 2, Chapter 14, Elsevier/North-Holland, Handbooks in Finance Series, pp. 235–289.

Houston, J., C. James and M. Ryngaert, 2001, "Where Do Merger Gains Come from? Bank Mergers from the Perspective of Insiders and Outsiders," *Journal of Financial Economics*, 60, (2/3, May/June), 285–331.

Hsieh, J. and R. A. Walking, 2005, "Determinants and Implications of Arbitrage Holdings in Acquisitions," *Journal of Financial Economics*, 77, 605–648.

Huang, Y.-S. and R. A. Walkling, 1987, "Abnormal Returns Associated with Acquisition Announcements: Payment Method, Acquisition Form, and Managerial Resistance," *Journal of Financial Economics*, 19, 329–349.

Jensen, M. C., 1986, "Agency Costs of Free Cash Flow, Corporate Finance, and Takeovers," *American Economic Review*, 76, 323–329.

Jensen, M. C. and R. S. Ruback, 1983, "The Market for Corporate Control," *Journal of Financial Economics*, 11, 5–50.

Jindra, J. and R. A. Walkling, 2004, "Speculation Spreads and the Market Pricing of Proposed Acquisitions," *Journal of Corporate Finance*, 10, 495–526.

Kini, O., W. Kracaw and S. Mian, 2004, "The Nature and Discipline by Corporate Takeovers," *Journal of Finance*, 59, 1511–1552.

Kothari, S. P. and J. B. Warner, 2007, "Econometrics of Event Studies," In: B. E. Eckbo (Ed.), *Handbook of Corporate Finance: Empirical Corporate Finance*, Vol. 1, Chapter 1, Elsevier/North-Holland, Handbooks in Finance Series, pp. 3–36.

Larcker, D. F. and T. Lys, 1987, "An Empirical Analysis of the Incentives to Engage in Costly Information Acquisition: The Case of Risk Arbitrage," *Journal of Financial Economics*, 18, 111–126.

Lehn, K. and M. Zhao, 2006, "CEO Turnover After Acquisitions: Are Bad Bidders Fired?" *Journal of Finance*, 61, 1759–1811.

Li, K. and N. R. Prabhala, 2007, "Self-Selection Models in Corporate Finance," In: B. E. Eckbo (Ed.), *Handbook of Corporate Finance: Empirical Corporate Finance*, Vol. 1, Chapter 2, Elsevier/North-Holland, Handbooks in Finance Series, pp. 37–86.

Maksimovic, V. and G. Phillips, 1998, "Asset Efficiency and Reallocation Decisions of Bankrupt Firms," *Journal of Finance*, 53, 1495–1532.

Maksimovic, V. and G. Phillips, 2001, "The Market for Corporate Assets: Who Engages in Mergers and Asset Sales and Are There Efficiency Gains?" *Journal of Finance*, 56, 2019–2065.

Malmendier, U. and G. Tate, 2008, "Who Makes Acquisitions? CEO Overconfidence and the Market's Reaction," *Journal of Financial Economics*, 89, 20–43.

Martynova, M. and L. Renneboog, 2008, "Spillover of Corporate Governance Standards as a Takeover Synergy in Cross-Border Mergers and Acquisitions," *Journal of Corporate Finance*, 74, 200–223.

Masulis, R. W., C. Wand and F. Xie, 2007, "Corporate Governance and Acquirer Returns," *Journal of Finance*, 62, 1851–1889.

Matvos, G. and M. Ostrovsky, 2008, "Cross-Ownership, Returns, and Voting in Mergers," *Journal of Financial Economics*, 89, 391–403.

Mitchell, M. and J. H. Mulherin, 1996, "The Impact of Industry Shocks on Takeover and Restructuring Activity," *Journal of Financial Economics*, 41, 193–229.

Mitchell, M. and T. Pulvino, 2001, "Characteristics of Risk and Return in Risk Arbitrage," *Journal of Finance*, 56 (6), 2135–2175.

Mitchell, M., T. Pulvino and E. Stafford, 2004, "Price Pressure Around Mergers," *Journal of Finance*, 59 (1), 31–63.

Moeller, T., 2005, "Let's Make a Deal! How Shareholders Control Impacts Merger Payoff," *Journal of Financial Economics*, 76, 167–190.

Moeller, S. B., F. P. Schlingemann and R. M. Stulz, 2004, "Firm Size and the Gains from Acquisitions," *Journal of Financial Economics*, 73, 201–228.

Moeller, S. B., F. P. Schlingemann and R. M. Stulz, 2005, "Wealth Destruction on a Massive Scale? A Study of Acquiring Firm Returns in the Recent Merger Wave," *Journal of Finance*, 60, 757–782.

Mulherin, J. H. and A. L. Boone, 2000, "Comparing Acquisitions and Divestitures," *Journal of Corporate Finance*, 6, 117–139.

Murphy, K. J., 1999, "Executive Compensation," In: O. Ashenfelter and D. Card (Eds.), *Handbook of Labor Economics, Vol. 3b of Handbook of Labor Economics*, Chapter 38, Elsevier/North-Holland, pp. 2485–2563.

Myers, S. C., 1984, "The Capital Structure Puzzle," *Journal of Finance*, 39, 575–592.

Myers, S. C. and N. S. Majluf, 1984, "Corporate Financing and Investment Decisions When Firms Have Information That Investors Do Not Have," *Journal of Financial Economics*, 13, 187–221.

Offenberg, D., 2009, "Firm Size and the Effectiveness of the Market for Corporate Control," *Journal of Corporate Finance*, 15, 66–79.

Officer, M. S., 2003, "Termination Fees in Mergers and Acquisitions," *Journal of Financial Economics*, 69, 431–467.

Pena, M. F. and H. Unal, 2004, "Gains in Bank Mergers: Evidence from the Bond Markets," *Journal of Financial Economics*, 74, 149–179.

Pulvino, T., 1999, "Effects of Bankruptcy Court Protection on Asset Sales," *Journal of Financial Economics*, 52, 151–186.

Rhodes-Kropf, M. and S. Viswanathan, 2004, "Market Valuation and Merger Waves," *Journal of Finance*, 59, 2685–2718.

Rhodes-Kropf, M., D. T. Robinson and S. Viswanathan, 2005, "Valuation Waves and Merger Activity: The Empirical Evidence," *Journal of Financial Economics*, 77, 561–603.

Roll, R., 1986, "The Hubris Hypothesis of Corporate Takeovers," *Journal of Business*, 59, 437–467.

Rose, M. J., 2009, "Heterogeneous Impacts of Staggered Boards by Ownership Concentration," *Journal of Corporate Finance*, 15, 113–128.

Ross, S., 1977, "The Determination of Financial Structure: The Incentive Signalling Approach," *Bell Journal of Economics*, 8, 23–40.

Rossi, S. and P. F. Volpin, 2004, "Cross-country Determinants of Mergers and Acquisitions," *Journal of Financial Economics*, 74, 277–304.

Schlingemann, F. P., 2004, "Financing Decisions and Bidder Gains," *Journal of Corporate Finance*, 10, 683–701.

Schwert, G. W., 2000, "Hostility in Takeovers: In the Eyes of the Beholder?" *Journal of Finance*, 55, 2599–2640.

Shahrur, H., 2005, "Industry Structure and Horizontal Takeovers: Analysis of Wealth Effects on Rivals, Suppliers, and Corporate Customers," *Journal of Financial Economics*, 76, 61–98.

Shenoy, J., 2008, "An Examination of the Efficiency, Foreclsore, and Collusion Rationales for Vertical Takeovers," Working Paper, Georgia State University.

Shleifer, A. and R. W. Vishny, 1986, "Large Shareholders and Corporate Control," *Journal of Political Economy*, 94, 461–488.

Shleifer, A. and R. W. Vishny, 1992, "Liquidation Values and Debt Capacity: A Market Equilibrium Approach," *Journal of Finance*, 47, 1343–1366.

Shleifer, A. and R. W. Vishny, 2003, "Stock Market Driven Acquisitions," *Journal of Financial Economics*, 70, 295–311.

Song, M. H. and R. A. Walkling, 2000, "Abnormal Returns to Rivals of Acquisition Targets: A Test of the Acquisition Probability Hypothesis," *Journal of Financial Economics*, 55, 143–172.

Stillman, R., 1983, "Examining Antitrust Policy Toward Horizontal Mergers," *Journal of Financial Economics*, 11, 225–240.

Stulz, R., 1988, "Managerial Control of Voting Rights: Financing Policies and the Market for Corporate Control," *Journal of Financial Economics*, 20, 25–54.

Travlos, N. G., 1987, "Corporate Takeover Bids, Method of Payment, and Bidding Firms' Stock Returns," *Journal of Finance*, 42, 943–963.

Walkling, R. A. and M. S. Long, 1984, "Agency Theory, Managerial Welfare, and Takeover Bid Resistance," *RAND Journal of Economics*, xx, 54–68.

Wulf, J., 2004, "Do CEOs in Mergers Trade Power for Premium? Evidence from Mergers of Equals," *Journal of Law, Economics and Organization*, 20, 60–101.

PART 1

SURVEYS OF BIDDING THEORY, AUCTIONS, AND TAKEOVER PREMIUM EVIDENCE

Chapter 1

MERGERS AND ACQUISITIONS: STRATEGIC AND INFORMATIONAL ISSUES*

DAVID HIRSHLEIFER

School of Business Administration, University of Michigan, Ann Arbor, Michigan, USA

Contents

* I thank the anonymous referee for extremely insightful comments, and James Ang, Mark Bagnoli, Henry Cao, Bhagwan Chowdhry, Kent Daniel, Michael Fishman, Milton Harris, Jack Hirshleifer, Barton Lipman, Rene Stulz, Sheridan Titman, Ralph Walkling, and J. Fred Weston for very helpful comments and discussions.

This article originally appeared in B. E. Eckbo (ed.), *Finance* (North-Holland Handbooks in Operation Research and Management Science Series), Ch. 26, 839–885 (1995).

Corporate Takeovers, Volume 2
Edited by B. Espen Eckbo
DOI: 10.1016/B978-0-12-381982-6.00001-X

Keywords

tender offer, share tendering decision, toehold acquisition, optimal bidding, pivotal shareholder, resistance strategies, voting power

JEL classification: C72, C79, G34

1. Introduction

A merger is a transaction that combines two firms, leaving one surviving entity. An acquisition is the purchase of one firm by another individual or firm. Both transactions fall under the more general heading of *takeovers*. Takeovers can play a constructive economic role, for example by removing inefficient management or by achieving economies of scale and complementarity. On the other hand, they can have the possibly less desirable effect of redistributing wealth, as in takeovers that exploit tax benefits or expropriate bondholders or stakeholders. Finally, takeovers may reduce efficiency if they reflect agency problems on the part of bidding managers, or result simply from misjudgments.

There are many important conflicts of interest and informational differences among parties to takeovers: bidding shareholders who only want an acquisition if the price of the target is not too high compared to underlying value, bidding management who may seek self-aggrandization through takeover, target shareholders who wish to obtain a price that fully reflects any possible takeover improvements, target management who wish to retain private benefits of control, and potential competing bidders deciding whether to make their own offers.

This essay describes the relationships between different models of the takeover process, and where possible provides analytical syntheses to integrate major trends in the literature. I focus mainly on three types of models: (1) models of tender offers, which examine the decisions of individual shareholders whether to tender (sell) their shares to a bidder, (2) models of competition among multiple bidders, and (3) models that examine the voting power of target managers who own shares.[1]

Beginning with (1), tender offers to purchase shares directly from shareholders are a crucial mechanism for overcoming management opposition to takeover, as contrasted with merger bids which require management approval. Models of the tender offer process may be classified according to whether (i) all parties are identically informed, or alternatively the bidder has superior information about the posttakeover value of the target; and whether (ii) individual target shareholders take the probability of offer success as given, or else recognize the influence of their individual tendering decisions upon offer success or failure.

Issues (i) and (ii) are important for understanding target managers' defensive measures and bidders' incentives to undertake mergers and acquisitions, and so for the design of regulatory policy. With regard to (i), superior bidder information presents target shareholders with an inference problem. One would expect that this informational disadvantage could lead target shareholders to be skeptical about the adequacy

---

[1] These categories are neither mutually exclusive nor exhaustive. In practice, however, most theoretical papers on takeovers have fallen into one of these categories. Many of the insights from these papers would also apply to other cases, such as the analysis of merger bid when there is little competitive threat, or the analysis of tender offers when there is competitive threat.

of the offer, and thus reluctant to tender their shares. I therefore examine the effect of bidder information on its probability of success and expected profits, and how defensive measures affect the informational advantage.

With regard to (ii), if target shareholders take probability of success as given, then their tendering decisions will be nonstrategic—being based on a simple comparison of gains from tendering or not. If a shareholder's decision influences the probability of success, however, she has a stronger incentive to tender in order to bring about success. This essay will therefore examine the determinants of how likely it is that individual shareholders will be pivotal in determining offer success, and the effect of this probability on the expected profitability of takeovers for bidders.

Turning to point (2), models of competition, any attempt to understand competitive takeover auctions must address the anomaly that bidding in takeover contests generally occurs in a few large jumps, rather than many small increments as predicted by the conventional analysis of bidding in costless English auctions. This essay therefore examines models of costly investigation and costly bid revision, wherein successive bids may increase by large increments when bidders try to intimidate their competitors into quitting. Since the intimidated bidder may be able to increase value more than the intimidator, this may not be a good thing. This leads to consideration of the effects of regulations that influence the cost of investigation and the ease of preemption. I will also consider how the choice of means of payment (cash, equity, or other securities) can signal information, and thus can be used as a tool for preempting competitors.

Finally, with regard to point (3) above, the share ownership and voting power of target management that values control can be important for the outcome of a tender bid and for the bidder's decision whether to undertake a tender offer or a proxy fight. It is therefore important to understand how a manager may be able to alter his effective control of voting rights either directly through share purchases or indirectly through changes in capital structure.

This essay mainly covers topics that have been the focus of several related models that yield divergent results. It is for these topics that integrated discussion and analysis seems most valuable and feasible. The cost of this approach is that many other important topics are not addressed here or are only briefly touched upon. Such topics include the analysis of why takeover occur, bidder/target bargaining, the effect on competition of bidding by well-informed target managers (as in leveraged buyouts), winner's curse effects when bidders with common valuations compete, and the effect of takeover threats on directorial oversight of managers and on investment and operating decisions. Section 7 discusses these issues briefly and gives some literature references.

The remainder of this essay is structured as follows. Section 2 gives a synopsis of empirical material. Section 3 discusses tender offers and share tendering decisions. Section 4 analyzes competitive bidding. Section 5 discusses the means of payment in takeover contests. Section 6 discusses target financing, managerial voting power and private benefits of control. Section 8 concludes.

2. An empirical synopsis

This section lays out some empirical evidence relevant for the theories discussed in this review. The summary will by no means be comprehensive, even for this limited purpose.

Target shareholders on average earn large positive abnormal returns from tender offers, while bidding shareholder abnormal returns are on average close to zero; see, for example, Weston et al. (1990) for summary of empirical evidence. High target returns reflect remarkably high and rising premia in successful contests. Nathan and O'Keefe (1989) report average successful premia for cash tender takeovers that rose from 41% to 75% in the 1963–1973 and 1974–1985 periods, and a rise from rose from 29% to 70% for cash merger premia.

The Williams Act of 1968 and associated legislation requires disclosure and delays completion of tender offers. Tender offer premia decreased after the Williams Act (Nathan and O'Keefe, 1989).[2]

Bradley et al. (1988) provide evidence that the joint market value increase of bidder and target is on average positive. Bradley et al. (1983) find that target stock market gains on average vanish in failed offers where the target is not later acquired by another bidder. Roll (1986) emphasized that stock returns may not accurately measure value improvements to the extent that making a takeover bid reveals information about the stand-alone value of the bidder (e.g., that the bidder has enough funds to afford the offer). However, Bhagat and Hirshleifer (1995) estimate value improvements to be on average positive and substantial using a method that disentangles value improvements from revelation effects.

Bradley et al. (1988) also find that US bidder abnormal stock returns were on average lower in the 1980s than in the 1960s and 1970s. They report that multiple bidder contests provide higher average abnormal target stock returns, and lower bidder returns (close to zero).

Tender offer success versus failure is often highly uncertain, as evidenced by the negative reaction of the target stock price to offer failure (see Bradley et al., 1983; Ruback, 1988; Samuelson and Rosenthal, 1986) and by the positive bidder stock price reaction to success and negative reaction to failure (see Bradley, 1980). Offer success is positively related to the bid premium and to the initial shareholding of the bidder in the target (Walkling, 1985).

Target management defensive measures on average reduce the probability of a takeover occurring (Pound, 1988; Walkling, 1985). The target stock price reaction to greenmail is on average negative (Bradley and Wakeman, 1983; Dann and DeAngelo, 1983), as is the average reaction to antitakeover amendments, poison pills, defensive

---

[2] A persistent upward trend in takeover premia and target abnormal returns began 5 years after the Williams Act. This timing suggests that the change was not related to the Williams Act. A similar increase occurred in the United Kingdom (Franks and Harris, 1989) during the 1970s and 1980s.

restructurings, and several other defensive measures (see, e.g., Bhagat and Jefferis, 1991; Dann and DeAngelo, 1988; Malatesta and Walkling, 1988; Ryngaert, 1988).

There is evidence that target managers can position their firms in ways that alter bidder behavior. Stulz et al. (1990) provide evidence that the bid level is on average higher when target management owns a greater share of the target. Palepu (1986) finds that the probability of a hostile takeover attempt is decreasing with the target's debt-equity ratio.

Certain items of evidence have provided sharp empirical challenges to theories of the takeover transaction process. The traditional solution to the English auctions model with multiple buyers involves many small bid increments. This has faced a glaring challenge from the evidence that takeover bidding occurs by small numbers of enormous jumps, a challenge taken up in Section 4. In Jennings and Mazzeo (1993), the majority of *initial* bid premia were over 20% of the market value of the target 10 days prior to the offer. Since price runup may occur earlier, this is likely to be an underestimate of premia relative to nontakeover value.

A second challenge is provided by the often puzzlingly low ownership in target firms accumulated by bidders prior to making a takeover bid. Given the very high premia paid in tender offers, we would expect bidders to buy up shares at the open market price prior to the bid up to the limits of market liquidity. In fact, the majority of tender offer bidders own no target shares (Bradley et al., 1988),[3] and even among those that do, the potential profit on these holdings appears to be modest compared to bidding costs (Bhagat and Hirshleifer, 1995). This challenge is taken up by theories discussed in Section 3.1.5.

A third empirical challenge is the mixed evidence regarding the effect of means of payment (stock vs. fixed payments) on bidder and target stock abnormal stock returns. There is evidence, consistent with the Myers and Majluf (1984) adverse selection problem with equity issuance, that bidder and target returns for stock offers are on average lower than for cash offers (see, e.g., Huang and Walkling, 1987 on target returns). However, the US result that average abnormal bidder returns are negative in stock offers does not apply in France, the United Kingdom, or Canada (Eckbo et al., 1990 and citations therein). Furthermore, Lang et al. (1991) report that the effect of means of payment in the United States is subsumed by a cash flow variable. The associated theoretical issues are discussed in Section 5.

3. Tender offers and share tendering decisions

A tender offer can be either conditional or unconditional. A conditional offer is not binding on the bidder unless a given number of shares are tendered. An offer may require acceptance of all tendered shares (an unrestricted offer), or alternatively the

---

[3] In a sample of successful post-1968 offers, Stulz et al. (1990) find a positive median bidder share ownership of 2.35% among successful offers, and a 4.75% ownership in successful single bidder contests.

bidder may not be obliged to purchase more than a prespecified number of shares (a restricted offer). An offer that is unconditional and unrestricted is often called an "any-or-all" offer.

Consider a bidder who can increase the value of the target only if he obtains control. Except where otherwise specified, in this essay the nontakeover value of the target firm is normalized to zero. Also, I assume that the bidder obtains no control unless he succeeds in buying a given fraction of target shares, in which event he obtains complete control. Let v be the posttakeover value of a firm's shares. Ignoring taxes, a risk-neutral target shareholder i should tender if the price offered for the firm's shares, b, exceeds the expected value of her share if she retains it:

$$\text{Tender if } b > \text{Pr}(\text{Success}|i \text{ Retain})v. \tag{1}$$

A target shareholder will be more willing to tender if she believes that posttakeover value v is low, and if she believes that her individual decision not to tender will reduce the takeover's probability of succeeding.

Section 3.1 presents a model (due to Grossman and Hart, 1980; Hirshleifer and Titman, 1990; Shleifer and Vishny, 1986a) in which each shareholder believes he will not be pivotal. This model allows for possible informational superiority of the bidder. Section 3.2 discusses models (by Bagnoli and Lipman, 1988; Holmström and Nalebuff, 1992) which allow for the fact that individual shareholders are sometimes pivotal, but assume symmetric information.

3.1. A nonpivotal shareholder model

3.1.1. The model under complete information

Consider a bidder who can increase the value of the target to $100 per share if he obtains control, which requires >50% of the target's shares. Assume the offer is conditional upon obtaining control. Under some circumstances, he will be unable to profit on the shares that he purchases owing to a free-rider problem among target shareholders (Bradley, 1980; Grossman and Hart, 1980). Suppose he makes a rather generous offer of $80 per share. Each shareholder reasons that if the offer fails, the value of her retained shares remains the same regardless of whether she tenders; while if the offer succeeds, she is better off receiving the posttakeover value of $100 than the offered price of $80. Thus, each shareholder will retain her shares, and the offer will fail, even though its success would be jointly profitable for shareholders. The paradoxical conclusion is that a bidder cannot succeed in a tender offer except at a price that gives all the potential profits to the target shareholders. If there is any cost of investigation or bidding, the bidder actually loses money. Empirically, the evidence cited earlier on bidder and target stock returns are fairly consistent with this conclusion, particularly in the 1980s.

Nevertheless, bidders may reap a profit if they can dilute the value of minority shares after a takeover (Grossman and Hart, 1980).[4] The threat of dilution may induce target shareholders to tender at a price low enough for the bidder to profit. Alternatively, if the bidder himself owns shares in the target prior to the offer, he can reap a profit even without dilution. By improving firm value, he increases the value of his own shares (Shleifer and Vishny, 1986a).[5]

To illustrate these points, let the posttakeover value of the target be v, the fraction that can be diluted be δ, the initial fractional shareholding of the bidder in the target be α, the level of the conditional tender offer be b, and the cost of bidding be c^B.[6] Under complete information, a risk neutral target shareholder will tender if the price offered exceeds the diluted posttakeover value, that is

Tender if $b > (1 - \delta)v$.   (2)

Assume that the bidder needs to buy an additional fraction of at least ω of the firm's shares, over and above his initial fraction α, to obtain control. The equilibrium strategy pair for the bidder is to offer just above $(1 - \delta)v$, and for all shareholders to tender at this price. If the offer is unrestricted (so that all tendered shares are purchased), he therefore purchases all $1 - \alpha$ shares, for a profit of

$$\alpha v + (1 - \alpha)(v - b) - c^B.$$ (3)

Combining Equation (2) with Equation (3) gives the following proposition.

Proposition 1   *Under complete information, the bidder's profit in a conditional unrestricted offer is*

$$\alpha v + (1 - \alpha)\delta v - c^B.$$

The first term is the improvement in value of the bidder's initial shareholding. The second term is the profit on the shares purchased in the tender offer. If follows trivially (letting α and δ approach zero) that:

Proposition 2   *Under complete information, if a bidder's initial shareholding (α) in the target and dilution opportunities (δ) are sufficiently small, then a conditional unrestricted tender offer is unprofitable.*

---

[4] In other words, the bidder can exclude (nontendering) minority target shareholders from part of the posttakeover value of the target firm. For example, the bidder, having obtained control, may be able to choose the price in a merger with the target (subject to legal constraints). Or the bidder may be able to buy assets of the target at a below-market price. A restricted two-tier offer can be profitable if nontendering minority shareholders can be forced to accept less than tendering shareholders. This will be the case if there is a credible dilution threat.

[5] Since this internalizes only a fraction of the value improvement, the bidder still has a suboptimal incentive to make a bid.

[6] Since the non-takeover value has been set to zero, the possibility that the bidder can extract value from the target's assets-in-place (rather than just appropriating part of the takeover improvement) has been excluded.

Four further points are worth noting. First, diluting target value may be costly, in the sense that the bidder's gain is less than target shareholder's loss. If so, then it is a dominant strategy for the bidder to make an unrestricted offer as assumed above.[7] Second, the second term in Proposition 1 shows that having an initial shareholding reduces the value of the dilution threat, because to some extent the bidder would be diluting his own holdings. Third, the profit deriving from initial shareholdings tends to be fairly small because of low shareholdings (see empirical synopsis). Fourth, if a shareholder may be pivotal, or if the offer is unconditional, then a threat by the bidder to reduce the target's nontakeover value would also encourage shareholders to tender.[8]

3.1.2. Share tendering decisions under asymmetric information

A bidder usually knows what he plans to do with the target better than target shareholders. Superficially, it might appear that a bidder could on average profit even without dilution or an initial shareholding, based on superior information about the posttakeover value of the target (v). However, rational expectations (or in game--theoretic terminology, perfect Bayesian equilibrium) implies that if the bidders were on average offering less than posttakeover value in tender offers, shareholders would be aware of this and would refuse to tender. Thus, the free-rider problem remains when asymmetric information is introduced.

In such a generalized model, two equilibria are of interest. In one, the price offered is uninformative, and offers always succeed (Shleifer and Vishny, 1986a). In the other, the level of the offer reveals the bidder's valuation, and the probability of offer success increases with the amount offered (Hirshleifer and Titman, 1990).[9]

3.1.2.1. Uninformative offer levels

If a bidder's information about posttakeover value or about potential dilution is superior to that of target shareholders, then shareholders must draw some inference about the bidder's valuation from the level of the offer. Shleifer and Vishny (1986a) provide a model in which the level of the offer is uninformative in equilibrium, because shareholders foresee perfectly the price that will be offered if a bid occurs. Since it is assumed that at any offer level the bidder knows with certainty whether shareholders will tender, the equilibrium price offered is set to be just high enough to induce shareholders to accept the offer. When indifferent, it is assumed that target shareholders tender. For simplicity, assume that there is no

---

[7] If there is no wastage, then whether the offer is restricted is a matter of indifference. Even if wastage is arbitrarily close to 100%, as Proposition 1 shows, the bidder benefits substantially from the threat of dilution since it allows him to buy shares cheaply.

[8] Gilbert and Newbery (1988) examine a model in which a bidder acquires cheaply because he can threaten to enter an industry and reduce the profits of a member of an oligopoly.

[9] In what follows, it is assumed that the only information asymmetry is about posttakeover value v; information is symmetric about the initial shareholding α. Regulations require the bidder to file information about share ownership with the S.E.C. at the time of the bid.

dilution ($\delta = 0$), that bidding is costless ($c^B = 0$), and that (possibly owing to financing costs) the offer is restricted to the minimum additional fraction of the firms shares needed for control, ω.

Then to persuade target shareholders to tender, a bidder must offer target shareholders at least

$$b^* = E[v|\text{Offer}], \tag{4}$$

where the RHS is the expected valuation of the bidder given that he makes an offer. In the proposed equilibrium, a bidder with low valuation cannot reduce the amount offered, because if he bid any less, $b < b^*$, shareholders would infer that his valuation was higher than the amount offered, $v > b$, and so would retain their shares. Thus, the probability of success $P(b)$ is a step function of the level of the offer, that is, $P(b) = 0$ if $b < E[v]$ and $P(b) = 1$ if $b \geq E[v]$ (as illustrated by the dark line segments in Figure 1).

Proposition 3 *Under asymmetric information, there is an equilibrium in which a bidder who makes an offer pays a price equal to the expected posttakeover valuation of the shares he purchases. His gain on the shares he buys is positive if the improvement v is high, and is negative if v is low. He derives an expected profit from the increase in value of his initial shareholding in the target.*

On average a bidder does not profit on the shares purchased in a tender offer. (If he did, shareholders would not want to tender!) A bidder with valuation v close to zero will not make an offer, because he takes a loss on the shares purchased in the offer of $v - b^*$, and his initial holding profit αv is low. For larger v, the bidder's profits both on shares purchased and on the initial holding increase. There is a critical value v^* such

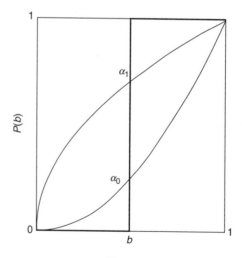

Fig. 1.

that profits are zero. The bidder makes an offer if and only if $v > v^*$. Thus, the bid in Equation (4) is $b^* = E[v|v > v^*]$.[10]

3.1.2.2. Revealing offer levels   The bidder's gain from succeeding is increasing with its valuation of the target. Since a low offer reduces the probability of offer success (Walkling, 1985), a low-valuation bidder has a stronger incentive to save money by defecting to a low offer than a high-valuation bidder.[11] The probability of a low offer succeeding is greater to the extent that the bidder can persuade shareholders that his improvement is small, since this encourages shareholders to tender (Equation (1)). Since high-valuation bidders have a stronger incentive to bid high, a bidder can reveal a lower valuation credibly by bidding less.

In order to examine the revealing equilibrium of the tender offer model, let $P(b; \alpha, \omega)$ be an offer's probability of success given a bid of b by a bidder with initial shareholding of α who needs a further ω shares to obtain control. The bidder chooses a bid level to maximize his expected profit, so he solves

$$\max_b [\alpha v + (v - b)\omega]P(b; \alpha, \omega). \tag{5}$$

The first-order condition for this problem is

$$P'(b)[\alpha v + (v - b)\omega] = P(b)\omega. \tag{6}$$

Assuming an interior solution for b, and parametrically differentiating Equation (6) with respect to v, implies the following proposition (see Hirshleifer and Titman, 1990).

Proposition 4   *Suppose that a bidder faces an exogenous probability of offer success function that is twice differentiable and increasing with the amount bid. If an interior optimal level of the bid exists for each bidder valuation, then the level of the bid is increasing in the bidder's valuation of the target (db/dv > 0). Therefore, the bidder's information is fully revealed by his bid.*

This proposition takes shareholder behavior as exogenous, so we cannot yet conclude that there is a revealing equilibrium. One is displayed later. Proposition 4, however, shows that almost any reasonable model of tender offers will lead to separation for at least a range of bidder types. For example, in a model in which target management can take defensive action but cannot with perfect effectiveness "just say no," we expect the intensity of opposition to the takeover to decrease with the amount

---

[10] If bidding is costly, the critical value increases. An empirical implication is that if the cost of bidding decreases, the critical level for bidding decreases, so premia on average decrease.

[11] A low-valuation bidder who makes a lower bid will profit under a wider set of shareholder responses than a high-valuation bidder. This suggests that investors should believe his valuation is low, and should accept his offer. Thus, the pooling equilibrium of the preceding section is removed by the strong refinement criterion of Banks and Sobel (1987). However, the pooling equilibrium survives several other criteria, such as those of Grossman and Perry (1986) and Cho and Kreps (1987).

bid, so the probability of offer success should increase smoothly. Such a model leads to full revelation. A steadily increasing probability of success as a function of the bid can also be derived from a model where shareholders have different capital gains bases (Bagwell, 1991; Stulz, 1988).[12] In the pooling equilibrium of the previous section, there is no revelation because it violates the assumption of a continuous probability of success.

In the model developed here, there is a unique equilibrium in which the level of the bid is a fully revealing signal of the bidder's valuation. In this equilibrium, the bidder offers his valuation, the minimum amounted needed to have a chance of succeeding, $b = v$ (compare with Equation (4)). Instead of assuming that indifferent shareholders always tender, let us now (consistent with evidence cited earlier) allow for the possibility that the outcome of the offer is uncertain from the viewpoint of the bidder. This uncertainty is modeled as arising from randomization by shareholders as to whether to tender in a mixed strategy equilibrium.[13] In the mixed strategy equilibrium, the bidder's uncertainty about his probability of success at different bid levels is such that he optimally makes a bid that leaves shareholders indifferent as to whether to tender. Imposing the indifference condition ($b = v$) in Equation (6) leads to a differential equation that determines the probability of success,

$$\frac{P'(b)}{P(b)} = \frac{\omega}{\alpha b}.$$

(7)

The relevant boundary condition is that the highest possible bid (made by the highest valuation bidder) always succeeds, $P(\bar{v}) = 1$. The solution,

$$P(b; \alpha) = \left(\frac{b}{\bar{v}}\right)^{\omega/\alpha},$$

(8)

is illustrated by the dark curves in Figure 1. The probability of an offer's success increases with the bid premium and with the initial holding α (consistent with evidence cited earlier) of Walkling (1985), and decreases with the number of additional shares needed for control ω.[14] Offer failure is caused by the informational superiority of the bidder. Shareholders recognize the bidder's temptation to offer less than the

---

[12] Pooling among the highest valuation types, however, remains a possibility because if a very high offer is sure to succeed, above this bid level $P(b)$ is no longer increasing.

[13] A mixed strategy equilibrium is a way of modeling the fact that, owing to small amounts of uncertainty about payoffs, the behavior of some players (target shareholders) seems uncertain from the point of view of another player (the bidder) (see Harsanyi, 1973). For example, the bidder may not know the liquidity or capital gains tax considerations that affect shareholders' tender decisions.

[14] Thus, a supermajority antitakeover amendment reduces the probability of offer success. An untested implication of the model is that the ratio of the target stock price increase at the announcement of the bid to the bid premium is increasing in both the bid level and α, and decreasing in ω. The model also implies that average premia are lower when the initial shareholding α is higher (consistent with evidence of Walkling and Edmister, 1985), and when the required number of shares ω is lower.

posttakeover value of their shares, and are therefore reluctant to tender at low prices (i.e., they tender with lower probability). The model therefore predicts that actions that improve the information of target shareholders will (by shifting the upper bound $\bar{v}$ in Equation (8) downward toward the true value $v < \bar{v}$) increase the probability of offer success.[15]

Like an initial shareholding, proportional dilution increases the benefit to achieving success. It therefore increases the incentive to bid high. This reduces shareholders' skepticism of the offer, and increases the probability of offer success.[16]

This model assumes that if the offer fails, the bidder does not acquire the target and hence loses a valuable profit opportunity. In reality, if an offer fails, the bidder can revise his offer upward. This opportunity can potentially eliminate the separating equilibrium. In order for a separating equilibrium to survive, it is crucial that failure impose an opportunity cost on the bidder that is increasing in the size of the potential value improvement. This can occur for several reasons: (1) initial failure gives entrenched managers more time to mobilize blocking defensive strategies, (2) failure may give target management time to announce changes that preempt the potential takeover improvement, (3) loss of time can involve the loss of a window of opportunity to exploit a synergy between the firms, and (4) rejection may give a competing bidder time to enter. The arrival of a competitor is costly to a bidder who hopes to profit by diluting minority shareholders (see Hirshleifer and Titman, 1990, section I.D.). In evaluating defensive measures in the next section, it should be kept in mind that the efficiency consequences of failure of an initial offer depend on which of the costs of failure listed above are relevant.

3.1.3. Management defensive strategies

We focus in this section on the revealing equilibrium, since it permits analysis of how defensive strategies affect the information revealed by the bid and the probability of offer success.

3.1.3.1. Effects on incentive to bid high A manager who values control may oppose takeover for his own purposes. As an extreme example, if a target manager is expected to be able to block any reasonable offer, then no offer will be made. The Grossman and

---

[15] This is consistent with Walkling's (1985) evidence that share solicitation activity increases the probability of success.

[16] Asquith (1991) extends this model by allowing for a probability that the bidding manager is afflicted with "hubris" (see Roll, 1986) in the sense that he incorrectly believes he can increase target value (i.e., he believes that $v > 0$ when actually $v = 0$). Asquith shows that the presence of hubristic bidders allows nonhubristic bidders to profit, even without dilution and without initial shareholdings. Target shareholders become willing to tender even if rational bidders offer below posttakeover value owing to the chance that the offer is from a hubristic bidder. Thus hubris can improve efficiency despite the obvious cost of inefficient takeovers.

Hart model without dilution (Section 3.1.1) suggests that defensive measures are undesirable, as there is already too little incentive to make an offer. They suggest that target shareholders, in order to attract later takeovers, will write corporate charters that encourage dilution, for example, the absence of defensive antitakeover provisions such as "fair price" amendments or classified boards (see Jarrell and Poulsen, 1987). However, the incentive of target shareholders to permit dilution is too weak, because extracting a high price from the bidder provides shareholders with a redistributive gain.

On the other hand, if a bidder has substantial opportunities for dilution, then target shareholders can benefit from defensive activity to force a higher bid (DeAngelo and Rice, 1983). There is a time-inconsistency problem here, however, in that the ex post benefit to shareholders of forcing a higher price conflicts with the ex ante benefit of encouraging potential bidders to investigate the target.

In practice, US courts have allowed firms to reject takeover offers at will based upon the "business judgement" of target management. Target management's incentive to block low-priced offers is greater when management's share ownership is high. The key exception in which the target management may be coerced into selling is if it has already begun negotiating sale of the firm to another buyer. Once the firm has been put in play in this fashion, management is obligated to auction the firm and attempt to get the best deal for shareholders.

Since a defensive measure can induce a high offer, when information is asymmetric defensive measures can reduce shareholders' skepticism, and thereby increase the probability of offer success. Consider a threat to block the offer unless an offer of over $\bar{v}$ is made. Since the bidder must then offer $b > \bar{v}$, shareholders should always tender, and the offer will always succeed. More generally, if the cost or risk of failure imposed on the bidder by the defensive strategy is greater when the bid is lower, then the bidder is encouraged to bid higher, so that shareholders probabilistically become more willing to tender (Hirshleifer and Titman, 1990).

These results are summarized as follows.

Proposition 5 *A management defensive strategy, by blocking takeover, can harm target shareholders and reduce efficiency. However, by increasing the incentive to bid high, such a measure can also increase the probability of offer success and improve efficiency.*

Other defensive measures reduce the incentive to bid high, and therefore reduce the probability of success. A poison pill, by increasing the value of nontendered shares after a successful offer, acts as the opposite of dilution (see Section 3.1.1 earlier). Thus, it reduces the incentive to ensure success by bidding high. More generally, strategies that impose greater costs on the bidder when his offer succeeds than when it fails reduce the incentive to bid high, since they reduce the gain from success. For example, an antitakeover amendment ("shark repellent") such as staggered board terms that delays transfer of control to the bidder in the event of offer success will reduce bid levels, and so the probability of success. Evidence cited earlier indicating that defensive measures tend to prevent takeover from occurring (Pound, 1988; Walkling, 1985) suggests that target managers may often be acting against shareholder interest by adopting those strategies that prevent takeovers.

3.1.3.2. Effects on asymmetry of information   A subtler effect of defensive strategies is to change the informational advantage of the bidder over target shareholders. Consider a value-reduction strategy, defined as a defensive activity that reduces the posttakeover value of the target. An example would be the sale of an asset that, as part of the target, could be improved by the bidder ("sale of the crown jewels," also known as the "scorched earth defense"). A value-reducing defensive measure can reduce or increase informational asymmetry. Suppose that the bidder can increase the value of the target by $v = x + y$, where x is an improvement that is known to shareholders perfectly while y is known to the bidder but not the target. If a value-reduction strategy eliminates the possibility of the unknown improvement y, then the informational asymmetry is removed, and the bidder can ensure success by offering just above x. Thus, a value-reduction strategy can reduce informational asymmetry and promote success.

Conversely, if a value-reduction strategy eliminates the known improvement x, then the probability of success is

$$P(b; \alpha) = \left(\frac{b}{\bar{y}}\right)^{\omega/\alpha}. \tag{9}$$

The probability of success at any level of the bid b is higher than in Equation (8).[17] However, the probability of success is reduced for a given bidder because he bids less when his valuation is reduced.[18]

Proposition 6   *A value-reduction defensive strategy, by decreasing (increasing) the importance of publicly known improvements relative to improvements known privately by the bidder, can decrease (increase) the probability of tender offer success.*

3.1.4. Target private information

The target as well as the bidder may have private information. If the target is undervalued by the market, then by signaling high value, managers can make shareholders less willing to tender. Increasing leverage and repurchasing shares, actions which can signal high value, are often used defensively. Ofer and Thakor (1987) analyze signaling through repurchase; Bagnoli et al. (1989) analyze repurchase signaling as a defensive strategy.

---

[17] This is not surprising, since a given level of the bid becomes more attractive when compared to a smaller posttakeover value.
[18] Without the value-reduction measure, the probability of a bidder with valuation v succeeding is $(v/\bar{v})^{\omega/\alpha}$. With the defensive measure, the probability is $[(v - x)/(\bar{v} - x)]^{\omega/\alpha}$.

3.1.5. Pretender offer share acquisition

Prior to announcing his offer, a takeover bidder has private information about an event that will increase the market price of the target's stock. This leads to an incentive to acquire shares of the target quietly at a lower price. Pretakeover share acquisition is limited by disclosure requirements and by the depth of the market, because in a thin market a large purchase of shares will more quickly reveal the information of an informed trader. Kyle and Vila (1991) point out that if the possibility of a takeover is foreseen, then a potential bidder can profit by either buying shares secretly before making a takeover bid or selling shares short and not making a bid.

In any case, the evidence mentioned in the empirical synopsis that the majority of actual tender offer bidders do not accumulate *any* target shares is puzzling. One explanation has to do with the desire to signal low valuation to target shareholders. Since a high-valuation bidder has an incentive to bid higher (see Section 3.1.2.2), he has a stronger incentive to accumulate shares prior to the offer. But this means that the disclosure of the initial shareholding required at the time of an offer for a US firm reveals the bidder's valuation. It follows that there is an incentive to accumulate fewer shares in order to persuade target shareholders to tender their shares at a lower price (Chowdhry and Jegadeesh, 1994).[19]

3.1.6. The general free-rider problem

The free-rider problem has been discussed in the context of conditional tender offers. However, the conclusion that in the absence of dilution and initial holdings the bidder cannot profit holds very generally, so long as target shareholders do not perceive themselves to be pivotal.

Let us define a *tender offer* as an offer to buy shares in which the same prespecified price is offered for all purchased shares, no share is purchased unless it is tendered by the shareholder, and if it is tendered, whether it is purchased is a function of the tendering decisions of all shareholders.[20] Suppose that there are two control states, bidder control and target control, leading to target firm values of v or 0, respectively. The state is determined by whether the critical fraction of shares is tendered.

If a shareholder is virtually never pivotal, then she perceives herself as being in a virtually constant-sum game with the bidder. Shareholders as a whole are in a

---

[19] Another possible explanation for low initial holdings is that the bidder wishes to keep the preoffer share price low, if the legally permissible amount of dilution in a freeze-out merger is constrained by this price (Ravid and Spiegel, 1991).

[20] These conditions hold for both conditional and unconditional offers, for either restricted or unrestricted offers, and for offers in which oversubscription leads to pro-rationing, first-come-first-serve, or to discrimination by the bidder amongst different shareholders in acceptance of shares.

nonconstant sum game with the bidder, but any individual shareholder partakes of only a vanishingly small fraction of the joint benefit derived from her decision to tender. Thus, any offer that gives the individual shareholder an expected profit will give the bidder an expected loss on purchases from that shareholder.

Let the cost of bidding be $c^B > 0$. For brevity and clarity of notation, let it be assumed that shareholders tender all or none of their shares; the result does not depend on this assumption.

Definition   A shareholder is *pivotal* if, given the actions of the other shareholders, her decision of whether to tender determines whether the bidder obtains control.

The word "pivotal" might seem to suggest that there is always exactly one pivotal shareholder. This is far from the case. For example, if there are three identical shareholders, and if all (or if none) tender, then none of them are pivotal. If one or two tender, then two are pivotal. One might expect that in a very widely held firm with small shareholders, shareholders will be very unlikely to be pivotal because it is unlikely that the number of shares tendered will be close to the borderline. The following result, which is in the spirit of Grossman and Hart (1980), shows that such a situation leads to zero gross profits for a takeover bidder. Net of bidding costs, the bidder's profit becomes negative, so no offer occurs.

Proposition 7   *Holding constant the value improvement v but allowing the distribution of target share ownership to vary, as the probability of any shareholder being pivotal approaches zero the bidder's expected gross profit becomes arbitrarily close to zero.*

Proof. See Appendix.

The conclusion of this proposition is not at all surprising given the critical premise that the probability of a shareholder being pivotal is small. This assumption is not valid in all models, as discussed in Section 3.2. If an individual shareholder's decision can cause an offer to succeed when otherwise it will fail or *vice versa*, that is, if he may be pivotal, then he should tender if the price offered exceeds the expected value of her shares *given that she does not tender*. This latter quantity may be below the expected value given that she does tender. This wedge allows the bidder to make a profit on purchased shares.

3.2.   When are shareholders pivotal?

This section discusses the conditions under which pivotality can be important. Section 3.2.1 points out that large shareholdings lead to pivotality. Sections 3.2.2 and 3.2.3 discuss equilibria in which pivotality is important even in widely held firms. Section 3.2.4 examines the effect on bidder profits of the ability to bid repeatedly. In Section 3.2.5, I argue that pivotality in widely held firms may not provide a plausible solution to the free-rider problem.

3.2.1. Block size

The larger the blocks held by target shareholders, the larger the probability of being pivotal, and so the greater the incentive to tender. Since in reality there are large blockholders even in many large firms, this is an important escape from the free-rider problem.[21]

Holmström and Nalebuff (1992) point out that the increased probability of offer success resulting from the tender of one share by a blockholder increases the expected value of retaining her other shares. A large blockholder therefore has a greater incentive to tender some of her shares than a small one, leading to an equilibrium that gets close to equalizing the number of nontendered shares by larger stockholders. By tendering only a fraction of her shares, a blockholder partly internalizes the benefit accruing to nontendering shareholders.

3.2.2. Pure strategy equilibria with pivotal shareholders

Under complete information, in either a conditional or an unconditional tender offer, there are many equilibria in which just enough shares are tendered to cause a transfer of control. Consider a conditional tender offer for 20,000 shares in a takeover that will increase value. Consider a set of shareholders whose shares total to exactly 20,000. An equilibrium is for these shareholders to tender all their shares, and for the others to retain their shares. In the equilibrium, If any shareholder were to tender one less share, the offer would fail, reducing the value of her nontendered shares. Thus, a bidder can succeed with a very small premium (Bagnoli and Lipman, 1988), apparently solving the free-rider problem.

Proposition 8 *Under complete information, and in the absence of management defensive measures, in both an unconditional tender offer and a conditional offer for the minimum number of shares required to shift control, there exist strong Nash equilibria in which the bidder offers just above zero and receives exactly enough shares to transfer control. Therefore the bidder can effect any desirable change in the target even if he owns no shares in the target and cannot dilute.*

3.2.3. Mixed strategy equilibria with pivotal shareholders

There are also many mixed strategy equilibria in which shareholders are sometimes pivotal. Continuing the assumption of complete information, let us focus on any-or-all offers. Intuitively, if other shareholders tender with high probability, then the offer is likely to succeed, in which case a given shareholder would do better to retain her shares; while if other shareholders tender with low probability, then the offer is likely

---

[21] This is related to the general principle, important in the theory of political pressure groups, that the small free-ride on the large (see Olson, 1965).

to fail, in which case a given shareholder does better by tendering. Thus, there is a stable outcome in which shareholders tender with intermediate probability (see Bagnoli and Lipman, 1988; Holmström and Nalebuff, 1992).[22]

To develop this point, I follow the presentation of Holmström and Nalebuff (1992). Consider a firm with N risk neutral shareholders each of whom owns a single share. Suppose that the bidder needs exactly K shares to obtain control. It is informative to focus on the symmetric equilibrium in which shareholders randomize with identical probabilities. Let the improved value of the target be $v = 1$. Shareholder i's tendering decision will be based on a comparison of the certainty of receiving the per-share offer price b/N versus a probability $P(b|i$ does not tender$)$ of the per-share improved value of the firm $1/N$. She will be indifferent if

$$b = P(b|i \text{ does not tender}). \tag{10}$$

Let $p(b)$ be the probability that a single shareholder tenders, and let $P(b)$ be the probability that the offer succeeds given equilibrium behavior by all shareholders. Then the bidder's expected surplus is the difference between the total expected surplus, $P(b)$, and the expected surplus going to shareholders, b. Thus, the bidder's expected surplus is

$$P(b) - b = P(b) - P(b|i \text{ does not tender }). \tag{11}$$

On the RHS, $P(b)$ is the probability that at least K shareholders tender, and $P(b|i$ does not tender$)$ is the probability that at least K shareholders other than i tender. The difference is therefore the probability that the other shareholders tender exactly $K - 1$ shares, and shareholder i also tenders, that is,

$$_{N-1}C_{K-1}p(b)^K[1 - p(b)]^{N-K}, \tag{12}$$

where $_{N-1}C_{K-1}$ is the number of combinations by which $K - 1$ tendering shareholders other than shareholder i can be selected from the $N - 1$ possible shareholders. Maximizing this quantity over p (which the bidder controls through b) gives the following proposition.

Proposition 9 *In the symmetric equilibrium of the any-or-all tender offer game of this section, the tendering probability is $p^* = K/N$, and the bidder's expected profit is positive. This profit approaches zero,* ceteris paribus, *as the number of shareholders N becomes large.*

By making the expected number of shares tendered equal to the number of shares needed for success, the bidder maximizes the probability that a given shareholder will be pivotal. The proposition's last statement is shown in Bagnoli and Lipman (1988).

---

[22] Intuitively, if an individual shareholder does not know the precise liquidity or capital gains situation of other shareholders, from her point of view their behavior is random. The logic described in the text causes shareholders to be near indifference, so that small uncertainties about payoffs lead to substantial uncertainty about behavior.

Holmström and Nalebuff examine a more general setting in which shareholders hold any number of shares. They find an equilibrium in which all sufficiently large shareholders tender down to a common range of either m or $m + 1$ shares. Large shareholders randomize between these two possibilities, the offer sometimes succeeds and sometimes fails, and the bidder makes a positive gross profit. Those with less than m shares do not tender. Since each large shareholder randomizes over just a single share, if the number of outstanding shares is large compared to the number of shareholders, the fraction of the firm tendered is always very close to the minimum needed to shift control.

If the number of shares is increased through stock splits, in the limit, even if the firm is widely held, the takeover almost surely succeeds, and the bidder's gross profit approaches fraction f of the takeover improvement, where f is the fraction of the shares needed to obtain control.[23] This equilibrium becomes very similar to the pure strategy equilibria of Section 3.2.2, in which just enough shares are tendered to ensure success and make shareholders pivotal. Here, the probability of failure must approach zero, because in equilibrium each shareholder can ensure success at low cost by tendering a vanishingly small additional fraction of her shares. Thus, they are always pivotal.

An implication of the Holmström-Nalebuff analysis is that if each shareholder holds a single share, then a supermajority antitakeover amendment, which increase the number of shares needed for control, increases the probability of offer success by increasing the probability that shareholders will be pivotal. The reason for this is that the probability that a shareholder is pivotal decreases with the variance in the total number of shares tendered. A supermajority rule corresponds to a higher probability of tendering in the mixed strategy equilibrium, which (with a tendering probability of greater than $1/2$) corresponds to a lower variance.[24]

3.2.4. The effects of offer revision with pivotal shareholders

The ability of a bidder to make repeated offers for a given target may be very important for the strategic structure of the takeover auction (see, e.g., the discussion at the end of Section 3.1.2.2). The option to bid a second time after failing to obtain control in an initial bid must benefit the bidder ex post, because he may obtain control on his second try. However, the possibility of a later offer reduces a shareholder's incentive to tender initially. The balance between these effects is not obvious. Harrington and Prokop (1993) find that with discounting, as the time between offers approaches zero, the expected gross profit to a tender offer bidder approaches zero. Their numerical

---

[23] In a widely held firm, notwithstanding the fact that shareholders retain some of their shares, each internalizes only a small fraction of total value improvement arising from takeover. This is offset by the fact that there are many such shareholders, and each has a significant chance of being pivotal.

[24] Empiricists should note that this implication is the opposite of that of Hirshleifer and Titman (1990) discussed in Section 3.1.2, in which supermajority amendments reduce the probability of offer success by reducing the incentive to bid high (see footnote 15).

simulations based on reasonable parameter values imply that bidders can obtain less than 1% of the takeover surplus.

3.2.5. Plausibility of equilibria with pivotal shareholders

The equilibria described in Sections 3.2.3 and 3.2.4, in which bidders profit on shares purchased because shareholders are often pivotal, are based on delicate coordination amongst shareholders. Realistically, in a firm with many small shareholders, it seems unlikely that shareholders perceive themselves to have a significant chance of being pivotal. Why don't the models match the *a priori* intuition?

In general, in games with many players, a plausible equilibrium (I contend) should be robust with respect to "misbehavior" by a small (though not necessarily infinitesimal) fraction of individuals. Consider a widely held firm of N shareholders, and suppose that h of the shareholders will not tender their shares in the relevant range of offer prices, where h is a discrete random variable, $0 \leq h \leq H$, and H/N is "small," but not infinitesimal (say 1/50).[25]

I make the quantitative conjecture that under mild conditions on the distribution of h, there will be no equilibrium in which shareholders have a significant chance of being pivotal. The reason is that, not knowing h, strategic shareholders have no way of knowing how many shares they must jointly tender in order to make the offer succeed. Suppose shareholdings are identical, for example, with $H = 100$, and $N = 5000$. Substantial exogenous uncertainty about the characteristics of even 100 shareholders would seem to make it exceedingly unlikely that the decision of a single shareholder will determine success or failure.

In experiments in which shareholders can tender all or none of their shares, Kale and Noe (1991) provide evidence that is only partly consistent with the argument provided here. They found that the probability of success in conditional tender offers to 41 shareholders was at some prices substantially below that predicted by a mixed strategy equilibrium with pivotal shareholders. However, the probability of success in any-or-all offers to 32 shareholders was greater than the equilibrium prediction.

4. Competitive bidding

Most models of the free-rider problem assume only one bidder for a given target. The models of competing bids discussed here generally makes the assumption that the target will always accept the highest offer made by any bidder, so long as it is above some minimum reservation price.

---

[25] This "misbehavior" could be rational, if their are costs of tendering such as locked in capital gains of size known only to the individual. The upper bound H could be quite low, for example, 1/50 of outstanding shares, but the argument may fail if probability bunches too close to zero. Thus, the plausibility concept suggested here differs in this respect from Selten's trembling hand equilibrium.

The analysis in this section should thus be viewed as referring to merger bids, or else to tender offers in which the threat of dilution limits free-riding. We focus on models of competitive bidding in which bidders have differing private valuations of a target, and examine the effects of investigation costs and bidding costs on auction outcomes.

Perhaps the simplest model of takeover bidding is the standard analysis of English auctions. In this model, bidders *costlessly* make offers and counteroffers, each bid incrementally higher than the previous one, until the bidder with highest valuation wins at a price equal to the valuation of the second highest bidder. I will call this outcome the *ratchet solution*.

In the conventional English auction analysis, rather than paying a substantial initial premium, an initial bidder should bid the minimum reservation price, and increase the offer only if a competitor actually arrives. Suppose that the first bidder (*FB*) has a known valuation of $v_1 = \$80$, and a potential competing bidder (*SB*) has a valuation of $v_2 = \$0, \$30$ or $\$100$ with equal probability. Normalize the reservation price of the target to zero. Then *FB* will begin with a bid of zero. If $v_2 = 0$, *FB* buys the target at this price. If $v_2 = \$30$, *FB* still wins, but the price is driven up to $30. If $v_2 = \$100$, then *SB* buys the target at a price of $80. Competition in the bidding process not only helps target shareholders, it increases total surplus, because of the possible realization of a larger improvement ($100).

The ratchet solution illustrates the potential gain to the target and society of competition. It is, however, not descriptive of actual takeover contests, in which initial bids are typically made at a substantial premium to the market price (see the empirical synopsis), and each successive bid typically involves a significant increase over the previous outstanding bid.

4.1. Costly investigation and preemptive takeover bidding

A possible explanation for a high initial bid in a takeover contest derives from the fact that takeover benefits are partly specific to the acquirer (e.g., complementarities), but partly common (e.g., gains derived from replacing inefficient target management). Owing to correlated valuations, an initial bid will alert potential competitors to the potential desirability of the target.[26] This suggests that in planning its initial offer, an initial bidder will consider the incentives created for potential competitors.

Specifically, such a bidder may wish to offer a substantial premium on his initial bid in order to deter potential competitors (Fishman, 1988; Png, 1985). In Fishman's model, an initial bid alerts a second potential bidder to a state of the world in which the target is potentially profitable. However, the model assumes that conditional upon this state of the world, the valuations of the first and second bidder are independent.

---

[26] See, for example, Grossman and Hart (1981).

FB and *SB* can acquire information about the target at a cost of c^I. By investigating, a bidder learns his private valuation of the target.[27] If both bidders enter, it is assumed that a costless English auction ensues, so that the target is sold to the highest valuation bidder at a price equal to the valuation of the second highest bidder, $\min(v_1, v_2)$ (i.e., the ratchet solution).

In the unique equilibrium in this game (applying the equilibrium concept of Grossman and Perry, 1986), the bidder offers the minimum reservation price for the target if his valuation is below a critical threshold level v^*. In this event *SB* investigates, and the target is sold in a costless English auction. If $v > v^*$, *FB* makes a high bid b^D that deters *SB* from investigating. The initial bid is therefore a coarse signal of the *FB*'s valuation.

Suppose that the valuations of *FB* and *SB* are independent and uniform on the unit interval $[0, 1]$. I assume directly that *SB* only arrives if *FB* bids. *FB*'s payoff after a bid of b_1 is $v_1 - b_1$ if *SB* does not investigate. If *SB* does investigate, *FB* makes:

$$
\begin{array}{ll}
v_1 - b_1 & \text{if } v_2 \leq b_1, \\
v_1 - v_2 & \text{if } b_1 < v_2 \leq v_1, \\
0 & \text{if } v_2 > v_1.
\end{array}
\tag{13}
$$

SB's payoffs are zero unless he investigates. If he does, he makes:

$$
\begin{array}{ll}
-c_2^I & \text{if } v_2 \leq v_1, \\
v_2 - v_1 - c_2^I & \text{if } v_2 > v_1.
\end{array}
\tag{14}
$$

SB as well as *FB* follows threshold behavior. If *FB* bids $b_1 < b_1^D$, *SB* infers that $v_1 < v^*$, so *SB* investigates and a costless English auction ensues. If *FB* bids $b_1 \geq b_1^D$, *SB* infers that $v_1 \geq v^*$, so *SB* quits.

To understand the equilibrium, first note that if *FB* offers less than b_1^D, he should bid zero, because *SB* will investigate and bid up to v_2 in any case. There is no gain to *FB* from bidding $b_1 > b_1^D$, because he can already win with certainty at b_1^D. The gain to *FB* of bidding b_1^D instead of 0 is increasing in v_1, because his cost of bidding zero is greater when his valuation is higher. This is because *FB* with a larger v_1 values certainty of victory more highly, and because paying v_2 to beat the competitor whenever $v_2 < v_1$ has a greater expected cost when v_1 is higher.

The high deterring bid does *not* deter *SB* through the direct means of forcing him to pay at least b_1^D. Since $b_1^D < v_1$, *SB* knows that if he investigates he must pay *more* than b_1^D to win. Rather, high b_1 *signals* to *SB* that $v_1 > v_1^*$, which makes *SB* pessimistic about his potential profit. Thus, it is reasonable for *SB* to follow a threshold rule in which he investigates if and only if the initial bid is below a critical value.

Specifically, *SB* is deterred if his expected profit from investigating is zero or negative, that is,

---

[27] Low valuations are assumed to be so likely that it does not pay to bid without investigating.

$$E\left[\prod_2(v_1, v_2)|v_1 > v_1^*\right] \leq 0. \tag{15}$$

where $\prod_2$ is *SB*'s profit as a function of the two valuations, and where *SB* believes that *FB* has valuation of at least v_1^*. *SB*'s profit does not depend directly on b^*, the level of the initial bid, only on the minimum valuation v_1^* communicated by the offer. Direct substitution from Equation (14) and differentiation with respect to v_1^* shows that the LHS of this inequality is decreasing with v_1^*, because higher v_1^* makes *SB* more likely to lose and makes him on average pay more when he wins. This monotonicity leads to the threshold rule for *SB*.

To make expectations and actions consistent, the deterring bid b_1^D is set as a function of v_1^*, $b_1^D(v_1^*)$, defined as the maximum amount that *FB* with $v_1 = v_1^*$ would be willing to bid in order to preempt competition. This just prevents mimicry by any *FB* with $v_1 < v_1^*$.

There are multiple equilibria of this type, based on a value of v_1^* and the implied deterring bid value b_1^D. The lowest possible value of v_1^* consistent with this equilibrium sets Equation (15) to 0 so that *SB* is *just* deterred.[28]

To calculate v_1^*, set Equation (15) to 0. Under the uniform assumption, this yields

$$c^I = \int_{v_1^*}^1 \int_{v_1}^2 \left(\frac{v_2 - v_1}{1 - v_1^*}\right) dv_2 dv_1, \tag{16}$$

so

$$v_1^* = 1 - \sqrt{6c^I}. \tag{17}$$

The deterring bid b_1^D makes *FB* with $v_1 = v_1^*$ indifferent between bidding to deter or to accommodate investigation. If he bids to deter, he gets

$$1 - \sqrt{6c^I} - b_1^D. \tag{18}$$

If he bids 0, he receives $v_1^* - v_2$ if $v_1^* > v_2$, and 0 otherwise, for an expected gain of

$$\int_0^{v_1^*} (v_1^* - v_2)f(v_2)dv_2 = \frac{1}{2}(v_1^*)^2. \tag{19}$$

Equating and solving for b_1^D gives

$$b_1^D = \frac{1}{2} - 3c^I. \tag{20}$$

The model has the following properties.

---

[28] Note that if *FB* is going to bid, he would prefer to pay the low $b_1^D(v_1^*)$ rather than some higher amount. This equilibrium is the sole one consistent with the "credibility" criterion of Grossman and Perry (1986).

Proposition 10   *In the Fishman model, SB investigates only after a low-premium bid, not after a high bid. The level of the bid needed to deter competition is decreasing with the investigation cost c^I. The expected profit of FB is increasing and SB decreasing with c^I.*

The expected profit of *FB* is increasing and *SB* decreasing with c^I, because it is more expensive for *SB* to compete and thus cheaper for *FB* to preempt competition.

As discussed in Spatt (1989), the Fishman model has the excessively strong implication that an initial bid at a premium will always deter competition. Fishman suggests that if *SB* has private information about his investigation costs or valuation, then attempts to deter will sometimes fail (as analyzed by Bhattacharyya, 1992).

Evidence consistent with the implication that a second bidder is less likely to compete after a high-premium bid than a low one has been provided by Jennings and Mazzeo (1993). A further implication of the model is that a reduction in *SB*'s cost of investigation leads to a higher expected price of the target. This results from two reinforcing effects. First, if the investigation cost is low, then higher value must be signaled to deter competition, and hence a higher preemptive bid b^D is needed by Equation (20). Thus, the bid is higher in single-bidder contests. Furthermore, since deterring competition is more costly, *FB* makes the deterring bid over a smaller range of valuations, so that the higher expected price associated with competition is more often realized.

Lower investigation cost also increases efficiency. The social cost of competition comes from *SB*'s investigation cost c^I. The social benefit from competition is max $(0, v_2 - v_1)$, derived from the possible realization of a higher valuation than that of *FB*'s. Since in the ratchet solution a victorious *SB* profits by difference between his valuation and *FB*'s *SB*'s decision of whether to investigate is socially as well as privately optimal. Therefore, taking the occurrence of the initial bid as given, lower investigation cost improves efficiency by permitting realization of higher valuations. However, there is a crucial countervailing effect on the incentive of *FB* to investigate in the first place. A greater threat of competition can lead to too little initial investigation, and the loss of takeover gains.

Proposition 11   *Taking FB's investigation as given, a reduction in SB's cost of investigation c^I leads to a higher expected price of the target and greater social efficiency.*

4.2. Costly bidding

Fishman's and Bhattacharyya's models show that predictions that are more realistic than those derived from the costless English auction model can be derived when there are investigation costs associated with an initial offer. However, both authors assume that once both bidders have investigated, the game reverts to a costless English auction and the ratchet solution ensues. Several more recent papers extending the Fishman model for different purposes have made a similar assumption.

The ratchet solution may at first seem appealing in postentry subgames, because of its tractability and because the costs of revising a bid upward are likely to be smaller than the setup and investigation costs needed for an initial offer. However, the conventional English auction analysis is extremely sensitive to small costs of bidding (Hirshleifer and Png, 1990). To see this, suppose that *FB*'s valuation is known to be $80, and *SB*'s is known to be $30. In the ratchet solution, *SB* has nothing to lose by bidding up to $30, which becomes the price paid by *FB*. Suppose now that there is a cost of bidding and of revising a bid of $c^B = \$.01$. Then the target will be sold at a price of *zero*, because *SB* quits rather than wasting bid costs in a contest he must lose. Thus, even an extremely low bid cost drastically reduces the price paid for the target.

A possible justification for the ratchet solution is imperfect information. If *SB* does not know whether *FB*'s valuation is higher or lower, then he should be willing to incur some bid cost to preserve his chance of winning. There are two important limitations to this argument.

First, *FB*'s offer may signal his valuation. If so, a *SB* who knows his own valuation can make a well-informed decision as to whether to bid again or to quit immediately (see Daniel and Hirshleifer, 1993).[29]

Second, there are costs associated with revising an offer that may be far from trivial. First is the extension of the period during which managers must devote time to the takeover contest. Second are possible costs of obtaining further financing. Third, if takeovers will be associated with restructuring of the bidder and target, then real investment and operating decisions of the bidder may continue to be influenced by uncertainty over whether merger will occur. Fourth, some mandated filings may have to be repeated.[30]

By changing auction strategies, bidding costs can crucially affect the implications of takeovers models (see, e.g., the discussion of target defensive strategies in Section 4.3). When bid revision costs are added to Fishman's preemptive bidding model, it is still the case that *FB* can preempt competition through a high initial bid. However, Hirshleifer and Png (1990) show that a reduction in the cost of investigation c^I can *reduce* both the expected price paid for the target and efficiency. With regard to price, the difference arises from the much lower gains to the target when a second bidder investigates. Instead of a price of min(v_1, v_2), the premium may go up by little. Because of this, even though lower c^I raises the price that must be offered when *FB* deters investigation, the greater frequency of low offers that do not deter competition can lead to a lower target price on average. The welfare advantage of greater competition is also ambiguous since, with costly bidding, *SB* may sometimes succeed even if his valuation is below that of *FB*.

---

[29] Note that even if the bid cost is small, more than a small amount of residual uncertainty about *FB*'s valuation may be required to induce *SB* to bid, because *FB*'s valuation must be sufficiently variable that it may be below *SB*'s valuation.

[30] Investigation as well as pure bid costs may be positive even after the initial bid, since more investigation may be required to justify the risk of a higher offer.

The Williams Act of 1968 and associated legislation discussed in the empirical synopsis has been widely viewed as reducing the cost to competitors of investigating after an initial bid (see, e.g., Jarrell and Bradley, 1980). Evidence discussed earlier that average tender offer premia decreased after passage of the Williams Act is consistent with the costly bidding analysis.[31]

An unrealistic implication of the assumption of costless bid revisions is that after a single initial jump, offers increase by infinitesimal increments. Daniel and Hirshleifer (1993) examine a model of costly sequential bidding in which the offered price jumps on each successive bid. In this model, since the initial bid signals *FB*'s valuation, *SB* either quits (if his valuation is below some critical value determined by *FB*'s signaled valuation), or else jumps to a bid high enough to induce *FB* to withdraw. Since *FB*'s offer reveals his valuation, any less conclusive response by *SB* would be wasteful of bidding costs without any corresponding gain. Daniel and Hirshleifer argue that the only plausible equilibrium in a sequential bidding model with bid costs has bids revealing valuation and substantial bid increments until the auction ends.

To understand why, consider the Fishman model with the investigation cost c^I replaced with a cost of bidding c^B that is incurred by a bidder *each time he bids*. This is a pure transaction cost (such as those described a few paragraphs earlier); paying c^B does not directly yield any information about valuations. It is simplest to analyze a limiting case of the Daniel-Hirshleifer model in which the bid cost is very close to zero. As the numerical example at the start of Section 4 suggests, the outcome will be very different from the conventional ratchet solution outcome with costless bidding.[32] Let $b_1(v_1)$ denote *FB*'s equilibrium bid as a function of his valuation. If this schedule is strictly monotonic, then the inverse function $\hat{v}_1 = \hat{v}(b_1) \equiv b_1^{-1}(v_1)$ is single-valued. This function is the inference schedule for *FB*, that is the valuation signaled by a bid of b_1.

Figure 2 illustrates the equilibrium geometrically when both bidders' valuations are drawn from a uniform distribution on $[0, 1]$. The horizontal axis represents *FB*'s valuation v_1 and his bid b_1. The vertical axis represents the inferred valuation of *FB*, $\hat{v}(b_1)$. In this example the inference schedule is a straight line. In equilibrium, *SB* quits if $v_2 < \hat{v}_1$, so *FB*'s probability of winning with his first bid is $\Pr(v_2 < \hat{v}_1) = \hat{v}_1$. The bold line is the inference schedule. Inscribed in the large triangle is a rectangle with width $v_1 - b_1$, *FB*'s gain if he wins, and height $\hat{v}(b_1)$, *FB*'s probability of winning with his first bid. Suppose (as will be verified later) that in equilibrium *FB* will make only a single bid.

---

[31] Even in the costless bid revision model, a decrease in average premia could be predicted since initial bids will be observed from a lower valuation pool of bidders.

[32] Daniel and Hirshleifer describe a hitherto unrecognized weak signaling equilibrium of a costless English auction game ($c^B = 0$). However, this is best viewed as a limit of strong equilibria as $c^B \to 0$. Suppose (as will be shown) that the initial bid signals the true valuation v_1. If there is a positive bidding cost, however small, then after v_1 is revealed, *SB* with $v_2 < v_1$ strongly prefers to quit. Hence, bidding ends at a price below $\min(v_1, v_2)$, the price under the ratchet solution.

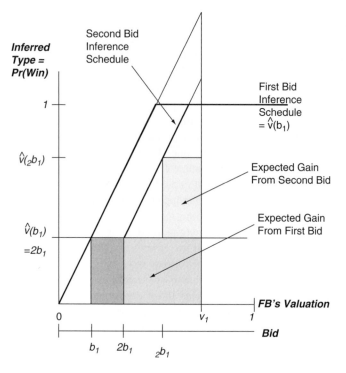

Fig. 2. Geometric interpretation of the signaling equilibrium.

Then the area of the inscribed rectangle is *FB*'s expected profit, and *FB*'s maximization problem is to set b_1 so as to maximize the area of this rectangle. Thus, *FB* solves

$$\max_{b_1} (v_1 - b_1)\hat{v}(b_1) = \max_{\hat{v}_1} [v_1 - b_1(\hat{v}_1)]\hat{v}_1.$$

This problem is identical to that solved by a bidder in a first price symmetric sealed bid auction (see, e.g., Riley and Samuelson, 1981). Differentiating with respect to $\hat{v}_1$ gives the first-order condition of the latter problem. In equilibrium $\hat{v}_1 = v_1$, which gives the differential equation

$$v_1 b_1'(v_1) + b_1(v_1) - v_1 = 0, \tag{21}$$

with the initial condition that a low valuation leads to a low bid, that is, $\lim_{v_1 \to 0} b_1(v_1) = 0$. The solution is $b_1(v_1) = v_1/2$, so the inference schedule is $\hat{v}(b_1) = 2b_1$, the straight line in Figure 2.

Interestingly, the bid is equal to the expected price paid by *FB* conditional on his winning in the ratchet solution,

$$E[\tilde{v}_2 | \tilde{v}_2 < v_1] = \frac{v_1}{2}. \tag{22}$$

Thus, *FB*'s expected profit as a function of his valuation,

$$\left(v_1 - \frac{v_1}{2}\right)\Pr(\tilde{v}_2 < v_1) = \frac{(v_1)^2}{2}, \tag{23}$$

is the same as in the ratchet solution.[33]

In response to the initial bid, *SB* withdraws if $v_2 \leq \hat{v}_1$, and wins with a bid of $b_2 = \hat{v}_1$ if $v_2 > \hat{v}_1$. *SB* does not bid less than $\hat{v}_1$ because in this equilibrium *FB* always infers skeptically that *SB*'s bid is virtually as high as *SB*'s valuation.[34] Thus, *SB*'s expected price paid and expected profit as a function of this valuation are respectively as given in Equation (22) and Equation (23) with subscripts 1 and 2 reversed.

Before analyzing *FB*'s possible defections in more detail, it is useful to summarize some implications.

Proposition 12   *If two risk neutral bidders have valuations that are uniformly distributed on the interval* [0, 1] *and the bid cost* $c^B = 0$, *then there exists a weak equilibrium in which the FB offers half his valuation as his initial offer. This offer is the same as FB's expected payment, given that he wins, in the ratchet solution. SB, if he wins, pays FB's valuation, the same amount as in a ratchet solution.*

In this special case of zero bid costs, the *FB*'s bid schedule is the same as that in a conventional first price sealed bid auction, and the bid schedule in Bhattacharyya (1992) (as the one-shot entry fee approaches zero). The *realized* price in the sealed first price auction differs, since the winning bid in this auction essentially never matches the ratchet solution outcome.

To see that this is an equilibrium when *FB* can bid repeatedly, note first that *FB* would never bid higher than the proposed bidding schedule because, if he did, and *SB* followed with his equilibrium response $b_2 = \hat{v} > v_1$, *FB* would quit. As was already shown, if *FB* plans to bid at most once, he will bid on the proposed schedule.

So consider instead a defection by *FB* of initially bidding low ($b_1 < v_1/2$), and if *SB* responds with a higher bid, bidding a second time to signal his true valuation v_1. The initial offer signals his type to be $v(b_1) < v_1$. *SB*'s equilibrium response to the initial offer is either to withdraw or else to win with a bid of $v(b_1)$. If *SB* bids, and *FB* responds, then *SB*'s bidding decision will depend on his inference after observing this off-equilibrium occurrence. Let us assume that *SB* interprets *FB*'s second bid as a new and (this time) truthful separating bid.[35] *FB*'s two-bid maximization problem is

---

[33] *FB*'s bidding schedule in Equation (22) depends not on the distribution of his own valuation, but on the distribution of his *opponent's* valuation. This is because the differential Equation (21) derives from *FB*'s choice problem, which weighs the extent to which raising his bid will reduce the probability that his opponent's valuation will lead to a competing bid.

[34] *FB* would top any bid below $\hat{v}_1$ in order to force out *SB*. Thus, *SB* will never bid below $\hat{v}(b_1)$. There are other equilibria in which *FB* is less skeptical about *SB*'s valuation; these are broadly similar to the equilibrium discussed here.

[35] This is a conservative assumption. If, once convinced by the first signal that $v_1 = \hat{v}_1$, *SB* would never change his mind, he would be less willing to withdraw, making *FB*'s defection even less profitable.

illustrated in Figure 2. *FB* expected profit derived from states of the world in which *SB* quits immediately after the initial bid is $2b_1(v_1 - b_1)$, the large lower rectangle. *SB*'s equilibrium responses are either to quit or to bid *FB*'s signaled valuation of $v(b_1) = 2b_1$. If *SB* bids, *FB* infers that *SB*'s type is distributed uniformly on $[2b_1, 1]$. Analogous to the equilibrium schedule on the first bid, to signal his type as v_1, *FB* must bid $b_1' = (v_1 + 2b_1)/2$. *FB*'s expected profit derived from states of the world in which he makes a second bid is therefore $(v_1 - 2b_1)^2 /2$, the smaller upper rectangle. Thus, the *total* expected profit from both bids, the sum of the rectangular areas, is $v_1^2/2$, which is *independent of the amount bid*, and the same as if *FB* did not defect. This confirms the proposed (weak) equilibrium.

By defecting to a low-bid strategy, *FB* pays less than with the truth-revealing strategy if *SB* quits. However, he pays considerably more if he wins on a second bid, so his expected profit is no higher with the low-bid strategy than with the truth-revealing strategy. As Daniel and Hirshleifer show, with a strictly positive bidding cost, his profit from the low-bid defection is *strictly* lower.[36]

Proposition 12 implies that the signaling equilibrium leads to a surprising identity of expected payoffs between the bidders, and with other auction mechanisms.

Proposition 13 *Both unconditionally and conditional on his own valuation, each bidder is indifferent between the signaling equilibrium and the ratchet solution. If target shareholders are risk neutral, then they are also indifferent. The two bidders earn the same expected profits, so who moves first is a matter of indifference.*

Thus, the revenue equivalence of optimal auctions (see Myerson, 1981; Riley and Samuelson, 1981) extends to the sequential bidding game (when bid costs approach zero). Since the ratchet solution provides the bidders and stockholders with the same expected revenue as a sealed bid first or second price auction, the signaling equilibrium described here provides the same expected revenues as well.[37]

When a specific level of the bid cost is considered (instead of the limit approaching zero), the Daniel-Hirshleifer model implies that a bidder with low valuation may wait one or several rounds before bidding. Suppose the game continues until one player makes a positive offer and the other player quits. If neither bidder makes an offer in the first round, *FB* gets another chance to bid in the second round. In this setting, a low-valuation bidder will wait rather than bid. To illustrate, consider the uniform example with a bid cost of 0.01. A bidder with valuation of 0.1 has a 0.1 probability of winning. If he bids 0 and wins, his gross profit is 0.1, so his expected

---

[36] *FB* could also contemplate a low bid followed by a contingency plan involving several possible further bids. It can be shown by similar reasoning that such defections are not profitable.

[37] Although the bidding process and strategic reasoning is different, the final outcome with arbitrarily small bid costs in every round is identical to a game with only a small entry fee (followed by the ratchet solution if *SB* enters). However, if there is a significant investigation cost or entry fee, the first bid will not fully reveal the bidder's valuation (Bhattacharyya, 1992; Fishman, 1988). In such settings, the introduction of small bid costs in later rounds drastically affects final outcomes as well as the bid process.

gross profit is $0.1 \times 0.1 = 0.01$, leaving him zero net profits. By waiting, he can obtain positive expected profits, so no type with $v_1 \leq 0.1$ will bid in the first round. If *SB* similarly passes, *FB* learns that *SB* valuation is low, which raises *FB*'s chance of winning. At this point *FB* may submit a bid. Each further round of waiting reveals lower valuations, increasing the incentive to bid. Eventually any bidder whose valuation exceeds the bid cost c^B will submit a bid, but he may need to wait many rounds before doing so.

Prices jump either once or twice in the version of the Daniel-Hirshleifer model discussed here. They also suggest when there will be a greater number of bids. First, further information disclosed during the contest can alter bidder valuations. Second, the target may undertake defensive measures that shift bidders' valuations (see Sections 3.1.3.2 and 4.3). Third, when there are n bidders, the price jumps up to n times, as each of the first $n - 1$ bidders either signals his type or quits.

Their signaling equilibrium suggests that bidders will make substantial bid jumps in order to drive out unmotivated competitors not just initially (as in Fishman and Bhattacharyya), but at every stage of a sequential auction. However, the existence of a signaling equilibrium does not rule out alternative equilibria in which pools of bidder types are gradually revealed through small bid increments. Daniel and Hirshleifer argue that reasonable equilibria in costly sequential bidding games have the property that bidders bid in substantial increments in order to signal in the minimum number of moves enough information to determine the contest winner. In this view, the outcomes of sequential bidding games with even modest bid costs will not resemble the conventional ratchet solution to the English auction.

The intuition is roughly as follows. If in equilibrium pooling disappears with certainty within a given number of rounds of bidding, then a backwards recursion argument indicates that it pays to bid to win earlier rather than risk incurring extra bid costs. Suppose instead the equilibrium calls for "dueling pools" that potentially last any number of rounds, gradually shrinking as offers grow. Then a bidder whose valuation is near the top of a pooling interval foresees a chance that, after his current bid, he will need to bid again. To avoid the extra bid cost, he will defect to a higher bid in the current round. If a high-valuation bidder has a stronger incentive to signal in this fashion than a low-valuation bidder, this defection can credibly deter the competitor. Profitable defection unravels the dueling pools from the top.

4.3. Managerial defensive measures and bidder elimination

In Section 3.1.3, management defensive measures were analyzed in single-bidder contests. In multiple-bidder contests, the possibility exists of using defensive measures as means of discriminating among bidders. The extreme case of discrimination between bidders is to take an action that eliminates one bidder but not others. Shleifer and Vishny (1986b) show that it is possible for a target firm to profit from payment of greenmail to a bidder, in order to signal to other potential bidders that the target does not have a hidden "white knight" bidder ready to top all offers.[38] This encourages investigation by other bidders. Since the fact that the target does not have a hidden white knight can be bad news for shareholders, the stock price reaction to greenmail can be negative (consistent with evidence cited earlier) even if it benefits target shareholders.[39]

Spatt (1989) describes and generalizes an example due to Sudipto Bhattacharya in which several potential bidders decide simultaneously whether to pay an entry fee in order to participate in bidding. Spatt concludes that even under full information the elimination of some members of a group of potential bidders can increase the expected profit of the target when an increase in the entry fee does not. The example assumes the conventional ratchet solution among those bidders that enter.

In summary, several models have demonstrated the theoretical possibility that the elimination of potential bidders can sometimes improve efficiency and help target shareholders. But since the conditions needed for elimination to be in shareholders' interests seem to be restrictive, it would be desirable to develop empirical tests to distinguish these models from the common view that greenmail promotes undesirable entrenchment of target management.

As these models show, even a defensive strategy that is good for target shareholders can reveal bad news. However, there are perhaps stronger reasons to expect defensive measures to convey favorable information (even if they are undesirable). One expects management to be more likely to oppose a takeover at a given price if it has favorable information about firm value, or about the likelihood of other bidders arriving. Furthermore, a defensive strategy can be good for shareholders given the arrival of a bid, and yet undesirable ex ante because it deters investigation. The negative average stock price reactions associated with various kinds of defensive measures cited earlier suggests that these actions are often undesirable for target shareholders.

Instead of buying off the bidder, the target can raise the cost to a bidder by repurchasing shares from other investors. Aside from signaling effects (see Section 3.1.4), a repurchase can force the bidder to offer more if the supply curve of shares slopes upward (Bagwell, 1991). For example, if different investors have different capital gains bases, repurchase takes out the shareholders with lowest reservation prices. Thus, the greater is shareholder heterogeneity, the more effective is repurchase in blocking takeover.

As emphasized by Jensen (1986), the distribution of cash through repurchase can be a good thing if management would otherwise be inclined to overinvest, and can reduce the gain from takeover. More generally, a management can help preserve its control by preempting the improvements that might otherwise be effected through a hostile

---

[38] Greenmail is the repurchase at a premium of the shareholdings of a potential takeover bidder, often combined with a standstill agreement that prevents the bidder from further purchases of target shares.

[39] This last implication is shared by the model of Giammarino and Heinkel (1990), which is based on greenmail signaling that the target has greater value under current management than if investment levels are cut by an acquirer.

takeover. The issue of whether the threat of takeover on the whole improves efficiency (by giving managers a "kick-in-the-pants") or harm it (by inducing risk avoidance and "short-termism") is a topic of current debate.[40]

Uncertainty about how much a firm's management values control affects the information conveyed by target resistance activity (Baron, 1982). If the manager is a shareholder, then he may reject an offer if he has private information indicating that the target is worth more than the price offered, or because he places high value on retaining control. In Baron's model, the expected value of making an offer to a manager who values control is negative because of an associated adverse selection problem, that the offer will only be accepted if it is too high. The rejection of an offer leads outsiders to revise upward their beliefs about the manager's value of control, discouraging further offers and causing bidders to shade their offers downward.

As with the analysis of takeover auctions in general, it is important to take into account bidding costs to arrive at robust conclusions about the effects of defensive strategies (see Section 4.2). Berkovitch and Khanna (1990) examine a model in which a target takes an action that reduces its value more to an initial bidder than to a potential second bidder. An example would be selling an asset that can be improved more by *FB* than *SB*. The advantage of this is that it encourages *SB* to compete, despite an entry cost, and forces the *FB* to make a higher offer to deter value reduction and competition.[41]

The following numerical example illustrates their model under full information. Suppose that *FB*'s valuation is \$80, and *SB*'s valuation is \$30. Suppose that *SB* has a cost of \$5 for its *initial* bid only, and that if *SB* enters, the ratchet solution of a costless English auction ensues thereafter. Assume no defensive measures. Then *FB* will succeed with an offer just above zero. Now allow the target, after the first bid, to reduce *FB*'s valuation by an arbitrary amount without changing *SB*'s valuation. *FB* will now win at a price of \$25.[42]

The outcome is very different when bid revision is slightly costly. Suppose that after *SB* enters, there is a further cost of bidding of \$0.01 for either bidder. Suppose in addition there is a cost of \$0.01 to the target of value reduction. (For example, value reduction is likely to be costly if there is a slight chance that no acquisition will take place.) Now, even with value-reduction strategies, *FB* will win at a price of \$0.[43] More generally, the gains from stimulating a competing bid are greatly reduced by even small bid costs in later rounds of bidding.

---

[40] See, for example, Stein (1988) and other models reviewed in Hirshleifer (1993a)

[41] Giammarino and Heinkel (1986) provide a related model in which an uninformed bidder is reluctant to compete against an informed bidder when valuations arc common. This leads to a gain to the target of committing to resist counteroffers by the informed bidder.

[42] If *FB* offered any less, \$20 say, then the target would reduce *FB*'s valuation of the target to just below \$25. *SB* would win the English auction at a price of just under \$25, to make a small profit.

[43] If the target responds to a first bid of \$0 by reducing *FB*'s valuation to below \$25, then *SB* will enter, *FB* will quit, and *SB* will win at a price just above \$0. But this means that the target has lost \$.01 from its value-reduction strategy. Hence, the threat to reduce value is not credible.

4.4. Bidder debt as a strategic positioning device

Debt can play an important strategic role in takeover contests. The role of target debt is discussed in Section 6; here I discuss the bidding side. Merging has a risk-combination effect that can benefit either bidder debt- or equity-holders, depending on capital structures, the probability distributions for separate and combined firm cash flows, and the means of payment. To disentangle other effects, consider acquisitions without merger.

High leverage increases the bidder's incentive to prefer risky investments (especially if financed by further debt). This increases the incentive to bid high. Thus, an initial bidder may obtain a strategic advantage by leveraging his firm, thereby committing to bidding aggressively. While this reduces the cost of deterring competition, if the *FB* is imperfectly informed about potential competition, in equilibrium a competitor will still sometimes investigate and bid. In such cases, an equity-value-maximizing bidder may buy the target above its value to the bidding firm as a whole (Chowdhry and Nanda, 1993).

Chowdhry and Nanda's conclusion that debt helps a bidder commit to aggressive bidding conflicts with the popular view that a bidder with high debt is "strapped for cash," hence unable to afford a high offer. The popular view is consistent with the underinvestment problem with debt (Myers, 1977); if debtholders absorb part of the value-improvement from takeover, shareholders may have insufficient incentive to undertake it.

Which view is correct? The advantage of issuing new debt to expropriate old debtholders (which does not occur in the Chowdhry/Nanda model) can be achieved without an acquisition, and so is not a benefit to bidding high. If the bid is financed internally, shareholders are sacrificing dividends to make the purchase, so the underinvestment problem will normally apply. However, some acquisitions probably create substantial risk of generating losses greater than the purchase price (reducing the value of the bidder's assets-in-place). In this case part of the potential loss from the investment is borne by debtholders, so overbidding may be profitable for equity-holders. Finally, the risk-combination effects of merger in redistributing wealth between debt and equity can operate in either direction.

4.5. Initial shareholdings as a strategic positioning device

Another way to commit to aggressive bidding in takeover contests is to accumulate an initial shareholding in the target (Burkart, 1994). A simple numerical example (developed independently of Burkart's paper) illustrates these incentives. Suppose there are two bidders with valuations known to be $100 and $200. If there are no initial shareholdings, the high-valuation bidder will win at a low price: $0 if there is even a small transaction cost of bidding (or $100 in the costless English auction solution). Suppose now that the low-valuation bidder owns an initial fraction $\alpha > 0$ of the target firm. He will now bid up to $200 - \varepsilon$, ($\varepsilon > 0$ small), in order to sell his stake to the winning bidder at the highest possible price. Thus, initial shareholdings can lead to drastic overbidding.

This threat of overbidding can deter potential new bidders from investigating. If the initial bidder has a low valuation, he may prefer not to deter competitors, since he would rather sell out at a higher profit. His initial offer may attract competition by conveying information about possible value improvements. Some corporate "raiders" have in fact been accused of making bids to put companies "in play," with the intention of selling out.

An initial bidder with a high valuation would like to deter low-valuation competitors. But deterrence may be incomplete, because it may be profitable for another bidder to accumulate a stake (even at prices elevated by takeover speculation), drive up the price further, and sell out to the *FB*. This possibility reduces the expected value to investigating and becoming an initial bidder. Thus, ironically, it seems that the potential to accumulate initial shareholdings may *reduce* takeover activity.

If the bidder does not know the valuation of his competitor, his incentive to overbid is weakened, because he runs the risk of driving out the competitor. A critical strategic factor then is whether the bidder is contractually committed to following through with an acquisition offer. Another limit to overbidding is the difficulty of obtaining financing for an offer that is likely to either lose money or just lose.

4.6. Bidding for multiple targets

Some bidders, such as corporate "raiders" or firms building conglomerates, have engaged in programs of repeated acquisition. In general, when a repeating player has private information about some strategically relevant characteristic, there can be an incentive to select actions in early rounds that help to build reputation (see, e.g., Fudenberg and Levine, 1989; Kreps et al., 1982). A repeated takeover bidder may want to bid relatively low in early contests, because if later targets believe he can bring about large improvements, they may insist on higher prices (Leach, 1992). Leach provides evidence which suggests that repeat bidders bid lower than nonrepeaters.

5. Means of payment

The means of payment (cash vs. debt or equity securities) in takeover contests has important consequences for the information revealed by the bidder and the target and the efficiency of the transaction outcome. Four key factors have been emphasized by recent theoretical research:

(i) *Value of equity in limiting overpayment* (Eckbo et al., 1990; Hansen, 1987). If the target has some private information about its value or the value of the takeover, then the bidder faces a tradeoff between the likelihood of paying too much, or of offering too little and being rejected. The latter case is inefficient. Equity makes the terms contingent on the target's value, mitigating adverse selection.

(ii) *Cash as an indicator of high value or valuation, and equity as an indicator of low value or valuation* (Berkovitch and Narayanan, 1990; Eckbo et al., 1990; Fishman, 1989; Hansen, 1987; Myers and Majluf, 1984). Equity (or risky debt) is cheaper for a bidder that is overvalued, or whose valuation of the target is low, so the offer of cash instead signals high value or valuation. For example, a bidder can preempt competitors by offering cash. However, empirically cash does not seem to be associated with less competition (Jennings and Mazzeo, 1993). With mixed offers value can be revealed fully. If the target has bargaining power, a bidder may offer equity to signal low valuation and induce the target to accept less.

(iii) *The use of equity to exploit the target's information* (Fishman, 1989). If the bidder is not sure whether a merger will create or destroy value, it is valuable to exploit the target's information. An equity offer gives the target a share of takeover gains or losses, so it will tend to reject undesirable transactions.

(iv) *Tax advantages of equity* (Brown and Ryngaert, 1991). In the United States, tax-free status depends on at least 50% of consideration being in the form of equity; many offers occur at or near 50%.

A stimulus to this theoretical research has been evidence (discussed in the empirical synopsis) of lower bidder and target returns for stock offers than for cash offers (see point (ii) above). The failure of the US result of negative average abnormal bidder returns to carry over to other countries is puzzling.[44] Further research will help clarify the source of the inconsistency between theory and evidence.

The use of securities as a means of payment is a case of what Riley (1988) refers to as use of ex post information to set auction payoffs. Riley shows that a *seller* who can set the payoff function, will want to use ex post information. This suggests that sellers may insist upon an appropriate debt-equity bundle in order to reduce the problems of asymmetric information about buyers' valuations. Applications of these ideas to takeovers may be of interest for further research.

6. Target financing, managerial voting power, and private benefits of control

6.1. Debt as a means of preempting takeover benefits

Debt is frequently increased by potential takeover targets either before or after the arrival of a bidder. A possible explanation is that the purpose of hostile takeovers is to cut expenses and investment. If there are agency problems associated with free cash flow that are reduced by debt (see Jensen, 1986), then the target can commit to

---

[44] Since stock is associated with mergers, and cash with tender offers, it is hard to distinguish acquisition form from means of payment. Since cash tender offers can be consummated more rapidly than stock offers, returns may also be related to the mood of the takeover and prospects for competition.

preempting the bidder's planned cutbacks by increasing debt.[45] Alternatively, if managers who value control are reluctant to risk financial distress to exploit heavily the tax advantage of debt, they may shift to higher debt when a takeover threat appears.

6.2. Debt as a means of capturing takeover benefits

An alternative theory is that high leverage allow the target to capture a greater fraction of a bidder's improvement through increases in the value of debt (Israel, 1992). The greater the improvement in firm value associated with a takeover, ceteris paribus the lower the probability of default on target debt. If the possibility of takeover-related improvement in debt value can be foreseen by purchasers of debt in advance, target shareholders can absorb this gain at the time of debt issuance. A limit to debt issuance is that this reduces the incentive of potential bidders to investigate the target (Israel, 1991),[46] consistent with evidence cited earlier that high debt targets are less likely to receive hostile tender offers. Similarly, going public can have the advantage of introducing a free-rider problem in tendering (Zingales, 1991). If dilution opportunities are limited, then public shareholders, by virtue of the free-rider problem, are effectively committed to bargaining tough with the bidder, allowing them to absorb more of the takeover gain than would a single firm owner. The owner can absorb these potential profits at the time of equity issuance.

6.3. Use of resistance strategies to influence contest form

Harris and Raviv (1988) describe how target management, through its resistance strategy, can influence the form of the takeover contest and the likelihood that control changes. They focus on the relationship between target debt levels and two alternative corporate control mechanisms: proxy fights and tender offers.[47] In their model, shifts in capital structure at the time of a control contest affect management's voting power and gains from a control change. Management's resistance strategy is based on a trade-off between value improvements brought about by control changes, and management's private interest in retaining control benefits.

Their model focuses on the behavior of incumbent management (*I*), a rival management team (*R*), and passive investors (*P*). Passive investors may vote in a proxy fight for *I* or *R*, but do not seek control for themselves. Both *I* and *R* may have either high or low ability. If ability is high, the NPV of the firm (Y_H) is greater than if ability

---

[45] However, on average investment was not reduced following successful hostile takeovers in the mid-1980s (see Bhagat et al., 1990; Bhide, 1989).

[46] It is also possible that an acquirer can expropriate target debt by shifting dividend or investment policy.

[47] A third mechanism of corporate control is dismissal of top executives by the board of directors.

is low (NPV $= Y_L$). Managers do not have any superior information about their ability. When R arrives, all agents assess a probability p that I is better than R, $1 - p$ that R is better than I, and 0 that they are equally able. Prior to R's arrival, p is distributed uniformly on $[0, 1]$. Each passive investor receives an i.i.d. signal about the relative abilities of I and R. If a proxy fight occurs, each passive investor votes for the control candidate he believes is better based on p and her signal. If I is actually of ability $i = H$, L, then $\pi_i(p)$ is the probability that a passive investor will vote for I, with $\pi_H(p) > \pi_L(p)$. With many small passive investors, $\pi_i(p)$ is also the fraction of small investors voting for I.

I and R have limited amounts of wealth available to invest in the firm's equity, W_I and W_R. When a potential rival for control of a firm appears, target management may initiate a debt-for-equity exchange to increase its voting power. Let D be the face value of debt issued when a takeover threat begins. Debt affects firm value only through its effect on who ends up managing the firm. Higher D reduces I's benefit from control, $K_i(D)$, as it increases the probability of bankruptcy. For any level of debt D, control benefits are greater for a high than for a low ability manager, $K_1(D) > K_2(D)$.

The sequence of events is as follows. Before R appears, the firm makes an initial investment of $1, financed by $ W_I from I and $1 - W_I$ from passive investors. I initially selects zero debt. When R appears, I decides on the size of a debt-for-equity exchange in order to maximize the sum of the value of his shares and his expected benefit from control. After any such exchange, R decides whether to purchase equity. Passive investors then observe their signals about managerial ability. A shareholder vote then determines control of the firm.

The value of the firm if no control change is possible is

$$Y_I \equiv pY_1 + (1 - p)Y_2. \tag{24}$$

Let α_I be the initial fraction of the firm owned by the incumbent. After issuing debt in exchange for nonmanagement equity, I's equity share becomes

$$\alpha_I(D) = \frac{\alpha_I Y(D)}{E(D)}, \tag{25}$$

where $Y(D)$ and $E(D)$ are the market values of the firm and of the firm's equity when the face value of the debt is D. The numerator is the value of the manager's old shares when it becomes known that debt will be increased, and the denominator is the total value of the firm's equity after recapitalization. Y and E depend on D because D, by affecting ownership fractions, affects the outcome of the control contest.

If the rival appears, he invests his wealth W_R in equity. An upper bound on his purchases is that he can buy no more than $1 - \alpha_I$, the holdings of passive shareholders. Thus, his purchase is

$$\alpha_R(D) = \min\left[\frac{W_R}{E(D)}, 1 - \alpha_I(D)\right]. \tag{26}$$

The remaining fraction of the firm's equity is held by P.

The incumbent's problem is then to set debt to solve

$$\max_{D \geq 0} \alpha_I Y(D) + K(D), \tag{27}$$

where $K(D)$ denotes the expected control benefit to the incumbent given debt level D. There are three possible cases:

1. R acquires enough shares to guarantee he obtains control.
2. Neither R nor I is certain of control.
3. I increases his fractional ownership so much that he is certain to retain control.

These three cases are suggestively termed *successful tender offer*, *proxy fight*, and *unsuccessful tender offer*, respectively. In a successful tender offer, R obtains control even if he is inferior to I. In an unsuccessful tender offer, I retains control even if he is inferior to R. In a proxy fight the superior candidate always wins, because passive investors in the aggregate always cast more votes in favor of the superior candidate.

I's total vote in a control contest is

$$\alpha_I(D) + \pi_i \alpha_P(D), \tag{28}$$

where $i = 1$ if I is better and $i = 2$ if R is better. Thus, an unsuccessful tender offer corresponds to a level of debt such that Equation (28) is at least 1/2 even when $i = 2$. A successful tender offer corresponds to a level of debt such that Equation (28) is less than 1/2 even when $i = 1$. A proxy fight corresponds to debt levels such that Equation (28) is less than 1/2 if $i = 2$, but at least 1/2 when $i = 1$.

If I selects a given case, he will optimally select the lowest debt level consistent with that case. This is because debt affects the control outcome only when it changes the case, while higher debt always reduces I's expected benefit of control. Thus, if I chooses to permit a successful tender offer, he will choose a debt level $D = 0$. It is assumed that a positive level of debt is needed to bring about an unsuccessful tender offer. A positive level of debt may be needed to force a proxy fight.

Because of the role of leverage in blocking control change, greater debt issuance is associated with those types of transactions that maintain incumbent control. Some implications of the model for leverage are now summarized.

Proposition 14 *In the Harris-Raviv model, leverage-increasing shifts in financial structure occur during control contests. Since greater incumbent shareholdings are required to prevent a control shift than to allow one, leverage increases are predicted to be on average smaller for targets of successful tender offers than for firms involved in proxy contests (in which control may not shift) or unsuccessful tender offers. So long as passive shareholders are sufficiently well-informed, the average increase in debt is lower among firms involved in proxy contests than in the unsuccessful tender offer case.*

The analysis also has implications for stock price reactions to control contests, summarized as follows.

Proposition 15

(1) *The average target abnormal stock return associated with successful tender offers (in which control change is certain) is larger than the abnormal returns associated with a proxy fight (in which a change in control is uncertain).*

(2) *The target stock price does not increase on average, in an unsuccessful tender offer.*

(3) *Thus, even an unsuccessful proxy fight is associated with positive abnormal stock return.*

(4) *The abnormal return associated with a successful proxy fight is higher than for an unsuccessful one.*

(1) holds because incumbent management will risk relinquishing control if the likelihood that the rival is more efficient is sufficiently large, since this increases the potential capital gain on management-owned shares. (2) holds because no value improvement is effected; it is consistent with the evidence of Bradley et al. (1983) discussed earlier. (3) holds because the winner of a proxy fight is the more efficient management team. (4) holds because success is associated with a lower ex ante probability that incumbent management is efficient, and thus a lower prior stock price.

6.4. Target management ownership and resistance when the supply of shares is upward sloping

Stulz (1988) offers related arguments concerning the defensive role of target management share ownership and capital structure in a model that focuses on tender offers. He considers an incumbent manager who wishes to retain control and owns shares of the firm. The greater his holdings, the smaller the remaining share fraction available for purchase by a potential bidder. (The incumbent's shareholding can be adjusted through changes in leverage and other means.) Under the assumptions of an upward sloping supply curve for shares, and that the target manager values control so much that he never tenders, it follow that the bidder must pay a larger premium for a given probability of success. (For a related argument, see Bagwell, 1991.)

Under these more adverse circumstances, the bidder will in fact offer more. To see this, consider a slightly modified Equation (5), so that the bidder's expected profit is

$$E\left[\prod\right] = P(b; m)(v - b), \tag{29}$$

where $P(b; m)$ is the bidder's probability of success as a function of the amount offered b and target management share ownership m, and where v is the bidder's valuation of the target. The first-order condition is

$$P'(b; m)(v - b) = P(b; m). \tag{30}$$

Suppose that the probability of offer success is linearly increasing in the bid and is linearly decreasing in the level of target management share ownership,

$$P(b; m) = a_0 + a_1 b - a_2 m. \tag{31}$$

This simplified equation reflects two considerations in Stulz's analysis. First, a higher offer increases the probability that the bid will exceed the unknown reservation prices of a large enough fraction of shareholders that the offer will succeed. Second, an increase in the fraction of shares not available for tendering m decreases the probability of success. Then substituting Equation (31) into Equation (30) and solving for b gives

$$b(v; m) = \frac{v}{2} - \frac{a_0}{2a_1} + \frac{a_2 m}{2a_1}. \tag{32}$$

By Equation (32), this argument implies the following proposition.

Proposition 16 *The level of the bid is increasing with target management share ownership, m.*

This result may seem surprising, because with an upward sloping supply curve for shares, a higher target management ownership raises the cost of purchasing shares. One might suppose that this higher cost could induce the bidder to reduce his offer and accept a lower expected number of tendered shares. The reason this does not occur is that, for any given offered price, the lower probability of success reduces the expected marginal cost of increasing the level of the bid (the price increment multiplied by the probability of success). Thus, the bid increases. The evidence of Stulz et al. (1990) discussed earlier that supports the prediction of Proposition 16, particularly for multiple bidder contests.

The paper goes on to examine the consequences of target management shareholding for firm value. Stulz finds that increased managerial ownership does not necessarily improve shareholder welfare because it facilitates the entrenchment of the incumbent manager in control contests. As the incumbent management's shareholding increases, the target loses from a reduction in the probability of a successful takeover, but benefits from a higher premium in the event of success. Private benefits of control in effect serve as a commitment not to tender. In general, such commitment can have strategic value (Schelling, 1960). Here, the manager is strategically positioned to force the bidder to raise the premium. This leads to an interior optimum from shareholders' point of view.

A number of different kinds of corporate actions can lead to effective increases in management control of voting rights. First, as in Harris and Raviv, shifts in capital structure can affect this end. Thus, the model predicts that the probability of a hostile takeover attempt is decreasing with the target's debt-equity ratio (consistent with evidence cited earlier). Another way of maintaining high management control of voting rights may be to delay the call of a convertible debt. The negative common stock price reaction to the announcement of forced conversion of debt into common stock could then be due to the fact that this reveals to the market that the firm is unlikely to be a takeover target. Since a supermajority rule make takeover more costly for the bidder, Stulz predicts that these can either increase or decrease firm value, but that a decrease is more likely when managerial shareholdings are high (consistent with evidence of Alexander, 1986 and Jarrell and Poulsen, 1987). Differential voting rights of stock and the purchase of shares by a firm's ESOP provide ways for managers to increase voting power at low personal cost.

7. Omitted topics and further references

With its focus on the transaction process, this essay has not addressed in detail the reasons that mergers and acquisitions occur. Some value-improving motives for takeovers include scale economies and complementarities, and remedying inefficient target management behavior. Some reasons for value-reducing takeovers include bidder agency problems, bidder overconfidence, and redistribution of wealth from target security holders or other stakeholders. Hirshleifer (1993b) reviews these issues and provides references.

I have by no means exhausted the application of economic theories of bargaining and of auctions to takeover modeling. Spatt (1989) provides an insightful survey that deals further with these issues. When target management has the power to reject a bidder, there is room for bargaining over the price. If delay is costly, there is pressure on both sides to reach agreement. This suggests the application of a Rubinstein-type model of bargaining between a bidder and a target in which an alternating sequence of offers determines the division of gains (see Berkovitch and Narayanan, 1990; Tiemann, 1985). Bulow and Klemperer (1993) examine the expected-price-maximizing choice between selling the company in an English auction versus negotiating with a bidder, and find that under mild conditions the public auction is superior. When the valuations of different competing bidders contain a common component, auction theory suggests a need for bidders to shade their offers downward to account for the winner's curse effect; see the evidence of Giliberto and Varaiya (1989).

Takeover threats can influence the behavior of a firm's top executives and its board of directors. Top executives may be forced to work harder, or may make investment or other operating decisions which are unprofitable but make the firm appear successful temporarily. A growing literature on such managerial reputational concerns has been stimulated by Holmström (1982); for a recent review, see Hirshleifer (1993a). Takeover markets can also interact with internal supervision by boards of directors, because arrival or nonarrival of a bid conveys information about how potential bidders view the manager (see Hirshleifer and Thakor, 1994).

8. Conclusion

Certain central ideas emerge from the models discussed here:

1. *The free-rider problem in tender offers.* A free-rider problem occurs among shareholders of a tender offer target whose value can be improved by the bidder. This occurs because an individual shareholder does not take into account that tendering his shares to the bidder increases the expected wealth of the other shareholders and the bidder. Since the free-rider problem encourages shareholders to retain their shares, it leads to higher prices in successful tender offers, and deters potential bidders. In the extreme case, a bidder cannot capture any of the takeover surplus. Free-riding is more severe if shareholders are small, hence less likely to be individually pivotal in determining the success or failure of an offer (Grossman and Hart, 1980; but see Bagnoli and Lipman, 1988; Holmström and Nalebuff, 1992), and if a bidder can revise his offers (Harrington and Prokop, 1993).

2. *The effect of noise on the likelihood of shareholders being pivotal.* Models in which shareholders overcome the free-rider problem are based on tendering strategies that are coordinated so that each shareholder has a substantial probability of being pivotal. It was conjectured that this degree of coordination may not be possible when plausible noise is added in the form of a fraction of the shareholders who are influenced by costs and benefits that are not observed by the others. Thus, there remains reason to expect the free-rider problem to be effective.

3. *Means of profit in tender offers.* Despite the free-rider problem, there exist means by which a value-improving bidder can profit in a tender offer. First, the bidder can succeed at a price below posttakeover value if he has a credible threat to dilute the posttakeover value of nontendered shares (Grossman and Hart, 1980). Second, the improvement in target value will increase the value of shares owned by the bidder or accumulated secretly prior to the offer (e.g., Chowdhry and Jegadeesh, 1994; Kyle and Vila, 1991; Shleifer and Vishny, 1986a). However, in many tender offers, profits derived from initial shareholdings do not justify the costs of bidding.

4. *Adverse selection among targets.* A disadvantage of cash tender offers is that there is an adverse selection problem arising from the information possessed by targets of merger bids: they will accept offers that are too generous, and reject offers that are too stingy (Hansen, 1987). This leads to a problem of efficiency as well as distribution, because potential bidders may be deterred from making offers, and because targets may accept offers even when their information indicates that the takeover will not increase underlying value (Fishman, 1989).

5. *Offer success and informational superiority of the bidder.* Informational superiority does not necessarily benefit the bidder, because this increases the skepticism of the target about the adequacy of the offer in comparison with the posttakeover value the bidder can generate. Thus, an informational advantage of the bidder can cause offer failure, and steps taken to reduce asymmetry of information can increase the probability of offer success (Hirshleifer and Titman, 1990).

6. *Communication and structuring of offers.* The terms of takeover bids (level of bid and the choice of means of payment) communicate part or all of the bidder's information about the target, and can be designed to mitigate inefficiencies that arise from informational advantages of the bidder or target (e.g., Berkovitch and Narayanan, 1990; Eckbo et al., 1990; Fishman, 1988, 1989; Hansen, 1987; Hirshleifer and Titman, 1990). Communication occurs through both the level of the bid and the means of payment chosen. A high offer generally indicates high valuation, because it indicates that the bidder places high value on increasing his probability of success. The use of equity rather than cash indicates low valuation, because of adverse selection problems with equity issuance (Myers and Majluf, 1984). Payment with equity makes the target partake in the bidder's gains and losses, so that overpayment by the bidder can be limited and the target's information can be exploited in determining whether the takeover will be completed.

7. *Information costs, bid costs and the efficiency of auction outcomes.* Costs of investigation and of bidding cause takeover auctions to proceed by a few jumps rather than many small increments, and can reduce the expected price at which the target is sold. The advantage of increasing the bid substantially is that this can communicate a high valuation, inducing a competitor to withdraw. Since both investigation and costs of bid revision limit the information conveyed in the auction process, the winner need not be the bidder with highest valuation of the target (e.g., Bhattacharyya, 1992; Daniel and Hirshleifer, 1993; Fishman, 1988, 1989; Hirshleifer and Png, 1990). The conventional analysis of competitive takeover auctions based on zero bid costs is extremely delicate; very different results emerge with positive but small costs. This is because in a costly auction, as information is communicated a bidder withdraws as soon as he believes he will lose; this can occur at an offer level well below the lowest bidder valuation.

8. *Ambiguous nature and effects of managerial defensive strategies.* Certain measures ordinarily regarded as defensive can promote bidder success by reducing asymmetry of information, and by driving the price up to a level that encourages shareholders to tender (Hirshleifer and Titman, 1990). Most target defensive measures and takeover regulations imposed upon bidders have theoretically ambiguous effects on the expected price paid and efficiency, because they (i) drive up price, (ii) cause failure, (iii) deter investigation of targets by initial bidders, and (iv) sometimes encourage competition by higher valuation bidders (numerous papers).

9. *Managerial voting rights as a takeover defense.* Target managerial control of voting rights provides a defense against tender offers by reducing the pool of voting shares available for purchase by the bidder (Harris and Raviv, 1988; Stulz, 1988). It therefore affects whether a rival for control will attempt a tender offer, a merger bid or a proxy fight (Harris-Raviv).

10. *The effect of target capital structure on managerial voting power.* Managerial control of voting rights and the fraction of gains appropriated by the bidder are influenced by target capital structure and other corporate decisions. A debt-for-

equity exchange in which managers do not participate will increase managers' fractional equity holdings (Harris and Raviv, 1988; Stulz, 1988). Thus, capital structure can be used as a strategic device to position the firm to absorb takeover gains.

11. *Other uses of capital structure as a device for strategic positioning.* A bidder can position himself to bid aggressively by adjusting his debt levels or his initial shareholdings in the target, deterring potential competitors (Burkart, 1994; Chowdhry and Nanda, 1993). A target can issue risky debt so that a value improvement effected by takeover will accrue partly to its debtholders rather than the acquirer (Israel, 1991).

I will conclude by mentioning three directions for further research. A problem that will require a combination of analytics and empiricism is to select among various possible explanations why bidders on average pay such high premia (see Berkovitch and Narayanan, 1991; Nathan and O'Keefe, 1989), and why average combined bidder-target equity holder value gains from takeover appear to be so large. (The much-noted phenomenon of high average target abnormal stock returns associated with takeover is of course a result of the high premia paid.)

A second direction is to explore the consequences of bid costs for the analysis of competitive bidding when there are management defensive measures, and when there is strategic commitment through capital structure or bidder share ownership. Our under-standing of these topics is based on models in which bidding is costless (except possibly for the initial bid), and the *FB*'s valuation is imperfectly revealed by his bid. In these models bidders ratchet up price a little at a time, instead of the large jumps in price actually observed in most takeovers. Auction outcomes in such settings will be sensitive to the inclusion of arbitrarily small bid costs. Thus, more realistic assumptions about bid costs are likely to lead to different conclusions about various corporate control issues.

A third direction is to explore more thoroughly the consequences of strategic target management behavior, in contrast with the passive or mechanistic assumptions of many models. It would be interesting to study the most dangerous competitor to a takeover bidder, the target management itself. Target management can use inside information about target value and potential improvements either indirectly, by encouraging a white knight (friendly) acquirer to make an offer, or directly by making an offer to purchase the company in a leveraged buyout. It seems possible that the threat of target management competition with potential bidders could be so intense that the feasibility of buyouts would *decrease* aggregate takeover activity, and the disciplinary power of takeover threats.

Appendix: Pivotality and bidder profits

Proof of Proposition 7. Let shareholder i own fraction θ_i of the target. Let v_R be the target firm value if a given shareholder retains her shares, for given actions by the other shareholders, and let v_T be the firm value if she tenders her shares. Let $\prod_S^i$ be the gain to a shareholder from tendering her share fraction given the actions of all other shareholders, that is, the difference in the share value if he retains her shares $\theta_i v_R$ and her revenue if she tenders (bid price b, if her share is purchased; $\theta_i v_R$ if not). Let $\prod_B^i$ be the profit made by a bidder from his transaction with given shareholder i, that is, 0 if the shareholder retains her share, 0 if the shareholder tenders but her share is not purchased, and the difference between the bid price and v_T if the share is purchased. The shareholder will not tender unless $E\left[\prod_S^i\right] \geq 0$.

I will show that as the probability that any shareholder is pivotal becomes small, the bidder's expected profits can be reduced below any given positive ε,

$$E\left[\sum_i \prod_B^i\right] < \varepsilon. \tag{33}$$

Thus, for a sufficiently low probability that shareholders are pivotal, if there is any positive bidding cost, no bid will occur. In obtaining this "sufficiently low" probability, we are allowing the ownership distribution (number of shareholders and sizes of θ_i's) to vary. I now verify that the tendering condition implies the no-bid condition Equation (33). $\prod_S^i = 0$ unless the shareholder actually sells her share, in which case $\prod_S^i = \theta_i(b - v_R)$. The bidder's profit from the shareholder $\prod_S^i$ is 0 unless the shareholder sells her share, in which case it is $\theta_i(v_T - b)$. Hence, the sum $\prod_B^i + \prod_S^i$ is 0 if the shares are not purchased, and is $\theta_i(v_T - v_R)$ if they are. Taking the expectation over the probability distribution of the equilibrium actions of the other players and summing over i, and recalling that the θ_is sum to 1,

$$E\sum_i\left[\prod_B^i\right] = \Pr(\text{Sale})E[v_T - v_R|\text{Sale}] - E\left[\sum_i \prod_S^i\right]. \tag{34}$$

As the probability that shareholder i is pivotal becomes arbitrarily small,

$$E[v_T - v_R|\text{Sale}] \to 0, \tag{35}$$

because $v_T = v_R$ unless the shareholder is pivotal. Since the target shareholder expected profit is nonnegative, it follows that the bidder's expected gross profit is arbitrarily close to zero. Therefore he never makes an offer. □

References

Alexander, C., 1986, "Ownership Structure, Efficiency and Entrenchment and Antitakeover Charter Amendments," Manuscript, UCLA.

Asquith, D., 1991, "Are Bad Bidders Good?" Working Paper, Tulane University.

Bagnoli, M. and B. Lipman, 1988, "Successful Takeovers Without Exclusion," *Review of Financial Studies*, 1, 89–110.

Bagnoli, M., R. Gordon and B. L. Lipman, 1989, "Stock Repurchase as a Takeover Defense," *Review of Financial Studies*, 2 (3), 423–443.

Bagwell, L. S., 1991, "Share Repurchase and Takeover Deterrence," *Rand Journal of Economics*, 22 (1), 72–88.

Banks, J. S. and J. Sobel, 1987, "Equilibrium Selection in Signalling Games," *Econometrica*, 55, 647–664.

Baron, D., 1982, "Tender Offers and Management Resistance," *The Journal of Finance*, 38, 331–342.

Berkovitch, E. and N. Khanna, 1990, "How Target Shareholders Benefit from Value-Reducing Defensive Strategies," *The Journal of Finance*, 45, 137–156.

Berkovitch, E. and M. P. Narayanan, 1990, "Competition and the Medium of Exchange in Takeovers," *Review of Financial Studies*, 3, 153–174.

Berkovitch, E. and M. P. Narayanan, 1991, "Negative Acquirer Returns in Takeovers: Agency or Error?" Working Paper No. 91-22, School of Business Administration, University of Michigan.

Bhagat, S. and D. Hirshleifer, 1995, "Do Takeovers Create Value? An Intervention Approach," Working Paper #9505-03, School of Business Administration, University of Michigan.

Bhagat, S. and R. Jefferis, 1991, "Voting Power in the Proxy Process: The Case of Antitakeover Charter Amendments," *Journal of Financial Economics*, 30 (1), 193–226.

Bhagat, S., A. Shleifer and R. Vishny, 1990, "Hostile Takeovers in the 1980's: The Return to Corporate Specialization," *Brookings Papers on Economic Activity, Special Issue*, 1–72.

Bhattacharyya, S., 1992, "The Analytics of Takeover Bidding: Initial Bids and their Premia," Working Paper, Carnegie Mellon University.

Bhide, A., 1989, "The Causes and Consequences of Hostile Takeovers," *Journal of Applied Corporate Finance*, 2, 36–59.

Bradley, M., 1980, "Interfirm Tender Offers and the Market for Corporate Control," *Journal of Business*, 53, 345–376.

Bradley, M. and L. Wakeman, 1983, "The Wealth Effects of Targeted Share Repurchases," *Journal of Financial Economics*, 11, 301–328.

Bradley, M., A. Desai and E. H. Kim, 1983, "The Rationale Behind Inter-Firm Tender Offers: Information or Synergy?" *Journal of Financial Economics*, 11, 141–153.

Bradley, M., A. Desai and E. H. Kim, 1988, "Synergistic Gains from Corporate Acquisitions and their Division Between the Stockholders of Target and Acquiring Firms," *Journal of Financial Economics*, 21, 3–40.

Brown, D. T. and M. D. Ryngaert, 1991, "The Mode of Acquisition in Tender Offers: Taxes and Asymmetric Information," *The Journal of Finance*, 46 (2), 653–670.

Bulow, J. and P. Klemperer, 1993, *Auctions vs. Negotiations*, Stanford University.

Burkart, M., 1994, "Overbidding in Takeover Contests," Discussion Paper No. 180, London Business School.

Cho, I.-K. and D. Kreps, 1987, "Signaling Games and Stable Equilibria," *The Quarterly Journal of Economics*, 102, 179–221.

Chowdhry, B. and N. Jegadeesh, 1994, "Optimal Pre-Tender Offer Share Acquisition Strategy in Takeovers," *Journal of Financial and Quantitative Analysis*, 29, 117–129.

Chowdhry, B. and V. Nanda, 1993, "The Strategic Role of Debt in Takeover Contests," *The Journal of Finance*, 48 (2), 731–746.

Daniel, K. and D. Hirshleifer, 1993, "A Theory of Costly Sequential Bidding," Manuscript, Anderson Graduate School of Management, UCLA.

Dann, L. and H. DeAngelo, 1983, "Standstill Agreements, Privately Negotiated Stock Repurchases, and the Market for Corporate Control," *Journal of Financial Economics*, 11, 275–300.

DeAngelo, H. and E. Rice, 1983, "Antitakeover Amendments and Stockholder Wealth," *Journal of Financial Economics*, 11, 329–360.

Eckbo, B. E., R. Giammarino and R. Heinkel, 1990, "Asymmetric Information and the Medium of Exchange in Takeovers: Theory and Evidence," *Review of Financial Studies*, 3, 651–676.

Fishman, M. J., 1988, "A Theory of Pre-Emptive Takeover Bidding," *RAND Journal of Economics*, 19 (1), 88–101.

Fishman, M. J., 1989, "Preemptive Bidding and the Role of Medium of Exchange in Acquisitions," *The Journal of Finance*, 44, 41–58.

Franks, J. and R. Harris, 1989, "Shareholder Wealth Effects of Corporate Takeovers: The U.K. Experience 1955–85," *Journal of Financial Economics*, August, 225–250.

Fudenberg, D. and D. K. Levine, 1989, "Reputation and Equilibrium Selection in Games with a Patient Player," *Econometrica*, 57 (4), 759–778.

Giammarino, R. M. and R. L. Heinkel, 1986, "A Model of Dynamic Takeover Behavior," *The Journal of Finance*, 41, 465–481.

Giammarino, R. M. and R. L. Heinkel, 1990, "The Evolution of Firm Value and the Allocative Role of Green Mail," School of Commerce, University of British Columbia.

Gilbert, R. J. and D. M. Newbery, 1988, "Entry, Acquisition, and the Value of Shark Repellents," Working Paper #8888, University of California.

Giliberto, S. and N. Varaiya, 1989, "The Winner's Curse and Bidder Competition in Acquisitions: Evidence from Failed Bank Auctions," *The Journal of Finance*, 44 (1), 59–76.

Grossman, S. J. and O. D. Hart, 1980, Takeover Bids, the Free-Rider Problem and the Theory of the Corporation," *Bell Journal of Economics*, 11, 42–64.

Grossman, S. J. and O. D. Hart, 1981, "The Allocational Role of Takeover Bids in Situations of Asymmetric Information," *The Journal of Finance*, 36, 253–270.

Grossman, S. J. and O. D. Hart, 1988, "One Share-One Vote and the Market for Corporate Control," *Journal of Financial Economics*, 20 (1/2), 175–202.

Grossman, S. J. and M. Perry, 1986, "Perfect Sequential Equilibrium," *Journal of Economic Theory*, 39, 97–119.

Hansen, R. G., 1987, "A Theory for the Choice of Exchange Medium in Mergers and Acquisitions," *Journal of Business*, 60, 75–95.

Harrington, J. E., Jr. and J. Prokop, 1993, "The Dynamics of the Free-Rider Problem in Takeovers," *Review of Financial Studies*, 6 (4), 851–882.

Harris, M. and A. Raviv, 1988, "Corporate Control Contests and Capital Structure," *Journal of Financial Economics*, 20 (1/2), 55–86.

Harsanyi, J. C., 1973, "Games with Randomly Disturbed Payoffs: A New Rationale for Mixed-Strategy Equilibrium Points," *International Journal of Game Theory*, 2 (1), 1–23.

Hirshleifer, D., 1993a, "Reputation, Incentives and Managerial Decisions," In P. Newman, M. Milgate and J. Eatwell (Eds.), *The New Palgrave Dictionary of Money and Finance*, Stockton Press, New York.

Hirshleifer, D., 1993b, "Takeovers," In P. Newman, M. Milgate and J. Eatwell (Eds.), *The New Palgrave Dictionary of Money and Finance*, Stockton Press, New York.

Hirshleifer, D. and I. P. L. Png, 1990, "Facilitation of Competing Bids and the Price of a Takeover Target," *Review of Financial Studies*, 2 (4), 587–606.

Hirshleifer, D. and A. Thakor, 1994, "Managerial Performance, Boards of Directors and Takeover Bidding," *Journal of Corporate Finance*, 1 (1), 63–90.

Hirshleifer, D. and S. Titman, 1990, "Share Tendering Strategies and the Success of Hostile Takeover Bids," *Journal of Political Economy*, 98 (2), 295–324.

Holmström, B., 1982, "Moral Hazard in Teams," *The Bell Journal of Economics*, 13, 324–340.

Holmström, B. and B. Nalebuff, 1992, "To the Raider Goes the Surplus? A Reexamination of the Free-Rider Problem," *Journal of Economics and Management Strategy*, 1 (1).

Huang, R. and R. Walkling, 1987, "Target Abnormal Returns Associated with Acquisition Announcements: Payment, Acquisition Form, and Managerial Resistance," *Journal of Financial Economics*, 19 (2), 329–350.

Israel, R., 1991, "Capital Structure and the Market for Corporate Control: The Defensive Role of Debt Financing," *The Journal of Finance*, 46 (4), 1391–1410.

Israel, R., 1992, "Capital and Ownership Structures and the Market for Corporate Control," *Review of Financial Studies*, 5 (2), 181–198.

Jarrell, G. and M. Bradley, 1980, "The Economic Effects of Federal and State Regulations of Cash Tender Offers," *The Journal of Law and Economics*, 23, 371–407.

Jarrell, G. and A. Poulsen, 1987, "Shark Repellents and Stock Prices: The Effects of Antitakeover Amendments Since 1980," *Journal of Financial Economics*, 19, 127–168.

Jennings, R. H. and M. A. Mazzeo, 1993, "Competing Bids, Target Management Resistance and the Structure of Takeover Bids," *Review of Financial Studies*, 6 (4), 883–910.

Jensen M., 1986, "Agency Costs of Free Cash Flow, Corporate Finance and Takeovers," *The American Economic Review*, 76, 323–339.

Kale, J. R. and T. H. Noe, 1991, *Unconditional and Conditional Takeover Offers: Theory and Experimental Evidence*, Department of Finance, Georgia State University.

Kreps, D., P. Milgrom, J. Roberts and R. Wilson, 1982, "Rational Cooperation in the Finitely Repeated Prisoners' Dilemma," *Journal of Economic Theory*, 27, 245–52, 486–502.

Kyle, A. S. and J. -L. Vila, 1991, "Noise Trading and Takeovers," *RAND Journal of Economics*, 22 (1), 54–71.

Lang, L. H. P., R. M. Stulz and R. A. Walkling, 1991, "A Test of the Free Cash Flow Hypothesis: The Case of Bidder Returns," *Journal of Financial Economics*, 29 (2), 315–336.

Leach, C., 1992, "Repetition, Reputation and Raiding," *Review of Financial Studies*, 5 (4), 685–708.

Malatesta, P. and R. Walkling, 1988, "Poison Pill Securities: Stockholder Wealth, Profitability and Ownership Structure," *Journal of Financial Economics*, 20 (1–2), 347–376.

Myers, S. C., 1977, "Determinants of Corporate Borrowing," *Journal of Financial Economics*, 5, 147–175.

Myers, S. C. and N. Majluf, 1984, "Corporate Financing and Investment Decisions when Firms have Information that Investors Do Not Have," *Journal of Financial Economics*, 13, 187–222.

Myerson, R., 1981, "Optimal Auction Design," *Mathematics of Operations Research*, 6 (1), 58–73.

Nathan, K. S. and T. B. O'Keefe, 1989, "The Rise in Takeover Premiums: An Exploratory Study," *Journal of Financial Economics*, 23 (1), 101–119.

Ofer, A. R. and A. V. Thakor, 1987, "A Theory of Stock Price Responses to Alternative Corporate Cash Disbursement Methods: Stock Repurchases and Dividends," *The Journal of Finance*, 42, 365–394.

Olson, M., 1965, *The Logic of Collective Action*, Harvard University Press, Cambridge.

Palepu, K., 1986, "Predicting Takeover Targets: A Methodological and Empirical Analysis," *Journal of Accounting and Economics*, 8, 3–37.

Png, I. P. L., 1985, "The Information Conveyed by a Takeover Bid," Working Paper #3-85, UCLA, AGSM.

Pound, J., 1988, "The Information Effects of Takeover Bids and Resistance," *Journal of Financial Economics*, 22 (2), 207–228.

Ravid, A. and M. Spiegel, 1991, "On Toeholds and Bidding Contests," Working Paper, Columbia University.

Riley, J., 1988, "Ex-post Information in Auctions," *The Review of Economic Studies*, 55, 409–430.

Riley, J. and W. Samuelson, 1981, "Optimal Auctions," *The American Economic Review*, 71, 381–392.

Roll, R., 1986, "The Hubris Hypothesis of Corporate Takeovers," *Journal of Business*, 59 (2, Part 1), 197–216.

Ruback, R. S., 1988, "Do Target Shareholders Lose in Unsuccessful Control Contests?" In A. J. Auerbach (Ed.), *Corporate Takeovers: Causes and Consequences*, University of Chicago Press (for NBER), Chicago, IL.

Ryngaert, M., 1988, "The Effect of Poison Pill Securities on Shareholder Wealth," *Journal of Financial Economics*, 20 (1/2), 377–417.

Samuelson, W. and L. Rosenthal, 1986, "Price Movements as Indicators of Tender Offer Success," *The Journal of Finance*, 41, 481–499.

Schelling, T., 1960, *The Strategy of Conflict*, Harvard University Press, Cambridge.

Shleifer, A. and R. W. Vishny, 1986a, "Large Shareholders and Corporate Control," *Journal of Political Economy*, 94 (3, Part 1), 461–488.

Shleifer, A. and R. W. Vishny, 1986b, "Greenmail, White Knights, and Shareholders' Interest," *RAND Journal of Economics*, 17, 293–309.

Spatt, C. S., 1989, "Strategic Analyses of Takeover Bids," In S. Bhattacharya and G. Constantinides (Eds.), *Financial Markets and Incomplete Information*, Rowman and Littlefield, Totowa, NJ, pp. 106–121.

Stein, J., 1988, "Takeover Threats and Managerial Myopia," *Journal of Political Economy*, 96 (1), 61–80.

Stulz, R. M., 1988, "Managerial Control of Voting Rights: Financing Policies and the Market for Corporate Control," *Journal of Financial Economics*, 20, 25–54.

Stulz, R. M., R. A. Walkling and M. H. Song, 1990, "The Distribution of Target Ownership and the Division of Gains in Successful Takeovers," *The Journal of Finance*, 45, 817–833.

Tiemann, J., 1985, "Applications of Bargaining Games in Mergers and Acquisitions," Working Paper, Harvard Business School.

Walkling, R., 1985, "Predicting Tender Offer Success: A Logistic Analysis," *Journal of Financial and Quantitative Analysis*, 20 (4), 461–478.

Walkling, R. and R. Edmister, 1985, "Determinants of Tender Offer Premiums," Financial Analysts Journal, 27, 27–37.

Weston, J. F., K. S. Chung and S. E. Hoag, 1990, *Mergers, Restructuring, and Corporate Control*, Prentice-Hall, Englewood Cliffs, NJ.

Zingales, L., 1991, "Insider Ownership and the Decision to go Public," Working Paper, MIT.

Chapter 2

AUCTIONS IN CORPORATE FINANCE[*]

SUDIPTO DASGUPTA

Department of Finance, Hong Kong University of Science and Technology, Clear Water Bay, Kowloon, Hong Kong

ROBERT G. HANSEN

Tuck School of Business, Dartmouth College, Hanover, New Hampshire, USA

Contents

[*] We thank Parimal K. Bag, Espen Eckbo, and Mike Fishman for comments and suggestions.

This article originally appeared in B. E. Eckbo (ed.), *Handbook of Corporate Finance: Empirical Corporate Finance, Volume 1*, (Elsevier/North-Holland, Handbooks in Finance Series), Ch. 3, pp. 87–143 (2007).
Corporate Takeovers, Volume 2
Edited by B. Espen Eckbo

Abstract

This paper reviews the applications of auction theory to corporate finance. It starts with a review of the main auction theory frameworks and the major results. It then goes on to discuss how auction theory can be applied, in the context of the market for corporate control, not only to "inform" a company's board or regulators, but also to understand some of the observed empirical evidence on target and bidder returns. It then considers the role of preemptive bidding, stock versus cash offers, the effect of toeholds on bidding behavior, the effect of bidder heterogeneity and discrimination in auctions, merger waves, bankruptcy auctions, share repurchases and "Dutch" auctions, IPO auctions, and the role of debt in auctions. It concludes with a brief discussion of the econometrics of auction data.

Keywords

bidders, targets, private value, common value, winner's curse, auctions, bidding, takeovers, mergers and acquisitions, toeholds, bankruptcy auctions, IPO auctions

JEL classifications: C72, C79, G34

1. Introduction

This paper reviews developments in auction theory, with a focus on applications to corporate finance. Auctions, viewed broadly, are economic mechanisms that transfer control of an asset and simultaneously determine a price for the transaction.[1] Auctions are ubiquitous across the world. Formal auctions are used to buy and sell goods and services from fish to mineral rights and from logging contracts to lawyers' services in class action lawsuits. In the world of finance, auctions are used to buy and sell entire firms (in bankruptcy and out of bankruptcy) as well as securities issued by governments and companies. In the most recent and public example of auctions in corporate finance, the Internet search firm Google sold its shares via a Dutch auction method in its initial public offering.

Auction theory has developed to explore a variety of issues, with the most important ones relating to pricing, efficiency of the allocation, differential information, collusion, risk aversion, and of course a very large topic, the effects of different auction rules (sealed-bids vs. open auctions, reserve prices, entry fees, etc.) on the revenue to the seller.[2] Concomitant with theoretical work, there has been significant work in applications of auction theory, with many of these being related in some way to corporate finance. On one level, application of auction theory to corporate finance is very natural, for corporate finance sometimes directly involves auctions (e.g., auctions in bankruptcy). At another level, though, auction theory should serve to inform corporate finance because the underlying primitive issues are the same: pricing of assets, exchange of control, uncertainty especially in regard to asset valuation, heterogeneity of agents, asymmetric or disparate information, and strategic behavior. Given this similarity in the underlying frameworks, one should expect auction theory to have significant influence, both direct and indirect, on corporate finance research. There has also been, particularly in recent years, much work in the estimation of auction models. The econometrics of this work is very sophisticated, utilizing structural estimation methods that can retrieve estimates of the underlying distribution of bidders' valuations from bid data. While these techniques have not yet been applied to data from finance-related auctions, there would seem to be room for application to, for instance, corporate bankruptcy auctions. The broad lesson from these econometric studies is also very relevant for empirical work in financial auctions: use the restrictions from the theory to learn more from the data than nonstructural methods will reveal. For this reason, empirical finance researchers studying auctions should have a good knowledge of auction theory.

[1] Throughout this survey, we will normally consider auctions where an item is being sold. Reverse auctions, where an auction is used to purchase an item, can generally be modeled by simply reversing the direction of payment.

[2] Krishna (2002) provides an excellent, comprehensive review of all existing auction theory. Klemperer (2000) is a shorter, recent review of auction theory, while McAfee and McMillan (1987) is thorough but a bit dated by now.

A careful review of the literature shows that auction theory has had a significant but not overwhelming influence on corporate finance. Perhaps the more insightful applications have been in the context of corporate takeover bidding: preemptive bidding, means-of-payment (takeover auctions are not always financed with cash), bidder heterogeneity, and discrimination amongst bidders. Application of auction theory to these contexts has at times produced new insights. Overall, however, while the applications have extended our understanding of the inefficiencies that are due to the underlying primitive construct of private information, they have not changed that understanding in any fundamental way.

The survey proceeds as follows. Section 2 reviews the simplest auction setting, that of independent private values. Many key insights can be developed from this simplest model: the basic pricing result that an auction's expected price equals the expected second-highest value; general solution methodology; effects of more bidders' risk aversion, reserve prices; revenue equivalence of the different auction forms; revenue enhancement from ex post means-of-payment; and the solution of auction models via the Revelation Principle. Section 3 considers the interdependence amongst bidders' valuations (including the special case of a "common value" for the object) and reviews Milgrom and Weber's (1982a,b) generalized auction model. Critical insights in this section pertain to the effects of the winner's curse; that lack of disclosure by the seller can lower expected prices; and that the different auction forms are no longer revenue-equivalent. With the basic theory developed in these sections, Section 4 turns to the applications most relevant to corporate finance. Section 5 ends with some thoughts about future applications and further development of auction theory that would make it more relevant for corporate finance.

2. The most basic theory: independent private values

2.1. Initial assumptions

Auction theory begins with assumptions on how bidders value the asset for sale; the model then shows how an auction converts valuations into a price and an exchange of control. Valuation assumptions are absolutely key to auction theory. However, as we will argue later, the existing paradigms are not complete as they do not consider certain sets of valuation assumptions that are particularly relevant in corporate finance.

Independent preference (sometimes called independent private values) assumptions are straightforward: each bidder is simply assumed to know her value for the asset. For bidder i, denote this value as v_i. While each bidder knows her own value, to make the situation realistic and interesting, we assume that a bidder does not know other bidders' values. To model this uncertainty, we assume that each bidder believes other bidders' values to be independent draws from a distribution $F(v)$. We have therefore introduced a degree of symmetry in the model, that of symmetric beliefs.[3]

---

[3] Several papers examine the effects of asymmetric beliefs, for example, Maskin and Riley (2000a,b). See also Krishna (2002).

Fix a particular bidder, and focus on the highest value among the remaining $N - 1$ values from the other $N - 1$ bidders, and denote this value as v_2. Since v_2 is the highest among $N - 1$ independent draws from the same distribution, its probability distribution $G(v_2)$ (i.e., the probability that $N - 1$ independent draws are less than a value v_2) is

$$G(v_2) = F(v_2)^{N-1}. \tag{1}$$

Notice that the distribution $G(v_2)$ has a density function $g(v_2) = (N - 1)F(v_2)^{N-2}f(v_2)$. If $F(v)$ is uniform over the unit interval, that is, $F(v) = v$ for $0 \leq v \leq 1$, then note that

$$G(v_2) = F(v_2)^{N-1} = v_2^{N-1}. \tag{2}$$

2.2. *First-price sealed-bid auctions*

We are now in a position to evaluate any specific set of auction rules. Turn first to the common first-price sealed-bid auction, where bidders submit sealed bids and the highest bidder wins and pays the amount of her bid (hence the "first-price" qualifier). For now we assume a zero reserve price (a price below which the seller will keep the asset rather than sell).

In placing a bid b, bidder i has expected profit of

$$E(\pi_i) = \Pr(\text{win})(v_i - b), \tag{3}$$

where one can note that in the case that bidder i loses, her profit is zero. While Equation (3) does not make it explicit, Pr(win) will be a function of b, normally increasing. This creates the essential tension in selecting an optimal bid: increasing one's bid increases the chance of winning, but the gain upon winning is less.

To solve this model, we need just a bit more structure. Let us use an intuitive version of the so-called Revelation Principle. Fix a bid function $b(v)$, and think of bidder i as choosing the v she "reports" rather than choosing her actual bid. So long as $b(v)$ is properly behaved, we have not restricted bidder i's choice in any way, for she could get to any bid b desired by simply "reporting" the requisite v.

Looking ahead, we are searching for a symmetric Nash equilibrium in bidding strategies. In terms of our $b(v)$ function, symmetry means that all bidders use the same $b(v)$. Nash equilibrium requires that, given other bidders' strategies, bidder i's bid strategy is optimal. In terms again of our $b(v)$ formulation, equilibrium requires each bidder to report $v = v_i$, that is, "honest" reporting. Our requirement for Nash equilibrium will therefore be as follows. Suppose that the other bidders are using $b(v)$ and honestly reporting, so that bidder j's bid is $b(v_j)$. If $b(v)$ represents a (symmetric) bidding equilibrium, then bidder i's optimal decision will be to report $v = v_i$, so that her bid is $b(v_i)$.

In the situation where the other $N - 1$ bidders are both using $b(v)$ and reporting honestly, we can rewrite Equation (3) as

$$E(\pi_i) = \Pr(\text{win})(v_i - b) = G(v)(v_i - b(v)), \tag{4}$$

where we assume bidder i is using $b(v)$ but not requiring $v = v_i$. Note that bidder i wins if all other $N - 1$ values are less than the v that bidder i reports, hence the conversion of Pr(win) into $G(v)$, the distribution for the highest value among the remaining $N - 1$ values.

Now we simply require that bidder i's optimum decision is also honest reporting. Taking the first derivative of Equation (4) with respect to v, we have

$$\frac{dE(\pi_i)}{dv} = g(v)(v_i - b(v)) - G(v)\frac{db(v)}{dv} = 0. \tag{5}$$

The first term of Equation (5) shows the marginal benefit of bidding higher while the second term shows the marginal cost. Rearranging, we have

$$G(v)\frac{db(v)}{dv} = g(v)(v_i - b(v)). \tag{6}$$

For equilibrium, we require that Equation (6) holds at $v = v_i$. Hence we get

$$G(v)\frac{db(v)}{dv} = g(v)(v - b(v)). \tag{7}$$

Equation (7) is a standard first-order differential equation that can be solved via integration-by-parts.[4] Doing this yields

$$b(v) = \frac{1}{G(v)}\int_0^v yg(y)dy. \tag{8}$$

Equation (8) can be easily interpreted. As $G(x)$ is the distribution for the highest value among the remaining $N - 1$ values, $g(x)/G(v)$ is the density of that value conditional on it being lower than v. Equation (8) tells a bidder to calculate the expected value of the highest value among the remaining $N - 1$ bidders, conditional on that value being less than bidder i's own, and to bid that amount. This is about as far as intuition can take us: the expected value of the second-highest value is in some sense bidder i's real competition, and equilibrium bidding calls for her to just meet that competition. (One other intuitive approach involves marginal revenue; we will turn to this view below.)

If beliefs on values are governed by the uniform distribution, then $G(v) = v^{N-1}$, $g(v) = (N - 1)v^{N-2}$, and Equation (8) becomes

$$\begin{aligned} b(v) &= \frac{1}{v^{N-1}}\int_0^v y(N - 1)y^{N-2}dy \\ &= \frac{N - 1}{v^{N-1}}\int_0^v y^{N-1}dy \\ &= \frac{N - 1}{N}v. \end{aligned} \tag{9}$$

---

[4] Rewrite Equation (7) as $G(y)db + b\,dG = y\,dG$ or $d(G(y)b(y)) = y\,dG$. Integrating, and using the fact that $G(0) = 0$, we get $b(v) = \int_0^v y\,dG/G(v) = \int_0^v yg(y)dy/G(v)$.

In the particular case when $N = 2$, Equation (9) implies that equilibrium bidding calls for bidding half of one's value—a significant "shading" of one's bid beneath true value. Note that in this case, however, the lowest the competitor's value could be is zero. If the distribution of values was instead uniform over [8, 10], the equilibrium bid would be $(8 + v)/2$—halfway between the lower bound and one's own valuation.

To see that in general, there is bid shading, notice that we can write

$$
\begin{aligned}
b(v) &= \frac{1}{G(v)} \int_0^v yg(y)dy = \frac{1}{G(v)} \int_0^v y\, dG(y) \\
&= \frac{1}{G(v)} \left[yG(y)\big|_0^v - \int_0^v G(y)dy \right] \\
&= v - \int_0^v \frac{G(y)}{G(v)}dy \\
&= v - \int_0^v [F(y)/F(v)]^{N-1}dy,
\end{aligned}
$$

where we have used integration-by-parts in the third line.[5] Notice that while $b(v) < v$, since $F(y) < F(v)$ within the integral, as $N \to \infty$, $b(v) \to v$. In other words, intense competition will cause bidders to bid very close to their true values, and be left with little surplus from winning.

How does the seller fare in this first-price auction? We can construct the seller's expected revenue by calculating the expected payment by one bidder and then multiplying that by N. Sticking to the uniform [0, 1] distribution for clarity, we have the expected payment by bidder i as

$$
\begin{aligned}
E(\text{Payment}_i) &= \int_0^1 \Pr(\text{win})b(y)dy \\
&= \int_0^1 y^{N-1}\frac{N-1}{N}y\, dy = \frac{N-1}{N(N+1)}.
\end{aligned}
\tag{10}
$$

Multiplying this by N gives the seller's expected revenue as

$$
E(\text{Revenue to seller}) = \frac{N-1}{N+1}.
\tag{11}
$$

Intuitively, since each bidder is bidding her expectation of the highest value among the remaining $N - 1$ bidders, conditional on her value being the highest, the expected payment received by the seller should be the unconditional expected value of the

---

[5] Since $d(uv) = u\, dv + v\, du$, we can write $\int u\, dv = uv - \int v\, du$. This handy trick is used very commonly in the auction literature.

second-highest value. In general, the density for the second-highest value is, from the theory of order statistics,[6]

$$f_2(y_2) = N(N-1)(1-F(y_2))F(y_2)^{N-2}f(y_2). \tag{12}$$

In the case of the uniform $[0, 1]$ distribution, the expected value of the second-highest value is then

$$E(y_2) = \int_0^1 xN(N-1)(1-x)x^{N-2}dx$$
$$= \frac{N-1}{N+1} \tag{13}$$

as expected.[7] To reiterate and emphasize, the seller's expected revenue from the auction is exactly the expected value of the second-highest value. This result, of course, extends beyond the uniform distribution.

2.3. Open and second-price sealed-bid auctions

As compared to the first-price sealed-bid auction, the open auction and second-price sealed-bid auctions are considerably easier to solve. For this reason, they are often chosen to model any kind of auction mechanism; the Revenue Equivalence Theorem discussed below ensures that, in many cases, the results for one auction form extend to others.

In an open auction, bidders cry out higher and higher bids until only one bidder, the winner, remains. It is easy to see that "staying in the auction" until the bid exceeds

---

[6] To see this, first note that the distribution function $F_2(y_2)$ of the second-highest value y_2 is the probability that either: (a) all N values are less than or equal to y_2 or (b) *any* $N-1$ values are less than y_2 and the remaining value is greater than y_2. Note that this latter event can happen in N possible ways. Thus, the probability is $F_2(y_2) = F^N(y_2) + NF^{N-1}(y_2)(1-F(y_2))$. Differentiating this expression with respect to y_2, we get the expression for $f_2(y_2)$.

[7] This interpretation of the expected revenue holds for any distribution. Notice that the expected payment from any bidder is

$$\int_0^{\bar{v}} [\text{Prob(win)} \cdot \text{Amount Bid}]f(v)dv = \int_0^{\bar{v}} G(v)b(v)f(v)dv = \int_0^{\bar{v}} \left(\int_0^{\bar{v}} yg(y)dy\right)dF(v)$$

from Equation (8). Integrating by parts, this expression becomes

$$\int_0^{\bar{v}} yg(y)dy - \int_0^{\bar{v}} F(v)vg(v)dv = \int_0^{\bar{v}} yg(y)dy - \int_0^{\bar{v}} F(y)yg(y)dy = \int_0^{\bar{v}} y(1-F(y))g(y)dy$$
$$= \int_0^{\bar{v}} y(1-F(y))(N-1)F^{N-2}.$$

N times this expression is the expected revenue to the seller in the auction, and is exactly the expected value of the second-highest valuation.

one's value is a dominant strategy.[8] Staying in the auction beyond the point of the bid equaling one's value cannot be rational. Likewise, if the item is about to be won by someone else at a bid less than v_i, then bidder i should be willing to bid a bit higher than the current bid, for if such a bid wins the auction it will yield a profit.

An open auction therefore will quite easily find the second-highest valuation and establish that as the price—for bidding will cease once the bidder with the second-highest valuation is no longer willing to bid more.[9] The expected price in the open auction is therefore the expected value of the second-highest valuation, the same as for the first-price sealed-bid auction. This result is an implication of the Revenue Equivalence Theorem; we return to a more general statement of that below.

Turn now to a second-price sealed-bid auction: in such an auction, sealed bids are submitted and rules call for the highest bid to win but that the price paid will be the second-highest bid submitted. With these rules it is again a dominant strategy to submit a bid equal to one's valuation. Bidding more than one's value would mean possibly winning at a price in excess of value. Bidding less than one's value will mean possibly forgoing an opportunity to buy the object at a price less than value. The key to understanding the second-price auction is to note that the linkage between one's bid and the price one pays has been severed; bidding equal to value to maximize the probability of profitable wins becomes optimal. Thus, as is the case for the open auction, the second-price sealed-bid auction will also yield as a price the second-highest value out of the N values held by the bidders.[10]

All three auctions therefore yield the same expected price.[11] Note, however, that the first-price and second-price (including the open auction as essentially a second-price auction) auctions have equilibrium strategies that are easy to compute for both the modeler and the bidder. Note also that the first-price auction gives a different (and less volatile) price for any given set of bidders. It is also important that all three auctions are efficient in that the bidder with the highest valuation is the winner. Auctions can be seen as accomplishing two distinct tasks: reallocating ownership of an asset and determining a price for the transfer of ownership. Efficiency is an important characteristic of any sales procedure, and auctions under private value

---

[8] A (weakly) dominant strategy in game theory is a strategy which does at least as well as any other strategy no matter what strategies other agents use.

[9] This neglects effects (usually unimportant) of a minimum bid increment.

[10] Therefore, the second-price and the open (also called English or Ascending) auctions are "equivalent" in the sense that they lead the bidders to bid or drop out at their private value for the object. However, this "equivalence" holds only in the private values setting. If the other bidders' signals or valuations are relevant for a given bidder's valuation of the object, this equivalence breaks down, as the open bids by the other bidders conveys additional information.

[11] The first-price auction is "strategically equivalent" to yet another auction known as the Dutch auction, which an open descending price auction in which the auctioneer starts with a high price and then gradually lowers the price until some bidder accepts the price. Provided that the object has not been sold yet, a bidder will accept an asking price that equals her bid in the first-price auction. Strategic equivalence is a stronger notion than the equivalence between the open and the second-price auctions.

assumptions should get the asset to its most highly valued use. Reserve prices, considered below, may hamper this efficient transfer. Efficiency of auctions under asymmetric beliefs is also not assured (see Krishna, 2002, for further discussion).

2.4. Revenue equivalence

The result that the second-price auctions and the first-price auction yield the same expected revenue to the seller is a consequence of the so-called "Revenue Equivalence Theorem." What is fascinating about the revenue equivalence of these two auctions is that such sophisticated models confirm a result which is really quite intuitive: different mechanisms all yield what is really a "competitive" price, that being the second-highest valuation. The seller cannot, under these standard auction rules, extract any more revenue than the valuation of the second-highest bidder.

The revenue equivalence result in this independent private value context can be generalized—not only to encompass a broader class of auctions, but also a more general value environment. Suppose that each bidder i privately observes an informational variable x_i. To simplify notation, we assume $N = 2$. Assume that x_1 and x_2 are independently and identically distributed with a distribution function $F(x_i)$ and density $f(x_i)$ over $[0, \bar{x}]$ for $i = 1, 2$. Let $v_i = v(x_i, x_j)$ denote the value of the object to bidder i, $i = 1, 2$ and $i \neq j$.

Consider a class of auctions in which the equilibrium bid function is symmetric and increasing in the bidder's signal, and let A denote a particular auction form. Let $\prod_i^A (z, x)$ denote the expected payoff to bidder i when she receives signal $x_i = x$ and bids as if she received signal z. Then

$$\Pi_i^A(z, x) = \int_0^z v(x, y) f(y) \mathrm{d}y - P_i^A(z),$$

where $P_i^A(z)$ denotes the expected payment conditional on bidding as if the signal were z, and we have used the assumption that the bidders have symmetric and increasing bid functions, so that i wins if and only if $x_j < z$. Differentiating with respect to z, we get:

$$\frac{\partial \prod_i^A (z, x)}{\partial z} = v(x, z) f(z) - \frac{\mathrm{d} P_i^A(z)}{\mathrm{d}z}.$$

In equilibrium, $\partial \prod_i^A (z, x) / \partial z = 0$ at $z = x$, and hence

$$\frac{\mathrm{d} P_i^A(y)}{\mathrm{d}y} = v(y, y) f(y).$$

Integrating, we get

$$P_i^A(x) = P_i^A(0) + \int_0^x v(y, y) f(y) \mathrm{d}y.$$

Notice that $P_i^A(0)$ is the expected payment made by bidder i with the lowest draw of the signal. Since the seller's expected revenue is simply two times $\int_0^{\bar{x}} P^A(x) f(x) \mathrm{d}x$, it follows that all auctions in which the bid functions are symmetric and increasing, and in which the bidder drawing the lowest possible value of the signal pays zero in expected value, are "revenue equivalent."[12]

The model considered here is one in which the values of the bidders are "interdependent" in the sense that one bidder's signal affects the value (estimate) of the other bidders. The signals themselves, however, are statistically independent. An example of the value function we considered here would be, for example, $v_1 = \alpha x_1 + (1 - \alpha)x_2$ and $v_2 = \alpha x_2 + (1 - \alpha)x_1$, where $1 \geq \alpha \geq 0$. Clearly, the independent private values model is a special case, in which $\alpha = 1$. The case of $\alpha = 1/2$ corresponds to a case of the "pure common value" model, for which $v(x, y) = v(y, x)$, that is, the bidders have identical valuations of the object as a function of both bidders' signals.

2.5. Reserve prices

As reserve prices have figured in some of the corporate finance literature, it is worthwhile to consider analysis of reserve prices in auctions. Sticking with independent private values, consider an open auction with two bidders. Suppose that bidder 1 has valuation $v_1 > 0$ and bidder 2 has valuation $v_2 = 0$. Then the open auction will yield a price of zero. Better in this case would be for the seller to have a reserve price set in-between 0 and v_1 so that bidder 1 would still win but pay the reserve. Of course, the problem with a reserve price is that if it is set above v_1 no sale will result.

To understand how the reserve price is chosen,[13] let us return to the independent private values model with N bidders. Consider any auction form A in the class of auctions with symmetric increasing bid functions. As above, denote by $P^A(z)$ the expected payment by a given bidder in auction A when she bids $b^A(z)$. If the bidder's private value of the object is v, her expected profit is

$$\Pi^A(z, v) = G(z)v - P^A(z),$$

where $G(z) = F^{N-1}(z)$. As above, in equilibrium, it must be optimal for the bidder with valuation v to bid $b(v)$, which requires that $\Pi^A(z, v)$ is maximized at $z = v$. This implies that

$$g(y)y = \frac{dP^A(y)}{dy}. \tag{14}$$

Let us suppose now that a bidder with private value v^* is indifferent between bidding and not bidding. For such a bidder (known as the "marginal bidder"), by definition $\Pi^A(v^*, v^*) = G(v^*)v^* - P^A(v^*) = 0$. Now from Equation (14), integrating, we get for $v \geq v^*$

---

[12] Absent reserve prices, the bidder drawing the lowest possible signal will typically be indifferent between bidding and not bidding.

[13] Our treatment of the problem here follows that in Riley and Samuelson (1981).

$$P^A(v) = P^A(v^*) + \int_{v^*}^{v} yg(y)dy$$

$$= G(v^*)v^* + \int_{v^*}^{v} ydG(y) \tag{15}$$

$$= vG(v) - \int_{v^*}^{v} G(y)dy,$$

where in the last step, we used integration-by-parts.

The expected revenue for the seller from a single bidder is $\int_0^{\bar{v}} P^A(v)f(v)dv$. Again, using integration-by-parts, this can be written as

$$
\begin{aligned}
E(R_i^A) &= \int_0^{\bar{v}} P^A(v)f(v)dv \\
&= \int_{v^*}^{\bar{v}} P^A(v)f(v)dv \\
&= \int_{v^*}^{\bar{v}} vG(v)f(v)dv - \int_{v^*}^{\bar{v}} \left[\int_{v^*}^{\bar{v}} G(y)dy \right] dF \\
&= \int_{v^*}^{\bar{v}} vG(v)f(v)dv - \int_{v^*}^{\bar{v}} G(y)dy + \int_{v^*}^{\bar{v}} F(v)G(v)dv \\
&= \int_{v^*}^{\bar{v}} [vf(v) - (1 - F(v))]G(v)dv.
\end{aligned}
\tag{16}
$$

Given equal treatment of all N buyers, the expected revenue to the seller is simply N times the above expression.

Notice that what we have shown is that all auction forms in the class of auctions being considered must provide the seller with the same expected revenue if the marginal bidder is the same. The reserve price will determine the marginal bidder. If no bidder has a valuation above that of the marginal bidder, the seller keeps the object. Assume that the seller values the object at v_0. Then for any auction, the seller should choose the marginal bidder to maximize

$$\int_{v^*}^{\bar{v}} [vf(v) - (1 - F(v))]G(v)dv + F(v^*)v_0.$$

From the first-order condition with respect to v^*, we get

$$v^* = v_0 + \frac{1 - F(v^*)}{f(v^*)}. \tag{17}$$

Since the optimal marginal bidder is the same in all auctions—all auctions in the class of auctions we are considering provide the seller with the same expected *profit* as well as revenue. The revenue equivalence result survives when a reserve price is introduced.

It remains to characterize the reserve prices in different auction settings. Suppose the reserve price is r. Notice that in both the first-price and the second-price auctions, no bidder with a value less than r can make any positive profit, as they have to bid at least r to win the object. On the other hand, the profit of a bidder with value greater than r must be strictly positive (in the second-price auction, if no other bidder bids higher than r, the bidder pays r). Thus, by continuity, the marginal bidder must have a value $v^* = r$.

Note from Equation (17) that the optimal reserve price exceeds the seller's own valuation and is independent of the number of bidders. This latter point makes sense given that the optimal reserve price is only aimed at making the high bidder pay more in the instance when all other valuations are beneath the reserve price. Note also that a reserve price destroys the assurance of an efficient allocation; in the case where the highest valuation among the bidders is less than v^* but greater than v_0, the seller will retain possession even though one of the bidders has a valuation greater than the seller.

Notice also that *entry fees* are an alternative way of implementing a positive reserve price. By setting an entry fee equal to the expected profit of a bidder with value r when the reserve price is 0,[14] the seller can ensure that a bidder participates if and only if her value exceeds r.

2.6. Optimal selling mechanisms

Auctions are best thought of as "selling mechanisms"—ways to sell an object when the seller does not know exactly how the potential buyers value the object. There is obviously a very large number of ways in which an object could be sold in such a situation: for example, the seller could simply post a price and pick one bidder randomly if more than one buyer is willing to pay that price; post a price and then negotiate; use any one of the common auctions; use any of the *less* common forms of auction such as an "all pay" auction in which all bidders pay their bids but only the highest bidder gets the object; impose nonrefundable entry fees; use a "matching auction" in which one bidder bids first and the other bidder is given the object if he matches the first bidder's bid, and so on. The search for an optimal selling scheme in a possibly infinite class of selling schemes would indeed seem like a daunting task. The major breakthrough, however, was the insight that without loss of generality, one could restrict attention to selling mechanisms in which each buyer is induced to report her valuation (often called "type") truthfully. This is the so-called "Revelation Principle" (Dasgupta et al., 1979; Harris and Raviv, 1981; Myerson, 1981), and it greatly simplified the formulation of the problem.

Armed with the Revelation Principle, one can attack the problem in a more general setting than we have discussed so far. While we will still remain within the confines of the independent private values framework,[15] we can dispense with the assumption that

---

[14] From Equation (15), this is, $\int_0^r G(y)dy$.

[15] Myerson's (1981) framework is slightly more general in that he allows the value estimate of a bidder as well as the seller to depend on the signals of all other bidders, that is, his model is one in which the signals are independent and private, but the valuations are interdependent.

all bidders' valuations are drawn from identical distributions, that is, one can accommodate asymmetries among bidders. Asymmetries are important in many real world situations—for example, in procurement, when both domestic and foreign bidders participate, and especially in corporate finance, in the context of takeover bidding.

Before proceeding further, however, we need to introduce some notation. Let $\mathbf{v} = (v_1, v_2, \ldots, v_N)$ denote the set of valuations for bidders $1, \ldots, N$ and let $\mathbf{v} \in \mathbf{V} \equiv (\times V_i)_{i=1}^{N}$, where V_i is some interval $[0, \bar{v}_i]$. Likewise, let $\mathbf{v}_{-\mathbf{i}} = (v_1, v_2, \ldots, v_{i-1}, v_{i+1}, \ldots, v_N)$, and $\mathbf{v}_{-\mathbf{i}} \in \mathbf{V}_{-\mathbf{i}} \equiv (\times V_i)_{i=1, j\neq i}^{N}$. Let $f(\mathbf{v})$ denote the joint density of the values; since the values are independently drawn, we have $f(\mathbf{v}) = f_1(v_1) \times f_2(v_2) \times \ldots \times f_N(v_N)$, and $f_{-i}(\mathbf{v}_{-i}) = f_1(v_1) \times \ldots \times f_{i-1}(v_{i-1}) \times f_{i+1}(v_{i+1}) \times \ldots \times f_N(v_N)$ is similarly defined.

The seller picks a mechanism, that is, an allocation rule that assigns the object to the bidders depending on messages sent by the latter. By appealing to the Revelation Principle, we can restrict attention to *direct* mechanisms, that is, mechanisms that ask the bidders to report their values v_i. Thus, the mechanism consists of a pair of functions $\langle Q_i(\mathbf{v}'), P_i(\mathbf{v}') \rangle_{i=1}^{N}$ for each i which states the probability Q_i with which the object would go to bidder i and the expected payment P_i that bidder i would have to make for any vector of *reported* values of the bidder valuations. Of course, the mechanism has to satisfy two conditions: (i) it must be Incentive Compatible, that is, it must be (weakly) optimal for each bidder to report her value truthfully given that all others are doing the same, and (ii) it must be Individually Rational, that is, the bidders must be at least as well off participating in the selling process than from not participating.

Thus, the probability that bidder i gets the object when she reports her value to be z_i and all other bidders report truthfully is

$$q_i(z_i) = \int_{\mathbf{V}_{-i}} Q_i(z_i, \mathbf{v}_{-i}) f_{-i}(\mathbf{v}_{-i}) d\mathbf{v}_{-i},$$

and the expected payment he makes is

$$p_i(z_i) = \int_{\mathbf{V}_{-i}} P_i(z_i, \mathbf{v}_{-i}) f_{-i}(\mathbf{v}_{-i}) d\mathbf{v}_{-i},$$

It can be shown[16] that (i) Incentive Compatibility is equivalent to the requirement that the $q_i(v_i)$ functions are nondecreasing, that is, the probability that a bidder gets the object is nondecreasing in her reported value of the object, and (ii) Individual Rationality is equivalent to the requirement that the $p_i(v_i)$ functions satisfy $p_i(0) \leq 0$, that is, the bidder with zero value has nonpositive expected payment. It can also be shown that in the optimal selling mechanism, the $Q_i(\mathbf{v})$ need to be chosen to maximize the following expression:

---

[16] For details, see Myerson (1981) or Krishna (2002).

$$\sum_{i=1}^{N} p_i(0) + \sum_{i=1}^{N} \int_{\mathbf{v}} \left(v_i - \frac{1 - F_i(v_i)}{f_i(v_i)} \right) Q_i(\mathbf{v}) f(\mathbf{v}) d\mathbf{v}$$

$$= \sum_{i=1}^{N} p_i(0) + \int_{\mathbf{v}} \left(\sum_{i=1}^{N} J_i(v_i) Q_i(v_i) \right) f(\mathbf{v}) d\mathbf{v} \tag{18}$$

and the payment made by bidder i needs to satisfy

$$P_i(\mathbf{v}) = Q_i(\mathbf{v}) v_i - \int_{0}^{v_i} Q_i(z_i, \mathbf{v}_{-i}) dz_i. \tag{19}$$

The quantities $J(v_i) = v_i - [(1 - F_i(v_i))/f_i(v_i)]$ are known as "virtual valuations" for reasons that will become clear below. Notice that $[1 - F_i(v_i)]/f_i(v_i)$ is the inverse of the hazard rate $f(v_i)/[1 - F_i(v_i)]$. If the hazard rate is increasing, then the virtual valuations are increasing in v_i. This is known as the "regular case" in the literature.

Ignoring the Incentive Compatibility and Individual Rationality constraints for the moment, it is clear that the objective function Equation (18) is maximized pointwise if $Q_i(\mathbf{v})$ is set equal to the maximum value (i.e., 1, since it is a probability) when $J_i(v_i)$ is the highest for any realized $\mathbf{v}$, and 0 otherwise. Two implications immediately follow.

First, notice that the allocation rule implies that if the bidders are symmetric (i.e., the private values are drawn from the same distribution $F(v_i)$ for all i), then the bidder with the highest value gets the object with probability one. Moreover, from Equation (19), any two selling procedures that have the same allocation rule must also result in the same expected payment made by the bidders and thus result in the same expected revenue for the seller. In particular, when the bidders are symmetric, all the standard auctions—since they result in the highest value bidder getting the object with probability 1—are optimal selling mechanisms and result in the same expected revenue for the seller.

Second, if the bidders are not symmetric, then the object need not go to the bidder with the highest v_i. For example, suppose $f_i(v_i) = 1/(b_i - a_i)$. Then $J_i(v_i) = 2v_i - b_i$. Thus, $v_i > v_j \rightarrow J_i(v_i) > J_j(v_j)$ if and only if $v_i - v_j > (b_i - b_j)/2$. In other words, the high-value bidder may not get the object if the upper bound on her value for the object is sufficiently high. The intuition is that the potential for such a bidder to under-represent her value is high; thus, by discriminating against her in terms of the likelihood of being awarded the object, the seller induces her to report truthfully when her valuation is high. The basic message here is of considerable importance, as we will see in more detail later: when bidders are asymmetric, it may pay to discriminate against the stronger bidder.[17]

---

[17] Notice that in the regular case, since the virtual valuations are nondecreasing, the q_i's are nondecreasing as well. Moreover, it is easily checked that $P_i(0, \mathbf{v}_{-i}) = 0$ for all $\mathbf{v}_{-i}$; hence $p_i(0) = 0$ for all i. Thus, incentive compatibility and individual rationality conditions are satisfied.

2.7. Interpreting the optimal auction: the marginal revenue view

Bulow and Roberts (1989) provide an intuitive interpretation of the "virtual valu-ations" $J_i(v_i)$ according to which the object is allocated in the optimal selling scheme. Interpret v_i as a "price" and $1 - F_i(v_i)$ as a demand curve: if a price p is set as a take-it-or-leave-it price, $1 - F_i(p)$ gives the probability of a sale, that is, the "quantity" $q(p)$ sold at price p. We can then calculate a marginal revenue curve in the usual way, but using $1 - F_i(v_i)$ as the demand curve:

$$\text{Total Revenue} = v_i q(v_i)$$

$$\Rightarrow (\text{Marginal Revenue}) = \frac{d(\text{Total Revenue})}{dq}$$

$$= v_i + q(v_i)\frac{dv_i}{dq}$$

$$= v_i + (1 - F_i(v_i))\frac{1}{dq/dv_i} \tag{20}$$

$$= v_i - \frac{1 - F_i(v_i)}{f_i(v_i)}.$$

Thus, the virtual valuations are marginal revenues, and the optimal mechanism awards the good to the bidder with the highest marginal revenue. Bulow and Roberts (1989) in fact provide the following "second marginal revenue" auction interpretation of the optimal selling scheme. Each bidder is asked to announce her value, and the value is converted into a marginal revenue. The object is awarded to the bidder with the highest marginal revenue (M_1), and the price she pays is the lowest value that she could have announced without losing the auction (i.e., $MR_1^{-1}(M_2)$).[18]

Why does the "second marginal revenue" auction call for the winner to pay the lowest value she could announce without losing the auction? This is, in fact, a property of the optimal selling mechanism discussed in the previous section. To see this, define $s_i(\mathbf{v}_{-i})$ as the smallest value (more precisely, the infimum) of v_i for which i's virtual valuation (marginal revenue) would be no less that the highest virtual valuation from the rest of the values. Clearly, $Q_i(z_i, \mathbf{v}_{-i}) = 1$ if $z_i > s_i(\mathbf{v}_{-i})$ and 0 otherwise. Thus, $Q_i(z_i, \mathbf{v}_{-i})$ is a step function, and this implies that $\int_0^{v_i} Q(z_i, \mathbf{v}_{-i})dz_i = v_i - s_i(\mathbf{v}_{-i})$ if $v_i > s_i(\mathbf{v}_{-i})$ and 0 otherwise. Since $v_i > s_i(\mathbf{v}_{-i})$ implies $Q_i(\cdot, \cdot) = 1$ and $\int_0^{v_i} Q(z_i, \mathbf{v}_{-i})dz_i = v_i - s_i(\mathbf{v}_{-i})$, from Equation (19) we get $P_i(v_i, \mathbf{v}_{-i}) = s_i(\mathbf{v}_{-i})$ for the winning bidder. Thus, the bidder with the highest marginal revenue pays the lowest value that would win against all other values when the object is allocated according to the marginal revenue rule.

---

[18] If no bidder has positive marginal revenue, the seller keeps the object; if only one bidder has a positive marginal revenue, then she pays the price at which her marginal revenue is zero. It is easy to check that truthful reporting is a dominant strategy in this auction.

3. Common-value auctions

3.1. Common-value assumptions

To this point we have mostly considered auctions where bidders' preferences were described by the independent private values assumptions. Clearly, in this framework, given their signals, bidders have complete information about the value of the object to themselves. We turn now to another class of models where each bidder has information that, if made public, would affect the remaining bidders' estimate of the value of the object. The general model could be described as each bidder having a value $V_i = v_i(t_1, t_2, \ldots, t_N)$, where t_i represents bidder i's signal. However, before we turn to the general model, it is useful to focus on a particularly important special case—the case of the "pure common value" model. In this scenario, every bidder has the same valuation for the item, hence the phrase "common value." In other words, we have

$$V_i = v(t_1, t_2, \ldots, t_N) \tag{21}$$

for each bidder i. Such an assumption is reasonable for auctions of many assets. The sale of a company, for instance, is sure to exhibit common value characteristics, for the company's underlying cash flows will be uncertain but, at least to the first consideration, will be the same for all potential acquirers.[19]

Common or interdependent-value auctions involve a certain form of adverse selection, which if not accounted for by bidders, leads to what has been called the "winner's curse." Auctions are wonderful at selecting as winner the bidder with the highest valuation. However, the highest of several value estimates is itself a biased estimate, and this fact would cause the winner to adjust downward her estimate of the value of the object. For example, suppose that there are two bidders, the object is worth $v = t_1 + t_2$ to each, where each t_i is an independent draw from the uniform $[0, 1]$ distribution. Based on her signal alone, each bidder's estimate of the value is $t_i + 1/2$. However, if the bidders are symmetric, after learning that she is the winner in a first-price auction, bidder i's estimate of the value will change to $t_i + E(t_j|t_j < t_i) = t_i + t_i/2 < t_i + 1/2$.

The point to emphasize here is that under almost any reasonable bidding scenario, the high bidder will be the one with the highest value estimate. While each bidder's estimate is an unbiased ex ante estimate of the common value, the highest of those estimates is biased high. Or to put it another way, winning an auction gives a bidder information that they had the highest estimate of value. If one respects the fact that the other bidders are as good at estimating value as oneself, then the information that

---

[19] The classroom "wallet game" mimics this particular common value auction model. In this game, two students are picked and each is asked to privately check the amount of money in his wallet. The teacher then announces that a prize equal to the combined amount of money in the wallets will be auctioned. The auction method is a standard ascending auction in which the price is gradually raised until one student drops out. The winner then gets the prize by paying that price. See Klemperer (1998).

$N - 1$ other bidders thought the item is worth less should give one pause for reflection (and of course this pause should have been taken before the bid was submitted).

3.2. Optimal bidding with a common value

We begin with the illustrative example introduced above, and show how the principles apply.

Suppose there are only two bidders and the value to each bidder is given as

$$v = t_i + t_j, \tag{22}$$

where t_i and t_j are each bidder's privately known signals. We will suppose that the signals are independently distributed according to a uniform distribution on $[0, 1]$.

Consider first a second-price auction. It is easy to show that in this auction, it is optimal for each bidder to bid $2t_i$. Suppose bidder j is following this strategy, and bidder i bids b. Then bidder i wins the auction if $2t_j = b_j < b$, that is, $t_j < b/2$. Her expected gain is $\int_0^{b/2} (t_i + \tilde{t} - 2\tilde{t})d\tilde{t} = t_i(b/2) - (1/2)(b^2/4)$. Maximizing with respect to b, one gets $b_i = 2t_i$, as claimed.

With two bidders, the second-price auction is equivalent to an ascending auction. Thus, it should be no surprise that the equilibrium bidding strategies in an ascending auction are identical to the one derived above. To see this, suppose bidder j has a bidding strategy of $b_j = 2t_j$. If bidder i continues to be in the auction at a price $b > 2t_i$, her profit if j ended the auction by dropping out would be $t_i + b/2 - b = t_i - b/2 < 0$, and thus it cannot be optimal for her to be in the auction at that price. Similarly, if $b < 2t_i$ her profit if j ends the auction would be $t_i + b/2 - b > 0$, and thus it cannot be optimal for her to quit at that price. Consequently, she must stay in the auction until the price reaches $2t_i$.

Notice that the bidders do take into account winner's curse in equilibrium. If the price reaches a level $b = 2t_i$, the value of the object is at least $t_i + b/2 = 2t_i$, since j is still in the auction. Thus, the expected value is strictly higher than $2t_i$. However, i would still quit at this price, because *if the auction had ended* at this price because j quit, she would be breaking even. As we saw above, she would lose if the auction ends at any higher price and she is the winner.

A first-price auction is more complicated, but similar results hold. One can think of the optimal bid in a first-price auction as being the result of a two-stage process: first, adjust one's expected value for the bias associated with being the highest out of N signals; and second, further lower the bid to account for the strategic nature of an auction.

3.3. Milgrom and Weber's (1982a,b) generalized model

3.3.1. Core assumptions

While both the independent private value and the pure common value model capture many key aspects of real auctions, they are obviously polar cases. Many real auctions will contain both private value and common value characteristics. In an auction of a company, for instance, the company's "core" cash flow will be a common value for all bidders, but synergies will likely differ across bidders and therefore contribute an element of independent private values. In a seminal paper, Milgrom and Weber (1982a,b) developed analysis of a generalized valuation model for auctions. The key valuation assumption in Milgrom and Weber's general *symmetric* model is that the value of the item to bidder i is given by

$$v_i = u(t_i, \mathbf{t}_{-i}).\tag{23}$$

In Equation (23), t_i is the signal privately observed by bidder i, and $\mathbf{t}_{-i}$ denotes the vector of signals $(t_i, t_2, \ldots, t_{i-1}, t_{i+1}, \ldots, t_N)$. The function $u(\cdot, \ldots)$ is nondecreasing in all its variables. The model is symmetric in the sense that interchanging the values of the components of $\mathbf{t}_{-i}$ does not change the value of the object to bidder i. In this symmetric model, note that both the private and pure common value models are special cases: if $v_i = u(t_i)$ for all i, we have the private value model, and if $v_i = u(t_1, t_2, \ldots, t_N)$ for all i (i.e., $u(\cdot, \ldots)$ is symmetric in *all* the signals, then the model is a common value model. The interdependent values model with independent signals discussed earlier is also obviously a special case, in which the signals are i.i.d.

The symmetric model assumes that the joint density of the signals, denoted by $f(\cdot, \ldots, \cdot)$ is defined on $[0, \bar{t}]^N$, and is a symmetric function of its arguments. The density functions are also assumed to have a statistical property known as "affiliation," which is a generalized notion of positive correlation among the signals.

It will be convenient to work in terms of the expected value of the object to bidder i conditional on her own signal t_i and the highest among the remaining $N-1$ signals. Without any loss of generality, we will focus on bidder 1, and accordingly, let us define

$$v(t, y) = E[v_i(\cdots)|t_1 = t, Y_1 = y],\tag{24}$$

where Y_1 is the highest signal among the remaining $N-1$ signals of bidders $2, \ldots, N$. We will denote the distribution function of Y_1 by $G(y)$ and its density by $g(y)$. Notice that because of symmetry, it does not matter who among the remaining bidders has the highest signal, and moreover, by virtue of symmetry with respect to the way in which a bidder's own signal affects the value of the object to the bidder, the function is the same for all bidders. Because of affiliation, it follows that $v(\cdot, \cdot)$ is nondecreasing function in t and y.

3.3.2. Equilibrium bidding

It is convenient to begin with the second-price auction. Generalizing the example in Section 3.2, we shall show that the symmetric equilibrium bid function is given by $v(t, t)$. Recall that the function $v(t, t)$ is the expected value of the bidder's valuation, conditional upon the bidder having signal t and on the bidder with the second-highest signal also having signal t.

To see that $v(t, t)$ is the symmetric equilibrium bid function, notice that if bidder 1 bids b_1 assuming that all other bidders are following the proposed equilibrium bidding strategy, then her expected payoff is

$$\int_0^{b^{S-1}(b_1)} (v(t, y) - v(y, y))g(y|t)dy.$$

Differentiating, it is immediate that the first-order condition is satisfied if $b_1 = b^S(t)$ so that $b^{S-1}(b_1) = t$.

Turning now to the ascending auction, suppose that the bidding is at a stage where all bidders are still active. Suppose bidder with signal t has the strategy that she will remain in the bidding until the price $b^N(t) = u(t, t, \ldots, t)$ is established, provided no bidder has dropped out yet. If the first bidder to drop out does so at the price p_N, let t_N be implicitly defined by $b^N(t_N) = p_N$. Then suppose every remaining bidder with signal t has the strategy of staying until the price reaches $b^{N-1}(t, p_N) = u(t, t, \ldots, t, t_N)$. Let p_{N-1} be the price at which the next bidder drops out. Then let t_{N-1} be implicitly defined by $b^{N-1}(t_{N-1}, P_N) = p_{N-1}$. Now every remaining bidder has a strategy of remaining in the bidding until the price reaches $b^{N-2}(t, p_{N-1}, p_N) = u(t, t, \ldots, t_{N-1}, t_N)$. Proceeding in this manner, the bidding strategies of the bidders after each round can be written down until two bidders remain. Clearly, these strategies entail that each bidder drops out at that price at which, given the information revealed by the bidding up to that point, the expected value of the object would be exactly equal to the price if all remaining bidder except herself were to drop out all at once at that price.

We shall argue that these strategies constitute an equilibrium of the ascending auction. If bidder 1 wins the auction, then t_1 must exceed all other signals. Now, from the construction of the bidding strategies, it is clear that the bidder with highest signal among the remaining bidders quits at a price $u(y_1, y_1, y_2, y_3, \ldots, y_{N-1})$, where y_i denotes the value of the ith highest signal among the rest of the bidders, that is, excluding bidder 1. Thus, bidder 1 gets $u(t, y_1, y_2, y_3, \ldots, y_{N-1}) - u(y_1, y_1, y_2, y_3, \ldots, y_{N-1})$, which is strictly positive. Quitting earlier, she would have obtained zero, and any other strategy that makes her drop out after the bidder with signal y_1 cannot give her any higher payoff. Consider now a situation in which bidder 1 does not have the highest draw. For her to win the auction, she must have to pay $u(y_1, y_1, y_2, y_3, \ldots, y_{N-1})$; however, this exceeds the value of the object to her, which is $u(t, y_1, y_2, y_3, \ldots, y_{N-1})$. Thus, she cannot do better than drop out as prescribed by the equilibrium strategy.

To find the equilibrium bid in the first-price auction, assume that each of the other $N - 1$ bidders follow a bidding strategy $b^F(z)$, and that bidder 1 bids as though her private signal were z. Since the bids are increasing, the expected profit for bidder 1 whose signal is t is

$$\prod(z, t) = \int_0^z (v(t, y) - b^F(z))g(y \mid t)dy.$$

The derivative of this expression with respect to z is

$$(v(t, z) - b^F(z))g(z \mid t) - b^{F'}(z)G(z \mid t),$$

which should be zero at $z = t$. Thus, we get

$$(v(t, t) - b^F(t))\frac{g(t \mid t)}{G(t \mid t)} = b^{F'}(t). \tag{25}$$

Since $v(0, 0) = 0$, we have the boundary condition $b^F(0) = 0$. The differential equation can then be solved[20]

$$b^F(t) = \int_0^t v(y, y)dL(y \mid t), \tag{26}$$

where

$$L(y \mid t) = \exp\left(-\int_y^t \frac{g(x \mid x)}{G(x \mid x)}dx\right).$$

It is easy to check that $L(\cdot \mid t)$ is in fact a probability distribution function on $[0, t]$, so that the expression for the equilibrium bid is an expected value with respect to some probability measure.

3.3.3. Revenue ranking and the linkage principle

With affiliated signals, revenue equivalence no longer holds. The ascending auction generates at least as much expected revenue to the seller as the second-price auction, which in turn generates at least as much expected revenue as the first-price auction. While a direct comparison is possible, the so-called "Linkage Principle" provides a fundamental insight. Consider an auction A in which a symmetric equilibrium exists, and suppose that all bidders are bidding in accordance with this symmetric equilibrium except possibly bidder 1, who has a signal t but bids as though her signal were z (z could equal t). Suppose $W^A(z, t)$ denotes the expected price that is paid by that bidder if she is the winning bidder. Then the Linkage Principle says that of any two auctions A and B with $W^A(0, 0) = W^B(0, 0)$, the auction for which $W_2^i(t, t)$ (i.e., the partial derivate with respect to the second argument evaluated with both arguments at t) is higher will generate the higher expected revenue for the seller.

With the benefit of the Linkage Principle, it is easy to see why the first-price auction generates higher revenue than the second-price auction. In the first-price auction, a bidder with signal t bidding as if the signal were z would pay $b^F(z)$ conditional on winning, that is, $W_2^F(z, t) = 0$ for all t and z. On the other hand, in the second-price auction, the corresponding expected payment is $E[b^S(Y_1)|t_1 = t, Y_1 < z]$, where Y_1 is

---

[20] The first-order condition is only a necessary condition. It can be shown that $P_i(z, t)$ is indeed maximized at $z = t$ if the signals are affiliated.

the highest signal among the other $N-1$ bidders. It can be shown that given that $b^S(\cdot)$ is an increasing function, affiliation implies that $E[b^S(Y_1)|t_1 = t, Y_1 < z]$ is increasing in t. Hence, the second-price auction generates higher expected revenue.

An important implication of the Linkage Principle—especially for corporate finance purposes—is that the seller can raise her expected price (revenue) by committing to release to all bidders any information relevant to valuations. More formally, if the seller releases an informative variable that is affiliated with the other variables, then the expected equilibrium price (for all auction forms) is at least as high as when the information is not released.

3.4. Limitations of the common-value and general symmetric auctions

For corporate finance situations especially, issues of information and efficiency in auctions should be important. Existing models do not allow for full consideration of some of these issues.

In the independent private values auction, efficiency has only one dimension: whether the item is sold to the bidder with the highest valuation. In the pure common value model, there is no real allocation problem so that from an efficiency standpoint, one might as well allocate the item randomly. While a random allocation may not provide optimal revenue for the seller, one should be suspicious of a model focused only on wealth-transfer and not efficiency considerations. One can imagine a variety of economic forces outside of the auction process itself that will tend to cause efficient processes to develop (competition between auctioneers, or even the law). Models that assume away any possibility of inefficiency may cause us to lose sight of the true economic issues in comparing alternative selling mechanisms.

The Milgrom and Weber (1982a,b) model brings an allocation problem back into the picture, in that bidders' valuations differ, so there are efficiency implications of the allocation. On another level, though, this relatively general model still fails to permit a complete role for economic efficiency. As pointed out by Hirshleifer (1971), information can have both private and social value. For information to have social value, it must have the capability to affect the allocation of resources. One would expect that in an auction context, information would not only allow bidders to refine their estimates of value, but since the bidders do have inherently different valuations, one would also expect that information would possibly change relative valuations. That is, with one information set, bidder i might have the highest expected value; but with a different information set, bidder j might have the highest expected value.

The Milgrom and Weber model does not permit this kind of role for information. A simple example suffices to show this as well as to illustrate why it is important to allow information to play an efficiency role. Consider the following two-bidder, two-state model:

	State	
	A	B
Bidder 1	100	200
Bidder 2	200	100

In State A, the asset is worth 100 to bidder 1 and 200 to bidder 2, with the valuations reversing for State B. Recall that a major result from the Milgrom and Weber (1982a,b) model is that the expected price increases upon the seller's release of additional information. In the example above this result does not hold. Consider an open auction, and let the information on state initially be diffuse, with each state believed to be equally likely. Then each bidder has an expected value of 150, and an open auction will yield a price of 150. Now let the seller release public information which discloses precisely which state prevails. In either state, an open auction will yield a sale price of only 100, the second-highest valuation. Release of information therefore lowers the expected price, contrary to the Milgrom and Weber findings. Interestingly, there is also now a tension between the seller's objective and economic efficiency: additional information improves efficiency by allocating the asset to its highest-valued use, but it lowers the seller's revenue. Little work has been done on the relative efficiency of auctions under circumstances such as this, but see Krishna (2002) for an excellent summary of efficiency in auctions. In corporate finance, it would seem that the issue of information and efficiency will be closely related: does additional information increase the efficiency of an auction (bearing in mind the cost of producing the information, possibly by multiple bidders) and does this create a conflict between revenue maximization and efficiency?

4. Applications of auction theory to corporate finance

4.1. Introduction

We now turn to survey the more important applications of auction theory to corporate finance. We begin with the market for corporate control and auctions in bankruptcy, which are the two largest areas of application. Then we turn to share repurchases, initial public offerings (IPOs), and a limited review of corporate finance issues in the Federal Communication Commission's auction of radio spectrum. We do not cover applications of auctions to capital markets finance, for instance to models of the stock trading process or to auctions of bonds by governments and companies. Our intent in this survey is to go beyond a simple review and to point out how well auction theory can actually be used to "inform" corporate finance.

4.2. Applications to the market for corporate control

Auctions of one form or another typically occur in the market for corporate control. The field has proved fruitful for a variety of auction-based models to be constructed that explain many aspects of the market. One aspect is to explain the wealth gains to bidders and targets, as well as the combined wealth gains, on announcements of acquisitions.

4.2.1. Returns to bidders and targets

Many studies have documented the evidence on stock returns to bidders and targets in corporate acquisitions, and the overall evidence is that returns to targets are large and positive, while returns to acquirers are generally negative but statistically insignificant. Jarrell et al. (1988) provide evidence prior to 1988; Andrade et al. (2001) provide a recent update: over the period 1973–1998, with a database of 3688 acquisitions, the average 2-day abnormal return around the announcement of an acquisition was 16% (statistically significant at the 5% level) for the target; -0.7% for the acquirer (statistically insignificant); and the combined gain was 1.8% (statistically significant at the 5% level). Boone and Mulherin (2003) further update the recent evidence; they find for a sample of acquisitions between 1989 and 1999 that target returns were on average 21.6%, and that the return to acquirers was an insignificant -0.7%.

Further cuts on the data provide interesting results on the returns to bidders. Returns to bidders are generally more negative the more is the competition from other bidders (although see Boone and Mulherin, 2006, discussed below). All-stock offers generally yield lower returns to bidders than do all-cash offers (see discussion below). Returns to bidders are generally more positive when the acquisition is large relative to the acquirer's size (Eckbo and Thorburn, 2000; Loderer and Martin, 1990; Moeller et al., 2004). One strong empirical regularity is that the total profit to bidders and targets (as measured by the event studies) is greater for auctions than for merger negotiations. This is true for both bidders and targets. This may point to a particular measurement problem: merger bids are often a more drawn-out and partially antici-pated takeover process than auctions—which means profits in auctions are more easily measured. It is also possible that tender offers are more profitable because they tend to remove old management (to a greater extent than mergers).

The most recent evidence come from the large-sample studies of Betton et al. (2008, 2009). They study more than 12,000 publicly traded targets of merger bids and tender offers over the period 1980–2004. Following the approach of Betton and Eckbo (2000), bids are organized sequentially to form contests for a given target, and they focus in particular on the first and on the winning bidder (which need not be the same). Since the surprise effect of the initial bid is greater than that of subsequent bids, and since the initial bidder starts the contest, studying abnormal returns to the initial bidder yields additional power to test hypotheses concerning the sign and magnitude of bidder gains. Moreover, since bids are studied sequentially in calendar time, they present a natural laboratory for testing auction-theoretic and strategic bidding propositions (toehold bidding, bid preemption, bid jumps, target defenses, etc.).

Initially, Betton, Eckbo, and Thorburn follow the tradition and report average abnormal returns for samples of offer outcomes, including "successful" and "unsuccessful" bids. In the traditional analysis, abnormal returns to "success" (AR_s) is found by cumulating abnormal returns from the first bid announcement through completion of the takeover process which may take several months. The lengthy cumulation adds noise to this estimate of AR_s. Therefore, Betton-Eckbo-Thorburn also report ex ante estimates of AR_s using the more precisely measured market reaction to the initial bid announcement only. To illustrate, let x denote a set of offer characteristics (e.g., bid premium, the payment method, toehold purchases) and $p(x)$ the probability that the bid will succeed as a function of x. The market reaction Γ in response to the initial announcement of bid i is

$$\Gamma_i(x_i) = AR_s p(x_i) + AR_u(1 - p(x_i)), \tag{27}$$

where AR_u is the average abnormal return conditional on the offer being unsuccessful. Here, AR_s and AR_u are estimated as regression parameters in a cross-sectional regression involving *all* sample bids, whether ultimately successful or not.[21] Using the right-hand side of Equation (27), they conclude that the expected value of the initial bid (conditional on x) is statistically indistinguishable from zero. As in the earlier literature, targets expected returns are positive and significant, as is the value of the sum of the gains to targets and bidders. Thus, the data do not support theories predicting value-destruction.

Betton, Eckbo, and Thorburn also report that the magnitude and distribution of abnormal returns to bidders and targets depends significantly on whether they are private or publicly traded companies. Bidder gains are larger, and target premiums smaller, when the bidder is public but the target is a private firm. Moreover, private bidder firms have a significantly lower probability of succeeding with their bids for public targets. They also report that, in contests where no bids succeed, the target share price reverts back to the level where it was three calendar months prior to the initial bid in the contest. As noted by Bradley et al. (1983) as well, this share price reversal is what one would expect if the market conditions the initial target stock price gain on a control change in fact taking pace (where control may be acquired by either the initial or some rival bidder).

Overall, the evidence suggests that auctions tend to yield great results for targets but that competition in the auction (or something else) tends to ensure that gains to bidders are at best minimal. From the standpoint of auction theory, this is surprising: certainly in a private values context, and even in a common-value context, the strategic equilibrium of an auction should still yield an expected profit for the winning bidder.

---

[21] The estimation is in three steps: (1) estimate AR_i using time series of returns to the bidder up to the first bid announcement, (2) estimate $p(x)$ using the cross-section of bids, and (3) run regression (27) to produce AR_s and AR_u.

The fact that gains to bidders are minimal suggests that the pure auction models do not capture the richness of the process, and that other forces are likely at play. As Boone and Mulherin (2003) suggest, the evidence is in favor of two-stage models such as that of French and McCormick (1984) which analyze costly entry. While pure auction models imply an expected surplus for participating bidders, entry of additional bidders will cause that expected surplus to be dissipated through costly entry.

Roll (1986) first used the idea of the winner's curse to explain the empirical evidence that acquiring firms appear to overbid for targets in that acquiring firms' stock prices fall (or stay at best constant) upon announcement of acquisitions. If bidders ignore the winner's curse, they may well overpay (in a common value setting, which is not unreasonable in the corporate acquisition market). The problem, of course, is that equilibrium theory does not permit expected overbidding, so Roll is relying upon acquirers making mistakes. Proponents of behavioral finance will find it quite convincing to think that bidders may not properly adjust their strategy for the pitfalls inherent in common-value auctions, for avoidance of the winner's curse requires some careful analysis. Those inclined towards rational, equilibrium-based models of behavior will be wary of models that assume incomplete strategic adjustment. Boone and Mulherin (2006) use unique data that allows them to characterize sales of companies as either auctions or negotiations, and for the auctions, to say how many potential bidders were contacted in the sales process and how many actually submitted bids. Finding no relationship between bidder returns and these measures of competition, Boone and Mulherin conclude that their findings do not support the existence of a winner's curse.

A large literature attributes the acquirer wealth losses to managerial agency problems or "empire building" tendencies. For example, in a sample of 326 US acquisitions between 1975 and 1987, Morck et al. (1990) find that three types of acquisitions have systematically lower and predominantly negative announcement period returns to bidding firms: diversifying acquisitions, acquisitions of rapidly growing targets, and acquisitions by firms whose managers performed poorly before the acquisition. The authors argue that these results are consistent with the view that managerial objectives may drive acquisitions that reduce bidding firms' values. Lang et al. (1991) present related results. Jensen (2004) provides a new angle to this argument by hypothesizing that high market valuations increase managerial discretion, making it possible for managers to make poor acquisitions when they have run out of good ones.

Another recent approach to overbidding is based on the idea that when bidders own initial stakes or "toeholds" in the target firm, they are essentially wearing two hats—that of a buyer for the target's remaining shares, and that of a seller of their initial stakes to the rival bidder. We review the theory-based work in this area more fully below. For now, we note that in an independent private values model, Burkart (1995) and Singh (1998) show that a bidder with toehold will bid above her private value in a second-price auction. Similar results are also obtained in alternative value environments and under alternative auction procedures (Bulow et al., 1999; Dasgupta and Tsui, 2003). Evidence on the empirical relevance of toeholds, however, is mixed.

In Jennings and Mazzeo's (1993) sample of 647 tender offers and mergers, the mean toehold is 3%, but only about 15% of the bidders own an initial stake. Betton and Eckbo (2000) study toeholds for initial and rival bidders in a sample of 1250 tender offer contests over the period 1972–1991. They find that toeholds increase the probability of single-bid success and lower the price paid by the winning bidders.

Betton et al. (2009) delve more deeply into the subtleties of various facts about toeholds. In their sample of 12,723 bids for control (3156 tender offers and 9034 mergers), 11% of the bids involved toeholds. The percentage was significantly higher for tender offers than for mergers, both for nonhostile targets (21% and 6%, respectively, for tender offers and mergers) and for hostile targets (62% and 31%, respectively). The mean and median toehold sizes conditional on being positive were 21% and 17%, respectively, for the overall sample. However, a majority of these toeholds were "long-term toeholds," that is, acquired before 6 months prior to the bid. The percentage of bids involving short-term toeholds for the entire sample was only about 2%. Betton et al. (2009) argue that since toeholds are likely to deter competition, the target might turn hostile if the bidder acquires toeholds when private negotiations might be going on. Thus, it is unclear to what extent toeholds are used strategically in bidding contexts. It is worth recalling in this context, however, Shleifer and Vishny's (1986) analysis of the role of large shareholders in the target firm: even when they are not bidders, the presence of large shareholders in the target firm who are willing to split the gains on their shares with a bidder has the same effect as the bidder having an initial stake in the target.

Another approach to reconciling the existing findings on loss of value to acquirers, the gains to targets, and joint value losses is presented by Jovanovic and Braguinsky (2004), even though their model is not explicitly auction-based. The model incorporates uncertainty over the skill of corporate managers, the value of projects that companies have, and the takeover market. In equilibrium, the takeover market facilitates the exchange of "good" projects from firms with "bad" managers to firms with "good" managers but "bad" projects. Ex ante values of firms represent investors' knowledge of management type but uncertainty over project type. If a firm puts itself up for sale, which it does only if its project is good and its management is bad, then investors learn that the firm does have the property right to a good project and its value increases—hence the positive return to targets. A firm becomes an acquirer only if its own project is bad. Upon learning that a firm will be an acquirer, investors learn that the firm's own project is bad—hence the negative return to acquirers. For reasonable parameter values, including a cost incurred in the takeover process, joint values of the target and acquirer fall. Even so, the mergers in the model are welfare-enhancing.

4.2.2. The auction process in the market for corporate control

As our previous discussion shows, takeover models help understand some of the observed empirical evidence on bidder and target returns. Another major role of auction theory, in so far as it facilitates our understanding of the takeover bidding process, has been to "inform" a company's board or regulators about the impact of selling processes or rules on shareholder wealth, efficiency and welfare. However, here, for the prescriptions to be useful, the auction models must at least reasonably mimic the takeover bidding environment. The question we address now is the extent to which this is the case.

First, it is important to note that auction theory has developed in the spirit of mechanism design, or the design of optimal selling schemes. Any auction model assumes a degree of commitment power on the part of the seller. There are clear "rules of the game" that the seller and the bidders are required to abide by. For example, in a first-price auction, in which bidders shade their bids, the losing bidders might want to submit a bid higher than the winning bid after the latter is disclosed. The seller must be able to commit not to entertain such bids. A similar argument applies to the reserve price. Casual observation, however, suggests that many bids (even when they are friendly) are not seller initiated. It might appear that many control contests are not really formal auctions, in which the seller is trying to secure the best price for the firm's shareholders by committing to a selling mechanism.

This perspective is misleading, for several reasons. First, the board has a formal responsibility to be an "auctioneer." Under Delaware law,[22] a company's board must act as "auctioneers charged with getting the best price for the stock-holders at a sale of the company." In several well-publicized cases, after potential bidders had indicated their interest in acquiring the company, the board of directors of the target company have conducted an auction.[23] Although procedures similar to the ascending auction are most commonly used, boards have also held single, and sometimes even multiple, rounds of sealed-bid auctions (e.g., in the well-documented case of RJR Nabisco).

The commitment issue discussed above may influence the board's choice of auction mechanism. For example, the board might have a preference for ascending auctions because, under alternative auction rules such as the sealed-bid auction, should a losing bidder offer a higher subsequent bid, it may be difficult to reject that bid if the board is required to obtain the "best price for the shareholders." In other words, it may be difficult to commit to a single round of bidding.

Legal scholars, however, have taken the view that whether or not it is feasible for the board to pursue a particular auction mechanism depends, ultimately, on how the courts view it. If, in a given context, the courts consider that a particular auction mechanism can generate higher revenue for the shareholders ex ante than the more commonly used ones, there is no reason why a board cannot adopt it as a selling scheme. Further, if the shareholders do not perceive a particular selling scheme to be against their interests ex ante, there is no reason why a board cannot secure shareholder approval prior to conducting a sale. It is exactly in this spirit that legal scholars have looked at

[22] The Delaware law is significant because many US public companies are incorporated in Delaware.

[23] For example, in the takeover battle for Paramount between Viacom and QVC, the Paramount board eventually conducted an auction in an effort to "select the bidder providing the greatest value to share-holders."

alternative selling procedures (see, e.g., Cramton and Schwartz, 1991). The focus of this literature has very much been on what one can learn from economic theory (in particular, auction theory) to "inform" takeover regulation or selling practices.

Second, the board's commitment power is sometimes underestimated. Boards can commit to awarding an object to a "winner" from a given round of bidding even when better bids might subsequently emerge—thereby undermining the auction—in a variety of ways. The most common practice is to enter into a lock-up arrangement[24] with the declared winner, together with an agreement to pay a break-up fee should the sale be terminated.[25] Another possibility is for the target board to refuse to rescind poison pills for any but the declared winning bidder. While it is unclear whether the courts will allow such poison pills to stand, the legal costs of challenging the poison pills and the possibility that the board might switch to an ascending auction (so that the challenger is by no means assured of winning the contest) may deter further challenge from a losing bidder.

Third, formal or informal auctions are much more common than is usually assumed. Boone and Mulherin (2007) analyze a sample of 400 takeovers of US corporations in the 1989–1999 period and find evidence consistent with the idea that boards act as auctioneers to get the best price for the shareholders in the sale of a company. Based on information from the SEC merger documents, the authors provide new information on the sale process. The most important evidence is that there is a significant *private* takeover market prior to the public announcement of a bid. The authors document that almost half of firms in their sample were auctioned among multiple bidding firms, and the rest conducted negotiations with a single bidder. A third of the firms in the former category went through a formal auction, in which the rules were clearly laid out. In all cases, the process usually began with the selling firm hiring an investment bank and preparing a list of potential bidders to contact. After the bidders agreed to sign a confidentiality/standstill agreement, they received nonpublic information. Subsequently, a subset of the bidders indicating preliminary interest was asked to submit sealed bids.[26]

---

[24] Lockups are "agreements that give the acquirer the right to buy a significant division, subsidiary or other asset of the target at an agreed (and generally favorable) price when a competing bidder acquires a stated percentage of the target's shares" (see Herzel and Shepro, 1990). They may also involve options to buy a block of target shares from the target that may make acquisition by a competing bidder more difficult. Lockup agreements are quite common in takeover contests. The legal status of lockups is unclear, as some courts have upheld them, while others have not. For an account of the legal literature on lockups, see Kahan and Klausner (1996a,b).

[25] For example, Viacom's initial offer for Paramount in 1993 was associated with (a) an option to buy 20% of Paramount's outstanding shares and (b) a termination fee of $150 million plus expenses, should the transaction not be concluded.

[26] Betton et al. (2009) show that of the 12,000 contests, about 3000 (25%) start out as tender offers (which subsequently turn into auctions). Some initial merger bids also end up in auctions, so the overall percentage of auctions maybe closer to 30%.

Another issue relevant for the applicability of auction models to control contests concerns the complexity of the environments in which takeovers are conducted, compared to the standard auction environments. Auction models are nicely classified as belonging to different value environments, and results differ depending on which value environment is under consideration. The takeover environment is considerably more complicated. The motives for takeover bids could be varied. The early takeover models (e.g., Grossman and Hart, 1980) assumed that the benefit from a takeover comes from an improvement in the operational efficiency of the target company. As the authors showed, this could lead to a "free-rider" problem and the market for corporate control could fail. However, later models have focused on "merger synergies" as the source of gain from takeovers. If the synergies accrue to the bidding firm, then the standard auction environment is more applicable. Here, however, there are issues about whether "private values" or "common values" assumptions are more relevant. Since bidders are different and the synergies are likely to have idiosyncratic components, a private values model does not appear unreasonable. However, common value elements will also undoubtedly exist. Synergies can have common-value components if their magnitudes depend on the quality of the target's assets, or if the bidders plan to bundle these assets with other assets that they own and eventually sell these assets.[27],[28]

Other complexities also arise when applying the auction framework to the analysis of takeover bidding. Bidders could bid for the company, or they could bid for a fraction of the company's shares. Different regulatory regimes permit different types of bids. Bids could be exclusionary, discriminatory, conditional, and so on. Bids can be in cash, or in shares of the target company. Bidders may have different toeholds, and they might have different degrees of expertise in the target industry (a factor that could affect the degree of information conveyed by their bids in common value environments). Finally, if the bidders are competing with each other in the same industries, then the outcome of the auction may impose externalities on the bidders. As we will argue below, while existing takeover models, drawing on auction theory, have evolved to deal with these many of these complexities, significant gaps still exist in the literature.

4.2.3. Auctions versus negotiations

Several papers use auction theory to further refine our theoretical and empirical understanding of the auction process in corporate takeovers. Starting at the most

---

[27] Models of takeover bidding, when making common values assumption about the target's "true worth," have often tended to assume away the free-rider problem. If a bidder obtains a large majority of the shares, she may be able to "freeze out" the remaining minority shareholders. Also, the loss of liquidity on any remaining shares can have the same effect as "dilution" (see Grossman and Hart, 1980) that reduce the post-takeover value of the minority shares.

[28] Betton and Eckbo (2000) show that the average number of days from the initial tender offer bid to the second bid is 15 days (counting only auctions with two or more bids). They suggest that this very short period is evidence of correlated values. Of course, the vast majority of all cases develop a single bid only, which may be taken as evidence of private (uncorrelated) values, or preemptive bidding (see below).

basic level, Bulow and Klemperer (1996) show that in an English auction, it is always better to have $N + 1$ bidders in a formal auction than to have N bidders but with a follow-on (optimal) negotiation between the winning bidder and the seller. If $N = 1$, this shows that it is better to have an auction with two bidders than to sell by posting a reserve price.[29] Very simply, the auction process is extremely efficient at extracting value from the high bidder, more so than even an optimally conducted negotiation. This theoretical result does conflict with a stylized fact that companies do frequently avoid auctions and instead negotiate with just one buyer (Boone and Mulherin, 2007).

4.2.4. Preemptive bidding

Fishman (1988, 1989) considers models where one bidder has incentive to make a "preemptive" bid. In the main model of Fishman, a first bidder has incentive to put in a high bid that discourages the second bidder from bidding. The reason for this is that a high bid can signal a high valuation on the part of the first bidder, and a second bidder will then infer that the gain from participating in the auction is low (they are not likely to win in the final English auction). Since participation in the auction requires a bidder to spend resources to determine her own value, the second bidder can be discouraged from even entering the auction. Fishman (1989) extends this initial work by including the possibility of noncash offers.

Fishman's (1988) model works as follows. The value of the target assets to the bidders depends in part on the realization of a state of nature which is observed only by the target. Conditional on the target's information, the value of the assets to the bidders is increasing in the bidders' independent private signals. The means-of-payment can be either cash or debt that is backed by the target's assets. Each bidder has to incur some cost to learn the private signal. Bidder 1 identifies a target by accident, and then incurs some cost to learn his signal (bidding is assumed to be not profitable if the true signal is unknown). If bidder 1 submits a bid, the target is "put in play," and a second bidder is aware of the target. This bidder then decides whether or not to compete for the target and incur the cost of learning her signal.

There is a stand-alone value of the target that is public information, and the target rejects all bids below this value. Since the bidders do not know completely how much the target assets are worth to them (recall that the target privately observes part of this information), bidders could end up overpaying for the target. Paying with debt mitigates the overpayment because the value of the debt is contingent on the value of the target assets (since the debt is backed by these assets). However, if bidder 1 draws a high private signal, a cash offer—though costly—will separate it from a bidder with low signal: the latter will prefer to pay only with debt since his own private signal is not sufficiently high. Thus, by bidding with cash, the first bidder can signal to the second bidder that the latter's likelihood of winning the ensuing auction is low: hence,

---

[29] See Krishna (2002) for an analysis of this case.

the second bidder may decide not to incur the cost of learning her signal. This, then, is a "preemptive" bid. On the other hand, if the first bidder's signal is low, bidding high with a cash offer is too costly. Thus, such a bidder would decide not to preempt and instead bid with debt to mitigate the potential loss from buying a target with low synergy. Notice that one prediction of this model is that more competing offers should be forthcoming with noncash offers than with cash offers.[30]

4.2.5. Modeling auctions of companies

Hansen (2001) reviews the formal auction process used for selling private companies and divisions of public companies. The model explains the common practices of limiting the number of bidders and limiting the disclosure of information to bidders (Boone and Mulherin, 2007), even though theory suggests that both practices would reduce prices. Hansen argues that some information in a corporate sale is competitive in nature, and that its broad release can destroy value in the selling company. The seller therefore faces a tradeoff between having many bidders and full disclosure versus protecting value by limiting disclosure, as well as the number of bidders. While not modeling negotiations formally, the analysis implies that negotiation with a single bidder may be optimal if the "competitive information cost" is high enough. The model also explains the practice of a two-stage auction, with a first stage calling for nonbinding "indications of interest" (value estimates for the target) which are used to select bidders for the second round and giving them access to more information on the selling company. If the selling company uses the initial value estimates for the target to set a reserve price that is an increasing function of the estimates, bidders in the initial round will reveal their private valuations honestly and the selling company can select the most highly valued bidders for the final, binding, round (see the discussion below on the process for pricing IPOs for an earlier similar finding).

4.3. Means-of-payment

Hansen (1985a,b, 1986) has considered the role of noncash means-of-payment in the market for corporate control; this work has now been extended by DeMarzo et al. (2005). In one model, Hansen shows that ex post means-of-payment can increase the seller's revenue beyond what cash payments can do. Take an independent private values context, where v_i represents bidder i's valuation of the target company. An ascending auction with cash as the means-of-payment will yield v_2—the second-highest value—as the price. Consider, however, bidding using bidders' stock as the means-of-payment. Let each bidder have a common value, v, of her stand-alone equity. Then each bidder will be willing to bid up to s_i, where s_i is the share of firm i offered

---

[30] Betton and Eckbo (2000) find that the average offer premium in successful single-bid contests is greater than the average offer premium in the *first* bid in multiple-bid contests. This what consistent with preemptive bidding.

(implicitly through an offer of equity) and is defined to make the postacquisition value of the bidder's remaining equity equal to its preacquisition value:

$$v = (v + v_i)(1 - s_i),$$

which implies

$$s_i = \frac{v_i}{v + v_i}. \tag{28}$$

The bidder with the highest valuation of the target will win this auction (s_i is increasing in v_i) and she will have to offer a share defined by v_2, the valuation of the second-highest bidder. However, the value of this bid to the target will be

$$s_2(v + v_1) = \frac{v + v_1}{v + v_2} v_2 > v_2$$

since $v_1 > v_2$. The stock-based bidding therefore extracts more revenue from the high-bidder than does cash bidding. DeMarzo et al. (2005) generalize this result, showing that expected revenues are increasing in the "steepness" of the security design, where steepness refers, roughly, to the rate of change of a security's value in relation to the underlying true state. This paper also compares auction formats in a world where bids can be noncash; it turns out that revenue equivalence does not always hold. Overall the paper concludes that the optimal auction is a first-price auction with call options as the means-of-payment.

Ex post pricing mechanisms also yield benefits in common-value contexts. The reason for this follows from the return of the adverse selection problem inherent in the winner's curse: the problem arises because the price for the asset is being determined before the value of the asset is known. Any kind of pricing mechanism that determines all or part of the price ex post can alleviate the problem. Using the acquiring firm's stock is an ex post pricing mechanism, for that stock's value will depend upon the actual value of the target firm. Hansen (1986) builds on this insight and shows that stock and cash/stock offers can be used efficiently in mergers and acquisitions. However, in offering stock as the means-of-payment, acquiring firms bring in their own adverse selection problem—acquiring firms may offer stock when they have information that their own value is low. Taking into account both the ex post pricing advantage of stock and the "reverse" adverse selection problem, it turns out that higher-valued acquirers will offer cash while low-valued acquirers offer stock. Fishman (1989) reaches a similar conclusion, in that noncash offers induce the target firm to make more efficient sell/don't sell decisions, but that cash offers have an advantage in preempting other bids.[31]

Several studies on US data show results consistent with Hansen and Fishman's work, that acquirers' returns are higher for cash offers than for stock offers (see Eckbo et al.,

---

[31] Rhodes-Kropf and Viswanathan (2000) consider a general model of noncash auctions for a bankrupt firm. We discuss this model later.

1990, for a brief summary). The first paper to explicitly model the choice of mixed offers is Eckbo et al. (1990). These authors prove the existence of a fully separating equilibrium in which the market's revaluation of the bidder firm is increasing and convex in the proportion of the offer that is paid in cash. Since one can estimate the revaluation, and since the proportion paid in cash is observable, this theory is testable. Using over 250 Canadian takeovers (where tax issues do not confound the choice of payment method), the authors find empirical support for the "increasing" part but not for convexity.

4.4. Toeholds

Recently, a number of theoretical papers have examined how toeholds affect takeover bidding. The main result that emerges from this literature is that the presence of makes bidders more aggressive, with the result that bidders can bid above the value of the object. The result holds for the second-price auction in both the independent private values as well as a common value environment.

Burkart (1995)[32] considers a two-bidder and independent private values model. The private values are best interpreted as synergies. The auction form is a second-price auction, which in this context is strategically equivalent to an ascending auction (Lemma 1 in the paper). From standard arguments, it follows that (i) it is a dominant strategy for the bidder with no toeholds to bid exactly her valuation, and (ii) it is a *dominated* strategy for the bidder with positive toehold to bid below her valuation. A general result is that any bidder with positive initial stake will bid strictly above her valuation. The model is then specialized to the case in which one bidder—call her bidder 1—has an initial stake of θ while the other bidder—bidder 2—has no initial stake.

Since bidder 2 will bid her value, we have $b_2(v_2) = v_2$. Thus, bidder 1's problem is to choose b_1 to maximize

$$\text{Max}_{b_1} \prod_1 (v_1, b_1, \theta) = \int_0^{b_1} [v_1 - (1 - \theta)v_2] f_2(v_2) dv_2 + \theta b_1 (1 - F_2(b_1)). \qquad (29)$$

The first-order condition is

$$(v_1 - (1 - \theta)b_1) f_2(b_1) + \theta(1 - F_2(b_1)) - \theta b_1 f_2(b_1) = 0.$$

Rearranging, we get

$$b_1 = v_1 + \theta \frac{1 - F_2(b_1)}{f_2(b_1)} > v_1. \qquad (30)$$

If one assumed that the hazard function $f_2(\cdot)/[1 - F_2(\cdot)]$ is increasing, then a number of results follows immediately. First, bidder 1's equilibrium bid is increasing in her valuation and the size of her toehold. Therefore, the probability that bidder 1

---

[32] Singh (1998) has essentially similar results.

wins the auction is also increasing in her toehold. It is also clear that the auction outcome can be inefficient: since bidder one bids more aggressively than bidder 2, it is clearly possible that $v_1 < v_2 < b_1(v_1)$, that is, bidder 1 has the lower valuation but wins the auction. This result is similar to the inefficiency in the standard auctions where the seller sets a reserve price. In fact, the intuition for the overbidding result is exactly that of an optimal reserve price from the point of view of a seller. Indeed, with a toehold, a bidder is a part-owner and we should not be surprised to find that she wants to "set a reserve price" in excess of her own value.

It is interesting to note that winning can be "bad news" for bidder 1. Suppose $v_1 = 0$ with probability 1. Then bidder 1 still bids a positive amount (equal to bidder 2's value) but since her bid exceeds the value of the synergy, she always overpays when she wins the auction. By continuity, the same conclusion holds for $\bar{v}_1$ (the upper bound of the support of the distribution of bidder 1's synergy) sufficiently small, and for bidder 2's valuation in some interval $[v_2', b_1(\bar{v}_1)]$.[33]

Bulow et al. (1999) examine the effect of toeholds in a pure common value environment. They make a significant contribution to the literature on toeholds by deriving bid functions for both the second and first-price auctions when both bidders have positive toeholds. They examine how (for small positive toeholds) bidder asymmetry affects the takeover outcome in each auction, and compare expected revenues in the two auctions when the toeholds are symmetric as well as asymmetric. We first discuss their setup in some detail, before discussing the intuition for the main results.

Bulow et al. (1999) consider a "pure common value" model with two bidders where each bidder draws an independent signal t_i from a uniform [0, 1] distribution. The value of the target to each bidder is $v(t_1, t_2)$. Bidder i owns initial stake θ_i in the target, where $1/2 > \theta_i > 0$, for $i = 1, 2$. Each bidder bids for the remaining $1 - \theta_i$ fraction of the shares of the target.

In the second-price auction, bidder i's problem is to choose b_i to maximize

$$\text{Max}_{b_i} \prod_i (t_i, b_i) = \int_0^{b_j^{-1}(b_i)} [v(t_i, \alpha) - (1 - \theta_i)b_j(\alpha)]d\alpha + \int_{b_j^{-1}(b_i)}^1 \theta_i b_i \, d\alpha. \tag{31}$$

The first-order condition is

$$\frac{1}{b_j'}[v(t_i, b_j^{-1}(b_i)) - (1 - \theta_i)b_j(b_j^{-1}(b_i))] + [1 - b_j^{-1}(b_i)]\theta_i - \theta_i b_i \frac{1}{b_j'} = 0.$$

Let us now define $\phi_j(t_i) = b_j^{-1}(b_i(t_i))$, that is, this defines the pair of signals for bidders i and j for which they have the same bid, since $b_j(\phi_j(t_i)) = b_i(t_i)$. Similarly, we can define $\phi_i(t_j) = b_i^{-1}(b_j(t_j))$. Using these definitions, we can rewrite the first-order condition as

---

[33] Using Burkart's private value setting with two bidders, Betton et al. (2009) also show optimal overbidding when the bidder has a lock-up agreement with the target. Moreover, they show optimal underbidding when the bidder has a breakup fee agreement with the target.

$$b'_j(\phi_j(t_i)) = \frac{1}{\theta_i} \frac{1}{1 - \phi_j(t_i)} [b_i(t_i) - v(t_i, \phi_j(t_i))], \tag{32}$$

where we have replaced t_j by $\phi_j(t_i)$.

The corresponding first-order condition for bidder j is

$$b'_i(\phi_i(t_j)) = \frac{1}{\theta_j} \frac{1}{(1 - \phi_i(t_j))} [b_j(t_j) - v(\phi_i(t_j), t_j)], \tag{33}$$

where we have used the fact that $v(\phi_i(t_j), t_j) = v(t_j, \phi_i(t_j))$. Consider a pair of t_i and t_j that in equilibrium bid the same, then we must have $t_i = \phi_i(t_j)$ and $t_j = \phi_j(t_i)$. Using this, the last equation can be rewritten as

$$b'_i(t_i) = \frac{1}{\theta_j} \frac{1}{(1 - t_i)} [b_j(\phi_j(t_i)) - v(t_i, \phi_j(t_i))]. \tag{34}$$

Since $b_j(\phi_j(t_i)) = b_i(t_i)$ and $b'_i(t_i) = b'_j(\phi_j(t_i))\phi'_j(t_i)$, dividing Equation (34) by Equation (32), we get

$$\phi'_j(t_i) = \frac{\theta_i}{\theta_j} \left[\frac{1 - \phi_j(t_i)}{1 - t_i} \right]. \tag{35}$$

Integrating, and using the boundary condition $b_i(0) = b_j(0)$ (see Bulow et al., 1999, for a proof), we get

$$\phi_j(t_i) = 1 - (1 - t_i)^{\theta_i/\theta_j}. \tag{36}$$

Since the probability that bidder i wins the object is $\int_0^1 \int_0^{\phi_j(t_i)} dt\, dt_i = \theta_i/(\theta_i + \theta_j)$, it is clear that bidder i is more likely to win the auction as her stake increases and that of bidder j decreases. Remarkably, a bidder's probability of winning goes to 0 as her stake becomes arbitrarily small, given that the other bidder has a positive stake. The intuition for this result is that while bidder i with zero stake has no incentive to bid above $v(t_i, \phi_j(t_i))$ given the equilibrium bidding strategy of j, as we shall see below, bidder j with $t_j = \phi_j(t_i)$ and a positive stake will strictly bid above this value.[34]

---

[34] Klemperer (1998) demonstrates in the context of the "Wallet Game" how a very small asymmetry in a common value model can give rise to very asymmetric equilibria. This is a consequence of the fact that in the standard Wallet Game, there are in fact a continuum of asymmetric equilibria. A small toehold—like a small bonus to one of the players in the Wallet Game—introduces a slight asymmetry that can have a major impact on the equilibrium, that is, one of the bidders essentially having a zero probability of winning. With a slight advantage, the stronger player bids slightly more aggressively, but that increases the winner's curse on the weaker player. The latter then bids less aggressively, which reduces the winner's curse on the stronger player, who then bids still more aggressively, and so on. With slight entry or bidding costs, this prevents the weaker player/players from entering the auction, so that very low prices result. Klemperer (1998) provides several illustrative examples from Airwaves Auctions.

Now, Equation (34) can be integrated to give

$$b_i(t_i) \frac{\int_{t_i}^{1} v(t, \phi_j(t))(1-t)^{(1/\theta_j)-1} dt}{\int_{t_i}^{1} (1-t)^{(1/\theta_j)-1} dt},$$ (37)

where the boundary condition $b_i(1) = b_j(1) = v(1, 1)$ is used (see Bulow et al., 1999). From Equation (36), we then get

$$b_i(t_i) = \frac{\int_{t_i}^{1} v(t, 1-(1-t)^{\theta_i/\theta_j})(1-t)^{(1/\theta_j)-1} dt}{\int_{t_i}^{1} (1-t)^{(1/\theta_j)-1} dt}.$$ (38)

Bidder j's bid function is derived similarly. From Equation (37), it is clear that for $t_i < 1$, $b_i(t_i) > v(t_i, \phi_j(t_i))$. Thus, when bidder i wins the auction, she is paying more than the target is worth to her. Moreover, bidder i's bid is increasing in her stake θ_i, that is, a higher stake makes the bidder act more like a seller and causes her to bid higher.

Bulow et al. (1999) extend the analysis in two main directions. First, they consider the effect of a more asymmetric distribution of the toeholds and find that subject to an overall constraint on the toeholds of the two bidders that is sufficiently small, a more uneven distribution of toeholds leads to lower expected sale price for the target. This result is a consequence of the fact that as the toeholds become more asymmetric, the bidder with the higher toehold bids more aggressively, that is, further away from the value. For the bidder with a smaller toehold, this implies that the target is worth less conditional on winning. Exposed to this "winner's curse," the bidder with the smaller toehold therefore bids lower. Since in the second-price auction the winner pays the lower of the two bids, the expected sale price is adversely affected when the toeholds become asymmetric.

Bulow et al. (1999) next consider first-price auction and derive the equilibrium bid functions using methods similar to those described above for the second-price auction. In this case, we have $\tilde{\phi}_j(t_i) = t_i^{(1-\theta_i)/(1-\theta_j)}$. The probability that bidder i with signal t_i and toehold θ_i wins the auction in this case is given by $(1 - \theta_j)/[(1 - \theta_i) + (1 - \theta_j)]$, which is increasing in θ_i. It is easily checked that for $\theta_i < \theta_j$, the probability of bidder i winning the auction is lower in the second-price auction than in the first-price auction. Since in both auctions the probability is exactly 1/2 when $\theta_i = \theta_j$, this implies that the winning probability falls more steeply with a decrease in a bidder's toehold the second-price auction than in the first-price auction.

The incentive for bidders with toeholds to bid high in the first-price auction are not as strong as in the second-price auction. This is because in the in the first-price auction (unlike the second-price auction), bidding high does affect the bidder's cost, although a higher toehold does lower that cost since fewer shares need to be purchased.

Unlike the second-price auction, the expected sale price can increase in the first-price auction as the toeholds become more asymmetric. Revenue comparisons indicate that with *symmetric* toeholds, the expected sale price is higher in the second-price auction. This is because as the winner's curse problem is mitigated with symmetric toeholds, both bidders can bid more aggressively and essentially set a higher reserve price for their stakes in the second-price auction. With asymmetric toeholds, as we saw above, the second-price auction generates low expected sale prices due to the winner's curse.[35]

4.5. Bidder heterogeneity and discrimination in takeover auctions

Bidder asymmetry is common in the context of corporate control contests and can take several forms. Asymmetry in initial stakes or toeholds, discussed in the previous section, is one form of bidder asymmetry. Bidder asymmetry can also arise when bidders draw their signals from different distributions, or when (in a common value environment) the bidder signals have asymmetric impact on the value function.

In Section 2.6, we saw that when bidders are asymmetric, the optimal mechanism may not allocate the object to the bidder with the highest valuation. For example, in the independent private value context, an allocation rule that discriminates against a stronger bidder may provide a higher expected profit to the seller. Thus, standard auctions are no longer optimal in the presence of various forms of bidder heterogeneity.

To increase the expected sale price when bidders are asymmetric, the seller has essentially two alternative responses. Both involve "leveling the playing field." When the asymmetry is due to differences in toeholds or access to information, the target's board may decide to restore symmetry by allowing the disadvantaged bidder increase his toehold cheaply or provide access to additional information.[36] Alternatively, the board may decide to design the auction rules in a way that discriminates against the strong bidder.

An especially simple way to discriminate is to impose an order of moves on the bidders. Since bidding games are price-setting games, there is usually a "second-mover advantage" associated with bidding games (see Gal-Or, 1985, 1987). Thus, to discriminate against the strong bidder, the seller could ask this bidder to bid first. This bid could then be revealed to a second bidder, who wins the auction if she agrees to match the first bid. Otherwise, the first bidder wins. In the context of takeover bidding, this "matching auction" has been studied by Dasgupta and Tsui (2003), who note that since courts are more concerned about shareholder value than whether the playing field

---

[35] The analysis of toeholds can be extended to models that include the private value model and the common value model of Bulow et al. (1999) as special cases. Dasgupta and Tsui (2004) analyze auctions where bidding firms hold toeholds in each other in the context of such a model.

[36] Betton and Eckbo (2000) note that when a rival (second) bidder enters the auction with a toehold, the toehold is of roughly the same magnitude as the initial bidder's toehold (about 5%). This is consistent with the "leveling the playing field" argument of Bulow et al. (1999).

is level or not, it is unlikely that the matching auction will run into trouble because it does not treat the bidders symmetrically.[37]

To see that the matching auction can generate a higher expected sale price than the second-price auction in the independent private value setting, let us return to the private values model introduced in Section 4.4. Assume that the private values of both bidders are drawn from the uniform [0, 1] distribution. From Equation (30), we get the bid of bidder 1 who has a toehold of θ to be

$$b_1(t_1) = \frac{t_1 + \theta}{1 + \theta}.$$

Thus, the expected bid from bidder 1 is

$$P_1 = \int_0^1 \int_0^{(t_1+\theta)/(1+\theta)} t_2 dt_2 dt_1 = \frac{1}{6} \left[\frac{3\theta^2 + 3\theta + 1}{(1 + \theta)^2} \right]$$

and that from bidder 2 is

$$P_2 = \int_0^1 \int_0^{(1+\theta)t_2-\theta} \frac{t_1 + \theta}{1 + \theta} dt_1 dt_2 = \frac{1}{6} \left[\frac{1 - 2\theta^2 + 2\theta}{1 + \theta} \right].$$

Thus, the expected sale price in the second-price auction is

$$P^S = P_1 + P_2 = \frac{(2\theta + 1)(2 + 2\theta - \theta^2)}{6(1 + \theta)^2}. \tag{39}$$

Now consider the matching auction. Given a bid b_1 from bidder 1, bidder 2 will match if and only if $t_2 > b_1$. Thus, bidder 1 chooses b_1 to maximize

$$\int_0^{b_1} (t_1 - (1 - \theta)b_1)dt_2 + \theta(1 - b_1)b_1.$$

From the first-order condition, one readily gets $b_1(t_1) = (1/2)t_1 + (1/2)\theta$. Thus, the expected sale price in the matching auction is

$$P^M = \frac{1}{4} + \frac{1}{2}\theta. \tag{40}$$

Comparing Equations (39) and (40), it can be verified that $P^M > P^S$ if and only if $\theta > 0.2899$. Thus, if the toeholds are sufficiently asymmetric, asking the strong bidder to move first increases the expected sale price.

The matching auction's properties in the context of a common value model with independent signals similar to Bulow et al. (1999) have been explored by Dasgupta and Tsui (2003). The authors show that there exists a perfect Bayesian Nash equilibrium in which bidder 1 with stake θ_1 bids

---

[37] Herzel and Shepro (1990) note: "Opinion in several cases in the Delaware Chancery court has noted that the duty and loyalty [of managers] runs to shareholders, not bidders. As a result, 'the board may tilt the playing field if it is in the shareholder interest to do so'."

$$b_1(t_1) = v(t_1, F_2^{-1}(\theta_1)) \tag{41}$$

and bidder 2 matches if and only if $t_2 \geq F_2^{-1}(\theta_1)$.[38] Here, bidder i's signal is drawn from the distribution $F_i(t_i)$. Notice that the expected sale price is then

$$P^M = E_{t_1}[v(t_1, F_2^{-1}(\theta_1))]. \tag{42}$$

Notice that (i) conditional on her bid, losing is better than winning for bidder 1, since her payoff in the former event is $\theta_1 v(t_1, F^{-1}(\theta_1))$, and her payoff in the latter event is at most $v(t_1, F^{-1}(\theta_1)) - (1 - \theta_1)v(t_1, F^{-1}(\theta_1))$, and (ii) as a consequence, winning is "bad news" for bidder 1, that is, if she wins, there would be a negative effect on the stock price. In contrast, winning is always "good news" for the second bidder.

It is also immediate that the expected sale price increases in the first bidder's toehold. In contrast, bidder 2's stake has no effect on the expected sale price. The probability of bidder 1 winning the auction is $F_2^{-1}(\theta_1)$ and is therefore increasing in θ_1. However, the common value feature of the model is apparent in that if bidder 1's toehold is 0, then her probability of winning is also 0; moreover, in this case, she bids $v(t_1, 0)$, that is, the lowest possible value conditional on her own signal. This is because the bidder who moves first is subjected to an extreme winner's curse problem.

How can the matching auction improve the expected sale price compared to the standard auctions? Recall that in the second-price auction with asymmetric toeholds, the smaller toehold bidder is exposed to an extreme winner's curse problem. The matching auction is a way to shield the low toehold bidder from this extreme winner's curse by asking her to move second. This, of course, imposes a winner's curse on the first bidder. However, if the asymmetry is large, the first bidder with a higher toehold will act more like a seller, and this the sale price will not suffer as much. Dasgupta and Tsui (2003) show that, for the case of a value function that is symmetric and linear in the signals (i.e., $v(t_1, t_2) = t_1 + t_2$) that are drawn from the uniform distribution, the matching auction generates a higher expected sale price than both the first- and the second-price auctions when the toeholds are sufficiently asymmetric and not too small.

Another type of bidder asymmetry arises in the common value framework if the value function is not symmetric, for example, $v(t_1, t_2) = \alpha t_1 + (1 - \alpha)t_2$ and $\alpha > 1/2$. Dasgupta and Tsui (2003) show that with symmetric toeholds, the matching auction generates a higher expected sale price than the first-price auction if the value function is sufficiently asymmetric (i.e., α sufficiently close to 0 or 1); and it generates a higher expected sale price than the second-price auction if the value function is sufficiently asymmetric and the toeholds are not too large. Povel and Singh (2006) characterize the optimal selling mechanism for the zero toeholds case and show that discrimination against the strong bidder is optimal. However, to implement the optimal mechanism, the seller needs to know the precise value of α as well as the distribution of the signals.

---

[38] For a derivation and a complete characterization of the equilibrium, see Dasgupta and Tsui (2003).

This is not required in the matching auction, for which only the identity of the stronger bidder is needed. In other words, the matching auction is a "detail-free" mechanism. This is an especially appealing property given that for sufficiently large asymmetry, the matching auction does almost as well as the optimal mechanism in extracting the surplus.

4.6. Merger waves

There is no question that merger and acquisition activity goes in waves. Rhodes-Kropf and Viswanathan (2004) give the following perspective: in 1963–1964, there were 3311 acquisition announcements while in 1968–1969 there were 10,569; during 1979–1980 and also from 1990 to 1991 there were only 4000 announcements while in 1999 alone there were 9278 announcements. The 1980s were generally a period of high merger and acquisition activity, and saw the emergence of the hostile takeover and corporate raiders, but activity dropped off in the early 1990s only to rebound again late in the 1990s. Holmstrom and Kaplan (2001) review the evidence on merger waves and offer a macro explanation based on changing regulatory and technological considerations which created a wedge between corporate performance and potential performance, along with developments in capital markets which gave institutional investors the incentives ands ability to discipline managers.

Rhodes-Kropf and Viswanathan (2004) offer an alternative explanation for merger waves based on an auction-theoretic model rich in informational assumptions. They note that periods of high merger activity tend to be periods of high market valuation, and the means-of-payment is generally stock. For example, the percentage of stock in acquisitions as a percentage of deal value was 24% in 1990, but 68% in 1998. They focus on mergers where stock is the means-of-payment. The essence of the argument is as follows: stock values of both targets and acquirers can become overvalued on a market-wide basis. These are economy-wide pricing errors that managers of neither targets nor acquirers have information on, but they do know they occur. Managers of targets know when their own stocks are overvalued; however, they do not know how much of that is due to economy-wide pricing errors and how much is firm-specific. When a stock offer is made *in an overvalued market*, target managers, knowing their own firms are overvalued but not knowing whether this is due to market-wide or firm specific factors, will overestimate potential synergies with acquirers. This is similar to search-based explanations of labor market unemployment, whereby workers think that a decrease in demand for their labor at one firm is firm-specific (when it is in fact business cycle related) and therefore accept unemployment, thinking that their economy-wide opportunities have not been affected. Thus, in times of economy-wide overvaluation, target firms will accept more bids, for they rationally infer that synergy with the bidder is high. Of course, with each merger, the market should rationally lower the price, taking the possibility of overvaluation into account. However, this does not rapidly lead to an end of a wave: if synergies are correlated, then merger waves can occur, because the market also revises upward the probability that synergies for *all* firms are high. Correlation of synergies can arise out of the sort of considerations that Holmstrom and Kaplan discuss, for example, changes in technology which increase the efficient scale of firms. Thus, a merger wave that begins when the market becomes overvalued may end only when the market realizes that the synergies that were anticipated are actually not there—that is, the wave ends with a market crash.

Rhodes-Kropf and Viswanathan's model is one of an open auction with bidders offering shares of the combined firm, similar to that of Hansen (1985a,b). Multiple bidders and cash offers are possible. High bids by other bidders imply more likely misvaluation in stock offers; however, since synergies are correlated, this does not cause the wave to end. Stock-based deals are also more likely than pure cash deals in times of economy-wide overvaluation because of the valuation errors that targets make given the information structure. Thus, the model explains not only merger waves but also the stylized fact that in times of intense merger activity, stock is more likely to be used as the means-of-payment.

Shleifer and Vishny (2003) propose a theory of mergers and acquisitions which has a similar flavor. They argue that merger activity is driven by the relative valuations of bidders and targets and perceptions of synergies from merger activity. Suppose that acquirer and target have K_1 and K units of capital, respectively. The current market valuations per unit of capital are Q_1 and Q, respectively, where $Q_1 > Q$. The long-run value of all assets is q per unit. If the two firms are combined, then the *short-run* value of the combined assets is $S(K + K_1)$, where S is the "perceived synergy" from the merger. In other words, "S is the story that the market consensus holds about the benefits of the merger. It could be a story about [the benefits of] diversification, or consolidation, or European integration." Suppose P is the price paid to the target in a merger. If the means-of-payment is stock, it is easily checked that *long-run* benefit to the bidding firms' shareholders is $qK(1 - P/S)$ and that to the target shareholders is qK $(P/S - 1)$.[39] Thus, if $S > P > Q$, bidding firms' shareholders benefit in the long run but target shareholders benefit in the short run. Shleifer and Vishny (2003) argue that if target shareholders or managers have shorter horizons, they may be willing to trade off the short run benefits for the long run losses. For example, target management may be close to retirement or own illiquid stock and options.[40] Shleifer and Vishny (2003)

---

[39] Since the synergy is only in the mind of the beholder (the market), the long term benefit to the bidding firms' shareholders from a cash offer would be $q(K + K_1) - PK < qK_1$ since $P > Q > q$. On the other hand, if the synergy were real, a bidding firm would have no reason to prefer stock over cash. Thus, a large number of stock offer during a particular period should reveal to the market that the synergies are more apparent than real. It is precisely this kind of inference that is carefully modeled in Rhodes-Kropf and Viswanathan's (2004) model discussed above. Shleifer and Vishny (2003) brush aside these issues by assuming that the market is irrational.

[40] Cai and Vijh (2007) find that in the cross-section of all firms during 1993–2001, CEOs with higher illiquidity discount are more likely to get acquired. Further, in a sample of 250 completed acquisitions, target CEOs with higher illiquidity discount accept lower premium and are more likely to leave after acquisition. They also put up lower resistance and speed up the process.

argue that the example of family firms selling to conglomerates and entrepreneurial firms selling to firms such as Cisco and Intel in the 1990s fit this story very well. Alternatively, the bidding firm could simply "bribe" target management—Hartzell et al. (2004) find that target management receive significant wealth gains in acquisitions, and acquisitions with higher wealth gains for target management are associated with lower takeover premia.

Overall, the theory predicts that cash offers will be made when perceived synergies are low but the target is undervalued ($Q < q$). This is likely to be a situation where the firm needs to be split up and/or incumbent management replaced to improve value, and will be associated with target management resistance and poor preacquisition target returns. In contrast, stock offers will be made when market valuations are high, but there is also significant dispersion in market values. Finally, for stock offers to succeed, there must be a widely accepted "story" about synergies, and target management must have shorter horizons. Notice that the model also predicts that the short term returns to bidders in stock offers would be negative if the synergies are not extremely high ($S > Q_1$, i.e., the bidder essentially has a money machine) and the long-run returns would also be negative. For cash offers, both short and long-term returns should be positive.

Shleifer and Vishny (2003) argue that the three most recent merger waves nicely fall into their framework. The conglomerate merger wave of the 1960s was fuelled by high market valuations and a story about the benefits of diversification through better management. The acquisition of firms in unrelated businesses might have been more attractive because target firms in the same industry would also have high market valuations. The targets were often family firms whose owners wished to cash out and retire. However, since there was really no synergy from diversification, the wave of the 1960s gave rise to the bust-up takeovers of the 1980s—acquisitions that were in cash, hostile, and of undervalued targets. Rising stock market prices ended this wave of takeover activity as undervalued targets became more difficult to find. The most recent wave of the 1990s was ushered in by the rising market valuations. The story of synergy was reinvented: technological synergies, the benefits of consolidation, and the European integration.

4.7. Auctions in bankruptcy

One of the most fruitful areas for the application of auction theory in corporate finance is in the context of corporate bankruptcy. The theoretical efficiency of auctions in allocating assets to their most highly valued use has led many scholars to propose auctions as a means to resolve some of the issues in bankruptcy. As an auction also yields a price for the corporation, the question of determining value (for the purpose of settling claims) is also solved. Unfortunately, the informational issues in bankruptcy are quite severe; so any complete auction-based model of the process which will yield predictions on total cost must include the cost of information acquired by bidders. There is also a fairly prevalent view that credit markets may not always allocate financing efficiently to potential buyers of bankrupt companies, so prices may be low because of a dearth of bidders. Some of these issues have been addressed empirically by examining the bankruptcy process in Sweden, where auctions of bankrupt companies are mandatory (see related discussion below).[41]

Baird (1986) was one of the first to point out that auctions may be preferable to the court-supervised reorganization process of the United States' Chapter 11 bankruptcy code. Baird, among others, used the auction processes and results of the corporate takeover market as an analogy to estimate the gains that may be achieved if auctions were used to transfer control of bankrupt companies' assets. Other researchers, Weiss (1990) in particular, turned to estimating the direct cost of Chapter 11 procedures—with those costs being estimated at between 2.8% and 7.5% of assets. Easterbrook (1990) argues against auctions, maintaining that the costs associated with the IPO process is a good analogy for estimating the costs of determining a firm's value, and calculates IPO direct costs at roughly 14% of proceeds. Hansen and Thomas (1998) argue that Easter-brook's figures need to be adjusted and put on a total asset, not proceeds, basis, and that the so-called "dealer's concession" built into IPO costs should also be subtracted as it is a cost of distribution, not of the auction process per se. Their resulting figure of 2.7% is then roughly equal to Weiss' estimates of the direct cost of bankruptcy. Thus, auctions and Chapter 11 would seem to have similar direct costs, leaving their relative efficiency to be determined by either theory or further empirical work.

On the empirical side, Thorburn (2000) has exploited the Swedish bankruptcy experience to draw important conclusions on the relative efficiency of cash auctions of bankrupt firms. In Sweden, the typical procedure has been for a bankrupt firm to be taken over by a court-appointed trustee who supervises a cash auction of the firm, either piecemeal or as an ongoing combination. These data therefore allow for direct examination of how auctions work in bankruptcy. Thorburn (2000) finds that three-quarters of the 263 bankrupt firms are auctioned as going-concerns, which compares favorably to Chapter 11 survival rates. As to cost, direct costs average 6.4% of prefiling assets, with the one-third largest firms experiencing costs of only 3.7% of assets. As to debt recovery, the recovery rates are comparable to Chapter 11 reorganizations of much larger firms: on average, creditors received 35% of their claims, with secured creditors receiving 69% and unsecured creditors only 25%. Thorburn finds that APR is maintained by the auction procedure.

Eckbo and Thorburn (2009) construct an auction-based model to examine the incentives of the main creditor bank in a bankruptcy auction. Their work addresses one fear of bankruptcy auctions, that credit market inefficiencies will sometimes limit credit and cause bankrupt companies to be sold at "fire-sale" prices, possibly to the benefit of the original owner/managers. Eckbo and Thorburn show that the main creditor bank has an incentive to provide financing to one bidder and to encourage

---

[41] See Eckbo and Thorburn (2003, 2009).

that bidder to bid higher than would be in their private interest. The reason for this follows from the analysis of an optimal reserve price (see also the discussion of toeholds in Section 4.4) in an auction, for the main creditor bank is essentially a partial owner of the bankrupt company. Just as an optimal reserve price exceeds the seller's own valuation (see above), the optimal bid for a main-bank financed bidder exceeds that bidder's own valuation. The equation specifying the optimal bid in Eckbo and Thorburn is exactly analogous to the equation for an optimal reserve price. Eckbo and Thorburn, examining again the Swedish data, find strong results for the overbidding theory and no evidence that auction prices are affected by industry-wide distress or business cycle downturns. They also demonstrate a surprising degree of competition in the automatic bankruptcy auctions, and that auction premiums are no lower when the firm is sold back to its own owners. Overall, their evidence—which is the first to exploit directly the cross-sectional variation in auction prices—fails to support either fire-sale arguments or the notion that salebacks are noncompetitive transactions.

Auction theory has also been applied to study the question of optimal bankruptcy procedures. Hart et al. (1997) propose an ingenious three-stage auction process for bankrupt companies. The first stage solicits cash and noncash bids for the firm, while the second and third stages determine prices and ownership of so-called "reorganization rights." Reorganization rights are new securities which consolidate all the various existing claims on the firm's assets. This proposal differs from Aghion et al. (1992) in that there is a public auction (the third auction) for the reorganization rights. The purpose here is to reduce any inefficiencies caused by liquidity constraints in determining prices and allocations of the new securities which replace the old claims.

Rhodes-Kropf and Viswanathan (2000) extend the limited work done on noncash bids in auctions discussed previously. While theory such as Hansen (1985a,b) shows that noncash bids such as equity can increase sales revenue, noncash bids are themselves subject to uncertain valuation. Building on these basic insights, Rhodes-Kropf and Viswanathan show that in any separating equilibrium, a security auction (the means-of-payment is a security the value of which depends on the bidder's type) generates higher expected revenue to the seller than a cash auction. The reason for this is that in a security auction, the low types have a greater gain from mimicking the high types, so to separate, the high types have to bid more. However, some securities will not separate the bidders. The authors show that there is no incentive compatible separating equilibrium with stock alone. Debt bids, or a minimum debt requirement, can achieve separation in some cases; in others, cash payments or large nonpecuniary bankruptcy costs are needed to achieve separation (so that the highest value bidder can be identified). However, relative to cash bids, bids that involve debt or equity distort ex post effort choices. Bids that involve high debt and low equity rank higher because they distort effort less. Convertibles can work better as they give the seller the option to affect the ex post capital structure of the target firm. The model thus is capable of explaining why debt and convertibles are often part of reorganization plans, and why companies often end up more highly levered than when they were distressed (Gilson, 1997).

Hansen and Thomas (1998) apply the model of French and McCormick (1984) to argue that uncertainty surrounding a bankrupt firm's assets can cause auction prices to be low. Using the French and McCormick model, with free entry of bidders, the auction price will be N^*C less than true value, where N^* is the equilibrium number of bidders and C is the prebid cost of entry (which they model as an information acquisition cost). Theoretically, then, the question is whether a court, by having to only obtain one (good) evaluation of the firm's assets, can hold costs below N^*C. They argue that the greater the uncertainty surrounding a firm's assets, the worse an auction will perform. By way of example, Reece (1978) shows that with high uncertainty, a common-value auction yields a price only 70% of true value.

4.8. Share repurchases

Companies frequently buy back their shares through either fixed-price tender offers or Dutch auction mechanisms. In a Dutch auction repurchase, a company determines a quantity of shares to buy back and asks shareholders to submit bids specifying a price and quantity of shares that they are willing to sell. The bids are ordered according to price (low to high), creating a supply curve. As the Securities and Exchange Commission prohibits price discrimination, a uniform price is set corresponding to the lowest price that enables the firm to buy the predetermined number of shares.

While there has been little formal modeling of the Dutch auction repurchase process itself (possibly because no real auction-theoretic issues are present) there is considerable empirical study, and their effects relative to fixed-price offers has been studied in a more traditional corporate finance setting. Bagwell (1992) studies 32 Dutch auction repurchases between 1988 and 1991. In one transaction, the highest bid was 14% above the preannouncement market price, while the lowest bid was only 2% above. Such disparities in bids are documented for the entire sample, showing that the firms did face upward-sloping supply curves for their shares, contrary to naive ideas of a perfect capital market. Bagwell mentions several possible explanations, including differences in private valuations (e.g., because of capital gains tax lock-ins), asymmetric information about a common value as in Milgrom and Weber (1982a,b), or differences in opinion (Miller, 1977). While tax considerations could play a large role, it is certainly not a stretch to assume that shareholders will have different information on the value of a company (even though they share the public information embedded in the current price).

Other work has explored signaling aspects of Dutch auction repurchases relative to fixed price tender offers (Persons, 1994) and relative to paying dividends (Hausch and Seward, 1993). Persons (1994) considers a situation in which shareholders demand a premium (perhaps due to capital gains tax frictions) to tender their shares, but this premium varies across shareholders, resulting in an upward sloping supply curve. Repurchases are costly to existing shareholders because the tendering shareholders must be offered a premium. Importantly, the slope of the supply curve is random. In a fixed-price tender offer, the price is fixed, while the quantity of shares tendered adjusts to the random slope of the supply curve; in a Dutch auction, exactly the opposite is the case. If the manager intends to signal the true value by maximizing a weighted average of the intrinsic value and the market value of the shares (as in the dividend signaling model of Miller and Rock, 1985), fixed-price offers are more effective signals of the manager's private information; on the other hand, if the manager needs to buy back a specific number of shares to prevent a takeover threat, a Dutch auction is better as it guarantees that the required number of shares will be tendered.

4.9. Auction aspects of initial public offerings (IPOs)

In the summer of 2004, the Internet search firm Google completed the world's largest initial public offering to be conducted via an auction procedure. Google sold 19.6 million shares at an offering price of $85 each, for a total of $1.67 billion raised. The auction method used was a variant of the Wall Street Dutch auction, covered immediately above. IPOs of equity shares would seem to be excellent candidates for an auction procedure: multiple units of the same item for sale, with uncertainty over value and ability of a seller to commit to a sales method.

Interestingly, however, the evidence suggests that formal auctions are not favored as a sales mechanism. Instead, the IPO procedure known as "bookbuilding" attracts most of the market in regions where multiple sales methods can legally exist (Degeorge et al., 2004; Jagannathan and Sherman, 2006; Sherman, 2005). A fair amount of theoretical work has been done to explore differences in sales mechanisms for IPOs as well as issues within any one sales method. There is also a literature examining relative performance of auctions versus other sales methods, for in some countries we do have different sales methods coexisting.

In applying auction theory to IPOs, the place to start is the literature on uniform price, multiple unit auctions. The main initial contributions here are Wilson (1979) and Back and Zender (1993). A recent contribution is by Kremer and Nyborg (2004a,b). The reason this literature is so important is that it shows how simple auction analysis yields the main underpricing result from IPO studies (i.e., that the initial stock market returns immediately after setting the IPO price are overwhelmingly positive).[42] The auction models show in fact that uniform price, multiple unit auctions have a multitude of equilibria with varying degrees of underpricing. The intuition of the underpricing result is quite simple: in a uniform price auction, bidders are asked to essentially submit demand schedules, specifying the number of shares they would be willing to buy at different prices. Wilson (1979) showed that instead of thinking of bidders as selecting a demand schedule to submit, a simple transformation allows us to model a bidder's decision as one of selecting the optimal "stop-out" price after subtracting other bidders' demands from the available supply. This makes each bidder a monopsonist over the residual supply and sets up the essential monopsonistic tension:

---

[42] For a detailed account of various theories of IPO underpricing, see Ljungqvist (2007).

a higher bid increases the quantity of shares purchased, but raises the price paid on all shares. Optimally, a bidder will submit a low stop-out bid, and as this will be the case for all bidders, a Nash equilibrium holds. Interestingly, the literature on underpricing in IPOs has not picked up on this simple explanation, relying instead on more complicated explanations.

While not relying on the Wilson/Back and Zender insights, Benveniste and Spindt (1989) nonetheless use an auction-based model to explain certain aspects of the IPO process. The basic idea is similar to that of Hansen (2001), as it involves conditions under which bidders reveal truthfully their information through bids that are nonbinding "indications of interest." The model asks under what conditions an investor will reveal her information to the investment banker collecting demand information for an IPO. Underpricing of the IPO guarantees a return to these investors; this is critical for otherwise there could be no incentive to honestly reveal information. Also, those investors who reveal high valuations must receive more of the undervalued shares, or again there would be no payoff from honestly revealing information (and there is a cost to honest revelation as it affects the offering price). Thus, this auction-based model explains two core features of the IPO process, underpricing and differential allocations of shares.

Biais and Faugeron-Crouzet (2002) present a complex and quite general model of the IPO process that compares auctions to fixed-price offerings. Unfortunately, the authors' conclusion that the book-building approach dominates the auction method is clouded by the assumption that the auction method will induce collusion between the bidders. It is not at all clear why collusion, if profitable, will occur only in one auction method. This paper also shows why it is extremely difficult to use auction theory to convincingly show that one method is more efficient than another: to do this, one must introduce a myriad of assumptions, covering everything from valuations to costs of information collection. The validity of all these assumptions is difficult to evaluate, and the chances that the ranking of the sales methods would change, or become indeterminate, is high if some of the assumptions were changed.

Sherman (2005) compares bookbuilding to auctions under the very reasonable assumption that entry by bidders is an endogenous decision. Her model yields a result similar in spirit to a core result that emerges from comparing the basic auction methods that while the expected price is the same in sealed-bids versus second-price auctions, the variance of prices is greater for the second-price auction. This result comes about because in the first-price auction, bidders put in their bids using their *expectation* of what other bidders' values are, while in the second-price auction, the high-bid is dependent on the *actual* value of the second-highest valuation. Sherman focuses on the uncertainty in the number of bidders caused by a mixed strategy equilibrium in the game of entry into an IPO auction. If bidders are free to enter the IPO auction, then if there is some cost to entering and some classes of bidders are ex ante identical, the equilibrium in the entry game has a probability of entry for at least some bidders; the result is uncertainty over the actual number of bidders. Sherman claims that this uncertainty over the actual number of bidders causes the IPO price to vary and in particular to vary in its relation to a "true" underlying value. Sherman observes that this additional uncertainty further worsens the "winners' curse" and considerably complicates the optimal "bid-shaving" calculation that is required when there is winners' curse. She also shows that each investor optimally collects less information in a uniform price rather than a discriminatory auction, because of the free rider (moral hazard) problem in the uniform price auction.[43]

Sherman assumes that in the bookbuilding process, the underwriter can select the number of investors to invite into an information-acquisition process; this makes the bookbuilding process more like the first-price auction in terms of the variance of its outcomes. Jagannathan and Sherman (2006) rely on this model to explain their findings of a worldwide abandonment of IPO auctions in favor of bookbuilding; they also support the theoretical model with evidence on the variance in number of participants for IPO auctions. The issues of number of bidders and information collection would seem to be key in an optimal IPO pricing/allocation mechanism. One wonders, however, if a slight twist on assumptions for the auction models—let the auctioneer control somehow the selection of bidders, à la Hansen (2001) would bring equivalence back to the two mechanisms. Sherman (2005, p. 619) does note that "If the term 'auction' is interpreted in a broad sense, it is almost a tautology that an appropriate auction could be designed for IPOs." This exemplifies a general difficulty in building theoretical models of two different institutions to explain their empirical performances: one can capture the sense of institutional differences by making clear assumptions (e.g., the underwriter can select the number of potential investors for bookbuilding but not for auctions) but one is left wondering if the assumptions really do justice to what actually happens in practice.

In anther recent attempt at comparing bookbuilding to auctions, Degeorge et al. (2004) show that bookbuilding seems to dominate empirically (they look at France, where for a time auctions and bookbuilding had roughly equal market shares, but now auctions are virtually extinct) and they offer a justification for issuers' preference for the bookbuilding method that is based not on the price performance of bookbuilding but on the investment bankers' preference for the method. While one might understand why investment bankers prefer a method that creates more demand for their services, the link to issuers' interests is less clear. Degeorge et al. hypothesize that bankers agree to provide research coverage for issuers in return for using the bookbuilding method. What is left unstated is that issuers must be unable to buy such research coverage on the open market at prices similar to the costs paid by investment bankers: the authors agree that auctions would yield issuers a better price, so one must wonder why issuers put up with an inefficient procedure simply to get a tied service.

On the empirical side of the auctions/IPO issue, Kandel et al. (1999) utilize a data set from Israel IPO auctions to document elasticity of demand and underpricing.

---

[43] In the uniform price auction, since the auction price is set by the actions of bidders who have already paid the information gathering and processing costs, there is an incentive for uninformed bidders to free ride and jump in with a high bid.

The underpricing of Israeli IPOs is intriguing, for those IPOs had their prices set by an explicit auction mechanism. In the period 1993–1996, Israeli IPOs were conducted much like Dutch auction share repurchases: investors submitted sealed-bids specifying prices and quantities, a demand curve was determined, and a uniform price was set at the highest price for which demand equaled the supply of shares available. Kandel, Sarig and Wohl document some elasticity of demand for the reported bids: the average elasticity at the clearing price, based on the accumulated demand curves, was 37 (relatively elastic). Interestingly, even in these IPO auctions, there was underpricing: the 1-day return between the auction price and the market trading price was 4.5%. Another interesting feature of the Israeli auctions is that after the auction but before the first day of trading, the underwriters announce the market clearing price corresponding to the offered quantity, as well as the oversubscription at the minimum price stipulated in the auction. This essentially means that the investor can estimate the price elasticity of demand based on two points on the demand curve. The authors find that the abnormal return on the first day of trading is positively related to the estimate of the elasticity. The authors argue that this reflects greater homogeneity in the estimates of value on the part of the participants in the auction; this is "good news" either because it implies greater accuracy of information about future cash flows and thus leads to a lower risk-premium demanded by investors, or because it signifies greater "market depth" and hence greater future liquidity.

Kerins et al. (2003) examine IPOs in Japan in the period 1995–1997, a time when Japanese firms had to use a discriminatory (bidders pay the amount of their bid) auction to sell the first tranche of newly issued shares. This first tranche of shares would be relatively small, and the sale by auction was restricted to outside investors only, with further limitations on the amount that could be bought by any investor. These restrictions could be interpreted as limiting the informational advantages of any one bidder. Under that interpretation, it is not surprising that the authors find relatively little "underpricing" of the shares for the auction tranche: for all the issues, the auction proceeds were only 1.6% below what proceeds would have been at the final aftermarket price. The second stage of the Japanese process was a more traditional fixed-price offer, and there was considerable underpricing of shares at this stage. While this might suggest that the auction was a better choice of mechanism, one must recognize that costs of a larger auction (to sell the entire issue) could well be larger than costs of just the first tranche.

4.10. The spectrum auctions and the role of debt in auctions

Beginning in 1994, the Federal Communications Commission in the United States auctioned licenses for the use of radio spectrum in designated areas. The licenses were auctioned using a novel auction format involving sequential rounds of sealed-bidding on numerous licenses simultaneously. At the end of each round, complete information on the level of bids for all licenses was revealed. The auction format was designed by economists, and at least in regard to the vast sums of money raised, was a great success. Numerous articles summarize all aspects of the auctions, including their design and performance: see, for example, McAfee and McMillan (1996), Milgrom (2000), and Salant (1997). For the empirical researcher, FCC auctions provide a wealth of information: for example, the FCC Web site (http://www.fcc.gov) lists all the bids in all the auctions. Moreover, many of the participating companies are publicly traded, so that company-specific information is also easily available. We focus here on one analysis which studied the effect of debt on the FCC auctions. Clayton and Ravid (2002) construct an auction model where bidders' debt induces lower bids than would otherwise be the case. In this model, bidders have outstanding debt that is large enough to induce bankruptcy if the auction is not won. Lower bids decrease the probability of winning, of course, but in this case guarantee some residual to the shareholders conditional on winning. In effect, in this model, preexisting debt holders are "third parties" who have a prior claim of a part of the pie. Thus, preexisting debt serves to reduce bidders' values and therefore reduces bids.[44] An empirical analysis of the FCC bidding data produces a negative but generally insignificant effect of a bidder's own debt on their bid but a negative and significant effect on a firm's bid of competitors' debt levels.

Che and Gale (1998) were the first to explicitly study the role of debt in auctions.[45] They have a result similar to Clayton and Ravid, although the models rely on different effects. In Che and Gale's framework, a second-price auction yields lower expected revenue than a first-price auction. To see how financial constraints affect revenue comparisons, suppose that due to budget constraints, bidders cannot bid more than a given budget, which is observed only by the bidder. The private valuations and budgetary endowments of each bidder are independently and identically distributed according to some joint distribution function. In this context, since bidders in the second-price auction bid their value, but in the first-price auction they bid *below* their value, bidding is more constrained in the second-price auction because of budget constraints, ceteris paribus. As a consequence, the first-price auction generates higher expected revenue. Che and Gale (1998) allow for financial constraints that are more general than we have considered here: for example, these could take the form of a marginal cost of borrowing that is increasing in the amount of the loan.

4.11. Advanced econometrics of auction data

There has been considerable progress in the application of econometric techniques to auction data. While the datasets used in these studies do not cover corporate finance directly, the techniques used should be of interest to corporate finance researchers, as they may be applicable to financial datasets and help resolve certain key issues.

---

[44] On the role of debt holders as "third parties" in the context of bilateral bargaining, see Dasgupta and Sengupta (1993). On the role of "third party" shareholders in the context of bilateral bargaining, see Dasgupta and Tao (1998, 2000).

[45] For a recent contribution on the role of financing in auctions, see Rhodes-Kropf and Viswanathan (2005).

One broad topic that has been covered in empirical auction studies and that also appears in corporate finance are auctions with one informed bidder and numerous uninformed bidders. In corporate finance, such a situation could reasonably be assumed when current management is allowed to bid for a corporation, either in a takeover or bankruptcy context. Certainly, in bankruptcy one concern has been that management, if allowed to bid in an auction, may be able to purchase the corporate assets at less than fair value. Hendricks and Porter (1988, 1992) have studied US government oil lease auctions of so-called "drainage" tracts—tracts that have a neighboring tract currently under lease to one of the bidders. For these drainage tracts, it is reasonable to assume that the owner of the neighboring tract would have better information than other bidders. The authors of several studies have found this assumption, and the related equilibrium bidding theory, to be consistent with the data. The econometrics used relies heavily on the underlying auction theory. For example, equilibrium with one informed bidder imposes restrictions on the distributions of the informed bidder's bid distribution and the uninformed bidders' bid distributions. Note that a test of this type requires that data on all bids be available.

Structural models are also being used successfully to examine auction data. The most exciting approach here is to use equilibrium theory in conjunction with data on all bids to estimate the underlying probability distribution of the valuations of bidders. The essence of the idea here is that an equilibrium bid function maps a valuation to a bid. If data on bids are available, then with suitable econometrics one can recover the distribution of the underlying valuations from the bid data. Li et al. (2002) provide a step-by-step guide to structural estimation of the affiliated private value auction model. One aim of this work in the economics literature has been to estimate the optimal selling mechanism for a real auction. For example, if valuations are affiliated, then revenue equivalence no longer holds. Also, the optimal reserve price depends upon the underlying distribution of values, so if that distribution can be estimated, we can also get an estimate of the optimal reserve price. Researchers in empirical corporate finance should be aware of the progress made in structural estimation of auctions, for some of the issues at the heart of finance auctions may be resolved through structural estimation (and in some finance auctions, there should be data on all bids). For example, in the bankruptcy area, questions of reserve prices and informational rents abound, and these are two issues that structural estimation can get at.[46]

---

[46] In the context of takeover auctions, Betton and Eckbo (2000) pursue an interesting line of empirical research. A takeover contest typically associated with an "event tree" beginning with the initial bid, possibly followed by the appearance of rival bidders, until the eventual success or failure of the initial bid. The market reaction to a bid (or indeed, at reaching any node) therefore represents the sum of the product of the probabilities of all subsequent events in the tree emanating from that node, and the associated payoffs. Since the probabilities and market reactions can be estimated, the payoff implications associated with the events (the "market prices") can be estimated. Betton and Eckbo (2000) find generally significant effects for the target, but less significant effects for the bidders.

5. Conclusion

Upon reflection, the accomplishments of auction theory are really quite amazing. The "black box" of the Walrasian auctioneer has been opened, studied in depth, and its perfection questioned. We can now say a lot about the process of actual price formation in many real markets. While modelers have been able to explore theoretically important topics such as revenue comparisons across auctions, their work has also enabled economists to consult with governments on the design of optimal auctions to sell public assets. And with only a slight time lag, empirical work in auctions is following in the footsteps of theory, with structural estimation methods setting a new standard for creativity and rigor. Similar to the way that theoretical developments made their way into the real world of auction design, empirical work is focusing on real world auctions such as those found on Ebay and other online auctions. There are not too many topics in economics that allow researchers to cover such a broad swath of analytical territory, from the highly theoretical to the highly empirical and practical. In this way, auction theory resembles developments in financial asset pricing, where for instance the development of the option pricing model led to a surge in theoretical and empirical work while at the same time the model was applied in real markets.

The application of auction theory in corporate finance really needs to be seen as the intersection of two fields, that of auction theory and of information-based corporate finance theory. Nobody should have been surprised to see auction theory have a bit of a field day in being applied to topics in corporate finance, and as we think this survey shows, this is clearly what has happened and continues to happen. The question before us, however, must be: what have we learned in the process? That there has been considerable learning cannot be doubted, with the most significant learning being in interpreting the returns to bidders and targets in the market for corporate control, and in understanding the real institutional practices used in financial markets, such as underpricing in the IPO market, noncash bids in takeover markets, and the role of asymmetries and discrimination against selected bidders. Perhaps the single best measure of auction theory's influence in corporate finance is that most PhD courses in corporate finance will include several papers, if not an entire module, on applications of auctions. As even a superficial study of auctions requires a fair amount of knowledge of game theory, the inclusion of auctions in PhD finance courses reinforces the study of games, itself a critical component of modern finance.

While auction theory deserves much credit for its inroads into corporate finance, two areas of concern do emerge. First, there are some phenomena in corporate finance for which we still lack sufficient understanding, and where one might have expected auction theory to lead the way. Yes, we have increased our understanding of returns to bidders and targets in the market for corporate control, but why are acquirers' returns so small? Any auction with heterogeneity of valuations or information leads to strategic behavior and expected profits for inframarginal bidders. And why do acquirers seem to do better when acquiring private companies? There is still a huge question as to whether auctions in bankruptcy are better than a court-supervised valuation and division of assets. Why are toeholds so seldom taken, if they lead to a bidding advantage? If auctions really are so good, why are they used so infrequently in the initial public offering market, and why do some sellers of companies bypass an auction in favor of a one-on-one negotiation?

The second unsatisfactory aspect of auctions in corporate finance is simply that no new fundamental insights have emerged. We do understand better how information, values, and strategic behavior combine to yield prices and allocations of assets in real financial markets. There has been no quantum leap forward, just incremental learning at the margin. This should, we suppose, actually be gratifying, for it shows the robustness of our primitive and most cherished assumptions. Unfortunately, at times the models that are developed and that are pushing back the frontier only marginally are incredibly complicated, and one has to wonder if the complexity is worth it. One doubts that quantum leaps in knowledge are going to come from models that need a myriad of questionable assumptions.

Where next for auctions in corporate finance? We would suggest three areas for focus. First, data will be key for further empirical discovery, and this could in turn lead to new theoretical developments. We believe that auctions of private companies and auctions in bankruptcy are two areas that may yield significantly better data in the future and where the returns to clever empirical work would be large. Second, on the theoretical side, it is clear that some of the best work to date has been on what might appear as the second-order institutional practices, such as noncash bids, toeholds, bidder discrimination, and reserve prices. Much progress has been made in understanding the role of these practices, while at the same time reinforcing the importance and validity of the overall auction-based framework. Third, we would like to see more work done with nonstandard informational and valuation assumptions. The general symmetric model is extremely powerful, but does it really capture many of the real settings that we observe? We should expect that heterogeneity of bidders will be manifested in many ways and will turn out to affect the equilibria quite strongly, especially in regard to bidders' profits. Efficiency of the allocation will also become inherently more interesting of a question, and initial work suggests it will be harder to achieve.

We would confidently make the prediction, though, that auctions in corporate finance will be a much-studied topic for years to come. Our very strong recommendation would be for all PhD students to get a thorough grounding in auction theory.

References

Aghion, P., O. Hart and J. Moore, 1992, "The Economics of Bankruptcy Reform," *Journal of Law, Economics and Organization*, 8, 523–546.

Andrade, G., M. Mitchell and E. Stafford, 2001, "New Evidence and Perspectives on Mergers," *Journal of Economic Perspectives*, 15, 103–120.

Back, K. and J. Zender, 1993, "Auctions of Divisible Goods: On the Rationale for the Treasury Experiment," *Review of Financial Studies*, 6, 733–764.

Bagwell, L. S., 1992, "Dutch Auction Repurchase: An Analysis of Shareholder Heterogeneity," *Journal of Finance*, 47, 71–105.

Baird, D. G., 1986, "The Uneasy Case of Corporate Reorganization," *Journal of Legal Studies*, 15, 127–147.

Benveniste, L. M. and P. A. Spindt, 1989, "How Investment Bankers Determine the Offer Price and Allocation of New Issues," *Journal of Financial Economics*, 24, 343–361.

Betton, S. and B. E. Eckbo, 2000, "Toeholds, Bid-Jumps, and Expected Payoffs in Takeovers," *Review of Financial Studies*, 13, 841–882.

Betton, S., B. E. Eckbo and K. S. Thorburn, 2009, "Merger Negotiations and the Toehold Puzzle," *Journal of Financial Economics*, 91, 158–178.

Betton, S., B. E. Eckbo and K. S. Thorburn, 2008, "Corporate Takeovers," In B. E. Eckbo (Ed.), *Handbook of Corporate Finance: Empirical Corporate Finance*, Vol. 2, Chapter 15, Elsevier/North-Holland, Amsterdam, Handbooks in Finance Series, 291–429.

Biais, B. and A. M. Faugeron-Crouzet, 2002, "IPO Auction: English, Dutch, …French and Internet," *Journal of Financial Intermediation*, 11, 9–36.

Boone, A. and H. Mulherin, 2003, "Corporate Restructuring and Corporate Auctions," Working Paper, College of William and Marry, Claremont McKenna College.

Boone, A. and H. Mulherin, 2007, "How are Firms Sold?" *Journal of Finance*, 62, 847–875.

Boone, A. and H. Mulherin, 2006, "Do Auctions Induce a Winner's Curse? New Evidence from the Corporate Takeover Market," Working Paper, University of Georgia.

Bradley, M., A. Desai and E. H. Kim, 1983, "The Rationale Behind Inter-Firm Tender Offers: Information or Synergy?" *Journal of Financial Economics*, 11, 141–153.

Bulow, J. and P. Klemperer, 1996, "Auction versus Negotiations," *American Economic Review*, 86, 180–194.

Bulow, J. and J. Roberts, 1989, "The Simple Economics of Optimal Auctions," *Journal of Political Economy*, 97, 1060–1090.

Bulow, J., M. Huang and P. Klemperer, 1999, "Toeholds and Takeovers," *Journal of Political Economy*, 107, 427–454.

Burkart, M., 1995, "Initial Shareholdings and Overbidding in Takeover Contests," *Journal of Finance*, 50, 1491–1515.

Cai, J. and A. M. Vijh, 2007, "Incentive Effects of Stock and Option Holdings for Target and Acquirer CEOs," *Journal of Finance*, 64, 1891–1933.

Che, Y. K. and I. Gale, 1998, "Standard Auctions with Financially Constrained Bidders," *Review of Economic Studies*, 65, 1–22.

Clayton, M. J. and S. A. Ravid, 2002, "The Effect of Leverage of Bidding Behavior: Theory and Evidence from the FCC Auction," *Review of Financial Studies*, 15, 723–750.

Cramton, P. and A. Schwartz, 1991, "Using Auction Theory to Inform Takeover Regulation," *Journal of Law, Economics and Organization*, 7, 27–53.

Dasgupta, S. and K. Sengupta, 1993, "Sunk Investment, Bargaining, and Choice of Capital Structure," *International Economic Review*, 34, 203–220.

Dasgupta, S. and Z. Tao, 1998, "Incomplete Contracts, Ownership Rights, and the Optimality of Equity Joint Ventures," *Journal of Economic Behavior and Organizations*, 37, 391–413.

Dasgupta, S. and Z. Tao, 2000, "Bargaining, Bonding, and Partial Ownership," *International Economic Review*, 41, 609–635.

Dasgupta, S. and K. Tsui, 2003, "A "Matching Auction" for Targets with Heterogeneous Bidders," *Journal of Financial Intermediation*, 12, 331–364.

Dasgupta, S. and K. Tsui, 2004, "Auction with Cross-Shareholdings," *Economic Theory*, 24, 163–194.

Dasgupta, P. S., P. J. Hammond and E. S. Maskin, 1979, "The Implementation of Social Choice Rules: Some General Results on Incentive Compatibility," *Review of Economic Studies*, 46, 185–216.

Degeorge, F., F. Derrien and K. L. Womack, 2004, "Quid Pro Quo in IPOs: Why Book-Building is Dominating Auctions," Working Paper, University of Lugano; University of Toronto; Dartmouth College.

DeMarzo, P. M., I. Kremer and A. Skrzypacz, 2005, "Bidding With Securities: Auctions and Security Design," *American Economic Review*, 95, 936–959.

Easterbrook, F. H., 1990, "Is Corporate Bankruptcy Efficient?" *Journal of Financial Economics*, 27, 411–417.

Eckbo, B. E. and K. S. Thorburn, 2000, "Gains to Bidder Firms Revisited: Domestic and Foreign Acquisitions in Canada," *Journal of Financial and Quantitative Analysis*, 35, 1–25.

Eckbo, B. E. and K. S. Thorburn, 2003, "Control Benefit and CEO Discipline in Automatic Bankruptcy Auctions," *Journal of Financial Economics*, 69, 227–258.

Eckbo, B. E. and K. S. Thorburn, 2009, "Creditor Financing and Overbidding in Bankruptcy Auctions: Theory and Tests," *Journal of Corporate Finance*, 15, 1029.

Eckbo, B. E., R. Giammarino and R. Heinkel, 1990, "Asymmetric Information and Medium of Exchange in Takeovers: Theory and Tests," *Review of Financial Studies*, 3, 651–675.

Fishman, M. J., 1988, "A Theory of Pre-Emptive Takeover Bidding," *RAND Journal of Economics*, 19, 88–101.

Fishman, M. J., 1989, "Preemptive Bidding and the Role of the Medium of Exchange in Acquisitions," *Journal of Finance*, 44, 41–57.

French, K. R. and R. E. McCormick, 1984, "Sealed Bids, Sunk Costs, and the Process of Competition," *Journal of Business*, 57, 417–441.

Gal-Or, E., 1985, "First Mover and Second Mover Advantages," *International Economic Review*, 649–653.

Gal-Or, E., 1987, "First Mover Disadvantages with Private Information," *Review of Economic Studies*, 279–292.

Gilson, S. C., 1997, "Transactions Costs and Capital Structure Choice: Evidence from Financially Distressed Firms," *Journal of Finance*, 52, 161–196.

Grossman, S. and O. Hart, 1980, "Disclosure Laws and Takeover Bids," *Journal of Finance*, 35, 323–334.

Hansen, R. G., 1985a, "Empirical Testing of Auction Theory," *American Economic Review*, 75, 156–159.

Hansen, R. G., 1985b, "Auction with Contingent Payments," *American Economic Review*, 75, 862–865.

Hansen, R. G., 1986, "Sealed Bid versus Open Auctions: The Evidence," *Economic Inquiry*, 24, 125–142.

Hansen, R. G., 2001, "Auction of Companies," *Economic Inquiry*, 39, 30–43.

Hansen, R. G. and R. S. Thomas, 1998, "Auctions in Bankruptcy: Theoretical Analysis and Practical Guidance," *International Review of Law and Economics*, 18, 159–185.

Harris, M. and A. Raviv, 1981, "Allocation Mechanisms and the Design of Auctions," *Econometrica*, 49, 1477–1499.

Hart, O., R. LaPorta, F. Lopez-de-Silanes and J. Moore, 1997, "A New Bankruptcy Procedure that Uses Multiple Auctions," *European Economic Review*, 41, 461–473.

Hartzell, J., E. Ofek and D. Yermack, 2004, "What's In It for Me? CEOs Whose Firms are Acquired," *Review of Financial Studies*, 17, 37–61.

Hausch, D. B. and J. K. Seward, 1993, "Signalling with Dividends and Share Repurchases: A Choice between Deterministic and Stochastic Cash Disbursements," *Review of Financial Studies*, 6, 121–154.

Hendricks, R. and R. Porter, 1988, "An Empirical Study of an Auction with Asymmetric Information," *American Economic Review*, 78, 865–883.

Hendricks, K. and R. Porter, 1992, "Joint Bidding in the Federal OCS Auctions," *American Economic Review*, 82, 506–511.

Herzel, L. and W. Shepro, 1990, *Bidders and Targets: Mergers and Acquisitions in the U.S.*, Blackwell, Cambridge, MA.

Hirshleifer, J., 1971, "The Private and Social Value of Information and the Reward to Inventive Activity," *American Economic Review*, 61, 561–574.

Holmstrom, B. and S. N. Kaplan, 2001, "Corporate Governance and Merger Activity in the United States: Making Sense of the 1980s and 1990s," *Journal of Economic Perspectives*, 15, 121–144.

Jagannathan, R. and A. Sherman, 2006, "Why Do IPO Auctions Fail?" NBER Working Paper.

Jarrell, G. A., J. A. Brikley and J. M. Netter, 1988, "The Market for Corporate Control: The Empirical Evidence Since 1980," *Journal of Economic Prospectives*, 2 (1), 49–68.

Jennings, R. H. and M. A. Mazzeo, 1993, "Competing Bids, Target Management Resistance, and the Structure of Takeover Bids," *Review of Financial Studies*, 6, 883–909.

Jensen, M. C., 2004, "The Agency Costs of Overvalued Equity," Harvard NOM Research Papar No. 04-26 (May 2004) and ECGI-Finance Working Paper No. 39/2004, http://ssrn.com/abstract=480421.

Jovanovic, B. and S. Braguinsky, 2004, "Bidder Discounts and Target Premia in Takeovers," *American Economic Review*, 94, 46–56.

Kahan, M. and M. Klausner, 1996a, "Lockups and the Market for Corporate Control," *Stanford Law Review*, 48, 1539–1571.

Kahan, M. and M. Klausner, 1996b, "Path Dependence in Corporate Contracting: Increasing Returns, Herding Behavior and Cognitive Biases," *Washington University Law Quarterly*, 74, 317–325.

Kandel, S., O. Sarig and A. Wohl, 1999, "The Demand for Stocks: An Empirical Analysis of IPO Stock Auctions," *Review of Financial Studies*, 12, 227–247.

Kerins, F., K. Kutsuna and R. Smith, 2003, "Why are IPO Underpriced? Evidence from Japan's Hybrid Auction-Method Offerings," Working Paper, Claremont Graduate University.

Klemperer, P. D., 1998, "Auctions with Almost Common Values," *European Economic Review*, 42, 757–769.

Klemperer, P. D., 2000, "Why Every Economist Should Learn Some Auction Theory," In M. Dewatripont, L. Hansen, S. Turnovsky (Eds.), *Advances in Economics and Econometrics*, Cambridge University Press, Cambridge.

Kremer, I. and K. G. Nyborg, 2004a, "Divisible Good Auctions: The Role of Allocation Rules," *RAND Journal of Economics*, 35, 147–159.

Kremer, I. and K. G. Nyborg, 2004b, "Underpricing and Market Power in Uniform Price Auctions," *Review of Financial Studies*, 17, 849–877.

Krishna, V., 2002, *Auction Theory*, Academic Press, San Diego, CA.

Lang, L., R. M. Stulz and R. A. Walkling, 1991, "A Test of the Free Cash Flow Hypothesis: The Case Bidder Returns," *Journal of Financial Economics*, 29, 315–335.

Li, T., I. M. Perrigne and Q. Vuong, 2002, "Structural Estimation of the Affiliated Private Value Model," *RAND Journal of Economics*, 33, 171–193.

Ljungqvist, A., 2007, "IPO Underpricing," in B. E. Eckbo (ed.), *Handbook of Corporate Finance: Empirical Corporate Finance, Volume 1*, (Elsevier/North-Holland, Handbooks in Finance Series), Ch. 7, pp. 377–422.

Loderer, C. and K. Martin, 1990, "Corporate Acquisitions by Listed Firms: The Experience of a Comprehensive Sample," *Financial Management*, 19, 17–33.

Maskin, E. and J. Riley, 2000a, "Asymmetric Auctions," *Review of Economic Studies*, 67, 413–438.

Maskin, E. and J. Riley, 2000b, "Equilibrium in Sealed High Bid Auctions," *Review of Economic Studies*, 67, 439–454.

McAfee, R. P. and J. McMillan, 1987, "Auctions and Biddings," *Journal of Economic Literature*, 25, 699–738.

McAfee, R. P. and J. McMillan, 1996, "Analyzing the Airwaves Auction," *Journal of Economic Perspectives*, 10, 159–175.

Milgrom, P. R., 2000, "Putting Auction Theory to Work: The Simultaneous Ascending Auction," *Journal of Political Economy*, 108, 245–272.

Milgrom, P. R. and R. J. Weber, 1982a, "A Theory of Auctions and Competitive Bidding," *Econometrica*, 50, 1089–1122.

Milgrom, P. R. and R. J. Weber, 1982b, "The Value of Information in a Sealed-Bid Auction," *Journal of Mathematical Economics*, 10, 105–114.

Miller, M., 1977, "Debt and Taxes," *Journal of Finance*, 32, 261–275.

Miller, M., K. Rock, 1985, "Dividend Policy under Asymmetric Information," *Journal of Finance*, 40, 1031–1051.

Moeller, S., F. Schlingemann and R. Stulz, 2004, "Firm Size and the Gains from Acquisitions," *Journal of Financial Economics*, 73, 201–228.

Morck, R., A. Shleifer and R. W. Vishny, 1990, "Do Managerial Objectives Drive Bad Acquisitions?" *Journal of Finance*, 45, 31–48.

Myerson, R., 1981, "Optimal Auction Design," *Mathematics of Operation Research*, 6, 58–73.

Persons, J., 1994, "Signaling and Takeover Deterrence with Stock Repurchases: Dutch Auctions versus Fixed Price Tender Offers," *Journal of Finance*, 49, 1373–1402.

Povel, P. and R. Singh, 2006, "Takeover Contests with Asymmetric Bidders," *Review of Financial Studies*, 19, 1399–1431.

Reece, D. K., 1978, "Competitive Bidding for Offshore Petroleum Lease," *Bell Journal of Economics*, 9, 364–384.

Rhodes-Kropf, M. and S. Viswanathan, 2000, "Corporate Re-Organization and Non-Cash Auctions," *Journal of Finance*, 55, 1807–1849.

Rhodes-Kropf, M. and S. Viswanathan, 2004, "Market Valuation and Merger Waves," *Journal of Finance*, 59, 2685–2718.

Rhodes-Kropf, M. and S. Viswanathan, 2005, "Financing Auction Bids," *RAND Journal of Economics*, in press.

Riley, J. and W. Samuelson, 1981, "Optimal Auctions," *American Economic Review*, 71, 381–392.

Roll, R., 1986, "The Hubris Hypothesis of Corporate Takeovers," *Journal of Business*, 59, 197–216.

Salant, D. J., 1997, "Up in the Air: GTE's Experience in the MTA Auction for Personal Communication Services Licenses," *Journal of Economics and Management Strategy*, 6, 549–572.

Sherman, A., 2005, "Global Trends in IPO Methods: Book Building versus Auctions with Endogenous Entry," *Journal of Financial Economics*, 78, 615–649.

Shleifer, A. and R. Vishny, 1986, "Large Shareholders and Corporate Control," *Journal of Political Economy*, 94, 461–488.

Shleifer, A. and R. Vishny, 2003, "Stock Market Driven Acquisitions," *Journal of Financial Economics*, 70, 295–311.

Singh, R., 1998, "Takeover Bidding with Toeholds: The Case of Owner's Curse," *Review of Financial Studies*, 11, 679–704.

Thorburn, K., 2000, "Bankruptcy Auctions: Costs, Debt Recovery, and Firm Survival," *Journal of Financial Economics*, 58, 337–368.

Weiss, L. A., 1990, "Bankruptcy Resolution: Direct Costs and Violation of Priority of Claims," *Journal of Financial Economics*, 27, 285–314.

Wilson, R., 1979, "Auctions of Shares," *Quarterly Journal of Economics*, 94, 675–689.

Chapter 3

BIDDING STRATEGIES AND TAKEOVER PREMIUMS: A REVIEW[*]

B. ESPEN ECKBO

Tuck School of Business at Dartmouth, Hanover, New Hampshire, USA

Contents

* This paper was written in conjunction with the broader review of corporate takeovers in Betton et al. (2008a). I am indebted to Sandra Betton and Karin Thorburn. I am also grateful for the suggestions and comments made by editors of the Journal of Corporate Finance's special issue on Corporate Control, Mergers and Acquisitions, in particular Jeffry Netter and Mike Stegemoller.

This article originally appeared in the *Journal of Corporate Finance*, Vol. 15, pp. 149–178 (2009).
Corporate Takeovers, Volume 2
Edited by B. Espen Eckbo
DOI: 10.1016/B978-0-12-381982-6.00003-3

Abstract

I review recent empirical research documenting offer premiums and bidding strategies in corporate takeovers. The discussion ranges from optimal auction bidding to the choice of deal payment form and premium effects of poison pills. The evidence describes the takeover process at a detailed level, from initial premiums to bid jumps, entry of rival bidders, and toehold strategies. Cross-sectional tests illuminate whether bidders properly adjust for winner's curse, whether target stock price runups force offer price markups, and whether auctions of bankrupt firms result in fire-sale discounts. The evidence is suggestive of rational strategic bidding behavior in specific contexts.

Keywords

takeover, merger, tender offer, auction, offer premium, bidder gains, toeholds, overbidding, markups, hostility, method of payment, fire-sale discounts, bankruptcy

JEL classification: G32, G33, G34

1. Introduction

This paper reviews recent empirical studies of takeover premiums and bidding behavior in corporate takeovers. There is growing research interest in the details of the takeover process from the initial bid through the final contest outcome. Succeeding with a takeover bid is difficult and involves strategies as the target may force the bidder to raise the offer price, reject all offers by the initial bidder in favor of a rival, and even reject all bidders. Betton et al. (2009) report that the initial bidder wins the target in only two-thirds of 10,000 initial control bids for US public targets 1980–2002. Moreover, it wins less often when the initial bid is in the form of an invitation to negotiate a merger as opposed to a tender offer, and when the initial bidder is private. Also, when a rival bidder enters the contest, the rival wins the auction twice as often as the initial bidder. In sum, initiating a takeover is risky business. With the substantial resources committed to the takeover process, bidders obviously need to think strategically in order to maximize the expected value of bid initiation.

With the emergence of machine-readable data sources such as Thomson Financial (SDC), researcher now have large-scale access to initial and final offer premiums to investigate the nature of observed bid strategies. A variety of questions are being examined: What determines the initial bid premium? If the initial bid is rejected, what should be the bid revision strategy (bid jump)? Do bidders fully account for the possibility of a winner's curse? Do bidders mark up the initially planned offer price in response to a runup in the target stock price ("markup pricing")? Should the bidder acquire a toehold in the target, and is there evidence of toehold-induced (rational) overbidding in offer premiums? Do auction bids for financially distressed firms reflect a "fire-sale" discount? How does the choice of payment method affect bid premiums? How do offer premiums respond to a target defensive mechanism such as a poison pill? Empirical evidence on all of these issues are reviewed below.

Empirical tests of bidding theories are also important for the broader debate over bidder rationality and the efficiency of the market for corporate control. As is well known, bidder abnormal stock returns are typically small and often negative around takeover announcements. Roll (1986) was the first to suggest that bidder overconfidence or "hubris" may go a long way in explaining the surprisingly low bidder takeover gains. The relatively poor bidder performance remains a pervasive and puzzling phenomenon also today. Since part of the problem is one of properly estimating and interpreting bidder announcement returns, however, direct evidence on offer premiums and bidding behavior is of key interest in this debate.[1]

Theory addresses optimal bid strategies when target shareholders free ride, and when the initial bid risks attracting competition and target resistance. In general, optimal strategies depend on the specifics of the takeover setting, such as the selling

---

[1] Bidder announcement returns are subject to attenuation bias due to partial anticipation, and they reflect valuation impacts of factors beyond the value of the takeover per se (including revelations about bidder managerial quality and exogenous changes in industry conditions).

mechanism (merger negotiations v. auction) and the information environment. In addition to the initial offer premium and subsequent bid revisions, strategic choices include acquiring a prebid ownership stake (toehold) in the target, and selecting an optimal payment method (mix of cash and securities).

The most important of these offer parameters is the *initial* bid premium, which is also the main focus of this paper. Bid initiation carries a first-mover advantage which the bid strategy presumably is designed to protect. To the extent that strategic bidding behavior exists, it is more likely to be evident in the first offer than in subsequent bids. After the initial bid, the race is on: bidder entry costs are sunk, toehold acquisitions are expensive (they take place at market prices reflecting the expected takeover premium), and it may be difficult to lower any cash portion that defines the payment method selected by the first bidder.

Much of the empirical tests use a basic auction setting to illustrate optimal bids. This is a natural approach in the context of corporate takeovers. Whether the bid is in the form of a tender offer or an invitation to negotiate a merger agreement, the takeover process resembles an auction setting in important ways. A public tender offer is an auction in the sense that bidding is open and target shareholders are allowed to tender their shares to the highest bidder within the tender period. However, takeover auctions initiated by the bidder are made complex by the fact that the seller reserve price is often unknown ex ante. This added complexity over standard auction settings initiated by the target helps explain the substantial number of takeover contests where no bidder wins.

The auction analogy is also useful when the bidder invites the target to negotiate a merger agreement to be put to a shareholder vote. Betton et al. (2009) and Aktas et al. (2008) present models of merger negotiations in which the outside option is a tender offer (auction). In a very real sense, merger negotiations occur in the shadow of an auction, so the expected auction outcome affects the bargaining power of the negotiating parties. In the United States, the bidder risks losing the target to a rival even *after* the target signs a merger agreement: Delaware case law on director fiduciary duties requires merger agreements to include a "fiduciary out" clause which permits target directors to evaluate competing offers before the shareholder vote. As indicated above, the data confirms that having signed a merger agreement is not a guarantee against the risk that the takeover process turns into an open auction for the target.

The paper is organized as follows. Section 2 presents summary information on total (bidder plus target) takeover gains, bidder announcement returns, and offer premiums. This helps set the stage for the subsequent discussion of bidding strategies and their implications for offer premiums and bidder returns. Section 3 discusses premium effects within the classical free-rider model, the model's empirical relevance for actual takeover settings, and evidence on the response of offer premiums to the introduction of mandatory disclosure. In Section 4, I focus on specific auction settings and discuss issues such as preemptive bidding, bid jumps, markup pricing, winner's curse, toehold-induced overbidding, the disappearing toehold phenomenon, and fire-sale discounts. Section 5 reviews several hypotheses for the bidder's choice of payment method, while Section 6 discusses premium effects of poison pills. Section 7 concludes the paper.

2. Takeover gains

Rational bidding requires that the total (bidder plus target) expected synergy gain from the takeover is positive. Thus, I begin by reviewing evidence on this fundamental requirement. I then summarize recent broad-based evidence on bidder announcement returns, which also serves as a link to the discussion of the valuation effects of the bidder's choice of payment method later in this paper. Finally, given the central focus on offer premiums in this survey, I provide a brief summary of recent large-sample evidence on the magnitude and cross-sectional determinants of initial and final offer premiums.

2.1. Total gains

In their classical survey, Jensen and Ruback (1983) conclude from the empirical evidence that the value-weighted sum of takeover-induced abnormal stock returns to bidders and targets is positive and significant.[2] In Betton et al. (2008a), we present estimates of total takeover gains using a comprehensive sample of 15,000 initial control bids for US targets over the period 1980–2005. The findings are replicated in Figure 1 which shows the daily cumulative abnormal returns from day −40 through day 10 relative to the initial offer announcement for both bidders and targets, classified by the respective firms' public status. The cumulative abnormal returns to targets are somewhat greater when the bidder is public than when the bidder is private. Several studies provide evidence of a valuation impact of the public status of the bidder and target firms in US takeovers,[3] and will be discussed further below.

The average target runup typically constitutes about one-third of the total runup plus the announcement abnormal returns, and the largest target abnormal returns occur in all-cash offers, where the sum of the runup and the announcement return is 28%. Using market capitalizations on day −42, the value-weighted sum of the runups of the bidder and target firms, and the value-weighted sum of the announcement-induced abnormal return are both positive and significant.[4] The sum the combined abnormal returns over

---

[2] Subsequent comprehensive surveys have reached a similar conclusion: Jarrell et al. (1988), Eckbo (1988), Andrade et al. (2001), Burkart and Panunzi (2008), Martynova and Renneboog (2007), and Betton et al. (2008a).

[3] Chang (1998), Fuller et al. (2002), Moeller et al. (2004), Bradley and Sundaram (2006), and Officer et al. (2009).

[4] Betton et al. (2008a) report that, for the 4803 pairs of listed bidders and targets, the average combined runup is 0.7% with a z-value of 4.3, while the average combined announcement return is 1.06% with a z-value of 14.6.

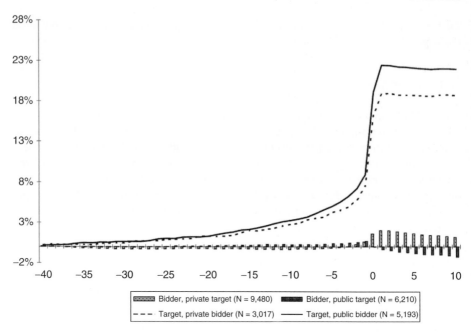

Fig. 1. Percent average cumulative abnormal stock returns to targets and initial bidders from day −40 through day 10 relative to the initial control bid date. US targets 1980–2005. Source: Betton et al. (2008a).

the runup and announcement periods averages a statistically significant 2%. Thus, total takeover gains are positive on average.[5]

2.2. Bidder announcement returns

Table 1 lists bidder announcement returns as reported by 19 large-sample studies, most of which are based on data from SDC. A typical finding is small (less than 1%) but significantly negative average bidder announcement returns, in particular if the bidder is large and offers all-stock as payment for the target in a merger proposal. Moreover, bidder announcement returns are typically positive and insignificant in tender offers. To get a sense of the magnitudes, when using the sample underlying Figure 1 the 3-day

[5] In Betton et al. (2008a) we also report estimates of 5-year postmerger abnormal stock returns. These estimates tend to be significantly negative when using the buy-and-hold, matched-firm estimation technique, and insignificantly different from zero when using the calendar-time portfolio technique. Long-run perform-ance estimates primarily address issues of market efficiency and the correct asset pricing model, and is therefore not discussed further here.

Table 1

Large-sample ($N > 1000$) estimates of announcement-induced average cumulative abnormal stock returns (ACAR) to US bidders

Study	Sample	ACAR(day τ_1, day τ_2)
Loderer and Martin (1990)	$N = 1135$ completed mergers, 274 completed tender offers, and 3296 "other" acquisitions (not classifiable as merger or tender offer) by public acquirers, where the offer is announced in the *Wall Street Journal*, 1996–1984	ACAR(-5, 0) is 1.7%[*] for 970 cases 1966–1968, 0.57%[*] for 3401 cases 1968–1980, and -0.1% for 801 cases 1981–1984. Bidder announcement returns smaller for larger bidders and decreasing in the relative size of the target firm
Eckbo and Thorburn (2000)	United States and Canadian bidders acquiring $N = 1846$ targets in Canada, 1964–1983	Announcement-month abnormal stock return are zero when the bidder is a US company and significantly positive when the bidder is a Canadian company (all acquiring Canadian targets). The relative size of the bidder is a key determinant of the different performance of United States and domestic Canadian bidders
Betton and Eckbo (2000)	Initial and rival bidders in $N = 1353$ tender offer contests for public targets, 1971–1990	(1) Day 0 is the initial bid date: ACAR(-60, 0) is 1.3% for initial bidders and 2.2% for rival bidders. (2) Day 0 is the second bid date: ACAR(-60, 0) is 1.2% for initial bidders, and 6.1%[*] for rivals
Fuller et al. (2002)	$N = 3135$ takeovers, 1990–2000, by 539 public acquirers with at least 5 successful control bids within 3 years. Minimum deal size is $1 million	ACAR(-2, 2) is 1.8%[*] for total sample of bidders, -1.0%[*] when target is public, 2.1%[*] when target is private, and 2.8%[*] when target is a subsidiary
Akbulut and Matsusaka (2003)	$N = 3466$ successful mergers between public firms, 1950–2002	ACAR(-2, 1) is 1.2% for "related" acquisitions (bidder and target have at least one three-digit SIC code in common) and 1.1%[*] for unrelated acquisition
Officer (2003, 2004)	$N = 2511$ attempted mergers and tender offers between public firms, 1988–2000 (Officer, 2003)	ACAR(-3, 3) is -1.2%[*] for the total sample
Moeller et al. (2004, 2005)	$N = 12{,}023$ acquisitions, 1980–2001. Minimum deal value is $1 million and 1% of the acquirer's assets	ACAR(-1, 1) is 1.1%[*] for total sample, 2.3%[*] for small acquirers, and 0.1% for large acquirers. Using dollar values, bidders loose a total of $221 billion in market capitalization over day -1 to $+1$. This aggregate loss is driven by a small number of very large deals concentrated to the 1998–2001 period
Bhagat et al. (2005)	$N = 1018$ tender offers for public targets	ACAR(-5, 5) is 0.2% with a median dollar return of -1.2 million
Song and Walkling (2005)	$N = 3389$ acquisitions, 1985–2001. Minimum deal value is $10 million	ACAR(-1, 0) for the first bidder after a 12-month dormant period in

(Continued)

Table 1 (*Continued*)

Study	Sample	ACAR(day τ_1, day τ_2)
		the industry is 0.7%*, and 0.04% for subsequent bidders. Consistent with an attenuation effect of partial anticipation of takeover activity
Bradley and Sundaram (2006)	$N = 12{,}476$ completed acquisitions by 4116 public companies, 1990–2000	ACAR(-2, 2) is 1.4% for the total sample, -0.7% for public targets, and 1.9% when the target is private. Bidding firms experience a large stock price runup over the 2-year period preceding the bid. This runup is greater for stock bids than for cash bids
Savor (2006)	$N = 1484$ (159 failed and 1335 successful) merger bids, 1990–2000. The bid is nonhostile and all-cash (359 successful cases) or all-equity (976 successful cases). Minimum deal size is 5% of bidder market value	ACAR(-1, 1) is $-3.5\%^*$ for all-stock bidders and 1.0%* for all-cash bidders. Similar results for the full sample of failed acquirers
Dong et al. (2006)	$N = 3137$ merger bids and tender offers between public firms, 1978–2000	ACAR(-1, 1) ranges from -0.2% (when target is ranked as relatively "undervalued") to -1.8% (when target is ranked as relatively "overvalued")
Moeller et al. (2007)	$N = 4322$ all-cash and all-stock bids, 1980–2002. Minimum deal value is $1 million and 1% of the acquirer's assets	ACAR(-1, 1) for the total sample is 0.8%. When target is public, ACAR (-1, 1) is -2.3% in all-stock deals and 0.7% in all-cash deals. When the target is private, ACAR(-1, 1) is 3.4% in all-stock deals
Bargeron et al. (2008)	$N = 1292$ completed all-cash takeovers of US public targets by private and public bidders, 1990–2005	Average target announcement CAR (-1,1) is 32% for public bidders and 22% for private bidders
Betton et al. (2008b, 2009)	$N = 10{,}806$ initial control bids for public targets: 7076 merger bids from 1980 to 2002 and 3730 tender offers from 1973 to 2002	ACAR(-1, 1) is $-1.2\%^*$ for total sample and $-0.15\%^*$ if the bidder has a toehold. In Betton et al. (2008b), ACAR(-1, 1) is $-1.9\%^*$ for merger offers, and an in significant 0.3% for tender offers
Betton et al. (2008c)	$N = 15{,}987$ initial control bids by public bidders for public or private targets, 1980–2005: 13,985 merger bids and 1468 tender offers	ACAR(-1, 1) is 0.69% with a significantly negative z-statistic of -3.9 for initial bidders in mergers, and 0.76 (insignificant) for initial bidders in tender offers. Large public bidders acquiring public targets and paying with all cash produces ACAR(-1, 1) of $-2.2\%^*$. Small public bidders acquiring private targets in all stock offers produces ACAR(-1,1) of 6.5%*

* significant at 10% level.

average abnormal stock return is 0.69% with a z-statistic of -3.9 for initial merger bids, and a statistically insignificant 0.76% for initial bidders making tender offers.[6]

The literature shows that two key drivers of negative bidder returns is the size of the bidder's total equity (Asquith et al., 1983; Eckbo and Thorburn, 2000; Moeller et al., 2004; 2005) and the target's status as a public or private firm (Bargeron et al., 2008; Betton et al., 2008c; Bradley and Sundaram, 2006). This average effect is summarized in Table 2 for the sample in Betton et al. (2008a). When the initial bidder (i) is relatively large (in the upper-size quartile), (ii) is bidding for a public target, and (iii) is offering all-stock as payment, the average 3-day announcement-period abnormal stock return is as low as -2.21%. Moreover, the "best-case" scenario is the combination of a small bidder (lower size quartile), private target, and, again, *all-stock* as payment, which produces an average bidder abnormal return of as much as 6.46%.

The finding fact that all-stock offers appear in both of these two samples with extreme bidder valuations is relevant for the discussion of the payment method choice later in this paper (Section 5). Bidder size and target public status appear to swamp the valuation effect of the payment method choice per se. Notice also the finding of Moeller et al. (2005) that bidder size—and the associated negative bidder returns—

Table 2

Summary of initial bidder 3-day announcement-period abnormal returns, 1980–2005

Source: Betton et al. (2008a). Initial bidder cumulative abnormal returns for the window $-1, 1$ relative to the initial control bid. Large bidders are bidders in the upper quartile of market capitalization on day -42 (in constant 2000 dollars) and small bidders are bidders in the lower quartile of market capitalization on day -42. The cutoff values for the upper and lower quartiles are \$134 million and \$2.2 billion, respectively. The method of payment is determined from the SDC 100% cash or 100% stock consideration field. The public status of the target is determined from SDC.

Sample	Public targets		Private targets	
	N	CAR$(-1, 1)$	N	CAR$(-1, 1)$
A: Large bidders				
All-stock	769	-0.0221^*	445	0.0010
All-cash	439	-0.0030^*	88	0.0026^*
B: Small bidders				
All-stock	495	-0.0006	872	0.0646^*
All-cash	190	0.0306^*	184	0.0176^*

* represents significance at the 1% level (two-sided test).

[6] The z-statistic is the average value of the t-statistic for the null of zero abnormal return multiplied by $\sqrt{N}$. A value of the average abnormal return that is positive but close to zero may have a negative z value due to skewness.

were particularly large in 1999 and 2000. Betton et al. (2008c) argue that the significant bidder size effect is largely confined to that particular time period.

2.3. Offer premiums

Prior to the availability of offer pries on SDC, the empirical takeover literature
conventionally used target cumulative abnormal stock returns around takeover bids
as a proxy for offer premiums. This proxy is, of course, problematic as target abnormal
stock returns reflect not only the offer price but also the probability of competition and
bid failure at the initial offer date. The attenuating effect of the residual uncertainty
about bid success at the initial offer announcement is important: it tends to produce
offer premium estimates in the vicinity of 25–30% in Figure 1 when, as shown in the
last two columns of Table 3, the true offer premium is about 45–50%.[7]

The availability of SDC has spurred large-sample studies based directly on offer
prices. With offer prices, premium estimation is reduced to finding the best "base"
price with which to scale the known offer price. In principle, the correct base price is
the preoffer secondary market price of the target which the bidder relies on in order to
determine the initial offer premiums. While this base price is unobservable, it is
common to select a target share price 2 or 3 months prior to the first bid (in Table 3
the base price is 42 trading days prior to the initial offer announcement). The usual
motivation, which is supported by Figure 1, is that a price this far back from the initial
bid is largely free of market anticipation of the pending offer.[8]

The last two columns of Table 3 show average initial and final offer premiums
relative to the target share price 42 days prior to the initial bid announcement (adjusted
for splits and dividends). The table uses the sample in Betton et al. (2009). Two-thirds
of 10,000 initial bids are from the period 1990 to 2002, and 72% of the sample
represents merger bids. The data is collected primarily from SDC which lists *official*
or public bids for the target only. As emphasized by Boone and Mulherin (2007b),
targets increasingly initiate takeovers on their own. That is, some targets privately
solicit bidder interest and select a negotiating partner among the respondents. Whenever this happens, the initial bid identified by the SDC (and listed in Table 3) is the
winner of the private round of target solicitations.

---

[7] The difference between actual premiums and abnormal return estimates is also affected by the estimation
error in the model generating expected stock returns. The estimation error is compounded when using target
stock returns over long windows to capture the final premium at the very end of the takeover process.

[8] Several pre-SDC studies report hand-collected offer prices. For example, Bradley (1980) presents the first
systematic offer price analysis in the context of public tender offers. Jarrell and Bradley (1980) and Eckbo
and Langohr (1989) study the impact of disclosure regulations on offer prices. Walkling (1985) uses offer
premiums to predict tender offer success. Eckbo and Langohr (1989) examine the effect of disclosure rules
and method of payment (cash vs. stock) on tender offer premiums, while Betton and Eckbo (2000) examine
bid jumps and offer premium determinants in more than 1200 tender offers.

Table 3

Deal characteristics and initial and final offer premiums in 10,806 control contests for public US targets, 1973–2002

Source: Betton et al. (2009). A control bid is defined as the bidder owning less than 50% of the target shares prior to the bid and seeking to own at least 50% of the target shares. Successive control bids for the same target are then grouped into a control contest. A given control bid initiates the contest if there are no other public control bids for the same target over the preceding 6 months. All subsequent control bids within 6 months of a previous bid belong to the same contest, and the contest ends when there are no additional control bids for the same target over the following 6-month period. The initial offer premium is $p_{ini}/p_{-41} - 1$, where p_{ini} is the first offer price, p_{-41} is the target stock price on day -41 adjusted for splits and dividends, and 0 is the day of the initial control bid. The final offer premium is $p_{fin}/p_{-41} - 1$, where p_{fin} is the last offer price in the contest.

Sample	Number of cases	Deal value ($ million)		% of contests where the winner is			Average offer premium (%)	
		Mean	Median	Initial bidder	Rival	No bidder wins	Initial bid	Final bid
All contests	10,806	715	89	66.6	3.7	29.7	44.5	46.1
1973–1989	3730	312	60	58.7	5.2	36.1	45.0	48.5
1990–2002	7076	903	108	70.7	3.0	26.4	44.2	45.0
Merger bid	7750	827	92	63.5	3.3	33.2	43.6	44.5
Tender offer	3056	433	78	74.8	4.8	20.4	46.5	50.2
Acquirer public	6726	902	112	75.6	3.2	21.3	46.1	47.5
Acquirer private	4080	285	52	51.7	4.6	43.7	40.1	42.6
Single bidder	9944	693	88	70.5	0.0	29.5	44.8	45.4
Multiple bidders	862	989	101	20.6	47.8	31.7	41.1	53.2
Target friendly	10,295	688	85	68.0	3.2	28.8	44.1	45.1
Target hostile	511	1204	183	34.4	16.3	49.2	49.0	60.9
All cash	4185	320	66	69.1	4.0	27.0	44.1	46.6
Stock/mixed	6621	1048	119	65.0	3.6	31.4	44.7	45.8

The average initial offer premium is 45% across the total sample with premium data (while not shown, the median offer premium is consistently a few percentage points lower than the mean). The final premium is almost identical (46%) reflecting the large portion of the sample where the initial price is also the final price (single-bid contests). There is a small difference in initial and final offer premiums in the first and the second part of the sample period. Initial (final) offer premiums are 44% (45%) in mergers and 47% (50%) in tender offers. Separating ex post single- and multiple-bidder contests, the average initial and final premiums in multiple-bidder contests is 41% and 53%, respectively. For single-bidder contests, the initial premium averages 45% (final 45%).

Table 3 also shows that initial (and final) offer premiums are somewhat lower when the bidder is private: 40% versus 46% for public acquirers, respectively. Average premiums are almost identical in all-cash and all-stock/mixed offers, however, the multivariate regressions discussed next indicate that all-cash bid premiums tend to be higher. Finally, contests with hostile targets have both the highest initial bid premium (49% vs. 44% for friendly targets) and final offer premium (61% vs. 45%).

Table 4

Determinants of the offer premium in 4889 control contests for US public targets 1980–2002

Source: Betton et al. (2008b). The table shows OLS estimates of the initial and final offer premium, defined as $\ln(p_{initial}/p_{-42})$ and $\ln(p_{final}/p_{-42})$, respectively, where $p_{initial}$ is the initial offer price, p_{final} is the final offer price in the contest, and p_{-42} is the stock price on day -42 adjusted for splits and dividends. Amihud liquidity is the average value of $|R_i|/(p_i\,S_i)$ over days $i \in \{-250, -42\}$, where R_i is the % holding period return, p_i is the closing price and S_i is the number of shares traded. Industry is the four-digit SIC code in CRSP. The sample is 4889 control bids 1980–2002 for US targets with a stock price $\geq$ \$1 and a market capitalization $\geq$ \$10 million. The p-values are in parenthesis.

	Initial offer premium		Final offer premium	
Mean	0.43		0.48	
Median	0.37		0.39	
S.D.	0.46		0.47	
Intercept	0.296 (0.000)	0.256 (0.000)	0.296 (0.000)	0.254 (0.000)
A: Target characteristics				
Size: ln of target market capitalization on day -42	−0.030 (0.000)	−0.027 (0.000)	−0.030 (0.000)	−0.027 (0.000)
Target book-to-market > industry median	0.025 (0.000)	0.029 (0.000)	0.024 (0.000)	0.029 (0.000)
Target runup: $\ln(p_{-1}/p_{-42})$	0.808 (0.000)	0.811 (0.000)	0.808 (0.000)	0.811 (0.000)
Amihud liquidity	8.55 (0.311)	13.29 (0.114)	8.71 (0.302)	13.46 (0.110)
Poison pill dummy	−0.016 (0.606)	0.000 (0.990)	−0.016 (0.604)	−0.001 (0.987)
B: Bidder characteristics				
Positive toehold (vs. zero toehold)	−0.023 (0.032)	−0.025 (0.024)	−0.023 (0.032)	−0.025 (0.024)
Acquiror public (vs. private)	0.015 (0.079)	0.023 (0.008)	0.015 (0.072)	0.023 (0.007)
Horizontal takeover (same industry)	−0.004 (0.608)	−0.004 (0.664)	−0.004 (0.618)	−0.004 (0.673)
C: Deal characteristics				
Tender offer (vs. merger)	−0.061 (0.000)	−0.066 (0.000)	−0.061 (0.000)	−0.066 (0.000)
All cash consideration (vs. stock or mixed)	0.019 (0.017)	0.021 (0.012)	0.019 (0.017)	0.021 (0.012)
Hostile target response (vs. friendly or neutral)	0.020 (0.185)	0.020 (0.185)	0.019 (0.216)	0.019 (0.216)
Multiple bidders (vs. single bidder contest)			0.009 (0.497)	0.008 (0.501)
Announced in 1980–1989 (vs. 1990–2002)	−0.016 (0.056)		−0.017 (0.050)	
Year fixed effects	No	Yes	No	Yes
Adjusted R^2	0.424	0.436	0.423	0.436
F-value	300.3 (0.000)	115.3 (0.000)	277.2 (0.000)	111.9 (0.000)

Table 4 shows cross-sectional determinants of the offer premiums using the offer premium data in Betton et al. (2008b). The explanatory variables are grouped into "Target characteristics," "Bidder characteristics," and "Deal characteristics." The regressions alternately use a time dummy for offers taking place in the early sample period (1980–1989) and year fixed effects. Notice also that the information in these variables is known at the time the offer premium was set. The variable "Hostile target response" is included as a determinant of the initial offer premium because this information is most likely known at the outset. However, the variable "multiple bidders" is not and is therefore included as a determinant of the final offer premium only.[9] The results are summarized as follows:

(1) The initial and final offer premiums are *higher* after the 1980s; when the bidder is a public company; when the initial bid is an all-cash offer; and the higher the prebid target runup.

(2) The initial and final offer premiums are *lower* the greater the target total equity capitalization prior to the initial bid; when the target's book-to-market ratio (B/M) exceeds the industry median B/M (i.e., when the target is a growth company relative to industry rivals); when the initial bid is a tender offer; and when the initial bidder has a positive toehold.

(3) The initial and final offer premiums are *unaffected* by the presence of a target poison pill; target hostility to the initial bid;[10] target stock liquidity; the presence of multiple bidders; and whether the takeover is horizontal.

The recent literature provides some additional offer premium evidence. For example, Officer (2003) and Bates and Lemmon (2003) show that offer premiums are significantly greater when the SDC indicates the existence of a target termination agreement, while Bargeron (2005) find lower premiums in the presence of a target board/management tender agreement. Moeller (2005) present evidence indicating that powerful entrenched target CEOs reduce takeover premiums. Chatterjee et al. (2008) find that takeover premiums are larger the greater the disagreement between the earnings forecasts of financial analysts following the target. Levi et al. (2008) use RiskMetrics Group data on board structure and find that bid premiums are affected by the gender composition of the board. Specifically, bid premiums are lower when the bidder CEO is female, and the higher the target board's proportion of female directors (provided that the female directors are independent appointees).[11]

I now turn to various bidding hypotheses and their implications for offer premiums.

---

[9] Not surprisingly (given the relative paucity of multiple-bid contest), the explanatory variables have similar coefficients and level of significance for both the initial and final offer premiums.

[10] Note that most of the hostile bids took place in the 1980s when the time dummy shows average premiums were significantly lower.

[11] Since several of the variables used to explain the offer premium are themselves endogenous choice variables (payment method, toehold, hostility, termination agreements, bidder's public status), some of the reported effects may not be robust to endogeneity. Betton and Eckbo (2000), Officer (2003), and Betton et al. (2009) use systems of equations and various corrections for self-selection. See Li and Prabhala (2007) for a comprehensive survey of self-selection models in corporate finance.

3. Free-riders and mandatory disclosure

3.1. Offer premiums and the free-rider problem

An early workhorse in the theoretical takeover literature is the free-rider model of Grossman and Hart (1980b) and Bradley (1980). They analyze the incentives of dispersed, noncooperative target shareholders to accept a tender offer from a single bidder, and the resulting inefficiency of the takeover market. To illustrate, suppose the target's preoffer (stand-alone) share price is equal to zero, and that it is common knowledge that the posttakeover share price will equal $v > 0$. The value-increase v may be thought of as synergy gains resulting from the bidder taking control of the target. The bidder makes a conditional unrestricted bid b for 50% of the target shares (sufficient to transfer control of the target to the bidder).[12] A risk-neutral target shareholder i tenders only if the offer price exceeds the expected value of her share if she retains it:

$$\text{Tender if } b \geq \Pr(\text{Success}|i \text{ Retain})v \tag{1}$$

where $\Pr(\cdot)$ denotes the probability that the offer succeeds given that the shareholder does not tender.[13]

By inspection of Equation (1), the target shareholder is more willing to tender the lower is the posttakeover value v, and the more she believes that retaining reduces the takeover's probability of success. As the number of target shareholder becomes large, however, the probability that any single shareholder is pivotal for the outcome of the bid becomes arbitrarily small. For such shareholders, the tender criterion in Equation (1) reduces to:

$$\text{Tender if } b \geq v \tag{2}$$

Since the bidder has no economic incentive to make the bid in Equation (2), these shareholders are in effect free riding on a decision by others to tender. Of course, if all shareholders behave this way, the takeover opportunity never materializes.[14]

Making every target shareholder pivotal by a conditional and restricted offer for 100% is unlikely to help. Because the bidder gains control after receiving 50% of the shares, refusing to purchase those shares if she is one share short of 100% is not credible. Also, allowing the bidder to be better informed than target shareholders

---

[12] "Conditional" means no shares will be purchased if less than 50% are tendered. "Unrestricted" means any or all tendered shares above 50% will be purchased.

[13] We are ignoring taxes. For example, when b is paid in cash, the offer may trigger a capital gains tax liability.

[14] Just as the free-rider problem can discourage value-increasing bids, value-reducing bids—bids where the posttakeover value of the target is less than its preoffer value—may be encouraged due to a "pressure-to-tender" problem (Bebchuk, 1985): Conditional on the offer succeeding, tendering may dominate retaining and receiving an even lower value. Thus, paradoxically, there may be "pressure-to-tender" when the bidder is value-reducing. The root cause of this result is, as above, that each target shareholder bases the tendering decision on a comparison between b and v, ignoring the pretakeover value.

(about v) does not solve the problem. Individual target shareholders now demand an offer price $b \geq E(v|\text{Offer})$ in order to tender, where the right-hand side is the expected valuation of the bidder given that he makes an offer. An offer below this expectation leads target shareholders to infer that $b < v$ and therefore to retain their shares. In this case, there does not exist a rational expectations (perfect Bayesian) equilibrium in which the bidder expects to make a profit from the takeover.[15]

There are a number of ways to mitigate the free-rider problem so that the bidder gains on the acquired target shares. Two frequently mentioned mechanisms are post-takeover dilution (Grossman and Hart, 1980b) and pretakeover toehold acquisition (Shleifer and Vishny, 1986). Posttakeover dilution reduces the "back-end" value of the takeover, and may be enforced through a two-tiered tender offer. The first tier is a bid b while the back end is a minority buyout (enforced by the bidder after acquiring control in the front end) at a lower value $v_d < v$. Alternatively, if fair price rules prevent the minority buyout to take place at a price below the front-end price, the bidder may resort to self-dealing ("asset tunneling") which is harmful to minority shareholders after the takeover. Examples of such dilution techniques are asset sales at prices below market value, transfer pricing favorable to the majority shareholder, excessive compensation schemes, and so on. These schemes create a wedge between the posttakeover share value to the acquirer and minority shareholders and enables the acquirer to make a profit. Although such transfers may enhance the ex ante efficiency of the takeover market, they are controversial and legally difficult to enforce ex post.[16]

A firm contemplating making a bid for the target may also decide to purchase target shares (a toehold) in the market at the prebid (no-information) target share price. The implications of such toehold acquisitions for optimal bidding are discussed in detail in the next section. In the context of the free-rider problem, the important point is that the toehold bidder may gain on the toehold while making zero profits on the shares acquired in the formal takeover bid. Let δ denote the fraction of the target posttakeover value that may be diluted ex post, and α the fraction of the target shares held by the bidder prior to the offer, respectively. The bidder makes the conditional unrestricted offer of

$$b^* = (1 - \delta)v \tag{3}$$

[15] Hirshleifer and Titman (1990) prove the existence of a separating equilibrium in which the offer price fully reveals v.

[16] Djankov et al. (2008) survey the opportunities for corporate insiders around the world to dilute minority shareholder value through self-dealings deemed *legal* under a country's corporate laws. Under the European Takeover Directive (article 14), member-states may grant acquirers a squeeze-out right, that is, the right to compel posttakeover minority shareholders to sell their shares after the acquirer has purchased 90% of the target shares.

which yields a bidder profit of

$$v - (1 - \alpha)b^* = \alpha v + (1 - \alpha)(v - b^*) = \alpha v + (1 - \alpha)\delta v \qquad (4)$$

The first term, αv, is the gain on the toehold shares, while the second term is the profits on the shares purchased in the takeover. The second term, $(1 - \alpha)\delta v$, shows that dilution is costly for the bidder in that it also reduces the value of the bidder's toehold shares. Thus, the larger the initial stake α, the lower the controlling shareholder's incentive to dilute ex post. In other words, a corporate insider with a larger equity stake is more prone to act in the outside (minority) shareholders' interest (Burkart et al., 1998; Jensen and Meckling, 1976).

3.2. Is the free-rider problem important in practice?

What is the empirical relevance of the free-rider problem in corporate takeovers? The most direct way to evaluate this question is to look at the frequency of (pivotal) blockholders in corporate shareownership structures. A large blockholder likely accounts for the possibility that her tendering decision affects the probability that the offer will succeed. In this case, shareholders are willing to tender at a price lower than indicated by expression (1) above (Bagnoli and Lipman, 1988; Holmstrom and Nalebuff, 1992).[17]

The evidence on corporate ownership structures around the world suggests that the existence or one or more large blockholder is the rule rather than the exception.[18] In the United States and elsewhere, small and midsized publicly traded companies typically have one or more large shareholder (defined as a minimum 5% holding).[19] In large-cap firms, individual (or family) block-holdings are less frequent in the United States; however, large blocks held by financial institutions such as pension funds are common for large firms. As highlighted by Holderness (2009), the evidence challenges

---

[17] In Holmstrom and Nalebuff (1992), there are N target shareholders of equal size, and the bidder needs K of these to tender in order to acquire control. They show that there exists a mixed strategy equilibrium where the takeover succeeds and the bidder makes a positive expected profit. In this equilibrium, individual target shareholders tender with a probability $p = K/N$. Expected profits go to zero when N becomes large.

[18] Following the early international evidence of La Porta et al. (1999), detailed information on corporate ownership structures has appeared for East Asia (Claessens et al., 2000), Western Europe (Faccio and Lang, 2002; Franks et al., 2005), and the United States (Dlugosz et al., 2006; Helwege et al., 2007; Holderness, 2009; Holderness et al., 1999).

[19] The definition of a block varies in the literature from 5% to 20%. Note that a relatively small block may become pivotal depending on the ownership distribution of the remaining shares. A natural empirical measure of pivotal is the Shapley transformation of the block (Shapley, 1953). The Shapley value is the probability that the block will be pivotal, computed using all possible shareholder coalitions (with the block) in which the coalition determines the voting outcome. See, for example, Eckbo and Verma (1994) and Zingales (1994) for applications in corporate finance.

the view—originating with Berle and Means (1932)—that US ownership is largely dispersed, and it suggests that free-rider problems in takeovers may be a rarity.[20]

A more indirect way to evaluate the empirical relevance of free-rider problems is to examine characteristics of observed takeover bids. First, the unequal distribution of takeover gains between target and bidder firms—with most if not all of the total gains typically accruing to the target—is often cited in support of the existence of the free-rider problem (Burkart and Panunzi, 2008; Hirshleifer, 1995). However, competition among bidders also lowers the winning bidder's share of synergy gains. Second, toehold bidding—perhaps the most obvious way to mitigate expected free-rider problems—is extremely rare in control-oriented acquisitions (Betton et al., 2009). Third, since merger negotiations per se avoid the free-rider problem,[21] it is interesting to compare offer premiums in mergers and tender offers. Recall from Table 4 that the marginal impact of a tender offer is to *lower* offer premiums. Overall, it is difficult to argue that the large initial offer premiums in takeovers are driven by free-rider problems.

3.3. Premium effects of the introduction of disclosure rules

The 1968 Williams Act, the main federal law governing public tender offers, requires an orderly auction mechanism: the tender offer must be open for a minimum 20 business days; competing bid and material bid revisions automatically extend the offer period by 10 days; target shareholders may withdraw all tendered shares for any reason (typically in response to a higher bid) within 15 days; and the bidder must purchase target shares on a pro rata basis among those who tenders.[22] The Williams Act also requires public information disclosure.[23]

---

[20] Holderness (2009) studies a random sample of 10% of the firms trading on the NYSE, Amex, and NASDAQ. Large shareholders (which include institutional holdings) on average own 39% of the voting power of the common stock. Moreover, 96% of the firms have at least one 5% + blockholder, and the average holding of the largest blockholder is 26%. Holderness also reports that 89% of the firms in the S&P 500 Index have large blockholders. Thus, free-rider problems are unlikely. Whether the evidence also challenges the seriousness of the Berle-Means warnings of agency costs associated with delegated management in public firms is, of course, a different issue. It is possible that a large block held by a financial institution (as opposed to an individual investor) carries with it serious agency problems when seen from the point of view of the firm's individual shareholders.

[21] Notice, however, that although the free-rider problem does not exist in terms of the negotiated offer premium, it may reappear during the subsequent shareholder vote over the proposed agreement.

[22] Contrary to takeover regulations in many Western countries (Berglof and Burkart, 2003), the Williams Act does not include a mandatory bid rule. A mandatory bid rule requires the bidder to proceed with an offer for 100% of the target shares after acquiring a certain stake in the target (Burkart and Panunzi, 2003). Mandatory bid rules do, however, exist in certain states, including Pennsylvania and Maine. The mandatory bid price varies with jurisdiction, but is typically a function of the price(s) the bidder paid for the initial stake.

[23] A tender offer is disclosed through a 14D filing with the SEC. Also, irrespective of any plans to acquire the target, an investor purchasing 5% or more of the target shares must file Form 13D with the SEC within a 10-day period. The 13D includes statements concerning the purchaser's intention with respect to the eventually purchase of control. Anti-fraud provisions were added to the Williams Act in 1970 to back up these disclosure requirements.

The Williams Act was in part a response to perceived takeover abuses in the 1960s, such as "midnight mergers" where the bidder quickly gained control of the target shares using all-cash purchases in the market and privately from blockholders. While the stated intention of the Act is the protection of target shareholders, a concern for potential bidders is that the mandatory disclosure rules also act to increase the ability of potential rival bidders to compete for the target. As pointed out by Grossman and Hart (1980a) and Jarrell and Bradley (1980), an active market for corporate control presupposes that initial bidders expect to have an advantage over potential rivals when search costs are sunk. Mandatory disclosure rules which increase expected competition among bidders possibly raise offer premiums and therefore deter some bids.[24]

Jarrell and Bradley (1980) examine whether the disclosure provisions of the Williams Act have raised tender offer premiums. They find that the average cash tender offer premium increased from 32% to nearly 53% following the passage of the Act in 1968. Consistent with higher premium costs, Schipper and Thompson (1983) present evidence indicating that a sample of frequent acquirers earned significantly negative abnormal returns over the months surrounding announcements of the introduction of the Williams Act. Also, Asquith et al. (1983), Loderer and Martin (1990) and others report that gains to bidder firms in mergers are on average lower after 1968.

Nathan and O'Keefe (1989) find that the premium increase after the introduction of the Williams Act is not restricted to cash tender offers: Cash *mergers* experienced an increase in the average premium from 30% to 67%, while security exchange mergers saw an increase in the average premium from 30% to 54%. They also show that the majority of the increase in the average offer premium takes place after 1972. This delay is puzzling and raises the question of whether the premium increase is due to the Williams Act (which was amended in 1970) or to some other economic phenomenon.

The Williams Act introduced both disclosure rules and a minimum 20-day offer period. Providing rival bidders with time to respond to the initial bid (the 20-day wait period) is obviously key to increased competition. Thus, the studies of the Williams Act do not isolate the premium impact of the disclosure rules. Specifically, studies of the Williams Act do not answer the fundamental question of whether the introduction of disclosure rules affect offer premiums in an environment where rival bidders already have time to respond.

Eckbo and Langohr (1989) provide evidence on this question using a different institutional setting. France introduced mandatory disclosure rules for public tender offers in 1970—much like those in the Williams Act. The difference is that France had already established a minimum (4-week) tender offer period much earlier (in 1966). Eckbo and Langohr (1989) find that the average offer premium in successful cash tender offers increased from 34% to nearly 61% after the 1970 disclosure regulations.

---

[24] However, severe penalties on the release of false (or misleading) information may benefit some bidder firms by making their otherwise voluntarily disclosed information more credible (Eckbo and Langohr, 1989). This positive effect is greater the lower the correlation between rival bidders' private valuations of the target (i.e., the more unique the bidder's contribution to total synergy creation).

Since the minimum tender offer period remained at 1 month throughout their sample period, this indicates that disclosure requirements *alone* can cause a substantial increase in average offer premiums. Eckbo and Langohr (1989) also study a contemporaneous control sample of privately negotiated controlling-block trades, exempt from the 1970 disclosure regulation. Premiums in these alternative control acquisitions did not increase after 1970.

4. Auctions and overbidding incentives

4.1. Takeover auctions

A second work horse in the theoretical literature on takeover bidding is the competitive auction. Here, the bidder faces a single seller in the form of a large target shareholder or a target management with sufficient authority to commit to selling in the auction. As Dasgupta and Hansen (2007) note in their survey, auction theory plays an important prescriptive role: to inform a company's board or regulators about the impact of selling processes or rules on shareholder wealth, efficiency, and welfare. They also note that, for such prescriptions to be useful, the auction model must reasonably mimic the actual takeover bidding environment. One important characteristic of any auction is the seller's commitment to stick to the rules of the game. For auction-theoretic results to apply, the seller must be trying to secure the best price for the firm's shareholders by committing to a selling mechanism.[25] As noted in the introduction, since a publicly traded target's board of directors has a fiduciary obligation to accept the highest offer (provided the board has placed the target "in play"), a takeover is arguably much like an auction even if the target initially negotiates a merger agreement.

The typical assumption is of an open, ascending (English) auction with zero entry and bidding costs, and where the winning bidder pays the second-highest bid.[26] Bidder valuations v (synergies) are private knowledge, but the seller knows the probability distribution function over v, $G(v)$. Since bidders tend to have different skill levels in terms of managing the target assets, it is often assumed that the valuations v are uncorrelated across bidders—a private value. Alternatively, bidder valuations may be correlated—a common value environment which requires bidders to shave their bids in anticipation of the winners curse.

In a common-value setting, bidders receive private and noisy signals as to the true (common) value of the target. Bidding the full value of the signal would cause the bidder with the largest positive signal error to win and overpay (the "curse"). Optimal

[25] For example, in a first-price auction, in which bidders optimally shave their bids, the seller must be able to commit not to allow further bid revisions by the losing bidder (who, after losing, may want to submit a bid higher than the winning bid).

[26] With zero entry and bidding costs, optimal bid increments are infinitesimal, so the winning bidder pays the second highest price whether or not the auction is defined formally as a firs-price or second-price auction.

bidding takes this possibility into account by reducing the bid to the point where the expected value of the bid *conditional on winning* is nonnegative. Thus, testing for the presence of a winner's curse is equivalent to testing the hypothesis that bidders are rational (properly shave the bids). This hypothesis is discussed further below. In a private value setting, bidders know their true valuations and thus do not face a winner's curse.

It is also commonly assumed that the bidder's outside option is status quo. That is, the payoff to the bidder is zero when losing the auction. This assumption is effectively relaxed when the bidder has a toehold (Betton et al., 2009; Bulow et al., 1999; Burkart, 1995), or a target termination agreement, or when the takeover is a response to changes in industry competition (Akdogu, 2007; Molnar, 2008; Morellec and Zhdanov, 2005). The toehold provides a positive payoff when the toehold bidder loses to a rival (who purchases the toehold). A termination contract also pays off when the bidder loses and no other bidder wins and the target remains independent. Also, a worsening of the competitive industry equilibrium can place the unsuccessful bidder at a competitive disadvantage vis a vis the winner.

4.2. Preemptive bidding and bid jumps

Takeovers are characterized by large bid jumps. The bid jump from the prebid (no-information) target share price to the initial offer price is by far the largest jump in a takeover contest. As shown in Table 5, which is reproduced from Betton and Eckbo (2000), there are significant bid jumps also following the initial bid.[27] The average jump from the initial to the second bid price in the contest is 10%, implying a 31% change in the initial offer premium. The jump from the first to the final bid average 14% (a 65% revision in the initial offer premium), and the average bid-jump throughout the entire contest is 5% (average premium increments of 17%). The evidence of significant bid jumps is consistent with the presence of bidding costs. This in turn support the notion in Fishman (1988) that initial bidders may strategically raise the first bid in an attempt to deter competition.[28]

The high premiums and jumps are consistent with the hypothesis that takeover benefits are in part common to several potential bidders, such as benefits emanating from replacing inefficient target management or using voting control to extract value from ex post minority shareholders in the merged firm. These and other forms of bidder-target complementarities often do not require specialized resources owned by a single potential bidder firm. As pointed out in Section 3.3 on premium effects of mandatory disclosure, in the absence of specialized resources, the first bidder is concerned that the initial bid will alert potential rivals to a profit opportunity.

---

[27] To my knowledge, this is the only systematic evidence on bid jumps published in the takeover literature.
[28] See also Hirshleifer and Ping (1990) and Daniel and Hirshleifer (2008) for implication of bidding costs for optimal bidding strategies.

Table 5

Median percentage bid-jumps in multibid tender offer contests, 1971–1990

Source: Betton and Eckbo (2000). $p_{initial}$ is the initial bid price and p is either the second or the final bid price (as indicated by the first column). Thus, the third column shows the percent change in the initial bid *price*. p_{-60} is the target share price 60 days prior to the initial bid. Thus, the fourth column shows the percent change in the initial bid *premium*.

	Sample size	% Offer price revision $(p - p_{initial})/p$	% Premium revision $(p - p_{initial})/$ $(p_{initial} - p_{-60})$
I. All multibid contests			
Jump from first to second bid	454	10.00	30.77
Jump from first to final bid	457	14.29	65.08
Average bid-jump throughout contest	457	5.43	16.67
II. Contests where second bid is by initial bidder			
Jump from first to second bid	264	7.91	24.40
Jump from first to final bid	264	13.21	35.93
Average bid-jump throughout contest	264	5.00	14.97
III. Contests where second bid is by rival bidder			
Jump from first to second bid	190	13.90	45.20
Jump from first to final bid	193	17.86	59.70
Average bid-jump throughout contest	193	6.67	22.99

In his model of preemptive bidding, Fishman (1988) assumes that bidders must pay an investigation cost in order to identify their private valuations of the target. If both bidders enter (so both investigation costs are sunk), an open English auction with costless bidding ensues and the winner pays $b = \min[v_1, v_2]$. However, there may exist an initial bid that deters the second bidder from paying the investigation cost and entering the auction. Specifically, a high initial (all-cash) bid signals that the initial bidder has a relatively high private valuation for the target, which reduces rival bidders' expected value of winning. For a sufficiently large investigation cost, the expected value is negative and the rival does not enter.

Testing preemption arguments is difficult since one obviously cannot observe deterred bids. One must look to auxiliary or related model predictions, and the following results seem relevant in this respect. First, as shown in Betton and Eckbo (2000) and Betton et al. (2008a), entry of a rival bidder is relatively rapid when it occurs (within 3 weeks in tender offers). Again, a rapid rival entry response is consistent with relatively low investigation costs—perhaps because takeover benefits are partly common to several potential bidders—requiring a relatively high initial premium to deter entry.

A rapid entry response will also result if potential rival bidders have been able to complete much of their evaluation *prior* to the initial bid. This is possible whenever the corporate resources required to produce synergy gains from the takeover have industry-specific components. In this case, potential rival bidders quickly update their priors of a takeover opportunity with the information in the initial offer—possibly resulting in a higher bid. This hypothesis suggests that takeover announcements are associated with positive industry wealth effects and that rival bidders tend to operate in the same industry as the target.[29]

As indicated earlier, auction outcomes are sensitive to bidder asymmetries. One important form of bidder asymmetry is uneven bidder toeholds. In theory, even small toehold differences can have a large impact on entry and competition (Bulow et al., 1999). In Betton and Eckbo (2000), we show that when a rival bidder enters a takeover contest with a positive toehold, the toehold size is on average of roughly the same size as that of the initial bidder (approximately 5%). It is as if the rival bidder realizes the initial bidder's toehold advantage and wants to neutralize it upon entry. This is also suggestive of correlated bidder private valuations and where the initial bidder may have (often unsuccessfully) attempted to deter competition through jump bidding and toehold acquisitions.

Finally, in Betton and Eckbo (2000) and Betton et al. (2009) we report that the average offer premium in tender offers where the initial bidder succeeds with the first bid is marginally higher than the average *initial* offer premium in takeover contests that develop multiple bids. This is consistent with the argument that the premiums in single-bid successful contests are preemptive in the sense of Fishman (1988). The premium effect is weak, however, as the probability of rival bidder entry appears unaffected by the initial offer premium (Betton et al., 2008b). Overall, additional work is needed to determine the extent of preemptive bidding in the offer premium data.

4.3. Do target runups cause offer price markups?

Initial takeover bids are typically preceded by substantial target stock price runups (Figure 1). Runups are typically thought to reflect takeover rumors generated from various public sources, such as Schedule 13(d) filings with the Securities and Exchange Commission (SEC) disclosing stake purchases of 5% or more in the target, media speculations and "street talk." In other words, the conventional view is that runups reflect information about the target that is known to the bidder.[30] Under this view, the runup simply substitutes for an already planned offer premium and does not require the bidder to raise the planned offer price before making the first bid ("the substitution hypothesis").

Schwert (1996) argue that the runup may alternatively reflect an increase in the target's *stand-alone* value and thus require the bidder to mark up the offer price. Since

[29] For evidence on intra-industry wealth effects of takeovers, see Eckbo (1983, 1992), Song and Walkling (2000), Fee and Thomas (2004), Shahrur (2005) and Section 6 in Betton et al. (2008a) for a review.

[30] Jarrell and Poulsen (1989) and King and Padalko (2005) conclude that runups are primarily a result of public information. Meulbroek (1992) and Schwert (1996) find greater target runups in cases where the SEC subsequently alleges insider trading.

the true cause of the runup is unknown to the negotiating parties, this possibility presents the initial bidder with a dilemma:

> Suppose that you are planning to bid for control of a company and, before you can announce the offer, the price of the target firm's stock begins to rise coincident with unusually high trading volume. You have not been buying the target company's stock, and there is no reliable evidence to show who has been buying. Do you go forward with the offer exactly as you had planned? Or do you take into account the recent movement in the target's stock price and adjust your bidding strategy? (Schwert, 1996, pp. 153–154)

Note that this dilemma exists for the *initial* bidder only as any second bidder responds to the initial bid and not to the initial runup per se.

Schwert (1996) examines this markup question by regressing the final offer premium on the prebid runup in a sample of 1814 mergers and tender offers from the period 1975 to 1991. In his analysis, the runup is the cumulative target abnormal stock return from day -42 through day -1 relative to the first bid for the target (day 0), while his proxy for the final premium is the target abnormal return over the event window $[-42, 126]$ (or until target delisting if before day 126). The coefficient on the runup variable in this regression is 1.13, which means that a dollar runup in the target stock price is associated with a final premium that is higher by approximately a dollar. Schwert infers from this evidence that bidders systematically mark up the offer price so that target runups are costly for bidders.

In Betton et al. (2008b), we revisit Schwert's markup pricing hypothesis using *initial offer prices* directly in more than 7000 bids for US targets over the period 1980–2002. The evidence indicates a strong positive association between offer premiums and runups: a dollar increase in the runup is associated with an increase of $0.8 in the initial offer price. The paper points out that neither this result nor the results in Schwert (1996) necessarily mean that the markup actually takes place *after* the runup. The "markup" may take place ex ante (before the runup), in which case we're back to the substitution hypothesis.

To illustrate, suppose that total (bidder plus target) takeover synergies are either "high" or "low." If bidders expect competition to drive most of the total gains to the target (as suggested by the evidence on bidder announcement returns), a preemption strategy is to raise the planned offer price for high-synergy targets ex ante. If takeover rumors allow outside investors to distinguish high and low synergy targets, target runups and total premiums will be highly correlated in the data even in the absence of any offer price markup ex post. That is, the substitution hypothesis does not rule out a positive cross-sectional correlation between and premiums and runups.

Absent detailed information about the bidder's price-setting process, it is difficult to empirically distinguish Schwert's ex post markup pricing hypothesis from the substitution hypothesis with ex ante markup. However, Betton et al. (2008b) show that regressions of *bidder* abnormal announcement returns on the *target* runup produces a positive and highly significant coefficient. That is, greater target runups (and thus offer premiums) are associated with greater bidder synergies from the takeover. In other words, the target runup is an empirical proxy for *total* takeover synergies in the cross-section. This result is interesting in out itself (we know of no other know proxies for total synergies), and it suggests that the target runup is unlikely to deter bidder toehold purchases during the runup period. Consistent with this view, Betton et al. (2008b) also report that while short-term toehold purchases tend to raise the runup, toeholds are associated with lower (not higher) initial and final offer premiums.

4.4. Do bidders properly adjust for "winner's curse"?

As summarized in Section 2.2, bidder gains are on average close to zero, and bidder shareholders have only a fifty-fifty chance of coming out ahead from the takeover announcement. In some cases, bidder losses are so substantial that they suggest a breakdown of the firm's corporate governance system. In light of the poor bidder returns, Roll (1986) suggests that bidder managements may exhibit "hubris" (over-confidence) when competing to win the target firm. While the data appears to reject the joint hypothesis of overbidding and zero total takeover gains (Section 2.1), the potential for falling prey to overconfidence and/or a winner's curse remains an interesting and ongoing research question.[31]

For example, Malmendier and Tate (2008) construct an empirical proxy of CEO overconfidence in 394 large US firms (1980–1994) based on the CEO's personal portfolio decisions (specifically, whether or not they delay executive option exercise beyond some threshold date suggested by rationality). They present two empirical hypotheses: First, the acquisition propensity of overconfident CEOs should be greater than for rational CEOs, in particular when the firm has sufficient internal resources to pay for the target (so the firm does not need to raise external financing). Second, the average merger undertaken by overconfident CEOs should generate less value for the acquirer than those by rational bidders. The sample CEOs undertake about 900 mergers and the two behavioral empirical predictions are supported by the data. The principle of conditioning the tests on some proxy for overconfidence is important. Additional research is needed, however, to indicate whether the same evidence also rejects rational bidder behavior.

To what extent do bidder returns reflect irrational overbidding? Several recent papers estimate bidder returns in successive takeover transactions and find diminishing returns on average.[32] This pattern of bidder abnormal return is consistent with behavioral arguments (overconfidence and a failure to learn from earlier mistakes). However, it is also consistent with neoclassical hypotheses (diminishing returns in a competitive market for corporate control). Moreover, serial acquirers are likely to

---

[31] Unlike a situation where a rational but entrenched CEO overinvests in mergers, the overconfident CEO actually thinks he or she maximizes shareholder value. Thus, while a compensation package exhibiting pay-performance sensitivity may correct the agency problem of the former, it may not work for a CEO exhibiting hubris.

[32] See, for example, Fuller et al. (2002), Billett and Qian (2005), Croci (2005), Ismail (2006), Ahern (2006), and Aktas et al. (2008).

generate partial anticipation of future takeover events which reduces abnormal stock returns around successive takeover announcements.[33] Overall, the evidence indicates that gains to serial acquirers are positive on average, and one cannot infer from this evidence whether bids properly adjust to a potential winner's curse.

The winner's curse is a concept developed for auction settings where bidder valuations have a common component. At the extreme, every bidder has the *same* valuation for the auctioned item—a "pure" common value setting. An example would be a target where bidders are going to use the target resources simply as a financing vehicle for future investments by the bidder. Or, the change of control may allow the bidder to simply replace inefficient target management. A third example would be that the bidder is purchasing the target purely as a speculation in its future resale value. The point is that specialized resources owned by the bidder is irrelevant for the production of takeover gains. If generating target gains in fact requires unique bidder resources, bidder valuations are to some extent private (not a pure common value).

To illustrate the winner's curse, let each bidder i receive a private signal t_i about the true value of the acquisition before bidding starts. With N bidders, each bidder's valuation is a common function of all the signals: $v_i = v(t_1, t_2, \ldots, t_N) \; \forall i$. That is, at the start of the auction, each bidder has information that, if made public, would affect the remaining bidders' estimate of the value of the acquisition. It is this valuation link between bidders' information signals which, if unaccounted for, leads to the winner's curse. Winning the auction means that the winner had the highest value estimate. Moreover, although each bidder's estimate is an unbiased ex ante estimate of the common value, the highest of those estimates is biased high.[34]

Suppose there are only two bidders and that the target is worth $v = t_i + t_j$ to each, where each t_i is an independent draw from the uniform [0, 1] distribution.[35] At the start of the auction, each bidder estimates the value of the target as:

$$v_i = t_i + E(t_j) = t_i + 1/2. \tag{5}$$

However, if the bidders are symmetric (each bidder uses the same bid strategy as a function of the signal), conditional on winning in a first-price ascending auction, this estimate changes to:

$$v_i | t_j < t_i = t_i + E\left(t_j | t_j < t_i\right) = t_i + t_i/2 < t_i + 1/2. \tag{6}$$

---

[33] See Malatesta and Thompson (1985) and Eckbo et al. (1990b) for models of partial anticipation. Schipper and Thompson (1983) find that firms that announce intentions to undertake entire acquisition programs on average earn significantly positive abnormal stock returns. Song and Walkling (2000, 2005) also present evidence that partial anticipation of takeover activity attenuates bidder announcement returns.

[34] In a private value auction setting, which is used extensively in Section 4.5 below on optimal toehold bidding, $v_i = v(t_i)$ for all i. That is, given their signals, bidders have complete information about the value of the acquisition to themselves, and there is no bias.

[35] Klemperer (1998) use this setting for the so-called "wallet game". In this game, two students bid for the sum of the cash in their two respective wallets. The price in the ascending auction is raised gradually until one student quits, at which point the winner pays that price for the two wallets.

That is, assuming the payoff from losing is zero, to avoid the winner's curse, the winner must replace the unconditional expected value of the signal with the lower expected signal conditional on winning, $t_i/2$.[36]

The bid adjustment necessary to correct for the winner's curse increases with the number of bidders and with the degree of uncertainty in the bidder valuations.[37] Conversely, failure to properly correct for the winner's curse causes bidder losses to increase in the degree of competition and valuation uncertainty. Boone and Mulherin (2008) examines these prediction using a sample of 308 completed takeovers, 1989–1999. Of these, 145 are classified as "auctions" and 163 are "negotiations." In the former, the seller contacted multiple potential buyers, while the latter refers to a sales process in which the selling firm focused on a single buyer. Presumably, final winning bid prices reflect the degree of competition in the private as well as in the subsequent public round of bidding. The authors use data from SEC filings to identify the number of private offers preceding the first public bid.

Accounting for the endogeneity between bidder returns and competition, they reject the hypothesis that bidder returns are negatively related to takeover competition and uncertainty in the value of the target. They also fail to find any negative effects of bidding competition on subsequent posttakeover operating performance. Moreover, they investigate the role of investment banks in the takeover process and conclude that prestigious banks hired by the bidder do not promote the winner's curse. Overall, the authors conclude that "the breakeven returns to bidders in corporate takeovers stem not from the winner's curse but from the competitive market for targets that occurs predominantly prior to the public announcement of bids." (Boone and Mulherin, 2009, p. 1).

4.5. Rational toehold-induced overbidding

Betton et al. (2009) and Aktas et al. (2008) derive optimal bids in a takeover setting where merger agreements are negotiated in the shadow of a competitive auction. As indicated in the introduction, merger agreements must include a fiduciary-out clause: the target board is legally obligated to remain open to higher offers from other bidders, until target shareholders have voted the proposed deal. Betton et al. (2009) also argue that the fiduciary-out clause has contributed to the widespread use of target termination agreements in merger proposals.[38]

---

[36] The symmetric equilibrium bid strategy is $b = 2t_i$. To see why, if both bidders follow this strategy, the bidder i wins if $2t_j < b$, or $t_j < b/2$. The expected gain from winning is $\int_0^{b/2} (t_i + \tilde{t} - 2\tilde{t}) d\tilde{t} = t_i(b/2) - (1/2)(b^2/4)$. The bid which maximizes this expected gain is $b = 2t_i$. See Klemperer (1998) for a discussion of other equilibria.

[37] See McAfee and McMillan (1987) for a review.

[38] A termination agreement provides the bidder with a compensation in the form of a fixed fee ("breakup fee") or an option to purchase target shares at a discount ("lock-up option") should the target withdraw from the agreement (Bates and Lemmon, 2003; Boone and Mulherin, 2007a; Burch, 2001; Officer, 2003).

Betton et al. (2009) derive optimal auction bids when the bidder has both a toehold and a termination agreement. It is instructive to review the optimal bids, as these form the basis for empirical tests also discussed below. The auction setting is one with two risk-neutral bidders with private valuations that are i.i.d. with distribution and density functions $G(v)$ and $g(v)$, respectively. The initial bidder (B1) has toehold $\alpha \in [0, 0.5)$ acquired at the normalized pretakeover target share price of zero. B1 has negotiated a merger agreement with the target management that includes a termination fee $t \in (0, v)$. A rival bidder (B2) challenges the agreement and forces an open auction. The termination fee is paid by B2 if B2 wins, or by the target if neither B1 nor B2 wins (the target remains independent). The no-bidder-wins outcome occurs with an exogenous probability θ.[39]

Since the termination fee represents a claim of t on the target, the fee reduces B2's private valuation to $v_2 - t$. B2's optimal bid is therefore $b_2^* = v_2 - t$: bidding less risks foregoing a profitable takeover, while bidding more risks overpaying for the target.[40] Given B2's optimal bid, and noting that the net termination fee paid to B1 if B2 wins is $(1 - \alpha)t$, B1's expected profits from bidding b is

$$E(\Pi) = \left\{ (v)G(b+t) - (1-\alpha) \int_t^{b+t} (v_2 - t)g(v_2) \, \mathrm{d}v_2 \right.$$
$$\left. + (t + \alpha b)[1 - G(b+t)] \right\}(1 - \theta) + t(1-\alpha)\theta$$

The right-hand side is the sum of four components. The first three (inside the curly brackets) are, respectively, B1's expected private value, the expected payment for the target, and the expected value from selling the toehold α and receiving t when B2 wins the auction. The fourth term is the expected payoff when no bidder wins. Using Equation (7), the first order condition for profit maximization, $\partial E(\Pi)/\partial b = 0$, implies an optimal bid for B1 of:[41]

$$b_1^* = v_1 - t + \alpha h(b_1^*), \tag{8}$$

where $h(b_1^*) \equiv [1 - G(b_1^*)]/g(b_1^*)$. Notice the following from Equation (8):

- The toehold induces "overbidding," that is, a bid greater than the private valuation v_1. This means that B1 may win even if B2 is the higher valuation bidder (when $v_1 < v_2 < b_1^*$).

---

[39] The probability θ captures exogenous factors that may derail merger negotiations or cause all bidders to abandon a takeover auction. For example, the market may revise upwards it's estimate of the target's stand-alone value during the contest, causing the takeover to be unprofitable for both B1 and B2. Betton et al. (2009) reports that close to 30% of the takeover contests end up in the no-bidder-wins state. This issue is discussed further below.

[40] This optimal bid is the "ratchet solution" in Hirshleifer (1995) adjusted for t.

[41] To ensure uniqueness, $G(v)$ must be twice continuously differentiable and satisfy the monotonicity condition $\partial(1 - G(v))/\partial g(v) \geq 0$.

- The effect of the termination fee is to induce "underbidding." For example, a bidder with zero toehold and a termination agreement walks away from the target when rival bids exceed $v_1 - t$ (quitting means receiving t while continued bidding implies an expect profit of less than t). Since B2's bid is also reduced by t (B2 finances the termination fee), t is effectively paid by target shareholders.
- Since B1's optimal bid is increasing in the toehold, the probability that B1 wins the auction is also increasing in the toehold. Since B2's optimal bid is $v_2 - t$, there is no corresponding reduction in the probability that B1 wins deriving from the existence of a termination fee.
- The optimal bid b_1^* is equivalent to the optimal reserve price by a monopolist seller in a "take-it-or-leave-it" offer. This is intuitive since the toehold bidder is part seller (of the toehold) when losing the contest to B2.

Bulow et al. (1999) and Dasgupta and Tsui (2003) examine toehold bidding in a pure common-value setting where both B1 and B2 have toeholds but of unequal size (asymmetric toeholds). Toehold bidding induces overbidding also in a common-value setting, and they show that holding B1's toehold constant, B2's probability of winning goes to zero as B2's toehold gets arbitrarily small. Even small differences in toeholds can produce significant benefits for the bidder with the greater toehold. Moreover, the expected winning sales prices are decreasing in the difference between the toeholds of B1 and B2. This suggests an incentive on the part of the target to sell a toehold to B2—and for B2 to purchase a toehold—in order to "even the playing field." Consistent with this, Betton and Eckbo (2000) find that when a rival bidder enters a takeover contest with a toehold, the toehold size is on average of roughly the same size as that of the initial bidder (approximately 5%).

4.6. Does toehold-induced overbidding exist?

In Equation (8), bidders optimally bid v adjusted for any toehold α and termination fee t. "Overbidding" occurs when $b^* - v > 0$, which is an unobservable quantity. Eckbo and Thorburn (2009) develop an overbidding test which does not require observations on $b^* - v > 0$. Their setting is bankruptcy auctions in Sweden, where firms filing for bankruptcy are automatically auctioned off. The auction is open and first-price, and the highest bid determines whether the firms will be continued as a going concern or liquidated piecemeal. As reported by Thorburn (2000), the auctions are quick—lasting an average of 2 months—and relatively cost-efficient. Moreover, three-quarters of the 260 sample filing firms survive the auction as a going concern. The average auctioned firm has $5 million in sales and assets of $2 million ($8 and $4 million, respectively, in 2007 dollars), and it has an average of 45 employees.[42]

---

[42] By comparison, a majority of Chapter 11 filings are also by small private firms: Chang and Schoar (2007) report average sales of $2 million and 22 employees in a large and representative sample of Chapter 11 filings between 1989 and 2003. Bris et al. (2006) report that the median firm filing for Chapter 11 has assets of $1 million.

In the sample of Swedish bankruptcies, the main creditor is always a single bank. The bankruptcy event effectively creates an instant "creditor toehold" of $\alpha = 1$ when the creditor's debt is impaired at filing. A value of $\alpha = 1$ follows because the bank, being the secured creditor with an impaired debt claim, is effectively the seller of the auctioned firm. As shown by Hotchkiss and Mooradian (2003) as well (in the context of Chapter 11 sales), a creditor toehold induces overbidding in the same manner as a bidder toehold outside of bankruptcy.

As a monopolist seller, the bank benefits from setting a reserve price in the auction. Swedish bank regulations prevent the bank from bidding directly (which would support a reserve price). However, Eckbo and Thorburn (2009) observe that the bank often finances the winning bidder and use this observation to motivate the following proposition: Bank financing of a bidder in the auction (say B1) allows the bank to induce B1 to submit a jointly optimized coalition bid b_1^* that implies overbidding. As in Section 4.5, overbidding forces a wealth transfer from B2 to the bank-bidder coalition whenever B2 wins the auction. This potential rent transfer raises expected auction revenue and the bank's expected debt recovery rate, and is in principle sufficiently large to induce B1 to participate in the coalition. One mechanism for the bank to compensate B2 for the cost of overbidding is by granting a lower interest on the loan if B1 wins.

Let f denote the face value of the bank's debt claim. The coalition's optimal bid is then:

$$b_c^* = \begin{cases} v_1 + h(b_c) & \text{if } v_1 \leq f - h(b_c) \quad \text{(unconstrained overbidding)} \\ f & \text{if } f - h(b_c) < v_1 < f \text{ (constrained overbidding)} \\ v_1 & \text{if } v_1 \geq f \qquad \text{(no overbidding)} \end{cases} \qquad (9)$$

Here, the unconstrained overbidding price is identical to the bid in Equation (8) but with $\alpha = 1$ and a termination fee $t = 0$. The key for testability is the constraining effect of the bank-debt face value f on the coalition's optimal bid. The constraint imposed by f is illustrated in Figure 2 which assumes the uniform distribution, $v \sim U[0, 1]$. The horizontal axis plots v_1 and the bold-faced line shows the coalition bids b_c. Each bold-faced segment corresponds to the optimal bids in Equation (9). The first segment is the unconstrained overbidding price, while the second (horizontal) segment is the constrained overbidding price. Constrained overbidding begins when v_1 is such that the unconstrained bid price equals the face value f. The third segment starts when $v_1 > f$. Here, the bank's debt is fully paid off without overbidding, so that $b_1^* = v_1$. In sum, the coalition optimally overbids *only* if the bank's debt claim is impaired at the outset of the auction as further overbidding just benefits junior creditors.

To develop the overbidding test, let l denote an estimate of the bankrupt firm's piecemeal liquidation value at the beginning of the auction. In Sweden, the bankruptcy trustee publicizes a professional estimate of l before the auction starts. Since l is the sum of the value of the firm's assets if each were sold individually, l effectively plays the role of a price floor for bidders attempting to purchase the firm as a going concern.[43]

---

[43] This is supported by the auction premium data: when the firm is liquidated piecemeal, auction prices average only 8% above l. In contrast, when the firm is purchased as a going concern, the final auction price more than doubles the value l on average. See Eckbo and Thorburn (2009)

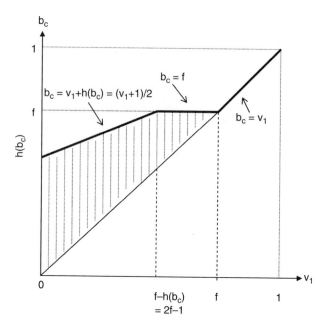

Fig. 2. The bank-bidder coalition's optimal bid, $b_1^*(v_1)$, and the expected amount of overbidding (shaded area), assuming a piecemeal liquidation value l of zero. The figure is drawn assuming bidder valuations are distributed uniform, $v_i \sim U[0, 1]$. The coalition-bidder's private valuation is v_1, f is the face value of the bank's debt, and $h(b_c)$ is the inverse hazard rate at b_c. When $v_1 \leq 2f - 1$, the coalition fully overbids: $b_1^* = (v_1 + 1)/2$. When $f > v_1 > 2f - 1$, the coalition partially overbids: $b_c^* = f$. When $v_1 \geq f$, the coalition does not overbid: $b_c^* = v_1$. Source: Eckbo and Thorburn (2009).

Introducing $l > 0$ lowers overbidding incentives by lowering the constrained overbidding price from f to $f - l$. This in turn lowers the expected amount of overbidding (the shaded area in Figure 2).

To test this cross-sectional prediction, Eckbo and Thorburn (2009) scale f with l and regress winning auction premiums on the bank's debt recovery rate *if the firm were to be liquidated piecemeal*: where $r \equiv \min[l/f, 1] \in [0, 1]$. Since r captures the degree of bank-debt impairment at the beginning of the auction, the model predicts that winning auction premiums are decreasing in r. The cross-sectional regressions provide robust support for this prediction in the subsample where firms are purchased as going concerns. Moreover, this test rejects overbidding when the theory says there should be none, such as for auctions where the bank's debt is unimpaired ex ante ($l \geq f$) or when the firm ends up being liquidated piecemeal.

The empirical analysis in Eckbo and Thorburn (2009) is a first step toward testing for the existence of overbidding directly based on auction prices. Empirical evidence on toehold-induced overbidding in takeovers more generally (outside of bankruptcy) is indirect. For example, theory implies that overbidding increases the probability of winning, which is supported by studies of corporate takeover bids with equity toeholds

(Betton and Eckbo, 2000; Betton et al., 2009). On the other hand, because one cannot directly verify the existence of the bank-bidder coalitions hypothesized in Eckbo and Thorburn (2009), one also cannot rule out the possibility that the auction-premium evidence in that paper is the result of other forms of bidding incentives. Eckbo and Thorburn (2009) formulate but rule out one such alternative, namely that entrenched bank managers attempt to hide nonperforming loans from their superiors by colluding with the acquirer to simply "roll over" the debt.

Finally, overbidding may (but need not) result in allocative inefficiency. The inefficiency occurs when the bank-bidder coalition wins against a higher valuation bidder. To examine this possibility, Eckbo and Thorburn (2009) estimate the post-bankruptcy operating performance of firms sold as going concern The evidence shows that postbankruptcy operating performance is independent of overbidding incentives and at par with that of the bankrupt firms' industry rivals.

4.7. The disappearing toehold phenomenon

The case for acquiring a toehold before initiating a takeover bid is compelling. The toehold not only reduces the number of shares that must be purchased at the full takeover premium, it may also be sold at an even greater premium should a rival bidder enter the contest and win the target. This expected toehold gain raises the bidder's valuation of the target, which in turn helps overcome free-rider problems (Section 3.1) and make the toehold bidder a more aggressive competitor in the presence of rivals (Section 4.5). Early empirical research supports the existence of toehold benefits. Walkling (1985), Jennings and Mazzeo (1993), and Betton and Eckbo (2000) show that toehold bidding increases the probability of winning the target. Consistent with entry deterrence effects of toeholds, Betton and Eckbo (2000) and Betton et al. (2008b) also find that toeholds are associated with lower offer premiums in winning bids.

However, toehold bidding has in fact been declining dramatically over the past two decades and is now rare. This decline is apparent in Figure 3 which plots toehold data from Betton et al. (2009). The toeholds in Figure 3 include target shares held by the bidder long term as well as shares purchased within 6 months of the actual offer date (short-term toeholds). Betton et al. (2009) report a sample-wide toehold frequency of 13%. Moreover, the sample-wide frequency of short-term toeholds—defined as target shares purchased within 6 months of the offer—is only 2%. In sum, toehold benefits notwithstanding, toeholds acquired as part of an active bidding strategy are almost nonexistent.

Presumably, rational bidders avoid toeholds as a response to large toehold costs. Several potential sources of toehold costs have been suggested in the literature, ranging from mandatory information disclosure and market illiquidity, to costs associated with target management resistance to the takeover.

Consider first the argument that mandatory disclosure rules make toeholds too costly because they reveal the bidder's intentions early in the takeover process. As discussed above, toehold purchases of 5% or more have triggered mandatory disclosure require-

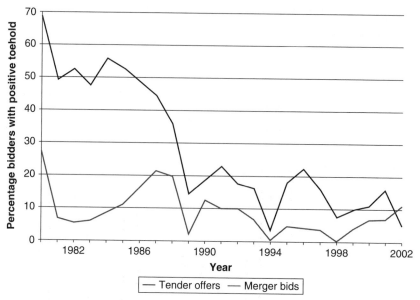

Fig. 3. Annual percentage of initial control bidders with a positive toehold in the target, classified by the type of the initial bid. US public targets. Source: Betton et al. (2009).

ments (13d filings with the Security and Exchange Commission) since the 1968 Williams Act. Also, under the 1976 Hart-Scott-Rodino Antitrust Improvements Act, share acquisitions exceeding a certain threshold ($60 million in 2007) trigger notification to the antitrust agencies. As shown in Figure 3, however, toehold bidding was relatively common in the early 1980s. The passage of disclosure rules in the 1970s cannot explain this time series pattern. Also, the decline in toehold bidding occurs despite a general increase in market liquidity over the entire sample period.[44] Furthermore, Betton et al. (2009) report that the average toehold size (when positive) is as large as 20%, and 13% for short-term toeholds. It is difficult to explain the observed bimodal toehold distribution (centered on either zero or large toeholds) by appealing to general market illiquidity.

Goldman and Qian (2005) point to a toehold cost when entrenched target management successfully thwarts the takeover bid. In their model, entrenched target managements may resist a bidder in order to retain private benefits of control. The degree of target entrenchment is unknown ex ante and, in equilibrium, signaled ex post through the size of the bidder's toehold in successfully resisted offers. The idea is that it is more

---

[44] Small toeholds, for which concerns with liquidity and disclosure are unimportant, can also have significant investment value as they retain many of the strategic benefits of larger ones. Toehold benefits arise as long as the toehold is greater than that of the rival bidder (Dasgupta and Tsui, 2004; Bulow et al., 1999).

difficult (requires greater target management entrenchment) to successfully defeat bidders with larger toeholds.[45] Successful resistance causes the target share price to drop, and the price drop is greater the greater the bidder's toehold (due to the greater negative signal about target management entrenchment). Bidders trade off expected toehold benefits (greater success probability) with expected toehold costs (greater target price decline when the bid fails), causing some bidders to select small or even zero toeholds. Betton et al. (2009) test this prediction and fail to find supporting evidence. They infer that the potential for a toehold loss in the event that all bids fail following target resistance is unlikely to explain the disappearing toehold phenomenon.

Betton et al. (2009) develop and test a model in which bidder toehold costs arise endogenously. As in Goldman and Qian (2005), some target managements oppose a takeover. However, the target decision to oppose is now a direct function of the toehold itself—capturing the notion often heard in practice that toehold bidding is "aggressive." The takeover game starts with the initial bidder approaching the target with an invitation to negotiate a merger. In line with the "fiduciary out" requirement discussed earlier, a merger agreement is followed by a wait period before the shareholder vote during which time the target board must reasonably consider any rival bids that emerges. The expected outcome of this "open auction" period determines the outcome of merger negotiations ex ante. Since a toehold affects the expected auction outcome (as per Equation (8) above), it also affects the willingness of entrenched target managements to accept the bidder's invitation to negotiate.

If the target management accepts merger negotiations, it issues a target termination agreement to the bidder. If the target management rejects negotiations, however, the bidder foregoes the benefit of the termination agreement and incurs resistance costs during the takeover process. These toehold-induced bidder costs make it optimal for some bidders to approach the target without a toehold. That is, the expected toehold cost creates a *toehold threshold* (a minimum toehold size) below which the optimal toehold is zero.

Betton et al. (2009) estimate the toehold threshold to be 9% for the average initial bidder. This threshold is consistent with the observation that the distribution of actual toeholds is bimodal, centered on either zero or large toeholds. While nearly 90% of initial bidders have zero toeholds, nonzero toeholds average as much as 20% of the target shares. Under the threshold model, bidders selecting zero toehold find that the toehold threshold is too costly to purchase in the market (e.g., due to market illiquidity). Bidder electing to go for the toehold "jump" the threshold hurdle, producing large average toeholds. The model also predicts that the likelihood of toehold bidding decreases in the toehold threshold estimate, which the empirical evidence supports.

---

[45] Recall that, with optimal bidding, greater toeholds increase the probability that the toehold bidder will win against rival bidders.

The toehold threshold model is consistent with another stylized fact, namely that toeholds are much more common in hostile than in friendly takeovers. Fifty percent of the initial bidders in hostile contests have toeholds. If target management is expected to resist irrespective of the toehold size, then acquiring a toehold is always optimal.[46] Thus, the toehold threshold model also predicts a higher toehold frequency in hostile bids. This prediction is supported by the evidence, and it is consistent with the observed decline in the frequency of toehold bidding over the 1990s (Figure 3). The decline coincides with a general reduction in hostile bids due to a widespread adoption of strong takeover defenses such as poison pills.

In the absence of synergistic opportunities with the target ($v = 0$), the owner of a toehold may contemplate making a (false) bid in an attempt to put the target in play. That is, the bidder may try to sell the toehold to a potential rival bidder or (anonymously) to an unwitting market anticipating a successful takeover. Bagnoli and Lipman (1996) presents a model with a single bidder selling the toehold shares to individual noise traders through a market maker before calling off the takeover bid. While charges of price manipulation go back at least to the greenmail episodes of the late 1970s, systematic empirical evidence on the feasibility of this type of price manipulation is virtually nonexistent. The context of hostile bids is potentially interesting since hostility may induce the target to produce a white knight committed to purchase the toehold.

4.8. Auctions and fire-sale discounts

A fire-sale discount results when the auction price is below the assets' fundamental value (the value in best alternative use). The literature highlights temporary demand-side conditions that may give rise to such a discount. For example, since financial distress tends to be contagious within an industry (Lang and Stulz, 1992), high-valuation industry rivals may themselves be financially constrained and unable to bid in the auction (Aghion et al., 1992; Shleifer and Vishny, 1992). Industry debt overhang may also attenuate industry rivals' incentive to invest in the distressed firm (Clayton and Ravid, 2002; Myers, 1977). As industry rivals are unwilling to bid, the risk increases that relatively low-valuation industry outsiders win the auction—at fire-sale prices. The chance of this happening is greater for unique or specific assets with few potential buyers (Williamson, 1988).[47]

Eckbo and Thorburn (2008) test the fire-sale hypothesis using automatic Swedish bankruptcy auctions. The Swedish auction setting is particularly interesting in this

[46] Similarly, toehold bidding occurs when the target's optimal strategy is to never resist.
[47] Several US studies present evidence on fire-sale discounts in voluntary asset sales, both in and out of Chapter 11. For example, Pulvino (1998, 1999) provides evidence of fire-sale discounts for the sale of individual aircrafts. Ramey and Shapiro (2001) and Officer (2007) study liquidity discounts associated with distressed plant closings and corporate targets outside of bankruptcy, and Acharya et al. (2007) examine recovery rates for US firms defaulting of their debt.

context as it represents mandatory auctions of entire bankrupt firms as going concerns. The paper estimates a cross-sectional model for the auctioned firm's fundamental value, and computes the difference between actual and model prices. A fire-sale discount is said to exist if this difference is adversely affected by measures of industry-wide illiquidity and financial distress. While there is evidence of fire-sale discounts in auctions that lead to *piecemeal liquidation*, the paper finds no evidence of fire-sale discounts in going-concern premiums. Also, there is no evidence of lower prices when the buyer is an industry outsider, or when the firm is sold back to its previous owner/manager (a saleback). The evidence also indicates that the main creditor (the bank) counters the potential for excessive liquidation by sometimes promoting a prefiling private workout (in the form of a sales proposal), or a "prepackaged" bankruptcy filing. In sum, the Swedish auction bankruptcy system appears to generate a degree of bidder competition that is sufficient to avoid serious concerns with auction fire-sales.

5. Strategies for the payment method

5.1. Frequency of payment forms

Takeovers are settled in cash and various forms of securities. The cash amount is typically financed using accumulated retained earnings (financial slack) or debt issues prior to the takeover. The merger agreement sets out how the bidder will settle any noncash portion of the merger payment. Frequently used contingent payment forms include stock swaps, collars, clawbacks, and earnouts.[48] Contingent payment forms allow bidder and target shareholders to share the risk that the target and/or bidder securities are overvalued ax ante.

When the bidder pays the target in the form of bidder stock, the merger agreement specifies the exchange ratio (the number of bidder shares to be exchanged for each target share). A collar provision provides for changes in the exchange ratio should the level of the bidder's stock price change before the effective date of the merger. This helps insulate target stockholders from volatility in the bidder's stock price. Collar bids may have floors and caps (or both), which define a range of bidder stock prices within which the exchange ratio is held fixed, and outside of which the exchange ratio is adjusted up or down. Thus, floors and caps guarantee the target a minimum and a maximum payment.

The total payment to target shareholders may also be split between an upfront payment and additional future payments that are contingent upon some observable measure of performance (earnouts, often over a 3-year period). This helps close the deal when the bidder is particularly uncertain about the true ability of the target to generate cash flow. It provides target managers with an incentive to remain with the firm over the earnout period, which may be important to the bidder. The downside is

---

[48] Officer (2004, 2006), Kohers and Ang (2000), and Cain et al. (2005).

that the earnout may distort the incentives of target managers (an emphasis on short-term over longer term cash flows), and it may induce the new controlling shareholder (the bidder) to manipulate earnings in order to lower the earnout payment. Thus, earnouts are not for everyone.

Betton et al. (2008a) show the distribution of all-cash, all-stock, and mixed cash-stock offers in their sample of 13,503 initial merger bids and 2678 initial tender offers from the 1980 to 2005 period. This information is reproduced in Figure 4. For the overall sample, 26% of the initial bidders use the all-cash method while the groups of all-stock and mixed offers each cover 37% of the initial bids. The use of the various payment methods clearly differs between merger bids and tender offers: the majority of tender offers use all-cash or a mix of cash and stock, while the majority of merger bids are in the form of all-stock (with the exception of the 1980–1985 period when 90% of the initial merger bids offered a mix of cash and securities). Importantly, comparing the two subperiods 1990–1995 and 1996–2000, the percentage all-stock offers in initial merger bids were approximately 55% in *both* periods. In other words: (1) nearly half of the initial merger bids in the 1990s use some cash as payment and (2) the percentage all-stock merger bids remained unaffected by the significant runup in overall market valuations in the 1996–2000 period.

Table 6 summarizes a number of economic hypotheses and related empirical evidence concerning the choice of payment method. The associated empirical evidence is a combination of determinants of the probability of a specific payment method choice (e.g., all-cash vs. all-stock), and announcement-induced abnormal stock returns as a function of the payment method. The hypotheses deal with tax effects, deal financing costs under asymmetric information, agency and corporate control motives, and behavioral arguments. These hypotheses are not necessarily mutually exclusive, so a given payment choice may reflect elements of several theories. I discuss each of these hypotheses next.

5.2. Taxes

The US Internal Revenue Code (IRC) requires target shareholders to immediately pay capital gains taxes in an all-cash purchase. If the merger qualifies as a tax-free reorganization under Section 368 of IRC, for example by using all-stock as method of payment, target shareholder capital gains taxes are deferred until the shares received in the deal are sold. Mixed cash-stock offers are treated as either all-cash bids or the stock part is treated as an all-stock bid depending on the cash portion and other characteristics of the deal. There is a carryover of the tax basis in the target to the acquiring company, unless a 338 election is made. Under a 338 election, there is a step-up of the tax-basis of the target assets to the price paid in the takeover (Bruner, 2004). Such elections imply a capital gains tax in the target, and are used only in rare circumstances such as when there are substantial target net operating losses (NOLs) due to expire, or when the target is a subsidiary.

Panel A: Distribution of mergers by time period and method of payment

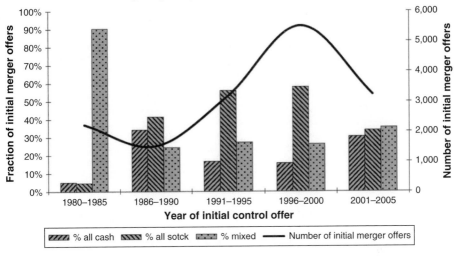

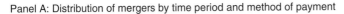

Panel B: Distribution of tender offers by time period by method of payment

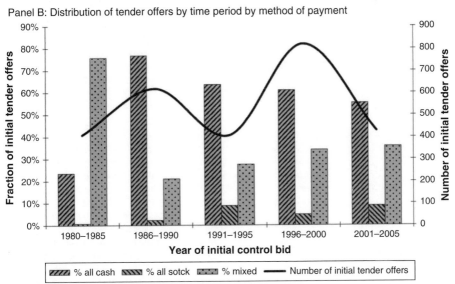

Fig. 4. The initial control bidder's use of all-cash, all-stock, and mixed cash-stock as method of payment. Total sample of 13,503 merger bids and 2678 tender offers with SDC information on payment method. US targets, 1980–2005. Source: Betton et al. (2008a).

Given these differences in the tax treatment, there is little doubt that taxes play an important role in the bidder's choice of payment method. The more difficult empirical issue is whether the bidder in all-cash offers must pay target shareholders a compensation up front both for the realization of a potential capital gains tax penalty and for

Table 6

Selected hypotheses and US evidence concerning the choice of payment method in takeovers.

Theories	Hypotheses	Evidence
A. Taxes and the payment method		
US Internal Revenue Code, Section 368 governing statutory merger	*H1: Cash deals may be relatively costly as the implied capital gains tax penalty forces higher target premiums*	Carleton et al. (1983): Probability of stock offer increases in bidder's market-to-book ratio
Gilson et al. (1988)	In a cash-for-stock deal, target shareholders pay capital gains tax immediately (the deal is taxable if target shareholders receive less than 50% of the deal in bidder stock). The buyer steps up the tax basis with the takeover premium. In a Stock deal, however, target capital gains taxes are deferred until shares received are sold. No step-up of tax basis for buyer. Buyer in stock deal may make a Section 338 election to be treated as cash deal (Bruner, 2004)	Huang and Walkling (1987), Hayn (1989): Target announcement returns in United States deals higher for taxable than tax-deferred transactions Franks et al. (1988): Reach similar conclusion for control-oriented takeovers in United Kingdom However, the all-cash premium effect is present also *before* the introduction on capital gains taxes Eckbo and Langohr (1989): Find higher target premiums in all-cash tenders offers for control as well as for minority buyouts in France Brown and Ryngaert (1991): Find empirical support for their proposition that stock should not be used by bidders selecting taxable offers
B. The payment method choice motivated by asymmetric information		
Myers and Majluf (1984)	*H2: One-sided information asymmetry: Investor concern with adverse selection produces a negative market reaction to the news of a stock deal*	Travlos (1987), Asquith et al. (1987), Servaes (1991), Brown and Ryngaert (1991), Smith and Kim (1994), Martin (1996), Emery and Switzer (1999), Heron and Lie (2004), Schlingemann (2004) and many others show that bidder announcement-induced abnormal stock returns are on average negative in all-stock offers for public targets However, bidder announcement returns are nonnegative in all-stock offers for private targets (Bradley and Sundaram, 2006; Chang, 1998; Fuller et al., 2002; Moeller et al., 2004; Officer 2007)
Hansen (1987)	*H3: Two-sided information asymmetry: Paying with securities induce targets to make more*	Hansen (1987): Probability of stock offer increases in bidder's asset size as well as in the size of its liabilities

(Continued)

Table 6 *(Continued)*

Theories	Hypotheses	Evidence
	efficient accept/reject decisions than with cash. Stock offers are less likely when (i) the bidder has a relatively large total equity size, and (ii) when the target undervalues the bidder's shares	Chemmanur and Paeglis (2003): Probability of stock offer increases in a measure of market mispricing of bidder shares and falls as the dispersion of analyst forecast of bidder earnings increases
		Betton and Eckbo (2000): Probability that the target accepts the initial bid in tender offer contests is lower for stock offers than for cash bids
Fishman (1989)	The value of a stock offer is contingent on the true values of both the bidder and the target. A cash offer that undervalues the target will be rejected, while an equivalent stock offer may be accepted because the stock offer will rise in value ex post. This ex post price effect is smaller the smaller the size of bidder's total equity relative to the target's	Travlos (1987): Bidder's announcement-induced abnormal stock returns lower for stock offers than for cash bids
	The more the target undervalues the bidder's stock, the more costly a given stock offer, and the more likely the bidder is to use cash	
Eckbo et al. (1990a)	*H4: Two-sided information asymmetry where bidders in equilibrium choose a mix of cash and stock. There exists a fully revealing separating equilibrium in which the greater the proportion of the deal paid in cash, the greater the true value of the bidder*	Eckbo et al. (1990a), Eckbo and Thorburn (2000): The average announcement-induced abnormal stock returns to bidders are highest for all-cash deals, lowest for all-stock deals, with mixed cash-stock deals in between
Berkovitch and Narayanan (1990)	In Eckbo et al. (1990a), target adverse selection pushes the bidder toward using stock as payment method, while target undervaluation of bidder shares pushes the bidder toward cash. The market uses the proportion of the deal paid in cash to separate low-value from high-value bidders. In equilibrium, bidder announcement-induced abnormal stock returns are an increasing	Eckbo et al. (1990a): In cross-sectional regressions, bidder announcement-induced abnormal stock returns are increasing in the cash portion of the deal as predicted. However, the data rejects convexity
		Betton et al. (2008c): Shows frequent use of mixed cash-stock offers in tender offers. Moreover, there is evidence that multiple bids raise the use of cash, however, the amount of

(Continued)

Table 6 (*Continued*)

Theories	Hypotheses	Evidence
	and convex function of the cash portion of the deal In Berkovitch and Narayanan (1990), the bidder's choice of cash-stock mix affects target returns as well. Greater potential bidder competition raises the optimal amount of cash, and with actual competition all but the lowest type make all-cash offers	stock used in competitive contests remains significant

C. Capital structure and corporate control motives for the payment method choice

Theories	Hypotheses	Evidence
Ross (1977)	*H5: The payment method is selected as part of a broader capital structure choice. More-over, some bidder managements select (possibly debt financed) cash over stock as payment method in order to avoid diluting their private benefits of control in the merged firm*	Capital structure: The cash portion of the bid must be financed internally or by a previous security issue. Schlingemann (2004), Toffanin (2005) find a link between the market reaction to takeover announcements and financing decision in the previous year
Jensen (1986) Harris and Raviv (1988)	In Ross (1977) increased leverage raises expected managerial-spe-cific bankruptcy costs. In Jensen (1986), paying with cash drains free cash flow and reduces agency costs. In Harris and Raviv (1988) and Stulz (1988), managers act to protect private benefits of control	Yook (2003) find greater bidder gains in all-cash offers when the takeover causes down-grading of the merged firm's debt (due to increased lever-age). The results are consistent with agency costs of free cash flow (Jensen, 1986)
Stulz (1988)		
		Control: Amihud et al. (1990), Martin (1996), and Ghosh and Ruland (1998) find that bidder man-agement shareholdings in the United States have negative effect on stock financing Studying European mergers, Faccio and Masulis (2005) find that corpor-ate control incentives to choose cash are particularly strong when in bidder firms with relatively concentrated shareownership structures. Marty-nova and Renneboog (2006) finds a link between the quality of a coun-try's corporate governance system and the market reaction to stock as payment form

(*Continued*)

Table 6 (*Continued*)

Theories	Hypotheses	Evidence
D. Behavioral motives for the payment method choice		
Shleifer and Vishny (2003)	*H6: Bidders are able to sell overpriced stock to less overpriced targets*	The propensity of all-stock offers increases with M/B ratios (Ang and Cheng, 2006; Dong et al., 2006; Rhodes-Kropf et al., 2005). This supports the behavioral argument provided M/B is a fundamental driver of takeovers
Rhodes-Kropf and Viswanathan (2004)	Bidders attempt to cash in on a temporary market overvaluation of their stocks. In Shleifer and Vishny (2003) they succeed because targets have "short time horizon." In Rhodes-Kropf and Viswanathan (2004) they succeed because targets accept more bids from overvalued bidders during market valuation peaks because they tend overestimate synergies during these periods	Harford (2005): A macroeconomic measure of capital liquidity (interest rate spreads) drives merger activity and drives out M/B as a predictor of merger activity. This is inconsistent with the behavioral argument Betton et al. (2008c): There are nearly as many mixed cash-stock offers as all-stock offers, also in the recent period of high market valuations and peak merger activity (1996–2000). Mixed offers are an enigma in the model of Shleifer and Vishny (2003). The fact that the substantial market runup prior to year 2000 did not induce a greater use of all-stock offers as a proportion of all merger bids is inconsistent with the behavioral argument

the value of the target's unused tax benefits. This depends, of course, on the relative bargaining power of the bidder and the target and is therefore transaction specific. For example, targets that have low-cost substitute ways of capitalizing on unused tax benefits will force bidders to pay for these in the deal (Gilson et al., 1988).

Hypothesis H1 in Table 6 holds that targets will receive higher offer premiums in all-cash bids than in all-stock offers, where the difference is compensation for the capital gains tax penalty inherent in the cash bid. Early studies that classify takeover premiums according to the payment method include Huang and Walkling (1987) and Hayn (1989) on US data, and Franks et al. (1988) and Eckbo and Langohr (1989) on acquisitions in the United Kingdom and France, respectively. This evidence shows that takeover premiums are indeed significantly greater in all-cash deals that in all-stock offers, which is consistent with H1. Also, Brown and Ryngaert (1991) find empirical support for their hypothesis that stock are less likely to be found in taxable offers (offers where less than 50% of the offer is to be paid in bidder stock).

On the other hand, Franks et al. (1988) show that takeover premiums in the United Kingdom were greater in cash deals even *before* the introduction of capital gains taxes.

Moreover, Eckbo and Langohr (1989) argue that for a tax compensation to induce tendering behavior, it must be included in the value of the option to tender (as opposed to keeping) the target shares. They approximate this option value with the difference between the offer price and the expected postoffer target share price, and find that this difference is indistinguishable across all-stock and all-cash offers. They also show that the larger total premium in all-cash offers carries over to minority buyouts which convey few if any bidder tax benefits (as the two firms are already consolidated for accounting purposes). This evidence does not support the view that the larger takeover premiums observed in all-cash deals are driven by the tax hypothesis H1.

5.3. Information asymmetries

Hypotheses H2-H5 in Panel B of Table 6 suggest that the payment method choice may be economically important—and give rise to premium effects—even in the absence of taxes. When the bidder and target are asymmetrically informed about the true value of their respective shares, the payment method may cause information revelation and affect both the division of synergy gains and the probability that the offer is successful. Hypothesis H2 is motivated by the adverse selection argument of Myers and Majluf (1984) and the associated financing "pecking order" suggested by Myers (1984). H2 focuses on the implication for the market's reaction to the all-stock versus all-cash announcement: Equity issues to relatively uninformed target shareholders may cause a negative market reaction as investors hedge against the possibility that the bidder's stock is overpriced.

There is substantial empirical evidence that seasoned equity offerings are on average met with a negative market reaction (approximately -3%)—even when the SEOs are fully underwritten by reputable investment banks. This is consistent with the hypothesis that outside investors are somewhat nervous that the typical equity issue may be overpriced—despite the substantial due diligence effort and reputational risk exposure of underwriters. The evidence on bidder returns by several of the studies summarized in Tables 1 and 6 indicates that all-equity acquisition announcements also tend to cause a statistically significant (approximately) 1% price bidder price drop when the target is a public company.[49] However, as discussed above (Table 2), bidder announcement returns are nonnegative (or even positive) in all-stock offers for *private* targets.

Thus, it appears that the overall information impact of the stock sale in all-stock takeovers is dominated by other offer characteristics for some bidders. Disentangling the information content of the payment method choice therefore requires cross-sectional restrictions on bidder announcement returns based on theory. Hansen (1987),

---

[49] See, for example, Travlos (1987), Asquith et al. (1987), Servaes (1991), Brown and Ryngaert (1991), Martin (1996), Emery and Switzer (1999), Heron and Lie (2004), and Schlingemann (2004). Because the level of communication between bidder and target management teams in merger negotiations is greater than that between underwriters and the market in SEOs, the potential for adverse selection is also smaller, thus the smaller price drop in all-equity bids than in SEOs.

Fishman (1989) and Eckbo et al. (1990a) provide theoretical analyses that incorporate adverse selection but where the bidder's choice of payment method is modeled explicitly.

An important insight of Hansen (1987) is that ex post means of payments such as stock can increase the seller's revenue beyond what cash payments can do.[50] This point is easily illustrated using our second-price, independent private value auction with two bidders ($v_1 > v_2$). If bidder 1 (B1) wins with an all-cash offer, the target receives v_2 (the second price). Alternatively, with all-stock as the payment method, the bidder offers the target the ownership fraction z_i in the merged firm. Suppose B1 and B2 have the same stand-alone value v. The optimal bid is the fraction z_i which satisfies

$$(v + v_i)(1 - z_i) = v, \tag{10}$$

or $z_i = v_i/(v + v_i)$. This leaves each bidder with a postacquisition value equal to the preacquisition (stand-alone) value. If B1 wins, the target receives

$$z_2(v + v_1) = \frac{v + v_1}{v + v_2} v_2 > v_2 \tag{11}$$

since $v_1 \geq v_2$. In other words, the all-stock offer extracts a higher revenue from the winning bidder than does the all-cash bid, resulting in more efficient sell decisions by the target.[51]

Another insight is that all-stock payment may increase the expected deal value for the bidder if there is little or no uncertainty concerning the true bidder value. Consider a single bidder B who has all the bargaining power. Denote B's with-synergy value as $v_B \equiv v + v_i$. Assume v_B is known to everyone, and that B1 only knows the probability distribution over the true target value, $v_T \in [\underline{v}_T, \bar{v}_T]$, where $\underline{v}_T < \bar{v}_T$. Moreover, suppose B's strategy is to ensure bid success.[52] The all-cash offer is therefore $c = \bar{v}_T$. This means that B expects to overpay for the target by the amount $\bar{v}_T - E(v_T \mid \text{accept})$, where the expectation is conditional on the target accepting the bid. The corresponding all-stock offer solves $z(v_B + \bar{v}_T) = \bar{v}_T$, or $z = \bar{v}_T/(v_B + \bar{v}_T)$. The expected overpayment cost is now

$$z[v_B + E(v_T|\text{accept})] - E(v_T|\text{accept}) = \frac{v_B}{v_B + \bar{v}_T}[\bar{v}_T - E(v_T|\text{accept})]. \tag{12}$$

Since $v_B/(v_B + \bar{v}_T) < 1$, the expected overpayment cost of securities is less than that of cash, reflecting the contingent nature of stock as payment form (payment in shares

---

[50] See also Hansen (1985), DeMarzo et al. (2005), and Dasgupta and Hansen (2007) for a review.

[51] In Fishman (1989), the alternative to cash is a debt instrument secured in the *target's* asset. This eliminates target uncertainty about the true value of the bidder's payment also for all-security offers and leads to efficient target accept/reject decisions.

[52] This bid strategy is maintained in the model of Eckbo et al. (1990a). In Hansen (1987), high-value bidders separate themselves by lowering their all-stock offers z, which is costly as it reduces the probability that the target will accept. The signaling cost is the reduction in the bidder's expected synergy gains from a reduction in z.

causes the target to share in the overpayment ex post). Cash, on the other hand, precommits the bidder to a target value ex ante.

If we allow also v_B to be private information (two-sided information asymmetry), then the above preference for a stock offer is reversed provided the bidder shares are sufficiently undervalued by the target. With two-sided information asymmetry, let $\hat{v}_B$ denote target beliefs about bidder value. In this case, the all-stock offer which guarantees success solves $z(\hat{v}_B + \bar{v}_T) = \bar{v}_T$, and the difference between the expected overpayment cost of an all-stock and an all-cash offer becomes

$$\bar{v}\frac{(v_B - \hat{v}_B) - (\bar{v}_T - E(v_T \mid \text{accept})}{v_B + E(v_T \mid \text{accept})} \tag{13}$$

which is positive or negative depending on whether the target undervalues ($v_B - \hat{v}_B > 0$) or overvalues ($v_B - \hat{v}_B < 0$) the bidder shares, respectively. Consistent with this, Chemmanur and Paeglis (2003) find that the probability of a stock offer falls when measures of bidder share underpricing increase.

As discussed earlier (Figure 4), mixed cash-stock offers are pervasive over the entire 1980–2005 period. Eckbo et al. (1990a) and Berkovitch and Narayanan (1990) model equilibrium mixed offers.[53] In the separating equilibrium of Eckbo et al. (1990a), bidder types are separated by the fraction of the total target payment that is paid in cash. Consistent with a separating equilibrium, Eckbo et al. (1990a) and Eckbo and Thorburn (2000) find that abnormal announcement returns are on average highest in all-cash offers, lowest in all-stock deals, with mixed offers in between.[54]

Eckbo et al. (1990a) present cross-sectional regressions tests of their signaling model. To illustrate, let γ_j denote the announcement-induced bidder abnormal return. The separating equilibrium implies that

$$\gamma_j = h_j\left(\frac{c_j}{v_T}\right), \; h'_j, \, h''_j > 0, \tag{14}$$

where c_j is the cash payment, v_T is the average prebid target value, and the superscripts denote first and second derivatives of the nonlinear signaling function h, respectively. That is, in the separating equilibrium, the market reaction to the takeover announcement is an increasing and convex function of the cash portion of the deal. Since the variables may be readily estimated, this theory is testable via a cross-sectional regression of the form

---

[53] In Hansen (1987) and Fishman (1989), bidders select between all-stock and all-cash offers, but do not mix the two.

[54] These two studies use mergers in Canada where offering less than 50% of the deal in cash does not trigger capital gains taxes. In the US, the tax code confounds the analysis as it in of itself discourages mixed offers where the cash portion exceeds 50% (Brown and Ryngaert, 1991).

$$\gamma_j = \delta_0 + \delta_1 \left(\frac{c_j}{v_T}\right) + \delta_2 \left(\frac{c_j}{v_T}\right)^2 + \cdots + u_j, \quad j = 1, \ldots, N. \tag{15}$$

The first regressor provides a test for the "increasing" part ($\delta_1 > 0$) and the second for convexity ($\delta_2 > 0$). The regression tests confirm $\delta_1 > 0$, however, the estimate of δ_2 is indistinguishable from zero across a number of different tests. Additional empirical tests are required to sort out why convexity fails.[55]

5.4. Capital structure and control motives

Under hypothesis H5 in Panel C of Table 6, the payment method is selected as part of a broader capital structure choice. Moreover, some bidder managements select cash over stock to avoid diluting private benefits of control. Attempts to link the payment method choice to financing sources for the cash portion of the bid are only starting to emerge. Schlingemann (2004) and Toffanin (2005) examine whether the market reaction to the payment method choice is a function of the type of cash financing. While the market is aware of any prebid public security issues, the acquisition bid announcement possibly resolves uncertainty regarding the use of the issue proceeds. If this resolution is economically important, the source of financing for the cash portion of the bid will affect the market reaction to the takeover attempt. The empirical results indicate a prior-cash-financing-source component in acquisition announcement returns.

Schlingemann (2004) reports that, after controlling for the form of payment, financing decisions during the year before a takeover play an important role in explaining the cross section of bidder gains. Bidder announcement period abnormal returns are positively and significantly related to the amount of ex ante equity financing. This relation is particularly strong for high Q firms. He further reports a negative and significant relation between bidder gains and free cash flow. This relation is particularly strong for firms classified as having poor investment opportunities. The amount of debt financing before a takeover announcement is not significantly related to bidder gains. Interestingly, Toffanin (2005) finds that the well-known positive market reaction to all-cash bids requires the cash to have been financed either using internal funds (retained earnings) or borrowing. All-cash acquisitions financed by a prior equity issue earn zero or negative abnormal returns.

Early theories incorporating private benefits of control in the contexts of takeovers and capital structure choice are Stulz (1988) and Harris and Raviv (1988). In our

---

[55] Note that the equilibrium signaling function h_j in Equation (14) holds for a *single* bidder j. Identifying h_j via cross-sectional tests therefore requires the additional assumption that bidder private information is independently and identically distributed across takeovers (so $h_j = h \forall j$). Violation of this cross-sectional assumption creates a family of convex signaling curves and thus an identification problem. For example, increases in the variance of the distribution over bidder j private information causes the theoretical h_j function to rotate in the (γ_j, h_j) space.

context, an all-cash offer preserves the bidder's control position, while an all-stock offer may significantly dilute this position (e.g., a "merger of equals"). The potential for control dilution may therefore drive the use of cash. Several empirical papers examine the payment method choice from this angle. For example, Amihud et al. (1990), Martin (1996), Ghosh and Ruland (1998) all find that bidder management shareholdings in the United States have negative effect on stock financing. Similarly, studying European mergers, Faccio and Masulis (2005) find that corporate control incentives to choose cash are particularly strong when in bidder firms with relatively concentrated shareownership structures. Overall, corporate control motives are likely to play a role in some all-cash mergers. Martynova and Renneboog (2006), who also examine acquisitions in Europe, find a link between the quality of a country's corporate governance system and the market reaction to stock as payment form. All-stock offers are more likely in countries with greater levels of shareholder rights protection.

5.5. Behavioral arguments for all-stock payment

Even in the absence of synergy gains, a merger may be in the interest of bidder stockholders if the alternative of no merger is worse:

> From our perspective, the central feature of this [AOL Time Warner] acquisition is not technological synergies, but rather the attempt by the management of the overvalued AOL to buy the hard assets of Time Warner to avoid even worse returns in the long run. (Shleifer and Vishny, 2003, p. 295)

This "market-driven merger" hypothesis is typically discussed in the context of merger waves, largely because merger waves are correlated with economic expansions and high stock market valuations.[56] The main idea is that bull markets may lead bidders with overvalued stock as currency to purchase the assets of undervalued (or less overvalued) targets (H6).

In Shleifer and Vishny (2003), target managements accept overpriced bidder stock as they are simply assumed to have a short-time horizon. In Rhodes-Kropf and Viswanathan (2004), rational (Bayesian) managers accept too many all-stock merger bids when the stock market booms and too few when the market is low. In their model, the market's pricing error has two components, one economy-wide and another that is firm specific. When receiving a bid, the target attempts to filter out the market-wide error component. The Bayesian update puts some weight on there being high synergies in the merger, so when the market-wide overvaluation is high, the target is more likely to accept the offer. In other words, bids tend to look better in the eyes of the target when the market is overvalued.

---

[56] There is substantial evidence of industry-clustering of mergers (Andrade and Stafford, 2004; Andrade et al. 2001; Harford, 2005; Maksimovic and Phillips, 2001; Mitchell and Mulherin, 1996; Mulherin and Boone, 2000). Merger waves are also affected by industry deregulations, such as that of the airline industry in 1970s (Slovin et al., 1991; Spiller, 1983) and of the utility industry in 1992 (Becher et al., 2008; Jovanovic and Rousseau, 2004).

Rhodes-Kropf et al. (2005), Ang and Cheng (2006), and Dong et al. (2006) find that merger waves coincide with high M/B ratios. One argument is that the M/B ratio is a reliable proxy for market overvaluation and that investor misvaluations tend to drive merger waves. High market valuations may be a fundamental driver of merger waves as bidders attempt to sell overpriced stock to targets (and succeed). Harford (2005) argues instead that the driver of merger waves is market liquidity, and that market liquidity is the fundamental driver of *both* M/B ratios and merger waves. He constructs a measure of aggregate capital liquidity based on interest rate (default) spreads, and uses this measure in a "horse race" with M/B ratios in predicting industry merger waves. He finds that waves are preceded by deregulatory events and high capital liquidity. More importantly, he shows that the capital liquidity variable eliminates the ability of M/B ratios to predict industry merger waves, and concludes that aggregate merger waves are caused by the clustering of shock-driven industry merger waves, not by attempts to time the market.

When evaluating market-driven merger hypotheses, it is also important to look at the proportion of all-stock mergers in the overall population. As pointed out earlier (Figure 4), there are nearly as many mixed cash-stock offers as all-stock offers, even in the recent period of high market valuations and peak merger activity (1996–2000). Because mixing cash and stock increases the ability of undervalued bidders to separate out from the pool of overvalued bidders (Eckbo et al., 1990a), the substantial presence of mixed offers undermines the pooling equilibrium of Shleifer and Vishny (2003). Also, the finding that the substantial market runup prior to year 2000 did *not* induce a greater use of all-stock offers as a proportion of all merger bids further undermines the behavioral argument. In sum, while some bidders undoubtedly get away with selling overpriced stock to their targets, there is little systematic evidence that this determines the form of payment in takeovers.

6. Offer premiums and poison pills

A poison pill ("shareholder rights plan") is a permanent threat to dilute the value of a blockholder—typically defined as one holding 15% or more of the company's stock. The dilution takes place by allowing shareholders other than the blockholder to purchase (or exchange old for) new shares at half price. As this right is akin to a dividend, the pill may be adopted by the board anytime (including the day after receiving an unsolicited bid—a "morning after pill") and without shareholder vote. Since, to my knowledge, no bidder has yet triggered a pill, the perceived cost of triggering must be high, effectively forcing the would be acquirer to negotiate with the target board and management. Should the target refuse to negotiate (appealing to the board's right to "just say no"), the only way around the pill appears to be to launch a proxy contest simultaneously with the offer. If the proxy contest succeeds, the bidder replaces the board with directors who are willing to rescind the pill. Board classification (staggered election of directors), however, prevents this strategy from working (Bebchuk and Cohen, 2005; Bebchuk et al., 2002; 2004).[57]

The number of hostile takeovers has declined dramatically after the 1980s—the decade where pill adoptions became popular (Betton et al., 2008a; Comment and Schwert, 1995). Defenders of poison pills argue that a pill enhances shareholder wealth by improving the target's bargaining strength (conditional on receiving a bid). This argument suggests that poison pills should be associated with higher takeover premiums. However, the evidence in Table 4 shows that targets with poison pills receive offer premiums that are on average indistinguishable from offer premiums received by nonpill targets. A similar result has been reported by several studies, including Comment and Schwert (1995), Field and Karpoff (2002), and Heron and Lie (2006).

What explains the surprising neutral impact of pills on observed offer premiums? Possible interpretations include the following:

H1 Poison pills do not convey bargaining power.
H2 Poison pills convey bargaining power and increases takeover premiums relative to what premiums would have been for the same target without a pill.
H3 Poison pills convey bargaining power which is used to benefit target management at the expense of target shareholders.
H4 Poison pills provide bargaining power, but "shadow" pills are as effective as adopted pills.

Hypotheses H2-H4 maintain that pills convey bargaining power, but that a comparison of offer premiums in samples of firms with or without pills is fraught with econometric difficulties. Pill adoptions are voluntary, which raises complex issues of endogeneity (H2). Controlling for self-selection is also difficult, however, because the marginal effect of a poison pill depends on the firm's entire governance system, including executive compensation (H3). Also, in order to isolate true premium effects of pills, empirical work relies on the existence of two samples, one representing "poison" and the other "placebo" effects (Comment and Schwert, 1995). This sampling is difficult if not impossible if as in H4 *all* firms effectively have ready access to the pill at any point in time (Coates, 2000).

As to H3, Heron and Lie (2006) find that targets of hostile bids are more likely to adopt poison pills when they have classified boards, suggesting that the two antitakeover devices are interdependent. Moeller (2005) concludes that targets with powerful CEOs receive lower takeover premiums. A key question is what package of capital gains, cash and subsequent employment do target CEOs accept in exchange for

---

[57] Masulis et al. (2007) report that acquisition announcement-period stock returns are significantly lower for bidders with staggered boards, possibly because board classification reduces forced board turnover and quality. On the other hand, Bates et al. (2008) find that board classification does not reduce the probability that a firm, once it is targeted, is ultimately acquired. Moreover, targets with classified boards appear to extract premiums equivalent to those of single-class boards. Rose (2009) concludes that the presence of staggered boards have more of a detrimental impact of firm value when management is relatively entrenched.

relinquishing control. Another important issue is whether target CEOs sacrifice premiums paid to their own outside shareholders in return for a favorable "golden handshake."[58] Walkling and Long (1984), Cotter and Zenner (1994), Wulf (2004), and Hartzell et al. (2004) all present evidence on acquisition-induced compensation of target firm CEOs. Hartzell et al. (2004) analyze a sample of 311 negotiated mergers between 1995 and 1997. They conclude from their evidence that "acquirers overtly pay certain CEOs to surrender managerial control over the firm's assets, or equivalently, that some CEOs 'purchase' executive jobs in the buyer by foregoing cash payments that they might otherwise have obtained" (p. 39). Also, they present some evidence indicating an inverse association between selling shareholder premia and unusual bonuses received by the target CEO as a reward to "step aside."[59]

H1 maintains that pills are ineffective as a bargaining tool. For example, the bidder may believe that target board is not committed to trigger the pill. As a case in point, consider the failed 1996 takeover attempt by US Surgical Corporation of medical device maker Circon Corporation. Exercising the Circon pill would have required Circon shareholder to pay approximately $800 million in cash into a company with a pretakeover total equity value of $150 million. In return for this massive (and expensive) cash infusion, Circon shareholders would lose a 70% takeover premium and stood to gain only $10 million from the resulting dilution of US Surgical's shareholding in Circon. In general, a pill with this structure may lack credibility and therefore have little effect on bargaining outcomes.[60]

As pointed out by Schwert (2000), the definition of target "hostility" used in the literature probably captures plenty of targets that are ready to negotiate with or without the pill. Bidders that are able to look beyond the pill and determine whether negotiations are possible (based on observable target characteristic or on the bidder's own ability to persuade a hostile target management), may reach a final bargaining outcome that is largely indistinguishable from that observed in samples of ex ante "friendly" targets. This may also help explain why empirical evidence shows that the probability of receiving a bid (and ultimate bid success) is either unaffected or only slightly lower for targets with strong antitakeover defenses.[61]

---

[58] Yermack (2006) presents evidence on severance packages more generally, in a sample of *Fortune 500* companies.

[59] As the authors recognize, since the study uses a sample of completed mergers only, it does not provide information on the sort of packages that other target CEOs turn down in attempted mergers that were not completed. Thus, the question of whether larger CEO packages come at the expense of target shareholders remains open.

[60] In the Circon case, Circon chairman and CEO Richard Auhll appeared to be protecting large private benefits of control. Using information on SDC, approximately half of all pills are cash pills (the exercise price is paid in cash rather than by an exchange of securities).

[61] Comment and Schwert (1995), Field and Karpoff (2002), and Heron and Lie (2006).

7. Conclusions

There is growing research interest in the details of the takeover process from the initial bid through the final contest outcome. This paper reviews empirical evidence on bid strategies, takeover premiums and associated bidder returns, with a particular emphasis on the initial bidder. Bidding theory addresses optimal bid strategies when target shareholders free ride, and when the initial bid risks attracting competition and target resistance. In addition to the initial offer premium and subsequent bid jumps, the initial bidder's strategic arsenal include postoffer dilution of minority target shareholders, use of state-contingent payment methods, markup pricing in response to new information, toeholds, termination agreements, and legal maneuvering when the target is hostile.

The evidence is suggestive of rational and strategic bidder behavior in specific contexts. For example, bid jumps are largest for the very first bid and when this bid ends up winning the target (consistent with preemptive bidding). Moreover, theory implies a deterrent effect of toeholds on competition, and the evidence suggests that bidders in fact trade off toeholds and offer premiums. In one auction setting (bankruptcy auctions) offer premiums are consistent with rational toehold-induced overbidding incentives, while in another (target takeover solicitations) bidders appear to avoid the winner's curse.

Large-sample evidence on offer premiums is only starting to emerge. The initial offer premiums average nearly 50% over the past three decades, with additional jumps when bid revisions are required. Notwithstanding the high initial offer premium, initial bids carry a substantial risk of failure (approximately 30% of all initial bids fail). The average offer premium in successful single-bid takeover contests is higher than the average initial offer premium in *multibid* contests. This is consistent with the greater premium preempting competition in ex post successful single-bid cases. Bid revisions are substantial when the initial bid attracts competition and/or is revised by the initial bidder. The average bid-jump from the first to the second bid in the contest of 10%, a 31% change in the offer premium. A "jump" of a different kind is the tendency for bidders to mark up the offer price so that it varies almost one-to-one with the target stock price runup prior to the first bid. Offer premiums (both initial and final) are greater after the 1980s, greater for public than for private bidders, and greater in all-cash offers than when the payment is all-stock in the bidder firm. Moreover, offer premiums are lower for toehold bidders, and unaffected by either the presence of a target poison pill or target hostility to the initial bid.

Toehold bidding fell dramatically after the 1980s. This fall coincides with the rise of structural takeover defenses beginning in the 1980s. In theory, toehold bidding conveys substantial strategic advantage of rival bidders, particularly in a common-value setting. Since many of these advantages come at the expense of the *target*, some targets may be reluctant to negotiate if the bidder has a toehold. If so, acquiring a toehold prior to attempting friendly merger negotiations may backfire: if the target refuses, the bidder foregoes not only things like a termination agreement but also the opportunity to examine the target books—which is crucial for pricing of the merger. Another way to put this is that a toehold must be large to be worth it—larger than 10% by some (conservative) estimates. This argument possibly explains the dual observation that toeholds are large when they exist, and that they occur mostly in hostile bids.

The choice of payment method is strategic for several reasons. Over the past three decades, bidders initiating takeover bids for US targets offered all-cash as payment in about one-quarter of the cases, all-stock in one-third and a mix of stock of cash also in one-third of the takeovers. The majority of tender offers are all-cash or a mix of cash and stock, while the majority of merger bids are in the form of all-stock. All-cash and mixed cash-stock offers are predominant in tender offers. Moreover, mixed stock-cash offers rose to become the most frequently used payment method in mergers by 2001. The percentage all-stock offers in initial merger bids were approximately 50% throughout the 1990s: the percentage all-stock merger bids did not increase with the substantial runup in market valuations toward the end of the 1990s. Consistent with information-based theories, offer premiums are greater in all-cash offers than in all-stock offers.

The pervasive negative market reaction to all-stock merger bids by public bidders is reminiscent of the negative market reaction typically observed in response to announcements of seasoned equity offers. The analogy is appealing since the timing of the equity issue is determined endogenously by the issuer in both events, and thus involve some degree of adverse selection. On the other hand, stock-swaps in mergers are closer to private placements than they are to an underwritten seasoned equity offering—and there is substantial evidence that the market reaction to private placement is positive on average (Eckbo et al., 2007). Moreover, the market reaction to merger stock swaps is positive when the target is private. Additional research is needed to establish the empirical relevance of asymmetric information arguments for the strategic payment choice.

Overall, the empirical evidence reviewed here is relevant for the broader debate over bidder rationality and the efficiency of the market for corporate control. While much remains to be done, the picture emerging is one where bidder behavior is consistent with optimizing behavior in certain contexts. Coupled with the fact that total (target plus bidder) takeover gains are positive on average, such behavior supports the neoclassical view of takeovers. While some bidders undoubtedly exhibit overconfidence and simply pay too much for control of the target, the evidence appears to indicate some degree of restraint in the bidding process—as if bidders act strategically.

References

Acharya, V. V., S. T. Bharath and A. Srinivasan, 2007, "Does Industry-Wide Distress Affect Defaulted Firms? Evidence from Creditor Recoveries," *Journal of Financial Economics*, 85, 787–821.

Aghion, P., O. Hart and J. Moore, 1992, "The Economics of Bankruptcy Reform," *Journal of Law, Economics and Organization*, 8, 523–546.

Ahern, K. R., 2006, "Markets Talk, Firms Listen: The Dynamics of Repeat Acquirers," Working Paper, UCLA.

Akbulut, M. E. and J. G. Matsusaka, 2003, "Fifty Years of Diversification Announcements," Working Paper, Marshall School of Business, University of Southern California.

Akdogu, E., 2007, "Value-Maximizing Managers, Value-Increasing Mergers and Overbidding," Working Paper, Southern Methodist University.

Aktas, N., E. de Bodt and R. Roll, 2008, "Negotiation Under the Threat of an Auction: Friendly Deals, Ex ante Competition and Bidder Returns," Working Paper, University of California at Los Angeles.

Amihud, Y., B. Lev and N. Travlos, 1990, "Corporate Control and the Choice of Investment Financing: The Case of Corporate Acquisitions," *Journal of Finance*, 45, 603–616.

Andrade, G. and E. Stafford, 2004, "Investigating the Economic Role of Mergers," *Journal of Corporate Finance*, 10, 1–36.

Andrade, G., M. Mitchell and E. Stafford, 2001, "New Evidence and Perspectives on Mergers," *Journal of Economic Perspectives*, 15, 103–120.

Ang, J. S. and Y. Cheng, 2006, "Direct Evidence on the Market-Driven Acquisition Theory," *Journal of Financial Research*, 29, 199–216.

Asquith, P., R. Bruner and D. Mullins, 1983, "The Gains to Bidding Firms from Merger," *Journal of Financial Economics*, 11, 121–139.

Asquith, P., R. Bruner and D. Mullins, 1987, "Merger Returns and the Form of Financing," *Proceedings of the Seminar on the Analysis of Securities Prices*, 34, 115–146.

Bagnoli, M. and B. L. Lipman, 1988, "Successful Takeover without Exclusion," *Review of Financial Studies*, 1, 89–110.

Bagnoli, M. and B. L. Lipman, 1996, "Stock Price Manipulation Through Takeover Bids," *RAND Journal of Economics*, 27, 124–147.

Bargeron, L., 2005, "Do Shareholder Tender Agreements Inform or Expropriate Shareholders?" Working Paper, University of Pittsburgh.

Bargeron, L., F. P. Schlingemann, R. M. Stulz and C. Zutter, 2008, "Why Do Private Acquirers Pay So Little Compared to Public Acquirers?" *Journal of Financial Economics*, 89, 375–390.

Bates, T. H. and M. L. Lemmon, 2003, "Breaking Up is Hard to Do? An Analysis of Termination Fee Provisions and Merger Outcomes," *Journal of Financial Economics*, 69, 460–504.

Bates, T. W., D. A. Becher and M. L. Lemmon, 2008, "Board Classification and Managerial Entrenchment: Evidence from the Market for Corporate Control," *Journal of Financial Economics*, 87, 656–677.

Bebchuk, L. A., 1985, "Toward Undistorted Choice and Equal Treatment in Corporate Takeovers," *Harvard Law Review*, 98, 1695–1808.

Bebchuk, L. A. and A. Cohen, 2005, "The Costs of Entrenched Boards," *Journal of Financial Economics*, 78, 409–433.

Bebchuk, L. A., J. C. Coates and G. Subramanian, 2002, "The Powerful Anti-Takeover Force of Staggered Boards: Theory, Evidence, and Policy," *Stanford Law Review*, 54, 887–951.

Bebchuk, L. A., A. Cohen and A. Ferrell, 2004, "What Matters in Corporate Governance?" Working Paper, Harvard University.

Becher, D. A., J. H. Mulherin and R. A. Walkling, 2008, "Industry Shocks and Merger Activity: An Analysis of U.S. Public Utilities," Working Paper, Drexel University.

Berglof, E. and M. Burkart, 2003, "European Takeover Regulation," *Economic Policy*, 36, 171–213.

Berkovitch, E. and M. Narayanan, 1990, "Competition and the Medium of Exchange in Takeovers," *Review of Financial Studies*, 3(2), 153–174.

Berle, A. A. and G. C. Means, 1932, *The Modern Corporation and Private Property*, Macmillan, New York, NY.

Betton, S. and B. E. Eckbo, 2000, "Toeholds, Bid Jumps, and Expected Payoff in Takeovers," *Review of Financial Studies*, 13, 841–882.

Betton, S., B. E. Eckbo and K. S. Thorburn, 2009, "Merger Negotiations and the Toehold Puzzle," *Journal of Financial Economics*, 91, 158–178.

Betton, S., B. E. Eckbo and K. S. Thorburn, 2008a, "Corporate Takeovers," In B. E. Eckbo (Ed.), *Handbook of Corporate Finance: Empirical Corporate Finance*, vol. 2, Chapter 15, Elsevier/North-Holland, Handbooks in Finance Series, pp. 291–430.

Betton, S., B. E. Eckbo and K. S. Thorburn, 2008b, "Markup Pricing Revisited," Working Paper, Tuck School of Business at Dartmouth, Hanover, NH.

Betton, S., B. E. Eckbo and K. S. Thorburn, 2008c, "Massive Wealth Destruction? Bidder Gains Revisited," Working Paper, Tuck School of Business at Dartmouth, Hanover, NH.

Bhagat, S., M. Dong, D. Hirshleifer and R. Noah, 2005, "Do Tender Offers Create Value? New Methods and Evidence," *Journal of Financial Economics*, 76, 3–60.

Billett, M. T. and Y. Qian, 2005, "Are Overconfident Managers Born or Made? Evidence of Self-Attribution Bias from Frequent Acquirers," Working Paper, Boston College.

Boone, A. L. and J. H. Mulherin, 2008, "Do Auctions Induce a Winner's Curse? New Evidence from the Corporate Takeover Market," *Journal of Financial Economics*, 89, 1–19.

Boone, A. L. and J. H. Mulherin, 2007a, "Do Termination Provisions Truncate the Takeover Bidding Process?" *Review of Financial Studies*, 20, 461–489.

Boone, A. L. and J. H. Mulherin, 2007b, "How are Firms Sold?" *Journal of Finance*, 62, 847–875.

Bradley, M., 1980, "Interfirm Tender Offers and the Market for Corporate Control," *Journal of Business*, 53, 345–376.

Bradley, M. and A. Sundaram, 2006, "Acquisitions and Performance: A Re-Assessment of the Evidence," Working Paper, Duke University.

Bris, A., I. Welch and N. Zhu, 2006, "The Costs of Bankruptcy: Chapter 7 Liquidation versus Chapter 11 Reorganization," *Journal of Finance*, 61, 1253–1303.

Brown, D. T. and M. D. Ryngaert, 1991, "The Mode of Acquisition in Takeovers: Taxes and Asymmetric Information," *Journal of Finance*, 46, 653–669.

Bruner, R. F., 2004, *Applied Mergers & Acquisitions*, Wiley, New York.

Bulow, J., M. Huang and P. Klemperer, 1999, "Toeholds and Takeovers," *Journal of Political Economy*, 107, 427–454.

Burch, T., 2001, "Locking Out Rival Bidders: The Use of Lockup Options in Corporate Mergers," *Journal of Financial Economics*, 60, 103–141.

Burkart, M., 1995, "Initial Shareholdings and Overbidding in Takeover Contests," *Journal of Finance*, 50, 1491–1515.

Burkart, M. and F. Panunzi, 2003, "Mandatory Bids, Squeeze-Out, Sell-Out and the Dynamics of the Tender Offer Process," Working Paper, European Corporate Governance Institute.

Burkart, M. and F. Panunzi, 2008, "Takeovers," In Ph. Hartmann, X. Freicas and C. Mayer (Eds.), *Financial Markets and Institutions: An European Perspective*, Chapter 9, Oxford University Press, USA.

Burkart, M., D. Gromb and F. Panunzi, 1998, "Why Takeover Premia Protect Minority Share-Holders," *Journal of Political Economy*, 106, 647–677.

Cain, M. D., D. Denis and D. K. Denis, 2005, "Earnouts: A Study of Contracting in Acquisition Agreements," Working Paper, Purdue University.

Carleton, W., D. Guilkey, R. Harris and J. Stewart, 1983, "An Empirical Analysis of the Role of the Medium of Exchange in Mergers," *Journal of Finance*, 38, 57–82.

Chang, S., 1998, "Takeovers of Privately Held Targets, Methods of Payment, and Bidder Returns," *Journal of Finance*, 53, 773–784.

Chang, T. and A. Schoar, 2007, "The Effect of Judicial Bias in Chapter 11 Reorganization," Working Paper, Massachusetts Institute of Technology.

Chatterjee, S., K. John and A. Yan, 2008, "Takeover Premium and Divergence of Opinions," Working Paper, School of Business, Fordham University.

Chemmanur, T. J. and I. Paeglis, 2003, "The Choice of the Medium of Exchange in Acquisitions: A Direct Test of the Double-Sided Asymmetric Information Hypothesis," Working Paper, Boston College.

Claessens, S., S. Djankov and L. H. P. Lang, 2000, "The Separation of Ownership and Control in East Asian Corporations," *Journal of Financial Economics*, 58, 81–112.

Clayton, M. J. and S. A. Ravid, 2002, "The Effect of Leverage on Bidding Behavior: Theory and Evidence from the FCC Auctions," *Review of Financial Studies*, 15, 723–750.

Coates, J. C., 2000, "Takeover Defenses in the Shadow of the Pill: A Critique of the Scientific Evidence," *Texas Law Review*, 79, 271–382.

Comment, R. and G. W. Schwert, 1995, "Poison or Placebo? Evidence on the Deterrent and Wealth Effects of Modern Antitakeover Measures," *Journal of Financial Economics*, 39, 3–43.

Cotter J. and M. Zenner, 1994, "How Managerial Wealth Affects the Tender Offer Process," *Journal of Financial Economics*, 35, 63–97.

Croci, E., 2005, "Why Do Managers Make Serial Acquisitions? An Investigation of Performance Predictability in Serial Acquisitions," Working Paper, Universit degli Studi di Milano-Bicocca.

Daniel, K. and D. Hirshleifer, 2008, "A Theory of Costly Sequential Bidding," Working Paper, Anderson Graduate School of Management, UCLA.

Dasgupta, S. and R. G. Hansen, 2007, "Auctions in Corporate Finance," In: B. E. Eckbo (Ed.), *Handbook of Corporate Finance: Empirical Corporate Finance*, vol. 1, Chapter 3, Elsevier/North-Holland, Handbooks in Finance Series, pp. 87–143.

Dasgupta, S. and K. Tsui, 2003, "A "Matching Auction" for Targets with Heterogeneous Bidders," *Journal of Financial Intermediation*, 12, 331–364.

Dasgupta, S. and K. Tsui, 2004, "Auctions with Cross-Shareholdings," *Economic Theory*, 24, 163–194.

DeMarzo, P. M., I. Kremer and A. Skrzypacz, 2005, "Bidding with Securities: Auctions and Security Design," *American Economic Review*, 95, 936–959.

Djankov, S., R. La Porta, F. Lopez-de-Silanes and A. Shleifer, 2008, "The Law and Economics of Self-Dealing," *Journal of Financial Economics*, 88, 430–465.

Dlugosz, J., R. Fahlenbrach, P. A. Gompers and A. Metrick, 2006, "Large Blocks of Stock: Prevalence, Size, and Measurement," *Journal of Corporate Finance*, 12, 594–618.

Dong, M., D. Hisrshleifer, S. Richardson and S. H. Teoh, 2006, "Does Investor Misvaluation Drive the Takeover Market?" *Journal of Finance*, 61, 725–762.

Eckbo, B. E., 1983, "Horizontal Mergers, Collusion, and Stockholder Wealth," *Journal of Financial Economics*, 11, 241–272.

Eckbo, B. E., 1988, "The Market for Corporate Control: Policy Issues and Capital Market Evidence," In R. S. Khemani, D. Shapiro and W. T. Stanbury (Eds.), *Mergers, Corporate Concentration and Corporate Power in Canada*, The Canadian Institute for Research on Public Policy, Montreal, Canada, pp. 143–225.

Eckbo, B. E., 1992, "Mergers and the Value of Antitrust Deterrence," *Journal of Finance*, 47, 1005–1029.

Eckbo, B. E. and H. Langohr, 1989, "Information Disclosure, Method of Payment, and Takeover Premiums: Public and Private Tender Offers in France," *Journal of Financial Economics*, 24, 363–403.

Eckbo, B. E. and K. S. Thorburn, 2000, "Gains to Bidder Firms Revisited: Domestic and Foreign Acquisitions in Canada," *Journal of Financial and Quantitative Analysis*, 35, 1–25.

Eckbo, B. E. and K. S. Thorburn, 2008, "Automatic Bankruptcy Auctions and Fire-Sales," *Journal of Financial Economics*, 89, 404–422.

Eckbo, B. E. and K. S. Thorburn, 2009, "Creditor Financing and Overbidding in Bankruptcy Auctions," *Journal of Corporate Finance*, 15, 10–29.

Eckbo, B. E. and S. Verma, 1994, "Managerial Shareownership, Voting Power, and Cash Dividend Policy," *Journal of Corporate Finance*, 1, 33–62.

Eckbo, B. E., R. M. Giammarino and R. L. Heinkel, 1990a, "Asymmetric Information and the Medium of Exchange in Takeovers: Theory and Tests," *Review of Financial Studies*, 3, 651–675.

Eckbo, B. E., V. Maksimovic and J. Williams, 1990b, "Consistent Estimation of Cross-Sectional Models in Event Studies," *Review of Financial Studies*, 3, 343–365.

Eckbo, B. E., R. W. Masulis and Ø. Norli, 2007, "Security Offerings," In B. E. Eckbo (Ed.), *Handbook of Corporate Finance: Empirical Corporate Finance*, vol. 1, Chapter 6, Elsevier/North-Holland, Handbooks in Finance Series, pp. 233–374.

Emery, G. and J. Switzer, 1999, "Expected Market Reaction and the Choice of Method of Payment for Acquisitions," *Financial Management*, 28(4), 73–86.

Faccio, M. and L. H. P. Lang, 2002, "The Ultimate Ownership of Western European Corporations," *Journal of Financial Economic*, 65, 365–395.

Faccio, M. and R. W. Masulis, 2005, "The Choice of Payment Method in European Mergers and Acquisitions," *Journal of Finance*, 60, 1345–1388.

Fee, C. E. and S. Thomas, 2004, "Sources of Gains in Horizontal Mergers: Evidence from Customers, Supplier, and Rival Firms," *Journal of Financial Economics*, 74, 423–460.

Field, L. C. and J. M. Karpoff, 2002, "Takeover Defenses at IPO Firms," *Journal of Finance*, 57, 1857–1889.

Fishman, M. J., 1988, "A Theory of Preemptive Takeover Bidding," *RAND Journal of Economics*, 19, 88–101.

Fishman, M. J., 1989, "Preemptive Bidding and The Role of the Medium of Exchange in Acquisitions," *Journal of Finance*, 44, 41–57.

Franks, J. R., R. S. Harris and C. Mayer, 1988, "Means of Payment in Takeovers: Results for the U.K. and the U.S." In A. Auerbach (Ed.), *Corporate Takeovers*, NBER, University of Chicago Press, USA.

Franks, J., C. P. Mayer and S. Rossi, 2005, "Ownership: Evolution and Regulation," Working Paper, London Business School.

Fuller, K., J. Netter and M. Stegemoller, 2002, "What Do Returns to Acquiring Firms Tell Us? Evidence from Firms that Make Many Acquisitions," *Journal of Finance*, 57, 1763–1793.

Ghosh, A. and W. Ruland, 1998, "Managerial Ownership and the Method of Payment for Acquisitions, and Executive Job Retention," *Journal of Finance*, 53(2), 785–797.

Gilson, R. J., M. S. Scholes and M. A. Wolfson, 1988, "Taxation and the Dynamics of Corporate Control: The Uncertain Case for Tax-Motivated Acquisitions," In: J. C. Coffe, L. Lowenstein and S. Rose-Ackerman (Eds.), *Knights, Raiders and Targets: The Impact of the Hostile Takeover*, Oxford University Press, New York.

Goldman, E. and J. Qian, 2005, "Optimal Toeholds in Takeover Contests," *Journal of Financial Economics*, 77, 321–346.

Grossman, S. and O. Hart, 1980a, "Disclosure Law and Takeover Bids," *Journal of Finance*, 35, 323–334.

Grossman, S. J. and O. D. Hart, 1980b, "Takeover Bids, the Free-Rider Problem, and the Theory of the Corporation," *Bell Journal of Economics*, 11, 42–64.

Hansen, R. G., 1985, "Auctions with Contingent Payments," *American Economic Review*, 75, 862–865.

Hansen, R. G., 1987, "A Theory for the Choice of Exchange Medium in the Market for Corporate Control," *Journal of Business*, 60, 75–95.

Harford, J., 2005, "What Drives Merger Waves?" *Journal of Financial Economics*, 77, 529–560.

Harris, M. and A. Raviv, 1988, "Corporate Control Contests and Capital Structure," *Journal of Financial Economics*, 20, 55–86.

Hartzell, J. C., E. Ofek and D. Yermack, 2004, "What's In It for Me? CEOs Whose Firms are Acquired," *Review of Financial Studies*, 17, 37–61.

Hayn, C., 1989, "Tax Attributes as Determinants of Shareholder Gains in Corporate Acquisitions," *Journal of Financial Economics*, 23, 121–153.

Helwege, J., C. Pirinsky and R. M. Stulz, 2007, "Why Do Firms Become Widely held? An Analysis of the Dynamics of Corporate Ownership," *Journal of Finance*, 62, 995–1028.

Heron, R. A. and E. Lie, 2004, "A Comparison of the Motivations for and the Information Content of Different Types of Equity Offerings," *Journal of Business*, 77, 605–632.

Heron, R. A. and E. Lie, 2006, "On the Use of Poison Pill and Defensive Payouts by Takeover Targets," *Journal of Business*, 79, 1783–1807.

Hirshleifer, D., 1995, "Mergers and Acquisitions: Strategic and Informational Issues," In R. A. Jarrow, V. Maksimovic and W. T. Ziemba (Eds.), *Finance*, vol. 9, Chapter 26, Elsevier/North-Holland, Handbooks in Operation Research and Management Science, pp. 839–885.

Hirshleifer, D. and I. P. L. Ping, 1990, "Facilitation of Competing Bids and the Price of a Takeover Target," *Review of Financial Studies*, 2, 587–606.

Hirshleifer, D. and S. Titman, 1990, "Share Tendering Strategies and the Success of Hostile Takeover Bids," *Journal of Political Economy*, 98, 295–324.

Holderness, C. G., 2009, "The Myth of Diffuse Ownership in the United States," *Review of Financial Studies*, 22, 1377–1408.

Holderness, C. G., R. S. Kroszner and D. P. Sheehan, 1999, "Were the Good Old Days that Good? Changes in Management Stock Ownership Since the Great Depression," *Journal of Finance*, 54, 435–469.

Holmstrom, B. and B. Nalebuff, 1992, "To the Raider Goes the Surplus? A Reexamination of the Free Rider Problem," *Journal of Economics and Management Strategy*, 1, 37–62.

Hotchkiss, E. S. and R. M. Mooradian, 2003, "Auctions in Bankruptcy," *Journal of Corporate Finance*, 9, 555–574.

Huang, Y. S. and R. A. Walkling, 1987, "Abnormal Returns Associated with Acquisition Announcements: Payment Method, Acquisition Form, and Managerial Resistance," *Journal of Financial Economics*, 19, 329–349.

Ismail, A., 2006, "Will Multiple Acquirers Ever Learn? The US Evidence from Single versus Multiple Acquirers," Working Paper, American University of Beirut.

Jarrell, G. A. and M. Bradley, 1980, "The Economic Effects of Federal and State Regulations of Cash Tender Offers," *Journal of Law and Economics*, 23, 371–407 (2, October).

Jarrell, G. A. and A. B. Poulsen, 1989, "Stock Trading Before the Announcement of Tender Offers: Insider Trading or Market Anticipation?" *Journal of Law, Economics and Organization*, 5, 225–248.

Jarrell, G. A., J. A. Brickley and J. M. Netter, 1988, "The Market for Corporate Control: The Empirical Evidence Since 1980," *Journal of Economic Perspectives*, 2, 49–68.

Jennings, R. H. and M. A. Mazzeo, 1993, "Competing Bids, Target Management Resistance, and the Structure of Takeover Bids," *Review of Financial Studies*, 6, 883–910.

Jensen, M. C., 1986, "Agency Costs of Free Cash Flow, Corporate Finance, and Takeovers," *American Economic Review*, 76, 323–329.

Jensen, M. C. and W. Meckling, 1976, "Theory of the Firm: Managerial Behavior, Agency Costs, and Capital Structure," *Journal of Financial Economics*, 3, 305–360.

Jensen, M. C. and R. S. Ruback, 1983, "The Market for Corporate Control," *Journal of Financial Economics*, 11, 5–50.

Jovanovic, B. and P. L. Rousseau, 2004, "Mergers as Reallocation," Working Paper, New York University.

King, M. R. and M. Padalko, 2005, "Pre-Bid Run-Ups Ahead of Canadian Takeovers: How Big is the Problem?" Working Paper 2005-3, Bank of Canada.

Klemperer, P. D., 1998, "Auctions with Almost Common Values," *European Economic Review*, 42, 757–769.

Kohers, N. and J. Ang, 2000, "Earnouts in Mergers: Agreeing to Disagree and Agreeing to Stay. *Journal of Business*, 73, 445–476.

Lang, L. and R. Stulz, 1992, "Contagion and Competitive Intra-Industry Effects of Bankruptcy Announcements," *Journal of Financial Economics*, 32, 45–60.

La Porta, R., F. Lopez-de-Silanes and A. Shleifer, 1999, "Corporate Ownership Around the World," *Journal of Finance*, 54, 471–518.

Levi, M., K. Li and F. Zhang, 2008, "Mergers and Acquisitions: The Role of Gender," Working Paper, Sauder School of Business, University of British Columbia.

Li, K. and N. R. Prabhala, 2007, "Self-Selection Models in Corporate Finance," In B. E. Eckbo (Ed.), *Handbook of Corporate Finance: Empirical Corporate Finance*, vol. 1, Chapter 2, Elsevier/North-Holland, Handbooks in Finance Series, pp. 37–86.

Loderer, C. and K. Martin, 1990, "Corporate Acquisitions by Listed Firms: The Experience of Comprehensive Sample," *Financial Management*, 19, 17–33.

Maksimovic, V. and G. Phillips, 2001, "The Market for Corporate Assets: Who Engages in Mergers and Asset Sales and are There Efficiency Gains?" *Journal of Finance*, 56, 2019–2065.

Malatesta, P. and R. Thompson, 1985, "Partially Anticipated Events: A Model of Stock Price Reaction with An Application to Corporate Acquisitions," *Journal of Financial Economics*, 14, 237–250.

Malmendier, U. and G. Tate, 2008, "Who Makes Acquisitions? CEO Overconfidence and the Market's Reaction," *Journal of Financial Economics*, 89, 20–43.

Martin, K., 1996, "The Method of Payment in Corporate Acquisitions, Investment Opportunities, and Management Ownership," *Journal of Finance*, 51, 1227–1246.

Martynova, M. and L. Renneboog, 2006, "Mergers and Acquisitions in Europe," In L. Renneboog (Ed.), *Advances in Corporate Finance and Asset Pricing*, Chapter 2, Elsevier, pp. 13–75.

Martynova, M. and L. Renneboog, 2007, "Sources of Transaction Financing in Corporate Takeovers," Working Paper, Tilburg University.

Masulis, R. W., C. Wand and F. Xie, 2007, "Corporate Governance and Acquirer Returns," *Journal of Finance*, 62, 1851–1889.

McAfee, P. and D. McMillan, 1987, "Auctions and Bidding," *Journal of Economic Literature*, 25, 699–738.

Meulbroek, L., 1992, "An Empirical Analysis of Illegal Insider Trading," *Journal of Finance*, 47, 1661–1699.

Mitchell, M. and J. H. Mulherin, 1996, "The Impact of Industry Shocks on Takeover and Restructuring Activity," *Journal of Financial Economics*, 41, 193–229.

Moeller, T., 2005, "Let's Make a Deal! How Shareholders Control Impacts Merger Payoff," *Journal of Financial Economics*, 76, 167–190.

Moeller, S. B., F. P. Schlingemann and R. M. Stulz, 2004, "Firm Size and the Gains from Acquisitions," *Journal of Financial Economics*, 73, 201–228.

Moeller, S. B., F. P. Schlingemann and R. M. Stulz, 2005, "Wealth Destruction on a Massive Scale? A Study of Acquiring Firm Returns in the Recent Merger Wave," *Journal of Finance*, 60, 757–782.

Moeller, S. B., F. P. Schlingemann and R. M. Stulz, 2007, "How Do Diversity of Opinion and Information Asymmetry Affect Acquirer Returns?" *Review of Financial Studies*, 20, 2047–2078.

Molnar, J., 2008, "Preemptive Horizontal Mergers: Theory and Evidence," Working Paper, Bank of Finland.

Morellec, E. and A. Zhdanov, 2005, "The Dynamics of Mergers and Acquisitions," *Journal of Financial Economics*, 77, 649–672.

Mulherin, J. H. and A. L. Boone, 2000, "Comparing Acquisitions and Divestitures," *Journal of Corporate Finance*, 6, 117–139.

Myers, S. C., 1977, "Determination of Corporate Borrowing," *Journal of Financial Economics*, 4, 147–175.

Myers, S. C., 1984, "The Capital Structure Puzzle," *Journal of Finance*, 39, 575–592.

Myers, S. C. and N. S. Majluf, 1984, "Corporate Financing and Investment Decisions When Firms Have Information that Investors Do Not Have," *Journal of Financial Economics*, 13, 187–221.

Nathan, K. S. and T. B. O'Keefe, 1989, "The Rise in Takeover Premiums: An Exploratory Study," *Journal of Financial Economics*, 23, 101–119.

Officer, M. S., 2003, "Termination Fees in Mergers and Acquisitions," *Journal of Financial Economics*, 69, 431–467.

Officer, M. S., 2004, "Collars and Renegotiations in Mergers and Acquisitions," *Journal of Finance*, 59, 2719–2743.

Officer, M. S., 2006, "The Market Pricing of Implicit Options in Merger Collars," *Journal of Business*, 79, 115–136.

Officer, M. S., 2007, "The Price of Corporate Liquidity: Acquisition Discounts for Unlisted Targets," *Journal of Financial Economics*, 83, 571–598.

Officer, M. S., A. B. Poulsen and M. Stegemoller, 2009, "Target-firm Information Asymmetry and Acquirer Returns," *Review of Financial Studies*, 467–493.

Pulvino, T., 1998, "Do Asset Fire-Sales Exist? An Empirical Investigation of Commercial Aircraft Transactions," *Journal of Finance*, 53, 939–978.

Pulvino, T., 1999, "Effects of Bankruptcy Court Protection on Asset Sales," *Journal of Financial Economics*, 52, 151–186.

Ramey, V. A. and M. D. Shapiro, 2001, "Displaced Capital: A Study of Aerospace Plant Closings," *Journal of Political Economy*, 109, 958–992.

Rhodes-Kropf, M. and S. Viswanathan, 2004, "Market Valuation and Merger Waves," *Journal of Finance*, 59, 2685–2718.

Rhodes-Kropf, M., D. T. Robinson and S. Viswanathan, 2005, "Valuation Waves and Merger Activity: The Empirical Evidence," *Journal of Financial Economics*, 77, 561–603.

Roll, R., 1986, "The Hubris Hypothesis of Corporate Takeovers," *Journal of Business*, 59, 437–467.

Rose, M. J., 2009, "Heterogeneous Impacts of Staggered Boards by Ownership Concentration," *Journal of Corporate Finance*, 15, 113–128.

Ross, S., 1977, "The Determination of Financial Structure: The Incentive Signalling Approach," *Bell Journal of Economics*, 8, 23–40.

Savor, P., 2006, "Do Stock Mergers Create Value for Acquirers?" Working Paper, Wharton School of Business.

Schipper, K. and R. Thompson, 1983, "Evidence on the Capitalized Value of Merger Activity for Acquiring Firms," *Journal of Financial Economics*, 11, 85–119.

Schlingemann, F. P., 2004, "Financing Decisions and Bidder Gains," *Journal of Corporate Finance*, 10, 683–701.

Schwert, G. W., 1996, "Markup Pricing in Mergers and Acquisitions," *Journal of Financial Economics*, 41, 153–192.

Schwert, G. W., 2000, "Hostility in Takeovers: In the Eyes of the Beholder?" *Journal of Finance*, 55, 2599–2640.

Servaes, H., 1991, "Tobin's *q* and the Gains from Takeovers," *Journal of Finance*, 46, 409–419.

Shahrur, H., 2005, "Industry Structure and Horizontal Takeovers: Analysis of Wealth Effects on Rivals, Suppliers, and Corporate Customers," *Journal of Financial Economics*, 76, 61–98.

Shapley, L., 1953, "A Value for n-Person Games," In H. Kuhn and A. Tucker (Eds.), *Contributions to the Theory of Games, Volume II*, vol. 28, Princeton University Press, Princeton, Annals of Mathematics Studies, pp. 307–317.

Shleifer, A. and R. W. Vishny, 1986, "Large Shareholders and Corporate Control," *Journal of Political Economy*, 94, 461–488.

Shleifer, A. and R. W. Vishny, 1992, "Liquidation Values and Debt Capacity: A Market Equilibrium Approach," *Journal of Finance*, 47, 1343–1366.

Shleifer, A. and R. Vishny, 2003, "Stock Market Driven Acquisitions," *Journal of Financial Economics*, 70, 295–311.

Slovin, M. B., M. E. Sushka and C. D. Hudson, 1991, "Deregulation, Contestability, and Airline Acquisitions," *Journal of Financial Economics*, 30, 231–251.

Smith, R. L. and J. H. Kim, 1994, "The Combined Effect of Free Cash Flow and Financial Slack on Bidder and Target Stock Return," *Journal of Business*, 67, 281–310.

Song, M. H. and R. A. Walkling, 2000, "Abnormal Returns to Rivals of Acquisition Targets: A Test of the Acquisition Probability Hypothesis," *Journal of Financial Economics*, 55, 143–172.

Song, M. H. and R. A. Walkling, 2005, "Anticipation, Acquisitions and Bidder Returns," Working Paper, LeBow College of Business.

Spiller, P. T., 1983, "The Differential Effect of Airline Regulation on individual firms and Markets: An Empirical Analysis," *Journal of Law and Economics*, 26, 655–689.

Stulz, R., 1988, "Managerial Control of Voting Rights: Financing Policies and the Market for Corporate Control," *Journal of Financial Economics*, 20, 25–54.

Thorburn, K. S., 2000, "Bankruptcy Auctions: Costs, Debt Recovery, and Firm Survival," *Journal of Financial Economics*, 58, 337–368.

Toffanin, M., 2005, "Examining the Implications of Financing Choice for Cash Acquisitions," Unpublished Master of Science Dissertation, Concordia University.

Travlos, N. G., 1987, "Corporate Takeover Bids, Method of Payment, and Bidding Firms' Stock Returns," *Journal of Finance*, 42, 943–963.

Walkling, R., 1985, "Predicting Tender Offer Success: A Logistic Analysis," *Journal of Financial and Quantitative Analysis*, 20, 461–478.

Walkling, R. A. and M. S. Long, 1984, "Agency Theory, Managerial Welfare, and Takeover Bid Resistance," *RAND Journal of Economics*, 15, 54–68.

Williamson, O. E., 1988, "Corporate Finance and Corporate Governance," *Journal of Finance*, 43, 567–592.

Wulf, J., 2004, "Do CEOs in Mergers Trade Power for Premium? Evidence from Mergers of Equals," *Journal of Law, Economics and Organization*, 20, 60–101.

Yermack, D., 2006, "Golden Handshakes: Separation Pay for Retired and Dismissed CEOs," *Journal of Accounting and Economics*, 41, 237–256.

Yook, K. C., 2003, "Larger Returns to Cash Acquisitions: Signaling Effect or Leverage Effect?" *Journal of Business*, 76, 477–498.

Zingales, L., 1994, "The Value of the Voting Right: A Study of the Milan Stock Exchange Experience," *Review of Financial Studies*, 7, 125–148.

PART 2

TOEHOLDS, COMPETITION, WINNER'S CURSE, AND OVERCONFIDENCE: DO BIDDERS BEHAVE STRATEGICALLY?

Chapter 4

MERGER NEGOTIATIONS AND THE TOEHOLD PUZZLE*

SANDRA BETTON

John Molson School of Business, Concordia University, Montreal, Quebec, Canada

B. ESPEN ECKBO

Tuck School of Business at Dartmouth, Hanover, New Hampshire, USA

KARIN S. THORBURN

Tuck School of Business at Dartmouth, Hanover, New Hampshire, USA

Contents

* We are grateful for the comments of Eric de Bodt, Arturo Bris, Diego Garcia, Dalida Kadyrzhanova, Kai Li, Jun Qian, Matthew Rhodes-Kropf, and an anonymous referee. We also appreciate suggestions made by seminar participants at Berkeley, Boston College, Dartmouth, London Business School, Rice, Stanford, the Norwegian School of Economics and Business Administration, the Norwegian School of Management (BI), the universities of Amsterdam, British Columbia, Exeter, Oslo, Texas at Dallas, and Vienna, and Vanderbilt University. This paper was presented at the 2006 Western, Northern, and European Finance Meetings, and the 2007 UNC/Jackson Hole finance conference.

This article originally appeared in the *Journal of Financial Economics*, Vol. 91, pp. 158–178 (2009).
Corporate Takeovers, Volume 2
Edited by B. Espen Eckbo
DOI: 10.1016/B978-0-12-381982-6.00004-5

Abstract

The substantial control premium typically observed in corporate takeovers makes a compelling case for acquiring target shares (a toehold) in the market prior to launching a bid. Moreover, auction theory suggests that toehold bidding may yield a competitive advantage over rival bidders. Nevertheless, with a sample exceeding 10,000 initial control bids for US public targets, we show that toehold bidding has declined steadily since the early 1980s and is now surprisingly rare. At the same time, the average toehold is large when it occurs (20%), and toeholds are the norm in hostile bids. To explain these puzzling observations, we develop and test a two-stage takeover model where attempted merger negotiations are followed by open auction. With optimal bidding, a toehold imposes a cost on target management, causing some targets to (rationally) reject merger negotiations. Optimal toeholds are therefore either zero (to avoid rejection costs) or greater than a threshold (so that toehold benefits offset rejection costs). The toehold threshold estimate averages 9% across initial bidders, reflecting in part the bidder's opportunity loss of a merger termination agreement. In the presence of market liquidity costs, a threshold of this size may well induce a broad range of bidders to select zero toehold. As predicted, the probability of toehold bidding decreases, and the toehold size increases, with the threshold estimate. The model also predicts a relatively high frequency of toehold bidding in hostile bids, as observed. Overall, our test results are consistent with rational bidder behavior with respect to the toehold decision.

Keywords

takeover premium, toehold, termination agreement, merger negotiation, auction, target resistance

JEL classification: G3, G34

1. Introduction

Given substantial takeover premiums, one would expect a large number of bidders to establish a toehold by purchasing target shares in the market prior to launching the bid. A toehold not only reduces the number of shares that must be purchased at the full takeover premium, it is sold at an even greater premium whenever a rival bidder wins the target. Moreover, since the expected toehold gain raises the bidder's valuation of the target, it induces more aggressive bidding which can help deter competition from rivals and overcome target free-rider problems.[1] Empirically, Walkling (1985), Jennings and Mazzeo (1993), and Betton and Eckbo (2000) report that toehold bidding increases the probability of winning the target. Moreover, Eckbo and Langohr (1989) and Betton and Eckbo (2000) report that toeholds are associated with lower offer premiums in winning bids, which is consistent with a deterrent effect of toeholds on bidder competition.[2]

Bidder toehold benefits notwithstanding, we document that toehold bidding has declined dramatically since the 1980s and is now rare. Over the period 1973–2002, only 13% of 10,000+ initial bidders seeking control of publicly traded US targets have toeholds. Even more striking, only 3% acquire toeholds during the 6-month period leading up to the initial offer announcement, the period when the actual bid strategy is being formulated. The annual toehold frequency reached a high in the early 1980s and has since been steadily declining, despite a general increase in market liquidity over the same period. At the same time, toeholds tend to be large when they exist—on average 20%—so actual toeholds center on either zero or a substantial fraction of the target shares. We also show that toehold bidding is the norm in hostile bids (50% frequency), more frequent when the initial bid is a tender offer rather than a merger bid, and more frequent when the bidder is a private company rather than a publicly traded firm.

To help explain these puzzling observations, we develop and test a novel two-stage takeover model in which merger negotiations explicitly take place in the "shadow" of an open auction. The target's willingness to enter negotiations and the terms of the merger agreement are determined by the expected auction outcome. This setup has two distinct advantages. First, it reflects an important fiduciary requirement under Delaware case law, namely that the target board of directors must consider any additional bids materializing in the interim period after concluding merger negotiations but before final shareholder approval of the merger agreement. Approval requires a target shareholder vote, a bidder shareholder vote if the bidder issues new shares of 20% or

---

[1] Grossman and Hart (1980), Shleifer and Vishny (1986), Hirshleifer and Titman (1990), and Bulow et al. (1999).

[2] Betton and Eckbo (2000) also show that rivals who enter the auction have toeholds of a similar size on average as the initial bidder—as if to level the playing field (Bulow et al., 1999; Dasgupta and Tsui, 2004). Eckbo and Thorburn (2009) show that the degree of debt impairment, which has incentive effects analogous to toeholds, affects takeover premiums in bankruptcy auctions.

more to pay for the target, and regulatory (such as antitrust) consent. The approval process averages 5 months for the successful initial bidders in our sample which gives potential rival bidders ample time to compete. The fact that the target board must have a "fiduciary out" during this waiting period has contributed to the widespread inclusion of provisions for target termination fees in merger agreements, which play a key role in our model as well.

The second advantage of our two-stage takeover game (merger negotiations followed by open auction) is that it allows us to solve explicitly for the optimal decision by target management to accept or reject the initial bidder's invitation to negotiate. The target decision criterion in turn dictates an equilibrium toehold strategy for the initial bidder which is testable—the ultimate goal of this paper. A key model feature is that approaching the target with a toehold may impede the bidder's attempt to start negotiations. Toeholds antagonize some targets because with optimal bidding toeholds directly reduce target management's expected private benefits of control (by increasing the probability that the initial bidder wins the second-stage auction). Thus, our model captures the notion frequently heard in practice that toehold bidding is "aggressive" towards the target. The implication is a "toehold threshold" strategy in equilibrium: approach the target with a zero toehold (to avoid rejection costs) or acquire a toehold greater than a certain threshold. The threshold is the toehold at which toehold-benefits equal toehold-induced rejection costs. To our knowledge, ours is the only model in the literature which delivers the bimodal toehold distribution (centered on either zero or large toeholds) observed in the data.

Cross-sectional tests of the toehold threshold model require estimating the threshold value for each initial bidder in the sample. An important input into this estimation is the cost to the bidder of the target refusing to negotiate. In practice, rejection costs range from extra due diligence costs whenever the target refuses to open its books to the bidder to wealth transfers from enforcing poison pills. We focus in this paper on a particular, quantifiable rejection cost: the opportunity loss of a target termination agreement. Termination provisions, which stipulate a form of bidder compensation if the target withdraws from the negotiated agreement, have evolved since the mid-1980s and is now common in friendly deals.[3] Our toehold threshold incorporates the opportunity loss of a breakup fee, fully accounting for the impact of the fee on the optimal auction bids. In this framework, toeholds and termination agreements arise endogenously as economic substitutes—in equilibrium you can have one but not necessarily both.

The theoretical threshold value function is increasing in the bidder's private valuation of the target, the size of the termination fee, and the probability that the target rejects all bids. The latter probability is as high as 30% across the full sample and (surprisingly) greater when the initial bid is a merger rather than a tender offer.

---

[3] The typical form of compensation, used below, is a fixed breakup fee (Bates and Lemmon, 2003; Boone and Mulherin, 2007a; Burch, 2001; Officer, 2003).

The no-bidder-wins probability plays an important role in the tradeoff between a toehold and a termination agreement because only the latter provides the bidder with a payment when the target rejects all offers. Thus, the greater no-bidder-wins probability, the greater the relative advantage of a termination agreement over a toehold, which is reflected in a greater toehold threshold value.

The estimated toehold threshold averages 9% across the total sample. In the presence of transaction costs of acquiring a toehold, a threshold of this size could well induce a broad range of bidders to prefer a zero toehold—as the data indicate. Cross-sectional regressions also confirm that the probability of toehold bidding decreases, and the actual toehold size increases, in the toehold threshold estimate.

Moreover, the toehold threshold model is consistent with the observed greater toehold frequency in hostile bids. Intuitively, given substantial toehold benefits, toehold bidding is always optimal when the target's decision to resist the takeover is *independent* of the bidder's toehold. When the target management is highly entrenched (enjoying substantial private benefits of control), it will defend itself against any bidder—toehold or not. In this case, the toehold opportunity cost is zero, making toehold bidding optimal. Interestingly, if toeholds are primarily used as a means to overcome hostile target managements, then we would also expect the overall toehold bidding frequency to decline along with a decline in the frequency of hostile takeovers, which is precisely what we observe.

Finally, we present new evidence on the valuation effects of toehold bidding. Of particular interest is the potential for a negative return on the toehold investment when all bids fail. While our model abstracts from this type of toehold loss, significant negative target returns in the no-bidder-wins outcome could also deter toehold purchases ex ante (Goldman and Qian, 2005). As in Bradley et al. (1983), we show that target abnormal stock returns through the entire contest is on average indistinguishable from zero when all bids are rejected. However, we also find that target returns in the no-bidder-wins outcome are increasing in bidder toeholds. Overall, the potential for negative toehold returns when all bids fail is unlikely to explain the pervasive bidder preference for zero toehold.

The paper is organized as follows. Section 2 develops the structure of the takeover game, explains the intuition behind the toehold threshold bidding, and presents the paper's main testable hypothesis. Section 3 explains the data collection and the construction of takeover contests, and describes our new evidence on toehold bidding frequencies. We test our toehold threshold theory in Section 4. Section 5 presents estimates of the impact of toeholds on bidder returns, and Section 6 concludes the paper.

2. Optimal toehold strategies

In this section, we develop the structure of our takeover game and discuss properties of the implied toehold threshold. All proofs are in the Appendix.

2.1. Game structure, payoffs, and optimal bids

The game structure is shown in Figure 1. In the first stage, target management accepts or rejects an invitation by the initial bidder (B1) to negotiate a merger. In the second stage, there is an auction for the target where B1 competes with a single rival bidder B2. If the target rejects B1's initial merger proposal (lower Stage-1 branch in Figure 1), B1 launches an unsolicited (hostile) tender offer in the second stage. If, however, the target accepts negotiations (upper Stage-1 branch), the second-stage auction is friendly, effectively taking place in the interim period until final shareholder approval of the negotiated agreement. The key parameters are as follows:

(1) *Toehold* (α): B1 bids with a toehold $\alpha \in [0, 0.5)$, acquired at the normalized pregame target share price of zero. B2's toehold is always zero.
(2) *Termination fee* (t): In merger negotiations, the target awards B1 a termination agreement with a breakup fee of $t \in [0, \nu]$, where $\nu \in [0, 1]$ is the bidder's private valuation of the target. The fee is payable to B1 whenever the target withdraws, which happens either if B2 wins or if the target rejects all bids.

STAGE 1: Merger negotiations **STAGE 2:** Public auction

Target's decision	Target is acquired (1-θ), or all bids fail (θ)	Who wins the auction?	Retention of private benefits β?	Target management utility U	Initial bidder payoff Π
Accept merger bid	1-θ	Initial bidder wins	no (no resistance)	p_2	$v-(1-\alpha)p_2$
		Rival bidder wins	no (breakup)	p^*	αp^*+t
	θ	No bidder wins	yes	$\beta-t$	$t(1-\alpha)$
Reject merger bid	1-θ	Initial bidder wins	no (target resists)	p_2	$v-r-(1-\alpha)p_2$
		Rival bidder wins	yes (white knight)	$\beta+p^*$	αp^*
	θ	No bidder wins	yes	β	0

Fig. 1. The takeover game: attempted merger negotiations (Stage 1) followed by auction (Stage 2). The pregame target share price is normalized to $p = 0$. The payoff to target management is $U \equiv \beta + p$, where β is private benefits of control and p is the price paid by the winner in the auction. The initial bidder B1's private valuation of the target is v and it has a toehold α. B1 approaches the target with an offer to negotiate a merger in which it receives a termination fee t if the target withdraws, and where B1 will remove β. The target's decision whether or not to accept merger negotiations is always followed by a sealed-bid second-price auction, where rival bidder B2 enters without a toehold and bids p_2 while B1 bids p^*. If the target accepts negotiations, B2 will remove β. If the target rejects negotiations, B1 makes a hostile tender offer while B2 is a white knight allowing target management to retain β. In the hostile auction, the target imposes a bidder-specific resistance cost r on B1. If all bids fail, which happens with probability θ, the target stock price falls back to zero.

(3) *Private benefits (β)*: The target management enjoys private benefits of control $\beta \in [0, 1]$. If the target accepts negotiations, the winner of the second-stage auction (B1 or B2) removes β. If the target rejects merger negotiations, however, the target brings in B2 as a white knight in the hostile auction. The white knight allows target management to retain β if it wins. For simplicity, we assume that the retention of β does not reduce B2's valuation of the target.

(4) *Resistance costs (r)*: When the target rejects negotiations and B1 launches a hostile bid, the target imposes a bidder-specific resistance cost $r \in [0, \nu]$ on B1, reducing B1's valuation from ν to $\nu - r$.[4]

(5) *No-bidder-wins probability (θ)*: The auction has three possible outcomes: B1 wins, B2 wins, or no bidder wins. The no-bidder-wins outcome occurs with probability θ, determined by exogenous factors that can derail merger negotiations or cause all bidders to abandon a takeover auction. θ is not to be confused with the conditional probability that B1 defeats B2 in the auction, which is determined endogenously by the bids.

This structure yields the payoff Π to B1 and the utility U of target management shown in Figure 1 for each of the six outcomes in the game. The total utility of target management is given by $U \equiv \beta + p$, where p is the price paid by the winning bidder in the auction. Thus, we assume that target management values the offer premium p as much as target shareholders do. However, target management's incentives are not fully aligned with shareholders: the risk of losing β means that management will refuse merger negotiations in some states where shareholders would have preferred to negotiate with B1.

To derive the payoffs, suppose the auction is second-price (the winner pays the loser's bid), and let p^* and p_2 denote the bids of B1 and B2, respectively:

- When the auction follows merger negotiations, B1 pays p_2 for the remaining $1 - \alpha$ target shares if it wins, resulting in $\Pi = \nu - (1 - \alpha)p_2$ and $U = p_2$.

  If B2 wins, it pays p^* for the target shares and the target pays t to B1, so $\Pi = \alpha p^* + t$ and $U = p^*$.

  If neither B1 nor B2 wins, the target pays t to B1 and the target share price falls back to $-t$ (the sum of the pretakeover price of zero and the cost of the termination fee), yielding $\Pi = t(1 - \alpha)$ and $U = \beta - t$.

- When the auction follows target rejection of merger negotiations, B1 makes a hostile tender offer without a termination agreement. In this case, if neither B1 nor B2 wins, $\Pi = 0$ and $U = \beta$.

---

[4] In our sample below, B2 wins six times more often when the target is hostile rather than friendly, possibly a direct effect of r reducing the initial bidder's valuation.

If B1 wins, $\Pi = v - r - (1 - \alpha)p_2$ and $U = p_2$, and if B2 wins (now as a white knight) $\Pi = \alpha p^*$ and $U = \beta + p^*$.

Given these payoffs, Proposition 1 shows the optimal bids in the Stage-2 auction with risk-neutral bidders. Bidder private valuations are i.i.d with distribution and density functions $G(v)$ and $g(v)$, respectively:

Proposition 1 (*Stage-2 auction bids*). *If the target agrees to negotiate in Stage 1, optimal Stage-2 bids are*

$$\text{B1:} \quad p^* = v + \alpha \left(\frac{1 - G(p^* + t)}{g(p^* + t)} \right) - t = \frac{v + \alpha}{1 + \alpha} - t,$$

$$\text{B2:} \quad p_2 = v_2 - t,$$

(1)

where the second equality for B1 invokes the uniform distribution $v \sim U[0, 1]$. If the target rejects merger negotiations in Stage 1, optimal Stage-2 bids are

$$\text{B1:} \quad p^* = v + \alpha \left(\frac{1 - G(p^*)}{g(p^*)} \right) - r = \frac{v + \alpha - r}{1 + \alpha},$$

$$\text{B2:} \quad p_2 = v_2.$$

(2)

As shown by Burkart (1995) as well, in this auction setting B1's optimal bid p^* increases with α as the toehold induces B1 to overbid relative to its private valuation v. In addition, Proposition 1 incorporates the effects of the termination fee t and the resistance cost r. The existence of the termination fee reduces p^* and p_2 by the full value of t (i.e., underbidding). Interestingly, although the fee is costly to B2 (who effectively pays t), t lowers B1's optimal bid to the point where t does *not* affect competition between the two bidders. This result contradicts the notion that termination fees are designed to help protect entrenched target managements against rival bidders. Instead, we view the fee simply as a device to protect the value of proprietary bidder information revealed during negotiations.

The resistance cost r reduces B1's bid but not the bid of B2 and therefore provides a competitive advantage for B2 when it is playing the role as a white knight. Notice also that, because there are no price-dependent payoffs to either B1 or B2 in the no-bidder-wins outcome, none of the optimal bids in Proposition 1 are affected by θ.

2.2. Target management's optimal response

It follows from Proposition 1 that B1's toehold raises $E(p)$ (through overbidding) and lowers the expected private benefit $E(\beta)$ (as overbidding raises the probability that B1 wins the auction). Moreover, a target rejection in Stage 1 lowers $E(p)$ by lowering B1's bid (reflecting the resistance costs and the absence of a termination fee that follow rejection). The relative importance of these effects for $E(U)$ gives rise to the three distinct regions for the private benefits of control β depicted in Figure 2, and which determine the optimal target response to B1's invitation to negotiate a merger:

1. Target managment's optimal response conditional on the bidder's toehold:

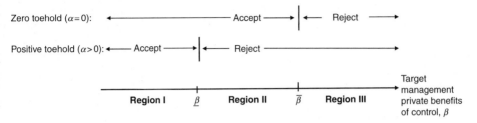

2. Bidder's optimal toehold strategy given the target's optimal response:

Fig. 2. Optimal target management response in Stage 1 of the takeover game, and the initial bidder's toehold strategy. The initial bidder decides on a zero or positive toehold α before approaching the target with an invitation to negotiate a merger. Target management's optimal response depends on its private benefits of control β and the bidder's toehold α. The bidder designs an optimal toehold strategy considering the target's optimal response.

Proposition 2 (*Target's decision in Stage 1*). *Suppose target management maximizes $E(U) \equiv E(\beta) + E(p)$ subject to the optimal Stage-2 auction bids in Proposition 1. The target accepts or rejects B1's offer to negotiate in Stage 1 as follows:*

$$\text{accept for any } \alpha \text{ when } \beta < \underline{\beta} \text{ (Region I)},$$
$$\text{accept if } \alpha = 0 \text{ and reject if } \alpha > 0 \text{ when } \underline{\beta} \le \beta \le \bar{\beta} \text{ (Region II)}, \qquad (3)$$
$$\text{reject for any } \alpha \text{ when } \beta > \bar{\beta} \text{ (Region III)},$$

where the limits when $v \sim U[0, 1]$ are

$$\underline{\beta} = \left[\frac{1}{2}r^2 + r(1-v) + \left(\frac{1}{2}t^2 - \frac{t}{1-\theta} \right)(1+\alpha)^2 \right]$$
$$\times \left(\frac{1}{(1-v+r)(1+\alpha)} \right),$$
$$\bar{\beta} = \left[\frac{1}{2}r^2 + r(1-v) + \frac{1}{2}t^2 - \frac{t}{1-\theta} \right]\left(\frac{1}{1-v+r} \right).$$

The optimal target response is illustrated in Figure 2. Targets that are only mildly entrenched (Region I with $\beta < \underline{\beta}$) value the expected takeover premium $E(p)$ sufficiently to always accept B1's invitation to negotiate. Conversely, highly entrenched targets (Region III where $\beta > \bar{\beta}$) always reject B1's invitation. This is because the reduction in $E(\beta)$ resulting from a takeover by B1 more than offsets the positive premium effect. In Region III, rejection is optimal despite the negative effect of the resistance cost r on $E(p)$ when B1 is forced to make a hostile bid.

However, B1's toehold plays a pivotal role for the target accept/reject decision when β falls in the middle range (Region II where $\underline{\beta} \leq \beta \leq \bar{\beta}$). In Region II, the marginal impact of the toehold is such that the target management optimally accepts negotiations if $\alpha = 0$ and rejects if $\alpha > 0$. Targets in this region are willing to negotiate a takeover with B1, but only if B1 has no toehold. In other words, in this region, B1's toehold *by itself* antagonizes (rational) target management enough to impede merger negotiations.

2.3. Optimal toehold strategy

B1's optimal toehold strategy follows from optimal bidding (Proposition 1) and the target's response (Proposition 2):

Proposition 3 (*Toehold strategy*). *Let $\hat{\alpha}$ denote a toehold threshold that makes B1 indifferent between a toehold of zero and of $\hat{\alpha}$ in Region II of Proposition 2. B1's optimal toehold α is such that*

$$\alpha > 0 \text{ if } \beta < \underline{\beta} \text{ (Region I)},$$
$$\alpha = 0 \text{ or } \alpha \geq \hat{\alpha} \text{ if } \underline{\beta} \leq \beta \leq \bar{\beta} \text{ (Region II)}, \qquad (4)$$
$$\alpha > 0 \text{ if } \beta > \bar{\beta} \text{ (Region III)},$$

where the toehold threshold when $v \sim U[0,1]$ is given by

$$\hat{\alpha}(\theta,t,v,r) = -k_1 + \sqrt{k_1^2 + k_2},$$
$$k_1 = v - r - \frac{1}{2}(v^2 - t^2) - \frac{t}{1-\theta}, \qquad (5)$$
$$k_2 = r(2v - r) + t\left(\frac{2}{1-\theta} - t\right).$$

Proposition 3 shows that in Region II toeholds are bimodal in equilibrium, centered on either zero or at least the threshold value $\hat{\alpha} > 0$. Figure 2 illustrates this strategy given the targets' optimal response. Obviously, when the target's response is independent of the toehold (Regions I and III), toehold bidding is always optimal. In this case, B1 captures toehold benefits without punity. Toehold benefits include reducing the fraction of the target shares that B1 must purchase at a premium to $1 - \alpha$, and providing a capital gain should B2 ultimately win the auction.

In Region II, however, the target rejects merger negotiations only if $\alpha > 0$. Because of this rejection, B1's choices are (i) approach the target with a zero toehold to avoid rejection or (ii) acquire a toehold which is large enough to offset the expected cost of toehold-induced target rejection of merger negotiations. Recall that target rejection implies that B1 foregoes the termination agreement (with a fee of t) and has to face resistance cost r when proceeding with the hostile auction in the second stage. The toehold threshold $\hat{\alpha}$ in Proposition 3 is the smallest toehold consistent with the choice under (ii). The choice between a zero toehold and one that exceeds the toehold threshold depends on the transaction costs of acquiring a toehold in the market (which are not included in Proposition 1). The greater the toehold transaction costs, the more likely one is to observe zero toeholds.

2.4. Toehold threshold properties and testable hypothesis

The toehold threshold $\hat{\alpha}$ in Proposition 3 is an increasing function of the four parameters θ, t, v, and r. Intuitively, because the termination fee but not the toehold provides B1 with a payment in the no-bidder-wins outcome, the advantage of termination agreements over toeholds increases with θ. Second, v and t both raise the payoffs under the termination contract. Since $\hat{\alpha}$ reflects the opportunity loss of this contract, it increases in t and v as well. Third, because the threshold must overcome the expected cost of rejection and target resistance, $\hat{\alpha}$ is also increasing in r.

In the empirical analysis, we replace the unknown resistance cost r with its minimum value $\bar{r}$ necessary for Region II to exist. From Proposition 2, Region II exists only if $\bar{\beta} > 0$. Setting $\bar{\beta} = 0$ and solving for r yields

$$\bar{r} = v - 1 + \sqrt{(1-v)^2 + 2t/(1-\theta) - t^2}. \tag{6}$$

Substituting $\bar{r}$ for r ensures that the estimated threshold value is consistent with the existence of Region II for each target. To see why, recall that Region II is where the target accepts negotiations if and only if B1's toehold is zero. Accepting negotiations is costly as it reduces $E(\beta)$ and it requires granting a termination agreement which reduces $E(p)$ (Proposition 1). Thus, if rejection were costless, the target would always reject, and Region II would not exist. The cost r ensures that rejection is also costly for the target because it reduces the expected takeover premium $E(p)$ by reducing B1's optimal bid. The minimum resistance cost $\bar{r}$ is such that rejection is sufficiently costly for targets to accept negotiations when α is zero.

We test for the existence of toehold threshold bidding using values of θ, t, and v estimated from the data, and $\bar{r}$ computed using Equation (6). The main empirical hypothesis is as follows:

H1 (*Toehold threshold bidding*). *Let $c(\alpha) > 0$ denote the transaction costs of acquiring a toehold of α, where $\partial c/\partial \alpha > 0$. The toehold strategy in Proposition 1 predicts that*

(i)   *the probability of observing $\alpha > 0$ decreases in the threshold $\hat{\alpha}$,*
(ii) *conditional on $\alpha > 0$, α increases in $\hat{\alpha}$,*
(iii) *the probability of observing $\alpha > 0$ is greater when the bidder expects target management to reject all bids irrespective of α.*

H1(i) and H1(ii) refer to Region II in Proposition 3, where bidders are indifferent between approaching the target with a zero toehold or with a toehold equal to the threshold $\hat{\alpha}$. The toehold transaction cost $c(\alpha)$ breaks this indifference in favor of selecting a zero toehold. The positive derivative $\partial c/\partial \alpha$ reflects the increasing nature of illiquidity and information costs that are part of $c(\alpha)$, and it renders toehold bidding less likely for greater thresholds. H1(iii) refers to Region III, in which target management is sufficiently entrenched to resist all bids regardless of the toehold.

For the purpose of the empirical tests of H1 below, recall that target hostility is endogenously triggered by B1's toehold in Region II only. This endogeneity is accounted for by modeling B1's toehold decision as a function of $\hat{\alpha}$. In Region III, however, target hostility is exogenous to B1 while at the same time inducing B1 to bid with a toehold. To account for Region III, we therefore include proxies for expected hostility in the regressions determining B1's toehold choice. Moreover, since the no-bidder-wins outcome follows target resistance to all bids (regardless of toeholds), we also include these proxies when estimating θ.[5]

3. Sample of takeover contests

3.1. Definition and construction of contests

As in Betton and Eckbo (2000), we group successive bids for the same target into a takeover contest. A contest can have a single control bid, multiple bids by a single bidder, or multiple bidders. Our use of the term "contest" emphasizes the fact that, ex ante, any attempt to acquire control of the target is subject to a competing bid (including competition from the target management itself). As explained in the Introduction, this is true also for signed merger agreements, as the target board has a fiduciary responsibility to consider any rival offer until the agreement is finally approved by shareholders. In our definition, a control bid initiates the contest if there are no other public control bids for the same target over the preceding 6 months. All subsequent control bids within 6 months of a previous bid belong to the same contest. The contest ends when there are no additional control bids for the same target over the following 6-month period.

To identify the initial control bidder, we first sample bids from the Thomson Financial SDC Merger and Acquisitions data base. From January 1980 through December 2002, SDC contains 13,896 control bids for US publicly traded firms with transaction form M (merger) or AM (acquisition of majority interest). A control bid is defined as the bidder owning less than 50% of the target shares prior to the bid and seeking to own at least 50% of the target shares after completion of the transaction. We further include 1106 tender offers for control identified by Betton and Eckbo (2000) that are not in SDC. In addition,

---

[5] Proposition 1 also predicts toehold bidding in Region I, where target managements driven largely by $E(p)$ always accept B1's invitation to negotiate. We do not pursue this prediction because we are essentially unable to empirically classify a target as being in Region I. However, we present some evidence suggestive of Region I by referring to private bidders below.

a search for tender offers in the Wall Street Journal (WSJ) identifies 200 control bids also not in SDC, producing a total of 15,197 bids for control. Reading the WSJ and the SDC history, we include any additional information on tender offer announcement dates, rival bids and toeholds. With our contest definition, the bids take place in 12,721 takeover contests. Finally, we require the target to be listed on the Center for Research in Security Prices (CRSP) data base, which eliminates 1915 contests, for a total sample of 10,806 control contests over the period 1973–2002.[6]

3.2. Sample characteristics

As shown in the second column of Table 1, two-thirds of the total number of initial bids (7076 cases) are from the period 1990–2002, and 7750 or 72% of the total are merger bids. A bid is a merger if it has transaction form M and is not flagged as a tender offer in SDC. All other bids are tender offers. A total of 6726 or 62% of the bidders are publicly traded.[7] The target receives publicly announced control bids from two or more bidders in 862 or 8% of the contests. The target management is hostile in 511 (5%) of the contests. (The target's response is classified as friendly if SDC or the WSJ characterize the response as positive or neutral, or a response is not recorded, and hostile otherwise.) While not shown in the table, targets are hostile in 10% of the cases prior to 1990 and in 2% after 1989. Moreover, tender offers trigger hostility four times as often as merger bids (10% vs. 2%), and multiple-bidder contests are associated with target hostility in 14% of the cases versus 4% in single-bidder contests. The initial bidder offers an all-cash payment to the target in 4185 cases (39%).

Columns 3 and 4 of Table 1 show the mean and median deal values. Deal value is available for 8271 targets, with missing information primarily for the no-bidder-wins outcome. The median is substantially smaller than the mean, indicating a skewed distribution. For the total sample, the average deal size is $715 million with a median of $89 million. The deal size is greater in the second part of the sample period, in merger deals (on average twice the size of tender offers), when the bidder is public, when the contest develops multiple bidders, and when the payment is all stock or mixed cash and securities. The largest average deal size in the sample occurs when the target is hostile: $1204 million versus $688 million in friendly deals.

We are able to classify the outcome for 10,619 contests. The initial bidder wins in 67% of the cases. The initial bidder fails either because a rival bidder wins (4% of all

---

[6] The formation of contests and the CRSP listing requirement reduces the number of non-SDC cases from 1306 to 400 (all tender offers), of which 395 are from Betton and Eckbo (2000) and five from the WSJ search. Moreover, of these 400 cases, three quarters are in the pre-SDC period 1973–1980 and the remainder from the early SDC years (the 1980s). These non-SDC cases have similar sample characteristics as the SDC sample and are not singled out below.

[7] The 4080 private bidders include 754 subsidiaries, four government-owned companies, 19 investor groups, 45 joint ventures, and eight mutual companies. Private bidders select a merger bid somewhat less often than public bidders (64% vs. 76%).

Table 1

The total sample of 10,806 control contests for public US targets, 1973–2002

The contest sample is constructed as follows: Between 1/1980 and 12/2002, the SDC Merger and Acquisitions data base contains 13,896 control bids for US publicly traded firms with transaction form "M" (merger) or "AM" (acquisition of majority interest). A control bid is defined as the bidder owning less than 50% of the target shares prior to the bid and seeking to own at least 50% of the target shares. Successive control bids for the same target are then grouped into a control contest. A "contest" can have a single control bid, multiple bids by a single bidder, or multiple bidders. A given control bid initiates the contest if there are no other public control bids for the same target over the preceding 6 months. All subsequent control bids within 6 months of a previous bid belong to the same contest, and the contest ends when there are no additional control bids for the same target over the following 6-month period. We also include 1106 tender offers for control identified by Betton and Eckbo (2000) that are not found in SDC, and we update another 610 SDC records with information from that paper. In addition, we search the WSJ for tender offers, which produces 200 control bids also not in SDC. Reading the WSJ and the SDC history, we include any additional information on tender offer announcement dates, rival bids, and toeholds. This leaves a total of 15,197 bids for control. With our contest definition, these bids take place in a total of 12,721 takeover contests. When we also require the target to be listed on CRSP, the total sample becomes 10,806 control contests. The deal value is available for 8271 contests and the final contest outcome is classified for 10,619 contests. The initial offer premium is $p_{ini}/p_{-41} - 1$, where p_{ini} is the first offer price, p_{-41} is the target stock price on day -41 adjusted for splits and dividends, and 0 is the day of the initial control bid. The final offer premium is $p_{fin}/p_{-41} - 1$, where p_{fin} is the last offer price in the contest. We have data on offer premiums for a total of 6886 contests from SDC, WSJ and Betton and Eckbo (2000).

Sample	Number of cases	Deal value ($ million)		% of contests where the winner is			Average offer premium (%)	
		Mean	Median	Initial bidder	Rival	No bidder wins	Initial bid	Final bid
All contests	10,806	715	89	66.6	3.7	29.7	44.5	46.1
1973–1989	3730	312	60	58.7	5.2	36.1	45.0	48.5
1990–2002	7076	903	108	70.7	3.0	26.4	44.2	45.0
Merger bid	7750	827	92	63.5	3.3	33.2	43.6	44.5
Tender offer	3056	433	78	74.8	4.8	20.4	46.5	50.2
Acquirer public	6726	902	112	75.6	3.2	21.3	46.1	47.5
Acquirer private	4080	285	52	51.7	4.6	43.7	40.1	42.6
Single bidder	9944	693	88	70.5	0.0	29.5	44.8	45.4
Multiple bidders	862	989	101	20.6	47.8	31.7	41.1	53.2
Target friendly	10,295	688	85	68.0	3.2	28.8	44.1	45.1
Target hostile	511	1204	183	34.4	16.3	49.2	49.0	60.9
All cash	4185	320	66	69.1	4.0	27.0	44.1	46.6
Stock/mixed	6621	1048	119	65.0	3.6	31.4	44.7	45.8

contests) or because the target rejects all bids (30%). Interestingly, the initial bidder wins more often with a tender offer than with a merger bid (75% vs. 64%). Initiating a merger bid is riskier than a tender offer primarily because targets are more likely to reject all bids in mergers: 33% versus 20% in tender offers. Not surprising, target hostility increases the percent of the sample where no bidder wins from 29% to almost half (49%). Notice also that, in the overall sample, the probability of the no-bidder-wins outcome is substantially greater for private than for public bidders: 44% versus 21%.

Conditional on a rival bidder entering, the rival wins the contest twice as often as the initial bidder (48% vs. 21%). The entry of a rival does not materially change the sample proportion of the no-bidder-wins outcome. Moreover, when the initial bid is hostile, rivals win in 16% of the contests compared to only 3% when the target is friendly towards the initial bid. Thus, hostility increases both the chance of a rival bidder winning and the chance of a no-bidder-wins outcome. Overall, in hostile cases, the initial bidder succeeds in only 34% of the bids compared to a 68% initial bidder success rate in friendly deals.

The last two columns of Table 1 show average initial and final offer premiums. We use the former in our estimation of the toehold threshold below. The initial offer premium is defined as $(p_{ini}/p_{-41}) - 1$, where p_{ini} is the initial offer price and p_{-41} is the target share price listed on CRSP on day -41 relative to the initial offer date (adjusted for splits and dividends). The final offer premium is $(p_{fin}/p_{-41}) - 1$, where p_{fin} is the final price offered. Thus, the final premium is the total premium relative to the precontest target share price. With SDC as our primary source, we have offer premium data on a total of 6886 contests. When the initial offer price is missing in SDC, and SDC reports no bid revision by the same bidder, we use the final price offered by this bidder as our initial price.

The median offer premium is consistently a few percentage points lower than the mean, and we report only the mean in Table 1. The average initial offer premium is 44.5% across the total sample with premium data. The final premium is almost identical (46.1%) due to the large portion of contests in which the initial price is also the final price (single-bid contests). There is no discernible difference in initial and final offer premiums in the first and second parts of the sample period. Initial (final) offer premiums are 43.6% (44.5%) in mergers and 46.5% (50.2%) in tender offers.

Separating ex post single- and multiple-bidder contests, the average initial and final premiums in multiple-bidder contests are 41.1% and 53.2%, respectively. For single-bidder contests, the initial premium averages 44.8% (final 45.4%). Thus, as also found by Betton and Eckbo (2000), the initial bid in contests that develop bidder competition is slightly lower than the final (single) price in contests where no rival bidder enters to compete. While not a test of preemptive bidding, this finding is consistent with the argument that single-bid contests have only one bid because the initial bidder strategically raises the initial bid enough to deter competition (Fishman, 1989).

Table 1 also shows that initial (and final) offer premiums are lower at 40.1% when the bidder is private, versus 46.1% for public acquirers. Premiums are almost identical in all-cash and all-stock/mixed offers. Finally, contests with hostile targets have both the highest initial bid premium at 49.0% (vs. 44.1% for friendly targets) and final offer premium at 60.9% (vs. 45.1% for friendly targets).

3.3. Toeholds

A toehold is an ownership stake in the target held at the announcement of the initial bid. With our definition of a control bid, toeholds are less than 50% of the target shares. Beginning in 1980, the primary source of our toehold data is SDC for both mergers and tender offers. There are a total of 1363 positive toeholds in the sample. Of these 1363 toeholds, 885 are from SDC and 180 are from the 400 non-SDC cases. Of the remaining 298 toeholds, 202 are from the tender offers in Betton and Eckbo (2000) that overlap with SDC. Another 83 are found in SDC records of acquisitions of partial interest (form AP) in the target by the bidder within 6 months of the initial control bid, and the remaining 13 toeholds are from the WSJ and the SDC history field.

Missing toehold data are classified as a toehold of zero. As indicated above, the hand-collected information in Betton and Eckbo (2000) and the WSJ search allow usto replace some toeholds that are missing from SDC in the early period. SDCs overall reporting accuracy increases over the sample period. In fact, the WSJ search for toeholds in tender offers during the 1990s failed to identify any toeholds missing from SDC. Note that our tests below, which condition on the toehold being positive, are unlikely to be affected by the potential for missing toeholds. Also, while missing toehold data will introduce noise into our estimates of the probability of toehold bidding, lack of power is not an issue in the subsequent empirical analysis.

Figure 3 shows the annual toehold frequency for the initial merger bids and tender offers in our sample. The toehold frequency in tender offers increases during the 1970s and starts declining in the mid-1980s. For merger bids, the toehold frequency peaks in 1980 and again in 1986–1988, and then falls steadily towards the end of the sample period. Notice that this decline coincides with a general increase in stock market liquidity. Notice also that the increase in toehold frequency throughout the 1970s continues well after the passage of the 1968 Williams Act (mandating information disclosure in public tender offers) and the 1976 Hart-Scott-Rodino Act (mandating prenotification of mergers for antitrust review).

Table 2 lists additional information on the toehold frequency and size across bid categories. Of the 10,806 initial bidders, 13% have toeholds. The toehold frequency is substantially lower in the second half of our sample period (7% vs. 22%), and it is lower in merger bids (7%) than in tender offers (26%). There are toeholds in 12% of single-bidder contests, versus 18% in multiple-bidder contests. Toeholds are four times more frequent in hostile bids (50%) than in friendly bids (11%). There are also more toeholds among private bidders than public bidders (16% vs. 11%), and when a rival wins the contest.

We classify toeholds as long- and short-term using the reporting practice of SDC. A long-term toehold is defined as target shares held 6 months prior to the initial bid date. A short-term toehold is the incremental toehold purchased during the 6-month period leading up to the bid. Note that the merger negotiation process in itself limits short-term toehold acquisitions as defined here. It is common practice for bidders to sign a standstill agreement at the start of the negotiations. The length of these

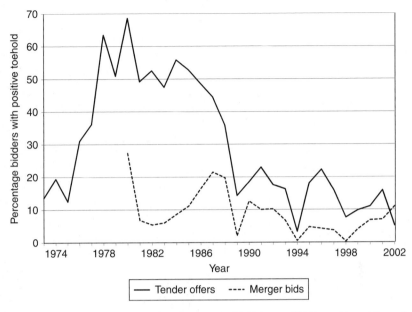

Fig. 3. Annual percentage of toehold bidders. Percentage of initial control bidders with positive toehold in the total sample of 3056 tender offers over the period 1973–2002, and in 7750 merger bids over the period 1980–2002. Targets are US domiciled and publicly traded.

negotiations, which take place prior to the public announcement of the merger, typically ranges from two to 6 months (Boone and Mulherin, 2007b; Bruner, 2004). Thus, for some bidders, negotiations could have prevented a short-term toehold acquisition in the 6-month look-back period prior to the announcement date. In the context of our threshold theory, signing a standstill agreement is itself a decision that involves the tradeoff between negotiations and an unsolicited bid. Thus, observing a zero short-term toehold carries information regardless of the constraint imposed by the negotiation process.

Of the 1363 toehold bidders, we are able to classify 970 toeholds as either long- or short-term. As shown in Table 2, 91% of these toehold bidders have a long-term toehold, and 22% acquire a short-term toehold. This means that in the overall sample of 10,000+ initial control bidders, only 3% have short-term toeholds. Moreover, 13% of the toehold bidders have both short- and long-term toeholds, and 14% of the bidders with a long-term toehold also acquire a short-term stake. Of the bidders with short-term toeholds, 41% have no long-term toehold. Table 2 also shows that the percentage of long-term toeholds is somewhat higher, and of short-term toeholds somewhat lower, in the second half of the sample period, in tender offers, and when the target is friendly.

Private toehold bidders have a high proportion of short-term toeholds at 25% versus 18% for public toehold bidders. Moreover, in hostile bids, 31% of toehold bidders have

Table 2

Characteristics of the initial control bidder's toehold, 1973–2002

The table shows the toehold of the initial control bidder in 10,806 contests for US targets listed on CRSP.
A toehold consists of target shares held by the acquirer prior to the announcement of the initial control bid.
The toehold information is from SDC, the WSJ, and Betton and Eckbo (2000). A long-term toehold is
purchased more than 6 months prior to the bid. A short-term toehold is purchased within the 6 months leading
up to the bid. For 393 tender offers, toeholds could not be classified as long- or short-term. The toehold size
reported in the table is conditional on a positive toehold.

Sample	Initial bidders with toehold		% of toehold bidders with[a]		Average toehold size in % of target shares		
	Number of cases	% of all bidders[b]	Long-term toehold	Short-term toehold	Total toehold	Long-term toehold	Short-term toehold
All contests	1363	12.6	91.1	21.6	20.0	20.2	12.6
1973–1989	832	22.3	88.2	25.4	18.7	18.2	11.2
1990–2002	531	7.5	93.7	18.4	22.0	21.9	14.2
Merger bid	558	7.2	89.1	26.0	19.0	18.9	11.1
Tender offer	805	26.3	93.9	15.8	20.6	21.8	15.8
Acquirer public	714	10.6	91.8	17.7	19.5	20.4	14.2
Acquirer private	649	15.9	90.6	24.9	20.4	20.1	11.6
Single bidder	1211	12.2	90.9	21.6	20.9	21.2	12.8
Multiple bidders	152	17.6	92.9	22.3	12.8	13.0	11.1
Target friendly	1106	10.7	92.0	20.4	21.9	21.6	13.1
Target hostile	257	50.3	85.1	30.6	11.5	10.0	10.1
Initial bidder wins	866	12.2	88.3	24.3	22.7	23.0	14.8
Rival wins	79	20.0	94.0	16.0	10.9	12.1	5.8
No bidder wins	354	11.2	97.6	15.0	16.4	16.6	6.7

[a]The percent of the total number of initial toehold bidders in the category specified by the row.
[b]The percent of the total number of initial bidders (with or without toehold) in the category specified
by the row.

a short-term toehold versus 20% in friendly bids with toeholds. Thus, 15% of all
bidders in hostile deals acquire a short-term toehold versus only 2% of all bidders in
friendly deals.

Conditional on being positive, the average toehold size is large: 20% of the target
shares. The average size of a long-term toehold is also 20% of the target equity, while
the average short-term toehold size is 13%. Since large toeholds can trigger significant
costs associated with liquidity and information disclosure (Bris, 2002; Ravid and
Spiegel, 1999), this short-term toehold size is particularly surprising. The average
toehold size increases somewhat from the 1980s to the 1990s. Toeholds are larger in
friendly than in hostile bids (22% vs. 11%), and in single-bidder contests versus
multiple-bidder contests (21% vs. 13%). Moreover, toeholds are on average greater
in contests where the initial bidder wins. The average size of long- and short-term
toeholds displays a similar pattern as the total toehold.

Panel A of Figure 4 plots the frequency distribution of the toehold size. About half of the toeholds exceed 15% of the target shares and are relatively evenly distributed between 15% and 50%. One-sixth of the toeholds are less than 5% with a peak in the distribution of toeholds between 5% and 10%. Panel B of Figure 4 shows the relative distribution of short- and long-term toeholds across different toehold sizes. Long-term toeholds have a fatter right tail than short-term toeholds, with two-thirds exceeding 10% of the target shares and one-third exceeding 25%. For short-term toeholds, 40% are greater than 10% and 10% exceed 25%.

4. Does toehold threshold bidding exist?

4.1. Estimating the Threshold

As discussed in Section 2, the toehold threshold $\hat{\alpha} = f(\theta,t,v,r)$ is estimated as a function of the first three parameters only, where the resistance cost r is replaced by its minimum value $\bar{r} = f(\theta, t, v)$ in Equation (6). With the estimates of θ, t and v discussed below, $\bar{r}$ averages 3% in the data, with a median of 2%. We begin the estimation with the probability θ of the no-bidder-wins outcome. Recall from Table 1 that 30% of all contests end up with no bidder winning the target. We estimate θ using binomial logit, where the dependent variable equals one if the target rejects all bids. The explanatory variables are defined in Table 3, while Table 4 shows the coefficient estimates. The variables represent target, bidder, and contest characteristics. Target characteristics include (log of) market value of equity (*Target size*), measures of target stock liquidity such as an indicator for a share price below $1 on day -41 (*Penny stock*), average stock turnover on days -166 through -42 (*Turnover*), and whether the target is listed on a major stock exchange (*NYSE/Amex*). Moreover, the logit regression contains a poison pill indicator.

We include as bidder characteristics the public status of the bidder (*Acquirer public*) and an indicator for the product market relation with the target. The acquisition is classified as horizontal if the two firms have the same primary four-digit SIC code (*Horizontal*). With this definition, 27% of the contests start with a horizontal bid. The regression further includes contest characteristics such as indicators for tender offer (*Tender offer*), the payment method being cash only (*Cash*), target hostility (*Hostile*), and the entry of a rival bidder (*Multiple bidders*). As discussed in Section 2.3 above, *Hostile* is included to capture targets in Region III of the takeover game, where target management reject all bids (irrespective of toeholds). Finally, we include industry fixed effects (not shown) for financial, manufacturing, trade, and service industries.

The process of takeover negotiations changes over time as the investment banking industry becomes more actively involved in promoting takeovers and develops new deal protection devices such as termination agreements. Since these changes are likely to affect θ, we estimate the model separately for the 1973–1989 and

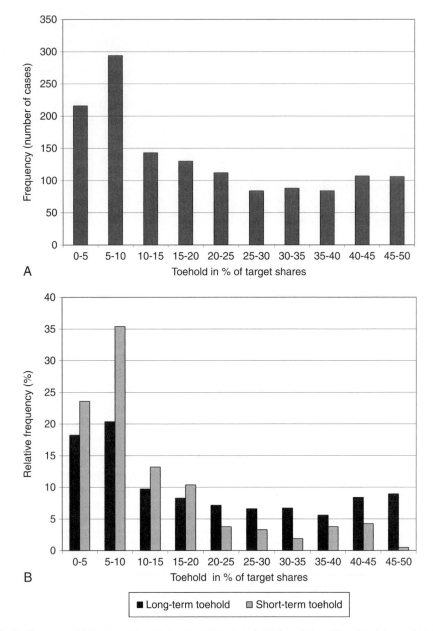

Fig. 4. Frequency distribution of the initial control bidder's toehold size when positive. Panel A uses the total sample of 1363 initial control bidders with positive toeholds for US public targets, 1973–2002 (with merger bids sampled from 1980 to 2002). A toehold with a size equal to the boundary between two intervals is included in the lower interval. Panel B is for the subsample of 970 initial control bidders whose toeholds could be classified as long- and short-term. A long-term toehold is purchased more than 6 months prior to the announcement of the initial control bid. A short-term toehold is purchased within 6 months of the initial bid. (A) Frequency distribution of the total toehold size. (B) Frequency distribution of long- and short-term toehold size.

Table 3

Summary of variables used in the cross-sectional analysis

Variable	Definition and estimation
A. Toehold bidding	
Toehold size	Fraction target shares owned by the initial control bidder prior to announcing the bid
Positive toehold	The acquirer has a positive toehold
Threshold	The minimum % toehold threshold $\hat{\alpha}$ required for the bidder to optimally acquire a toehold (Proposition 3): $\hat{\alpha} = -k_1 + \sqrt{k_1^2 + k_2}$, where $k_1 = v - r - \frac{1}{2}(v^2 - t^2) - t/(1 - \theta)$ and $k_2 = r(2v - r) + t(2 / (1 - \theta) - t)$. The estimation uses the initial offer premium as a proxy for bidder private valuations v and assumes $v \sim U[0,1]$. The termination fee t is the average fee for control bids in the same industry and year. The probability θ that no bidder wins is the predicted value from Table 4. The resistance cost r is replaced by $\bar{r} = -(1 - v) + \sqrt{(1 - v)^2 + 2t/(1 - \theta) - t^2}$, the minimum r for Region II to exist (Equation (6))
B. Target characteristics	
Target size	Natural logarithm of the target market capitalization in $ million on day -41 relative to the announcement day of the initial bid (day 0)
Target run-up	Target average cumulative abnormal return over the period $[-41, -2]$ using a value-weighted market model estimated over $[-291, end]$ with a dummy for the run-up window. The contest ends on the earlier of target delisting and 126 trading days after the last control bid in the contest
Penny stock	$p_{-41} < 1$, where p_{-41} is the target share price on day -41
Turnover	Average daily trading volume as a fraction of target shares over the period $[-166, -42]$
NYSE/Amex	The target is listed on NYSE or Amex
Poison pill	The target has a shareholder rights plan
Industry	Vector of industry dummies for financial, manufacturing, trade, and service industries
C. Bidder characteristics	
Horizontal	Bidder and target has the same four-digit primary SIC code
Acquirer public	The bidder is publicly traded
D. Contest characteristics	
Tender offer	Bid for at least 50% of the target shares (i) with SDC transaction form AM, (ii) with SDC transaction form M and flagged as a tender offer, or (iii) identified by the WSJ or Betton and Eckbo (2000) as a tender offer
Cash	Payment method is cash only
1973–1989	The contest is announced in the period 1973–1989 (vs. 1990–2002)
Hostile	Target management's response is recorded as hostile, as opposed to friendly/ neutral or response not recorded
Multiple bidders	A rival bidder enters the contest
No bidder wins	Indicates the no-bidder-win contest outcome

1990–2002 time periods. Moreover, to check the sensitivity of our results to the inclusion of *Hostile* and *Multiple bidders*, we use two model specifications for θ, as reported in Table 4.

Table 4

Determinants of the probability θ of the no-bidder-wins outcome

The table shows logit estimates of the coefficients for variables determining the probability θ that no bidder
wins the contest. The estimations use initial control bids for targets listed in CRSP, 1973–2002. Variables are
defined in Table 3. All regressions control for industry fixed effects (using the vector *Industry*). The *p*-values
are in parentheses.

Variable	Sample period 1973–1989		Sample period 1990–2002	
	Model I	Model II	Model I	Model II
Constant	0.847	0.911	0.495	0.445
	(0.009)	(0.006)	(0.062)	(0.097)
Target characteristics				
Target size	−0.015	−0.016	0.020	0.022
	(0.550)	(0.504)	(0.274)	(0.242)
Penny stock	−0.728	−0.615	0.473	0.483
	(0.074)	(0.135)	(0.001)	(0.001)
Turnover	0.024	0.025	0.003	0.003
	(0.163)	(0.138)	(0.506)	(0.423)
NYSE/Amex	−0.247	−0.367	−0.223	−0.253
	(0.029)	(0.002)	(0.015)	(0.006)
Poison pill	1.058	0.645	1.951	1.117
	(0.000)	(0.036)	(0.000)	(0.010)
Bidder characteristics				
Acquirer public	−0.567	−0.545	−1.693	−1.708
	(0.000)	(0.000)	(0.000)	(0.000)
Horizontal	0.024	−0.036	−0.279	−0.287
	(0.827)	(0.752)	(0.001)	(0.001)
Contest characteristics				
Tender offer	−0.574	−0.766	−0.942	−0.927
	(0.000)	(0.000)	(0.000)	(0.000)
Cash	−0.337	−0.364	−0.821	−0.887
	(0.000)	(0.000)	(0.000)	(0.000)
Hostile		1.070		1.831
		(0.000)		(0.000)
Multiple bidders		−0.299		−0.032
		(0.019)		(0.814)
Number of cases	2344	2344	5285	5285
Nagelkerke R^2	0.087	0.117	0.208	0.226
χ^2	156.7	212.7	803.1	876.7
	(0.000)	(0.000)	(0.000)	(0.000)

The regressions are all significant at the 1% level. For both time periods, the
estimated probability of the no-bidder-wins outcome θ increases with target hostility
(both *Hostile* and *Poison pill*). In other words, target hostility to the *initial* bid lowers
the probability of success of *all* bids. This is consistent with hostility reflecting high
target management entrenchment, as predicted in Region III of Proposition 1. It is also

interesting that having a poison pill by itself increases θ. Since we show below that poison pills have no discernible impact on offer premiums, this means that pills reduce expected premiums. This result extends the finding of Comment and Schwert (1995) on the impact of pills.

Moreover, θ decreases when the initial bidder is publicly traded and if the target is listed on NYSE/Amex. After 1989, θ is also greater for penny stocks and lower for horizontal bids. These results indicate that targets are more likely to accept an offer the more liquid the bidder (public status) and target shares. Moreover, targets are more likely to be acquired in tender offers and when the payment method is cash. In the following, we use the predicted value of θ for each initial bidder, using either Model I or II.

Second, the threshold requires an estimate of the target termination fee t. Target termination agreements come in two forms: a fixed dollar payment or a lockup option to purchase target assets below market value. We restrict our attention to fixed breakup fees which are also the most prevalent in the data. Using SDC information, termination agreements are rare prior to 1990, increasing to 50% of our control bidders in the late 1990s. The average termination fee is $34 million or 4% of the deal value. In our sample, target termination agreements are observed almost three times as often for public bidders (33% of the bids) as for private bidders (13%).

We require an estimate of t for each initial bidder in the sample, regardless of whether or not an agreement is observed ex post. Since B1 makes the toehold decision prior to initiating the takeover, it must predict t. We use the average fee for the target's four-digit industry and year of takeover bid as the predictor. The conclusions below do not change if we instead use the actual termination fee received ex post by B1. SDC does not report any termination agreement before 1985, and we set $t = 0$ for takeover bids prior to this year. The average industry-estimate of t in the sample is 3%. Note that this estimation benefits from the substantial standardization of termination contracts in the 1990s.

Third, we approximate the initial bidder's private valuation v with the initial bid premium $(p_{\text{ini}}/p_{-41}) - 1$. Thus, bidders are assumed to differ in their synergy gains with the target (giving rise to different offer premiums), while the stand-alone, no-information target share value (p_{-41}) is common across bidders. As in the model, we fit the premium observations to the uniform cumulative distribution function. As robustness checks, we replace the initial offer premium with the initial bidder's *final* offer premium (whether or not this is the last premium in the contest), and use the normal rather than the uniform distribution for v. These alterations do not change our conclusions below.

Figure 5 shows the frequency distribution of the threshold estimate. The threshold is estimated for a total of 6155 initial bidders with available offer premiums. The estimate averages 9% (median 8%) for the total sample. While not shown, the threshold distribution shifts to the right over the sample period, averaging 7% (median 4%) over 1973–1989 and 11% (median 9%) over 1990–2002. As discussed above, offer premiums (used to estimate v) do not change materially between the two periods. Moreover, the probability of the no-bidder-wins outcome decreases after the first

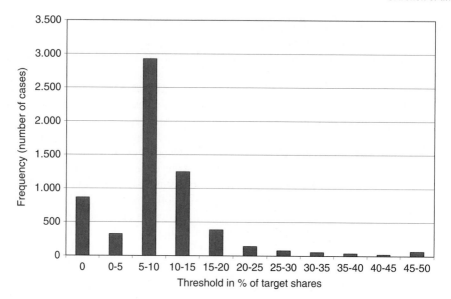

Fig. 5. Toehold threshold frequency distribution for 6155 initial bidders, 1973–2002. Frequency distribution of the toehold threshold $\hat{\alpha} = -k_1 + \sqrt{k_1^2 + k_2}$, where $k_1 = v - r - \frac{1}{2}(v^2 - t^2) - t/(1 - \theta)$ and $k_2 = r(2v - r) + (2/(1 - \theta) - t)$. The estimation uses the initial offer premium as a proxy for bidder private valuations v and assumes $v \sim U[0, 1]$. The termination fee t is the average fee for control bids in the same industry and year. The probability θ that no bidder wins is the predicted value from Model II in Table 4. The resistance cost r is replaced by $\bar{r} = -(1 - v) + \sqrt{(1 - v)^2 + 2t/(1 - \theta) - t^2}$. A threshold with a size equal to the boundary between two intervals is included in the lower interval.

subperiod. Therefore, the shift in the sample toehold threshold distribution is most likely driven by the absence of termination contracts prior to the mid-1980s.

4.2. Testing the toehold threshold hypothesis

Table 5 shows the coefficients in regressions for the probability of observing a toehold (logit estimates) and for the toehold size (OLS estimates). The explanatory variables are as in the earlier regressions for the probability θ with the addition of our estimate of the toehold threshold $\hat{\alpha}$. *Thresholds* I and II refer to estimates of $\hat{\alpha}$ using Models I and II in Table 4, respectively, for the probability θ. The regressions are significant and yield several interesting results. First, recall that the main prediction of H1 is that the probability of observing toehold bidding is greater for lower values of $\hat{\alpha}$. The logit regressions provide strong support for this prediction. In the first two regressions, the coefficients on *Thresholds* I and II are both negative and significant at the 1% level. Second, toehold bidding is more likely when liquidity costs are lower, here indicated by the target trading on NYSE or Amex. Liquidity does not seem to play a role beyond stock exchange listing, as the variable *Turnover* enters with a small but negative coefficient and *Penny stock* is statistically insignificant.

Table 5

Determinants of the probability of toehold bidding and the toehold size

The table shows coefficient estimates in logit regressions for the probability that the initial control bidder has a toehold, and OLS regressions for the percent toehold size. Sample of initial control bids for targets listed in CRSP, 1973–2002. *Thresholds* I and II are computed using the predicted value of θ using Models I and II in Table 4, respectively. Variables are defined in Table 3. All regressions control for industry fixed effects (*Industry*). The *p*-values are in parentheses.

Variable	Probability of toehold (logit)		% toehold size (OLS)	
Constant	−0.970	−1.175	3.377	3.723
	(0.001)	(0.000)	(0.000)	(0.000)
Toehold bidding				
Threshold I	−0.025			
	(0.000)			
Threshold I × *Positive toehold*			1.004	
			(0.000)	
Threshold II		−0.017		
		(0.005)		
Threshold II × *Positive toehold*				0.842
				(0.000)
Target characteristics				
Target size	−0.031	−0.034	−0.029	−0.033
	(0.148)	(0.125)	(0.571)	(0.517)
Penny stock	−0.434	−0.408	−1.782	−1.765
	(0.182)	(0.215)	(0.005)	(0.006)
Turnover	−0.032	−0.025	−0.047	−0.052
	(0.001)	(0.012)	(0.002)	(0.001)
Nyse/Amex	0.670	0.512	0.653	0.786
	(0.000)	(0.000)	(0.003)	(0.000)
Poison pill	1.654	0.897	−4.379	−2.456
	(0.000)	(0.002)	(0.000)	(0.008)
Bidder characteristics				
Acquirer public	−1.098	−0.985	−0.982	−1.114
	(0.000)	(0.000)	(0.000)	(0.000)
Horizontal	−0.069	−0.170	−0.227	−0.186
	(0.469)	(0.089)	(0.285)	(0.391)
Contest characteristics				
Tender offer	1.146	1.050	2.916	3.193
	(0.000)	(0.000)	(0.000)	(0.000)
Cash	0.324	0.395	−0.477	−0.370
	(0.000)	(0.000)	(0.030)	(0.099)
Hostile		1.621		−2.089
		(0.000)		(0.000)
Multiple bidders		0.174		−0.874
		(0.186)		(0.014)
Number of cases	5828	5828	5859	5859
Nagelkerke/adjusted R^2	0.194	0.235	0.292	0.262
χ^2/F-value	668.3	821.2	173.5	130.9
	(0.000)	(0.000)	(0.000)	(0.000)

Third, the univariate information in Table 2 suggests that toehold bidding is frequent in hostile takeovers. This is also the prediction of H1(iii) (Region III in Proposition 3). As shown in Table 5, toehold bidding is significantly more likely when the target has a poison pill (*Poison*) and when the target response to the initial bid is hostile (*Hostile*). Importantly, the inclusion of *Hostile* in the second regression does not materially alter the significance level of *Threshold*. Thus, *Threshold* and *Hostile* provide two independent and important sources of toehold bidding behavior, again as implied by our takeover model (Regions II and III, respectively).

Fourth, toehold bidding is significantly less likely when the bidder is a public firm (*Acquirer public*) and more likely when the payment method is all cash (*Cash*). Since a private bidder is less likely to offer stock as payment, this all-cash effect likely also emanates from the private status of the bidder. While public bidders offer all cash (all stock) as the payment method in 32% (36%) of the cases, private bidders use all-cash offers in 50% of the deals and all stock in only 3%. Recall that the targets are all publicly traded so accepting stock from a private bidder means converting a liquid target stock into an illiquid bidder stock, which is generally unattractive to target shareholders.

Our finding of a significantly greater toehold bidding probability for private bidders is intriguing. Recall that toehold bidding is optimal when the target's accept/reject criterion is independent of the toehold (Regions I and III in Proposition 3). Target hostility (Region III) is unlikely to explain the greater toehold propensity of private bidders, however, as there is no discernible difference in the sample proportions of public and private bidders that are hostile (5% in both categories). Alternatively, private bidders could have a comparative advantage over public bidders in identifying less entrenched target managements whose accept/reject decision is driven primarily by the offer price (Region I). Thus, a consistent interpretation is that the greater toehold frequency for private bidders reflects a greater proportion of the targets belonging to Region I.

Turning to the bidder's decision on the toehold size, recall from Table 2 that the average toehold conditional on being positive is 20%. As expected under threshold bidding, the average threshold estimate conditional on $\hat{\alpha} > 0$ is lower: 11%. The last two columns of Table 5 examine whether the toehold size is also increasing in the threshold. For this test we condition on the toehold being positive. The coefficients on *Threshold* I * *Positive toehold* and *Threshold* II * *Positive toehold* are both positive and highly significant. Thus, when bidders elect to bid with a positive toehold, the toehold size is increasing in the toehold threshold, as predicted by H1(ii).

The impact of the remaining explanatory variables for the toehold size is somewhat weaker than their effect on the probability of observing a positive toehold. For example, neither target hostility nor cash payment impact the average toehold size. Toehold size does increase, however, when the target is traded on NYSE/Amex and when the initial bid is a tender offer. The average toehold size is smaller when the target has a poison pill, possibly reflecting the constraint on the toehold of the pill itself (pills are often triggered for toeholds greater than 15%) and when the auction attracts multiple bidders. The latter finding is consistent with the proposition that relatively large initial bidder toeholds help deter competition from rival bidders with smaller or no toeholds (Bulow et al., 1999; Dasgupta and Tsui, 2004).

5. Toeholds and takeover gains

The analysis so far has focused on the likelihood and size of toehold bidding. Our tests indicate that actual toehold bidding is consistent with the existence of a toehold threshold. In this section, we examine two additional issues of interest to the overall toehold puzzle. First, we examine whether toehold bidding impacts takeover gains, either directly through prices or indirectly through the probability that the bidder wins the contest. Second, we study valuation effects of toeholds in the no-bidder-wins outcome. This allows us to examine the assumption in Section 2 that the target share price falls back to its pretakeover level when all bids fail. A greater price drop in the no-bidder-wins outcome implies an additional source of toehold costs that in itself could deter toehold bidding.

5.1. Toeholds and average abnormal stock returns

We estimate abnormal stock returns from trading day -41 relative to the first bid through the contest end. The ending date is the earlier of the target delisting date and the day of the last bid in the contest plus 126 trading days. Let AR_k denote the average daily abnormal stock return over the kth event window, $k = 1, 2, 3$. The first event window covers trading days $[-41, -2]$ (the run-up period), the second is $[-1, 1]$ (the announcement period), and the third is $[2, \text{end}]$ (the postannouncement period). The three event parameters AR_k are estimated using the following market model:

$$r_{jt} = \alpha_j + \beta_j r_{mt} + \sum_{k=1}^{3} AR_{jk}d_{kt} + \varepsilon_{jt}, \tag{7}$$

$$t = \text{day}(-291), \ldots, \text{day(contest ends)},$$

where r_{jt} is the return to firm j over day t, r_{mt} is the value-weighted market return, and d_{kt} is a dummy variable that takes a value of one if day t is in the kth event window and zero otherwise. We estimate the event parameter for the total contest window $[-41, \text{end}]$ separately using the market model with a single event parameter for the entire event period. To be included in this analysis, a firm must have at least one valid return observation in each of the event windows and the preevent period. The estimation uses ordinary least squares with White's heteroskedastic-consistent covariance matrix. The cumulative abnormal return for event period k is $CAR_{jk} = \omega_k AR_{jk}$, where ω_k is the number of trading days in the event window. In a sample of N firms, the average cumulative abnormal return is $ACAR_k = (1/N)\Sigma_j CAR_{jk}$, which is reported in Table 6. The table also reports the z-value for ACAR, where $z = (1/\sqrt{N})\sum_j AR_{jk}/\sigma_{AR_{jk}}$ and $\sigma_{AR_{jk}}$ is the estimated standard error of AR_{jk}. Under the null of $ACAR_k = 0$, z is distributed standard normal for large N.

Table 6

Average abnormal returns to bidders and targets sorted on toehold bidding

The sample is 9418 control contests for US targets with return data on CRSP, 1973–2002. The average daily abnormal stock return for firm j over event window k is estimated directly as the event parameter AR_{jk} in the value-weighted market model

$$r_{jt} = \alpha_j + \beta_j r_{mt} + \sum_{k=1}^{3} AR_{jk} d_{kt} + \varepsilon_{jt}, \quad t = \text{day} (-291), \ldots, \text{day (contest ends)},$$

where r_{jt} is the return to firm j over day t, r_{mt} is the value-weighted market return, and d_{kt} is a dummy variable that takes a value of one if day t is in the kth event window and zero otherwise. Day 0 is the day of the initial control bid and the ending date is the earlier of the target delisting date and the day of the last bid in the contest plus 126 trading days. The three event windows are $[-41, -2]$ (the run-up period), $[-1, 1]$ (the announcement period), and $[2, \text{end}]$ (the postannouncement period). The estimation uses ordinary least squares with White's heteroskedastic-consistent covariance matrix. The cumulative abnormal return to firm j over event period k is $CAR_{jk} = \omega_k AR_{jk}$, where ω_k is the number of trading days in the event window. In a sample of N firms, the average cumulative abnormal return is $ACAR_k = (1/N) \sum_j CAR_{jk}$. The z-values are in parentheses, where $z = (1/\sqrt{N}) \sum_j AR_{jk}/\sigma_{AR_{jk}}$ and $\sigma_{AR_{jk}}$ is the estimated standard error of AR_{jk}. Under the null of $ACAR = 0$, $z \sim N(0, 1)$ for large N.

Sample	Bidder ACAR (%)				Target ACAR (%)			
	No. of cases	Run-up [−41, −2]	Announcement [−1, 1]	Total [−41, end]	No. of cases	Run-up [−41, −2]	Announcement [−1, 1]	Total [−41, end]
Panel A: All contests								
All	5297	0.36	−1.24	−10.19	9418	6.84	13.43	17.17
		(0.20)	(−18.40)	(−12.71)		(25.61)	(105.20)	(37.45)
Zero toehold	4.731	0.48	−1.38	−10.92	8.146	6.83	13.39	16.98
		(0.55)	(−18.22)	(−12.76)		(22.80)	(95.88)	(34.00)
Positive toe-hold	566	−0.68	0.00	−4.05	1272	6.90	13.69	18.39
		(−1.00)	(−3.61)	(−1.97)		(11.99)	(43.62)	(15.85)
Panel B: Contests where the target is ultimately acquired								
All	4190	0.63	−1.24	−7.96	6520	8.47	14.93	26.90
		(0.82)	(−17.06)	(−9.90)		(25.15)	(90.65)	(44.47)
Zero toehold	3757	0.78	−1.39	−8.54	5639	8.61	15.07	27.91
		(1.11)	(−17.10)	(−10.11)		(23.01)	(83.52)	(41.76)
Positive toe-hold	433	−0.75	0.00	−2.88	881	7.57	14.05	20.39
		(−0.71)	(−2.70)	(−1.00)		(10.21)	(35.33)	(15.34)
Panel C: Contests where no bidder wins								
All	1107	−0.66	−1.21	−18.64	2898	3.18	10.06	−4.71
		(−1.17)	(−7.05)	(−8.55)		(8.45)	(53.67)	(0.80)
Zero toehold	974	−0.69	−1.36	−20.11	2507	2.83	9.62	−7.60
		(−0.96)	(−6.56)	(−8.28)		(6.59)	(47.57)	(−1.34)
Positive toe-hold	133	−0.46	−0.15	−7.83	391	5.40	12.88	13.90
		(−0.78)	(−2.58)	(−2.27)		(6.30)	(25.64)	(5.56)

Starting with bidder abnormal returns, the ACAR for the total sample of 5297 publicly traded bidders in Panel A is negative and strongly significant over the announcement period (−1.24%, z-value −18.40) and over the total contest period (−10.19%, z-value −12.71). Our announcement-return estimate is similar to the significant −1% bidder abnormal return reported by Fuller et al. (2002) in acquisitions of public targets.[8] In our subsample of 566 toehold bidders, however, the bidder ACAR is close to zero over the announcement period and a marginally significant −4.05% (z-value −1.97) for the total contest period. The difference between the bidder ACAR in the zero-toehold sample and in the positive-toehold sample is statistically significant at the 1% level. Furthermore, sorting on toehold bidding generates the largest relative benefit of toeholds for the subsample of 1107 contests where no bidder wins. In Panel C, the bidder ACAR in the zero-toehold sample is −20.11% for the total contest (z-value −8.28) compared to −7.83% (z-value −2.27) for 133 toehold bidders. The difference of 12.28% in these two ACARs is again statistically significant at the 1% level. In sum, the univariate sorts in Table 6 indicate that toehold bidders on average outperform bidders without toeholds, and particularly so when the target rejects all bids.

Turning to the sample of 9418 target firms with sufficient data for CAR estimation, the target ACAR is a significant 6.84% for the run-up period, 13.43% over the announcement period, and 17.17% over the entire contest. The total contest gain for the 6520 successful targets is a significant 26.90%, while the corresponding ACAR for 2898 contests where no bidder wins is a statistically insignificant −4.71% (z-value 0.80). The latter finding updates the evidence on failed contests first presented by Bradley et al. (1983): the target share price on average falls back to its precontest level when all bids fail. Note that while Bradley et al. estimate the price drop over 2 years following the initial bid, our event window ends within 126 days of the final offer.

Table 6 further shows that there is no discernible impact of toehold bidding on the target ACAR for either the total sample or the sample of successful targets. The contest-period ACAR for unsuccessful targets, however, is a significantly positive 13.90% (z-value 5.56) when the bidder has a toehold. In other words, when no bidder wins, the target stock price falls back to the precontest level only if the initial bidder has a zero toehold. This finding is of particular interest as the target price decline represents an ex post toehold cost by reducing the market value of the toehold investment. Panel C of Table 6 suggests that toehold bidding itself is correlated with factors that lower this cost. We return to this issue below.

5.2. Cross-sectional determinants of bidder gains

Table 7 presents parameter estimates in two sets of cross-sectional regressions with either bidder abnormal returns (CAR[−41, 1] and CAR[−41, end]) or offer premiums (initial and final) as dependent variables. The bidder abnormal return regressions use WLS, while the premium regressions use OLS. The last column of the table shows

---

[8] For a comprehensive review of bidder returns in takeovers, see Betton et al. (2008a).

Table 7

Determinants of bidder abnormal returns, initial and final offer premiums, and the probability π that the initial bidder wins the contest

Sample of initial control bids for US public targets with stock return data on CRSP, 1973–2002. The table reports WLS estimates of bidder cumulative abnormal returns (CAR) over the run-up and announcement period $[-42, 1]$ and over the entire contest $[-41, end]$, respectively, using σ_{AR} as weights. Columns 3 and 4 report OLS estimates of log of the initial and final offer premium, $\ln(p_{ini}/p-41)$ and $\ln(p_{fin}/p-41)$, respectively, where p_{ini} is the initial offer price, p_{fin} is the final offer price in the contest, and p_{-41} is the target stock price on day -41 adjusted for splits and dividends. The last column shows a logit estimation of the probability π that the initial control bidder wins the contest. Variables are defined in Table 3. All regressions control for industry fixed effects. The p-values are in parentheses.

Variable	Bidder CAR $[-41, 1]$	Bidder CAR $[-41, end]$	Initial offer premium	Final offer premium	Probability π that initial bidder wins
Constant	−0.032	−0.173	0.168	0.156	−0.217
	(0.169)	(0.009)	(0.000)	(0.000)	(0.290)
Toehold bidding					
Toehold size	−0.001	0.014	−0.105	−0.106	1.863
	(0.978)	(0.914)	(0.024)	(0.033)	(0.000)
Target characteristics					
Target size	0.000	−0.001	0.000	0.001	−0.018
	(0.893)	(0.859)	(0.809)	(0.575)	(0.213)
Target run-up	0.150	0.144	0.740	0.754	0.806
	(0.000)	(0.000)	(0.000)	(0.000)	(0.000)
Penny stock	0.091	0.214	−0.111	−0.136	−0.506
	(0.000)	(0.000)	(0.000)	(0.000)	(0.000)
Turnover	−0.002	−0.008	−0.001	−0.001	0.002
	(0.000)	(0.000)	(0.082)	(0.101)	(0.704)
NYSE/Amex	0.010	0.098	0.021	0.026	0.211
	(0.104)	(0.000)	(0.020)	(0.005)	(0.002)
Poison pill	0.018	0.038	−0.001	0.018	−1.694
	(0.562)	(0.676)	(0.986)	(0.649)	(0.000)
Bidder characteristics					
Acquirer public			0.026	0.021	1.197
			(0.015)	(0.059)	(0.000)
Horizontal	0.017	0.013	−0.005	0.003	0.121
	(0.008)	(0.457)	(0.539)	(0.779)	(0.060)
Contest characteristics					
Tender offer	0.000	0.004	−0.036	−0.032	0.704
	(0.988)	(0.868)	(0.000)	(0.002)	(0.000)
Cash	0.009	0.075	0.039	0.049	0.450
	(0.252)	(0.000)	(0.000)	(0.000)	(0.000)
1973–1989	−0.003	0.052	0.014	0.016	−0.783
	(0.739)	(0.018)	(0.115)	(0.108)	(0.000)
Hostile		0.048		0.062	
		(0.260)		(0.000)	

(Continued)

Table 7 (*Continued*)

Variable	Bidder CAR [−41, 1]	Bidder CAR [−41, end]	Initial offer premium	Final offer premium	Probability π that initial bidder wins
Multiple bidders		−0.045		0.059	
		(0.198)		(0.000)	
No bidder wins		−0.113			
		(0.000)			
Number of cases	4417	4417	5825	5926	7470
Nagelkerke/adjusted R^2	0.050	0.048	0.286	0.271	0.197
χ^2/F-value	16.5	13.4	147.0	123.6	1139.6
	(0.000)	(0.000)	(0.000)	(0.000)	(0.000)

logit-estimates of the determinants of the probability π that the initial bidder wins the contest. Note that π differs from the probability θ estimated earlier in Table 4, as $1 - \theta$ is the probability that either the initial or rival bidder wins.

There are several interesting results. We follow Betton et al. (2008b) and include the target stock price run-up prior to the initial bid as a determinant for the bidder CARs and premiums. The significantly positive effect of the variable *Target run-up* suggests that takeovers associated with relatively large target run-ups are also relatively profitable for both bidders and targets. Also, the greater the target run-up, the greater is the probability π that the initial bidder succeeds. Moreover, bidder CARs measured over the total contest are significantly lower when no bidder wins. This result, which is consistent with the average CARs reported earlier in Table 6, indicates that winning is marginally better than losing for the bidder. While this does not explain why the overall market reaction to takeover bidding is negative for acquiring firms, it does indicate that withdrawing from the takeover attempt could be suboptimal once the bid has been launched.

In addition to *Target run-up* and *No bidder wins*, significant determinants of total contest-induced bidder CARs include the liquidity variables (*Penny stock, Turnover, NYSE/Amex*), the payment method, and the bid occurring prior to 1990. With the exception of *Penny stock*, these variables tend to affect offer premiums in the same direction as bidder CARs. Notice also that *Hostile* increases the final offer premium but does not impact total bidder CARs. As discussed earlier in Table 1, offer premiums are greater for public than for private bidders (see also Bargeron et al., 2008). Moreover, the size of the target is insignificant across the board. *Toehold size* also receives a statistically insignificant coefficient in the bidder CAR regressions. This suggests that the other variables in the cross-sectional regression pick up the tendency for toehold bidding to be associated with greater (less negative) bidder CARs shown in Panels A and C of Table 6.

Finally, Table 7 shows that greater toeholds lower offer premiums (both initial and final premiums) and increase the probability π that the initial bidder wins. Thus, toeholds play two potentially opposing roles related to the no-bidder-wins outcome. On the one hand, this outcome reduces the value of the toehold itself (Panel C of

Table 6). On the other hand, toehold bidding increases the probability π, which generally reduces the probability of the no-bidder-wins outcome. It appears that the net effect on bidder gains is zero at the margin as the coefficients on *Toehold size* in the two bidder CAR regressions are statistically insignificant.[9]

5.3. When all bids fail

Recall from Section 2.1 that, in our model, toeholds are assumed to be acquired at the pregame target share price of zero, which is also the final target share price if all bids fail. Consequently, as also shown in Figure 1, the toehold bidder's payoff in this outcome is $\Pi = 0$ if the target rejects the initial invitation to negotiate. Furthermore, B1's payoff is $\Pi = t(1 - \alpha)$ if the target rejects all bids after having accepted merger negotiations and awarded B1 a termination agreement. However, what if the target stock price falls to a level below the toehold acquisition price? As theorized by Goldman and Qian (2005), outside investors might react negatively to news that the target management has defeated all bids. If so, the negative market reaction possibly reduces the target's stand-alone value and result in a loss on the initial bidder's toehold investment.

What is the likely importance of this potential toehold cost? If we assume that toeholds are acquired at the precontest target market price p_{-41}, then the average abnormal returns to targets shown earlier in Table 6 fail to support this toehold-cost argument: on average, the target stock price falls back to the precontest level when all bids fail. To examine this question in greater detail, Table 8 shows the results of regressing the target's total contest return in the no-bidder-wins outcome on the bidder's toehold. We are particularly interested in whether this target return is (1) greater for toehold bidders and (2) increasing in the toehold size, conditional on the other target and bidder characteristics used in the empirical analysis above.

---

[9] We use the estimation technique developed in Betton and Eckbo (2000) to further check for a toehold impact on bidder CARs. Notice first that market rationality implies

$$\text{CAR}[-41,1] = \mu_u(1 - \pi(x)) + \mu_s\pi(x),$$

where μ_u and μ_s are the expected bidder returns conditional on the bid failing or succeeding, respectively, and x is a vector of offer characteristics, including *Toehold size*. We estimate μ_u and μ_s using the full sample of $N = 7470$ bidders in Table 7 as coefficients in the following cross-sectional regression:

$$\text{CAR}_i[-41,1] = \mu_u + (\mu_s - \mu_u)\hat{\pi}_i(x_i) + \varepsilon_i, \ i = 1,\ldots,N,$$

where $\hat{\pi}_i(x_i)$ is bidder i's predicted $\hat{\pi}_i$ from Table 7 and ε_i is a mean-zero error term. Here, the estimated values $\hat{\mu}_s$ and $\hat{\mu}_u$ are the average expected abnormal bidder returns in the two outcomes. Weighted with $\hat{\pi}_i$, these estimates provide a prediction model for each initial bidder's expected return conditional on x_i, $\text{E}(\text{CAR}_i[-41,1]|x_i)$. We find that the partial derivative of this expected return with respect to *Toehold size* is positive. Since $\hat{\mu}_s$ and $\hat{\mu}_u$ are constants, this effect is a manifestation of the positive impact of *Toehold size* on $\hat{\pi}$ and therefore on $\text{E}(\text{CAR}_i[-41,1]|\ x_i)$. This partial derivative is of particular interest because it controls for the effect on bidder CARs of the other explanatory variables in $\hat{\pi}(x)$

Table 8

Determinants of target abnormal returns when no bidder wins

The table shows WLS estimates of the target total cumulative abnormal return CAR[−41, end], using σ_{AR} as weights, and OLS estimates of the target total raw return $\ln(p_{end}/p_{−41})$, where p_{end} is the target stock price 126 days after the last control bid in the contest and $p_{−41}$ is the closing price 41 days prior to the initial control bid, adjusted for splits and dividends. The sample is control contests for targets listed in CRSP 1973–2002 where no bidder wins. The explanatory variables are defined in Table 3. All regressions control for industry fixed effects. The p-values are in parentheses.

Variable	Target total CAR[−41, end]		Target raw return $\ln(p_{end}/p_{−41})$	
Constant	−0.349	−0.353	5.342	5.309
	(0.005)	(0.005)	(0.000)	(0.000)
Toehold bidding				
Toehold size	0.917		0.450	
	(0.001)		(0.505)	
Positive toehold		0.233		0.255
		(0.000)		(0.084)
Target characteristics				
Target size	−0.011	−0.011	−0.486	−0.485
	(0.244)	(0.246)	(0.000)	(0.000)
Target run-up	1.305	1.302	0.275	−0.271
	(0.000)	(0.000)	(0.126)	(0.132)
Penny stock	0.066	0.067	−3.007	−3.003
	(0.192)	(0.181)	(0.000)	(0.000)
Turnover	−0.010	−0.010	−0.011	−0.011
	(0.000)	(0.000)	(0.072)	(0.075)
Nyse/Amex	0.195	0.188	0.600	0.594
	(0.000)	(0.000)	(0.000)	(0.000)
Poison pill	0.172	0.165	0.552	0.538
	(0.237)	(0.256)	(0.078)	(0.086)
Bidder characteristics				
Acquirer public	−0.062	−0.058	−0.189	−0.181
	(0.147)	(0.177)	(0.117)	(0.135)
Horizontal	0.146	0.150	0.118	0.123
	(0.002)	(0.002)	(0.348)	(0.325)
Contest characteristics				
Tender offer	−0.007	−0.015	−0.596	−0.612
	(0.873)	(0.740)	(0.000)	(0.000)
Cash	0.216	0.213	−0.244	−0.262
	(0.000)	(0.000)	(0.017)	(0.011)
1973–1989	0.020	0.013	0.188	0.181
	(0.627)	(0.750)	(0.055)	(0.065)
Hostile	0.138	0.097	0.663	0.616
	(0.071)	(0.209)	(0.000)	(0.001)
Multiple bidders	−0.119	−0.123	−0.013	−0.019
	(0.048)	(0.041)	(0.932)	(0.906)
Number of cases	2292	2292	2026	2026
Adjusted R^2	0.391	0.392	0.233	0.234
F-value	82.59	82.93	35.12	35.31
	(0.000)	(0.000)	(0.000)	(0.000)

In the first two regressions in Table 8, the dependent variable is the target CAR[−41, end]. For robustness, we also use as a dependent variable the total target raw return ln (p_{end}/p_{-41}), where p_{end} is the target stock price 6 months following the date of the last bid in the contest (the results do not change if we instead define p_{end} as the target price on the last bid date plus either 3 months or 12 months). The raw return avoids the estimation error in the market model parameters embedded in CAR[−41, end], which could be nonnegligible given the long contest duration of some defeated contests (on average 130 trading days, median 127).

The variable *Toehold size* receives a positive and statistically significant coefficient in the CAR regression, as does the dummy variable *Positive toehold*. There is also no evidence of a negative price impact of toeholds when using the target's raw return. This finding complements the results reported earlier in Panel C of Table 6, which show that the target CAR[−41, end] averages a statistically significant 14% when all bids fail and the bidder has a toehold. Importantly, the evidence fails to support the notion that toehold bidding is deterred by the expected target price drop when no bidder wins.

Several of the other regressors in Table 8 are also significant. The target CAR in ultimately defeated contests increases with target characteristics such as run-up and NYSE/Amex listing. The CAR—but not the premium measure—is also greater if the bid is horizontal and is an all-cash offer. Notice that while several extant empirical studies report positive effects on target gains from an all-cash payment, the evidence in Table 8 further shows that such valuation effects are also present in total target returns when all bids are defeated.

6. Conclusions

With control premiums averaging 45% in our sample, the case for toehold bidding is compelling. If the toehold bidder succeeds, or if the toehold is sold to a rival bidder, the return on the toehold investment approaches the takeover premium itself. Also, bidding theory points to a potential deterrent effect of toeholds on competing bids. Nevertheless, we show that toehold bidding in US mergers and tender offers has been steadily declining since the early 1980s and is now surprisingly rare. In the sample of 10,000+ initial control bidders, only 13% bid with a toehold. Moreover, as few as 3% acquire toehold shares in the 6-month period leading up to the initial offer. In mergers, bidders by and large reject the idea of acquiring toeholds.

The puzzle extends beyond a surprising aversion to toehold bidding. When bidders do have toeholds, we find that they are large, on average 20% of the target, with toeholds purchased within 6 months of the bid averaging 13%. Thus, a theory purporting to explain the puzzle must produce a form of threshold bidding centered on either zero or a substantial toehold size. Also, the theory should explain our finding that toehold bidding is the norm for hostile bids, and greater for private than for publicly traded acquirers.

We develop and test a takeover model that addresses all of these findings. The model formalizes the often-heard notion that toehold bidding is "aggressive", antagonizing entrenched (but rational) target managements. The model makes this notion explicit as a toehold increases the probability that the bidder succeeds in winning control of the target and proceeds to eliminate target management's private benefits of control. As a result, some target managements who would otherwise accept merger negotiations refuse to negotiate with a toehold bidder, opting instead for the open auction. Bidders trade off toehold gains with costs of target rejection. Rejection is costly because it forces bidders to launch unsolicited tender offers without the benefit of a termination agreement should a rival win the target or should the target withdraw. In equilibrium, bidders either approach the target with a zero toehold to avoid rejection or acquire a toehold with expected benefits that outweigh expected rejection costs.

In addition to being an increasing function of the termination fee, our toehold threshold increases with the initial takeover premium, and with the probability that no bidder wins. In our sample, this probability is 30%, and higher for mergers than for tender offers. The toehold threshold increases with the no-bidder-wins probability because only the termination agreement provides the bidder with a positive payoff when all bids fail. The toehold threshold estimate averages 9% across the total sample. In the presence of toehold transaction costs, a threshold of this magnitude could well cause the typical bidder to prefer a zero toehold (and avoid rejection). We find that toehold bidding is more likely the lower is the threshold estimate. Moreover, when the observed toehold is positive, the toehold size increases with the threshold value, again as predicted.

Our model also highlights the point that, for sufficiently large private benefits of control, target management will reject any bid, regardless of bidder toeholds. In this case, toehold bidding is optimal, provided of course that the bidder is prepared to make a hostile offer. Our finding of a 50% toehold frequency in hostile bids is consistent with this argument. The argument is also supported by the marked decline in toehold frequency after the mid-1980s. This decline coincides with a widespread adoption of structural takeover defenses, and a concomitant decline in hostile takeovers. Moreover, our finding of a greater toehold frequency and lower takeover premiums for private than for public bidders is suggestive of private bidders having a comparative advantage in identifying targets with a low level of managerial entrenchment.

Finally, we present evidence on the valuation effects of toeholds, focusing in particular on the return on the toehold investment when all bids fail. Target abnormal stock returns through the entire contest average zero when all bids are rejected. If toeholds are purchased at the precontest target share price (which the threshold model assumes), this evidence suggests that toehold losses ex post are negligible. Since we also find that target abnormal returns in the no-bidder-wins outcome are increasing in bidder toeholds, we conclude that the potential for negative toehold returns when all bids fail is very unlikely to deter toehold purchases ex ante.

Appendix A: Proof of propositions

A.1. Proposition 1: optimal Stage-2 auction bids

Starting with B2, if the target rejects merger negotiations, B1 does not have a termination agreement, and B2 bids its private valuation, $p_2 = v_2$. This follows because a bid less than v_2 risks forgoing a profitable takeover, while bidding more than v_2 risks overpaying for the target. If the target accepts merger negotiations, B1 has a termination agreement which reduces B2's valuation and optimal bid to $p_2 = v_2 - t$. We assume that B1 wins the target and pays a price of zero when $v_2 < t$. B1's expected profit from bidding p with a termination agreement, and given B2's optimal bid, is

$$
\begin{aligned}
\mathrm{E}(\Pi) &= \left\{ (v)G(p + t) - (1 - \alpha) \int_t^{p+t} (v_2 - t)g(v_2) \, dv_2 + (t + \alpha p)[1 - G(p + t)] \right\} \\
&\quad \times (1 - \theta) + t(1 - \alpha)\theta \\
&= [v(p + t) - \frac{1}{2}(1 - \alpha)p^2 + (t + \alpha p)(1 - (p + t))] \times (1 - \theta) + t(1 - \alpha)\theta,
\end{aligned}
\tag{8}
$$

where, again, the second equality invokes the uniform distribution. The right-hand side of the first equation is the sum of four components. The first three (inside the curly bracket) are, respectively, B1's expected private value, the expected payment for the target, and the expected value from selling the toehold α and receiving t when B2 wins the auction. The fourth term is the expected payoff when no bidder wins. Using Equation (8), the first-order condition for profit maximization, $\partial \mathrm{E}(\Pi)/\partial p = 0$, implies the optimal bid conditional on acceptance in Proposition 1. (To ensure uniqueness, $G(v)$ must be twice continuously differentiable and satisfy the monotonicity condition $\partial(1 - G(v))/\partial g(v) \geq 0$. With the uniform distribution, this condition is satisfied.) If the target rejects negotiations and imposes the resistance cost r, B1's expected profit is

$$
\begin{aligned}
\mathrm{E}(\Pi) &= \left\{ (v - r)G(p) - (1 - \alpha) \int_0^p v_2 g(v_2) \, dv_2 + \alpha p[1 - G(p)] \right\}(1 - \theta) \\
&= [(v - r)p - \frac{1}{2}(1 - \alpha)p^2 + \alpha p(1 - p)](1 - \theta),
\end{aligned}
\tag{9}
$$

which leads to the optimal bid conditional on rejection in Proposition 1.

A.2. Proposition 2: optimal target response in Stage 1

If the target management accepts the invitation to merge, its expected utility is

$$E(U_{\text{accept}}) = (\beta - t)\theta + \left\{ \int_t^{p^*+t} (v_2 - t)g(v_2)dv_2 + p^*[1 - G(p^* + t)] \right\}(1 - \theta)$$

$$= \beta\theta + \left[\frac{v+\alpha}{1+\alpha} - \frac{1}{2}\left(\frac{v+\alpha}{1+\alpha}\right)^2 \right](1-\theta) - t\left(1 - \frac{1-\theta}{2}t\right), \qquad (10)$$

where the second equality invokes the uniform distribution as before. The first term after the second equality is the expected private benefits (retained only when no bidder wins), and the remainder of the expression is the expected auction revenue net of t. If the target rejects,

$$E(U_{\text{reject}}) = \beta[\theta + (1 - G(p^*))(1-\theta)] + \left\{ \int_0^{p^*} v_2 g(v_2)dv_2 + p^*[1 - G(p^*)] \right\}(1-\theta)$$

$$= \beta\left[1 - \frac{v-r+\alpha}{1+\alpha}(1-\theta)\right] + \left[\frac{v-r+\alpha}{1+\alpha} - \frac{1}{2}\left(\frac{v-r+\alpha}{1+\alpha}\right)^2\right](1-\theta), \quad (11)$$

where β is retained either if B2 wins or if no bidder wins. The target accepts negotiations if $E(U_{\text{accept}}) > E(U_{\text{reject}})$. If $\alpha = 0$, this condition holds for $\beta < \bar{\beta}$. If $\alpha > 0$, this holds for $\beta < \underline{\beta}$. To complete the proof, it is also necessary that $\underline{\beta} < \bar{\beta}$. By inspection of the limits shown in the lemma, this condition always holds.

A.3. Proposition 3: optimal toehold strategy

Assuming optimal bidding, if the target accepts merger negotiations, B1's expected profits are as follows:

$$E(\Pi^*) = \left\{ (v)G(p^* + t) - (1-\alpha)\int_t^{p^*+t} (v_2 - t)g(v_2)dv_2 + (t+\alpha p^*)[1 - G(p^* + t)] \right\}$$

$$\times (1-\theta) + t(1-\alpha)\theta$$

$$= \frac{1}{2}\left[\frac{(v+\alpha)^2}{1+\alpha} - (1-\alpha)t^2\right](1-\theta) + t(1-\alpha), \qquad (12)$$

where the second equality invokes the uniform distribution. If the target rejects merger negotiations,

$$E(\Pi^*) = \left\{ (v-r)G(p^*) - (1-\alpha)\int_0^{p^*} v_2 g(v_2)dv_2 + \alpha p^*[1 - G(p)] \right\}(1-\theta)$$

$$= \frac{1}{2}\frac{(v-r+\alpha)^2}{1+\alpha}(1-\theta). \qquad (13)$$

Using Equation (12), in Region I where target management accepts negotiations (Proposition 2), we have $E(\Pi^*_{\alpha>0}|\text{accept}) > E(\Pi^*_{\alpha=0}|\text{accept})$, so it is optimal to acquire a toehold in Region I. Similarly, using Equation (13), in Region III where target management rejects negotiation, $E\left(\Pi^*_{\alpha>0}|\text{reject}\right) > E\left(\Pi^*_{\alpha=0}|\text{reject}\right)$ and it is optimal for the bidder to acquire a toehold. Finally, in Region II, target management accepts negotiations if $\alpha = 0$ and rejects if $\alpha > 0$. In this region, B1 is indifferent between bidding with a zero and a positive toehold when $E\left(\Pi^*_{\alpha=0}|\text{accept}\right) = E\left(\Pi^*_{\alpha>0}|\text{reject}\right)$. Solving for the toehold that satisfies this condition yields the toehold threshold $\hat{\alpha}$ stated in Proposition 3.

References

Bargeron, L., F. P. Schlingemann, R. M. Stulz and C. J. Zutter, 2008, "Why Do Private Acquirers Pay So Little Compared to Public Acquirers?" *Journal of Financial Economics*, 89, 375–390.

Bates, T. H. and M. L. Lemmon, 2003, "Breaking Up is Hard to Do? An Analysis of Termination Fee Provisions and Merger Outcomes," *Journal of Financial Economics*, 69, 460–504.

Betton, S. and B. E. Eckbo, 2000, "Toeholds, Bid Jumps, and Expected Payoff in Takeovers," *Review of Financial Studies*, 13, 841–882.

Betton, S., B. E. Eckbo and K. S. Thorburn, 2008a, "Corporate Takeovers," In B. E. Eckbo (Ed.), *Handbook of Corporate Finance: Empirical Corporate Finance*, vol. 2, Chapter 15, Elsevier, North-Holland, Amsterdam, Handbooks in Finance Series, pp. 291–430.

Betton, S., B. E. Eckbo and K. S. Thorburn, 2008b, "Markup Pricing Revisited," Working Paper, Tuck School of Business at Dartmouth.

Boone, A. L. and J. H. Mulherin, 2007a, "Do Termination Provisions Truncate the Takeover Bidding Process?" *Review of Financial Studies*, 20, 461–489.

Boone, A. L. and J. H. Mulherin, 2007b, "How Are Firms Sold?," *Journal of Finance*, 62, 847–875.

Bradley, M., A. Desai and E. H. Kim, 1983, "The Rationale Behind Inter-Firm Tender Offers: Information or Synergy?" *Journal of Financial Economics*, 11, 141–153.

Bris, A., 2002, "Toehold, Takeover Premium, and the Probability of Being Acquired," *Journal of Corporate Finance*, 8, 227–253.

Bruner, R. F., 2004, *Applied Mergers and Acquisitions*, Wiley, New York.

Bulow, J., M. Huang and P. Klemperer, 1999, "Toeholds and Takeovers," *Journal of Political Economy*, 107, 427–454.

Burch, T., 2001, "Locking Out Rival Bidders: The Use of Lockup Options in Corporate Mergers," *Journal of Financial Economics*, 60, 103–141.

Burkart, M., 1995, "Initial Shareholdings and Overbidding in Takeover Contests," *Journal of Finance*, 50, 1491–1515.

Comment, R. and G. W. Schwert, 1995, "Poison or Placebo? Evidence on the Deterrent and Wealth Effects of Modern Antitakeover Measures," *Journal of Financial Economics*, 39, 3–43.

Dasgupta, S. and K. Tsui, 2004, "Auctions with Cross-Shareholdings," *Economic Theory*, 24, 163–194.

Eckbo, B. E. and H. Langohr, 1989, "Information Disclosure, Method of Payment, and Takeover Premiums: Public and Private Tender Offers in France," *Journal of Financial Economics*, 24, 363–403.

Eckbo, B. E. and K. S. Thorburn, 2009, "Creditor Financing and Overbidding in Bankruptcy Auctions: Theory and Tests," *Journal of Corporate Finance*, 15, 10–29.

Fishman, M. J., 1989, "Preemptive Bidding and the Role of the Medium of Exchange in Acquisitions," *Journal of Finance*, 44, 41–57.

Fuller, K., J. Netter and M. Stegemoller, 2002, "What Do Returns to Acquiring Firms Tell Us? Evidence from Firms that Make Many Acquisitions," *Journal of Finance*, 57, 1763–1793.

Goldman, E. and J. Qian, 2005, "Optimal Toeholds in Takeover Contests," *Journal of Financial Economics*, 77, 321–346.

Grossman, S. J. and O. D. Hart, 1980, "Takeover Bids, the Free-Rider Problem, and the Theory of the Corporation," *Bell Journal of Economics*, 11, 42–64.

Hirshleifer, D. and S. Titman, 1990, "Share Tendering Strategies and the Success of Hostile Takeover Bids," *Journal of Political Economy*, 98, 295–324.

Jennings, R. H. and M. A. Mazzeo, 1993, "Competing Bids, Target Management Resistance, and the Structure of Takeover Bids," *Review of Financial Studies*, 6, 883–910.

Officer, M. S., 2003, "Termination Fees in Mergers and Acquisitions," *Journal of Financial Economics*, 69, 431–467.

Ravid, S. A. and M. Spiegel, 1999, "Toehold Strategies, Takeover Laws and Rival Bidders," *Journal of Banking and Finance*, 23, 1219–1242.

Shleifer, A. and R. W. Vishny, 1986, "Large Shareholders and Corporate Control," *Journal of Political Economy*, 94, 461–488.

Walkling, R., 1985, "Predicting Tender Offer Success: A Logistic Analysis," *Journal of Financial and Quantitative Analysis*, 20, 461–478.

Chapter 5

DO AUCTIONS INDUCE A WINNER'S CURSE? NEW EVIDENCE FROM THE CORPORATE TAKEOVER MARKET[*]

AUDRA L. BOONE

School of Business, University of Kansas, Lawrence, Kansas, USA

J. HAROLD MULHERIN

Terry College of Business, University of Georgia, Athens, Georgia, USA

Contents

* We thank Laura Field, Bob Hansen, Ron Harstad, Michelle Lowry, Qingzhong Ma, Micah Officer, seminar participants at Boston College, Dartmouth College, Georgia State University, North Carolina State University, Pennsylvania State University, the University of Alabama, the University of Iowa, the University of Missouri, and the University of Pittsburgh, and an anonymous referee for comments on prior drafts.

This article originally appeared in the *Journal of Financial Economics*, Vol. 89, pp. 1–19 (2008).
Corporate Takeovers, Volume 2
Edited by B. Espen Eckbo
DOI: 10.1016/B978-0-12-381982-6.00006-9

Abstract

We contrast the winner's curse hypothesis and the competitive market hypothesis as potential explanations for the observed returns to bidders in corporate takeovers. The winner's curse hypothesis posits suboptimal behavior in which winning bidders fail to adapt their strategies to the level of competition and the amount of uncertainty in the takeover environment and predicts that bidder returns are inversely related to the level of competition in a given deal and to the uncertainty in the value of the target. Our measure of takeover competition comes from a unique data set on the auction process that occurs prior to the announcement of a takeover. In our empirical estimation, we control for the endogeneity between bidder returns and the level of competition in takeover deals. Controlling for endogeneity, we find that the returns to bidders are not significantly related to takeover competition. We also find that uncertainty in the value of the target does not reduce bidder returns. Related analysis indicates that prestigious investment banks do not promote overbidding. Analysis of posttakeover operating performance also fails to find any negative effects of takeover competition. As a whole, the results indicate that the breakeven returns to bidders in corporate takeovers stem not from the winner's curse but from the competitive market for targets that occurs predominantly prior to the public announcement of bids.

Keywords

mergers and acquisitions, auction, negotiation

JEL classification: G34, D44

1. Introduction

Auctions are regularly used to transfer the ownership of assets, to assign procurement contracts, to privatize government-owned assets, and to facilitate corporate takeovers. Because of their importance, auctions have been widely studied at the theoretical, empirical, and experimental level. McAfee and McMillan (1987), Laffont (1997), and Klemperer (1999) survey the many facets of the research on auctions. Dasgupta and Hansen (2007) review the auctions used in corporate finance.

An especially provocative topic in the research on auctions is the winner's curse. While subject to some variations (Cox and Isaac, 1984), the essence of the winner's curse is that the highest (and winning) bidder in an auction paid too much. The central prediction is that the incidence and the magnitude of the winner's curse is a direct function of the number of bidders in the auction (Kagel and Levin, 1986). A related prediction is that the winner's curse is heightened by the uncertainty in the value of the assets being sold (Bazerman and Samuelson, 1983).

If at play, the winner's curse implies suboptimal behavior in which market participants fail to adapt their bidding strategy to the level of competition and the amount of uncertainty. Conceptually, therefore, a contentious behavioral question is whether the presence of information asymmetry leads to market-wide mistakes as modeled by Akerlof (1970) or whether market participants have the incentive and ability to devise solutions to informational complexities as suggested by Barzel (1977). Because of these two distinct conceptual views, Thaler (1988, pp. 192–193) notes that "it is an empirical question whether bidders in various contexts get it right or are cursed."

Prior empirical and experimental research has produced mixed evidence on the existence of a winner's curse. In empirical field studies, one difficulty in definitively determining the presence of the winner's curse is the lack of a benchmark market value for auctioned assets such as an untapped oil field (Capen et al., 1971; Hendricks and Porter, 1988) or a highway construction contract (Thiel, 1988). Hence, results for or against the winner's curse are often sensitive to the functional form used in the empirical model (Levin and Smith, 1991). As a response, research has often turned to controlled experiments in labs (Roth, 1991). However, Hansen and Lott (1991) show that even carefully constructed experiments are often subject to biases that influence the results on the winner's curse, and Dyer and Kagel (1996) note that experiments often do not capture the richness of institutional features that arise to mitigate the winner's curse.

In this paper, we provide new evidence on the winner's curse in the setting of the corporate takeover market. Because of a market benchmark for the value of the winning bidding firm, such a setting avoids many of the estimation obstacles in prior empirical research. We use conventional event study techniques to determine whether winning bidders fare worse as the level of competition in a corporate takeover increases and as the uncertainty in the value of the target firm rises.

Surveys of behavioral finance (Baker et al., 2007; Barberis and Thaler, 2003; Thaler, 1988) conclude that the winner's curse holds in the corporate takeover market. This can be traced to the persuasive hubris hypothesis posed by Roll (1986) in which overconfident managers fall prey to the winner's curse and overbid when acquiring other corporations. Thaler (1988), in particular, draws on Roll (1986) to argue that the nonpositive return to bidders shown in empirical research is consistent with the winner's curse. Yet the breakeven returns could simply stem from the zero profits of a competitive takeover market and not reflect overvaluation by the winning bidder (Asquith, 1983; Mandelker, 1974; Travlos, 1987).

Definitive tests of the winner's curse would directly relate bidder returns to the extent of competition during the entire takeover bidding process. However, the extant research limits its measurement of takeover competition to the number of publicly announced bidders in a takeover and finds inconsistent effects on bidder returns. As a representative sample of this research, we review the following papers that conduct regression analysis of the relation between bidder returns and the number of public bidders in a takeover: Bradley et al. (1988), Varaiya (1988), Morck et al. (1990), Franks and Harris (1989), Servaes (1991), Schwert (2000), Kale et al. (2003), and Moeller et al. (2004). Of these eight papers, only Morck et al. (1990) and Schwert (2000) find a significant relation between bidder returns and the number of public bidders, and the Schwert (2000) results were sensitive to the sample employed in the analysis. In addressing these inconsistent results, both Varaiya (1988, p. 216) and Moeller et al. (2004, p. 210) attribute the lack of a significant effect on bidder returns to the fact that the number of public bidders is a noisy and incomplete measure of takeover competition.

Our research provides direct tests of the winner's curse that are not found in the prior analysis. Our innovation is the use of new data from Securities and Exchange Commission documents that more accurately measure the competitiveness of takeover deals. Rather than simply base the competitiveness of a takeover on the number of publicly announced bidders, our measure gauges takeover competition by determining the number of bidders in the private process prior to the announcement of the deal. As we show, this process ranges from sealed-bid auctions with multiple bidders to one-on-one negotiations between the target and a single bidder and provides a more accurate indication of the level of competition in takeovers during the 1990s. We use this novel data to study the relation between bidder returns and the level of takeover competition.

Another important feature of our analysis is that we model the endogeneity between takeover competition and bidder returns. Because the level of competition in takeovers and the wealth effects of bidders are jointly determined, we develop two-stage models to avoid the biased estimates produced by ordinary least squares (OLS). Similar to related auction research (Hansen, 1985; Smith, 1987), we show that models that control for endogeneity alter some of the inferences of the OLS models.

For a sample of 308 major takeovers announced in the 1989–1999 period, we test for the winner's curse by estimating whether bidder returns are negatively and significantly related to takeover competition and to the uncertainty in the value of the target. While we find some evidence of an inverse relation between bidder returns and takeover competition using OLS, we find no evidence of this inverse relation in two-stage models that account for the endogeneity between bidder returns and takeover competition. We also find no evidence of an inverse relation between bidder returns and the uncertainty in the value of the target. Analysis of posttakeover operating performance also fails to find any negative effects of takeover competition. We interpret the evidence to be inconsistent with the winner's curse.

As part of our analysis, we also analyze the market mechanisms and takeover characteristics that cross-sectionally affect the level of takeover competition. In particular, we study the role of investment banks (IBs) in impacting takeover competition as well as inducing or mitigating the winner's curse. Our results indicate that prestigious investment banks hired by the bidder do not promote the winner's curse.

To present our analysis, Section 2 describes our novel measure of takeover competition and develops our tests of the winner's curse. Section 3 reports the characteristics of the sample. Section 4 reports the OLS analysis of bidder returns and tests of the winner's curse. Section 5 reports analysis of the factors affecting the level of takeover competition. Section 6 synthesizes the analysis by reporting results from two-stage regressions that jointly model bidder returns and the level of takeover competition. Section 7 reports the operating performance following the takeovers in our sample and measures whether this ex post benchmark varies by the level of competition in the deals. Section 8 summarizes the paper and discusses the implications of our results.

2. Developing tests of the winner's curse

Our tests of the winner's curse examine whether the returns to a winning bidder are related to the level of competition in a takeover. The novel aspect of our analysis is that it includes data from the private sales process that occurs prior to the public announcement of a deal. This private sales process, which ranges from multiple-bidder auctions to one-on-one negotiations with a single bidder, is described by Herzel and Shepro (1990) and Wasserstein (2000), has been formally modeled by Hansen (2001), and has been empirically studied in the context of takeover targets by Boone and Mulherin (2007). By incorporating the private sales process, we have a better measure of takeover competition than is found in conventional studies such as Varaiya (1988), Moeller et al. (2004), and Schwert (1996, 2000), which narrowly measure takeover competition as the number of firms that make a public bid for the target.

2.1. Measuring takeover competition

To gauge competition, we use hand-collected information from SEC documents to determine the number of bidders in a given takeover. Two examples serve to illustrate the variety in the depth of competition across the corporate takeovers that we study. An example of an auction is the acquisition of Beneficial Corporation by Household International in 1998. The details of the auction are described in an S-4 filing related to the merger by Household International on June 1, 1998. In February 1998, the Beneficial board decided to consider strategic alternatives, including the possible sale of the company. Following this decision, Beneficial's investment banks, Goldman Sachs and Merrill Lynch, contacted or were contacted by 29 companies that expressed interest in a transaction. Confidentiality agreements were signed with 23 prospective bidders. In March 1998, Beneficial received preliminary indications of interest from several parties and continued discussions with the five parties with the highest indications of interest. These five parties engaged in extensive due diligence and were notified that the deadline for definitive proposals was April 6, 1998. In accordance with these bidding procedures, Household International delivered a definitive proposal on this date and the other four interested parties indicated that they were not willing to submit a superior proposal. The merger was executed on April 7, 1998. In spite of the active auction process for Beneficial indicated by the 29 companies contacted and the 23 signing confidentiality agreements, Household International was the only bidder making a formal public offer. Data from the Securities Data Corporation (SDC) report that the Beneficial deal had only one public bidder.

The merger between Honeywell and Allied Signal in 1999 provides an example of a negotiation. The background of the merger is provided in the merger proxy filing (DEFM 14A) by Honeywell Inc. dated July 29, 1999. After initial meetings between the two chief executive officers (CEOs) of the companies in February 1998, Honeywell indicated that it was not interested in pursuing a business combination. Talks were reinitiated in February 1999. As the talks heightened in May 1999, the two companies signed a confidentiality agreement that restricted the disclosure of confidential information and a standstill agreement that restricted the purchase of the other company's common stock. In conjunction with these agreements, the two companies pursued a 30-day exclusivity arrangement, agreeing not to enter discussion with any other party regarding a possible business combination. A draft merger agreement was distributed on May 26, 1999. The boards of the two companies approved the merger on June 4, 1999, and a press release announcing the merger was issued prior to trading on June 7, 1999.

To systemize the variety in takeover competition suggested by these two examples, we study 308 takeovers that were announced in the 1989–1999 period. Most of our observations are taken from Mulherin and Boone (2000). That paper began with the firms listed on the Value Line Investment Survey as of 1990 and determined those that were the object of a takeover during the 1990–1999 period. In the prior paper, 281 takeovers entailed US publicly traded bidders with available data on bidder returns. The current sample adds 27 observations for takeovers that were announced in 1999 but were completed in the year 2000. There are 251 mergers and 57 tender offers.

The sample has 290 completed takeovers and 18 unsuccessful deals. From a scrutiny of the news media, 10 of the unsuccessful deals can be attributed to antitrust or regulatory obstacles, four entailed hostile bids rebuffed by the target, and four lapsed due to financial changes at the target or the bidder. In results not reported in the paper, our findings are robust to whether or not we include the unsuccessful deals in the analysis.

For each observation, we use SEC documents to characterize the depth of bidder competition prior to the public announcement of the takeover. We analyze the number of firms that the target and its investment bank contacted, we determine the number of potential buyers signing confidentiality agreements that allowed the receipt of nonpublic information about the target, and we measure the number of firms that made private written offers for the target as well as the number of firms that announced formal bids in the public media. With some exceptions, the number of firms in each category declines sequentially with the number contacted being greater than the number signing confidential agreements, which is greater than private bidders, which usually is greater than or equal to the number of public bidders. The latter variable, the number of public bidders, is the measure of deal competition traditionally reported by SDC and in prior research such as Schwert (1996, 2000).

From this analysis, we classify the takeovers into auctions and negotiations. Auctions are takeovers in which the selling firm contacts multiple potential buyers and usually signs confidentiality agreements with more than one possible buyer. Negotiations are takeovers in which the selling firm focuses on a single buyer. In effect, our classification follows Fama and Laffer (1972) in modeling competition in deals with two or more active bidders. Our classification indicates that 145 (47%) of the takeovers are auctions and 163 (53%) are negotiations.

Table 1 summarizes the level of competition during the private sales process for the sample firms, reporting the mean, maximum, median, and minimum number of firms in each of the sales process categories. For the full sample reported in panel A, the average target firm and its investment bank contact roughly seven firms. An average of three potential bidders signs confidentiality agreements. The average number of bidders making private written bids is 1.24 and the average number of public bidders is 1.12.

Panel B of Table 1 contrasts the private sales process for auctions and negotiations. In an average auction, roughly 14 firms are contacted by the target. An average of six firms signs confidentiality agreements. The average number of firms making private written bids is 1.51 and the average number of public bidders is 1.23.

For negotiations, by construction, the depth of the competition in the private takeover process is much less than that for auctions. The average number of potential buyers contacted is 1.13. This value is greater than one because of some cases in which informal discussions did not develop, an initial negotiation fell through, or the target rebuffed an unsolicited bidder. For negotiations, the number of firms signing confidentiality agreements and making private written offers is always one. The average number of public bidders is slightly greater than one, and is greater than the average number of private bidders, because of a few cases in which another bidder made an unsolicited offer that was rebuffed by the target.

2.2. Tests of the winner's curse

The winner's curse is an empirical possibility in a common value environment in which, with full information, all bidders would assign the same value to the asset. However, each bidder has an imperfect signal as to the actual value of the asset. If the winner's curse is at play, even though the average value across bidders could be correct, the winning bidder is the one who most overvalued the auctioned asset.

Table 1

Summary of the sales process

This table summarizes the sales process for the sample of 308 takeovers. Panel A describes the sales process for the full sample. Contact reports the number of potential buyers with which the selling firm and its investment bank were in contact. Confidential reports the number of potential buyers that engaged in a confidentiality agreement with the selling firm. Private bidders reports the number of potential buyers that submitted a private written offer. Public bidders reports the number of potential buyers that announced a formal bid for the firm in the financial media. Panel B compares the sales process for auctions and negotiations. Auction refers to cases in which the selling firm contacted multiple potential buyers. Negotiation refers to a sales process in which the selling firm focused on a single buyer.

	Mean	Maximum	Median	Minimum
Panel A. Full sample (N = 308)				
Contact	7.10	150	2	1
Confidential	3.25	50	1	1
Private bidders	1.24	6	1	1
Public bidders	1.12	2	1	1
Panel B. By sales method				
Auction (N = 145)				
Contact	13.81	150	3	2
Confidential	5.77	50	2	1
Private bidders	1.51	6	1	1
Public bidders	1.23	2	1	1
Negotiation (N = 163)				
Contact	1.13	3	1	1
Confidential	1.00	1	1	1
Private bidders	1.00	1	1	1
Public bidders	1.02	2	1	1

The takeover market for publicly traded corporations has many attributes of the common value environment that potentially gives rise to the winner's curse. As noted by Schwert (1996), the marketable nature of publicly traded target firms implies a common value component. In general, auctions of assets that have liquid markets for resale involve common values (Bajari and Hortacsu, 2003; Kagel et al., 1995).

A possible criticism of assuming common values for corporate takeovers is the presence of synergies. However, synergies could also have a common value element (Varaiya, 1988), as two different bidders could both be able to reap the equivalent costs savings from acquiring a particular target. Empirically, the standard interpretation of data on the gains in mergers is that the sources of synergies are unique to targets and imply no special synergies, on average, to bidders (see, e.g., Asquith, 1983).

Even relaxing the assumption of a purely common value environment does not eliminate the potential for a winner's curse in corporate takeovers. Klemperer (1998) and Bulow and Klemperer (2002) note that allowing for some bidder asymmetry such as differential synergies can compound the potential winner's curse. But the presence of possible bidder asymmetries also heightens the importance of the choice of auction design in a given deal, a factor that we model as part of our analysis.

Given the assumption of a common value element in corporate takeovers, we offer several direct tests of the winner's curse. A central prediction is that any overvaluation of the auctioned asset is a function of the number of participants in a given auction. Hence, if the winner's curse is at play in the corporate takeover market, theory predicts that the returns to the winning bidder are inversely related to the magnitude of bid competition (Kagel and Levin, 1986). We implement this test by analyzing the relation between the announcement returns for the winning bidders in our sample and the level of competition in a given deal. The winner's curse predicts a significant, negative relation between bidder returns and the level of competition in a deal.

A second prediction of the winner's curse is that the return to the winning bidder is inversely related to the uncertainty in the value of the auctioned asset (Bazerman and Samuelson, 1983). We test this prediction by regressing bidder returns on variables that proxy for the uncertainty in the value of the target firms. The winner's curse predicts that bidder returns are negatively and significantly related to target uncertainty.

We supplement our tests of bidder returns with data on postmerger changes in operating performance. Roll (1986) argues that hubris and the winner's curse induce some takeovers that are mistakes that do not create synergies. Similarly, Thaler (1988, p. 192) notes that the winner's curse implies that the winning bidder would be disappointed in doing the deal. We examine this depiction of the winner's curse by estimating whether the operating performance of winning bidders is a function of the level of competition. The winner's curse predicts that operating performance is negatively and significantly related to takeover competition.

An alternative to the winner's curse predictions for bidder returns is the hypothesis of a competitive takeover market. Takeover competition has often been cited as an explanation of breakeven bidder returns (Asquith, 1983; Mandelker, 1974; Travlos, 1987). The takeover competition hypothesis argues that the presence of actual or potential competition leads to a pricing of the target that results in zero profits to the winning bidder. This hypothesis relies on the underlying structure of the takeover market and makes no prediction about the relation between the returns to the bidder and the number of bidders in a given deal. As noted by Fama and Laffer (1972, p. 674), "When there are at least two noncolluding firms in an industry, there is no clear-cut relationship between the number of firms and the degree of competition."

In the context of our empirical tests, the takeover competition hypothesis posits a model in which winning bidders rationally respond to the number of bidders and the uncertainty in the value of the target. For this hypothesis, the winning bidder does not make systematic errors and no relation should exist between bidder returns and either the number of bidders or the uncertainty in target value. Moreover, the takeover competition hypothesis predicts that the ex post operating performance of winning bidders would not be negative and, in particular, that the performance following auctions would not be different from that following negotiations.

3. Sample characteristics

This section reports the characteristics of the sample of takeovers used in our analysis. Table 2 reports the distribution of the takeovers by year for the sample period of 1989–1999. The takeovers cluster in the second half of the sample, with two-thirds of the observations occurring in the 1995–1999 period. Both auctions and negotiations have a similar distribution over time. For example, 48% of the deals in the 1989–1994 subperiod are auctions and 46% of the deals in the 1995–1999 subperiod are auctions. This indicates that, although the level of takeover activity varies during our sample period, the underlying depth of competition in the takeover market, as measured by the probability of an auction in any given deal, is similar over time.

Table 3 reports summary statistics for the different variables to be used in our analysis. Data are reported for the full sample as well as for the auction and negotiation subsamples. The final column presents the p-value from the test that the mean values of the auction and negotiation subsamples are equal.

Panel A of Table 3 reports data on target and bidder size. The bidder data refer to the winning bidder in the takeover. Targets have a mean value of $2.96 billion. Bidders are larger and have a mean value of $10.58 billion. The average size of the target relative to the bidder is 45%, which indicates that the deals in our sample have a significant magnitude of importance to the bidding firms. As also reported in panel A, both targets and bidders in auctions are significantly smaller than in negotiations, although the relative size of targets is comparable across the two takeover procedures.

Table 2

Sample by year

This table reports the number of takeovers per year in the sample period of 1989–1999. Takeovers are classified by year of initial announcement. Data are reported for the full sample and for the two sales procedures. Auction refers to cases in which the selling firm contacted multiple potential buyers. Negotiation refers to a sales process in which the selling firm focused on a single buyer.

Year	Full sample	Auction	Negotiation
1989	5	4	1
1990	20	9	11
1991	16	8	8
1992	20	11	9
1993	12	4	8
1994	22	10	12
1995	43	18	25
1996	33	17	16
1997	51	23	28
1998	52	21	31
1999	34	20	14
Total	308	145	163

Table 3

Sample statistics

This table reports summary statistics on size and deal characteristics for the sample of 308 takeovers. Data are reported for the full sample and for auctions and negotiations. Auction refers to cases in which the selling firm contacted multiple potential buyers. Negotiation refers to a sales process in which the selling firm focused on a single buyer. Panel A reports the mean and median values of firm size. Target and bidder size are the equity value (stock price × shares outstanding) in billions of dollars measured 64 days prior to the initial takeover announcement. Relative size is calculated as target size divided by bidder size. Bidder data are for the winning bidder. Panel B reports deal characteristics. Stock reports the fraction of cases in which the method of payment was at least partially in stock. Unsolicited reports the fraction of cases in which the event was initiated by the winning bidder or a third party. Panel C reports target firm characteristics. Intangible assets is one minus the ratio of the target's property, plant, and equipment divided by its assets in the year prior to the merger. Antitakeover state is a dummy variable equal to one if the target is located in a state with strong antitakeover regulation. Industry count represents the number of firms in the same Fama and French industry as the target with a market value greater than the target in the year prior to the merger. Target CEO gets a job is a dummy variable equal to one if the target chief executive officer (CEO) gets a job in the merged firm. Panel D reports investment bank characteristics. Bidder hires no IB is a dummy variable equal to one if the bidder does not use an investment bank (IB) as its adviser. Bidder Hires Top IB is a dummy variable equal to one if the bidder hires a top-tier investment bank as its adviser. Target hires top IB is a dummy variable equal to one if the target hires a top-tier investment bank as its adviser. Panel E reports bidder return values. Bidder returns are measured using net-of-market returns for the $(-1, +1)$ window in which day 0 is the initial announcement date for the bidder and the market index is the Center for Research in Security Prices value-weighted index. The final column presents the p-value of a means test that tests the null that the mean of the auction and negotiation samples are equal.

Variable	Full sample ($N = 308$)		Auction ($N = 145$)		Negotiation ($N = 163$)		p-Value
	Mean	Median	Mean	Median	Mean	Median	
Panel A. Firm size							
Target size	2.96	0.87	1.86	0.51	3.94	1.23	0.010
(billions of dollars)							
Bidder size	10.58	3.41	6.94	3.03	13.82	4.01	0.003
(billions of dollars)							
Relative size	45%	27%	46%	21%	44%	29%	0.837
Panel B. Deal characteristics							
Percent Stock	74		62		85		0.000
Percent Unsolicited	16		25		7		0.000
Panel C. Target characteristics							
Intangible assets	65%		68%		63%		0.116
Antitakeover state	14%		10%		17%		0.055
Industry count	69		81		59		0.010
Target CEO gets job	58%		42%		72%		0.000
Panel D. Investment bank characteristics							
Bidder hires no IB	26%		37%		15%		0.000
Bidder hires top IB	39%		28%		49%		0.000
Target hires top IB	57%		58%		56%		0.711
Panel E. Bidder returns $(-1, +1)$							
Bidder returns	−0.70%		−0.69%		−0.71%		0.985

Panel B of Table 3 reports deal characteristics of the sample takeovers. Seventy-four percent of the sample takeovers use some or all stock as a method of payment while the remaining 26% use all cash. Sixteen percent of the takeovers are unsolicited, defined as being initiated by the winning bidder or a third party. The deal characteristics vary between auctions and negotiations. Auctions are significantly more likely to use cash and to be unsolicited.

Panel C of Table 3 reports the characteristics of the target firms in the sample. The first variable, intangible assets, equals one minus the ratio of plant, property, and equipment to assets and proxies for the uncertainty in the value of the target. The variable averages 65% for the full sample. The second variable, strong antitakeover state, is a dummy variable equal to one for the 14% of the targets incorporated in states determined by Bebchuk and Ferrell (2002) to have heavy takeover impediments: Idaho, Indiana, Maryland, Nevada, Ohio, Pennsylvania, South Dakota, Tennessee, and Wisconsin. The third variable, industry count, is the number of firms on Compustat in the target's (Fama and French, 1997) industry with a value greater than the target in the year prior to the takeover announcement. This variable gauges the potential depth of the takeover market for a target and averages 69 for the full sample. The fourth variable, CEO gets job, is a dummy variable equal to one for cases in which the CEO of the target firm retains a position in the merged firm and depicts an ongoing relation between the target and the winning bidder. We follow Harford (2003) in measuring target CEO retention using the first proxy statement following the takeover. In 58% of the takeovers, the target CEO retains a position in the merged firm. Comparing the data in panel C across auctions and negotiations, auctions tend to be associated with target firms with a greater fraction of intangible assets, weaker antitakeover states, a higher industry count, and a lower likelihood that the target CEO gets a job at the merged firm.

Panel D in Table 3 provides information on the use of investment banks by the target and the winning bidder. We use SEC documents to determine whether the target and winning bidder use any investment bank and, if so, whether the investment bank is a top-tier firm. We classified as top tier the five banks appearing most often in the sample: Goldman Sachs, Morgan Stanley, Merrill Lynch, CS First Boston (including First Boston on its own), and Salomon Smith Barney (including Salomon Brothers on its own). The investment banks that we designate as top tier resemble prior research such as Bowers and Miller (1990) and Servaes and Zenner (1996). As reported in panel D, in 26% of the deals, winning bidders chose not to hire any investment bank, while in 39% of the takeovers the winning bidders hire a top-tier investment bank. In data not reported in Table 3, we find that all of the target firms used an investment bank. In 57% of the deals the targets used a top-tier bank. Comparing the data in panel D, auctions tend to have a slightly greater use of top-tier investment banks by the target firm and a measurably lower likelihood that the winning bidding firm uses a top-tier bank.

4. OLS analysis of bidder returns

In this section, we report our initial cross-sectional analysis of bidder returns. The bidder data refer to the winning bidder. The estimates of bidder returns are net-of-market returns for the $(-1, +1)$ window in which day zero is the initial announcement date for the bidder and the market is the Center for Research in Security Prices value-weighted index.

We first report simple comparisons of bidder returns in auctions versus negotiations. We then study how bidder returns interact with the investment banks employed by the targets and bidders. We then report OLS regression analysis that controls for other factors related to bidder returns. We also consider the robustness of the analysis for various proxies for takeover competition and for longer event periods.

4.1. Average bidder returns in auctions and negotiations

Panel E of Table 3 reports the basic event study analysis of bidder returns. For the full sample of 308 takeovers, the average bidder return is -0.70% (p-value $= 0.106$). The small, negative return for bidders is consistent with prior research such as Andrade et al. (2001).

Panel E of Table 3 also reports the bidder returns for the auction and negotiation subsamples. The mean bidder returns are virtually identical for the two sales procedures. The means test reported in the far right column indicates no significant difference between the bidder returns in auctions and negotiations. Because the results indicate no relation between bidder returns and the extent of takeover competition, the results are inconsistent with the presence of a winner's curse in our sample.

4.2. Modeling investment banking

To begin to understand some of the factors that affect bidder returns in the cross-section, we study the impact of investment banks. In particular, we study whether prestigious investment banks affect the potential winner's curse faced by bidders in the takeover process. Two distinct schools of thought exist on the relation between investment bank prestige and the winner's curse. Rau (2000) argues that prestigious investment banks are more concerned with deal completion than with bidder wealth maximization, suggesting that prestigious investment banks accentuate the winner's curse for bidding firms. By contrast, Kale et al. (2003) argue that investment banks with a high reputation have the incentive to mitigate the winner's curse.

Prior research provides useful guidance for modeling the relation between bidder returns and investment banks. Kale et al. (2003) point out that, because the target or the bidder or both can potentially hire a prestigious investment bank, one must account for the prestige of the investment bank used by both the bidder and the target. The Fernando et al. (2005) model of the initial public offering process indicates that the association between a firm and an investment bank is a joint matching decision that is based on the quality of both the firm and the bank. Servaes and Zenner (1996) note that some firms could have enough in-house expertise so as to elect not to use an investment bank, and Kale et al. (2003, p. 483) argue that such in-house expertise should be accounted for when studying the bargaining between targets and bidders.

Following the guidance of prior research, Table 4 reports initial data on how the interaction between target and bidder investment banks affects bidder returns. Because all target firms employ an investment bank in our sample, the data are stratified by whether the target employs a top- or low-tier investment bank. The data are also

Table 4

Investment bank quality and bidder returns

This table reports the returns of the 308 bidder firms over the $(-1, +1)$ window by the use and quality of investment banks employed by both the bidder and target companies. Bidder data refer to the winning bidder. Bidder no bank refers to cases in which the bidder firm did not hire any outside investment bank to assist it in the takeover. All target firms in the sample hired an investment bank. Lo bank refers to mergers in which either the bidder or target firm employed an investment bank but did not hire a top-tier bank. Top bank refers to mergers in which either the bidder or target firm hired a top-tier investment bank. Top-tier banks were classified as the five banks appearing most often in the sample: Goldman Sachs, Morgan Stanley, Merrill Lynch, CS First Boston (including First Boston on its own), and Salomon Smith Barney (including Salomon Brothers on its own). The means test compares whether the returns across the given investment bank subsamples are statistically different.

	Full sample	Target lo bank	Target top bank	Means test: lo target bank versus top target bank [t-statistic/ (p-value)]
Full sample	−0.70%	0.80%	−1.90%	3.109
	($N = 308$)	($N = 133$)	($N = 175$)	(0.002)
Bidder no bank	0.80%	2.10%	−0.80%	1.773
	($N = 79$)	($N = 43$)	($N = 36$)	(0.080)
Bidder yes bank	−1.20%	0.20%	−2.10%	2.296
	($N = 229$)	($N = 90$)	($N = 139$)	(0.023)
Bidder lo bank	−2.20%	0.00%	−3.70%	2.470
	($N = 109$)	($N = 44$)	($N = 65$)	(0.015)
Bidder top bank	−0.30%	0.40%	−0.80%	0.843
	($N = 120$)	($N = 46$)	($N = 74$)	(0.401)
Means tests across bidder investment bank categories [t-statistic/(p-value)]				
No bank versus yes bank	1.985	1.132	1.110	
	(0.048)	(0.260)	(0.269)	
No bank versus lo bank	2.592	1.064	2.262	
	(0.010)	(0.291)	(0.026)	
No bank versus top bank	1.012	0.874	−0.048	
	(0.313)	(0.384)	(0.962)	
Lo bank versus top bank	−1.850	−0.196	−2.538	
	(0.066)	(0.845)	(0.012)	

stratified by whether the bidder employs an investment bank and, if so, whether the chosen investment bank is top tier or low tier. This presentation of the data reveals some interesting regularities. First, the choice of a top-tier bank by the target is negatively associated with bidder returns. Second, bidder returns are lower when the bidder employs an investment bank. However, a further parsing of the data indicates that this result is associated with the cases in which the bidder employs a low-tier investment bank.

4.3. OLS regression analysis of bidder returns

We next perform OLS regression analysis of bidder returns. While OLS analysis in our setting has potential biases due to endogeneity (Hansen, 1985; Smith, 1987), we report these results in the interests of full disclosure and to also enable comparisons with the two-stage analysis reported later in the paper.

We use two explanatory variables to test for the winner's curse. The first variable is a dummy variable that takes a value of one if the target was sold via an auction. The winner's curse predicts that the coefficient of this dummy variable should be negative and statistically significant from zero. The second variable that we use is intangible assets, which proxies for the uncertainty in the value of the targets assets. If the winner's curse is at play, bidder returns should be negatively and significantly related to intangible assets.

In our analysis, we follow conventional practice and report two-tailed statistical tests. While the alternative hypothesis of the winner's curse makes unidirectional predictions that a negative relation exists between bidder returns and both takeover competition and target uncertainty, the winner's curse is not the only alternative hypothesis. For example, Officer et al. (2009) offer an optimal contracting hypothesis that predicts a positive relation between bidder returns and the uncertainty in the value of the target, an alternative hypothesis that is the opposite sign of the winner's curse. Officer et al. (2009) also provide supporting evidence for their alternative hypothesis. The presence of competing alternative hypotheses suggests the use of two-tailed tests.

However, because our analysis emphasizes tests of the winner's curse, a case could be made that one-tailed tests are more appropriate.[1] Because we provide *p*-values for all of our results, the reported two-tailed tests can be readily converted to one-tailed tests by dividing by two. We note in the text any cases in which the distinction between one- and two-tailed tests is important.

We include as control variables in the regression analysis, variables shown in prior research to be related to bidder returns: the size of the target relative to the bidder, bidder size, whether the method of payment included some stock, and whether the deal was unsolicited. Prior research by Asquith et al. (1983) and Jarrell and Poulsen (1989) find a positive relation between bidder returns and the relative size of the target.

---

[1] We acknowledge the referee for making this point.

Moeller et al. (2004) find that bidder returns are negatively related to bidder size. Travlos (1987) finds that bidder returns are inversely related to the use of stock as a method of payment. Schwert (2000) reports that bidder returns are negatively related to his composite measure of unsolicited deals.

We also include variables capturing the role of investment banks in the takeover process. From the guidance in prior research and our own findings in Table 4, we use three investment bank variables. The first two variables account for both the bidder's joint choice as to whether to use an investment bank and, if so, whether to use a top-tier bank. The first variable, bidder hires no IB, is a dummy variable equal to one in the cases in which the bidder does not use an investment bank (IB). The second variable, bidder hires top bank, is a dummy variable equal to one when the bidder uses a top-tier investment bank and zero if the bidder either uses a low-tier investment bank or does not use an investment bank. The third variable, target hires top bank, is a dummy variable equal to one when the target uses a top-tier investment bank.

The results of the OLS regression are reported in Table 5. In the regression, the coefficient on the auction dummy variable is negative but not significantly different from zero. Like the simple means test in panel E of Table 3, this result is inconsistent with the winner's curse. The coefficient on intangible assets is positive and significant. This implies that bidder returns are more positive when the assets of the target are more intangible, which is the opposite of the prediction of the winner's curse. Our results for intangible assets resemble the Officer et al. (2009) analysis of the acquisition of private targets, which also finds that bidder returns are positively related to the uncertainty in the value of the target. For the four control variables, relative size, bidder size, stock, and unsolicited, the coefficients generally have the sign and significance reported in prior research.

In Table 5, the signs of the coefficients of the bidder hires no IB variable and the bidder hires top bank variable are both positive and significant. These findings indicate that the use of an investment bank by the bidder has a negative effect on bidder returns but, consistent with Kale et al. (2003), the choice of a top-tier investment bank has an incremental positive effect on bidder returns. The results suggest that bidders that lack in-house expertise and that are not clients of top-tier investment banks fare relatively worse in a takeover transaction, along the lines of the sorting model of Fernando et al. (2005). We also find that the use of a top-tier bank by the target firm has a negative effect on bidder returns, which is also consistent with Kale et al. (2003), who argue that investment banks with greater reputations favorably affect their client during the bargaining in a particular deal.

4.4. Other proxies for takeover competition

The analysis in Table 5 uses a discrete variable (auction vs. negotiation) to proxy for the level of competition in a given takeover. To test for the robustness of the results, we repeat the analysis using four continuous measures of takeover competition summar-

Table 5

Ordinary least squares regression analysis of bidder returns, $(-1, +1)$ window

This table reports regression analysis of bidder returns on variables that capture the sales procedure, deal size, payment method, and acquisition form. Bidder data are for the winning bidder. The dependent variable is net-of-market bidder returns for the $(-1, +1)$ window in which day 0 is the first date the bidder is announced in the financial press and the market index is the Center for Research in Security Prices value-weighted index. Auction is a dummy variable equal to one when the sales procedure is an auction. Intangible assets is one minus the ratio of the target's property, plant, and equipment divided by its assets in the year prior to the merger. Relative size is the natural log of the equity value of the target divided by the equity value of the bidder 64 days prior to the initial announcement date. Bidder size is the natural log of bidder equity value measured 64 days prior to the initial takeover announcement. Stock is a dummy variable equal to one for acquisitions in which the payment is at least partially made in stock. Unsolicited is a dummy variable equal to one for deals that were initiated by the bidder or a third party. Bidder hires no IB is a dummy variable equal to one when the bidder does not use an investment bank (IB). Bidder hires top bank is a dummy variable equal to one when the bidder uses a top-tier investment bank and zero if the bidder either uses a lower tier investment bank or no investment bank at all. Target hires top bank is a dummy variable equal to one if the target uses a top-tier investment bank and zero if the target uses a lower tier investment bank. The p-values of the regression coefficients are reported in parentheses. The model p-value and adjusted R^2 are reported at the bottom of the table. The regression employs 308 observations.

Variable	$(-1, +1)$ Window
Intercept	0.213
	(0.000)
Auction	−0.010
	(0.281)
Intangible assets	0.033
	(0.024)
Relative size	0.011
	(0.007)
Bidder size	−0.009
	(0.002)
Stock	−0.038
	(0.000)
Unsolicited	−0.024
	(0.044)
Bidder hires no IB	0.036
	(0.002)
Bidder hires top bank	0.028
	(0.003)
Target hires top bank	−0.016
	(0.060)
Model p-value	0.000
Adjusted R^2	0.145

ized in Table 1: the number of bidders contacted by the target firm, signing confidentiality agreements, making written private bids, and publicly making a bid.

The results of this analysis are reported in Table 6. Each of the four regressions uses one continuous measure of takeover competition with the control and investment bank

Table 6

Ordinary least squares regression analysis, other proxies for takeover competition

This table reports regression analysis of bidder returns on variables that include various proxies for takeover competition. Bidder data are for the winning bidder. The dependent variable is net-of-market bidder returns for the $(-1, +1)$ window in which day 0 is the first date the bidder is announced in the financial press and the market index is the Center for Research in Security Prices value-weighted index. Contact is the natural log of the number of buyers contacted by the selling firm and its investment bank. Confidential is the natural log of the number of buyers that engaged in a confidentiality agreement. Private bidders is the natural log of the number of buyers that submitted a private written offer. Public bidders is the natural log of the number of buyers that announced a formal bid in the financial media. Intangible assets is one minus the ratio of the target's property, plant, and equipment divided by its assets in the year prior to the merger. Relative size is the natural log of the equity value of the target divided by the equity value of the bidder 64 days prior to the initial announcement date. Bidder size is the natural log of bidder equity value measured 64 days prior to the initial takeover announcement. Stock is a dummy variable equal to one for acquisitions in which the payment is at least partially made in stock. Unsolicited is a dummy variable equal to one for deals that were initiated by the bidder or a third party. Bidder hires no IB is a dummy variable equal to one when the bidder does not use an investment bank (IB). Bidder hires top bank is a dummy variable equal to one when the bidder uses a top-tier investment bank and zero if the bidder either uses a lower tier investment bank or no investment bank at all. Target hires top bank is a dummy variable equal to one if the target uses a top-tier investment bank and zero if the target uses a lower tier investment bank. The p-values of the regression coefficients are reported in parentheses. The model p-value and adjusted R^2 for each regression are reported at the bottom of the table. Each regression employs 308 observations.

Variable	(1)	(2)	(3)	(4)
Intercept	0.209	0.214	0.209	0.201
	(0.000)	(0.000)	(0.000)	(0.000)
Contacted	−0.003	-	-	-
	(0.410)			
Confidential	-	−0.006	-	-
		(0.193)		
Private bidders	-	-	−0.020	-
			(0.109)	
Public bidders	-	-	-	−0.017
				(0.391)
Intangible assets	0.033	0.032	0.033	0.032
	(0.028)	(0.027)	(0.026)	(0.032)
Relative size	0.011	0.011	0.011	0.012
	(0.006)	(0.005)	(0.004)	(0.003)
Bidder size	−0.009	−0.009	−0.008	−0.008
	(0.003)	(0.002)	(0.003)	(0.004)
Stock	−0.037	−0.038	−0.038	−0.037
	(0.000)	(0.000)	(0.000)	(0.000)
Unsolicited	−0.024	−0.024	−0.026	−0.024
	(0.042)	(0.043)	(0.024)	(0.047)
Bidder hires no IB	0.037	0.038	0.037	0.037
	(0.002)	(0.001)	(0.002)	(0.002)
Bidder hires top bank	0.029	0.029	0.029	0.029
	(0.002)	(0.002)	(0.002)	(0.002)
Target hires top bank	−0.017	−0.017	−0.017	−0.018
	(0.048)	(0.052)	(0.042)	(0.038)
Model p-value	0.000	0.000	0.000	0.000
Adjusted R^2	0.144	0.147	0.149	0.144

variables. In each regression, the coefficient on the measure of takeover competition is negative. Assuming a two-tailed test, none of the coefficients for the competition measures is statistically significant. However, if one instead assumes a one-tailed test, the coefficients in two of the four regressions, for the confidential and private bidders measures of competition, would be significant at the 10% level. Hence, assuming a one-tailed test, these two cases show some evidence of the winner's curse in the OLS specifications using continuous measures of takeover competition.

The other variables in Table 6 have signs and significance similar to that in Table 5. In particular, the coefficient on intangible assets is positive and significant, which is the opposite sign of the winner's curse hypothesis.

4.5. Longer event windows

As a further robustness check, we report regression results for bidder returns estimated over longer event periods, the $(-20, +20)$ and $(-63, +126)$ windows. The longer windows possibly capture information not reflected at the time of the specific takeover announcement but introduce noise relative to the $(-1, +1)$ window (Fama, 1991).

The results for the two longer event windows can be quickly summarized and more detailed results are available upon request. For the $(-20, +20)$ window, the results resemble those for the narrower event window reported in Table 5. The coefficient on the auction dummy variable is negative but statistically insignificant assuming either two- or one-tailed test. The coefficient on intangible assets is positive and significant. For the $(-63, +126)$ window, the coefficient on the auction dummy flips to a positive sign while the coefficient on intangible assets is positive but is no longer significant. These results for the longer windows are not consistent with the winner's curse.

5. Modeling the level of competition in a takeover

While not broad based, the results in the Section 4 report some evidence consistent with the winner's curse, specifically in two of the four specifications in Table 6. However, the analysis using OLS suffers from potential biases due to endogeneity (Hansen, 1985; Smith, 1987). In the auction setting that we study, the wealth effects for bidders and the level of competition in a deal are jointly determined. To account for endogeneity, this section uses auction theory to develop an empirical model of the cross-sectional variation in the level of competition in the takeovers in our sample. Summary statistics on the variables that we use are provided in Table 3.

5.1. The explanatory variables

In contrast to classical auction theory, which assumes zero information costs and symmetric bidders, the theories on auction design model the effects of information costs and bidder asymmetry on the sales process. Hansen (2001, p. 33) lays out the general framework, representing the sales process for corporate targets as a balance between the benefits of obtaining more bidders and the information costs of takeover deals. He argues (p. 36) that if information costs are low, the target seeks many bidders, while if information costs are high, the target negotiates with a single bidder.

Related research identifies particular factors that affect auction design and the number of bidders. French and McCormick (1984) provide a model in which the selling firm balances the costs and benefits of adding potential bidders in an auction. They argue (p. 430) that the greater the uncertainty in the asset being sold, the greater the benefit of having more bidders incur the costs of valuing the assets. To test this prediction, we use the intangible assets of the target firm as an explanatory variable and predict that this variable is positively related to the level of competition in a corporate takeover.

French and McCormick (1984) suggest that uncertainty in the value of the target can also be proxied by whether the buyer and the seller have an ongoing relation and argue (p. 433) that a buyer and a seller with an ongoing relation is more likely to conduct a negotiated sale. We proxy for an ongoing relation with a dummy variable that takes a value of one when the target CEO retains a job at the merged firm.

Uncertainty in valuation can also cause interactions between takeover competition and other deal characteristics such as the method of payment. Hansen (1987) models how the method of payment is a function of the adverse selection between the bidder and the target and predicts that stock is used the greater is this adverse selection. Hence, to the extent that the use of stock indicates the presence of adverse selection, we would expect the use of stock as the method of payment to be negatively related to the occurrence of auctions. In a related vein, given that a bidder in a stock deal would have to reveal more information to the target, that bidder would prefer a negotiation rather than an auction so as to protect confidential information as modeled by Hansen (2001). Empirically, prior research by both Houston and Ryngaert (1997) and Officer (2004) provides evidence that the use of stock is inversely related to takeover competition.

Prior research suggests other target characteristics that could affect the level of competition in a takeover. Comment and Schwert (1995) provide evidence that the more stringent is a state's antitakeover law, the greater is the bargaining power of the target. The greater bargaining power would lessen the likelihood that the target would sell itself via an auction. Hence, we predict that the level of competition in a takeover is lower for targets in strong antitakeover states as classified by Bebchuk and Ferrell (2002).

Prior research also suggests that the quality of financial advisers used by the target and the bidder affects the level of competition in a takeover transaction. Ma (2005) argues that high-quality investment banks maintain longer client lists and that the use of a high quality bank by a target firm would thereby be associated with a greater number of potential bidders. Kale et al. (2003) argue that the use of a high-quality investment bank by the bidding firm should increase the bargaining power of the bidder and thereby lessen the number of other bidders.

Theory also suggests that the level of competition is a function of bidder characteristics. Bulow and Klemperer (2002) point to asymmetry between bidders as an important determinant of auction design (see also Klemperer, 1998; Povel and Singh, 2006). In their model, the presence of a strong bidder would heighten the possibility of a winner's curse for other possible bidders and would scuttle any gains from conducting an auction. Hence, bidder asymmetry implies gains from limiting takeover competition. We use the size of the bidder as a proxy for this asymmetry and predict that the level of competition is inversely related to bidder size.

Klemperer (2002) more generally points to the number of potential bidders as a determinant of auction design. He argues that the actual level of competition in a takeover is directly related to the number of potential bidders. We proxy for the number of potential bidders with industry count, which is the number of firms in the same Fama and French (1997) industry that have a value greater than the target. We predict that the level of competition in a takeover is positively related to industry count.

A final deal characteristic that we study is whether the takeover was initially unsolicited. Theory by Fishman (1988) and empirical work by Betton and Eckbo (2000) indicate that target managers are more likely to resist low-premium offers. Schwert (2000) finds that deals identified as hostile in the financial media are more likely to have multiple public bidders. This suggests that unsolicited offerings are likely to induce the target firm to conduct an auction.

5.2. Empirical analysis of the choice of sales procedure

Our empirical analysis of the factors affecting the level of takeover competition is reported in Table 7. In the analysis, the dependent variable is the dichotomous variable of the choice of the sales procedure, which takes a value of one for auctions and a value of zero for negotiations. We choose this basic depiction of takeover competition out of a desire for simplicity and also because the extant theory does not provide guidance on the functional form for the continuous measures of competition.

The results in Table 7 are generally consistent with the predictions taken from auction theory. As predicted by French and McCormick (1984), the sign on the coefficient of target intangible assets is positive and significant, indicating that firms with more intangible assets are more likely to conduct an auction. The coefficient on the dummy for the target CEO retaining a job is negative and significant, indicating that a bidder and a target in an ongoing relation are more likely to conduct a negotiated sale.

The results in Table 7 also indicate that the level of takeover competition interacts with the method of payment. As predicted by Hansen (1987), stock is used less in auctions. Bargaining power also appears to be an important determinant of the level of competition in corporate takeovers. As suggested by Comment and Schwert (1995), targets incorporated in strong antitakeover states are less likely to conduct an auction.

We find some evidence that the quality of the financial advisers used in a transaction affects the level of takeover competition. The results indicate that the use of a high-quality investment bank by the bidding firm is inversely related to takeover

Table 7

Choice of sales procedure

This table reports a probit regression analysis of the choice of sales procedure. The dependent variable, auction, equals one if the target firm is sold via an auction and equals zero if the target is sold via a negotiation. Intangible assets is one minus the ratio of the target's property, plant, and equipment divided by its assets in the year prior to the merger. Target CEO gets a job is a dummy variable equal to one if the target chief executive officer (CEO) gets a job in the merged firm. Stock is a dummy variable equal to one for acquisitions in which the payment is at least partially made in stock. Antitakeover state is a dummy variable equal to one if the target is located in a state with strong antitakeover regulation. Bidder hires top IB is a dummy variable equal to one if the bidder hires a top-tier investment bank (IB) as its adviser. Target hires top IB is a dummy variable equal to one if the target hires a top-tier investment bank as its adviser. Bidder size is the natural log of bidder equity value measured 64 days prior to the initial takeover announcement. Bidder data are for the winning bidder. Industry count is the natural log of the number of firms in the same Fama and French industry as the target with a market value of greater than the target in the year prior to the merger. Unsolicited is a dummy variable equal to one for deals that were initiated by the bidder or a third party. The p-values of the regression coefficients are reported in parentheses. The likelihood ratio chi-square value, the chi-square p-value, and pseudo-R^2 for the regression are reported at the bottom of the table. The marginal effects report the change in the probability for an infinitesimal change in each continuous independent variable and the discrete change in the probability for dummy independent variables.

Variable	Coefficients	Marginal effects
Intercept	1.249	–
	(0.195)	
Intangible assets	0.504	0.201
	(0.073)	
Target CEO gets a job	−0.568	−0.224
	(0.001)	
Stock	−0.350	−0.139
	(0.072)	
Antitakeover state	−0.470	−0.180
	(0.051)	
Bidder hires top bank	−0.477	0.092
	(0.003)	
Target hires top bank	0.234	−0.187
	(0.152)	
Bidder size	−0.107	−0.043
	(0.044)	
Industry count	0.150	0.060
	(0.054)	
Unsolicited	0.663	0.257
	(0.005)	
Likelihood ratio chi-square	73.89	
p-Value of chi-square	(0.000)	
Pseudo-R^2	0.174	

competition, which supports the arguments in Kale et al. (2003). The coefficient on the dummy variable equal to one for targets using a high-quality investment bank is positive but is not statistically significant (p-value $= 0.152$) and therefore differs from the evidence in Ma (2005), which relies on a measure of takeover competition based on the number of publicly reported bidders.

The results in Table 7 also indicate that bidder characteristics are a significant determinant of takeover competition. The coefficient on bidder size is negative and significant, consistent with the model of Bulow and Klemperer (2002) in which bidder asymmetry lessens the value of conducting a full-scale auction. The coefficient on industry count is positive and significant, which supports the Klemperer (2002) point that the likelihood of an auction is directly related to the potential depth of the bidder pool.

Table 7 also reports that auctions are more likely to be used in unsolicited deals that are initiated by the bidder or a third party. Hence, a natural response of a target faced by an unsolicited bid is to seek other buyers. This finding could suggest one cost to conducting an unsolicited takeover in the 1990s environment that we study.

6. Regression analysis that incorporates selection

The results in Section 5 indicate that the choice of the sales procedure in a corporate takeover is not a random event but is instead related to target, bidder, and deal characteristics. Because of this apparent selection, our OLS regressions of bidder returns that test for the winner's curse might not produce consistent estimators (Li and Prabhala, 2007). To account for selection, this section reports analysis using two-step regressions as well as a simultaneous equations system.

6.1. Two-step regression analysis

Our first method of dealing with selection is a two-step treatment method that has been used in related corporate finance applications such as Bris et al. (2006) and Campa and Kedia (2002). The first-step estimates procedure*, the predicted sales procedure, using the probit model in Table 7. The second step uses this predicted value in our regressions of bidder returns. The winner's curse predicts that the coefficient of procedure* is negative and significantly different from zero.

This method accounts for the factors affecting the choice of sales procedure but assumes that this choice is exogenous to bidder returns. Although not necessary for identification under our assumptions, the model is clearly identified because the probit model in Table 7 has several variables that are not in our model of bidder returns: CEO gets a job, antitakeover state, and industry count. Moreover, our analysis indicates that these variables are individually and jointly significantly related to the choice of the sales procedure but are neither individually nor jointly significantly related to bidder returns. The estimation method in the Stata statistical package relies on the parameters and covariance matrix in Heckman (1979) to produce consistent estimators.

The results of the second stage of the two-step analysis are reported in Table 8. For all three event windows, the coefficient on procedure*, the predicted value of the sales procedure from the model in Table 7, is negative but not statistically significant. These results are similar to the OLS regression in Table 5. The coefficients of the other explanatory variables in the regressions generally retain the sign and significance reported in the OLS regressions. In two of the three regressions, the coefficient on intangible assets is positive and significant, which is inconsistent with the winner's curse.

The lack of difference between our OLS regression in Table 5 and the two-step analysis reported in Table 8 is reflected in values of Lambda, which is the product of the correlation between the error terms in the two equations in the two-step analysis and the standard error of the second regression. We test for null that there is no selection bias, that is, Lambda equal to zero. As reported by the p-values reported toward the bottom of Table 8, we cannot reject the null that Lambda equals zero.

6.2. Simultaneous equations analysis

Thee two-step analysis reported above assumes that there is selection in the choice of sales procedure but that this choice is exogenous to bidder returns. Yet, on the assumption that bidders choose to participate in a particular sales procedure to maximize returns, the chosen procedure and the wealth effects for a bidder are jointly determined. Hence, a simultaneous equations system is arguably the more appropriate framework. Lowry and Shu (2002), Officer (2003), and Smith (1987) also use simultaneous equations analysiss in related applications.

To implement the simultaneous equations system, we first regress the two dependent variables, bidder returns and the sales procedure (i.e., auction or negotiation), on a set of exogenous variables. In the second stage, we use the fitted value for a given dependent variable as an explanatory variable for the other dependent variable. In particular, in the first stage we estimate procedure*, the fitted value for the choice of the sales procedure, and then regress that estimate on bidder returns in the second stage. The winner's curse predicts that procedure* is negatively and significantly related to bidder returns. Because the regression for the sales procedure is a qualitative choice model, care must be taken in estimating the standard errors (Maddala, 1983, pp. 244–245). Our estimation uses the Stata statistical package as described in Keshk (2003).

As exogenous variables in the model, we use the intersection of the variables that prior research has shown to affect bidder returns as well as the variables that auction theory predicts affect the choice of the sales procedure. These variables are intangible assets, the relative size of the target to the bidder, bidder size, whether the method of payment includes some stock, whether the deal was unsolicited, a dummy for deals in which the target hires a high-quality investment bank, a dummy for when the bidder hires any investment bank, a dummy for when the bidder hires a high-quality invest-

Table 8

Treatment regression of bidder returns to control for self-selection

This table reports two-step treatment regression analysis using Heckman's two-step consistent estimates for bidder returns. Bidder data are for the winning bidder. Returns are measured using net-of-market returns for the $(-1, +1)$, $(-20, +20)$, and $(-63, +126)$ windows, in which day 0 is the initial announcement date and the market index is the Center for Research in Security Prices value-weighted index. Procedure* is the predicted value of the choice of sales procedure from the first stage in which the inputs are the same as in Table 7. Intangible assets is one minus the ratio of the target's property, plant, and equipment divided by its assets in the year prior to the merger. Relative size is the natural log of the equity value of the target divided by the equity value of the bidder 64 days prior to the initial announcement date. Bidder size is the natural log of bidder equity value measured 64 days prior to the initial takeover announcement. Stock is a dummy variable equal to one for acquisitions in which the payment is at least partially made in stock. Unsolicited is a dummy variable equal to one for deals that were initiated by the bidder or a third party. Bidder hires no IB is a dummy variable equal to one when the bidder does not use an investment bank (IB). Bidder hires top bank is a dummy variable equal to one when the bidder uses a top-tier investment bank and zero if the bidder either uses a lower tier investment bank or no investment bank at all. Target hires top bank is a dummy variable equal to one if the target uses a top-tier investment bank and zero if the target uses a lower tier investment bank. The p-values of the regression coefficients are reported in parentheses. The Lambda coefficient (test for selection bias) and its p-value, along with the model p-value are reported at the bottom of the table. There are 308 observations for the $(-1, +1)$ and $(-20, +20)$ windows, but 307 for the $(-63, +126)$ window due to missing data.

	Window		
Variable	$(-1, +1)$	$(-20, +20)$	$(-63, +126)$
Intercept	0.213	0.161	0.506
	(0.000)	(0.118)	(0.103)
Procedure*	−0.007	−0.023	−0.197
	(0.827)	(0.684)	(0.243)
Intangible assets	0.033	0.052	0.094
	(0.031)	(0.039)	(0.221)
Relative size	0.011	−0.006	−0.030
	(0.007)	(0.283)	(0.098)
Bidder size	−0.009	−0.009	−0.030
	(0.012)	(0.109)	(0.065)
Stock	−0.037	−0.032	−0.087
	(0.001)	(0.088)	(0.122)
Unsolicited	−0.024	−0.022	−0.018
	(0.080)	(0.334)	(0.792)
Bidder hires no IB	0.037	0.049	0.078
	(0.001)	(0.008)	(0.138)
Bidder hires top bank	0.028	0.037	0.041
	(0.007)	(0.033)	(0.430)
Target hires top bank	−0.016	−0.029	0.012
	(0.070)	(0.051)	(0.782)
Lambda	−0.001	0.011	0.158
	(0.950)	(0.741)	(0.125)
Model p-value	0.000	0.000	0.126

ment bank, a dummy for when the target CEO retains a job with the merged firm, a dummy for targets in strong antitakeover states, and industry count, the number of firms in the target's industry that are larger than the target. The system is identified because of the lack of a complete intersection in the variables that have been found to affect bidder returns and the variables that are in our empirical model of the sales procedure.

Table 9 reports the simultaneous equations analysis for the $(-1, +1)$ window. The table presents both the first- and second-stage regressions for bidder returns and the choice of sales procedure. Our main variable of interest is procedure*, the fitted value of the choice of sales procedure. The coefficient of this variable is positive and statistically insignificant, which is not consistent with the winner's curse.

The other variables in the second-stage regressions for bidder returns tend to retain the sign and statistical significance reported in the OLS specification in Table 5. In particular, the coefficient on intangible assets is positive and significant, which is also inconsistent with the winner's curse.

We also conducted simultaneous equations analysis using the four continuous measures of competition. Table 10 reports the second-stage regressions for bidder returns. For three of the competition variables (contacted, confidential, and public bidders), the coefficient is positive and insignificant. The coefficient on the private bidders variable is negative, but not statistically significant whether using a two- or a one-tailed test. The results in Table 10 differ from the results of the OLS regressions using the continuous measures of competition in Table 6. In the OLS analysis, two of the four measures had statistically negative coefficients using a one-tailed test. The lack of statistical significance in the analysis in Table 10 that controls for endogeneity is evidence against the winner's curse and suggests that the two cases consistent with the winner's curse in Table 6 were due to biases in the OLS analysis.

As a further robustness check, we perform simultaneous regression analysis for the two longer event windows, the $(-20, +20)$ period and the $(-63, +126)$ period and with the auction dummy as the dependent variable. In results not reported in the tables, we find that for both event windows the coefficient on procedure* in the second-stage regression for bidder returns is negative and insignificant. These results continue to be inconsistent with the winner's curse.

6.3. Robustness analysis

We conduct a further battery of robustness analyses that are reported in Table 11. The table reports the coefficients and p-values of the auction and uncertainty variables. These variables are part of second-stage regressions of two-stage least squares simultaneous equations analysis of bidder returns in the $(-1, +1)$ window that contain the same variables as in Table 9 except as noted.

Panel A reports regressions that estimate abnormal bidder returns with two different benchmarks: size-adjusted deciles and the Fama and French (1993) three factors. For both of these alternative benchmarks, the coefficient of the fitted value of the auction

Table 9

Simultaneous regression analysis, $(-1, +1)$ window

This table reports two-stage least squares simultaneous equations analysis for bidder returns and for the choice of sales procedure. Bidder data are for the winning bidder. Returns are measured using net-of-market returns for the $(-1, +1)$ window, in which day 0 is the initial announcement date and the market index is the Center for Research in Security Prices value-weighted index. Procedure* is the predicted value of the choice of sales procedure. Returns* is the predicted value of bidder returns. Intangible assets is one minus the ratio of the target's property, plant, and equipment divided by its assets in the year prior to the merger. Relative size is the natural log of the equity value of the target divided by the equity value of the bidder 64 days prior to the initial announcement date. Bidder size is the natural log of bidder equity value measured 64 days prior to the initial takeover announcement. Stock is a dummy variable equal to one for acquisitions in which the payment is at least partially made in stock. Unsolicited is a dummy variable equal to one for deals that were initiated by the bidder or a third party. Bidder hires no IB is a dummy variable equal to one when the bidder does not use an investment bank (IB). Bidder hires top IB is a dummy variable equal to one if the bidder hires a top-tier investment bank as its adviser. Target hires top IB is a dummy variable equal to one if the target hires a top-tier investment bank as its adviser. Target CEO gets a job is a dummy variable equal to one if the target chief executive officer (CEO) gets a job in the merged firm. Antitakeover state is a dummy variable equal to one if the target is located in a state with strong antitakeover regulation. Industry count is the natural log of the number of firms in the same Fama and French industry as the target with a market value of greater than the target in the year prior to the merger. The analysis uses the 308 takeovers with available bidder equity data. (*p*-Values are in parentheses).

Variable	Bidder returns		Sales procedure	
	First stage	Second stage	First stage	Second stage
Intercept	0.257	0.192	2.135	0.105
	(0.000)	(0.001)	(0.043)	(0.951)
Procedure*		0.002		
		(0.895)		
Returns*				4.831
				(0.425)
Intangible assets	0.031	0.031	0.473	0.367
	(0.038)	(0.046)	(0.096)	(0.262)
Relative size	0.009	0.011	−0.016	
	(0.024)	(0.007)	(0.843)	
Bidder size	−0.011	−0.008	−0.125	−0.045
	(0.001)	(0.039)	(0.043)	(0.637)
Stock	−0.062	−0.036	−0.324	−0.204
	(0.002)	(0.003)	(0.103)	(0.441)
Unsolicited	−0.029	−0.027	0.645	0.795
	(0.015)	(0.065)	(0.006)	(0.006)
Bidder hires no IB	0.034	0.035	0.271	-
	(0.004)	(0.006)	(0.236)	
Bidder hires top bank	0.030	0.030	−0.370	−0.572
	(0.002)	(0.005)	(0.042)	(0.004)
Target hires top IB	−0.018	−0.018	0.271	0.317
	(0.038)	(0.062)	(0.106)	(0.101)
Target CEO gets a job	−0.011	-	−0.520	−0.508
	(0.214)		(0.002)	(0.005)
Antitakeover state	0.003	-	−0.431	−0.476
	(0.830)		(0.076)	(0.047)
Industry count	−0.007	-	0.134	0.192
	(0.112)		(0.105)	(0.040)
Adjusted R^2	0.148	0.142	0.178	0.175
Model *p*-value	0.000	0.000	0.000	0.000

Table 10

Simultaneous regression analysis, $(-1, +1)$ window, other proxies for takeover competition

This table reports the second stage of a two-stage least squares simultaneous equations analysis of bidder returns on variables that include various proxies for takeover competition. Bidder data are for the winning bidder. The dependent variable in each regression is net-of-market bidder returns for the $(-1, +1)$ window in which day 0 is the first date the bidder is announced in the financial press and the market index is the Center for Research in Security Prices value-weighted index. Contact* is the predicted value of the number buyers contacted by the selling firm and its investment bank. Confidential* is the predicted value of the number of buyers that engaged in a confidentiality agreement. Private bidders* is the predicted value of the number of buyers that submitted a private written offer. Public bidders* is the predicted value of the number of buyers that announced a formal bid in the financial media. Intangible assets is one minus the ratio of the target's property, plant, and equipment divided by its assets in the year prior to the merger. Relative size is the natural log of the equity value of the target divided by the equity value of the bidder 64 days prior to the initial announcement date. Bidder size is the natural log of bidder equity value measured 64 days prior to the initial takeover announcement. Stock is a dummy variable equal to one for acquisitions in which the payment is at least partially made in stock. Unsolicited is a dummy variable equal to one for deals that were initiated by the bidder or a third party. Bidder hires no IB is a dummy variable equal to one when the bidder does not use an investment bank (IB). Bidder hires top IB is a dummy variable equal to one if the bidder hires a top-tier investment bank as its adviser. Target hires top IB is a dummy variable equal to one if the target hires a top-tier investment bank as its adviser. The p-values of the regression coefficients are reported in parentheses. The model p-value and adjusted R^2 for each regression are reported at the bottom of the table. Each regression employs 308 observations.

Variable	(1)	(2)	(3)	(4)
Intercept	0.106	0.111	0.193	0.064
	(0.143)	(0.149)	(0.005)	(0.627)
Contacted*	0.007	-	-	-
	(0.695)			
Confidential*	-	0.009	-	-
		(0.767)		
Private bidders*	-	-	−0.136	-
			(0.218)	
Public bidders*	-	-	-	0.406
				(0.569)
Intangible assets	0.031	0.032	0.037	0.042
	(0.041)	(0.036)	(0.032)	(0.156)
Relative size	0.012	0.011	0.012	−0.007
	(0.007)	(0.005)	(0.008)	(0.833)
Bidder size	−0.007	−0.007	−0.011	−0.008
	(0.122)	(0.111)	(0.005)	(0.075)
Stock	−0.035	−0.034	−0.0349	−0.026
	(0.001)	(0.004)	(0.002)	(0.292)
Unsolicited	−0.030	−0.029	−0.029	−0.079
	(0.059)	(0.059)	(0.033)	(0.047)
Bidder hires no IB	0.032	0.033	0.045	0.004
	(0.029)	(0.022)	(0.003)	(0.942)
Bidder hires top bank	0.030	0.030	0.029	0.033
	(0.002)	(0.002)	(0.008)	(0.049)
Target hires top bank	−0.018	−0.018	−0.018	−0.004
	(0.043)	(0.046)	(0.067)	(0.894)
Model p-value	0.000	0.000	0.000	0.007
Adjusted R^2	0.121	0.123	−0.082	−1.178

Table 11

Simultaneous regression analysis, $(-1, +1)$ window, robustness analysis

This table reports a variety of robustness analyses of regressions of bidder returns. Bidder data are for the winning bidder and are for the $(-1, +1)$ window. The table reports the coefficients and p-values for the auction and uncertainty variables. These variables are part of second-stage regressions of a two-stage least squares simultaneous equations analysis of bidder returns that contain the same variables as in Table 9 except as noted. Panel A contains alternative specifications of the benchmark return. Size-adjusted returns are measured by assigning each bidder to size decile in the year of the announcement and then subtracting the corresponding return of the size decile from the bidder's return for the $(-1, +1)$ window. Fama and French three-factor uses the Fama and French (1993) factors as the benchmark return for the $(-1, +1)$ window. Panel B contains alternative measures of the uncertainty about the value of target assets. Return standard deviation is calculated as the standard deviation of target stock returns in the period -317 to -64 days prior to the initial announcement of the takeover. R & D/sales is the amount of research and development (R & D) expenditures divided by sales for the target in the year prior to the merger. Market/book is defined as the sum of the target firm's market value of equity plus book value of debt dividend by the book value of equity and debt in year prior to the merger. Panel C contains additional or alternative variables as controls in the two-stage regressions. Fixed-exchange and collar is a dummy variable equal to one if the merger deal includes either a fixed-exchange or collar as part of the stock deal. Strong antitakeover state is a dummy variable equal to one if the target is located in a state with strong antitakeover regulation and is included in the return regression as an additional control variable. Any state with antitakeover provision is a dummy variable equal to one if the target is located in a state any antitakeover regulation and is included as an alternative to the antitakeover state dummy in the sales procedure regression. Bidder size in top industry quartile is a dummy variable equal to one if the bidder is in the top size decile of all firms in the same Fama and French industry in the year prior to the merger. It is used as a substitute measure of firm size in the sales procedure regression. Deregulation is a dummy variable equal to one if the target firm is in an industry that underwent deregulation in the 1990s, including utilities, banks, and telecommunications firms. Panel D breaks the sample into two parts based on the announcement of the merger: 1989–1994 and 1994–1999. Panel E reports the analysis for particular subsamples of the data. Deals in which bidder announcement date is merger announcement date is a dummy variable equal to one if the first date that the bidder is announced is also the first date of any announcement about the takeover. Auction deals runs the analysis on only the subset of deals conducted via an auction in which the dependent variable in the sales procedure is now the log number of firms signing confidentiality agreements. Cash deals runs the analysis on only the subset of deals that uses 100% cash.

	Auction coefficient (p-value)	Uncertainty coefficient (p-value)
Panel A. Alternative measures of abnormal returns		
Size-adjusted	0.001	0.032
	(0.943)	(0.038)
Fama and French three factors	0.002	0.025
	(0.879)	(0.123)
Panel B. Alternative proxies for target uncertainty		
Return standard deviation	0.002	−0.257
	(0.876)	(0.570)
R&D/sales	0.001	−0.114
	(0.967)	(0.031)
Market-to-book	0.003	−0.005
	(0.839)	(0.415)
Panel C. Other additional and alternative variables		

(Continued)

Table 11 (*Continued*)

	Auction coefficient (p-value)	Uncertainty coefficient (p-value)
Fixed exchange and collar	−0.003	0.036
	(0.823)	(0.038)
Strong antitakeover state (as explanatory variables in return regression)	0.004	0.030
	(0.771)	(0.061)
Any state with antitakeover provision (in sales procedure regression)	0.004	0.031
	(0.771)	(0.055)
Bidder size in top industry quartile	0.009	0.027
	(0.448)	(0.086)
Deregulation	0.003	0.028
	(0.810)	(0.070)
Panel D. Analysis by time period		
1989–1994 ($N = 95$)	0.028	0.066
	(0.376)	(0.036)
1995–1999 ($N = 213$)	−0.008	0.018
	(0.559)	(0.324)
Panel E. Subsample analysis		
Deals in which bidder announcement date is merger announcement date ($N = 215$)	−0.011	0.037
	(0.401)	(0.046)
Auction subsample ($N = 145$) (for confidential variable)	0.041	0.053
	(0.546)	(0.112)
Cash deals ($N = 80$)	0.008	0.036
	(0.781)	(0.440)

dummy is positive but insignificant, resembling the result in Table 9, which used net-of-market bidder returns. For both of the alternative measures of abnormal returns, the coefficient on the uncertainty measure is positive, although it is not statistically significant in the Fama and French (1993) three-factor regression.

Panel B of Table 11 reports regressions that employ alternative proxies for the uncertainty in the value of the target: the target's return standard deviation, the target's research and development/sales (R&D/sales), and the target's market-to-book ratio. The use of these alternative proxies for uncertainty did not alter the insignificance of the auction dummy variable. The coefficients on the three different proxies for uncertainty in the value of the target are all negative in sign, which is the opposite of the results for the intangible assets of the target that was used in our primary specification. The coefficient on R&D/sales is negative and statistically significant, which is consistent with the predictions of the winner's curse. However, in results not reported in the table, we also ran the regressions for bidder returns estimated over the $(−20, +20)$ and $(−63, +126)$ event windows and found no significant relation between bidder returns and any of the three alternative proxies for the uncertainty in the value of the target. Our conclusion is that no reliable relation exists between bidder returns and the alternative proxies of the uncertainty in target value.

Panel C reports the results from specifications that either added other explanatory variables or used alternative variables in place of our primary specification. For example, we also control for whether the deal was a fixed-exchange stock transaction and whether the transaction had a stock collar. Mitchell et al. (2004) provide evidence that fixed-exchange deals and collar deals have generally more negative bidder returns at announcement. In our sample, 56% of the takeovers are fixed-exchange deals for stock and 21% of the deals have a collar. Auctions are less likely to be fixed-exchange deals but are more likely to have a collar. Consistent with Mitchell et al. (2004), we find in regression analysis that the coefficients on dummy variables for the fixed-exchange and collar deals are both negative and significant. But even after controlling for these additional deal factors, the coefficient on the auction dummy variable is not significantly different from zero.

We also include the dummy variable for strong antitakeover states, taken from Bebchuk and Ferrell (2002), in the second stage of the bidder returns regression. However, the dummy for strong antitakeover states is not significantly related to bidder returns and the addition of this variable does not alter our main results. We also use an alternative antitakeover dummy variable that takes a value of one for target firms incorporated in any state with at least one antitakeover statute (as reported in Table 9 of Bebchuk and Cohen, 2003), but this alternative specification does not change our main findings. Similarly, in results not reported in the table, an interaction between the antitakeover and unsolicited dummies does not significantly impact bidder returns.

We also use a different proxy for bidder size, a dummy variable equal to one if a bidder is in the top size decile of its industry. The use of this variable does not change the result of an insignificant relation between bidder returns and takeover competition.

In the final additional specification in panel C of Table 11, we add a deregulation dummy variable for firms in three industries experiencing major federal deregulation in the 1990s: banking, electric utilities, and telecommunications. In results not reported in the table, we find that the deregulation dummy is negatively and significantly related to bidder returns but is not significantly related to the choice of sales procedure. As reported in the table, the addition of this variable does not alter the result of an insignificant relation between bidder returns and takeover competition.

As reported in panel D of Table 11, we rerun the results by time period. We study the relatively less active 1989–1994 period, with 95 deals in 6 years, and the relatively more active 1995–1999 period, with 213 deals in 5 years. In neither period is the relation between bidder returns and takeover competition statistically significant; in the 1989–1994 period the coefficient on the auction variable is positive but insignificant, and in the 1995–1999 period the coefficient is negative but insignificant.

In panel E of Table 11, we report analyses of other subsamples of the data. We consider the 215 deals in which the announcement date is the same as the formal merger agreement date. We also analyze the subsample of 145 deals conducted as an auction, using the number of firms signing confidentiality agreements as the measure of takeover competition. We also study the subsample of the 80 all cash deals. As for the full sample, the analysis of these subsamples indicates an insignificant relation between bidder returns and takeover competition.

In summary, the robustness analysis in Table 11 reports the results of 15 different specifications of the effect of takeover competition on bidder returns. Twelve of the coefficients for the auction variable are positive and three are negative, but in none of the regressions is the coefficient on the auction variable statistically significant. These results are not consistent with the winner's curse.

7. Operating performance

Our empirical analysis has used event study techniques to test for the winner's curse. This analysis relies on the assumption of semi-strong market efficiency in which the market reaction to the announcement of a takeover is an unbiased assessment of the wealth consequences of bidder decisions (Fama, 1991).

As an alternative test we use an ex post measure based on operating performance. This test is motivated by Roll (1986), who argues that hubris and the winner's curse induce some takeovers that are mistakes and would not provide synergies. Similarly, Thaler observes (1988, p. 192) that the winner's curse implies that the winning bidder would be disappointed in the deal. Our basic question in this test is whether the posttakeover operating performance of bidders depends on whether the takeover procedure was an auction or a negotiation. The winner's curse predicts that winning bidders in auctions would suffer poorer operating performance following a takeover vis-à-vis winning bidders in negotiations.

In structuring our analysis of operating performance, we follow the general recommendations of Barber and Lyon (1996) as well as the approach in papers more specific to takeovers including Ghosh (2001), Heron and Lie (2002), and Powell and Stark (2005). As our measure of performance, we use operating income scaled by sales. We estimate changes in this performance measure around takeovers by comparing the combined performance of the target and bidder in the year prior to the takeover with the performance of the bidder in the years following the merger. As the main benchmark of performance, we use matched firms based on industry and pretakeover performance, although we also report the unadjusted performance changes and changes adjusted only for industry performance. In our statistical tests, we focus on median changes and use Wilcoxon tests of significance.

The estimates of operating performance are reported in Table 12. The full sample for the performance analysis is reported in panel A and reflects completed mergers in which data are available in the year prior to the merger. Panel B reports the subsample of negotiations with available data while Panel C reports the subsample of auctions. In Panels A, B, and C, three measures of operating income are reported: unadjusted

Table 12

Levels and changes of median operating income scaled by sales

This table reports the unadjusted, industry-adjusted, and performance-adjusted median operating performance for bidders in completed takeovers. Year 0 is the year of takeover completion. Operating performance data must be available for both the bidder and target in Year −1 for the takeover to be included in the calculations. Data and matching in year −1 reflect the combined operating performance of the bidder and the target. Data in other years reflect the operating performance of the bidder. Unadjusted income is operating income scaled by sales. Industry-adjusted income is unadjusted income minus the income of the median firm in the same Fama and French industry. Performance-adjusted income is unadjusted income minus the income of a benchmark firm matched on Fama and French industry and pretakeover performance. Panel A reports the results for the full sample of completed takeovers with available data. Panel B reports the results for the subsample of negotiations. Panel C reports the results for the subsample of auctions. (Numbers in parentheses in Panels A, B, and C present the number of firms used in the analysis.) Panel D reports the difference in medians between the negotiation and auction subsamples and *p*-values (in parentheses) from Wilcoxon tests.

Performance measure	Median income level					Median income changes		
	−1	0	+1	+2	+3	−1 to +1	−1 to +2	−1 to +3
Panel A. Full sample								
Unadjusted income	0.187	0.181	0.189	0.189	0.185	0.008	0.012	0.013
	(230)	(224)	(221)	(209)	(204)	(221)	(209)	(204)
Industry-adjusted income	0.011	0.020	0.023	0.023	0.014	0.008	0.010	0.013
	(230)	(224)	(221)	(209)	(204)	(221)	(209)	(204)
Performance-adjusted income	0.001	0.001	0.016	0.016	0.018	0.014	0.012	0.013
	(230)	(206)	(187)	(168)	(148)	(187)	(168)	(148)
Panel B. Negotiation								
Unadjusted income	0.193	0.206	0.201	0.196	0.184	0.007	0.009	0.000
	(121)	(117)	(116)	(111)	(108)	(116)	(111)	(108)
Industry-adjusted income	0.009	0.022	0.025	0.023	0.011	0.008	0.008	−0.001
	(121)	(117)	(116)	(111)	(108)	(116)	(111)	(108)
Performance-adjusted income	0.001	0.000	0.021	0.011	0.027	0.018	0.008	0.023
	(121)	(103)	(93)	(81)	(73)	(93)	(81)	(73)
Panel C. Auction								
Unadjusted income	0.166	0.163	0.176	0.184	0.187	0.011	0.018	0.027
	(109)	(107)	(105)	(98)	(96)	(105)	(98)	(96)
Industry-adjusted income	0.015	0.014	0.022	0.024	0.020	0.010	0.014	0.018
	(109)	(107)	(105)	(98)	(96)	(105)	(98)	(96)
Performance-adjusted income	0.001	0.005	0.012	0.017	0.004	0.008	0.014	0.002
	(109)	(103)	(94)	(87)	(75)	(94)	(87)	(75)
Panel D. Differences								
Unadjusted income	0.027	0.043	0.025	0.012	−0.003	−0.004	−0.009	−0.027
	(0.378)	(0.035)	(0.139)	(0.280)	(0.454)	(0.941)	(0.256)	(0.083)
Industry-adjusted income	−0.006	0.008	0.003	−0.001	−0.009	−0.002	−0.006	−0.019
	(0.724)	(0.478)	(0.965)	(0.549)	(0.546)	(0.819)	(0.353)	(0.048)
Performance-adjusted income	0.000	−0.005	0.009	−0.006	0.023	0.010	−0.006	0.021
	(0.252)	(0.721)	(0.662)	(0.634)	(0.768)	(0.638)	(0.586)	(0.759)

income, income adjusted for the median in an industry, and income adjusted for matched firms based on both industry and pretakeover performance.

In all three panels, the order of magnitude for unadjusted income levels is comparable to prior studies. Also, by design, the performance-adjusted income level in year -1 is virtually zero in all three panels. Consistent with prior research, the median operating income changes for unadjusted income, industry-adjusted income, and performance-adjusted income tend to be positive.

Our main interest is whether there are differences in the median income changes following the takeovers between the negotiation and auction subsamples. Evidence from statistical tests of these differences is reported in Panel D of Table 12. Focusing first on median changes in performance-adjusted income, the recommended performance measure in the literature, Panel D indicates that there is no significant difference between negotiations and auctions. For the other two measures, unadjusted income and industry-adjusted income, the differences also tend to be statistically insignificant. For the two cases in which the p-values report significance at the 0.10 level, the performance of auctions exceeds that of negotiations. As a whole, the results in Table 12 indicate that auctions do not have lower posttakeover operating performance than negotiations. Similar to our analysis of shareholder wealth effects, the evidence on operating performance is not consistent with the presence of the winner's curse.

8. Summary and conclusion

As succinctly stated by Levitt and List (2006, p. 32), "The Winner's Curse represents a disequilibrium behavior in which bidders systematically overbid and thus earn a negative payoff upon winning." Possibly due to the persuasive arguments by Roll (1986), an article cited more than 950 times on Google Scholar, a common perception is that the winner's curse holds in the corporate takeover market. Yet there have been few if any direct tests for the winner's curse in corporate takeovers, in part because of the difficulty in measuring takeover competition with readily available proxies.

We use a novel data set of the private takeover process to provide direct tests of the winner's curse in mergers and acquisitions. Our central tests of the winner's curse study whether bidder returns are inversely related to takeover competition and the uncertainty in the value of the target. While we find some evidence of an inverse relation between bidder returns and takeover competition in OLS regressions, we find no evidence of this inverse relation in two-stage models that account for the endogeneity between bidder returns and takeover competition. We also do not find an inverse relation between bidder returns and the uncertainty in the value of the target. Related analysis of posttakeover operating performance also fails to find any negative effects of takeover competition. The results do not support the presence of a winner's curse in the corporate takeover market.

We also empirically model the factors affecting takeover competition and the potential for the winner's curse. In particular, we consider how the potential of a winner's curse is affected by the prestige of the investment banks used in the takeover bidding process. In doing so, we provide new evidence on the contrasting findings previously reported by Rau (2000) and Kale et al. (2003). We find that the use of a prestigious bank by the bidding firm does not promote overbidding.

Our detailed treatment of the private auction process in corporate takeovers resolves the extant puzzle as to why bidders tend to only break even. Andrade et al. (2001, p. 118) note that a competitive takeover market is a potential answer to this puzzle, but they discount this possibility for the 1990s, a period that they show usually has only a single public bidder per takeover. Our analysis indicates that this focus on public bidders significantly underestimates the depth of competition in the corporate takeover process during the 1990s. Even though only 12% of the transactions in our sample have multiple public bidders, roughly half of the target firms entertained serious discussion, often in private, with more than one potential buyer. Such underlying competition provides a straightforward explanation for breakeven bidder returns.

Our results also have important implications for securities law. Some commentators suggest that the potential for the winner's curse in corporate takeovers might motivate mandated constraints on takeover auctions (Black, 1989; Hechler, 1997). Our results indicate that bidders do not fall prey to the winner's curse, thereby mitigating any motivation for a visible hand in auction design by securities law.

Our analysis is also pertinent to ongoing debates in behavioral finance. Thaler (1988), for example, cites the data on acquirer returns in corporate takeovers as a real-world example of bidder irrationality. The absence of the winner's curse in our tests suggests instead that the decisions of bidders in corporate takeovers are consistent with rational behavior. Our results indicate that participants in the takeover market devise strategies to surmount potential bidding pitfalls.

References

Akerlof, G., 1970, "The Market for 'Lemons': Quality Uncertainty and the Market Mechanism," *Quarterly Journal of Economics*, 84, 488–500.

Andrade, G., M. Mitchell and E. Stafford, 2001, "New Evidence and Perspectives on Mergers," *Journal of Economic Perspectives*, 15, 103–120.

Asquith, P., 1983, "Merger Bids, Uncertainty, and Stock Returns," *Journal of Financial Economics*, 11, 51–83.

Asquith, P., R. Bruner and D. Mullins, 1983, "The Gains to Bidding Firms from Merger," *Journal of Financial Economics*, 11, 121–139.

Bajari, P. and A. Hortacsu, 2003, "The Winner's Curse, Reserve Prices, and Endogenous Entry: Empirical Insights from eBay Auctions," *Rand Journal of Economics*, 34, 329–355.

Baker, M., R. Ruback and J. Wurgler, 2007, "Behavioral Corporate Finance: A Survey," In E. Eckbo (Ed.), *The Handbook of Corporate Finance*, Elsevier/North-Holland, New York, pp. 145–186.

Barber, B. and J. Lyon, 1996, "Detecting Abnormal Operating Performance: The Empirical Power and Specification of Test Statistics," *Journal of Financial Economics*, 41, 359–399.

Barberis, N. and R. Thaler, 2003, "A Survey of Behavioral Finance," In G. Constantinides, M. Harris and R. Stulz (Eds.), *Handbook of the Economics of Finance*, Elsevier, New York, pp. 1052–1121.

Barzel, Y., 1977, "Some Fallacies in the Interpretation of Information Costs," *Journal of Law and Economics*, 20, 291–307.

Bazerman, M. and W. Samuelson, 1983, "I Won the Auction but Don't Want the Prize," *Journal of Conflict Resolution*, 27, 618–634.

Bebchuk, L. and A. Cohen, 2003, "Firms Decisions Where to Incorporate," *Journal of Law and Economics*, 46, 383–425.

Bebchuk, L. and A. Ferrell, 2002, "On Takeover Law and Regulatory Competition," *Business Lawyer*, 57, 1047–1068.

Betton, S. and E. Eckbo, 2000, "Toeholds, Bid Jumps, and Expected Payoffs in Takeovers," *Review of Financial Studies*, 13, 841–882.

Black, B., 1989, "Bidder Overpayment in Takeovers," *Stanford Law Review*, 41, 597–653.

Boone, A. and H. Mulherin, 2007, "How are Firms Sold?" *Journal of Finance*, 62, 847–875.

Bowers, H. and R. Miller, 1990, "Choice of Investment Banker and Shareholders' Wealth of Firms Involved in Acquisitions," *Financial Management*, 19, 34–44.

Bradley, M., A. Desai and H. Kim, 1988, "Synergistic Gains from Corporate Acquisitions and Their Division Between the Stockholders of Target and Acquiring Firms," *Journal of Financial Economics*, 21, 3–40.

Bris, A., I. Welch and N. Zhu, 2006, "The Costs of Bankruptcy: Chapter 7 Liquidation Versus Chapter 11 Reorganization," *Journal of Finance*, 61, 1253–1303.

Bulow, J. and P. Klemperer, 2002, "Prices and the Winner's Curse," *Rand Journal of Economics*, 33, 1–21.

Campa, J. and S. Kedia, 2002, "Explaining the Diversification Discount," *Journal of Finance*, 57, 1731–1762.

Capen, E., R. Clapp and W. Campbell, 1971, "Competitive Bidding in High-Risk Situations," *Journal of Petroleum Technology*, 23, 641–653.

Comment, R. and W. Schwert, 1995, "Poison or Placebo? Evidence on the Deterrence and Wealth Effects of Modern Anti-Takeover Measures," *Journal of Financial Economics*, 39, 3–43.

Cox, J. and M. Isaac, 1984, "In Search of the Winner's Curse," *Economic Inquiry*, 22, 579–592.

Dasgupta, S. and R. Hansen, 2007, "Auctions in Corporate Finance," In E. Eckbo (Ed.), *The Handbook of Corporate Finance: Empirical Corporate Finance*, Elsevier/North-Holland, New York, pp. 87–143.

Dyer, D. and J. Kagel, 1996, "Bidding in Common Value Auctions: How the Commercial Construction Industry Corrects for the Winner's Curse," *Management Science*, 42, 1463–1475.

Fama, E., 1991, "Efficient Capital Markets: II," *Journal of Finance*, 46, 1575–1617.

Fama, E. and K. French, 1993, "Common Risk Factors in the Returns of Stocks and Bonds," *Journal of Financial Economics*, 33, 3–56.

Fama, E. and K. French, 1997, "Industry Costs of Equity," *Journal of Financial Economics*, 43, 153–193.

Fama, E. and A. Laffer, 1972, "The Number of Firms and Competition," *American Economic Review*, 62, 670–674.

Fernando, C., V. Gatchev and P. Spindt, 2005, "Wanna Dance? How Firms and Underwriters Choose Each Other," *Journal of Finance*, 60, 2437–2469.

Fishman, M., 1988, "A Theory of Preemptive Takeover Bidding," *Rand Journal of Economics*, 19, 88–101.

Franks, J. and R. Harris, 1989, "Shareholder Wealth Effects of Corporate Takeovers: The UK Experience, 1955–1985," *Journal of Financial Economics*, 23, 225–249.

French, K. and R. McCormick, 1984, "Sealed Bids, Sunk Costs, and the Process of Competition," *Journal of Business*, 57, 417–441.

Ghosh, A., 2001, "Does Operating Performance Really Improve Following Corporate Acquisitions?" *Journal of Corporate Finance*, 7, 151–178.

Hansen, R., 1985, "Empirical Testing of Auction Theory," *American Economic Review*, 75, 156–159.

Hansen, R., 1987, "A Theory of Choice of Exchange Medium in Mergers and Acquisitions," *Journal of Business*, 60, 75–95.

Hansen, R., 2001, "Auctions of Companies," *Economic Inquiry*, 39, 30–43.

Hansen, R. and J. Lott, 1991, "The Winner's Curse and Public Information in Common Value Auctions: A Comment," *American Economic Review*, 81, 347–361.

Harford, J., 2003, "Takeover Bids and Target Directors' Incentives: The Impact of a Bid on Directors' Wealth and Board Seats," *Journal of Financial Economics*, 69, 51–83.

Hechler, M., 1997, "Towards a More Balanced Treatment of Bidder and Target Shareholders," *Columbia Business Law Review*, 1997, 319–397.

Heckman, J., 1979, "Sample Selection Bias As a Specification Error," *Econometrica*, 47, 153–162.

Hendricks, K. and R. Porter, 1988, "An Empirical Study of an Auction with Asymmetric Information," *American Economic Review*, 78, 865–883.

Heron, R. and E. Lie, 2002, "Operating Performance and the Method of Payment in Takeovers," *Journal of Financial and Quantitative Analysis*, 37, 137–155.

Herzel, L. and R. Shepro, 1990, *Bidders and Targets: Mergers and Acquisitions in the US*, Basil Blackwell, Cambridge, MA.

Houston, J. and M. Ryngaert, 1997, "Equity Issuance and Adverse Selection: A Direct Test Using Conditional Stock Offers," *Journal of Finance*, 52, 197–219.

Jarrell, G. and A. Poulsen, 1989, "The Returns to Acquiring Firms in Tender Offers: Evidence from Three Decades," *Financial Management*, 18, 12–19.

Kagel, J. and D. Levin, 1986, "The Winner's Curse and Public Information in Common Value Auctions," *American Economic Review*, 76, 894–920.

Kagel, J., D. Levin and R. Harstad, 1995, "Comparative Static Effects of Number of Bidders and Public Information on Behavior in Second-Price Common Value Auctions," *International Journal of Game Theory*, 24, 293–319.

Kale, J., O. Kini and H. Ryan, 2003, "Financial Advisors and Shareholder Wealth Gains in Corporate Takeovers," *Journal of Financial and Quantitative Analysis*, 38, 475–501.

Keshk, O., 2003, "CDSIMEQ: A Program to Implement Two-Stage Probit Least Squares," *Stata Journal*, 3, 1–11.

Klemperer, P., 1998, "Auctions with Almost Common Values: The 'Wallet Game' and Its Applications," *European Economic Review*, 42, 757–769.

Klemperer, P., 1999, "Auction Theory: A Guide to the Literature," *Journal of Economic Surveys*, 13, 227–286.

Klemperer, P., 2002, "What Really Matters in Auction Design?" *Journal of Economic Perspectives*, 16, 169–189.

Laffont, J., 1997, "Game Theory and Empirical Economics," *European Economic Review*, 41, 1–35.

Levin, D. and J. Smith, 1991, "Some Evidence on the Winner's Curse: Comment," *American Economic Review*, 81, 370–375.

Levitt, S. and J. List, 2006, "What Do Laboratory Experiments Tell Us About the Real World?" Unpublished Working Paper, University of Chicago and National Bureau of Economic Research, Chicago, IL, Cambridge, MA.

Li, K. and N. Prabhala, 2007, "Self-Selection Models in Corporate Finance," In E. Eckbo (Ed.), *The Handbook of Corporate Finance: Empirical Corporate Finance*, Elsevier/North-Holland, New York, pp. 37–86.

Lowry, M. and S. Shu, 2002, "Litigation Risk and IPO Underpricing," *Journal of Financial Economics*, 65, 309–335.

Ma, Q., 2005, "Mergers and Investment Banks: How Do Banks Help Targets?" Unpublished Working Paper, Cornell University, Ithaca, NY.

Maddala, G., 1983, *Limited Dependent and Qualitative Variables in Econometrics*, Cambridge University Press, Cambridge, MA.

Mandelker, G., 1974, "Risk and Return: The Case of Merging Firms," *Journal of Financial Economics*, 1, 303–335.

McAfee, P. and J. McMillan, 1987, "Auctions and Bidding," *Journal of Economic Literature*, 25, 699–738.

Mitchell, M., T. Pulvino and E. Stafford, 2004, "Price Pressure Around Mergers," *Journal of Finance*, 59, 31–63.

Moeller, S., F. Schlingemann and R. Stulz, 2004, "Firm Size and the Gains from Acquisitions," *Journal of Financial Economics*, 73, 201–228.

Morck, R., A. Shleifer and R. Vishny, 1990, "Do Managerial Objectives Drive Bad Acquisitions?" *Journal of Finance*, 45, 31–48.

Mulherin, H. and A. Boone, 2000, "Comparing Acquisitions and Divestitures," *Journal of Corporate Finance*, 6, 117–139.

Officer, M., 2003, "Termination Fees in Mergers and Acquisitions," *Journal of Financial Economics*, 69, 431–467.

Officer, M., 2004, "Collars and Renegotiations in Mergers and Acquisitions," *Journal of Finance*, 59, 2719–2743.

Officer, M., A. Poulsen and M. Stegemoller, 2009, "Target-firm Information Asymmetry and Acquirer Returns," *Review of Finance*, 13, 467–493.

Povel, P. and R. Singh, 2006, "Takeover Contests with Asymmetric Bidders," *Review of Financial Studies*, 19, 1399–1431.

Powell, R. and A. Stark, 2005, "Does Operating Performance Increase Post-Takeover for UK Takeovers? A Comparison of Performance Measures and Benchmarks," *Journal of Corporate Finan.ce*, 11, 293–317.

Rau, R., 2000, "Investment Bank Market Share, Contingent Fee Payments, and the Performance of Acquiring Firms," *Journal of Financial Economics*, 56, 293–324.

Roll, R., 1986, "The Hubris Hypothesis of Corporate Takeovers," *Journal of Business*, 59, 197–216.

Roth, A., 1991, "Game Theory As a Part of Empirical Economics," *Economic Journal*, 101, 107–114.

Schwert, W., 1996, "Markup Pricing in Mergers and Acquisitions," *Journal of Financial Economics*, 41, 153–192.

Schwert, W., 2000, "Hostility in Takeovers: In the Eyes of the Beholder?" *Journal of Finance*, 55, 2599–2640.

Servaes, H., 1991, "Tobin's q and the Gains from Takeovers," *Journal of Finance*, 46, 409–419.

Servaes, H. and M. Zenner, 1996, "The Role of Investment Banks in Acquisitions," *Review of Financial Studies*, 9, 787–815.

Smith, R., 1987, "The Choice of Issuance Procedure and the Cost of Competitive and Negotiated Underwriting: An Examination of the Impact of Rule 50," *Journal of Finance*, 42, 703–720.

Thaler, R., 1988, "Anomalies: The Winner's Curse," *Journal of Economic Perspectives*, 2, 191–202.

Thiel, S., 1988, "Some Evidence on the Winner's Curse," *American Economic Review*, 78, 884–895.

Travlos, N., 1987, "Corporate Takeover Bids, Methods of Payment, and Bidding Firms' Stock Returns," *Journal of Finance*, 42, 943–963.

Varaiya, N., 1988, "The 'Winner's Curse' Hypothesis and Corporate Takeovers," *Managerial and Decision Economics*, 9, 209–219.

Wasserstein, B., 2000, *Big Deal*, Warner Books, New York.

Chapter 6

WHO MAKES ACQUISITIONS? CEO OVERCONFIDENCE AND THE MARKET'S REACTION[*]

ULRIKE MALMENDIER

University of California, Berkeley, California, USA

GEOFFREY TATE

University of California at Los Angeles, Los Angeles, California, USA

Contents

[*] We are indebted to Brian Hall, Kenneth Froot, Mark Mitchell, and David Yermack for providing us with essential parts of the data. We are very grateful to Jeremy Stein and Andrei Shleifer for their invaluable support and comments. We also thank Gary Chamberlain, David Laibson, and various participants in seminars at Harvard University, Stanford University, University of Chicago, Northwestern University, Wharton, Duke University, University of Illinois, Emory University, Carnegie Mellon University, INSEAD and Humboldt University of Berlin for helpful comments. Becky Brunson, Justin Fernandez, Jared Katseff, Camelia Kuhnen, and Felix Momsen provided excellent research assistance. The authors acknowledge support from the Russell Sage Foundation, the Division of Research of the Harvard Business School (Malmendier) and the Center for Basic Research in the Social Sciences at Harvard (Tate).

This article originally appeared in the *Journal of Financial Economics*, Vol. 89, pp. 20–43 (2008).
Corporate Takeovers, Volume 2
Edited by B. Espen Eckbo
DOI: 10.1016/B978-0-12-381982-6.00007-0

Abstract

Does CEO overconfidence help to explain merger decisions? Overconfident CEOs overestimate their ability to generate returns. As a result, they overpay for target companies and undertake value-destroying mergers. The effects are strongest if they have access to internal financing. We test these predictions using two proxies for overconfidence: CEOs' personal overinvestment in their company and their press portrayal. We find that the odds of making an acquisition are 65% higher if the CEO is classified as overconfident. The effect is largest if the merger is diversifying and does not require external financing. The market reaction at merger announcement (-90 basis points (bp)) is significantly more negative than for nonoverconfident CEOs (-12 bp). We consider alternative interpretations including inside information, signaling, and risk tolerance.

Keywords

mergers and acquisitions, returns to mergers, overconfidence, hubris, managerial biases

JEL classification: D80, G14, G32, G34

1. Introduction

Many managements apparently were overexposed in impressionable childhood years to the story in which the imprisoned handsome prince is released from a toad's body by a kiss from a beautiful princess. Consequently, they are certain their managerial kiss will do wonders for the profitability of Company T[arget] ... We've observed many kisses but very few miracles. Nevertheless, many managerial princesses remain serenely confident about the future potency of their kisses-even after their corporate backyards are knee-deep in unresponsive toads.

-Warren Buffet, Berkshire Hathaway Inc.

Annual Report, 1981[1]

US firms spent more than \$3.4 trillion on over 12,000 mergers during the last two decades. If chief executive officers (CEOs) act in the interest of their shareholders, these mergers should have increased shareholder wealth. Yet, acquiring shareholders lost over \$220 billion at the announcement of merger bids from 1980 to 2001 (Moeller et al., 2005). While the joint effect of mergers on acquiror and target value may be positive, acquiring shareholders appear to be on the losing end.[2] In this paper, we ask whether CEO overconfidence helps to explain the losses of acquirors.

Overconfidence has long had popular appeal as an explanation for failed mergers.[3] Roll (1986) first formalized the notion, linking takeover contests to the winner's curse. The implications of overconfidence for mergers, however, are more subtle than mere overbidding. Overconfident CEOs also overestimate the returns they generate internally and believe outside investors undervalue their companies. As a result, they are reluctant to raise external finance and may forgo mergers if external capital is required. The effect of overconfidence on merger frequency, then, is ambiguous. Overconfident managers are unambiguously more likely to conduct mergers only if they have sufficient internal resources. Moreover, if overconfidence increases merger frequency, it also lowers average deal quality and induces a lower average market reaction to the announcement of merger bids.

We test these hypotheses using a sample of 394 large US firms from 1980 to 1994. We use CEOs' personal portfolio decisions to elicit their beliefs about their companies' future performance. Previous literature shows that risk-averse CEOs should reduce their exposure to company-specific risk by exercising in-the-money

---

[1] Quote taken from Weston et al. (1998).

[2] Andrade et al. (2001) find average stock price reactions of -0.4% and -1.0% over a 3-day window for acquirors during the 1980s and 1990s; see also Dodd (1980), Firth (1980), and Ruback and Mikkelson (1984). Targets may gain from merger bids; see Asquith (1983) and Bradley et al. (1983). Jensen and Ruback (1983) and Roll (1986) survey earlier studies.

[3] Recent business press articles include *CFO Magazine*, June 1, 2004 ("Avoiding Decision Traps"); *US Newslink*, December 13, 2001 ("Enron's Bust: Was It the Result of Over-Confidence or a Confidence Game?"); *Accenture Outlook Journal*, January, 2000 ("Mergers & Acquisitions: Irreconcilable Differences").

executive stock options prior to expiration.[4] A subset of CEOs in our data persistently fails to do so. They delay option exercise all the way until expiration, even when the underlying stock price exceeds rational exercise thresholds such as those derived in Hall and Murphy (2002). Moreover, they typically make losses from holding their options relative to a diversification strategy.

We link the beliefs CEOs reveal in their personal portfolio choices to their merger decisions. We find that CEOs who fail to diversify their personal portfolios are significantly more likely to conduct mergers at any point in time. The results hold when we identify such CEOs with a fixed-effect ("Longholder") or allow for variation over time ("Post-Longholder" and "Holder 67"). They are robust to controlling for standard merger determinants like Q, size, and cash flow, and using firm fixed effects to remove the impact of time-invariant firm characteristics. The effect is largest among firms with abundant internal resources and for diversifying acquisitions. Taking diversification as a proxy for value destruction,[5] these results confirm the overconfidence hypothesis.

We also analyze the market's reaction to merger announcements, which provides a more direct measure of value creation. We find that investors react significantly more negatively to merger bids of Longholder CEOs. Over the 3 days around announcements, they lose on average 90 basis points (bp), compared to 12 bp for other CEOs. The result holds controlling for relatedness of target and acquiror, ownership stake of the acquiring CEO, board size of the acquiror, and method of financing. While announcement effects may not capture the overall value created by mergers, due to market frictions and inefficiencies (Mitchell et al., 2004; Shleifer and Vishny, 2003), the differential reaction to bids of Longholder CEOs is likely to be orthogonal to these factors and, thus, to capture value differences.

We consider several explanations for the link between late option exercise and mergers: positive inside information, signaling, board pressure, risk tolerance, taxes, procrastination, and overconfidence. Only positive CEO beliefs (inside information or overconfidence) and risk preferences (risk tolerance), however, provide a straightforward explanation for both personal overinvestment and excessive merger activity. Among these explanations inside information (or signaling) is hard to reconcile with the losses CEOs incur on their personal portfolios by delaying option exercise and with the more negative reaction to their merger bids. Similarly, risk-seeking is difficult to reconcile with the observed preference for cash financing and diversifying mergers. Overconfidence, instead, is consistent with all findings.

To further test the overconfidence interpretation, we hand-collect data on CEO coverage in the business press. We identify CEOs characterized as "confident" or "optimistic" versus "reliable," "cautious," "conservative," "practical," "frugal," or

[4] See, e.g., Lambert et al. (1991).
[5] Graham et al. (2002) and Villalonga (2004), among others, question the interpretation of the diversification discount and attribute the effect to preexisting discounts or econometric and data biases. Schoar (2002), however, confirms the negative impact of diversification via acquisition using plant-level data.

"steady." Characterization as confident or optimistic is significantly positively correlated with our portfolio measures of optimistic beliefs. And, our main results replicate using a press-based measure of overconfidence.

Our results suggest that a significant subset of CEOs is overconfident about their future cash flows and engages in mergers that do not warrant the paid premium. Overconfidence may create firm value along some dimensions—for example, by counteracting risk aversion, inducing entrepreneurship, allowing firms to make credible threats, or attracting similarly minded employees[6]—but mergers are not among them.

Our paper relates to several strands of literature. First, we contribute to research on the explanations for mergers. Much of the literature focuses on the efficiency gains from mergers (e.g., Lang et al., 1989; Mulherin and Poulsen, 1998; Servaes, 1991). Overconfidence, instead, is closest to agency theory (Jensen, 1986, 1988). Empire-building, like overconfidence, predicts heightened acquisitiveness to the detriment of shareholders, especially given abundant internal resources (Harford, 1999). Unlike traditional empire-builders, however, overconfident CEOs believe that they are acting in the interest of shareholders, and are willing to personally invest in their companies. Thus, while excessive acquisitiveness can result both from agency problems and from overconfidence, the relation to late option exercise, that is, CEOs' personal overinvestment in their companies, arises only from overconfidence.

The paper also contributes to the literature on overconfidence. Psychologists suggest that individuals are especially overconfident about outcomes they believe are under their control (Langer, 1975; March and Shapira, 1987) and to which they are highly committed (Weinstein, 1980; Weinstein and Klein, 2002).[7] Both criteria apply to mergers. The CEO gains control of the target. And a successful merger enhances professional standing and personal wealth.

We also contribute to the growing strand of behavioral corporate finance literature considering the consequences of biased managers in efficient markets (Barberis and Thaler, 2003; Baker et al., 2006; Camerer and Malmendier, 2007). A number of recent papers study upward biases in managers' self-assessment, focusing on corporate finance theory (Heaton, 2002), the decision making of entrepreneurs (Landier and Thesmar, 2003), or indirect measures of "hubris" (Hayward and Hambrick, 1997). We complement the literature by using the decisions of CEOs in large companies to measure biased managerial beliefs and their implications for merger decisions. Seyhun (1990) also considers insider stock transactions around mergers, though overconfidence is not his primary focus. Our approach is most similar to Malmendier and Tate

---

[6] See Bernardo and Welch (2001), Goel and Thakor (2000), Schelling (1960), and Van den Steen (2005).

[7] The overestimation of future outcomes, as analyzed in this literature, is sometimes referred to as "optimism" rather than "overconfidence," while "overconfidence" is used to denote the underestimation of confidence intervals. We follow the literature on self-serving attribution and choose the label "overconfidence" for the overestimation of outcomes related to own abilities (such as IQ or managerial skills) and "optimism" for the overestimation of exogenous outcomes (such as the growth of the US economy).

(2005), but improves the identification and test of overconfidence in two important ways: by directly measuring the value consequences of corporate decisions and by constructing an alternative media-based proxy.

The paper is organized as follows. Section 2 derives the empirical predictions of managerial overconfidence for mergers. Section 3 introduces the data. Section 4 develops our empirical measures of delayed option exercise. Section 5 describes the empirical strategy and relates late option exercise to heightened acquisitiveness and more negative market reactions to merger bids. Section 6 discusses alternative interpretations of the link between late exercise and mergers and derives a press-based measure of overconfidence. Section 7 concludes.

2. Empirical predictions

We analyze the impact of overconfidence on mergers in a general setting that allows for market inefficiencies, such as information asymmetries, and managerial frictions, such as agency costs and private benefits.[8] We assume that these frictions and the quality of merger opportunities do not vary systematically between overconfident and rational CEOs, that is, that overconfident and rational CEOs sort randomly across firms over time. When we test the resulting predictions, we account for violations of this assumption using a host of firm and manager level controls.

Overconfident managers overestimate their ability to create value. As a result, they overestimate the returns they can generate both in their own company and by taking over other firms. These two manifestations of overconfidence generate a trade-off when considering potential mergers. The overestimation of merger synergies induces excessive willingness to acquire other firms. But, the overestimation of stand-alone value generates perceived financing costs: potential lenders demand a higher interest rate and potential new shareholders demand lower issuance prices than the CEO deems appropriate given future returns. As a result, the CEO may forgo value-creating mergers he perceives to be too costly to finance, even if investors evaluate the company and the merger correctly. Thus, the net effect of overconfidence on merger frequency is ambiguous. A positive net effect would indicate that overconfidence is an important explanation of merger activity in practice, but is not a necessary implication of overconfidence.

Overconfidence unambiguously predicts more mergers, however, when the CEO does not need to access external capital markets to finance the deal. In firms with large cash stocks or spare riskless debt capacity, only the overestimation of synergies impacts the merger decisions of overconfident CEOs. We obtain the following prediction:

---

[8] We derive these and further predictions formally in a more stylized setting in Malmendier and Tate (2004).

Prediction 1 *In firms with abundant internal resources, overconfident CEOs are more likely to conduct acquisitions than nonoverconfident CEOs.*

Overconfidence also has implications for the value created by mergers. Since overconfident managers overestimate merger synergies, they misperceive some merger opportunities with negative synergies to be value-creating. As a result, they are more likely to undertake value-destroying projects that rational managers would forgo. Moreover, overconfident managers may have too high a reservation price for the target firm. Thus, if they compete with another bidder or if the target has significant bargaining power, they may overpay.[9]

Overconfident CEOs may also forgo some value-creating mergers due to perceived financing costs. Abstaining from a value-creating deal lowers shareholder value (though it improves average deal quality if the forgone deal is below average). Hence, we have the following prediction:

Prediction 2 *If overconfident CEOs do more mergers than rational CEOs, then the average value created in mergers is lower for overconfident than for rational CEOs.*

Note that overconfidence does not necessarily predict a negative reaction to merger bids. Rational managers may do some value-destroying deals or forgo some value-creating deals due to other frictions. In the latter case, some of the extra mergers of overconfident CEOs may create value (as in Goel and Thakor, 2000). However, as long as overconfident CEOs undertake more mergers, the average announcement effect for bids by overconfident CEOs will be lower than the average announcement effect among rational CEOs.

3. Data

Our starting sample consists of 477 large publicly traded US firms from 1980 to 1994. The core of the data set is described in detail in Hall and Liebman (1998) and Yermack (1995). To be included in the sample, a firm must appear at least four times on one of the *Forbes* magazine lists of largest US companies from 1984 to 1994.[10] The virtue of this data set is its detailed information on CEOs stock and option holdings. We observe, in each sample year, the number of remaining options from the grants the CEO received in each of his prior years in office as well as the remaining duration and strike price. The data provide a fairly detailed picture of the CEOs portfolio rebalancing over his tenure.

---

[9] Note that, contrary to Roll's (1986) theory, an overconfident CEO does not always bid higher than a rational bidder. A CEO who is more overconfident about the value of his firm than about the merger may lose the contest due to perceived financing costs.

[10] This criterion excludes IPOs from our sample. Thus, the more stringent restrictions on trading associated with such firms, such as lockup periods, do not apply.

We also collect data on articles about the CEOs in *The New York Times, Business-Week, Financial Times,* and *The Economist* using LexisNexis and in the *The Wall Street Journal* using Factiva.com. For each CEO and sample year, we record (1) the total number of articles, (2) the number of articles containing the words "confident" or "confidence," (3) the number of articles using "optimistic" or "optimism," (4) the number of articles using "reliable," "cautious," "conservative," "practical," "frugal," or "steady." We hand-check that the terms describe the CEO and separate out articles in which "confident" or "optimistic" are negated.[11]

We use the Securities Data Company (SDC) and Center for Research in Security Prices (CRSP) merger databases to obtain announcement dates and merger financing information for completed deals by our sample firms. The CRSP data set covers only mergers with CRSP-listed targets. We use SDC to supplement the data with acquisitions of private firms, large subsidiaries, and foreign companies.[12] We require that the acquiring company obtains at least 51% of the target shares (and, hence, control) and omit acquisitions in which the acquiror already holds at least 51% of the target before the deal. Finally, following Morck et al. (1990), we omit acquisitions worth less than 5% of acquiror value.[13]

We supplement the data with various items from the Compustat database. We measure firm size as the natural logarithm of assets (item 6) at the beginning of the year, investment as capital expenditures (item 128), cash flow as earnings before extraordinary items (item 18) plus depreciation (item 14), and capital as property, plants and equipment (item 8). We normalize cash flow by beginning-of-the-year capital. Given that our sample is not limited to manufacturing firms (though it mainly consists of large, nonfinancial firms), we check the robustness of our results to normalization by assets (item 6). We measure Q as the ratio of market value of assets to book value of assets. Market value of assets is defined as total assets (item 6) plus market equity minus book equity. Market equity is defined as common shares outstanding (item 25) times fiscal year closing price (item 199). Book equity is calculated as stockholders' equity (item 216) [or the first available of common equity (item 60) plus preferred stock par value (item 130) or total assets (item 6) minus total liabilities (item 181)] minus preferred stock liquidating value (item 10) [or the first available of redemption value (item 56) or par value (item 130)] plus balance sheet deferred taxes and investment tax credit (item 35) when available minus postretirement assets (item 330) when available. Book value of assets is total assets (item 6).[14] We use fiscal year closing prices (item 199) adjusted for stock splits (item 27) to calculate annual stock

---

[11] Our search procedure also ensures that the words "overconfidence," "overconfident," "overoptimistic," and "overoptimism" (with or without hyphenation) will show up in categories (2) and (3).

[12] All results are robust to using only CRSP data, that is, mergers involving publicly traded US targets.

[13] This criterion is important when using SDC data since acquisitions of small units of another company differ substantially from those of large NYSE firms and may not require active involvement of the acquiror's CEO.

[14] Definitions of Q and its components as in Fama and French (2002).

returns. Our calculation of annual returns excludes dividends; we consider the impact of capital appreciation and dividend payments separately in Section 6. We use CRSP to gather stock prices and Standard Industrial Classification (SIC) codes. Missing accounting data (largely of financial firms) leaves us with a final sample of 394 firms. As in Malmendier and Tate (2005), we trim cash flow at the 1% level to ensure that our results are not driven by outliers. However, all results replicate with the full data.

In addition, we collect personal information about the CEOs using Dun and Bradstreet (1997) and Who's Who in Finance and Industry (1980/81–1995/96). We broadly classify a CEOs educational background as financial, technical, or miscellaneous. CEOs have finance education if they hold undergraduate or graduate degrees in accounting, finance, business (including an MBA), or economics. They have technical education if they hold undergraduate or graduate degrees in engineering, physics, operations research, chemistry, mathematics, biology, pharmacy, or other applied sciences.

Table 1 presents summary statistics of the data. Panel A presents firm-specific variables. Our sample firms are large, and most (48%) are in the manufacturing industry. Panel B shows CEO-specific variables, both for the full set of CEOs and for the subset of CEOs whom we classify as overconfident based on their option-exercise behavior ("Longholder," see Section 4). The means, medians, and standard deviations of all variables are remarkably similar for Longholder and non-Longholder CEOs. Only the number of vested options that have not been exercised is considerably higher among Longholder CEOs. This difference could stem from overconfidence, as we will see later. But, regardless, we will control for the level of vested options in all of our regressions. Panel C presents the summary statistics of the CEOs' press coverage. While the mean and median number of annual mentions are relatively high (8.89 and 3), mentions with the attributes "confident" or "optimistic" or any of "reliable," "cautious," "conservative," "practical," "steady," and "frugal" are infrequent (the means are below 0.1 and the medians are 0). Our analysis will use dummy variables, which indicate differences in the number of mentions of each type, in lieu of the raw numbers of articles in each category. Finally, Panel D presents summary statistics of the mergers undertaken by CEOs in our sample. Notably, the acquiror's stock has a negative cumulative abnormal return of 29 bp on average over the 3 days window surrounding the announcement of a merger bid.

4. Measuring overconfidence

We use the panel data on CEOs' personal portfolios to identify differences across managers in executive option exercise. Executive options give the holder the right to purchase company stock, usually at the stock price on the grant date. Most executive options have a 10-year life span and are fully exercisable after a 4-year vesting period. Upon exercise, the holder receives shares of company stock. These shares are almost always immediately sold (Ofek and Yermack, 2000).

Table 1
Summary statistics

Financial variables are reported in $ millions. Q is the market value of assets over the book value of assets. Cash flow is earnings before extraordinary items plus depreciation. Stock ownership is the fraction of company stock owned by the CEO and his immediate family. Vested options are the CEOs holdings of options that are exercisable within 6 months, as a fraction of common shares outstanding, and multiplied by 10 (so that the mean is roughly comparable to Stock ownership). Efficient board size is a binary variable where 1 signifies that the board has between 4 and 12 directors. Technical industry is an indicator variable for firms with primary SIC codes 1000–1799, 8711; Financial industry indicates firms with primary SIC codes 6000–6799; Manufacturing industry indicates primary SIC codes 2000–3999; Transportation industry primary SIC codes 4000–4999; Trade industry primary SIC codes 5000–5999; and Service industry primary SIC codes 7000–8710, 8712–8720, 8722–8999. Assets, Capital, Q, Stock ownership, and Vested options are measured at the beginning of the fiscal year; all other variables are at the end. Finance education is binary and equal to 1 for CEOs with an undergraduate or graduate degree in accounting, finance, business (incl. MBA), or economics. Technical education is binary and equals 1 for CEOs with an undergraduate or graduate degree in engineering, physics, operations research, chemistry, mathematics, biology, pharmacy, or other applied sciences. The press data comes from *BusinessWeek*, *The New York Times*, *Financial Times*, *The Economist*, and *The Wall Street Journal* using LexisNexis and Factiva.com. Relatedness is a dummy variable which takes the value 1 when acquiror and target belong to the same Fama-French 48 industry group. Cumulative abnormal returns to the acquiror are calculated for an event window of −1 to +1 using a modified market model with the daily S&P 500 return as proxy for expected returns.

Panel A. Summary statistics of firm data

	Full sample (394 firms)			
	Obs.	Mean	Median	S.D.
Assets	3911	5979.06	2248.15	13,985.26
Capital (PPE)	3911	2278.64	877.20	5587.07
Investment (CAPX)	3704	385.00	153.44	952.94
Cash flow	3911	450.76	192.31	968.87
Cash flow normalized by lagged capital	3911	0.37	0.26	0.36
Cash flow normalized by lagged assets	3911	0.11	0.10	0.07
Q	3911	1.42	1.12	0.88
Efficient board size	3911	0.55	1	0.50
Technical industry	3894	0.04	0	0.19
Manufacturing industry	3894	0.48	0	0.50
Transportation industry	3894	0.24	0	0.43
Trade industry	3894	0.10	0	0.31
Financial industry	3894	0.09	0	0.29
Service industry	3894	0.04	0	0.20

Panel B. Summary statistics of CEO data

	Full sample (738 CEOs)				Longholder CEOs (80 CEOs)			
	Obs.	Mean	Median	S.D.	Obs.	Mean	Median	S.D.
Age	3910	57.57	58	6.73	662	57.54	58	6.31
President and chairman	3911	0.38	0	0.48	662	0.36	0	0.48
Tenure	3873	8.50	6	7.39	639	10.68	9	7.07
Founder	3350	0.16	0	0.37	591	0.12	0	0.32
Stock ownership	3911	0.02	0.001	0.07	662	0.02	0.003	0.04
Vested options	3911	0.02	0.005	0.11	662	0.07	0.020	0.25
Finance education	2302	0.34	0	0.47	422	0.42	0	0.49
Technical education	2302	0.55	1	0.50	422	0.47	0	0.50

Panel C. Summary statistics of press data

	Full sample (393 firms, 738 CEOs)			
	Obs.	Mean	Median	S.D.
Total mentions	3889	8.89	3	22.03
"Confident" mentions	3889	0.08	0	0.36
"Optimistic" mentions	3889	0.07	0	0.32
"Not confident" mentions	3889	0.002	0	0.06
"Not optimistic" mentions	3889	0.004	0	0.07
"Reliable, cautious, conservative, practical, steady, frugal" mentions	3884	0.05	0	0.27

Panel D. Summary statistics of merger bids

	Obs.	Mean	Median	S.D.
Relatedness	808	0.386	0	0.487
Cumulative abnormal return to acquiror [−1, +1]	808	−0.003	−0.005	0.048
Acquiror in technical industry	808	0.026	0	0.159
Acquiror in manufacturing industry	808	0.314	0	0.465
Acquiror in transportation industry	808	0.099	0	0.299
Acquiror in trade industry	808	0.071	0	0.256
Acquiror in financial industry	808	0.444	0	0.497
Acquiror in service industry	808	0.046	0	0.209

Merton (1973) shows that investors should not exercise options early since the right to delay purchasing the underlying stock has nonnegative value and investors are free to diversify. This logic does not apply to executive options. Executive options are nontradeable, and CEOs cannot hedge (legally) the risk of their holdings by short-selling company stock. CEOs are also highly exposed to company risk since a large part of their compensation is equity based and their human capital is invested in their firms. As a result, risk-averse CEOs should exercise options early if the stock price is sufficiently high (Hall and Murphy, 2002; Lambert et al., 1991), that is, when the marginal cost of continuing to hold the option (risk exposure) exceeds the marginal benefit (option value). The exact threshold for exercise depends on remaining option duration, individual wealth, the degree of underdiversification, and risk aversion.

In our sample of FORBES 500 CEOs, the high degree of underdiversification implies fairly low thresholds, given reasonable calibrations of wealth and risk aversion. A subset of CEOs, however, persistently fails to exercise highly in-the-money vested options. One interpretation of this failure to exercise is overconfidence, that is, overestimation of the firm's future returns. Other interpretations include positive inside information, signaling, board pressure, risk tolerance, taxes, and procrastination. After relating late option exercise to merger decisions (Section 5), we will discuss these alternative interpretations (Section 6.1).

We construct three indicator variables, which partition our CEOs into "late" and "timely" option exercisers:

Longholder: Our first indicator variable identifies CEOs who, at least once during their tenure, hold an option until the year of expiration, even though the option is at least 40% in-the-money entering its final year. The exercise threshold of 40% is calibrated using the model of Hall and Murphy (2002) with a constant relative risk aversion (CRRA) of three and 67% of wealth in company stock, and refines the Longholder measure in Malmendier and Tate (2005). The particular choice of parameter values is not important for our results: the median percentage in-the-money entering the final year for options held to expiration is 253. Any assumption from no threshold at all to a threshold of 100% yields similar results.[15] We apply this measure as a managerial fixed effect, denoted Longholder.

We construct two alternative indicators of late exercise which (1) allow for time variation over a manager's sample years and (2) eliminate forward-looking information from the classification.

Pre-/Post-Longholder: First, we split the Longholder indicator into two separate dummy variables. Post-Longholder is equal to 1 only after the CEO for the first time holds an option until expiration (provided it exceeds the 40% threshold). Pre-Longholder is equal to 1 for the rest of the CEO-years in which Longholder is equal to 1.

[15] See Figure 1 in the NBER Working Paper version, Malmendier and Tate (2004). We do not calculate a separate threshold for every option package, depending on the CEOs wealth, diversification, and risk aversion, as we cannot observe these characteristics. Individual calibration would introduce observation-specific noise into the estimation without clear benefits.

One shortcoming of Post-Longholder is its lack of power. Only 42% of the observations in which Longholder is 1 fall into the Post-Longholder category, capturing 74 mergers. This effectively excludes the Post-Longholder measure from tests that require us to subdivide mergers into finer categories (cash versus stock or diversifying versus intraindustry mergers).

Holder 67: We construct a second backward-looking measure, Holder 67, which relaxes the requirement that CEOs hold their options all the way until expiration.[16] Instead, we focus on the exercise decision in the 5th year prior to expiration. Five years before expiration is the earliest point we can consider since most options in our sample have a 10-year duration and are fully vested only after year 4. We drop the small number of option packages with 5 years remaining duration that are not fully vested.[17] Maintaining the previous assumptions on CRRA and diversification, the new exercise threshold in the Hall-Murphy framework is 67%. We set Holder 67 equal to 1 if a CEO fails to exercise options with 5 years remaining duration despite a 67% increase in stock price (or more) since the grant date. As above, the results are robust to variation in the value of the threshold.

When we use this proxy, we consider only CEOs who could have been classified as Holder 67. That is, a CEO enters the sample once he has an option with 5 years remaining duration that is at least 67% in-the-money. Once he postpones the exercise of such options he is classified as Holder 67 and retains that label for his remaining sample years. The selection criterion controls for the impact of past performance: all CEOs experienced (at least) a 67% appreciation in stock prices between the grant and vesting dates of their options. Overall, the sample restrictions leave 1667 of our original 3911 observations. Because of the less stringent requirements of Holder 67, there are more late-exercise CEO-years and completed mergers (232) than under Post-Longholder, making the measure more appropriate for split-sample estimations.

In Table 2, we report the pairwise correlations between the Longholder measure and firm and CEO characteristics. (The patterns are similar for the other portfolio measures.) The correlations are generally low. The only two variables with correlations higher than 0.1 with Longholder are Vested options and Tenure. These correlations may arise mechanistically since classification as Longholder requires the CEO to hold options for 10 years (typically) to expiration. The correlation with Tenure does not arise for Holder 67. The (untabulated) correlation between Holder 67 and Tenure is −0.012. However, the correlation with vested options is also large for Holder 67 (0.21). Vested option holdings, then, might also proxy for excessive exposure to company risk. However, exposure due to vested option holdings reflects both the CEOs choice and board choices on compensation and contract provisions. Longholder and Holder 67 instead only reflect the CEOs choice not to diversify. We will control

---

[16] The definition of Holder 67 differs from the definition in Malmendier and Tate (2005), most importantly in removing all forward-looking information.

[17] These rare cases are options with fewer than 10 years duration.

Table 2

Correlations of portfolio measures

Longholder is a binary variable where 1 signifies that the CEO at some point during his tenure held an option package until the last year before expiration, provided that the package was at least 40% in-the-money entering its last year. Size is the log of assets, Q the market value of assets over the book value of assets. Cash flow is earnings before extraordinary items plus depreciation, normalized by beginning-of-the-year capital. Stock ownership is the fraction of company stock owned by the CEO and his immediate family. Vested options are the CEOs holdings of options that are exercisable within 6 months, as a fraction of common shares outstanding, and multiplied by 10 (so that the mean is roughly comparable to Stock ownership). Efficient board size is a binary variable equal to 1 if the board has between 4 and 12 directors. Size, Q, Stock ownership, and Vested options are measured at the beginning of the year; all other variables are at the end. Finance education is binary and equal to 1 for CEOs with an undergraduate or graduate degree in accounting, finance, business (incl. MBA), or economics. Technical education is binary and equals 1 for CEOs with an undergraduate or graduate degree in engineering, physics, operations research, chemistry, mathematics, biology, pharmacy, or other applied sciences.

Panel A. Correlations with firm characteristics (N = 3911)

	Longholder	Size	Q	Cash flow	Stock ownership	Vested options	Efficient board size
Longholder	1						
Size	−0.09	1					
Q	0.09	−0.32	1				
Cash flow	0.10	−0.13	0.39	1			
Stock ownership	−0.04	−0.18	0.10	0.11	1		
Vested options	0.19	−0.17	0.09	0.17	0.10	1	
Efficient board size	0.04	−0.38	0.13	0.06	0.19	0.08	1

Panel B. Correlations with CEO characteristics (I) (N = 3872)

	Longholder	Age	Pres. and chm.	Tenure
Longholder	1			
Age	0.00	1		
President and chairman	−0.02	−0.03	1	
Tenure	0.13	0.40	0.004	1

Panel C. Correlations with CEO characteristics (II) (N = 2078)

	Longholder	Fin. ed.	Tech. ed.
Longholder	1		
Finance education	0.08	1	
Technical education	−0.07	−0.10	1

for option holdings and tenure in our estimations to prevent their direct effects from contaminating our results.

Finally, we find that the different measures of failure to exercise are significantly correlated with each other: the correlation between Longholder and Holder 67 is 0.47.

5. Overconfidence and acquisitiveness

Our empirical analysis relates CEOs' personal portfolio decisions to their corporate decisions. We test whether CEOs in cash-rich firms who maintain high personal exposure to company risk are more acquisitive and whether their mergers create less value on average.

We begin by measuring the unconditional relation between late option exercise and merger frequency. In Figure 1, we plot merger frequency among Longholder CEOs and their peers over time. The fraction of Longholder CEOs making at least one acquisition is higher in most years (up to 414%), often significantly so. Overall, Longholder CEOs do at least one merger in 108 out of 662 firm-years. For almost five times as many (3249) firm-years, their peers do mergers in only three times as many (343) years. Aggregating over time, the odds of a Longholder CEO making at least one acquisition are 1.65 times the odds of other CEOs (significant at 1%).[18] The pattern in the number of mergers per CEO is even stronger (Figure 2). Longholders surpass their peers in all but 2 years. The pictures are also similar using merger bids instead of completed mergers or using our other measures of late exercise: the odds ratio for making at least one acquisition is 1.48 for Post-Longholder (significant at 10%) and 1.62 for Holder 67 (significant at 1%). This strong unconditional relation between late exercise and merger frequency suggests that overconfidence may be a significant determinant of mergers.

5.1. Merger frequency and internal resources

We formalize this evidence and test Prediction 1 using the following regression specification:

$$\Pr\{Y_{it} = 1 | O_{it}, X_{it}\} = G(\beta_1 + \beta_2 O_{it} + X'_{it}B).$$ (1)

O is the overconfidence measure and X a set of controls. Y is a binary variable that takes the value 1 if the CEO made at least one successful merger bid in a particular firm-year. Throughout the paper, we assume that G is the logistic distribution.[19] The null hypothesis is that β_2, the coefficient on the overconfidence proxy, is equal to zero.

---

[18] The odds are 0.195 for Longholder CEOs and 0.118 for the rest.
[19] Wherever econometrically possible, we confirm the robustness to the assumption that G is normal.

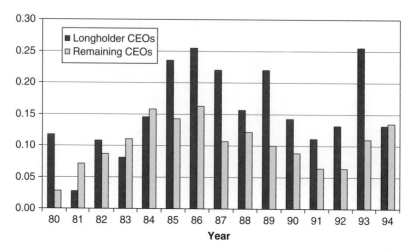

Fig. 1. Merger frequency (I): probability of completing a merger. The figure displays year-by-year merger frequencies, separately for Longholder CEOs and the remaining sample of CEOs. For each subgroup, the frequency is calculated as the number of CEOs who completed at least one merger divided by the total number of CEOs in that subgroup in a given year. Years are fiscal years.

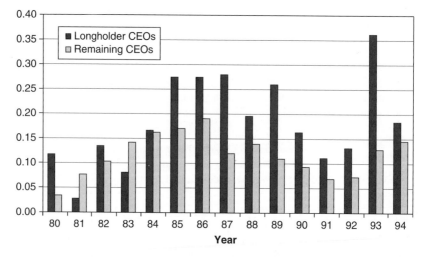

Fig. 2. Merger frequency (II): average number of mergers. The figure displays year-by-year merger frequencies, separately for Longholder CEOs and the remaining sample of CEOs. For each subgroup, the frequency is calculated as the number of mergers divided by the number of CEOs in that subgroup in a given year. Years are fiscal years.

We report the results of two-tailed tests even though the overconfidence theory motivates one-sided hypothesis tests. Thus, significance at the 10% level can be interpreted as significance at the 5% level for the theoretically derived one-sided test.

As described in Section 4, we use several proxies for O. Our first measure, Longholder, uses two types of variation: cross-sectional and within-firm variation. As an example for cross-sectional identification, consider the case of Wayne Huizenga, CEO of Blockbuster Entertainment Group for all 7 years the firm appears in our data. Since he holds some options until the year of expiration, we classify him as overconfident. He also conducts seven acquisitions during those 7 years. Similarly, David Farrell is the CEO of May Department Stores—the holding company of Lord & Taylor, Filene's, and Robinsons-May, among others—for the 15 years the firm appears in our sample and is classified as overconfident. He conducts five mergers during those 15 years. By contrast, J. Willard Marriott is the CEO of Marriott International for all 15 years of our sample, but never holds an option until expiration. He also never conducts an acquisition. By comparing these two types of CEOs, we can identify a cross-sectional effect of overconfidence on acquisitiveness.

As an example of within-firm variation, consider Colgate Palmolive. For the first 4 years, the CEO is Keith Crane. Crane never holds an option until expiration and he never conducts an acquisition. Reuben Mark succeeds him as CEO in 1984. Over the next 11 years, he holds some options until the year of expiration and he also conducts four acquisitions. By comparing overconfident and rational CEOs within the same firm, we might also identify the effect of overconfidence on acquisitiveness.

The Holder 67 measure, on the other hand, can vary within CEO. It exploits changes in CEOs' option-exercise behavior in addition to the two sources of variation described above. Longholder Wayne Huizenga, for example, does not exercise two option packages that have passed the 67% threshold with 5 years remaining duration. From 1987 to 1989, before he is classified as Holder 67, he does four acquisitions. From 1990 through 1994, he does another three. Similarly, David Farrell, a Longholder, fails to exercise an option that has reached the 67% threshold in 1986. From 1980 to 1986, he completes two acquisitions. From 1987 through 1995, after he becomes a Holder 67, he does three more.

We estimate Equation (1) using three procedures. First, we estimate pooled logit regressions, which use all types of variation. Second, we estimate logit regressions with random effects, which also use all sources of variation, but explicitly model the effect of the firm on acquisitiveness. If the estimated effects of overconfidence in the pooled specification were due to firm effects, the estimates should decline when we include random effects. Third, we estimate logit regressions with firm fixed effects. This specification makes use only of within-firm and within-CEO variation. That is, we estimate the effect of overconfidence on acquisitiveness using only variation between overconfident and rational CEOs within firms and (in the case of Holder 67) between CEOs' overconfident and rational years. To address the incidental parameters problem, we estimate the fixed-effects model with a conditional logit regression. Conditioning the likelihood on the number of successes in each panel, we avoid estimating the coefficients of the fixed effects and obtain consistent estimates of the remaining coefficients. The advantage of the fixed-effects approach is that it eliminates any time-invariant firm effect on acquisitiveness. The disadvantage is that it induces sample selection. Only firms that conduct at least one merger during the sample period are included in the conditional logit estimation, and only firms that had at least one overconfident and one nonoverconfident CEO during the sample period (or a CEO who switches from not overconfident to overconfident under Holder 67) are used to identify β_2. We cluster standard errors in the pooled and fixed-effects logits to account for heteroskedasticity and autocorrelation at the firm level.[20] We tabulate only the most stringent, fixed-effects specification, except in the split-sample analyses where the number of identifiable cases is too small. In these cases, we tabulate the random-effects specification. In all other cases, the results are robust across estimation procedures.

Table 3 presents two sets of results. In the left half of the table, we test the robustness of the unconditional patterns in Figures 1 and 2 to the inclusion of firm- and CEO-level controls. We include the following firm-level controls[21]: the logarithm of assets at the beginning of the year as a control for firm size, Tobin's Q at the beginning of the year as a control for investment opportunities, cash flow as a measure of internal resources, an indicator for efficient board size (4-12 members)[22] as a measure of corporate governance, and firm fixed effects. At the CEO level, we include two controls for the incentive effects of stock and options: the percent of company stock held by the CEO at the beginning of the year and the number of options exercisable within 6 months of the beginning of the year, normalized by total shares outstanding.[23] We include year effects to control for time trends in the likelihood of conducting a merger. The coefficient estimates are presented as odds ratios. Thus, to test for a positive effect on acquisitiveness, we compare the reported estimates to 1.

Among the controls, we consistently find that firms with lower Tobin's Q are more acquisitive, suggesting that acquisitions may substitute for profitable investment opportunities.[24] More cash flow generally leads to more merger activity, as expected if cash eases financing constraints. Vested option holdings predict fewer mergers. The within-firm effect of size on acquisitiveness is positive; however, the relationship may be mechanistic since the assets of a firm must increase during a merger. We rerun

---

[20] We verify the robustness of the results to clustering at the CEO rather than the firm level. Firm-level clustering is more stringent since it allows for the possibility that all of the firm's errors are correlated. CEO-level clustering instead assumes that observations of different CEOs within the same firm are independent.

[21] We use the standard firm-level controls from the investment literature as our regression is a binary investment model.

[22] The results are robust to using the logarithm of board size or the number (or percentage) of CEOs of other firms sitting on the board. The firm fixed effects capture most of the remaining variation in governance since firm governance is very stable over our sample period. (See Guner et al. (2008) for a detailed analysis of board composition in a closely related data set.) Recent measures such as the Gompers et al. (2003) index are not available for our 1980–1994 sample period.

[23] We multiply vested option holdings by 10 so that the mean is similar to stock ownership.

[24] This effect appears to be nonmonotonic. For example, we find a positive and marginally significant effect when we include a dummy variable for "high Tobin's Q" ($Q > 1$). Alternatively, including the square of Tobin's Q reverses the direction of the level effect (though it becomes insignificant).

Table 3

Do late-exercisers complete more mergers?

The dependent variable is binary where 1 signifies that the firm made at least one merger bid that was eventually successful in a given year. Size is the log of assets, Q the market value of assets over the book value of assets. Cash flow is earnings before extraordinary items plus depreciation, normalized by beginning-of-the-year capital. Stock ownership is the fraction of company stock owned by the CEO and his immediate family. Vested options are the CEOs holdings of options that are exercisable within 6 months, as a fraction of common shares outstanding, and multiplied by 10 (so that the mean is roughly comparable to Stock ownership). Efficient board size is a binary variable where 1 signifies that the board of directors has between 4 and 12 members. Longholder is a binary variable where 1 signifies that the CEO at some point during his tenure held an option package until the last year before expiration, provided that the package was at least 40% in-the-money entering its last year. Post-Longholder is a dummy equal to 1 for all CEO-years after the CEO for the first time holds options to expiration. Pre-Longholder are all years classified as 1 under Longholder, but 0 under Post-Longholder. Holder 67 is a dummy equal to 1 for all CEO-years after the CEO for the first time fails to exercise a 67% in-the-money option with 5 years remaining duration. In the Holder 67 regressions, the sample is limited to CEO-years after the CEO for the first time had a 67% in-the-money option with 5 years remaining duration. Size, Q, Stock ownership, and Vested options are measured at the beginning of the year; all other variables are at the end. The fixed-effects logit model is estimated consistently using a conditional logit specification and standard errors are robust to heteroskedasticity and arbitrary within-firm serial correlation. In Columns (4)–(6), we use the cash-reserves model of Harford (1999) to identify cash-rich and cash-poor firms. In the untabulated first stage, we regress cash and short-term investments scaled by (net) sales on the following independent variables: the level and the t to $t + 1$ and $t + 1$ to $t + 2$ changes in net cash flow to sales, defined as operating cash flow (operating income before depreciation − interest − taxes − Δ noncash working capital) minus investment (capital expenditures) over sales; the change in the risk premium, defined as the spread in interest rates between AAA and Baa bonds, measured in the month the fiscal year ends; NBER recession, defined as an indicator variable for fiscal years that end within an NBER-defined recession; Q, defined as the market value of assets over the book value of assets; cash flow volatility, defined as the coefficient of variation of firm-specific operating cash flows; and size, defined as the market value of the firm (fiscal-year end stock-price times common shares outstanding). Column (4) shows the results of the random-effects estimation on the full sample of firm-years, for which all variables of the Harford (1998) cash-reserves model are available. Column (5) shows the results for the subsample of Cash-rich firm-years, in which cash reserves at the beginning of the year are at least 1.5 standard deviations above the predicted value from the first-stage cash-reserves regression. The relevant standard deviation is the firm-specific standard deviation of cash reserves. Column (6) contains the random-effects estimation for the remaining subsample of Cash-poor firm-years. All coefficients are presented as odds ratios.

| | Fixed-effects logit | | | Random-effects logit | | |
| | | | | Baseline | Cash rich | Cash poor |
	(1)	(2)	(3)	(4)	(5)	(6)
Size	0.6537	0.6600	0.3278	0.9022	0.9480	0.9177
	(2.50)**	(2.42)**	(3.42)***	(1.49)	(0.50)	(1.03)
Q	0.7135	0.7154	0.9062	0.7019	0.7686	0.6839
	(2.20)**	(2.18)**	(0.45)	(2.96)***	(1.25)	(2.70)***
Cash flow	2.0231	2.0377	1.6607	1.5427	0.9948	1.8719
	(1.72)*	(1.72)*	(0.67)	(2.07)**	(0.01)	(2.35)**
Stock ownership	0.3840	0.3813	0.0418	1.4084	21.4335	0.7232
	(0.95)	(0.96)	(0.70)	(0.36)	(1.80)*	(0.29)

(Continued)

Table 3 (*Continued*)

	Fixed-effects logit			Random-effects logit		
	(1)	(2)	(3)	Baseline (4)	Cash rich (5)	Cash poor (6)
Vested options	0.4566	0.4595	0.6384	1.2165	4.2168	1.3186
	(3.97)***	(3.93)***	(0.51)	(0.46)	(0.91)	(0.63)
Efficient board size	1.0817	1.0811	1.8488	0.8012	0.575	0.9184
	(0.40)	(0.40)	(2.10)**	(1.55)	(2.44)**	(0.48)
Longholder	2.1891			1.7447	1.9728	1.5471
	(2.70)***			(3.21)***	(2.53)**	(2.10)**
Post-Longholder		1.8642				
		(1.91)*				
Pre-Longholder		2.3305				
		(2.72)***				
Holder 67			2.5159			
			(2.49)**			
Firm fixed effects	Yes	Yes	Yes	No	No	No
Year fixed effects	Yes	Yes	Yes	Yes	Yes	Yes
Observations	2568	2568	853	3540	1227	2313
Number of firms	225	225	124	322	282	314

z-Statistics in parentheses. Constant included.
*Significant at 10%; **significant at 5%; ***significant at 1%.

the regressions without size and verify that this effect does not change the estimates of β_2. Finally, the effects of efficient board size and stock ownership are typically insignificant.

Turning to the coefficient of interest, the effect of late exercise on merger frequency remains positive after including all the controls and fixed effects. CEOs who persistently hold options are significantly more acquisitive, even when we identify β_2 using only variation across CEOs or (for Holder 67) within CEOs in the same firm.

In the right half of Table 3, we test Prediction 1: are overconfident CEOs more acquisitive in firms with abundant internal resources? Since overconfident CEOs both overestimate the returns to mergers and perceive their stand-alone firms to be undervalued, they view issuing equity or taking risky debt to be costly, even when investors evaluate their firms correctly. The perceived costs do not affect the decision to merge only if the merger can be financed internally. We test whether CEOs who fail to exercise in-the-money options are more acquisitive than their peers when in cash-rich firms.

Note that traditional agency theory generates a different prediction. Empire-building CEOs also waste free cash flow on bad acquisitions (Harford, 1999). But, unlike overconfident CEOs, they are aware that their mergers destroy shareholder value. As a result, they should minimize their personal investment in the company by exercising in-the-money options at the earliest opportunity. Personal investment in the company, as measured by our controls for stock and option holdings, should decrease an empire-building CEOs propensity to acquire since it aligns CEO and shareholder interests. Our measures of late exercise, instead, isolate the active decision of the CEO not to divest company risk. This behavior and the link to increased acquisitiveness distinguishes overconfidence from traditional agency theory.

We identify cash-rich and cash-poor firms using the model of Harford (1999). In a first stage, we regress cash reserves (cash stock normalized by sales) on the change in the risk premium between AAA and Baa bonds, a dummy for NBER recession years, the ratio of market to book value of assets, the coefficient of variation of operating cash flows, firm size (market value), and the level of and changes from year t to $t + 1$ and $t + 1$ to $t + 2$ in operating cash flow net of investment (normalized by sales). In our sample, the model explains 84% of the variation in cash reserves. Following Harford, we call firm-years "cash rich" if beginning-of-the-year cash reserves are at least 1.5 standard deviations above the value predicted by the baseline model, where the standard deviation is the time series deviation in firm cash reserves.

We estimate random-effects logit regressions of Equation (1) on all firm-years for which the Harford model is defined (Column (4)), on "cash rich" firm-years (Column (5)), and on the remaining firm-years (Column (6)).[25]

Among the controls, the estimated effect of Tobin's Q is similar to the full-sample estimation: firms with lower Tobin's Q are more acquisitive. The effect of cash flow on acquisitiveness depends on whether the firm is cash-rich or cash-poor. Cash flow increases acquisitiveness among cash-poor firms. But, among cash-rich firms there is no significant effect of cash flow on acquisitiveness suggesting that cash constraints do not bind. This result corroborates the classification of the Harford model. The effects of Stock ownership and Vested options are insignificant in all specifications except Column (5) (cash-rich subsample), in which the Stock ownership odds ratio appears to "blow up." The Longholder effect is robust to excluding this control variable. Finally, efficient board size predicts less acquisitiveness in cash-rich firms, but not in cash-poor firms, consistent with traditional agency theory.

Turning to the coefficient of interest, we find that Longholder CEOs are significantly more likely to make acquisitions than other CEOs not only in the full sample, but also in the subsample of cash-rich firm-years as predicted by the overconfidence model (odds ratio = 1.97, significant at 5%). We also find a significant effect in the cash-poor subsample (odds ratio = 1.55, significant at 5%). A Wald test fails to reject equality of the estimates in the two subsamples. The latter finding neither confirms nor rejects the overconfidence hypothesis: the CEOs decision in constrained firms depends on the unobservable relation between overestimated gains to merging and perceived own-company undervaluation. Hence, overconfidence may or may not have a significant impact on acquisitiveness in cash-poor firms. The results are similar using Holder 67 (cash-rich odds ratio = 2.14, significant at 5%; cash-poor odds ratio = 1.39, insignificant).

---

[25] Splitting the sample leaves us with too few identifiable cases in the subsamples to use fixed-effects logit.

We find similar results if we measure internal resources using the Kaplan-Zingales index rather than the Harford model. The index, based on logit estimates from Kaplan and Zingales (1997), is defined as

$$KZ_{it} = -1.001909 \times \frac{CF_{it}}{K_{it-1}} + 0.2826389 \times Q_{it} + 3.139193 \times Lev_{it} - 39.3678$$

$$\times \frac{Div_{it}}{K_{it-1}} - 1.314759 \times \frac{C_{it}}{K_{it-1}}$$

where CF/K is cash flow to capital, Lev is debt to total capital, Div/K is dividends to capital, and C/K is cash holdings to capital.[26] Higher values imply higher constraints. Following recent research (Baker et al., 2003; Lamont et al., 2001; Malmendier and Tate, 2005), we use the twice-lagged value of the index to split sample firms into quintiles and estimate random-effects logit regressions of Equation (1) separately on each quintile. The Longholder coefficient is positive and significant in the "least constrained" quintile (odds ratio = 2.03, significant at 5%) and insignificant in the "most constrained" quintile (odds ratio = 1.07). Again, the cross-quintile difference is not significant at conventional levels (p-value = 0.133).[27]

Finally, we test the effect of perceived undervaluation directly by looking at merger financing. We find that, conditional on conducting a merger, Longholder CEOs are more likely to finance it using cash (Panel A, Table 4). The odds ratio of using cash versus any mixture of risky securities with cash is 1.10. It is even stronger for the Holder 67 measure (1.38; untabulated). We also examine the effect in a regression framework, controlling for above- or below-average firm valuation (relative to its industry), Tobin's Q, CEO stock and vested option ownership, merger size, the availability of internal funds, and year effects in various combinations (Panel B). The odds ratio increases to 1.2 but is insignificant. It is 1.7 and significant at the 10% level for Holder 67. It is also significant for Longholder CEOs when the firm is unlikely to be (objectively) overvalued, that is, when Tobin's Q is less than the (within-sample) industry average. The interaction of "undervaluation" and Longholder is significant in all specifications.

The financing results allow us to disentangle the two manifestations of overconfidence in the context of mergers: managers who are overconfident about the returns they generate overestimate both the value they create in their own firm and the value they create by taking over other firms. The overconfidence hypothesis predicts that the two types of overestimation are linked and that their relative importance varies with the market valuation of the own company. In times of high market valuation, captured

---

[26] For this test, we use the definition of Q employed by Kaplan and Zingales (1997) to avoid rendering the weights meaningless. The Compustat data items are: cash flow to capital = (item 18 + item 14)/item 8; Q = [item 6 + (item 24 * item 25)—item 60—item 74]/item 6; debt to total capital (leverage) = (item 9 + item 34)/(item 9 + item 34 + item 216); dividends to capital = item 21 + item 19)/item 8; cash to capital = item 1/item 8. Item 8, capital, is always taken at the beginning of the year (lagged).

[27] There are too few observations in quintiles of the Holder 67 sample to allow a similar analysis.

Table 4

Merger financing

The sample includes all successful merger bids. The dependent variable in Panel B is binary and equals 1 if the merger was financed using only cash. Q below industry is a binary variable where 1 indicates that Q at the beginning of the year was less than or equal to industry Q. Industries are the 48 Fama-French industry groups. Q is the market value of assets over the book value of assets. Stock ownership is the fraction of company stock owned by the CEO and his immediate family. Vested options are the CEOs holdings of options that are exercisable within 6 months, as a fraction of common shares outstanding, and multiplied by 10 (so that the mean is roughly comparable to Stock ownership). Merger size is the amount the acquiror paid for the target as a fraction of acquiror value. (For SDC mergers, amount paid is the value of the transaction; for CRSP mergers, it is the market value of the target the day after the announcement. When both variables are present, we use the minimum.) Cash rich is a dummy variable equal to 1 if cash reserves at the beginning of the year are at least 1.5 standard deviations above the predicted value from the cash-reserves regression. The relevant standard deviation is the firm-specific standard deviation of cash reserves. In the cash-reserves regression (which follows Harford, 1999), we regress cash and short-term investments scaled by (net) sales on the following independent variables: the level and the t to $t + 1$ and $t + 1$ to $t + 2$ changes in net cash flow to sales, defined as operating cash flow (operating income before depreciation − interest − taxes − Δ noncash working capital) minus investment (capital expenditures) over sales; the change in the risk premium, defined as the spread in interest rates between AAA and Baa bonds, measured in the month the fiscal year ends; NBER recession, defined as an indicator variable for fiscal years that end within an NBER-defined recession; Q, defined as the market value of assets over the book value of assets; cash flow volatility, defined as the coefficient of variation of firm-specific operating cash flows; and size, defined as the market value of the firm (fiscal-year end stock-price times common shares outstanding). Longholder is a binary variable where 1 signifies that the CEO at some point during his tenure held an option package until the last year before expiration, provided that the package was at least 40% in-the-money entering its last year. Q below industry, Q, Stock ownership, Vested options, and Cash rich are measured at the beginning of the year; all other variables are at the end. Standard errors are robust to heteroskedasticity and arbitrary within-firm serial correlation. Coefficients are presented as odds ratios. z-Statistics in parentheses. Constant included.

Panel A. All mergers with disclosed method of payment

	Total mergers	Cash (%)	Debt OR cash and debt (%)	Stock AND cash and/or debt (%)	Stock (%)	Odds (cash vs. stock)	Odds (cash vs. other)	Odds ratio (vs. stock)	Odds ratio (vs. other)
Longholder = 1	188	38.8	6.9	19.7	34.6	1.12	0.63	1.09	1.10
Longholder = 0	708	33.5	8.3	25.6	32.6	1.03	0.58		

Panel B. Logit regressions

	(1)	(2)	(3)	(4)	(5)
Q Below industry		1.7215	1.8457	1.9274	1.1035
		(2.72)***	(3.02)***	(3.11)***	(0.39)
Q	0.8018		1.2618	1.0288	0.6457
	(1.28)		(1.26)	(0.14)	(1.90)*
Stock ownership	2.818		1.7263	1.6837	0.1726
	(0.87)		(0.41)	(0.42)	(1.30)

(*Continued*)

Table 4 (*Continued*)

	(1)	(2)	(3)	(4)	(5)
Vested options	0.3403		0.5818	0.4279	0.2214
	(1.54)		(0.75)	(1.21)	(1.04)
Merger size	0.9934		0.981	0.9927	0.9924
	(0.58)		(1.37)	(0.58)	(0.73)
Cash rich					1.3895
					(1.55)
Longholder	1.2001	0.7423	0.7685	0.7766	0.8383
	(0.77)	(0.84)	(0.76)	(0.72)	(0.45)
(*Q* Below industry) × (Longholder)		2.3096	2.2577	1.9555	2.0647
		(2.09)**	(2.06)**	(1.71)*	(1.67)*
Year fixed effects	Yes	No	No	Yes	Yes
Observations	772	772	772	772	427

*, **, and *** significant at 10%, 5%, and 1%, respectively.

by high Q relative to the industry, the CEO is less likely to perceive his own company to be undervalued. In this case, even overconfident managers are willing to finance deals using equity. The results are also consistent with the view that investor sentiment affects merger financing decisions, as in Shleifer and Vishny (2003).

5.2. Value consequences

Next we test Prediction 2. We ask whether the heightened acquisitiveness of late-exercising CEOs leads to an increased propensity to take projects with negative expected returns. We first use deal characteristics as a rough measure of quality. We then measure differences in the market's reaction to bids by Longholder and other CEOs.

5.2.1. Diversification

First, we use diversification as a proxy for deal quality. Many prior studies find evidence of a diversification discount.[28] Plant-level data confirm the negative impact of diversification via acquisition and address concerns about econometric and data biases.[29] Moreover, the market seems to anticipate that many diversifying bids are unwise. Morck et al. (1990) measure negative announcement effects to diversifying deals, an effect we confirm in our data.[30]

---

[28] See, for example, Lang and Stulz (1994), Berger and Ofek (1995), Servaes (1996), and Lamont and Polk (2002).

[29] Schoar (2002), addressing Graham et al. (2002) and Villalonga (2004) among others.

[30] Further suggestive evidence comes from Lys and Vincent (1995) and Shefrin (2000), who chronicle AT&T's 1990 acquisition of NCR using exactly this paradigm. Interestingly, both the Longholder and Holder 67 measures identify AT&T's CEO (Robert Allen) as overconfident.

We reestimate Equation (1) with a dependent variable that indicates diversifying merger bids and, separately, with a dependent variable that indicates intraindustry bids.[31] We classify deals as diversifying if acquiror and target are not members of the same Fama-French 48 industry group.[32] The results are in Column (1) of Table 5. We find that Longholder CEOs are significantly more likely than other CEOs to do diversifying mergers (odds ratio = 2.54, significant at 1%), but not within-industry deals (odds ratio = 1.66, insignificant). This result suggests that the extra mergers of late-exercisers may be disproportionately low quality. However, the cross-regression difference in coefficients is not significant. The (untabulated) results are similar using the Holder 67 measure (odds ratio = 2.72, significant at 5% for diversifying mergers; odds ratio = 0.84, insignificant for within-industry mergers).

We also measure differences in the propensity to diversify among cash-rich firms. As in Section 5.1, we measure internal resources using the model of Harford (1999) and estimate a random-effects model. In the full sample, the logit results replicate: Longholder CEOs are particularly likely to do diversifying deals (odds ratio = 2.01, significant at 1%), but are no more likely to do within-industry deals (odds ratio = 1.30, insignificant). We find similar results for Longholder CEOs in cash-rich firms: the odds ratio is 2.50, significant at 5%, for diversifying mergers, but insignificant for within-industry mergers. In the cash-poor subsample, the pattern is similar, though weaker for diversifying deals (odds ratio = 1.78, significant at 5%). The same is true for Holder 67 (cash-rich diversifying odds ratio = 2.15, significant at 10%; cash-poor diversifying odds ratio = 1.86, significant at 5%; no significant effects within industries).

In unreported estimations, we check the robustness of these patterns to the inclusion of further controls for the agency effects of free cash flow. In addition to our controls for incentive misalignment (stock and option ownership), we include a measure of CEO power (consolidation of the titles CEO, Chairman of the Board, and President) and a continuous measure of the availability of cash reserves. The controls are typically insignificant and the effect of late exercise is largely unchanged.

In summary, we find that the point estimates for the effect of late exercise on excess acquisitiveness are always largest in the sample of cash-rich firms and for diversifying deals. The results suggest a mechanism by which overconfidence destroys shareholder value. However, we must be cautious in interpreting the results since the cross-sample differences are typically not significant. In the next subsection, we use different methodology to provide additional evidence.

---

[31] As before, we analyze merger bids that were ultimately successful. However, since the likelihood of failure may differ across diversifying and intraindustry mergers, we also perform the estimations including unsuccessful merger bids. None of our conclusions in this section (as elsewhere in the paper) are affected.

[32] See Ken French's website http://mba.tuck.dartmouth.edu/pages/faculty/ken.french/data_library.html.

Table 5

Diversifying and same-industry mergers

The dependent variable in Panel 1 (Panel 2) is binary where 1 signifies that the firm made a diversifying (within-industry) merger bid that was eventually successful in a given year. Diversification is measured using the 48 Fama and French industry groups. Size is the log of assets, Q the market value of assets over the book value of assets. Cash flow is earnings before extraordinary items plus depreciation, normalized by beginning-of-the-year capital. Stock ownership is the fraction of company stock owned by the CEO and his immediate family. Vested options are the CEOs holdings of options that are exercisable within 6 months, as a fraction of common shares outstanding, and multiplied by 10 (so that the mean is roughly comparable to Stock ownership). Efficient board size is a binary variable where 1 signifies that the board of directors has between 4 and 12 members. Longholder is a binary variable where 1 signifies that the CEO at some point during his tenure held an option package until the last year before expiration, provided that the package was at least 40% in-the-money entering its last year. Size, Q, Stock ownership, and Vested options are measured at the beginning of the year; all other variables are at the end. The fixed-effects logit model is estimated consistently using a conditional logit specification, and standard errors are robust to heteroskedasticity and arbitrary within-firm serial correlation. The random-effects estimations employ the cash-reserves model of Harford (1999) to identify cash-rich and cash-poor firms. In the untabulated first stage, we regress cash and short-term investments scaled by (net) sales on the following independent variables: the level and the t to $t +$ 1 and $t + 1$ to $t + 2$ changes in net cash flow to sales, defined as operating cash flow (operating income before depreciation − interest − taxes − Δ noncash working capital) minus investment (capital expenditures) over sales; the change in the risk premium, defined as the spread in interest rates between AAA and Baa bonds, measured in the month the fiscal year ends; NBER recession, defined as an indicator variable for fiscal years that end within an NBER-defined recession; Q, defined as the market value of assets over the book value of assets; cash flow volatility, defined as the coefficient of variation of firm-specific operating cash flows; and size, defined as the market value of the firm (fiscal-year end stock-price times common shares outstanding). The baseline estimation uses the full sample of firm-years, for which all variables of the Harford cash-reserves model are available. The Cash-rich subsample contains all firm-years in which actual cash reserves at the beginning of the year are at least 1.5 standard deviations above the predicted value from the baseline cash-reserves regression. The relevant standard deviation is the firm-specific standard deviation of cash reserves. The cash-poor subsample contains all remaining firm-years. All coefficients are presented as odds ratios. z-Statistics in parentheses. Constant included.

	Fixed-effects logit	Random-effects logit		
		Baseline	Cash rich	Cash poor
Panel 1. Diversifying mergers				
Size	0.7592	1.065	1.1462	1.0689
	(1.29)	(0.73)	(0.95)	(0.64)
Q	0.8437	0.718	0.7241	0.7092
	(0.86)	(2.08)**	(1.05)	(1.87)*
Cash flow	2.1685	1.5963	0.8767	2.0797
	(1.53)	(1.84)*	(0.28)	(2.32)**
Stock ownership	0.1268	2.5704	98.2692	1.2053
	(1.48)	(0.81)	(2.10)**	(0.13)
Vested options	0.8589	1.5657	4.3008	1.6552
	(0.50)	(1.01)	(0.54)	(1.11)
Efficient board size	0.9737	0.7331	0.4504	0.8741
	(0.11)	(1.71)*	(2.62)***	(0.60)

(Continued)

Table 5 (*Continued*)

		Random-effects logit		
	Fixed-effects logit	Baseline	Cash rich	Cash poor
Longholder	2.5376	2.0108	2.5042	1.781
	(3.31)***	(3.29)***	(2.56)**	(2.27)**
Firm fixed effects	Yes	No	No	No
Year fixed effects	Yes	Yes	Yes	Yes
Observations	1832	3540	1227	2313
Number of firms	159	322	282	314

Panel 2. Within-industry mergers

Size	0.4656	0.6992	0.7031	0.7302
	(2.77)***	(3.42)***	(2.40)**	(2.45)**
Q	0.5359	0.6864	0.7664	0.6572
	(2.43)**	(2.23)**	(1.02)	(2.02)**
Cash flow	2.496	1.3048	1.096	1.483
	(1.50)	(0.84)	(0.20)	(0.94)
Stock ownership	0.8916	0.819	1.1449	0.6252
	(0.10)	(0.14)	(0.06)	(0.30)
Vested options	0.1853	0.6936	3.6528	0.7161
	(3.71)***	(0.66)	(0.78)	(0.54)
Efficient board size	1.1113	0.844	0.7228	0.9176
	(0.36)	(0.82)	(1.11)	(0.33)
Longholder	1.6646	1.2965	1.3161	1.1471
	(1.03)	(1.01)	(0.82)	(0.43)
Firm fixed effects	Yes	No	No	No
Year fixed effects	Yes	Yes	Yes	Yes
Observations	1467	3540	1227	2313
Number of firms	127	322	282	314

*, **, and *** significant at 10%, 5%, and 1%, respectively.

5.2.2. Market reaction

Next we use announcement effects to test Prediction 2 more directly. When overconfident CEOs engage in more deals than other CEOs, their deals have lower average quality. Moreover, they may overbid, even in (otherwise) value-creating deals. As a result, the market reaction to merger bids should be significantly lower for overconfident than for nonoverconfident CEOs.

We calculate the cumulative abnormal return to the acquiring firm's stock over a 3-day window around the announcement of the merger bid,[33] using the daily return on the S&P 500 index as our proxy for expected returns. This approach is appropriate

---

[33] We find similar results using a window of 5 days (-2 to $+2$).

since our sample consists of large US companies that comprise a substantial portion of market returns.[34]

The average announcement effect in our sample is −29 bp in Panel A, Table 6. The market reaction to merger bids by Longholder CEOs is three times as negative as for the rest of the sample: among Longholder CEOs, the average effect is −90 bp (significant at 1%) and among other CEOs it is −12 bp (insignificant). We can decompose these effects further based on the means of financing. Among non-Longholder CEOs, the reaction to cash bids is significantly positive (70 bp) and the reaction to stock bids is significantly negative (−75 bp).[35] Bids of Longholder CEOs, instead, always trigger a negative average reaction, though it is four times as large and significant only for stock bids (−135 bp). Moreover, the negative reaction for Longholder CEOs is most pronounced in the subsample of firm-years classified as Post-Longholder. Here, the average effect is −160 bp (and −277 bp for stock bids).[36]

We test whether the negative contribution of overconfidence to cumulative abnormal returns holds controlling for firm and CEO characteristics using the following model:

$$CAR_i = \gamma_1 + \gamma_2 O_i + X_i' G + \varepsilon_i. \tag{2}$$

O is the overconfidence proxy. The set of controls X includes standard predictors of the market's reaction to merger bids: relatedness (an indicator for within-industry mergers) and cash financing. We continue to include controls for stock and option ownership and corporate governance (efficient board size). Lastly, we include year effects to control for time trends in the market reaction to merger bids and potential clustering of overconfident and nonoverconfident bids in different merger waves. Since the dependent variable is continuous rather than binary, we switch from a logit specification to a linear regression. The null hypothesis is $\gamma_2 = 0$.

Panel B of Table 6 presents the results. The coefficient estimates of all controls have the expected signs. The two consistently significant controls are Cash Financing and Vested Options. Cash deals are, on average, viewed more favorably by the market. The effect of vested option holdings on cumulative abnormal returns is nonlinear. The effect is positive at lower values, possibly due to improved incentives, and negative at high values, possibly due to entrenchment or excessive CEO power. We include a quadratic term to capture the nonlinearity.

Most importantly, the market reaction to merger bids of Longholders is negative, confirming Prediction 2. Compared to the simple averages, the difference between Longholder CEOs and the remaining sample increases from −78 bp (significant at 5%) to −112 bp, or −115 bp with year effects (both significant at 1%). The results are

---

[34] The standard market-model results (using a preestimation period to identify α and β) are almost identical.

[35] We define stock bids as bids in which any portion is financed using equity.

[36] Under the Holder 67 measure, the results are sensitive to the window of evaluation (i.e., $(-1, +1)$ versus $(-2, +2)$) and also to the inclusion or exclusion of failed merger bids. Inclusion gives us more power and leads to results more in line with the Longholder estimates.

Table 6

Market response

The event window is from the day before through the day after the announcement of the bid. The dependent variable in Panel B is the Cumulative abnormal return on the bidder's stock from the day before the announcement of the bid through the day after. Cumulative abnormal returns are calculated by taking the daily return on the bidder's common equity and subtracting expected returns. Expected returns are the daily return on the S&P 500 index. Cash bids are financed with any combination of cash and debt. Stock bids are financed with any portion of equity. Stock ownership is the fraction of company stock owned by the CEO and his immediate family at the beginning of the year in which the bid occurs. Vested options are the CEOs holdings of options that are exercisable within 6 months of the beginning of the year of the bid, as a fraction of common shares outstanding, and multiplied by 10 (so that the mean is roughly comparable to Stock ownership). Relatedness is 1 for acquisitions in which the bidder and target firms are in the same industry, measured using the Fama-French 48 industry groups. Cash financing is a binary variable where 1 indicates that the acquisition was financed using some combination of cash and debt. Efficient board size is a binary variable where 1 signifies that the board of directors has between 4 and 12 members. Longholder is a binary variable where 1 signifies that the CEO at some point during his tenure held an option until the last year before expiration, provided that the package was at least 40% in-the-money entering its last year. Post-Longholder is a dummy equal to 1 for all CEO-years after the CEO for the first time holds options to expiration. Pre-Longholder are all years classified as 1 under Longholder, but 0 under Post-Longholder. All standard errors in Panel B are clustered by event date to account for cross-sectional correlation of stock returns. *t*-Statistics in parentheses. Constant included.

Panel A

	Average CAR [−1, +1]		
	All bids	Cash bids	Stock bids
Full sample	−0.0029	0.0045	−0.0087
	(808; 1.73)*	(354; 1.82)*	(454; 3.94)***
Longholder = 0	−0.0012	0.0070	−0.0075
	(611; 0.62)	(265; 2.21)**	(346; 3.03)***
Longholder = 1	−0.0090	−0.0032	−0.0135
	(178; 2.73)***	(78; 0.88)	(100; 2.64)***
Pre-Longholder = 1	−0.0052	−0.0033	−0.0066
	(115; 1.26)	(48; 0.81)	(67; 1.02)
Post-Longholder = 1	−0.0160	−0.0031	−0.0277
	(63; 2.91)***	(30; 0.45)	(33; 3.49)***

Number of observations and *t*-statistics in parentheses.

Panel B. OLS regressions

	(1)	(2)	(3)	(4)	(5)
Stock ownership		0.052	0.0561	0.051	0.0555
		(1.41)	(1.51)	(1.39)	(1.49)
Vested options		0.1039	0.1071	0.105	0.1066
		(2.64)***	(2.59)***	(2.65)***	(2.58)**
(Vested options)^2		−0.0322	−0.0329	−0.033	−0.0332
		(2.67)***	(2.59)***	(2.72)***	(2.62)***

(*Continued*)

Table 6 (*Continued*)

	(1)	(2)	(3)	(4)	(5)
Relatedness		0.0035	0.0034	0.0039	0.0037
		(1.02)	(0.98)	(1.13)	(1.07)
Efficient board size		0.0053	0.0058	0.0056	0.006
		(1.31)	(1.42)	(1.38)	(1.47)
Cash financing		0.0119	0.0155	0.0119	0.0155
		(3.39)***	(4.03)***	(3.41)***	(4.02)***
Longholder	−0.0078	−0.0112	−0.0115		
	(2.02)**	(2.72)***	(2.80)***		
Post-Longholder				−0.0198	−0.0193
				(3.46)***	(3.29)***
Pre-Longholder				−0.0065	−0.007
				(1.34)	(1.50)
Year fixed effects	No	No	Yes	No	Yes
Observations	789	789	789	789	789
R^2	0.00	0.05	0.08	0.06	0.08

*, **, and *** significant at 10%, 5%, and 1%, respectively.

stronger for Post-Longholder firm-years (Columns (4) and (5)). One interpretation is that the market discounts the bids of Longholder CEOs only after they have revealed their overconfidence through their portfolio decisions. Moreover, the results are robust to including additional controls for agency concerns, as in Section 5.2.1.

We can use the announcement effects to quantify the loss in shareholder wealth through merger bids by late-exercising CEOs. The Longholder measure identifies 10.8% of CEOs as overconfident. If we calculate the value creation or destruction to acquiring-company shareholders as announcement effect times market capitalization before announcement, we find that this 10.8% of CEOs causes 44% of value destruction around merger bids. Per bid, Longholders destroy on average $7.7 million more value than other CEOs. Over the sample period, Longholder CEOs are responsible for the loss of $2.15 billion to acquiring shareholders (out of $4.39 billion total).

6. Discussion

There are many reasons why CEOs may hold options even when rational models suggest exercise. We first assess several such reasons in light of their consistency with the evidence and their ability to link late exercise to merger decisions. We then offer an additional measure of overconfidence, which further tightens the interpretation of the observed CEO behavior.

6.1. Alternative explanations

1. *Taxes and dividends.* CEOs may delay the exercise of in-the-money options to postpone the payment of taxes on their profits. Personal income tax deferral,

however, makes no direct prediction for merger decisions. Similarly, CEOs may accelerate option exercise to capture the dividend payments on the underlying shares. If firms are less likely to pay dividends around mergers, time series variation in dividend payments might link late exercise to merger decisions. We verify that our results are robust to including dividend payments as an additional control.

2. *Board pressure (and corporate governance)*. Board pressure can explain both delay in option exercise and merger decisions. Directors may pressure CEOs to hold in-the-money options to signal the high quality of the firm's merger deals to the market. If this signaling is effective, the market should prefer the merger deals of option-holders to exercisers. We find in Section 5.2.2, however, that the opposite is the case.

Two possibilities remain: boards have incorrect beliefs about the signaling value of holding options; or, option holding does have positive signaling value and the market would have reacted even worse had the CEOs exercised their options. We have no evidence that directly addresses these stories. However, the inclusion of firm fixed effects largely controls for differences in board influence since board composition is remarkably stable over time in our data. More generally, it removes the influence of any unspecified firm-level variation in corporate governance.

3. *Past performance (and market inefficiencies)*. If good past performance reflects good opportunities, then CEOs in firms with a recent run-up in stock prices may both hold options and engage in acquisitions. Alternatively, if good past perform-ance leads to overvaluation in an inefficient market, then CEOs may trade over-valued equity for the (real) assets of target firms (Dong et al., 2006; Shleifer and Vishny, 2003). Moreover, they may delay option exercise to reap the benefits of the bubble. Or they may want to avoid "popping" the bubble, if option exercise conveys a negative signal to the market. To address this possibility, we check whether merger frequency covaries with past performance and whether controlling for this effect reduces the coefficient of late exercise. We add five lags of stock returns ($t-1$ to $t-5$) to the controls in Equation (1). We find a positive relation between the ($t-1$) lag of returns and acquisitiveness in most specifications. The coefficient of late exercise, however, is not materially affected.

We also verify the robustness of our results to including fixed effects for the Fama-French 48 industry groups and the interaction of industry and year effects, adjusting standard errors for industry clustering. This specification controls for clustering of mergers within industries over time (Andrade et al., 2001) and the possibility that mergers of late-exercisers and their peers cluster in different waves. The effect on the results is negligible.

4. *CEO preferences (risk tolerance; inertia)*. Some CEOs may be more risk-tolerant than we assume in calibrating the CRRA utility function, or manage to hedge the risk of their options despite the prohibition of trading and short sales. These CEOs

may delay option exercise and may also be inclined to undertake risky projects like mergers. However, absent other frictions, risk-neutral CEOs use first-best investment rules and the market should react positively to their merger bids. We find the opposite. Thus, risk-tolerance can explain the results only if (1) option-holding CEOs are risk-seeking; or (2) some other friction induces value-destroying mergers, and less risk-averse managers are more susceptible to it. Neither interpretation, though, predicts that such managers are more averse to stock financing (Section 5.1) or more prone to undertake diversifying mergers (Section 5.2.1).

Though not a preference-based explanation per se, variation in volatility could affect option exercise in the same way as variation in risk tolerance: higher volatility increases option value and induces later exercise. Moreover, acquisitiveness may increase stock volatility. Alternatively, CEOs in highly volatile firms may engage in mergers to diversify the corporate account (Amihud and Lev, 1981). Our results are robust to adding annual volatility as a control.

Late exercise may also be due to inertia in the sense of O'Donoghue and Rabin (2001). However, over 68% of Longholders conduct other transactions on their personal portfolios in the 2 years prior to the year their "longheld" options expire. Moreover, inertia cannot explain the link to increased merger frequency.

Finally, we test whether other CEO characteristics, which may capture individual preferences, drive both suboptimal option exercise and excess acquisitiveness. We consider educational background, age, CEO tenure, and title accumulation (President and Chairman of the Board in addition to CEO). Tenure is a particularly important control given the correlation with Longholder (Table 2). We find that finance education has a positive impact on acquisitiveness, but is orthogonal to late exercise. The other CEO characteristics negatively impact the market reaction to merger bids, but do not affect the estimated impact of late exercise.

5. *CEO beliefs (inside information; signaling).* CEOs may delay option exercise because they believe that their stock will perform strongly and they want to profit personally from the expected appreciation.[37] These beliefs may be correct: CEOs may have persistently positive inside information that their companies' stock is undervalued. Or, they may be incorrect: nonexercising CEOs are overconfident. In both cases, if the positive beliefs include potential mergers, they can link late exercise to merger decisions.

Several pieces of evidence help to distinguish information from overconfidence. If inside information drives late option exercise, the returns from holding the options should be positive. In Panel A of Table 7, we calculate the hypothetical returns that Longholder CEOs could have realized had they exercised their options 1 year before

---

[37] As a rough measure of the stakes involved for the CEO, we multiply the current stock price times the number of options remaining in the package entering the expiration year. The average value is $5,465,086.

Table 7

Are Longholders right to hold their options?

In Panel A, we calculate the return the CEO would have earned from exercising the option 1 year earlier and investing in the S&P 500 for each option that is held until expiration and that is at least 40% in-the-money at the beginning of its final year. We assume exercise both in the final year and in the hypothetical year occur at the maximum stock price during that year. In Panel B, the dependent variable is binary where 1 signifies that the firm made at least one merger bid that was eventually successful in a given year. Size is the log of assets, Q the market value of assets over the book value of assets. Cash flow is earnings before extraordinary items plus depreciation, normalized by beginning-of-the-year capital. Stock ownership is the fraction of company stock owned by the CEO and his immediate family. Vested options are the CEOs holdings of options that are exercisable within 6 months, as a fraction of common shares outstanding, and multiplied by 10 (so that the mean is roughly comparable to Stock ownership). Efficient board size is a binary variable where 1 signifies that the board of directors has between 4 and 12 members. Longholder is a binary variable where 1 signifies that the CEO at some point during his tenure held an option package until the last year before expiration, provided that the package was at least 40% in-the-money entering its last year. Longholder: did OK is 1 for CEOs for whom Longholder is 1 and who did better by holding at least as many times as they would have done better by exercising longheld options a year earlier and investing in the S&P 500. Longholder: should have exercised is 1 for CEOs for whom Longholder is 1 and who would have done better by exercising a year earlier more times than they did better by holding. Size, Q, Stock ownership, and Vested options are measured at the beginning of the year; all other variables are at the end. The fixed-effects logit model is estimated consistently using a conditional logit specification. Standard errors are robust to heteroskedasticity and arbitrary within-firm serial correlation. Coefficients are presented as odds ratios. z-Statistics in parentheses. Constant included.

Panel A. Returns to diversifying

Percentile	Return
10th	−0.24
20th	−0.15
30th	−0.10
40th	−0.05
50th	−0.03
60th	0.03
70th	0.10
80th	0.19
90th	0.39
Mean	0.03
S.D.	0.27

Panel B. Do "mistaken" holders drive the acquisitiveness result?

	Fixed-effects logit
Size	0.6757
	(2.20)**
Q	0.7147
	(2.14)**
Cash flow	2.052
	(1.71)*

(Continued)

Table 7 (*Continued*)

	Fixed-effects logit
Stock ownership	0.3502
	(0.97)
Vested options	0.3026
	(1.03)
Efficient board size	1.111
	(0.54)
Longholder: did OK	1.4259
	(0.76)
Longholder: should have exercised	3.4042
	(3.47)***
Year fixed effects	Yes
Observations	2515
Number of firms	221

*, **, and *** significant at 10%, 5%, and 1%, respectively.

expiration and invested the proceeds in the S&P 500. Allowing for maximum insider knowledge, we assume that both the hypothetical exercise and the actual exercise occur at the maximum stock price during the fiscal year. We find that, on average, Longholder CEOs did not profit from holding until expiration compared to this alternative strategy. The average return to exercising a year earlier is positive, though statistically insignificant. We also replicate the test for hypothetical exercise 2, 3, 4, and 5 years before expiration.[38] The average CEO would have done better under all four alternative strategies than by holding to expiration. Similarly, we calculate the hypothetical returns for Holder 67 CEOs from exercising in year 5, when the options pass the 67% threshold, and investing the proceeds in the S&P 500, rather than holding until the next year in which they exercise any options in the package. The mean difference in returns is -0.0049 with a standard deviation of 0.2997. Thus, CEOs who delay option exercise do not earn abnormal returns over the S&P 500 index on average, and the link between Longholder (or Holder 67) and mergers is unlikely due to inside information.

Nevertheless, we consider the possibility that some late exercise decisions reflect inside information and that these are precisely the cases that link to excessive merger activity. To address this possibility, we decompose Longholder into CEOs who profit from not exercising and CEOs who do not. The "winning" CEOs may indeed have positive inside information; the behavior of "losing" CEOs is more plausibly due to incorrect beliefs (overconfidence). We categorize Longholders into the group "Did OK" if, more often than not, they earned positive profits over the S&P 500 by holding

---

[38] We increase the threshold for exercise by 0.05 per year earlier to account for the increase in the Hall-Murphy (2002) threshold as remaining duration on the option increases.

an option to expiration. The remaining Longholder CEOs are classified as "Should have exercised." We reestimate Equation (1) replacing Longholder with these two component variables. We find that the increased acquisitiveness of Longholders is not concentrated among the CEOs who profit from holding their options (Table 7, Panel B). To the contrary, only the coefficient of Longholders who "should have exercised" is significant. While the difference between the two groups is not significant (p-value $= 0.14$), the significant effect of the loser group suffices to show that inside information cannot fully explain our results.

Finally, the Post-Longholder measure isolates differences in acquisitiveness among late-exercising CEOs which occur after their options expire. The disjoint timing of option-holding and mergers is difficult to reconcile with an information story since the information causing late exercise cannot be information about the merger itself. This measure also addresses the possibility that CEOs hold options to signal positive information about mergers. Signaling is unlikely to be effective for mergers occurring after the (held) options expire.

In summary, many potential explanations for the delay in option exercise do not affect our analysis since they do not predict increases in merger activity. Other theories make additional predictions that are not supported by the data. A third set of explanations can be accounted for directly in our merger regressions by including variables such as cash flow, stock returns, dividends, or volatility. Overconfidence, instead, is consistent with all of our evidence.[39] It is important to stress, though, that our analysis does not rule out other determinants of option exercise. Rather, we argue that, after conducting the preceding tests and including a wide array of controls, the residual relation between late option exercise and mergers is most consistent with overconfidence.

As a final test of the overconfidence interpretation, we introduce a second, media-based proxy that is unlikely to be confounded by explanations like tax exposure and board pressure.

6.2. Overconfidence and the press

So far, we have used CEOs' personal portfolio decisions to identify differences in beliefs between managers and outsiders about the firms' future prospects. We now ask which CEOs outsiders perceive to be "confident" and "optimistic." Our proxy for market perception uses press coverage in leading business publications: *The Wall Street Journal, The New York Times, BusinessWeek, Financial Times,* and *The Economist.* This proxy provides direct insight into the type of person we classify as over-

---

[39] Alternatively, one may call a CEO who overinvests in his company and who does too many and bad mergers simply "stupid" or low-skilled. Since the managerial decisions point to systematic overestimation of future returns, overconfidence characterizes the type of the mistake more tightly.

confident. While necessarily noisy and less precise than the portfolio measures, its strength is that it measures CEO beliefs as assessed by outsiders.

As described in Section 3, we retrieve all articles during the sample period that characterize sample CEOs as "Confident" (confident, confidence, optimistic, optimism) or "Cautious" (cautious, reliable, practical, conservative, frugal, steady, or negating one of the "Confident" terms). For all such articles, we determine (1) the article type, that is, whether the article focuses on the CEO, the firm, or the market or industry as a whole and (2) the source of the assessment, that is, the identity of the person who characterized the CEO. We refine the article type for articles about the firm, which make up 80% of the sample, into articles mainly about a company product, earnings, mergers and acquisitions, company culture, or other firm events (e.g., lawsuits or financial policy). We perform both classifications separately on the subsamples of articles using "Confident" and "Cautious" terms. As a third step, we refine the Confident references and identify articles that attribute a high or excessive degree to the CEO.

The descriptive statistics (Panel A, Table 8) provide several important insights. First, the distribution of article types in the Confident and Cautious subsamples are similar, alleviating concerns that the articles in each subgroup focus on systematically different events. In particular, articles about mergers and acquisitions are not more likely for CEOs in the Confident category. Second, in 55% of the Confident articles the CEO himself expresses confidence, while only 30% of the Cautious articles are classified based on a CEO quote. Thus, the CEOs in the Confident group fit the image of outgoing and assertive managers. The majority of CEO characterizations, however, come from the journalist or other outsiders.

Finally, 21% of the Confident articles describe the trait as "high" or "excessive." Many of these characterizations follow a big corporate decision (like a merger) with a bad outcome. Our empirical duration model eliminates this source of endogeneity since it excludes these articles from the analysis. Nevertheless, the statistic confirms that outsiders attribute excessive confidence or optimism to sample CEOs and often precisely as our theory would predict: following value-destroying acquisitions.[40]

To illustrate the typical context of Confident and Cautious mentions, we return to our example from Section 5.1, Wayne Huizenga of Blockbuster. Huizenga, a late option exerciser, is twice described as "optimistic" and once as "conservative." The first article is from *The Wall Street Journal* and falls into the "excessive confidence" category (Waldman, 1989). It discusses company stock performance amidst concerns about the company's accounting practices. The article notes that Huizenga "says he feels misunderstood" and uses optimism as follows:

Mr. Huizenga remains ebullient in his optimism, determined to make life miserable for the "disbelievers" who have invested short in Blockbuster stock.

---

[40] Thirty-seven percent of the "over" confident mentions occur for CEOs who have already been described in prior sample years as "confident" or "optimistic."

Table 8
Press data

Descriptive statistics of all articles in *BusinessWeek, The New York Times, Financial Times, The Economist,* and *The Wall Street Journal* during the 1980 to 1994 sample period that describe the sample CEOs using the terms "confident" or "confidence," "optimistic" or "optimism," or "reliable," "cautious," "practical," "conservative," "frugal," or "steady." More than one Article type and Classification source category may apply so that percentages need not add to 100. Subcategories of Article type "About the firm" (e.g., About a company product) give percentages out of all articles About the firm. The "CEO confident" column contains the subsample of articles describing the CEO using "confident," "confidence," "optimistic," or "optimism." The "CEO cautious" column contains the subsample of articles describing the CEO as "reliable," "cautious," "practical," "conservative," "frugal," or "steady" and any article containing negated confidence terms.

TOTALconfident is a dummy variable equal to 1 when the number of "confident" and "optimistic" mentions for a CEO in the LexisNexis and *The Wall Street Journal* searches exceeds the number of "not confident," "not optimistic," and "reliable, cautious, practical, conservative, steady, frugal" mentions. TOTALmentions is the total number of articles mentioning the CEO in both sets of searches. Both dummies consider all articles over the sample period up to the previous year. Longholder is a binary variable where 1 signifies that the CEO at some point during his tenure held an option package until the last year before expiration, provided that the package was at least 40% in-the-money entering its last year. Holder 67 is a dummy equal to 1 for all CEO-years after the CEO for the first time fails to exercise a 67% in-the-money option with 5 years remaining duration. In the Holder 67 panel, the sample is limited to CEO-years after the CEO for the first time had a 67% in-the-money option with 5 years remaining duration. Size is the natural logarithm of assets; *Q* the market value of assets over the book value of assets. Cash flow is earnings before extraordinary items plus depreciation, normalized by beginning-of-the-year capital. Stock ownership is the fraction of company stock owned by the CEO and his immediate family. Vested options are the CEOs holdings of options that are exercisable within 6 months, as a fraction of common shares outstanding, and multiplied by 10 (so that the mean is roughly comparable to Stock ownership). Efficient board size is a binary variable where 1 signifies that the board of directors has between 4 and 12 members. Size, *Q*, Stock ownership, and Vested options are measured at the beginning of the year; all other variables are at the end. Finance education is binary and equal to 1 for CEOs with an undergraduate or graduate degree in accounting, finance, business (incl. MBA), or economics. Technical education is binary and equals 1 for CEOs with an undergraduate or graduate degree in engineering, physics, operations research, chemistry, mathematics, biology, pharmacy, or other applied sciences.

Panel A. Descriptive statistics of CEO articles

	Full sample	CEO confident	CEO cautious
Number of articles	1200	895	305
Article type			
About the CEO (%)	11	9	18
About the firm (%)	80	83	72
About a company product (%)	10	10	11
About company earnings (%)	53	56	46
About a merger or acquisition (%)	17	15	22
About the company's culture (%)	6	5	12
Other (lawsuit, financial policy, etc.) (%)	16	17	12
About the market or industry (%)	13	12	16
Classification source			
CEO quote	n.a.	55%	30%

(Continued)

Table 8 (Continued)

	Full sample	CEO confident	CEO cautious
Journalist's assessment	n.a.	41%	62%
Other assessment (colleague, business expert, etc.)	n.a.	8%	11%
Reference specifies excessive confidence	n.a.	21%	n.a.

Panel B. Correlations with Longholder (N = 3328) and Holder 67 (N = 1698)

	Longholder	TOTconf.	TOTmen.	Holder 67	TOTconf.	TOTmen.
Longholder	1					
TOTALconfident	0.10	1				
TOTALmentions	0.02	0.36	1			
Holder 67				1		
TOTALconfident				0.05	1	
TOTALmentions				-0.01	0.32	1

Panel C. Correlations with firm characteristics (N = 3328)

	TOTALconfident	TOTALmentions	Size	Q	Cash flow	Stock ownership	Vested options	Efficient board size
TOTALconfident	1							
TOTALmentions	0.36	1						
Size	0.23	0.32	1					
Q	0.06	0.02	-0.32	1				
Cash flow	0.01	0.05	-0.13	0.39	1			
Stock ownership	0.09	0.09	-0.18	0.10	0.11	1		
Vested options	0.02	0.01	-0.17	0.09	0.17	0.10	1	
Efficient board size	-0.07	-0.08	-0.38	0.13	0.06	0.19	0.08	1

Panel D. Correlations with CEO characteristics (N = 3293)

	TOTconf.	TOTmen.	Age	Pres. & chm.	Tenure
TOTALconfident	1				
TOTALmentions	0.36	1			
Age	0.00	0.12	1		
President and chairman	0.03	0.01	-0.03	1	
Tenure	0.14	0.12	0.40	0.004	1

Panel E. Correlations with CEO education (N = 2017)

	TOTconf.	TOTmen.	Finance education	Technical education
TOTALconfident	1			
TOTALmentions	0.36	1		
Finance education	0.02	-0.02	1	
Technical education	0.00	0.05	-0.10	1

The second article, from *BusinessWeek*, uses the term "optimistic" with respect to Huizenga's projections of the spread of the VCR into American households (Engardio and Fins, 1989):

With VCR sales tailing off, entertainment analyst Peter Ting of Richard Blum Associates believes even 80% penetration is optimistic.

The quotes are representative of the typical "confident" or "optimistic" reference: either the CEO expresses optimism about future company performance (often in the context of an earnings announcement) or an outsider assesses a CEOs forecast as optimistic.

The article using "conservative" appears 4 years later in *BusinessWeek* (DeGeorge, 1993). It describes Huizenga's "ambitious plans to transform the ... video-rental giant into a full-scale entertainment company" through diversifying acquisitions. The article characterizes his approach to acquiring movie studios—first building up stakes—as conservative. Generally, Cautious references apply to company strategy, though not always tied to a specific policy.[41]

To use this data in our merger analysis, we compare, for each year, the number of articles that refer to the CEO with (*a*) the "Confident" terms and (*b*) the "Cautious" terms or negated "Confident" terms. We then construct the following indicator for each CEO *i* in year *t*:

$$
\text{TOTALconfident}_{it} = \begin{cases} 1 & \text{if } \sum_{s=1}^{t-1} a_{is} > \sum_{s=1}^{t-1} b_{is}; \\ 0 & \text{otherwise.} \end{cases}
$$

Like the Holder 67 measure, TOTALconfident captures not only between-firm and within-firm variation in CEO types, but also variation within CEO. When using this measure, we control for the total number of press mentions over the same period (TOTALmentions), that is, all sample years up to the previous year,[42] since a press bias towards positive stories might imply a higher number of mentions as "confident" or "optimistic" when the total number of mentions is high.

Press coverage suffers from an important endogeneity problem: mergers may change the tenor of press coverage. The press may perceive acquiring CEOs as more confident, or managers may try to convey confidence during merger bids. Even though the descriptive statistics (Table 8, Panel A) alleviate this concern, we eliminate any remaining endogeneity by employing a duration model that restricts the sample to observations up to each CEOs first merger (if any). That is, we identify out of articles only up to the year prior to the first merger. In addition, we drop executives who

---

[41] For the other examples of late exercisers in Section 5.1, we find four Confident articles and only one Cautious article for David Farrell and two Confident articles and one Cautious article for Reuben Mark. For the examples of CEOs not classified as late exercisers, we find two Confident and three Cautious articles in the case of J. Willard Marriott and no articles about Keith Crane. The context of the mentions follows the pattern described above.

[42] Alternatively, we calculate both TOTALconfident and TOTALmentions for the past year.

became CEO before the beginning of the sample period, for whom we cannot identify the first merger (and all press mentions during their tenure). The duration model tests whether press coverage as "optimistic" or "confident" shifts up the hazard for exiting the "no past mergers" state and includes dummy variables for each year prior to exit. We also address the concern that other personal characteristics may induce differential press coverage. We use hand-collected data, described in Section 3, to control for educational background, age, and title accumulation (Chairman, President). Adding these controls reduces the sample size; thus, we report specifications with and without CEO-level controls.

Panel B of Table 8 displays the correlations of the press measures and the portfolio-based overconfidence measures. The correlations of TOTALconfident with Longholder and Holder 67 are positive (0.1 and 0.05, respectively) and statistically significant at the 1% level. Though the magnitudes appear low, it is important to note that the correlations are between noisy proxies for a managerial trait (overconfidence) that is not directly observable and are constructed from different data sources. For comparison, even the correlations between observable firm characteristics constructed from Compustat data are relatively low. The highest correlation (0.39) occurs between Q and cash flow, two variables which both, at least partially, measure firm performance. As a placebo comparison, the correlations of the TOTALmentions control with the late-exercise measures are, instead, insignificant and near zero.

Panels C, D, and E display the correlations of TOTALconfident with various firm and CEO characteristics. As with the portfolio measures, there are few strong patterns. Unlike the portfolio measures, TOTALconfident is not correlated with vested option holdings. It is, however, strongly correlated with firm size, confirming the importance of the size control.

We repeat the analysis of merger frequency, substituting TOTALconfident for the portfolio measures and adapting the econometric specification to the duration model. Given the reduced sample size, we do not partition the sample based on internal resources and focus instead on the full sample tests. We find that CEOs portrayed as (net) "confident" and "optimistic" have 1.8 times higher odds of conducting their first merger at any point in time (Table 9). Controls for CEO characteristics increase the odds ratio to 2.5. Both estimates are significant, the latter at the 5% level. The odds ratio is similar in magnitude after including firm fixed effects, but the test is not sufficiently powerful (with only 371 identifiable observations and 79 firms) to reject the null hypothesis of a zero marginal effect.[43]

---

[43] The coefficient estimates for Vested Options are unstable and blow up when we add CEO controls. We therefore test for multicollinearity or extreme outliers driving the results. We find no evidence that the Vested Options control affects the TOTALconfident coefficient estimates. Similarly, the baseline hazards blow up in the within-industry, no-CEO-controls specification. This effect appears to arise from multicollinearity with the size variable. Excluding the size control, however, has no impact on the TOTALconfident coefficient estimate.

Table 9

Press coverage and mergers

The dependent variable is binary where 1 signifies that the firm made at least one merger bid that was eventually successful in a given year. It is restricted to diversifying mergers in Columns (3) and (4) and to intraindustry mergers in Columns (5) and (6). Diversification is measured using the Fama-French 48 industries. Size is the log of assets, Q the market value of assets over the book value of assets. Cash flow is earnings before extraordinary items plus depreciation, normalized by beginning-of-the-year capital. Stock ownership is the fraction of company stock owned by the CEO and his immediate family. Vested options are the CEOs holdings of options that are exercisable within 6 months, as a fraction of common shares outstanding, and multiplied by 10 (so that the mean is roughly comparable to Stock ownership). Efficient board size is a binary variable where 1 signifies that the board of directors has between 4 and 12 members. CEO age is measured in years. CEO chairman & president is a dummy variable and equal to 1 if the CEO is also chairman of the board and president of his company. Finance education is binary and equal to 1 for CEOs with undergraduate or graduate degrees in accounting, finance, business (incl. MBA), or economics. Technical education is binary and equals 1 for CEOs with undergraduate or graduate degrees in engineering, physics, operations research, chemistry, mathematics, biology, pharmacy, or other applied sciences. Size, Q, Stock ownership, and Vested options are measured at the beginning of the year; all other variables are at the end. TOTALconfident is a dummy variable equal to 1 when the number of "confident" and "optimistic" mentions for a CEO in the LexisNexis and *The Wall Street Journal* searches exceeds the number of "not confident," "not optimistic," and "reliable, cautious, practical, conservative, steady, frugal" mentions. TOTALmentions is the total number of articles mentioning the CEO in both sets of searches. Both dummies consider all articles over the sample period up to the previous year. The "No past merger" state dummies capture time in the initial state and run from "Second year as CEO" to "Fourteenth year as CEO." The sample is restricted to all firm-years up to the first merger for a given CEO (and drops all firm-years under that CEO after the first merger, if any). It is also restricted to CEOs whose tenure begins between 1980 and 1994 so that press coverage is all-inclusive. Standard errors are robust to heteroskedasticity and arbitrary within-firm serial correlation. Coefficients are presented as odds ratios. z-Statistics in parentheses. Constant excluded.

	All mergers		Diversifying mergers		Intraindustry mergers	
	(1)	(2)	(3)	(4)	(5)	(6)
Size	0.8919	0.8580	0.9411	0.813	0.7757	0.8897
	(1.03)	(0.97)	(0.41)	(0.93)	(1.72)*	(0.52)
Q	0.5967	0.6876	0.6963	0.7351	0.3837	0.523
	(2.19)**	(1.18)	(1.23)	(0.67)	(2.67)***	(1.66)*
Cash flow	1.7996	1.5027	1.7200	1.0514	2.2824	3.0977
	(2.28)**	(1.17)	(1.75)*	(0.11)	(2.28)**	(2.27)**
Stock ownership	2.2172	0.6546	4.4640	1.3446	0.6097	0.0589
	(0.65)	(0.28)	(1.05)	(0.17)	(0.29)	(0.78)
Vested options	7.0257	130.212	27.5615	7409.64	0.1693	0.0008
	(0.95)	(0.93)	(0.72)	(1.76)*	(0.42)	(0.65)
Efficient board size	0.8396	0.7450	0.8600	0.7204	0.8038	0.7434
	(0.78)	(0.95)	(0.50)	(0.82)	(0.75)	(0.76)
CEO age		1.0047		1.0036		1.0156
		(0.18)		(0.12)		(0.32)
CEO chairman and president		0.9431		0.7984		1.2737
		(0.21)		(0.68)		(0.57)
Finance education		1.5721		1.9397		1.1161
		(1.62)		(1.98)**		(0.24)

(Continued)

Table 9 (*Continued*)

	All mergers		Diversifying mergers		Intraindustry mergers	
	(1)	(2)	(3)	(4)	(5)	(6)
Technical education		0.9185		0.9385		1.0711
		(0.31)		(0.19)		(0.15)
TOTALmentions	1.0009	1.0003	1.0019	1.0028	0.9985	0.9946
	(0.37)	(0.09)	(0.70)	(0.88)	(0.39)	(0.95)
TOTALconfident	1.7972	2.5442	2.1734	3.2492	1.4250	1.6670
	(1.74)*	(2.36)**	(1.83)*	(2.35)**	(0.75)	(0.86)
"No past merger" state dummies	Yes	Yes	Yes	Yes	Yes	Yes
Year fixed effects	Yes	Yes	Yes	Yes	Yes	Yes
Observations	1144	716	1144	716	1040	548

*, **, and *** significant at 10%, 5%, and 1%, respectively.

In Columns (3)–(6), we replicate the test of Prediction 2 from Section 5.2.1, using diversification as a proxy for negative expected value, in the duration framework. The odds ratios are 2.2 (no CEO controls) and 3.2 (with CEO controls) for diversifying mergers, significant at the 10% and 5% levels, but 1.4 and 1.7 and insignificant for within-industry mergers. Hence, TOTALconfident predicts heightened odds of exiting the "no merger" state by conducting a diversifying deal, but not by conducting an intraindustry merger.

To address the concern that "confident" press portrayal proxies for good past performance, we also reestimate all regressions with controls for five lags of company stock returns. The results are unchanged and none of the return variables have consistent predictive power. As a further corroboration of the press measure, we note that it not only predicts acquisitiveness, but also investment-cash flow sensitivity. Malmendier and Tate (2005) show that similar portfolio measures of overconfidence predict heightened investment-cash flow sensitivity, particularly among equity-dependent firms. In untabulated results, we replicate these analyses with a simplified version of the TOTALconfident measure (calculated once for the full sample period).

These results corroborate the overconfidence explanation for mergers. Whether we measure differences in beliefs between the manager and the market using managerial portfolio decisions or press portrayal, the effect on merger activity is the same. Moreover, the press measure directly captures characterizations of executive personality features, providing insight into the type of executive identified by our portfolio measures of overconfidence.

7. Conclusion

We analyze the impact of overconfidence on merger decisions. Overconfidence does not necessarily predict more acquisitions—that depends on the trade-off between CEOs' perceived undervaluation of their company as a stand-alone and overestimation of future returns from acquisitions. However, overconfident CEOs are unambiguously more likely to make lower quality acquisitions when their firm has abundant internal resources.

We measure overconfidence in two ways. First, we use CEOs' private investment decisions to capture their "revealed beliefs." Second, we use the press to measure outsiders' perceptions of the CEOs. Our empirical analysis confirms the overconfidence predictions. We also find that overconfident CEOs are more acquisitive unconditionally. Our results point to overconfidence as an important element of a unified theory of corporate mergers.

Much of the existing evidence in favor of the hubris hypothesis comes from interpreting the average announcement effects to merger bids: shareholders of target companies seem to gain while acquiring shareholders lose. However, these aggregate effects are open to many interpretations. A key contribution of our analysis is to directly measure which CEOs are prone to overconfidence (or hubris) and to show that those CEOs, in particular, destroy value for their shareholders through acquisitions. Our field evidence complements the vast experimental and psychological evidence on individual overconfidence.

Our results also have implications for contracting practices and organizational design. Overconfidence provides an alternative interpretation of agency problems in firms and of the origin of private benefits. Unlike CEOs with empire-building preferences, who consciously disregard shareholders' interests, overconfident CEOs believe they are maximizing value. Thus, standard incentive contracts are unlikely to correct their suboptimal decisions. However, overconfident CEOs do respond to financing constraints. Overconfidence therefore further motivates the constraining role of capital structure. In addition, independent directors may need to play a more active role in project assessment and selection to counterbalance CEO overconfidence.

References

Amihud, Y. and B. Lev, 1981, "Risk Reduction as a Managerial Motive for Conglomerate Mergers," *Bell Journal of Economics*, 12, 605–617.

Andrade, G., M. Mitchell and E. Stafford, 2001, "New Evidence and Perspectives on Mergers," *Journal of Economic Perspectives*, 15, 103–120.

Asquith, P., 1983. "Merger Bids, Uncertainty, and Stockholder Returns," *Journal of Financial Economics*, 11, 51–83.

Baker, M., J. Stein and J. Wurgler, 2003, "When Does the Market Matter? Stock Prices and the Investment of Equity-Dependent Firms," *Quarterly Journal of Economics*, 118, 969–1006.

Baker, M., R. Ruback and J. Wurgler, 2006, "Behavioral Corporate Finance: A Survey," In E. Eckbo (Ed.), *Handbook of Corporate Finance: Empirical Corporate Finance*, North Holland, Amsterdam, pp. 145–186.

Barberis, N. and R. Thaler, 2003, "A Survey of Behavioral Finance," In G. Constantinides, M. Harris and R. Stulz (Eds.), *Handbook of the Economics of Finance: Financial Markets and Asset Pricing*, North Holland, Amsterdam, pp. 1053–1124.

Berger, P. and E. Ofek, 1995, "Diversification's Effect on Firm Value," *Journal of Financial Economics*, 37, 39–66.

Bernardo, A. and I. Welch, 2001, "On the Evolution of Overconfidence and Entrepreneurs," *Journal of Economics and Management Strategy*, 10, 301–330.

Bradley, M., A. Desai and E. Kim, 1983, "The Rationale Behind Interfirm Tender Offers: Information or Synergy?" *Journal of Financial Economics*, 11, 183–206.

Camerer, C. and U. Malmendier, 2007, "Behavioral Economics of Organizations," In P. Diamond and H. Vartiainen (Eds.), *Behavioral Economics and Its Applications*, Princeton University Press, Princeton, NJ, pp. 235–290.

DeGeorge, G., 1993, "Wayne's World: Busting Beyond Video," *Business Week*, 3343, 122.

Dodd, P., 1980, "Merger Proposals, Managerial Discretion and Stockholder Wealth," *Journal of Financial Economics*, 8, 105–138.

Dong, M., D. Hirshleifer, S. Richardson and S. Teoh, 2006, "Does Investor Misvaluation Drive the Takeover Market?" *Journal of Finance*, 61, 725–762.

Dun & Bradstreet Reference Book of Corporate Managements, 1997, Dun & Bradstreet, Inc., Bethlehem, PA.

Engardio, P. and A. Fins, 1989, "Will This Video Chain Stay on Fast-Forward?" *BusinessWeek*, 3109, 72.

Fama, E. and K. French, 2002, "Testing Tradeoff and Pecking Order Predictions About Dividends and Debt," *Review of Financial Studies*, 15, 1–33.

Firth, M., 1980, "Takeovers, Shareholder Returns and the Theory of the Firm," *Quarterly Journal of Economics*, 94, 235–260.

Goel, A. and A. Thakor, 2000, "Rationality, Overconfidence and Leadership," Business School Faculty Working Paper No. 00–022, University of Michigan.

Gompers, P., J. Ishii and A. Metrick, 2003, "Corporate Governance and Equity Prices," *Quarterly Journal of Economics*, 118, 107–155.

Graham, J., M. Lemmon and J. Wolf, 2002, "Does Corporate Diversification Destroy Value?" *Journal of Finance*, 57, 695–720.

Guner, A., U. Malmendier and G. Tate, 2008, "Financial Expertise of Directors," *Journal of Financial Economics*, 88, 323–354.

Hall, B. and J. Liebman, 1998, "Are CEOs Really Paid Like Bureaucrats?" *Quarterly Journal of Economics*, 113, 653–691.

Hall, B. and K. Murphy, 2002, "Stock Options for Undiversified Executives," *Journal of Accounting and Economics*, 33, 3–42.

Harford, J., 1999, "Corporate Cash Reserves and Acquisitions," *Journal of Finance*, 54, 1969–1997.

Hayward, M. and D. Hambrick, 1997, "Explaining the Premiums Paid for Large Acquisitions: Evidence of CEO Hubris," *Administrative Science Quarterly*, 42, 103–127.

Heaton, J. B., 2002, "Managerial Optimism and Corporate Finance," *Financial Management*, 31, 33–45.

Jensen, M., 1986, "Agency Costs of Free Cash Flow, Corporate Finance, and Takeovers," *American Economic Review (Papers & Proceedings)*, 76, 323–329.

Jensen, M., 1988, "Takeovers: Their Causes and Consequences," *Journal of Economic Perspectives*, 2, 21–48.

Jensen, M. and R. Ruback, 1983, "The Market for Corporate Control: The Scientific Evidence," *Journal of Financial Economics*, 11, 5–50.

Kaplan, S. and L. Zingales, 1997, "Do Investment-Cash Flow Sensitivities Provide Useful Measures of Financing Constraints?" *Quarterly Journal of Economics*, 112, 169–215.

Lambert, R., D. Larcker and R. Verrecchia, 1991, "Portfolio Considerations in Valuing Executive Compensation," *Journal of Accounting Research*, 29, 129–149.

Lamont, O. and C. Polk, 2002, "Does Diversification Destroy Value? Evidence from Industry Shocks," *Journal of Financial Economics*, 63, 51–77.

Lamont, O., C. Polk and J. Saá-Requejo, 2001, "Financial Constraints and Stock Returns," *Review of Financial Studies*, 14, 529–554.

Landier, A. and D. Thesmar, 2003, "Financial Contracting with Optimistic Entrepreneurs: Theory and Evidence," Working Paper, New York University.

Lang, L. and R. Stulz, 1994, "Tobin's Q, Corporate Diversification, and Firm Performance," *Journal of Political Economy*, 102, 1248–1280.

Lang, L., R. Stulz and R. Walkling, 1989, "Managerial Performance, Tobin's Q, and the Gains from Successful Tender Offers," *Journal of Financial Economics*, 24, 137–154.

Langer, E., 1975, "The Illusion of Control," *Journal of Personality and Social Psychology*, 32, 311–328.

Lys, T. and L. Vincent, 1995, "An Analysis of Value Destruction in AT&T's Acquisition of NCR," *Journal of Financial Economics*, 39, 353–378.

Malmendier, U. and G. Tate, 2004, "Who Makes Acquisitions? CEO Overconfidence and the Market's Reaction," NBER Working Paper #10807.

Malmendier, U. and G. Tate, 2005, "CEO Overconfidence and Corporate Investment," *Journal of Finance*, 60, 2661–2700.

March, J. and Z. Shapira, 1987, "Managerial Perspectives on Risk and Risk Taking," *Management Science*, 33, 1404–1418.

Merton, R., 1973, "Theory of Rational Option Pricing," *The Bell Journal of Economics and Management Science*, 4, 141–183.

Mitchell, M., T. Pulvino and E. Stafford, 2004, "Price Pressure Around Mergers," *Journal of Finance*, 59, 31–63.

Moeller, S., F. Schlingemann and R. Stulz, 2005, "Wealth Destruction on a Massive Scale? A Study of Acquiring-Firm Returns in the Recent Merger Wave," *Journal of Finance*, 60, 757–782.

Morck, R., A. Shleifer and R. Vishny, 1990, "Do Managerial Objectives Drive Bad Acquisitions?" *Journal of Finance*, 45, 31–48.

Mulherin, J. and A. Poulsen, 1998, "Proxy Contests and Corporate Change: Implications for Shareholder Wealth," *Journal of Financial Economics*, 47, 279–313.

O'Donoghue, T. and M. Rabin, 2001, "Choice and Procrastination," *Quarterly Journal of Economics*, 116, 121–161.

Ofek, E. and D. Yermack, 2000, "Taking Stock: Equity-Based Compensation and the Evolution of Managerial Ownership," *Journal of Finance*, 55, 1367–1384.

Roll, R., 1986, "The Hubris Hypothesis of Corporate Takeovers," *Journal of Business*, 59, 197–216.

Ruback, R. and W. Mikkelson, 1984, "Corporate Investments in Common Stock," *Proceedings of the Seminar on the Analysis of Security Prices*, 29, 179–209.

Schelling, T., 1960, *The Strategy of Conflict*, Harvard University Press, Cambridge, MA.

Schoar, A., 2002, "Effects of Corporate Diversification on Productivity," *Journal of Finance*, 57, 2379–2403.

Servaes, H., 1991, "Tobin's Q and the Gains from Takeovers," *Journal of Finance*, 46, 409–419.

Servaes, H., 1996, "The Value of Diversification During the Conglomerate Merger Wave," *Journal of Finance*, 51, 1201–1225.

Seyhun, H., 1990, "Do Bidder Managers Knowingly Pay Too Much for Target Firms?" *Journal of Business*, 63, 439–464.

Shefrin, H., 2000, *Beyond Greed and Fear: Understanding Behavioral Finance and the Psychology of Investing*, Harvard Business School Press, Cambridge, MA.

Shleifer, A. and R. Vishny, 2003, "Stock Market Driven Acquisitions," *Journal of Financial Economics*, 70, 295–311.

Van den Steen, E., 2005, "Organizations Beliefs and Managerial Vision," *Journal of Law, Economics, and Organization*, 21, 256–283.

Villalonga, B., 2004, "Diversification Discount or Premium? New Evidence from the Business Information Tracking Series," *Journal of Finance*, 59, 479–506.

Waldman, P., 1989, "Huizenga Says Blockbuster Won't Bomb," *The Wall Street Journal*, May, 19, Section 2; Page 7, Column 1.

Weinstein, N., 1980, "Unrealistic Optimism About Future Life Events," *Journal of Personality and Social Psychology*, 39, 806–820.

Weinstein, N. and W. Klein, 2002, "Resistance of Personal Risk Perceptions to Debiasing Interventions," In
    T. Gilovich, D. Griffin and D. Kahneman (Eds.), *Heuristics and Biases: The Psychology of Intuitive
    Judgment*, Cambridge University Press, Cambridge, UK.
Weston, J., K. Chung and J. Sui, 1998, *Takeovers, Restructuring, and Corporate Governance*, Prentice Hall,
    Upper Saddle River, NJ.
Who's Who in Finance and Industry, 1980/81–1995/96, Marquis Who's Who in America, Chicago, IL.
Yermack, D., 1995, "Do Corporations Award CEO Stock Options Effectively?" *Journal of Financial
    Economics*, 39, 237–269.

PART 3

BIDDING FOR DISTRESSED TARGETS: FIRE-SALES AND CREDITOR INCENTIVES

Chapter 7

ACQUISITIONS AS A MEANS OF RESTRUCTURING FIRMS IN CHAPTER 11

EDITH S. HOTCHKISS

Boston College, Fulton Hall, Chestnut Hill, Massachusetts, USA

ROBERT M. MOORADIAN

College of Business Administration, Northeastern University, Boston, Massachusetts, USA

Contents

Abstract

This paper provides empirical evidence that takeovers can facilitate the efficient redeployment of assets of bankrupt firms. Bidders for bankrupt firms are generally in related industries and often have some prior relationship to the target, suggesting they are well

*We thank David Brown, Gayle Erwin, Chris James, and Anjan Thakor for helpful suggestions.

This article originally appeared in the *Journal of Financial Intermediation*, Vol. 7, pp. 240–262 (1998).
Corporate Takeovers, Volume 2
Edited by B. Espen Eckbo
DOI: 10.1016/B978-0-12-381982-6.00008-2

informed with respect to both the value and best use of the target's assets. For a sample of 55 acquisitions in Chapter 11, we find that firms merged with bankrupt targets show significant improvements in operating performance, while matching nonbankrupt transactions show no significant improvement. We also find positive and significant abnormal stock returns for the bidder and bankrupt target at the announcement of the acquisition.

Keywords

bankruptcy, chapter 11, 363 sales, acquisition, merger, post-bankruptcy operating performance

JEL classification: G33, G34

1. Introduction

There remains considerable debate whether Chapter 11 bankruptcy provides an efficient mechanism under which the assets of financially distressed firms are effectively redeployed. For example, Hotchkiss (1995) finds that many firms that emerge from Chapter 11 continue to experience poor operating performance and more than one-third must undergo a second restructuring. Baird (1993) and Bradley and Rosenzweig (1992) argue that Chapter 11 fails to provide managers with appropriate incentives to allocate corporate resources to their highest-valued uses. To mitigate this and other agency conflicts associated with operating a firm in bankruptcy, critics of Chapter 11 suggest that bankruptcy law should be reformed to encourage an immediate sale of the firm through an auction.[1] Jensen (1991, 1993) also argues that acquisitions are an important mechanism to induce the efficient redeployment of assets of bankrupt firms.

Since acquisitions have been suggested as an effective means for resolving financial distress, interesting questions arise concerning how the acquisition process works for firms in bankruptcy. In this paper we investigate two questions central to understanding the bankruptcy and acquisition processes. First, do the current structure of Chapter 11 or asymmetric information problems impede acquisitions? Because an acquisition is a substitute for a reorganization in Chapter 11, we address this question by providing a comparison of firms acquired in Chapter 11 to firms which are reorganized as independent companies. Since both the number and the type of bidders for a bankrupt firm can impact the effectiveness of a sale as an efficient means of resolving financial distress, we further examine whether acquisitions in Chapter 11 occur in a competitive environment. The second important question is: do acquisitions in bankruptcy create value? To address this question we examine several *ex post* measures of the success of the transaction, as well as bidder and target stock price reactions to the announcement of the acquisition.

To begin thinking about these questions, note that the current structure of Chapter 11 may discourage acquisitions in several ways. Incumbent management remains in control when the firm enters Chapter 11. As described by Baird (1993), it is not clear that self-interested managers can be counted on to conduct a sale of the firm even if it is in the interest of shareholders and creditors for them to do so. Furthermore, an acquisition in Chapter 11 is typically part of a reorganization plan, and this requires creditor approval.[2] For bankrupt firms with more complex debt structures, gaining creditor approval for an acquisition is likely to be difficult because of possible disagreements among creditor groups over the distribution of the proceeds from the

---

[1] Specific proposals for reforming Chapter 11 are described by Aghion et al. (1992) and Bebchuk and Chang (1992).

[2] As discussed in Brown (1989), Gertner and Scharfstein (1991), and Mooradian (1994), the voting rules in Chapter 11 mitigate coordination problems within a class of creditors. However, a potential acquirer must negotiate with each creditor group over not only the sale price but also the distribution of the proceeds from the sale.

sale. If the bias toward incumbent management and the requirement of creditor approval make hostile acquisitions of Chapter 11 firms difficult, takeover activity will be more likely for firms whose management has already been replaced and for firms with less complex debt structures.

Industry conditions may also deter an acquisition. Shleifer and Vishny (1992) argue that industry conditions will affect the type of bidders and the prices paid for distressed firms. The highest valuation potential buyers of bankrupt firms are likely to be other firms in the industry. For example, Federated successfully acquired Macy's in the first hostile acquisition by a major corporation in Chapter 11 in 1994. Federated's valuation was higher than management's valuation of Macy's as an independent company because of the projected gains from combining operations of the two retailers. In general, however, Shleifer and Vishny (1992) point out that potential bidders in the same industry are also likely to be financially distressed and thus constrained in their ability to raise funds to acquire the bankrupt firm.[3] Not only may the price bid for a bankrupt firm be low, but in Shleifer and Vishny's model the winning bidder may not be the firm that values the assets the most.

Our comparison of firms acquired in Chapter 11 to those reorganized as independent companies shows that firms acquired are less likely to have public debt outstanding and that they have fewer debt contracts outstanding. This is consistent with the idea that coordination problems among creditors (proxied by the number of debt contracts and the existence of public debt) deter acquisitions. Variables which proxy for management entrenchment or industry conditions are not significantly related to the probability of acquisition. Our analysis also shows there is no evidence that differences in postbankruptcy performance of firms reorganizing as independent companies from those acquired in Chapter 11 are driven by differences in prebankruptcy characteristics.

Gertner and Picker (1992) argue that asymmetric information may also impede acquisitions of distressed firms. Potential bidders, in particular those from outside the target's industry, may be uninformed with respect to not only the firm value but also with respect to the best use of the target's assets. In general, however, even bidders with operations in the same industry face a "lemons problem." Bankrupt firms with better future prospects (good firms) are likely to choose to reorganize as independent companies rather than attempt a sale in a market where good firms, pooled with firms with poor prospects (bad firms), sell at a low price. Given a "lemons" market we would expect to find only the bad firms for sale.

We examine in detail the characteristics of 55 transactions where firms in bankruptcy are acquired by another public company and find evidence consistent with the idea that asymmetric information deters bidding by potentially less well informed firms. Bankrupt targets are most often acquired by firms in the same industry. While

---

[3] Consistent with Shleifer and Vishny's model, Hotchkiss and Mooradian (1997) present evidence of the frequency of takeover activity by buyers without related operations. However, such takeover activity is excluded from the sample examined in this paper, because the acquirers, vulture investors who specialize in the acquisition and management of distressed firms, are financial buyers and not operating companies.

Kaplan and Weisbach (1992), in a study of nonbankrupt acquisitions, find that the bidder and target have at least one matching primary line of business for only 35% of the transactions, we find a match for 66% of the transactions involving bankrupt targets.[4] Furthermore, for a large number of transactions the target and acquirer have some prior relationship: for example, in several cases the bidder has previously purchased some assets of the target. An asymmetric information problem is unlikely for bidders with a prior relationship or for bidders operating a related line of business.

For a bankrupt firm that receives an offer to purchase its assets, there is frequently competitive bidding. In our sample of 55 transactions, 18 have multiple bidders. The percentage of transactions with multiple bidders for bankrupt targets is at least as large as found in previous empirical studies of nondistressed targets such as Bradley et al. (1988) and Bange and Mazzeo (1997). When we compare our sample to 55 nonbankrupt acquisitions matched based on industry and on size and date of the transaction, we find that only 11 nonbankrupt matching transactions have multiple bidders. Despite efforts by the court to encourage competitive bidding, the prices paid by bidders for bankrupt firms (as a multiple of target sales or assets) are lower than prices paid in matching transactions for nonbankrupt firms. Bankrupt targets are on average purchased at a 45% discount relative to prices paid for nonbankrupt targets in the same industry.[5] Although the transactions are at discount prices, the high proportion of acquirers operating in the same industry as the target, as well as the competitive bidding environment, does not support the conclusion that acquisitions in bankruptcy are sales to lower value users.

To address the issue of whether the sale of firms in bankruptcy produces economic gains, we examine the postmerger cash flow performance of firms acquired in Chapter 11. The postmerger performance of firms combined with bankrupt targets is better than that of firms that emerged from Chapter 11 without being acquired based on the findings of Hotchkiss (1995). As noted above, this difference does not appear to be driven by differences in prebankruptcy firm characteristics. Furthermore, we find improved postmerger cash flows of the combined firm (bidder plus target) relative to the year prior to the transaction for firms acquired in Chapter 11 but not for the matching sample of 55 nonbankrupt acquisitions. The increase in profitability for bankrupt targets is associated with a decrease in operating expenses and decreases in employment.

Also consistent with the idea that acquisitions of bankrupt firms create value, we find positive and significant abnormal stock returns for both bidders and bankrupt targets for the days surrounding the announcement of an acquisition. For the nonbankrupt matching transactions, we find positive abnormal returns to the target but not to the bidding firm. One possible explanation for the difference in the bidder's stock price reaction is that empire-building managers (i.e., those less concerned about

---

[4] A match of a primary line of business is a match of at least one of the first four SIC codes at the three- or four-digit level.

[5] In comparison, Pulvino (1998) finds that financially distressed airlines sell relatively liquid assets, used aircraft, at a 9.5-37% discount to the average market price.

shareholder wealth) find acquiring bankrupt firms less desirable because they require complex negotiations with creditors and the courts. Thus, it seems reasonable that there are fewer "bad bidders" in a sample of bankrupt acquisitions. Free cash flow problems, as discussed in Jensen (1986a), are also less likely for these bidders because they are often in distressed industries.

Overall, our evidence of gains from acquisitions of bankrupt firms supports the idea that takeovers can facilitate an efficiency-enhancing redeployment of assets. The evidence is consistent with the hypothesis that firms operating in the same industry as the target possess better information and/or expertise concerning the efficient redeployment of the assets of the bankrupt firm. Moreover, despite the fact that many acquirers of bankrupt firms are highly levered and operate in a distressed industry, acquisitions still result in an improvement on average in operating performance.

The paper proceeds as follows: Section 2 describes the sample selection process and provides a comparison of firms reorganized in Chapter 11 as independent companies to those acquired. Section 3 examines bidder, target, and transaction characteristics for acquisitions in bankruptcy. Section 4 examines the postmerger performance, and Section 5 concludes.

2. Sample selection and the probability of acquisition

The initial sample used to identify firms acquired in Chapter 11 consists of 1200 public companies which filed for Chapter 11 between October 1979 and December 1992. These firms were reported to be in Chapter 11 by the Securities and Exchange Commission, and were included on Compustat prior to filing. For each firm, the status or outcome of the filing is determined from a number of sources including the Wall Street Journal, press releases, and individual 10K and 8K reports. We identify 339 firms which reorganized as independent public companies and 111 firms which were acquired by another operating company.[6] For much of our analysis, we further restrict the sample to 55 firms acquired by public companies included on Compustat in order to obtain postmerger financial data for the acquirer.

Table 1 provides a comparison of the firms reorganized as public companies to those which were acquired in Chapter 11. We also report descriptive statistics for the subsample of 55 firms for which postmerger financial data are available. These firms are quite similar to the full acquisition sample based on all reported measures.

Panel A provides some basic prebankruptcy characteristics of these groups. For both firms independently reorganized and firms acquired, financial condition and operating performance is poor. Firms acquired in Chapter 11 are somewhat smaller based on the book value of total assets at filing. Leverage is high for both groups; firms are generally

---

[6] Firms are classified as reorganized as independent companies, acquired by another operating company, liquidated, emerged as a private company, or unknown. A more complete description of the outcomes of Chapter 11 filings is provided by Hotchkiss (1993).

Table 1

Comparison of firms acquired in Chapter 11 to firms reorganized as independent public companies

Note: The sample consists of 550 firms filing for Chapter 11 between 1979 and 1992. Firms are identified as reorganized as an independent public company or acquired in Chapter 11 based on news searches and SEC filings. Growth in industry operating income (EBITDA/sales) and employment are calculated as the change in the 2 years preceding the bankruptcy filing. Financial data are obtained from Compustat, 10K and proxy reports and Moody's manuals for the fiscal year end prior to filing. EBITDA: Earnings before interest, taxes, depreciation, and amortization.

	Firms reorganized as independent public companies ($n = 339$)		Firms acquired ($n = 111$)		Firms acquired by another public company ($n = 55$)	
	Mean	Median	Mean	Median	Mean	Median
A. Firm characteristics						
Total assets ($ million)	284.6*	38.9	160.0	30.3	141.4	36.3
Total liabilities/total assets	1.19	0.91	1.16	1.0	1.08	0.940
EBITDA/total assets	−0.170	−0.011	−0.169	−0.031	−0.127	−0.024
Industry-adjusted EBITDA/total assets	−0.256	−0.113	−0.283	−0.133	−0.234	−0.117
Months spent in Chapter 11	19.9***	17.0**	16.1	14.0	16.0	13.7
B. Management turnover and ownership						
CEO retained through filing	0.490	0.000	0.537	1.000	0.456	0.000
% stock held by officers and directors	26.5	22.1	26.2	22.8	25.1	18.3
% stock held by CEO	12.9	5.6	13.4	4.2	12.4	3.9
C. Debt structure						
Dummy $= 1$ if firm has public debt	0.46***	0.00	0.31	0.00	0.32	0.00
Public debt/total long-term debt	0.192**	0.00	0.117	0.000	0.166	0.000
Bank debt/total long-term debt	0.246	0.086	0.227	0.016	0.248	0.032
Number of long-term debt contracts	5.7***	5.0*	4.2	4.0	4.3	4.0
D. Industry performance						
Growth in industry EBITDA/sales	−0.028	−0.013	−0.016	−0.011	−0.016	−0.012
Growth in industry employment	0.016**	0.010	0.031	0.020	0.037	0.033

*, **, *** Mean (median) significantly different between firms reorganized as independent companies and firms acquired at the 10%, 5%, and 1% level, respectively, based on t-test (Wilcoxon rank sum test).

insolvent based on the ratio of book value of liabilities to assets. Firms are economically distressed based on negative median cash flow, and profitability as measured by the ratio of operating cash flow (EBITDA) to total assets. We also examine industry-adjusted cash flow by subtracting the median EBITDA/total assets of industry portfolios constructed using all other Compustat firms with the same three-digit SIC code. Negative industry-adjusted cash flow return on assets indicates that these firms underperform relative to the industry groups.[7] Overall, except for firm size, the

---

[7] The firm's primary SIC code is verified in the year prior to filing from 10K reports and other SEC filings.

prebankruptcy characteristics of firms independently reorganized versus firms acquired in Chapter 11 are not significantly different. Panel A also shows that acquired firms spend a median time in bankruptcy of 14 months, compared to 17 months for the independently reorganized firms. Therefore, the characteristics of bankrupt firms examined in this study are similar to those of firms considered in previous studies such as Hotchkiss (1995) and Gilson (1996).

Panels B, C, and D of Table 1 describe proxies for whether management entrenchment, the potential for disagreement among creditor groups, or industry conditions are related to the probability of acquisition. Data on management turnover and insider ownership are obtained from proxy and 10K statements prior to filing. The variable "CEO retained through filing" indicates whether the CEO in office 2 years prior to filing is still in office at the time of filing. CEO turnover is similar to levels found in previous studies of distressed firms and is close to 50% for both groups.[8] It does not appear that firms which have replaced their CEO early in the restructuring process are more likely to be targets of acquisitions. The level of CEO and insider stockholdings is also similar between groups, suggesting that management is no more or less entrenched for the acquisition group.

Panel C shows that 46% of the firms which are independently reorganized have public debt outstanding, in contrast to 31% for the acquired firms. The ratio of public to total long-term debt is also greater for the independently reorganized group, though there is no significant difference in the proportion of bank debt. The higher proportion of public debt suggests a more complex debt structure for the independently reorganized firms. The number of long-term debt contracts described in the Moody's manual prior to filing directly measures the complexity of the capital structure, and is higher for the independently reorganized group. Although the somewhat more complex capital structure for the independently reorganized group is consistent with the idea that disagreement among creditors over the distribution of proceeds from a sale impedes acquisitions, it may also be explained by the larger size of these firms.

Panel D of Table 1 provides two measures of industry performance, based on the median performance of all other firms on Compustat with the same three-digit SIC code as the bankrupt firm prior to filing. Based on Shleifer and Vishny's (1992) arguments, we expect acquisitions to be more common in better performing industries. However, firms in both groups frequently belong to poorly performing industries. The mean and median changes in operating income/sales are negative, suggesting that industry performance has been declining. Only the mean employment growth is significantly higher for the acquired firms' industries at the 5% level.

We also examine a series of logistic regressions (not reported) where the dependent variable equals 1 for firms which are acquired and 0 otherwise, and the independent

---

[8] For example, Betker (1994) finds 51% of CEOs are replaced by the time of filing. Turnover at the resolution of the Chapter 11 case is, however, substantially higher. Hotchkiss (1995) finds that CEOs are replaced for 70% of firms reorganized as independent companies by the time they emerge. For the subsample of 55 firms acquired by public companies, the original CEO never appears as a top manager of the combined firm, but is retained as a division manager in at least five cases.

variables include the measures described above. Attempts to correctly classify acquired versus independently reorganized firms are generally unsuccessful. The only variable which has a significant relationship to the probability of acquisition is the dummy variable indicating firms with public debt outstanding, providing weak evidence consistent with the idea that coordination problems deter acquisitions.

In the following analysis, we attempt to characterize acquisitions as successful or unsuccessful based on improvements in postmerger cash flow performance and based on qualitative assessments of postmerger performance. If assets are redeployed to more efficient use through mergers, we expect the postmerger performance to show a greater proportion of successful turnarounds than was found by Hotchkiss (1995) for firms independently reorganized. It is possible that firms that are acquired in bankruptcy are those with the best prospects. It is equally plausible that the firms sold in bankruptcy suffer from a "lemons" problem or are those whose prospects are sufficiently poor that management has abandoned efforts to survive as an independent company. However, there is no evidence to suggest that differences in postbankruptcy performance of firms reorganizing as independent companies from those which are acquired are driven by differences in prebankruptcy characteristics.

3. Analysis of transactions in Chapter 11

3.1. Characteristics of acquirers and bankrupt targets

Table 2 provides a more detailed description of the sample of 55 acquisitions of bankrupt firms for which postmerger financial data are available. The size of the target relative to the combined acquirer and target is on average 25.8% based on total assets and 30.2% based on sales (medians are 16.6% and 21.3%, respectively). The average relative size is the same as in the sample of mergers studied by Clark and Ofek (1994) and only slightly lower than Healy's et al. (1992) sample (29%), though the medians for this sample are lower. There are five cases where the target is less than 10% of combined assets. However, all empirical results in this paper are unchanged if we exclude these five observations from the analysis.[9] Table 2 shows that acquirers are more profitable than the targets, though some acquirers are also highly levered. In contrast to studies that do not focus on distressed firms (e.g., Palepu, 1986), prior to the acquisition, bidding firms experience declining levels of EBITDA/sales as well as declining performance relative to the industry.

Table 3 reports additional characteristics of the acquisitions in bankruptcy as well as nonbankrupt matching transactions. For each firm in the sample, we determine the closest matching transaction from Securities Data Corporation based on the three- or four-digit SIC code, size of the target, and date of acquisition. Targets in the matching

---

[9] We are less likely to detect economic gains if the target is small relative to the acquirer. However, in Section 4 we look both at cash flow changes and at qualitative measures of the success of the transaction.

Table 2

Characteristics of bidders and targets acquired in Chapter 11

Note. Sample consists of 55 firms acquired by a public company while in Chapter 11 between 1983 and 1992. Financial data are obtained from Compustat, 10K reports, and Moody's manuals for the fiscal year end prior to announcement of the acquisition. EDITDA: Earnings before interest, taxes, depreciation, and amortization. Industry-adjusted: subtracts the median EBITDA/sales of all other firms on Compustat having the same three-digit SIC code as the sample firm.

	Mean	Median	Min	Max
Relative size of target to combined firm				
Book value target/combined book value (%)	25.8	16.6	0.1	74.5
Sales target/combined sales (%)	30.2	21.3	0.1	82.2
Acquirer characteristics				
Total assets ($ million)	2020.3	242.3	1.4	37,134.0
Sales	2132.6	249.5	0.8	47,679.0
Book value leverage	0.57	0.60	0.08	0.94
EBITDA/sales	0.12	0.11	−0.96	0.75
EBITDA/sales minus industry	0.02	0.02	−1.04	0.57
Change in EBITDA/sales (year −3 to −1) (%)	−2.2	−0.1	−95.7	2.3
Change in industry-adjusted EBITDA/sales (year −3 to −1) (%)	−4.2	−0.1	−187.6	24.6
Target characteristics				
Total assets ($ million)	157.0	35.5	3.4	3390.9
Sales	144.2	46.9	0.6	1376.9
Book value leverage	1.37	1.07	0.39	4.90
EBITDA/sales	−0.03	−0.05	−0.81	0.67
EBITDA/sales minus industry	−0.13	−0.13	−1.20	0.60
Change in EBITDA/sales (year −3 to −1) (%)	−1.2	−1.2	−12.2	8.2
Change in industry-adjusted EBITDA/sales (year −3 to −1) (%)	−6.2	−0.7	−76.2	3.8

transactions are in less serious financial condition than the bankrupt targets (not reported), but since they are matched on industry they are also frequently distressed. Acquirers in the matching transactions are also slightly more profitable than acquirers of the bankrupt companies.

To measure the relatedness of an acquisition, we follow the methodology used by Kaplan and Weisbach (1992) based on SIC codes listed in the Standard and Poor's Register of Corporations. An acquisition is related at the three-digit level if one of the four most important businesses (ranked by sales) of the acquirer and target match at the three-digit level. We find 36 (out of 55) cases where the target and acquirer match at least one three-digit SIC code. There are only nine cases identified as unrelated transactions where there is no match (at any level of SIC code) for the target and acquirer.[10] The matching transactions have a similarly low proportion of cases where

---

[10] In contrast, Kaplan and Weisbach (1992) find at least one match at the three-digit level for only 35% of the transactions and no match for 45% of the transactions in their sample.

Table 3

Transaction characteristics for firms acquired in Chapter 11

Note. Match at three- or four-digit SIC code is based on the first four SIC codes listed for each firm in Standard & Poor's Register of Corporations in the year prior to the acquisition; no match indicates there is no overlap at any level of SIC code. Data are obtained from Compustat, 10K reports, Securities Data Corporation, and news stories at the time of the acquisition. Transaction value is defined as the total consideration paid by the acquirer, excluding fees, and expenses. Enterprise value is the transaction value plus all liabilities assumed by the acquirer. Industry median ratios are determined using all transactions reported by Securities Data Corporation for targets with the same three-digit SIC code within 1 year (+ or −) of the Chapter 11 acquisition. Matching transactions are identified from Securities Data Corporation as a single transaction with the same target three-digit SIC code and with target total assets and transaction date closest to the Chapter 11 acquisition. Discount measures the percentage difference between the actual price paid for the bankrupt target (enterprise value) and the "benchmark" price obtained by multiplying the bankrupt target sales (or book value of assets) by the industry median or matching transaction ratio of enterprise value/sales (or enterprise value/book value of assets).

	Chapter 11 targets		Matching transactions	
	#	%	#	%
A. Transaction characteristics				
Multiple bidders	18	32.7	11	20.0
Hostile transaction	0	0.0	4	7.3
Target and acquirer match at three- or four-digit SIC code	36	65.5	34	61.8
No match in target and acquirer SIC codes	9	16.4	10	18.2
	Mean	Median	Min	Max
B. Valuation of target				
Transaction value ($ million)	103.183	13.600	0.400	3194.000
Enterprise value ($ million)	106.219	12.170	0.400	3194.000
Multiple of sales				
Bankrupt target enterprise value/sales	1.1	0.4	0.01	7.5
Industry median enterprise value/sales	1.6	1.1	0.4	8.7
Matching transaction enterprise value/sales	2.3	1.1	0.2	33.2
Multiple of book value				
Bankrupt target enterprise value/book value of assets	0.7	0.5	0.01	3.1
Industry median enterprise value/book value of assets	1.3	1.2	0.6	3.3
Matching transaction enterprise value/book value of assets	1.9	1.2	0.05	16.4
C. Price paid versus value based on benchmark				
Discount calculated based on:				
Industry median enterprise value/sales (%)	45.1	60.5	−109.4	99.4
Matching transaction enterprise value/sales (%)	43.5	68.8	−342.5	99.3
Industry median enterprise value/book value of assets (%)	45.7	64.7	−104.6	99.8
Matching transaction enterprise value/book value of assets (%)	40.2	59.6	−149.7	99.6

the acquirer and target are in unrelated industries. This result is similar to that of Clark and Ofek (1994), who find that acquirers of distressed firms are frequently in the same industry. Acquirers in the same industry as the target are more likely to be informed with respect to the best use of the target's assets and are more likely to benefit from a consolidation of operations.

Asymmetric information is less likely to impede an acquisition in bankruptcy if the target and acquirer have a prior relationship. There are a relatively large number of cases where the acquirer and bankrupt target have some prior relationship (not reported). In five cases the acquirer has previously purchased assets of the target, in one case the acquirer CEO is the former target CEO, in one case the acquirer is a large customer of the target, and in one case the acquirer managed the target's operations just prior to the acquisition.

3.2. Bidding in Chapter 11

There are two ways in which a firm can sell substantially all of its assets in Chapter 11, through a Section 363 (of the US Bankruptcy Code) sale or as part of a confirmed plan of reorganization.[11] First, under a Section 363 sale, management must first obtain an offer and then notify the court. The bankruptcy court in turn notifies creditors and shareholders. Many courts also require a marketing effort. The Bankruptcy Code invalidates any "no shop" agreements. With court approval and at the expense of the debtor firm, creditors can retain advisers to seek other possible buyers. Any sale must be approved by the judge at a hearing; if there are competing bids, the court conducts an auction in the courtroom. Second, a sale can be accomplished by way of a plan of reorganization. One plan can incorporate multiple bids. In this case, creditors and shareholders vote on the plan and then on the bid preference. Alternatively, bidders can present competing plans for a vote once the exclusivity period for management to propose a plan has expired. In the case of Public Service Co. of New Hampshire, once the exclusivity period expired, three bidders presented their own plans of reorganization.[12]

Consistent with a competitive bidding environment, Table 3 reports multiple bidders for 18 (32.7%) of 55 bankrupt targets. In contrast, there are only 11 (20%) of 55 matching transactions with multiple bidders. The number of multiple bidders for bankrupt targets is also at least as large as found in previous research for nondistressed targets.[13] We also examine (not reported) the proportion of Chapter 11 transactions with multiple bidders for sales under Section 363 and for sales completed as part of a reorganization plan. Eight of the 24 (33.3%) Section 363 sales involve multiple

---

[11] For further information regarding the law with respect to acquisitions in Chapter 11, see McBride (1996).
[12] Sales involving a plan of reorganization generally take longer to complete because of requirements for creditor approval.
[13] For example, Bange and Mazzeo (1997) find multiple bidders for 103 (23.6%) of 436 transactions from 1979 to 1991 and Bradley et al. (1988) find multiple bidders for 73 (31%) of 236 transactions from 1963 to 1984.

bidders, while 10 of the 31 (32.3%) sales as part of a reorganization plan involve multiple bidders. Section 363 sales and sales as part of a reorganization plan appear to involve equally competitive bidding.

Although none of the acquisitions in bankruptcy are hostile, some acquisitions are unsolicited. The target actively seeks a buyer in 23 cases; in 10 of these the search for a buyer starts prior to filing for Chapter 11.[14] For the matching transactions, we find only four hostile transactions. The relatively low proportion of hostile acquisitions contrasts with studies of nondistressed targets (e.g., Martin and McConnell, 1991 find that 50% of transactions in their sample are hostile).

Previous research (see e.g., Jensen 1986b) examines the premium paid relative to the preoffer share price of the target, and cites the gains to the target as evidence of the value created in mergers. However, this measure is not meaningful for transactions involving bankrupt targets because target shareholders often receive little or no distribution in the transaction. Furthermore, for many of the targets, the common stock has ceased trading in bankruptcy.

For our purposes, a more useful measure is the price paid for the assets of the bankrupt firm relative to two benchmarks. The first benchmark compares the price paid for the bankrupt firm to all other acquisitions in the same industry reported by Securities Data Corporation within 1 year (+ or −) of the sample transaction. The second benchmark compares the price paid for the bankrupt firm to the matching transaction.

Specifically, the price paid is equal to the implied enterprise value of the target company; enterprise value is defined as the transaction price (total value of consideration paid by the acquirer, excluding fees and expenses) plus all liabilities assumed by the acquirer. These values are determined from news sources, 10K reports of the acquirer, and Securities Data Corporation. For the benchmark firms, we calculate the ratio of the enterprise value to target sales (or to book value of assets); this yields the benchmark price paid as a multiple of sales (or assets). This multiple times the bankrupt target sales (or assets) tells us the price that would have been paid for the bankrupt firm if it had been valued similarly to the benchmark. The "discount" for the bankrupt firm is the percentage difference between the actual price paid (enterprise value) and the price that would have been paid based on the benchmark multiple.

Table 3 (Panel B) shows that relative to these two benchmarks, acquirers pay substantially lower multiples of book value; this might be expected if assets of the target are to be written down subsequent to the transaction. However, the mean and median multiple of sales are also lower than the two benchmarks. Although there are some outliers, particularly based on matching transactions, the mean (median) discounts (Panel C) using either multiples of sales or book value of assets are approximately 45% (60%). These discounts are larger than the 9.5-37% discounts in Pulvino's (1998) study of sales of used aircraft by distressed firms. However, the size of the discounts in our study relative to the Pulvino study is not surprising. While we examine

---

[14] In three Chapter 11 cases, a buyer was solicited by a trustee who had replaced target management.

sales of substantially all of the assets of the bankrupt firms, Pulvino (1998) calculates discounts for piecemeal sales of highly standardized assets (used aircraft) by distressed but not necessarily bankrupt firms in a generally liquid market.

We also use multivariate regressions to examine how the prices paid (as a multiple of sales or assets) vary with characteristics of the target (not reported). Prices will be higher if there is more to gain from combining the operations of a distressed target with an acquirer. On the other hand, prices will be lower if bankrupt targets have less bargaining power in the takeover process due to their weak financial condition or a limited number (if any) of competing bidders. Prices paid are greater for firms with better preacquisition industry-adjusted profitability (EBITDA/sales greater than the sample median). Prices paid are also greater for targets with public debt outstanding. However, we find no significant differences based on the size of the target or the number of long-term debt contracts outstanding. The mean and median multiples paid are also not significantly different when there is more than one bidder for the target, although in some individual cases the purchase price increases substantially when a second bidder appears.[15]

In summary, although prices paid are generally lower when compared to the two benchmarks, Chapter 11 does encourage competitive bidding. While asymmetric information is a deterrent to bidding by unrelated firms from outside the industry of the target, firms related in some way to the target frequently bid. Most acquirers are firms with a prior relationship to the target and/or firms operating in the same industry as the target. Given the relationship between the acquirer and target, the acquirer is more likely to possess the information and/or expertise necessary to effectively redeploy the assets of the bankrupt target.

4. Postmerger performance

4.1. Cash flow performance

We use pretax operating cash flow return on sales to measure improvements in operating performance. Operating cash flows are measured as earnings before interest, taxes and depreciation (EBITDA). We deflate EBITDA by sales to provide a measure comparable across firms. Results are similar based on cash flow return on assets; we choose to report the return on sales because it is not affected by differences in accounting treatment across transactions and differences in the degree of asset write-downs which can be substantial for these transactions. Before the merger, the combined cash flow ratio is calculated as the sum of acquirer and target EBITDA divided by the sum of acquirer and target revenues. After the merger, we use the acquirer's cash flow ratio. If the premerger acquirer and target are not in the same industry, the

---

[15] In protracted bidding for Financial News Network, the winning bid was 70% higher than the first bid for the company (New York Times, 5/10/91).

combined industry median is calculated as the weighted average of the industry medians for the acquirer's and target's industries (weighted respectively by the acquirer or target revenues divided by the combined revenues).

Table 4 reports median levels of firm and industry-adjusted cash flows from 3 years before the merger to 3 years after the merger for the combined firm. For the firms acquired in Chapter 11, the combined firms' cash flow returns decline in the years prior to the merger and improve somewhat in the postmerger years. For matching transactions, the level of these returns appears similar across the entire time period. The median levels, however, do not provide information about whether there is an improvement in cash flow for specific transactions.

Panel A of Table 5 shows more directly the changes in cash flow relative to the year prior to the merger. For the firms acquired in bankruptcy, we observe positive and significant changes from the year prior to the merger to years $+1$ and $+2$.[16] Relative to

Table 4

Cash flow performance of combined target and acquirer

Note. Median cash-flow performance of 55 combined targets and acquirers in the years surrounding the acquisition. Combined performance for years -1 to -3 relative to the year the merger takes place is measured as the sum of the bidder's and target's earnings before interest, taxes, depreciation, and amortization (EBITDA) divided by the combined revenues of the target and bidder. Performance for years $+1$ to $+3$ relative to merger completion is measured as the ratio of EBITDA to revenues of the bidder. Industry adjustment subtracts the median ratio of EBITDA to revenues of all firms with the same three-digit SIC code. If the bidder and target have different SIC codes, the industry median cash flow is the weighted average of the median ratios in each of the bidder's and target's industries.

Year relative to merger	Firm median	% positive	Industry-adjusted median	% positive	N
Firms acquired in Chapter 11					
−3	0.116	87.5	0.016	59.6	48
−2	0.080	77.1	0.009	51.1	48
−1	0.073	77.6	−0.004	44.7	49
1	0.081	90.4	0.012	56.9	52
2	0.079	94.0	0.011	57.1	50
3	0.085	91.5	0.003	58.5	47
Matching transactions					
−3	0.120	91.7	0.028	68.8	48
−2	0.132	98.1	0.031	71.2	52
−1	0.130	92.3	0.033	69.2	52
1	0.140	87.0	0.049	70.4	54
2	0.142	90.7	0.040	79.6	54
3	0.148	91.1	0.030	68.9	45

[16] Observations exclude matching transactions if data for the corresponding bankrupt firm is missing. Results are unchanged when all matching firms are included.

Table 5

Postmerger abnormal performance

Note: Median cash-flow performance of combined targets and acquirers in the years following the acquisition relative to the year preceding the acquisition. Combined performance for year -1 relative to merger completion is measured as the sum of the bidder's and target's earnings before interest, taxes, depreciation, and amortization (EBITDA) divided by the combined revenues of the target and bidder. Performance for years $+1$ to $+3$ relative to merger completion is measured as the ratio of EBITDA to revenues of the bidder. $CR_{t,i}$ is the cash flow return on sales in year t for the combined targets and acquirers. The intercept of the cross-sectional regressions of postmerger cash flow returns on corresponding premerger returns provides a measure of abnormal performance. Regressions also include the change in industry cash flow return (ΔICR) over the same time period.

A. Change in combined cash flow performance (EBITDA/sales) relative to year prior to merger

Years	Median change	Median % change	% positive	Median change	Median % change	% positive	N
Firms acquired in Chapter 11							
-1 to $+1$	0.010	8.09**	58.7	0.018	29.70	59.1	46
-1 to $+2$	0.011	9.40**	61.4	0.015	44.90	59.5	44
-1 to $+3$	0.010	11.70	58.5	0.010	42.27	60.0	41
Matching transactions							
-1 to $+1$	0.006	5.62	56.9	0.010	20.69	58.8	49
-1 to $+2$	0.003	2.39	52.9	0.005	17.57	54.9	48
-1 to $+3$	0.007	6.38	53.5	0.009	15.74	53.5	45

B. Abnormal postmerger cash flow returns (t-values in parentheses)

							Adj R^2	N
Firms acquired in Chapter 11								
$CR_{+1,i}$	$=$	5.2% (2.25)**	$+$	0.48 $CR_{-1,i}$ (3.90)***			0.25	46
$CR_{+1,i}$	$=$	4.9% (2.24)**	$+$	0.53 $CR_{-1,i}$ (4.10)***	$+$	0.27 $\Delta ICR_{+1,i}$ (0.95)	0.26	45
$CR_{+2,i}$	$=$	6.5% (3.03)***	$+$	0.34 $CR_{-1,i}$ (2.91)***			0.16	44
$CR_{+2,i}$	$=$	5.9% (2.83)***	$+$	0.45 $CR_{-1,i}$ (4.01)***	$+$	0.55 $\Delta ICR_{+1,i}$ (1.68)*	0.27	43
							Adj R^2	N
Matching transactions								
$CR_{+1,i}$	$=$	2.0% (0.52)	$+$	0.87$CR_{-1,i}$ (3.92)***			0.22	49
$CR_{+1,i}$	$=$	1.9% (0.49)	$+$	0.90 $CR_{-1,i}$ (4.02)***	$+$	0.24 $\Delta ICR_{+1,i}$ (0.97)	0.23	49
$CR_{+2,i}$	$=$	4.6% (1.40)	$+$	0.79 $CR_{-1,i}$ (4.21)***			0.25	48
							0.25	48
$CR_{+2,i}$	$=$	4.6% (1.38)	$+$	0.82 $CR_{-1,i}$ (4.26)***	$+$	0.11 $\Delta ICR_{+1,i}$ (0.64)	0.25	48

*, **, *** Significance at 10%, 5%, and 1% level, respectively.

industry performance, the median change is also positive but not significantly different from zero. In contrast, Hotchkiss (1995) finds poor postbankruptcy cash flow performance of firms independently reorganized. Hotchkiss and Mooradian (1997) find improved postrestructuring performance of firms where a vulture investor gains control and argue that vulture investors possess the expertise needed to improve performance. It is possible that both vulture investors and acquirers of bankrupt firms merely select firms likely to experience improved performance. However, since most acquirers of bankrupt firms operate a business related to the target, it is likely the improved operating performance can be attributed to the combination of the businesses. Changes for the matching firms in Table 5 are not significant.

Panel B of Table 5 provides an alternative measure to assess cash flow performance.[17] Postmerger performance is influenced by economy-wide as well as industry factors. It will also reflect a continuation of firm-specific performance before the merger, particularly when the target is a smaller proportion of the combined assets. Therefore, we measure abnormal performance as the intercept in the following cross-sectional regression of postmerger cash flow returns on the corresponding premerger returns,

$$CR_{post,i} = \alpha + \beta CR_{pre,i} + \varepsilon_i,$$

where CR is the cash flow return on sales. We also report regressions which include the change in the industry cash flow return over the same time period.[18] The slope coefficient β captures any correlation in cash flow returns between the pre- and postmerger years so that $\beta CR_{pre,i}$ measures the effect of the premerger performance on postmerger returns. For each regression the intercept indicating abnormal performance is positive and significant. The magnitude of cash flow improvements range from approximately 5% to year +1 and 6% to year +2. In contrast, the matching transactions show no significant improvement. This evidence is consistent with the hypothesis that mergers of firms in Chapter 11 can create value.

Table 6 suggests that potential sources of operating gains for the bankrupt acquisitions are reductions in operating expenses and employment. Based on the changes in expenses (measured as cost of goods sold plus sales and general administrative expense) relative to sales, there is a significant decline in expenses for the bankrupt acquisitions, but not for the matching transactions. We also observe a significant decline in industry-adjusted employment for the Chapter 11 acquisitions; the matching firms in contrast are increasing employment, though not significantly relative to their

---

[17] A similar approach is described in Healy et al. (1992). Barber and Lyon (1995) also suggest the use of these measures to detect abnormal operating performance.

[18] Missing observations in Panel B are due to seven firms which are missing preacquisition cash flow data and two (four) firms which are missing data for year +1 (+2) acquirer performance. Of these 11 firms, only three transactions are qualitatively characterized as failures as described below, either because the acquirer subsequently files bankruptcy or because the target's operations are subsequently divested.

Table 6

Sources of operating gains

Note. Changes in operating expenses, employment and revenues for combined targets and acquirers in years following the acquisition relative to the year preceding the acquisition.

Years	Median % change	% positive	Industry adjusted		N
			Median % change	% positive	
A. (Cost of goods sold + SG&A expense)/sales					
Firms acquired in Chapter 11					
−1 to +1	−6.6**	31.9	−12.6**	31.9	43
−1 to +2	−2.9**	34.2	−57.1**	34.1	41
−1 to +3	−1.7*	35.9	−11.1	46.2	39
Matching transactions					
−1 to +1	0.2	51.2	−0.4	48.8	43
−1 to +2	0.1	51.2	−1.4	43.9	41
−1 to +3	−0.8	47.4	−1.3	47.4	38
B. Employment growth					
Firms acquired in Chapter 11					
−1 to +1	−3.5	45.2	−13.6*	35.7	42
−1 to +2	−3.1	45.9	−18.6*	32.4	37
−1 to +3	−5.9*	39.5	−36.8***	31.6	38
Matching transactions					
−1 to +1	13.7***	66.7	1.5	50.0	42
−1 to +2	19.6***	70.0	11.1	55.0	40
−1 to +3	24.5***	73.7	7.1	55.3	38
C. Revenue growth					
Firms acquired in Chapter 11					
−1 to +1	12.3***	70.2	−10.6*	29.8	47
−1 to +2	15.0***	66.7	−25.2	35.6	45
−1 to +3	15.2**	61.9	−31.4*	26.2	42
Matching transactions					
−1 to +1	24.6***	78.0	4.6	62.0	50
−1 to +2	38.2***	77.6	3.5	57.1	49
−1 to +3	49.7***	78.2	9.9	54.4	46

*, **, *** Median significantly different from 0 at 10%, 5%, and 1% level, respectively.

industries. Despite the fact that distressed firms generally sell assets and reduce their size in Chapter 11 (Brown et al., 1994; Hotchkiss, 1995), revenues increase for the combined firms, though these increases are of smaller magnitude than observed for the matching transactions and are lower than industry increases. We also examine changes in capital expenditures and asset turnover (not reported), and find no significant changes for either the Chapter 11 or matching transactions.

4.2. Qualitative measures of performance

Information from news stories is used to determine whether the cash flow returns adequately characterize "successful" transactions. We identify 11 cases from the acquirer's annual report or news stories where the acquirer specifically reported the acquired assets are performing well. In six cases the target is later divested, though this does not necessarily indicate failure (Kaplan and Weisbach, 1992). In contrast, we find seven cases where the acquirer either reports operating problems related to the acquisition or write-offs (unrelated to the initial transaction) due to the performance of these assets. For 11 cases the acquirer (or the target as a subsidiary of the acquirer) later files bankruptcy, though the bankruptcy is not directly related to the acquisition.[19]

Based on these descriptions, we make a qualitative assessment of whether the acquisition is successful. We classify 22/55 (40%) as clearly successful, 14/55 (25%) as marginally successful, and 19/55 (35%) as failures. This measure of performance is highly correlated with our measures of cash flow improvement. The failure rate is somewhat lower than the 53% found by Clark and Ofek (1994) using similar classifications. When we perform the same exercise for the matching transactions, we classify 19/55 (35%), as clearly successful, 21/55 (38%) as marginally successful, and 15/55 (27%) as failed. While we detect improvements in cash flow performance on average, there are clearly a significant number of failures. However, our failure rates are not surprising given the failure rates for acquisitions of nonbankrupt firms. In a study of acquisitions followed by divestitures, Kaplan and Weisbach (1992) report that 34-50% of acquisitions in their sample are unsuccessful.

4.3. Stock price effects at announcement of acquisition

We also perform an event study (Table 7) to determine whether the market perceives the acquisition as favorable for both the acquirer and target shareholders. Abnormal returns are market model residuals using common stock returns from the period 250 to 30 days prior to the announcement. Test statistics are calculated as in Mikkelson and Partch (1986). Test results based on medians are qualitatively similar.

For announcements of acquisitions in Chapter 11, Panel A shows that there are positive significant returns to the bidder in the days surrounding the announcement of the acquisition. This contrasts with most studies of announcement returns to bidding firms which are generally negative or insignificant (see Jensen, 1986b or Jensen and Ruback, 1993 for a survey). There are only 22 firms for which the target stock is traded and has data available on CRSP at the announcement of the acquisition. Target shareholders also benefit from large, positive, and significant gains. These results are consistent with the hypothesis that acquisitions in Chapter 11 create value for both the acquirer and target firm.

---

[19] In nine cases the acquirer subsequently files; in two cases only a subsidiary (the former target) files.

Table 7

Stock price effects at announcement of acquisition

Note: Daily abnormal returns (AR) and cumulative abnormal returns (CAR) for companies acquired in Chapter 11 and matching nonbankrupt transactions, from day prior to 5 days following the announcement of the offer. Abnormal returns are market model residuals using common stock returns from the period 250 to 30 days prior to the announcement. Test statistics (shown in parentheses) are calculated as in Mikkelson and Partch (1986).

Acquisitions in Chapter 11								
	Bidder (*n* = 41)					Target (*n* = 22)		
	AR (%)		CAR (%)			AR (%)		CAR (%)
−1	−0.5	(−0.51)	−0.5		−1	5.3	(5.14)	5.3	
0	1.2	(0.21)	0.7	(0.22)	0	12.9	(13.81)	18.2	(13.40)
1	1.8	(2.66)	2.5	(1.36)	1	2.9	(4.72)	21.1	(16.74)
2	0.4	(1.88)	3.0	(2.12)	2	1.0	(−0.04)	22.1	(16.72)
3	0.4	(0.13)	3.3	(1.95)	3	−0.6	(−1.61)	21.4	(15.58)
4	0.3	(1.19)	3.6	(2.27)	4	−2.0	(−1.52)	19.4	(14.51)
5	0.4	(1.02)	4.0	(2.48)	5	−0.3	(−0.24)	19.1	(14.34)
Matching transactions								
	Bidder (*n* = 50)					Target (*n* = 50)		
−1	−0.5	(−1.65)	−0.5		−1	2.9	(5.99)	2.9	
0	0.1	(0.21)	−0.3	(−1.02)	0	10.4	(16.88)	13.2	(18.24)
1	−0.1	(−0.54)	−0.4	(−1.14)	1	1.5	(3.16)	14.7	(20.47)
2	0.8	(1.98)	0.3	(0.00)	2	−0.1	(0.54)	14.7	(20.85)
3	−0.5	(−0.41)	−0.2	(−0.18)	3	−0.5	(−1.52)	14.1	(19.78)
4	−0.1	(−1.64)	−0.3	(−0.84)	4	0.1	(−0.30)	14.2	(19.57)
5	−0.8	(−1.77)	−1.2	(−1.45)	5	0.1	(−0.14)	14.3	(19.47)

Panel B provides a similar analysis for the matching transactions. While returns to the target company are again positive, in this case we do not observe gains for the bidding firms. As described in the introduction to this paper, acquisitions of bankrupt firms may be less desirable to empire-building managers because they require complex negotiations. While it is difficult to directly test whether this leads to less "bad bidders" for bankrupt companies, one might expect managers of bidders for bankrupt firms to hold large equity stakes if these managers are more disciplined. In our sample, acquirers of bankrupt firms have higher average CEO ownership than acquirers in the matching sample (11% vs. 7.5%), but the median CEO ownership is similar (3.4% vs. 3.7%); holdings by all officers and directors are also similar between these groups. The comparison of management stock ownership does not suggest that bidders for bankrupt firms have incentives that are more strongly aligned with their stockholders'.

5. Summary and conclusions

This paper provides empirical evidence that takeovers can facilitate the efficient redeployment of assets of bankrupt firms. We first examine whether the current structure of Chapter 11 or asymmetric information problems impede acquisitions. Comparing firms acquired in Chapter 11 to firms which are independently reorganized, we find that firms with more complex debt structures are less likely to be acquired. Based on a detailed analysis of 55 transactions in Chapter 11, we also find that bidders for bankrupt companies are often in the same industry as the target, have performed poorly prior to the acquisition, and frequently have some prior relationship with the target. Our evidence is consistent with the idea that asymmetric information deters bidding by firms potentially less well informed with respect to the target firm value and the best use of the target's assets. The prices paid by bidders for bankrupt firms are at substantial discounts when compared to prices paid for matched nonbankrupt firms, in spite of efforts by the court to encourage competitive bidding.

We also provide evidence that acquisitions in bankruptcy can create value. The postmerger performance of firms acquired in bankruptcy is better than the postbankruptcy performance of firms independently reorganized in Chapter 11 based on the findings of Hotchkiss (1995). The postmerger performance of firms acquired in bankruptcy is also better than that of matching nonbankrupt transactions. The potential sources of operating gains for the bankrupt acquisitions are reductions in operating expenses and employment. Furthermore, we find positive abnormal stock returns to both the bidder and bankrupt target at the announcement of the acquisition. In contrast, for matching nonbankrupt transactions we find positive returns to the target but not to the bidding firm.

The evidence presented in this paper is useful in the ongoing debate over the efficiency of the Chapter 11 mechanism and proposals to reform the process. However, one cannot conclude from the evidence that a bankruptcy law that mandates the sale of all bankrupt firms enhances efficiency relative to a bankruptcy law that encourages (but does not mandate) takeovers. Before one can conclude that bankruptcy law ought to be reformed to mandate a sale, one must consider the impact of the reform on the choice to seek bankruptcy and, as suggested in Mooradian (1994), the impact on out-of-court restructurings.

References

Aghion, P., O. Hart and J. Moore, 1992, "The Economics of Bankruptcy Reform," *Journal of Law Economics and Organization*, 8, 523–546.

Baird, D., 1993, "Revisiting Auctions in Chapter 11," *Journal of Law and Economics*, 36, 633–653.

Bange, M. and M. Mazzeo, 1997, *When Do Bidders By-Pass Target Management?*, Michigan State University, Michigan.

Barber, B. and J. Lyon, 1995, *Detecting Abnormal Operating Performance: The Empirical Power and Specification of Test-Statistics*, University of California-Davis, California.

Bebchuk, L. and H. Chang, 1992, "Bargaining and the Division of Value in Corporate Reorganization," *Journal of Law Economics and Organization*, 8, 253–279.

Betker, B., 1994, "Management's Incentives, Equity's Bargaining Power and Deviations from Absolute Priority in Chapter 11 Bankruptcies," *Journal of Business*, 68, 161–183.

Bradley, M. and M. Rosenzweig, 1992, "The Untenable Case for Chapter 11," *Yale Law of Journal*, 101, 1043–1095.

Bradley, M., A. Desai and E. Kim, 1988, "Synergistic Gains from Corporate Acquisitions and Their Division Between the Stockholders of Target and Acquiring Firms," *Journal of Financial Economics*, 21, 3–40.

Brown, D., 1989, "Claimholder Incentive Conflicts in Reorganization: The Role of Bankruptcy Law," *Review of Financial Studies*, 2, 109–123.

Brown, D., C. James and R. Mooradian, 1994, "Asset Sales by Financially Distressed Firms," *Journal of Corporate Finance*, 1, 233–257.

Clark, K. and E. Ofek, 1994, "Mergers as a Means of Restructuring Distressed Firms: An Empirical Investigation," *Journal of Financial Quantitative Analysis*, 29, 541–565.

Gertner, R. and R. Picker, 1992, *Bankruptcy and the Allocation of Control*, University of Chicago, Chicago.

Gertner, R. and D. Scharfstein, 1991, "A Theory of Workouts and the Effects of Reorganization Law," *Journal of Finance*, 46, 1189–1222.

Gilson, S., 1996, "Transactions Costs and Capital Structure Choice: Evidence from Financially Distressed Firms," *Journal of Finance*, 52, 161–196.

Healy, P., K. Palepu and R. Ruback, 1992, "Does Corporate Performance Improve After Mergers?" *Journal of Financial Economics*, 31, 135–175.

Hotchkiss, E. S., 1993, "Investment Decisions Under Chapter 11 Bankruptcy," Ph.D. dissertation, New York University.

Hotchkiss, E. S., 1995, "Post-Bankruptcy Performance and Management Turnover," *Journal of Finance*, 50, 3–21.

Hotchkiss, E. and R. Mooradian, 1997, "Vulture Investors and the Market for Control of Distressed Firms," *Journal of Financial Economics*, 43, 401–432.

Jensen, M., 1986a, "The Agency Costs of Free Cash Flow: Corporate Finance and Takeovers," *American Economic Review*, 76, 323–329.

Jensen, M., 1986b, "The Takeover Controversy: Analysis and Evidence," *Midland Corporate Finance Journal*, 4, 6–32.

Jensen, M., 1991, "Corporate Control and the Politics of Finance," *Journal of Applied Corporate Finance*, 4, 13–33.

Jensen, M., 1993, "The Modern Industrial Revolution, Exit, and the Failure of Internal Control Systems," *Journal of Finance*, 48, 831–880.

Jensen, M. and R. Ruback, 1983, "The Market for Corporate Control: The Scientific Evidence," *Journal of Financial Economics*, 11, 5–50.

Kaplan, S. and M. Weisbach, 1992, "The Success of Acquisitions: Evidence from Divestitures," *Journal of Finance*, 47, 107–138.

Martin, K. and J. McConnell, 1991, "Corporate Performance, Corporate Takeovers, and Management Turnover," *Journal of Finance*, 46, 671–687.

McBride, J. M., 1996, *Purchase and Sale of Assets in Bankruptcy*, Wiley, New York.

Mikkelson, W. and M. Partch, 1986, "Valuation Effects of Security Offerings and the Issuance Process," *Journal of Financial Economics*, 15, 31–56.

Mooradian, R., 1994, "The Effect of Bankruptcy Protection on Investment: Chapter 11 as a Screening Device," *Journal of Finance*, 49, 1403–1430.

Palepu, K., 1986, "Predicting Takeover Targets: A Methodological and Empirical Analysis," *Journal of Accounting Economics*, 8, 3–35.

Pulvino, T., 1998, "Do Asset Fire-Sales Exist? An Empirical Investigation of Commercial Aircraft Transactions," *Journal of Finance*, 53, 939–978.

Shleifer, A. and R. Vishny, 1992, "Liquidation Values and Debt Capacity: A Market Equilibrium Approach," *Journal of Finance*, 47, 1343–1366.

Chapter 8

EFFECTS OF BANKRUPTCY COURT PROTECTION ON ASSET SALES[*]

TODD C. PULVINO

Kellogg Graduate School of Management, Northwestern University, Evanston, Illinois, USA

Contents

[*] I am grateful to George Baker, Ben Branch, Charles Calomiris, Miguel Cantillo, Richard Caves, Ken Froot, Bill Schwert (the editor), Andrei Shleifer and Jerry Warner (referee) for helpful comments. I would also like to thank Chris Allen for helping with data collection. Financial support from the Harvard Business School Division of Research is gratefully acknowledged.

This article originally appeared in the *Journal of Financial Economics*, Vol. 52, pp. 151–186 (1999).

Abstract

This paper uses commercial aircraft transactions to determine whether prices obtained from asset sales are greater under Chapter 11 reorganization than under Chapter 7 liquidation. Results indicate that prices obtained under both bankruptcy regimes are substantially lower than prices obtained by nondistressed airlines. Furthermore, there is no evidence that prices obtained by firms reorganizing under Chapter 11 are greater than those obtained by firms liquidating under Chapter 7. An analysis of aircraft sales indicates that Chapter 11 is also ineffective in limiting the number of aircraft sold at discounted prices.

Keywords

bankruptcy, asset sales

JEL classification: G33

1. Introduction

When a firm files for protection under Chapter 11 of the US Bankruptcy Code, an automatic stay is imposed on creditors. Payments to creditors and suppliers are suspended until management generates, and creditors approve, a plan of reorganization. This removes much of the pressure to meet principal and interest payments with cash raised via quick liquidation of assets.

Whether the reduction in the pressure to liquidate provided by the automatic stay is desirable has been the subject of debate by both policymakers and academicians. On one side of the debate are those who argue that the current US reorganization law (Chapter 11) fails to provide adequate incentives for managers to sell assets to higher value users (Bradley and Rosenzweig, 1992; Wruck, 1990). According to this view, distressed firms' managers faced with the prospect of unemployment have strong incentives to keep their firms operating, whether profitably or not. The complex bargaining process fostered by the current reorganization law creates severe holdup problems and allows incumbent managers to avoid liquidation, even if liquidation would maximize firm value. Consequently, in addition to direct bankruptcy costs, reorganization (rather than liquidation via Chapter 7) often results in gross investment inefficiencies and substantial wealth transfers from creditors to managers and equity holders (Altman, 1984, 1993; Betker, 1995; Franks and Torous, 1994; Warner, 1977; Weiss, 1990; Weiss and Wruck, 1998; Wruck, 1990). Some authors argue that immediate cash liquidation of insolvent firms' assets would result in a superior allocation of resources compared to the allocation obtained by allowing managers to choose the lengthy and potentially costly option of reorganization (Baird, 1986; Thorburn, 1997).

On the other side of the debate are those who argue that forced liquidation of insolvent firms' assets would result in an inefficient allocation of resources. They point out that forced liquidation can result in the dismantling of economically viable firms. Furthermore, they argue that in the presence of capital market imperfections, assets will not necessarily be allocated to the highest value users. This will be particularly true when forces that caused the insolvent firm's distress also affect others in the industry. In this case, direct competitors might not be able to pay fundamental value for the insolvent firm's assets. Assets will then be allocated to firms outside the industry who, if the assets are industry specific, are lower value users. Not only will this result in a socially inefficient allocation of resources, but it can also fail to maximize the amount of cash available for distribution to the insolvent firm's creditors (Aghion et al., 1992; Shleifer and Vishny, 1992). Evidence from commercial aircraft transactions presented in Pulvino (1998) supports these concerns. Outside of bankruptcy, financially distressed airlines receive lower prices when selling assets; they are also more likely to sell to firms outside the industry. Brown (2000) and Strömberg (1998) provide additional evidence that liquidation is costly for distressed firms that have industry specific assets. Conversely, Thorburn (1997) finds no evidence that distressed firms liquidate assets at discounted prices. However, her analysis does not focus on industries with industry specific assets.

This paper makes further use of data on commercial aircraft sales by US airlines to assess the effects of both Chapters 11 and 7 protection on asset-sale revenues.

Asset-sale revenues can be affected by bankruptcy court protection by (1) increasing prices at which assets are sold and (2) reducing the quantity of assets sold at distress-sale discounts. This paper examines both of these effects.

The advantage of using aircraft transactions to assess the effect of bankruptcy court protection on asset-sale revenues is that transaction data are readily available. Prior to 1992, prices at which US airlines sold their aircraft had to be disclosed to the Department of Transportation. Thus, both prices and quantities of sales are available. Another advantage of using aircraft transactions is that bankruptcy is common in the US airline industry. Analyses presented in this paper are based on nine bankruptcy filings by major US airlines between 1978 and 1992: Air Florida (July 1984), America West (June 1991), Braniff (May 1982), Continental (September 1983), Continental (December 1990), Eastern (March 1989), Midway (March 1991), Pan Am (January 1991), and TWA (January 1992).

Analyses of transaction prices suggest that prices obtained by airlines reorganizing under Chapter 11 are not significantly higher than those obtained by airlines liquidating under Chapter 7. Bankrupt carriers, whether operating under Chapter 11 or liquidating under Chapter 7, sell assets at discounts that average between 14% and 46%. Because aircraft account for a large portion of airlines' total assets, the dollar magnitude of this discount can be substantial. For example, net flight equipment (flight equipment less depreciation) accounted for more than $700 million of Braniff Airlines' $1 billion in prebankruptcy assets. An average discount of only 15% would have reduced the amount available for distribution to creditors by more than $100 million. Moreover, because airplanes are among airlines' most liquid assets, these discounts are likely to underestimate the average discount associated with a complete liquidation of an airline's assets.

Regardless of bankruptcy venue (i.e., Chapter 7 or Chapter 11), prices that bankrupt airlines receive for their used aircraft are generally lower than prices received by distressed but nonbankrupt firms. For example, distressed but nonbankrupt airlines sell aircraft at discounts ranging from 12% to 28%. The magnitude of this discount increases as the rate of aircraft sales increases. Consistent with the literature on the price impact of large-block stock transactions, evidence presented in this paper and in Pulvino (1998) suggests that the price decreases by 1.5% for each additional aircraft sold in the calendar quarter.[1] Because it is not uncommon for distressed firms to sell 10 or more aircraft per quarter, this incremental discount can be substantial. However, once bankruptcy court protection is obtained, the sensitivity of the price discount to the number of sales disappears in that bankrupt airlines sell aircraft at substantial discounts regardless of the number of aircraft being sold.

---

[1] In stock transactions, the large-block discount is usually associated with asymmetric information. However, information asymmetries are not likely to be severe for used aircraft transactions. Liquidity costs have also been suggested as an explanation for price declines around large-block trades; this explanation is likely to be more applicable to used aircraft. Effects of large-block transactions are discussed in Holthausen et al. (1987, 1990), Chan and Lakonishok (1993, 1995), Mikkelson and Partch (1985), and Kraus and Stoll (1972).

There are at least two reasons that bankrupt airlines receive lower prices for their aircraft than distressed but nonbankrupt carriers. First, bankruptcy status attracts "low-ball" bids from opportunistic buyers. Second, the structure of the bankruptcy law encourages managers to accept these low bids. For 120 days after filing for Chapter 11, incumbent management has the exclusive right to propose a reorganization plan. Acceptance of the plan requires approval by each *impaired* creditor class (including shareholders) or a decision by the bankruptcy judge to force the plan on dissenting classes (commonly referred to as a "cram down"; see Section 1126 of Chapter 11 of the US bankruptcy code for a complete discussion of the conditions under which this option is viable). As Wruck (1990, p. 441) points out, the fact that only impaired creditors and shareholders vote means that "the plan determines who votes and which claimants vote together." Thus, managers interested in securing their jobs have a strong incentive to raise capital so that they can satisfy certain claims (within the confines of the bankruptcy code), thereby selecting the most favorable voters to pass judgment on the reorganization plan.

Furthermore, proceeds from asset sales can be used to finance operations. Weiss and Wruck (1998) describe Eastern Airline's use of asset-sale proceeds to fund operations while operating under Chapter 11 protection. Bankrupt firms that are severely cash constrained can avoid immediate shutdown by accepting low bids, even if doing so fails to maximize firm value.

The rate of asset sales provides additional evidence that Chapter 11 is ineffective in helping distressed firms search for high-value buyers for their assets. Rather than decreasing, the rate of asset sales increases after firms file for Chapter 11 protection. This is particularly true for firms that eventually liquidate under Chapter 7. These firms experience very high rates of asset sales in the 2 years preceding Chapter 11 filing, and an increased rate of sales after the filing date. For firms that eventually emerge from bankruptcy, the rate of asset sales is low in the 2 years preceding bankruptcy and increases slightly after bankruptcy court protection is obtained. Results from both this analysis and the pricing analysis suggest that providing sellers with time to find high-value buyers for their assets is not a benefit provided by Chapter 11 protection.

The remainder of this paper proceeds as follows. Section 2 describes the sample of aircraft transactions used in the empirical analyses. Section 3 examines the effect of bankruptcy court protection on prices that airlines receive for their assets. Section 4 presents an analysis of the effect of bankruptcy court protection on the rate of asset sales and Section 5 concludes.

2. Data description

Department of Transportation and Federal Aviation Administration records of used commercial aircraft transactions between 1978 and 1991 are used to examine asset sales in bankruptcy. These data were collected by Avmark, Inc., an aircraft appraisal firm, and consist of transaction date, aircraft model, serial number, transaction price, engine type, seller identity, and buyer identity.

Using aircraft transactions has a number of advantages. First, bankruptcy filings are common in the US airline industry. Of the 27 major US airlines examined in this paper, eight went bankrupt between 1978 and the end of 1992 (Continental filed for Chapter 11 protection twice during this period). Second, compared to other observable asset sales by distressed firms (for example, sales of manufacturing plants or corporate divisions), aircraft are relatively homogeneous. This makes it much easier to isolate the effects of bankruptcy on transaction prices and quantities. Finally, because the Department of Transportation required price disclosure for aircraft transactions that occurred prior to 1992, aircraft sales provide a sample that is free from selection bias.

This paper presents two analyses. The first examines prices that bankrupt airlines receive for their assets and the second analyzes the rate of aircraft sales. The first analysis includes only aircraft models for which at least 15 transactions occurred between 1978 and 1991 and for which transactions are not dominated by a single airline. For example, Airbus 300B4-100s are omitted because 13 of the 16 transactions that occurred were sales by Eastern Airlines. Eliminating infrequently traded models helps to ensure accuracy in estimating market prices.

Table 1 presents the airlines and number of aircraft sales included in the pricing analysis. The sample comprises 582 (87%) narrow-body transactions and 86 (13%) wide-body transactions. Bold-faced airlines in Table 1 filed for bankruptcy protection sometime in the 1978–1992 time period. Of the bankrupt airlines, Eastern Airlines has the greatest number of sales (21% of the total sample). In addition to sales by airlines listed in Table 1, sales by non-US airlines (i.e., leasing companies, banks, and regional airlines) are used to estimate asset prices. However, these transactions are not used to assess the effects of bankruptcy status on prices.

Table 2 presents the number and timing of aircraft sales by bankrupt airlines. It lists the number of sales by firms operating under Chapters 7 and 11 as well as transactions that occurred up to 2 years prior to the Chapter 11 filing date. There are two numbers in each cell of Table 2. The first number is the total number of aircraft sales and the number in parentheses is the number of sales included in the pricing analysis. Differences between the two numbers represent sales of aircraft models for which there were few transactions. For example, two calendar quarters before filing for Chapter 11 protection, Eastern Airlines sold 13 aircraft. Only four of these aircraft are used to examine the effects of bankruptcy on asset-sale prices. The other nine transactions consist of sales of Airbus 300B4-100 aircraft. As noted above, there are an insufficient number of non-Eastern sales of this particular model to establish reliable market prices.

Bankruptcy sales are dominated by Eastern and Braniff. Table 2 shows that, of the 130 bankruptcy sales analyzed in this paper, 73 (56%) were by Eastern and 49 (38%) by Braniff (including Braniff Liquidating Trust). Table 2 also shows that the majority of sales by airlines that filed for bankruptcy occurred after the Chapter 11 filing date. The general pattern revealed in Table 2 is that bankrupt firms that are eventually liquidated sell large numbers of aircraft both before and after filing for bankruptcy court protection. Conversely, bankrupt airlines that eventually emerge sell few aircraft, regardless of their bankruptcy status.

Table 1

Numbers of narrow-body and wide-body aircraft sales (not including sale/leasebacks) for selected airlines and aircraft models, 1978–1991.

Only aircraft models for which at least 15 transactions occurred over the 1978–1991 time period are included. Airlines that filed for bankruptcy at least once between 1978 and 1992 are in bold face.

	No. of narrow-body sales (1978–1991)	No. of wide-body sales (1978–1991)	Total number of sales (1978–1991)
Air Florida	10	0	10
Alaska	6	0	6
Aloha	2	0	2
America West	8	0	8
American	38	3	41
Braniff	54	1	55
Braniff Liq. Trust	26	0	26
Continental	12	0	12
Delta	50	16	66
Eastern	123	20	143
Hawaiian	4	0	4
Midway	6	0	6
Northwest	38	0	38
Ozark	2	0	2
PSA	17	0	17
Pan Am	33	30	63
People Express	0	1	1
Piedmont	5	0	5
Republic	4	0	4
TWA	40	4	44
United	54	8	62
US Air	25	0	25
Western	25	3	28
Total	582	86	668

In addition to aircraft prices, data describing airlines' fleets, financial characteristics, operating statistics, and bankruptcy filing dates are used (quarterly data when available and annual data otherwise). Fleet descriptions are obtained from companies' annual and quarterly reports. Financial data are obtained from Compustat, and operating statistics are obtained from *Air Carrier Traffic Statistics* published by the Department of Transportation and the Civil Aeronautics Board. Bankruptcy filing dates are obtained from the *Capital Changes Reporter* (published by Commerce Clearing House).

3. Effect of bankruptcy court protection on asset prices

The analysis presented in this section assesses the degree to which bankruptcy laws affect prices that distressed sellers receive for their assets. If reorganization laws like

Table 2

Number of aircraft sales before and during bankruptcy for airlines that filed for bankruptcy court protection between 1978 and the end of 1992.

Transactions listed under "Chpt. 11" occurred while the firm was operating under Chapter 11 protection; those listed under "Chpt. 7" occurred while the firm was liquidating under Chapter 7 of the bankruptcy code. Numbers of prebankruptcy sales in each of the eight calendar quarters preceding the Chapter 11 filing date are also presented. For example, transactions listed under the heading "1" occurred no more than 3 months prior to Chapter 11 filing; those listed under "2" occurred between 3 and 6 months prior to filing. There are two numbers per cell in this table. The first number is the total number of sales. The second number (in parentheses) is the number of sales used in the pricing analyses presented in Tables 4 and 5. Differences between the two numbers result from omitting aircraft models for which there were an insufficient number of sales to estimate market prices. Bold-faced airlines are those that were eventually liquidated. Table Entries: Total number of aircraft sales (Number of sales for models included in pricing analysis).

Airline(Chapter 11 date)	Chpt. 7	Chpt 11	No. of calendar quarters prior to Chapter 11 filing							
			1	2	3	4	5	6	7	8
Air Florida (7/84)	3 (3)	0 (0)	2 (2)	2 (2)	0 (0)	0 (0)	0 (0)	0 (0)	0 (0)	1 (0)
America West (6/91)	n.a.	0 (0)	0 (0)	0 (0)	0 (0)	0 (0)	1 (1)	0 (0)	0 (0)	0 (0)
Braniff (5/82)	9 (9)	15 (14)	1 (1)	1 (1)	7 (7)	0 (0)	5 (5)	9 (8)	3 (2)	1 (1)
Braniff Liquidating Trust (n.a.)	26 (26)	n.a.	n.a.	n.a.	n.a.	n.a.	n.a.	n.a.	n.a.	n.a.
Continental (9/83 and 12/90)	n.a.	7 (3)	1 (1)	1 (0)	0 (0)	0 (0)	0 (0)	0 (0)	0 (0)	0 (0)
Eastern (3/89)	2 (2)	83 (71)	3 (3)	13 (4)	7 (4)	5 (5)	3 (1)	0 (0)	0 (0)	2 (2)
Midway (3/91)	0 (0)	2 (2)	0 (0)	0 (0)	0 (0)	0 (0)	0 (0)	0 (0)	0 (0)	0 (0)
Pan Am (1/91)	3 (0)	0 (0)	2 (2)	0 (0)	0 (0)	0 (0)	0 (0)	0 (0)	0 (0)	0 (0)
TWA (1/92)	n.a.	0 (0)	0 (0)	0 (0)	0 (0)	1 (1)	0 (0)	1 (1)	3 (3)	0 (0)
Total	43 (40)	107 (90)	9 (9)	17 (7)	14 (11)	6 (6)	9 (7)	10 (9)	6 (5)	4 (3)

Chapter 11 of the US bankruptcy code are better at promoting orderly dispositions of assets than are liquidation proceedings such as Chapter 7, then we should observe smaller price discounts for asset sales conducted under Chapter 11 than for those conducted under Chapter 7. Furthermore, because the bankruptcy code's automatic stay provision reduces pressure to meet debt obligations via quick asset sales, we should observe smaller discounts for transactions by bankrupt airlines than for transactions by distressed but nonbankrupt airlines. In order to make this comparison, sellers' levels of distress must be characterized. Consequently, this section proceeds in three steps. First, price discounts are calculated. Second, the degree of seller distress is characterized. Third, the effects of bankruptcy status and distress on price discounts are estimated.

3.1. Step #1: hedonic price calculation

The first step involves calculating "hedonic prices," that is, prices that are functions of only aircraft attributes and time. Hedonic regressions are often used to study real estate prices. They also have been used in a number of other industries including rigid disk drives (Lerner, 1995), automobiles (Ohta and Griliches, 1986), and computers (Chow, 1967). Essentially, this procedure estimates an equilibrium price for each aircraft model in every calendar quarter between 1978 and the end of 1991. The following specification is used to calculate hedonic prices:

$$\log(\text{PRICE}) = \beta_0 + \sum_1^I \beta_i \text{QTR}_i + \sum_1^J \beta_j \text{MODEL}_j + \sum_1^K \beta_k \text{STAGE}_k$$

$$+ \beta_{\text{AGE}} \log(1 + \text{AGE}) + \varepsilon, \tag{1}$$

where PRICE is the transaction price, QTR are the dummy variables representing calendar quarters, MODEL are the dummy variables representing aircraft models, STAGE are the dummy variables representing engine stage categories, and AGE is the aircraft age at time of transaction.

All aircraft sales, including those by non-US airlines (i.e., leasing companies, banks, and regional airlines) but excluding sale/leasebacks, are used to estimate Equation (1). The logarithm of transaction price is used as the dependent variable to impose a (price) nonnegativity constraint on the model. Price levels depend significantly on the aircraft model. For example, the average transaction price for 727-100s is $3 million (in 1992 dollars). The average price for 747-200s is $39 million. In general, wide-body aircraft and late-model aircraft with quiet engines command the highest prices. All prices are in 1992 dollars. Inflation adjustments are made using the producer price index. Including additional dummy variables to represent engine type substantially reduces the number of degrees of freedom but increases the adjusted R^2 by less than 0.5%. Therefore, engine variant dummies are omitted from the analysis. Stage categories refer to engine noise output characteristics. Stage 1 aircraft are the loudest—they are no longer allowed to fly in the United States. Stage 2 engines are quieter, but they too will be outlawed by the year 2000. Stage 3 aircraft are the quietest.

Equation (1) is estimated separately for narrow-body and wide-body aircraft. Segmenting the data in this way allows coefficients on calendar quarter dummies, stage dummies, and the age variable to differ for these two aircraft classes, thus improving the accuracy of hedonic price estimates. Appendix A presents results from this regression for both narrow- and wide-body aircraft. Both regression models have significant explanatory power—the adjusted R^2 is 0.76 for the narrow-body regression and 0.74 for the wide-body regression. The AGE coefficient of -0.16 in the narrow-body regression implies that narrow-body aircraft depreciate by 16% per year in the first year of operation and by 1% per year after 10 years. The coefficient is slightly larger in absolute value for wide-body aircraft, suggesting that they depreciate at a more rapid rate than narrow-body aircraft. Calendar quarter dummies are highly variable and generally signify the health of the airline industry. For example, dummy variables representing calendar quarters between 1982 and the middle of 1984 are small. During this time period, the US airline industry was ailing and aircraft values were low. In the later 1980s, the airline industry was relatively healthy. Aircraft values, represented by the calendar quarter dummy variables from 1985 through

1989, were relatively high during this period. When a severe recession hit the airline industry in 1991, aircraft values dropped significantly.

Residuals from estimation of Equation (1) are used as the dependent variable in many of the analyses that follow. A positive residual implies that the aircraft sold for a premium whereas a negative residual indicates that the aircraft sold at a discount to the hedonic price. Because of the logarithmic specification, residuals can be interpreted (approximately) as percentages. For example, a residual of -0.15 implies that the actual transaction price is 14% ($=1 - e^{-0.15}$) lower than the hedonic price. An alternative to the two-stage analysis presented in this paper would be to perform a single-stage analysis by including explanatory variables from the second stage directly in the hedonic regression. The primary problem with this approach is that transactions for which second-stage explanatory variables are unavailable (e.g., leasing companies) would have to be omitted. Omission of these transactions would result in less accurate hedonic prices.

3.2. Step #2: characterizing sellers' distress levels

The second step of the analysis consists of classifying transactions according to the level of distress of the seller. The following categories are constructed:

1. *Chapter 7 transactions*: Transactions that occur while the seller is liquidating under Chapter 7.
2. *Chapter 11 transactions*: Transactions that occur while the seller is operating under Chapter 11.
3. *Prebankruptcy transactions*: Transactions that occur during the 2 years preceding the seller's Chapter 11 filing date.
4. *Nonbankruptcy transactions*: Transactions that occur more that 2 years prior to the seller's Chapter 11 filing date or transactions by firms that never file for bankruptcy court protection.

Transactions classified under Category 4 are further segmented according to the selling firm's bankruptcy probability. This is accomplished by estimating the following airline-specific probit model, where each observation consists of one firm-quarter:

$$
\begin{aligned}
\Pr(\text{BKRPT} = 1) = {} & \alpha + \beta_1 \text{NETLEV} + \beta_2 \text{ISS} + \beta_3 \text{OPINC} \\
& + \beta_4 \text{COST} + \beta_5 \text{REV} + \beta_6 \ln(\text{ASSETS}) \\
& + \beta_7 \text{INDEX} + \beta_8 (\text{Med.NETLEV}) \\
& + \beta_9 (\text{Med.COST}) + \beta_{10} (\text{Med.REV}) + \varepsilon,
\end{aligned}
\tag{2}
$$

where BKRPT is 1 if the firm files for bankruptcy in the following quarter and 0 otherwise, NETLEV is the book value of long-term debt less working capital divided by the sum of book value of debt and market value of equity, ISS are the number of debt issues outstanding, OPINC is the operating income divided by sales, COST is the cost of goods sold divided by available seat-miles, REV is the load factor multiplied by revenue per revenue-passenger-mile, ASSETS is the book value of assets, INDEX is the index of narrow-body prices, Med.NETLEV is the median of NETLEV across firms in each calendar quarter, Med.COST is the median of COST across firms in each calendar quarter, and Med.REV is the median of REV across firms in each calendar quarter.

Explanatory variables in Equation (2) fall into three categories: (1) proxies for financial distress, (2) proxies for economic distress, and (3) control variables. Proxies for financial distress include NETLEV and ISS. NETLEV measures the effect of financial condition on bankruptcy probability. The coefficient on NETLEV should be positive; as financial leverage increases and financial liquidity decreases, bankruptcy probability increases. ISS proxies for creditor dispersion. Because debt renegotiation is likely to be more difficult as the number of creditors increases, the likelihood of bankruptcy should increase as creditor dispersion increases (Asquith et al., 1994; Gertner and Scharfstein, 1991). Thus, the sign on ISS should be positive.

OPINC, COST, and REV are all intended to measure economic distress. Firms with favorable economic prospects are likely to have low bankruptcy probabilities, whereas firms with poor economic prospects are likely to have high bankruptcy probabilities. Thus, we would expect coefficients on OPINC and REV to be negative and the coefficient on COST to be positive.

Control variables include firm size, INDEX, Med.NETLEV, Med.COST, and Med. REV. Including firm size, measured by ln(ASSETS), controls for the possibility that firms of different sizes have inherently different bankruptcy probabilities. The remaining variables control for the effect of the overall condition of the airline industry on the probability of bankruptcy. INDEX is calculated from the calendar quarter dummy variables in the narrow-body hedonic regression presented in Appendix A.

Equation (2) is estimated for 27 airlines over the 1978–1991 time period. Because of mergers, entry, and liquidations, not all airlines are represented in every calendar quarter. The final sample consists of 980 firm-quarters. High predicted values from this regression correspond to firm-quarters in which the chances of bankruptcy in the near future are high. Low predicted values correspond to firm-quarters in which bankruptcy is unlikely.

Table 3 presents results from estimating Equation (2). As expected, the NETLEV coefficient is positive and statistically significant, implying that bankruptcy probability increases as the level of financial distress increases. Airlines' cost efficiencies and revenue-generating capabilities also significantly influence bankruptcy probability. The coefficient on COST indicates that as cost of goods sold per available seat-mile increases, bankruptcy probability increases. Similarly, the coefficient on REV in Table 3 indicates that bankruptcy probability decreases as airlines' abilities to fill their planes with high-revenue passengers increases. Although none of the other coefficients are statistically significant at conventional levels, most have the expected signs. Furthermore, the pseudo-R^2 of 0.58 indicates that the model has substantial explanatory power.

Table 3

Probit analysis used to estimate the bankruptcy probability for 27 airlines between 1978 and 1991:

$$\text{Pr(Bankrupt} = 1) = \alpha + \beta_1 \text{NETLEV} + \beta_2 \text{ISS} + \beta_3 \text{OPINC} + \beta_4 \text{COST}$$
$$+ \beta_5 \text{REV} + \beta_6 \ln(\text{ASSETS}) + \beta_7 \text{INDEX}$$
$$+ \beta_8 (\text{Med.NETLEV}) + \beta_9 (\text{Med.COST}) + \beta_{10} (\text{Med.REV}) + \varepsilon.$$

Total sample size is 980 firm-quarters. The dependent variable takes a value of 1 if the firm files for Chapter 11 protection in the calendar quarter and 0 otherwise. NETLEV equals long-term debt plus current liabilities minus current assets all divided by the sum of book value of debt and market value of equity; ISS equals number of outstanding debt issues; OPINC equals operating income divided by sales; COST equals cost of goods sold divided by available seat-miles; REV equals load factor times revenue per revenue-passenger-mile; ASSETS equals book value of assets; INDEX measures relative prices of used aircraft; Med.NETLEV equals the median net leverage across firms in the calendar quarter; Med.COST equals median cost of goods sold divided by available seat miles in each quarter; Med.REV equals median load factor times revenue per revenue-passenger-mile in each quarter. All independent variables are lagged one calendar quarter. Standard errors are in parentheses.

Dependent variable equals 1 in the calendar quarter in which Chapter 11 filing occurs, 0 otherwise; 980 observations.

Net le-verage	ISS	OPINC	COST	REV	ln(As-sets)	INDEX	Median net leverage	Med. COST	Med. REV	Constant	Adj. R^2
10.53	−0.05	3.51	118.64	−90.18	−0.14	0.19	4.81 (4.24)	−56.74	17.19	−12.71	0.58
(3.89)[b]	(0.052)	(6.14)	(50.99)[a]	(43.28)[a]	(0.368)	(0.437)		(84.36)	(76.85)	(7.19)	

[a]Significant at 0.05 level.
[b]Significant at 0.01 level.

3.3. Step #3: price comparisons

The third and final step of the analysis involves comparing price residuals from the hedonic regressions for each of the four transaction categories listed above, that is, Chapters 11 and 7, prebankruptcy, and nonbankruptcy. This comparison is made by regressing hedonic regression residuals on indicator variables that represent each category. To control for potential misspecification associated with omitted variables in Equations (1) and (2), the regression also includes firm-specific indicator variables. Southwest Airlines provides a good example of why firm effects should be included. Because their planes do not have kitchens, Southwest aircraft would likely sell at a discount compared to sales of otherwise similar aircraft by other airlines (since the Avmark database contains no records of used aircraft sales by Southwest Airlines between 1978 and the end of 1991, the expected effect of Southwest's unique aircraft configuration on transaction price cannot be verified). Another example of a firm--

specific effect involves airlines' abilities to find high-value buyers for their assets. Until the mid-1990s, there was no organized market for used airplanes. Transactions were privately negotiated and the prices that airlines received for their planes were affected, at least in part, by the talents of those responsible for negotiating the sales. Many smaller airlines relied on third-party brokers to locate potential buyers. Conversely, George "Bud" Dutton of Eastern Airlines was reputed to be a particularly talented aircraft salesman (based on discussions with Morten Beyer of Morten Beyer Associates). Therefore, ceteris paribus, Eastern would be expected to receive relatively high prices for their aircraft. The mid-1990s saw the development of organized auctions of used aircraft, but these auctions have not been particularly successful. Most aircraft transactions continue to be privately negotiated deals.

Given a large enough sample of transactions by bankrupt carriers, the "Eastern" effect would not bias the relation between asset prices and bankruptcy status. Hence, there would be no need to control for firm-specific effects. However, as previously discussed, Chapter 11 transactions are dominated by Eastern Airlines (71 out of 90) and Chapter 7 transactions are dominated by Braniff and its liquidating trust (35 out of 40). Including firm-specific dummy variables allows bankruptcy effects to be isolated from the "Eastern" and "Braniff" effects. Therefore, the following model is estimated:

$$\text{RES} = \alpha + \beta_1 \text{Ch}\,7 + \beta_2 \text{Ch}\,11 + \beta_3 T_{-1} + \beta_4 T_{-2} + \beta_5 \text{PBR}_5$$
$$+ \beta_6 \text{PBR}_4 + \beta_7 \text{PBR}_3 + \beta_8 \text{PBR}_2 + \beta_9 \text{NSALE} \tag{3}$$
$$+ \text{FirmEffects} + \varepsilon,$$

where RES is the residual from hedonic regressions, Chapter 7 is a dummy variable equal to one if the transaction occurred under Chapter 7 liquidation, Chapter 11 is a dummy variable equal to one if the transaction occurred when the selling firm was operating under Chapter 11 protection, T_{-1} is a dummy variable equal to one if the transaction occurred in the year preceding the seller's Chapter 11 filing date, T_{-2} is a dummy variable equal to one if the transaction occurred between 1 and 2 years prior to the seller's Chapter 11 filing date, PBR_j are the dummy variables indicating bankruptcy probability quintiles based on predicted values from Equation (2); PBR_5 takes the value of 1 if the firm-quarter is in the highest bankruptcy probability quintile and 0 otherwise and PBR_2 takes the value of 1 if the firm-quarter is in the second lowest bankruptcy probability quintile and 0 otherwise (PBR_1 is omitted to avoid collinearity) and, NSALE is the number of used aircraft sold by the airline in the current calendar quarter.

To test statistically for the effects of bankruptcy court protection on asset-sale prices, this regression is estimated in both restricted and unrestricted forms. The restricted form imposes the condition that coefficients on the Chapter 7 dummy variable, the Chapter 11 dummy variable, and dummy variables representing distressed (but not bankrupt) airlines are equal (i.e., H_0: $\beta_1 = \beta_2 = \beta_3 = \beta_5$). An *F*-test is used to determine the statistical significance of this restriction.

3.3.1. Univariate results

Table 4 presents average price residuals for various categories of transactions. Panel A contains price residuals for bankrupt firms and Panel B contains residuals for non-bankrupt firms. Because the dependent variable in the hedonic regression used to calculate residuals is the logarithm of price, entries in Table 4 approximate percentage deviations from the hedonic price. For example, Panel A shows that sales by Chapters 7 and 11 firms are transacted at average discounts of 11% and 10% from the hedonic price, respectively.[2] Although both of these average discounts are significantly different from zero at the 0.1% level, they are not different from each other. This evidence suggests that the current reorganization law is no more effective than court-supervised liquidation in helping distressed sellers locate high-value buyers for their assets. Prior to entering Chapter 11, there is no discernible pattern (over time) in prices that airlines receive for their assets. However, as will be reported in subsequent regressions that control for firm effects, there is evidence of substantial price discounting in the year preceding Chapter 11 filing.

Panel B uses predicted values from the airline-specific bankruptcy probability model of Equation (2) to summarize price residuals according to the bankruptcy probability of the seller. Only transactions by firms that do not file for Chapter 11 protection within 2 years of the transaction are included in Panel B. Transactions by firms with bankruptcy probabilities in the lowest quintile receive prices that average 5% above the hedonic price. This premium decreases, although not monotonically, with bankruptcy probability. Sales by firms in the second-highest bankruptcy-probability quintile and the highest bankruptcy-probability quintile are transacted at discounts of 11% and 8%, respectively. The null hypothesis that average residuals are the same for the low and high bankruptcy-probability quintiles is rejected at the 5% level. Similarly, tests that average residuals are the same for sales by bankrupt firms (Chapters 11 and 7) and sales by firms in the low bankruptcy-probability quintile reject at the 0.1% level. However, there is no evidence of differences in discounts for bankrupt airlines and distressed (but not bankrupt) airlines. Discounts for all of these groups average between 8% and 11%. Differences between groups are not statistically significant at conventional levels. Thus, simply comparing price residuals indicates that although distressed airlines receive lower prices for their aircraft, this particular cost of distress is mitigated neither by Chapter 11 nor Chapter 7 protection.

---

[2] Table 4 entries approximate price discounts. To get an exact estimate of the discount requires exponentiating the table entries. For example, Chapter 7 transactions occur at a discount of $1 - e^{-0.11}$ or 10.4%. As this example shows, the approximation is accurate for small residuals.

Table 4

Average residuals (ε) from the following hedonic price regression using aircraft transactions that occurred between 1978 and 1991:

$$\log(\text{PRICE}) = \beta_0 + \sum_1^I \beta_i \text{QTR}_i + \sum_1^J \beta_j \text{MODEL}_j + \sum_1^K \beta_k \text{STAGE}_k + \beta_{\text{AGE}} \log(1 + \text{AGE}) + \varepsilon$$

where PRICE equals transaction price, QTR_i are a series of 56 dummy variables representing calendar quarters between 1978 and 1991, MODEL_j are dummy variables representing aircraft models, STAGE_k are dummy variables representing engine noise categories, and AGE is aircraft age (in years) at the time of the transaction. Results from estimating the hedonic regression using 1333 used-aircraft transactions are presented in Appendix A. Residuals (ε) summarized in this table can be interpreted as percent deviations from hedonic price. Positive residuals imply that the aircraft were sold for prices above the hedonic price; negative residuals imply that the aircraft were sold for prices below the hedonic price. Panel A presents average residuals for transactions by airlines that are liquidating under Chapter 7, reorganizing under Chapter 11, and transactions that occur within 2 years prior to Chapter 11 filing. Panel B presents residuals for transactions by airlines that remained solvent throughout the 1978–1992 time period. Bankruptcy probability is calculated using predicted values from the bankruptcy model presented in Table 3.

Panel A: Mean price residuals for bankrupt firms

| | While in | | No. of calendar quarters prior to Chapter 11 filing | | | | | | | |
	Ch 7	Ch 11	1	2	3	4	5	6	7	8
Mean price residual	−0.11	−0.10	−0.002	0.05	−0.24	0.08	0.07	0.06	−0.06	−0.06
Standard deviation of mean	0.020[c]	0.026[c]	0.056	0.042	0.081[a]	0.065	0.011[c]	0.016[b]	0.058	0.002
No. of observations	40	90	9	7	11	6	7	9	5	3

Panel B: Mean price residuals for nonbankrupt firms

| | Bankruptcy probability quintile | | | | |
| | High probability | | | | Low probability |
	5	4	3	2	1
Mean price residual	−0.08	−0.11	−0.04	0.03	0.05
Standard deviation of mean	0.048	0.051[a]	0.040	0.022	0.035
No. of observations	97	98	94	96	96

[a]Significant at 0.05 level.
[b]Significant at 0.01 level.
[c]Significant at 0.001 level.

3.3.2. Multivariate results

As previously discussed, simply comparing average residuals across groups controls for neither the number of aircraft sold in a calendar quarter (the large-block effect) nor firm fixed effects. Results from estimating Equation (3), which includes these controls, are presented in Panel A of Table 5. To account for the possible lack of independence of the error terms, standard errors presented in Table 5 are calculated assuming that observations are independent across firms. No assumptions are made regarding independence of observations across or within firm-quarters. The effect of this assumption is that standard error estimates are conservatively high. True standard errors are likely to be smaller than those reported in Table 5.

Specification 1 in Table 5 controls for the rate of asset sales but does not include firm fixed effects. Results indicate that after controlling for the rate of asset sales, the difference in price residuals between bankrupt and distressed (but solvent) firms is slight. More importantly, there are no significant differences in prices obtained by firms operating under Chapter 11 and those liquidating under Chapter 7. A test of the null hypothesis that coefficients on the Chapters 7, 11, T_{-1}, and Bankruptcy Quintile 5 variables are equal fails to reject at conventional levels. The effect of the number of aircraft sales in a calendar quarter contributes only slightly to the price discount. For each additional aircraft sold, the price decreases by approximately one-half of one percent.

Specification 2 in Panel A of Table 5 controls for the rate of asset sales as well as firm fixed effects. Results from this specification indicate that firms with low bankruptcy probabilities receive higher prices for their aircraft than do firms with high bankruptcy probabilities. Transactions that occur in the year preceding bankruptcy filing occur at an average discount of 32% compared to sales by airlines with the lowest bankruptcy probabilities. Discounts are slightly smaller for transactions by airlines selling while in Chapter 11 (30%) and slightly larger for airlines liquidating under Chapter 7 (38%). While it appears that firms liquidating under Chapter 7 receive lower prices than firms operating under Chapter 11, the difference is not statistically significant. The effect of the number of sales per calendar quarter increases slightly when firm-specific effects are included, but the effect is not statistically significant.

To further examine the effects of Chapters 11 and 7 protection on distress-sale discounts, the effect of the number of sales per quarter is allowed to vary depending on bankruptcy venue (Chapter 11 vs. Chapter 7). Specifications 3 and 4 of Panel A in Table 5 include interaction terms to accomplish this. The effect of these interactions is most significant when firm-specific effects are included in the model (Specification 4). Discounts associated with Chapters 11 and 7 are higher, but again, they are not significantly different from one another. In addition, discounts increase with the number of aircraft sales per quarter, but only when the seller is without bankruptcy court protection. For each additional aircraft sold in the calendar quarter, the price discount increases by approximately 1.5%. When the firm has either Chapter 11 or Chapter 7 protection, the increased discount associated with large-block sales

Table 5

Ordinary least-squares regressions of the effect of bankruptcy court protection on transaction price, 1978–1991.

The dependent variable is the residual from estimating the following hedonic price regression:

$$\log(\text{PRICE}) = \beta_0 + \sum_1^I \beta_i \text{QTR}_i + \sum_1^J \beta_j \text{MODEL}_j + \sum_1^K \beta_k \text{STAGE}_k + \beta_{\text{AGE}} \log(1 + \text{AGE}) + \varepsilon,$$

where PRICE equals transaction price, QTR_i are a series of 56 dummy variables representing calendar quarters between 1978 and 1991, $MODEL_j$ are dummy variables representing aircraft models, $STAGE_k$ are dummy variables representing engine noise categories, and AGE is aircraft age (in years) at the time of the transaction. Results from estimating the hedonic regression using 1333 used-aircraft transactions are presented in Appendix A. Independent variables characterize the selling firm's bankruptcy status and are defined as follows: Ch 7 is a dummy variable equal to one if the transaction occurred while the firm was liquidating under Chapter 7 of the bankruptcy code; Ch 11 is a dummy variable equal to one if the firm was operating under Chapter 11 of the code; T_{-1} is a dummy variable equal to one if the transaction occurred within 1 year prior to Chapter 11 filing; T_{-2} is a dummy variable equal to one if the transaction occurred more than 1 year but less than 2 years prior to Chapter 11 filing; bankruptcy probability quintile dummies correspond to predictions from the Probit regression in Table 3; INDEX measures the relative strength of the used aircraft market at the time of the transaction and is obtained from the calendar quarter dummy variable coefficients in the hedonic regression; Number of sales equals the total number of used aircraft sales by the selling firm in the quarter. Panel A presents OLS regressions; Panel B presents results after inclusion of the Inverse Mills Ratio to control for sample selection bias. The dummy variable representing the lowest bankruptcy probability quintile is omitted to avoid collinearity. Standard errors (in parentheses) are calculated assuming independence across firms. No assumptions are made regarding the independence of transactions that have common sellers.

Panel A: OLS regression, dependent variable is hedonic price residual; 668 observations

Specification	While in:		Years before Chapter 11 filing:		Bankruptcy probability quintile				No. of sales	Ch 7 × no. of sales	Ch 11 × no. of sales	Constant	Adj. R^2
	Ch 7	Ch 11	T_{-1}	T_{-2}	(High probability) 5	4	(Low probability) 3	2					
1	−0.15 (0.102)	−0.08 (0.143)	−0.09 (0.142)	−0.002 (0.103)	−0.13 (0.168)	−0.16 (0.111)	−0.08 (0.067)	−0.01 (0.094)	−0.006 (0.007)			0.07 (0.089)	0.02
2	−0.48 (0.186)[a]	−0.35 (0.195)	−0.38 (0.169)[a]	−0.17 (0.177)	−0.34 (0.213)	−0.30 (0.145)	−0.12 (0.137)	−0.03 (0.102)	−0.01 (0.009)			Firm effects	0.26

(Continued)

Table 5 (*Continued*)

Specification	While in: Ch 7	Ch 11	Years before Chapter 11 filing: T_{-1}	T_{-2}	Bankruptcy probability quintile (High probability) 5	4	3	(Low probability) 2	No. of sales	Ch 7 × no. of sales	Ch 11 × no. of sales	Constant	Adj. R^2
3	-0.22 (0.129)	-0.23 (0.118)	-0.08 (0.148)	0.02 (0.117)	-0.13 (0.166)	-0.16 (0.111)	-0.06 (0.063)	0.01 (0.098)	-0.01 (0.011)	0.02 (0.016)	0.02 (0.011)	0.10 (0.083)	0.03
4	-0.62 (0.200)[b]	-0.52 (0.228)[a]	-0.35 (0.153)[a]	-0.14 (0.161)	-0.33 (0.195)	-0.28 (0.133)[a]	-0.10 (0.120)	-0.004 (0.093)	-0.02 (0.009)[a]	0.03 (0.017)	0.02 (0.09)[a]	Firm effects	0.27

Panel B: Heckman two-step second-stage regression, dependent variable is Hedonic price residual; 668 observations

Specification	While in: Ch 7	Ch 11	Years before Chapter 11 filing: T_{-1}	T_{-2}	Bankruptcy probability quintile (High probability) 5	4	3	(Low probability) 2	No. of sales	Ch 7 × no. of sales	Ch 11 × no. of sales	Inverse Mills ratio	Constant	Adj. R^2
1	-0.27 (0.101)[a]	-0.01 (0.153)	-0.07 (0.148)	-0.005 (0.095)	-0.08 (0.163)	-0.14 (0.098)	-0.06 (0.065)	-0.004 (0.094)	-0.003 (0.007)			0.22 (0.089)[a]	-0.20 (0.032)	0.05
2	-0.45 (0.260)	-0.33 (0.258)	-0.36 (0.198)	-0.16 (0.206)	-0.32 (0.248)	-0.28 (0.193)	-0.12 (0.156)	-0.02 (0.107)	-0.01 (0.009)			0.05 (0.181)	Firm effects	0.26
3	-0.26 (0.099)[a]	-0.15 (0.123)	-0.06 (0.155)	0.02 (0.110)	-0.07 (0.161)	-0.14 (0.098)	-0.05 (0.061)	0.01 (0.097)	-0.01 (0.011)	0.002 (0.021)	0.01 (0.012)	0.22 (0.088)[a]	-0.17 (0.135)	0.05
4	-0.61 (0.275)[a]	-0.51 (0.296)	-0.35 (0.185)	-0.13 (0.193)	-0.32 (0.235)	-0.28 (0.188)	-0.10 (0.143)	-0.003 (0.100)	-0.02 (0.010)[a]	0.03 (0.017)[a]	0.02 (0.009)[a]	0.01 (0.183)	Firm effects	0.26

[a]Significant at 0.05 level.
[b]Significant at 0.01 level.

disappears. However, this is not as much of a benefit as it might first appear. Regression coefficients in Specification 4 of Panel A in Table 5 imply that, because of the large "fixed" discount associated with bankruptcy, only firms selling more than nine aircraft per calendar quarter would receive higher prices with bankruptcy court protection than without it. This is true regardless of bankruptcy venue—there is little evidence that reorganization proceedings allow firms to obtain better prices for their assets than liquidation proceedings.

Firm fixed effects (not reported) are highly variable and range in magnitude from a statistically insignificant −0.21 (American Airlines) to a significant 0.55 (Pacific Southwest Airlines). Only two firms (American and US Air) have negative intercepts. Of the bankrupt airlines, TWA has the smallest intercept (0.10) and Air Florida has the largest (0.53). Both Eastern and Braniff have positive intercepts (0.47 and 0.34, respectively). The variability in firm effects suggests that, because the other independent variables in Equations (1) and (2) do not fully explain variation in price, firm effects should be included in the specification. Furthermore, the fact that all of the bankrupt firms have positive intercepts is inconsistent with the notion that airlines that file for bankruptcy are inherently more likely to sell aircraft at discounted prices, regardless of their financial condition.

3.4. Specification tests

This section describes three specification tests used to assess the robustness of the conclusions drawn from the pricing analysis summarized in Tables 4 and 5. The first test involves an assessment of the degree to which the results depend on the specific bankruptcy model used to define firm-quarter bankruptcy-probability quintiles. The second tests for sample selection biases. The third test assesses the degree to which predicted prices obtained from the hedonic regressions described by Equation (1) are affected by the large number of Eastern and Braniff sales.

Because there are only nine bankruptcies in this analysis, there is a possibility that the bankruptcy probability model described by Equation (2) inaccurately places firms into bankruptcy probability quintiles. To determine whether results presented in Tables 4 and 5 are dependent on the specific bankruptcy probability model used, bankruptcy probabilities are calculated using two alternative approaches. Both of the alternative approaches are based on Altman's (1993) Z-score methodology. The first uses Z-scores to categorize firm-quarters into bankruptcy probability quintiles:

$$Z = 1.2X_1 + 1.4X_2 + 3.3X_3 + 0.6X_4 + 1.0X_5, \qquad (4)$$

where X_1 is working capital/total assets, X_2 is the retained earnings/total assets, X_3 is the earnings before interest and taxes/total assets, X_4 is market value equity/book value of liabilities, and X_5 is sales/total assets.

Firm-quarters with low Z-scores are assumed to have high bankruptcy probabilities; those with high Z-scores are assumed to have low bankruptcy probabilities.

The second approach uses a probit model similar to that described by Equation (2), except that Altman's (1993) independent variables (X_1–X_5) are used:

$$\Pr(\text{BKRPT} = 1) = \alpha + \beta_1 X_1 + \beta_2 X_2 + \beta_3 X_3 + \beta_4 X_4 + \beta_5 X_5. \tag{5}$$

All three of the bankruptcy probability models provide reasonable assessments of relative bankruptcy probabilities. Regardless of the model used, airlines approaching bankruptcy (e.g., Eastern Airlines in 1988) are consistently in the highest bankruptcy-- probability quintiles and financially healthy airlines (e.g., Southwest Airlines) are consistently in the lowest bankruptcy-probability quintiles. Furthermore, pricing ana- lyses using all of the bankruptcy-probability models yield similar results. Therefore, there is no evidence that observed similarities in price discounts for Chapters 7 and 11 transactions are driven by the specific bankruptcy model used.

The second specification issue addressed in this section involves sample selection bias. Although bankruptcy court protection fails to mitigate discounts at which dis- tressed firms sell assets, it can help firms avoid liquidation in the first place (liquidation avoidance is addressed in more detail in the following section). This raises questions concerning the accuracy of the price discount analyses presented in Table 5. In particular, since we only observe discounts for airlines that choose to sell, previously reported coefficient estimates might be biased because of the sample selection pro- cedure. To address this possibility, Heckman's (1979) two-step correction is imple- mented. In the first step, the inverse Mills ratio is calculated from a probit model that predicts the probability that an airline will sell an aircraft in a given calendar quarter. In the second step, the inverse Mills ratio is included as a regressor in Equation (3), the price discount regression. The inverse Mills ratio is calculated using the following probit model, estimated over 1021 firm-quarters:

$$\Pr(\text{SALE} = 1) = \alpha + \sum_{j=2}^{5} \beta_j \Pr(\text{BR})_j + \beta_6 T_{-1} + \beta_7 T_{-2} + \beta_8 \text{BKRPT}$$
$$+ \beta_9 \text{INDEX} + \beta_{10} \text{NDEL} + \beta_{11} \text{NBUY} + \beta_{12} \log(\text{NOWN}), \tag{6}$$

where SALE is 1 if the firm sells at least one aircraft in the calendar quarter and 0 otherwise, $\Pr(\text{BR})_j$ are dummy variables indicating bankruptcy probability quintiles, calculated using Equation (2), BKRPT is 1 if the transaction occurred when the firm was operating under Chapter 11 or liquidating under Chapter 7 and 0 otherwise, INDEX is the used aircraft price index calculated from hedonic regression calendar quarter dummy variable coefficients, NDEL is the number of new aircraft delivered in the quarter, NBUY is the number of used aircraft purchased in the quarter, and NOWN is the number of aircraft owned at the beginning of the quarter.

Estimation results from Equation (6) are presented in Appendix B.

Panel B of Table 5 presents analyses of hedonic regression residuals when the inverse Mills ratio is included as a regressor. Results are very similar to those obtained when the inverse Mills ratio is excluded (Panel A), especially if firm effects are included in the model. A test of the null hypothesis that Chapters 7, 11, T_{-1}, and Bankruptcy Quintile 5 coefficients are equal still fails to reject at conventional levels. This suggests that sample selection bias is not driving the conclusion that there is little difference in the effects of Chapters 11 and 7 protection on asset-sale prices.

The third and final specification test addresses the possibility that similarities in price discounts for Chapters 7 and 11 transactions are caused by the hedonic regression methodology. Specifically, because Chapters 7 and 11 sales are dominated by Braniff and Eastern, respectively, these transactions may be causing a downward bias in hedonic prices. Therefore, even if bankruptcy transactions occur at severe discounts to true fundamental value, discounts from hedonic prices would not be detected, additionally impeding the ability to detect differences in price discounts for Chapters 7 and 11 transactions. To determine whether this concern is valid, analyses presented in Tables 4 and 5 are repeated after omitting Eastern and Braniff transactions from the hedonic regression. Results are similar to those reported in Tables 4 and 5. Even when Braniff and Eastern sales are omitted from the hedonic regression, there is little statistical evidence that discounts are different for Chapters 7 and 11 transactions.

3.5. Aircraft quality

An alternative explanation for observed effects of bankruptcy status on price is that bankrupt airlines sell aircraft of lower quality. Although the FAA enforces maintenance requirements, airlines are nevertheless able to choose which aircraft in their fleets to sell. To reduce maintenance expenses, bankrupt airlines might choose to sell aircraft that have little time remaining until the next maintenance overhaul. In this case, we would see lower transaction prices for bankrupt sellers simply because of aircraft quality differences. To control for this possibility, one would need information describing time until next airframe overhaul, number of hours on engines, and compliance with FAA airworthiness directives for each aircraft at the time of the transaction. Unfortunately, these data are generally unavailable. Aircraft maintenance records are transferred to aircraft buyers; duplicates are maintained neither by the selling airline nor the FAA. Maintenance expense is reported to the Department of Transportation on a quarterly basis, but after controlling for aircraft type and calendar quarter, maintenance expense is an insignificant predictor of price. Furthermore, bankruptcy and distress variable coefficients are not substantially affected by including maintenance expense as an independent variable.

Although quality-adjusted prices are not available for the entire sample, they are available for a small subsample of Braniff sales that occurred in April 1984 when that airline was operating under Chapter 7 protection. Braniff sold 11 727-200 ADV aircraft to People Express Airlines, which financed the $54.3 million purchase by issuing secured debt. Included in the prospectus for this secured debt issue are appraised values for each of the 11 Braniff aircraft. Appraised values, provided by Avmark, Inc., an independent aircraft appraisal firm, take variability in aircraft quality into consideration. Based on Avmark's appraisals, values for these 11 727-200 ADVs averaged $7.3 million. Braniff sold the airplanes for an average price of $4.9 million, corresponding to a 32.6% discount. This discount, which is in excess of the cost of refurbishment incurred by People Express Airlines, is close to the 24% discount implied by predicted values from Specification 4 of Panel A in Table 5. Thus, based on this small subsample of aircraft, controlling for aircraft quality variation would not significantly alter reported results.

Institutional details also help to alleviate the concern that quality differences are driving results presented in Table 5. Because FAA-approved maintenance plans are carrier specific, airlines have an incentive to sell used aircraft that are in need of scheduled overhauls. By doing so, the buyer's (rather than the seller's) maintenance procedures can be followed, thereby avoiding costly duplication of maintenance. Therefore, it is likely that even financially healthy airlines are prone to sell aircraft in need of maintenance. This reduces the likelihood that differences in observed prices are driven by differences in aircraft quality.

4. Effect of bankruptcy court protection on the rate of sales

The rate of asset sales provides further evidence that bankruptcy court protection is ineffective in helping distressed firms conduct orderly dispositions of their assets. Although firms reorganizing under Chapter 11 receive prices that are no greater than prices received by firms liquidating under Chapter 7, Chapter 11 protection may help airlines limit the number of aircraft sold at discounted prices. The number of aircraft sales in a given calendar quarter for firms operating under Chapter 11 protection is compared to the number of sales for the same firms prior to Chapter 11 filing. If Chapter 11 is effective, there should be a noticeable drop in the rate of sales after the filing date.

Table 2 shows the number of sales for each of the bankrupt airlines both during bankruptcy and in the 2 years preceding bankruptcy filing. The pattern revealed in Table 2 is that firms that eventually enter liquidation proceedings (Air Florida, Braniff, Eastern, Midway, and Pan Am) also sell a significant number of aircraft in the 2 years preceding bankruptcy. After these firms file for Chapter 11, the number of aircraft sales *increases*. However, airlines that eventually emerge from bankruptcy (America West, Continental, and TWA) sell few aircraft in the months leading up to bankruptcy and experience only a slight increase in the number of sales after bankruptcy filing. Therefore, it does not appear that Chapter 11 protection allows firms to reduce the number of aircraft sales. The data are more consistent with sample selection, whereby the sickest airlines liquidate and the healthier airlines restructure their liabilities (not their assets) in Chapter 11.

There are two potential problems with conclusions drawn from Table 2. The first is that, while Table 2 documents the total number of sales in bankruptcy, it does not document the *rate* of sales for bankrupt firms. The second problem is that there are no controls for other factors that contribute to the rate of sales. For example, larger airlines are likely to sell more aircraft per quarter, as are airlines in the process of upgrading their fleets. To control for these factors, a regression model of the number of aircraft sold in a calendar quarter is constructed.

The dependent variable in the analysis that follows is the number of aircraft sales by a particular firm in a given quarter. Because the dependent variable is a "count" variable with many observations equal to zero, I assume a Poisson model for aircraft sales. Unlike ordinary least squares (OLS), this specification is particularly well suited to modeling nonnegative integers. Another approach would be to use a probit estimation where the dependent variable takes the value of 1 if the airline sold a positive number of aircraft in the quarter and 0 otherwise. This approach suppresses information contained in the number of sales per quarter. Nevertheless, it yields results similar to those presented. A drawback of the Poisson model is its assumption that the mean and variance of the dependent variable are equal. To avoid imposing this restriction on the data, I use a negative-binomial maximum likelihood procedure pioneered by Hausman et al. (1984, p. 922, Equation (3.1)). Pulvino (1998), Appendix C, uses the same approach to analyze aircraft purchases. Following this approach, the expected number of sales by firm i during quarter t, $E(n_{it})$, equals the parameter λ_{it}, which is gamma distributed with a mean of γ_{it} and variance δ_{it}. Because the expected number of sales is nonnegative, I assume the following exponential form:

$$\gamma_{it} = e^{X_{it-1}\beta}. \tag{7}$$

X is a matrix of the following explanatory variables:

PBR_j	= dummy variables indicating bankruptcy probability quintiles per Equation (2), which only take the value of 1 if the firm is solvent and does not go bankrupt within the next 2 years,
Ch 7	= dummy variable equal to one if the firm is currently liquidating under Chapter 7,
LIQ	= dummy variable equal to one if the firm is currently operating under Chapter 11 and is eventually liquidated,
LIQ_{-1}	= dummy variable equal to one if the calendar quarter is within 1 year preceding the seller's Chapter 11 filing date and the seller is eventually liquidated,
LIQ_{-2}	= dummy variable equal to one if the calendar quarter is within 2 years, but more than 1 year, preceding the seller's Chapter 11 filing date and the seller is eventually liquidated,
NOLIQ	= dummy variable equal to one if the firm is currently bankrupt but eventually emerges from bankruptcy,
$NOLIQ_{-1}$	= dummy variable equal to one if the calendar quarter is within 1 year preceding the seller's Chapter 11 filing date and the seller eventually emerges from bankruptcy,
$NOLIQ_{-2}$	= dummy variable equal to one if the calendar quarter is within 2 years, but more than 1 year, preceding the seller's Chapter 11 filing date and the seller eventually emerges from bankruptcy,
INDEX	= used aircraft price index calculated from calendar quarter dummy variable coefficients in the narrow-body hedonic regression,
NBUY	= number of used aircraft purchased in the quarter,
NDEL	= number of new aircraft delivered in the quarter, and
log(NOWN)	= logarithm of the number of aircraft owned at the beginning of the quarter.

The effect of bankruptcy court protection on the rate of asset sales can be inferred by examining differences in the coefficients multiplying the bankruptcy variables (Ch7, LIQ, NOLIQ) and the prebankruptcy variables (LIQ_{-1}, LIQ_{-2}, $NOLIQ_{-1}$, $NOLIQ_{-2}$). For example, a finding that the NOLIQ coefficient is significantly smaller than the $NOLIQ_{-1}$ coefficient would imply that bankruptcy court protection reduces the rate of asset sales.

Control variables in the negative binomial model include INDEX, NBUY, NDEL, and NOWN. INDEX is included to control for the effect of the strength of the used aircraft market on firms' propensities to sell aircraft. NBUY and NDEL control for the possibility that airlines sell used airplanes because they have commitments to buy other planes, and NOWN controls for the possibility that firms that own more aircraft tend to sell more aircraft.

Panel A of Table 6 presents results from estimating the negative binomial model. These results are consistent with patterns observed in Table 2. Coefficients on the bankruptcy probability dummy variables indicate that the rate of asset sales is positively related to the degree of distress. Compared to firm-quarters in the lowest bankruptcy probability quintile, those in the highest quintile sell approximately twice as many aircraft per quarter ($e^{0.76} = 2.14$). For firms that are eventually liquidated, the rate of sales increases dramatically in the 2 years before the Chapter 11 filing. Further increases in the rate of sales are evident during Chapter 11. The rate of sales in Chapter 11 is seven times greater than the rate observed for financially healthy firms ($e^{2.03} = 7.61$) and is almost identical to the rate observed in Chapter 7 liquidation.

Results are much less dramatic for firms that emerge from bankruptcy. In the 2 years prior to filing for bankruptcy, the rate of sales for these firms is indistinguishable from the rate at which healthy airlines sell aircraft. After Chapter 11 filing, the rate of sales jumps to a rate that is 1.8 times greater than the rate at which the most healthy airlines sell assets, but this effect is not statistically significant at conventional levels. The bottom line is that there is no evidence that Chapter 11 protection *reduces* the rate of asset sales.

To determine whether the negative binomial results presented in Panel A are sensitive to specification, I use OLS to assess the effect of bankruptcy status on "net sales," defined to be the number of used aircraft sales per calendar quarter minus the sum of new and used aircraft purchases in the same calendar quarter. Results from the OLS analysis are presented in Panel B of Table 6. Consistent with results from the negative binomial model, Chapter 11 does not reduce the rate of aircraft sales.

5. Conclusions

This paper uses a sample of commercial aircraft transactions to assess the effects of reorganization and liquidation proceedings on revenues from asset sales. The evidence indicates that neither protection under Chapter 11 of the bankruptcy code nor court-supervised liquidation under Chapter 7 of the code is effective at eliminating

This table presents determinants of the number of aircraft transactions

The dependent variable in Panel A is the number of aircraft sold in a calendar quarter. In Panel B, the dependent variable is the number of net sales (sales minus the sum of new and used aircraft purchases) per calendar quarter. Independent variables are defined as follows: Ch 7 is a dummy variable equal to one if the firm is liquidating under Chapter 7 in the current calendar quarter; LIQ is a dummy variable equal to one if the firm is operating under Chapter 11 in the calendar quarter and is eventually liquidated; LIQ_{-1} is a dummy variable equal to one if the calendar quarter is within 1 year preceding the Chapter 11 filing date and the firm is eventually liquidated; LIQ_{-2} is a dummy variable equal to one if the firm is operating under Chapter 11 in the calendar quarter is within 2 years, but more than 1 year, preceding the Chapter 11 filing date and the firm is eventually liquidated; NOLIQ equals one if the firm is operating under Chapter 11 in the current calendar quarter but eventually emerges from bankruptcy; $NOLIQ_{-1}$ is a dummy variable equal to one if the calendar quarter is within 1 year preceding the Chapter 11 filing date and the firm eventually emerges from bankruptcy; $NOLIQ_{-2}$ is a dummy variable equal to one if the calendar quarter is within 2 years, but more than 1 year, preceding the Chapter 11 filing date and the firm eventually emerges from bankruptcy; and bankruptcy probability quintile dummies (lagged one period) correspond to predictions from the Probit regressions reported in Table 3. Index, calculated from hedonic regression calendar quarter dummy variables, measures the relative strength of the used aircraft market in the given calendar quarter. NBUY equals the number of used aircraft purchases in the quarter; NDEL equals the number of new aircraft delivered in the firm-quarter; NOWN equals the number of aircraft owned at the beginning of the quarter. Low probability of bankruptcy firm-quarters are omitted to avoid collinearity. Panel A presents maximum likelihood estimates, based on a Poisson specification with an adjustment to allow for differences in the distribution's mean and variance. The estimated variance/mean ratio equals $(1 + \delta)/\delta$. Standard errors are in parentheses.

Panel A: Maximum likelihood estimates of the determinants of the number of used aircraft sales per calendar quarter; 1021 observations

	Liquidating firms			Emerging firms			Bankruptcy probability quintile									
							5 (High probability)	4	3 (Low probability)	2				ln		
Ch 7	LIQ	LIQ_{-1}	LIQ_{-2}	NOLIQ	$NOLIQ_{-1}$	$NOLIQ_{-2}$					Index	NBUY	NDEL	(NOWN)	$\ln(\delta)$	Constant
2.18	2.03	1.74	1.12	0.58	0.09	0.09	0.76	0.54	−0.01	0.36	0.02	0.07	0.02	0.65	−0.98	−4.73
(0.38)[c]	(0.32)[c]	(0.34)[c]	(0.39)[b]	(0.42)	(0.70)	(0.59)	(0.21)[c]	(0.21)[a]	(0.25)	(0.21)	(0.07)	(0.03)[a]	(0.02)	(0.07)[c]	(0.13)[c]	(0.42)[c]

Panel B: OLS estimates of the determinant of the number of "net sales" per calendar quarter; 1021 observations

	Liquidating firms			Emerging firms			Bankruptcy probability quintile							
							5 (High probability)	4	3 (Low probability)	2		ln		
Ch 7	LIQ	LIQ_{-1}	LIQ_{-2}	NOLIQ	$NOLIQ_{-1}$	$NOLIQ_{-2}$					Index	(NOWN)	Constant	Adj. R^2
5.33	7.80	4.21	2.69	2.44	2.45	2.24	1.91 (0.37)[c]	1.62 (0.37)[c]	0.34 (0.37)	0.37	0.18	−0.64	−0.40	0.16
(1.09)[c]	(0.88)[c]	(0.82)[c]	(0.82)[c]	(0.84)[b]	(0.91)[b]	(0.90)				(0.36)	(0.14)	(0.09)[c]	(0.60)	

[a] Significant at 0.05 level.
[b] Significant at 0.01 level.
[c] Significant at 0.001 level.

distress-sale discounts. Airlines operating under supervision of the bankruptcy court sell assets at greater discounts than do distressed but nonbankrupt carriers. Furthermore, the magnitude of the discount is not significantly lower for transactions occurring in reorganization proceedings than in liquidation proceedings. Therefore, the data do not support the contention that Chapter 11 of the current bankruptcy law (rather than liquidation via Chapter 7) helps to mitigate distress-sale discounts and improve resource allocation.

Bankruptcy court protection also does not appear to affect the rate of asset sales. Distressed firms that eventually liquidate experience a high rate of asset sales prior to entering bankruptcy and an even higher rate after Chapter 11 filing. Airlines that eventually emerge from bankruptcy refrain from selling assets before filing for Chapter 11 and experience a slight increase in selling activity during bankruptcy proceedings. As far as asset sales are concerned, Chapter 11 does not appear to provide significant benefits to distressed firm's claimholders—it neither increases prices at which assets are sold nor limits the number of aircraft sold at discounted prices. Therefore, whether bankruptcy systems that encourage reorganization are superior to those that require liquidation depends on the ability of reorganization laws to allow the continuation of financially distressed firms and promote liquidation of economically distressed firms. To date, studies that have examined this question have failed to reach a consensus. Hotchkiss (1995, p. 3) concludes that the current bankruptcy code provides "... economically important biases toward continuation of unprofitable firms." The opposite conclusion is reached by Alderson and Betker (1995), who find that of 88 firms that reorganized under Chapter 11, over 80% created more wealth by continuing rather than liquidating. Additional research on the relative efficiencies of reorganization and liquidation bankruptcy venues is clearly needed.

Appendix A

The following table presents results from estimating the following hedonic regression:

$$\log(\text{PRICE}) = \beta_0 + \sum_1^I \beta_i \text{QTR}_i + \sum_1^J \beta_j \text{MODEL}_j + \sum_1^K \beta_k \text{STAGE}_k$$
$$+ \beta_{\text{AGE}} \log(1 + \text{AGE}) + \varepsilon.$$

The dependent variable is the natural logarithm of transaction price. Panel A presents results using narrow-body transactions; Panel B presents results using wide-body transactions. Dummy variables for Airbus 300B4-200 for the narrow-body regression and B-747-100 for the wide-body regression, Stage 3 engines, and the third quarter of 1991 are omitted to avoid collinearity. Standard errors are in parentheses and are corrected for heteroskedasticity using the methods of Huber (1967) and White (1980). Missing entries are due to a lack of transactions and collinearity (e.g., B-737-100 and B-707-320C are the only Stage 1 narrow-body aircraft in the sample). Significance at the 0.001, 0.01, and 0.05 levels is denoted by ***, **, and *, respectively.

	Independent variables	Panel A: narrow-body sales	Panel B: wide-body sales
Model dummies (narrow-body/ wide-body)	DC-9-10/DC-10-10	−0.40 (0.073)***	0.17 (0.071)*
	DC-9-30/DC-10-30	0.19 (0.066)**	0.38 (0.079)***
	DC-9-50/B-747-100	0.76 (0.092)***	–
	B-707-320C/B-747-200	−0.71 (0.151)***	0.49 (0.072)***
	B-727-100/L-1011-1	−0.63 (0.069)***	−0.51 (0.088)***
	B-727-100QC/L-1011-500	−0.34 (0.071)***	0.11 (0.110)
	B-727-200	−0.07 (0.081)	–
	B-727-200 ADV	0.46 (0.077)***	–
	B-737-100	–	–
	B-737-200	0.14 (0.073)*	–
	B-737-200 ADV	0.77 (0.110)***	–
	B-737-300	−0.51 (0.170)***	–
Quarter dummies	1978.1	1.34 (0.221)***	–
	1978.2	1.32 (0.205)***	0.95 (0.166)***
	1978.3	1.54 (0.247)***	1.01 (0.175)***
	1978.4	1.23 (0.199)***	0.74 (0.171)***
	1979.1	1.62 (0.230)***	–
	1979.2	1.34 (0.214)***	–
	1979.3	1.40 (0.219)***	–
	1979.4	1.52 (0.211)***	–
	1980.1	1.28 (0.200)***	–
	1980.2	1.36 (0.198)***	0.82 (0.159)***
	1980.3	1.49 (0.230)***	–
	1980.4	1.22 (0.192)***	–
	1981.1	1.05 (0.192)***	0.66 (0.170)***
	1981.2	1.16 (0.197)***	0.03 (0.210)
	1981.3	1.14 (0.202)***	0.20 (0.158)
	1981.4	1.03 (0.200)*	–
	1982.1	0.65 (0.226)**	0.57 (0.150)***
	1982.2	0.95 (0.208)***	–
	1982.3	0.92 (0.223)***	−0.15 (0.161)
	1982.4	0.75 (0.240)***	−0.12 (0.150)
	1983.1	0.88 (0.226)***	0.29 (0.148)*
	1983.2	0.98 (0.202)***	−0.19 (0.146)
	1983.3	0.57 (0.220)**	−0.08 (0.165)
	1983.4	0.73 (0.194)***	0.11 (0.164)
	1984.1	0.75 (0.191)***	−0.21 (0.147)
	1984.2	0.90 (0.193)***	0.09 (0.166)
	1984.3	0.94 (0.211)***	0.14 (0.172)
	1984.4	1.00 (0.192)***	0.30 (0.157)
	1985.1	1.11 (0.190)***	0.38 (0.147)**
	1985.2	1.04 (0.192)***	0.24 (0.146)
	1985.3	1.40 (0.193)***	0.39 (0.146)**

(Continued)

Appendix A (*Continued*)

Independent variables	Panel A: narrow-body sales	Panel B: wide-body sales
1985.4	1.31 (0.193)***	0.49 (0.164)**
1986.1	1.40 (0.206)***	0.40 (0.144)**
1986.2	1.08 (0.243)***	0.41 (0.163)*
1986.3	1.30 (0.221)***	0.41 (0.141)**
1986.4	1.20 (0.195)***	0.52 (0.150)***
1987.1	1.38 (0.191)***	0.54 (0.181)**
1987.2	1.42 (0.206)***	0.56 (0.171)***
1987.3	1.23 (0.186)***	0.43 (0.154)**
1987.4	1.34 (0.190)***	0.56 (0.157)***
1988.1	1.22 (0.236)***	0.39 (0.170)*
1988.2	1.28 (0.200)***	0.46 (0.145)**
1988.3	1.28 (0.191)***	0.37 (0.171)*
1988.4	1.17 (0.196)***	0.29 (0.170)
1989.1	1.14 (0.195)***	0.41 (0.151)**
1989.2	1.09 (0.189)***	0.39 (0.166)*
1989.3	1.20 (0.197)***	0.49 (0.170)**
1989.4	1.24 (0.185)***	0.74 (0.142)***
1990.1	0.96 (0.222)***	0.71 (0.139)***
1990.2	1.10 (0.192)***	0.55 (0.146)***
1990.3	1.03 (0.203)***	0.63 (0.163)***
1990.4	1.05 (0.214)***	0.04 (0.219)
1991.1	0.90 (0.195)***	0.30 (0.173)
1991.2	0.69 (0.214)**	0.45 (0.234)
1991.4	−0.08 (0.409)	0.17 (0.198)
$\log(AGE + 1)$	−0.16 (0.057)***	−0.33 (0.089)***
St1 Dummy	−2.16 (0.277)***	–
St2 Dummy	−1.73 (0.146)***	–
Constant	2.83 (0.247)***	3.61 (0.309)***
Number of observations	1079	254
Adjusted R^2	0.76	0.74

Appendix B: Heckman two-stage regression

The following table presents results from the first-stage probit estimation used in the Heckman two-stage sample selection correction procedure:

$$\Pr(\text{SALE} = 1) = \alpha + \sum_{j=2}^{5} \beta_j \text{PBRj} + \beta_6 T_{-1} + \beta_7 T_{-2}$$
$$+ \beta_8 \text{BKRPT} + \beta_9 \text{INDEX} + \beta_{10} \text{NDEL}$$
$$+ \beta_{11} \text{NBUY} + \beta_{12} \log(\text{NOWN}).$$

The dependent variable takes the value of 1 if the airline sold at least one airplane in the calendar quarter and 0 otherwise. PBR2, PBR3, PBR4, and PBR5 are dummy variables representing bankruptcy probability quintiles generated from Equation (2). PBR1 is omitted from the regression to avoid collinearity. T_{-1} and T_{-2} are dummy variables indicating whether the firm files for bankruptcy within the next 1 and 2 years, respectively; BKRPT takes the value of 1 if the firm is bankrupt in the quarter, 0 otherwise; INDEX uses the hedonic regression calendar quarter dummy coefficients to measure the relative strength of the used aircraft market in the calendar quarter; NDEL equals the number of new aircraft deliveries and NBUY equals the number of used aircraft purchases in the calendar quarter; and NOWN equals the number of aircraft owned at the beginning of the calendar quarter. All independent variables, except for NDEL and NBUY, are lagged one period. Predicted values from this regression are used to calculate the Inverse Mills Ratios:

$$\text{Inverse Mills Ratio} = \frac{\phi(\alpha)}{1 - \Phi(\alpha)},$$

where α is predicted value from the probit regression, ϕ is probability density function for the normal distribution, and Φ is cumulative function for the normal distribution. Standard errors are in parentheses.

Heckman first-stage probit: dependent variable equals 1 if number of sales is positive, 0 otherwise. Significance at the 0.001, 0.01, and 0.05 levels is denoted by ***, **, and *, respectively.

Independent variables	
PBR1	–
PBR2	0.33 (0.155)*
PBR3	0.01 (0.168)
PBR4	0.51 (0.156)***
PBR5	0.62 (0.155)***
T_{-1}	0.63 (0.259)*
T_{-2}	0.44 (0.262)
BKRPT	1.00 (0.227)***
INDEX	0.04 (0.057)
NDEL	0.02 (0.015)
NBUY	0.05 (0.027)
log(NOWN)	0.37*** (0.044)
Constant	−2.70 (0.283)***
Number of observations	1021
Pseudo-R^2	0.13

References

Aghion, P., O. Hart and J. Moore, 1992, "The Economics of Bankruptcy Law Reform," *Journal of Law, Economics, and Organization*, 8, 523–546.

Alderson, M. and B. Betker, 1995, "Liquidation Versus Continuation: Did Reorganized Firms Do the Right Thing?" Unpublished Working Paper, Ohio State University.

Altman, E., 1984, "A Further Empirical Investigation of the Bankruptcy Cost Question," *Journal of Finance*, 39, 1067–1089.

Altman, E., 1993, *Corporate Financial Distress and Bankruptcy*, 2nd edition, Wiley, New York.

Asquith, P., R. Gertner and D. Scharfstein, 1994, "Anatomy of Financial Distress: An Examination of Junk-Bond Issuers," *Quarterly Journal of Economics*, 109, 625–658.

Baird, D., 1986, "The Uneasy Case for Corporate Reorganizations," *Journal of Legal Studies*, 15, 127–147.

Betker, B., 1995, "Management's Incentives, Equity's Bargaining Power, and Deviations from Absolute Priority in Chapter 11 Bankruptcies," *Journal of Business*, 68, 161–183.

Bradley, M. and M. Rosenzweig, 1992, "The Untenable Case for Chapter 11," *Yale Law Journal*, 101, 1043–1095.

Brown, D., 2000, "Liquidity and Liquidation: Evidence from Real Estate Investment Trusts," *Journal of Finance*, 55, 469–485.

Chan, L. and J. Lakonishok, 1993, "Institutional Trades and Intraday Stock Price Behavior," *Journal of Financial Economics*, 33, 173–199.

Chan, L. and J. Lakonishok, 1995, "The Behavior of Stock Prices Around Institutional Trades," *The Journal of Finance*, 50, 1147–1174.

Chow, G., 1967, "Technological Change and the Demand for Computers," *American Economic Review*, 57, 1117–1130.

Franks, J. and W. Torous, 1994, "A Comparison of Financial Recontracting in Distressed Exchanges and Chapter 11 reorganizations," *Journal of Financial Economics*, 35, 349–370.

Gertner, R. and D. Scharfstein, 1991, "A Theory of Workouts and the Effects of Reorganization Law," *The Journal of Finance*, 46, 1189–1222.

Hausman, J., B. Hall and Z. Griliches, 1984, "Econometric Models for Count Data with an Application to the Patents–R&D Relationship," *Econometrica*, 52, 909–938.

Heckman, J., 1979, "Sample Selection Bias as a Specification Error," *Econometrica*, 47, 153–162.

Holthausen, R., R. Leftwich and D. Mayers, 1987, "The Effect of Large Block Transactions on Security Prices," *Journal of Financial Economics*, 19, 237–267.

Holthausen, R., R. Leftwich and D. Mayers, 1990, "Large Block Transactions, the Speed of Response, and Temporary and Permanent Stock-Price Effects," *Journal of Financial Economics*, 26, 71–95.

Hotchkiss, E., 1995, "Postbankruptcy Performance and Management Turnover," *Journal of Finance*, 50, 3–21.

Huber, P., 1967, "The Behavior of Maximum Likelihood Estimates Under Non-Standard Conditions," *Proceedings of the Fifth Berkeley Symposium on Mathematical Statistics and Probability*, 1, 221–233.

Kraus, A. and H. Stoll, 1972, "Price Impacts of Block Trading on the New York Stock Exchange," *Journal of Finance*, 27, 569–588.

Lerner, J., 1995, "Pricing and Financial Resources: An Analysis of the Disk Drive Industry, 1980-1988," *Review of Economics and Statistics*, 77, 585–598.

Mikkelson, W. and M. Partch, 1985, "Stock Price Effects and Costs of Secondary Distributions," *Journal of Financial Economics*, 14, 165–194.

Ohta, M. and Z. Griliches, 1986, "Automobile Prices and Quality: Did the Gasoline Price Increases Change Consumer Tastes in the US?" *Journal of Business and Economic Statistics*, 4, 187–198.

Pulvino, T., 1998, "Do Asset Fire-Sales Exist?: An Empirical Investigation of Commercial Aircraft Transactions," *Journal of Finance*, 53, 939–978.

Shleifer, A. and R. Vishny, 1992, "Liquidation Values and Debt Capacity: A Market Equilibrium Approach," *Journal of Finance*, 47, 1343–1366.

Strömberg, P., 1998, "Conflicts of Interest and Market Illiquidity in Bankruptcy Auctions: Theory and Tests," Unpublished Working Paper, University of Chicago.

Thorburn, K., "Cash Auction Bankruptcy: Costs 1997, Recovery Rates and Auction Premiums," Unpublished Working Paper, Stockholm School of Economics.

Warner, J., 1977, "Bankruptcy Costs: Some Evidence," *Journal of Finance*, 32, 337–347.

Weiss, L., 1990, "Bankruptcy Resolution: Direct Costs and Violation of Priority Claims," *Journal of Financial Economics*, 27, 285–314.

Weiss, L. and K. Wruck, 1998, "Information Problems, Conflicts of Interest, and Asset Stripping: Chapter 11's Failure in the Case of Eastern Airlines," *Journal of Financial Economics*, 48, 55–97.

White, H., 1980, "A Heteroskedasticity-Consistent Covariance Matrix Estimator and a Direct Test for Heteroskedasticity," *Econometrica*, 48, 817–830.

Wruck, K., 1990, "Financial Distress, Reorganization, and Organizational Efficiency," *Journal of Financial Economics*, 27, 419–444.

Chapter 9

AUTOMATIC BANKRUPTCY AUCTIONS AND FIRE-SALES*

B. ESPEN ECKBO

Tuck School of Business at Dartmouth College, Hanover, New Hampshire, USA

KARIN S. THORBURN

Tuck School of Business at Dartmouth College, Hanover, New Hampshire, USA

Contents

* We thank Viral Acharya, Ken Ayotte, Lucian Bebchuk, James Brander, Alex Stomper, Clas Whilborg, Youchang Wu, Yishay Yafeh, Valerie Ramey (the referee), and seminar participants at Dartmouth College, Helsinki School of Economics, the Norwegian School of Economics and Business Administration, the CEPR Conference on Corporate Finance and Risk Management (Norway 2007), the UBC Summer Finance Conference (Canada 2007), the Workshop on Private and Public Resolution of Financial Distress at the Vienna Institute for Advanced Studies (Austria 2007), and the Ninth Annual SNEE European Integration Conference (Sweden 2007). Part of this research was supported by a grant from the Norwegian National Research Council (Grant no. 125105/510) and Tuck's Center for Corporate Governance.

This article originally appeared in the *Journal of Financial Economics*, Vol. 89, pp. 404–422 (2008).
Corporate Takeovers, Volume 2
Edited by B. Espen Eckbo
DOI: 10.1016/B978-0-12-381982-6.00010-0

Abstract

We test for fire-sale tendencies in automatic bankruptcy auctions. We find evidence consistent with fire-sale discounts when the auction leads to piecemeal liquidation, but not when the bankrupt firm is acquired as a going concern. Neither industry-wide distress nor the industry affiliation of the buyer affect prices in going-concern sales. Bids are often structured as leveraged buyouts, which relaxes liquidity constraints and reduces bidder underinvestment incentives in the presence of debt overhang. Prices in "prepack" auctions (sales agreements negotiated prior to bankruptcy filing) are on average lower than for in-auction going-concern sales, suggesting that prepacks may help preempt excessive liquidation when the auction is expected to be illiquid. Prepack targets have a greater industry-adjusted probability of refiling for bankruptcy, indicating that liquidation preemption is a risky strategy.

Keywords

bankruptcy, auction, going-concern sale, piecemeal liquidation, fire-sale

JEL classification: G33, G34

1. Introduction

Will a bankruptcy system that automatically puts bankrupt firms up for auction produce fire-sales? While direct evidence on this issue is sparse, legal and financial scholars have expressed skepticism toward the workings of automatic bankruptcy auctions. For example, the perceived risk of auction fire-sales helped motivate the 1978 US bankruptcy reform introducing court-supervised debt renegotiations under Chapter 11. Provisions for court-supervised reorganization were also adopted in several member states of the European Union in the 1990s. Observing the reform process in Europe, Hart (2000) comments that "I'm not aware of any group—management, shareholders, creditors, or workers—who is pushing for cash auctions." The auction mechanism is unpopular in large part due to widespread—but largely untested—concerns with illiquidity and fire-sales.[1]

Since a debt renegotiation system such as Chapter 11 involves costs of its own, the comparative efficiency of automatic auctions is an empirical issue.[2] Interestingly, there is growing use of relatively low-cost, market-based mechanisms to resolve bankruptcy in the United States, indicating substantial concern with traditional Chapter 11 proceedings. These include "prepackaged" bankruptcies with a reorganization plan in place at filing (Betker, 1995; Lease et al., 1996), acquisition of distressed debt by "vulture" investors in order to make voting more efficient (Hotchkiss and Mooradian, 1997), and voluntary sales in Chapter 11 (Hotchkiss and Mooradian, 1998; Maksimovic and Phillips, 1998). Baird and Rasmussen (2003) report that more than half of all large Chapter 11 cases resolved in 2002 used the auction mechanism in one form or another, and that another quarter were prepacks.

This paper presents the first comprehensive empirical analysis of the tendency for automatic bankruptcy auctions to induce fire-sale discounts in prices and debt recovery rates. We study bankruptcies in Sweden, where filing firms are automatically turned over to a court-appointed trustee who organizes an open, cash-only auction. All targets are subject to a single uniform selling mechanism (open, first-price auction), and the bids alone determine the auction outcome (continuation sale or piecemeal liquidation). As a result, the cross-sectional variation in auction prices is determined largely by demand-side conditions, which is ideal for the identification of fire-sale discounts. Our sample of 258 bankrupt firms are all private (bankruptcies among publicly traded Swedish firms were rare over the sample period), and the average prefiling sales is

---

[1] Shleifer and Vishny (1992) formalize this concern in a model of industry illiquidity and conclude that, "We agree with Easterbrook (1990) that the policy of automatic auctions for the assets of distressed firms, without the possibility of Chapter 11 protection, is not theoretically sound." (p. 1344).

[2] The literature on Chapter 11 points to costs associated with conflicts of interests and excessive continuation resulting from managerial control over the restructuring process. For early warnings of agency problems in Chapter 11, see, for example, Baird (1986), Bebchuk (1988), Jensen (1989), Aghion, Hart, and Moore (1992), Bebchuk and Chang (1992), Bradley and Rosenzweig (1992), and Baird (1993).

about $8 million (2007 dollars). This is similar to the average sales for firms filing for Chapter 11 (Chang and Schoar, 2007).

A fire-sale discount results when the observed auction price is lower than an estimate of the assets' fundamental value (taken to represent the value in best alternative use). The literature highlights temporary demand-side conditions that may give rise to such a discount. For example, since financial distress tends to be contagious within an industry (Lang and Stulz, 1992), high-valuation industry rivals may themselves be financially constrained and unable to bid in the auction (Aghion et al., 1992; Shleifer and Vishny, 1992). Industry debt overhang may also attenuate industry rivals' incentive to invest in the bankrupt firm (Clayton and Ravid, 2002; Myers, 1977). As industry rivals are unwilling to bid, the risk increases that relatively low-valuation industry outsiders win the auction—at fire-sale prices. The chance of this happening is greater for unique or specific assets with few potential buyers (Williamson, 1988).

Several US studies present evidence on fire-sale discounts in voluntary asset sales, both in and out of Chapter 11. For example, Pulvino (1998, 1999) provides evidence of fire-sale discounts for the sale of individual aircrafts. Ramey and Shapiro (2001) and Officer (2007) study liquidity discounts associated with distressed plant closings and corporate targets outside of bankruptcy, and Acharya et al. (2007) examine recovery rates for US firms defaulting on their debt. Our empirical setting differs fundamentally from these studies in that we examine *mandatory* auctions of entire bankrupt firms.

Much is known about the workings of the Swedish auction bankruptcy system. Thorburn (2000) presents evidence that the auctions are speedy (lasting on average 2 months) and have low direct bankruptcy costs. Moreover, she finds that recovery rates are similar to those reported by Franks and Torous (1994) for a sample of Chapter 11 cases with market value data for the new debt securities. She also reports that direct bankruptcy costs are lowest for bankruptcy filings where the target has privately worked out an acquisition agreement just prior to filing. These "auction prepacks" play an important role in the empirical analysis below. Eckbo and Thorburn (2003) show substantial CEO turnover and wealth decline following bankruptcy filing, and find that firms sold as going concern typically perform at par with industry rivals. Eckbo and Thorburn (2009) find that the bankrupt firm's main creditor (always a bank) actively promotes auction liquidity by financing a bidder. The bank also has an incentive to use bid financing to engineer greater auction premiums (and therefore higher debt recovery rates), which the evidence supports.

Strömberg (2000) develops and tests a model for the decision of the previous owner to repurchase the bankrupt firm (a saleback). He finds that salebacks are more likely to occur when industry financial distress is high, and conjectures that salebacks help preempt excessive liquidation. The auction price data presented below (not available in Strömberg's analysis) directly addresses this conjecture. If the transacting parties view piecemeal liquidation as the relevant alternative to a saleback, prices will on average be lower in salebacks than in nonsaleback going-concern sales. Instead, we show that prices in these two categories of going-concern sales are indistinguishable. There is no evidence that saleback prices resemble those in piecemeal liquidations. Instead, we find significant average price discounts in *auction prepacks* relative to other going-concern sales, which is consistent with liquidation preemption.

Since severe economic decline causes firms to exit their industries at low prices (efficient liquidation), studies of fire-sale discounts face a fundamental identification problem: is a given low sales price due to temporary financial- or permanent-economic distress? Similar to Pulvino (1998), we deal with this problem by estimating a cross-sectional model for the asset's fundamental value. This value estimate accounts for the tendency for firms that are liquidated piecemeal to have significantly lower economic value than firms that are acquired as going concerns. We then compute the difference between actual and model prices, also referred to as the "price residual." A fire-sale discount is said to exist if the price residual is adversely affected by measures of industry-wide illiquidity and financial distress. Since this fire-sale test is joint with the fundamental value model, we check for robustness to alternative model specifications, including a model that allows for endogenous selection of the going concern versus piecemeal liquidation outcomes.

The main empirical results are as follows. First, there is evidence of conditional fire-sale discounts in auctions that lead to *piecemeal liquidation*. This conclusion holds for both auction prices and debt recovery rates, and it is robust to a model that allows the liquidation outcome to be endogenously specified. A 1% increase in industry distress reduces piecemeal liquidation prices by 2%. The probability of piecemeal liquidation is higher for targets with relatively tangible assets, and higher when industry-wide leverage ratios are high and the business cycle is in a downturn. Thus, industry-wide distress appears to simultaneously increase the odds of a piecemeal liquidation and reduce piecemeal liquidation prices, as predicted by the fire-sale hypothesis.

Second, price- and recovery-rate residuals in going-concern sales are unaffected by industry distress, and there is no evidence of lower prices when the buyer is an industry outsider. This important conclusion holds for salebacks as well, suggesting there is little scope for bypassing the discipline of the auction mechanism even if the buyer is the former target owner. The typical going-concern auction attracts five interested bidders and three actual bids, which appears sufficient to counter potential fire-sale tendencies.

Third, we observe that buyers in going-concern sales frequently structure the acquisition as a leveraged buyout as opposed to a merger. In a merger, the buyer finances the auction cash payment using retained earnings and the proceeds from securities issued on the acquiring firm. Thus, a merger requires internal financial slack. In a buyout, however, the target assets are placed in a new company, and the cash payment is raised by issuing securities directly on this buyout firm. The latter method is equivalent to the "project financing" method, which Myers (1977) shows will resolve the underinvestment problem caused by debt overhang. We find that bidders employ the buyout mechanism to the point where price- and recovery-rate residuals in buyouts and mergers are statistically indistinguishable and independent of industry-wide distress. This suggests that the buyout method increases liquidity and promotes auction competition in continuation sales.

Fourth, facing the prospect of fire-sale discounts in liquidations, we hypothesize that the main creditor (the bank) counters excessive liquidation by promoting a prefiling private workout (in the form of a sales proposal). As indicated above, prices in prepacks are significantly lower than prices in regular going-concern sales, which is consistent with the liquidation preemption hypothesis. Interestingly, despite the lower prepack prices, the bank's own recovery rate is no lower in prepacks than in regular going-concern auctions. It appears that the bank strategically promotes a prepack agreement when it is in its interest to do so.

Finally, we ask whether the target firms that are continued via prepacks, or are purchased by industry outsiders, are operated less efficiently than other going-concern sales. If prepacks represent attempts to avoid excessive liquidation, the target assets may be in relatively bad shape and difficult to restructure as a going concern. We find the postbankruptcy operating performance of prepack targets and targets of industry outsiders to be at par with industry rivals. However, the probability of bankruptcy refiling over the 2 years following the auction is significantly greater for prepacks, suggesting that liquidation preemption is a risky strategy.

The paper is organized as follows. Section 2 provides sample information and key auction characteristics. Section 3 presents our cross-sectional evidence on the existence of a fire-sale discount for the total sample. Section 4 focuses on potential price impacts of industry distress in auction prepacks and salebacks. Section 5 produces evidence on postbankruptcy operating performance and bankruptcy refiling rates, while Section 6 concludes the paper.

2. Auction data and characteristics

2.1. The auction bankruptcy system

A Swedish firm may enter bankruptcy if it is insolvent.[3] Upon bankruptcy filing, control of the firm is transferred to an independent, court-appointed trustee with fiduciary responsibility to creditors. The trustee's main task is to organize the sale of the firm in an open, cash-only auction. Trustees are certified and supervised by a government agency ("Tillsynsmyndigheten i Konkurs"), which reviews the trustees' compensation and ability to hold a proper arms-length auction. The filing triggers an automatic stay of debt payments and prevents repossession of collateral. The firm's employees, including the management team, run the firm until it is auctioned off.

---

[3] If the firm files the petition, insolvency is presumed and the filing approved automatically. If a creditor files, insolvency must be proven, a process that takes on average 2 months. In our sample, about 90% of the filings are debtor-initiated.

Expenses incurred while operating in bankruptcy are paid as you go, effectively granting such expenses super-priority.[4]

The bids in the auction determine whether the firm will be liquidated piecemeal or continued as a restructured going concern. As indicated above, a going-concern sale takes place by merger, where the target is fused with the operations of the acquiring firm, or through a buyout, where the target assets are placed in an empty company set up by the buyer. In either case, the target's assets are transferred to the buying company while the debt claims remain on the books of the bankrupt firm. The cash auction proceeds are distributed to creditors strictly according to absolute priority.

A prepackaged bankruptcy filing is subject to approval by secured creditors. Since the firm remains insolvent following the prepack sale—the cash proceeds from the sale are necessarily less than the face value of debt—it must file for bankruptcy. In a prepack filing, the trustee checks for conflicts of interest in the proposed asset sale. If the sale is overturned, the contract is voided and the trustee continues with the auction (where the prepack bidder may participate). In practice, prepack filings are almost never overturned (Thorburn, 2000).

The Swedish bankruptcy code also has provisions for renegotiating *unsecured* debt claims (so-called composition). A composition must offer full repayment of secured debt and priority claims (taxes, wages, etc.) and at least 25% of unsecured creditors' claims. In practice, composition is rare as the priority claims tend to be highly impaired in bankruptcy.

2.2. Sample characteristics

We start with the sample information on 263 bankruptcies compiled by Strömberg and Thorburn (1996) and Thorburn (2000). This sample originates from a population of 1159 Swedish firms with at least 20 employees that filed for bankruptcy over the period January 1988 through December 1991. We expand the original data to include firm- and auction characteristics required for our fire-sale hypotheses. Of the 263 original auctions, three are excluded because the final outcome cannot be unambiguously classified as a going-concern sale or a piecemeal liquidation, and another two auctions are dropped due to lack of target financial data. Thus, our final sample contains 258 bankruptcy auctions. Of the 258 targets, 31% are manufacturing companies, 33% are wholesale and retail companies, 14% are construction companies, 11% are in the transportation industry, and another 11% are hotels and restaurants.

Table 1 lists asset characteristics of the target firms, industry liquidity conditions, and auction outcome variables. Target asset characteristics and industry liquidity

---

[4] The trustee may raise super-priority debt to finance the firm's activities until the final sale. Since the auctions are speedy there is little demand for such financing. There is a government wage guarantee applicable to unpaid wages for up to 6 months prior to bankruptcy filing, as well as up to 6 months following filing depending on the employee's tenure with the firm. During our sample period, the maximum guarantee was approximately $55,000 per employee.

Table 1

Sample characteristics and variable definitions for automatic bankruptcy auctions

The sample contains 258 auctions from January 1988 to December 1991. "*GC*" and "*PL*" indicate going-concern sale and piecemeal liquidation, respectively. Financial information and book values are either "at filing" (from the bankruptcy case file), or "last reported" (from the most recent financial statement prior to bankruptcy filing, dated on average 16 months earlier). The target industry is defined using the four-digit SIC industry code of the target, and requires a firm to have at least 20 employees. All industry information is for the year of the bankruptcy filing.

Variable	Definition	All mean	*GC* mean	*PL* mean
N	Sample size	258	200	58
A. Target asset characteristics				
Size	Log (book value of assets), last reported[a]	2.30	2.33	2.23
Asset sales	Indicator for asset sales within 2 years prior to filing, trustee's file	0.26	0.28	0.19
Profit	Operating profitability: EBITDA/sales, last reported	−0.00	0.00	−0.02
Specific	Book value of (machinery and equipment)/(total assets), last reported	0.15	0.16	0.12
Intangible	Fraction intangible assets: (unsecured debt)/(total debt), at filing	0.61	0.62	0.58
B. Industry liquidity conditions				
Ind Profit	Median industry firm operating profitability: EBITDA/sales	0.05	0.05	0.05
Bus Cycle	Change in a quarterly, composite business cycle index[b]	−0.48	−0.33	−0.93
Ind Distress	Fraction of industry firms reporting an interest coverage ratio < -1 or file for bankruptcy the following year[c]	0.34	0.34	0.32
Ind Leverage	Median industry firm leverage: book value of debt/assets	0.78	0.78	0.80
No. of firms	Number of firms in the industry	267	268	262
C. Auction outcomes				
PL	Indicator for piecemeal liquidation of the target	0.22		
GC	Indicator for going-concern sales	0.78		
Outsider	Indicator for going-concern buyer being a target industryoutsider[d]		0.26	
Buyout	Indicator for going-concern buyer using the buyout method (vs. merger)		0.71[e]	
Prepack	Indicator for going-concern buyer agreeing to acquire target prefiling	0.21	0.27	
Saleback	Indicator for going-concern buyer being a former target owner		0.63[f]	
Recovery	Debt recovery rate: (net auction revenue)/(total face value of debt)[g]	0.35	0.37	0.26

[a]For illustration, the numbers reported in this row are in US dollars million (not the logarithm).
[b]The change is from the quarter prior to the quarter of the bankruptcy filing. The index is composed of the gross national product (+), producer price index (+), aggregate consumption (+), unemployment rate (−), and number of corporate bankruptcy filings (−). The variables are normalized with their respective mean and standard deviation before entering the index with equal weight and the sign indicated in parentheses.
[c]Interest coverage ratio = (EBITDA + interest income)/(interest expense).
[d]We define insider sales as cases where the buyer (i) has the same three-digit SIC code as the sample firm; (ii) is identified as a competitor of the sample firm; or (iii) is a former owner or employee of the bankrupt firm.
[e]The *Buyout* variable is identified for a total of 146 continuation sales, so 71% is 104/146.
[f]The *Saleback* variable is identified for a total of 193 continuation sales, so 63% is 122/193.
[g]Net auction revenue is the total proceeds from bankruptcy minus cost of the trustee's services.

conditions combine to determine bidder demand and thus the auction outcome. As discussed below, we use the asset characteristics to model the target's fundamental value, and industry characteristics largely to examine the sensitivity of auction prices to fire-sale conditions.

2.2.1. Target asset characteristics

The literature on asset sales shows that distressed firms prefer to sell off relatively tangible, less productive (noncore) assets when raising cash to stave off bankruptcy.[5] This means that, at the time of the bankruptcy filing, some targets will have a high proportion of intangible and illiquid assets. Highly specialized assets require unique managerial skills and have limited redeployment options, affecting both the fundamental value and the type of bidder that is likely to submit a continuation bid in the auction. To capture these effects, we employ five proxies for the state of the target assets, listed in Panel A of Table 1. The first is the prefiling target book value, *Size*, defined as the logarithm of the book value of the target firm's assets as reported in the last financial statement prior to bankruptcy filing.[6] The bankrupt firms, which are all privately held, are typically small with an average book value of assets of $2.3 million.[7]

Extensive prefiling asset sales and general revenue decline cause *Size* to overstate the actual size of the bankrupt firm at the time of filing. In fact, total proceeds from the bankruptcy sale average only half of the prefiling book-asset size. To capture some of the cross-sectional variation in the size reduction caused by prefiling asset sales, we include the binary variable *Asset sales*. This variable, which is constructed from information in the bankruptcy trustee's report, takes a value of one if the report indicates significant prefiling asset sales, and zero otherwise. Overall, larger firms and targets with more of its original assets intact are expected to generate higher auction prices.

We also include three proxies for the quality of the target assets. The first is the prefiling operating profitability (*Profit*) defined as earnings before interest, taxes, depreciation, and amortization (EBITDA) divided by sales, as reported in the last financial statement prior to filing. Moreover, as Strömberg (2000), we capture asset uniqueness with the variable *Specific*, defined as book value of machinery and equipment over total assets (from the last financial statement). Third, the variable *Intangible*, defined as the fraction of total debt at filing that is unsecured, is used as a proxy for asset intangibility in the absence of market value data for our private firms. We expect the three proxies for asset quality to affect auction prices as well as the probability that the target will be sold as a going concern.

---

[5] See, for example, Asquith et al. (1992), Ofek (1993), John and Ofek (1995), Kim (1998), and Maksimovic and Phillips (2001).

[6] The time from the last financial statement to the bankruptcy filing date is on average 16 months.

[7] As is common for small firms, ownership concentration is high. The average CEO owns 60% of the equity (Eckbo and Thorburn, 2003).

2.2.2. Industry liquidity conditions

Under the fire-sale hypothesis, industry liquidity affects bidder demand in the auction and hence the final auction price. Tests of the fire-sales hypothesis therefore amount to examining whether sales prices are correlated with measures of industry liquidity and distress. Our analysis uses the four-digit Standard Industrial Classification (SIC) code for the target firms' industry. Industry benchmarks are created for each target firm using financial information for the Swedish population of 16,000 firms with at least 20 employees provided by Upplysnings Centralen AB.

We use five proxies for industry conditions, listed in Panel B of Table 1. All industry information is measured in the year of the bankruptcy filing. Of the five variables, industry profitability and business cycle change are used to estimate the fundamental value of the target. Industry operating profitability, *Ind Profits*, is defined as EBITDA/ sales of the median industry firm. The variable *Bus Cycle* measures the most recent change in the quarterly value of a composite business cycle index. The index components include gross national product (entering the index with a positive sign), producer prices (+), aggregate consumption (+), unemployment rate (−), and the aggregate number of corporate bankruptcy filings (−).[8]

The remaining three proxies are used to capture effects of industry financial distress on auction demand. We measure industry distress, *Ind Distress*, as the fraction of industry firms that file for bankruptcy the following year or has an interest coverage ratio (the ratio of EBITDA and interest income to total interest expense) less than one. On average, one-third of the industry rivals are classified as financially distressed in this sense. We measure industry leverage, *Ind Leverage*, using the median firm leverage (book value of debt over total assets) in the industry. The average industry leverage ratio is high: 0.78 for the overall sample. Finally, we include the number of firms in the four-digit target industry, *No. of firms*, as an indicator of potential demand for the target assets in the auction. As shown in Table 1, the average industry consists of 267 rivals.

2.2.3. Auction outcomes

Panel C of Table 1 shows six binary variables representing different auction outcomes. These outcomes indicate the nature of the asset restructuring (going-concern sale *GC* vs. piecemeal liquidation *PL* of the target), whether the buyer is an industry outsider (*Outsider*), whether the buyer uses the buyout acquisition method (*Buyout*), whether a bidder was identified prior to filing and the filing came with a prepackaged takeover agreement (*Prepack*), and whether the buyer is a former owner of the target (*Saleback*). Finally, Panel C lists the total debt recovery rate (*Recovery*).

---

[8] This data is from Statistics Sweden. The components are normalized with their respective mean and standard deviation and enter the index with equal weight.

As shown in the top line of Table 1, of the 258 auctions, 200 targets are sold as going concerns, while 58 targets are liquidated piecemeal. The corresponding sample proportions (0.78 and 0.22) are shown in Panel C, using the indicator variables *GC* and *PL*. The variable *Prepack* shows that 27% or 53 of the 200 going-concern auctions are prepack filings.[9] The bankruptcy files contain information on prior links between the buyer and the bankrupt firm. Using this information, 63% or 122 of 193 going-concern sales are identified as salebacks to a former owner of the target firm. A total of 32 cases are both a prepack and a saleback, an interesting subsample which we examine in some detail below. The overall saleback propensity is similar across prepacks and regular bankruptcy filings.

We follow Strömberg (2000) and classify a buyer as an industry outsider if the buyer (i) is neither a former owner or employee of the target, and (ii) does not have the same three-digit SIC code as the target, and is not otherwise identified as a direct target competitor. Strömberg also classifies piecemeal liquidations as sales to outsiders. However, we restrict the outsider indicator variable to going-concern sales, because the identity of the buyer is rarely identifiable from the bankruptcy file when the auction results in piecemeal liquidation. As shown in Panel C, *Outsider* has an average value of 0.26, indicating that 26% of the going-concern sales result in sales to an industry outsider.[10] It is reasonable to expect target industry insiders to have an advantage over industry outsiders in terms of their ability to create synergy gains from the takeover.

For 146 of the 200 continuation sales, we are able to classify the acquisition method as either merger or buyout. As shown in Panel C, a majority (71%) are buyouts. Buyouts occur in 74% of nonprepack going-concern sales and in 64% of prepacks (not shown in Table 1). In the remaining cases the target firm is merged into the preexisting bidder company. Saleback transactions occur in 55% of the mergers and 66% of the buyouts.

The debt recovery rate is defined as net auction revenue divided by total face value of debt. Note that, since auction revenue is determined in an open auction and paid in cash, this recovery rate is effectively measured using market values. The recovery rate averages 37% in going-concern sales and 26% in piecemeal liquidations.

2.2.4. Bidder competition

We obtain bid information from the auction files and through direct communication with auction trustees. In addition to maintaining a record of the actual bids, the trustees keep track of parties expressing a serious interest in participating in the auction. Some of the interested bidders proceed with a formal offer, while others are deterred by competition and never move beyond the expression of interest. The existence of a pool of interested bidders is interesting as it indicates the level of potential competition in the auction.

[9] While not shown in Table 1, in prepacks the median CEO owns 100% of the equity, possibly because prepacks require a voluntary coordination among the distressed firm's claimholders.

[10] While not shown in the table, the buyer is an industry outsider in 19% or 36% of the prepacks, indicating that a prepack often involves a wide search for a buyer prior to filing.

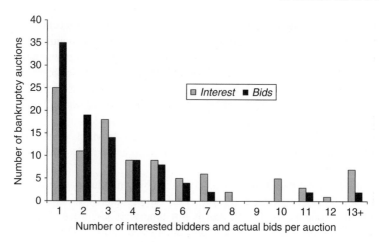

Fig. 1. Frequency distributions of the number of interested bidders and actual bids in automatic bankruptcy auctions. The average number of interested and actual bidders are 5.5 and 3.5, respectively. Sample of Swedish firms filing for bankruptcy, 1988–1991, and sold as going concerns in the bankruptcy auction (excluding auction prepacks).

We have information on bidder interest in 102 of the 147 nonprepack going-concern sales. We do not track bid frequencies in prepacks nor in piecemeal liquidations since these are largely missing. In piecemeal liquidations, the number of bidders depends arbitrarily on the number of assets sold. In auction prepacks, the bid data are incomplete since the trustee approves the firm's sales agreement after the prepack buyer has been selected. Tracking a subsample of 33 prepacks with bid data, we find direct evidence of bid competition in only five (15%) of the cases.

Figure 1 shows the frequency distribution of actual and interested bidders across the subsample of nonprepack continuation sales. The number of actual bids ranges from one to 22, with a mean of 3.5. The number of interested bidders (which includes the actual bids) ranges from 1 to 40, with an average of 5.5 (median 3.0). There are multiple actual bids in a majority (63%) of the going-concern auctions. The bid frequency reported here for automatic bankruptcy auctions is somewhat higher than the number of bids per target in US tender offers found by Betton and Eckbo (2000), and the number of bidders involved in premerger talks with targets found by Boone and Mulherin (2007). In sum, our auctions attract substantial bidder competition.

3. Do auction fire-sales exist?

3.1. The fire-sale hypothesis and two-step test approach

In this section, we test for the existence of fire-sale discounts in auction prices and debt recovery rates. As stated in the introduction, industry distress may temporarily reduce auction demand and lower auction proceeds. Severe liquidity constraints could also result in the winning bidder being a relatively inefficient industry outsider. Let P denote the total proceeds from the auction. The analysis is carried out using auction prices p in logarithmic form, so $p \equiv \ln(P)$. Total debt recovery rate is defined as $r \equiv (P - C)/D$, where C is direct bankruptcy costs and D is the face value of the target's total debt. The following hypothesis summarizes our key predictions:

H1 (*Fire-sale hypothesis*). Fire-sale discounts in auction prices and debt recovery rates increase with industry-wide financial distress, and are greater when the winning bidder is an industry outsider.

We follow Pulvino (1998) and use a two-step procedure to test the fire-sale hypothesis. The first step identifies the fundamental values (absent industry liquidity constraints) by regressing p and r on a vector X_1 of target asset quality factors as follows:

$$p = \beta'_{1p}X_1 + \varepsilon_{1p},$$
$$r = \beta'_{1r}X_1 + \varepsilon_{1r}, \tag{1}$$

where ε_{1p} and ε_{1r} are first-step error terms assumed i.i.d. with mean zero. The fundamental prices and recovery rates are defined as the predicted values $p^* \equiv \hat{\beta}_{1p}' X_1$ and $r^* \equiv \hat{\beta}_{1r}' X_1$, where the hat indicates ordinary least square (OLS) estimate. In the second step, the residuals $p - p^*$ and $r - r^*$ from the first step are standardized with the regression standard error and regressed on a vector X_2 containing proxies for fire-sale conditions:

$$p - p^* = \beta'_{2p}X_2 + \varepsilon_{2p},$$
$$r - r^* = \beta'_{2r}X_2 + \varepsilon_{2r}. \tag{2}$$

The second-step error terms ε_{2p} and ε_{2r} are assumed i.i.d. with mean zero. The vectors X_1 and X_2 are nonoverlapping (except for PL, see below). We then use the OLS parameter estimates $\hat{\beta}_{2p}$ and $\hat{\beta}_{2r}$ to test whether the fire-sale factors in X_2 drive the final auction prices and recovery rates below their estimated fundamental values.

This two-step approach allows us to use the full sample in the first regression, while the second step may be restricted to subsamples. Also, since the two-step approach fixes the estimated coefficients $\hat{\beta}_1$ from the first step in the second-step regression, it highlights the first-step as a fundamental pricing model. Moreover, it allows easy interpretation of the second-step coefficients as the marginal impact of industry liquidity conditions.

As a robustness test, we also report results for a single-equation estimation to allow a direct comparison with the two-step approach. Moreover, we implement a procedure to control for potential self-selection bias in OLS estimates given that bidders' choice between going-concern sale and piecemeal liquidation is endogenous. The results of the self-selection procedure indicate that OLS estimates are consistent, hence we report OLS estimates unless otherwise indicated.

3.2. The fundamental pricing model

Table 2 shows the results of the first-step regressions for p^* and r^* using the full sample of 258 auctions. The explanatory variables X_1 include a constant plus the following three groups of fundamental target valuation characteristics:

$$X_1 \begin{cases} \text{Target assets: } \textit{Size, Asset sales, Profit, Specific, Intangible} \\ \text{Industry conditions: } \textit{Ind Profits, Bus Cycle} \\ \text{Auction outcome: } \textit{GC,PL.} \end{cases} \qquad (3)$$

All variables are as defined in Table 1. We argue that asset specificity and intangibility affect the value of the target as a going concern, regardless of industry liquidity conditions. Moreover, the fundamental target value is hypothesized to depend on contemporaneous industry profitability and the most recent quarterly change in the business cycle index.

Twenty-two percent of our targets end up being liquidated piecemeal, and it is imperative not to confound the absence of a going-concern premium in liquidations with a fire-sale discount. The typical going-concern premium in our data is 125% measured relative to a professional estimate of the piecemeal liquidation value made public by the trustee at the beginning of the auction. Our targets have similar book-asset sizes 1 year prior to bankruptcy filing, so book-asset size is not a predictor of the piecemeal liquidation outcome.

Since piecemeal liquidation occurs only when no bidder values the target as a going concern, the ex post liquidation outcome is a proxy for the lower fundamental bidder valuations ex ante. Consistent with this view, the average realized piecemeal liquidation price exceeds the trustee's piecemeal liquidation value estimate by only 8%. Moreover, whenever an auction leads to piecemeal liquidation, we observe no going-concern bids for the target—as if the liquidation outcome is apparent to all bidders.[11] We therefore include the indicator PL in the fundamental pricing model.

The regression models in Table 2 are all statistically significant with R^2 of 0.50 for the two auction price regressions. The regressions in Panel A show that the final auction price increases in Size and falls with Asset sales, as expected. Auction prices decrease in Intangible, which suggests that bankruptcy is more costly for firms with a high proportion of intangible assets, as predicted by, for example, Williamson (1988). Auction prices are significantly lower in piecemeal liquidations.

We run separate regressions to test which variables in X_1 have coefficients that are significantly different across the outcomes PL and GC. The variable Specific is the only one to pass this test and is therefore entered with separate coefficients for the two auction outcomes.[12] The interaction variable Specific * GC has a significantly negative coefficient while Specific * PL receives a positive coefficient. There is no significant

---

[11] The reverse is not true: when the target is sold as a going concern, we sometimes observe competing bids for individual assets that lost out to the higher continuation bid.

[12] Each of the remaining variables is constrained to a single coefficient across the two auction outcomes.

Table 2

Estimation of the fundamental auction price (p^*) and auction debt recovery rate (r^*)

The cross-sectional regression models in Panels A and B are, respectively, $p = \beta_{1p}X_1 + \varepsilon_{1p}$ and $r = \beta_{1r}X_1 + \varepsilon_{1r}$, where $p \equiv \ln(P)$, P is the total proceeds from the bankruptcy proceeding, and r is the debt recovery rate ($r = (P - C)/D \in [0, 1]$, where D is the face value of the target's debt and C is the direct costs of the bankruptcy proceedings). The fundamental auction price is defined as $p^* \equiv \hat{\beta}_{1p}X_1$, and the fundamental recovery rate is $r^* \equiv \hat{\beta}_{1r}X_1$. The table shows the OLS coefficient estimates $\hat{\beta}_{1p}$ and $\hat{\beta}_{1r}$. Total sample of 258 Swedish firms filing for auction bankruptcy 1988–1991. Variable definitions for the regressors in X_1 are given in Table 1 (p-values in parentheses).

	Target asset characteristics										Industry conditions			
Constant	Size	Asset sales	Profit	Profit * GC	Profit * PL	Specific * GC	Specific * PL	Intangible	PL	Ind Profit	Bus Cycle	Adjusted R^2	F-value
A. Auction price regressions													
5.44	0.67	-0.56	-0.46			-0.86	1.77	-1.61	-1.06			0.50	37.51
(0.000)	(0.000)	(0.000)	(0.309)			(0.048)	(0.055)	(0.000)	(0.000)				(0.000)
5.56	0.66	-0.56	-0.47			-0.91	1.67	-1.64	-1.07	1.99	-0.02	0.50	29.22
(0.000)	(0.000)	(0.000)	(0.295)			(0.078)	(0.039)	(0.000)	(0.000)	(0.433)	(0.435)		(0.000)
B. Auction recovery-rate regressions													
0.73	-0.01	-0.04		0.30	-0.25	-0.09	0.28	-0.29	-0.18			0.18	8.22
(0.001)	(0.461)	(0.121)		(0.020)	(0.031)	(0.303)	(0.123)	(0.000)	(0.000)				(0.000)
0.76	-0.01	-0.04		0.25	-0.22	-0.10	0.20	-0.30	-0.18	1.03	-0.00	0.19	7.18
(0.001)	(0.275)	(0.138)		(0.058)	(0.061)	(0.218)	(0.262)	(0.000)	(0.000)	(0.040)	(0.306)		(0.000)

impact on the final auction price of the prefiling target profits, the contemporaneous industry profits, or business cycle change. Given the insignificance of the two industry conditions for the target fundamental value, we use the first regressions in Panel A as our model for the fundamental price $p*$.

Turning to the two debt recovery-rate regressions in Panel B of Table 2, the regressions have an R^2 of 0.18 and 0.19, respectively. The reduction in R^2 from Panel A is primarily driven by the positive correlation between firm size and debt face value D (larger firms have more debt). This positive relation produces a negative correlation between size and the inverse of D, which is sufficient to offset the positive correlation between price and size, thus the insignificant coefficient on size.

The recovery-rate regressions maintain the significantly negative effect of asset intangibility and piecemeal liquidation. As in Panel A, we run separate regressions to test which variables in X_1 have coefficients that are significantly different across the outcomes *PL* and *GC*. For the total recovery rate, *Profit* and *Specific* pass this test and are entered with separate coefficients for the two auction outcomes. There is now a significant impact of *Profit*, and this variable enters with a positive sign in the subsample of going-concern sales and with a negative sign in the piecemeal liquidation subsample. There is, however, no significant impact of asset specificity on the recovery rate. Finally, there is some evidence that recovery rates are greater when contemporaneous industry profitability is high, but with no impact from the business cycle change. In the remaining empirical analysis, we use the first of the two regressions in Panel B as our model for the fundamental price $r*$.[13]

3.3. Residual regression tests

Recall that the dependent variable in the second step of the analysis is the standardized regression residuals from Table 2. The second-step vector X_2 of explanatory variables contains a constant plus the following two categories of variables:

$$X_2 \begin{cases} \text{Industry liquidity: } \textit{Ind Distress, Ind Leverage, No. of firms} \\ \text{Auction outcome: } \textit{GC, PL, Outsider, Buyout.} \end{cases} \qquad (4)$$

Our primary industry liquidity variable is *Ind Distress*, which is based on bankruptcy filing frequencies and interest coverage ratios of rival firms in the target industry at the time of the auction (as defined in Table 1). Moreover, we complement this variable with *Ind Leverage* in order to further capture adverse investment incentive effects of industry-wide debt overhang.

The third indicator of industry liquidity is *No. of firms*. There are two potentially offsetting effects on auction prices of this variable. First, the greater the number of

---

[13] Our main conclusions are unaffected whether we use the first or the second regression model for $r*$. Also, inclusion of industry dummies in the regressions in Table 2 does not alter our conclusions below concerning the existence of fire-sale discounts.

firms in the target's industry, the greater the degree of potential competition in the auction, which tends to increase auction prices. On the other hand, profit margins in highly competitive industries tend to be smaller, which reduces bidder valuations. The net effect on auction prices is an empirical issue.

3.3.1. Going-concern sale versus piecemeal liquidation

Table 3 shows the results of the second-step residual regressions for the full sample of 258 auctions. Although the overall explanatory power of the regressions is low, there are several interesting results. First, the regressions yield statistically insignificant coefficients for the industry distress variables *Ind Distress* and *Ind Leverage* in the overall sample (first regressions in Panels A and B). The number of firms in the target industry receives a negative coefficient that is significant at the 6% level. Thus, targets in larger industries tend to be associated with lower auction prices, possibly because profit margins and asset values in highly competitive industries are relatively small.

Second, as in step 1 above, we run separate regressions to test which variables in X_2 have coefficients that are significantly different across the auction outcomes *PL* and *GC*. *Ind Distress* is the only variable to pass this test and is therefore entered with separate coefficients for the two outcomes (*Distress * GC* and *Distress * PL*).[14] Importantly, there is no evidence of a negative effect of *Ind Distress* in the subsample of going-concern sales, whether we use auction price residuals or recovery-rate residuals as dependent variable.

Third, there is a statistically significant and negative interaction effect between industry distress and piecemeal liquidations. The coefficient on *Distress * PL* is approximately -1.9 in the auction price regressions of Panel A, and -1.7 in the recovery-rate regressions of Panel B. The p-values for this coefficient are approximately 0.03 in Panel A and 0.05 in Panel B. In each regression, the coefficient on *Distress * PL* is also significantly different from the coefficient on *Distress * GC*. The negative and significant interaction effect between *Distress* and piecemeal liquidation persists throughout the remaining tables with price and recovery regression specifications.

Fourth, the binary variable for the buyer being an industry outsider is not significant. If the outside buyer is less efficient than an industry insider (as presumed in the model of Shleifer and Vishny, 1992) the outsider may attempt to counter this inefficiency by rehiring a high-quality CEO. This happens rarely in our sample, however. Of the 39 cases where the buyer is an industry outsider and the new CEO could be identified, only four (10%) rehire the old CEO.[15] The absence of fire-sale discounts in outsider

---

[14] We include the dummy *PL* to allow the two interaction effects *Distress * GC* and *Distress * PL* to have different intercept terms. As shown in the table, *PL* is insignificant here.

[15] In contrast, the old CEO is rehired in 82 (62%) of 133 insider sales where CEO retention could be identified.

Table 3

Determinants of auction price residuals $(p - p^*)$ and recovery-rate residuals $(r - r^*)$

Coefficient estimates from OLS regressions of the standardized auction price residuals $p - p^*$ (Panel A) and total debt recovery-rate residuals (Panel B). The standardized residuals are from the first regression models in Panels A and B of Table 2, respectively. The explanatory variables are defined in Table 1 (p-values are in parentheses).

		Industry liquidity conditions				Auction outcomes					
Constant	Ind Distress	Distress * GC	Distress * PL	Ind Leverage	No. of firms	PL	Outsider	Buyout	Adjusted R^2	F-value	N
A. Auction price residual $(p - p^*)$											
1.07	−0.50			−0.95	−0.57				0.01	1.52	258
(0.103)	(0.286)			(0.273)	(0.067)					(0.196)	
0.88		−0.04	−1.88	−0.91	−0.59	0.60			0.02	1.92	258
(0.181)		(0.946)	(0.033)	(0.294)	(0.055)	(0.091)				(0.092)	
0.88		−0.07	−1.88	−0.86	−0.59	0.57	−0.10		0.01	1.66	258
(0.181)		(0.895)	(0.033)	(0.319)	(0.056)	(0.118)	(0.541)			(0.132)	
0.56		0.12	−2.03	−0.29	−0.69	0.50	−0.11	−0.12	0.02	1.51	204
(0.454)		(0.854)	(0.020)	(0.756)	(0.051)	(0.211)	(0.558)	(0.489)		(0.167)	
B. Auction recovery-rate residual $(r - r^*)$											
0.97	−0.67			−0.88	−0.21				0.00	1.11	258
(0.138)	(0.158)			(0.312)	(0.495)					(0.350)	
0.83		−0.32	−1.70	−0.84	−0.23	0.45			0.00	1.28	258
(0.209)		(0.554)	(0.054)	(0.331)	(0.456)	(0.207)				(0.272)	
0.83		−0.35	−1.71	−0.81	−0.23	0.42	−0.08		0.00	1.11	258
(0.209)		(0.520)	(0.053)	(0.355)	(0.461)	(0.247)	(0.599)			(0.355)	
0.31		−0.01	−1.76	−0.40	−0.18	0.63	−0.10	0.10	−0.01	0.69	204
(0.704)		(0.985)	(0.060)	(0.694)	(0.631)	(0.149)	(0.631)	(0.583)		(0.677)	

purchases, combined with the outsiders' decision not to rehire the old CEO, challenges the notion that industry outsiders are less efficient buyers than industry insiders.

The insignificance of the buyer's industry affiliation for auction prices contradicts a conclusion of Strömberg (2000) that sales to outsiders tend to have lower prices than sales to insiders (and which he labels a fire-sale cost). However, while we are comparing prices paid by industry insiders and outsiders in going-concern sales, Strömberg's comparison mixes continuation sales and piecemeal liquidations. In his analysis, sales to insiders are exclusively going-concern sales (40 cases), while sales to outsiders are primarily piecemeal liquidations (60 of 86 cases). The lack of a going-concern premium in piecemeal liquidations produces greater average prices in his group of insider sales regardless of any liquidity constraints and fire-sale discounts. Table 3 shows that there is no price impact of the industry affiliation of the buyer for continuation sales.

Fifth, average price residuals when the acquisition method is a buyout are indistin-guishable from price residuals in mergers. As discussed above, buyouts allow otherwise liquidity-constrained buyers to finance the cash bid externally. Moreover, the buyout method overcomes the underinvestment incentive resulting from debt overhang emphasized by Myers (1977). Absent liquidity constraints, or if the buyout method is available to all bidders, competition between buyers is expected to drive prices to the point where there is no impact of the acquisition method on final auction prices, which is what we observe in Table 3. Combined with the finding that bidders use the buyout method in the majority of the going-concern sales, we conclude that the buyout mechanism is important for promoting auction liquidity.

We next test whether there is a differential price effect of distress in the subsamples of continuation sales to industry insiders and outsiders, respectively.

3.3.2. Industry affiliation of buyer

The first two regressions in Panels A and B of Table 4 explore effects of buyer industry affiliation. This is done by creating the interaction variables *Distress * Outsider* and *Distress * Insider*. *Insider* is defined as the complement to *Outsider* in continuation sales, so that *Outsider + Insider + PL = 1*. Table 4 displays the results of estimating the following system of two equations (shown here only with the variables interacting with industry distress):

$$
p - p^* = \begin{cases} {}_1\beta_2 \ Distress^* \ Outsider +_1 \beta_3 \ Distress^* \ Insider \\ +_1\beta_4 \ Distress^* \ PL + \cdots \\ {}_2\beta_1 \ Distress +_2 \beta_3 \ Distress^* \ Insider \\ +_2\beta_4 \ Distress^* PL + \cdots . \end{cases} \tag{5}
$$

The first equation tests whether the industry distress coefficients are individually different from zero for the three subsamples *Outsider*, *Insider*, and *PL*. The second equation provides a direct test of whether the coefficients are also different from each

Table 4

Tests for the impact of industry distress on price and recovery-rate residuals conditional on buyer industry affiliation

The dependent variable in Panel A is the standardized auction price residuals $p - p^*$ from the first regression in Panel A of Table 2. In Panel B, the dependent variable is the standardized recovery-rate residuals $r - r^*$ from the first regression model in Panel B of Table 2. Insider is the complement to Outsider in continuation sales, so that $Outsider + Insider + PL = 1$. All other variables are defined in Table 1 (p-values in parentheses).

Constant	Ind Distress	Distress * Outsider	Distress * Insider	Distress * PL	Ind Leverage	No. of firms	Outsider	PL	Adjusted R^2	F-value	N
					Industry liquidity conditions		Auction outcomes				
A. Tests for the impact on the auction price residual ($p - p^*$)											
1.15	1.17	−0.54		−1.84	−1.01	−0.56	−0.66	0.39	0.02	1.76	258
(0.092)	(0.231)	(0.381)		(0.036)	(0.249)	(0.071)	(0.102)	(0.301)		(0.096)	
1.15	1.17		−1.72	−3.02	−1.01	−0.56	−0.66	0.39	0.02	1.76	258
(0.092)	(0.231)		(0.129)	(0.018)	(0.249)	(0.071)	(0.102)	(0.301)		(0.096)	
B. Tests for the impact on the recovery-rate residual ($r - r^*$)											
0.95	0.22	−0.56		−1.69	−0.87	−0.21	−0.34	0.34	0.00	1.02	258
(0.165)	(0.826)	(0.369)		(0.056)	(0.321)	(0.491)	(0.403)	(0.372)		(0.418)	
0.95	0.22		−0.78	−1.91	−0.87	−0.21	−0.34	0.34	0.00	1.02	258
(0.165)	(0.826)		(0.493)	(0.137)	(0.321)	(0.491)	(0.403)	(0.372)		(0.418)	

other. Specifically, $_2\beta_3 \neq 0$ implies that $_1\beta_3 \neq {}_1\beta_2$, and $_2\beta_4 \neq 0$ indicates that $_1\beta_4 \neq {}_1\beta_2$.[16]

The regression results in Panel A show that the coefficients $_1\beta_2$ and $_1\beta_3$ are both statistically insignificant, indicating that prices in sales to outsiders and insiders, respectively, do not depend on industry distress. The coefficient $_1\beta_4$ for *Distress* * *PL* remains negative and significant (as in Table 3), and significantly different from the distress coefficient $_1\beta_2$ conditional on an outsider sale. The conclusion is similar when using the recovery-rate residual as dependent variable (Panel B). Auction prices in going-concern sales are unaffected by industry distress, also when allowing for different effects across buyer industry affiliation.[17]

In sum, the fire-sale hypothesis H1 is rejected for auctions leading to sale of the target as a going concern, a conclusion that contradicts Strömberg (2000). There is, however, evidence of conditional fire-sale discounts in auctions that lead to piecemeal liquidations. Controlling for the lower average fundamental value in a liquidation, price and recovery residuals in piecemeal liquidations are shown to interact negatively with industry-wide distress: a 1% increase in *Ind Distress* is associated with a 2% decrease in piecemeal liquidation prices. Conditional on our fundamental pricing model being correct, this is evidence of a fire-sale discount. Overall, our finding of fire-sale discounts in piecemeal liquidations is comparable to conclusions in the extant literature on distressed asset sales (Pulvino, 1998, 1999; Ramey and Shapiro, 2001).

3.4. The probability of a going-concern sale

The previous analysis indicates a significant price impact of industry distress only when the auction leads to piecemeal liquidation of the bankrupt firm. In Table 5, we examine determinants of the probability that the target is purchased as a going concern versus liquidated piecemeal. The explanatory variables Z in the model are the target asset characteristics and industry liquidity conditions observable at the beginning of the auction. Panel A shows binomial logit estimates, where the choice is between going-concern sale ($N = 200$) and piecemeal liquidation ($N = 58$). Panels B and C provide trinomial estimates, where the choice is between two types of going-concern transactions as well as piecemeal liquidation.

---

[16] To see why, note that the second equation can be rewritten as

$$p - p^* = {}_2\beta_1 \; Distress(Outsider + Insider + PL)$$
$$+ {}_2\beta_3 \; Distress^* \; Insider + {}_2\beta_4 \; Distress^* \; PL + \cdots .$$

Comparing these coefficients with the coefficients of the first equation, it follows that $_2\beta_1 = {}_1\beta_2$, $_2\beta_3 + {}_2\beta_1 = {}_1\beta_3$ and $_2\beta_4 + {}_2\beta_1 = {}_1\beta_4$.

[17] When performing tests analogous to those in Table 4 for the acquisition method, the coefficients on *Distress* * *Buyout* and *Distress* * *Merger* are also insignificantly different from zero.

Table 5

Determinants of the probabilities of the going concern (GC) and piecemeal liquidation (PL) outcomes

Panel A of the table reports the coefficients estimates γ in binomial logit regressions with explanatory variables Z for the probability π of a GC (vs. PL). In Panels B and C the GC outcome is split in two parts, industry Outsider or Insider in Panel B, and Buyout or Merger in Panel C. These two Panels report the partial derivatives $\partial\pi_n/\partial z_k = \pi_n\left(\gamma_{nk} - \sum_{m=1}^3 \gamma_{mk}\pi_m\right)$, where γ_{nk} is the parameter for explanatory variable k in the vector γ_n determining probability π_n. The characteristics vector Z is the same across Panels. Sample of firms auctioned in Swedish bankruptcy, 1988–1991. Variable definitions are in Table 1 (p-values in parentheses).

Dependent variable	Constant	Target asset characteristics				Industry liquidity conditions				Probability at mean vector	N
		Size	Profit	Specific	Intangible	Bus Cycle	Ind Distress	Ind Leverage	No. of firms		
A. Binomial parameter estimates (γ) for the probability π of GC versus PL											
	-0.15	0.20	0.76	1.99	1.31	0.11	1.99	-4.45	0.32		258
	(0.966)	(0.229)	(0.468)	(0.087)	(0.052)	(0.070)	(0.104)	(0.054)	(0.676)		(200 GC + 58 PL)
$N = 258$, Log likelihood $= 260.3$, $\chi^2 = 14.69$, df $= 8$ ($p = 0.065$)											
B. Derivatives $\partial\pi/\partial Z$ for the probabilities of GC-Outsider, GC-Insider, and PL											
GC-Outsider	-0.02	-0.01	-0.13	-0.01	-0.07	-0.01	-0.23	0.30	0.05	0.210	53
	(0.971)	(0.605)	(0.470)	(0.947)	(0.548)	(0.487)	(0.246)	(0.442)	(0.682)		
GC-Insider	-0.11	0.05	0.28	0.34	0.29	0.03	0.58	-1.06	-0.00	0.578	147
	(0.884)	(0.166)	(0.254)	(0.106)	(0.038)	(0.036)	(0.023)	(0.027)	(0.990)		
PL	0.13	-0.03	-0.15	-0.33	-0.23	-0.02	-0.34	0.76	-0.05	0.212	58
	(0.827)	(0.220)	(0.388)	(0.082)	(0.043)	(0.059)	(0.091)	(0.046)	(0.694)		
$N = 258$, Log likelihood $= -242.2$, $\chi^2 = 21.85$, df $= 16$ ($p = 0.148$)											
C. Derivatives $\partial\pi/\partial Z$ for the probabilities of GC-Buyout, GC-Merger, and PL											
GC-Buyout	-1.49	0.10	0.21	0.58	0.35	0.03	0.36	-0.62	0.37	0.516	104
	(0.085)	(0.015)	(0.454)	(0.017)	(0.049)	(0.018)	(0.227)	(0.251)	(0.052)		
GC-Merger	0.54	-0.03	-0.05	-0.17	0.01	-0.01	0.11	-0.10	-0.17	0.212	42
	(0.415)	(0.282)	(0.804)	(0.384)	(0.921)	(0.431)	(0.647)	(0.806)	(0.267)		
PL	0.94	-0.07	-0.16	-0.41	-0.36	-0.02	-0.47	0.72	-0.20	0.272	58
	(0.200)	(0.050)	(0.477)	(0.072)	(0.016)	(0.047)	(0.069)	(0.120)	(0.235)		
$N = 204$, Log likelihood $= -195.5$, $\chi^2 = 27.78$, df $= 16$ ($p = 0.034$)											

Let π_n denote the probability of outcome n. With three outcomes, the multinomial logit model is

$$\pi_n = \frac{\exp(\gamma_n'Z)}{\sum_{m=1}^{3}\exp(\gamma_m'Z)}, \tag{6}$$

where γ_n is the vector of coefficients to be estimated for auction outcome n. We are primarily concerned with the derivative of the probability of outcome n with respect to characteristic k in the vector Z, $\partial \pi_n / \partial z_k$. With two outcomes only (binomial estimation), $\pi_1 = 1 - \pi_2$ and this partial is simply given by the coefficient estimate γ_k in the vector γ. In the multinomial case, however, a change in z_k changes all probabilities simultaneously, so that

$$\frac{\partial \pi_n}{\partial z_k} = \pi_n \left(\gamma_{nk} - \sum_{m=1}^{3} \gamma_{mk} \pi_m \right), \tag{7}$$

where γ_{nk} is the parameter for explanatory variable k in the vector γ_n.

Panel A provides the coefficient estimates γ and their p-values. The likelihood ratio test statistic (LRT) indicates that the regression model is significant at the 6.5% level. None of the individual coefficients are significant at the 5% level, while four coefficients are significant at the 10% level. These four coefficients are for the variables *Specific*, *Intangible*, *Bus Cycle*, and *Ind Leverage*. The probability of a going-concern sale is hence greater the more specific and intangible the target assets. This makes intuitive sense as firm-specific rents tend to be greater for such asset characteristics and a piecemeal liquidation eradicates going-concern rents. Thus, bidders are more likely to submit continuation bids when the loss in value from a piecemeal liquidation is relatively high. Moreover, the probability of the auction resulting in a going-concern sale increases with the recent uptick in the business cycle.

Interestingly, while the industry distress variable played an important role in the above price-residual regressions for piecemeal liquidation, this variable does not affect the decision to liquidate. The coefficient on *Ind Distress* is 1.99 with a p-value of only 0.10. Piecemeal liquidation is, however, significantly more likely when industry leverage is high. The coefficient on *Ind Leverage* is -4.45 with a p-value of 0.05. Industry distress and industry leverage are, of course, correlated: the Pearson correlation coefficient between these two variables is a significant 0.29. Thus, according to Panel A, the odds in favor of continuing the target as a going concern (relative to piecemeal liquidation) are lower when the auction takes place during industry-wide distress. Together with the earlier price-residual results, the evidence indicates that industry-wide distress simultaneously increases the odds of a piecemeal liquidation and reduces piecemeal liquidation prices. It is possible that industry-wide economic (not just financial) distress accelerates industry exit and lowers liquidation sales prices.

In the model framework of Shleifer and Vishny (1992), fire-sale prices are the result of relatively inefficient industry outsiders winning the auction for the target. We have already shown that auction prices in going-concern sales are statistically independent of the industry association of the buyer. Panel B of Table 5 further shows that the probability that an industry outsider wins the target in a going-concern bid ($N = 53$) is unaffected by the distress variables *Ind Distress* and *Ind Leverage*). In contrast, several of the coefficients for the buyer being an industry insider ($N = 147$) are significant: buyers are more likely to be an insider when the target assets are relatively intangible, and in periods of business cycle upturns. In terms of industry distress, however, the evidence is mixed. The probability that the buyer is an insider is increasing in *Ind Distress* and falling in *Ind Leverage*. While the net impact of industry distress is ambiguous, it does appear that industry insiders are willing to bid during industry distress provided that there has also been a recent uptick in the business cycle.[18]

Finally, Panel C separates going-concern sales via merger ($N = 42$) versus buyout ($N = 104$). This regression is statistically significant with a p-value of 0.03. Buyers are more likely to select the buyout method the greater the target asset size, the more specific and intangible the target assets, and during a business cycle increase. The choice of the buyout mechanism is, however, statistically unrelated to industry distress variables. *Ind Distress* is a predictor of the piecemeal liquidation outcome (p-value of 0.07) but not of the acquisition method in going-concern sales.

3.5. Robustness tests

Recall that the two-step approach fixes the estimated coefficients $\hat{\beta}_1$ on the fundamental asset quality variables in X_1 in the second-step regression. As a result, the estimated coefficients $\hat{\beta}_2$ on the fire-sales variables in X_2 measure the marginal impact of industry illiquidity on auction prices and recovery rates. To examine the impact on $\hat{\beta}_2$ of relaxing this constraint, we estimate the following single-step regression:

$$
\begin{aligned}
p &= \beta'_{1p}X_1 + \beta'_{2p}X_2 + \varepsilon_p, \\
r &= \beta'_{1r}X_1 + \beta'_{2r}X_2 + \varepsilon_r,
\end{aligned}
\tag{8}
$$

where the error terms are again assumed i.i.d. with mean zero, and the coefficients are estimated using OLS. The explanatory variables are the fundamental asset characteristics X_1 from Table 2, and the industry liquidity conditions X_2 from Table 3 (without the piecemeal liquidation indicator PL in X_2). The coefficient estimates for the auction price (p) are shown in the first row of Panel A in Table 6, while the estimates for the recovery rate (r) are in the first row of Panel B. The key result, that auction prices are affected by industry distress in piecemeal liquidations but not in going-concern sales, is robust to this single-equation specification.

---

[18] The results of Panel B should be interpreted with caution, however, as the regression χ^2 statistic has a p-value of only 0.15.

Table 6

Tests for fire-sale discounts in auction prices and debt recovery rates with correction for self-selection of the auction outcome

The right-hand side variables in this table combine the fundamental asset characteristics from Table 2 and the industry liquidity conditions from Table 3 in a single regression. In Panel A the dependent variable is the logarithm of the auction price (p), while in Panel B it is the debt recovery rate (r). The first regression in both Panels shows coefficient estimates using OLS. The second regression is estimated using WLS, and it includes the term λ correcting for self-selection of the auction outcome, where $\lambda = \phi/\Phi$ if the auction outcome is a going-concern sale and $\lambda = -\phi/(1-\Phi)$ if piecemeal liquidation. ϕ and Φ are the standard normal density and cumulative distribution functions, respectively, evaluated at $\hat{\gamma}'Z$. $\hat{\gamma}'Z$ is the predicted value from a probit regression for the probability of going-concern sale (vs. piecemeal liquidation), where the explanatory variables Z are the same as in Panel A of Table 5. Total sample of 258 Swedish firms filing for auction bankruptcy 1988–1991. Variable definitions for the explanatory variables are in Table 1 (p-values in parentheses).

A. Dependent variable: logarithm of auction price (p)

				Fundamental price characteristics						Industry liquidity conditions					
Constant	Size	Asset sales	Profit	Specific * GC	Specific * PL	Intangible	Ind Profits	Bus Cycle	Distress * GC	Distress * PL	Ind Leverage	No. of firms	λ	Adjusted R^2	F-value
6.90	0.66	−0.61	−0.33	−0.82	1.67	−1.53	−0.41	−1.88	−0.02	−0.16	−2.11	−1.25	−0.64	0.51	21.4
(0.000)	(0.000)	(0.000)	(0.466)	(0.076)	(0.079)	(0.000)	(0.301)	(0.540)	(0.392)	(0.792)	(0.024)	(0.221)	(0.049)		(0.000)
6.38	0.69	−0.60	−0.14	−0.50	2.25	−1.27	0.72	−1.96	0.22	−1.63	−2.12	−0.55	0.70	0.51	21.3
(0.000)	(0.000)	(0.000)	(0.766)	(0.360)	(0.042)	(0.001)	(0.521)	(0.525)	(0.744)	(0.102)	(0.116)	(0.096)	(0.294)		(0.000)

B. Dependent variable: debt recovery rate (r)

Constant	Size	Asset sales	Profit * GC	Profit * PL	Specific * GC	Specific * PL	Intangible PL	Ind Profit	Bus Cycle	Distress * GC	Distress * PL	Ind Leverage	No. of firms	λ	Adjusted R^2	F-value
0.87	−0.01	−0.05	0.25	−0.19	−0.08	0.19	−0.29	−0.08	0.60	−0.01	−0.05	−0.34	−0.09	0.06	0.19	5.41
(0.003)	(0.292)	(0.096)	(0.055)	(0.117)	(0.349)	(0.301)	(0.000)	(0.299)	(0.320)	(0.232)	(0.637)	(0.065)	(0.638)	(0.623)		(0.000)
0.69	−0.00	−0.05	0.29	−0.12	0.00	0.34	−0.22	0.24	0.70	0.06	−0.19	−0.33	−0.01	0.20	0.20	5.68
(0.021)	(0.837)	(0.096)	(0.034)	(0.306)	(0.972)	(0.102)	(0.002)	(0.261)	(0.255)	(0.654)	(0.303)	(0.213)	(0.907)	(0.120)		(0.000)

Next, recall from Table 5 that bidders use target asset characteristics such as *Specific* and *Intangible* (in addition to various unobservable characteristics) in the selection of a going-concern sale over piecemeal liquidation. Moreover, the explanatory variable X_1 in our fundamental pricing model includes the indicator *PL* for the auction outcome, which is endogenous. This raises the possibility that the OLS estimation of the pricing model yields biased coefficients due to self-selection (Heckman, 1979; Li and Prabhala, 2007; Maddala, 1983).

To deal with this issue, let $\gamma'Z$ be the bidder's choice model, where a going-concern bid (gc) is selected over a piecemeal liquidation (pl) if $\gamma'Z \geq \eta$, and where η is a mean zero error term with $Var(\eta) = 1$. The bidder switches between two pricing regressions:

$$
\begin{aligned}
p_{gc} &= \beta'X + \varepsilon_{gc} \text{ iff } \gamma'Z \geq \eta, \\
p_{pl} &= \beta'X + \varepsilon_{pl} \text{ iff } \gamma'Z < \eta,
\end{aligned}
\tag{9}
$$

where $X = X_1 + X_2$ and η is correlated with ε_{gc} and ε_{pl}. Due to this correlation, $E(\varepsilon_{gc}|\eta \leq \gamma'Z) \neq 0$ and $E(\varepsilon_{pl}|\eta > \gamma'Z) \neq 0$.

The standard procedure to yield unbiased estimates is to include the inverse Mills ratio based on the choice model $\gamma'Z$ as an additional explanatory variable in the pricing model regression. We use as our selection model the variables Z as listed in Panel A of Table 5, and where the coefficients γ are estimated using probit. Define the inverse Mills ratio λ such that $\lambda = \phi/\Phi$ if the auction outcome is a going-concern sale and $\lambda = -\phi/(1 - \Phi)$ if piecemeal liquidation, where ϕ ($\gamma'Z$) and $\Phi(\gamma'Z)$ are the standard normal density and cumulative distribution functions, respectively, evaluated at the predicted value $\hat{\gamma}'Z$. If the coefficient on λ is statistically significant, OLS-estimations are biased.

The regression results are shown in the second row of both Panels A and B in Table 6. These two regressions are estimated using weighted least squares (WLS) to correct for heteroskedasticity, and include the correction term λ for self-selection. The WLS estimate for λ is statistically insignificant in both regressions. This means that correcting for self-selection of the auction outcome is not required and that the OLS estimates are unbiased with respect to the going-concern choice. Thus, we maintain our earlier conclusions of a conditional fire-sale effect in piecemeal liquidations but not in going-concern sales.

4. Auction prepacks and liquidation preemption

In theory, pervasive bidder illiquidity may eliminate the prospect of any going-concern bids in the auction, and cause excessive or inefficient liquidation of financially distressed but economically viable firms. As mentioned in the introduction, a major motivation behind the introduction of Chapter 11 was to reduce the risk of this happening relative to an auction-based system. Direct tests for the presence of excessive liquidation are difficult if not impossible to design. Below, we examine this issue from the opposite angle: is there evidence that key parties to the bankrupt firm work to *preempt* excessive liquidation?

The idea pursued below is that auction prepacks anticipate and therefore preempt some liquidations. Prepacks are private workouts prior to filing, so they naturally respond to anticipations of excessive liquidation. Prepacks are also important in the auction system, as they constitute approximately one-quarter of our continuation sales. We first propose and test a price implication of the liquidation preemption hypothesis. We then present measures of postbankruptcy performance in prepacks versus other going-concern sales as further evidence on the likelihood of liquidation preemption.

4.1. The liquidation preemption hypothesis

If market conditions create expectations of excessive liquidation in the bankruptcy auction, the bank lender may take action to prevent it. Once the firm has filed for bankruptcy, the auction eliminates the bank's bargaining power, and severe auction illiquidity may produce a price close to or at the piecemeal liquidation value. Anticipating this, it may be in the bank's best interest to initiate a voluntary workout involving sale of the target firm's operations followed by a prepackaged bankruptcy filing. Our predictions for auction prepacks are as follows:

H2 (*Liquidation preemption hypothesis*). A creditor anticipating inefficient liquidation due to auction illiquidity has an incentive to work out a continuation sale prior to bankruptcy filing—an auction prepack. Auction prepacks designed to preempt liquidation have prices that are higher than the piecemeal liquidation value but lower than prices in regular going-concern auctions. Prepacks are more likely to occur the more specific and intangible the target assets.

Under H2, the prepack prevents a loss of the firm's going-concern value implied by inefficient piecemeal liquidation. Because some going-concern value is retained, the buyer accepts paying a price exceeding the expected piecemeal liquidation value in the auction. Moreover, because a prepack tends to occur in response to the threat of liquidation, the bidder's bargaining power is greater than normal, so average prepack prices are lower than in regular auction going-concern sales. As to the second part of H2, target asset specificity and intangibility generate rents that will be dissipated in a piecemeal liquidation. Given a high risk of liquidation and the greater the expected loss of rents, the more likely we are to observe a prepack. We next turn to empirical tests of these predictions.

4.2. Price and recovery residuals in prepacks

Table 7 shows coefficient estimates in price- and recovery-residual regressions for auction prepacks and salebacks. We single out salebacks along with prepacks because liquidation destroys private benefits of control, which in turn may prompt target insiders to support liquidation preemption (Strömberg, 2000). Notice first that the

Table 7

Determinants of auction price residuals (p − p*) and debt recovery residuals (r − r*) in prepacks and salebacks

The standardized residuals p − p* and r − r* are from the first regression models in Panels A and B, respectively, reported in Table 2. The explanatory variables are defined in Table 1 (p-values are in parentheses).

	Industry liquidity conditions						Auction outcomes					
	Distress * GC	Distress * PL	Ind Leverage	No. of firms	PL	Prepack Saleback	Prepack * Saleback	Prepack * Nonsale	Nonprepack * Saleback	Adjusted R²	F-value	N
Constant												
A. Auction price residual (p − p*)												
0.90	−0.09	−1.89	−0.74	−0.56	0.45	−0.52				0.06	3.55	258
(0.164)	(0.858)	(0.028)	(0.383)	(0.062)	(0.202)	(0.001)					(0.002)	
1.06	−0.14	−1.89	−0.77	−0.57	0.31	−0.56	−0.17			0.06	3.37	251
(0.112)	(0.794)	(0.030)	(0.375)	(0.066)	(0.392)	(0.001)	(0.232)				(0.002)	
1.06	−0.14	−1.89	−0.77	−0.57	0.31		−0.73	−0.56	−0.17	0.06	2.94	251
(0.113)	(0.795)	(0.030)	(0.377)	(0.066)	(0.401)		(0.001)	(0.041)	(0.296)		(0.004)	
B. Total recovery-rate residual (r − r*)												
0.83	−0.33	−1.71	−0.80	−0.22	0.41	−0.12				0.00	1.17	258
(0.207)	(0.537)	(0.053)	(0.355)	(0.470)	(0.251)	(0.433)					(0.323)	
0.99	−0.30	−1.70	−0.86	−0.23	0.29	−0.15	−0.18			0.01	1.27	251
(0.144)	(0.593)	(0.056)	(0.334)	(0.463)	(0.428)	(0.350)	(0.231)				(0.264)	
0.99	−0.28	−1.70	−0.88	−0.23	0.32		−0.35	−0.06	−0.15	0.00	1.13	251
(0.148)	(0.616)	(0.057)	(0.321)	(0.461)	(0.396)		(0.117)	(0.823)	(0.396)		(0.342)	

coefficient on *Distress * PL* is negative and significant as before. The first regression in Panel A includes an indicator for prepack. It enters with a significantly negative coefficient of −0.52 (*p*-value of 0.00), suggesting lower prices in prepack sales. In separate regressions (not shown here), we include a dummy for nonprepack going-concern sales in our fundamental pricing regression (Table 2). This dummy receives a significantly positive coefficient, while the coefficient for *PL* is still negative and significant. This means that average prices in prepacks are lower than in other going-concern sales but higher than in piecemeal liquidations, as predicted by our liquidation preemption hypothesis.

The second regression in Table 7 adds the indicator variable *Saleback*, which is insignificant. In the third regression, we replace the indicators for prepack and saleback with indicators for the nonoverlapping subsamples *Prepack * Saleback*, *Prepack * Nonsaleback*, and *Nonprepack * Saleback*. The average price-residual in the subsample of prepack-salebacks is strong and negative, with a coefficient value of −0.73 and a *p*-value of 0.00. The subsample of prepack-nonsalebacks also shows a negative coefficient, significant at the 5% level. The average price-residual is, however, insignificantly different from zero for salebacks that take place in the regular auction: the coefficient for *Nonprepack * Saleback* is −0.17 with a *p*-value of 0.30. In sum, prepacks produce negative price-residuals on average, and more so when the prepack is also a saleback. Salebacks, however, have no significant price-residuals when occurring in the regular auction. It is the private workout that matters, not the saleback transaction in and of itself.[19]

Turning to debt recovery rates, in Panel B of Table 7, none of the coefficients involving prepacks or salebacks are significant. Thus, while prepacks on average produce lower prices, this category does not affect total debt recovery rates. This is as expected if the bank promotes the prepack mechanism over piecemeal liquidation only when it is advantageous to do so. Consistent with this self-selection argument, rerunning the regressions in Panel B with the bank's own recovery rate (instead of the total debt recovery rate) yields results that are indistinguishable from those reported in Panel B (available upon request). That is, the bank's recovery in prepacks is statistically similar to that of nonprepack continuation sales.

4.3. Prepack and saleback probabilities

We next examine the determinants of the prepack and saleback decisions. Hypothesis H2 further predicts that prepacks are more likely to occur the more specific and intangible the target assets. Table 8 reports the total derivative with respect to each regression variable (as in Table 5). Consistent with H2, Panel A shows that the prepack

---

[19] We also examine the effect of industry distress in the subsamples of prepacks and salebacks, using the structure of Equation (5). The results show that the price-residuals in prepacks, salebacks, nonprepacks, and nonsalebacks do not interact with *Ind Distress*.

Table 8

Determinants of the probabilities of an auction prepack, a saleback, and a piecemeal liquidation

The probability π_n of auction outcome n is assumed to be determined by the value of $\gamma_n'Z$ ($n = 1, 2, 3$), where γ_n is the parameter vector and Z is a vector of characteristics. We estimate γ_n using multinomial logit, and the table reports estimated partial derivatives $\pi_n/z_k = \pi_n(\gamma_{nk} - \sum_{m=1}^{3} \gamma_{mk}\pi_m)$, where γ_{nk} is the parameter for explanatory variable k in Z. Sample of firms auctioned in Swedish bankruptcy, 1988–1991. Variable definitions are in Table 1 (p-values in parentheses).

Dependent variable	Constant	Target asset characteristics				Industry liquidity conditions			No. of firms	Probability at mean vector	N
		Size	Profit	Specific	Intangible	Bus Cycle	Ind Distress	Ind Leverage			
A: The prepack decision											
Prepack	−1.37	0.06	0.09	0.33	0.29	−0.00	−0.08	0.13	0.05	0.192	53
	(0.014)	(0.029)	(0.644)	(0.021)	(0.008)	(0.702)	(0.671)	(0.733)	(0.694)		
Nonprepack	1.28	−0.02	0.03	−0.01	−0.08	0.02	0.41	−0.88	0.00	0.593	147
	(0.074)	(0.439)	(0.880)	(0.955)	(0.564)	(0.062)	(0.095)	(0.061)	(0.991)		
PL	0.09	−0.03	−0.13	−0.32	−0.22	−0.02	−0.33	0.75	−0.05	0.215	58
	(0.877)	(0.250)	(0.463)	(0.099)	(0.056)	(0.065)	(0.106)	(0.052)	(0.694)		

$N = 258$, Log likelihood $= -238.3$, $\chi^2 = 26.40$, df $= 16$ ($p = 0.049$)

Dependent variable	Constant	Size	Profit	Specific	Intangible	Bus Cycle	Ind Distress	Ind Leverage	No. of firms	Probability at mean vector	N
B: The saleback decision											
Saleback	0.09	0.02	0.27	0.38	0.31	0.03	0.79	−1.06	0.10	0.488	122
	(0.902)	(0.511)	(0.309)	(0.075)	(0.039)	(0.019)	(0.003)	(0.032)	(0.527)		
Nonsaleback	−0.26	0.01	−0.10	−0.04	−0.05	−0.01	−0.41	0.27	−0.04	0.293	71
	(0.697)	(0.715)	(0.622)	(0.828)	(0.674)	(0.344)	(0.080)	(0.544)	(0.768)		
PL	0.17	−0.03	−0.16	−0.34	−0.25	−0.02	−0.38	0.80	−0.06	0.219	58
	(0.783)	(0.217)	(0.364)	(0.084)	(0.030)	(0.063)	(0.068)	(0.042)	(0.640)		

$N = 251$, Log likelihood $= -249.6$, $\chi^2 = 26.10$, df $= 16$ ($p = 0.053$)

probability increases with firm size, asset specificity, and asset intangibility. Notice also that there is no effect of industry liquidity conditions on the prepack probability. This suggests that fundamental target asset characteristics—not industry conditions *per se*—drive the basic prepack decision.

Target liquidation eliminates private benefits, if any, of target insiders. While a value-maximizing creditor has an incentive to preempt inefficient liquidation, target insiders may be willing to pay to continue the target as a going concern even when liquidation is efficient—up to the value of the private benefits. This is consistent with our observation that salebacks occur in both regular auctions and prepacks. We expect the probability of a saleback to have some of the same determinants as the prepack probability. This is confirmed by the multinomial logit estimates in Panel B of Table 8. As for prepacks, the saleback probability increases with target asset specificity and intangibility. In addition, there is a positive impact on the saleback probability from the recent change in the business cycle.

The greatest impact on the saleback probability comes from the two industry distress indicators. *Ind Distress* has a large and positive coefficient, a result also shown by Strömberg (2000). However, this coefficient is to a large extent countered by a negative impact of *Ind Leverage*. The net effect is difficult to interpret. As argued by Strömberg (2000), it is possible that salebacks are designed to avoid auction illiquidity during industry-wide distress (thus the positive effect of *Ind Distress*). On the other hand, the negative and offsetting effect of *Ind Leverage* may suggest that the target owner's incentive to invest is severely attenuated in periods with substantial industry debt overhang.

5. Postbankruptcy performance

To the extent that auction prepacks are attempts to avoid piecemeal liquidation, successful restructuring of the target may be relatively difficult. If so, we would expect to see poorer postbankruptcy performance for targets in such transactions. Similarly, if industry outsiders bring fewer managerial skills to the table than do industry insiders (as presumed under the fire-sale hypothesis), then the inferior managerial quality may also result in subpar postbankruptcy performance.[20]

Eckbo and Thorburn (2003) conclude that firms restructured under Swedish bankruptcy auctions overall have a postbankruptcy operating performance at par with that of nonbankrupt industry rivals. Because the sample firms are all private, they use operating profitability and bankruptcy refiling rates to indicate the economic viability of the firms' operations. Here, we use the same performance metrics but

---

[20] Studies of Chapter 11 show that postbankruptcy operating cash flows tend to be below industry standards, suggesting inefficient restructurings (Alderson and Betker, 1995; Chang and Schoar, 2007; Hotchkiss, 1995). One reason for the apparent inefficiency may be inferior quality of managers retained through the Chapter 11 process.

focus on the performance of our subsamples of auction prepacks and sales to industry outsiders.

Postbankruptcy performance estimation requires the identity of the newly restructured firm. We have this information in the first year after bankruptcy ("year 1") for a total of 150 of our targets sold as going concern, which is the sample we use to compute cumulative refiling probabilities. Within this subsample, postbankruptcy financial statements are available for a total of 106 firms in year 1. Table 9 reports annual industry-adjusted operating profitability (EBITDA/sales) in Panel A, book value of total debt to total assets in Panel B, and cumulative bankruptcy refiling probabilities (Panel C) for 4 years following the bankruptcy auction. Panels A and B report the median industry-adjusted value, computed as the difference between the firm and its median industry rival, where a rival is a firm with at least 20 employees in the same four-digit SIC industry as the target.

Using a Wilcoxon signed-rank test, the median industry-adjusted operating profitability is statistically indistinguishable from zero for the first 3 years following bankruptcy. Moreover, the p-values for the difference between prepacks and nonprepacks, and outsiders versus insiders, are all high. We conclude that the postbankruptcy operating performance of auctioned targets is indistinguishable from the corresponding performance of industry rivals, and that it is unaffected by whether the filing is a prepack or whether the buyer is an industry outsider.

Panel B shows that targets in prepacks as well as nonprepacks have postbankruptcy leverage ratios that are significantly higher than that of industry peers in years 1 and 2. There is no difference in the use of leverage in prepacks versus nonprepack acquisitions, however. Targets that are acquired by industry insiders (but not outsiders) have significantly higher leverage ratios than rivals in all 4 years shown in the table. Moreover, inside buyers show a greater reliance on leverage than outside buyers in years 3 and 4 (with p-values for the difference in those years of 0.03 and 0.00, respectively).

Panel C shows the difference between the bankruptcy refiling rates of our auctioned targets and the industry-weighted bankruptcy filing rate. Interestingly, targets in prepacks have a significantly greater industry-adjusted refiling probability than targets in nonprepack going-concern sales. By year 4, the cumulative industry-adjusted refiling rate is 35% for prepacks compared to 8% for nonprepack targets. In contrast, targets where the buyer in the auction was an industry outsider on average refile for bankruptcy at a rate that is statistically indistinguishable from the refiling rate of targets purchased by industry insiders (4% vs. 18% by year 4, with a p-value of 0.24 for the difference).

Intrigued by the relatively low average refiling rate when the buyer is an industry outsider, we estimate the probability of bankruptcy refiling within 2 years of the auction. Table 10 shows the coefficient estimates in the logit-regressions. In the first regression, the refiling probability is shown to increase with asset specificity, but is independent of the target size and asset tangibility at the time of the auction. Moreover, targets that are auctioned during a business cycle upturn are less likely to refile.

Table 9

Industry-adjusted postbankruptcy operating performance and cumulative bankruptcy refiling rates for targets sold as going concern, classified by filing method (prepack vs. nonprepack) and buyer industry affiliation (outsider vs. insider)

The table reports operating margin, debt ratios and cumulative refiling rates for bankrupt firms auctioned as going concerns. "Industry-adjusted" is the difference between the target firm's value and the corresponding median value in the target's four-digit SIC industry code. "Year 1" is the first calendar year after auction bankruptcy, etc. Superscript ** (*) indicates that the sample median is different from the industry median at the 1% (5%) level, using a Wilcoxon signed-ranks test. The p-value for the difference in industry-adjusted medians is from a two-sided Mann-Whitney U-test and for the difference in cumulative refiling rates a two-sided t-test. Variable definitions are in Table 1. Sample of 150 Swedish firms filing for auction bankruptcy and sold as going concern during 1988–1991.

Year after bankruptcy		1	2	3	4
A: Industry-adjusted operating margin (EBITDA/sales)					
Prepack	Median	0.01	−0.03	−0.02	0.00
	n	23	20	15	12
Nonprepack	Median	−0.01	−0.02	−0.00	0.02**
	n	83	74	58	44
p-Value of difference: prepack vs. nonprepack		(0.138)	(0.416)	(0.069)	(0.140)
Outsider	Median	0.01	−0.02	−0.00	0.05
	n	29	26	19	11
Insider	Median	−0.00	−0.02	−0.01	0.02*
	n	77	68	54	45
p-Value of difference: outsider vs. insider		(0.918)	(0.906)	(0.841)	(0.657)
B: Industry-adjusted debt ratio (book value of debt/total assets)					
Prepack	Median	0.16**	0.15**	0.13	0.07
	n	23	21	15	12
Nonprepack	Median	0.11**	0.08**	0.08*	0.05
	n	83	75	60	45
p-Value of difference: prepack vs. nonprepack		(0.797)	(0.364)	(0.474)	(0.625)
Outsider	Median	0.10	0.04	−0.02	−0.16
	n	29	27	20	12
Insider	Median	0.12**	0.12**	0.11**	0.07**
	n	77	69	55	45
p-Value of difference: outsider vs. insider		(0.280)	(0.119)	(0.033)	(0.004)
C: Industry-adjusted cumulative bankruptcy refiling rate					
Prepack	$n = 39$	0.17	0.33	0.34	0.35
Nonprepack	$n = 111$	−0.01	0.08	0.10	0.08
p-Value of difference: prepack vs. nonprepack		(0.014)	(0.010)	(0.017)	(0.023)
Outsider	$n = 36$	0.03	0.07	0.07	0.04
Insider	$n = 114$	0.04	0.17	0.18	0.18
p-Value of difference: outsider vs. insider		(0.862)	(0.230)	(0.230)	(0.236)

Table 10

Bankruptcy refiling probability for targets sold as going concern

Coefficients in logit estimations of the probability that the surviving firm refiles for bankruptcy within 2 years of the auction. The sample is 150 Swedish firms sold as going concern in auction bankruptcy 1988–1991. p-Values are in parentheses. Variable definitions are in Table 1.

	Target asset characteristics					Industry conditions				Auction outcomes			
Constant	Size	Profit	Specific	Intangible	Bus Cycle	Ind Distress	Ind Leverage	$p - p^*$	Outsider	Prepack	Cox Snell R^2	Chi-square
−2.42	−0.14	0.43	2.83	−1.12	−0.22	−5.32	6.90	−0.06			0.14	22.96
(0.628)	(0.577)	(0.837)	(0.015)	(0.260)	(0.012)	(0.003)	(0.022)	(0.794)				(0.003)
−2.79	−0.14	−0.66	2.78	−1.15	−0.22	−6.25	8.00	0.02	−1.46	1.35	0.21	35.01
(0.599)	(0.601)	(0.778)	(0.037)	(0.149)	(0.017)	(0.001)	(0.012)	(0.932)	(0.016)	(0.007)		(0.000)

The two industry distress variables, *Ind Distress* and *Ind Leverage*, have significant but opposite effects, with industry distress lowering the probability and industry leverage increasing the probability. Our fire-sale discount estimate has no impact on the refiling probability: the coefficient on the price residual $p - p^*$ is statistically insignificant. A consistent interpretation is that the fire-sale discount is economically unimportant (as concluded above), or that a fire-sale discount, if present, does not affect the quality of the restructuring of the target.

In the second regression of Table 10, we have added the binary variables *Prepack* and *Outsider*. Being a prepack target significantly increases the refiling probability, while a target acquired by an industry outsider has a significantly lower probability of refiling within 2 years of the auction. Both results are interesting. Consistent with our liquidation preemption hypothesis H2, prepacks appear to be more risky than nonprepacks in terms of the chance of having to refile within several years after the auction. This makes intuitive sense if "rescuing" a target from inefficient liquidation involves a relatively complex restructuring. As to the lower refiling probability for industry outsiders, it could reflect a selection of less risky targets or the presumption that industry outsiders are less efficient buyers may be wrong. The latter interpretation is consistent with the evidence above that outsiders pay no lower auction prices than do insiders, and they show no lower postbankruptcy operating performance.

6. Conclusions

Proponents of a renegotiation-based bankruptcy system such as Chapter 11 argue that the alternative auction mechanism carries an unacceptable risk of fire-sale and excessive liquidation. Sweden's system of automatic bankruptcy auctions represents an interesting setting for testing this argument as there are no effective provisions for renegotiations under court supervision. The auctions are mandatory for all filing firms, standardized in form, and the seller has little or no influence over the outcome. The bids alone determine whether the firm will be continued as a going concern or liquidated piecemeal. A creditor concerned with auction illiquidity leading to excessive liquidation must take preventative measures by means of a private workout (before filing). Private workouts are target acquisition agreements that are submitted along with the bankruptcy filing (prepack auction).

We study prices, debt recovery rates, acquisition mechanisms, and postbankruptcy performance across the entire range of auction outcomes in this system. The bankrupt firms are all private and with an average prefiling asset size close to the average size of private firms filing for Chapter 11. We specify a fundamental pricing model based on target asset characteristics and test whether final auction prices deviate from fundamentals during periods of severe industry distress. Conditional on the fundamentals, significantly lower auction prices during periods of industry-wide illiquidity are considered evidence of fire-sale discounts. Thus, our tests of fire-sale discounts are joint tests of the fundamental pricing model and the hypothesized pricing effects of temporary demand-side illiquidity.

A key—and perhaps surprising—finding is that fire-sale discounts exist *only* when the auction leads to piecemeal liquidation of the target (the outcome in one-fifth of our sample auctions). Prices in going-concern sales are unaffected by measures of industry-wide illiquidity and distress. For piecemeal liquidations, however, higher industry-wide financial distress lowers both prices and debt recovery rates. This result is robust to endogenous selection of the auction outcome by bidders in the auction. Moreover, our finding of a fire-sale discount for piecemeal liquidations is comparable to studies of voluntary asset sales by US companies both in and out of bankruptcy.

It appears that auctions where the buyer continues the target as a going concern are sufficiently competitive to yield prices that are indistinguishable from fundamentals. In going-concern sales, there are typically multiple bids, and there is no evidence that prices or recovery rates interact with measures of industry-wide distress, or with the industry affiliation of the buyer (outsider vs. insider)—two central indicators of fire-sale conditions used in the extant literature. We further show that bidders make frequent use of a leveraged buyout acquisition method which likely increases competition. Buyouts relax liquidity constraints and reduce bidder underinvestment incentives in the presence of industry-wide debt overhang. Possibly as a result, buyout prices are indistinguishable from prices in mergers, the alternative acquisition method.

We also argue that auction prepacks play an important role as a mechanism to preempt excessive liquidation when the auction is expected to be illiquid. There is substantial evidence to support this proposition. Prepack prices are somewhat higher than in piecemeal liquidations but lower than in regular, in-auction going-concern sales. The industry-adjusted postbankruptcy operating performance of prepacks is on average similar to nonprepack going-concern sales. However, prepack targets have a significantly greater probability of refiling for bankruptcy after the auction. Thus, liquidation preemption appears to be a relatively risky strategy. Overall, as prepacks constitute one-quarter of our going-concern sample, the automatic auction mechanism produces substantial activity to avoid excessive liquidation.

We have shown in this paper that the Swedish automatic auction bankruptcy system works particularly well when the bankrupt firm is purchased as a going concern. There is no systematic evidence of fire-sales nor excessive liquidation. An interesting issue for future research is whether automatic auctions would also work well in the context of US bankruptcies. It is possible that mandatory auctions are particularly well suited for the unique legal and corporate governance tradition in Sweden. On the other hand, as mentioned in the introduction, US capital markets have moved in the direction of what Baird and Rasmussen (2003) characterize as "auction mechanisms in one form or another" for large bankruptcies also. This trend is likely to continue if auctions are in fact able to resolve the often complex corporate capital structures observed in the US—something that the Swedish experience does not address.

References

Acharya, V. V., S. T. Bharath and A. Srinivasan, 2007, "Does Industry-Wide Distress Affect Defaulted Firms? Evidence from Creditor Recoveries," *Journal of Financial Economics*, 85, 787–821.

Aghion, P., O. Hart and J. Moore, 1992, "The Economics of Bancruptcy Reform," *Journal of Law, Economics and Organization*, 8, 523–546.

Alderson, M. J. and B. L. Betker, 1995, "Liquidation Costs and Capital Structure," *Journal of Financial Economics*, 39, 45–69.

Asquith, P., R. Gertner and D. Scharfstein, 1992, "Anatomy of Financial Distress: An Examination of Junk-Bond Issuers," *Quarterly Journal of Economics*, 109, 625–658.

Baird, D. G., 1986, "The Uneasy Case for Corporate Reorganizations," *Journal of Legal Studies*, 15, 127–147.

Baird, D. G., 1993, "Revisiting Auctions in Chapter 11," *Journal of Law and Economics*, 36, 633–653.

Baird, D. G. and R. K. Rasmussen, 2003, "Chapter 11 at Twilight," *Stetson Law Review*, 56, 673–699.

Bebchuk, L. A., 1988, "A New Approach to Corporate Reorganizations," *Harvard Law Review*, 101, 775–804.

Bebchuk, L. A. and H. F. Chang, 1992, "Bargaining and the Division of Value in Corporate Reorganization," *Journal of Law, Economics and Organization*, 8, 253–279.

Betker, B. L., 1995, "An Empirical Examination of Prepackaged Bankruptcy," *Financial Management*, 24, 3–18.

Betton, S. and B. E. Eckbo, 2000, "Toeholds, Bid Jumps, and Expected Payoff in Takeovers," *Review of Financial Studies*, 13, 841–882.

Boone, L. and J. H. Mulherin, 2007, "How Are Firms Sold?" *Journal of Finance*, 62, 847–875.

Bradley, M. and M. Rosenzweig, 1992, "The Untenable Case for Chapter 11," *Yale Law Journal*, 101, 1043–1095.

Chang, T. and A. Schoar, 2007, "The Effect of Judicial Bias in Chapter 11 Reorganization," Working Paper, Massachusetts Institute of Technology.

Clayton, M. J. and S. A. Ravid, 2002, "The Effect of Leverage on Bidding Behavior: Theory and Evidence from the FCC Auctions," *Review of Financial Studies*, 15, 723–750.

Easterbrook, F. H., 1990, "Is Corporate Bankruptcy Efficient?" *Journal of Financial Economics*, 27, 411–418.

Eckbo, B. E. and K. S. Thorburn, 2003, "Control Benefits and CEO Discipline in Automatic Bankruptcy Auctions," *Journal of Financial Economics*, 69, 227–258.

Eckbo, B. E. and K. S. Thorburn, 2009, "Creditor Financing and Overbidding in Bankruptcy Auctions: Theory and Tests," *Journal of Corporate Finance*, 15, 10–29.

Franks, J. and W. Torous, 1994, "A Comparison of Financial Recontracting in Distressed Exchanges and Chapter 11 Reorganizations," *Journal of Financial Economics*, 35, 349–370.

Hart, O., 2000, "Different Approaches to Bankruptcy," Working Paper, Harvard University, Massachusetts.

Heckman, J. J., 1979, "Sample Selection Bias as a Specification Error," *Econometrica*, 47, 153–161.

Hotchkiss, E. S., 1995, "Post-Bankruptcy Performance and Management Turnover," *Journal of Finance*, 50, 3–21.

Hotchkiss, E. S. and R. M. Mooradian, 1997, "Vulture Investors and the Market for Control of Distressed Firms," *Journal of Financial Economics*, 43, 401–432.

Hotchkiss, E. S. and R. M. Mooradian, 1998, "Acquisitions as a Means of Restructuring Firms in Chapter 11," *Journal of Financial Intermediation*, 7, 240–262.

Jensen, M. C., 1989, "Eclipse of the Public Corporation," *Harvard Business Review*, 67, 61–74.

John, K. and E. Ofek, 1995, "Asset Sales and Increase in Focus," *Journal of Financial Economics*, 37, 105–126.

Kim, C. E., 1998, "The Effects of Asset Liquidity: Evidence from the Contract Drilling Industry," *Journal of Financial Intermediation*, 7, 151–176.

Lang, L. and R. Stulz, 1992, "Contagion and Competitive Intra-Industry Effects of Bankruptcy Announcements," *Journal of Financial Economics*, 32, 45–60.

Lease, R., J. McConnell and E. Tashjian, 1996, "Prepacks: An Empirical Analysis of Prepackaged Bankruptcies," *Journal of Financial Economics*, 40, 135–162.

Li, K. and N. R. Prabhala, 2007, "Self-Selection Models in Corporate Finance," In B. E. Eckbo (Ed.), *Handbook of Corporate Finance: Empirical Corporate Finance*, vol. 1, Chapter 2, Elsevier/North-Holland, Amsterdam, Handbooks in Finance Series, pp. 37–86.

Maddala, G. S., 1983, *Limited-Dependent and Qualitative Variables in Econometrics*, Econometric Society Monographs, vol. 3, Cambridge University Press, UK.

Maksimovic, V. and G. Phillips, 1998, "Asset Efficiency and Reallocation Decisions of Bankrupt Firms," *Journal of Finance*, 53, 1495–1532.

Maksimovic, V. and G. Phillips, 2001, "The Market for Corporate Assets: Who Engages in Mergers and Asset Sales and are There Efficiency Gains?" *Journal of Finance*, 56, 2019–2065.

Myers, S. C., 1977, "Determination of Corporate Borrowing," *Journal of Financial Economics*, 4, 147–175.

Ofek, E., 1993, "Capital Structure and Firm Response to Poor Performance: An Empirical Analysis," *Journal of Financial Economics*, 34, 3–30.

Officer, M. S., 2007, "The Price of Corporate Liquidity: Acquisition Discounts for Unlisted Targets," *Journal of Financial Economics*, 83, 571–598.

Pulvino, T., 1998, "Do Asset Fire-Sales Exist? An Empirical Investigation of Commercial Aircraft Transactions," *Journal of Finance*, 53, 939–978.

Pulvino, T., 1999, "Effects of Bankruptcy Court Protection on Asset Sales," *Journal of Financial Economics*, 52, 151–186.

Ramey, V. A. and M. D. Shapiro, 2001, "Displaced Capital: A Study of Aerospace Plant Closings," *Journal of Political Economy*, 109, 958–992.

Shleifer, A. and R. W. Vishny, 1992, "Liquidation Values and Debt Capacity: A Market Equilibrium Approach," *Journal of Finance*, 47, 1343–1366.

Strömberg, P., 2000, "Conflicts of Interests and Market Illiquidity in Bankruptcy Auctions: Theory and Tests," *Journal of Finance*, 55, 2641–2692.

Strömberg, P. and K. S. Thorburn, 1996, "An Empirical Investigation of Swedish Corporations in Liquidation Bankruptcy," EFI Research Report, Stockholm School of Economics.

Thorburn, K. S., 2000, "Bankruptcy Auctions: Costs, Debt Recovery, and Firm Survival," *Journal of Financial Economics*, 58, 337–368.

Williamson, O. E., 1988, "Corporate Finance and Corporate Governance," *Journal of Finance*, 43, 567–592.

Chapter 10

CREDITOR FINANCING AND OVERBIDDING IN BANKRUPTCY AUCTIONS: THEORY AND TESTS*

B. ESPEN ECKBO

Tuck School of Business at Dartmouth, New Hampshire, USA

KARIN S. THORBURN

Tuck School of Business at Dartmouth, New Hampshire, USA

Contents

* Beginning with the first draft of this paper (Eckbo and Thorburn, 2000) we have benefited from the comments of numerous people, including Sandra Betton, Julian Franks, Andres Almazan, Diego Garcia, Robert G. Hansen, Edith Hotchkiss, Ronen Israel, Craig Lewis, Paul Povel, Kose Riis, Kristian Rydqvist, Keun Kwan Ryu, Matthew Rhodes-Kropf, Chester Spatt, and Matthew Spiegel, and the seminar participants at the following universities: Dartmouth, Boston College, Emory, the Finish School of Economics, Georgetown, NYU, the Norwegian School of Economics, the Norwegian School of Management, Oxford, Rutgers, Montreal, Rochester, Simon Fraser, SMU, the Swedish School of Economics, Toronto, Utah, UBC, and Vanderbilt. The paper has also been presented at the annual meetings of the American Law and Economics Association, the American Finance Association, the European Finance Association, the Financial Management Association, and at CEPR and NBER conferences. Partial financial support from Tuck's Center for Corporate Governance, the Norwegian National Research Council (grant no. 125105/510) and the Swedish National Council for Crime Prevention is gratefully acknowledged.

This article originally apperaed in the *Journal of Corporate Finance*, Vol. 15, pp. 10–29 (2009).
Corporate Takeovers, Volume 2
Edited by B. Espen Eckbo
DOI: 10.1016/B978-0-12-381982-6.00011-2

Abstract

We present unique empirical tests for auction overbidding using data from Sweden's auction bankruptcy system. The main creditor (a bank) can neither bid in the auction nor refuse to sell in order to support a minimum price. However, we argue that the bank may increase its expected revenue by financing a bidder in return for a joint bid strategy, and we show that the optimal coalition bid exceeds the bidder's private valuation (overbidding) by an amount that is increasing in the bank's ex ante debt impairment. We find that bank-bidder financing arrangements are common, and our cross-sectional regressions show that winning bids are increasing in the bank-debt impairment as predicted. While, in theory, overbidding may result in the coalition winning against a more efficient rival bidder, our evidence on postbankruptcy operating performance fails to support such allocative inefficiency effects. We also find that restructurings by bank-financed bidders are relatively risky as they have greater bankruptcy refiling rates, irrespective of the coalition's overbidding incentive.

Keywords

bankruptcy, auction, overbidding, creditor financing, allocative efficiency, going-concern sale, piecemeal liquidation, operating performance

JEL classification: G33, G34

1. Introduction

In Sweden, a firm filing for bankruptcy is turned over to a court-appointed trustee who puts the firm up for sale in an auction. This mandatory auction system has an attractive simplicity. All debt claims are stayed during the auction period and the bids determine whether the firm will be continued as a going concern or liquidated piecemeal. Payment must be in cash, allowing the auction proceeds to be distributed to creditors strictly according to absolute priority. Moreover, the auctions are quick (lasting an average of 2 months) and relatively cost-efficient, and as much as three-quarters of the filing firms survive the auction as a going concern (Thorburn, 2000). A going-concern sale takes place by merging the assets and operations of the auctioned firm into the bidder firm, or into an empty corporate shell—much like a leveraged buyout transaction.

There is an ongoing debate over the relative efficiency of auction bankruptcy versus Chapter 11 in the United States, where firms are reorganized in bankruptcy. Proponents of a more market-oriented auction system point to costs associated with conflicts of interests and excessive continuation of operations due to managerial control over the restructuring process in Chapter 11.[1] Perhaps as a result, there is a trend toward increased use of market-based mechanisms in the United States, as evidenced by prepackaged bankruptcies (Betker, 1995; Lease et al., 1996), participation by distressed investors (Hotchkiss and Mooradian, 1997), and sales in Chapter 11 (Hotchkiss and Mooradian, 1998; Maksimovic and Phillips, 1998). In fact, Baird and Rasmussen (2003) report that more than three-quarters of all large Chapter 11 cases resolved in 2002 involved the sale of company assets or a prepackaged bankruptcy procedure.

On the other hand, proponents of Chapter 11 argue that the time pressure of an auction system is costly as it possibly causes excessive liquidation of economically viable firms when potential bidders in the auction are themselves financially constrained. However, Eckbo and Thorburn (2008) fail to find auction fire-sale discounts in going-concern sales, and the three-quarters survival rate reported for the Swedish auction system is similar to that of Chapter 11.[2] Also, in Eckbo and Thorburn, (2003) we show that firms purchased as going concerns in the auction tend to perform at par with nonbankrupt industry rivals.

In this paper, we study an empirical issue of importance for the workings of the auction system: the incentives and opportunities of the bankrupt firm's major creditor to influence the auction outcome. We show that creditor incentives have the potential for affecting both the liquidity and allocative efficiency of bankruptcy auctions. Our empirical evidence is based on 260 private Swedish firms auctioned in bankruptcy.

---

[1] See, for example, Baird (1986), Bebchuk (1988), Jensen (1989), Aghion et al. (1992), Bebchuk and Chang (1992), Bradley and Rosenzweig (1992), and Baird (1993). Hotchkiss (1995) finds that firms emerging from Chapter 11 tend to underperform their industry rivals which is consistent with excessive continuation.

[2] See, for example, White (1984), Franks and Torous (1989), Weiss (1990), LoPucki and Whitford (1993), and Hotchkiss et al. (2008) for a review.

The average firm has $5 million in sales and assets of $2 million ($8 and $4 million, respectively, in 2007 dollars), and it has an average of 43 employees. This small-firm evidence is of interest to the US debate as a majority of Chapter 11 filings are also by small private firms: Chang and Schoar (2007) report average sales of $2 million and 22 employees in a large and representative sample of Chapter 11 filings between 1989 and 2003. Bris et al. (2006) report that the median firm filing for Chapter 11 has assets of $1 million.

In our sample, as is common for small firms, the bankrupt firm's secured creditor is a bank. Upon filing, whenever the bank's debt claim is impaired, the bank becomes the firm's residual claimant and therefore effectively the seller in the auction. Auction rules and banking regulations prevent the bank from openly enforcing a seller reserve price (it can neither bid directly nor refuse to sell). However, we observe that the bank often finances the winning bidder in the auction. We postulate that the bank uses this bid financing as a vehicle for engineering a (bank-bidder) coalition to get around the auction bidding constraint. Under certain conditions, the coalition optimally overbids, that is, bids more than the private valuation of the bank's coalition partner. We show that the optimal coalition bid mimics the sales price of a monopolist seller when the bank's debt is greatly impaired. In this situation, the bank effectively enforces a reserve price and raises its expected debt recovery. This also raises the possibility that the bankrupt firm ends up being acquired by a relatively inefficient bidder. Allocative inefficiency occurs when the bank-bidder coalition wins against a rival bidder that has a higher private valuation of the target.[3]

Our empirical analysis addresses both the overbidding and efficiency aspects of the auctions. First, we present a unique test for the existence of overbidding based directly on auction premiums. To characterize the test approach, it is instructive to think of the bankruptcy event as creating an instant "bank toehold" equal to one (100% bank ownership of the auctioned firm) when bank debt is impaired. As with toehold bidding in general, toeholds raise the bidder's reserve price above and beyond its private valuation—referred to as "overbidding" (Bulow et al., 1999; Burkart, 1995). In our bankruptcy auction setting, bank-bidder coalition overbidding increases the expected auction revenue flowing to the bank.[4] Hotchkiss and Mooradian (2003) also examine creditor overbidding incentives, but in the context of voluntary sales in Chapter 11 of the US bankruptcy code.

---

[3] Issues of auction efficiency also arise in the context of fire-sales (Eckbo and Thorburn, 2008; Shleifer and Vishny, 1992), the choice of auction versus renegotiation (Hansen and Thomas, 1998; Hotchkiss and Mooradian, 2003), the payment method (Aghion et al., 1992; Rhodes-Kropf and Viswanathan, 2000), and managerial investment in human capital (Berkovitch et al., 1997). In Berkovitch et al. (1997), participation in the bankruptcy auction by a relatively informed creditor produces underinvestment in managerial human capital ex ante. Our argument below does not rely on the bank having an informational advantage over other bidders.

[4] Burkart (1995) alludes to the analogy between an impaired debt claim and a toehold: "When a bankrupt firm's assets are auctioned off, the firm's creditors are in a similar position to that of a large shareholder" (p. 1506).

Importantly, the coalition optimally overbids *only* if the bank's debt claim is impaired at the outset of the auction (further overbidding just benefits junior creditors). It is this cross-sectional restriction that makes overbidding testable in our setting. This restriction does not exist for takeovers outside of bankruptcy. Extant empirical evidence on toehold-induced overbidding is therefore indirect. For example, theory implies that overbidding increases the probability of winning, which is supported by studies of corporate takeover bids with equity toeholds (Betton and Eckbo, 2000).

Our tests require a measure of the degree of bank-debt impairment at the beginning of the auction, capturing the bank's overbidding incentive. We use the *ex ante liquidation recovery rate*, defined as the firm's expected piecemeal liquidation value scaled by the face value of the bank's debt. At the beginning of every auction, the bankruptcy trustee publishes an industry estimate of the piecemeal liquidation value, which we use directly. Bidders appear to rely on this estimate as well: when the auction does lead to piecemeal liquidation, the average price paid by the winning bidder is close to (on average 8% above) the trustee's estimate. In contrast, when the bankrupt firm is purchased as a going concern, the average auction premium more than doubles the trustee's piecemeal liquidation-value estimate.

In theory, the greater the liquidation recovery rate, the lower is the incentive to overbid and, in turn, the lower is the expected premium paid by the winning bidder. We find that when the firm is sold as a going concern, auction premiums are decreasing in the liquidation recovery rate, as predicted. Equally important, there is no evidence of overbidding in auction premiums for subsamples where the theory implies zero overbidding incentive. There are two such subsamples, representing 40% of the total sample. The first subsample consists of auctions that result in a going-concern sale, but where the bank's debt is not impaired at the ex ante liquidation value. In this case, the bank has no incentive to push for a coalition-bidding strategy since any revenue increase flows to junior creditors. Second, overbidding for targets that are expected to be liquidated piecemeal is suboptimal because these targets have only negligible going-concern value. When no bidder values the target as a going concern, there are no rents to be extracted from rival bidders through overbidding. We detect no evidence of overbidding in either subsample. Overall, our test results provide surprisingly robust support for our coalition overbidding theory.

Our main overbidding theory presumes that that bank managers act in the interest of the bank's shareholders by attempting to maximize auction revenue. We also consider an alternative coalition-bidding strategy, dubbed "debt rollover". Here, entrenched bank managers use the first-price auction to roll over impaired bank debt at face value in order to hide nonperforming loans from their superiors. Under the rollover hypothesis, the coalition's bid equals the face value of the bank debt (plus any debt senior to the bank), effectively establishing a price floor in the auction. While the rollover hypothesis also implies overbidding, it predicts an auction revenue that is approximately equal to the face value of the bank's debt when the coalition wins. The data rejects this prediction.

Overbidding results in allocative inefficiency whenever the bank-bidder coalition wins against a higher valuation bidder. Thus, a second objective of our empirical analysis is to shed light on whether the auction system tends to produce inefficient outcomes due to overbidding. Previous work shows that firms restructured under Swedish bankruptcy auctions typically perform at par with nonbankrupt industry rivals (Eckbo and Thorburn, 2003). However, the previous evidence does not condition on bank financing and overbidding incentives. The intersection of bank financing of the winning bidder and high overbidding incentives is the ideal place to look for ex post allocative inefficiency. We find postbankruptcy operating performance to be at par with industry rivals for these subgroups of auctions as well. If anything, the operating performance is higher in the subsample where the bank-bidder coalition wins and overbidding incentives are high ex ante.

Finally, we show that the probability of bankruptcy refiling over the 2 years following the auction is significantly greater when the bank finances the winning bidder. This refiling probability is, however, independent of overbidding incentives and therefore cannot be attributed to inefficiencies in the auction *per se*. A consistent interpretation is that banks tend to finance relatively high-risk restructuring prospects. In sum, bank financing of bidders increases auction liquidity, and seem to result in overbidding without significantly distorting the restructuring process.

The paper is organized as follows. Section 2 develops the coalition-bidding model and the model's central empirical implications. Section 3 describes the data selection and sample characteristics. Section 4 performs the main cross-sectional tests for overbidding. Section 5 shows postbankruptcy performance statistics, while Section 6 concludes the paper.

2. Bank-bidder coalition overbidding

In this section, we develop the overbidding hypothesis, its key empirical prediction (Proposition 3), and we comment on factors that may attenuate overbidding incentives in our Swedish setting.

2.1. The auction setting

The Swedish bankruptcy code mandates an open bid first-price auction. As is common in the toehold literature, we use the sealed-bid second-price analogy for analytical tractability.[5] We assume the existence of two bidders who are risk neutral and have unaffiliated private valuations of the target firm. Bidder i's private valuation of the auctioned firm's asset is denoted $v_i \in [0, 1]$ ($i = 1, 2$). Private valuations are i.i.d. with distribution and density functions $G(v)$ and $g(v)$, respectively. The bids determine whether the firm's assets will be purchased individually (piecemeal liquidation) or at the higher price required to continue the target as a going concern.

---

[5] With zero bidding costs, the sealed-bid second-price auction is revenue-equivalent to the open first-price auction and it produces identical asset allocation (Dasgupta and Hansen, 2007; Klemperer, 2000).

Denote the piecemeal liquidation value by l, and the going-concern premium by p, so that the total price paid by the winning bidder is $p + l$. The trustee provides bidders with a professional industry estimate of l at the start of the auction. Our auction premium data below suggest that bidders tend to treat l as a minimum price in the auction: when the auction results in piecemeal liquidation, the price paid is on average 8% higher than the estimate l. In contrast, when the auction outcome is a sale of the target as a going concern, the price paid averages 2.25 times l, or a going-concern premium of $p = 125\%$. For simplicity, we treat l as a known constant, and derive optimal bids b_i determining the auction premium p. We reintroduce l in Section 2.6 when deriving testable restrictions of the theory.

2.2. The coalition's optimal bid

While the bank cannot bid directly in the auction, there are no regulatory restrictions on the bank's ability to issue debt to a bidder. Suppose the bank approaches a randomly selected bidder (henceforth bidder 1) and offers to finance the acquisition should the bidder win the auction. Bidding alone, the optimal bid of bidder 1 is $b_1 = v_1$.[6] Assuming $l = 0$, the following represents an incentive-compatible coalition bid strategy.

Proposition 1 (optimal coalition bid strategy). *Let $l = 0$ and suppose the bank is the bankrupt firm's only senior creditor, holding a debt claim with face value f. The following represents a revenue-maximizing coalition bid strategy:*

$$b_c \begin{cases} v_1 + h(b_c) & \text{if } v_1 \le f - h(b_c) & \text{(unconstrained overbidding)} \\ f & \text{if } f - h(b_c) < v_1 < f & \text{(constrained overbidding)} \\ v_1 & \text{if } v_1 \ge f, & \text{(no overbidding)} \end{cases} \tag{1}$$

where $h(b_c) \equiv [1 - G(b_c)]/g(b_c)$ is the inverse of the hazard function at b_c.

Proof. Starting with the coalition bid under unconstrained overbidding, the expected revenue π_c to the bank-bidder coalition from unconstrained bidding is

$$\pi_c = \int_{b_c}^{1} b_c g(v_2)\, dv_2 + \int_0^{b_c} v_1 g(v_2)\, dv_2 = b_c[1 - G(b_c)] - v_1 G(b_c), \tag{2}$$

where the first term on the right-hand side is the expected revenue if the coalition loses to bidder 2, and the second term is the net payoff of $(v_1 - b_2) + b_2 = v_1$ times the probability of winning, $G(b_c)$. The first-order condition with respect to b_c is

---

[6] Dropping out of the auction when $b_1 < v_1$ means foregoing a positive expected profit from winning at a price less than v_1. Moreover, a bid of $b_1 > v_1$ implies a negative expected profit conditional on winning.

$$\frac{\partial \pi_c}{\partial b_c} = 1 - G(b_c) - b_c g(b_c) + v_1 g(b_c) = 0, \tag{3}$$

which yields the optimal coalition bid $b_c = v_1 + h(b_c)$.[7]

Turning to the constrained overbidding price in Equation (1), this bid reflects the effect of the bank-debt face value f. As the senior claimant, the bank has no incentive to help generate an auction revenue that exceeds f, as every dollar of additional overbidding is transferred directly to junior creditors. Thus, when $f - h(b_c) < v_1 < f$, the coalition bids $b_c = f$. Finally, when $v_1 \geq f$, the creditor toehold is effectively zero, and the coalition optimally bids bidder 1's private valuation, $b_c = v_1$.

By raising the price in the auction, overbidding produces a wealth transfer from bidder 2 to the coalition when $v_2 > b_c > v_1$. The optimal coalition bid strategy is illustrated in Figure 1 for the case of the uniform distribution, $v_i \sim U[0, 1]$.

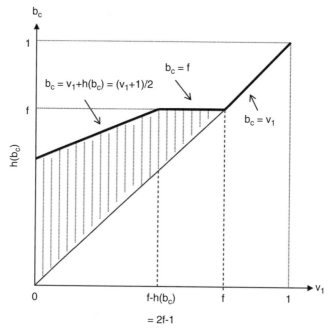

Fig. 1. The bank-bidder coalition's optimal bid, $b_c(v_1)$, and the expected amount of overbidding (shaded area), assuming a piecemeal liquidation value l of zero. The figure is drawn assuming bidder valuations are distributed uniform, $v_i \sim U[0, 1]$. The coalition-bidder's private valuation is v_1, f is the face value of the bank's debt, and $h(b_c)$ is the inverse hazard rate at b_c. When $v_1 \leq 2f - 1$, the coalition fully overbids: $b_c = (v_1 + 1)/2$. When $f > v_1 > 2f - 1$, the coalition partially overbids: $b_c = f$. When $v_1 \geq f$, the coalition does not overbid: $b_c = v_1$.

[7] To ensure uniqueness, G must be twice continuously differentiable and satisfy the monotonicity condition $\partial h^{-1}(v)/\partial v \geq 0$.

The horizontal axis plots v_1 and the bold-faced line shows the coalition bid b_c. The first segment of the bold-faced line is the unconstrained overbidding price, $b_c = v_1 + h(b_c)$ $= (v_1 + 1)/2$. The second (horizontal) segment is the constrained overbidding price, $b_c = f$, which occurs when $f - h(b_c) < v_1 < f$. The segment starts when v_1 is such that the unconstrained bid price equals the face value f. The third segment starts when $v_1 > f$. Here, the bank's debt is fully paid off without overbidding, so that $b_c = v_1$.

2.3. Incentive compatibility and bid delegation

Coalition overbidding is ex post costly for bidder 1 unless the highest-valuation bidder wins. Since bidder 1 is responsible for paying the bid, the coalition agreement must include a compensating transfer to bidder 1. Proposition 2 holds that there exists a positive transfer from the bank to bidder 1, which satisfies the participation constraint by both coalition parties.

Proposition 2 (incentive compatibility). *Let c denote the cost to bidder 1 of participating in the coalition, and t the bank's net revenue from coalition bidding (net of the bank's revenue without coalition bidding). Conditional on the optimal coalition bid strategy b_c in Proposition 1, $E(t) > E(c)$ so coalition formation is incentive compatible.*

Proof. We have that

$$
c = \begin{cases}
0 & \text{if } v_2 \le v_1 \le b_c & \text{(coalition wins and pays } v_2 \le v_1) \\
v_2 - v_1 & \text{if } v_1 < v_2 \le b_c & \text{(coalition wins and pays } v_2 > v_1) \\
0 & \text{if } v_1 \le b_c < v_2 & \text{(coalition loses)}
\end{cases}
\tag{4}
$$

The expected overbidding cost to bidder 1 is

$$
E(c) = \int_{v_1}^{b_c} (v_2 - v_1) g(v_2) \, dv_2.
\tag{5}
$$

The bank's net revenue t is given by

$$
t = \begin{cases}
0 & \text{if } v_2 \le v_1 \le b_c & \text{(coalition wins and pays } v_2 \le v_1) \\
v_2 - v_1 & \text{if } v_1 < v_2 \le b_c & \text{(coalition wins and pays } v_2 > v_1) \\
b_c - v_1 & \text{if } v_1 \le b_c < v_2 & \text{(coalition loses)}
\end{cases}
\tag{6}
$$

The expected net revenue is

$$
E(t) = \int_{v_1}^{b_c} (v_2 - v_1) g(v_2) dv_2 + (b_c - v_1)(1 - G(b_c))
$$

$$
= E(c) + (b_c - v_1)(1 - G(b_c)).
\tag{7}
$$

Since, with overbidding, $b_c > v_1$, it follows that $E(t) > E(c)$ and the bank's expected net revenue is sufficient to cover the coalition partner's expected overbidding cost.

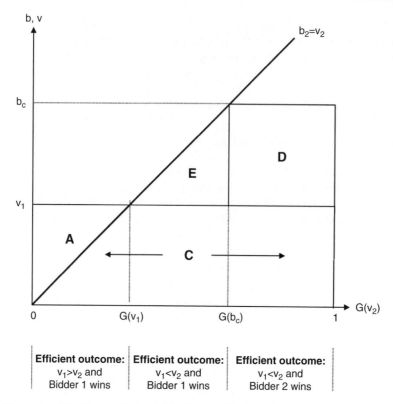

Fig. 2. Expected profits with and without coalition bidding. The figure is drawn assuming bidder valuations are distributed uniform, $v_i \sim U[0, 1]$. $G(v_2)$ is the cumulative distribution over v_2. Bidder 2's optimal bid is $b_2 = v_2$ (the diagonal line) and the coalition's optimal bid is b_c. Area A is the expected profits to Bidder 1 and C is the bank's expected revenue under noncooperative bidding. With coalition bidding, area E is bidder 1's expected cost of overbidding (the minimum transfer), and area $E + D$ is the bank's expected net revenue from overbidding. Thus, area D is the coalition's expected net surplus from overbidding (which equals the expected wealth transfer from bidder 2).

Figure 2 illustrates the gains and losses from coalition bidding for the uniform case. The vertical axis is bidder 2's valuation v_2 and the horizontal axis is $G(v_2)$. Area A equals bidder 1's expected profit from bidding alone. Area C is the bank's expected revenue without coalition formation. Area E is the expected cost to bidder 1 from overbidding (the minimum transfer), while the bank's expected net revenue $E(t)$ equals area $D + E$. Area D is the expected wealth transfer from bidder 2 resulting from coalition overbidding and thus the coalition's net surplus (which motivates coalition formation).

To induce participation by bidder 1 in the coalition, the coalition agreement may stipulate a transfer of an amount at least equal to $E(c)$ (area E) ex ante (at the beginning of the auction). Alternatively, the agreement may arrange for at least $v_2 - v_1$ to be paid to bidder 1 conditional on winning against a less efficient bidder ($v_1 < v_2$). Since the loan takes effect only if the coalition wins, a simple way to effectuate this ex post transfer is for the bank to reduce the interest on the loan.

After establishing the optimal coalition bid strategy and a compensating transfer to bidder 1, the bank may fully delegate bidding to its coalition partner. This follows because the transfer to bidder 1 increases its private valuation of the auctioned firm. Since it is a dominant strategy for bidder 1 to bid its private valuation (when bidding alone), the transfer causes bidder 1 to voluntarily raise its bid. Thus, the transfer plays the dual role of inducing bidder 1 to participate and to delegate the coalition-bidding strategy.

2.4. The bank as monopolist seller

As mentioned in Section 1, although the bank is effectively a monopolist seller in the auction, regulatory constraints prevent it from enforcing a seller reserve price. By forming a coalition, however, the bank gets around the regulatory constraint. To see why, let b_m denote the price charged by a monopolist seller in a take-it-or-leave-it offer to sell the bankrupt firm, and suppose the monopolist seller's alternative use is worth v_1, so the expected opportunity cost of selling is $v_1[1 - G(b_m)]$. Moreover, the expected sales revenue is $b_m[1 - G(b_m)]$. Equating the expected marginal revenue $1 - G(b_m) - b_m g(b_m)$ with expected marginal cost $-v_1 g(b_m)$ yields a monopolist selling price of $b_m = v_1 + h(b_m)$ which is identical to the unconstrained coalition bid in Proposition 1. In other words, the coalition bid b_c allows the bank to achieve its expected revenue objective despite the institutional restriction preventing the bank from directly enforcing its seller reserve price.

2.5. Factors attenuating overbidding

A number of factors may work to attenuate the degree of coalition overbidding. If the bank is not the sole member of its creditor class, its toehold is reduced from a value of one to the proportion $\theta < 1$ of the creditor class owned by the bank (Hotchkiss and Mooradian, 2003). This scales down the overbidding amount, as terms involving $h(b_c)$ in Equation (1) are replaced by $\theta h(b_c)$.[8] Empirically, the case with $\theta < 1$ is irrelevant for our Swedish data where the bank is always the sole member of its debt class.

---

[8] As in Burkart (1995), the coalition's maximization problem (unconstrained by f) is now

$$\text{Max}_{b_c} \, \pi_c = \int_0^{b_c} [v_1 - (1 - \theta)v_2] g(v_2) \, dv_2 + \theta b_c(1 + G(b_c)).$$

The first term is the expected profit if the coalition wins and acquires the remaining $1 - \theta$ portion of the firm at a price of v_2. The second term is the expected profit when bidder 2 wins and purchases the coalition's toehold at the price b_c. The first-order condition is $(v_1 - (1 - \theta)b_c)g(b_c) + \theta[1 - G(b_c)] - \theta b_c g(b_c) = 0$. Rearranging yields an optimal (unconstrained) coalition bid of $b_c = v_1 + \theta h(b_c)$.

Second, in small- and medium-sized Swedish companies, it is common for the bank to demand a personal loan guarantee from the owner-manager. Such loan guarantee effectively makes the owner a residual claimant in the auction—with a concomitant reduction in the impairment of the bank's debt. The loan guarantee provides the old owner with an incentive to overbid even without formation of a coalition. In a saleback coalition, where the old owner is attempting to buy back the firm, the existence of a personal guarantee eliminates the need for a transfer to induce coalition overbidding. We address this possibility by treating salebacks as a separate category in parts of the empirical analysis.

Third, our analysis presumes that bidder 1, following coalition formation, fully reveals v_1 to the bank. Full revelation is a standard assumption in the literature on reorganization of financially distressed firms.[9] It can be shown, however, that the transfer necessary to induce bidder 1 to participate in the coalition is decreasing in v_1.[10] As a result, the bidder may have an incentive to understate v_1 in order to increase the transfer under the coalition agreement. In this case, bidder 1 seeks to capture informational rents which reduces the bank's profit and the overall incentive to form a coalition, possibly to the point where coalition formation is no longer incentive compatible for the bank.

Again, with symmetric information, the bank's coalition profit exceeds the minimum transfer necessary to induce participation by bidder 1. The bank has an incentive to allocate some or all of this excess profits toward reducing the information advantage of bidder 1, for example, by purchasing an audit. Alternatively, the bank may approach a bidder with whom it has a prior banking relationship. Thus, the degree of information asymmetry between the bank and its coalition partner may well be limited in practice.

2.6. A testable restriction on overbidding

We now bring the piecemeal liquidation value l back into the analysis. Let $r \equiv l/f \in [0, 1]$ denote the bank's recovery rate at the piecemeal liquidation value. Thus, r is the fraction of the face value expected to be recovered by the bank if the firm is liquidated piecemeal.

---

[9] See, for example, Bulow and Shoven (1978), Brown (1989), Gertner and Scharfstein (1991), Strömberg (2000), and Hotchkiss and Mooradian (2003).
[10] The partial derivatives with respect to v_1 of the participation constraints for the bidder (Equation (5)) and the bank (Equation (7)) are, respectively,

$$\frac{\partial E(c)}{\partial v_1} = (b_c - v_1)g(b_c)\frac{\partial b_c}{\partial v_1} - [G(b_c) - G(v_1)] \leq 0$$

$$\frac{\partial E(t)}{\partial v_1} = [1 - G(b_c)]\frac{\partial b_c}{\partial v_1} - [1 - G(v_1)] \leq 0$$

given the monotonicity condition $\partial h^{-1}(v)/\partial v \geq 0$.

Proposition 3 (expected going-concern premium). *Given the optimal coalition bid b_c in* Equation (1), *the expected going-concern premium $E(p)$ paid by the winner in the auction decreases as the bank's liquidation recovery rate r increases.*

Proof. The proposition is that r affects $E(p)$ via its impact on the expected coalition bid $E(b_c)$ so that

$$\frac{\partial E(p)}{\partial r} = \frac{\partial E(p)}{\partial E(b_c)} \frac{\partial E(b_c)}{\partial r} < 0 \tag{8}$$

We proceed by showing that $\partial E(p)/\partial E(b_c) > 0$ and that $\partial E(b_c)/\partial r < 0$. Notice first that coalition overbidding increases the expected premium paid by the winning bidder: if the coalition wins, the expected premium is $E(v_2|b_c) > E(v_2|v_1)$, and if it loses, bidder 2 pays $b_c > v_1$. In other words, $\partial E(p)/\partial E(b_c) > 0$. Second, using the integral limits defined in Equation (1), we have that

$$E(b_c) = \int_0^{f-h(b_c)} [v_1 + h(b_c)]g(v_1)\,dv_1 + \int_{f-h(b_c)}^f fg(v_1)\,dv_1 + \int_f^1 v_1 g(v_1)\,dv_1 \tag{9}$$

Replacing f with $f(r) \equiv l/r$, and defining $k(r) \equiv f(r) - h(b_c)$:

$$E(b_c) = \int_0^{k(r)} [v_1 + h(b_c)]g(v_1)\,dv_1 + f(r)[G(f(r)) - G(k(r))]$$
$$+ \int_{f(r)}^1 v_1 g(v_1)\,dv_1 \tag{10}$$

The first-order condition with respect to r is

$$\frac{\partial E(b_c)}{\partial r} = [k(r) + h(b_c)]g(k(r))k'(r) + f'(r)[G(f(r)) - G(k(r))]$$
$$+ f(r)[g(f(r))f'(r) - g(k(r))k'(r)] - f(r)g(f(r))f'(r) \tag{11}$$

Since $f'(r) = k'(r) = -l/r^2 < 0$ and $f(r) > k(r)$:

$$\frac{\partial E(b_c)}{\partial r} = f'(r)[G(f(r)) - G(k(r))] < 0 \tag{12}$$

Thus, $\partial E(p)/\partial r < 0$.

Intuitively, increases in the piecemeal liquidation value l effectively reduce the face value at risk for the bank. Figure 3 illustrates how changes in l affect the liquidation recovery rate r and the expected amount of overbidding $E(b_c - v_1)$ for $f = 0.8$ and the uniform distribution. Here, $E(b_c - v_1)$ equals the shaded area above the diagonal line and below $f - l$. Increases in l increase r and decrease $E(b_c - v_1)$. The figure shows three alternative values of l: $l = 0.0$, $l = 0.1$, and $l = 0.2$. The corresponding expected amounts of overbidding are represented by the shaded areas below $f - l = 0.8, f - l = 0.7$, and $f - l = 0.6$, respectively. The downward shifts in $f - l$ reduce the region for overbidding.

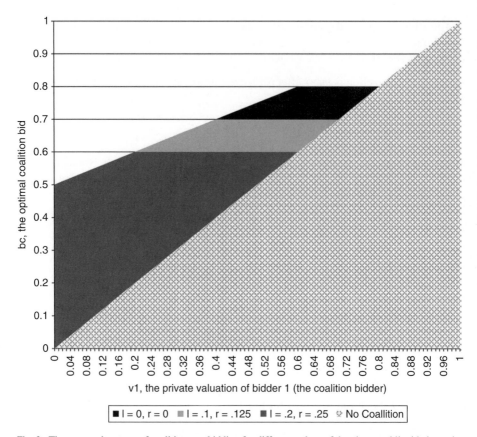

Fig. 3. The expected amount of coalition overbidding for different values of the piecemeal liquidation value
l. The figure illustrates how changes in l affect the expected amount of overbidding $E(b_c - v_1)$, where b_c is
the coalition's optimal bid and v_1 is the coalition-bidder's private valuation (distributed uniform). The face
value of the bank's debt claim is set to $f = 0.8$. $E(b_c - v_1)$ equals the shaded area above the diagonal line (v_1,
bidder 1's optimal bid with no overbidding) and below $f - l$. As l increases, the bank's liquidation recovery
rate $r = \min[l/f, 1]$ increases and $E(b_c - v_1)$ decreases. The figure is drawn for three alternative values of
l: $l = 0.0$, $l = 0.1$, and $l = 0.2$. The corresponding expected amounts of overbidding are the shaded areas
below $f - l = 0.8$, $f - l = 0.7$, and $f - l = 0.6$, respectively. Thus, the downward shifts in $f - l$ reduce the
region for overbidding.

Proposition 3 forms the basis for our cross-sectional empirical tests of overbidding.
If the firm is sold as a going concern (reflecting $v_i > 0$ and therefore $p > 0$), and
provided that the bank's debt is impaired ex ante at the piecemeal liquidation value (so
that $r < 1$), the proposition holds that r affects the final winning price through $E(b_c)$. A
first-order test of the theory is therefore achieved by regressing p on r. Overbidding
implies a negative coefficient on r in this regression. Specifics of the test approach are
found in Section 4 below.

3. Data and sample characteristics

3.1. The auction setting

When a company files for Swedish bankruptcy, the control rights are transferred to a court-appointed trustee who puts the firm up for sale in an open first-price auction. Buyers are free to place bids for individual assets (piecemeal liquidation) or for the entire firm (going-concern sale). The highest bid wins, so going-concern offers dominate competing piecemeal liquidation bids. We do not observe auctions with a mix of piecemeal liquidation and going-concern bids, possibly because it is common knowledge among bidders when a company's going-concern value is close to zero and the firm should be liquidated piecemeal. In general, the bidding process is open for 1 month and the firm is sold within 2 months of filing (Thorburn, 2000).

The firm and its business operations receive protection during the auction bankruptcy procedure, much as in Chapter 11. Debt payments and collateralized assets are stayed. The incumbent management team is often retained to run the operations under the trustee's supervision until the sale is completed. Bankruptcy law permits operating costs incurred while in bankruptcy to be paid in cash, effectively granting these costs super-priority status. While the law also permits debtor-in-possession financing, such debt issues are never observed, reflecting the swift auction process.

Bidders are required to pay in cash. They often form a shell company that, financed by debt and equity, acquires the bankrupt firm's assets much like in an LBO. Alternatively, the bidder merges the bankrupt target with its own operations. The cash proceeds from the auction, net of the trustee's fees and expenses, are distributed to creditors strictly according to the absolute priority of the debt claims. For the average sample firm, the debt structure is as follows (Thorburn, 2000): rent and audit costs (senior to the bank) 1%, bank debt 39%, tax and wage claims (junior to the bank) 28%, and trade credits (junior to all other claims) 32%.

The trustee's fiduciary duty is to creditors. The auction process and outcome are monitored by a government supervisory agency (TSM). If an insider of the bankrupt firm is the only bidder (attempting a saleback of the firm), the trustee is required to search for competing bids. Moreover, firms sometimes negotiate a sale of the assets right before filing. While such prepackaged arrangements (refereed to below as "auction prepacks") are subject to approval by the trustee and secured creditors, they are rarely overturned (Thorburn, 2000). The trustee does not provide the piecemeal liquidation-value estimate *l* for auction prepacks. We return to the implication of this in the empirical analysis below.

3.2. Characteristics of auctioned firms

We use a sample of 260 bankruptcy cases between 1/1988 and 12/1991 originally compiled by Strömberg and Thorburn (1996) and Thorburn (2000), drawn from the population of 1159 bankrupt Swedish companies with at least 20 employees.

The sample is restricted to bankruptcies in the four largest administrative provinces in Sweden, including the country's four main metropolitan areas, Stockholm, Gothenburg, Malmö and Uppsala. We expand the sample information with auction characteristics—including final auction prices—required to test our overbidding hypotheses. Liquidation-value estimates and bid information are obtained from trustee reports and in direct communication with trustees. Data on bank financing of bidders are from the national register of corporate floating charge claims ("Inskrivningsmydigheten for Foretagsinteckning") and complemented by the trustees. Company financial statements for all Swedish firms with at least 20 employees are obtained from UpplysningsCentralen (UC) AB. As described below, this information is used to construct a measure of industry-wide financial distress.

As shown in Panel A of Table 1, 53 firms (20% of the sample) are sold as going concerns in a prepack. Of the remaining 207 firms auctioned off in bankruptcy,

Table 1

Characteristics of the sample of 260 firms filing for bankruptcy in Sweden, 1988–1991

		Total sample	Prepack filing	Going-concern sale	Piecemeal liquidation
A: Distribution of sample firms across industries					
Manufacturing		81	13	50	18
Construction		37	7	22	8
Transport		28	3	13	12
Trade and retail of goods		45	15	23	7
Hotels and restaurants		28	9	12	7
Services		41	6	27	8
Total		260	53	147	60
B: Firm financial characteristics and CEO ownership[a]					
Total assets ($ million)	Mean	2.3	2.6	2.2	2.2
	Median	1.2	1.4	1.1	1.1
Sales ($ million)	Mean	4.7	6.2	4.1	4.7
	Median	2.5	2.7	2.5	2.2
Number of employees	Mean	43	47	44	36
	Median	29	28	29	29
EBITDA/sales (%)	Mean	−0.2	0.3	0.2	−1.7
	Median	1.8	1.7	1.7	2.3
Debt/assets	Mean	0.92	0.88	0.94	0.94
	Median	0.93	0.92	0.93	0.95
CEO equity ownership (%)	Mean	60	66	56	63
	Median	72	100	60	81

[a]The financial data is from the last financial statement reported prior to filing. CEO ownership is from the bankruptcy filing documents.

147 (61%) are sold as a going concern and 60 (29%) are liquidated piecemeal. Panel A also shows the distribution of sample firms across different industries. Almost one-third of the sample (81 firms) is in the manufacturing industry. The remaining firms are distributed between construction (37 firms), transport (28 firms), hotels and restaurants (28 firms), trade and retail of goods (45 firms), and services (41 firms). A relatively large fraction of firms in the transport industry (12 firms or 43%) are liquidated piecemeal, while a relatively large fraction of firms in hotels and restaurants (9 firms or 32%) and trade and retail of goods (15 firms or 33%) are sold in prepacks.

Panel B of Table 1 shows selected firm characteristics from the last financial statement reported prior to bankruptcy filing. The sample firms are small, with an average book value of assets of $2.3 million (median $1.2 million) and sales of $4.7 million. The mean (median) number of employees is 43 (29). Operating profitability is generally poor, with a mean (median) ratio of EBITDA/sales of −0.2% (1.8%), and firms are highly leveraged with typical debt levels exceeding 90% of book value of assets. All firms in the sample are privately held and have concentrated ownership. At bankruptcy filing, the CEO owns on average 60% of the equity. There is no discernible difference in the financial ratios between firms sold in prepacks, auctioned as going concerns or liquidated piecemeal.

3.3. Bid activity and auction premiums

The trustees keep records of potential bidders who show an interest in buying the firm's assets. These potential rivals induce competitive bidding also when their interest fails to translate into an actual bid, since a low offer may encourage entry. In the empirical analysis below, we condition premium regressions on the level of potential competition in the auction.

We have data on bidder interest in 195 cases. As shown in Panel A of Table 2, in 77 (75%) of 102 going-concern sales in bankruptcy, multiple bidders express an interest in participating in the auction. In the sample of auction prepacks, we find bid competition in only 5 (15%) of 33 cases. This data may, however, be incomplete since the trustee in prepacks approves the firm's purchase agreement after the buyer has been selected. In piecemeal liquidations, where bids are for individual assets, there is multiple bidder interest in 16 (80%) of 20 auctions.

The filing firm's bank can help increase liquidity in the auction by offering financing to bidders. Panel A of Table 2 presents information on the bank financing of the winning bidder for a total of 130 going-concern sales. The bank finances the winning bidder in half (49%) of the cases, distributed as 20 of 35 auction prepacks and 44 of 95 going-concern auctions. When the old bank does not finance the winning bidder, it either finances a losing bid or none of the bids. There are, however, no public records of bank financing commitments for losers in the auction. Overall, we conclude that the bankrupt firm's bank adds liquidity to the bankruptcy auctions.

Panel B of Table 2 lists the average and standard error of the mean for the auction premium and bank-debt recovery rates. The auction premium is the price paid by the

Table 2

Bidder interest, bank financing, premiums, and recovery rates

		Total sample[a]	Prepack filing[b]	Going-concern sale	Piecemeal liquidation
A: Auction demand					
Multiple buyers expressing an interest in placing a bid	Number	98	5	77	16
	Total	195	33	102	20
	Percent	50	15	75	80
Bankrupt firm's bank financing the winning bidder	Number	64	20	44	
	Total	130	35	95	n/a
	Percent	49	57	46	
B: Premiums and recovery rates					
Auction premium $(p-1)^c$	Average	94%		125%	8%
	S.E.	18%	n/a	24%	8%
	N	175		130	45
Bank liquidation recovery rate $(r)^d$	Average	0.60		0.66	0.45
	Median	0.68	n/a	0.77	0.39
	S.E.	0.03		0.03	0.05
	N	196		141	55
Bank realized recovery rate[e]	Average	0.69	0.77	0.76	0.46
	Median	0.83	0.91	0.89	0.40
	S.E.	0.02	0.05	0.02	0.05
	N	236	40	141	55

[a]Sample of 260 firms filing for bankruptcy in Sweden, 1988–1991.

[b]In prepacks, the trustee typically does not report a piecemeal liquidation-value estimate, hence the missing information on the auction premium and the bank liquidation recovery rate.

[c]The auction premium is the price paid by the winning bidder in excess of the trustee's piecemeal liquidation-value estimate l^a of the auctioned assets. If the auction excludes some liquid assets (such as cash balances, accounts receivables and real estate), then $l^a < l$, where l is the trustee's estimate of the total piecemeal liquidation value of the bankrupt firm's assets.

[d]The liquidation recovery rate r is the bank's recovery rate on its debt if the winning bidder pays the trustee's piecemeal liquidation-value estimate l. Specifically, $r = \min[(l - s)/f, 1]$, where f is the face value of the bank's debt and s is the face value of all debt senior to the bank.

[e]Realized payoff to the bank divided by the face value of its claim f on the bankrupt firm.

winning bidder in the auction in excess of the trustee's liquidation-value estimate for the assets sold in the auction (l^a). This value estimate, which is the sum of the individual second-hand values of the assets, is produced by industry experts. Noncore assets such as real estate holdings, accounts receivables, securities, cash holdings, etc., are often sold or collected separately also when the firm's core operations are auctioned as a going concern. Thus $l^a < l$, where l denotes the trustee's estimate of the target's total piecemeal liquidation value at the start of the auction (used to define r). We use the bankruptcy file to infer the asset exclusion in l^a.

The premium p averages 8% for piecemeal liquidations with a standard error of 0.08. Using a standard t-test, we cannot reject the hypothesis that $p = l^a$ in piecemeal liquidations. In contrast, the premium paid in going-concern auctions averages 125% with a standard error of 0.24. The p-value for the difference in average premiums across going-concern sales and piecemeal liquidations is 0.00. Competition to run the surviving firm may explain the substantially greater premiums when the firm is sold as a going concern. The trustee typically does not report a piecemeal liquidation-value estimate for auction prepacks, precluding a premium comparison for this subsample.

Turning to recovery rates, Panel B shows the bank's liquidation recovery rate r as well as the actual debt recovery rate. Recall that Proposition 3 defines r as $\min[l/f, 1]$, where f is the face value of the bank's debt. This definition assumes that the bank is the firm's only senior creditor. In our data, however, there is on average 1% of total debt outstanding that is senior to the bank's claim. Denoting this debt as s, we modify the definition of the liquidation recovery rate to $r \equiv \min[(l - s)/f, 1]$. The rescaling of l is purely for empirical purposes and does not affect the above theoretical predictions involving r.

The average value of r is 45% in piecemeal liquidations and 66% in going-concern auctions. This difference is statistically significant at the 1% level, indicating that firms that are liquidated piecemeal tend to have more impaired bank debt at the outset of the auction. The frequency distribution of r for going-concern auctions and piecemeal liquidations is plotted in Figure 4. The bank receives full recovery at the trustee's

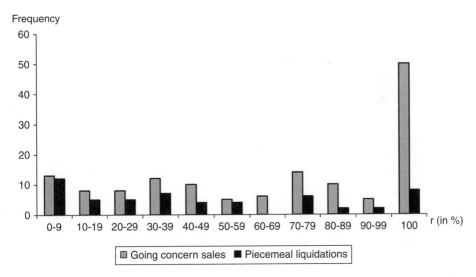

Fig. 4. Frequency distribution of the liquidation recovery rate r at the beginning of the auction. The liquidation recovery rate is $r = \min[l/f, 1]^* 100\%$, where l is the bankruptcy trustee's estimate (provided at the beginning of the auction) of the bankrupt firm's piecemeal liquidation value and f is the face value of the bank's debt. Sample of 196 bankruptcy auctions, excluding auction prepack filings.

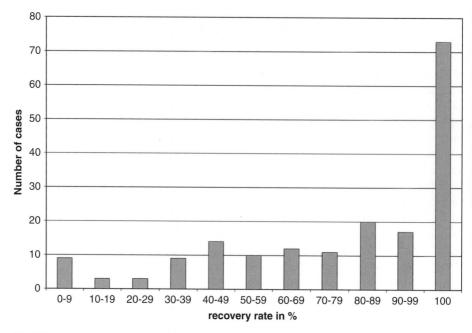

Fig. 5. Frequency distribution of the bank's realized debt recovery rate. The bank's realized recovery rate is its payoff in bankruptcy as a fraction of the face value of its debt claim on the bankrupt firm. Sample of 181 Swedish firms auctioned as a going concern or filing a prepackaged bankruptcy, excluding piecemeal liquidation, 1988–1991.

piecemeal liquidation-value estimate in 58 bankruptcy filings (30%). The 138 cases with less than full liquidation recovery are evenly distributed across the range of r from 0% to 99%.

The actual distribution to banks (bank realized recovery rate) averages 69% (median 83%) of the face value of bank debt. Bank recovery rates are on average significantly higher in prepacks and going-concern auctions (77% and 76%, respectively) than in piecemeal liquidations (46%), again reflecting the additional value created in auctions where the going-concern value of the firm is preserved. The distribution of the realized bank recovery rate in going-concern sales and prepacks are shown in Figure 5.

4. Does coalition overbidding exist?

4.1. Testing the overbidding theory

Our approach to testing Proposition 3 is summarized in hypothesis H1:

H1 (Overbidding). *In a regression of the ex post going-concern premium p on the bank's ex ante liquidation recovery rate $r \equiv min[(l - s)/f, 1]$, let β denote the* *regression coefficient on r.* Proposition 3 *predicts that* $\beta < 0$ *when the auction results in a going-concern sale. Moreover,* $\beta = 0$ *when* $r = 1$ *(the bank debt is not impaired ex ante), and when the firm is liquidated piecemeal (there is no going-concern premium).*

We use a cross-sectional regression framework to test H1, where the log-auction premium $\ln(p)$ is regressed on r as well as on a vector X of control variables. Structurally, the direction of causality in this cross-sectional regression runs from r (observed at the beginning of the auction) to the auction premium (determined ex post) through the hypothesized incentive to overbid. Also, in our institutional setting, it is safe to assume that r is exogenous to the bank.[11]

Table 3 lists the variable definitions for the cross-sectional regressions. The control variables in X include *Piecemeal* (indicator for piecemeal liquidation), *Size* (natural logarithm of book value of total assets), *Profit margin* (prefiling industry-adjusted operating profitability), and *Tangible* (fraction of secured debt in the capital structure). Assuming that firms tend to lever up their tangible assets, *Tangible* is a proxy for asset tangibility.[12]

Table 4 shows our main test results for the overbidding hypothesis. Panel A uses the total sample of 175 going-concern sales and piecemeal liquidations with available data on l and p.[13] The first row of Table 4 shows the impact of r on $\ln(p)$ for the full sample of auctions. The regression has an adjusted R^2 of 0.15. The coefficient on r is -0.90 with a p-value of 0.00, which is consistent with H1: auction premiums decrease in the bank's *ex ante* liquidation recovery rate. As for the control variables, the coefficient for *Piecemeal* is always negative and significant, which confirms the earlier evidence in Table 2. Auction premiums are on average lower in piecemeal liquidations than in going-concern sales, reflecting the absence of a going-concern premium. Of the remaining control variables, only *Tangible* is statistically significant. The negative coefficient indicates that bidders pay lower premiums for targets that have a relatively high proportion tangible assets.

Overbidding is restricted to going-concern sales as there is no rents to be extracted from bidders when the target is liquidated piecemeal. To check for this effect of the auction outcome, the second and the third regressions of Panel A permit r to have different impacts across going-concern sales (indicated by the binary variable *Concern*) and piecemeal liquidations. The two regression specifications are as follows:

$$\ln(p) = \begin{cases} \alpha + \beta_2 r \times \text{Piecemeal} + \beta_3 r \times \text{Concern} + \gamma X + \varepsilon \\ \alpha + \beta_1' r + \beta_2' r \times \text{Piecemeal} + \gamma X + \varepsilon \end{cases} \tag{13}$$

---

[11] A bidder anticipating the bankruptcy event might attempt to acquire the bank's toehold by purchasing the distressed debt ahead of bankruptcy filing. However, there was no secondary market for bank debt in Sweden during our sample period.

[12] This argument holds a *fortiori* for cash-constrained distressed firms. These firms often use all available debt capacity by borrowing against tangible assets.

[13] As indicated earlier, l is unavailable for the 53 auction prepacks. We return to the auction prepacks below.

Table 3

Definitions of variables used in cross-sectional regressions for overbidding

Variable name	Definition
A: Variables for direct tests of overbidding	
P	Auction premium: the price paid in the auction divided by the trustee's estimate of the piecemeal liquidation value l^a of the auctioned assets.[a] The auction determines p
R	Bank's liquidation recovery rate: $r = \min[(l - s)/f, 1]$, where f is the face value of the bank's debt and s is the face value of any debt senior to the bank. r is the bank's debt recovery obtained in the event that the bankruptcy proceeds equal l, the trustee's estimate of the firm's total piecemeal liquidation value. $r < 1$ implies incentive to overbid
r^*	$r^* = (l - s)/f$ for $r = 1$, and $r^* = 0$ for $r < 1$. $r^* \geq 1$ implies no incentive to overbid
r_{low}	Indicates that $0 < r \leq 0.5$, which implies incentives to overbid
r_{high}	Indicates that $r = 1$, which implies no incentives to overbid
B: Controls for firm characteristics[b]	
Size	Log of the book value of prefiling assets
Profit margin	Difference between the firm's prefiling operating margin (EBITDA/sales) and the industry median operating margin[c]
Tangible	Fraction secured debt to total debt at filing, a proxy for the fraction of tangible assets
C: Controls for auction demand	
Piecemeal	Binary indicator variable for the target firm being liquidated piecemeal
Concern	Indicator for the firm being sold as a going concern ($1 - Piecemeal$)
Industry distress	Fraction of industry firms reporting an interest coverage ratio ICR < 1 or file for bankruptcy the following year, where ICR = (EBITDA + interest income)/interest expense[c]
Saleback	Indicator that the firm is sold as a going concern to a target insider (owner and/or manager)
Multiple interest	Indicator that more than one potential bidder express an interest in placing a bid
Bank	Indicator that the bankrupt firm's bank finances the winning going-concern bid

[a]If the auction excludes some liquid assets (such as cash balances, accounts receivables, or real estate), then $l^a < l$, where l is the trustee's estimate of the total piecemeal liquidation value of the bankrupt firm's assets.
[b]Prefiling characteristics are from the last financial statement reported prior to filing.
[c]The bankrupt firm's industry consists of all Swedish firms with at least 20 employees and that operate in the same four-digit SIC code as the bankrupt firm.

where α is the constant term, γ is the vector of regression coefficients for the control variables in X, and ε is an error term. In the first regression, β_2 and β_3 capture the separate effects of overbidding in piecemeal liquidations and going-concern auctions. The second regression directly tests whether the two coefficient estimates are significantly different from each other. To see why, note that the second regression can be rewritten as $\alpha + \beta_1' r(Piecemeal + Concern) + \beta_2' r \times Piecemeal + \gamma X + \varepsilon$. Comparing the two regressions, we have $\beta_2' \equiv \beta_3$ and $\beta_2' \equiv \beta_2 - \beta_1' \equiv \beta_2 - \beta_3$. H1 predicts that $\beta_2 = 0$, $\beta_3 < 0$, and $\beta_2' > 0$ (i.e., that $\beta_2 > \beta_3$).

All of these predictions are borne out in the data. In the second regression of Panel A, the coefficient β_2 for $r \times Piecemeal$ is indistinguishable from zero (p-value 0.68),

Table 4

Regressions testing the overbidding hypothesis

OLS coefficient estimates in regressions of the auction premium $\ln(p)$ on the bank's ex ante liquidation recovery rate r, where $r \equiv \min[(l - s)/f, 1]$, l is the trustee's ex ante estimate of the piecemeal liquidation value, s is the face value of debt senior to the bank, and f is the face value of the bank's debt. The overbidding hypothesis predicts a negative coefficient for r. See Table 3 for remaining variable definitions. Sample of 175 Swedish firms auctioned in bankruptcy 1988–1991 and with data on p and l (p-values and degrees of freedom in parentheses).

Constant	r	$r \times$ Piecemeal	$r \times$ Concern	Piecemeal	Size	Profit margin	Tangible	Adjusted R^2	F-value	N
A: Sample of going-concern sales and piecemeal liquidations										
0.915	−0.900			−0.604	0.018	−0.303	−0.588	0.146	6.96	175
(0.350)	(0.000)			(0.000)	(0.770)	(0.461)	(0.055)	(df = 5)	(0.000)	
1.195		−0.147	−1.156	−1.152	0.012	−0.224	−0.633	0.172	7.03	175
(0.219)		(0.677)	(0.000)	(0.000)	(0.839)	(0.582)	(0.036)	(df = 6)	(0.000)	
1.195	−1.156	1.009		−1.152	0.012	−0.224	−0.633	0.172	7.03	175
(0.219)	(0.000)	(0.013)		(0.000)	(0.839)	(0.582)	(0.036)	(df = 6)	(0.000)	
B: Sample of going-concern sales and piecemeal liquidations where $r < 1$										
0.884	−0.832			−0.744	0.027	−0.361	−0.761	0.177	6.13	120
(0.459)	(0.002)			(0.000)	(0.722)	(0.410)	(0.042)	(df = 5)	(0.000)	
0.944		−0.225	−1.088	−1.113	0.032	−0.270	−0.802	0.187	5.55	120
(0.427)		(0.640)	(0.001)	(0.000)	(0.673)	(0.539)	(0.032)	(df = 6)	(0.000)	
0.944	−1.088	0.863		−1.113	0.032	−0.270	−0.802	0.187	5.55	120
(0.427)	(0.001)	(0.134)		(0.000)	(0.673)	(0.539)	(0.032)	(df = 6)	(0.000)	

suggesting that there is no overbidding in piecemeal liquidations. The coefficient β_3 for $r \times$ Concern is negative and highly significant, confirming the prediction of an overbidding effect in going-concern sales. In the third regression of Panel A, $\beta_2' = 1.01$ with a p-value of 0.01, confirming that the impact of r on the auction premium is significantly different across going concerns and piecemeal liquidations.

According to our theory, overbidding is limited to cases where the bank's debt is impaired at the liquidation recovery rate. Panel B of Table 4 repeats the regressions from Panel A on the subsample of auctions where $r < 1$. This eliminates 55 cases. All but one of the regression coefficients in Panel B are close to those in Panel A, both in terms of magnitude and significance levels. Specifically, the coefficient estimate for r is again negative and highly significant ($p = 0.00$) for the full sample of 120. Moreover, the coefficients for $r \times$ Concern (β_2) is negative and significant ($p = 0.00$), while the coefficient for $r \times$ Piecemeal (β_1) is not significantly different from zero. The estimate of β_2', however, is now 0.89 with a p-value of 0.13. Overall, the regression results in Table 4 strongly suggest that lower values of the liquidation recovery rate r result in higher auction premiums for going-concern sales, while no such effect is discernible for piecemeal liquidations, as predicted by H1.

4.2. Robustness tests

The coefficient estimate on r in the above regressions ignores the potential for estimation error in the liquidation-value estimates l and l^a. The auction price data shows that this estimation error is small on average: recall from Table 2 that final market prices in the piecemeal liquidation category are on average only 8% higher than the piecemeal liquidation-value estimate l^a.[14] A more important issue is the fact that the liquidation value appears on both sides of the regression equation ($\ln(p)$ contains $1/l^a$ and r contains l) and may therefore in part be driving the negative coefficient estimate on r. Below, we resolve this issue by isolating the range of r where overbidding does not exist in theory but in which the mechanical correlation remains present, and by orthogonalizing the effect of l on r. Second, we examine the robustness of our overbidding evidence with respect to the exclusion of prepack auctions (for which we do not have data on l). Third, since the theoretical overbidding function (Proposition 1) is nonlinear, we test whether the data rejects the linearity assumption behind our cross-sectional regressions. Our main conclusions appear robust to all of these specification issues.

4.2.1. The role of the piecemeal liquidation value

Recall from Equation (1) that when the bank's debt is not impaired, $(l - s)/f \geq 1$ so $r = 1$ and there is no overbidding. Since r is truncated at one, it does not capture the cross-sectional variation in $(l - s)/f$ when this value exceeds one. Define the variable r^* such that:

$$r^* = \begin{cases} (1 - s)/f & \text{if } r = 1 \\ 0 & \text{if } r < 1 \end{cases} \tag{14}$$

While Proposition 3 predicts a coefficient value of zero for r^*, the negative correlation between $\ln(1/l^a)$ and l affects r and r^* equally. Therefore, if this correlation is in fact driving the negative coefficient estimate for r reported in Table 4, we should observe a negative coefficient estimate for r^* as well.

We test this hypothesis in Table 5. In the first regression, which uses the full sample, the coefficient on r is -1.01 ($p = 0.00$). This estimate is close to that reported earlier for the full sample in Table 4. More importantly, the coefficient estimate for r^* is only 0.02 with a p-value of 0.39. The finding of an insignificant coefficient estimate for r^* is reinforced by the results in Panels B and C. In Panel B, where the sample is restricted to going-concern sales, the coefficient on r is again negative and significant, while the

---

[14] Even with estimation error, the impact on the coefficient on r is likely to be negligible. Write $l = \hat{l}\, u$, where $\hat{l}$ is the true liquidation value and u is a (multiplicative) measurement error. Let P denote the price paid in the auction, and consider a regression of the form $\ln(P/l) = \alpha + \beta \ln(l/f) + e$. Taking the logarithm, $P - \hat{l} - u = \alpha + \beta(\hat{l} - u - f) + \ln(e)$. If we assume that $\text{Cov}(P - \hat{l}, \hat{l} - f) = 0$, then the bias in β from the measurement error in l is small—on the order of $\sigma_u^2(\sigma_{f-\hat{l}}^2 + \sigma_u^2)$, where σ^2 is the variance.

Table 5

Robustness tests for the overbidding hypothesis

OLS coefficient estimates in regressions of the auction premium $\ln(p)$ on the overbidding variable r and a robustness test variable r^*, where $r^* = (l - s)/f$ when $r = 1$ and $r^* = 0$ when $r < 1$. The variable r^* captures the impact on auction premiums of the cross-sectional variation in $(l - s)/f$ when there is no scope for overbidding. The overbidding hypothesis predicts a negative coefficient for r and a zero coefficient for r^*. The table also adds control variables for industry liquidity, auction demand, and a saleback to the auctioned firm's previous owner. Variable definitions are in Table 3. Sample of 175 firms auctioned in Swedish bankruptcy 1988–1991 (p-values and the degrees of freedom in parentheses).

Constant	r	r^*	Piecemeal	Industry distress	Multiple interest	Saleback	Size	Profit margin	Tangible	Adjusted R^2	F-value	N
A: Sample of going-concern sales and piecemeal liquidations												
1.171	-1.010	0.024	-0.617	-0.597			0.018	-0.297	-0.569	0.149	5.35	175
(0.241)	(0.000)	(0.391)	(0.000)	(0.180)			(0.777)	(0.470)	(0.063)	(df = 7)	(0.000)	
B: Sample of going-concern sales												
1.770	-1.313	0.031		-0.721			-0.003	-0.532	-0.643	0.174	5.52	130
(0.126)	(0.000)	(0.264)		(0.166)			(0.966)	(0.436)	(0.070)	(df = 6)	(0.000)	
2.007	-1.416	0.029		-0.801	-0.323		0.017	-0.886	-1.136	0.173	3.68	91
(0.151)	(0.000)	(0.334)		(0.212)	(0.131)		(0.839)	(0.282)	(0.014)	(df = 7)	(0.002)	
1.740	-1.328	0.034		-0.840		0.226	-0.007	-0.580	-0.625	0.180	4.98	128
(0.136)	(0.000)	(0.219)		(0.118)		(0.119)	(0.921)	(0.395)	(0.080)	(df = 7)	(0.000)	
C: Sample of going-concern sales where $r = 1$												
1.289		0.040		-0.911			-0.070	0.586	0.060	-0.028	0.74	48
(0.500)		(0.172)		(0.317)			(0.562)	(0.775)	(0.927)	(df = 5)	(0.594)	
D: Sample of piecemeal liquidations												
-0.604	-0.126			-0.036			0.050	-0.075	-0.541	-0.104	0.17	45
(0.758)	(0.755)			(0.967)			(0.690)	(0.890)	(0.378)	(df = 5)	(0.973)	

coefficient on r^* is close to zero and insignificant. In Panel C, where we restrict the sample to cases where $r = 1$ (no overbidding), the coefficient estimate for r^* remains close to zero. These results suggest that the negative correlation between $\ln(1//l^a)$ and l has only a negligible effect on the coefficient estimate for r. This evidence strengthens the empirical support for the overbidding hypothesis.

Turning to the control variables, the inclusion of r^* does not change the impact on auction premiums of *Piecemeal* and *Tangible*, both of which receive negative and significant coefficients as before. The table also includes regressors controlling for auction demand conditions. The variable *Industry distress* measures the degree of industry-wide distress in the year of the bankruptcy filing. This variable is defined as the fraction of firms with the same four-digit SIC industry code as the sample firm that report an interest coverage ratio less than one or files for bankruptcy in the subsequent year. The interest coverage ratio is defined as (EBITDA + interest income)/interest expense. The coefficient estimate for *Industry distress* is insignificant across all regression specifications.[15]

Panel B, which is restricted to going-concern sales, also controls for the degree of competition and a saleback of the firm to target insiders. The former is represented by the binary variable *Multiple interest* which indicates the presence of at least two firms expressing a serious interest in bidding for the target, while the latter is the binary variable *Saleback*. Neither variable affect auction premiums and their inclusion has only a negligible effect on the coefficient estimates for r and r^*, respectively. In Section 2, we argue that since it is common for owner-managers of small firms to issue a personal guarantee of the company's bank debt, owner-managers may have their own incentives to overbid. The insignificance of *Saleback* reported here suggests that any such incentives do not on average have a separate premium impact—beyond what is already captured by our measure of bank-debt impairment r. The regressions in Panel D show that inclusion of *Industry distress* does not affect the coefficient estimate for r in the sample of piecemeal liquidations. In this regression, and consistent with the overbidding theory, r receives an insignificant coefficient.

Table 6 provides a final robustness check of whether the coefficient estimate for r is driven by the negative correlation between $\ln(1//l^a)$ and l. In this table, we first estimate the impact of l on r through an OLS regression $r = \gamma_0 + \gamma_1 \ln(l) + r_\varepsilon$. By construction, the residuals r are orthogonal to $\ln(l)$. We then replace r with r_ε in the premium regressions. As shown in the table, r_ε receives a negative coefficient estimate of the same magnitude as r and is highly significant with $p = 0.00$ across the full sample (Panel A) and going-concern auctions (Panel B), and it is insignificant for piecemeal liquidations (Panel C). These results are again as predicted by our overbidding theory, and they rule out a confounding effect of the correlation between $\ln(1//l^a)$ and l.

---

[15] Eckbo and Thorburn (in press) provide further evidence on the impact of industry illiquidity on bankruptcy auction prices.

Table 6

Tests for overbidding after orthogonalizing the liquidation recovery rate r and the piecemeal liquidation value l

OLS coefficient estimates in regressions of the auction premium $\ln(p)$ on r_ε. By construction, the variable r_ε is orthogonal to $\ln(l)$ as it is the residual from the following regression: $r = \gamma_0 + \gamma_1 \ln(l) + r_\varepsilon$. The overbidding hypothesis predicts a negative coefficient on r_ε. Variable definitions are in Table 3. Sample of 175 Swedish firms auctioned in bankruptcy 1988–1991 (p-values and the degrees of freedom in parentheses).

Constant	r_ε	Piecemeal	Industry distress	Multiple Interest	Saleback	Size	Profit margin	Tangible	Adjusted R^2	F-value	N
A: Sample of going-concern sales and piecemeal liquidations											
2.016	−1.042	−0.542				−0.083	−0.258	−0.713	0.131	6.23	175
(0.059)	(0.000)	(0.000)				(0.211)	(−0.534)	(0.028)	(df = 5)	(0.000)	
2.275	−1.088	−0.557	−0.483			−0.089	−0.246	−0.716	0.132	5.39	175
(0.038)	(0.000)	(0.000)	(0.279)			(0.183)	(0.553)	(0.027)	(df = 6)	(0.000)	
B: Sample of going-concern sales											
2.813	−1.316					−0.130	−0.338	−0.801	0.134	5.97	130
(0.026)	(0.000)					(0.096)	(0.627)	(0.034)	(df = 4)	(0.000)	
3.138	−1.359		−0.613			−0.137	−0.400	−0.787	0.136	5.06	130
(0.015)	(0.000)		(0.247)			(0.079)	(0.566)	(0.038)	(df = 4)	(0.000)	
3.440	−1.483		−0.673	−0.348		−0.125	−0.690	−1.244	0.139	3.41	91
(0.031)	(0.000)		(0.300)	(0.109)		(0.192)	(0.410)	(0.012)	(df = 6)	(0.005)	
3.133	−1.373		−0.716		0.221	−0.143	−0.448	−0.788	0.142	4.50	128
(0.016)	(0.000)		(0.190)		(0.136)	(0.070)	(0.519)	(0.039)	(df = 6)	(0.000)	
C: Sample of piecemeal liquidations											
−0.449	−0.151					0.036	−0.076	−0.566	−0.077	0.21	45
(0.824)	(0.760)					(0.779)	(0.884)	(0.372)	(df = 4)	(0.930)	
−0.443	−0.153		−0.014			0.036	−0.075	−0.567	−0.105	0.16	45
(0.831)	(0.769)		(0.987)			(0.782)	(0.889)	(0.381)	(df = 5)	(0.974)	

4.2.2. Auction prepack selection

As discussed above, because the trustee typically does not provide a piecemeal liquidation-value estimate l for auction prepacks, our premium regressions exclude this category of auctions. When approaching bankruptcy, however, the firm self-selects whether to do an ordinary bankruptcy filing or to find a buyer and file an auction prepack. For example, the firm may prefer to work out a private auction prepack agreement if the bankruptcy auction itself is expected to be illiquid and produce low prices (Eckbo and Thorburn, 2008). If so, since the sample truncates observations for l in prepacks, the OLS estimates of the coefficient vector β reported in earlier tables may be biased.

We use a two-step Heckman (1979) procedure to control for this truncation problem. To illustrate, suppose the firm selects the prepack filing based on $\gamma'Z$, where Z is a vector of explanatory variables and γ is a vector of coefficients. If so, the true data generating process is

$$\ln(p) = \begin{cases} \beta'X + u & \text{if } \gamma'Z > u_z \quad \text{(nonprepack filing)} \\ \beta_1'X + u_1 & \text{if } \gamma'Z \leq u_z \quad \text{(prepack filing)} \end{cases} \tag{15}$$

where u_z is the residual from the choice model $\gamma'Z$. To account for this self-selection, we first estimate the coefficients γ using probit for a regular (nonprepack) filing, where Z contains *Industry distress*, *Size*, *Profit margin*, and *Tangible*. These variables reflect the effect of industry-wide distress on auction illiquidity and the going-concern value that may be lost if the auction is illiquid, both of which may induce an auction prepack. We then perform the following second-step regression using weighted least squares:

$$\ln(p) = \beta'X + \eta \frac{\phi(\gamma'Z)}{\Phi(\gamma'Z)} + u, \tag{16}$$

where ϕ_i and Φ in the inverse Mill's ratio are the values of the standard normal density and the cumulative normal distribution functions, respectively, evaluated at $\gamma'Z$.

The estimate of η and the coefficient vector β are shown Table 7. In Panel A, we use the full sample of 175 firms auctioned in bankruptcy, while Panel B is restricted to 130 going concern auctions. The Mill's ratio receives an insignificant coefficient in all specifications, suggesting that it is not necessary to control for prepack selection to generate unbiased estimates of β. The estimates of β in Table 7 are similar to those reported above, with the exception of the coefficient for *Tangible* which is now insignificant. Importantly, the coefficient estimate for r again supports the overbidding hypothesis H1.

4.2.3. Linearity of the overbidding function

We have so far presumed a linear relationship between the winning auction premium and the coalition's overbidding incentive. As depicted in Figure 3, the relationship is

Table 7

Regressions for overbidding with correction for self-selection of auction prepack filing

WLS coefficient estimates in regressions of the auction premium $\ln(p)$ on r and the inverse Mill's ratio $\varphi(\gamma'Z)/\Phi(\gamma'Z)$ for the choice of a regular (nonprepack) filing. Z contains the variables *Industry distress*, *Size*, *Profit margin*, and *Tangible*, and a constant, and ϕ_i and Φ_i are the standard normal density and cumulative normal distribution functions, respectively, evaluated at $\gamma'Z$. The remaining variables are defined in Table 3. Sample of 175 Swedish firms filing for bankruptcy 1988–1991 (p-values and the degrees of freedom are in parentheses).

Constant	r	Piecemeal	Multiple interest	Saleback	Size	Profit margin	Tangible	$\dfrac{\varphi(\gamma'Z)}{\Phi(\gamma'Z)}$	Adjusted R^2	F-value	N
A: Sample of going-concern sales and piecemeal liquidations											
-0.191	-0.834	-0.537			0.245	0.341	-2.766	-4.332	0.114	4.71	175
(0.879)	(0.000)	(0.000)			(0.188)	(0.520)	(0.122)	(0.186)	(df = 6)	(0.000)	
B: Sample of going-concern sales											
-0.236	-1.202				0.259	-0.713	-2.753	-3.495	0.169	6.24	130
(0.928)	(0.000)				(0.484)	(0.336)	(0.353)	(0.468)	(df = 5)	(0.000)	
2.779	-1.262			-0.291	-0.175	-0.503	0.408	2.244	0.159	3.87	91
(0.209)	(0.000)			(0.178)	(0.625)	(0.604)	(0.894)	(0.618)	(df = 6)	(0.002)	
-0.416	-1.189		0.180		0.360	-0.669	-3.964	-5.643	0.164	5.16	128
(0.854)	(0.000)		(0.214)		(0.352)	(0.353)	(0.248)	(0.326)	(df = 6)	(0.000)	

linear for the case of the uniform distribution and $v_1 < f - h(b_c)$. However, the relationship may be nonlinear (concave) for other distributions $G(v)$. Since our theoretical model does not identify the functional form G, we apply a Box-Cox transformation to r.[16] A Box-Cox transformation of the variable r, denoted $r^{(\lambda)}$, is defined as

$$r^{(\lambda)} = \begin{cases} (r^\lambda - 1)/\lambda & \lambda \neq 0 \\ \ln r & \lambda = 0. \end{cases} \tag{17}$$

The resulting maximum likelihood estimate of λ determines the functional form of the relationship with auction premiums, where $\lambda = 1$ implies linearity. Using the subsample of auctions where $r < 1$, the Box-Cox transformation results in an estimated value of λ of 1.53 with a p-value of 0.69. This estimate is statistically indistinguishable from either zero or one.

As a sensitivity analysis, we rerun the premium regression using a transformation of r with $\lambda = 1.53$ and $\lambda = 0$. The results are shown in Table 8. For the subsample of going-concern sales (Panel A), the coefficient estimate for $r^{(\lambda)} = (r^{1.53} - 1)/1.53$ is -1.48 with a p-value of 0.00. In Panel B, we repeat the regression with $\lambda = 0$, which results in a coefficient estimate for $r^{(\lambda)} = \ln(r)$ of -0.35 and a p-value of 0.00. Finally, in Panel C, we again use $\lambda = 0$ but the sample is now restricted to piecemeal liquidations. The coefficient estimate for $r^{(\lambda)} = \ln(r)$ is now an insignificant -0.12 (p-value of 0.74). This evidence is uniformly consistent with the overbidding hypothesis H1 also when we allow a nonlinear functional form for the overbidding variable r.

4.3. Agency and overbidding through bank-debt rollover

In the overbidding theory of Section 2, bank managers are assumed to work in the bank's interest: the coalition bid strategy maximizes expected auction revenue. Alternatively, suppose bank managers are entrenched. If revealing credit losses lowers bank managers' reputation, they may try to rig the auction outcome by getting the bidder to roll over the bank's debt at face value. Using the notation from Section 2, and ignoring the piecemeal liquidation value ($l = 0$), the coalition agreement is for bidder 1 to offer $b'_c = \max[f + , v_1]$ and for the bank to transfer the overpayment amount $\max[f + s - v_1, 0]$ to bidder 1 conditional on winning.[17]

Under the rollover hypothesis, the bank is effectively trying to enforce a price floor (a seller reserve price) of $f + s$. Therefore, the auction must now be strictly first-price. The central implication of this setup hypothesis is that the bank will always achieve full repayment f of its debt. Notice also that the rollover strategy implies greater expected overbidding than under our overbidding hypothesis in Section 2. In terms

---

[16] See, for example, Judge et al. (1988, pp. 555–563).
[17] Since the transfer $f + s - v_1$ increases dollar for dollar as v_1 falls below $f + s$, the bank manager has an incentive to select a partner with high private valuation v_1. In contrast, in Section 2, the coalition is "bidding to lose," so the bank prefers coalition partners with low private valuations v_1.

Table 8

Overbidding tests assuming nonlinear bidding functions

The table uses a Box-Cox transformation $r^{(\lambda)}$ of r defined as

$$r^{(\lambda)} = \begin{cases} (r^\lambda - 1)\lambda & \text{for } \lambda \neq 0 \\ \ln r & \text{for } \lambda = 0. \end{cases}$$

Our estimate of λ is 1.53 with a p-value of 0.69. This estimate is indistinguishable from one (linearity) and from zero. The table reports OLS coefficient estimates for the auction premium $\ln(p)$ with the overbidding variable r transformed using $\lambda = 1.53$ (Panel A) and $\lambda = 0$ (Panels B and C). Sample of 124 firms auctioned in Swedish bankruptcy 1988–1991 with a liquidation recovery rate $r < 1$. Variable definitions are in Table 3. p-Values and the degrees of freedom are in parentheses.

Constant	$r^{(\lambda)}$	Size	Profit margin	Tangible	Adjusted R^2	F-value	N
A: Box-Cox transformation of r using $\lambda = 1.53$. Sample of going-concern auctions with $r < 1$							
0.090	−1.478	0.031	0.426	−1.123	0.184	4.28	80
(0.950)	(0.000)	(0.738)	(0.665)	(0.013)	(df = 4)	(0.004)	
B: Box-Cox transformation of r using $\lambda = 0$. Sample of going-concern auctions with $r < 1$							
−0.692	−0.346	0.093	−0.321	−1.310	0.146	4.24	76
(0.638)	(0.001)	(0.322)	(0.747)	(0.004)	(df = 4)	(0.004)	
C: Box-Cox transformation of r using $\lambda = 0$. Sample of piecemeal liquidations with $r < 1$							
−0.620	−0.124	0.050	−0.103	−0.542	−0.076	0.22	44
(0.746)	(0.741)	(0.686)	(0.842)	(0.368)	(df = 4)	(0.926)	

of Figure 1, the additional expected amount of overbidding—which the bank must transfer *ex post* to its coalition partner—is equal to the area of the triangle between the lines for f and b_c. This aggressive overbidding also results in a higher probability that the coalition wins against more efficient rivals ($b_c > v_2 > v_1$).

The prediction of full recovery for the bank is testable. Starting with the full sample of 236 auctions with data on bank recovery rates, the bank receives full debt recovery in 34% of the total sample. Focusing on the 181 going-concern sales and prepacks (excluding piecemeal liquidations), the bank receives full recovery in 40% of the cases. As shown in Figure 5, for the 60% of the sample with less than full bank recovery, realized bank recovery rates are evenly distributed between 0.40 and 0.90. Cases where the bank receives less than full recovery are inconsistent with debt rollover.

The most interesting place to look for debt rollover is when the bank-bidder coalition wins and the coalition partner is a former owner-manager (i.e., a saleback). In the total sample of 111 salebacks, the bank finances the bidder in 42 cases. In 22 of these cases (52%), the bank receives full recovery. Are these 22 cases the result of debt rollover? Within this group of 22, the average auction price exceeds $f + s$ by 91% (median 40%). That is, the bank's coalition partner pays a price in the auction than on average nearly doubles the bank's face value f. The bank receives full recovery because bidder 1's valuation is high ($v_1 \approx 2(f + s)$)) and not because of an attempt to rig the auction. Our overall conclusion is therefore that debt rollover is not an important characteristic of these bankruptcy auctions.

5. Overbidding and postbankruptcy performance

Our empirical analysis suggests that creditor overbidding incentives manifest themselves in actual auction prices. As shown in Section 2 (Figure 2), overbidding may lead to an inefficient auction outcome. When the bank-bidder coalition overbids and lose, bidder 2 has the highest private valuation, and the outcome is efficient. However, when the coalition overbids and wins, there are two possibilities: if $v_1 > v_2$ the outcome is efficient, while allocative inefficiency occurs when $v_1 < v_2$.

What is the likely empirical relevance of the case where the coalition wins and bidder 2's private valuation exceeds that of bidder 1? As bidder private valuations are unobservable, this question can only be assessed indirectly. Since severe allocative inefficiency arguably results in poor postbankruptcy performance, we provide performance evidence as a function of our measure of overbidding incentive r. Because the sample firms are all private, we use operating profitability and bankruptcy refiling rates as measures of performance.

H2 (Overbidding and performance). *Since the overbidding incentive is decreasing in the liquidation recovery rate r (Proposition 3), the likelihood of the inefficient auction outcome is also decreasing in r. If overbidding impacts allocative efficiency, average postbankruptcy operating performance and bankruptcy refiling rates are expected to be greater following auctions with a high value of r than in auctions with a low value of r.*

5.1. Postbankruptcy operating performance

Postbankruptcy performance estimation requires the identity of the newly restructured firm. We have this information for a total of 111 of our targets sold as a going concern and excluding prepacks. Within this subsample, postbankruptcy financial statements are available for a total of 83 firms in the first year postbankruptcy (year 1). Panel A of Table 9 reports median annual industry-adjusted operating profitability (EBITDA/sales) for groups of auctions with high and low values of the overbidding incentive r, and for the difference between two groups. As defined in Table 3, r_{high} indicates that $r = 1$, and r_{low} indicates that $0 < r \leq 0.5$. This eliminates 27 observations with $0.5 < r < 1$ and an additional five observations with missing information on r.

Moreover, we compare the performance across firms sold in auctions where the bank finances the winning bidder ($Bank = 1$) and auctions where the bank did not finance the buyer (Bank = 0). When using the variable $Bank$, 21 of the 83 firms with postbankruptcy financial statements are eliminated due to missing information. Industry-adjusted is defined as the difference between the firm and its median industry

Table 9

Industry-adjusted postbankruptcy operating performance and leverage

The table reports operating margins and debt ratios for firms auctioned as going concerns in bankruptcy, classified by the level of the bank's liquidation recovery rate r and whether the bankrupt firm's bank finances the winning bidder. "Industry adjusted" is the difference between the target firm's value and the corresponding median value for the target's four-digit SIC industry. "Year 1" is the first calendar year after auction bankruptcy, etc. Superscript **(*) indicate that the sample median is different from the industry median at the 1% (5%) level, using a Wilcoxon signed ranks test. The p-value for the difference in industry-adjusted performance and debt medians is from a two-sided Mann-Whitney U-test. Variable definitions are in Table 3. Sample of 83 Swedish firms sold as going concerns in auction bankruptcy during 1988–1991.

Year after bankruptcy		1	2	3	4
A: Industry-adjusted operating margin (EBDITA/sales)					
$r_{high} = 1$	Median	−0.004	−0.012	−0.011	0.018
	n	35	28	23	16
$r_{low} = 1$	Median	−0.005	−0.017	0.004	0.018
	n	24	21	14	13
Difference: r_{high} vs. r_{low}		0.001	0.005	−0.015	0.000
		(0.963)	(0.840)	(0.639)	(0.930)
Bank = 1	Median	−0.009	−0.010	−0.008	0.020
	n	36	29	23	20
Bank = 0	Median	0.014	−0.018	−0.001	0.040
	n	42	39	30	19
Difference: Bank = 1 vs. Bank = 0		−0.023	0.008	−0.007	−0.020
		(0.183)	(0.548)	(0.693)	(0.448)
$r_{high} = 1$ and Bank = 1	Median	−0.027	−0.034*	−0.032	0.019
	n	16	11	9	5
$r_{low} = 1$ and Bank = 1	Median	0.100	0.062	0.008	0.022
	n	7	6	4	5
Difference: r_{high} vs. r_{low}|Bank = 1		−0.128	−0.096	−0.040	−0.003
		(0.038)	(0.016)	(0.355)	(0.754)
B: Industry-adjusted debt ratio (book value of debt/total assets)					
$r_{high} = 1$	Median	0.114*	0.079*	0.004	0.026
	n	27	23	19	13
$r_{low} = 1$	Median	0.121**	0.069*	0.143	0.136**
	n	24	21	15	13
Difference: r_{high} vs. r_{low}		−0.010	0.010	−0.139	−0.110
		(0.610)	(0.934)	(0.591)	(0.144)
Bank = 1	Median	0.132**	0.100**	0.090	0.062
	n	36	28	23	20
Bank = 0	Median	0.112**	0.073*	0.151	0.026
	n	42	40	32	19
Difference: Bank = 1 vs. Bank = 0		0.020	0.027	−0.061	0.036
		(0.568)	(0.794)	(0.621)	(0.482)
$r_{high} = 1$ and Bank = 1	Median	0.145**	0.140**	0.097	0.083
	n	16	11	9	5
$r_{low} = 1$ and Bank = 1	Median	0.089	0.052	0.012	0.068
	n	7	6	4	5
Difference: r_{high} vs. r_{low}|Bank = 1		0.056	0.088	0.085	0.014
		(0.316)	(0.191)	(0.537)	(0.754)

rival, where a rival is a firm with at least 20 employees and with the same four-digit SIC industry code as the target.

Using a Wilcoxon signed-rank test, the typical sample firm has an operating profitability that is statistically indistinguishable from its median industry rival for each of the 4 years following bankruptcy. The p-values for the difference between auctions with high and low values of r are also high in all 4 years. The same holds when we condition the sample on the indicator *Bank*.

In principle, the greatest potential for an inefficient outcome occurs when the coalition wins (Bank = 1) and the overbidding incentives are high ($r_{low} = 1$). The third group of observations in Panel A focuses on this subsample by comparing the operating performance across cases with r_{high} and with r_{low} conditional on Bank = 1. If overbidding leads to an inefficient outcome, we expect the performance differences shown in the last row of Panel A to be positive and significant. Instead, they are significantly negative for years 1 and 2, and insignificant thereafter.

We conclude from Panel A of Table 9 that the median postbankruptcy operating performance of auctioned targets is typically (1) indistinguishable from the performance of industry rivals, (2) unaffected by whether the bank's ex ante incentive to overbid is high or low, and (3) higher when the coalition wins following high overbidding incentives. This evidence fails to support the joint hypothesis H2 of overbidding and allocative inefficiency.

Panel B of Table 9 shows that the postbankruptcy leverage ratios of the auctioned firms are significantly higher than that of industry peers in years 1 and 2. There is, however, no difference in the use of leverage across auctioned firms with high or low overbidding incentive r and with or without old bank financing of the winning bidder. The greater leverage ratios after emerging from bankruptcy may, however, carry with it a greater probability of refiling for bankruptcy, in particular if the firm is restructured by a relatively inefficient buyer. We turn to the refiling rate next.

5.2. Bankruptcy refiling rates

Table 10 presents logit-estimates of the probability of bankruptcy refiling within 2 years of the auction. The regressions use as explanatory variables the overbidding incentive r and its variants r^*, r_{low}, and r_{high}, as well as the industry- and firm characteristics *Industry distress*, *Saleback*, *Bank*, *Size*, *Profit margin*, and *Tangible*. The sample contains 106 of the 111 surviving firms, reflecting the missing information on r for five cases.

Of the nine regression specifications in Table 10, only the last four are statistically significant using a standard Chi-square test. All nine regressions produce statistically insignificant coefficients for all of the overbidding variables r. In other words, the bankruptcy refiling rate is unaffected by the bank's *ex ante* incentive to form a coalition and overbid. The only variable which affects the refiling probability is *Bank*. That is, the refiling rate is significantly greater in the subsample where the bank finances the winning bidder in the auction. Note also that the refiling rate is

Table 10

Bankruptcy refilling probability for targets sold as going concern

Coefficients in logit estimations of the probability that the surviving firm refiles for bankruptcy within 2 years of the auction. The variables are defined in Table 3. The sample is 106 Swedish firms sold as going concerns in auction bankruptcy 1988–1991. p-Values are in parentheses.

Constant	r	r^*	r_{low}	r_{high}	Industry distress	Saleback	Bank	Size	Profit margin	Tangible	Cox Snell R^2	χ^2	N
1.21 (0.776)	0.29 (0.695)							−0.15 (0.568)	2.59 (0.339)	−0.35 (0.785)	0.02	1.74 (0.783)	106
0.94 (0.826)		−0.09 (0.582)						−0.14 (0.608)	2.63 (0.331)	−0.41 (0.757)	0.02	2.16 (0.826)	106
1.92 (0.665)	0.24 (0.773)				−2.51 (0.182)			−0.14 (0.600)	2.56 (0.340)	−0.19 (0.885)	0.04	3.99 (0.677)	106
1.75 (0.679)		−0.07 (0.669)			−2.74 (0.140)			−0.15 (0.573)	2.64 (0.329)	−0.21 (0.868)	0.05	5.07 (0.534)	106
0.72 (0.868)			0.68 (0.296)	0.58 (0.365)	−3.44 (0.078)	0.83 (0.162)		−0.12 (0.670)	1.63 (0.580)	−0.05 (0.946)	0.07	7.16 (0.413)	106
1.03 (0.839)	−0.48 (0.635)				−3.54 (0.113)		2.22 (0.001)	−0.19 (0.557)	−0.40 (0.895)	1.89 (0.274)	0.16	15.37 (0.031)	85
−0.28 (0.955)		0.17 (0.539)			−3.37 (0.118)		2.17 (0.002)	−0.14 (0.639)	−0.13 (0.964)	1.29 (0.432)	0.18	16.81 (0.019)	85
−0.35 (0.947)	−0.37 (0.688)		0.76 (0.253)	0.60 (0.353)	−4.50 (0.058)	1.09 (0.128)	2.24 (0.002)	−0.14 (0.672)	−1.88 (0.594)	2.21 (0.196)	0.19	17.67 (0.014)	84
0.36 (0.951)			1.07 (0.195)	0.70 (0.395)	−3.26 (0.119)		2.14 (0.002)	−0.15 (0.628)	−0.17 (0.955)	1.66 (0.296)	0.16	14.98 (0.010)	85

independent of whether the auction results in a saleback. The important factor appears to be bank financing *per se*, and not whether the buyer is the firm's old owner.[18]

However, when we introduce the interaction variables r_{low}* Bank and r_{high}* Bank (not shown in Table 10), we cannot reject the hypothesis that these two interaction variables have identical coefficients. This means that, while refiling rates are higher when the bidder is financed by the old bank, this effect of Bank is unrelated to whether the overbidding incentives are high or low in the auction. Overall, we conclude that when the bank-bidder coalition wins the auction, the coalition appears to have selected a relatively risky restructuring project (in terms of the refiling rate). Moreover, since the operating performance indicates bidder efficiency also when the bank finances the winner, the greater refiling risk occurs even if the bank's coalition partner is relatively efficient.

6. Conclusions

The Swedish automatic auction system has an attractive simplicity, and it provides an important laboratory for examining the effectiveness of auctions to resolve bankruptcy. Previous research has shown that the auctions result in a speedy and relatively low-cost restructuring of the filing firms with no evidence of excessive liquidation (three-quarters survive as going concerns) or fire-sale discounts in going-concern sales. In this paper, we focus on the incentives and opportunities for the bankrupt firm's main creditor—the bank—to influence the auction outcome in order to increase expected bank-debt recovery. Regulatory constraints prevent banks from bidding in the auction. However, we observe that the old bank frequently finances bidders, and we postulate that the financing arrangement leads to joint bank-bidder offer strategies. The optimal bank-bidder coalition strategy implies overbidding and mimics a monopolist seller's reserve price. Thus, a bank-bidder coalition strategy may allow the bank to circumvent the institutional constraint on bank bidding in the auction.

We test for overbidding using cross-sectional regressions of the final auction premium on a measure of the bank's expected debt recovery rate if the firm is liquidated piecemeal (r). The lower the value of r, the more impaired is the bank's debt claim ex ante, and the greater the bank's incentive to form a coalition and overbid. We find robust evidence that auction premiums are decreasing in r. This inverse relationship is statistically significant and as predicted by the overbidding hypothesis. The estimated relationship is robust to the inclusion of various firm and industry characteristics in the cross-sectional regressions, and to a correction for bidder self-selection of the auction outcome. Moreover, evidence of overbidding occurs only for the relevant range of r (where theory suggests overbidding). To our knowledge, this is the first test of auction overbidding based directly on final auction prices.

---

[18] Inclusion of additional variables such as asset specificity, business cycle, and industry leverage does not alter this conclusion.

Since overbidding by the bank-bidder coalition may lead to inefficient auction outcome (when the coalition wins against a higher valuation rival bidder), we also examine the postbankruptcy performance of the auctioned firms. The hypothesis is that larger overbidding incentives in the auction (lower values of r) may lead to lower postbankruptcy operating performance and/or bankruptcy refiling probability. However, we find that postbankruptcy operating performance is independent of the ex ante overbidding incentive and whether or not the bank finances the winning bidder. While the bankruptcy refiling rate is greater following bank financing of the winner, this effect is independent of overbidding incentives. We infer from this that the bank's coalition partner tends to be relatively efficient in terms of restructuring and operating the bankrupt firm's assets. Moreover, bank financing appears to be more likely in auctions where the bankrupt firm's future prospects are relatively risky.

In the United States, there is a growing use of relatively low-cost, market-based mechanisms to resolve bankruptcy. An interesting question for future research is whether moving toward greater use of auctions would be beneficial in Chapter 11. The answer depends in part on to what extent the Swedish auction mechanism is uniquely suited to the country's legal and corporate governance tradition. For example, there does not appear to be any serious risk of corruption of the auction mechanism itself. Also, the auction mechanism may be better suited for firms with relatively simple capital structures than for the more complex structures involving public ownership of debt. However, the active market for corporate control in the United States suggests that neither firm size nor capital structure complexity necessarily impede takeover auctions outside of bankruptcy.

References

Aghion, P., O. Hart and J. Moore, 1992, "The Economics of Bankruptcy Reform," *Journal of Law, Economics and Organization*, 8, 523–546.

Baird, D. G., 1986, "The Uneasy Case for Corporate Reorganizations," *Journal of Legal Studies*, 15, 127–147.

Baird, D. G., 1993, "Revisiting Auctions in Chapter 11," *Journal of Law and Economics*, 36, 633–653.

Baird, D. G. and R. K. Rasmussen, 2003, "Chapter 11 at Twilight," *Stetson Law Review*, 56, 673–699.

Bebchuk, L. A., 1988, "A New Approach to Corporate Reorganizations," *Harvard Law Review*, 101, 775–804.

Bebchuk, L. A. and H. F. Chang, 1992, "Bargaining and the Division of Value in Corporate Reorganization," *Journal of Law, Economics and Organization*, 8, 253–279.

Berkovitch, E., R. Israel and J. Zender, 1997, "Optimal Bankruptcy Law and Firm-Specific Investments," *European Economic Review*, 41, 487–497.

Betker, B. L., 1995, "An Empirical Examination of Prepackaged Bankruptcy," *Financial Management*, 24, 3–18.

Betton, S. and B. E. Eckbo, 2000, "Toeholds, Bid Jumps, and Expected Payoff in Takeovers," *Review of Financial Studies*, 13, 841–882.

Bradley, M. and M. Rosenzweig, 1992, "The Untenable Case for Chapter 11," *Yale Law Journal*, 101, 1043–1095.

Bris, A., I. Welch and N. Zhu, 2006, "The Costs of Bankruptcy: Chapter 7 Liquidation Versus Chapter 11 Reorganization," *Journal of Finance*, 61, 1253–1303.

Brown, D. T., 1989, "Claimholder Incentive Conflicts in Reorganization: The Role of Bankruptcy Law," *Review of Financial Studies*, 2, 109–123.

Bulow, J. and J. Shoven, 1978, "The Bankruptcy Decision," *Bell Journal of Economics*, 9, 436–445.

Bulow, J., M. Huang and P. Klemperer, 1999, "Toeholds and Takeovers," *Journal of Political Economy*, 107, 427–454.

Burkart, M., 1995, "Initial Shareholdings and Overbidding in Takeover Contests," *Journal of Finance*, 50, 1491–1515.

Chang, T. and A. Schoar, 2007, "The Effect of Judicial Bias in Chapter 11 Reorganization," Working Paper, Massachusetts Institute of Technology.

Dasgupta, S. and R. G. Hansen, 2007, "Auctions in Corporate Finance," In B. E. Eckbo (Ed.), *Handbook of Corporate Finance: Empirical Corporate Finance*, vol. 1, Chapter 3, Elsevier/North-Holland, Amsterdam, pp. 87–143, Handbooks in Finance Series.

Eckbo, B. E. and K. S. Thorburn, 2000, "Toeholds and Fire-Sales in Bankruptcy Auctions," Working Paper 00–07, Tuck School of Business at Dartmouth.

Eckbo, B. E. and K. S. Thorburn, 2003, "Control Benefits and CEO Discipline in Automatic Bankruptcy Auctions," *Journal of Financial Economics*, 69, 227–258.

Eckbo, B. E. and K. S. Thorburn, 2008, "Automatic Bankruptcy Auctions and Fire-Sales," *Journal of Financial Economics*, 89, 404–422.

Franks, J. and W. Torous, 1989, "An Empirical Investigation of U.S. Firms in Reorganization," *Journal of Finance*, 44, 747–770.

Gertner, R. H. and D. S. Scharfstein, 1991, "A Theory of Workouts and the Effects of Reorganization Law," *Journal of Finance*, 46, 1189–1222.

Hansen, R. G. and R. S. Thomas, 1998, "Auctions in Bankruptcy: Theoretical Analysis and Practical Guidance," *International Review of Law & Economics*, 18, 159–185.

Heckman, J. J., 1979, "Sample Selection Bias as a Specification Error," *Econometrica*, 47, 153–161.

Hotchkiss, E. S., 1995, "Post-Bankruptcy Performance and Management Turnover," *Journal of Finance*, 50, 3–21.

Hotchkiss, E. S. and R. M. Mooradian, 1997, "Vulture Investors and the Market for Control of Distressed Firms," *Journal of Financial Economics*, 43, 401–432.

Hotchkiss, E. S. and R. M. Mooradian, 1998, "Acquisitions as a Means of Restructuring Firms in Chapter 11," *Journal of Financial Intermediation*, 7, 240–262.

Hotchkiss, E. S. and R. M. Mooradian, 2003, "Auctions in Bankruptcy," *Journal of Corporate Finance*, 9, 555–574.

Hotchkiss, E. S., K. John, R. Mooradian and K. S. Thorburn, 2008, "Bankruptcy and the Resolution of Financial Distress," In B. E. Eckbo (Ed.), *Handbook of Corporate Finance: Empirical Corporate Finance*, vol. 2, Chapter 14, Elsevier/North-Holland, Amsterdam, Handbooks in Finance Series.

Jensen, M. C., 1989, "Eclipse of the Public Corporation," *Harvard Business Review*, 67, 61–74.

Judge, G. G., R. C. Hill, W. E. Griffiths, H. Lutkepohl and T. C. Lee, 1988. *Introduction to the Theory and Practice of Econometrics*, 2nd edition, Wiley, New York.

Klemperer, P., 2000, "Auction Theory: A Guide to the Literature," *Journal of Economic Surveys*, 13, 227–286.

Lease, R., J. McConnell and E. Tashjian, 1996, "Prepacks: An Empirical Analysis of Prepackaged Bankruptcies," *Journal of Financial Economics*, 40, 135–162.

LoPucki, L. and W. Whitford, 1993, "Corporate Governance in the Bankruptcy Reorganization of Large, Publicly Held Companies," *University of Pennsylvania Law Review*, 141, 669–800.

Maksimovic, V. and G. Phillips, 1998, "Asset Efficiency and Reallocation Decisions of Bankrupt Firms," *Journal of Finance*, 53, 1495–1532.

Rhodes-Kropf, M. and S. Viswanathan, 2000, "Corporate Reorganizations and Non-Cash Auctions," *Journal of Finance*, 55, 1807–1849.

Shleifer, A. and R. W. Vishny, 1992, "Liquidation Values and Debt Capacity: A Market Equilibrium Approach," *Journal of Finance*, 47, 1343–1366.

Strömberg, P., 2000, "Conflicts of Interests and Market Illiquidity in Bankruptcy Auctions: Theory and Tests," *Journal of Finance*, 55, 2641–2692.

Strömberg, P. and K. S. Thorburn, 1996, "An Empirical Investigation of Swedish Corporations in Liquidation Bankruptcy," EFI Research Report, Stockholm School of Economics.

Thorburn, K. S., 2000, "Bankruptcy Auctions: Costs, Debt Recovery, and Firm Survival," *Journal of Financial Economics*, 58, 337–368.

Weiss, L., 1990, "Bankruptcy Resolution: Direct Costs and Violations of Priority of Claims," *Journal of Financial Economics*, 27, 285–314.

White, M., 1984, "Bankruptcy Liquidation and Reorganization," In L. Dennis and J. Seward (Eds.), *Handbook of Modern Finance 2*, Chapter E7, pp. 1–44, Warren, Gorham & Lamont, Boston.

PART 4

DO DEAL PROTECTION DEVICES AFFECT TAKEOVER PREMIUMS?

Chapter 11

TERMINATION FEES IN MERGERS AND ACQUISITIONS*

MICAH S. OFFICER

Marshall School of Business, University of Southern California, Los Angeles, California, USA

Contents

* This paper is a modified version of one chapter of my dissertation completed at the University of Rochester. I thank my dissertation committee, Gregg Jarrell, Bill Schwert (Chair), and Cliff Smith, for help and encouragement. I also thank Andreas Gintschel, Laurie Hodrick, Ken Kotz, David Ravenscraft, seminar participants at the University of Rochester, and especially Harry DeAngelo and Espen Eckbo (the referee) for helpful suggestions.

This article originally appeared in the *Journal of Financial Economics*, Vol. 69, pp. 431–467 (2003).
Corporate Takeovers, Volume 2
Edited by B. Espen Eckbo

Abstract

The paper provides evidence on the effects of including a target termination fee in a merger contract. I test the implications of the hypothesis that termination fees are used by self-interested target managers to deter competing bids and protect "sweetheart" deals with white knight bidders, presumably resulting in lower premiums for target shareholders. An alternative hypothesis is that target managers use termination fees to encourage bidder participation by ensuring that the bidder is compensated for the revelation of valuable private information released during merger negotiations. My empirical evidence demonstrates that merger deals with target termination fees involve significantly higher premiums and success rates than deals without such clauses. Furthermore, only weak support is found for the contention that termination fees deter competing bids. Overall, the evidence suggests that termination fee use is at least not harmful, and is likely beneficial, to target shareholders.

Keywords

mergers and acquisitions, takeovers, termination fees, takeover premiums

JEL classification: G34, K22

SDL would have to pay JDS Uniphase $1 billion if it decides to abandon the merger plan and become part of another company, giving new meaning to the phrase 'breaking up is hard to do—CNNFn, July 10, 2000.

1. Introduction

Almost two-thirds of the merger agreements announced between 1997 and 1999 included a target termination fee clause. A target termination, or breakup, fee clause requires that the target pay the bidder a fixed cash fee if the target does not consummate the proposed merger. Termination fees are of current interest in the area of mergers and acquisitions in light of the large termination fee recently paid by Pfizer/Warner-Lambert to American Home Products (AHP), following Warner-Lambert's decision to cancel its merger with AHP in favor of a union with Pfizer. Natural questions stem from the publicity surrounding this fee (see, e.g., *The Wall Street Journal*, February 7, 2000, p. A3), such as what target managers hope to gain by agreeing to pay a termination fee to the bidder, and in particular whether the use of a termination fee benefits or harms target stockholders on average.

This empirical setting has the potential to contribute to the extensive literature devoted to ascertaining, usually from the stock market reaction, whether decisions made by corporate managers appear to be motivated by "managerial entrenchment" or "shareholder interest." One particularly fertile area for studying entrenchment versus efficiency is mergers and acquisitions, as the act of selling a firm typically entails the selling managers losing their jobs, or at least sacrificing some degree of control. Evidence of behavior indicative of managerial entrenchment or shareholder interests in mergers and acquisitions is mixed. On the one hand, Hadlock et al. (1999) interpret high rates of management turnover following bank acquisitions as evidence that target managers actively oppose takeover attempts, and Chang (1990) finds that firms adopting ESOPs as takeover defenses suffer significant stock price declines, supporting the entrenchment hypothesis. Furthermore, Harford (1999) finds that cash-rich firms are more likely to make diversifying, value-destroying acquisitions with poor postacquisition performance.

On the other hand, Mulherin and Boone (2000) report evidence of positive wealth effects associated with acquisitions and divestitures, inconsistent with managerial entrenchment. Moreover, Schwert (2000) concludes that target managerial "hostility" toward potential acquirers is associated with outcomes that are most consistent with "strategic bargaining" on the part of target managers, and that this bargaining strategy is beneficial to target shareholders on average. Comment and Schwert (1995) reach a similar conclusion about the adoption of poison pill antitakeover provisions.

As a target termination fee agreement could be considered prima facie evidence that target managers have distorted the acquisition process to the detriment of their shareholders, the incidence of termination fee use has the potential to provide further evidence on the entrenchment and efficiency hypotheses. In this context, the entrenchment hypothesis presumes that termination fees are effective deterrents to competing bids for the target firm, and therefore allow entrenched target managers to selectively deal with one particular bidder in return for some benefit (e.g., job security). The agency cost to target shareholders is the assumed loss of takeover premium resulting from the curtailment of a full auction for the target firm.

The alternative "shareholder interests" hypothesis is that target termination fees serve a less exploitative role as contractual devices that efficiently solve contracting problems between the bidder and target. For example, a bidder could be reluctant to reveal valuable private information about its postmerger plans for the target's assets if another bidder is able to free ride on such information and submit a more valuable proposal, or reluctant to commit to premerger integration with the target without a tangible commitment that the merger will proceed. Target termination fees can protect these deal-related investments made by the bidder and increase the willingness of the bidder to make such investments, potentially to the benefit of target shareholders.

My evidence suggests that, on average, target termination fee use is not detrimental to target shareholders' interests. Specifically, target termination fee use is associated with approximately 4% higher takeover premiums after controlling for correlated deal characteristics. Furthermore, target termination fees increase the likelihood that the deal is successfully completed by almost 20% on average. Hence target shareholders receive the premium more often when a target termination fee is included in the merger terms. There is some evidence that the average incidence of competing bids is lower (by 3%, compared to a full sample average competition rate of 5%) following merger bids including a termination fee. However, several factors diminish the importance of competing bid deterrence of this magnitude. First, this effect appears to be largely driven by correlated deal and bidder characteristics (namely the fact that termination fees are more likely to appear in friendly deals) rather than the nature of the fees per se. Second, the economic impact on the value of the target's shares (from a 3% lower probability of receiving a competing offer) is small when second-bid jumps only average around 14% of the target's market value of equity (Betton and Eckbo, 2000).

Two extant papers, Burch (2001) and Coates and Subramanian (2000), empirically examine the role of lockup options and termination fees in merger bids. Stock or asset lockup options (generically referred to as "lockups") are similar to target termination fees. The difference between the two is that in a lockup the incumbent bidder is granted a call option on either the common shares or some important asset of the target firm, exercisable only if the target initiates termination to pursue a merger with another bidder. Coates and Subramanian show that the median stock lockup is priced slightly in-the-money, with the bulk of the distribution priced at-the-money and few lockups priced out-of-the-money. Furthermore, the median stock lockup represents an option on 19.9% of the target's equity, because most major exchanges require a stockholder vote on contractual provisions affecting more than 20% of the firm's equity capital.

While Burch (2001) does not specifically examine termination fees, his study of lockups is relevant to this paper. Burch finds that deals including a stock lockup result in higher abnormal announcement returns for target shareholders than those that do not, consistent with the shareholder interests hypothesis. Furthermore, the target abnormal return results are robust to controlling for other factors that could be correlated with lockup use, such as the size of the target and target managerial attitude toward the bid. Burch also examines one hundred randomly selected merger agreements from 1988 to 1989 for evidence of "abusive" (i.e., detrimental to target shareholders) use of lockup options. He reports that secretly negotiated lockup deals containing evidence of such abuse (e.g., guaranteeing target managers employment in the merged firm) are actually associated with higher average target returns than comparable deals with a lockup. Burch concludes that while lockups can be employed to benefit managers in a way that harms shareholders, lockups are not systematically used by target managers in this exploitative fashion. This evidence supports the contention that lockups are employed to improve the bargaining position of the target.

In a theoretical corporate law paper, Fraidin and Hanson (1994) appeal to the Coase Theorem to argue that a termination fee will not deter a higher valuing bidder from competing to acquire the target (i.e., termination fees will not affect allocative efficiency) as long as the transaction costs of arranging a deal with an incumbent lower valuing bidder are not prohibitively high. Coates and Subramanian (2000) test this hypothesis against several "buy side" distortions. They claim that these distortions diminish the incentive for low-valuing bidders protected by a termination fee to cede control of the target, even if such an action would increase the low-valuing bidder's profit from bidding. One example of a buy side distortion is *bidder* agency costs, where managers at an incumbent publicly held bidder accept a lower payoff from the bidding process simply because winning control of the target increases the size of the enterprise under their control.

Coates and Subramanian's (largely univariate) results demonstrate that both lockups and, particularly, termination fees are significantly associated with increases in the probability that the incumbent bidder acquires the target firm, but not with bid competition. They also examine the determinants of lockup and termination fee use and find that target termination fees are more likely to be used in pooling-of-interests deals, mergers involving large targets, and deals in which a tender offer was one of the modes of acquisition used by the bidder.

My focus is solely on termination fees, partly because Coates and Subramanian (2000) report that lockups are used approximately half as often as cash termination fees in merger agreements. This paper is one of the first to provide direct evidence on the effect of these devices on the target premium. This is also the first paper to provide multivariate evidence on the effect of termination fee use on the incidence of competing bids and offer success.[1] Evidence on premiums, competition, and offer outcome is important in determining whether, on average, the use of target termination fees is detrimental or beneficial to target shareholders. Furthermore, evidence on each of these outcomes individually has the potential to significantly increase our understanding of the merger negotiation process compared to the inferences from an examination of abnormal returns (as in Burch, 2001).

---

[1] In contemporaneous work unknown to the current author through much of the submission process, Bates and Lemmon (2003) examine similar issues as those covered in the current paper. They find, as I do, that target shareholders in termination fee deals benefit from higher completion rates and premiums, and interpret this as consistent with termination fees serving as efficient contracting devices.

I also attempt to control for the endogeneity problems that are largely ignored in prior literature. Endogeneity is a concern in this setting because the bid premium and the contractual clauses included in the merger agreement are both decided during merger negotiations between the bidder and target. Therefore, neither is truly exogenous, and simple OLS regression coefficients could be biased and inconsistent. Specifically, while a positive association between bid premiums and termination fee use will show up in a regression with either as the dependent variable, considerable care must be taken when inferring causality from such models. I use a simultaneous-equations system to demonstrate the robustness of the directional relation between termination fee use and premiums, namely that target managers appear to be able to improve their bargaining position and extract higher premiums from bidders through the use of a target termination fee.

The paper proceeds as follows. Section 2 describes the contractual structure and legal ramifications of termination fees. My principal hypotheses are discussed in Section 3. Section 4 describes my sample and provides descriptive statistics while the main results are discussed in Section 5. Section 6 discusses some endogeneity issues, and Section 7 concludes the paper.

2. The contractual structure and legal ramifications of termination fees

Appendix A contains an excerpt from the merger agreement signed by the boards of directors of Compaq Computer (the bidder) and Digital Equipment (the target) in January 1998. The salient terms of the target termination fee agreement require Digital to pay Compaq a $240 million fee (3.5% of Digital's market value of equity) if Digital's board rescinds or adversely alters its support for the combination for any reason, or if Digital's shareholders reject the proposed merger in favor of another acquisition proposal. In the latter case, half the termination fee is payable upon termination of the current agreement, with the balance owed once the alternate merger is consummated. A perusal of many recent merger agreements suggests that, while the language varies from contract to contract, the economic content of the Compaq/Digital termination agreement is reasonably common in large business combinations.

However, even the economic content of termination fee clauses included in merger agreements is not completely homogenous. For example, Appendix B contains the target termination clause from the merger agreement signed by the boards of COMSAT and Radiation Systems (RSI) in January 1994. This clause differs in an important way from that included in the Compaq/Digital merger agreement. Specifically, the termination clause stipulates that RSI agrees to pay COMSAT a $5 million fee (about 4.5% of RSIs market value of equity) if RSI agrees to be acquired by another bidder within the following 12 months. Notably, the COMSAT/RSI target termination fee arrangement does not allow for a punitive financial penalty if RSIs managers simply change their mind about the benefits of the proposed merger in favor of staying independent. It is also important to note that neither termination fee clause in the appendices penalizes the target when its shareholders reject the merger proposal in the absence of a concurrent alternate merger proposal.

Termination fees can be considered "punitive" because almost all merger agreements have separate clauses requiring compensation for the spurned party's actual documented costs associated with the failed merger proposal (up to $2.5 million in the COMSAT/RSI deal and up to $25 million for Compaq/Digital). Therefore, target termination fees typically provide the bidder with compensation from a failed bid process in excess of compensation for out-of-pocket costs. One notable exception I have encountered is the target termination fee included in the 1996 merger agreement between Healthsouth Corp. and Professional Sports Care Management, Inc. (PSCM). That termination clause specified a termination fee of 5% of the "aggregate merger consideration," payable by PSCM to Healthsouth if PCSM is subject to a third party acquisition attempt at any point within 1 year following PSCMs termination of the merger agreement. The termination clause claims that the 5% fee " ... represents the parties' best estimates of the out-of-pocket costs incurred by Healthsouth and the value of management time, overhead, opportunity costs and other unallocated costs of Healthsouth incurred ... in connection with this plan of merger."

Merger agreements sometimes also require the bidder to pay the target a fee if the bidder initiates termination. However, bidder termination fees are not nearly as common in practice as the target termination fees that are the focus of this paper.[2] Furthermore, bids including a bidder termination fee have a significantly lower ratio of bidder market-capitalization to target market-capitalization, suggesting that bidder termination fees appear principally in merger-of-equals deals. Bidder termination fees, therefore, are perhaps best thought of as one half of a reciprocal agreement in a class of merger bids where the titles "bidder" and "target" are almost meaningless.

Delaware courts have been suspicious of termination fees (and lockups) because of the possibility that targets could employ these contractual devices to favor one bidder over others, in return for some benefit provided to target managers. The obvious example of such a side payment is job security. In fact, Dhaya and Powell (1998) report that top managerial turnover is dramatically lower in a sample of friendly takeovers than in hostile acquisitions. Termination fees can considerably increase the cost of acquiring the target to a second (possibly hostile) bidder. It is therefore conceivable that target termination fees deter competing bids, thereby protecting a sweetheart deal made between a "white knight" bidder and the target. However, a termination fee did not deter Pfizer from making an initially hostile bid for Warner-Lambert.[3]

---

[2] Bates and Lemmon (2003) examine bidder termination fees in greater detail than that afforded here.

[3] However, Pfizer's bid for Warner-Lambert was conditional on the voiding of a lockup that would have allowed AHP to purchase 14.9% of Warner-Lambert's stock. Lockups are frequently contested because the issue of stock under the lockup would prevent the winning bidder from using the pooling method of merger accounting.

The judicial response to such concerns has generally been to enforce only those auction-ending termination fee agreements that are offered in exchange for a substantial bid increase. The opinion of the Delaware court is summarized in its final ruling in the *Revlon, Inc. v. MacAndrews & Forbes Holdings, Inc.* (1986). The court noted that termination fee agreements " ... are permitted under Delaware law where their adoption is untainted by director interest or other breaches of fiduciary duty."

Coates and Subramanian (2000) argue that target termination fee use has responded to the tone of two judicial decisions concerning the use of such devices. In particular, Coates and Subramanian contend that the 1994 decision in *Paramount Communications, Inc. v. QVC Network, Inc.* is weakly supportive of the validity of termination fees (while especially critical of stock lockups), and that the 1997 decision in *Brazen v. Bell Atlantic* strongly endorses termination fee use (conditional on the size of the fee).

3. Hypotheses and empirical predictions

I present evidence related to two hypotheses about *why* target termination fees are included in merger contracts. The first hypothesis assumes that target managers act in their own interests and use target termination fees to secure their tenure at the merged firm at the expense of their shareholders.[4] The second hypothesis presumes that target managers act in their shareholders' interests, and use target termination fees to efficiently solve a contracting problem between the bidder and target.

3.1. H1: Agency costs and target managers

The agency problems inherent in the relationship between shareholders and their professional managers have received considerable attention in the finance and corporate law literature (e.g., Fraidin and Hanson, 1994; Jensen, 1986; Jensen and Meckling, 1976). Target managers acting in their own interests, but forced for some reason to sell their firm, could select an acquirer who is most likely to offer them job security (a white knight). In return for continued tenure, the target managers could offer the white knight bidder the bid protection afforded by a target termination fee. Such a fee increases the bid costs of potential competing acquirers, thus circumventing a potential auction for the target firm that would have presumably resulted in a higher premium for target shareholders.

The agency cost to target stockholders under this hypothesis is the loss of takeover premium resulting from the deterrence of potential competing bids. Fraidin and Hanson's (1994) theoretical objection to this agency-cost hypothesis (noted above) focuses principally on the effect such agency problems might have on allocative

---

[4] Any other type of side payment from an initial bidder to the target managers would also fit into this hypothesis, but would be more blatantly contrary to the manager's fiduciary duty than a side payment of job security.

efficiency. However, even if we accept the notion that termination fees will not prevent the highest valuing bidder from acquiring the target, it is unlikely that target shareholders will earn as high a premium as would be the case if a target termination fee did not deter competing bidders from participating in the auction. At the very least, some of the rents that could have been earned by target shareholders are paid to the initial bidder in the form of the termination fee.

The role played by outside directors should help to mitigate this agency problem. The duty of care owed to target shareholders requires that outside directors hire their own legal and financial counsel in the process of negotiating a merger if insiders on the board face obvious conflicts of interest.[5] Indeed, Hatrzell et al. (2000) present evidence that, on average, there is only a very weak negative relation between the target premium and the value of pecuniary benefits negotiated by target CEOs who intend to remain employed in the merged entity.

3.2. H2: Termination fees as an efficient solution to a contracting problem

An alternative hypothesis is that target managers act in their shareholders best interests and use target termination fees to help solve a contracting problem between bidder and target.[6] Specifically, after agreeing to merge, the bidder and target must wait for regulatory and shareholder approval before consummating the union, a process that takes almost 6 months at the median (see Officer, 2003). In the intervening time period, competing bidders can free ride on the information released by the announced bid, including the sources of synergies between the bidder and target and the bidder's postmerger plans for the target's assets.

A target termination fee must generally only be paid by a winning bidder with a superior acquisition proposal submitted after an initial bidder has already revealed its plans, and the payment of this fee effectively internalizes the public good created by the initial bidder's efforts. I hypothesize that the "price" provided by a target termination fee acts as deterrent to this kind of free riding, thereby encouraging the bidder to reveal valuable private information to convince target shareholders of the benefits of the merger. The revelation of private information, such as the bidder's postmerger strategy for the target's assets, is potentially important to target shareholders contemplating the benefits of a proposed merger, especially when the bidder plans to pay for the target's shares using stock in the combined firm.

The arguments offered here are closely related to those in Jarrell and Bradley (1980). Jarrell and Bradley argue that the notice-and-pause provisions of the 1968 Williams Act impose a "tax" on mergers and acquisitions activity by allowing competitors to free ride on the information gathering and processing activities of initial bidders. For agreed mergers the same arguments apply to the shareholder approval

---

[5] See, for example, Lederman and Bryer (1989).
[6] I thank Espen Eckbo (the referee) for substantial help in refining this hypothesis.

process and the regulatory provisions of the Hart-Scott-Rodino Antitrust Improvements Act of 1976.[7] An unprotected initial bidder is unable to fully internalize the benefits of the public good created by the bid (the sources and magnitude of economic gains with the proposed target resulting from the acquirer's plans). Hence, target termination fees can be viewed as devices that help reduce the tax on acquisition--related investments.[8]

As noted in Section 2, the economic content of target termination fees varies across observed contracts. The principal difference among the observed fees is whether the fee is payable if target managers simply change their mind about the benefits of the proposed merger before recommending the deal to their shareholders, in the absence of a competing bid. The fact that some termination fees are payable under these circumstances (such as the Compaq fee) significantly undermines the agency-cost hypothesis that termination fees are designed to protect sweetheart deals between target managers and white knight bidders. If this hypothesis were true, why would the punitive fee still be payable if target managers decided it was now in their best interests to remain independent? Conversely, this fee structure is compatible with the logic of the contracting hypothesis. Target managers (as well as other bidders) are able to free ride on any private information revealed by the bidder during merger negotiations if they decide to cancel the proposed deal in favor of remaining independent.

Neither of the hypotheses is easily testable in a large sample, as the available empirical proxies for the mind-set of target managers do not typically work well in practice. For example, Burch (2001) employs target free-cash-flow and institutional ownership as proxies for agency costs and reports inconsistent evidence. While, as expected under an agency-cost hypothesis, free-cash-flow is positively associated with lockup use in some specifications, free-cash-flow is also highly correlated with operating profitability. Profitability is not a choice variable in the same way that free-cash-flow is hypothesized to be, and is likely correlated with the number of potential bidders for the target. This confounds our conclusions about the association between agency costs and lockup use. Furthermore, institutional ownership of the target firm is positively associated with lockup option use, not negatively associated as would be expected if institutional monitoring reduces agency costs.

I avoid these problems by reporting evidence on the outcomes of acquisition proposals (premiums offered, the incidence of competition, and success rates). This evidence will be suggestive of the sample average motivation for the use of termination fees in merger contracts. Consider the relation between termination fee use and target premiums. If agency problems are the primary reason termination fees are included in merger agreements, I would expect to see lower premiums paid by acquirers when a target termination fee is included in the merger contract.

---

[7] 15 U.S.C. Section 18a.

[8] Also see Berkovitch and Khanna (1990).

However, if target termination fees are principally used to solve a contracting problem between the bidder and target, premiums in termination fee deals should be no lower than in the rest of the sample. In fact, premiums should be higher if the target possesses the bargaining power to obtain a share of the rents created by the revelation of the bidder's private information. If the target believes that a termination fee will deter competing bidders from making higher valued offers (i.e., the target is unable to exploit its knowledge of the source of takeover gains, as in Eckbo and Langohr, 1989), the target board could bargain for a higher premium than otherwise would have been received from the bidder. A higher premium under these circumstances can be viewed as compensation paid by the bidder to the target for the loss of potential competing bids, and could be necessary for the target board to justify the merger terms to their shareholders.

The hypothesis that information revelation creates valuable rents that can be shared by target stockholders is consistent with the findings in Eckbo and Langohr (1989). Eckbo and Langohr report that an increase in disclosure requirements surrounding tender offers in France (without an increase in the minimum tender offer time period) significantly increased observed takeover premiums. The cross-sectional relation between termination fee use and target premiums depends, however, on the composition of the sample of deals without a termination fee. Bids in the sample of nonfee merger deals are likely to fall into one of two categories: (1) those where the exploitation of potential takeover gains requires resources controlled exclusively by the incumbent bidder and (2) those where the bidder has no valuable information to protect. Targets of the first type of bid are likely to have low bargaining power and hence expect low premiums. However, if the source of takeover gains is not valuable private information (e.g., a change of management), targets could exploit (implicit) competition among bidders to extract for their own shareholders a large share of the value increase created by the merger.

Of course, target managers faced with a bidder proposing to extract gains by firing the incumbent managers could defend themselves by deterring a deal completely, or by agreeing to be acquired by a white knight. In the case of a white knight bidder, a bid could potentially end up with both low premium (as a result of the agency costs noted in H1) and a termination fee. As this discussion illustrates, the relation between termination fee use and observable outcomes (such as the premium) is complicated by the fact that the two motivations for termination fee use (entrenchment and efficiency) are not mutually exclusive in the cross-section, and the lack of a termination fee can be reasonably associated with a variety of predictions. However, a large sample study such as this is able to shed light on the motivation that dominates the sample average premiums, and competition and completion rates. Furthermore, by carefully selecting relevant subsamples and control variables, my evidence should provide some clarity about the effect of certain bidder and target characteristics (e.g., white knight bidders) on offer outcomes.

4. Data and descriptive statistics

My sample of bids is taken from the Securities Data Corporation (SDC) Mergers and Acquisitions database for the 1988–2000 period. The first target termination fee reported by Dow Jones News Retrieval (DJNR) in an announced merger or acquisition is in the 1983 acquisition of Financial Corp. of Santa Barbara by Vagabond Hotels, Inc.[9] However, there are no target termination fees recorded on SDC for deals announced prior to 1988.[10] Therefore, to avoid a potential sample-selection bias because of time variation in premiums and bid competition, I only consider bids announced after 1988. Each bidder is required to be seeking to own at least 50% of the target firm. I also eliminate bids if both the bidder and target are not in the CRSP and Compustat databases for the announcement year of the bid.

My final sample contains 2511 merger and tender offer bids, and the distribution of these bids across years (panel A) and industries (panel B) is shown in Table 1. There is a marked increase over time in the number of deals in which the target agrees to pay a termination fee to the bidder. The years 1994 and 1997 are highlighted in Table 1, panel A, because Coates and Subramanian (2000) identifies two crucial judicial decisions (*Paramount* in 1994 and *Brazen* in 1997) in favor of termination fee use in those years. As can be seen, the fraction of deals employing target termination fees roughly doubles at each of these important break points.

The use of bidder termination fees has also increased over the sample period, but in every sample year there are considerably fewer bidder termination fees than target termination fees, and the fraction of deals including a bidder termination fee is correspondingly lower. Interestingly, the use of bidder termination fees increases markedly in 1994, most likely in response to the *Paramount* decision, but is unresponsive to the *Brazen* decision in 1997.

Table 1, panel B shows that target firms in my sample are concentrated in the machinery and equipment, financial, and recreation and entertainment industries, although all industries are reasonably well represented. More importantly, the use of target termination fees is relatively constant across the industry groups, except for the unusually low use rate in the financial industry.

Table 2 contains descriptive statistics for bidder and target termination fees. Target termination fees average $35.24 million, although the distribution is highly skewed. The median target termination fee is just $8 million. However, the *relative* size of a target termination fee is more interesting than its dollar value. The distribution of target termination fee amounts scaled by the market value of equity of the target 43 days prior to bid announcement has a mean of 5.87% and a median of 4.95%. Target termination fees as a percentage of total deal value (the total of the cash and securities

---

[9] It is not surprising that the use of target termination fees postdates the passing of the Williams Act in 1968, for reasons discussed in Section 3. It is somewhat surprising, however, that this contracting technology does not appear to have evolved earlier.

[10] An SDC representative claims that the data is back-filled, but only as far as 1988.

Table 1

Merger and tender offer bid sample

The sample consists of 2511 successful and unsuccessful merger and tender offer bids from 1988 to 2000 identified from the Securities Data Corporation (SDC) Mergers and Acquisitions Database. Bids are eliminated from the sample if either the target or bidder is not on both the CRSP and Compustat databases, or if the bidder is seeking to own less than 50% of the target firm. Bids are assigned to industries in Panel B using the target's primary SIC code from CRSP.

Panel A. Distribution across years

Year	No. of bids	No. (%) of bids including a target termination fee	No. (%) of bids including a bidder termination fee
1988	101	1 (0.99%)	0 (0.00%)
1989	93	2 (2.15%)	1 (1.08%)
1990	64	4 (6.25%)	1 (1.56%)
1991	61	13 (21.31%)	1 (1.64%)
1992	55	12 (21.82%)	3 (5.45%)
1993	123	22 (17.89%)	4 (3.25%)
1994	**191**	**68 (35.60%)**	**22 (11.52%)**
1995	231	88 (38.10%)	25 (10.82%)
1996	249	85 (34.14%)	40 (16.06%)
1997	**348**	**213 (61.21%)**	**53 (15.23%)**
1998	345	214 (62.03%)	46 (13.33%)
1999	371	221 (59.57%)	44 (11.86%)
2000	279	115 (41.22%)	34 (12.19%)
Total	2511	1058 (42.13%)	274 (10.91%)

Panel B. Distribution across industries

Target industry	No. of bids	No. of bids including a target termination fee	% of bids including a target termination fee
Agriculture, forestry, fishing, and mining	107	44	41.12
Construction and basic materials	113	52	46.02
Food and tobacco	35	17	48.57
Textiles, clothing, and consumer products	50	19	38.00
Logging, paper, printing, and Publishing	51	25	49.02
Chemicals	116	59	50.86
Petroleum	4	1	25.00
Machinery and equipment supply (incl. computers)	437	204	46.68
Transportation	77	27	35.06
Utilities and telecommunications	169	66	39.05
Wholesale distributors and retail	196	93	47.45
Financial services	679	193	28.42
Recreation, entertainment, services, and conglomerates	469	256	54.58
Other	8	2	25.00
Total	2511	1058	42.13

Table 2

Descriptive statistics for termination fees

This table contains descriptive statistics for bidder and target termination fees in a sample of 2511 successful and unsuccessful acquisition bids from 1988 to 2000. The termination fee amounts are in $ millions as recorded in the SDC Mergers and Acquisitions database. The market value of the bidder and target firms' equity is measured 43 days prior to the bid announcement date. Deal value is value of the cash and securities offered to the target shareholders, computed using data from SDC.

Variable	No. of obs.	Mean (S.E.)	Median	5%	95%
Target termination fee amount ($ millions)	1052	35.24 (4.66)	8.00	0.75	135.00
Bidder termination fee amount ($ millions)	264	70.61 (22.44)	10.00	0.50	225.00
Target termination fee as % of target market value of equity	1051	5.87% (0.15%)	4.95%	1.63%	12.52%
Target termination fee as % of deal value	853	3.80% (1.00%)	3.27%	1.20%	7.55%
Bidder termination fee as % of bidder market value of equity	262	4.51% (2.02%)	1.14%	0.06%	5.90%
Bidder termination fee as % of deal value	221	3.64% (0.24%)	3.10%	0.58%	7.71%

offered to target shareholders) average 3.80%. On average, therefore, targets agreeing to a termination fee commit to paying bidders almost 6% of their stand-alone market value, or almost 4% of the deal value, if the target terminates the merger agreement (typically by the acceptance of another bidder's offer).[11] Bidder termination fees are equal to $10 million at the median, and when scaled by deal values are of similar magnitude to the termination fees payable by the target.

Panel A in Table 3 contains descriptive statistics for the target premium. SDC offers several different data sources for a premium computation. The first is what I call "component" data, where the aggregate amount of each form of payment offered to target shareholders (cash, equity, debt, etc.) is individually recorded in the SDC database. The second is "price" data, where SDC reports a valuation of both the initial and final price per share of target stock offered by the bidder without noting the method of payment (or how the price is calculated). I compute premium measures using both component and price estimates of the offer made by the bidder, and the bid value is then compared to the target's market value of equity 43 days prior to the bid announcement to compute the premium.

Ideally, use of these different data definitions from SDC would result in consistent premium estimates, but the results in panel A of Table 3 suggest that they do not.

---

[11] Interestingly, the *Financial Times* notes that the Takeover Code in the United Kingdom explicitly limits the size of termination fees to 1% of the target market value of equity (February 4, 2002).

Table 3

Descriptive statistics for premiums offered to target shareholders

This table contains means and medians (in parentheses) for various measures of the premium offered to target shareholders (Panel A), and the premium in competition-based subsamples (Panel B), for 2511 successful and unsuccessful acquisition bids from 1988 to 2000. The statistics in the first column in both panels employ the full sample, while the final two columns use subsamples of bids divided by target termination fee use. The different premium measures included in Panel A are all based on SDC data. The target premium is defined as {(Bidder's offer/Target's prebid market value of equity) − 1}. Three different methods are used for computing the value of the bidder's offer. The first uses component data, where SDC records individually the aggregate value of cash, stock, and other securities offered by the bidder to target shareholders. The second and third methods use price data. SDC reports both "initial" and "final" offer prices per target share, and the second premium measure uses the final offer price. The third measure uses the initial price data only (where available). The denominator for all premium measures is the target's market value of equity 43 days prior to bid announcement. As these premium measures result in extreme positive and negative outliers, a fourth measure, combined premium, is computed. Combined premium is based on the component data if that data results in a value between zero and two, and if not relies on initial price data (or final price if initial price data is missing) if that data provides a value between zero and two. If neither condition is met, the combined premium is left as a missing observation. This combined premium measure is used in the remaining analysis in this paper and is denoted PREMIUM. Prebid (postbid) competition is determined by the incidence of a competing offer for the target in the 6 months before (after) the current bid. The number of observations in each cell is in brackets.

Panel A: Premiums

Premium definition	Full sample	No target termination fee	Target termination fee
Premium based on *component* data	63.41%	57.98%	70.00%
	(45.05%)	(40.76%)	(49.69%[a])
	[1890]	[1036]	[854]
Premium based *final price* data	48.65%	46.19%	51.89%[a]
	(41.96%)	(39.03%)	(44.69%[a])
	[2396]	[1361]	[1035]
Premium based on *initial price* data	47.83%	41.59%	53.90%[a]
	(40.49%)	(37.22%)	(44.68%[a])
	[1342]	[661]	[681]
Combined premium (PREMIUM)	55.10%	52.21%	58.78%[a]
	(47.46%)	(44.82%)	(51.04%[a])
	[2212]	[1240]	[972]

Panel B: Average PREMIUM in competition-based subsamples

Bid competition	Full sample	No target termination fee	Target termination fee
No competition	54.87%	51.45%	58.94%[a]
	(47.10%)	(44.27%)	(51.13%[a])
	[2004]	[1090]	[914]
Prebid competition only	61.11%	62.79%*	56.97%
	(53.91%)	(58.50%*)	(48.98%)
	[97]	[69]	[28]

(Continued)

Table 3 (*Continued*)

Bid competition	Full sample	No target termination fee	Target termination fee
Postbid competition only	54.89%	55.40%	53.41%
	(46.27%)	(45.35%)	(48.78%)
	[100]	[74]	[26]
Both pre- and postbid competition	46.11%	33.38%	68.38%[a]
	(54.46%)	(43.46%)	(67.58%)
	[11]	[7]	[4]

[a]Indicates that the Target termination fee mean or median premium is significantly different from the No target termination fee statistic in the same row at the 5% level.

In panel B, * indicates that a competition subsample mean or median premium is significantly different from the No competition statistic in the same column at the 5% level.

The component-based premiums in the first row are consistently higher than the premium estimates generated from price data in the second and third rows, especially in the extremes of the distribution (as reflected in the means). In fact, the sample correlation between the component and final (initial) price premium measures is just 0.22 (0.57). All premium measures also result in troubling outliers, with a substantial fraction of each distribution lying below zero (an economically meaningful bound) and above two (an arbitrary bound).

Therefore, I compute a composite premium estimate that I call the combined premium. This measure integrates the component and price premium measures in a way that eliminates the extremes of both distributions. Specifically, the combined premium is equal to the premium from the component data if that number is between zero and two. If it is not, the combined premium is equal to the initial price data premium (or final price data premium if the initial price is missing) if that provides a number between zero and two. If neither condition is met, the combined premium is left as a missing observation.[12]

Using this combined premium measure, the median set of target shareholders in the full sample is offered a 47% premium by the bidder. Bidders in deals with a target termination fee as part of the merger terms offer a 51% premium over the prebid market value of the target at the median, while in deals without a target termination fee the median set of target shareholders only receive a 45% premium. The median premium difference between the termination fee subsamples (51% vs. 45%) is statistically significantly different from zero, as is the difference in mean premiums (59% vs. 52%).

---

[12] While this premium measure is used throughout the rest of this paper, inferences about the determinants of the bid premium are qualitatively insensitive to the choice between the various premium measures represented in Panel A of Table 3. Inferences about the effect of termination fees on premiums are also unchanged if a measure of the premium based on target abnormal returns over the bid period is used (as in Schwert, 2000, among others).

These results are the first evidence that the use of a target termination fee in a merger agreement is, at least on average, not detrimental to target shareholders. Rather than generating agency costs from the perspective of target shareholders, as the entrenchment hypothesis suggests, termination fees appear to be associated with higher takeover premiums. Of course, the higher premiums in the target termination fee subsample may simply reflect correlated variables that influence both the use of target termination fees and the premium offered (e.g., bidder toeholds). Multivariate regressions that have the potential to address this concern are discussed in Section 5.

Panel B in Table 3 shows descriptive statistics for the premium offered by the bidder for subsamples based on bid competition. Prebid (postbid) competition is defined as the incidence of a competing bid for the target in the 6 months before (after) the current bid. The evidence in panel B of Table 3 has the potential to address the issue of whether white knight bidders with termination fee agreements in place offer significantly lower premiums to target shareholders (as in H1 above).

The evidence does not suggest that second (and final, i.e., white knight) bidders with termination fees pay significantly lower premiums relative to either other bidders in merger agreements with target termination fees or other second (and final) bidders. However, it appears that target shareholders do not receive the extra premium that a competing bid generates if their managers have agreed to a termination fee with the second bidder. In the subsample of bids without a target termination fee, the competition caused by the fact that another bid has already been observed for the target results in significantly higher premiums for target shareholders (63% vs. 51%). The same cannot be said for bids in the target termination fee subsample. In deals with a target termination fee, the fact that the target has already received a competing offer from another bidder is associated with slightly lower (but not significantly different) mean premium (57% vs. 59%).

However, termination fees do appear to elicit higher bids from bidders in highly competitive bargaining situations. When both pre- and postbid competing offers are observed, termination fee use is associated with significantly higher average bid premiums (68% vs. 33%). One interpretation of this result is that target termination fee use is beneficial to target shareholders in contested auctions for the target. This is consistent with H2, as the contracting hypothesis predicts that the rents created via the information protection afforded by a termination fee are increasing in the potential for other bidders to free ride on private information released by the current bidder. However, the small sample size somewhat limits the interpretation of this result.

Table 4 contains abnormal announcement returns for both bidder and target. Abnormal returns are measured over a seven trading-day interval centered on bid announcement, and relative to expectations from a market model estimated using 200 trading-days of returns ending 53 days prior to bid announcement. The inclusion of a target termination fee in the merger terms is associated with significantly more positive target abnormal returns at the mean and median and significantly more negative average bidder abnormal returns. It is conceivable that these abnormal return results

Table 4

Descriptive statistics for bidder and target abnormal announcement returns

This table contains means and medians (in parentheses) for bidder and target abnormal announcement returns in 2511 successful and unsuccessful acquisition bids from 1988 to 2000. The statistics in the first column employ the full sample, while the final two columns use subsamples of bids divided by target termination fee use. The bidder and target abnormal return measures are cumulative abnormal returns over the period from event day -3 to event day $+3$, where event day 0 is the bid announcement date. The abnormal returns are measured relative to a market model estimated for the bidder and target individually over a 200-day period ending 53 days prior to bid announcement. The number of observations in each cell is in brackets

Variable	Full sample	No target termination fee	Target termination fee
7-day bidder abnormal announcement returns $(-3, +3)$	-1.16%***	-0.83%***	-1.62%[a],***
	(-1.24%)***	(-1.12%)***	(-1.35%)***
	[2458]	[1423]	[1035]
7-day target abnormal announcement returns $(-3, +3)$	22.16%***	20.90%***	23.88%[a],***
	(17.99%)***	(16.90%)***	(19.74%[a])***
	[2487]	[1441]	[1046]

[a]Indicates that the Target termination fee mean or median abnormal return is significantly different from the No target termination fee statistic in the same row at the 5% level.
***, **, * indicate that the particular mean or median is significantly different from zero at the 1%, 5%, or 10% level, respectively.

largely reflect the significant premium differences noted in Table 3, but again the veracity of this hypothesis can only be established through the use of multivariate regressions.

Table 5 contains descriptive statistics for other bidder, target, and deal characteristics that are likely correlated with termination fee use and will be controlled for in the multivariate regressions presented in the next section. These control variables are taken from many prior papers explaining takeover premiums, including Huang and Walkling (1987), Bradley et al. (1988), Comment and Schwert (1995), Betton and Eckbo (2000), and Schwert (2000), among others. Specifically, this literature finds that takeover premiums are higher when competing bidders also attempt to acquire the target, the target has a poison pill in place, the method of payment is cash, target managers are hostile toward proposed acquirers, and the bid takes the form of a tender offer. Premiums are significantly lower when the bidder holds a substantial toehold in the target firm, the target has high market-capitalization, and the target has a high market-to-book ratio.

Virtually none of the deals including a target termination fee are hostile (as recorded by SDC) or affected by the use of a poison pill, as termination fees are included as part of agreed merger contracts. Somewhat surprisingly, however, the use of tender offers is more common in deals that include a termination fee (24%) than in acquisitions that do not (16%). SDC codes a deal as involving a tender offer if any of the target shares are

Table 5

Descriptive statistics for bidder, target, and deal characteristics

This table contains means and medians, and associated test statistics, for bidder, target, and deal characteristics in a sample of 2511 successful and unsuccessful acquisition bids from 1988 to 2000. The dummy variable SUCCESS is equal to one if the bidder successfully acquires the target and zero otherwise. HOSTILE is equal to one if the bid is recorded by SDC as "hostile" or "unsolicited" and zero otherwise. PRECOMP (POSTCOMP) is a dummy variable equal to one if another bid by a different bidder is recorded by SDC in the 6 months before (after) the current bid and zero otherwise. TENDER and CASH are dummy variables equal to one if the bid involved a tender offer or a payment of cash (even if mixed with other securities) to target shareholders and zero otherwise. SIND is equal to one if the bidder is from the same industry as the target (where industry definitions are taken from Fama and French, 1997) and zero otherwise. POISON is a dummy variable equal to one if a poison pill affects the bidder's acquisition attempt and zero otherwise. PHELD is the fraction of the target's common stock owned by the bidder on the bid announcement date. TOEHOLD is a dummy variable equal to one if PHELD is greater than 5% and zero otherwise. CLEANUP is a dummy variable equal to one if PHELD is greater than 50% and zero otherwise. BMVE (TMVE) is the market value of the bidder (target) firm (in $000's) on event day -1, or the closest trading-day prior to day -1 for which the bidder (target) market value can be computed from CRSP. BM2B (TM2B) is the ratio of market-to-book value of stockholders equity for the bidder (target) computed using data from COMPUSTAT from the year of the bid. The Tests column contains test statistics for the null hypothesis of zero difference in mean (median) between the two subsamples. Medians are only reported where appropriate.

	Full sample Mean [Median]	No target termination fee Mean [Median]	Target termination fee Mean [Median]	Tests t-test [Wilcoxon test]
HOSTILE	0.08	0.13	0.01	10.88***
TENDER	0.20	0.16	0.24	5.34***
CASH	0.35	0.37	0.31	2.90***
SIND	0.52	0.52	0.53	0.90
POISON	0.02	0.02	0.00	4.08***
CLEANUP	0.04	0.07	0.00	8.14***
TOEHOLD	0.09	0.13	0.03	9.12***
PHELD	0.04	0.06	0.01	8.89***
	[0.00]	[0.00]	[0.00]	
BMVE	8,071,221.18	4,766,675.47	12,609,505.61	6.90***
	[1,217,495.50]	[814,886.31]	[1,985,434.78]	[10.92]***
TMVE	711,254.26	512,864.59	983,711.90	3.48***
	[124,333.75]	[91,658.69]	[193,777.78]	[11.27]***
BM2B	3.52	2.76	4.56	3.47***
	[2.32]	[2.05]	[2.84]	[9.48]***
TM2B	3.81	3.94	3.64	0.16
	[1.69]	[1.58]	[1.89]	[6.79]***
SUCCESS	0.83	0.75	0.94	13.31***
PRECOMP	0.05	0.06	0.03	2.92***
POSTCOMP	0.05	0.06	0.03	3.59***

***, **, * indicate significance at the 1%, 5%, or 10% level, respectively, using a two-tailed test.

acquired in this manner, including two tier offers and aborted unsolicited acquisition attempts. Therefore, many deals coded as "tender offers" in this study also involve definitive merger agreements between the bidder and target (often follow-on stock swaps).

There are almost no cleanup offers in the termination fee subsample, where a cleanup offer is defined as a bid by a bidder already holding more than 50% of the target's stock. In fact, it appears that target termination fees and bidder toeholds are substitutable. Only 3% of the bidders in the termination fee subsample possess a toehold greater than 5% of the target's outstanding shares at bid announcement, while 13% of bidders announcing unprotected deals hold a stake of more than 5%. This is an intuitive result under the contracting hypothesis discussed above, as both termination fees and toeholds allow the incumbent bidder to capture a return on acquisition-related investments should another suitor free ride on valuable private information released by the initial bidder as part of the merger process.

Table 5 also demonstrates that deals including a target termination fee are significantly more likely to be successful, and bidders in such deals experience significantly less postbid competition (defined as another bid for the target by a different bidder in the 6 months following the current bid). This is potentially evidence of bid deterrence, but the targets in deals including termination fees are also less likely to have received a bid in the 6 months prior to contracting with the current bidder. It seems likely, therefore, that the targets in termination fee deals are simply less attractive acquisition candidates.

Table 6 contains a correlation matrix for the principal variables in my analysis. There is a significant, albeit small, sample correlation between the bid premium and the use of target termination fees, as noted in Table 3. As might be expected, bid success is positively correlated with the premium, and, consistent with previous results, also with the use of termination fees. Premiums are significantly higher in cash deals, potentially because of the tax-related consequences of cash bids (Huang and Walkling, 1987), and significantly lower if the bidder owns a substantial stake in the target firm at bid announcement. The latter result is consistent with Betton and Eckbo's (2000) finding that bidder toeholds have a negative impact on target premiums.

Bidders appear to acquire significantly greater toeholds in hostile deals, including those influenced by a poison pill, and when postbid competition is anticipated. The positive correlation between the use of cash and bid competition confirms the intuition that the existence of multiple competing suitors for the same target makes it more likely that a bidder offers cash to target shareholders (Fishman, 1989).

5. The effect of target termination fee agreements

5.1. The relation between target termination fees and premiums

Table 7 contains the results of regressions of target premiums on bidder, target, and deal characteristics. Only prima facie "exogenous" explanatory variables are chosen

Table 6

Correlation coefficients

This table contains Pearson correlation coefficients for a sample of 2511 successful and unsuccessful acquisition bids between 1988 and 2000. TTERMF is a dummy variable equal to one if the bid resulted in a merger agreement containing a termination fee payable by the target to the bidder and zero otherwise. All other variable definitions are contained in previous tables.

	TTERMF	SUCCESS	HOSTILE	PRECOMP	POSTCOMP	TENDER	POISON	CASH	CLEANUP	TOEHOLD
PREMIUM	0.09***	0.06***	0.00	0.03	-0.01	0.14***	0.02	0.10***	-0.13***	-0.13***
TTERMF		0.26***	-0.21***	-0.06***	-0.07***	0.11***	-0.08***	-0.06***	-0.16***	-0.18***
SUCCESS			-0.46***	-0.15***	-0.32***	0.06***	-0.15***	-0.02	0.03	-0.04*
HOSTILE				0.19***	0.20***	0.16***	0.35***	0.17***	0.06***	0.15***
PRECOMP					0.05**	0.10***	0.03*	0.07***	-0.02	0.01
POSTCOMP						0.06***	0.11***	0.08***	-0.02	0.04**
TENDER							0.17***	0.58***	0.05***	0.09***
POISON								0.14***	-0.01	0.11***
CASH									0.12***	0.21***
CLEANUP										0.66***

***, **, * indicate that the correlation coefficient is significantly different from zero at the 1%, 5%, or 10% level, respectively, using a two-tailed test.

Table 7

The determinants of target premium

The regressions are based on a sample of 2511 successful and unsuccessful merger and tender offer bids between 1988 and 2000. The dependent variable is PREMIUM. BTERMF is a dummy variable equal to one if the bid resulted in a merger agreement containing a termination fee payable by the bidder to the target and zero otherwise. FINSERV is a dummy variable equal to one if both the bidder and target are in the financial services industry (as defined in Table 1). All other independent variables are defined in previous tables. Heteroskedasticity-consistent standard errors are in parentheses.

Independent variable	Model 1	Model 2	Model 3
Intercept	0.56***	0.54***	0.61***
	(0.07)	(0.07)	(0.07)
TTERMF	0.07***	0.04**	0.03
	(0.02)	(0.02)	(0.02)
BTERMF		−0.01	−0.00
		(0.03)	(0.03)
PRECOMP		0.05	0.06
		(0.04)	(0.04)
POISON		0.06	0.09
		(0.06)	(0.06)
CASH		0.02	0.03
		(0.02)	(0.02)
SIND		0.03**	0.02
		(0.02)	(0.02)
HOSTILE		0.02	0.02
		(0.03)	(0.03)
TENDER		0.10***	0.10***
		(0.03)	(0.03)
TOEHOLD		−0.14***	−0.11***
		(0.03)	(0.03)
CLEANUP		−0.13***	−0.13***
		(0.04)	(0.04)
FINSERV		−0.07***	−0.05**
		(0.02)	(0.02)
Log(BMVE)	0.04***	0.04***	0.03***
	(0.01)	(0.01)	(0.01)
Log(TMVE)	−0.05***	−0.05***	−0.05***
	(0.01)	(0.01)	(0.01)
Log(BM2B)			0.08***
			(0.01)
Log(TM2B)			−0.01
			(0.02)
Number of observations	2204	2204	1972
Adjusted R^2	0.04	0.09	0.10

***, **, and * indicate that the parameter estimate is significantly different from zero at the 1%, 5%, and 10% levels, respectively.

as regressors in Table 7. For example, deal success is not included as a right-hand side variable (as it is in Burch, 2001). However, the regressions in Table 7 arguably suffer from several endogeneity issues, some of which are addressed in Section 6.

The only explanatory variables in the first regression in Table 7 are a dummy variable indicating whether the particular merger agreement contained a target termination fee and the logs of the market-capitalizations of the bidder and target. The coefficient on the target termination fee dummy variable is consistent with the results in Table 3, with targets in termination fee deals earning 7% higher bid premiums. This coefficient is statistically significant at the 1% level. The market values of the bidder and target also appear to affect the bid premium, with large bidders paying higher premiums and large targets earning lower premiums.

Termination fee deals may involve higher target premiums even in the absence of the fee because of correlated omitted variables, which are controlled for in Models 2 and 3. The magnitude of the effect of target termination fee inclusion on the bid premium is roughly halved when these control variables are included in the regression, and statistically indistinguishable from zero in Model 3. Bidder termination fee agreements do not seem to have any significant effect on premiums, although the lack of significance could be driven by the fact that bidder and target termination fee use is highly correlated (Table 11).

This evidence is not supportive of an agency-cost explanation for termination fee use. At worst, target premiums are unaffected by target termination fee inclusion (Model 3), and at best they are significantly higher if the bidder's investment in the deal process is protected by a punitive fee. This conclusion is, however, consistent with termination fees being used to solve one of the contracting problems between the bidder and target, as described in H2 above. The higher premium earned by the target is likely to be motivated by perceived deterrence of competing bids as a result of putting a price (the termination fee) on the free riding activities of potential bidders. Interestingly, however, results discussed later suggest that termination fees only weakly deter competing bids, if at all.

Many of the control variables in Models 2 and 3 are significant in explaining premiums. Premiums are higher in intraindustry mergers than in interindustry deals, except in the financial services industry. In fact, bank mergers appear to involve significantly lower premiums than deals in other industry sectors. Premiums are higher if the bidder uses a tender offer during the acquisition process, but significantly lower when the bidder has a toehold of more than 5% of the target's outstanding equity.[13] As might be expected, cleanup offers involve premiums that are significantly lower than premiums in other deals. Bidders with ample growth opportunities (high market-to-book, see Smith and Watts, 1992) agree to pay significantly higher premiums.

---

[13] Betton and Eckbo (2000) also report a significantly negative relation between toeholds and target premiums, but use a very different (simultaneous-equations) estimation technique.

5.2. The relation between target termination fees and abnormal announcement returns

Table 8 provides multivariate evidence on the abnormal returns associated with bid announcements. Cumulative abnormal stock returns are measured over a 7-day window centered on bid announcement. The results are largely consistent with the premium evidence offered in Table 7. The first column in Table 8 indicates that the target's abnormal announcement return is significantly more positive when a target termination fee is included in the deal terms, with the point estimate of a 3% higher abnormal announcement return.

However, the coefficient on the termination fee dummy becomes insignificantly different from zero once the control variables (including the bid premium) are included in the model (second column). Bidder abnormal stock returns do not appear to be at all related to target termination fee use, and neither abnormal announcement return is significantly associated with a dummy variable indicating bidder termination fee inclusion. Therefore, the effect of target termination fee use on target stockholder wealth is at worst neutral and potentially positive. This suggests that the market does not believe, at least on average, that termination fees are used to the detriment of target shareholders.

Some of the control variables have notable coefficients. The target's abnormal return is significantly positively associated with the bid premium, as would be expected in a reasonably specified model. However, the point estimate of the coefficient is just 0.25.[14] The dummy variable PRECOMP indicates whether the target received any bids from different bidders in the preceding 6-month period. This dummy variable is significantly negatively associated with the target's abnormal return, most likely because prior bids reduce the surprise associated with the current bid. Interestingly, the prior competition dummy is not associated with the bidder's abnormal announcement return, as might be expected if bidders in multiple bidder auctions fare substantially worse than uncontested bidders do (Bradley et al., 1988).

5.3. The relation between target termination fees and competition

Table 9 presents the determinants of postbid competition. The probit models directly address the ability of target termination fee to deter competing bidders. The marginal effects in brackets are computed by first calculating the probability of postbid competition using the sample means for all continuous independent variables and zeroes for all dummy independent variables (the base predicted probability). The probability of competition is then recomputed by changing each independent variable (in turn) by adding one standard deviation to the mean of continuous variables (or using a one for each dummy variable). The marginal effects reported in the tables are the differences between the new and base probability and represent the change in the

---

[14] This coefficient should equal the cross-sectional average rate of bid success if none of the independent variables are measured with error, there is no prebid information leakage, and the market does not anticipate higher premium competing offers. See Officer (2003).

Table 8

The determinants of the market reaction to merger and tender offer bids

The regressions are based on a sample of 2511 successful and unsuccessful merger and tender offer bids between 1988 and 2000. The dependent variables are the cumulative abnormal returns for the target and bidder over the seven trading-day period centered on bid announcement. All independent variables are defined in previous tables. Heteroskedasticity-consistent standard errors are in parentheses.

Independent variable	Target 7-day abnormal return		Bidder 7-day abnormal return	
Intercept	0.21***	0.04	0.09***	0.04**
	(0.04)	(0.04)	(0.02)	(0.02)
TTERMF	0.03***	−0.00	−0.00	−0.00
	(0.01)	(0.01)	(0.01)	(0.01)
BTERMF		−0.01		−0.00
		(0.01)		(0.01)
PREMIUM		0.25***		0.00
		(0.02)		(0.01)
PRECOMP		−0.09***		0.00
		(0.02)		(0.01)
POISON		0.02		−0.02
		(0.04)		(0.01)
CASH		0.03**		0.01*
		(0.01)		(0.00)
SIND		0.01		−0.00
		(0.01)		(0.00)
HOSTILE		0.02		−0.01
		(0.02)		(0.01)
TENDER		0.05***		0.02***
		(0.01)		(0.01)
TOEHOLD		0.02		0.01
		(0.02)		(0.01)
CLEANUP		−0.04		0.02
		(0.03)		(0.01)
FINSERV		−0.03***		−0.01
		(0.01)		(0.00)
Log(BMVE)	0.03***	0.02***	−0.00	0.00
	(0.00)	(0.00)	(0.00)	(0.00)
Log(TMVE)	−0.04***	−0.02***	−0.01***	−0.01***
	(0.00)	(0.00)	(0.00)	(0.00)
Log(BM2B)		−0.00		−0.01**
		(0.01)		(0.00)
Log(TM2B)		−0.01**		−0.00
		(0.01)		(0.00)
Number of observations	2476	1968	2450	1958
Adjusted R^2	0.05	0.25	0.02	0.05

***, **, and * indicate that the parameter estimate is significantly different from zero at the 1%, 5%, and 10% levels, respectively.

Table 9

The determinants of postbid competition

The probit regressions are based on a sample of 2511 successful and unsuccessful merger and tender offer bids between 1988 and 2000. The dependent variable in all columns is POSTCOMP, a dummy variable equal to one if another bidder bids for the target in the 6-month period following the current bid. The first two columns use all bids in the sample with sufficient data, while the third column only includes bids that have a target termination fee as part of the merger agreement. TTERMFPCT is the target termination fee as a percentage of the target's market value of equity, as in Table 2. All other independent variables are defined in previous tables. The marginal effects of a change from the sample means of continuous independent variables, and from zero for dummy independent variables, are in brackets. Base pred. prob. of comp is the base case predicted probability of postbid competition. Quasi-ML robust standard errors are in parentheses.

Independent variable	All bids				Bids including a target termination fee only	
Intercept	−1.60***		−1.50***		−1.49**	
	(0.31)		(0.37)		(0.68)	
TTERMF	−0.34***		−0.19			
	(0.10)	[−0.03]	(0.12)	[−0.01]		
TTERMFPCT					−0.93	
					(2.87)	[−0.00]
BTERMF			−0.07		0.11	
			(0.17)	[−0.01]	(0.19)	[0.01]
PREMIUM			−0.02		−0.09	
			(0.13)	[−0.00]	(0.25)	[−0.00]
PRECOMP			0.11		0.60**	
			(0.20)	[0.01]	(0.28)	[0.05]
POISON			0.10		0.66	
			(0.27)	[0.01]	(0.72)	[0.06]
CASH			0.13		0.06	
			(0.12)	[0.01]	(0.25)	[0.00]
SIND			−0.00		0.08	
			(0.10)	[−0.00]	(0.17)	[0.00]
HOSTILE			0.71***		0.70	
			(0.15)	[0.12]	(0.50)	[0.07]
TENDER			−0.05		0.03	
			(0.14)	[−0.00]	(0.26)	[0.00]
TOEHOLD			0.29		0.52	
			(0.19)	[0.03]	(0.40)	[0.04]
CLEANUP			−0.70*		−6.56***	
			(0.37)	[−0.04]	(0.41)	[−0.02]
FINSERV			−0.24*		−0.19	
			(0.12)	[−0.02]	(0.26)	[−0.01]
Log(BMVE)	−0.14***		−0.10***		−0.09**	
	(0.03)	[−0.03]	(0.03)	[−0.02]	(0.04)	[−0.01]
Log(TMVE)	0.16***		0.10***		0.07	
	(0.03)	[0.04]	(0.03)	[0.02]	(0.06)	[0.01]
Number of observations	2499		2204		957	
Base pred. prob. of comp	0.06		0.04		0.02	
McFadden R^2	0.04		0.11		0.06	

***, **, and * indicate that the parameter estimate is significantly different from zero at the 1%, 5%, and 10% levels, respectively.

probability of postbid competition resulting from a one-standard-deviation change in each continuous independent variable or a change from zero to one for each dummy independent variable. The same technique is used to compute marginal effects for all probit models in this paper.

The first column in Table 9 suggests that target termination fees do curb competing bids, with the termination fee dummy variable having a significantly negative coefficient. The marginal economic impact of termination fee use is a 3% reduction in the probability that an alternate offer emerges. This is quite a substantial effect when compared to the 6% base predicted probability of competition without a termination fee. However, the product of a 3% reduction in the probability of a competing bid and the expected incremental premium from such a bid is unlikely to be economically significant.

Furthermore, the statistical significance of the deterrence effect diminishes once the control variables are introduced. In particular, hostile bids are 12% more likely to attract competitors, and the friendly nature of termination fee deals seems to explain much of the lower incidence of competition in that subsample. As noted in Schwert (2000), however, conjectures about the causality between hostility and competition are treacherous, as perceived competition could induce target managers to play "hard to get."

The point estimates in the first-two columns of Table 9 must be interpreted with caution. Comment and Schwert (1995) examine the bid deterrence effect of poison pills and argue that it will appear as if poison pills actually attract merger bids if pills are adopted when the potential target suspects a bid will be forthcoming. The same is true of target termination fees. If target termination fees are included in merger agreements when the bidder and target suspect a competing bidder will make an offer, and that offer eventuates despite the fee, it will appear as if termination fees attract, rather than deter, competing bidders. Hence the coefficients in the first-two columns of Table 9 could be biased upward (i.e., biased against a finding of bid deterrence). However, applying the self-selection adjustments from either Comment and Schwert (1995) or Heckman (1979) does not alter the inferences from the regressions in the first-two columns of Table 9.

Therefore, the last column in Table 9 attempts to measure the deterrence effect in another way. If termination fees do deter competing bids, then the deterrence effect should be increasing in the size of the termination fee payable to the incumbent bidder.[15] Termination fee size as a percentage of the target's market value of equity, as in Table 2, is included as an explanatory variable in a probit regression using deals that included a target termination fee. While the coefficient on fee size in the postbid competition regression is negative, implying that bigger fees are more of a deterrent to competing bids, the coefficient is not significantly different from zero. Interestingly, in this sample of termination fee deals, bid competition exhibits "serial correlation." Specifically, the

---

[15] Of course, bidders anticipating greater competition could self-select larger termination fees, leading again to difficulties in interpreting the reported coefficients.

probability of another bidder making an offer for the target is 5% higher if a bid was received by the target in the 6 months prior to the current deal being announced.

The evidence in Table 9 is also not supportive of the agency-cost hypothesis for target termination fee use. Deterrence of competition is a key assumption in the agency-cost rationale for including a termination fee in a merger agreement, as this is the supposed benefit offered to white knight bidders in return for potential job security for target managers.

5.4. The relation between target termination fees and bid success

Table 10 contains results from probit regressions explaining the likelihood that a merger bid or tender offer results in a completed transaction. The inclusion of a target termination fee in the deal terms is associated with a significantly higher probability that the bidder is successful in acquiring the target. Even when the control variables are included, the point estimate of the effect of a target termination fee is an 11% increase in the predicted the success rate (from a base of 84%). Both target termination fee coefficients in Table 10 are significant at the 1% level. The bid premium also has a significantly positive impact on the probability of success, while competing bids and hostility toward the bidder reduce the likelihood that the current bid is successful. Deals involving large target firms are less likely to be successful, all else equal, while large bidders are more likely to complete proposed transactions.

The evidence suggests that the most striking effect of target termination fee use is an increase in probability that the bidder successfully acquires the target. The significantly higher success rates in termination fee deals are potentially the result of bidders making more substantial investments in the bid process, including the release of nonpublic information about postbid strategies for the target's assets, because such investments are protected with a termination fee from free riding by other bidders. The bidder's plans for the target's assets are conceivably important to target shareholders deciding whether to vote in favor of the proposed union, especially when the bidder plans to pay for their shares using stock in the combined firm.

6. Endogeneity and the determinants of target termination fee agreements

The prior sections contain evidence on the *effect* of target termination fees on premiums, returns, competition, and success rates, in an effort to discern the underlying motivation for termination fee use and whether this motivation is detrimental to target shareholders. More direct evidence on the determinants of target termination fee use is presented in Table 11. The dependent variable in the probit regressions is a dummy variable indicating whether a bid resulted in a merger agreement containing a target termination fee.

The results demonstrate the strong correlation between bidder and target termination fee use. Target termination fees are more than twice as likely to be found in a merger

Table 10

The determinants of bid success

The probit regressions are based on a sample of 2511 successful and unsuccessful merger and tender offer bids between 1988 and 2000. The dependent variable is SUCCESS, a dummy variable equal to one if the merger or tender offer bid results in a successful acquisition and zero otherwise. All independent variables are defined in previous tables. The marginal effects of a change from the sample means of continuous independent variables, and from zero for dummy independent variables, are in brackets. Base pred. prob. of success is the base case predicted probability of success. Quasi-ML robust standard errors are in parentheses.

Independent variable				
Intercept	−0.39		−0.59*	
	(0.25)		(0.35)	
TTERMF	0.90***		0.67***	
	(0.08)	[0.17]	(0.10)	[0.11]
BTERMF			−0.04	
			(0.15)	[−0.01]
PREMIUM			0.20*	
			(0.12)	[0.02]
PRECOMP			−0.55***	
			(0.16)	[−0.17]
POSTCOMP			−1.37***	
			(0.18)	[−0.49]
POISON			−0.02	
			(0.30)	[−0.00]
CASH			−0.05	
			(0.10)	[−0.01]
SIND			−0.07	
			(0.08)	[−0.02]
HOSTILE			−1.82***	
			(0.15)	[−0.64]
TENDER			0.96***	
			(0.17)	[0.13]
TOEHOLD			0.18	
			(0.17)	[0.04]
CLEANUP			0.64**	
			(0.32)	[0.11]
FINSERV			0.49***	
			(0.10)	[0.09]
Log(BMVE)	0.27***		0.20***	
	(0.02)	[0.13]	(0.03)	[0.08]
Log(TMVE)	−0.22***		−0.11***	
	(0.03)	[−0.13]	(0.03)	[−0.05]
Number of observations	2499		2204	
Base pred. prob. of success	0.78		0.84	
McFadden R^2	0.15		0.36	

***, **, and * indicate that the parameter estimate is significantly different from zero at the 1%, 5%, and 10% levels, respectively.

Table 11

The determinants of target termination fee agreements

The probit regressions are based on a sample of 2511 successful and unsuccessful merger and tender offer bids between 1988 and 2000. The dependent variable is TTERMF, a dummy variable equal to one if the merger agreement contains a termination fee payable by the target to the bidder and zero otherwise. D94 and D97 are dummy variables equal to one if the bid is announced in or following 1994 or 1997, respectively, and zero otherwise. All other independent variables are defined in previous tables. The marginal effects of a change from the sample means of continuous independent variables, and from zero for dummy independent variables, are in brackets. Base pred. prob. of TTERMF is the base case predicted probability that the merger agreement contains a target termination fee. Quasi-ML robust standard errors are in parentheses.

Independent variable				
Intercept	−2.87***		−3.04***	
	(0.21)		(0.28)	
BTERMF	1.67***		1.51***	
	(0.11)	[0.55]	(0.14)	[0.54]
PREMIUM			0.18**	
			(0.09)	[0.02]
PRECOMP			−0.03	
			(0.16)	[−0.01]
POISON			0.14	
			(0.34)	[0.04]
CASH			−0.23***	
			(0.09)	[−0.05]
SIND			0.04	
			(0.06)	[0.01]
HOSTILE			−1.72***	
			(0.20)	[−0.16]
TENDER			0.62***	
			(0.10)	[0.19]
TOEHOLD			−0.36**	
			(0.17)	[−0.07]
CLEANUP			−1.79***	
			(0.38)	[−0.16]
FINSERV			−0.65***	
			(0.08)	[−0.11]
D94			0.85***	
			(0.11)	[0.28]
D97			0.42***	
			(0.07)	[0.12]
Log(BMVE)	0.13***		0.05***	
	(0.02)	[0.10]	(0.02)	[0.03]
Log(TMVE)	0.06***		0.10***	
	(0.02)	[0.04]	(0.03)	[0.04]
Number of observations	2499		2204	
Base pred. prob. of TTERMF	0.36		0.16	
McFadden R^2	0.14		0.31	

***, **, and * indicate that the parameter estimate is significantly different from zero at the 1%, 5%, and 10% levels, respectively.

agreement if that agreement also contains a bidder termination fee. This evidence reinforces the interpretation of bidder termination fees as half of a reciprocal termination agreement between the bidder and target in merger-of-equals deals. The size of each individual firm also matters: target termination fees are significantly more likely to be used when the bidder or target has high market-capitalization. In this context size potentially proxies for the opportunity cost of managerial time (making protection of bid-specific investments more important), or the availability of sophisticated financial and legal advisors.

The results in Table 11 also confirm many of the univariate conclusions from Table 5. Target termination fees are significantly more likely to be found in deals that include a tender offer component, and each of the landmark case-law decisions concerning termination fees increase the probability of target termination fee use. The 1994 *Paramount* ruling appears to be especially important in determining termination fee use, as merger agreements signed during or after 1994 are 28% more likely than those announced prior to 1994 to include a target termination fee. Target termination fees are also considerably less likely to be found in mergers involving financial service firms, potentially because of the effect that the payment of a cash breakup fee would have on the target bank's compliance with regulatory capital requirements.[16]

Table 11 also suggests that target termination fees and toeholds are substitutable. This evidence is, however, consistent with both the contracting and entrenchment hypotheses. Under the contracting (or shareholder interests) hypothesis, termination fees are used to protect the bid-specific investments made by a bidder from free riding by competing bidders. A substantial toehold offers an alternate means of capturing value created for others bidders by the revelation of the current bidder's plans for the target's assets. However, initial bidder toeholds deter competing bids and lower the probability of target managerial resistance (Betton and Eckbo, 2000). The finding of substitutability would therefore also be consistent with termination fees being used as target-management entrenchment devices.

The coefficient on the premium variable is statistically significant and positive. However, termination fee use and the premium are almost certainly endogenous, as both are determined during merger negotiations between the bidder and target. Coates and Subramanian (2000) also use the bid premium as an explanatory variable for target termination fees. They interpret the positive correlation as implying that "...the bidder often pays for deal protection with a higher deal premium" (p. 325). But given that both are determined simultaneously during negotiations between the bidder and target, it is tenuous to conclude that bidders offer higher premiums in return for deal protection (a causal statement). The most we can infer from this coefficient is that, as noted earlier, premiums and termination fee use are positively associated (without inferring causality). The essential issue here is that stand-alone probit or logit regres-

---

[16] See Coates and Subramanian (2000, p. 394).

sions provide biased coefficient estimates when dependent and independent variables are endogenous.

Therefore, I estimate a simultaneous-equations system with the bid premium and a dummy variable indicating target termination fee use as the two endogenous variables. The estimation of this system is complicated by the fact that the bid premium is continuous,[17] while target termination fee use is dichotomous, making standard linear approaches to estimating systems of equations inappropriate. I employ the estimation technique for observed/dichotomous systems outlined in Maddala (1983, p. 245). Several independent variables are omitted from each equation to ensure that the system is identified.

The results from the system estimation are contained in Table 12. The positive association between premiums and target termination fees is principally driven by termination fee use resulting in higher premiums for target shareholders. The robustness of this result, first shown in Table 7, suggests that target shareholders can expect a 4% higher premium on average when the merger agreement with the bidder includes a target termination fee. This evidence further supports the contention that agency problems at the target firm are not the average motivation for termination fee use. My evidence is more consistent with the contracting hypothesis and substantiates the conclusion that target termination fees are not harmful to target shareholders on average.

7. Conclusion

I provide empirical evidence on effects of, and motivations for, the inclusion of target termination fees in merger agreements. The conventional wisdom is that target termination fees can be used by self-serving target managers to ensure that the target is acquired by a selected bidder offering target managers continued employment. The assumed cost to target shareholders under this hypothesis is the loss of takeover premium because the imposition of a termination fee deters potential competing bidders resulting in a lower price paid for the target's shares.

However, target termination fees can also serve a less exploitative role by enabling the target to commit to a particular bidder in order to induce that bidder to invest fully in the acquisition process. In particular, a termination fee can be used to encourage the bidder to reveal valuable private information in bilateral negotiations with the target. Bidders would be reluctant to reveal, for example, posttakeover plans for the target's assets if other bidders could free ride on such information and submit a more valuable competing bid. Termination fees internalize the public good component of a takeover bid by forcing competing bidders to pay for the information revealed by an incumbent bidder.

---

[17] The premium earned by target shareholders is theoretically and empirically truncated at zero (see Roll, 1986). While such truncation is not entirely consistent with the estimation method employed here (which assumes that the premium is continuous), I am unaware of a practical way of resolving this issue. See Maddala (1983, p. 246) for a discussion of the complexities of a censored/dichotomous model.

Table 12

The robustness of determinants of target premiums and target termination fee agreements

The regressions are based on a sample of 2511 successful and unsuccessful merger and tender offer bids between 1988 and 2000. The TTERMF instrument in the first column is the fitted value from a first-stage probit regression with TTERMF as the dependent variable, and all other variables listed in this table as independent variables (omitted for brevity). The PREMIUM instrument in the second column is the fitted value from a first-stage OLS regression with PREMIUM as the dependent variable, and all variables listed in this table as independent variables (omitted for brevity). Standard errors (in parentheses) in both columns are adjusted for the fact that both instruments are generated regressors, as described in Maddala (1983). All independent variables are defined in previous tables. The marginal effects of a change from the sample means of continuous independent variables, and from zero for dummy independent variables, are in brackets. Base pred. prob. of TTERMF is the base case predicted probability that the merger agreement contains a target termination fee.

	Second-stage regressions		
Independent variable	Dep. var. = PREMIUM (OLS)	Dep. var. = TTERMF (probit)	
Intercept	0.57***	−3.78***	
	(0.08)	(1.26)	
PREMIUM or TTERMF Instrument	0.04***	1.49	
	(0.01)	(2.11)	[0.04]
BTERMF		1.49***	
		(0.13)	[0.53]
PRECOMP	0.05	−0.09	
	(0.04)	(0.20)	[−0.02]
POISON	0.07		
	(0.06)		
CASH	0.02	−0.24**	
	(0.02)	(0.10)	[−0.05]
SIND	0.03*		
	(0.02)		
HOSTILE		−1.73***	
		(0.19)	[−0.15]
TENDER	0.10***	0.48*	
	(0.02)	(0.24)	[0.14]
TOEHOLD	−0.14***	−0.16	
	(0.04)	(0.35)	[−0.03]
CLEANUP	−0.13**	−1.61***	
	(0.06)	(0.50)	[−0.15]
FINSERV	−0.07***	−0.56***	
	(0.02)	(0.17)	[−0.10]
D94	−0.08***	0.95***	
	(0.03)	(0.19)	[0.32]
D97	0.04**	0.36***	
	(0.02)	(0.13)	[0.10]
Log(BMVE)	0.04***	0.00	
	(0.00)	(0.09)	[0.00]
Log(TMVE)	−0.05***	0.16	
	(0.01)	(0.10)	[0.07]
Number of observations	2204	2204	
Base pred. prob. of TTERMF	-	0.15	
Adjusted R^2	0.09	-	

***, **, and * indicate that the parameter estimate is significantly different from zero at the 1%, 5%, and 10% levels, respectively.

The evidence presented in this paper is supportive of the more benign explanation for target termination fee use. Controlling for deal, bidder, and target characteristics that could influence the cross-sectional distribution of premiums, I find that takeover premiums are not lower when a target termination fee is included in the merger terms and are potentially as much as 7% higher. However, univariate averages do suggest that bidders do not offer target shareholders a competition premium when a merger agreement with a target termination fee (potentially a white knight bid) is announced subsequent to an existing bid for the target firm.

The evidence that termination fees deter bid competition is surprisingly weak. While deterrence is evident in univariate results, termination fee deals do not involve significantly lower rates of postbid competition once I control for the publicly revealed attitude of target managers toward the bidder (see Schwert, 2000). Furthermore, conditional on the inclusion of a target termination fee in a merger agreement, the size of the fee does not appear to deter competing acquirers.

Weighing the implications of the point estimates presented in this paper suggests that termination fees offer a net benefit to target shareholders. Specifically, Betton and Eckbo (2000) report that the average competing second-bid jump is a 31% increase in the premium from an initial premium of roughly 45%. Back-of-the-envelope calculations suggest that the average premium gain from termination fee use (4%) is an order of magnitude higher than the average expected loss of premium resulting from the diminished probability of an auction (roughly 0.4%).[18]

Overall, therefore, my evidence on the effects of termination fee use on deal outcomes suggests that target termination fees are not detrimental to target stockholders. This conclusion is consistent with the hypothesis that target termination fees are used to induce the bidder to make investments in a deal with the target the public benefit of which cannot be fully internalized. From a policy perspective, while specific instances of abuse may occur, on average target shareholders (and by extension the courts) have little to fear from the inclusion of a target termination fee in a merger contract per se.

Appendix A: Excerpt from Compaq/digital merger agreement

This appendix contains an excerpt from the merger agreement between Compaq Computer Corporation (the "Parent") and Digital Equipment Corporation (the "Company"), signed January 25, 1998.

---

[18] The 0.4% figure is computed by multiplying a 3% decline in the probability of an auction by an expected incremental premium from the auction of 14% (0.31×0.45).

ARTICLE 9
TERMINATION

SECTION 9.1. Termination. Notwithstanding anything contained in this Agreement to the contrary, this Agreement may be terminated and the Merger may be abandoned at any time prior to the Effective Time (notwithstanding any approval of this Agreement by the Board of Directors of the Company or Parent or the stockholders of the Company):

(a) by mutual written agreement of the Company and Parent;
(b) by either the Company or Parent, if
   (i)   the Merger has not been consummated on or before November 1, 1998; provided that the right to terminate this Agreement pursuant to this clause 9.01(b)(i) shall not be available to any party whose breach of any provision of this Agreement results in the failure of the Merger to be consummated by such time;
   (ii) there shall be any law or regulation that makes consummation of the Merger illegal or otherwise prohibited or if any judgment, injunction, order or decree enjoining any party from consummating the Merger is entered and such judgment, injunction, order or decree shall have become final and non-appealable; provided, that the party seeking to terminate this Agreement pursuant to this clause 9.01(b)(ii) shall have used its reasonable best efforts to remove such injunction, order or decree; or
   (iii) the Common Stockholder Approval shall not have been obtained by reason of the failure to obtain the required vote at a duly held meeting of stockholders or any adjournment thereof; or
(c) by Parent, if (x) the Board of Directors of the Company shall have withdrawn or modified in a manner adverse to Parent its approval or recommendation of the Merger or (y) there shall have been any material breach of any provision of Section 5.02(a) or 5.03.

The party desiring to terminate this Agreement pursuant to this Section 9.01 (other than pursuant to Section 9.01 (a)) shall give notice of such termination to the other party.

SECTION 9.2. Effect of Termination. If this Agreement is terminated pursuant to Section 9.01, this Agreement shall become void and of no effect with no liability on the part of any party hereto, except that (i) the agreements contained in Sections 7.07 (b), 10.04, 10.05, 10.06, 10.07, and 10.08 shall survive the termination hereof and (ii) no such termination shall release any party of any liabilities or damages resulting from any willful or grossly negligent breach by that party of any provision of this Agreement.

ARTICLE 10
MISCELLANEOUS

SECTION 10.4. Expenses. (a) Except as otherwise provided in this Section, and except for all transfer taxes which shall be paid by the Company, all costs and expenses incurred in connection with this Agreement shall be paid by the party incurring such cost or expense.

(b) The Company agrees to pay Parent in immediately available funds by wire transfer an amount equal to $240 million (the "TERMINATION FEE") if:

   (i)   this Agreement is terminated by Parent pursuant to Section 9.01(c);

   (ii)   (A) prior to the termination of this Agreement, a bona fide Acquisition Proposal is commenced, publicly proposed or publicly disclosed and (B) this Agreement is terminated by the Company pursuant to Section 9.01(b)(i) or by the Company or Parent pursuant to Section 9.01(b)(iii); or

   (iii)   (A) this Agreement is terminated by Parent pursuant to Section 9.01(b)(i), (B) the Company Stockholder Meeting shall not have been held prior to the date of such termination, and (C) the Company shall have delayed the holding of the Company Stockholder Meeting pursuant to the final sentence of Section 5.02.

The Company shall pay the Termination Fee promptly, but in no event later than two business days, after the termination of this Agreement pursuant to clause (i), (ii) or (iii) above. Notwithstanding the previous sentence, in the event of a termination of the Agreement by Parent pursuant to clause (ii) or (iii) above, 50% of the Termination Fee shall be payable at the time set forth in the immediately preceding sentence and 50% of the Termination Fee shall be payable concurrently with the consummation of a Significant Acquisition Proposal within 12 months of the termination of this Agreement. "SIGNIFICANT ACQUISITION PROPOSAL" means an Acquisition Proposal involving the acquisition of at least 50% of the Company Common Stock or at least 50% of the assets of the Company.

   (c) The Company agrees to pay Parent in immediately available funds by wire transfer an amount equal to Parent's reasonable expenses incurred in connection with this transaction (but not to exceed $25 million) if (x) this Agreement shall have been terminated pursuant to Section 9.01(b)(i), (y) any representation or warranty made by the Company in this Agreement shall not have been true and correct as of the date hereof, and (z) the condition in Section 8.02 relating to representations and warranties shall not have been satisfied; provided, however, that in no event shall any payment be due pursuant to this subsection (c) in the event that a Termination Fee is payable pursuant to subsection (b) above. Such payment shall be made promptly, and in no event later than two business days, after such termination.

   (d) Parent agrees to pay the Company in immediately available funds by wire transfer an amount equal to the Company's reasonable expenses incurred in connection with this transaction (but not to exceed $25 million) if (x) this Agreement shall have been terminated pursuant to Section 9.01(b)(i), (y) any representation or warranty made by Parent in this Agreement shall not have been true and correct as of the date hereof, and (z) the condition in Section 8.03 relating to representations and warranties shall not have been satisfied. Such payment shall be made promptly, and in no event later than two business days, after such termination.

Appendix B: Excerpt from COMSAT/radiation systems merger agreement

This appendix contains an excerpt from the merger agreement between COMSAT Corporation and Radiation Systems, Inc, signed January 30, 1994.

ARTICLE VIII
TERMINATION

Section 8.1 Termination Events. Subject to the provisions of Section 8.2, this Agreement may, by written notice given at or prior to the Closing (in the manner provided by Section 9.9 herein) be terminated and abandoned only as follows:

8.1.1 Breach. By either COMSAT or RSI upon written notice if a material default or breach shall be made by the other, with respect to the due and timely perform-ance of any of the other party's respective covenants and agreements contained herein, or with respect to the due compliance with any of the other party's respective representations and warranties contained in Article III or IV herein, as applicable, and such default cannot be cured prior to Closing and has not been waived;

8.1.2 Mutual Consent. By mutual written consent of the parties hereto; or

8.1.3 Failure of Conditions to Close. By either COMSAT or RSI, if by reason of failure of their respective conditions to close contained in Article VI or VII herein, as applicable, and such conditions have not been satisfied or waived by December 31, 1994, or such later date as may be agreed upon by the parties hereto, provided that the right to terminate this Agreement under this Subsection 8.1.3 shall not be available to a party whose failure to fulfill any obligation or perform any covenant under this Agreement has been the cause of or resulted in the failure of any of the conditions to close of the other party hereto by such date.

Section 8.2 Effect of Termination. In the event this Agreement is terminated pursuant to Section 8.1 herein, all further rights and obligations of the parties here-under shall terminate, provided that if RSI at any time prior to 31 December, 1994 is acquired by, merges, effectuates a business combination with, or sells substantially all of its assets to any person or entity not controlled by COMSAT, or agrees to do any of the foregoing, RSI shall immediately upon such action or agreement pay to COMSAT Five Million Dollars ($5,000,000), plus all of COMSAT's costs, fees and expenses incurred in connection with this Agreement and the Merger as contemplated hereby, including fees and expenses of its accountants, investment advisers and counsel, and provided further that the total payment RSI shall pay to COMSAT immediately upon such action or agreement shall not in any event exceed Seven Million, Five Hundred Thousand Dollars ($7,500,000).

Section 8.3 Fees and Expenses; Damages. Except as otherwise provided in Section 8.2 herein, in the event this Agreement is terminated for any reason and the Merger is not consummated each party shall be responsible for its own costs, fees and expenses, including fees and expenses of its accountants, investment advisers and counsel, provided, however, that if the termination is caused by the breach of COMSAT and CTS on the one hand, or the breach of RSI on the other hand, the breaching party(ies) shall pay to the non-breaching party(ies) as liquidated damages (and as its sole and exclusive remedy) the actual costs and expenses of the non-breaching party(ies), including the fees and expenses of its accountants, investment advisers and counsel, not to exceed Two Million Five Hundred Thousand Dollars ($2,500,000).

References

Bates, T. and M. Lemmon, 2003, "Breaking Up is Hard to Do? An Analysis of Termination Fee Provisions and Merger Outcomes," *Journal of Financial Economics*, 69, 469–504.

Berkovitch, E. and N. Khanna, 1990, "How Target Shareholders Benefit from Value-Reducing Defensive Strategies in Takeovers," *Journal of Finance*, 45, 137–156.

Betton, S. and B. Eckbo, 2000, "Toeholds, Bid Jumps, and Expected Payoffs in Takeovers," *Review of Financial Studies*, 13, 841–882.

Bradley, M., A. Desai and E. Kim, 1988, "Synergistic Gains from Corporate Acquisitions and Their Division Between the Stockholders of Target and Acquiring Firms," *Journal of Financial Economics*, 21, 3–40.

Burch, T., 2001, "Locking Out Rival Bidders: The Use of Lockup Options in Corporate Mergers," *Journal of Financial Economics*, 60, 103–141.

Chang, S., 1990, "Employee Stock Ownership Plans and Shareholder Wealth: An Empirical Investigation," *Financial Management*, 19, 48–58.

Coates IV, J. and G. Subramanian, 2000, "A Buy-Side Model of M&A Lockups: Theory and Evidence," *Stanford Law Review*, 53, 307–396.

Comment, R. and G. Schwert, 1995, "Poison or Placebo? Evidence on the Deterrence and Wealth Effects of Modern Antitakeover Measures," *Journal of Financial Economics*, 39, 3–43.

Dhaya, J. and R. Powell, 1998, "Ownership Structure, Managerial Turnover, and Takeovers: Further UK Evidence on the Market for Corporate Control," *Multinational Finance Journal*, 2, 1–24.

Eckbo, B. and H. Langohr, 1989, "Information Disclosure, Methods of Payment, and Takeover Premiums: Public and Private Tender Offers in France," *Journal of Financial Economics*, 24, 363–403.

Fama, E. and K. French, 1997, "Industry Costs of Equity," *Journal of Financial Economics*, 43, 153–193.

Fishman, M., 1989, "Preemptive Bidding and the Role of the Medium of Exchange in Acquisitions," *Journal of Finance*, 44, 41–57.

Fraidin, S. and J. Hanson, 1994, "Toward Unlocking Lockups," *Yale Law Journal*, 103, 1739–1834.

Hadlock, C., J. Houston and M. Ryngaert, 1999, "The Role of Managerial Incentives in Bank Acquisitions," *Journal of Banking and Finance*, 23, 221–249.

Harford, J., 1999, "Corporate Cash Reserves and Acquisitions," *Journal of Finance*, 54, 1969–1997.

Hatrzell, J., E. Ofek and D. Yermack, 2000, "What's in It for Me? Personal Benefits Obtained by CEOs Whose Firms are Acquired," Unpublished Working Paper, New York University.

Heckman, J., 1979, "Sample Selection Bias As a Specification Error," *Econometrica*, 47, 153–161.

Huang, Y. and R. Walkling, 1987, "Target Abnormal Returns Associated with Acquisition Announcements: Payment, Acquisition form, and Managerial Resistance," *Journal of Financial Economics*, 19, 329–349.

Jarrell, G. and M. Bradley, 1980, "The Economic Effects of Federal and State Regulations of Cash Tender Offers," *Journal of Law and Economics*, 23, 371–407.

Jensen, M., 1986, "Agency Costs of Free Cash Flow, Corporate Finance, and Takeovers," *American Economic Review*, 76, 323–329.

Jensen, M. and W. Meckling, 1976, "Theory of the Firm: Managerial Behavior, Agency Costs, and Ownership Structure," *Journal of Financial Economics*, 3, 305–360.

Lederman, L. and B. Bryer, 1989, "Representing a Public Company in a Leveraged Buyout Transaction," In Y. Amihud (Ed.), *Leveraged Management Buyouts*, Dow Jones-Irwin, New York, pp. 111–174.

Maddala, G., 1983, *Limited-Dependent and Qualitative Variables in Econometrics*, Cambridge University Press, Cambridge.

Mulherin, J. and A. Boone, 2000, "Comparing Acquisitions and Divestitures," *Journal of Corporate Finance: Contracting, Governance, and Organization*, 6, 117–139.

Officer, M., 2003, "Collars and Renegotiation in Mergers and Acquisitions," Unpublished Working Paper, University of Southern California, Los Angeles.

Roll, R., 1986, "The Hubris Hypothesis of Corporate Takeovers," *Journal of Business*, 59, 197–216.

Schwert, G., 2000, "Hostility in Takeovers: In the Eyes of the Beholder?," *Journal of Finance*, 55, 2599–2640.

Smith, C. and R. Watts, 1992, "The Investment Opportunity Set and Corporate Financing, Dividend, and Compensation Policies," *Journal of Financial Economics*, 32, 263–292.

Chapter 12

POISON OR PLACEBO? EVIDENCE ON THE DETERRENCE AND WEALTH EFFECTS OF MODERN ANTITAKEOVER MEASURES[*]

ROBERT COMMENT

William E. Simon Graduate School of Business, University of Rochester, Rochester, New York, USA
US Securities and Exchange Commission, Washington, District of Columbia, USA

G. WILLIAM SCHWERT

William E. Simon Graduate School of Business, University of Rochester, Rochester, New York, USA
National Bureau of Economic Research, Cambridge, Massachusetts, USA

Contents

* The Bradley Policy Research Center, William E. Simon Graduate School of Business Administration, University of Rochester, provided support for this research. We are grateful for suggestions from Michael Bradley, Jim Brickley, Harry DeAngelo, Craig Dunbar, Ken French, Stuart Gilson, Paul Gompers, Gregg Jarrell, Michael Jensen (the editor), Steve Kaplan (the referee), E. Han Kim, Glenn MacDonald, Wayne Mikkelson, Mitchell Peterson, Roberta Romano, Robert Vishny, Marc Zenner, Jerold Zimmerman, and participants in seminars at the American Finance Association, the NBER Summer Institute, and the Universities of Chicago, Michigan, Rochester, and Southern California. This paper is part of NBER's research program in Asset Pricing. The Securities and Exchange Commission, as a matter of policy, disclaims any responsibility for any private publication or statements by any of its employees. The views expressed herein are those of the authors and do not necessarily reflect the views of the Commission, or of the authors' colleagues on the staff of the Commission, or of the National Bureau of Economic Research.

This article originally appeared in the *Journal of Financial Economics*, Vol. 39, pp. 3–43 (1995).
Corporate Takeovers, Volume 2
Edited by B. Espen Eckbo
Copyright © 1995 Published by Elsevier Science B.V.
DOI: 10.1016/B978-0-12-381982-6.00013-6

Abstract

This paper provides large-sample evidence that poison pill rights issues, control share laws, and business combination laws have not systematically deterred takeovers and are unlikely to have caused the demise of the 1980s market for corporate control, even though 87% of all exchange-listed firms are now covered by one of these antitakeover measures. We show that poison pills and control share laws are reliably associated with higher takeover premiums for selling shareholders, both unconditionally and conditional on a successful takeover, and we provide updated event-study evidence for the three-quarters of all poison pills not yet analyzed. Antitakeover measures increase the bargaining position of target firms, but they do not prevent many transactions.

Keywords

poison pill, antitakeover law, merger, tender offer, takeover premium

JEL classification: G34, G38

1. Introduction

At the end of the 1980s, the level of takeover activity fell dramatically. Many commentators have speculated that the demise of the market for corporate control was caused by the evolution of sophisticated antitakeover measures. This paper analyzes data on all exchange-listed firms from 1975 to 1991 and casts doubt on the hypothesis that antitakeover measures shut down the market for corporate control.

The 1980s saw many improvements in corporate antitakeover methods. More than 1500 firms adopted shareholder rights plans (poison pills) during the second half of the decade. These securities, issued as dividends, serve to create impossibly burdensome obligations for anyone who buys a controlling block of shares without management approval (Bruner, 1991, provides a detailed review of the mechanics of poison pills). Separately, states developed several forms of antitakeover statute able to pass constitutional muster: *control share laws* that restrict the voting rights of a controlling shareholder and *business combination* (merger-moratorium or freeze-out) *laws* that delay any business combination. In either variant, the prohibitions last for three to 5 years and, like poison pills, apply to the buyer of a controlling block of shares who buys without management approval. Ohio adopted the first business combination law in 1982 and New York adopted the first control share law in 1985. Many states have both types of law. The US Supreme Court upheld Indiana's control share law in April 1987, and an appellate court upheld Wisconsin's business combination law in June 1989.[1] The appellate court ruled that investors have no constitutional right to receive tender offers and that state law need not leave bidders a meaningful opportunity for success.

The demise of the 1980s market for corporate control is closely associated with the spread of these new antitakeover methods. Figure 1 plots the percentage of all firms listed on the New York (NYSE) or American Stock Exchange (Amex) that received initial takeover offers in each month from January 1975 to December 1991, along with the proportion covered by the three kinds of modern antitakeover measures. Coverage by business combination statutes jumped from 15% to 63% when Delaware adopted its law in January 1988 (half the exchange-listed firms are incorporated in Delaware) and reached 80% by 1991. Coverage by control share laws increased gradually to reach 24% by 1991. Coverage by poison pills, trivial before 1986, increased gradually to reach 35%. By 1991, 87% exchange-listed firms were covered by a poison pill, a business combination law, or a control share law. In comparison, takeover rates started at levels below 0.5% per month in 1975 and increased to a peak of about 1.5% per month during 1987 and 1988. A long, gradual rise in merger and acquisition activity culminated in a sharp reversal during 1989. Takeover rates were again below 0.5% per month in 1990 and 1991.

The association seen in Figure 1 suggests that incumbent managers used their enhanced decision rights to deter takeovers systematically. This interpretation is

---

[1] See CTS Corp. v. Dynamics Corp. of Am., 481 US 69, 86–87 (1987); Amanda Acquisition Corp. v. Universal Foods Corp., 877 F. 2d 496, 504–505 (7th Cir.), cert. denied, 110 S. Ct.367 (1989).

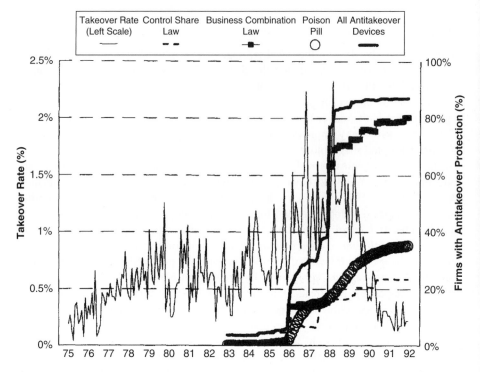

Fig. 1. Monthly time series plot of proportion of all exchange-listed firms that are covered by (1) control share laws, (2) business combination laws, (3) poison pill rights issues, (4) any of the above, and (5) the proportion of all exchange-listed firms that received initial merger proposals, merger agreements, or interfirm tender offers each month during 1975–1991 (left-hand scale).

consistent with (1) a substantial literature that portrays managers as more interested in entrenchment than in maximizing shareholder wealth, (2) anecdotal evidence from well-publicized cases of managers relying on antitakeover measures to defeat premium-priced takeover offers, and (3) indirect evidence from many event studies that find average reductions in shareholder wealth from adoption of antitakeover measures. The aim of this study is to use large-sample evidence to test whether modern takeover defenses have been used systematically to deter takeovers.

The evidence from our direct test of deterrence provides little support for the proposition that modern antitakeover measures have been used to deter takeovers systematically. We infer from this evidence that firm-specific antitakeover measures played a minor role in ending the 1980s merger wave. Our evidence points instead to broad-scale political or economic forces that manifest themselves as secular variation. In addition, our review of the major takeover-related court decisions suggests that this secular variation is not due to an evolution in takeover jurisprudence.

While systematic evidence is scarce, practitioners and researchers have long acknowledged that antitakeover measures could enhance the bargaining power of incumbent management versus bidders, thereby yielding higher takeover premiums for selling shareholders. We find that selling shareholders do receive premium prices for their shares when antitakeover measures are in place. Since higher prices surely deter buyers, this result is consistent with deterrence, and yet we fail to detect such deterrence. Moreover, we find that expected premiums are higher with an antitakeover measure in place even with expected premiums calculated to account for the possibility of added deterrence. Finally, we update previous studies of the stock price effects of announcements of adoptions of poison pills and closely replicate their results. Overall, our evidence casts doubt on the view that antitakeover measures are used primarily to entrench incumbent management.

Section 2 discusses some a priori grounds for skepticism regarding the deterrent effect of antitakeover measures, and offers several alternate explanations, notably the credit crunch that began with the dismantling of Drexel Burnham Lambert, for the sharp reduction in takeover activity that occurred in the late 1980s. We describe our data sources in Section 3. Section 4 updates the existing evidence on the wealth effect of poison pills. In Section 5, we exploit the firm- and time-specific nature of coverage by poison pills and state antitakeover laws to decide if deterrence is observable in the takeover experience of individual firms. In Section 6, we estimate the relation between antitakeover measures and conditional and unconditional takeover premiums. Section 7 discusses various specification checks that assure the insensitivity of our results to reasonable changes in the definition of the variables or tests. In particular, evidence for deterrence is not materially enhanced when we analyze hostile takeovers rather than all transactions. Section 8 presents our conclusions. The Appendix contains a brief history of case law in Delaware and Federal courts as it pertains to takeover defenses.

2. Takeover defenses as placebos

There is much a priori ground for skepticism about the deterrent effect of modern antitakeover measures. To begin with, incumbent managers wielded considerable influence over takeover outcomes even before modern antitakeover measures, as shown by the predominance of negotiated transactions during the first half of the 1980s. Considering all takeover attempts involving tender offers for exchange-listed firms between 1981 and 1984, Comment and Jarrell (1987) report that half of all bidders obtained a merger agreement before starting an offer, 22% of all transactions started as hostile but were superseded by negotiated bids, while another 12% started as hostile but ended with no shares purchased by any bidder. Few bids (the remaining 16%) were executed without management's approval. This evidence shows that deterrence is not management's main interest (eventually two-thirds of all offers were approved), and that management wielded considerable bargaining power versus bidders throughout the 1980s and not just after the spread of modern antitakeover measures.

Moreover, the burden imposed on buyers by a control share law (i.e., restricted voting rights) may be avoidable at low cost. As noted by Gilson and Black (1992), this type of law provides for a shareholder vote to decide if the law's restrictions on voting rights are to apply in a given instance. These elections are paid for by the buyer, triggered by a disclosure of intent to seek control, held within 55 days, and require a simple majority to grant the buyer full voting rights. Thus, the minimal burden imposed by a control share law is the cost of a special election and a 55-day delay (where the minimum tender-offer period is 20 days in any event). As a practical matter, bidders can make their offers conditional on the outcome of this vote, just as they might on the outcome of an antitrust review. Bidders might prefer such a vote since it would be viewed as an expression of shareholder preference that would undermine any claim of coercion as a legal rationale for antitakeover measures. For example, as an adjunct to its unnegotiated tender offer for Kansas Gas & Electric in 1990, Kansas City Power & Light sought a court order to force the target firm to comply with the Kansas Control Share Acquisitions Act by calling a special election to approve voting rights for any shares it might buy in its offer.

A corresponding provision for a shareholder vote occurs in business combination laws, but with the crucial difference that the vote is triggered by an actual purchase of shares, rather than by a stated intent to purchase. Thus, a buyer must win a vote among nontendering shareholders, rather than among all holders, to avoid the burden imposed by a business combination law (a 5-year delay before cleanup mergers).

Event studies of the stock price effects of adoptions of antitakeover measures provide considerable indirect evidence regarding deterrence, and although stock prices fall, implying deterrence, the size of the decline is inconsistent with strong deterrence. The typical decline is less than 1% for most types of antitakeover measures.[2] Ryngaert (1988) examines 283 poison pills adopted through 1986 and finds an average 2-day announcement return of -0.34%. Malatesta and Walkling (1988) examine 132 poison pills adopted through March 1986 and find an average 2-day return of -0.92%. Romano (1993) reviews 13 studies of the wealth effects of adoptions of antitakeover laws by individual states. Pooling these events, Karpoff and Malatesta (1989) examine the average stock price effect for a sample of 1505 firms affected by 40 different instances of an introduction of a law to a state legislature in 26 different states, and find a 2-day announcement return of -0.29%. In addition, Jarrell and Poulsen (1987) report an average announcement return of -1.25% for 649 fair-price, classified-board, and supermajority-voting charter amendments from 1980 to 1985, although other studies

---

[2] Exceptional results are reported by Szewczyk and Tsetsekos (1992). They find an average return of -9.09% for 56 Pennsylvania firms during the legislative process (from October 10, 1989 through April 27, 1990) for the adoption of that state's cash out law. When cumulated over key dates, a methodology comparable to that used by Karpoff and Malatesta, the average return is -3.33%. This law requires a buyer of more than 20% of the shares to purchase at fair value any remaining shares that holders wish to put to them. This type of antitakeover law appears late in our sample period and only Maine and South Dakota have followed Pennsylvania in adopting a cash out law, so we lack sufficient experience with this type of law to estimate its deterrence effects.

find little evidence of an adverse reaction to antitakeover charter amendments (e.g., DeAngelo and Rice, 1983; Linn and McConnell, 1983).

In juxtaposition to these studies, Nathan and O'Keefe (1989) show that shareholder gains of 50% are typical in takeovers and thus typical of what is forgone with deterrence. For instance, if the probability of a takeover decreases by 10% with the adoption of an antitakeover measure, and if a 50% gain is lost, then the wealth decline on adoption should be about 5%. The empirical estimates of wealth loss generally do not approach this level. Thus, the size of the average wealth decline on the adoption of an antitakeover measure is consistent with only a modest change in takeover probability.

A substantial literature relating merger waves and business cycles provides further grounds for skepticism (see Weston et al., 1990, ch. 11, for a review of this evidence). It is possible that the 1980s restructuring boom, like earlier booms, simply succumbed to market forces. The National Bureau of Economic Research marks the start of a recession in July 1990, which lags the decline in takeover activity in Figure 3, but there is evidence of an earlier credit crunch. As reported by Putnam (1991), US flow of funds data show a collapse in net new lending to the nonfinancial business sector by commercial banks from $33 billion in 1989 to $2 billion in 1990. Commercial banks were the dominant providers of bridge or transaction financing for large, cash acquisitions. The Securities and Exchange Commission (1986) shows that commercial banks provided over three-quarters of the immediate financing for 272 successful tender offers from 1981 to 1985.

The availability of long-term and subordinated financing had shriveled before 1990 due to declining prices, illiquidity, and government intervention in the market for junk bonds in 1989 (see Yago, 1991, for a detailed discussion). In September 1988, the S.E.C. sued Drexel Burnham Lambert, the investment bank most active in financing takeovers, alleging a secret alliance with Ivan Boesky. The impact on Drexel's ability to serve as a financial intermediary was immediate. By October, the $570 million, Drexel-financed leveraged buyout of Wickes was canceled and Drexel had to cover out of its own capital almost half its "highly confident" commitment to raise $1.4 billion for an offer for Interco. In a December 1988 attempt at damage control, Drexel dismissed Michael Milken, pleaded guilty to six felony counts, and paid a $650 million fine. In August 1989, Congress passed the Financial Institutions Reform, Recovery and Enforcement Act (FIRREA), which penalized savings and loans for holding junk bonds and mandated their sale, while regulators issued guidelines barring commercial bank participation in highly leveraged transactions (including all acquisition loans that raised liabilities to 75% of assets, or doubled the debt ratio while raising it to 50% of assets). The junk bond market crashed in September 1989 when Campeau, which had become a major issuer of (non-Drexel) junk bonds, revealed the extent of its liquidity crisis and when UAL failed to secure buyout financing. The decline in the value of Drexel's portfolio of junk bonds triggered its declaration of bankruptcy and dissolution in February 1990. Finally, the National Association of Insurance Commissioners adopted guidelines in June 1990 requiring insurance companies to increase reserves against junk bonds not in default.

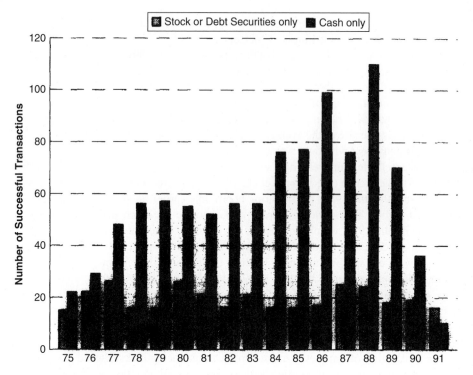

Fig. 2. Number of cash-only and securities-only successful takeovers of exchange-listed firms in the period 1975–1991, by year of announcement.

Although a formal test of a credit crunch model is beyond the scope of this paper, we do provide two illustrative charts. Figure 2 plots the number of cash-only transactions and the number of securities-only transactions (common and preferred stock, debt, and combinations), year-by-year, from 1975 to 1991. The number of securities-only transactions remains steady at 15–25 transactions per year, so both boom and bust are attributable to cash transactions. Figure 3 plots monthly the yield spread between long-term low-quality corporate bonds (rated below Baa) and high-quality bonds (rated Aaa), along with the takeover rates from Figure 1.[3] The most noticeable change in the yield spread is a jump after 1988. Combined, this evidence suggests that the demise of the takeover market coincided with tighter credit.[4] In the formal tests below,

[3] Long-term monthly bond yields are from Salomon Brothers and Ibbotson Associates. The gradual increase in the junk bond yield spread from 1975 to 1988 probably reflects a shift in the composition of the below-Baa group of bonds due to the gradual addition of a large number of original issue bonds issued in the early and mid-1980s to fund takeovers and restructurings.

[4] Tight credit conditions for takeovers could outlast any economy-wide problem. Neither Viacom nor QVC were able to borrow enough to make an all-cash offer for Paramount Communications in 1994.

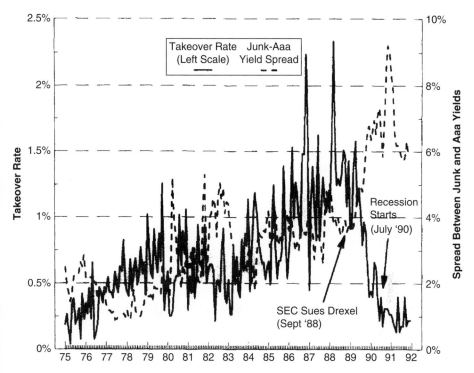

Fig. 3. Monthly time series plot of the spread between the junk (<Baa) and Aaa corporate bond yields and the proportion of all exchange-listed firms that received initial merger proposals, merger agreements, or interfirm tender offers each month, 1975–1991 (left-hand scale).

we represent changing economic conditions (from 1986 on) with yearly dummy variables.

3. Data sources and descriptive statistics

The information on merger and acquisition announcements comes from our proprietary mergers and acquisitions (M&A) database, which covers all exchange-listed target firms in the period 1975–1991. These announcements were obtained through various keyword searches of the *Dow Jones News Retrieval* (*DJNR*) database, inspection of the *Wall Street Journal Index*, and from Commerce Clearing House's *Capital Changes Reporter* [the original source for Center for Research in Security Prices (CRSP) delisting codes]. In this study, we use the subset of records covering merger proposals, merger agreements, and interfirm tender offers. Merger proposals are distinguished from merger talks by a public disclosure of terms of purchase. We use these data to identify (1) successful takeovers, (2) announcement dates, (3) method of payment (cash vs. stock), and (4) whether a target is bought in an auction (multiple, publicly revealed bidders). An announcement qualifies as the initial one (that puts the firm in play) if there has been no other qualifying announcement in the prior year.

We use data from CRSP to calculate takeover premiums as the compound difference between the returns to target firms' stock and the value-weighted NYSE and Amex market portfolio during announcement periods that vary in length from target to target. We know from event-study evidence that on average the wealth effect of takeovers occurs in a period from about 10 trading days before to 10 trading days after the initial announcement of a takeover. To ensure that we capture any run-up, we begin our periods 20 trading days before the initial takeover announcements. To ensure that we capture the wealth effects of multiple bids or auctions, we end our periods 5 days after the announcement of the successful offer.

Our information on adoptions of state antitakeover laws comes from the Investor Responsibility Research Center, and our information on states of incorporation (and reincorporations) comes from various issues of *Moody's Manuals*. Our information on adoptions of poison pills is from annual compilations contained in *Corporate Control Alert*, from various *DJNR* keyword searches, from *Capital Changes Reporter*, and from *Moody's Manuals*. We identify a total of 1584 original poison pill rights issues made through December 1991. Of these, 60% were issued by firms listed on the NYSE or Amex at the time of issue. For purposes of determining antitakeover coverage when predicting takeovers, we account for pills adopted before exchange listing and for the handful of pills redeemed without being replaced. It is likely that we fail to account for most opt outs from state laws due to the difficulty of identifying these events. Because they have not been enforced by federal courts, we ignore provisions in some state laws that attempt to extend coverage to firms incorporated in other states.[5]

3.1. Evolution of the legal market for poison pill securities

Figure 4 shows the number of new pills adopted each year from 1984 to 1991. Pill adoptions became common after 1985, with 1988 and 1989 being the peak years. The number of adoptions declines after this, and 1991 had the fewest adoptions since 1985. It is unlikely that the falloff in pill adoptions is due to saturation, as two-thirds of all exchange-listed firms remain without pills, consistent with our analysis of the legal treatment of antitakeover devices (in the Appendix). Because the legality of antitakeover devices depends only on the carefulness of the deliberations of the board of directors at the time that a pill is used, pills are no less valid when adopted on short notice, and the adoption itself is not a complex legal matter.

---

[5] The US Supreme Court found such extraterritorial effects unconstitutional in Edgar v. Mite Corp., 457 US 624 (1982).

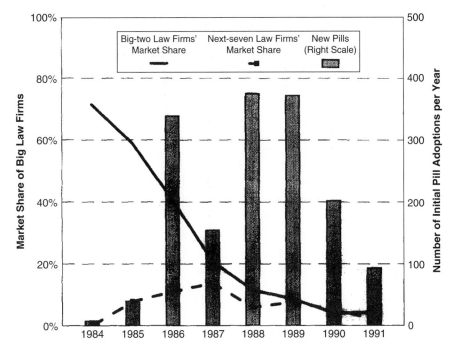

Fig. 4. Number of initial poison pill adoptions by year for all exchange-listed firms in the period 1984–1991. Also, market share of large law firms used in pill adoptions. The "big-two" law firms are Wachtell Lipton and Skadden Arps. The "next-seven" law firms are Fried Frank Harris, Sullivan Cromwell, Cravath Swaine, Paul Weiss, Wilkie Farr, Shearman Sterling, and Jones Day.

We can get a sense of the extent of specialization in the legal market for poison pills from information in *Corporate Control Alert* on the identity of the law firm that advised on the adoption. Figure 4 shows the market shares of several large law firms that frequently advise on pill adoptions. The "big-two" law firms are Wachtell Lipton and Skadden Arps, the market leaders. Wachtell Lipton invented the poison pill and Skadden Arps developed a popular variation. The "next-seven" group includes the next-seven firms most commonly retained to advise on pill adoptions: Fried Frank, Sullivan Cromwell, Cravath Swaine, Paul Weiss, Wilkie Farr, Shearman Sterling, and Jones Day. The big-two firms advised on about two-thirds of the pills adopted in 1984 and 1985, when pills were rare and experimental. The market shares of the two leaders fell continuously as pills became common place, ending at 7% in 1991. The market share of the next-seven law firms fell from 10% through 1986 to 7% afterward, so that the shift over time was toward the use of in-house counsel and local law firms, suggesting that poison pills did not present complex legal issues for long.

3.2. Accounting and stock market predictors of takeover activity

Palepu (1986) uses several accounting and stock market performance measures to predict takeovers. Following his approach, we create a sample of all firm-years with data available on Compustat for exchange-listed firms with fiscal years that end December 1976 through December 1990, yielding 21, 887 fiscal-year forecast periods that begin between January 1977 and January 1991. This sample approximates the population. We exclude firm-years without 4 years' worth of previous accounting data on Compustat, and we exclude a handful of firm-years that begin after the year of an initial takeover announcement. We use accounting and stock return variables in our prediction models to account for variation, across time and firms, in business conditions that affect the likelihood of takeovers. The variables are all calculated over the 4 years before each fiscal-year forecast period, and include:

abnormal stock return for firm i and day t, $u_{it} = R_{it} - \alpha_i - \beta_i R_{mt}$, averaged over 4 years before the forecast period (where the market model parameters α_i and β_i for the CRSP value-weighted portfolio are estimated in the 5th year before the forecast period),

sales growth measured as the proportional change in sales over 4 years [Compustat item 12],

liquidity measured as a 4-year average of the ratio of net liquid assets to total assets [Compustat items (4–5)/6],

debt/equity measured as a 4-year average of the ratio of debt to equity [Compustat items 9/60],

market/book (sometimes called the "q-ratio") measured as a 4-year average of the ratio of the year-end market value of common stock to the book value of equity [Compustat items 24 · 25/60],

price/earnings measured as a 4-year average of the ratio of the year-end stock price to earnings per share [Compustat items 24/58], and

size measured as the log of total assets at the start of the forecast period in millions of dollars [Compustat item 6].

Extreme outliers, such as market/book, price/earnings, or debt/equity ratios greater than 100, were omitted from the sample.

Table 1 shows means and standard deviations for these variables, along with t-tests for whether mean values differ for the 669 takeover firm-years compared with the full sample of 21,887 firm-years. Consistent with Palepu (1986), there are some modest differences. The average abnormal stock return is slightly higher for takeover targets. This could be due to anticipatory, prebid run-ups in the target's stock price, although by construction this prior return excludes any run-up within the fiscal year of the announcement. In addition, target firms have below-average sales growth, higher cash positions, and lower debt/equity ratios. These results imply that target firms are poor performers that make inefficient use of their financial capital, consistent with Jensen (1986) discussion of free cash flow. While their price/earnings ratios are not unusual,

Table 1

Means and standard deviations of accounting and stock market performance variables, antitakeover protection, and takeover characteristics for 21,887 firm-years beginning January 1977 through January 1991 for NYSE- and Amex-listed stocks with necessary data available in Compustat

Abnormal return is the average daily prediction error in percent from a market model regression using the CRSP value-weighted portfolio, where the parameters are estimated in the year before the measurement period (year −5 relative to the forecast fiscal year). Sales growth is the average growth rate in sales over the 4 years before the fiscal year. Liquidity is the 4-year average of net working capital divided by total assets. Debt/equity is the 4-year average ratio of debt to equity. Market/book is the 4-year average ratio of the year-end market value of stock to the book value of equity. Price/earnings is the 4-year average ratio of the year-end stock price to earnings per share. Size is the log of total assets at the start of the forecast period. The control share law and business combination law dummy variables are both defined in two ways: (a) they equal one if the forecast fiscal year occurs after the effective date of the law for the state in which the company is incorporated or (b) they equal one if that company's state has a law which is effective for the forecast period and there has already been a major judicial precedent indicating that such a law is likely to be upheld if challenged. Poison pill equals one if the firm has a shareholder rights plan in effect before the forecast period. The dummy variables 1986 through 1991 equal one in these years to show variation in the last part of the sample period. Successful takeover equals one when an initial tender offer or merger proposal that leads to a successful takeover occurs during the forecast firm-year. Auction equals one when more than one bidder tries to takeover the target firm. Cash equals one when the payment to target shareholders is in the form of cash. Tender offer equals one when the winning bid occurs in the form of a tender offer. The market-adjusted premium in successful takeovers is the compounded difference in the returns to target firm's stock and the CRSP value-weighted NYSE/Amex market portfolio during the period from 20 trading days before the first merger proposal or tender offer through 5 trading days after the successful offer; it equals zero for firm-years in which no takeover occurs.

Variable	Full sample, 21,887 firm-years		Takeover sample, 669 firm-years		t-Test for equal means
	Mean	S.D.	Mean	S.D.	
Abnormal return (in % over 4 years)	0.0117	0.1777	0.0256	0.1776	2.06
Sales growth (4-year average)	0.0867	0.1272	0.0768	0.1127	−2.30
Liquidity (4-year average)	0.2470	0.2061	0.2767	0.2190	3.57
Debt/equity (4-year average)	0.7410	1.8455	0.6063	0.9939	−3.43
Market/book (4-year average)	1.4814	1.7316	1.3718	1.0951	−2.57
Price/earnings (4-year average)	11.1357	11.0488	10.6688	10.4521	−1.17
Size	5.6291	1.8596	5.1638	1.4927	−8.12
Proportion of firm-years covered by:					
Control share law:					
Date law became effective	0.0577	0.2332	0.0553	0.2287	−0.28

(*Continued*)

Table 1 (Continued)

Variable	Full sample, 21,887 firm-years		Takeover sample, 669 firm-years		t-Test for equal means
	Mean	S.D.	Mean	S.D.	
Supreme Court upheld IN law (April 1987)	0.0404	0.1969	0.0389	0.1934	−0.21
Business combination law:					
Date law became effective	0.1561	0.3629	0.1345	0.3415	−1.66
Circuit Court upheld WI law (June 1989)	0.0742	0.2622	0.0314	0.1745	−6.33
Poison pill	0.0811	0.2731	0.0957	0.2944	1.30
1986	0.0632	0.2433	0.0912	0.2881	2.57
1987	0.0611	0.2396	0.0658	0.2481	0.49
1988	0.0589	0.2354	0.0822	0.2749	2.24
1989	0.0562	0.2304	0.0628	0.2427	0.71
1990	0.0495	0.2169	0.0329	0.1785	−2.43
1991	0.0462	0.2100	0.0075	0.0862	−11.00
Successful takeover (=1)	0.0306	0.1721			
Auction (=1 if multiple bidders)			0.2407	0.4278	
Cash (=1)			0.6741	0.4690	
Tender offer (=1)			0.4499	0.4979	
Market-adjusted premiums in successful takeovers	0.0107	0.0828	0.3489	0.3263	

targets do have lower than average market/book ratios, consistent with several inter-pretations. One interpretation is that targets have more assets in place and fewer growth options (Myers, 1977). Another is that firms become targets because they are undervalued in the stock market, and market/book measures this undervaluation. Third, takeover targets could be run less efficiently (Lang et al., 1989). In any event, the largest *t*-statistic by far is for (the log of) size, confirming the well-known fact that small firms are more likely to be acquired. Overall, these comparisons provide some reason to think that these accounting and stock market measures of performance can help predict takeover activity.

3.3. Coverage by antitakeover laws and poison pills

Since state antitakeover laws represent a legal innovation, there is ambiguity about when coverage took effect. It can be argued that control share laws took effect only after the US Supreme Court ruled on the Indiana law in April 1987, and that business combination laws took effect only after the appellate court ruled on the Wisconsin law in June 1989. The fact that the S.E.C. filed a friend-of-the-court brief challenging the Wisconsin law as unconstitutional implies that some uncertainty remained even after the Supreme Court ruling. We report descriptive statistics for alternate specifications of a pill coverage dummy variable in Table 1. In our subsequent analysis we define the effective dates of these laws using the dates of these two important judicial decisions, although this choice does not much affect the results. We ignore the issue of important court decisions for pills since the relevant decision, *Moran*, occurred in 1985 before all but a handful of pills were adopted.

Table 1 reports means and standard deviations for dummy variables that equal one when a firm is covered by a law or a poison pill at the beginning of the forecast fiscal year, so that mean values represent proportions of the sample covered (i.e., exchange-listed firms). Using adoption dates yields a total of 1263 firm-years of experience with control share laws (5.8% of the sample) and 3417 firm-years of experience with business combination laws (15.6%). When coverage is defined to begin after the judicial decisions, for laws adopted before these decisions, coverage drops to 884 firm-years for control share laws (4.0%) and to 1625 firm-years for business combination laws (7.4%). There are 1779 firm-years of experience with poison pills in the sample (8.1%). We treat firm-years as covered only when an antitakeover measure is in place at the start of the year, ignoring part-year coverage from mid-year adoptions.

Foreshadowing the estimates from our prediction model reported in Table 3, which show almost no deterrence, the univariate results in Table 1 show that coverage by control share laws is as frequent in the takeover sample as in the full sample (5.5% vs. 5.8%, *t*-statistic of −0.28), while coverage by business combination laws is slightly lower in the takeover sample than in the full sample (13.5% vs. 15.6%, *t*-statistic of −1.66). Coverage by poison pills is more frequent in the takeover sample than in the full sample (9.6% vs. 8.1%, *t*-statistic of 1.30). The only possible evidence of deterrence in Table 1 is in business combination laws for which coverage is assumed to begin only after the June 1989 appeals court decision that validated these laws. Here, coverage is less frequent in the takeover sample than in the full sample (3.1% vs. 7.4%, t-statistic of -6.33). However, this difference could also reflect a seculiar decline in the takeover market, rather than deterrence. Takeovers were unusually infrequent for fiscal years beginning in 1990 (t-statistic of -2.43) and 1991 (t-statistic of -11.00), confirming the evidence in Figure 1.

3.4. Characteristics of successful takeovers

Table 1 describes some variables that are only defined for takeovers. Exchange-listed firms were acquired at a rate of 3.1% per year. Auctions account for 24.1% of the 669 takeovers, cash is the only consideration paid in 67.4%, and tender offers are used 45.0% of the time. Net-of-market premiums received by target shareholders average 34.9%. We refer to this below as the conditional mean premium, conditioning on the occurrence of a successful takeover. We also calculate an unconditional mean premium using all 21,887 firm-years, assigning a takeover premium of zero to all of the firm-years with no initial announcement leading to a successful takeover. There are 669 firm-years with a mean premium of 34.5%, and 21,218 firm-years with a mean premium of zero, aggregating to a population or unconditional mean premium of 1.1% per firm-year.

The unconditional mean premium suggests the economic gain that could be forgone if the takeover market remains dormant, although future losses would be mitigated through alternate ways of regulating managerial slack, such as proxy fights or incentive pay schemes. The demise of the takeover market is often cited as a justification for greater involvement by institutional investors in corporate decisions and governance. Partly in response to the demands of institutional investors, the S.E.C. revised its proxy statement rules in October 1992 to expand disclosure of management compensation, to ease disclosure rules for communications among investors, and to facilitate partial slates of nominees to corporate boards.

4. New evidence on the wealth effect of poison pills

4.1. Poison pill announcement effects, 1983–1991

In contrast to event studies of the wealth effects of adoptions of state antitakeover laws, which have been conducted for most of the firms covered by such laws, existing event studies of pill adoptions have been done for only the earliest one-quarter of all the pills adopted to date. We update the event studies of Ryngaert (1988) and Malatesta and Walkling (1988), drawing on the entire population of 1577 original poison pills adopted through December 1991. Of these, we exclude 118 with inadequate stock return data available from CRSP.

The wealth effect of a pill adoption is a combination of a stock price decline amounting to the expected present value of future takeover premiums forgone due to deterrence, offset by the expected present value of any increase in premiums due to a gain in bargaining power versus bidders. In addition, prices can change due to a revelation of management's private information. Some managers probably wait to adopt pills until they know that an offer is imminent. They could be engaged in merger talks, for which public disclosure is not usually required, they could be aware that an investment bank is shopping the company, or they could anticipate a takeover based on undisclosed corporate performance. A good indication that investors suspect managers of basing their decisions to adopt pills on private information is that 56% of our *DJNR* stories on pill adoptions include a denial by management of knowledge of any pending takeover.

Information effects make it difficult to measure deterrence using stock prices. To address this problem, previous researchers have analyzed the subset of pill adoptions made after the market is already aware of a merger interest. Presumably, management's informational advantage regarding any outstanding merger interest is diminished when a merger interest has already been revealed. We refer to these cases below as the "control premium" subset of pill adoptions. Even in this subset, however, it can be difficult to separate deterrence and information effects. During merger negotiations, the announcement of a pill is tantamount to a disclosure of the bad news that a deal has yet to be struck, so a decline in stock price does not necessarily imply deterrence. Subject to this caveat, our evidence on the wealth effects of pill adoptions confirms earlier studies (i.e., it is consistent with deterrence, but not strong deterrence).

Table 2 shows estimates of the effect of poison pill adoptions on shareholder wealth, measured by the 3-day return on the common stock of the issuing firm, centered on the day of the announcement. To adjust for market movements, we subtract the prediction from a market model regression using the CRSP value-weighted portfolio, as estimated over the previous 253 trading days. If the *DJNR* time-stamp for a story is later than 4:00 p.m., we treat the following day as the announcement date. When we cannot find a *DJNR* mention, which happens in 8.5% of the cases, the announcement date is from the *Wall Street Journal Index* or from *Corporate Control Alert*. The *DJNR* text often provides information about coincident confounding news, pending takeover proposals, and rumors. We also check the *Wall Street Journal Index* for such items. Our sample includes 242 control premium cases (16.6% of the sample) in which the adoption was preceded within 12 months by a 13D filing, a published story about merger rumors, or an explicit takeover bid, and where no M&A event was announced simultaneously with the pill. There are 100 cases (6.9% of the sample) with a simultaneous M&A announcement.

Table 2 contains two estimates of average abnormal returns associated with announcements of poison pill adoptions. The fourth column shows the average abnormal return for each subset of the sample, and the second column shows the coefficients

Table 2

Least-squares regression showing the average wealth effect of initial poison pill rights issues announced in the period 1983–1991 for NYSE-, Amex-, and NASDAQ-listed stocks, by whether a 13D filing, rumors of a bid, or an explicit takeover bid make it likely that a control premium is built into the issuer's stock price at the time of announcement

Another variable measures whether merger and acquisition (M&A) news is announced at the same time as the pill. A different dummy variable indicates NASDAQ-listed firms. Dummy variables for the year of adoption represent the intercepts for each year (to distinguish the early pills from the later ones). The dependent variable is measured as the cumulative abnormal return over days -1 to $+1$ using a market model estimated with the CRSP value-weighted market portfolio during the year (trading days -255 to -2) prior to the pill announcement. The third column shows the proportion of the sample for which the respective dummy variables are nonzero. The right column shows the average abnormal return for each subset of the sample. White's (1980) heteroskedasticity-consistent t-statistics are in parentheses.

Variable	Regression coefficients (t-statistic)	Proportion of sample	Average return (t-statistic)
Prior control premium (=1)	−0.0209	0.1659	−0.0155
	(−6.60)		(−5.20)
Contemporaneous M&A news (=1)	0.0326	0.0685	0.0404
	(3.16)		(4.81)
NASDAQ-listed firm (=1)	−0.0076	0.3633	−0.0022
	(−2.40)		(−0.92)
Year-by-year intercepts			
1984	−0.0232	0.0062	−0.0285
	(−1.71)		(−1.56)
1985	0.0068	0.0254	0.0017
	(0.81)		(0.23)
1986	0.0032	0.2255	0.0005
	(1.31)		(0.20)
1987	0.0038	0.0987	0.0022
	(0.81)		(0.45)
1988	0.0098	0.2358	0.0072
	(3.29)		(2.98)
1989	0.0023	0.2282	−0.0014
	(0.66)		(−0.50)
1990	0.0036	0.1206	0.0032
	(0.74)		(0.71)
1991	0.0087	0.0596	0.0060
	(1.18)		(1.09)
$\bar{R}^2$	0.048		
Standard error of regression	0.0537		
Degrees of freedom	1448		

from a multiple regression that accounts for interaction effects among the variables. Most of the results are similar, but we focus on the multiple-regression estimates because they account for interactions among the subsamples.

The regression in Table 2 includes dummy variables for control premium cases, for simultaneous M&A news, for NASDAQ listing, and for the year of adoption. We include adoption-year dummy variables in case there is a different market reaction to more recent pills. Principally, we find that a prior control premium decreases the pill announcement effect by -2.09% (*t*-statistic of -6.60). This finding confirms Ryngaert (1988), who reports an average return of -1.51% (*t*-statistic of -2.77) for his control premium group, implying either deterrence or bad news about the progress of takeover negotiations.

NASDAQ companies have lower announcement effects, all else equal, by -0.8%. with a *t*-statistic of -2.40. This result could reflect larger fractional inside ownership. McWilliams (1990) shows that the stock market reaction to adoptions of antitakeover charter amendments is negatively related to the fraction of insider ownership, based on 763 announcements by exchange-listed firms in the period 1980–1984. Brickley et al. (1994) show that the stock market reaction to 247 pill adoptions depends on the composition of the board of directors: firms with insider-dominated boards had more negative announcement effects. They find no evidence that the takeover rate is lower for firms with insider-dominated boards. We include only NYSE- and Amex-listed companies in our analyses of deterrence and premiums (Tables 3 and 4), and this differential announcement effect for NASDAQ companies implies that our conclusions may not apply to smaller companies.

Among the yearly dummy variables, the only negative intercept estimate (-2.3% *t*-statistic of -1.71) is for 1984, which covers the first nine pills (including two from 1983). The earliest adopters may have been more likely to use poison pills to the detriment of target stockholders, or the market may have initially overestimated the deterrence effect of pills. Finally, average abnormal returns are higher by 3.3% (*t*-statistic of 3.16) when pills are announced jointly with M&A news. This effect is small compared to initial takeover announcements because these are usually cases in which a pill is announced after an initial takeover announcement, often as part of an announcement of management's response to a takeover attempt.

4.2. Can deterrence be measured for poison pills?

Figure 5 shows the endogenous nature of decisions to adopt poison pills (i.e., managers often adopt pills when a takeover attempt is unusually likely). It plots (in daily event time) the cumulative proportion of pill adopters that received an initial takeover attempt within 1 year on either side of the adoption date. The sample consists of all 960 adoptions of original poison pills by exchange-listed firms in the period 1983–1990. We exclude pills adopted after 1990 to ensure a year's worth of M&A data after every adoption. Takeover attempts include the first occurrence of a merger proposal, merger agreement, or interfirm tender offer. The plotted value for the *n*th event day is a count of the total number of takeover announcements in a period starting 250 trading days before an adoption and ending with the *n*th day relative to the

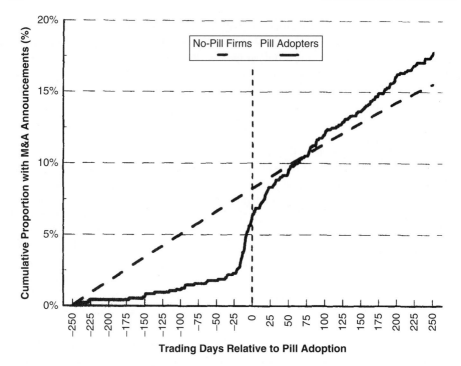

Fig. 5. Event study showing the cumulative proportion of firms receiving merger and acquisition (M&A) announcements within a year of the date of adoption of an initial poison pill, for 960 exchange-listed firms that adopted pills in the period 1983–1990. The dotted line shows the cumulative fraction, over corresponding 2-year periods, for exchange-listed firms that never adopted a poison pill. M&A announcements include merger proposals, merger agreements, and interfirm tender offers, regardless of success.

adoption. This count is divided by the sample size, so the plotted values represent the cumulative proportion of pill adopters put into play within 1 year of adoption.

For comparison, we also plot the average proportion of no-pill firms that are put into play over coincident intervals. No-pill firms are all those exchange-listed firms that did not adopt a pill. For each of the 960 adoptions, we calculate the cumulative proportion of no-pill firms in play as of the nth day relative to that adoption. We average these values across events to produce a series of n (plotted) values that can be interpreted as the proportion of firms expected to be in play as of each event day, allowing for secular variation in takeover frequency and an uneven distribution of pill adoptions over time. Since two-thirds of the exchange-listed firms are in the no-pill group, the cumulative proportion of no-pill firms that are put into play should be a smooth and continuous curve over any given 2-year period. Because we average these over 960 pill-adoption periods to get the cumulative proportion of no-pill firms that are put into play in the typical period, our expected values plot as a straight line.

The tendency for managers to adopt pills when the likelihood of a takeover is unusually high shows up in Figure 5 as a steeper slope for pill firms (solid line) than for no-pill firms (dashed line) near pill adoptions. The proportion of pill adopters that are in play increases from 2.4% 1 month before (day −25) to 19.4% 1 year after (day 250). Since the corresponding proportions for no-pill firms are 7.8% and 16.2%, the change among pill firms is about double that no-pill firms. Most of the difference arises near the pill adoption, with 6.4% of pill adopters put in play between days −25 and 25 compared with 1.7% of no-pill firms. Figure 5 also shows a curious deficit in merger and acquisition activity before poison pills are adopted, compared with the coincident experience among no-pill firms (2.7% vs. 7.8% as of day −25). This deficit is largely eliminated during the month before adoption and eliminated about 3 months after adoption. The proximity of the endpoints of the two curves (at the far right of Figure 5) is consistent with a long-run rate of receiving takeover bids that is largely independent of pill adoption, and consistent with the results of our prediction analysis in Section 5. Ken French has pointed out that the low level of M&A activity before pill adoptions may be an artifact of the decision to adopt pills when management perceives that M&A activity is likely, given that the long-run rate of receiving takeover bids is not strongly related to pill adoption.

This tendency for managers to adopt poison pills when takeovers are unusually likely is less of an issue with adoptions of state antitakeover laws because these laws are less under the control of a target firm's management, although they can switch their state of incorporation, lobby for new legislation, or opt out of existing legislation. Romano (1987) notes that antitakeover laws are sometimes adopted to protect a particular firm that is already in play. Since all of the firms domiciled in that state become covered, though few in play at the time, law adoptions are endogenous for a small fraction of firms. Thus, in Section 5, we implement a two-stage statistical procedure to address endogeneity in pill coverage, but use a standard procedure for law coverage.

5. Direct evidence of deterrence

5.1. Previous studies

Pound (1987) provides direct evidence that takeover frequency is lower for firms with antitakeover charter provisions. He compares the postadoption takeover experience of a sample of 100 NYSE firms that adopted supermajority and classified-board charter amendments (as a package) in the period 1973–1979 and the takeover experience of a time-matched sample of 100 NYSE firms that did not adopt either type of amendment. Over periods that run from adoption through 1984 (averaging 8 years in length), the takeover frequency is 28% for adopters and 38% for nonadopters. Ambrose and Megginson (1992) estimate a logit model using cross-sectional data on a sample of 117 exchange-listed target firms in the period 1981–1986 and a time-matched sample of 214 exchange-listed firms. Their model includes (among other things) dummy variables for whether each firm has a classified-board, fair-price charter provision, dual class capitalization, blank check preferred stock authorization, or poison pill. Preferred stock authorizations provide the only evidence of deterrence. Bhagat and Jefferis (1993) study classified-board charter provisions, poison pills, and fair-price amendments adopted in 1984–1985 and test whether they deterred takeovers over the following 2 years for 344 firms, and find little evidence that takeover defenses reduce takeover activity.

Other prediction studies do not include antitakeover measures as predictors. Hasbrouck (1985) uses a logit model to predict takeovers for a sample of 86 targets and a sample of 344 time-, size-, and industry-matched nontargets, and finds that larger market/book ratios and larger size reduce the likelihood of a takeover, but that liquidity and leverage are unimportant. Palepu (1986) provides logit estimates based on a sample of 163 target and 256 nontarget firms in the period 1971–1979 using the accounting and stock-based predictors described in Section 3. He obtains negative coefficient estimates for abnormal return, sales growth, leverage, and size, so these reduce the likelihood of a takeover. He obtains a positive coefficient estimate for a growth-resource mismatch dummy variable, so mismatched firms face a higher likelihood of a takeover. Market/book, price/earnings, and liquidity do not affect the likelihood of a takeover. Mørck et al. (1988) estimate a probit model using 1980 data for 454 Fortune-500 firms, of which 82 were takeover targets between 1981 and 1985, and find that larger size and q-ratio deter hostile takeovers, but not friendly ones. Mikkelson and Partch (1989) use a logit model and pool data as of 1973, 1978, and 1983 for 240 exchange-listed firms. They find that larger size and affiliate-firm cross-holdings deter acquisitions, but that leverage and managerial stockholdings do not affect the likelihood of a successful takeover. Shivdasani (1993) estimates a logit model using data on 193 hostile targets and 194 nontarget firms from 1980–1988 and finds that size, managerial stockholdings, and affiliate-firm cross-holdings deter hostile takeovers, but that earnings growth and board composition do not matter. Size is the only predictor that is consistently successful in these studies, while mixed success has been achieved with abnormal return, sales growth, leverage, q-ratio, or market/book, and certain ownership variables.

5.2. Predicting poison pills

If managers adopt poison pills when takeovers are unusually likely, as suggested by the evidence in Figure 5 and Table 2, then this tendency will mask the estimated deterrence effect of pills. If the tendency is severe, pills could appear to cause takeovers. Using a medical analogy, the consumption of aspirin might be a good predictor of the visible symptoms of the common cold, not because aspirin causes colds, but because people often take aspirin when they feel a cold coming on. Similarly, managers may adopt pills when they feel that a takeover is unusually likely. We mitigate this possibility by following a suggestion of Maddala (1983, p. 246). We first estimate a

Table 3

Probit estimates of the dependence of takeover probability on accounting and stock price data, state antitakeover laws, and poison pills (left panel), and the dependence of poison pill adoptions on accounting and stock price data and state antitakeover laws (right panel), using pooled time-series cross-sectional data for exchange-listed firms and for fiscal-year forecast periods beginning January 1977 through January 1991 (21,887 firm-years)

The dependent variable is either a dummy that equals one if a successful tender offer, merger proposal, or merger agreement is announced during the forecast period, or a dummy that equals one if a firm adopts an original poison pill during the forecast period. The predictor variables are all defined as of the start of the forecast period.

	Takeover dummy			Pill adoption dummy		
	Probit coefficient	Adjusted *t*-statistic	Marginal effect	Probit coefficient	*t*-Statistic	Marginal effect
Poison pill	0.345	4.60	0.0234			
Predicted pills (from probit)	−0.735	−2.01	−0.0498			
Surprise pills (error from probit)	0.418	5.23	0.0283			
Control share law	0.184	1.55	0.0124	0.277	5.49	0.0233
Business combination law	0.267	1.74	0.0181	0.573	7.88	0.0481
Abnormal return (in % over 4 years)	0.177	1.42	0.0120	−0.054	−0.46	−0.0045
Sales growth (4-year average)	−0.086	−0.51	−0.0059	−0.450	−3.28	−0.0378
Liquidity (4-year average)	0.073	0.64	0.0048	0.453	4.59	0.0380
Debt/equity (4-year average)	−0.024	−1.30	−0.0017	−0.011	−0.99	−0.0009
Market/book (4-year average)	−0.012	−0.70	−0.0008	0.011	0.96	0.0009
Price/earnings (4-year average)	−0.001	−0.62	−0.0001	0.003	2.33	0.0003
Size	−0.048	−3.24	−0.0032	0.231	20.79	0.0194
Constant	−1.602	−11.81	−0.1086	−4.997	−31.39	−0.4199
1986	0.216	1.61	0.0147	1.188	7.52	0.0998
1987	0.155	1.17	0.0105	2.374	17.29	0.1995
1988	0.300	2.20	0.0204	2.577	18.85	0.2165
1989	0.234	1.41	0.0159	2.866	21.04	0.2408
1990	−0.114	−0.58	−0.0077	2.689	18.22	0.2260
1991	−0.681	−2.58	−0.0462	2.746	18.19	0.2307
Log-likelihood		−2922.89			−3291.12	
Degrees of freedom		21,869			21,871	

model to predict pill coverage, using variables that are likely to predict management's choice of whether and when to adopt a pill. This yields "predictable" and "surprise" components of pill coverage. The logic is that pills that are a surprise (to researchers) are the ones most likely to have been adopted when management has information about a pending takeover attempt. We hope to isolate the deterrence effect of pill coverage, in a second-stage analysis discussed below, after stripping away the surprise component.

Candidates for inclusion in the first-stage (pill) prediction model are the accounting and stock return variables listed in Table 1, along with law coverage. Since poison pills represent an innovation, we include yearly dummy variables (for 1986–1991) to reflect the spread of pill coverage over time. The right panel of Table 3 shows estimates of a probit model that predicts pill coverage for all 21,887 firm-years. Since probit coefficients are difficult to interpret, Table 3 reports the marginal effect of a change in each predictor variable calculated at its sample mean (i.e., similar to the least-squares coefficient in a linear probability model).[6]

Being incorporated in a state with an antitakeover law is a good predictor of whether a firm has a poison pill. A control share law increases the likelihood of having a pill by 2.33% (t-statistic of 5.49) and a business combination law increases it by 4.81% (t-statistic of 7.88). These variables will be negatively related if one form of protection substitutes for another, and positively related if managers who prefer protection choose to both incorporate in a state with an antitakeover law and also to adopt a pill. The positive sign on these estimates implies that state laws and poison pills are more complements than substitutes.

Among the accounting and stock market predictors, only firm size is both statistically and economically significant. Larger firms are less likely to be acquired, as detailed in the next section, and more likely to have pills. An increase of just $1.7 million (t-statistic of 20.79) in total assets, which average $280 million, increases the probability of having a pill by 1%. For the average firm-year in our sample, this means an increase from 8.1% to 9.1% in the probability of having a pill. This positive relation between size and the probability of pill adoption is understandable if there are economies of scale in buying pill protection due to fixed costs in adopting pills, but the rapid trend toward in-house and local counsel to advise on pill adoptions (seen in Figure 4) suggests that the costs of adopting a pill, fixed or otherwise, are small. A positive relation could also occur if small firms have a natural or incidental immunity, perhaps due to ownership structures that are more concentrated, so that their demand for pill protection is low. By this reasoning, however, the demand for pill protection would be lower for larger firms because (as detailed below) size itself seems to be a natural or incidental deterrent.

Coefficient and t-statistic for the *poison pill* dummy variable are from a regression including all the other explanatory variables, except predicted pills and surprise pills. By definition, the sum of the predicted and surprise components of pills equals "*poison pill.*" For other variable definitions, see the note to Table 1. The marginal effect column transforms the probit coefficient into the marginal effect of the variable on the estimated probability, evaluated at the sample means of the explanatory variables. t-Statistics in the takeover prediction model have been adjusted to account for the fact that explanatory variables are estimates from another statistical model (i.e., the pill prediction model in the right panel); see Maddala (1983, p. 247).

---

[6] See, for example, Greene (1993, p. 639) for a description of this calculation. The predictions from a probit model estimated using data after 1983 (when poison pills were invented) are virtually identical to those from the full sample of firm-years.

The next-best predictors after size are sales growth and liquidity. A 1% increase in the probability of having a pill requires a decease in sales growth of 26% per year (*t*-statistic of -3.28), where typical sales growth is 8.7% per year. The same effect requires an increase of 27% (*t*-statistic of 4.59) in the ratio of net liquid assets to total assets, which would involve doubling the typical ratio of 24.7%. We do not judge either of these effects to be economically important.

5.3. Predicting takeovers

We test for the deterrence effect of antitakeover measures by including dummy variables defined on antitakeover coverage in a takeover prediction model. The power of this research design depends on dispersion in antitakeover coverage. At each time, we want some firms to be covered, while others are not. Because half of all exchange-listed firms became covered *en masse* when Delaware adopted its business combination law in January 1988, the deterrence effect of business combination laws could show up as a post-1987 drop in takeover frequency, rather than as a firm-specific phenomenon. Conversely, a late-1980s shift in takeover frequency, perhaps due to recession or regulatory intervention in credit markets, could show up as deterrence due to business combination laws. Our review of the events of the late 1980s in Section 2 favors the latter interpretation and persuades us to control for year-by-year variation in takeover frequency. Thus, our dummy variables for pills and laws tell us whether antitakeover measures had an effect *beyond* a probable secular decline in takeover activity. With one exception noted below and discussed in Section 7.2, our conclusions do not depend on the inclusion of yearly dummy variables.

The left-hand panel of Table 3 shows estimates of a model that predicts takeovers among exchange-listed firms with fiscal years beginning 1977–1991 (the sample described in Section 3). We predict a dummy variable equaling one if a successful merger proposal, merger agreement, or interfirm tender offer is announced during a fiscal year. The predictors include dummy variables for coverage by antitakeover measures, seven accounting and stock market predictors, and 6 yearly dummy variables (1986 through 1991).

The first row of Table 3 shows that the marginal deterrence effect of a pill is 2.34% (*t*-statistic of 4.60). A literal interpretation of the positive sign on this estimate is that a pill increases the likelihood of a takeover, but a more plausible interpretation is that pills tend to be adopted in anticipation of a takeover attempt, and that this (private) information is not captured by the (public) accounting and stock market factors that we include. To deal with any tendency for managers to adopt pills when a takeover is unusually likely, we break the dummy variable for pills into surprise and predictable components, based on estimates of the first-stage pill prediction model reported in the right panel of Table 3. We use these components as predictors in a second-stage takeover prediction model, reported in the left panel of Table 3. Thus, the predictable component of pill coverage is an estimate of the probability of pill coverage, and the surprise component is the difference between the pill dummy variable and this prediction.

The coefficient estimate for the surprise component of pills is positive, as expected, and implies that the annual probability of takeover is higher by 2.83% (*t*-statistic of 5.23) when a pill is a total surprise (i.e., the predicted probability of having a pill is zero, based on publicly available accounting and stock price data). The corresponding estimate for the predictable component of pill coverage is negative and implies that the annual probability of takeover is lower by 4.98% (*t*-statistic of −2.01) when a pill is completely predictable (i.e., the prediction of pill coverage = 1.0). None of the pills in our sample are completely predictable, however. Even in 1991, the year with the highest average predicted pill coverage (44.2%), the pill-induced decrease in annual takeover probability is only 2.15% per year (4.87% times 44.2%) for the typical firm.[7] Moreover, when we omit the yearly dummy variables that control for secular variation, the *t*-statistic for the predictable component of pill coverage falls to −0.84 (see Section 7.2).

The estimated coefficients for control share laws and business combination laws are positive (*t*-statistics of 1.55 and 1.74), so antitakeover laws appear to increase takeover probabilities slightly, holding other factors constant (including secular variation). Since the law adoptions are motivated by takeover expectations for only a few firms, we conclude from these estimates that managers have not used these laws to deter takeovers systematically, and infer that antitakeover laws played a minor role in depressing the 1980s market for corporate control.

Few of the accounting and stock market performance variables are reliable predictors of takeovers. Size is the one exception. Larger firms are less likely to be acquired (*t*-statistic of −3.24) and the economic significance of the estimated coefficient is not trivial. A decrease of $23 million from the average level of total assets (of $280 million) increases the annual likelihood of takeover by 1%. The probability of takeover falls reliably below the sample period norm only for fiscal years that start in 1991 (*t*-statistic of −2.58). As discussed in Section 2, these forecast periods follow the bankruptcy of Drexel Burnham Lambert and coincide roughly with the onset of recession and the credit crunch.

6. Predicting takeover premiums

Table 4 shows estimates of the dependence of takeover premiums on antitakeover measures, the accounting and stock market performance variables (described in Section 3), and certain takeover characteristics. Huang and Walkling (1987) estimate

---

[7] The standard errors have been corrected to account for the fact that this explanatory variable is an estimate from another statistical model. See Maddala (1983, p. 247). In earlier drafts of our paper we reported uncorrected logit estimates that differed little from the corrected probit estimates reported here. Since the same variables are used to predict pills and then takeovers, there is substantial collinearity between the pill predictions and the other variables in the takeover prediction model (except for surprise pills). In fact, identification is achieved in these models only because of the nonlinearity of the prediction models.

Table 4

Least-squares estimates of the relation of takeover premiums with state antitakeover laws, poison pills, accounting and stock price data, and characteristics of the takeover

Takeover premiums are measured as the compounded difference in the returns to target firm's stock and the CRSP value-weighted NYSE/Amex market portfolio during the period from 20 trading days before the first merger proposal or tender offer through 5 trading days after the successful offer. In the left panel, the sample consists of pooled time-series cross-sectional data for exchange-listed firms with fiscal-year forecast periods beginning January 1977 through January 1991 (21,887 firm-years). The right panel uses the 669 firm-years when a subsequently successful takeover begins. The predictor variables are all defined as of the start of the forecast period. The dates when important legal precedents established the effectiveness of control share laws (April 1987) and of business combination laws (June 1989) are used to define coverage by these laws (i.e., the dummy variable equals one for firm-years in which the firm was covered by a law that had already been certified by a major judicial decision). The t-statistics use White's (1980) heteroskedasticity-consistent standard errors.

Predictors	Full sample		Successful takeover sample	
	Coefficient	t-Statistic	Coefficient	t-Statistic
Poison pill	0.0144	4.38	0.1627	2.95
Predicted pills (from probit)	0.0024	0.30	0.4588	1.60
Surprise pills (error from probit)	0.0151	4.33	0.1453	2.31
Control share law	0.0080	1.96	0.1094	1.61
Business combination law	0.0054	2.22	0.0269	0.29
Abnormal return (in % over 4 years)	0.0059	1.71	0.0439	0.61
Sales growth (4-year average)	0.0048	1.27	0.3964	3.48
Liquidity (4-year average)	0.0096	3.18	0.0813	1.33
Debt/equity (4-year average)	−0.0003	−1.77	−0.0167	−1.37
Market/book (4-year average)	−0.0005	−2.52	−0.0212	−2.00
Price/earnings (4-year average)	−0.0001	−1.46	−0.0012	−0.97
Size	−0.0008	−2.38	0.0020	0.20
Constant	0.0137	5.31	0.2048	3.02
1986	0.0020	0.92	−0.1214	−3.74
1987	−0.0012	−0.48	−0.1665	−2.78
1988	0.0119	2.66	0.0198	0.29
1989	−0.0007	−0.18	−0.2400	−2.30
1990	−0.0103	−3.97	−0.3008	−4.42
1991	−0.0144	−4.21	−0.3300	−2.08
Auction (=1 if multiple bidders)			0.1137	3.61
Cash (=1)			0.0857	3.53
Tender offer (=1)			0.1296	5.27
$\bar{R}^2$	0.005		0.192	
Standard error of regression	0.0826		0.2933	
Degrees of freedom	21,869		648	

a regression model in a sample of 204 exchange-listed target firms acquired by merger or tender offer in the period 1977–1982, and find that premiums are reliably higher in all-cash transactions, but not in tender offers. Bradley et al. (1988) estimate a similar model for 236 tender offers for exchange-listed firms in the period 1963–1984, and find that premiums are higher in auctions. Thus, we include dummy variables defined by whether the transaction is (1) an auction with multiple, publicly revealed bidders, (2) an all-cash transaction, and (3) a tender offer.

The right panel of Table 4 reports estimates based on the sample of 669 successful takeover targets (conditional premiums) and the left panel of Table 4 reports estimates of the same model using all 21,887 firm-years with the takeover premium set to zero in nontakeover firm-years (unconditional premiums). The estimated effect of antitakeover measures on the unconditional premium (left column) is of interest because it is a net effect of a decrease in the premium if antitakeover devices deter offers and an increase if they increase premiums in successful offers. The first line of Table 4 shows (*in italics*) estimates for the coefficient on a dummy variable that combines the predictable and surprise components of pill coverage (described in the previous section). These estimates imply that both conditional and unconditional premiums are higher with a pill in place. Since we control for the (positive) effect of auctions on premiums, these estimates understate the effect of pills on premiums to the extent that pills cause auctions, as their proponents claim.[8]

Coefficient and *t*-statistic for the *poison pill* dummy variable are from a regression including all the other explanatory variables, except predicted pills and surprise pills. The other coefficients from that regression are not shown. The pill predictions come from the model shown in Table 3. By definition, the sum of predicted and surprise pills equals "poison pill." For other variable definitions, see the note to Table 1.

The surprise component of pill coverage is reliably related to higher premiums. For pills that are a total surprise (i.e., the predicted probability of pill coverage = 0.0), conditional premiums are higher by 14.5% (*t*-statistic of 2.31) and unconditional premiums by 1.5% (*t*-statistic of 4.33). Not only are takeovers more frequent the more surprising is pill coverage (from Table 3), average premiums are higher as well. With the predictable component of pills, the most we can conclude is that shareholders are not harmed, but this conclusion is important in view of the weak evidence in Table 3 that predictable pills deter takeovers. Specifically, the positive effect on conditional premiums is large, at 45.9%, but quite imprecise (*t*-statistic of 1.60). The effect on unconditional premiums is small but positive, 0.24% (*t*-statistic of 0.30), reflecting a large increase in conditional premiums and a smaller decrease in the probability of a takeover.

A control share law raises conditional premiums by 10.9% (*t*-statistic of 16.1) and a business combination law has almost no effect (*t*-statistic of 0.29). Control share and business combination laws have small positive effects on unconditional premiums, 0.8% and 0.5%, respectively (*t*-statistic of 1.96 and 2.22). In tests that are not reported here, we find that neither law has an effect on premiums reliably different from zero

---

[8] Using probit models, similar to Table 3, to predict which successful takeovers involve auctions shows an insignificant effect on the predictable component of pills (*t*-statistic of −1.77) and the surprise component (*t*-statistic of 0.14), but reliable positive effects of control share laws (*t*-statistic of 3.50) and business combination laws (*t*-statistic of 2.10).

when coverage is defined using the dates these laws took effect instead of judicial decision dates.

The accounting and stock market performance variables predict premiums better than they do takeovers. Recent sales growth has a modest positive effect on conditional premiums. A deviation in sales growth of 2.5% per year (from a sample mean of 7.7%) increases conditional premiums by 1% (*t*-statistic of 3.48), but unconditional premiums are not reliably related to sales growth (*t*-statistic of 1.27). Although liquidity has no reliable effect on conditional premiums, it is associated with larger unconditional premiums (*t*-statistic of 3.18). A higher market/book ratio reduces conditional premiums (*t*-statistic of −2.00) and unconditional premiums (*t*-statistic of −2.52). Although size has only a small positive effect on conditional premiums, size does predict lower unconditional premiums (*t*-statistic of −2.38). This finding is no surprise since size is the one variable with reliable predictive power for takeovers. The fact that the estimates for yearly dummy variables are generally reliably negative for the years 1989–1991 means that takeover premiums became much lower for unprotected targets after antitakeover protection became the norm, suggesting either a shift in the composition of the group of unprotected firms or a growing association between antitakeover measures and management bargaining power versus bidders.

We confirm a result reported by Bradley et al. (1988) with our finding that an auction is associated with an added takeover premium of 11.4% (*t*-statistic of 3.61), compared with their estimate of 13% (*t*-statistic of 4.23). We also confirm a result reported by Huang and Walkling (1987) with our finding that all-cash transactions are associated with an added premium of 8.6% (*t*-statistic of 3.53), compared with their estimate of 12.9% (*t*-statistic of 3.68). Our evidence contradicts another of their results, however, since we find that tender offers are associated with an added takeover premium of 13.0% of (*t*-statistic of 5.27), after controlling for method of payment, compared with their estimate of −0.2%.

7. Sensitivity analysis

As a check, we estimate alternate specifications for the tests in Tables 2, 3, and 4. In the interests of parsimony, we summarize these tests below but do not report detailed results.

7.1. Hostile takeovers

There are arguments in the literature that hostile takeovers are different from friendly takeovers in the sense that the sources of gain from the two kinds of transactions are likely to be different (e.g., Mørck et al., 1988, 1989). The takeover prediction estimates in Table 3 do not distinguish, however, between hostile and friendly transactions. By definition, antitakeover measures add nothing to management's ability to reject friendly transactions, that is, those conditioned implicitly on management approval, so including such transactions cannot help us measure the deterrence effect of antitake-over measures. Depending on how well we can measure friendliness, filtering out friendly transactions could reduce noise. Considering how large our sample is, how-ever, our concern over bias outweighs our concern over efficiency. Filtering would introduce a bias if stronger takeover defenses cause a substitution of negotiated for unnegotiated transactions, rather than a reduction in the frequency of transactions. Since some substitution is likely, a test of whether takeover defenses deter hostile transactions alone overstates the costs of antitakeover measures.

Despite these reservations, we estimate the effect of antitakeover measures on hostile takeovers alone using specifications of hostility that are, at least, replicable. Hostility is hard to measure in a replicable way because most initially hostile takeovers end as friendly (negotiated) transactions through a process of negotiation and compe-tition. Thus, the stage at which hostility is measured, within this process, determines whether transactions are classified as hostile. Moreover, these negotiations typically are confidential. When they are revealed before settlement, it is often because one of the negotiating parties sees its bargaining position enhanced by presettlement publi-city, and this presettlement publicity is the raw material for any measurement of hostility. We know of no way to define hostility that does not suffer from these practical difficulties.

Nonetheless, we treat takeovers as hostile if:

(1) during the 12 months before an initial merger or tender offer bid, a 13D statement is filed in which the buyer discloses an intent to seek control, or there are significant merger rumors about the target firm (suggesting an effort to put the firm in play), or there is a targeted share repurchase for more than 5% of the target company's stock;
(2) the initial bid is either an unnegotiated tender offer for control of the target firm, or a merger proposal specifying a price (a "bear hug").

Our full sample includes 438 takeovers that fit the first description, with hostility based on prebid events, and 172 that fit the second description, with hostility based on the character of the opening bid.

When we replicate our takeover prediction analysis for hostile takeovers, neither of these definitions yields results (not shown here) that differ substantively from those in Table 3, although the smaller number of successful takeovers resulting from these two definitions of hostility results in less precise estimates of all of the coefficients in the model.

7.2. Controlling for a secular trend

Our takeover prediction model in Table 3 includes yearly dummy variables for 1986–1991 because there is reason to expect a decline due to general business conditions, particularly a cash crunch, in the last few years of our sample period.

When we replicate this analysis without yearly dummy variables, the estimated effects of the state antitakeover law variables are stronger. t-Statistics for the control share and business combination law variables in the pill prediction equation are 19.16 and 37.78 (compared with 5.49 and 7.88 in Table 3). The marginal effect of coverage by control share and business combination laws increases the probability of pill coverage by 10.14% and 15.14%, respectively (compared with 2.33% and 4.81% in Table 3). The t-statistic for the predictable component of pill coverage in the takeover prediction model is smaller (-1.17 compared with -2.01 without the yearly dummy variables). Thus, there is no reason to believe that the yearly dummy variables substitute for the effects of the antitakeover laws or for pills to reduce the evidence for deterrence in the takeover prediction models.

Since poison pills were not introduced until 1983, and the significant legal precedents supporting state antitakeover laws also occurred after 1983, we also estimate our tests using only firm-years after 1983. The negative coefficient of the predicted component of pills and the positive coefficients for the surprise components of pills and for coverage by control share or business combination laws in the takeover prediction models are all larger and the t-statistics are larger, but the general conclusions described in Sections 5 and 6 are unchanged.

Also, Table 3 reports yearly dummy variables for only the last 6 years in the sample period in Table 3 to economize on the results we report. When we estimate a version of the takeover prediction model that includes dummy variables for all years (and no constant), the estimates of the yearly intercepts from 1977 to 1985 are between -1.379 and -1.628 with no discernible pattern. Constraining these coefficients to be equal in Table 3 does not affect the estimates of the other coefficients in the model.

Finally, the failure of the accounting and stock market performance measures, other than size, to help explain takeovers is due neither to the inclusion of the poison pill nor state law variables nor to the inclusion of the yearly dummy variables. We estimate models using only the accounting and stock market variables separately for each year from 1977 to 1991, and find only size helps predict takeovers in most years.

7.3. Wealth effect of pills

Szewczyk and Tsetsekos (1992, Table 4) provide evidence that the wealth effect of the adoption of the Pennsylvania antitakeover law was less negative for firms that already had a poison pill, the presumption being that the added deterrence from a state antitakeover law is lower in these cases. Reversing this, we test whether the wealth effect of the adoption of a pill is less negative for firms that are already covered by a law. Adding a dummy variable to the regression in Table 2, we find that the stock price reaction to pill announcements does not depend on whether a firm is already covered by a law (coefficients of 0.00003 and -0.0009, with t-statistics of 0.01 and -0.19, for business combination and control share laws, respectively). Also, since hiring expensive outside counsel to implement a pill could signal litigiousness, we included dummy variables equaling one if the adopting company retained a big-two or next-seven law firm, but these coefficients are not different from zero (coefficients of -0.0020 and 0.0026, with t-statistics of -0.57 and 0.41, respectively).

7.4. Effective dates for state antitakeover laws

We estimate versions of the models in Table 3 using the dates that the individual state antitakeover laws took effect (when these precede the relevant judicial decision dates). These results show even less evidence of deterrence for state laws, probably because they include more firm-years in the mid-1980s when takeover activity is high. Using the judicial decision dates, which are closer to the beginning of the crash in the market for corporate control, as we have done in Tables 3 and 4, gives the state laws a better chance to explain the time-series and cross-sectional behavior of takeover rates, but that advantage still yields no reliable evidence of deterrence.

7.5. Morning-after pills and success rates

The endogeneity problem, or the tendency for managers to adopt poison pills shortly before impending takeover attempts (seen in Figure 5 and discussed in Sections 4 and 5), would be worse if our measurement interval were narrower than 1 year. Figure 5 shows that many poison pills are adopted close to the time of tender offers or merger bids. We call these "morning-after pills." When we include these pills in our takeover prediction model, after subtracting the predictable component of these pills, they have positive effects similar to those of the surprise component of pill coverage, but about half as large. As for takeover premiums, in a regression similar to Table 4 the coefficient for the surprise component of morning-after pills is 0.0366 (t-statistic of 0.61) for conditional premiums and 0.0277 (t-statistic of 4.01) for unconditional premiums. Thus, morning-after pills affect premiums much as does the surprise component of pill coverage.

We do not report on takeover success rates elsewhere in this study, but we find that takeover success rates are lower for morning-after pills than for the predictable and surprise components of pill coverage, which are in place at the start of forecast fiscal years. In Table 3 we predict successful bids within the whole sample. We can predict takeover success rates by replicating our analysis on the subset of firm-years containing initial bids, regardless of success. Doing so, the marginal effect of the surprise component of pills is 4.8% (t-statistic of 0.80) and -17.0% (t-statistic of -2.95) for the surprise component morning-after pills. Of the 50 firms with morning-after pills, half are acquired in the following 12 months. This compares with a 76% success rate for the 875 firm-years in which a target firm receives a tender offer or merger proposal (resulting in the 669 firm-years with successful takeovers). In summary, although takeover bids are less likely to succeed when target firm management adopts a pill after the initial bid, expected takeover premiums remain positive even for these pills, so that from the selling shareholders' point of view, it is never too late to adopt a poison pill, nor is there a clear gain from preemptive adoption.

7.6. Clinical experience

Clinical experience leaves little doubt that some takeovers were deterred by antitakeover measures. For example, there were 27 instances from 1985 through 1990 in which a court upheld a poison pill challenged by a bidder. Since this sample excludes negotiations that settle quickly (before lawsuits are filed or before courts rule), these tend to be deals with difficult negotiations, where pills matter. Of these target firms, 11 remained independent 1 year after the decision and 16 were acquired by the plaintiff or some third party.[9] Clearly, total deterrence is the less common outcome even among these obviously hostile takeovers.

8. Conclusions

If the 1980s merger wave was ended by modern antitakeover measures, evidence of deterrence should be seen in the experience of individual firms following adoption of these measures, and this evidence should survive attempts to control for secular trends in takeover activity. Otherwise, it is more likely that broad-scale political or economic forces are responsible for the demise of the market for corporate control. We find no evidence of deterrence from control share or business combination laws. There is weak evidence of deterrence from poison pills that are predictable based on publicly available information about the firm's performance. Poison pills adopted by firms that do not fit the pattern in the market (which we call surprise pills) are associated with reliably higher takeover rates. This finding probably reflects the choice by management to adopt a poison pill when it has private information that a bid is imminent. The net effect of these two motivations for adopting poison pills is a positive association with takeover rates.

Anecdotal evidence and clinical experience strongly suggest that some potential takeovers were deterred by modern antitakeover measures, but this conclusion is not supported by our systematic evidence. In its decision upholding the Indiana control share law, the US Supreme Court noted that the case against the law ultimately rested on an unsubstantiated empirical claim of deterrence, and our results validate the Court's skepticism.

Our new evidence on how stock prices change with poison pill adoptions does not suggest an economically meaningful degree of deterrence. Controlling for other

---

[9] Firms whose pills were upheld in court, and who stayed independent for a year following the decision (date), include CTS (4/23/86), DeSoto (2/5/90), Household International (1/19/85), Johnson Controls (3/25/85), Phillips Petroleum (6/3/86), Property Trust of America (10/2/89), Revlon (10/9/85), Sea Containers Ltd (11/27/89), Universal Foods (3/18/89), Santa Fe-Southern Pacific (3/11/88), and USG (4/28/88). Firms that were acquired within a year include Allied Stores (10/24/86), Damon (9/16/88), Facet Enterprises (4/15/88), Federated Department Stores (3/18/88), Gelco (11/10/86), Great Northern Nekoosa (12/12/89), Hayes Albion (11/25/86), Holly Farms (12/30/88), Koppers (4/1/88), Milton Roy (11/9/89), Prime Computer (12/20/88), Ryan Homes (10/24/86), Southwest Forest (3/20/85), Staley Continental (5/9/88), T W Services (3/2/89), and Vermont American (10/13/89).

measures of information that reflect the likelihood of a subsequent takeover bid, only the earliest pills (before 1985) are associated with large declines in shareholder wealth on the adoption of these measures. There is a negative reaction to pill announcements when the firm is already in play through some prior public announcement that is likely to foreshadow M&A activity. This effect could represent either deterrence or negative information about the process of ongoing negotiations.

Our new evidence that takeover premiums are higher when target firms are protected by state laws or by pills suggests that the relative bargaining positions of bidders and targets are altered by these antitakeover devices, raising the costs to the bidder and the gains to the target. This implies deterrence, but we find that target shareholders gain even after accounting for deals that are never completed.

The combination of the event-study evidence in Table 2, the previous event studies on antitakeover devices in the literature, and the takeover premium evidence in Table 4 raises an interesting puzzle. Why is there ever a negative reaction to poison pills or to antitakeover laws when, based on the evidence through 1991, the net effect of takeover protection from laws and pills is positive? One possible answer is that the market misestimated the eventual effect of pills and laws, overestimating the costs of deterrence and underestimating the benefits of added bargaining power. Even in an efficient market, after all, we do not presume that investors have perfect foresight about the future evolution of takeover strategies. From this perspective, the evidence we provide about the actual takeover rate and premiums paid as a function of antitakeover devices outweighs the event-study evidence in judging deterrence.

The most plausible explanations for the collapse of the market for corporate control at the end of the 1980s are that (1) the spread of modern antitakeover measures made absolute deterrence feasible and that (2) the 1990 recession and credit crunch greatly affected this market. The first explanation is buttressed by our evidence that 87% of exchange-listed firms are now covered by one or another form of modern antitakeover measure (35% by poison pills, 80% by business combination laws, and 24% by control share laws), but refuted by our failure to find direct evidence of deterrence using all available data through 1991. We therefore conclude that the demise of the market for corporate control was caused by secular trends and not the introduction, spread, and legal acceptance of poison pill rights plans, control share laws, or business combination laws. An interesting test to discriminate between these alternate hypotheses will be to see whether the market for corporate control comes back from its recent doldrums. If state laws and pills are effective deterrents, the market will not recover unless firms rescind poison pills and opt out of state law protection (or switch to states like Texas and California that do not have antitakeover laws).[10]

---

[10] Since the first version of this paper in January 1993, the mergers and acquisitions market has become much more active. A front page story in the October 14, 1993 *Wall Street Journal* discussed the recent merger boom, and led to a brief summary of this paper on the front page of the October 21, 1993 *Wall Street Journal*.

Appendix: Case law about takeover defenses

The Delaware Supreme Court established the legality of defensive measures in May 1985 when it decided that Unocal's board of directors could exclude Mesa Petroleum from a defensive self-tender offer. This decision set a standard by which courts should focus solely on the nature of the deliberative process followed by the board of directors and ignore the optimality or "fairness" of the antitakeover measure that they happen to use. According to this (Unocal) standard, there are no legally defective antitakeover devices, only defective deliberations. This ruling explains why the takeover litigation of the 1980s never yielded a list of proscribed defensive measures, and why adjudications of takeover defenses have been commonplace and seemingly repetitive.

Specifically, the Unocal standard took the business judgment rule, the well-established principle that ordinary business decisions ought not be subject to judicial review, and extended it to court decisions regarding antitakeover measures. In takeover situations, however, the standard would allow for "special scrutiny," where boards of directors would need to show (1) reasonable grounds for believing that a "danger to corporate policy and effectiveness" existed and (2) that their actions are based on "good faith and reasonable investigation." The active involvement of independent, outside directors would show such a good faith deliberation.

The Delaware Supreme Court found an immediate application for the Unocal standard in its 1985 Moran decision, in which it upheld the adoption of a poison pill but noted that "[t]he ultimate response to an actual takeover bid must be judged by the Directors" actions at that time, and nothing we say here relieves them of their basic fundamental duties to the corporation and its stockholders'.[11] The Unocal standard was subsequently adopted by most other courts. For example, in 1986, a US District Court blocked a pill adopted by CTS because the board did not adequately consider the bidder's offer and acted without sufficient independent investigation. CTS cured its defect by forming a special committee of outside directors and by obtaining advice from outside counsel and investment bankers, and then adopted another pill, which the Court upheld. In the Buckhorn case in 1987, a US District Court blocked a poison pill and an ESOP-based defense because had the board made reasonable inquiries, it would have discovered that the investment bankers "relied too much" on management's assumptions and optimistic profit projections in computing fair value.[12]

The Delaware Supreme Court added a nuance to the Unocal standard in 1986 to address the proper conduct of an auction. In its Revlon decision, the Court overturned Revlon's lockup agreement with an LBO group led by Forstmann Little. In exchange for the lockup, Forstmann agreed in part to assume certain notes that Revlon had issued in a defensive exchange offer several months earlier, and that had fallen in value. "In reality," the Court said, "the Revlon board ended the auction in return for very little

---

[11] Unocal Corp. v. Mesa Petroleum Co., DelSupCt 5/17/85; Moran v. Household International Inc., DelSupCt 11/19/85.

[12] Dynamics Corp. v. CTS Corp., DC NIll 6/20/86; Buckhorn, Inc. v. Ropak Corp., DC SOhio, 2/11/87.

actual improvement in the final bid. The principal benefit went to the directors, who avoided personal liability to a class of creditors [note holders] to whom the board owed no further duty under the circumstances." The added nuance was that, once the board decided that the firm would not survive in its current form, "[t]he directors' role changed from defenders of the corporate bastion to auctioneers charged with getting the best price for the stockholders at a sale of the company." The Delaware Supreme Court applied similar reasoning in its MacMillan decision in 1989, in which it denounced the "illicit manipulation of a board's deliberative processes" and over-turned a lockup agreement granted to a management buyout group, adding that the board's hostility toward the competing bidder was unjustified once it decided to abandon its restructuring attempts and sell the entire company.[13]

Takeovers were completed so quickly in the 1980s that most court cases were either settled or rendered moot before they were appealed. This left the Delaware Supreme Court with only a few opportunities to reinforce the notion of a corporate bastion. In its Newmont decision, in 1987, it allowed a special dividend and rapid open-market purchases (a street sweep) to block a takeover bid. The Court found it significant that these actions did not constitute an abandonment of the corporation's continued existence, that most of the directors were outsiders, and that their investment banker estimated the foreclosed bid to be 8.7% below "fair" value.[14] This seemed to leave premium-priced offers open to question, but in the Time-Warner decision in 1990, the Delaware Supreme Court ruled that Time's board of directors could reject a premium offer, saying that "directors are not obliged to abandon a deliberately conceived corporate plan for a short-term shareholder profit unless there is clearly no basis to sustain the corporate strategy."[15] The Court also identified several previous lower court decisions that it thought were in error, but which had passed without review, saying that "the Court of Chancery has suggested that an all-cash, all-shares offer, falling within a range of values that a shareholder might reasonably prefer, cannot constitute a legally recognized 'threat' to shareholder interests sufficient to withstand a Unocal analysis." This view "represents a fundamental misconception of our standard of review under Unocal principally because it would involve the court in substituting its judgment for what is a 'better' deal for that of a corporation's board of directors." Again, the Court was impressed by the deliberative approach taken by Time's directors to a decision "made only after what could be fairly characterized as an exhaustive appraisal of Time's future as a corporation."[16]

In another noteworthy case, the Delaware Supreme Court acquiesced when the Chancery Court allowed Polaroid to deter an unnegotiated tender offer by Shamrock

---

[13] Revlon Inc. v. MacAndrews & Forbes Holdings Inc., DelSupCt, 3/13/86; MacMillan, DelSupCt, 5/3/89.

[14] Ivanhoe Partners v. Newmont Mining Corp., DelSupCt, 11/18/87.

[15] Paramount Communications Inc. v. Time Inc., DelSupCt, 2/26/90 (oral ruling 7/24/89).

[16] The lower court decisions that the Delaware Supreme Court identified as erroneous were Grand Metropolitan, PLC, v. Pillsbury Co., Del. Ch., 12/16/88, and City Capital Associates v. Interco, Inc., Del. Ch., 1988.

in 1989. The main issue was Polaroid's creation of an ESOP to hold 14% of its stock, which the lower court did not see as "unfair." Rather, it found that Polaroid's directors acted in good faith after a reasonable investigation, noting that all but two of Polaroid's 13 board members were independent outsiders, and that the board met at least six times in a 4-month period to review Shamrock's various offers and to discuss appropriate actions with financial and legal advisers.[17] Finally, the Unocal standard applies in the latest decisions. In 1993, the Delaware Chancery Court blocked a lockup provision of the merger agreement between Paramount Communications and Viacom, saying: "In connection with [Paramount CEO] Davis's efforts to entrench himself through the Viacom merger, Paramount's directors failed adequately to inform themselves of the relevant facts and circumstances. As a result, Davis was able to secure the approval of Paramount's directors for the Lockup Agreements in breach of the directors" fiduciary duties .... [T]he question finally becomes whether the directors have demonstrated that they were sufficiently informed to have a reasoned basis for favoring Viacom's offer. (Interestingly, regarding the lockup agreement, the Court asked: "Why such redundancy? They already had pill protection." The implication is that the Court believed the pill was sufficient to defeat the offer.)[18]

As an aside, we should note that courts overturned some pills because their "flip-in" features were found to conflict with general provisions in state corporation laws that require equal treatment of shareholders.[19] The affected states subsequently modified these provisions to exclude the discriminatory effect of pills, and we ignore these "pro-pill" antitakeover laws in our analysis.

This review of the important legal decisions regulating the use of defensive measures shows that directors have not been significantly constrained in their use of poison pills (or other measures) to deter takeovers; it also shows that the treatment of antitakeover measures was stable after 1985 (see also Greene, 1991). Consequently, we take the dates that poison pills were adopted to be the dates that they became effective, and estimate the deterrence effect of poison pills as a constant over the sample period. Overall, it leaves us disinclined to attribute the secular variation that we observe in takeover rates to any discontinuity in the legal environment.

References

Ambrose, B. W. and W. L. Megginson, 1992, "The Role of Asset Structure, Ownership Structure, and Takeover Defenses in Determining Acquisition Likelihood," *Journal of Financial and Quantitative Analysis*, 27, 575–589.

Bhagat, S. and R. H. Jefferis, 1993, "Is Defensive Activity Effective?," Working Paper, University of Colorado, Boulder, CO.

---

[17] See Shamrock Holdings, Inc. v. Polaroid Corp., Del. Ch., 1/6/89, and Del SupCt, 3/23/89.

[18] QVC Network v. Paramount Communications, Del. Ch., 10/21/93.

[19] See, for example, Amalgamated Sugar Co. v. NL Industries, Inc., DC SNY, 8/5/86.

Bradley, M., A. Desai and E. Han Kim, 1988, "Synergistic Gains from Corporate Acquisitions and Their Division Between the Stockholders of Target and Acquiring Firms," *Journal of Financial Economics*, 21, 3–40.

Brickley, J. A., J. L. Coles and R. L. Terry, 1994, "The Board of Directors and the Adoption of Poison Pills," *Journal of Financial Economics*, 35, 371–390.

Bruner, R. F., 1991, *The Poison Pill Anti-Takeover Defense: The Price of Strategic Deterrence*, Institute of Chartered Financial Analysts, Charlottesville, VA.

Comment, R. and G. A. Jarrell, 1987, "Two-Tier and Negotiated Tender Offers: The Imprisonment of the Free-Riding Shareholder," *Journal of Financial Economics*, 19, 283–310.

DeAngelo, H. and E. M. Rice, 1983, "Antitakeover Charter Amendments and Stockholder Wealth," *Journal of Financial Economics*, 11, 329–359.

Gilson, R. J. and B. S. Black, 1992, *The Law and Finance of Corporate Acquisitions: 1992 Supplement*, Foundation Press, Westbury, NY.

Greene, E. F., 1991, "Regulatory and Legislative Responses to Takeover Activity in the 1980s: The United States and Europe," *Texas Law Review*, 69, 1539–1593.

Greene, W. H., 1993, *Econometric Analysis*, 2nd edition, Macmillan, New York, NY.

Hasbrouck, J., 1985, "The Characteristics of Takeover Targets," *Journal of Banking and Finance*, 9, 351–362.

Huang, Y. -S. and R. A. Walkling, 1987, "Target Abnormal Returns Associated with Acquisition Announcements: Payment, Acquisition form, and Managerial Resistance," *Journal of Financial Economics*, 19, 329–349.

Jarrell, G. A. and A. B. Poulsen, 1987, "Shark Repellents and Stock Prices: The Effects of Antitakeover Amendments Since 1980," *Journal of Financial Economics*, 19, 127–168.

Jensen, M. C., 1986, "Agency Costs of Free Cash Flow, Corporate Finance, and Takeovers," *American Economic Review*, 76, 323–329.

Karpoff, J. M. and P. H. Malatesta, 1989, "The Wealth Effects of Second Generation State Takeover Legislation," *Journal of Financial Economics*, 25, 291–322.

Lang, L. H. P., R. M. Stulz and R. A. Walkling, 1989, "Managerial Performance, Tobin's Q, and the Gains from Successful Tender Offers," *Journal of Financial Economics*, 24, 137–154.

Linn, S. C. and J. J. McConnell, 1983, "An Empirical Investigation of the Impact of 'Antitakeover' Amendments on Common Stock Prices," *Journal of Financial Economics*, 11, 361–399.

Maddala, G. S., 1983, *Limited-Dependent and Qualitative Variables in Econometrics*, Cambridge University Press, Cambridge.

Malatesta, P. H. and R. A. Walkling, 1988, "Poison Pill Securities: Stockholder Wealth, Profitability, and Ownership Structure," *Journal of Financial Economics*, 20, 347–376.

McWilliams, V. B., 1990, "Managerial Share Ownership and the Stock Price Effects of Antitakeover Amendment Proposals," *Journal of Finance*, 45, 1627–1640.

Mikkelson, W. H. and M. Megan Partch, 1989, "Managers' Voting Rights and Corporate Control," *Journal of Financial Economics*, 25, 263–290.

Mørck, R., A. Shleifer and R. W. Vishny, 1988, "Characteristics of Targets of Hostile and Friendly Takeovers," In A. J. Auerbach (Ed.), *Corporate Takeovers: Causes and Consequences*, National Bureau of Economic Research, Chicago, IL, pp. 101–129.

Mørck, R., A. Shleifer and R. W. Vishny, 1989, "Alternative Mechanisms for Corporate Control," *American Economic Review*, 89, 842–852.

Myers, S. C., 1977, "Determinants of Corporate Borrowing," *Journal of Financial Economics*, 5, 147–176.

Nathan, K. S. and T. B. O'Keefe, 1989, "The Rise in Takeover Premiums: An Exploratory Study," *Journal of Financial Economics*, 23, 101–119.

Palepu, K. G., 1986, "Predicting Takeover Targets: A Methodological and Empirical Analysis," *Journal of Accounting and Economics*, 8, 3–35.

Pound, J., 1987, "The Effects of Antitakeover Amendments on Takeover Activity: Some Direct Evidence," *Journal of Law and Economics*, 30, 353–367.

Putnam, B. H., 1991, "Regulation and Capital Market Efficiency: Some Evidence from the U.S. Credit Crunch of 1990," *Journal of Applied Corporate Finance*, 4, 92–95.

Romano, R., 1987, "The Political Economy of Takeover Statutes," *Virginia Law Review*, 73, 111–199.

Romano, R., 1993, "Competition for Corporate Charters and the Lesson of Takeover Statutes," *Fordham Law Review*, 61, 843–864.

Ryngaert, M., 1988, "The Effect of Poison Pill Securities on Shareholder Wealth," *Journal of Financial Economics* 20, 377–417.

Securities and Exchange Commission, 1986, *Noninvestment Grade Debt As a Source of Tender Offer Financing*, Office of the Chief Economist, U.S. Securities and Exchange Commission, Washington, DC.

Shivdasani, A., 1993, "Board Composition, Ownership Structure, and Hostile Takeovers," *Journal of Accounting and Economics*, 16, 167–198.

Szewczyk, S. H. and G. T. Tsetsekos, 1992, "State Intervention in the Market for Corporate Control: The Case of Pennsylvania Senate Bill 1310," *Journal of Financial Economics*, 31, 3–24.

Weston, J. F., K. S. Chung and S. E. Hoag, 1990, *Mergers, Restructuring, and Corporate Control*, Prentice-Hall, New York, NY.

White, H., 1980, "A Heteroskedasticity-Consistent Covariance Matrix Estimator and a Direct Test for Heteroskedasticity," *Econometrica*, 48, 817–838.

Yago, G., 1991, "The Credit Crunch: A Regulatory Squeeze on Growth Capital," *Journal of Applied Corporate Finance*, 4, 96–100.

Chapter 13

BOARD CLASSIFICATION AND MANAGERIAL ENTRENCHMENT: EVIDENCE FROM THE MARKET FOR CORPORATE CONTROL[*]

THOMAS W. BATES

Department of Finance, Eller College of Management, University of Arizona, Tucson, Arizona, USA

DAVID A. BECHER

Department of Finance, LeBow College of Business, Drexel University, Philadelphia, Philadelphia, USA

MICHAEL L. LEMMON

Department of Finance, David Eccles School of Business, University of Utah, Salt Lake City, Utah, USA

Contents

* We thank an anonymous referee, Jeffrey Coles, Olubunmi Faleye, Michael Hertzel, Mark Huson, Kathy Kahle, Jim Linck, Bill Maxwell, Wayne Mikkelson, Scott Schaefer, and seminar participants at the University of Alberta, the University of Alabama, Arizona State University, Hong Kong University of Science and Technology, Lehigh University, National University of Singapore, Rice University, Simon Fraser University, Singapore Management University, the Stockholm School of Economics, the University of Utah, and the Empirical Research in Corporate Finance Conference at the University of Oregon for comments that were helpful in developing this work. We also thank Kinjal Desai and Wenjing Ouyang for their research assistance.

This article originally appeared in the *Journal of Financial Economics*, Vol. 87, pp. 656–677 (2008).
Corporate Takeovers, Volume 2
Edited by B. Espen Eckbo
Copyright © 2007 Elsevier B.V. All rights reserved.
DOI: 10.1016/B978-0-12-381982-6.00014-8

Abstract

This paper considers the relation between board classification, takeover activity, and transaction outcomes for a panel of firms between 1990 and 2002. Target board classification does not change the likelihood that a firm, once targeted, is ultimately acquired. Moreover, shareholders of targets with a classified board realize bid returns that are equivalent to those of targets with a single class of directors, but receive a higher proportion of total bid surplus. Board classification does reduce the likelihood of receiving a takeover bid, however, the economic effect of bid deterrence on the value of the firm is quite small. Overall, the evidence is inconsistent with the conventional wisdom that board classification is an antitakeover device that facilitates managerial entrenchment.

Keywords

merger, acquisition, takeovers, classified board, staggered board, boards, directors, antitakeover provisions, corporate governance, antitakeover provisions

JEL classification: G30, G34, K22

1. Introduction

Board classification is a corporate governance structure that staggers the annual election of director slates. In the absence of a classified board, all continuing and nominated directors of a corporation stand for election annually. In contrast, corporations with a classified board, also referred to as a staggered board, assemble directors into distinct classes (typically three) with successive annual elections occurring only for a single class of directors. Therefore, under a classified structure, directors are elected to terms equal in length to the number of classes. Board classification is a common feature of US corporate governance today. For example, among the approximately 3000 publicly traded firms covered by the Investor Responsibility Research Center (IRRC) between 1990 and 2002, a majority have a classified board.[1]

The literature has largely emphasized the antitakeover properties of classified boards when motivating their adoption and maintenance. For example, in establishing a corporate governance index, Gompers et al. (2003) suggest that board classification is "one of the few provisions that clearly retains some deterrent value in modern takeover battles." Daines and Klausner (2001) also reason that board classification has "no justification except to ward off challenges for control." A classified board presents a formidable obstacle to a change-in-control bid contested by target management because staggered elections make it impossible for a hostile bidder to remove a majority of incumbent directors without waiting for a minimum of two elections cycles.[2] Therefore, as summarized in Bebchuk and Cohen (2005), target board classification can raise the expected costs of bidders contemplating a hostile change-in-control bid. While firms can employ a number of alternative antitakeover provisions, arguably none presents as prohibitive of an expense for prospective acquirers.

Evidence in Bebchuk and Cohen (2005) and Bebchuk et al. (2004) indicates that board classification is systematically associated with lower firm value. The general supposition in these papers is that board classification insulates management from the market for corporate control and is therefore a causal antecedent to agency conflict in firms. Consistent with this view, Faleye (2007) finds that firms with classified boards have a lower sensitivity of both chief executive officer (CEO) pay and CEO turnover to firm performance. Masulis et al. (2007) also show that bidding firms with classified boards have lower announcement period returns in takeover transactions. This evidence has sparked a vigorous academic and policy debate, with some calling for a wholesale abolition of the structure on the grounds that it facilitates managerial entrenchment. Despite these claims, however, the extant literature offers no direct evidence that target board classification is reliably associated with characteristics of

---

[1] The IRRC governance database has 10,121 total firm and year observations between 1990 and 2002 of which 5911 observations are recorded as having a classified board structure.

[2] The proxy process and interval required to replace incumbent directors depends upon the ability of shareholders to call special meetings and replace directors without cause, conditions typically restricted in firms with a classified board. See Bebchuk et al. (2002) for a summary of these constraints.

the market for corporate control. Our study fills this void. Specifically, this paper evaluates the relation between board classification and the likelihood of takeover bidding, bid outcomes, and concomitant shareholder wealth effects.

The first component of the analysis considers whether target board classification is reliably associated with bid outcomes or self-dealing by target managers in observed change-in-control bids. Over 10% of the initial bids for targets with a classified board in our sample elicit a hostile response from management, roughly twice the rate of bid hostility (4.94%) for targets with a single class of directors. Controlling for transaction and target firm characteristics, however, we find that targets with a classified board are ultimately acquired at an equivalent rate as targets with a single class of directors. This result is not consistent with the premise that board classification is systematically used by entrenched managers to defeat takeover bids.

To evaluate whether board classification enables incumbent managers to extract private benefits during change-in-control events, we identify the posttransaction employment outcomes for target CEOs following the completed transactions in our sample. The CEOs of targets with classified boards are employed by the acquiring firm, either as a manager or director, at a statistically equivalent rate as the CEOs of targets with a single class of directors. This finding does not comport with the notion that board classification facilitates self-dealing by incumbent managers during takeover bids.

Finally, we analyze the shareholder wealth effects associated with observed change-in control bids conditioned on the target's use of a classified board. Controlling for bid and target firm characteristics, board classification has an insignificant impact on the cumulative abnormal returns (CARs) realized by target shareholders estimated either over the bid announcement period or from the bid announcement through the eventual culmination of a transaction. Announcement CARs for bidding shareholders, however, are 2.7% lower in bids involving target classified boards. An analysis of the distribution of transaction surplus between target and bidding shareholders in completed deals indicates that target shareholders of firms with classified boards receive a larger proportional share of the total value gains to mergers relative to the gains to target shareholders of firms with a single class of directors. Overall, the evidence is inconsistent with the view that board classification is associated with managerial entrenchment and instead suggests that classification improves the relative bargaining power of target managers on behalf of their constituent shareholders.

The second component of our analysis evaluates the extent of any bid deterrence attributable to classified boards. Controlling for the potentially endogenous decision to maintain a classified board, classification is associated with a 1.0% reduction in the likelihood of receiving a takeover bid. This effect is substantial relative to the observed bid frequency of 3.6% for the subsample of targets with classified boards, leading us to infer that deterrence is the primary channel through which a classified board alters a firm's exposure to the market for corporate control. We parameterize the hypothetical gain to eliminating bid deterrence for firms with a classified board and benchmark these potential gains to the differences in value between firms with and without classified boards. In keeping with prior research, we find that the average value of firms with a classified board, as proxied by Tobin's Q, is approximately 11% lower than the average Q for firms with a single class of directors. Our analysis indicates, however, that bid deterrence can explain only about one tenth of the difference in firm value between firms with and without classified boards.

This work makes several contributions to the existing literature. First, the evidence suggests that classified boards neither entrench managers in the context of takeover bidding nor facilitate managerial self-dealing in completed bids. Given this evidence, we question the basis for calls to enhance the standard of regulatory or judicial scrutiny over transactions involving targets with classified boards. Second, our analysis identifies a significant bid deterrence effect associated with classified board provisions, however, deterrence provides an incomplete explanation for the differences in firm value commonly attributed to managerial entrenchment. Furthermore, given the observed bid outcomes for the transactions in our study, it remains unclear whether the takeover bids that might obtain in the absence of board classification would be efficient for target shareholders. Finally, while board classification is a potent antitakeover mechanism, it is just one of many factors commonly indexed when evaluating the quality of corporate governance and the extent of shareholder rights in corporations. The results of this paper challenge the common perception that these factors, independently or as indexed, provide a reliable proxy for managerial entrenchment or a firm's exposure to the market for corporate control. Given a notable dearth of research concerning the possible shareholder benefits of classified boards that might accrue outside of the market for corporate control, our results suggest that a circumspect policy approach be applied when considering the adoption or dissolution of this common governance provision.[3]

The remainder of this paper is structured as follows. In Section 2, we summarize the theoretical literature concerning board classification and characteristics of the market for corporate control. Section 3 reviews the empirical literature on board classification, change-in-control transactions, and firm value, and it highlights corollary policy implications. Section 4 describes the sampling of firm-year observations for governance characteristics and takeover activity. In Section 5 we examine bid outcomes and the wealth gains to target and bidding shareholders conditioned on the target firm's use of a classified board. In Section 6 we estimate the likelihood of receiving a takeover bid as a function of board classification and parameterize the value loss attributable to bid deterrence. We provide concluding remarks in Section 7.

---

[3] Other explanations for the economic efficiency of board classification also exist. For example, extended director terms might promote autonomy between board members and management. Extended and overlapping director terms can also ensure continuity in decision making in instances involving managerial turnover or for firms with investments requiring long-horizon or sequential investment decisions.

2. Theory: board classification and the market for corporate control

Board classification can affect the market for corporate control in two ways. First, classification can be utilized at the discretion of target managers to negotiate with a bidder or to reject a transaction outright. Second, board classification can raise the expected cost of bids for prospective acquirers, altering the rate at which bids are observed. In this section we summarize the theoretical relation between board classification and these distinct characteristics of the market for corporate control in the context of two alternative hypotheses previously derived in the literature.

2.1. Managerial discretion

The managerial discretion hypothesis suggests that board classification facilitates, or is a byproduct of, managerial entrenchment.[4] Classification can preserve management's private benefits of control, either preemptively through bid deterrence or after a bid has been received through bid hostility and a lower incidence of bid or auction completion. Managerial discretion can also account for outcomes in friendly and completed bids. Evidence in Hartzell et al. (2004) and Wulf (2004) indicates that target managers can engage in self-dealing in negotiations with acquirers at the expense of their constituent shareholders. If board classification endows management with leverage in negotiating for private benefits, the managerial discretion hypothesis predicts that target board classification is associated with a lower incidence of explicit bid negotiation, a higher rate of self-dealing by target management in completed transactions, and lower transaction gains to target shareholders.

2.2. Shareholder interest

A second hypothesis, shareholder interest, suggests that board classification allows target management to deter opportunistic bids while improving target shareholder outcomes during merger and acquisition negotiations. Consistent with this perspective, DeAngelo and Rice (1983) and Stein (1988) infer that antitakeover provisions dissuade opportunistic bidding in instances in which the value of a firm's projects cannot be accurately conveyed to outside investors. Prior work has established the efficacy of alternative antitakeover provisions during change-in-control negotiations. For example, Comment and Schwert (1995) find that state antitakeover laws and poison pill provisions do not systematically deter bids but do increase the premiums received by target shareholders. Furthermore, evidence in Harford (2003) and Yermack (2004) suggests

---

[4] Our characterization of the managerial discretion hypothesis in the context of change-in-control bidding is drawn from a substantial volume of prior work first summarized in DeAngelo and Rice (1983). Bebchuk and Cohen (2005) provide a recent discussion of the potential for managerial entrenchment afforded by board classification.

that external incentives could be sufficient to mitigate managerial self-dealing and encourage directors (particularly unaffiliated directors) to proactively represent the interests of target shareholder during a change-in-control bid.

If board classification is used to increase the bargaining power of target managers, the shareholder interest hypothesis predicts that board classification is used to enhance the share of transaction surplus allocated to target shareholders in change-in-control bids. By raising the expected costs of bidding for prospective acquirers, however, the shareholder interest hypothesis also suggests that board classification is associated with a degree of bid deterrence as low value potential suitors refrain from bidding.

3. Literature and policy review

In this section we summarize the literature relating board classification to the value of the firm and characteristics of the market for corporate control. We then review current policy recommendations concerning the adoption and maintenance of board classification generally and in the context of corporate control bids.

3.1. Board classification, firm value, and the market for corporate control

Gompers et al. (2003) identify a systematic empirical relation between an index of 24 corporate governance characteristics, including board classification, and firm value and stock returns. In follow-on work, Bebchuk et al. (2004) suggest that a six factor entrenchment index that includes board classification yields the most significant negative correlation with Tobin's Q and long-run equity returns. Bebchuk and Cohen (2005) directly examine the cross-sectional relationship between board classification and firm value, and they find that board classification is negatively correlated with industry-adjusted Tobin's Q. In interpreting their findings, these authors infer that board classification insulates management from the market for corporate control and, by extension, exacerbates principal-agent conflict between stockholders and managers. In related research, Klock et al. (2005) find that the cost of corporate debt is decreasing in a firm's use of various antitakeover provisions, including board classification. Given their evidence, they conclude that these governance features reduce the exposure of debt holders to change-in-control transactions.

Complementary work has considered various channels through which agency problems associated with board classification might manifest in corporations. For example, Masulis et al. (2007) find that announcement period returns are 0.57–0.91% lower for bidding firms with a classified board. They attribute this finding to the self-serving behavior of acquiring firm managers, who themselves are insulated from the market for corporate control. In keeping with the notion that board classification facilitates managerial entrenchment, Faleye (2007) finds that classification reduces the probability of forced CEO turnover, is associated with a lower sensitivity of CEO turnover to firm performance, and is correlated with a lower sensitivity of CEO compensation to changes in shareholder wealth. Faleye, however, censors turnover observations attributable to mergers and acquisitions and therefore does not consider the efficacy of the implied mechanism of managerial discipline, that is, the market for corporate control.

Despite broad support for the notion that board classification insulates managers from the market for corporate control, the empirical evidence relating this governance feature to the likelihood that a firm receives a takeover bid is mixed. Pound (1987) identifies a lower incidence of takeover bids for firms adopting both supermajority and classified board amendments between 1974 and 1984. Alternatively, Ambrose and Megginson (1992) find that the likelihood of takeover bidding between 1981 and 1986 is insignificantly correlated with board classification.

Evidence on the relation between board classification and shareholder welfare in the context of observed takeover bids is also incomplete. Pound (1987) finds that 68% of target firms adopting classified boards and supermajority provisions resist bids, compared with 38% for a control sample. Announcement period returns to target shareholders, however, do not differ across the two groups of firms, leading Pound to conclude that these antitakeover provisions fail to improve target shareholder welfare in takeover contests. Case law concerning the use of antitakeover provisions developed substantially between 1985 and 1990 beginning with *Moran v. Household International*.[5] This and subsequent decisions bolstered the ability of target management to utilize antitakeover defenses in the context of a contested bid, suggesting that any antitakeover properties associated with classified boards should be more pronounced after 1989. Accordingly, Bebchuk et al. (2002) examine 92 hostile bids between 1996 and 2000. Of the 45 targets with classified boards, 60% (27) remain independent in the 9 months following a bid announcement, while 32% (16) of the 47 target firms without a classified board remain independent. Bebchuk, Coates, and Subramanian also do not find that premiums of hostile bids for firms with and without a classified board are significantly different. Given this evidence they infer that, conditioned on bid hostility, classification (particularly in conjunction with a poison pill) increases the likelihood of target independence but does not yield significantly higher premiums for target shareholders.

In contrast Heron and Lie (2006) find that board classification has an insignificant effect on the likelihood of bid success or target shareholder returns for a sample of hostile and unsolicited acquisition attempts announced between 1985 and 1998. Gordon (2002) also notes that the sample used in Bebchuk, Coates, and Subramanian omits bid outcomes for a far larger subset of friendly bids, deals in which managers could have successfully leveraged antitakeover mechanisms to either negotiate higher value deals for target shareholders or private benefits for themselves. Given this omission, it is difficult to accurately draw inferences regarding the ex ante shareholder welfare implications of board classification using only hostile change-in-control contests.

---

[5] See *Moran v. Household International Inc*. 500 A.2d 1346 DelSupCt (1985). We refer interested readers to the text of Bebchuk et al. (2002) and the appendix of Comment and Schwert (1995) for summaries of the case law concerning antitakeover provisions.

3.2. Board classification: a policy perspective

Board classification has become the subject of increasing investor scrutiny. Institutional Shareholder Services (ISS) provides a blanket recommendation in its 2006 proxy voting guidelines that its membership vote against proposals to classify a board or alter board structure in the context of a change-in-control bid and vote for proposals to repeal classified board provisions. ISS also recommends withholding votes for directors who have ignored shareholder resolutions to declassify, and ISS lowers its governance score for firms with a classified board. The basis for the ISS position is summarized by Patrick McGurn, senior vice president, who states that studies and empirical evidence show "pretty conclusively that unlike poison pills, there is no evidence that boards use a classified structure to enhance shareholder value. In fact the opposite appears to be true." (See Wall Street Journal, 2005) ISS is not alone in its critique. The largest public pension fund in the US, CalPERS, has targeted firms including Sears, Roebuck & Company and the Maytag Corporation, for shareholder votes to remove board classification from their corporate charters. The proxy voting guidelines of various mutual fund companies including TIAA-CREF and Fidelity Investments also call for voting against the adoption and for the removal of classified board provisions. The TIAA-CREF guidelines, for example, note that "A classified-board structure at a public company can be a significant impediment to a free market for corporate control."

Reform minded critics have also sought relief from the perceived entrenchment properties of board classification through the courts. Bebchuk et al. (2002) suggest that the election of a single slate of directors proposed by a hostile bidder is equivalent to a successful shareholder referendum on the bid. In this context, they argue for changing the legal rules to mandate the redemption of a poison pill following such an election and to allow the bidder to proceed with a bid. While such a proposal would eliminate the possibility of entrenchment, the revocation of an antitakeover feature, precisely in the context of a contested bid, can have an unintended consequence of reducing overall bid quality (e.g., Gordon, 2002).

In the wake of recent institutional and academic scrutiny, proposals to eliminate classified board provisions from corporate charters are at an all time high. ISS reports that as of October 2005 more than 65 firms had a repeal proposed in the annual proxy, while the proportion of firms covered by ISS with classified boards declined from 55.10% in 2003 to 52.60% in 2005 (see Institutional Shareholder Services, 2005). In response to external pressure, directors and management sponsored the majority of board-declassification proposals through the first half of 2005.

4. Data and summary statistics

Our sample includes US public corporations covered in at least one of the volumes published by the IRRC between 1990 and 2002. The IRRC volumes include information on a set of 24 governance provisions for firms in the Standard & Poor's 1500 and other major US corporations and are published for the years 1990, 1993, 1995, 1998,

2000, and 2002. This sample consists of 3121 unique firms and 10,121 firm-year observations. We match firm-year observations from IRRC to Compustat and retain those with nonmissing book value of assets. Following Gompers et al. (2003) we assume that a firm's governance provisions (excluding classification) remain in place from the publication date of an IRRC volume until the next publication date. Applying the requirement of nonmissing assets data for intervening years our panel consists of 20,335 firm-year observations for 3087 unique firms from 1990 to 2002.

Data on the year of adoption for board classification is obtained from IRRC. In the absence of IRRC information, we rely on Security and Exchange Commission filings from Edgar or on the fiche Q files from 1981 forward. In the event that we cannot identify the adoption date we assume that the firm classified its board at the initial public offering proxied by the first trading date on the Center for Research in Securities Prices (CRSP).

4.1. Sampling takeover attempts

Takeover attempts involving IRRC firms are obtained from the mergers and acquisitions database maintained by Securities Data Corporation (SDC). To account for multibid auctions and follow-on bidding we sample transactions from SDC announced from 2 years prior (1988) through 2 years following (2004) the panel interval. Targets are matched to CRSP/Compustat GVKEY identifiers using reported SDC target CUSIPs. Given variation in SDC and Compustat CUSIP codes we verify positive matches comparing the SDC reported company name against the historical name structure on CRSP. For a subset of targets not matched by CUSIP, we match using the target corporation's name from SDC and the name structure on CRSP.

Our sample of 3087 IRRC firms is associated with 1390 merger and acquisitions transaction reports on SDC between 1988 and 2004. These deals are screened to include only deal forms coded as "mergers", "acquisitions", and "acquisitions of majority interest" and exclude spin-off "acquisitions" where the acquirers are the firm's own shareholders. To discriminate between the economic effects of initial and follow-on bids, we define an auction sequence following Bates and Lemmon (2003). A bid is considered an initial bid if no bid for the target is identified for 365 calendar days before the announcement. Bids are part of an auction if announced within 365 calendar days of a prior bid announcement for a target. In the event that there is no follow-on bidding, an auction consists of only a single initial bid. We retain initial bids announced between 1990 and 2002. To ensure that we observe a complete auction sequence, we retain follow-on bids announced after 2002 provided the auction was initiated before the end of 2002. Initial bids in each auction are matched to the merged IRRC/Compustat data by calendar year. The final data set consists of 757 initial bids and 103 follow-on bids (860 bids in total).

Table 1 summarizes a subset of the governance characteristics compiled by IRRC for each sample year that corresponds to the publication of an IRRC volume. We refer readers to Appendix A in Gompers et al. (2003) for further detail regarding the governance features covered by IRRC. The governance characteristics in Table 1 are

Table 1

Corporate governance provisions

The table summarizes a subset of the governance characteristics for 10,121 firm-year observations obtained from the Investor Responsibility Research Center (IRRC) volumes published for the years 1990, 1993, 1995, 1998, 2000, and 2002. This sample includes US public corporations covered in at least one of the volumes and includes 3121 unique firms. Firm-year observations are screened to include only observations in which the book value of total assets for a firm, matched in calendar time to the publication of the IRRC volume, is nonmissing from Compustat.

	1990	1993	1995	1998	2000	2002
Number of observations	1396	1445	1493	1883	1696	1849
Entrenchment provisions						
Board classification	0.565	0.582	0.595	0.575	0.580	0.600
Poison pill	0.513	0.535	0.530	0.512	0.544	0.550
Super majority	0.169	0.182	0.173	0.142	0.154	0.158
Limits to bylaw amendment	0.142	0.155	0.156	0.176	0.194	0.222
Limits to charter amendment	0.032	0.031	0.031	0.029	0.032	0.024
Golden parachute	0.497	0.527	0.535	0.554	0.637	0.674
Other provisions						
Limited special meetings	0.239	0.287	0.310	0.331	0.365	0.479
Limited written consent	0.242	0.282	0.311	0.318	0.343	0.437
Blank check	0.766	0.794	0.847	0.874	0.890	0.903
Dual share classes	0.076	0.082	0.083	0.107	0.119	0.118
Business combination law	0.850	0.884	0.889	0.903	0.913	0.916
No cumulative vote	0.172	0.156	0.142	0.117	0.108	0.094
Fair price law	0.329	0.337	0.324	0.262	0.251	0.209
G-index	8.933	9.184	9.284	8.748	8.971	9.034
Delaware incorporation	0.479	0.505	0.527	0.574	0.575	0.605

delineated by whether or not they are included in the entrenchment index compiled by Bebchuk et al. (2004). The majority of firms (56.5–60%) utilize a classified board. Among the other entrenchment provisions, poison pills and golden parachutes are also adopted by a majority of firms, while supermajority provisions and limits to bylaw and charter amendments are less pervasive. Of the other governance provisions, blank check preferred stock and business combination laws are the most prevalent features. The average value of the Gompers et al. (2003) G-index, a cumulative index of 24 governance provisions, is about nine. Between 48% and 60% of the firms are incorporated in Delaware in a given year. In an unreported analysis we examine intrafirm variation in the G-index and its associated provisions. The average standard deviation of the G-index in our sample is 0.54 indicating that elements of the G-index are stable within firms over time. The intrafirm variation in the G-index observed in our sample is driven mainly by variation in three provisions: golden parachutes (0.121), poison pills (0.083), and limits on special meetings (0.056).

Panel A of Table 2 presents summary statistics of deal characteristics obtained from SDC transaction summaries, delineated by target board structure. The statistical

Table 2

Summary of bid and target firm characteristics in merger bids 1990–2002

The table summarizes transaction characteristics of 860 acquisition bids announced and either completed or withdrawn between 1990 and 2002 for firms covered by Investor Responsibility Research Center. Panel A summarizes bid frequency, bid rank, and general bid characteristics from Securities Data Corporation (SDC). Bid frequency and characteristics are reported only for first bids in auction sequences (757 bids). An auction is composed of all bids for a target beginning with the first observed bid and including any successive bids made within 365 calendar days of a prior announcement. Deal value is reported by SDC. Toehold is the bidding firm's ownership in the target at the announcement date. Bids receive a hostile classification from SDC if target managers rebuff the offer. A bid is equity if any portion of compensation paid to target shareholders includes bidder equity. Target termination fee is an indicator variable equal to one if the bid includes a target payable termination fee. Tender offer is an indicator variable equal to one for initial bids structured as a tender offer and zero otherwise. Bid completion is an indicator variable equal to one when for completed initial bids and zero if the initial bid is withdrawn. Target firm characteristics are reported in Panel B and are computed using firm data from the fiscal year immediately preceding an initial bid in an auction. Firm size is the log of total assets, and debt includes short- and long-term debt issues. Tobin's Q is proxied by market-to-book measured as total assets minus book equity plus market equity divided by total assets for the target. Ownership is measured as the proportional holding of equity cash flow rights for target chief executive officers (CEOs) and officers and directors measured in the fiscal year prior to an initial bid. The positions of the CEO and Chairman of the board are identified in fiscal year prior to an initial bid. Where appropriate we report statistical medians in parentheses and the number of observations for missing variables in brackets. The symbols *,**, and *** indicate that the subsample means (medians) for the classified board subsample is significantly different from that of the no-classified board subsample at the 10%, 5%, and 1% level, respectively.

	Targets with a classified board	Targets without a classified board
Panel A. Bid characteristics		
Bid frequency	3.60%	3.86%
Bid rank in auction sequence:		
1	428	329
2	55	33
3	7	6
4	1	0
5	1	0
Number of days in auction	171.05	171.61
	(134)	(126)
Deal value: (millions of dollars)	3677.28	3671.98
[Number of observations]	(1088.40)	(951.10)
	[392]	[305]
Toehold at announcement	1.12%	1.58%
	(0.00)	(0.00)
Bid hostility	10.43%	4.94%***
Proportion of equity bids	53.50%	61.42%
Target payable termination fee	51.64%	57.14%
Proportion of bids structured as tender offer	19.16%	15.20%
Bid completion	71.96%	76.29%

(Continued)

Table 2 (*Continued*)

	Targets with a classified board	Targets without a classified board
Panel B. Target characteristics		
Size (log total assets)	7.32	7.09**
	(7.16)	(6.84)**
Debt/assets	0.29	0.27
	(0.26)	(0.25)
Market-to-book (Tobin's Q)	1.50	1.67**
	(1.22)	(1.23)
CEO ownership	2.32%	3.89**
	(0.52%)	(0.55%)
	[423]	[317]
Officer and director ownership	9.24%	11.83%**
	(4.07%)	(4.70%)*
	[426]	[321]
CEO is also chairman (CEO duality)	68.72%	68.20%
	[422]	[327]

significance of differences in means (medians) between targets with and without classified boards is defined by asterisks in the far right column. Firms with a classified board receive 428 initial takeover bids during the sample period corresponding to 3.60% of the firm-year observations, compared with 329 bids or 3.86% of the firm-year observations for firms with a single class of directors. Follow-on bids in an auction sequence are slightly more common for firms with classified boards. Specifically, 13.01% of bids (64) involving classified targets are follow-on bids in an auction, while 10.59% (39) are follow-on bids for targets with a single class of directors. The average (median) number of days from the announcement to the conclusion of an auction is 171.05 days (134 days) for targets with a classified board and 171.61 days (126 days) for targets with a single class of directors.

Differences in mean (median) deal value and toeholds are not significantly different from zero. Bid hostility is observed at twice the rate for targets with classified boards (10.43%) compared with targets with a single class of directors (4.94%). Consistent with the higher rate of hostility, bids for targets with classified boards are less likely to involve termination fees or bidder equity and more likely to be tender offers. Approximately 71% of the initial bids for targets with classified boards are completed, somewhat lower than the 76% completion rate for targets with a single class of directors. With the exception of bid hostility, however, none of the differences in bid characteristics or completion rates is significantly different from zero across the two groups.

Panel B of Table 2 summarizes accounting and ownership characteristics of the target firms in our sample computed in the fiscal year prior to the initial bid. Accounting data are compiled from Compustat and ownership data are collected from the firms' proxy statements. Targets with classified boards are larger in terms of total assets compared with targets with a single class of directors. Differences in debt-to-assets are not significant. We measure Tobin's Q as the market-to-book assets ratio for the firm. The mean value of Tobin's Q for targets with classified boards is 1.50, significantly lower than the corresponding value for targets with a single class of directors (1.67). Differences in median Q are not significant.

The mean (median) CEO ownership of targets with classified boards is 2.32% (0.52%) compared with 3.89% (0.55%) for CEOs of targets with a single class of directors. A similar difference is observed for the total ownership of all officers and directors. The average (median) ownership of officers and directors is 9.24% (4.07%) of targets with classified boards, compared with 11.83% (4.70%) of those without. The differences in ownership characteristics are statistically different from zero with the exception of the median CEO ownership for the two groups of firms. Finally, we also identify whether a target's CEO serves as the chairman of the board, commonly referred to as CEO duality. This feature is observed in 68.72% of the targets with classified boards and 68.20% of targets with a single class of directors with the difference between the subsamples insignificantly different from zero.

5. Target board classification and the outcomes of observed takeover bids

In this section we examine whether board classification of targets is systematically associated with the outcomes of observed takeover bids. First, we investigate whether board classification is correlated with the likelihood that a bid, once initiated, results in a successful change-in-control event. Second, we consider whether board classification facilitates self-dealing by target managers in the context of completed bids. Finally, we examine whether target board classification is reliably associated with the wealth effects realized by target and bidding shareholders during change-in-control events.

5.1. Bid and auction completion

As shown in Table 2, initial bids for targets with classified boards elicit a hostile response at roughly twice the rate observed for initial bids involving targets with a single class of directors. A plausible explanation for the positive relation between board classification and bid hostility is that entrenched managers utilize the classified-board structure to repel change-in-control bids and preserve their private benefits of control (e.g., Bebchuk et al., 2002). Alternatively, consistent with Stulz (1988) and Schwert (2000) bid hostility could simply reflect the willingness and ability of target management to negotiate publicly for higher bid values.

To consider these divergent perspectives, Table 3 reports the results of logistic regressions modeling the likelihood of completing a bid or auction as a function of target board structure, bid disposition, and other governance, bid, and target characteristics. Of the 757 initial bids 559 (73.8%) are completed, while 590 (78%) of the auctions ultimately result in a completed transaction. We report marginal effects for coefficients in brackets, which

Table 3

Logistic regressions modeling the completion of an initial acquisition bid or auction

The table reports logistic regression modeling the likelihood that an initial bid or auction in the sample is completed. The sample consists of 757 initial merger bids and auctions for targets between 1990 and 2002 for firms covered in the Investors Responsibility Research Center handbook with total assets data available on Compustat. In each model the dependent variable is an indicator equal to one if an initial bid (or auction in Model 3) is ultimately completed and is set equal to zero otherwise. Target classified board is an indicator variable equal to one if the target firm employs the governance feature. The net G-index is the G-index reported by Gompers et al. (2003) minus one if the firm employs a classified board. Bids receive a hostile classification from Securities Data Corporation if target managers reject the offer. Target characteristics are computed using firm data from the fiscal year immediately preceding an initial bid in an auction. Firm size is the log of total assets, and debt includes long-term debt and current maturities. Tobin's Q is proxied by the market-to-book assets ratio measured as total assets minus book equity plus market equity divided by total assets for the target. Toehold is the bidder's ownership stake in the target at the announcement date. Target termination fee is an indicator variable equal to one if the bid includes a target payable termination fee. Tender offer is an indicator variable equal to one if the initial bid is structured as a tender offer. A bid is equity if any portion of compensation paid to target shareholders includes bidder equity. Ownership is measured as the proportional holding of equity cash flow rights for target officers and directors measured in the fiscal year prior to an initial bid. The position of the chief executive officer (CEO) and chairman of the board are identified in fiscal year prior to an initial bid. p-Values based on robust standard errors are in parentheses, and marginal effects computed at the mean values of the independent variables are provided in brackets. Marginal effects are the change in the probability of completing an acquisition bid for a one standard deviation change in a continuous variable or a shift from zero to one for an indicator variable. For interacted variables we report the mean interaction effect computed as in Ai and Norton (2003).

	Model 1	Model 2	Model 3
Bidding interval	First bids only	First bids only	Auctions
Number of observations	750	733	733
Intercept	1.286	0.657	2.259
	(0.019)	(0.314)	(0.001)
Target classified board	0.020	0.181	0.113
	(0.920)	(0.409)	(0.628)
	[0.004]	[0.029]	[0.016]
Net G-index	0.013	−0.036	0.013
	(0.725)	(0.424)	(0.753)
	[0.002]	[−0.006]	[0.002]
Hostile	−1.510	−1.011	−1.538
	(0.002)	(0.108)	(0.004)
	[−0.343]	[−0.201]	[−0.303]
Hostile × classified board	−1.076	−1.555	−0.422
	(0.090)	(0.041)	(0.506)
	[−0.240]	[−0.335]	[−0.067]
Size (log total assets)	−0.042	−0.114	−0.119
	(0.452)	(0.068)	(0.062)
	[−0.008]	[−0.018]	[−0.017]
Debt/assets	−0.316	−0.350	−0.681
	(0.409)	(0.424)	(0.120)
	[−0.059]	[−0.056]	[−0.096]

(Continued)

Table 3 (*Continued*)

Bidding interval Number of observations	Model 1 First bids only 750	Model 2 First bids only 733	Model 3 Auctions 733
Market-to-book (Tobin's Q)	0.171 (0.200) [0.032]	−0.113 (0.360) [−0.018]	0.076 (0.567) [0.011]
Toehold		0.015 (0.287) [0.002]	
Target payable termination fee		1.064 (0.000) [0.177]	
Tender offer		1.649 (0.000) [0.192]	
Stock deal		1.914 (0.000) [0.334]	
Officer and director ownership		0.935 (0.250) [0.151]	0.929 (0.246) [0.130]
CEO duality		0.161 (0.474) [0.026]	0.211 (0.350) [0.030]
Chi-squared	56.67	145.31	50.62
(Probability chi-squared)	(0.000)	(0.000)	(0.000)
Pseudo r^2	0.084	0.249	0.075

represent the change in the probability of bid or auction completion for a change in an indicator variable from zero to one or a one standard deviation change in a continuous variable, holding all other variables constant at their mean values. For interacted variables we compute the marginal effects following Ai and Norton (2003) and report the mean value of the marginal effect. For the statistical significance of the coefficient estimates we report p-values based on robust standard errors in parentheses. Missing firm-level data impart sample restrictions across the specifications.

Model 1 of Table 3 examines the likelihood that an initial bid is completed as a function of the target firm's governance characteristics and bid hostility. We model the effects of board classification with an indicator variable equal to one for targets with a classified board and zero otherwise. We aggregate the remaining governance characteristics using a net G-index computed as the Gompers et al. (2003) governance index minus one for targets with a classified board and equal to the G-index for targets without classified boards. The model also incorporates control variables for target size (log of total assets), leverage, and the market-to-book ratio, all measured in the fiscal year prior to the takeover bid.

The coefficient on the classified board variable in Model 1 is insignificantly different from zero, indicating that the likelihood of observing a completed initial bid is equivalent for targets with and without classified boards. Notably, the net G-index is also uncorrelated with the likelihood of completing a bid, indicating that indexed governance features commonly associated with managerial entrenchment are not reliably associated with the likelihood of initial bid completion. In an otherwise identical unreported specification we replace the net G-index with the independent elements of the entrenchment index. None of the coefficients on board classification or the other elements of the entrenchment index are statistically significant in this specification. The elements of the entrenchment index are also not jointly significant.

Model 1 of Table 3 also includes an indicator variable equal to one for initial bids that are met with a hostile response by target management, as well as an interaction term that isolates the joint effect of board classification and hostility on the likelihood of completion. The negative and significant (p-value <0.01) coefficient on hostility suggests that hostile bids are 34.3% less likely to be completed relative to unsolicited or friendly bids. The term interacting hostility and target board classification is negative (p-value $= 0.09$) and the effect is economically large. The incremental effect of a classified board in the context of a hostile bid suggests an additional 24% reduction in the likelihood of initial bid completion for this subset of target firms. None of the coefficients on the control variables are significantly different from zero.

Model 2 incorporates additional controls for deal characteristics, including the bidder toehold, indicator variables equal to one for deals with target payable termination fees, tender offers, and equity bids as well as target officer and director ownership and CEO duality. Officer and director ownership provides a measure of the direct incentives of target managers to accept bids. Bange and Mazzeo (2004) find that targets characterized by CEO duality are less likely to engage in public negotiations with a bidder but are more likely to be involved in completed transactions. Similar to results reported in Bates and Lemmon (2003), bids structured as tender offers, bids involving target payable termination fees, and equity bids are more likely to be completed. The coefficient estimates on bidder toeholds, ownership by officers and directors, and CEO duality are not statistically significant. In unreported specifications we replace officer and director ownership with CEO ownership, the coefficient of which is also insignificantly different from zero. The fundamental conclusions regarding board classification, bid tenor, and the likelihood of initial bid completion derived from Model 1 remain unchanged in this specification.

Overall, the results in Models 1 and 2 of Table 3 indicate that board classification of targets is not reliably associated with the likelihood of initial bid completion in cases in which bids are not met with a hostile response by target management. In contrast, hostile bids are significantly less likely to be completed and the negative incremental effect associated with the interaction between board classification and bid hostility suggests that board classification is an effective mechanism for defeating change-in-control bids opposed by incumbent management. However, completion rates for initial bids overstate the likelihood that a target firm ultimately remains independent if initial bid hostility is associated with follow-on bidding. To assess the importance of this issue, Model 3 of Table 3 examines the likelihood that a target is ultimately acquired in an auction. In this specification we control for the tenor of the initial bid, characteristics of the target firm, officer and director ownership, and CEO duality, but exclude initial bid characteristics.

The determinants of auction completion generally resemble those of initial bids. The likelihood of auction completion is not significantly associated with target board classification, but it is 35.0% lower when an initial bid receives a hostile response. In contrast to the results in Models 1 and 2, however, the coefficient on the interaction between board classification and initial bid response is insignificantly different from zero. This indicates that the likelihood of completing an auction, when the initial bid is hostile, is equivalent for targets with and without classified boards. These results are consistent with the notion that bid resistance by targets with classified boards is likely to be a precursor to follow-on negotiation instead of an indication of target management's preference for independence.

Bebchuk et al. (2002) argue that the classified board mechanism is an especially potent antitakeover device if the firm also employs a poison pill. Their reasoning is that the pill prevents the acquisition of target shares, relegating a potential acquirer to the uncertainty associated with a minimum of two proxy elections with no voting shares. However, as noted in Coates (2000) and Bebchuk and Cohen (2005), firms that do not currently have a pill in place can generally adopt one when confronted with a bid. In fact, Heron and Lie (2006) find that hostile acquisition targets with classified boards are more likely to adopt poison pill plans than firms with a single class of directors. This suggests that most change-in-control bids are effectively negotiated in the shadow of a poison pill and a joint poison pill and classified board defense for targets with classified boards. Nevertheless, to assess the independent and joint impact of a preexisting poison pill and a classified board we compute in unreported results the completion rates for auctions in our sample conditioned on whether or not the target has a classified board, a poison pill, both, or neither immediately prior to the bid. We do not find that the likelihood that a target remains independent at the culmination of an auction is significantly different across the four subsets of target firms, regardless of the tenor of the initial bid. These results cohere with Heron and Lie (2006), who also report that the combination of a classified board and poison pill defense has an insignificant effect on the likelihood of observing a successful takeover bid.

In sum, consistent with the shareholder interest hypothesis, board classification allows incumbent managers to negotiate vigorously with prospective acquirers, increasing the incidence of hostility and multibid auctions, while not perceptibly changing the likelihood that an initial bid ultimately yields a successful change-in-control transaction.

5.2. Auction completion and negotiated benefits for target management

Although board classification does not increase the likelihood that a target ultimately remains independent, it is plausible that it endows target managers with the leverage to

Table 4

Posttransaction target chief executive officer (CEO) employment with acquirer, completed bids only

The table summarizes posttransaction employment status for target CEOs involved in 618 completed acquisition bids between 1990 and 2002 for firms covered in the Investors Responsibility Research Center handbook that also have total assets data available on Compustat. The samples are delineated in the first row by whether or not the target utilized a classified-board structure. Indicator variables equal to one are constructed if the target CEO is an employee of the acquirer postmerger for a minimum of 6 months and if the target CEO is a director of the acquirer postmerger for at least 6 months. The *p*-values of the difference in the mean percentage of CEO retention (employee or director) are reported in the last column.

Posttransaction CEO employment	Targets without classified board	Targets with classified boards	*p*-Value for difference
Target CEO becomes an employee of acquirer	37.36%	37.54%	0.64
Target CEO becomes a director of acquirer	32.60%	38.71%	0.12
Number of observations	274	344	

negotiate with acquirers for self-serving side payments in completed transactions. For example, Hartzell et al. (2004) and Wulf (2004) find that target managers often receive additional benefits, negotiated directly with acquirers, in completed change-in-control transactions, the most prevalent being postacquisition employment with an acquirer. To consider this possibility, we identify instances in which target CEOs are employed by acquirers following successful change-in-control transactions. We define postacquisition employment as employment for a minimum of 6 months following the dissolution of the target determined using the 10 K and proxy filings of the acquiring firm and Factiva searches on the target CEOs name over a 48-month period following the completion of the deal.

The postacquisition employment of target CEOs is summarized in Table 4. Of the 618 completed auctions in our sample, CEOs of acquired firms with classified boards become an employee of the acquirer following 37.54% of the transactions. This is insignificantly different from the employment rate of 37.36% for the CEOs of acquired targets with a single class of directors (*p*-value = 0.64). CEOs of targets with classified boards become directors of the acquiring firm following 38.71% of the transactions, a slightly higher rate than the 32.60% incidence observed for the CEOs of targets with a single class of directors, although the difference is not statistically significant (*p*-value = 0.12). These results do not suggest that board classification is associated with a higher rate of self-dealing by target managers, as proxied by their postacquisition employment in the acquiring firm.

5.3. Board classification and shareholder wealth effects associated with takeover bids

Despite the evidence concerning postacquisition employment, incumbent management could use board classification to negotiate other (unobserved) private benefits in merger transactions at the expense of target shareholders. Alternatively, the classified board mechanism could facilitate bargaining on behalf of target shareholders. To evaluate whether board classification of target firms moderates shareholder welfare in takeover bids, we estimate changes in target and bidder shareholder wealth at the announcement of initial bids and over auction intervals. Announcement period CARs are computed as the firm's return minus the return on the CRSP value-weighted NYSE/AMEX/Nasdaq index cumulated over the 3 trading day period $\{-1, +1\}$ relative to the bid announcement. Announcement period CARs are estimated only for initial bids with nonmissing returns data over the event window yielding a sample of 749 announcement CARs for targets and 583 for the publicly traded bidders in our sample. We estimate auction CARs to target shareholders as daily net-of-market returns cumulated from 42 trading days prior to the initial bid and ending either 1 day after the withdrawal of the final bid or on the effective date of the acquisition.

Table 5 summarizes the results of ordinary least squares regressions modeling target and bidder returns. These specifications control for bidder toeholds, initial bid hostility, bid or auction completion, tender offers, and equity bids. Target firm variables include a classified board indicator and controls for the net G-index, firm size, market-to-book, leverage, and prebid stock price performance measured over the 40-day period $\{-42, -2\}$ prior to the bid announcement. In regressions of auction CARs, bid and target firm characteristics coincide with the initial bid. All specifications include year fixed effects (1990 is the excluded year).

Models 1 and 2 of Table 5 summarize regressions of target announcement period CARs. In both models the coefficient associated with target board classification is insignificantly different from zero as is the coefficient on the net G-index. The overall effect of hostility on target announcement CARs, however, is substantial. The coefficient in Model 1 indicates that target CARs are 6.2% (p-value $= 0.022$) higher for hostile bids. Model 2 estimates the joint effect of classification and hostility on target announcement CARs. The coefficient on the interaction term is insignificantly different from zero, suggesting that the announcement period CARs to target shareholders in hostile bids are similar for firms with and without classified boards. Consistent with other studies, target announcement CARs are higher in tender offers and are negatively correlated with bidder toeholds, equity bids, target firm size, the market-to-book ratio, and prebid target returns.

In Model 3 of Table 5 we estimate the determinants of target auction CARs. Auction CARs incorporate the wealth effects associated with prebid deal anticipation as well as the returns to any follow-on bidding not anticipated at the time of the announcement. Target auction CARs do not vary with target board classification but are significantly higher if the initial bid receives a hostile response. The interaction term again suggests that the effect of initial bid hostility on target abnormal returns is not significantly different for targets with a classified board. Overall, we find no evidence that board classification is reliably correlated with the returns to target shareholders.

Model 4 of Table 5 examines the determinants of announcement period bidder CARs. If board classification is systematically used by target management to negotiate

Table 5

Ordinary least squares (OLS) regressions on target and bidder announcement and auction cumulative abnormal returns (CARs)

The table presents OLS regressions of target CARs measured at the announcement of initial bids and over an auction sequence. Announcement CARs are measured as the firm's stock return less the return on the Center for Research in Security Prices (CRSP) value-weighted index beginning 1 trading day prior to the initial bid announcement and ending 1 day following the announcement date. Auction CARs are computed as the difference between the firm's stock return less the return on the CRSP value-weighted index cumulated from 42 trading days prior to the announcement of the initial bid to either 1 day after the withdrawal of the final bid in an unsuccessful auction or through the effective date of the acquisition for successful auctions. Target classified board is an indicator variables equal to one if the target firm employs the governance feature. The net G-index is the G-index reported by Gompers et al. (2003) minus one if the firm employs a classified board. Bids receive a hostile classification from Securities Data Corporation (SDC) if target managers rebuff the offer. A bid is equity if any portion of compensation paid to target shareholders includes bidder equity. Tender offer is an indicator variable equal to one obtained from SDC for those deals announced via a tender offer. Toehold is the bidder's ownership stake in the target at the announcement date. Target termination fee is an indicator variable equal to one if the bid includes a target payable termination fee. Target characteristics are computed using firm data from the fiscal year immediately preceding an initial bid in an auction. Firm size is the log of total assets, and debt includes long-term debt plus current maturities. Tobin's Q is proxied by the market-to-book assets ratio measured as total assets minus book equity plus market equity divided by total assets for the target. Prebid target abnormal return is measured as the rolling mean monthly abnormal return over the 12 months prior to the calendar year of the observation in the panel. p-Values based on robust standard errors are in parentheses.

Return estimate Daily CAR interval	Model 1 Target announcement CAR $(-1, +1)$	Model 2 Target announcement CAR $(-1, +1)$	Model 3 Target auction CAR $(-42,\text{end})$	Model 4 Bidder announcement CAR $(-1, +1)$
Number of observations	743	743	743	579
Intercept	0.253	0.254	0.150	−0.006
	(0.000)	(0.000)	(0.139)	(0.833)
Target classified board	−0.011	−0.006	0.014	−0.027
	(0.483)	(0.698)	(0.685)	(0.002)
Net G-index	0.004	0.004	0.005	−0.001
	(0.170)	(0.169)	(0.305)	(0.804)
Hostile	0.062	0.108	0.168	−0.023
	(0.022)	(0.027)	(0.019)	(0.379)
Hostile × classified board		−0.067	−0.055	0.032
		(0.214)	(0.499)	(0.202)
Deal (auction) status (1 = completed, 0 = withdrawn)	0.067 (0.002)	0.065 (0.003)	0.383 (0.000)	0.014 (0.324)
Stock offer indicator	−0.056	−0.056	−0.068	−0.040
	(0.007)	(0.007)	(0.059)	(0.000)
Tender offer indicator	0.092	0.092	0.048	0.019
	(0.000)	(0.000)	(0.255)	(0.081)

(Continued)

Table 5 (*Continued*)

Return estimate Daily CAR interval	Model 1 Target announcement CAR (−1, +1)	Model 2 Target announcement CAR (−1, +1)	Model 3 Target auction CAR (−42,end)	Model 4 Bidder announcement CAR (−1, +1)
Bidder toehold	−0.003	−0.003	−0.004	−0.001
	(0.005)	(0.005)	(0.050)	(0.378)
Target termination fee	0.017	0.018	−0.034	0.004
	(0.417)	(0.398)	(0.322)	(0.676)
Size (log total assets)	−0.017	−0.017	−0.020	−0.137
	(0.001)	(0.001)	(0.049)	(0.006)
Debt/assets	−0.010	−0.008	0.050	−0.002
	(0.790)	(0.821)	(0.533)	(0.868)
Market-to-book (Tobin's Q)	−0.022	−0.022	−0.035	0.001
	(0.012)	(0.012)	(0.055)	(0.956)
Prebid target abnormal return	−0.178	−0.175		
(%)	(0.000)	(0.000)		
Year indicators	Yes	Yes	Yes	Yes
F-statistic (p-value)	6.20	6.01	8.10	3.41
	(0.000)	(0.000)	(0.000)	(0.000)
Adjusted r^2	0.180	0.181	0.203	0.142

for private benefits in exchange for lower takeover premiums, then bidding shareholders should earn higher returns in these deals. In contrast to this prediction, the coefficient estimate on board classification is negative and significant, indicating that announcement period returns to bidding shareholders are 2.7% (p-value <0.01) lower when the bid involves a target with a classified board. The coefficient associated with the net G-index and bid hostility are insignificantly different from zero, as is the coefficient on the interaction term estimating the joint effect of board classification and hostility on the returns to bidding shareholders. These results are not consistent with the notion that classification, on average, facilitates self-dealing by incumbent managers at the expense of target shareholders. Instead, the findings indicate that, consistent with the shareholder interest hypothesis, bidders fare worse when negotiating takeover bids with targets with a classified-board structure.

To provide additional evidence concerning the welfare of transaction participants, we follow Bates et al. (2006) and examine the relative distribution of transaction surplus between bidding and target shareholders in completed deals. To avoid measurement issues arising from follow-on bids, we limit the sample to first bids in an auction sequence and completed bids. We also exclude transactions in which total wealth losses exceed $2 billion. As in Malatesta (1983), we estimate the abnormal change in market value by multiplying the prebid market value of bidding and target firms (as of day −2 relative to the announcement day) by the announcement CAR.

In unreported results we find that the average total wealth gain to target shareholders at the announcement of a bid is $249.5 million for targets with classified boards and $312.5 millions for targets with a single class of directors. Consistent with the results reported in Table 5, the wealth gains of target shareholders are not statistically different between firms with and without a classified board. Bidding shareholder wealth effects, however, are significantly different for the two subsamples. Bidding shareholders, on average, lose $94.37 million at the announcement of a bid for a target with a classified board but gain $197.4 million at the announcement of a bid for a target with a single class of directors. These results indicate that, consistent with the shareholder interest hypothesis, board classification by targets is associated with a larger proportional distribution of total bid surplus for target shareholders relative to the distributions that obtain for targets represented by a single class of directors. We caution against a strong interpretation of this result, however, as bidder returns could also reflect revisions in the market's assessment of the stand-alone value of the bidder.

6. Board classification and the likelihood of change-in-control bidding

Bid deterrence is a final dimension along which board classification can moderate the observed characteristics of the market for corporate control. A rational potential acquirer, anticipating that target managers use board classification to oppose a takeover or negotiate for a larger proportion of bid surplus, will simply refrain from bidding if the expected costs associated with the takeover exceed the expected benefits. In this section we evaluate the potential bid deterrence effects of board classification and estimate the impact of bid deterrence on firm value.

6.1. The likelihood of receiving a takeover bid

In Table 6 we summarize the results of probit regressions estimating the likelihood of a takeover bid for a firm-year observation as a function of the firm's governance provisions. The regressions also include controls for firm size, market-to-book, leverage, and abnormal performance measured as the rolling mean monthly net-of-market return on the firm's stock computed over the 12 months prior to the calendar year of the observation in the panel.[6] The regressions also control for industry using the 30 industry classification of Fama and French and year fixed effects (1990 is the excluded year). Missing firm-level data impart sample restrictions across the specifications.

Models 1 and 2 of Table 6 summarize the results of individual probit models with dependent variables equal to one for firm-year observations involving an initial takeover bid and zero otherwise. Statistical significance is evaluated using robust

---

[6] Several prior papers estimate takeover likelihoods as a function of firm-specific characteristics and antitakeover provisions including Ambrose and Megginson (1992), Comment and Schwert (1995), Hasbrouck (1985), and Palepu (1986).

Table 6

Probit regressions modeling the probability of being a bid target in a particular year

The table reports probit regressions modeling the likelihood that a firm receives an initial takeover bid in a given year as a function of governance and firm characteristics. Models 1 and 2 estimate the likelihood of a takeover attempt, while Model 3 is a bivariate probit simultaneously estimating the likelihood of a takeover attempt and the likelihood that a sample firm maintains a classified board. The full sample consists of 20,335 firm-year observations between 1990 and 2002 for firms covered in the Investors Responsibility Research Center (IRRC) handbook that also have total assets data available on Compustat. The dependent variable in the regression is set equal to one for firm years in which a firm receives a takeover bid and is set equal to zero otherwise. Target classified board, poison pill, super majority, limits to bylaw amendment, limits to charter amendment, and golden parachute are indicator variables equal to one if the target firm employs these governance feature as reported by IRRC. The net G-index is the G-index reported by Gompers et al. (2003) minus one if the firm employs a classified board. Target characteristics are computed using firm data from the fiscal year immediately preceding an initial bid in an auction. Firm size is the log of total assets, and debt includes long-term debt plus current maturities. Tobin's Q is proxied by the market-to-book assets ratio measured as total assets minus book equity plus market equity divided by total assets for the target. Prebid target abnormal return is measured as the rolling mean monthly abnormal return over the 12 months prior to the calendar year of the observation in the panel. Board size is the log of the total number of directors on the target board preceding the initial acquisition announcement. The p-values based on robust standard errors adjusted for clustering at the firm level are in parentheses, and marginal effects computed at the mean values of the independent variables are provided in brackets. Marginal effects reflect the change in the probability of receiving an acquisition bid for a one standard deviation change in a continuous variable, or a shift from zero to one for an indicator variable.

	Model 1	Model 2	Model 3	
Number of observations	19,465	19,465	18,293	
Estimated likelihood(s)	Takeover target	Takeover target	Classified board	Takeover target
Intercept	−1.528	−1.588	0.027	−1.850
	(0.000)	(0.000)	(0.921)	(0.000)
Target classified board	−0.076	−0.083		−0.259
	(0.048)	(0.031)		(0.047)
	[−0.005]	[−0.006]		[−0.010]
Net G-index	0.016			0.029
	(0.030)			(0.000)
	[0.001]			[0.001]
Target poison pill		−0.009		
		(0.825)		
		[−0.001]		
Super majority		−0.067		
		(0.174)		
		[−0.004]		
Limits to bylaw amendment		−0.018		
		(0.708)		
		[−0.001]		
Limits to charter amendment		0.152		
		(0.110)		
		[0.011]		

(Continued)

Table 6 (*Continued*)

	Model 1	Model 2	Model 3	
Number of observations	19,465	19,465	18,293	
Estimated likelihood(s)	Takeover target	Takeover target	Classified board	Takeover target
Golden parachute		0.280		
		(0.000)		
		[0.018]		
Size (log total assets)	−0.069	−0.064	−0.030	−0.059
	(0.000)	(0.000)	(0.151)	(0.000)
	[−0.005]	[−0.004]		[−0.002]
Debt/assets	0.147	0.120	−0.084	0.194
	(0.015)	(0.051)	(0.500)	(0.053)
	[0.010]	[0.008]		[0.006]
Market-to-book (Tobin's Q)	−0.091	−0.081	−0.036	−0.101
	(0.000)	(0.000)	(0.016)	(0.000)
	[−0.006]	[−0.005]		[−0.004]
Prebid target abnormal return (percent)	−1.829	−1.807	0.883	−2.653
	(0.062)	(0.064)	(0.206)	(0.022)
	[−0.123]	[−0.118]		[−0.088]
Board size (log)			0.204	
			(0.000)	
Industry indicators	Yes	Yes	Yes	Yes
Year indicators	Yes	Yes	Yes	Yes
Wald test of rho = 0 (probability chi-squared)			2.019	
			(0.155)	
Chi-squared (probability chi-squared)	402.13	459.61		4882.10
	(0.000)	(0.000)		(0.000)
Pseudo r^2	0.066	0.075		

clustered standard errors adjusted for nonindependence of observations by firm, and *p*-values assessing statistical significance are reported in parentheses. Marginal effects computed at the mean values of the independent variables are reported in brackets. In Model 1, the coefficient on the classified board indicator is negative and statistically different from zero (*p*-value = 0.048). The marginal effect suggests that firms with classified boards are 0.5% less likely to receive a bid in a particular year relative to comparable firms with a single class of directors. Coefficients on the control variables indicate that larger firms and firms with higher market-to-book ratios and stock returns are less likely to receive takeover bids, while leverage increases the likelihood of becoming a bid target. We control for other governance characteristics in Model 1 using the net G-index. Notably, the coefficient estimate for the net G-index is positive and statistically significant (*p*-value <0.01). Thus, controlling for board classification, firms with more antitakeover provisions are more likely to receive a takeover bid. However, the marginal effect associated with this result is economically small. A one standard deviation increase in net G-index is associated with a 0.1% increase in the likelihood of receiving a bid.

To examine the independent effects of other governance characteristics on the likelihood of receiving a takeover bid, Model 2 of Table 6 incorporates the individual elements of the Bebchuk et al. (2004) entrenchment index. In this specification, the coefficient on board classification remains negative and statistically significant, and the marginal effect on the likelihood of a takeover bid is −0.6%. Poison pills have an insignificant impact on the likelihood of takeover bidding, a result that differs from Comment and Schwert (1995), who find that poison pills are associated with an increase in the likelihood of a takeover bid. We infer that this difference is likely a function of the relative proliferation of poison pill provisions during our sample period, as well as the ease with which firms without a pill might adopt one during a change-in-control bid. Of the remaining governance characteristics, the presence of a golden parachute has the most significant impact on the likelihood of receiving a bid, increasing it by 1.8%. Golden parachutes are often thought to decrease the incidence of takeover bids by increasing transaction costs for acquirers, however, the positive coefficient estimate instead suggests that the adoption of golden parachutes could occur in anticipation of takeover bidding. None of the other components of the entrenchment index has a significant effect on the likelihood of a takeover bid for the firm. Statistical tests (unreported) indicate that the coefficient estimates associated with the individual elements of the entrenchment index are not jointly significant in Model 2.

We are aware of the potential for an endogenous relation between the likelihood of a bid and the decision to adopt antitakeover provisions such as poison pills (e.g., Comment and Schwert, 1995) or a classified-board structure. Poison pills are a relatively new bid defense, only coming into general usage following the 1985 Delaware Chancery Court decision in *Moran v. Household International*. In contrast, board classification is an established governance arrangement incorporated into Delaware law as early as the 19th century. Furthermore, classification is typically adopted by firms when they go public (e.g., Field and Karpoff, 2002) instead of in response to some imminent takeover threat. For example, in our sample we find that for the 428 bids involving firms with a classified board, the average length of time between the adoption date (or IPO date) of board classification and the announcement of a change-in-control bid is 12.51 years, with only four firms adopting a classified-board structure in the calendar year prior to an initial bid announcement. We therefore infer that board classification is not a mechanism adopted by managers anticipating a takeover bid.

A second concern is that firms adopting and maintaining classified boards might also be more likely to be the targets of takeover attempts. Despite our extensive use of control variables, if firms with a greater ex ante exposure to change-in-control bids are also more likely to maintain classified boards, estimated takeover likelihoods suffer from a self-selection bias and understate the deterrent effect of board classification. To address self-selection we follow the methodology outlined in Greene (2003) and estimate a bivariate probit model for the likelihood functions associated with the decision to adopt and maintain a classified board and the firm's receipt of a change-in-control bid, allowing for correlation in the estimation errors in the two equations. Board size provides a unique instrument in determining the likelihood of board classification. Our conjecture is that board classification reduces the transactions costs associated with nominating and electing a large slate of directors, while board size per se should not change the costs associated with a takeover attempt. Data on board size is obtained from IRRC for the years 1998–2002 and supplemented in earlier years with board data obtained from Compact Disclosure.[7] Data for board size are missing for 2042 firm-year observations.

Model 3 of Table 6 summarizes the simultaneous estimation of the likelihood of board classification and a takeover bid. Consistent with our hypothesis, the likelihood of board classification is increasing in board size. The table also reports the results from a Wald test of whether the error correlation (rho) between the two equations is equal to zero. The p-value associated with the Wald test is 0.155, providing weak evidence that accounting for self-selection is appropriate in this context. In the corresponding equation modeling takeover likelihood, the coefficient on board classi-fication is negative and statistically significant (p-value $= 0.047$), indicating that board classification reduces the likelihood that a firm receives a takeover bid. In this specification the marginal effect of classification on the likelihood of receiving a change-in-control bid is -1.0%. The relative magnitude of the estimated effect is substantial in light of an observed bid frequency of 3.6% for the subsample of targets with classified boards. Given the evidence in Table 6 we infer that bid deterrence is the primary channel through which classified boards alter a firm's exposure to the market for corporate control.

6.2. Board classification, bid deterrence, and firm value

To gauge the economic significance of bid deterrence we use our estimate of the expected change in takeover activity to evaluate the commensurate implied change in market value associated with the elimination of a classified-board structure. Uncondi-tioned on the receipt of a bid, average Tobin's Q (proxied by market-to-book assets) in our panel is 1.94 for firms with a single class of directors and 1.75 for the subsample of firms with a classified board. This difference is consistent other empirical studies including Faleye (2007) who finds that classification is associated with a 0.16–0.19 reduction in Tobin's Q. Bebchuk and Cohen (2005) do not report univariate statistics, however, in panel regressions they find that classification is associated with a 0.17 reduction in industry-adjusted Tobin's Q.

We assume that the observed market value of the firm reflects the present value of a series of cash flows obtained under incumbent management, as well as the expected cash flow improvements attributable to an acquirer. We assume that current manage-ment generates constant cash flows of x each year in perpetuity. However, if a takeover attempt occurs in year t, cash flows are expected to be improved to $y = x(1 + k)$ in all

---

[7] We thank Jim Linck for providing us with the merged data set of board characteristics used in Linck et al. (2008).

future years, where k is a takeover premium that reflects the value of cash flow improvements attributable to the acquisition. For simplicity we also assume that all bids are completed and that value improvements and premiums are fully capitalized for target shareholders. Given a probability (p) that a takeover bid occurs in year (t), and a discount rate (r), the present value of the firm can be written as

$$V_0 = x\left(\frac{1+r}{r+p}\right) + \left(\frac{y}{r}\right)\left(\frac{p(1+r)}{r+p}\right). \tag{1}$$

In this framework the value of the firm is equivalent to a perpetual stream of cash flows under incumbent management [the first term in Equation (1)], plus an additional premium resulting from the value improvements from an acquisition [the second term in Equation (1)]. Restating the cash flow improvement (y) in terms of the bid premium (k), firm value is

$$V_0 = x(1+r)\left[\left(\frac{1}{r+p}\right) + \left(\frac{(1+k)}{r}\right)\left(\frac{p}{r+p}\right)\right]. \tag{2}$$

We normalize the book value of assets to one, which equates firm value as given in Equation (2) with Tobin's Q.

We parameterize the model using observed premiums obtained from our sample of bids. The bid premium is computed as the final bid price per share from SDC divided by the target's share price 42 trading days prior to the initial bid, less one. Given missing data, premiums can be computed for 667 of the 757 initial bids in our sample. The average bid premium is 39.09% for firms with a classified board and 35.93% for firms with a single class of directors, although the difference in premiums is not significantly different from zero. We therefore assume that takeover bids yield a 39.09% premium for target shareholders in the model. We calibrate the model to the average Q of 1.75 for firms in the classified board subsample assuming a discount rate of 12% and an observed annualized probability of takeover of 3.6% for firms with classified boards. This yields a value for cash flow under incumbent management of 0.172.

The estimate of takeover deterrence associated with a classified board computed from the bivariate probit Model 3 in Table 6 is 1.0%, roughly twice the effect observed in Models 1 and 2. Increasing the likelihood of a takeover bid by 1.0% per year from the observed rate of 3.6%, the implied change in Tobin's Q associated with the elimination of deterrence is 0.03, suggesting that the average Q for the classified board subsample would be 1.78 if the boards of these firms were declassified. Thus under reasonable parameters, eliminating the deterrence effect associated with board classification increases the implied value of firms by only 1.1%, or approximately one tenth of the difference between the value of firms with and without a classified-board structure. This inference is relatively insensitive to the parameters chosen. For example, a 50% increase in takeover premiums to 58.64% yields an increase in implied Q for firms with classified boards to 1.87 in the absence of bid deterrence which, again, is substantially below the average value of Tobin's Q for the subsample of firms with a single class of directors (1.94). Alternatively, tripling the imputed deterrence effect to 3.0%, raising the overall probability of acquisition for classified board firms to 6.6%, increases the average implied Tobin's Q, absent bid deterrence, to 1.83. We conclude that bid deterrence, while statistically significant, is unlikely to account for the large differences in firm value that have commonly been attributed to the antitakeover properties of classified boards.

6.3. Board declassification and takeover activity

Firms covered by IRRC rarely change their board structure, although anecdotal evidence suggests that declassification is occurring at an increasing rate. Of the 20,335 firm-year observations in our panel, 49 firms are identified as declassifying their board, while 78 classify their board. Nine of the 49 firms that declassified (18.37%) became the target of a takeover bid at some point up through the end of the calendar year 2002, and eight of these bids ultimately result in a completed transaction. Of the 49 firms that classified their board, 17 became the subject of takeover bidding (22.79%) and 13 of these bids are ultimately completed. These results are inconsistent with the notion that firms that declassify are subject to an extraordinary rate of takeover bidding. They also do not suggest that the decision to classify precludes subsequent takeover bidding. The small size of these subsamples precludes a more systematic analysis of takeover likelihoods or outcomes.

6.4. Charter-based versus bylaw-based classified boards

Board classification can be established either in the corporate charter or in the company's bylaws. Bebchuk and Cohen (2005) argue that charter-based staggered boards are potentially more effective as an antitakeover device because the bylaws can be amended by shareholders, whereas the charter cannot be amended without board initiative. Notably, however, many firms restrict shareholder's ability to alter board characteristics established in the corporate bylaws without the consent of the board itself. In our sample, just over 90% of classified board provisions are based in the corporate charter, with the rest established in the bylaws. To assess the robustness of our findings to this distinction we repeat our analyses summarized in Sections 5.2, 5.3, and 6.1 using only charter-based classified boards to define board classification. All of the results are qualitatively identical to those reported using the more general definition of a classified board.

7. Summary and concluding remarks

Critics of board classification contend that the governance arrangement endows management with a device to dissuade value-increasing change-in-control bids, overcome unsolicited takeover attempts, or negotiate self-serving deals with friendly acquirers at the expense of target shareholders. This conjecture is frequently extended to support the notion that board classification is a causal antecedent to agency conflict in firms. An alternative perspective, ascribed to antitakeover devices generally, suggests that classification is efficient in the context of corporate control events because it endows target managers with leverage sufficient to deter opportunistic bidding, negotiate for higher value bids, or pursue higher value third-party suitors. In this paper we explore the veracity of these divergent views by examining the empirical relation between board classification, takeover activity, and transaction outcomes for a panel of firms between 1990 and 2002.

Conditioned on observing a bid, targets with classified boards are ultimately acquired at an equivalent rate as targets with a single class of directors, all else equal. An analysis of target CEO employment following completed bids does not suggest that managers of targets with classified boards are more likely to engage in self-dealing during negotiations with prospective acquirers. Target shareholder returns are equivalent in deals involving targets with a classified board relative to targets with a single class of directors. However, bidding shareholder returns are 2.7% lower at the announcement of a takeover bid for classified board targets. An analysis of the distribution of transaction surplus between target and bidding shareholders in completed deals indicates that target shareholders of firms with classified boards receive a larger proportional share of the total surplus to mergers relative to the target shareholders of firms with a single class of directors. Overall, the evidence is inconsistent with the notion that board classification is systematically associated with managerial entrenchment or self-dealing and suggests that classified boards could improve the relative bargaining power of target managers on behalf of their constituent shareholders.

We extend our analysis to consider the potential for bid deterrence associated with board classification. Controlling for possible endogeneity between a firm's decision to maintain a classified board and its exposure to the market for corporate control, our empirical specification suggests that board classification reduces a firm's likelihood of becoming a takeover target by 1.0% which is a significant effect given an average annual rate of takeover bidding of 3.6% for firms with classified boards generally. Our analysis indicates, however, that bid deterrence can explain only a small fraction of the difference in firm value between firms with and without classified boards.

Several broad conclusions can be derived from our results. First, given our findings we question the empirical basis for recent calls to enhance the standard of regulatory or judicial scrutiny over transactions involving targets with classified boards. We also reiterate a concern that proposals to dismantle antitakeover measures such as a classified board, specifically in the context of bid negotiation, are likely to lead to a reduction in bid quality for target shareholders. Second, our analysis suggests that bid deterrence provides, at best, an incomplete explanation for the differences in firm value commonly attributed to managerial entrenchment facilitated via board classification. Furthermore, given the observed bid outcomes for the transactions in our study, it remains unclear whether the takeover bids that might obtain in the absence of board classification would be efficient for target shareholders. Finally, board classification is just one of many factors commonly indexed when evaluating governance quality and shareholder rights in corporations. The results of this paper challenge the perception that these factors, either independently or as indexed, provide a reliable proxy for a firm's exposure to the market for corporate control. In closing, we note that the research to date has done little to empirically evaluate the potential shareholder benefits associated with classified board provisions or establish the causal nature of the relation between board classification and firm value. In this light we suggest a more circumspect policy approach be adopted by some governance practitioners and academics whose recent calls for the abolition of this common governance provision seem unwarranted and potentially damaging for shareholders.

References

Ai, C. and E. C. Norton, 2003, "Interaction Terms in Logit and Probit Models," *Economic Letters*, 80, 123–129.

Ambrose, B. W. and W. L. Megginson, 1992, "The Role of Asset Structure, Ownership Structure, and Takeover Defenses in Determining Acquisition Likelihood," *Journal of Financial and Quantitative Analysis*, 27, 575–589.

Bange, M. M. and M. A. Mazzeo, 2004, "Board Composition, Board Effectiveness, and the Observed form of Takeover Bids," *Review of Financial Studies*, 17, 1185–1215.

Bates, T. W. and M. L. Lemmon, 2003, "Breaking Up is Hard to Do? An Analysis of Termination Fee Provisions and Merger Outcomes," *Journal of Financial Economics*, 69, 469–504.

Bates, T. W., M. L. Lemmon and J. M. Linck, 2006, "Shareholder Wealth Effects and Bid Negotiation in Freeze-Out Deals: Are Minority Shareholders Left Out in the Cold?," *Journal of Financial Economics*, 81, 681–708.

Bebchuk, L. A. and A. Cohen, 2005, "The Costs of Entrenched Boards," *Journal of Financial Economics*, 78, 409–433.

Bebchuk, L. A., J. C. Coates and G. Subramanian, 2002, "The Powerful Anti-Takeover Force of Staggered Boards: Theory, Evidence, and Policy," *Stanford Law Review*, 54, 887–951.

Bebchuk, L. A., A. Cohen and A. Ferrell, 2004, "What Matters in Corporate Governance?" Unpublished Working Paper, Harvard University, John M. Olin Center for Law, Economics, and Business, Cambridge, MA.

Coates, J. C., 2000, "Takeover Defenses in the Shadow of the Pill: A Critique of the Scientific Evidence," *Texas Law Review*, 79, 271–382.

Comment, R. and G. W. Schwert, 1995, "Poison or Placebo? Evidence on the Deterrence and Wealth Effects of Modern Anti-Takeover Measures," *Journal of Financial Economics*, 39, 3–43.

Daines, R. and M. Klausner, 2001, "Do IPO Charters Maximize Firm Value? Anti-Takeover Protection in IPOs," *Journal of Law, Economics, and Organization*, 17, 83–120.

DeAngelo, H. and E. M. Rice, 1983, "Anti-Takeover Charter Amendments and Stockholder Wealth," *Journal of Financial Economics*, 11, 329–360.

Faleye, O., 2007, "Classified Boards, Firm Value, and Managerial Entrenchment," *Journal of Financial Economics*, 83, 501–529.

Field, L. C. and J. M. Karpoff, 2002, "Takeover Defenses of IPO Firms," *Journal of Finance*, 57, 1857–1889.

Gompers, P., J. Ishii and A. Metrick, 2003, "Corporate Governance and Equity Prices," *Quarterly Journal of Economics*, 118, 107–155.

Gordon, M., 2002, "Takeover Defenses Work. Is That Such a Bad Thing?" *Stanford Law Review*, 55, 819–837.

Greene, W. H., 2003, *Econometric Analysis*, Prentice-Hall, Upper Saddle River, NJ.

Harford, J., 2003, "Takeover Bids and Target Directors' Incentives: Retention, Experience, and Settling Up," *Journal of Financial Economics*, 69, 51–83.

Hartzell, J., E. Ofek and D. Yermack, 2004, "What's in It for Me? Personal Benefits Obtained by CEOs Whose Firms are Acquired," *Review of Financial Studies*, 17, 37–61.

Hasbrouck, J., 1985, "The Characteristics of Takeover Targets: Q and Other Measures," *Journal of Banking and Finance*, 9, 351–362.

Heron, R. A. and E. Lie, 2006, "On the Use of Poison Pills and Defensive Payouts by Takeover Targets," *Journal of Business*, 79, 1783–1807.

Institutional Shareholder Services, 2005, Governance at a crossroads. 2006 Proxy Season Preview/2005 review, October.

Klock, M., S. Mansi and W. Maxwell, 2005, "Does Corporate Governance Matter to Bondholders?" *Journal of Financial and Quantitative Analysis*, 40, 693–719.

Linck, J., J. Netter and T. Yang, 2008, "The Determinants of Board Structure," *Journal of Financial Economics*, 87, 308–328.

Malatesta, P. H., 1983, "The Wealth Effect of Merger Activity and the Objective Functions of Merging Firms," *Journal of Financial Economics*, 11, 155–181.

Masulis, R. W., C. Wang and F. Xie, 2007, "Corporate Governance and Acquirer Returns," *Journal of Finance*, 62, 1851–1889.

Palepu, K. G., 1986, "Predicting Takeover Targets: A Methodological and Empirical Analysis," *Journal of Accounting and Economics*, 8, 3–35.

Pound, J., 1987, "The Effects of Antitakeover Amendments on Takeover Activity: Some Direct Evidence," *Journal of Law and Economics*, 30, 353–367.

Schwert, G. W., 2000, "Hostility of Takeovers: In the Eyes of the Beholder," *Journal of Finance*, 55, 2599–2640.

Stein, J. C., 1988, "Takeover Threats and Managerial Myopia," *Journal of Political Economy*, 96, 61–80.

Stulz, R., 1988, "Managerial Control of Voting Rights: Financing Policies and the Market for Corporate Control," *Journal of Financial Economics*, 20, 25–54.

Wall Street Journal, 2005, "More Boards May End Staggered Terms," *Bhattiprolu Murti*, June 8.

Wulf, J., 2004, "Do CEOs in Mergers Trade Power for Premium? Evidence from Mergers of Equals," *Journal of Law, Economics, and Organization*, 20, 60–101.

Yermack, D., 2004, "Remuneration, Retention, and Reputation Incentives for Outside Directors," *Journal of Finance*, 59, 2281–2308.

PART 5

DOES LARGE SHAREHOLDER VOTING IMPROVE TAKEOVER GAINS?

Chapter 14

LET'S MAKE A DEAL! HOW SHAREHOLDER CONTROL IMPACTS MERGER PAYOFFS*

THOMAS MOELLER

Rawls College of Business Administration, Texas Tech University, Lubbock, Texas, USA

Contents

* I thank Ty Callahan, Jay Hartzell, John Robinson, Laura Starks, Sheridan Titman, Kimberly Rodgers, Wanda Wallace, James Weston, an anonymous referee, and seminar participants at the University of Texas at Austin, University of Cincinnati, College of William and Mary, Cornerstone Research, Louisiana State University, Rice University, Santa Clara University, The Brattle Group, University of Texas at Dallas, University of Toronto, Washington State University, and the 2002 Frank Batten Young Scholars Conference at the College of William and Mary for helpful comments. Large parts of the research were conducted while I was at the University of Texas at Austin, The Brattle Group, and Rice University. All errors are my own.

This article originally appeared in the *Journal of Financial Economics*, Vol. 76, pp. 167–190 (2005).
Corporate Takeovers, Volume 2
Edited by B. Espen Eckbo
DOI: 10.1016/B978-0-12-381982-6.00015-X

Abstract

Mergers and acquisitions are well-suited events for a detailed study of the valuation effects of corporate governance structures. Using a sample of 388 takeovers announced in the friendly environment of the 1990s, I empirically show that target shareholder control, proxied by low target chief executive officer share ownership, low fractions of inside directors, and the presence of large outside blockholders, is positively correlated with takeover premiums. In contrast, studies of takeovers in the hostile environment of the 1980s have shown a negative relation between target shareholder control and takeover premiums.

Keywords

mergers, acquisitions, agency, governance

JEL classification: G34

1. Introduction

How much control of a firm should rest in the hands of its managers, and how much should be retained by its shareholders? This question, and how to implement the optimal balance of power, has long been central not only to the corporate governance literature, but also to active investors and securities legislation. In this paper, I empirically examine how the balance of power between target chief executive officers (CEOs) and target shareholders affects takeover premiums in mergers and acquisitions in the 1990s.

Mergers and acquisitions are in many ways ideal natural experiments to test the valuation effects of corporate governance structures.[1] First, a merger generally requires the active participation of all decision makers, namely, managers, directors, and shareholders. Managers usually negotiate the merger, directors have to endorse it and are sometimes involved in the negotiations, and shareholders have to either vote on it or decide whether to tender their shares. Second, the effect of the corporate governance structure on the value of the target, given adequate control for other influences, is immediately observable in the takeover premium. Third, a merger announcement is a clearly defined and, in most cases, a surprising event.

Intuitively, higher shareholder control should lead to higher shareholder value. Therefore, we should only observe corporate governance structures with high levels of shareholder control in the long run. However, maximum shareholder control might not be optimal in all situations. In an environment without takeover defenses, for example, the United States before the late 1980s, even if a target CEO is opposed to a takeover, large takeover premiums help hostile bids succeed by inducing target shareholders to fight the CEOs resistance. The more powerful the target CEO and the weaker the target shareholders, the higher the takeover premium that is required to motivate shareholders to overturn the CEOs opposition. Shleifer and Vishny (1986) and Stulz (1988) provide theoretical rationales for this result, and Song and Walkling (1993) have empirical evidence. Therefore, giving target CEOs power to make decisions that are costly to overturn for shareholders can be valuable. However, a great change is evident in the characteristics of mergers and acquisitions over the past two decades. Merger and acquisition activity in the 1980s was characterized by spectacular hostile transactions, while in the 1990s the vast majority of transactions were done on friendly terms.[2]

In the 1990s, effective takeover defenses were widely available and hostile offers had only a small chance of success. With this shift in the balance of power toward target CEOs, bidders had to focus their efforts on convincing target CEOs to agree to

---

[1] I use the terms "merger," "acquisition," and "takeover" synonymously.

[2] The friendliness of the transactions is initially surprising, because, as Agrawal and Walkling (1994) find, CEOs of target firms who lose their jobs generally fail to find another senior executive position in any public corporation within 3 years after a bid. Schwert (2000) finds little economic difference between friendly and hostile transactions.

deals versus enticing target shareholders through large takeover premiums. One way to solicit a target CEOs merger approval at a reduced takeover price is for the bidder to offer private benefits to the target CEO, for example, positions in the merged firm and improved retirement packages.[3] Instead of negotiating the highest possible takeover premium, target CEOs bargain over their private benefits with the bidder. Target shareholders can intervene and block these transactions, but intervention is costly. The cost of target shareholder intervention is largely determined by the balance of power between the target CEO and the target shareholders. The more powerful the target CEO and the weaker the target shareholders, the higher the cost of shareholder intervention and the larger the reduction in the takeover premium that the target CEO can allow in return for private benefits. Therefore, in the 1990s the relationship between target shareholder control and takeover premium should be positive, while it appears to have been negative in the 1980s.

Given that the level of shareholder control is not directly observable, I must rely on various proxies in my empirical analysis. I consider CEOs to be strong when they own large fractions of their firms' stock, there are small outside blockholdings, or a large fraction of directors are insiders. I empirically show that these proxies for low target shareholder control are related to lower takeover premiums in the 1990s. Combining several of the shareholder control variables to identify distinct cases, I develop a proxy for high shareholder control. I find that bidder returns are lower and target returns are higher when target shareholders have more control. These results eliminate an important argument for high managerial power and discretion.[4]

Financial incentives, in particular the use of options, could substitute for direct shareholder control. I use the target CEOs' option holdings and the sensitivity of their value to the underlying stock price as proxies for financial incentives to maximize shareholder wealth. I find little evidence that the CEOs' stock options affect takeover premiums.

The results here are of substantial economic significance. The various proxies for low shareholder control and strong CEOs reduce takeover premiums by 5–16% points. With an average target market value of $1.2 billion, this premium reduction frees up significant amounts that can be distributed as rents to other parties.

There are some related studies. Hartzell et al. (2004) examine target CEOs' trade-offs between financial gains, including augmented golden parachutes and merger-related bonuses, and executive positions in the merged firm. They find that financial gains are reduced when target CEOs receive executive positions. Generally, target

---

[3] The idea that strong target CEOs are susceptible to bidder-provided incentives also appears in Morck et al. (1988a). They determine that targets in friendly transactions have higher share ownership by board members and are more likely to be run by a founder.

[4] Because shareholders in CEO-dominated target firms are in similar positions as minority shareholders, this result is consistent with findings in international comparisons of corporate governance features by LaPorta et al. (2000, 2002). They, among others, have shown that better minority shareholder protection is associated with higher valuations of corporate assets.

CEOs' payoffs are comparable to the net present value of what they would have received without the merger. Takeover premiums, however, seem to be smaller in cases in which target CEOs received extraordinary treatment.

My study differs from Hartzell et al. (2004) in three ways. First, they focus on the target CEOs' trade-off between financial gains and executive positions in the merged firm, while I relate the level of target shareholder control to bidder and target announcement returns. Second, they examine only the benefits of target CEOs and do not consider bidder returns. Third, my proxies, covering various aspects of the targets' corporate governance structures, are much broader than their variables that measure payments to the target CEO in great detail.

The analysis here is also related to Wulf (2004), who shows that target managers receive preferential treatment in mergers of equals compared with mergers of non-equals. In a detailed analysis of 40 transactions, she finds higher bidder returns and lower target returns in mergers of equals, which is consistent with my results. My sample, a broader selection of 388 mergers and acquisitions, allows more powerful tests and more general and robust results. In addition, my study is less sensitive to the accurate classification of bidders and targets, a difficult task in mergers of equals.

The remainder of the paper is organized as follows. Section 2 presents my main hypothesis. Section 3 develops the proxies for shareholder control. The sample description follows in Section 4. I discuss my takeover premium measures in Section 5. Section 6 presents the empirical results, and Section 7 examines various robustness checks. Section 8 concludes.

2. Main hypothesis

Takeover defenses shift power from target shareholders to target managers. If target managers trade takeover premiums in return for private benefits, target shareholders lose part of the potential premium they could have received in a successful hostile transaction. Therefore, target shareholders could wish to force target managers to maximize takeover premiums. Exerting influence on the target management's decisions is easier, the more powerful the shareholders are relative to the target management. For example, large outside blockholders with board representation can intervene at a low cost. Hence, strong target CEOs, or weak target shareholders, should be associated with reduced takeover premiums.[5] I test this hypothesis. It is the opposite of the prediction derived in the environment of hostile transactions of the 1980s.

---

[5] An important assumption necessary to translate predictions of merger payoffs to announcement returns is that the deals are not perfectly predictable. If investors already fully expected the merger, abnormal announcement returns should be zero. However, I believe that merger and acquisition announcements are, at least to a large degree, surprises. The relatively low frequency of these transactions and the significant stock price movements associated with them support this assumption. In addition, I control for preannouncement period returns in my regressions.

3. Description of proxies

The proxies represent the target firm's ownership structure, board composition, and position of the CEO.

3.1. Target CEO share ownership

The most direct way for a CEO to control the firm and make shareholder intervention costly is to own a large fraction of the firm. For example, large ownership will allow the CEO to have a disproportionate impact on board assignments. Therefore, I use target CEO share ownership, collected from Securities and Exchange Commission (SEC) filings, as a proxy for CEO power and expect it to be negatively related to takeover premiums. An alternative view would be that managerial shareholdings align CEOs' and shareholders' goals. In that case, higher ownership would lead to higher takeover premiums. However, because compensating target CEOs directly through bidder-provided incentives is always more efficient than indirectly through increased takeover premiums, I expect the control aspect of share ownership to dominate.

3.2. Outside blockholders

As a result of the free-rider problem described in Grossman and Hart (1980), shareholder intervention is more feasible when firms have large blockholders. I define shareholders that are listed in the target's SEC filings as beneficial owners of at least 5% of the target's stock as blockholders. (The 5% cutoff is commonly used. For example, the SEC requires firms to identify the owners of 5% or more of a firms' stock.) The larger the blockholdings, the smaller the potential value improvements that are required to trigger blockholder intervention. Because inside blockholders can be expected to support the CEO, the outside blockholdings determine the degree of shareholder control. Therefore, I expect higher outside blockholdings to lead to higher takeover premiums.

3.3. Board composition

Blockholders' influence can be significantly reduced when they lack board representation. The board of directors makes several critical decisions with respect to takeover offers. For example, it usually has to approve a deal. I define insiders as directors who, according to the target's SEC filings, have an executive position in the firm, had such a position in the past, or are related to an executive. Outsiders are all board members without such a connection. I assume that insiders' incentives are aligned with the CEOs goals. Then, large fractions of insiders on the board make shareholder intervention more costly, and the fraction of inside directors should be negatively related to takeover premiums.

3.4. Target CEOs' financial incentives

Shareholders can control CEOs directly or use financial incentives that reduce the need for shareholder intervention by aligning CEOs' objectives with shareholders' goals. I use the number of the target CEOs' stock options as a fraction of the firms' outstanding shares, the options' Black and Scholes value, and their value sensitivity to changes in the target's stock price as proxies. In most cases, all options vest once the deal closes, and restricted options become exercisable immediately. Consequently, large option holdings should motivate target CEOs to negotiate the maximum takeover premium. Age, however, might distort these incentives. Gibbons and Murphy (1992), for example, show that implicit incentives from career concerns to maximize shareholder wealth are lower for CEOs who are close to retirement.[6]

3.5. High shareholder control proxy

Only dominant and established target CEOs should have sufficient clout to effectively influence takeover premiums, for example, in return for bidder-provided incentives. A CEO should be under less strict supervision when she has had her position for several years because either she convinced shareholders of her worthiness or shareholders are unable to remove her. Therefore, a short tenure as CEO indicates higher shareholder control. Similarly, when the executive power is concentrated in the CEO, the CEO presumably has more far-reaching decision power. Therefore, shareholder control should be higher when there is a separate chairman or president. The CEOs control increases with her equity stake, and shareholder control is lower when insiders dominate the board. To identify distinct cases in which suboptimal takeover premiums are highly unlikely, I define my high shareholder control indicator variable to equal one when firms have a separate chairman or president, when CEOs are not large blockholders, when large fractions of board members are outsiders, and when CEOs have had a short tenure.

4. Sample description

The sample consists of mergers and acquisitions with an announcement date between January 1, 1990 and December 31, 1999. The deals are identified in the Securities Data Company (SDC) Mergers and Acquisitions database. I include only completed

---

[6] I examine the influence of the target CEOs' age on takeover premiums in various specifications without finding any significant relation (results not reported). Similarly, a CEO with a long tenure at the firm could have built up more firm-specific human capital that she could lose in a takeover. She might seek compensation, potentially through private benefits. Alternatively, longer tenure could indicate more CEO control. I emphasize the latter interpretation in the remainder of the paper.

transactions with a transaction value of at least $100 million, when both the bidder and the target are US firms. Furthermore, the bidder must acquire at least 25% of the target shares in the transaction and must own at least 50% of the target's shares afterward. This initial screening gives 5077 observations. In addition, I exclude transactions when bidder and target were closely related before the merger announcement, for example, firms with the same parent company, and when the SDC describes the bidder as "Shareholders," "Investor Group," "Investor," or "Creditors." This reduces the sample to 2039 observations. I exclude financial institutions and real estate trusts and require that both bidder and target are identifiable by the Center for Research in Security Prices (CRSP) and Compustat. These requirements leave 855 transactions. Checking if data items for bidder and target for the relevant dates are available on CRSP and Compustat reduces the sample to 704 observations. I am able to find proxy statements or 10-Ks for bidder and target for 609 deals. Because I measure the effect of the merger on the bidder, I require that the target's market value of equity is at least 5% of the bidder market value of equity. This requirement eliminates 152 transactions. To prevent miscoding of bidder and target from affecting my results, I exclude deals in which the target's market value of equity exceeds the bidder's equity by more than 50% (nine observations). To keep outliers or potential data errors from driving the results, I eliminate observations in which the target's excess announcement return exceeds 100% (nine observations) or is lower than −50% (one observation). I also eliminate 25 observations of highly leveraged targets with long-term debt more than three times as large as the market value of equity. Collectively, these restrictions reduce the sample size by 178, to 431 observations. Missing data items reduce the final sample size to 388. I am able to calculate the takeover premium for 373 observations.

Announcement dates are taken from the SDC Mergers and Acquisitions database. The SDC database also provides data on the deal attitude, the acquisition mode, and the fraction of the takeover price that was paid in cash. Standard industrial classification (SIC) codes and some control variables are from Compustat. The focus of my analysis, however, is on the corporate governance variables that I collect from SEC filings.

The proxy statements provide the data on the CEO, the board, and blockholders. For the CEO, I record the tenure in her position, her share ownership, whether she is the founder, her option holdings, and whether the firm has a separate chairman or president. I also calculate the Black and Scholes value of her options and the sensitivity of the value of her option holdings to a 1% price change in the underlying stock price using the procedure described in Core and Guay (1999, 2002). Core and Guay's method allows an estimation of the Black and Scholes value of executive option holdings using the data provided in a single proxy filing. I record the number of insiders and outsiders on the board and blockholdings for each target firm.

I also conduct a search for deal-related announcements in the Wall Street Journal and Public Relations (PR) Newswire using the Dow Jones News Retrieval (DJNR). I use DJNR to verify the accuracy of the announcement dates. I record any deal-related rumors prior to the announcement date, mentioning of competitive bidders, changes to the offer after the announcement (offer increased, offer decreased), unexpected regulatory approval problems, and indications regarding the friendliness of the transaction (clearly friendly). Furthermore, I record if the CEO is expected to assume, or is offered, an executive or board position in the merged firm.

5. Takeover premium measurement

I calculate the announcement return as the excess return over the CRSP equally weighted index from 5 days before to 5 days after the announcement date. This measure has several advantages. It takes expected movements in the bidder stock price into account, which is important when the bidder pays with stock. The short event window ensures that most of the return can be attributed to the merger event. However, the announcement return represents a combination of the takeover price and the probabilities that the transaction closes, fails, or that another bidder emerges. (This problem is mitigated because the vast majority of the sample involve clearly friendly transactions and all deals eventually close.)

Therefore, I eliminate the probability of the offer success by using

$$\text{Takeover premium} = \frac{\text{price per share offered by bidder}}{\text{target's share price 6 days prior to announcement}} - 1.$$

In stock offers, I determine the offered price by multiplying the number of bidder shares offered per target share by the bidder's closing price on the announcement date. When offers specify price ranges that depend on the bidder's or target's stock price or both prior to the closing of the deal, I use the exchange ratios that would result if current stock prices at the end of the announcement date prevailed. Unfortunately, some stock offers, through imbedded options, are so complicated that calculating an accurate takeover price is extremely difficult, or the exact exchange ratios are simply not available. My sample loses 15 observations that way.

6. Empirical results

Table 1 shows the majority of mergers in the sample occurred in the second half of the 1990s. Bidder announcement returns average −2.9%. Target announcement returns and takeover premiums average 21.3% and 30.8%, respectively. The combined market value of bidder and target increases on average by about 2%. According to SDC

Table 1

Summary statistics, indicator variables, and number of observations

Panel A shows selected summary statistics. The announcement returns are in excess of the equally weighted Center for Research in Security Prices index. The announcement return period spans 11 trading days starting 5 days before the announcement. Target realized return covers the period from 5 days before the announcement to the earlier of the effective or the target's delisting date. Takeover premium is calculated as the price per share offered by the bidder, using the closing prices at the announcement date for stock offers, divided by the target's closing price 6 days prior to the announcement date minus one. Combined announcement return is the total percentage change in the market value of equity of bidder and target. The market values of equity and option values are calculated as of 6 days before the announcement date. The data on chief executive officer (CEO) share ownership, board composition, and blockholdings are from the latest available proxy filing or 10-K before the announcement date. Governance index is calculated from Investor Responsibility Research Center (IRRC) data as in Gompers et al. (2003). Panel B shows the fractions of the observations in which the indicator variables are equal to one. Hostile, clearly friendly, tender offer, competitive bidder, and merger of equals are from the Securities Data Company Mergers and Acquisitions database. Offer increased, offer decreased, and prior rumors are hand-collected from *Wall Street Journal* and Public Relations Newswire articles. Poison pill is from IRRC data. Delaware corporation and staggered board are from proxy and 10-K filings. Distressed target equals one when the target's total liabilities exceed total assets. Same industry equals one when the bidder and the target share the same primary industry. Panel C shows the distribution of observations over time. About 83% of the observations are in the second half of the sample period.

Panel A. Selected summary statistics

Variable	Mean	Median	Standard deviation	Number of observations
Target announcement return	0.2131	0.1848	0.2017	388
Takeover premium	0.3081	0.2766	0.2240	373
Target realized return	0.2097	0.1893	0.3271	388
Bidder announcement return	−0.0291	−0.0303	0.0989	388
Combined announcement return	0.0173	0.0164	0.0963	388
Target market value equity (millions of dollars)	1166	291	4349	388
Bidder market value equity (millions of dollars)	4732	1472	13,200	388
Ratio of target to bidder market value of equity	0.3167	0.2234	0.2695	388
Percent CEO share ownership	0.0677	0.0200	0.1188	387
Amount CEO share ownership (thousands of dollars)	31,640	7882	108,952	387
Percent inside directors	0.3112	0.2857	0.1612	388
Percent outside blockholdings	0.2442	0.2356	0.1757	387
Option value (thousands of dollars)	9273	2923	24,583	305
Option price sensitivity (thousands of dollars/1% price change)	122	40	331	305
Governance index	9.08	9.00	2.93	173
Fraction paid with cash	0.2740	0.0000	0.3861	388
Excess return 200 days prior	−0.0745	−0.1056	0.3019	388
Days to effective or delisting date	148	112	130	388

(*Continued*)

Table 1 (*Continued*)

Panel B: statistics on indicator variables

Indicator variable	Number of observations in which indicator variable equals 1	Percent of sample	Number of observations
Hostile	14	3.6	388
Clearly friendly	358	92.7	386
Tender offer	73	18.8	388
Competitive bidder	23	6.0	386
Merger of equals	7	1.8	388
Offer increased	24	6.2	386
Offer decreased	11	2.8	386
Prior rumors	34	8.8	386
Poison pill	89	51.4	173
Delaware corporation	223	57.8	386
Distressed target	7	1.8	388
Same industry	276	71.1	388
CEO is founder	77	19.9	387
Percent CEO share ownership $\geq 5\%$	119	30.7	387
Percent inside directors $\geq 40\%$	123	31.7	388
Outside blockholdings $\leq 10\%$	94	24.3	387
CEO options $<1\%$	160	48.6	329
Option price sensitivity $<\$20,000$	107	35.1	305
Separate chairman or president	207	53.4	388
Tenure ≥ 5 years	199	53.8	370
Staggered board	190	49.4	385
Percent inside director $<40\%$ and percent CEO share ownership $<20\%$ and separate chairman or president and tenure <5 years	62	16.8	369

Panel C: observations by year

Year	1990	1991	1992	1993	1994	1995	1996	1997	1998	1999	Total
Number of observations	12	12	8	11	24	49	39	80	87	66	388

classifications, only seven mergers of equals are in the sample, less than 4% of deals are hostile, and tender offers occur in roughly 19% of the observations. Of all deals, about 93% have no indication of any hostility, only 6% face competitive bidders, and less than 2% involve financially distressed targets, that is, firms with total liabilities exceeding total assets. CEOs control on average 6.8% of the targets' equity. The target market value of equity averages about 32% of the bidder's market value. Table 2 shows the correlation between my proxies and the control variables. The magnitudes of the correlations do not suggest any problems stemming from multicollinearity.

Table 2
Correlation matrix

The table shows the pairwise correlation coefficients among the target shareholder control proxies and between the target shareholder control proxies and control variables. Bold coefficients indicate significance at the 0.05 level or higher. CEO = chief executive officer. MV = market value.

Variable	Percent CEO share ownership ≥5%	Log (percent CEO share ownership)	Log (amount CEO share ownership +1)	Percent inside directors ≥40%	Log (percent inside directors)	Outside blockholdings ≤10%	CEO options <1%	High shareholder control proxy
Percent CEO share ownership ≥5%	1.000							
Log (percent CEO share ownership)	**0.732**	1.000						
Log (amount CEO share ownership +1)	**0.511**	**0.720**	1.000					
Percent inside directors ≥40%	**0.351**	**0.341**	**0.196**	1.000				
Log (% inside directors)	**0.420**	**0.439**	**0.216**	**0.755**	1.000			
Outside blockholdings ≤10%	−0.025	−0.096	**0.107**	−0.050	−0.091	1.000		
CEO options <1%	0.039	**−0.193**	−0.003	−0.105	−0.083	**0.155**	1.000	
High shareholder control proxy	**−0.251**	**−0.241**	**−0.225**	**−0.310**	**−0.158**	**−0.152**	**0.100**	1.000
Log (amount CEO option value +1)	**−0.267**	**−0.181**	0.095	**−0.137**	**−0.190**	−0.070	**−0.460**	0.078
Option price sensitivity <$20,000	**0.213**	**0.117**	**−0.170**	0.025	0.094	0.025	**0.440**	−0.047
CEO is founder	**0.467**	**0.489**	**0.383**	**0.271**	**0.313**	−0.011	−0.002	**−0.172**
Hostile	**−0.129**	−0.090	0.002	−0.072	−0.021	**0.116**	0.038	0.025
Tender offer	**−0.107**	−0.024	**−0.174**	−0.045	−0.008	−0.073	−0.034	**0.112**
Ratio of target to bidder MV equity	−0.048	**−0.120**	0.068	0.010	−0.028	0.040	0.029	0.015
Log (target total assets)	**−0.365**	**−0.504**	0.057	**−0.271**	**−0.375**	**0.277**	**0.197**	**0.105**
Long-term debt/MV equity	−0.023	−0.026	−0.047	−0.041	−0.058	0.076	−0.097	−0.061
Competitive bidder	−0.047	−0.059	0.005	−0.008	0.017	0.010	−0.034	0.052
Fraction paid with cash	−0.054	0.024	**−0.127**	0.001	0.011	−0.053	0.016	0.078
Prior rumors	0.013	−0.039	−0.021	0.023	0.009	0.036	−0.005	0.046
Excess return 200 days prior	0.072	0.064	**0.179**	0.057	0.057	0.073	0.017	0.006
Days to effective or delisting date	**−0.128**	**−0.334**	**−0.190**	**−0.113**	**−0.194**	**0.331**	**0.143**	−0.021
Same industry	−0.097	**−0.123**	−0.075	−0.067	**−0.104**	0.079	−0.058	0.000
Distressed target	−0.006	0.028	0.048	0.074	0.028	0.014	−0.059	−0.009
Sales/total assets	**0.144**	**0.178**	0.093	**0.165**	**0.212**	−0.035	−0.015	−0.028
Net income/total assets	0.045	0.024	0.072	0.099	0.076	0.065	−0.004	**−0.139**
Regulatory problems	−0.048	−0.038	−0.012	−0.010	−0.053	0.058	−0.022	−0.010

6.1. Influence of control variables

Table 3 shows ordinary least squares (OLS) regressions of the takeover premium on my proxies.[7] The coefficients on the control variables are similar in all estimations.

CEO is founder indicates the target CEO being the founder or a member of the founder's family or having been the CEO since the inception of the firm. The point estimates appear to be positive but are generally insignificant.

Hostile indicates that the SDC Mergers and Acquisitions database designates a deal as hostile. Only 3.6% of all transactions are hostile, but the targets in these hostile transactions receive about 10% points higher takeover premiums than targets in friendly deals. Takeover premiums are significantly lower when the SDC database describes a deal as a tender offer (tender offer).

The larger the target relative to the bidder, the lower is the takeover premium, as indicated by the highly significant and negative coefficient on ratio of target to bidder market value of equity. The size of the target, measured by the logarithm of total assets, is not significant. The target's leverage seems to increase the takeover premium, but long-term debt/market value of equity is marginally insignificant.

Only 6% of the sample transactions involve a competitive bidder. The existence of a competitive bidder does not affect takeover premiums in my sample. Consistent with the prior literature, for example, Travlos (1987), paying for the target with cash (fraction paid with cash) is a positive signal that significantly increases takeover premiums. This effect could also be the result of the individual investors' inability to defer capital gains taxes in cash offers.

Prior rumors indicates evidence of rumors regarding the merger prior to the announcement, but its coefficient is insignificant. A better proxy for the anticipation of a takeover seems to be the target's excess return over the 200 trading days prior to the announcement window. Excess return 200 days prior has a highly significant and negative impact on takeover premiums. Not all of excess return 200 days prior's negative influence can necessarily be attributed to rumors of a takeover. For example, it could also be driven by a target's particularly poor performance prior to the merger announcement. Regardless of what is the main contributor to excess return 200 days prior's significance, it serves its purpose as a control for effects on the takeover premium that are unrelated to my proxies for the level of target shareholder control.

Days to effective or delisting date records the number of days between the announcement date and the earlier of the merger's effective date and the target's delisting date. It serves to control for the influence on the takeover premium of any remaining uncertainty regarding the successful completion of the transaction. The time to the completion of the deal appears to reduce takeover premiums but is insignificant.

---

[7] I check the takeover premium measures for nonnormality and left-truncation. The distributions seem close to normal, and little evidence emerges of truncation. Therefore, using OLS as the estimation method is appropriate. I also conduct my analyses using a truncated regression model. The results are qualitatively unchanged from those presented here.

Table 3

Impact of target characteristics on takeover premiums

Takeover premium is the dependent variable. All equations are estimated using ordinary least squares regressions with the heteroskedasticity adjustment by Davidson and MacKinnon (1993). In addition to the reported control variables, the coefficients of the following control variables, which either are insignificant or have no relevant interpretation in the context of this study, are not reported: industry dummies, an indicator for bidder and target in the same industry, year dummies for 1995–1999, a dummy when Dow Jones News Retrieval articles indicate problems with the regulatory approval of the transaction, a financial distress dummy (total liabilities exceed total assets), a proxy for the target's profitability (net income as a fraction of total assets), and a proxy for the target's efficiency (sales as a fraction of total assets). The last row shows the result of an F-test of the three target shareholder control proxies being jointly equal to zero. This hypothesis is rejected at the 0.01 level for the larger sample that does not require option data and at the 0.10 level for the sample with option data. High target chief executive officer (CEO) share ownership, large fractions of inside directors, and low outside blockholdings are associated with lower takeover premiums. Target CEO option holdings do not affect takeover premiums. T-statistics are in parentheses. ***, **, and * denote significance at the 0.01, 0.05, and 0.10 level, respectively. MV = market value.

Takeover premium	(1)	(2)	(3)	(4)	(5)	(6)
Percent CEO share ownership ≥5%	-0.0662** (-2.37)			-0.0546* (-1.90)		-0.0362 (-1.23)
Percent inside directors ≥40%		-0.0687** (-2.44)		-0.0614** (-2.15)		-0.0572* (-1.91)
Outside blockholdings ≤10%			-0.0499* (-1.78)	-0.0452 (-1.62)		-0.0275 (-0.87)
CEO options <1%					-0.0157 (-0.54)	-0.0118 (-0.41)
CEO is founder	0.0326 (0.97)	0.0178 (0.54)	0.0074 (0.23)	0.0441 (1.33)	-0.0148 (-0.44)	0.0184 (0.54)
Hostile	0.0968* (1.68)	0.0969* (1.70)	0.1130* (1.93)	0.1102* (1.87)	0.0962* (1.72)	0.1043* (1.77)
Tender offer	-0.1066** (-2.25)	-0.1005** (-2.12)	-0.0986** (-2.04)	-0.1099** (-2.36)	-0.0794 (-1.54)	-0.0894 (-1.76)
Ratio of target to bidder market value of equity	-0.2007*** (-4.69)	-0.1938*** (-4.60)	-0.2096*** (-4.98)	-0.1951*** (-4.74)	-0.1786*** (-4.16)	-0.1708*** (-3.97)
Log (target total assets)	-0.0055 (-0.50)	-0.0046 (-0.43)	0.0043 (0.39)	-0.0062 (-0.54)	0.0045 (0.41)	-0.0016 (-0.13)
Long-term debt/MV of equity	0.0462 (1.50)	0.0361 (1.19)	0.0360 (1.16)	0.0432 (1.42)	0.0340 (0.98)	0.0366 (1.07)
Competitive bidder	-0.0493 (-0.74)	-0.0472 (-0.73)	-0.0521 (-0.77)	-0.0509 (-0.78)	-0.0797 (-1.26)	-0.0836 (-1.38)
Fraction paid with cash	0.1276*** (2.61)	0.1288*** (2.59)	0.1204** (2.40)	0.1293*** (2.71)	0.1340*** (2.66)	0.1401*** (2.84)
Prior rumors	-0.0097 (-0.19)	-0.0150 (-0.29)	-0.0136 (-0.26)	-0.0125 (-0.25)	-0.0582 (-0.92)	0.0538 (0.88)
Excess return 200 days prior	-0.1564*** (-3.71)	-0.1582*** (-3.65)	-0.1546*** (-3.63)	-0.1500*** (-3.49)	-0.1827*** (-4.13)	-0.1729*** (-3.83)
Days to effective or delisting date	-0.0002 (-1.36)	-0.0002 (-1.34)	-0.0002 (-1.26)	-0.0001 (-1.02)	-0.0003 (-1.52)	-0.0002 (-1.16)
Intercept	0.2903*** (3.16)	0.2774*** (3.14)	0.2387*** (2.65)	0.2953*** (3.21)	0.2086** (2.36)	0.2360** (2.54)
Adjusted R^2	0.18	0.17	0.17	0.19	0.19	0.20
Number of observations	372	373	372	372	315	315
Pr (F-test)				0.0042***		0.0753*

In addition to the control variables reported in Table 3, I use industry dummies, an indicator for bidder and target in the same industry (same industry), year dummies for 1995–1999, a dummy when DJNR articles indicate problems with the regulatory approval of the transaction (regulatory problems), a financial distress dummy when total liabilities exceed total assets (distressed target), a proxy for the target's profitability (net income/total assets), and a proxy for the target's efficiency (sales/total assets).[8] These control variables are either insignificant or have no relevant interpretation in the context of this study (e.g., the industry and year dummy variables). However, they control for characteristics that have been shown to affect stock returns.

6.2. Impact of target characteristics on takeover premiums

The influence of CEO share ownership is likely nonlinear. A change in ownership from 1% to 6% is arguably more relevant than a change from 35% to 40%. To reduce the potential impact of the nonlinearities, I use indicator variables. Percent CEO share ownership $\geq 5\%$ equals one when the target CEO controls at least 5% of the target's shares.[9] The CEO is a blockholder in about 31% of the sample firms. Table 3 shows that the coefficient on this indicator variable is significantly negative. The point estimate indicates that high target CEO share ownership reduces takeover premiums by almost 7% points.

When at least 40% of board members are classified as insiders, the takeover premium is significantly reduced by almost 7% points. I choose the 40% cutoff because it identifies about one-third of the sample. The negative impact of high fractions of inside directors is consistent with the result for the CEO share ownership. The more control the target CEO has, the lower is the takeover premium.

I measure outside blockholdings as total percentage holdings of blockholders, that is, holders of at least 5% of the firm's stock, minus the CEOs percentage holdings. This variable faces the same nonlinearity issues as CEO share ownership and board composition. Therefore, I only report the impact of an indicator variable that equals one when outside blockholdings do not exceed 10%, a condition satisfied by about 24% of the sample. As expected, low outside blockholdings significantly decrease takeover premiums by almost 5% points.

Next, I jointly estimate the effect of the indicator variables for high CEO share ownership, a high fraction of inside directors, and low outside blockholdings on takeover premiums. Column 4 of Table 3 shows that all three proxies retain their

---

[8] The industry classification I use is based on Table 1 in Teoh et al. (1998) that distinguishes 17 industries and allocates firms based on two-digit SIC codes.
[9] The cutoff level for the indicator variables are determined to accomplish two goals. First, the resulting indicator variable should equal one for a sufficiently large portion of the sample to have statistical power. Second, the resulting indicator variable should be restricted to equal one for a sufficiently small portion of the sample to represent distinct cases. While the 5% cutoff is arbitrary, Morck et al. (1988b) use the same level and the SEC defines blockholders as owners of 5% or more of a firm's equity. More important, small changes in the cutoff of this and all other proxies in my paper do not affect my results qualitatively. Table 1 shows the proportions of observations in which the various indicator variables are equal to one.

signs, but their statistical significance is somewhat lower with the proxy for low outside blockholdings becoming marginally insignificant. However, an F-test shows the joint significance of the three proxies at the 1% level.

Why is CEO share ownership still an important determinant of entrenchment when the presence of takeover defenses indicates that most managers are entrenched? Here, CEO share ownership is a measure of managerial power, not entrenchment. Because large equity stakes convey power, they measure aspects of the CEOs power that are not necessarily picked up by other proxies, such as insiders on the board. More target CEO power makes target shareholder intervention more costly and therefore increases the magnitude by which takeover premiums can be reduced without triggering shareholder actions.

One proxy for financial incentives is the target CEOs total option holdings as a fraction of shares outstanding. Again, I create an indicator variable that equals one when the CEO option holdings are less than 1%. Opposing effects might confound the impact on the takeover premium. If options serve their purpose of motivating managers to maximize shareholder wealth, they would increase the takeover premium. However, large holdings of exercisable options can be converted into common stock. As shown above, high levels of CEO share ownership reduce takeover premiums because they give the CEO control.[10] Column 5 shows no effect of the target CEOs' low option holdings indicator on the takeover premium. When the other proxies for target shareholder control are included with the low option holdings indicator, the low option holdings indicator remains insignificant and the significance of the other proxies is reduced, likely as a result of the lower number of observations caused by missing option data. Still, an F-test shows that high target CEO share ownership, high fractions of inside directors, and low outside blockholdings remain jointly significant.

Overall, Table 3 provides strong support that the three proxies for lower target shareholder control (percent CEO share ownership $\geq 5\%$, percent inside directors $\geq 40\%$, and outside blockholdings $\leq 10\%$) are associated with lower takeover premiums. The target CEOs' option holdings do not seem to affect takeover premiums.

6.3. Bidder effects

My high shareholder control indicator variable for targets with very high levels of shareholder control equals one when the fraction of inside directors is smaller than 40%, the target CEOs share ownership is less than 20%, the target CEOs tenure in her position has been less than 5 years, and the target has a chairman or president separate from the CEO. This variable selects the 17% of the sample firms with the highest levels of target shareholder control. Table 4 shows that the high shareholder control indicator

[10] In addition, large numbers of options might have been granted in the special case when a merger or takeover could have been anticipated. For example, occasionally CEOs are hired specifically to sell a target firm that is in a crisis. While it could be efficient to compensate the CEO with highly sensitive options, the takeover premium should be low in these cases because financial distress weakens the target's negotiating power.

Table 4

Impact of high shareholder control on takeover premiums, bidder returns, and target chief executive officer (CEO) benefits

Takeover premium is the dependent variable in Column 1 and bidder announcement return in Column 2. Columns 1 and 2 are estimated using ordinary least squares regressions with the heteroskedasticity adjustment by Davidson and MacKinnon (1993). High target shareholder control is associated with higher takeover premiums and lower bidder announcement returns. The dependent variable in the probit estimation in Column 3 equals one when the bidder offers an executive or board position to the target CEO, and zero otherwise. This information is available only for a subset of the sample. The reported coefficients represent marginal effects (dF/dX). High target shareholder control reduces the probability of the target CEOs receiving a job offer in the merged firm by almost 21%. In addition to the reported control variables, the coefficients of the following control variables, which either are insignificant or have no relevant interpretation in the context of this study, are not reported: long-term debt as a fraction of the market value of equity, indicator for the existence of a competitive bidder, indicator for merger rumors prior to the announcement date, time between the announcement date and the earlier of the effective or the target's delisting date, industry dummies, an indicator for bidder and target in the same industry, year dummies for 1995–1999, a dummy when Dow Jones News Retrieval articles indicate problems with the regulatory approval of the transaction, a financial distress dummy (total liabilities exceed total assets), a proxy for the target's profitability (net income as a fraction of total assets), and a proxy for the target's efficiency (sales as a fraction of total assets). *T*- and *Z*-statistics are in parentheses. ***, **, and * denote significance at the 0.01, 0.05, and 0.10 level, respectively.

	(1) Takeover premium	(2) Bidder return	(3) Target CEO position
Percent inside directors <40% and percent CEO share ownership <20% and separate chairman or president and tenure <5 years	0.0780**	−0.0361***	−0.2075**
	(2.25)	−(2.60)	−(2.02)
Hostile	0.1090*	−0.0163	−0.5685*
	(1.81)	−(0.55)	−(1.91)
Tender offer	−0.1031**	0.0181	−0.0348
	−(2.08)	(0.82)	−(0.21)
Ratio of target to bidder market value of equity	−0.2043***	−0.0071	−0.2303
	−(4.46)	−(0.29)	−(1.55)
Log (target total assets)	−0.0009	0.0031	−0.0034
	−(0.08)	(0.73)	−(0.10)
Fraction paid with cash	0.1158**	0.0292	−0.2072
	(2.26)	(1.35)	−(1.29)
Excess return 200 days prior	−0.1624***		0.0338
	−(3.47)		(0.24)
Intercept	0.2484***	−0.0571*	
	(2.68)	−(1.71)	
Adjusted R^2/log likelihood	0.17	0.03	−109.67
Number of observations	354	354	200

variable has a significantly positive effect on the takeover premium and a significantly negative effect on bidder announcement returns. This result suggests that target CEOs who lack such high shareholder control are susceptible to agree to merger terms that are more favorable to bidders.

Why would target CEOs agree to lower takeover premiums? One explanation could be bidder-provided incentives for the target CEO. My only proxy here is an indicator variable that equals one when the target CEO is offered an executive or board position in the merged firm.[11] I am able to collect this information for 200 deals. High target shareholder control significantly reduces the probability of a target CEO receiving the benefit of a job offer by about 20%. Arguably, this is a weak and incomplete proxy for bidder-provided private benefits for the target CEO. However, while clearly no proof, the results are at least consistent with the intuition that some target CEOs trade takeover premium for private benefits.

7. Robustness

I conduct several tests to verify the robustness of the results.

7.1. Cutoff levels of indicator variables

Several of my proxies are indicator variables that rely on somewhat arbitrary cutoff levels. One concern could be that the results obtain only for a very narrow range of cutoffs. I examine the robustness of my results by varying the cutoff levels.[12] For example, I vary the high CEO share ownership indicator (5% cutoff in the paper) between 2.5% and 20%, the high inside director indicator (40% cutoff in the paper) between 30% and 50%, and the large outside blockholdings indicator (10% cutoff in the paper) between 5% and 15%. The point estimates and significance levels depend on the cutoff levels, but signs never reverse. Qualitatively, the results stay the same and are robust to small changes in the cutoff levels. Furthermore, Table 5 shows that the logarithm of the target CEOs' share ownership is negatively correlated with the takeover premium and significant at the 5% level. The logarithm of the fraction of inside directors seems to be negatively correlated with the takeover premium, but in contrast to the corresponding indicator variable it is marginally insignificant. Firms that have both a low fraction of inside directors and large outside blockholdings achieve about 8% points higher takeover premiums, an effect that is statistically significant at the 1% level.

---

[11] Matsusaka (1993) finds higher bidder returns when the target management is retained. He explains his result as investors putting positive value on the target management's expertise remaining with the merged firm. His sample period coincides with the conglomerate merger wave of the late 1960s and has a large portion of diversifying acquisitions. Because diversifying mergers were rare in the 1990s and retaining target managers' expertise was arguably less important, viewing executive positions in the merged firm as perks instead of retained expertise seems more plausible during my sample period.

[12] Results and tables are available upon request from the author.

Table 5

Robustness of share ownership, board composition, and chief executive officer (CEO) options

Takeover premium is the dependent variable. All equations are estimated using ordinary least squares regressions with the heteroskedasticity adjustment by Davidson and MacKinnon (1993). In addition to the reported control variables, the coefficients of the following control variables, which either are insignificant or have no relevant interpretation in the context of this study, are not reported: long-term debt as a fraction of the market value of equity, indicator for the existence of a competitive bidder, indicator for merger rumors prior to the announcement date, time between the announcement date and the earlier of the effective or the target's delisting date, industry dummies, an indicator for bidder and target in the same industry, year dummies for 1995–1999, a dummy when Dow Jones News Retrieval articles indicate problems with the regulatory approval of the transaction, a financial distress dummy (total liabilities exceed total assets), a proxy for the target's profitability (net income as a fraction of total assets), and a proxy for the target's efficiency (sales as a fraction of total assets). Columns 1–3 show that the results for CEO share ownership and board composition do not depend on the specific definition of indicator variables. Columns 4 and 5 test whether target CEO stock or option holdings have a stronger affect on takeover premiums. T-statistics are in parentheses. ***, **, and * denote significance at the 0.01, 0.05, and 0.10 level, respectively.

Takeover premium	(1)	(2)	(3)	(4)	(5)
Log (percent CEO share ownership)	−0.0195** −(2.46)				
Log (percent inside directors)		−0.0358 −(1.50)			
Percent inside directors <40% and outside blockholdings >10%			0.0790*** (3.39)		
Log (amount CEO share ownership +1)				−0.0148* −(1.76)	
Log (amount CEO option value +1)				0.0001 (0.02)	
Percent CEO share ownership ≥5%					−0.0555* −(1.87)
Option price sensitivity <$20,000					−0.0450 −(1.44)
Hostile	0.1034* (1.74)	0.1033* (1.74)	0.1169** (2.03)	0.0693 (1.30)	0.0701 (1.37)
Tender offer	−0.1059** −(2.09)	−0.0976** −(2.03)	−0.1041** −(2.21)	−0.0892* −(1.74)	−0.0869* −(1.79)
Ratio of target to bidder market value of equity	−0.1994*** −(4.47)	−0.1991*** −(4.63)	−0.1980*** −(4.87)	−0.1862*** −(4.11)	−0.1904*** −(4.26)
Log (target total assets)	−0.0111 −(0.97)	−0.0038 −(0.35)	0.0000 (0.00)	0.0136 (1.14)	0.0048 −(0.42)
Fraction paid with cash	0.1309*** (2.58)	0.1252** (2.48)	0.1242** (2.54)	0.1258** (2.50)	0.1367*** (2.82)
Excess return 200 days prior	−0.1590*** −(3.69)	−0.1573*** −(3.66)	−0.1526*** −(3.53)	−0.1798*** −(3.82)	0.1956*** −(4.24)
Intercept	0.2388*** (2.62)	0.2173** (2.35)	0.1913** (2.19)	0.2696** (2.32)	0.2609** (2.56)
Adjusted R^2	0.17	0.16	0.19	0.21	0.22
Number of observations	364	373	372	294	294

7.2. Effect of CEO share ownership and option holdings

Table 3 shows a strong negative effect of the target CEOs' percentage share ownership on takeover premiums, but no effect of the percentage CEOs option holdings. Column 4 of Table 5 presents a horse race between the logarithm of the value of target CEOs' stock and the logarithm of the Black and Scholes value of the target CEOs' options. Again, CEO share ownership is significantly associated with lower takeover premiums, while options have no effect. Column 5 repeats the analysis with the indicators for high CEO share ownership and low sensitivity of option prices to underlying stock price (change in option value <$20,000 per 1% change in stock price). Again, the high share ownership indicator is significantly negative, while the effect of the options' sensitivity is insignificant. One explanation for the stronger effect of CEO share ownership is that in my sample the average value of the CEOs' stock is about three times higher than the value of their options.

7.3. Takeover defenses

Takeover defenses could affect takeover premiums. However, they appear to have little impact in my sample.

7.3.1. Staggered boards

Bebchuk et al. (2002) point out that staggered boards are effective antitakeover tools, often to the detriment of target shareholders when bids fail. They find that "effective" staggered boards, that is, boards that cannot be dismantled without having control of the board, have the strongest antitakeover effects. Cotter et al. (1997) find that independent boards and poison pills increase takeover premiums. Comment and Schwert (1995) determine not only that poison pills and share control laws are associated with higher takeover premiums, but also that these antitakeover measures do not seem to prevent takeovers.

My sample does not allow any inferences on the effect of antitakeover measures on the probability of receiving a bid or the probability of deal success. Columns 1 and 2 of Table 6 show that staggered boards by themselves do not seem to affect takeover premiums and that the fraction of insiders on the board appears to be a more important influence. However, when an indictor for insider-controlled staggered boards is added, staggered boards seem to increase takeover premiums as long as they are independent. Insider-controlled staggered boards are associated with lower takeover premiums. It appears that the antitakeover effect of a staggered board can be used for and against target shareholders' interests, depending on who the directors are. This result provides some insight as to why some studies find positive and others find harmful effects of antitakeover measures. It also relates to Black and Kraakman's (2002) "hidden value" model. If a target's true value is only visible to directors and hidden to target shareholders and potential bidders, then a staggered board might prevent target shareholders from selling their shares at too low a price.

Table 6

Impact of takeover defenses on takeover premiums

Takeover premium is the dependent variable. All equations are estimated using ordinary least squares regressions with the heteroskedasticity adjustment by Davidson and MacKinnon (1993). In addition to the reported control variables, the coefficients of the following control variables, which either are insignificant or have no relevant interpretation in the context of this study, are not reported: long-term debt as a fraction of the market value of equity, indicator for the existence of a competitive bidder, indicator for merger rumors prior to the announcement date, time between the announcement date and the earlier of the effective or the target's delisting date, industry dummies, an indicator for bidder and target in the same industry, year dummies for 1995–1999, a dummy when Dow Jones News Retrieval articles indicate problems with the regulatory approval of the transaction, a financial distress dummy (total liabilities exceed total assets), a proxy for the target's profitability (net income as a fraction of total assets), and a proxy for the target's efficiency (sales as a fraction of total assets). The results show that staggered boards with high fractions of inside directors decrease takeover premiums while Delaware incorporation, poison pills, and the governance index seem to have no effect. T-statistics are in parentheses. ***, **, and * denote significance at the 0.01, 0.05, and 0.10 level, respectively.

Takeover premium	(1)	(2)	(3)	(4)	(5)
Percent inside directors ≥40%	−0.0654**	−0.0247			
	−(2.29)	−(0.69)			
Staggered board	0.0295	0.0576**			
	(1.20)	(2.09)			
Staggered board and inside directors ≥40%		−0.0907*			
		−(1.72)			
Delaware corporation		0.0079 (0.32)			
Governance index			−0.0005		
			−(0.07)		
Poison pill				−0.0319	
				−(0.77)	
Hostile	0.0978*	0.1005*	0.0975*	0.1055	0.1036
	(1.73)	(1.85)	(1.69)	(1.30)	(1.25)
Tender offer	−0.1050**	−0.1051**	−0.0984**	−0.2035***	−0.2125***
	−(2.21)	−(2.19)	−(1.99)	−(2.86)	−(2.95)
Ratio of target to bidder market value of equity	−0.1948***	−0.1875***	−0.2052***	−0.3069***	−0.3089***
	−(4.60)	−(4.48)	−(4.77)	−(3.45)	−(3.44)
Log (target total assets)	−0.0065	−0.0068	0.0008 (0.07)	0.0322**	0.0341**
	−(0.60)	−(0.63)		(1.99)	(2.19)
Fraction paid with cash	0.1296***	0.1305***	0.1272**	0.2533***	0.2613***
	(2.60)	(2.59)	(2.44)	(3.56)	(3.56)
Excess return 200 days prior	−0.1493***	−0.1494***	−0.1594***	−0.0991	−0.1023
	−(3.48)	−(3.51)	−(3.70)	−(1.17)	−(1.18)
Intercept	0.2726***	0.2603***	0.2444***	0.1313	0.1359
	(3.09)	(2.94)	(2.71)	(0.86)	(1.08)
Adjusted R^2	0.17	0.18	0.16	0.25	0.25
Number of observations	370	370	371	169	169

7.3.2. State of incorporation

State laws differ substantially in the degree of takeover defenses they provide or allow. Most firms are able to choose their state of incorporation based on tax and legal considerations. Delaware law, for example, allows a host of takeover defenses and about 58% of my sample firms are incorporated in that state. Incorporation in Delaware could be a takeover defense, but Column 3 of Table 6 shows that being incorporated in Delaware does not affect takeover premiums. (Daines, 2001, finds that being incorporated in Delaware increases firms' Tobin's Q and their probability of receiving a takeover bid and being acquired.)

7.3.3. Governance index

Gompers et al. (2003) find that firms with a lower governance index (constructed from the Investor Responsibility Research Center, IRRC, dataset), that is, stronger shareholder rights, outperformed firms with weaker shareholder rights in the 1990s. The governance index does not affect takeover premiums (Column 4 of Table 6), probably because my sample includes only firms that were taken over successfully.

7.3.4. Poison pills

Given that Comment and Schwert (1995) cover a different time period than my sample, it is instructive to examine if the impact of poison pills has changed. I collect poison pill data from the IRRC database. Unfortunately, the database covers less than half of my sample. Of the target firms covered by IRRC, about 52% have poison pills in place. However, Column 5 of Table 6 shows that the presence of poison pills has no effect on takeover premiums in my sample. The reduced sample size might be one reason for the insignificance, another might be that the IRRC data have been updated only every 2–3 years. Moreover, poison pills can usually be deployed on short notice as need arises, reducing the importance of having poison pills in place.

7.4. Long-run returns

I calculate the excess return from 5 days before the announcement date to the earlier of the deal's effective or the target's delisting date (target realized return). It eliminates all uncertainty but has long event windows that vary substantially from deal to deal. The length of the event window, the longest extends for almost two and a half years, introduces large variances and noise that are unrelated to the merger event. Furthermore, if target shareholders tendered their shares before the delisting date, this measure perhaps is not representative of shareholders' payoffs.[13] I repeat the analyses of Table 3 using this measure, and significance levels are reduced.[14] The signs of the

---

[13] I thank the referee for pointing this out.

[14] Results are available from the author upon request.

coefficients appear unchanged, but all individual target shareholder control proxies are insignificant. Still, F-tests of the joint significance of my proxy variables reject that they equal zero.

7.5. Friendly and hostile deals

I also test the robustness of my results with two subsamples. The first contains only clearly friendly deals that the SDC database does not classify as hostile and in which the *Wall Street Journal* announcements do not indicate any hostility. The second contains only clearly friendly deals without revisions of the original offers that closed within 180 days of the announcement. The results using both subsamples are qualitatively similar to those presented here.

8. Conclusion

In the 1980s, target shareholder control and takeover premiums were negatively related. I show, however, that this relation is positive in the 1990s. Shareholder control is beneficial in the important market for corporate control.

My results suggest that direct shareholder control through outside blockholders and outside directors is most effective, while large share ownership of the target CEO can be harmful to target shareholders. Indirect financial incentives, such as executive stock options, do not seem to mitigate the principal-agent problem. Targets that are highly controlled by shareholders are associated with lower abnormal bidder returns, and CEOs of these targets are less likely to receive executive positions in the merged firm. This evidence suggests that powerful entrenched target CEOs reduce takeover premiums, possibly in return for bidder-provided incentives. Large equity ownership appears to be an inappropriate incentive for CEOs, in particular when the firm becomes a target.

The results here and in the related studies have important implications for the potential rent extraction by managers. Clearly, targets with powerful CEOs receive lower takeover premiums. However, premiums are generally positive and average more than 20%, while target CEOs generally lose large amounts of their human capital in takeovers. Given the current abundance of takeover defenses, allowing some rent extraction by managers might be beneficial for shareholders when it increases the probability of receiving profitable takeover offers. The more fundamental question becomes: Why are CEOs allowed to extract large rents when shareholders on their own, for example, through blockholders, could presumably extract those rents for themselves? Additional research is needed to answer this question.

References

Agrawal, A. and R. A. Walkling, 1994, "Executive Careers and Compensation Surrounding Takeover Bids," *Journal of Finance*, 49, 985–1014.

Bebchuk, L., J. Coates IV and G. Subramanian, 2002, "The Powerful Antitakeover Force of Staggered Boards: Theory, Evidence and Policy," *Stanford Law Review*, 54, 887–951.

Black, B. and R. Kraakman, 2002, "Delaware's Takeover Law: The Uncertain Search for Hidden Value," *Northwestern University Law Review*, 96, 521–566.

Comment, R. and G. W. Schwert, 1995, "Poison or Placebo? Evidence on the Deterrence and Wealth Effects of Modern Antitakeover Measures," *Journal of Financial Economics*, 39, 3–43.

Core, J. and W. Guay, 1999, "The Use of Equity Grants to Manage Optimal Equity Incentive Levels," *Journal of Accounting and Economics*, 28, 151–184.

Core, J. and W. Guay, 2002, "Estimating the Value of Employee Stock Option Portfolios and Their Sensitivities to Price and Volatility," Unpublished Working Paper, University of Pennsylvania.

Cotter, J. F., A. Shivdasani and M. Zenner, 1997, "Do Independent Directors Enhance Target Shareholder Wealth During Tender Offers?," *Journal of Financial Economics*, 43, 195–218.

Daines, R., 2001, "Does Delaware Law Improve Value?," *Journal of Financial Economics* 62, 525–558.

Davidson, R. and J. G. MacKinnon, 1993, *Estimation and Inference in Econometrics*, Oxford University Press, New York.

Gibbons, R. and K. J. Murphy, 1992, "Optimal Incentive Contracts in the Presence of Career Concerns: Theory and Evidence," *Journal of Political Economy*, 100, 468–505.

Gompers, P. A., J. L. Ishii and A. Metrick, 2003, "Corporate Governance and Equity Prices," *Quarterly Journal of Economics*, 118, 107–155.

Grossman, S. J. and O. Hart, 1980, "Takeover Bids, the Free-Rider Problem and the Theory of the Corporation," *Bell Journal of Economics*, 11, 42–64.

Hartzell, J., E. Ofek and D. Yermack, 2004, "What's in It for Me? CEOs Whose are Acquired," *Review of Financial Studies*, 17, 37–61.

LaPorta, R., F. Lopez-De-Silanes, A. Shleifer and R. Vishny, 2000, "Investor Protection and Corporate Governance," *Journal of Financial Economics*, 58, 3–27.

LaPorta, R., F. Lopez-De-Silanes, A. Shleifer and R. Vishny, 2002, "Investor Protection and Corporate Valuation," *Journal of Finance*, 63, 1147–1170.

Matsusaka, J. G., 1993, "Takeover Motives During the Conglomerate Merger Wave," *RAND Journal of Economics*, 24, 357–379.

Morck, R., A. Shleifer and R. W. Vishny, 1988a, "Characteristics of Targets of Hostile and Friendly Takeovers," In A. J. Auerbach (Ed.), *Corporate Takeovers: Causes and Consequences*, University of Chicago Press, Chicago, pp. 101–129.

Morck, R., A. Shleifer and R. W. Vishny, 1988b, "Management Ownership and Market Valuation," *Journal of Financial Economics*, 20, 293–315.

Schwert, G. W., 2000, "Hostility in Takeovers: In the Eyes of the Beholder?," *Journal of Finance*, 55, 2599–2640.

Shleifer, A. and R. W. Vishny, 1986, "Large Shareholders and Corporate Control," *Journal of Political Economy*, 94, 461–488.

Song, M. H. and R. H. Walkling, 1993, "The Impact of Managerial Ownership on Acquisition Attempts and Target Shareholder Wealth," *Journal of Financial and Quantitative Analysis*, 28, 439–457.

Stulz, R., 1988, "Managerial Control of Voting Rights: Financing Policies and the Market for Corporate Control," *Journal of Financial Economics*, 20, 25–54.

Teoh, S. H., I. Welch and T. J. Wong, 1998, "Earnings Management and the Long-Run Market Performance of Initial Public Offerings," *Journal of Finance*, 53, 1935–1974.

Travlos, N. G., 1987, "Corporate Takeover Bids, Methods of Payment, and Bidding' Stock Returns," *Journal of Finance*, 42, 943–963.

Wulf, J., 2004, "Do CEOs of Target Trade Power for Premium? Evidence from "Mergers of Equals"," *Journal of Law, Economics, and Organization*, 20, 60–101.

Chapter 15

CROSS-OWNERSHIP, RETURNS, AND VOTING IN MERGERS[*]

GREGOR MATVOS

Graduate School of Business, University of Chicago, Chicago, Illinois, USA

MICHAEL OSTROVSKY

Graduate School of Business, Stanford University, Stanford, California, USA

Contents

* We thank Anne Anderson, John Campbell, John Friedman, Randall Morck, David Scharfstein, Michael Schwarz, Andrei Shleifer, Luigi Zingales, the anonymous referee, and especially Jeremy Stein for helpful comments and suggestions. Leonid Pekelis and Alexander Ostrovsky provided excellent research assistance. Earlier drafts of this paper were circulated under the titles "Cross-ownership and returns to shareholders in mergers" and "Cross-ownership, returns, and voting in mergers: Conflicts of interest among shareholders."

This article originally appeared in the *Journal of Financial Economics*, Vol. 89, pp. 391–403 (2008).
Corporate Takeovers, Volume 2
Edited by B. Espen Eckbo
DOI: 10.1016/B978-0-12-381982-6.00016-1

Abstract

We show that institutional shareholders of acquiring companies on average do not lose money around public merger announcements, because they hold substantial stakes in the targets and make up for the losses from the acquirers with the gains from the targets. Depending on their holdings in the target, acquirer shareholders generally realize different returns from the same merger, some losing money and others gaining. This conflict of interest is reflected in the mutual fund voting behavior: In mergers with negative acquirer announcement returns, cross-owners are significantly more likely to vote for the merger.

Keywords

mergers and acquisitions, bidder returns, proxy voting

JEL classification: G34, G23

1. Introduction

On October 27, 2003, Bank of America (BAC) announced plans to acquire Fleet-Boston Financial (FBF). In the week following the announcement, the market capitalization of BAC decreased by $9 billion, from $122 billion to $113 billion, while the market capitalization of FBF increased by approximately the same amount, from $33.5 billion to $42.5 billion.[1] The 10 largest shareholders of BAC owned 24% of the company and so lost more than $2 billion dollars on their BAC holdings. The merger was subsequently approved by the BAC shareholders. This is somewhat unsettling. Why would the shareholders of BAC agree to lose almost 10% on their holdings, especially given that the 10 largest shareholders control almost a quarter of the company voting stock?

This example, while striking, is by no means an exception. Many studies show that average returns to acquiring-firm shareholders are negative, or at best slightly positive, while average returns to target-firm shareholders are positive and high, when both companies are publicly traded (Andrade et al., 2001; Jarrell et al., 1988; Jensen and Ruback, 1983; Moeller et al., 2004, 2005; Morck et al., 1990). Proposed explanations of negative announcement returns for the acquirers include overconfidence of their managers (Malmendier and Tate, 2008; Roll, 1986), empire-building and other personal objectives of managers (Jensen, 1986; Morck et al., 1990; Shleifer and Vishny, 1988, 1989), and a price pressure effect on acquirer's stock price around mergers (Mitchell et al., 2004). These papers, however, do not explain why shareholders of the acquiring firms remain largely inactive and do not try to block mergers.

In this paper we show that the incentives for many shareholders of acquiring firms to block negative-return mergers are often blunted or even reversed: Institutional investors do not lose nearly as much money as the simple computation above might suggest, because they frequently also own large stakes in the target companies.[2] Table 1 illustrates the effect of cross-ownership for the Bank of America-Fleet merger. Panel A lists the 10 largest shareholders of BAC and the 10 largest shareholders of Fleet prior to the merger. Eight out of 10 shareholders are on both lists. Panel B shows dollar returns of the 10 largest shareholders of BAC on their holdings in the two stocks. Instead of losing more than $2 billion, these shareholders gained more than $300 million. Even without the most successful shareholder, Capital Research and Management Company (CRMC), the remaining nine lost only around $200 million, that is, an order of magnitude less than the $2 billion suggested by the simple calculation.

---

[1] On the day of the announcement, the changes were −$12.4 billion and +$7.8 billion, respectively.

[2] Easterbrook and Fischel (1982) and Hansen and Lott (1996) also point out that diversified shareholders could hold shares in both the acquirer and the target in a merger and, hence, could care about the total return to their portfolio instead of individual returns to its components. These papers, however, do not estimate the average returns to share-holders in mergers taking this effect into account, do not discuss the conflict of interest among the shareholders, and do not present evidence on shareholders' voting behavior.

Table 1

Top institutional investors' holdings and announcement returns in the merger of Bank of America (BAC) and FleetBoston Financial (FBF)

This table describes the returns of top institutional shareholders around the announcement of the Bank of America-FleetBoston Financial merger on Monday, October 27, 2003. Panel A lists 10 largest share-holders of BAC and FBF and their holdings (as a percentage of all shares outstanding). Panel B shows the losses from BAC holdings, gains from FBF holdings, and net returns of the 10 largest shareholders of BAC around the announcement. Panel C shows aggregate holdings and returns of all institutional shareholders of BAC around the announcement. Holdings are as of September 30, 2003. Gains and losses in millions of dollars are from Friday, October 24 to Friday, October 31, 2003. Data are from Thomson Financial and the Center for Research in Security Prices.

Panel A. 10 largest shareholders of BAC and FBF

Shareholder	Percent owned
Shareholders of Bank of America	
Barclays	4.77
Fidelity	3.69
State Street	3.00
Axa	2.97
CRMC	2.16
Vanguard	1.87
Mellon	1.52
Northern Trust	1.31
Deutsche Bank	1.27
Morgan Stanley	1.15
Shareholders of FleetBoston Financial	
CRMC	8.50
Barclays	5.14
Axa	3.13
State Street	2.91
Fidelity	2.23
Vanguard	1.88
Bank of America	1.82
MFS	1.77
Deutsche Bank	1.18
Northern Trust	1.10

Panel B. Returns of the 10 largest shareholders of Bank of America

Shareholder	BAC return	FBF return	Net return
Barclays	−430	461	31
Fidelity	−332	200	−133
State Street	−270	261	−9
Axa	−268	281	13
CRMC	−195	763	568
Vanguard	−170	168	−2

(Continued)

Table 1 (*Continued*)

Shareholder	BAC return	FBF return	Net return
Mellon	−137	90	−47
Northern Trust	−118	99	−19
Deutsche Bank	−115	106	−9
Morgan Stanley	−103	39	−64
Total	−2139	2469	329

Panel C. Aggregate holdings and returns of all institutional shareholders of Bank of America

Holdings and returns	Value
BAC shares held by institutional shareholders (millions)	861
Percent of BAC shares owned by institutional shareholders	57.5
FBF shares held by institutional shareholders of BAC (millions)	647
Percent of FBF shares owned by institutional shareholders of BAC	61.5
Loss of institutional shareholders of BAC on BAC shares	−5277
Gain of institutional shareholders of BAC on FBF shares	5558
Net gain	281

This observation points to a conflict of interest between Acquirer-only (A-only) shareholders, who do not hold shares of the target and bear the full loss, and cross-owners, who are compensated by the gains in the target. We first demonstrate that the Bank of America-Fleet merger is not an exception. In a sample of mergers between publicly traded US firms from 1981 to 2003, the amount of institutional cross-ownership is substantial. Without taking cross-ownership into account, average returns to acquiring-firm shareholders are negative and significant, in line with previous studies. Announcement returns to cross-owners, meanwhile, are on average positive. The returns realized in the target for this group of shareholders on average more than make up for the losses incurred from their holdings in the acquirer. Overall, taking target-firm holdings of acquiring-firm shareholders into account, we find that returns to institutional investors in the acquirer on average do not significantly differ from zero.

Because the returns to A-only shareholders and to cross-owners are so different, their incentives to approve or disapprove a merger are also different, and so it is natural to expect that their behavior when they vote on a merger proposal is different as well. We test this conjecture using a data set containing mutual fund votes in a sample of mergers announced in years 2003–2006. We show that mutual funds that hold shares in the target company are more likely than A-only shareholders to vote for a merger with negative acquirer announcement returns. There is no difference in voting behavior between the two groups of shareholders when acquirer announcement returns are positive.

The rest of the paper is organized as follows. Section 2 examines the impact of cross-ownership on institutional investor returns in mergers. We first work out in detail the effects of cross-ownership on returns of institutional investors on the example of the Bank of America-Fleet merger and then we extend the analysis to a sample of mergers from 1981 to 2003. Section 3 provides the details of the construction of the data set on mutual fund voting and presents evidence on the effect of cross-ownership on mutual fund voting in mergers. Section 4 concludes.

2. Institutional investors' holdings and returns around merger announcements

In this section, we describe the holdings of institutional investors and their returns around merger announcements, and then we show that taking into account holdings in the target firms makes a large and significant difference to the returns to the acquiring firms' investors. After taking these holdings into account, the average returns to institutional owners are statistically indistinguishable from zero.

2.1. Data

Our sample includes completed mergers of publicly traded US companies reported in Center for Research in Security Prices (CRSP) and Thomson Financial SDC Platinum (SDC) merger databases. The sample starts in 1981, when ownership data became available, and ends in 2003. We restrict the sample to mergers in which the acquiring firm owns less than 50% of the target prior to the announcement date and 100% after the completion of transaction. We also require that the market capitalization of the target be greater than $1 million (inflation-adjusted, 2003 dollars) and also greater than 1% of that of the acquirer. Finally, we exclude mergers involving firms that have multiple classes of shares traded, mergers involving bidding wars, mergers for which CRSP and SDC databases report announcement dates that differ by more than one trading day, and records that could not be matched with price and return data. The information on institutional ownership comes from the Thomson Financial CDA/ Spectrum Institutional (13f) Holdings database. We consider only mergers for which institutional ownership in both participating companies is positive.

The resulting sample contains 2529 observations. Panel A of Table 2 shows summary statistics for the sample. On average, institutional investors hold 43.1% of the shares of acquiring companies and 29.5% of the shares of target companies. Of these, slightly less than a third (12.1%) of shares of acquiring companies held by institutional holders is held by cross-owners, who also own slightly more than a half (15.5%) of institutional holdings of target companies' shares. The average market capitalizations of the acquirer and the target are approximately $6 billion and $816 million, respectively (in 2003 dollars), and the market capitalization of the target is on average 22% of the market capitalization of the acquirer.

Moeller et al. (2004) show that size is an important determinant of merger returns and that the shareholders of acquiring firms earn significantly lower abnormal returns in large mergers than they do in small mergers. In Panel B of Table 2, we show the same summary statistics as in Panel A, but only for the largest one hundred mergers

Table 2

Institutional ownership and cross-ownership of acquirer and target shares before merger announcements from 1981 to 2003

Panel A presents summary statistics on institutional ownership for a sample of 2529 completed mergers and acquisitions of public US companies between 1981 and 2003 in which institutional ownership in both the acquirer and the target is positive. Returns are market-model abnormal returns relative to the CRSP equally weighted index benchmark over the $(-5, +5)$ trading days event window, in percentages. Holdings are in percentages of all shares outstanding, as of the end of the last quarter prior to the merger. Market capitalization is in millions of 2003 dollars. Panel B presents summary statistics for the subsample of 100 largest mergers, by inflation-adjusted market capitalization of the target. Data are from the Center for Research in Security Prices and Thomson Financial SDC Platinum merger databases and the Thomson Financial CDA/Spectrum Institutional (13f) Holdings database.

Variable	Mean	Median	SD
Panel A. Full sample			
Market-model abnormal acquirer (A) return	−1.64	−1.65	10.50
Market-model abnormal target (T) return	21.93	18.16	24.87
Acquirer market capitalization	5973	1407	17,417
Target market capitalization	816	139	3747
Shares of acquirer held by institutions	43.09	43.03	24.15
Shares of target held by institutions	29.53	24.07	23.31
Shares of A held by T's institutional investors	12.13	6.99	13.53
Shares of T held by A's institutional investors	15.49	9.59	16.56
Relative size	0.22	0.13	0.23
Panel B. The one hundred largest mergers			
Market-model abnormal acquirer (A) return	−4.70	−4.52	9.82
Market-model abnormal target (T) return	16.48	15.45	14.59
Acquirer market capitalization	39,957	18,895	52,258
Target market capitalization	11,985	6650	14,819
Shares of acquirer held by institutions	56.21	57.38	17.22
Shares of target held by institutions	58.12	60.91	18.03
Shares of A held by T's institutional investors	42.23	41.81	15.65
Shares of T held by A's institutional investors	45.71	44.58	16.25
Relative size	0.44	0.41	0.25

(by the market capitalization of the target, in 2003 dollars). Institutional holdings and the degree of cross-ownership are much higher in this subsample. On average, institutions hold more than 50% of shares of each company (56.2% of acquirer and 58.1% of target) and cross-owners own three-quarters of acquirer (42.2%) and target (45.7%) institutional holdings.

2.2. Shareholders' gains and losses: an example

We estimate the average returns to shareholders around merger announcements using the standard event study methodology (Brown and Warner, 1985), with and without adjustment for cross-ownership. We first illustrate our adjustment procedure using the Bank of America-Fleet merger as an example (Table 1, Panel C). The weekly announcement return on the BAC shares was -7.5%. With the market capitalization of $122 billion, this translates into a return of $-7.5\% \times \$122{,}488$ million $= -\$9172$ million to BAC shareholders (the numbers in equations are rounded to the nearest tenth for percentages and to the nearest million for dollar amounts). The institutional ownership of BAC was 57.5%, so institutional owners lost $57.5\% \times \$9172$ million $-\$5277$ million on their investment in BAC. Without taking cross-ownership into account, this loss might be interpreted as the loss to the institutional shareholders of BAC from the transaction.

This calculation ignores the fact that the institutional shareholders of BAC also held 61.5% of all Fleet shares and partook in its 27% gain. With the market capitalization of $33 billion, this amounts to a return of $(27.0\% \times 61.5\% \times \$33{,}462 \text{ million}) = \$5558$ million. These gains exceeded the losses the institutional investors of BAC suffered on their positions in BAC by $5558 million $-\$5277$ million $= \$281$ million. We calculate adjusted announcement returns by taking into account the total holdings of acquirer institutional owners, including their investment in the target.[3] Then the total investment of institutional holders of BAC is $(57.5\% \times \$122{,}488 \text{ million} + 61.5\% \times \$33{,}462 \text{ million}) = \$91{,}040$ million and the adjusted return on this investment is $281 million/$91,040 million $= 0.3\%$. This simple calculation puts the BAC-FBF merger in a different light for the average institutional owner. Instead of losing 7.5%, it makes 0.3%.

The return calculation can also be applied to cross-owners, not all institutional owners of the acquirer (i.e., excluding the institutional shareholders of the acquirer who do not hold any shares in the target). They owned 53.8% of BAC and 61.5% of FBF, thus realizing smaller losses on the acquirer and earning the returns over a smaller overall investment. Their total investment was $(53.8\% \times \$122{,}488 \text{ million} + 61.5\% \times \$33{,}462 \text{ million}) = \$86{,}417$ million. They made $(-7.5\% \times 53.8\% \times \$122{,}488 \text{ million}) = -\$4931$ million on the acquirer and $(27.0\% \times 61.5\% \times \$33{,}462 \text{ million}) = \$5558$ million on the target, earning an overall return of $627 million. Their percentage return is then $627 million/$86,417 million $= 0.7\%$, which is significantly higher than the -7.5% earned by investors holding only the acquirer. This difference in returns also suggests that these two groups of shareholders could have very different incentives in whether this merger should take place.

Comparing the adjusted returns from the BAC-FBF example with the unadjusted returns to BAC, we see that the cross-ownership adjustment can be substantial. Section 2.3 applies the basic calculations above, with some variations and robustness checks, to the sample of 2529 mergers described in Section 2.1.

---

[3] An alternative way to normalize the cross-ownership-adjusted (adjusted) abnormal returns is to divide the dollar returns by the value of institutional investments in the acquirer only. The results do not change significantly because the target is on average much smaller than the acquirer.

2.3. Shareholders' gains and losses: results from 1981 to 2003

In this section, we show that, when cross-holdings are taken into account, the mean abnormal return to institutional shareholders around merger announcements is statistically indistinguishable from zero. Mean acquirer abnormal returns unadjusted for cross-ownership in our sample are consistent with the previous literature: They are negative at around -1% and highly statistically significant.[4] Table 3 presents the unadjusted and adjusted abnormal and raw returns to institutional shareholders over the $(-5, +5)$ days window. We use three different ways of estimating returns: market-model abnormal returns, market-adjusted returns (raw return minus the CRSP equally weighted index), and raw returns. The market-model abnormal return on the acquirer is -1.64%, and the market-adjusted abnormal return is -1.36%. Both are statistically significant at the 1% level. The raw return is -0.26%, statistically insignificant. Thus, by looking only at the abnormal returns to the acquirer shares, one might conclude that an acquisition of a public target is, on average, bad news for acquirers' shareholders.

Once we adjust for cross-ownership, the abnormal returns to acquirers' institutional shareholders around merger announcements are not statistically different from zero. Column 3 of Panel A shows that the average of adjusted market-model abnormal returns is -0.29% and statistically insignificant, as is the average of market-adjusted returns (-0.04%). The average of raw returns, once adjusted for acquirer holdings in the target, is positive (1.06%). Regardless of return specifications, on average the institutional owners of the acquirer do not seem to realize a negative announcement return in public mergers. Table 3 also demonstrates that the difference between adjusted and unadjusted acquirer returns is not a consequence of behavior in the tails. The results hold for the medians of adjusted and unadjusted returns. Table 4 shows that the results over the $(-1, +1)$ and $(-20, +20)$ days windows are similar to those over the $(-5, +5)$ days windows.

Another way to understand the impact of cross-ownership on merger announcement returns is to look at the average cross-ownership adjustment to acquirer announcement returns. This difference between the unadjusted and adjusted returns is presented in the last column. It is very stable, ranging from 1.33% for market-adjusted returns to 1.35% for market-model abnormal returns. All changes are statistically significant at the 1% level. These results show that the magnitude of the adjustment is comparable to the negative returns calculated without taking cross-ownership into account.

The results are even more striking if we restrict the analysis to the sample of one hundred largest mergers (by the inflation-adjusted market capitalization of the target), which are presented in Panel B. These mergers are on average worse for the acquirer than the average merger from the full sample. The magnitudes of the acquirer returns

---

[4] Andrade et al. (2001) report -0.7% return for the acquirer over the $(-1, +1)$ event window and -3.8% for the acquirer from 20 days before the announcement to the completion of the merger, for a sample of mergers of publicly traded companies from 1973 to 1998. Moeller et al. (2004) also report that acquirers of public companies lose, on average, 1% around announcement, for the sample of mergers from 1980 to 2001.

Table 3

Returns to institutional investors around merger announcements

The sample in Panel A contains 2529 completed mergers and acquisitions of public US companies between 1981 and 2003 in which institutional ownership in both the acquirer and the target is positive. The sample in Panel B contains the 100 largest mergers, by inflation-adjusted market capitalization of the target. All returns are over the (−5, +5) trading days event window. Market-adjusted and market-model abnormal returns are relative to the CRSP equally weighted index benchmark. Return to cross-holders is computed as the dollar return to shareholders who have shares both in the target and the acquirer, divided by the total value of their holdings in both the acquirer and the target. Adjusted return to the shareholders of an acquirer is computed as the total dollar return to the shareholders of the acquirer from their holdings in both the acquirer and the target, divided by the total value of their holdings in the acquirer and the target. *Significant at 10%; **significant at 5%; ***significant at 1%. Data are from the Center for Research in Security Prices and Thomson Financial SDC Platinum merger databases, Thomson Financial CDA/Spectrum Institutional (13f) Holdings database, and CRSP stock price database.

Returns	Return on acquirer stock (1)	Return to cross-holders (2)	Cross-ownership adjusted return (3)	Return difference (2 − 1)	Return difference (3 − 1)
Panel A. Full sample					
Market-model abnormal return					
Mean (%)	−1.64	2.29	−0.29	4.04	1.35
Standard error (%)	0.21	0.23***	0.20	0.14***	0.05***
Median (%)	−1.65	1.62	−0.26	2.02	0.35
Market-adjusted return					
Mean (%)	−1.36	2.49	−0.04	4.00	1.33
Standard error (%)	0.21***	0.23***	0.20	0.14***	0.05***
Median (%)	−1.49	1.79	−0.37	1.98	0.34
Raw return					
Mean (%)	−0.26	3.53	1.06	3.94	1.33
Standard error (%)	0.22	0.23***	0.22***	0.13***	0.05***
Median (%)	−0.35	2.75	0.65	1.99	0.34
Panel B. The one hundred largest mergers					
Market-model abnormal return					
Mean (%)	−4.70	0.80	−0.27	5.51	4.43
Standard error (%)	0.98***	0.87	0.86	0.46***	0.37***
Median (%)	−4.52	0.81	0.07	5.21	4.58
Market-adjusted return					
Mean (%)	−3.69	1.64	0.59	5.34	4.29
Standard error (%)	1.04***	0.98*	0.97	0.44***	0.36***
Median (%)	−3.65	1.03	0.31	5.07	4.37
Raw return					
Mean (%)	−2.80	2.51	1.47	5.31	4.27
Standard error (%)	1.10**	1.07**	1.05	0.44***	0.36***
Median (%)	−3.15	2.46	1.05	5.07	4.37

Table 4

Returns to institutional investors around merger announcements over the $(-1, +1)$ and $(-20, +20)$ days windows

The sample contains 2529 completed mergers and acquisitions of public US companies between 1981 and 2003 in which institutional ownership in both the acquirer and the target is positive. Panel A presents returns over the $(-1, +1)$ trading days event window. Panel B presents returns over the $(-20, +20)$ trading days event window. Market-adjusted and market-model abnormal returns are relative to the CRSP equally weighted index benchmark. Return to cross-holders is computed as the dollar return to shareholders who have shares both in the target and the acquirer, divided by the total value of their holdings in both the acquirer and the target. Adjusted return to the shareholders of an acquirer is computed as the total dollar return to the shareholders of the acquirer from their holdings in both the acquirer and the target, divided by the total value of their holdings in the acquirer and the target. *Significant at 10%; **significant at 1%.

Returns	Return on acquirer stock (1)	Return to cross-holders (2)	Cross-ownership adjusted return (3)	Return difference (2 − 1)	Return difference (3 − 1)
Panel A. (−1, +1) event window					
Market-model abnormal return					
Mean (%)	−1.49	1.99	−0.29	3.58	1.20
Standard error (%)	0.16**	0.19**	0.16*	0.14**	0.05**
Market-adjusted return					
Mean (%)	−1.42	2.04	−0.23	3.57	1.19
Standard error (%)	0.16**	0.19**	0.16	0.14**	0.05**
Raw return					
Mean (%)	−1.13	2.26	0.06	3.51	1.19
Standard error (%)	0.17**	0.19**	0.16	0.12**	0.05**
Panel B. (−20, +20) event window					
Market-model abnormal return					
Mean (%)	−3.05	1.64	−1.52	4.76	1.53
Standard error (%)	0.39**	0.38**	0.38**	0.17**	0.07**
Market-adjusted return					
Mean (%)	−1.76	2.52	−0.36	4.48	1.40
Standard error (%)	0.34**	0.35**	0.33	0.16**	0.06**
Raw return					
Mean (%)	2.71	6.97	4.11	4.42	1.40
Standard error (%)	0.37**	0.38**	0.36**	0.15**	0.06**

are -3.69% for market-adjusted returns and -4.70% for market-model abnormal returns. The average adjusted returns are similar to the ones calculated in the full sample, statistically indistinguishable from zero. These mergers are not only worse for the acquirer shareholders on average, but, as pointed out in Section 2.1, they also have a higher degree of cross-ownership. This is reflected in the difference between un-adjusted returns and adjusted returns in the last column. Regardless of return calculation, the difference is greater than 4%, statistically significant at the 1% level.

While the average announcement return to institutional investors from the merger is statistically indistinguishable from zero, these investors are not a homogeneous group and have potentially very different incentives in a merger. The investors who hold only acquirer stock on average realize negative abnormal returns. Cross-owners, meanwhile, realize positive returns (Table 3, Column 2). Their announcement abnormal returns are 2.29% for market-model abnormal returns and 2.49% for market-adjusted returns.[5] Column 4 in the same table shows that cross-owners on average realize announcement returns that are 4% points higher than the returns to institutional investors who hold only shares in the acquirer. These results suggest a potential conflict of interest between these two groups of shareholders, which is the focus of our analysis of shareholder voting behavior in Section 3.

Table 5 shows the results for cash, stock, and mixed mergers separately. The adjustment for cross-ownership is substantial and similar in magnitude for all three merger types. In contrast (and consistent with the previous literature), the unadjusted returns are very different for different merger types, and so the adjusted returns are different as well. Notably, cross-owners realize positive average announcement returns of 0.7% even in pure equity mergers, which have the lowest adjusted and unadjusted returns for the acquirers, once again showing that, in mergers, different shareholders of the acquirer receive very different payoffs, depending on their holdings in the target.

We do not have data for individual investors and therefore cannot estimate the impact of the cross-holding adjustment on their returns. Also, we do not take into account the fact that even if, say, a mutual fund holds shares only in the acquirer, an individual investor in that fund could hold shares in other mutual funds, which, in turn, could hold shares in the target. This individual investor would also get some benefit from cross-ownership, thus potentially reducing the conflict of interest between institutions that hold shares only in the acquirer and those that hold shares in both the acquirer and the target. The basic arithmetic, however, is the same: Diversified investors who hold shares in both acquiring and target firms lose less, and possibly even gain, while investors who hold shares only in acquiring firms bear the full loss around merger announcements.

3. Voting

In Section 2 we show that, while shareholders who hold shares only in the acquiring company on average realize negative announcement returns, institutional investors on average realize returns that are close to zero. Moreover, a subgroup of institutional shareholders, the cross-owners, in fact realize positive returns, even in equity mergers. This suggests a potential conflict of interest between the shareholders who hold only shares in the acquirer and the cross-owners. The former should never want bad mergers

[5] There are 122 mergers in our sample that do not have any cross-owners. For these mergers, the return to cross-owners is not defined and so the numbers in Columns 2 and 4 are reported only for the remaining 2407 mergers. Restricting the analysis to this sample changes the results in Columns 1, 3, and 5 only slightly.

Table 5

Returns to institutional investors around merger announcements by form of payment

The subsamples in this table are from the sample of 2529 completed mergers and acquisitions of public US companies between 1981 and 2003 in which institutional ownership in both the acquirer and the target is positive. The subsamples are drawn based on the method of payment: Panel A cash; Panel B stock; Panel C mixed. Returns are market-model abnormal returns relative to the CRSP equally weighted index benchmark over the $(-5, +5)$ trading days event window. Return to cross-holders is computed as the dollar return to shareholders who have shares both in the target and the acquirer, divided by the total value of their holdings in both the acquirer and the target. Adjusted return to the shareholders of an acquirer is computed as the total dollar return to the shareholders of the acquirer from their holdings in both the acquirer and the target, divided by the total value of their holdings in the acquirer and the target. *Significant at 5%; **significant at 1%.

	Return on acquirer stock (1)	Return to cross-holders (2)	Cross-ownership adjusted return (3)	Return difference (2 − 1)	Return difference (3 − 1)
Panel A. Cash					
Mean (%)	1.38	5.38	2.22	4.16	0.83
Standard error (%)	0.38**	0.54**	0.37**	0.41**	0.08**
Number of mergers	570	542	570	542	570
Panel B. Stock					
Mean (%)	−2.88	0.70	−1.55	3.62	1.32
Standard error (%)	0.32**	0.31*	0.30**	0.18**	0.08**
Number of mergers	1268	1213	1268	1213	1268
Panel C. Mixed					
Mean (%)	−1.86	2.67	−0.04	4.73	1.82
Standard error (%)	0.37**	0.38**	0.35	0.25**	0.12**
Number of mergers	691	652	691	652	691

to go through, while the latter might like such mergers if they own sufficiently large stakes in the target.

In principle, other conflicts of interest could arise among shareholders, due to different tax situations, risk attitudes, and time horizons. However, the specific conflict of interest that we identify is reflected in investors' behavior exceptionally clearly and directly. We show that, in a given merger, mutual funds that hold shares in both the acquirer and the target are more likely to vote for the merger than the ones that hold shares only in the acquirer. Furthermore, we show that this effect is present only in mergers with negative announcement effects, showing that, as expected, the conflict arises only in mergers with negative returns in the acquirer. It is in the interest of both shareholder groups to pass mergers with positive announcement returns.

3.1. Data

Until recently, voting in shareholder meetings in the US was confidential. Mutual funds and other investors did not have to disclose how they voted unless they wished to do so. Beginning in 2003, however, the Securities and Exchange Commission (SEC) required all mutual funds to disclose their votes in N-PX and N-PX/A filings. Our data set was collected from the filings submitted by the funds to the SEC between August 2004 and December 2006. These filings contain information on votes in shareholder meetings that took place between July 1, 2003 and June 30, 2006.

Each fund is required to report the names and identifiers of the companies in which voting took place, meeting and record dates, short descriptions of the proposals being voted on, management recommendations on the issues, and the fund's votes. The proposals range from mergers and acquisitions to election of directors and shareholder resolutions. The SEC, however, does not specify a particular format in which these reports should be submitted. As a result, funds submit their filings in a wide variety of different formats, and moreover, for the same fund the format often changes from one year to the next. Fortunately, some formats are relatively common. We downloaded all funds' filings and searched through a subsample of them (the subsample included the one hundred largest funds as well as a number of popular fund families) to identify the different formats present there. We identified 46 different formats and wrote Perl scripts to extract data from them.

From that voting data, we extracted the records with votes on mergers and acquisitions and combined them with a list of mergers and acquisitions obtained from SDC Platinum database for the corresponding time period (2003–2006) using firm identifiers (tickers and CUSIPs), keeping the deals for which voting data were present for both the acquirer and the target. For each fund and each merger in which the fund voted, we then identified whether the fund voted only in the acquirer, only in the target, or in both. Because we are interested in shareholder voting in acquiring firms, we focus on the records in which either the fund reported votes only in the acquirer (in which case we classify it as an A-only shareholder) or in both the acquirer and the target (in which case we classify it as a cross-owner).

Next, we combined our voting data with the data on mutual fund holdings. In their filings, the funds were not required to include any fund-specific identifiers. They only included fund family-specific identifiers as well as fund names. More precisely, they included the Central Index Key (CIK) numbers that the SEC assigned to fund families and groups. Multiple CIK numbers could correspond to the same fund family.

Because fund names can be written in many different ways, we could not match the voting data to the holdings data from other databases based directly on them. What we did instead is as follows. In a separate database, for the funds in which it can be done reliably, the SEC reports fund ticker symbols corresponding to fund names.[6] Because this is a different database, fund names in it do not have to match exactly to the names in NP-X and NP-X/A forms submitted by funds (in fact, they can be quite different, because funds' names sometimes change). Fortunately, both databases contain CIK

---

[6] For example, ticker symbols for Vanguard Index Funds can be obtained at http://www.sec.gov/cgi-bin/browse-edgar?CIK=0000036405&action=getcompany&scd=series.

numbers, and so our matching procedure consisted of two steps. First, we matched each group of funds with the same CIK number in one database to the group of funds with the same CIK number in the other database. Then, we manually matched the funds in each group by their names. We then matched the ticker symbols for the funds to their portfolio codes in CRSP Mutual Fund database, which allowed us to obtain mutual fund holdings.[7] The resulting data set contains 7322 records, which include 114 mergers and 1457 mutual funds. To calculate announcement returns we obtained stock prices from the CRSP stock price database and merged them with the voting and holdings data on six-digit CUSIPs. We obtained family membership from the CRSP ICDI mappings database, which we merged on portfolio codes.

3.2. Summary statistics

The summary statistics for the voting data are presented in Tables 6 and 7. The average acquirer market capitalization ($27.5 billion) and target market capitalization ($11.4 billion) are larger than in the sample analyzed in Section 2 ($6.0 billion and $0.8 billion, respectively). Because the merger has to have come up for a vote in the acquirer to be included in the sample, the targets are also on average much larger relative to the acquirer (0.55) than in Section 2 (0.22). Announcement returns are lower. Market-model abnormal returns from a $(-5, +5)$ event window for the acquirer are -5.2% and 13.3% for the target. In 36% of observations the fund is a cross-owner, holding both the acquirer and the target.

Table 7, Panel A shows that mutual funds overwhelmingly approve mergers: 97.4% of votes are "for" the acquisition, only 1.7% are "against," and 0.9% are "did not" or "abstain." A large number of funds in our sample never oppose the management and always vote "for." This is in line with the findings of Matvos and Ostrovsky (2008), who show that a large heterogeneity exists among funds in terms of their propensity to oppose the management in board of director elections and that a large fraction of funds votes "for" management-recommended directors 100% of the time. In Panel B of Table 7, we drop these "nonresponsive" funds. We look at "responsive" ones, which have cast an "against" or "did not" vote in at least one merger in our sample. These funds support mergers to a much smaller degree. They cast 90.3% of votes "for" mergers, 6.3% "against," and 3.5% "did not."

In principle, funds that hold shares in both the acquirer and the target should cast the same vote in both companies, either helping to approve the merger or trying to prevent it. Nevertheless, we observe several instances in which funds cast a "for" vote on one side of the deal and an "against" vote on the other. For example, in the merger between Boise Cascade and OfficeMax, Schwab Total Stock Market Index Fund voted "for" the merger in OfficeMax and "against" the merger in Boise Cascade.

---

[7] Another potential complication is that the same fund could have multiple ticker symbols for different share classes. This, however, turns out not to be a major issue, because the same group of tickers corresponding to the fund in the SEC database usually corresponds to it in the CRSP database as well.

Table 6

Voting behavior: summary statistics of holdings and returns

The sample contains 7322 mutual fund votes in acquirers in 114 completed mergers and acquisitions of public US companies between 2003 and 2006 in which mutual funds voted on the merger in the acquirer and the target. Returns are market-model abnormal returns relative to the CRSP equally weighted index benchmark over the $(-5, +5)$ trading days event window. Market capitalization is in millions of US dollars. Fund return is calculated as the abnormal dollar return to the fund from its holdings in the acquirer and the target divided by the total value of its holdings. Target holding is a dummy variable that takes the value of one if the mutual fund voting in the acquirer also has holdings in the target. Data are from the Securities and Exchange Commission Edgar database (N-PX filings), Thomson Financial SDC Platinum merger database, CRSP mutual fund holdings database, and CRSP stock price database.

Variable	Mean	Median	S.D.
Acquirer return (%)	−5.15	−5.91	9.14
Target return (%)	13.29	10.70	12.34
Fund return (%)	−3.23	−2.38	10.21
Acquirer market capitalization	27,503	8387	41,417
Target market capitalization	11,397	4919	15,478
Relative size (target/acquirer)	0.55	0.52	0.32
Target holding	0.36	0.00	0.48

Table 7

Voting behavior: distribution of votes

The sample in Panel A contains 7322 mutual fund votes in acquirers' shareholder meetings in 114 completed mergers and acquisitions of public US companies between 2003 and 2006. Panel B presents summary statistics for the subsample of responsive funds. Responsive funds are funds that have cast at least one "did not" or "against" vote in our sample.

Vote	Frequency	Percent
Panel A. Full sample		
Against	123	1.68
Did not	68	0.93
For	7131	97.39
Total	7322	100
Panel B. Responsive funds		
Against	123	6.26
Did not	68	3.46
For	1773	90.27
Total	1964	100

This voting behavior is inconsistent with the fiduciary duty of the funds. The funds are fiduciaries of their shareholders and not of the acquirer shareholders or the target shareholders. These inconsistent votes could be due to funds following recommendations of outside advisers or internal guidelines and procedures that do not take cross-ownership into account. We adopt a conservative approach and do not remove them from the data. Removing them would make our results stronger.

3.3. Results

The effect of cross-ownership on voting of mutual funds in mergers can be easily seen from basic descriptive statistics. In Table 8, Panel A, cross-owners are more than twice as likely to vote "against" the merger as A-only funds: 2.2% versus 0.8%. The difference is more striking when we restrict our attention to responsive funds in Panel B. Among these funds, 11.9% of A-only owners vote "against" the merger and 82.6% vote "for," while 2% of cross-owners vote "against" and 96.1% vote "for." Table 9 confirms the descriptive results by estimating the linear probability, logit, and conditional logit (fixed effects logit) models on the full sample. The linear probability model in Column 1 of Panel A and the logit model in Column 1 of Panels B and C yield similar results. Cross-owners are 1.6% points more likely to vote "for" the merger than A-only shareholders, and the results are statistically significant at 1%.

Table 8

Distribution of fund votes by holdings in the target

The sample in Panel A contains 7322 mutual fund votes in acquirers' shareholder meetings in 114 completed mergers and acquisitions of public US companies between 2003 and 2006. Panel B presents summary statistics for the subsample of responsive funds. Responsive funds are funds that have cast at least one "did not" or "against" vote in our sample. The dummy for holdings in the target is one if the fund has had a positive holding in the target at recording, announcement, or voting date.

	Dummy for holdings in the target				
	0		1		
Vote	Frequency	Percent	Frequency	Percent	Total
Panel A. Full sample					
Against	101	2.17	22	0.82	123
Did not	47	1.01	21	0.79	68
For	4507	96.82	2624	98.39	7131
Total	4655	100	2667	100	7322
Panel B. Responsive funds					
Against	101	11.90	22	1.97	123
Did not	47	5.54	21	1.88	68
For	701	82.57	1072	96.14	1773
Total	849	100	1115	100	1964

Table 9

Estimating probability of voting for the merger from cross-ownership

The sample contains 7322 mutual fund votes in acquirers' shareholder meetings in 114 completed mergers and acquisitions of public US companies between 2003 and 2006. The dependent variable is a dummy that takes the value of one if the vote in the acquirer is "for" and zero otherwise. Holdings in the target is a dummy variable that takes the value of one if the fund holds shares in the target. Panel A presents a linear probability model. Panel B presents logit and conditional logit models. Panel C presents the marginal effects of models in Panel B. Regression specifications (2) and (3) include merger and fund fixed effects, respectively. Standard errors are in parentheses. *Significant at 5%; **significant at 1%. Data are from the Securities and Exchange Commission Edgar database (N-PX filings) and Thomson Financial SDC Platinum merger database.

	(1) Vote (for)	(2) Vote (for)	(3) Vote (for)
Panel A. Linear probability model			
Holdings in the target	0.016	0.008	0.025
	(0.004)**	(0.003)*	(0.006)**
Constant	0.968	0.971	0.965
	(0.003)**	(0.002)**	(0.003)**
Merger fixed effects		Yes	
Fund fixed effects			Yes
Observations	7322	7322	7322
R^2	0.00	0.28	0.24
Panel B. Logit and conditional logit models			
Holdings in the target	0.695	0.498	1.096
	(0.175)**	(0.219)*	(0.214)**
Constant	3.416		
	(0.084)**		
Merger fixed effects		Yes	
Fund fixed effects			Yes
Observations	7322	4343	1876
Panel C. Logit and conditional logit models (marginal effects)			
Holdings in the target	0.016	0.122	0.249
	(0.004)**	(0.051)**	(0.040)**
Merger fixed effects		Yes	
Fund fixed effects			Yes
Observations	7322	4343	1876

If cross-ownership is correlated with merger or fund characteristics, our estimates could be biased. The presence of a bias is very likely, because acquirer size is positively correlated with cross-ownership and negatively correlated with acquirer announcement returns. Estimating models with merger and fund fixed effects in Columns 2 and 3 controls for this possibility. The results using linear probabilities and conditional logit confirm that when funds are cross-owners they are more likely to vote for the merger. While all models yield statistically significant results of the same sign, the magnitudes of the cross-ownership effect differ. They are much larger in the conditional logit model. The cross-holders are 12.2% points more likely to vote for the merger than A-only holders in the merger fixed effects model and 24.9% points in the fund fixed effects model.

This should not be surprising, given that cross-ownership can have an impact only on the behavior of responsive funds, and the conditional logit model with fund fixed effects automatically restricts the sample to that group. The magnitude of the cross-ownership effect in other regressions also changes when we focus on responsive funds. Table 10 presents these results. The effect ranges from 7.7% to 13.6% in the linear

Table 10

Estimating probability of voting for the merger from cross-ownership for responsive funds

The sample contains 1964 mutual fund votes in acquirers' shareholder meetings in 113 completed mergers and acquisitions of public US companies between 2003 and 2006 for funds who cast at least one "did not" or "against" vote in our sample. The dependent variable is a dummy that takes the value of one if the vote in the acquirer is "for" and zero otherwise. Holdings in the target is a dummy variable that takes the value of one if the fund holds shares in the target. Panel A presents a linear probability model. Panel B presents logit and conditional logit models. Panel C presents the marginal effects of models in Panel B. Regression specifications (2) and (3) include merger and fund fixed effects, respectively. Standard errors are in parentheses. *Significant at 1%.

	(1) Vote (for)	(2) Vote (for)	(3) Vote (for)
Panel A. Linear probability model			
Holdings in the target	0.136	0.108	0.077
	(0.014)*	(0.015)*	(0.016)*
Constant	0.826	0.842	0.859
	(0.013)*	(0.012)*	(0.013)*
Merger fixed effects		Yes	
Fund fixed effects			Yes
Observations	1964	1964	1964
R^2	0.05	0.45	0.28
Panel B. Logit and conditional logit models			
Holdings in the target	1.661	1.979	1.096
	(0.180)*	(0.249)*	(0.214)*
Constant	1.555		
	(0.090)*		
Merger fixed effects		Yes	
Fund fixed effects			Yes
Observations	1964	1092	1876
Panel C. Logit and conditional logit models (marginal effects)			
Holdings in the target	0.136	0.379	0.249
	(0.014)*	(0.027)*	(0.040)*
Merger fixed effects		Yes	
Fund fixed effects			Yes
Observations	1964	1092	1876

probability specifications and from 13.6% to 37.9% for the logit. In all specifications, it is statistically significant at the 1% level. For the remainder of the paper, we use the full voting sample. The results get stronger if we restrict the sample to responsive funds.

If the effect of cross-ownership is to blunt the incentives of funds to prevent mergers that are bad for the acquirer, then cross-ownership should not have an effect in mergers that are good for the acquirer, because the incentives of cross-owners and A-owners are aligned. One way to proxy for good mergers is to see whether they have positive announcement returns. This proxy is not perfect: Stock prices can move for reasons unrelated to the merger or because of speculative behavior by arbitrageurs. Nevertheless, good mergers should be more likely to result in positive returns to the acquirer (and vice versa), and our results below indicate that this is the case.

Table 11 shows descriptive statistics for the subsamples of mergers split according to their market-model abnormal announcement returns around the $(-5, +5)$ trading days window. In mergers with positive announcement returns presented in Panel A, A-only holders are no more likely to vote against mergers than cross-owners. When announcement returns are positive, only 0.7% of the shareholders vote "against." In mergers with negative announcement returns presented in Panel B, A-only holders are notably more likely than cross-owners to vote "against." Cross-owners are no more

Table 11

Distribution of fund votes by holdings in the target and acquirer announcement returns

The sample contains 7322 mutual fund votes in acquirers' shareholder meetings in 114 completed mergers and acquisitions of public US companies between 2003 and 2006. The sample in Panel A contains mutual fund votes in mergers with positive acquirer announcement returns. The sample in Panel B contains mutual fund votes in mergers with negative acquirer announcement returns. Returns are market-model abnormal returns relative to the CRSP equally weighted index benchmark over the $(-5, +5)$ trading days event window.

| | Dummy for holdings in the target | | | | |
| | 0 | | 1 | | |
Vote	Frequency	Percent	Frequency	Percent	Total
Panel A. Mergers with positive acquirer returns					
Against	3	0.34	7	1.36	10
Did not	3	0.34	7	1.36	10
For	887	99.33	501	97.28	1388
Total	893	100	515	100	1408
Panel B. Mergers with negative acquirer returns					
Against	98	2.60	15	0.70	113
Did not	44	1.17	14	0.65	58
For	3620	96.23	2123	98.65	5743
Total	3762	100	2152	100	5914

likely to oppose mergers with negative returns than the ones with positive returns: 0.7% vote against the merger when returns are negative versus 1.4% when returns are positive. The A-only holders, however, are much more likely to oppose negative-return mergers. In mergers with positive announcement returns, only 0.3% vote against the merger. In mergers with negative announcement returns, that number increases by almost an order of magnitude to 2.6%. As before, the magnitudes would be more pronounced if we restricted our sample to responsive funds.

That cross-ownership affects voting in bad mergers, but has no impact in good ones, is confirmed in Table 12 by estimating linear, logit, and conditional logit probability models. Positive and significant coefficients appear only in the subsample of mergers with negative announcement returns. Furthermore, as expected, the size of the coefficients in mergers with negative announcement returns is larger than the coefficients of corresponding regressions estimated on the complete sample in Table 9. The marginal effect in the pooled logit shows that cross-holders are 2.4% points more likely to vote for a merger with negative returns than A-only holders. The effect is larger in the conditional logit with merger fixed effects at 14.0%. These results demonstrate that cross-owners are more likely to vote "for" than A-only shareholders in mergers with negative returns but not in the ones with positive returns. The effect goes in the opposite direction for positive-return mergers, but it is not robust to the inclusion of merger fixed effects.

Realized fund announcement returns incorporate more salient information about funds' incentives than the simple cross-ownership dummy. Unfortunately, their magnitudes are plagued with an endogeneity problem, because they depend on the expected probability of merger approval, which itself depends on funds' voting and their attitudes toward the merger. The correlation of realized returns to the funds within a merger to their voting decision is nevertheless informative and serves as an additional robustness check of the results presented above.

In mergers with higher acquirer announcement returns, funds are no more likely to vote "for" (Column 1, Table 13). However, taking cross-ownership into account and calculating overall announcement returns, funds with higher overall returns are more likely to vote for the merger (Column 2, Table 13).[8] The endogeneity problem of returns should be reduced in the merger fixed effects specification, in which the fixed effects absorb the average return to the fund and with it some of the common component of the feedback from expected votes on returns. Column 3 shows that within a merger, funds with higher overall returns are more likely to vote "for." A 10% point increase in the overall return to a fund increases the (linear) probability of voting for the merger by 3.3% points. Similar conclusions can be reached from the logit and conditional logit estimations presented in Panels B and C.

---

[8] The acquirer announcement returns in the acquirer are highly correlated with the actual returns to the funds, making the coefficients in a pooled regression using both variables hard to interpret.

Table 12

Estimating probability of voting for the merger from cross-ownership, by announcement returns

The sample contains 7322 mutual fund votes in acquirers' shareholder meetings in 114 completed mergers and acquisitions of public US companies between 2003 and 2006. The dependent variable is a dummy that takes the value of one if the vote in the acquirer is "for" and zero otherwise. Holdings in the target is a dummy that takes the value of one if the fund holds shares in the target. Returns are market-model abnormal returns relative to the CRSP equally weighted index benchmark over the $(-5, +5)$ trading days event window. The regressions are a linear probability, logit, and conditional logit models for subsamples based on whether the abnormal announcement return to acquirer was positive or not. Panel C presents the estimated marginal effects models. Regression specifications (3) and (4) include merger fixed effects. Robust standard errors are in parentheses. *Significant at 5%; **significant at 1%. Data are from the Securities and Exchange Commission Edgar database (N-PX filings), Thomson Financial SDC Platinum merger database, and CRSP stock price database.

Merger abnormal return	(1) Vote (for) negative	(2) Vote (for) positive	(3) Vote (for) negative	(4) Vote (for) positive
Panel A. Linear probability model				
Holdings in the target	0.024	−0.020	0.009	−0.001
	(0.004)**	(0.008)**	(0.004)*	(0.004)
Constant	0.962	0.993	0.980	1.001
	(0.003)**	(0.003)**	(0.018)**	(0.004)**
Merger fixed effects			Yes	Yes
Observations	5914	1408	5914	1408
R^2	0.00	0.01	0.27	0.35
Panel B. Logit and conditional logit models				
Holdings in the target	1.055	−1.419	0.575	−0.146
	(0.206)**	(0.491)**	(0.235)*	(0.677)
Constant	3.238	4.996		
	(0.086)**	(0.410)**		
Merger fixed effects			Yes	Yes
Observations	5914	1408	3867	476
Panel C. Logit and conditional logit models (marginal effects)				
Holdings in the target	0.024	−0.020	0.140	−0.036
	(0.004)**	(0.008)**	(0.054)**	(0.168)
Merger fixed effects			Yes	Yes
Observations	5914	1408	3867	476

In our analysis of the effect of fund returns on voting in Tables 11–13, we use the market-model abnormal announcement returns over the $(-5, +5)$ trading days window. Our results remain largely unchanged if we use the $(-1, +1)$ window or market-adjusted returns instead. An alternative way to measure returns is to use longer return windows, for example, from the announcement date until the voting date. This has the benefit of incorporating all information available to the shareholders when casting their vote but also has the disadvantage of incorporating a substantial amount of information

Table 13

Estimating probability of voting for the merger from announcement returns

The sample contains 7322 mutual fund votes in acquirers' shareholder meetings in 114 completed mergers and acquisitions of public US companies between 2003 and 2006. The dependent variable is a dummy that takes the value of one if the vote in the acquirer is "for" and zero otherwise. Returns are market-model abnormal returns relative to the CRSP equally weighted index benchmark over the $(-5, +5)$ trading days event window. Actual fund return is calculated as the dollar return to the fund from its holdings in the acquirer and the target divided by the total value of its holdings. Panel A presents a linear probability model, Panel B presents logit and conditional logit models, and Panel C presents the marginal effects of models in Panel B. Regression specification (3) includes merger fixed effects. Robust standard errors are in parentheses. *Significant at 5%; **significant at 1%. Data are from the Securities and Exchange Commission Edgar database (N-PX filings), Thomson Financial SDC Platinum merger database, CRSP mutual fund holdings database, and CRSP stock price database.

	(1) Vote (for)	(2) Vote (for)	(3) Vote (for)
Panel A. Linear probability model			
Acquirer return	−0.021		
	(0.020)		
Actual fund return		0.107	0.333
		(0.044)*	(0.049)**
Constant	0.973	0.977	1.025
	(0.002)**	(0.002)**	(0.020)**
Merger fixed effects			Yes
Observations	7322	7322	7322
R^2	0.00	0.00	0.29
Panel B. Logit and conditional logit models			
Acquirer return	−0.827		
	(0.781)		
Actual fund return		2.008	7.206
		(0.410)**	(0.240)**
Constant	3.580	3.710	
	(0.081)**	(0.079)**	
Merger fixed effects			Yes
Observations	7322	7322	4343
Panel C. Logit and conditional logit models (marginal effects)			
Acquirer return	−0.021		
	(0.020)		
Actual fund return		0.050	1.746
		(0.010)**	(0.055)**
Merger fixed effects			Yes
Observations	7322	7322	4343

unrelated to the merger. In our case, the disadvantage seems to outweigh the benefit. Most "against" votes cast by A-only shareholders are associated with mergers that have positive abnormal returns over the $(-1$, voting date$-1)$ and $(-5$, voting date$-1)$

windows. This suggests that using longer return windows leads to a misclassification of mergers in our sample. Furthermore, unlike with shorter windows, some of the regression results in Tables 12 and 13 become sensitive to exactly how the abnormal returns are calculated. However, our last result that, within a merger, funds with higher announcement returns are more likely to vote "for" (Column 3, Table 13) remains valid and statistically significant at the 1% level. This is not surprising, because merger fixed effects absorb the additional noise introduced by the longer windows. The results with alternative window lengths and return specifications are available upon request.

Proxy voting decisions could also be taken at the fund family level rather than at the level of an individual fund. Therefore, the overall family holdings could have an impact on voting. The regressions in Table 14 explore this possibility. The results are similar in all specifications. If the fund itself does not hold shares in the target but another fund in the family does, the probability of voting for the merger in the acquirer increases. If, however, the fund is a cross-owner itself, the additional target holdings by other funds in the same family do not increase the probability of voting "for." While family cross-ownership influences voting, funds within a family do disagree. For example, when Sprint acquired Nextel in 2004, Fidelity Advisor Equity Income Fund voted against the merger, while Fidelity Advisor Equity Value Fund voted for it.

4. Conclusion

Taking cross-ownership into account can often change an assessment of whether a merger is beneficial to shareholders of the acquiring company. Even though mergers in our sample on average have negative acquirer announcement returns, the total announcement returns to institutional shareholders are on average not negative. We can identify two groups of institutional shareholders in the acquirer with potentially opposing incentives in the merger: the A-only shareholders, who realize negative announcement returns, and cross-owners, who realize positive returns.

Using a data set on mutual fund voting in mergers, we confirm the existence of a conflict of interest between these two types of shareholders. Cross-owners are much more likely to vote for a merger with negative announcement acquirer returns than A-only holders. There is no difference in voting behavior between the two groups in mergers with positive acquirer returns.

The literature on conflicts of interest in the United States mostly focuses on the agency relationship between the management and shareholders. Our results show that conflicts within the shareholder group, even in large public companies, are also important. It is not clear whether and how such conflicts should be addressed: After all, mutual funds are fiduciaries of their shareholders, and therefore they should vote to maximize the value of their combined holdings in the acquirer and the target, even if a merger is not good for the acquiring company.

Table 14

Estimating probability of voting for the merger from family cross-ownership

The sample contains 6369 mutual fund votes in acquirers' shareholder meetings in 114 completed mergers and acquisitions of public US companies between 2003 and 2006. The dependent variable is a dummy that takes the value of one if the vote in the acquirer is "for" and zero otherwise. Holdings in the target is a dummy variable that takes the value of one if the fund holds shares in the target. Family and cross takes the value of one if the fund holds shares in the target and some other fund in the same family holds shares in the target as well. Family and no cross takes the value of one if the fund does not hold shares in the target but some other fund in the same family does. Regression specifications (2) and (3) include merger and fund fixed effects, respectively. Standard errors are in parentheses. *Significant at 5%; **significant at 1%. Data are from the Securities and Exchange Commission Edgar database (N-PX filings), Thomson Financial SDC Platinum merger database, CRSP mutual fund holdings database, and Investment Company Data, Inc. (ICDI) mappings database.

	(1) Vote (for)	(2) Vote (for)	(3) Vote (for)
Panel A. Linear probability model			
Holdings in the target	0.029	0.017	0.036
	(0.006)**	(0.005)**	(0.009)**
Family and cross	0.000	0.003	0.01
	(0.005)	(0.005)	(0.009)
Family and no cross	0.028	0.018	0.024
	(0.005)**	(0.005)**	(0.007)**
Constant	0.956	0.962	0.952
	(0.004)**	(0.003)**	(0.005)**
Merger fixed effects		Yes	
Fund fixed effects			Yes
Observations	6369	6369	6369
R^2	0.01	0.30	0.25
Panel B. Logit and conditional logit models			
Holdings in the target	1.135	1.010	1.376
	(0.318)**	(0.367)**	(0.372)**
Family and cross	−0.008	0.236	0.258
	(0.369)	(0.410)	(0.441)
Family and no cross	1.021	0.952	0.720
	(0.235)**	(0.278)**	(0.317)*
Constant	3.081		
	(0.094)**		
Merger fixed effects		Yes	
Fund fixed effects			Yes
Observations	6369	3600	1617
Panel C. Logit and conditional logit models (marginal effects)			
Holdings in the target	0.023	0.212	0.282
	(0.006)**	(0.067)**	(0.069)**
Family and cross	−0.000	0.051	0.051
	(0.009)	(0.086)	(0.085)
Family and no cross	0.019	0.0190	0.123
	(0.003)**	(0.041)**	(0.042)**
Merger fixed effects		Yes	
Fund fixed effects			Yes
Observations	6369	3600	1617

Cross-ownership could also have an impact on which mergers are proposed to begin with. If managers do not propose mergers that are likely to be blocked by the shareholders, then mergers with low cross-ownership and low expected support for the merger cannot be observed. Therefore, cross-ownership potentially leads not only to a higher probability of passing a bad merger, but also to a higher number of bad mergers proposed by managers.

Finally, it is fascinating to consider why such a large fraction of A-only shareholders vote "for" the mergers, even when a merger appears to be bad for the acquiring company, and why so many funds never vote "against." This could be due to the beliefs of these shareholders that those mergers are good for the company (and the value of their investment in it) in the long term. Alternatively, it could be due to some unobserved costs of disagreeing with the management. In the latter case, these costs could be especially large if most other shareholders vote "for" the merger, giving rise to coordination games with peer effects. Matvos and Ostrovsky (2008) show that peer effects play an important role in corporate director elections. We leave to future research the analysis of the causes and consequences of the high average level of shareholder support in mergers and acquisitions, as well as the implications of (and the potential remedies to) the conflict of interest among the shareholders identified in this paper.

References

Andrade, G., M. Mitchell and E. Stafford, 2001, "New Evidence and Perspectives on Mergers," *Journal of Economic Perspectives*, 15, 103–120.

Brown, S. J. and J. B. Warner, 1985, "Using Daily Stock Returns, the Case of Event Studies," *Journal of Financial Economics*, 14, 3–31.

Easterbrook, F. H. and D. R. Fischel, 1982, "Corporate Control Transactions," *Yale Law Journal*, 91, 698–737.

Hansen, R. G. and J. R. Lott, 1996, "Externalities and Corporate Objectives in a World with Diversified Shareholder/Consumers," *Journal of Financial and Quantitative Analysis*, 31, 43–68.

Jarrell, G. A., J. A. Brickley and J. M. Netter, 1988, "The Market for Corporate Control: The Empirical Evidence Since 1980," *Journal of Economic Perspectives*, 2, 49–68.

Jensen, M. C., 1986, "Agency Costs of Free Cash Flow, Corporate Finance, and Takeovers," *American Economic Review*, 76, 323–329.

Jensen, M. C. and R. S. Ruback, 1983, "The Market for Corporate Control: The Scientific Evidence," *Journal of Finance*, 11, 5–50.

Malmendier, U. and G. Tate, 2008, "Who Makes Acquisitions? CEO Overconfidence and the Market's Reaction," *Journal of Financial Economics*, 89, 20–43.

Matvos, G. and M. Ostrovsky, 2008, "Heterogeneity and Peer Effects in Mutual Fund Proxy Voting," Unpublished Working Paper, University of Chicago.

Mitchell, M., T. Pulvino and E. Stafford, 2004, "Price Pressure Around Mergers," *Journal of Finance*, 59, 31–63.

Moeller, S. B., F. P. Schlingemann and R. M. Stulz, 2004, "Firm Size and the Gains from Acquisitions," *Journal of Financial Economics*, 73, 201–228.

Moeller, S. B., F. P. Schlingemann and R. M. Stulz, 2005, "Wealth Destruction on a Massive Scale? A Study of Acquiring-Firm Returns in the Recent Merger Wave," *Journal of Finance*, 60, 757–782.

Morck, R., A. Shleifer and R. W. Vishny, 1990, "Do Managerial Objectives Drive Bad Acquisitions? *Journal of Finance*, 45, 31–48.

Roll, R., 1986, "The Hubris Hypothesis of Corporate Takeovers," *Journal of Business*, 59, 197–216.

Shleifer, A. and R. W. Vishny, 1988, "Value Maximization and the Acquisition Process," *Journal of Economic Perspectives*, 27, 7–20.

Shleifer, A. and R. W. Vishny, 1989, "Management Entrenchment: The Case of Manager-Specific Investments," *Journal of Financial Economics*, 25, 123–139.

Chapter 16

INVESTOR ACTIVISM AND TAKEOVERS[*]

ROBIN GREENWOOD

Harvard Business School, Boston, Massachusetts, USA

MICHAEL SCHOR

Morgan Stanley, New York, New York, USA

Contents

* We appreciate funding from the Harvard Business School Division of Research and from the Faculty of Arts and Sciences. We are grateful to an anonymous referee and to Daniel Bergstresser, Lucian Bebchuk, Alon Brav, Lauren Cohen, Julian Franks, Mila Getmansky, April Klein, André Perold, Richard Ruback, Stefano Rossi, Andrei Shleifer, Erik Stafford, Emmanuel Zur, and seminar participants at the Bank of England, Harvard Business School, and Harvard Law School for useful comments. We also benefited from the advice of Colin Kingsnorth at Laxey Partners, Daniel Loeb at Third Point, Nick Panos at the Securities and Exchange Commission, and Barry Rosenstein and Scott Olson at JANA Partners. We thank Sonya Lai for research assistance.

This article originally appeared in the *Journal of Financial Economics*, Vol. 92, pp. 362–375 (2009).
Corporate Takeovers, Volume 2
Edited by B. Espen Eckbo
DOI: 10.1016/B978-0-12-381982-6.00017-3

Abstract

Recent work documents large positive abnormal returns when a hedge fund announces activist intentions regarding a publicly listed firm. We show that these returns are largely explained by the ability of activists to force target firms into a takeover. For a comprehensive sample of 13D filings by portfolio investors between 1993 and 2006, announcement returns and long-term abnormal returns are high for targets that are ultimately acquired, but not detectably different from zero for firms that remain independent. Firms targeted by activists are more likely than control firms to get acquired. Finally, activist investors' portfolios perform poorly during a period in which market-wide takeover interest declined.

Keywords

investor activism, event studies, hedge funds, corporate control

JEL classifications: G14, G32, G34

1. Introduction

Theory predicts that large shareholders should be effective monitors of the managers of publicly listed firms, reducing the free-rider problem (e.g., Grossman and Hart, 1980; Shleifer and Vishny, 1986). Yet the evidence that large shareholders increase shareholder value is mixed. In two recent surveys, Karpoff (2001) and Romano (2001) conclude that activism conducted by large institutional shareholders has had little impact on firm performance. Karpoff et al. (1996), Wahal (1996), and Gillan and Starks (2000) report that shareholder proposals have historically done little to improve firms' operations. On the few occasions when investors have attempted to remove managers from their jobs, they generally encountered resistance (Brav et al., 2008) or faced high costs (Bainbridge, 2005; Black, 1990; Kahan and Rock, 2006; Roe, 1994), and as a result were unsuccessful (Bebchuk, 2007; Black, 1998; Karpoff, 2001; Romano, 2001).

Recent research suggests that hedge funds might be up to the task of monitoring management. Brav et al. (2008) find that the announcement of hedge-fund activism generates abnormal returns of more than 7% in a short window around the announcement. In addition, the authors document modest changes in operating performance around the activism. Klein and Zur (2009) and Clifford (2007) also document significant positive abnormal returns around the announcement of activism.[1] Many of these studies also document positive abnormal returns in a longer period after the initial filing.

What accounts for the returns to hedge-fund activism? While the studies listed above go to great lengths to document changes in performance measures following activism, it is still largely unanswered where the announcement premium (and the upward drift in stock prices thereafter, for that matter) comes from. A reasonable starting hypothesis might be that activism creates value by improving the firm as a going concern, either by firing management or by forcing management to institute operational, financial, or governance reforms. Brav et al. (2008) and Klein and Zur (2009) document modest increases in leverage and the payout ratio following activism, but have less success finding evidence of other improvements.

In this paper, we suggest and test a simple alternate hypothesis: returns to investor activism are driven by activists' success at getting target firms taken over. Under this hypothesis, the high returns documented around the announcement of activism reflect investors' expectations that target firms will be acquired at a premium to the current stock price. From the perspective of the activist, exiting the position in the stock via a merger or a takeover is doubly beneficial: it generates a high premium, as well as allowing the activist to avoid the price pressure associated with an exit in the public

---

[1] Becht et al. (2009) also find that activist investments of the UK pension fund Hermes significantly outperformed benchmarks. Clifford (2007) shows that hedge funds earn a significantly higher return on their activist positions compared to their passive positions, suggesting that hedge funds may use these higher returns to counteract the costs of managing and monitoring an activist holding.

markets (in a merger or acquisition, the activist exits in cash or with stock of a larger, more liquid company).

We construct a comprehensive database of activist filings with the Securities and Exchange Commission (SEC) from 1993 to 2006, focusing on instances where the target is a US firm. Our main result is that activism targets earn high returns primarily when they are eventually taken over. However, the majority of activism targets are not acquired and these firms earn average abnormal returns that are not statistically distinguishable from zero. These findings apply both to announcement returns and to the drift in long-term returns following the initial activist filing. Thus, the returns associated with activism are largely explained by the ability of activists to force target firms into a takeover, thereby collecting a takeover premium. An interesting observation, in our view, is that in many of the events in which we eventually observe a takeover, the initial demands of the activist were quite different. For example, in 15.7% of incidents in which the activist targeted "corporate governance" issues, the final result was a takeover.

Our evidence is consistent with many hedge funds' characterizations of their activism. The activist Robert Chapman, for example, seeks out companies that are "digestible" in the sense that they are easy to market to bidders as potential takeover targets.[2] However, our characterization differs markedly from previous research on investor activism, which tends to attribute high announcement returns to improvements in operational performance, increases in the leverage or payout ratio, or reductions in agency costs. The evidence in our paper helps explain why there is no significant correlation between accounting-based measures of operational change and subsequent returns—the most "successful" targets of activism are those that leave the public markets (and hence the Compustat database) soon after the activist becomes involved. Thus, there is a significant selection bias, in that the firms with the largest returns tend to drop out of the sample by way of takeover.

In addition to our hypothesis, we consider a closely related explanation. Suppose that activist investors make no changes, but that the returns associated with their involvement reflect an ability to pick undervalued stocks. Suppose also that these undervalued stocks are probable acquisition targets regardless of activist intervention. Put differently, perhaps the path of the target and its ultimate takeover would have been no different absent the activist intervention. Consistent with this, activist targets tend to be small firms with low valuation ratios and thin analyst coverage, and have underperformed relative to other firms in their industry. These characteristics could all reasonably be associated with a higher probability of takeover. To address this concern, we form a matching portfolio based on industry, size, and preactivism return. We show that matching firms are less likely to be acquired within the next year, compared with firms that are targets of activism. In our full sample, activists increase

[2] Marcia Vickers, "Companies Beware … It's Shark Season," BusinessWeek, June 10, 2002.

the probability of takeover by about 11 percentage points. That is, activists put firms into play.

One implication of our work is that the announcement returns to investor activism should depend on the overall takeover interest in the market. Evidence from the credit crunch period from July to September 2007 confirms this intuition. During this time, private equity interest in debt-financed buyouts declined dramatically due to changes in credit market conditions. Many activists saw corresponding drops in the value of their holdings of target firms whose stock had been purchased in the hope of a takeover, the probability of which declined when rates increased. In the final section of the paper, we gather data on the positions of all serial activists during the time of the crisis. We show that the value of these activists' largest positions declined sharply during this short period, especially surrounding news of failed takeover attempts. This evidence is consistent with our hypothesis that activism targets were bought in the expectation of a takeover.

The paper proceeds as follows. Section 2 describes our data. Section 3 relates activism event returns to takeover outcomes and also examines the incidence of takeovers in our sample. Section 4 studies the implications of the credit crisis in mid-2007 for the performance of activists' portfolios. The final section concludes.

2. Data

2.1. Constructing the sample

We merge all Schedule 13D and DFAN14A filings from the SEC's EDGAR database for the 13-year period from the third quarter of 1993 through the third quarter of 2006. 13Ds are filed with the SEC within 10 days of an entity attaining 5% or greater share in any class of a company's securities. The filing documents the size of the purchase and summarizes the investors' intentions. Starting in 2000, activists began occasionally attaching a letter to a target firm's management or board in their SEC filing.

13Ds must be filed by institutional money managers and hedge funds, as well as for crossholdings formed when two firms merge or form business alliances. Several papers, starting with Mikkelson and Ruback (1985), note that mergers and takeovers are often preceded by the acquisition of a minority stake in the target. Since our focus is on portfolio investments, we restrict our sample by cross-referencing the 13D filings with a list of investment managers that have filed a Schedule 13F holdings report at some point in their history. We do this so as not to confuse corporate crossholdings with activism from portfolio investors. This restriction limits our data somewhat, because only institutions holding more than $100 million in US stocks file 13F reports. However, this step is necessary to facilitate the separation of the activist filings from the larger universe of 13D filings—a total of 173,078 for our period of study.

We add to our sample of 13Ds by including all definitive proxy statements filed by nonmanagement (DFAN14As). DFAN14As are filed with the SEC by investors who intend to or are engaged in a proxy fight with a firm's management. A proxy fight can be initiated with a stake in a company's securities that comprises less than 5% of the shares outstanding, although the mean for our sample is 10.8%, implying that these activists usually show up on both filings.

Our initial sample includes 20,771 filings. From these, we exclude targets that are closed-end funds, and firms that are not identifiable on the Center for Research in Security Prices (CRSP) files at the time of the initial filing. To arrive at a list of events, we read the "purpose of transaction" section of each 13D filing to identify whether or not the filer is pursuing an activist strategy. The overwhelming majority of transactions are for the purposes of passive investment only, and we exclude them. However, these nonactivist filings serve as a useful control group in some of the tests that follow.[3]

For each activist-target pair, there are typically multiple filings. These result from small changes in the activist position or from formal communication between the investor and management. We exclude repeat filings for an activist-target pair for which the purpose of the transaction is essentially unchanged—but if there is a meaningful change in the purpose of transaction over the course of several 13D filings for the same target-investor pair, we code these as separate events. Our results are not much affected by whether we throw out these follow-on events, which we do in some tests that require unique activist-target pairings.

Following the process described above, we find a total of 980 activist events covering 811 unique target-activist pairs. We use company Web sites, newspaper articles, and the Center for International Securities and Derivatives Markets (CISDM) hedge-fund database to determine whether or not the activist is a hedge fund or another type of investor (i.e., a mutual fund, pension fund, or investment management company). Some of the activists classified as nonhedge funds may indeed have a hedge fund, but the fund is not its main product offering to investors. We classify these as nonhedge funds.[4]

Panel A of Table 1 summarizes the sample. A total of 784 events were initiated by 139 unique hedge funds, and 196 events were initiated by 38 unique nonhedge funds. Over our sample period, almost four times more hedge funds engaged in activism using 13D filings than did other institutional investors. The table also shows that hedge-fund filings grow in number, relative to nonhedge-fund filings, in later sample years. Most of the nonhedge-fund filings can be traced to the Ontario Teachers Pension Plan Board, Franklin Mutual Advisers and Franklin Resources, and Gabelli Asset

---

[3] We also exclude several hundred events from Gabelli Investments in which the 13D states the firm's intention to "engage management." Our reasoning is that Gabelli appears to file identical 13Ds when acquiring large stakes, thus we have no reason to believe that these filings are activist. However, when press releases or further clarifications on the 13D spell out specific activist demands, then we do include the Gabelli event. Our final dataset includes 70 Gabelli events (including filings from Gabelli Funds, GAMCO Investors, and Gabelli Asset Management).

[4] For example, Gabelli Asset Management is an investment management company that offers mutual funds to retail investors in addition to a number of investment advisory services and products to institutional and high-net worth individual investors. These products include hedge funds.

Table 1

Summary statistics: investor activism 1994–2006

An event is defined as an instance in which an activist files a 13D filing announcing 5% ownership and an intention to influence the management of the company. Events are separated by hedge fund and nonhedge-fund activists, where a hedge fund is defined according to CISDM data. Panel A tabulates events by year. Panel B tabulates events based on the activist's initial set of demands. Event classifications are as follows: *engage management* (the activist intends to engage management or discuss issues with management to increase shareholder value, or makes a general statement that shares are undervalued without including specific proposals); *capital structure* (the activist requests a recapitalization, stock or debt issuance, restructuring of debt, dividends or a stock repurchase); *corporate governance* (the activist seeks to declassify the board, remove a poison pill, elect activist-selected directors, fire a company officer or board member, or target other governance issues); *business strategy* (the activist critiques excess diversification and the level of investment in some business lines or cites poor operating strategy at the target); *strategic alternatives* (the activist requests that the target pursue various strategic alternatives for the firm, including a spin off of an underperforming division); *asset sale* (the activist calls for the target to sell itself or certain assets in order to maximize shareholder value); *block merger* (the activist tries to block a merger with another firm or seeks to increase the bid made for the target); *financing/bankruptcy* (the activist provides financing for the target during bankruptcy or financial distress, and may also include an offer to finance the target's growth or acquisition strategies); *proxy contest* (the activist files under Schedule 14A with intention to solicit proxies from shareholders). Panel C shows sample means for various event characteristics.

	Hedge fund	Nonhedge fund	Full sample
Panel A: events by year			
1994	8	2	10
1995	8	2	10
1996	18	12	30
1997	45	21	66
1998	58	16	74
1999	63	27	90
2000	61	23	84
2001	66	17	83
2002	63	26	89
2003	53	14	67
2004	73	14	87
2005	141	12	153
2006	127	10	137
Total	784	196	980
Panel B: events by type of demand			
Engage management—asset undervalued	357	44	401
Capital structure	79	12	91
Corporate governance	172	95	267
Business strategy	36	12	48
Strategic alternatives	19	10	29
Asset sale	142	26	168
Block merger	44	20	64
Financing/bankruptcy	11	4	15
Proxy contest	71	6	77

(Continued)

Table 1 (*Continued*)

	Hedge fund	Nonhedge fund	Full sample
Panel C: other descriptive statistics			
Activist assets under management ($m)	1775	24,200	6793
Market value of stake in target ($m)	59.2	81.7	63.7
Percent of target shares outstanding (%)	9.83	12.97	10.47
Mean size decile of positions	2.71	3.23	2.82
Number of analysts covering target	3.79	3.29	3.69
Target market-to-book ratio	1.54	1.29	1.49
Target 24-month return net of industry return (%)	−13.13	−23.56	−15.12

Management, which each participated in 10 or more events. There are considerably more serial activists among hedge funds. For example, the hedge funds Farallon Capital, Steel Partners, ValueAct Partners, Wynnefield, Blum Capital, Carl Icahn, Chapman Capital, Newcastle Partners, JANA Partners, Third Point, and Pirate Capital constitute more than two-thirds of the sample.

2.2. Classification of activist demands

Every Schedule 13D filing includes a "purpose of transaction" section, in which the filer discloses any plans or proposals that could relate to or result in a significant change at the company, whether this is a call for the election of an independent director or a bid to acquire the target. This section can signal to the market the plan the investor intends to follow with regard to its position. Often, the investor has no activist plans, but files a Schedule 13D to reserve the right to engage in future activism. Any subsequent change in holdings or intention is then reported in an amended 13D filing.[5] If the filer has no activist intentions, the SEC allows for the filing of a Schedule 13G (instead of a 13D), which indicates that the large shareholder is a passive investor.

In addition to the information contained in the "purpose of transaction" section, the SEC allows investors to file additional materials as exhibits. These materials, along with the formal remarks in the 13D, provide the market with detailed explanations of the course of action the activist wants the firm to take. Our reading of the 13D statements suggests that activist demands fall into approximately nine well-defined categories: (1) intention to "engage" with management because the stock is undervalued, (2) capital structure issues, (3) corporate governance issues, (4) business strategy issues, (5) "strategic alternatives," (6) explicitly calling for the sale of all or part of the target, (7) blocking a proposed merger or acquisition because of unfavorable pricing, (8) financing for a firm in distress or other bankruptcy-related issues, and (9) the intention to engage in a proxy contest. In recent years, "strategic alternatives"

---

[5] If the filer has no activist intentions, the SEC allows for the filing of a Schedule 13G (instead of a 13D), which indicates that the large shareholder is a passive investor.

appears to be synonymous with a spin off or acquisition. Note that activist classifications are based on what is stated in the 13D filing, and *not* on the target company response. Additionally, we avoid classifying events as either hostile or friendly because potentially friendly investments may become hostile when management resists activist demands. An event can be assigned to multiple categories; however, most events have unique classifications.

Panel B of Table 1 categorizes events according to the activist demands. Because the categories are nonexclusive, the number of events in each category sums to more than 980. The table reveals important differences in the demands of hedge funds and nonhedge fund investors. Aside from making general "undervalued" statements or expressing an intention to engage with management, hedge-fund activists frequently demand that the target sell off all or part of its assets. In practice, activists that declare the target to be undervalued often try to locate a buyer for the firm, creating some overlap between the two demand categories of calling for an asset sale and making a general "undervalued" statement about a target. Governance-related activism is also fairly common and targets policies relating to poison pills, confidential voting, or board structure.

2.3. Activist and target characteristics

We collect detailed information on the activist portfolio, summarized in Panel C of Table 1. CDA/Spectrum makes available quarterly holdings information for institutional investors compiled from their 13F filings with the SEC. These filings include all holdings of domestic equities for funds that manage $100 million or more. We aggregate reported long positions to get a measure of the assets under management at the time of the event. The table shows that hedge funds tend to manage smaller portfolios than nonhedge funds. Yet the market value of the stake in the target is similar across the two types of institutions, implying that hedge funds tend to take more concentrated positions.

Panel C also highlights a few other important characteristics of activism targets: they tend to be small stocks (in the second or third size decile) with low market-to-book ratios and little or no analyst coverage, and have underperformed their industry over the previous 24 months. Both hedge funds and nonhedge funds target small firms, although hedge-fund targets are even smaller than nonhedge-fund targets. Finally, we observe a fair amount of industry concentration of these events (not tabulated).

2.4. Abnormal returns classified according to activist demand

Abnormal returns around the announcement of the 13D filing are measured by the difference between the return on the target stock and the return on a matching portfolio:

$$\mathrm{AR}_{it} = R_{it}^{\mathrm{Target}} - R_t^{\mathrm{Match}} \tag{1}$$

Ideally, we would identify matching stocks for each target based on size, industry, and book-to-market ratio. Compustat accounting data are not available for all firms in our sample, however. We consider cutting the sample down to include only Compustat firms, but this would result in the removal of smaller activism targets. Therefore, we form a surrogate matched portfolio as follows. We start with 100 days of returns in the interval $[t-110, t-10]$, where t denotes the date of the initial 13D filing, and we estimate loadings of target firm returns on the Fama and French (1993) HML, SMB, and market return factors:

$$R_{it}^{\text{Target}} - R_t^F = a_i + b_i \text{HML}_t + c_i \text{SMB}_t + d\left(R_t^M - R_t^M\right) + u_{it} \tag{2}$$

Our matching portfolio return in $t+1$ is then the factor loading weighted return on the HML, SMB, and market portfolios:

$$R_{it+1}^{\text{Match}} - R_{t+1}^F = \hat{b}_i \text{HML}_{t+1} + \hat{c}_i \text{SMB}_{t+1} + \hat{d}\left(R_{t+1}^M - R_{t+1}^M\right) \tag{3}$$

where $\hat{b}$, $\hat{c}$, and $\hat{d}$ are the estimates from the first-stage regression in Equation (1). On the few occasions where there is insufficient preevent return data to estimate factor loadings, we substitute the CRSP value-weighted portfolio for the match portfolio.[6]

The final step is to cumulate abnormal returns from Equation (3). These results are shown for the complete sample, as well as by type, in Panel A of Table 2. The table reveals that immediate returns to activism are large—approximately 3.5% over the 15-day event window. Note that announcement returns accrue starting a few days before the filing date, which we attribute to the 10-day window during which investors are required to file the 13D. Returns are positive when the activist indicates a desire to "engage management," when the activist requests an asset sale or tries to block a merger, and when the activist wages a proxy fight. In contrast, returns are not significantly different from zero when the activist targets capital structure issues, corporate governance, or corporate strategy, or proposes a spin off. These results are broadly consistent with our hypothesis that activists generate significantly positive returns only when they effectively put a company in play; other activist demands do not seem to garner the same favorable market reaction.

Monthly abnormal returns surrounding investor activism are computed following the same methodology. We start with 24 months of returns in the interval $[t-25, t-1]$ where t denotes the month of the initial 13D filing, and estimate loadings of target firm returns on the Fama and French (1993) HML, SMB, and market return factors. Our matching monthly return is the factor loading weighted monthly return on the HML, SMB, and market portfolios. Cumulative abnormal monthly returns for the period starting 1 month before the activism and ending 18 months later are shown in Panel B of Table 2. For the full sample of events, abnormal returns for the 18-month period are

---

[6] One drawback of our procedure is that it is inappropriate if factor exposures are changing quickly over time (a problem that does not arise if we assign matched firms to each stock). We are less concerned with this because we track performance for a fairly short window after the event.

Table 2

Returns by activism type

Panel A shows cumulative daily abnormal returns; Panel B shows cumulative monthly abnormal returns, estimated as follows. We form a matching portfolio as the factor-loading weighted return on the HML, SMB, and market portfolios. Abnormal returns are the difference between the daily or monthly return and the return on the matching portfolio. Cumulative averages are shown for the full sample and for the various types of activism, classified at time of the 13D filing. These event classifications are defined as follows: *engage management* (the activist intends to engage management or discuss issues with management to increase shareholder value, or makes a general statement that shares are undervalued without including specific proposals); *capital structure* (the activist requests a recapitalization, stock or debt issuance, restructuring of debt, dividends or a stock repurchase); *corporate governance* (the activist seeks to declassify the board, remove a poison pill, elect activist-selected directors, fire a company officer or board member, or target other governance issues); *business strategy* (the activist critiques excess diversification and the level of investment in some business lines or cites poor operating strategy at the target); *strategic alternatives* (the activist requests that the target pursue various strategic alternatives for the firm, including a spin off of an underperforming division); *asset sale* (the activist calls for the target to sell itself or certain assets in order to maximize shareholder value); *block merger* (the activist tries to block a merger with another firm or seeks to increase the bid made for the target); *financing/bankruptcy* (the activist provides financing for the target during bankruptcy or financial distress, and may also include an offer to finance the target's growth or acquisition strategies); *proxy contest* (the activist files under Schedule 14A with intention to solicit proxies from shareholders). *t*-Statistics are in brackets.

	All events		Engage management		Capital structure		Corporate governance		Corporate strategy		Asset sale		Block merger		Financing related to bankruptcy		Strategic alternatives		Proxy contest	
% Acquired	26.1%		23.7%		20.9%		15.7%		20.8%		35.7%		78.1%		26.7%		31.0%		18.2%	
	CAR (%)	[t]	CAR (%)	[t]	CAR (%)	[t]	CAR (%)	[t]	CAR (%)	[t]	CAR (%)	[t]	CAR (%)	[t]	CAR (%)	[t]	CAR (%)	[t]	CAR (%)	[t]
Panel A: cumulative daily abnormal returns																				
−10 days	−0.08	[−0.3]	0.43	[1.1]	−1.95	[−2.2]	−1.14	[−2.1]	−1.48	[−0.9]	−0.21	[−0.4]	2.80	[1.8]	4.68	[0.6]	−1.71	[−1.5]	0.55	[0.8]
−5 days	0.10	[0.2]	0.73	[1.1]	−2.34	[−1.7]	−0.24	[−0.3]	−2.82	[−1.0]	−0.13	[−0.2]	2.67	[1.5]	−1.75	[−0.5]	−1.90	[−1.6]	1.77	[1.4]
−4 days	0.29	[0.7]	1.01	[1.5]	−2.17	[−1.6]	−0.42	[−0.5]	−2.08	[−0.7]	0.10	[0.1]	2.67	[1.5]	−2.71	[−0.7]	−0.94	[−0.5]	2.42	[1.7]
−3 days	0.44	[0.9]	1.24	[1.7]	−2.21	[−1.4]	−0.50	[−0.6]	−2.55	[−0.9]	−0.05	[−0.1]	3.27	[1.6]	−1.89	[−0.5]	−0.18	[−0.1]	3.05	[2.0]
−2 days	0.67	[1.4]	1.18	[1.6]	−1.68	[−1.1]	−0.10	[−0.1]	−2.43	[−0.8]	1.01	[1.1]	3.17	[1.4]	1.29	[0.3]	−0.78	[−0.4]	3.00	[2.0]
−1 day	1.27	[2.5]	1.40	[1.9]	−0.63	[−0.4]	0.98	[1.0]	−2.25	[−0.7]	2.09	[2.0]	3.16	[1.3]	5.87	[0.8]	−0.10	[−0.0]	3.24	[2.2]
Filing date	2.41	[4.5]	2.28	[3.0]	−0.51	[−0.3]	1.48	[1.4]	−1.26	[−0.4]	5.21	[4.8]	4.54	[1.7]	8.37	[1.2]	1.40	[0.7]	3.98	[2.5]

(Continued)

Table 2 (*Continued*)

	All events		Engage management		Capital structure		Corporate governance		Corporate strategy		Asset sale		Block merger		Financing related to bankruptcy		Strategic alternatives		Proxy contest	
% Acquired	26.1%		23.7%		20.9%		15.7%		20.8%		35.7%		78.1%		26.7%		31.0%		18.2%	
	CAR (%)	[t]	CAR (%)	[t]	CAR (%)	[t]	CAR (%)	[t]	CAR (%)	[t]	CAR (%)	[t]	CAR (%)	[t]	CAR (%)	[t]	CAR (%)	[t]	CAR (%)	[t]
+1 day	3.22	[6.1]	3.34	[4.6]	0.72	[0.4]	2.12	[2.1]	−1.49	[−0.4]	6.00	[5.4]	4.69	[1.8]	9.08	[1.4]	0.99	[0.5]	4.81	[2.9]
+5 days	3.61	[6.2]	4.18	[5.0]	1.68	[1.0]	2.30	[2.1]	−2.32	[−0.5]	6.83	[5.7]	5.91	[2.4]	2.31	[0.4]	1.73	[0.8]	4.56	[2.8]
Panel B: cumulative monthly abnormal returns																				
−1 month	−0.59	[−1.2]	−0.90	[−1.2]	−1.03	[−0.7]	0.18	[0.2]	−3.07	[−1.3]	−1.23	[−1.2]	3.39	[1.6]	−9.34	[−1.6]	0.99	[0.5]	2.09	[1.3]
Filing month	3.84	[5.3]	2.25	[2.0]	1.30	[0.6]	4.85	[3.4]	−2.67	[−0.8]	5.34	[3.6]	10.62	[4.0]	−9.38	[−1.2]	3.11	[0.9]	8.82	[3.7]
+1 month	4.20	[4.5]	2.26	[1.6]	−0.95	[−0.3]	5.75	[2.9]	−4.62	[−1.0]	7.63	[4.2]	11.02	[4.1]	−17.85	[−1.7]	0.11	[0.0]	10.74	[3.3]
+6 months	5.32	[3.0]	4.08	[1.6]	−0.62	[−0.1]	6.39	[1.6]	−0.46	[−0.1]	6.04	[1.6]	14.42	[4.0]	5.13	[0.3]	−1.44	[−0.2]	8.41	[1.2]
+12 months	7.78	[2.9]	6.15	[1.9]	4.59	[0.6]	7.40	[1.0]	12.96	[1.5]	10.10	[2.2]	16.60	[3.7]	13.91	[0.5]	7.41	[0.5]	15.94	[1.7]
+18 months	10.26	[3.4]	5.90	[1.6]	7.24	[0.8]	13.75	[1.6]	12.56	[1.2]	11.04	[2.2]	21.02	[3.8]	16.52	[0.6]	8.11	[0.5]	14.93	[1.5]

significant and just over 10%. A large portion of these returns accrue in the [+3 months, +18 months] window. In other words, only a modest portion comes from the period around announcement, suggesting that the market underreacts, on average, to the announcement of activism. Another possibility is that the long-term abnormal positive returns reflect general undervaluation of the target, which reverts to fundamentals over the subsequent months. The remaining columns break down returns by activism category. Firms targeted for a sale or for which the activist tries to block a merger earn the largest abnormal returns. For the remaining categories, abnormal returns are positive but insignificant.

3. Analysis

In this section, we document the results of investor activism, focusing on both qualitative accounts based on press articles as well as more formal quantitative accounts based on Compustat accounting data. Our objective is to identify a correlation between the result of the activism and stock market performance. We are most interested in the correlation between an eventual takeover and stock market performance. However, we also check whether hedge-fund activists: (a) make operating or governance changes that are reflected in shareholder value even when the target remains independent or (b) simply pick undervalued stocks that are more likely to be acquired regardless of activist intervention. In other words, we try to shed light on the question of whether the activist investor *causes* the takeover or is simply effective at picking a stock that was likely to be taken over in the first place.

3.1. Outcomes

To understand the actions that the target firm takes in response to an activist's requests, we collect data on what happened after each event by reading the subsequent 13D filings and communications between management and the activist, as well as by searching the newswires for information on the outcome. To identify whether the firm merged or was acquired in the year after activism, we look at the CRSP delisting code and delisting date and check whether it falls within 18 months of the initial complaint filing. We classify a target as merged if its delisting date falls within 18 months of the initial filing, where the CRSP delisting code has a first digit of 2 (Mergers) or 3 (Exchanges).

Table 3 shows the results of this classification. We classify the outcomes into four broad outcomes comprising 16 subcategories. The four broad outcomes include: asset sales and spin offs, capital structure, corporate governance, and other. We cutoff our searches 18 months after the first filing. Classifications are nonexclusive: for example, if a target repurchases shares and gives board seats to the activist, this event will be categorized with two outcomes. Table 3 gives the number of exclusive classifications (i.e., where no other outcome was recorded) in parentheses to the right of the non-exclusive outcome number.

Table 3

Outcomes of activism

Outcomes apply to news announced no later than 18 months after the initial 13D activist filing. Each event can have more than one classification; uniquely classified outcomes are in parentheses. The sample is restricted to initial activist filings.

Outcome	Number (uniquely classified)
No news	379 (379)
News	
Asset sale related	
Merger or asset sale completed	178 (178)
Merger or asset sale announced	48 (25)
Merger called off or bid increased	12 (8)
Spin off completed or announced	7 (2)
Activist takes over target	7 (0)
Target hires IB or begins auction	14 (5)
Capital structure (non asset sale related)	
Shares repurchased/Special Dividend	23 (9)
Greenmail	4 (3)
Corporate governance	
Removal of poison pill	15 (10)
Resignation of CEO/CFO/Chairman	25 (5)
Board seats granted to activist	96 (69)
Proxy defeated	14 (10)
Other	
Activist cuts position below 5%	35 (31)
Financing/bankruptcy agreement	17 (10)

For nearly half of the activist events, we find no additional news following the first filing. Not surprisingly, these events tend to be concentrated among smaller targets. This raises the concern that these firms are less newsworthy than larger firms, generating fewer search results from the newswires. However, in the 18 months subsequent to filing, these events earn average abnormal returns close to zero.

The first group of outcomes for which we find news comprises events in which an asset sale or spin off is announced or completed. In 178 cases, the target is acquired. In 48 cases, a merger or asset sale is announced. The other outcomes in this category include completion of a spin off (seven events), the activist taking over the target entirely (seven events), and the target hiring an investment bank to solicit potential buyers (14 events).

Our main question is whether the returns to activism depend on whether the target is eventually acquired or not. These results are shown in Table 4 and plotted in Figure 1. The left-hand columns show average returns following the initial 13D filing for the 226 events for which an acquisition was announced or completed within 18 months of the initial 13D filing. The table shows that these events earn abnormal announcement

Table 4

Daily and monthly abnormal returns by outcome

Daily and monthly cumulative abnormal returns for activism targets, grouped according to the outcome. Abnormal returns are the difference between the daily or monthly return and the daily or monthly return on the matching portfolio. Outcomes are defined as follows: *acquisition announced/completed* (the target completed or announced a merger or sale of either all or part of its assets); *no news* (indicates no news of an outcome); *board or resignations* (indicates the announcement of resignations by the target's CEO and/or CFO and/or chairman of the board and/or the announcement that the activist gains seats on the target's board of directors, either through a proxy contest or a deal with the target); *reduces stake to <5%* (indicates that the activist reduced its stake in the target to below 5% of the shares outstanding, thereby ending its 13D filing requirements). Outcomes apply to news announced no later than 18 months after the initial 13D activist filing. *t*-Statistics are in brackets.

| | Events in which target is acquired within 18 months of initial filing: | | Events in which target remains independent: | | | | | | | | | | | |
| | | | All | | No news | | Board/ resignations | | Spin off | | Share repurchase | | Activist reduces stake <5% | |
	CAR (%)	[t]	CAR (%)	[t]	CAR (%)	[t]	CAR (%)	[t]	CAR (%)	[t]	CAR (%)	[t]	CAR (%)	[t]
Panel A: daily returns														
−10	1.29	[1.7]	−0.56	[−1.7]	−0.23	[−0.6]	−0.78	[−1.0]	0.36	[0.4]	−0.67	[−0.6]	−0.28	[−0.2]
−5	0.87	[1.0]	−0.37	[−0.7]	−0.01	[−0.0]	−0.83	[−0.8]	3.27	[1.0]	−1.54	[−0.7]	−0.55	[−0.2]
−4	1.23	[1.4]	−0.20	[−0.4]	0.10	[0.2]	−1.17	[−0.9]	2.96	[1.0]	−1.13	[−0.5]	1.50	[0.5]
−3	1.69	[1.7]	−0.19	[−0.3]	0.25	[0.4]	−1.48	[−1.1]	3.36	[1.1]	0.17	[0.1]	−0.13	[−0.0]
−2	2.00	[1.9]	−0.10	[−0.2]	0.13	[0.2]	−1.15	[−0.7]	3.73	[1.5]	−0.26	[−0.1]	1.97	[0.5]
−1	2.78	[2.5]	0.34	[0.5]	0.47	[0.6]	−0.32	[−0.2]	5.01	[4.0]	−0.36	[−0.1]	1.63	[0.4]
Filing	4.14	[3.6]	1.41	[2.1]	1.36	[1.8]	0.57	[0.3]	4.50	[2.4]	0.20	[0.1]	4.02	[1.1]
+1	4.75	[4.2]	2.12	[3.1]	2.02	[2.7]	1.24	[0.8]	5.56	[2.8]	0.08	[0.0]	5.56	[1.5]
+5	5.72	[4.9]	2.36	[3.0]	2.51	[2.9]	1.34	[0.8]	6.40	[4.5]	1.36	[0.5]	4.75	[1.2]
Panel B: monthly returns														
−1	1.39	[1.3]	−1.69	[−2.9]	−2.25	[−3.4]	−0.67	[−0.6]	−6.52	[−1.1]	3.34	[0.9]	1.35	[0.5]
Filing	7.88	[5.7]	1.78	[1.8]	0.86	[0.8]	4.71	[2.2]	8.76	[2.6]	5.95	[1.0]	−1.32	[−0.4]
+1	8.85	[5.4]	1.81	[1.4]	0.45	[0.3]	5.46	[2.1]	8.29	[1.0]	8.01	[1.0]	−0.59	[−0.1]
+6	16.84	[6.1]	0.64	[0.3]	−1.15	[−0.4]	−0.57	[−0.1]	12.20	[1.7]	18.53	[1.0]	−3.41	[−0.3]
+12	22.40	[6.8]	1.50	[0.4]	−2.63	[−0.5]	−0.93	[−0.1]	8.34	[0.4]	30.50	[0.9]	−1.64	[−0.1]
+18	25.85	[7.9]	2.85	[0.6]	0.00	[0.0]	−5.62	[−0.7]	−3.41	[−0.1]	29.97	[0.8]	−2.83	[−0.2]

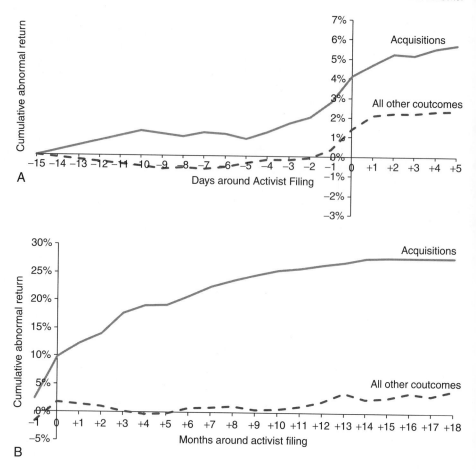

Fig. 1. Abnormal returns around activist filing by outcome. Average cumulative abnormal returns plotted separately for activism targets that were acquired and for activism targets that remained independent 18 months after the first filing of the 13D. We first estimate factor loadings on HML, SMB, and the market excess return using 100 days of returns prior to the first filing of the 13D. The matching portfolio is the factor-loading weighted return on the HML, SMB, and market portfolios. Abnormal returns are the difference between the target return and the return on the matching portfolio. Panel A shows cumulative daily abnormal returns during a 20-day interval around the announcement of activism. Panel B shows cumulative monthly abnormal returns during a 19-month interval around the announcement of activism. Panel A: short-term cumulative abnormal returns and Panel B: long-term cumulative abnormal returns.

returns of more than 5%. The rest of the table sorts the remaining nontakeover events by outcome. The average announcement return, over all of these events, is 2.36%, about half of that earned by firms that are eventually taken over. The right-hand columns further separate these events into categories based on the outcome. Events that result in changes to the board or a share repurchase do not cause significant positive returns. Events that result in a spin off earn significantly positive announcement returns of 6.4%.

The results in Panel B are more interesting because they show the long-term returns to activism, conditional on the outcome. Events in which an acquisition was announced or completed earn postfiling abnormal monthly returns of 25.85%, reflecting the takeover premium paid by the acquirer. For the full set of events that do not end in acquisition, post-13D filing returns are not significantly different from zero. These returns do not seem to depend on what actually happened—events for which there is no news do not have significantly different monthly returns than events for which good news is announced (i.e., board resignations or a spin off). The possible exception is the few events in which the firm agrees to repurchase shares. Monthly returns here are positive but not significant.

To summarize, classifications of activism based on the outcome reveal that a takeover is one of the most likely events. Both announcement returns and long-term returns in the event of a takeover are high. For the remaining outcomes, long-term abnormal returns can be positive but are not significantly different from zero.

3.2. Do targets that remain independent experience any improvement?

Another way to track the performance of firms postactivism is to study accounting measures before and after the activist request (see e.g., Brav et al., 2008; Klein and Zur, 2009). This is potentially problematic for a few reasons. First, the most significant outcome for a target firm is a takeover, in which case it is dropped from Compustat. Second, a few of the firms in our sample do not supply Compustat data even before the event, making a before-versus-after comparison impossible. These caveats notwithstanding, the left-hand column of Table 5 shows changes in accounting-based measures of operating performance following activist filings for the subset of targets that remain independent. In our discussion, we focus primarily on measures over which management has the most control, such as leverage, share repurchases, and payout policy. For example, a finding that activist targets with positive earnings shocks experience high returns would not necessarily teach us anything about the success of the activist as these shocks could be independent of the activist demands.

Performance changes are measured by the difference between the fiscal year after the 13D filing and the fiscal year before the filing. The accounting variables are constructed as follows: *capital expenditures* is capital expenditures (Compustat item 128) over lagged net property, plant, and equipment (item 8); *dividends/earnings* is the ratio of the sum of common dividends (item 21) and preferred dividends (item 19) to earnings before depreciation, interest, and tax (item 13); *leverage* is the sum of long-term debt (item 9) and current liabilities (item 34) divided by the sum of long-term debt, current liabilities, and the book value of common equity (item 60); *operating return on assets* is operating cash flow (item 308) lagged total assets (item 6); *return on assets* is the ratio of EBITDA (item 18) to lagged total assets; and $\Delta A/A_{t-1}$ denotes the percentage change in balance sheet assets; $\Delta S/S_{t-1}$ denotes the percentage change in

Table 5

Operating changes following activist filings for nonacquired targets

Descriptive statistics of changes in accounting-based measures of financial policy and performance between the fiscal year prior to the initial filing of an activist Schedule 13D and the fiscal year following the initial filing. The accounting variables are constructed from Compustat as follows: *leverage* is the sum of long-term debt (item 9) and current liabilities (item 34) divided by the sum of long-term debt, current liabilities, and the book value of common equity (item 60); *capital expenditures* is capital expenditures (item 128) divided by lagged net property, plant, and equipment (item 8); *dividends/earnings* is the ratio of the sum of common dividends (item 21) and preferred dividends (item 19) to earnings before depreciation, interest, and tax (item 13); *change in assets* is equal to the percentage change in assets for the year after activism (item 6) and the year prior to activism; *change in shares* is equal to the percentage change in shares outstanding (from CRSP) four quarters after activism and four quarters before activism; *return on assets* is the ratio of EBITDA (item 18) to lagged total assets (item 6); and *operating return on assets* is the ratio of operating cash flow (item 308) to lagged total assets (item 6). All accounting variables are winsorized at the 1% and 99% levels to reduce the influence of outliers. Long-term abnormal returns are calculated 18 months after the activist filing. t-Statistics and p-values are in brackets.

	All nonacquired targets		Correlation with long-term abnormal return	
	$\Delta_{-1,1}$	$[t]$	ρ	[p-Value]
Leverage	0.408	[2.69]	−0.031	[0.58]
Capital expenditures	−0.144	[−4.11]	−0.053	[0.34]
Dividends/Earnings	0.019	[1.31]	−0.067	[0.25]
$\Delta A/A_{t-1}$	0.079	[0.59]	0.022	[0.67]
$\Delta S/S_{t-1}$	−0.203	[−1.06]	0.051	[0.24]
Return on assets	−0.001	[−0.15]	0.165	[0.00]
Operating ROA	0.010	[0.70]	0.018	[0.74]

adjusted shares outstanding. All scaled variables are winsorized at the 1% and 99% levels to reduce the influence of outliers.

The left-hand column of Table 5 shows that for the full sample of events, there is no significant change in ROA, operating ROA, the payout ratio, asset growth, or share growth. We do find, however, that firms reduce investment levels—capital expenditures scaled by property, plant, and equipment falls from 36.5% to 22.1% for the average firm in the sample. The table also shows that surviving firms increase their leverage ratio by nearly 40 percentage points. This effect is far more pronounced when the activist initially targets "capital structure" issues in its initial 13D filing. In these instances, targets more than double their leverage ratios from the year before the activist filing to the year after.

The more important question is whether any of these operating changes are associated with high stock returns. Our objective is to find evidence of stock price appreciation for targets that execute operational or financing changes demanded by activists yet ultimately remain independent. These correlations, and their associated p-values, are shown in the right-hand column of Table 5. Any changes in operating ROA, leverage, capital expenditures, dividends, assets, and shares outstanding seem to have no significant correlation with returns, consistent with our hypothesis that activists have few levers in creating shareholder value over the long term other than a takeover. Return on assets is the only operational change that has a significant correlation with long-term abnormal returns, but it is not obvious that this has any relation to the demands raised by the activist.

3.3. Do activists increase the probability that firms are taken over?

While the evidence thus far is consistent with our hypothesis that activists create value by bringing about an acquisition of the target, it is also consistent with another explanation: the returns associated with activists' involvement reflect their ability to pick undervalued stocks that are inherently more likely to be acquired (with or without an activist intervention). And to the extent that the activists ask target firms to make operating changes, these are changes that were apt to happen anyway. Consistent with this alternate hypothesis, activist targets tend to have similar characteristics: they are small stocks with little or no analyst coverage and low market-to-book ratios, and have underperformed relative to other firms in their industry.

We compare the probability that target firms are acquired with the counterfactual probability that they would have been acquired in the absence of activism. We obtain a counterfactual probability by matching each activism target with a firm in the same industry that is of similar size and has experienced similar past returns. The premise of our matching procedure is that the matched firm is also a candidate for investor activism. We then track each of these firms for a period of 1 year (or 18 months) following the initial activist filing, keeping track of whether the firm is delisted, acquired, or still trading at the end of this window.

Table 6 shows these results. In our sample, 22.6% of firms are delisted within a year of the first filing. Of these, 18.1% are acquired by another firm and stop trading. In the matched sample, only 10.6% of firms are delisted within a year and only 7.2% are acquired. Thus, activists increase the probability of takeover by about 11 percentage points.

One drawback of our matching procedure is the potential omitted variable bias: perhaps activists select targets on the basis of unobserved characteristics that do not enter our match. Put differently, we cannot control for some heterogeneity between the firms that the activist actually targeted and the firms that, albeit similar, are not ultimately targeted. While there is no way to fully rule out the importance of unobserved characteristics, we try another matched sample that is based on 13D filings in which no activist intentions are stated. Thus, this sample comprises a group of firms that also represent large positions in the activist investors' portfolios but about which no formal issues were raised. The table shows that for this sample, 15.4% of firms are delisted and 12.6% are subsequently acquired within a year of the first activism complaint filing. Finally, we calculate the probability that stocks in the same size cohort as the target stocks are delisted. The table shows that only 7.4% of these stocks are delisted in a given year, with 4.7% of these being acquired.

Table 6

Delisting outcomes for targets and other companies

Statistics on the delisting of the target companies for all activist filings made between 1994 and 2006, hedge-fund activist filings only, other companies in an industry, size, and prior-return matched sample, targets of nonactivist 13D filings excluding those that delisted within 2 months of the filing, and the universe of all small CRSP stocks. Delisting information is from CRSP. Delisting data for "all small stocks" are based on an event date of December 31, 2004 for firms in the CRSP NYSE third size decile or less.

	All activist events	Hedge fund activist events	Industry-size-return matched sample	Nonactivist 13D filings	All small stocks
Panel A: within 12 months of first 13D filing					
Still in sample on CRSP	77.4%	77.1%	89.4%	84.6%	92.6%
Delisted	22.6%	22.8%	10.6%	15.4%	7.4%
Acquired	18.1%	18.6%	7.2%	12.6%	4.7%
Other	4.4%	4.3%	3.5%	2.8%	2.6%
Panel B: Within 18 months of first 13D filing					
Still in sample on CRSP	72.5%	72.6%	85.7%	80.4%	89.2%
Delisted	27.5%	27.4%	14.3%	19.6%	10.8%
Acquired	21.9%	21.9%	9.1%	16.1%	7.2%
Other	5.5%	5.5%	5.2%	3.4%	3.6%

An interesting exercise is to see whether the increase in takeover probability can be related to the abnormal returns on announcement of activism. A back-of-the-envelope calculation suggests that it is: activists increase the probability of takeover by about 11 percentage points. Multiplied by an expected takeover premium of 30% (e.g., Cremers et al., 2007) yields 3.3% abnormal returns on announcement, commensurate with what we observe in the data.

To sum up, based on a variety of control samples, activists increase the probability that a firm will be acquired. Panel B shows similar results but extends the window in which we track the target firm and its control firm to 18 months.

In addition to the matched sample analysis, there are other reasons to think that activists increase the probability that firms are acquired. First, announcement returns are related to the specific concerns of the activist. As we showed earlier, announcement returns are particularly high when the activist requests that the target look into the sale of all or some of the business. Since presumably all activist positions are motivated by undervaluation of the target, it would follow that those positions that specifically call for the sale of the target should see higher announcement returns only if the market believes that the activist will be able to follow through on its demands. Thus, the market rationally bids up the price of the target stock in anticipation of a takeover premium.

Finally, there is revealing evidence in the statements made by third-party buyers of activist targets. As Thomas H. Lee, a private equity fund manager, acknowledged in a speech in 2007, "I'd like to thank my friends Carl Icahn, Nelson Peltz, Jana Partners, Third Point ... for teeing up deals because ... many times [activist targets] are being driven into some form of auction."[7]

4. Implications: the credit crisis of mid-2007

One implication of our findings is that returns to investor activism should depend on overall takeover interest in the market. Shocks to financing availability resulting from credit market turmoil from July through September 2007 provide an opportunity to confirm or reject this hypothesis.

After a series of defaults by hedge funds and lenders on subprime-related investments, credit spreads widened during the late summer of 2007. The spread between the yield on a Moody's AAA bond and the yield on the 10-year Treasury bond increased from approximately 11 basis points in early June 2007 to over 60 basis points in September 2007. The Merrill Lynch aggregate credit market option adjusted spread over Treasuries increased from 94 basis points to 150 basis points over the same window; widening also occurred in the CDX and syndicated loan markets. Brunner-meier (2009) provides an overview of market conditions during this time.

From the perspective of a strategic buyer or private equity firm attempting to complete a debt-financed acquisition, the widening of spreads was an exogenous shock to the cost of funding. This shock was soon reflected in the withdrawal of large buyouts. On July 26, 2007, Alliance Boots and Chrysler both announced that buyers had been unable to secure financing for more than $20 billion of debt. The next day, Cadbury announced that it would delay the sale of its US drinks division, blaming turmoil in the credit markets. News accounts in July provide additional color—the *New York Times* reports in late July that many bankers and private equity firms were "trying to figure out what to do with dozens of pending deals that are now faced with the higher cost of debt."[8] News reports also confirmed that the stock prices of firms that were being considered as takeover targets were adversely affected.

What are the implications of this for activism? If activists are primarily focused on operating and governance improvements, the shocks to credit conditions should not affect the value of their positions. On the other hand, if activists' main objective is to foster an acquisition, we predict negative abnormal portfolio returns around the time of the credit crisis.

We assemble evidence on the performance of activist positions during this time to check whether activist investments are disproportionately affected by the credit market shocks. We isolate all activists that have been involved in 10 incidents or more, additionally requiring each activist to have been involved in at least one incident in

---

[7] Andrew Ross Sorkin, "Will Credit Crisis End the Activists' Run?" *New York Times*, August 27, 2007.
[8] Vikas Bajaj and Eric Dash, "Monday on Wall Street: A Day Filled with Jitters Rather than Mergers," New York Times, July 30, 2007.

2005 or 2006. Each of these activists must file quarterly 13F reports on their holdings. We study reported positions at the end of June 2007. For each of these activists, we collect the 10 largest positions under the reasoning that these positions are most likely subject to activism. A few of the targets have already been delisted by early July and are thus not available on CRSP. Our final sample includes 144 target companies owned by 16 activist investors.[9] This sample is a conservative place to start, since the investors had surely not taken an activist role in all of these positions.

We analyze returns over four periods of interest: (1) the precrisis period, (2) the week during which credit spreads first spiked and Chrysler and Boots fail to find adequate funds to secure buyouts, (3) the week during which Home Depot slashed its price in a buyout, and (4) the full "crisis" period covering July and August.

We weight returns in two ways, with our baseline results equal-weighted. We also show the returns to the portfolio in which positions are first value-weighted within each activist portfolio and then equal-weighted across activists. This more elaborate procedure ensures that activists that manage more assets do not receive more weight, but places more focus on the activists' most important positions. (A simpler value weighting produces nearly identical results, but overweights activists with more assets under management.) Table 7 shows that stocks in activist portfolios lost an average of approximately 5% during the week of July 25.

While the raw abnormal returns are suggestive, they are confounded by volatility in both market returns and abnormal returns accruing to value-growth and momentum--based strategies during this time (e.g., Brunnermeier, 2009; Khandani and Lo, 2007). Both value and momentum stocks underperformed growth stocks in July, August, and September. Identifying the benchmark is particularly important in this exercise because of the overlapping nature of the event returns. We take a nonparametric approach to matching, following Daniel et al. (1997) and form 125 value-weighted matching characteristic portfolios based on size, market-to-book equity, and momentum.[10] Abnormal returns for each target stock are measured by the excess over the returns on the matched portfolio. Figure 2 confirms that activism targets perform poorly during this time relative to their style-adjusted benchmarks. From mid-July to the end of September, the activist portfolio underperforms by more than 3 percentage points.

Somewhat more formally, Table 7 presents the abnormal returns over several periods of interest along with the corresponding t-statistics. Abnormal returns are not significantly different from zero during the "precrisis" period. However, the portfolio

---

[9] The funds include Blum Capital Partners, Cannell Capital, Farallon Capital, Franklin Resources, Gamco Investors, Jeffrey Halis, Icahn & Company, JANA Partners, Newcastle Capital, Nierenberg Investment Management, Oracle Investment Management, Pirate Capital, Soros Fund Management, Steel Partners, Third Point, and ValueAct Capital.

[10] It is possible that we *over control* for value and momentum exposure, in which case the results shown in Figure 2 and reported in Table 7 are attenuated. This is because many market participants claimed that the underperformance of value stocks was precisely because many of these stocks had been considered as takeover targets. In this case, we simply want to de-mean cumulative returns by the market return, yielding slightly stronger results (not tabulated).

Table 7

The stock market performance of activism targets during the 2007 credit crisis

Cumulative abnormal returns on the portfolio of stocks held by the 16 most active activist investors between June and September 2007, as reported in their 13F disclosures in June 2007. The portfolio contains the top 10 positions of these activists, 144 stocks in total. We consider four periods over which to calculate event returns: (1) the precrisis period between June 1 and July 25; (2) the week during which Chrysler and Boots failed to secure funding for $20 billion of buyouts; (3) the week during which Home Depot agreed to slash its price during a buyout; and (4) the period encompassing (2) and (3). The table shows both equal- and value-weighted results. In the value-weighted results, stocks are first value-weighted according to position size within activist portfolios, then equal-weighted across activists. In each panel, the left-hand columns show the average cumulative return (CR); the right-hand columns show the cumulative abnormal return (CAR), which is the average cumulative return minus the return on the corresponding Daniel et al. (1997) characteristic portfolio. The 125 characteristic portfolios are based on lagged size, book-to-market equity, and momentum.

	Equal-weighted		Value-weighted	
	CR (%)	CAR (%)	CR (%)	CAR (%)
June 1-July 24, 2007	−1.05	−0.21	−0.14	0.24
(precrisis period)	[−1.17]	[−0.25]	[−0.15]	[0.28]
July 25-July 31, 2007	−4.71	−1.01	−4.67	−1.13
(Chrysler and Boots fail to secure buyout funds)	[−11.30]	[−2.51]	[−14.15]	[−3.39]
August 25-August 29, 2007	−0.40	−0.40	−0.35	−0.46
(Home Depot slashes price in buyout)	[−1.26]	[−1.20]	[−1.31]	[−1.62]
July 25-August 29, 2007	−4.83	−2.04	−5.57	−2.97
(Extended period of credit spread widening)	[−6.25]	[−2.72]	[−7.79]	[−4.32]

significantly underperforms during the week in which Chrysler and Boots fail to secure funding for their buyouts. We also find weak evidence of underperformance during the week in which Home Depot announced that it would cut its price in a proposed buyout. The bottom lines of the table consider the full "crisis" period, from the end of July to the end of August, and confirm that the underperformance shown in Figure 2 is statistically significant.

To summarize, many activists saw drops in the value of their portfolios during a period when market-wide takeover interest fell, consistent with the idea that their portfolio firms had been purchased in the hope of securing a takeover.

5. Conclusions

In their survey of shareholder activism, Gillan and Starks (1998) define an activist as an investor who tries to "change the status quo through 'voice' without a change in control of the firm." While activist investors do not take controlling stakes in firms, we show that— ironically, from the perspective of value creation—activists are most successful at creating value when they are able to effect a change in control. In addition, we show that activism

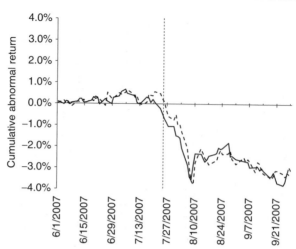

Fig. 2. The performance of activism targets during the July-August 2007 credit crisis. Equal- and value--weighted Daniel et al. (1997) adjusted abnormal returns on the portfolio of stocks held by the most active activists between June and September 2007. Matching portfolios are formed based on size, market-to-book equity, and momentum. The portfolio includes the 10 largest holdings for each activist. In the value-weighted results, stocks are first value-weighted within activist portfolios, then equal-weighted across activists. The dashed line at the end of July 2007 marks the public announcement that Chrysler and Boots failed to get adequate financing for their respective buyouts (solid—equal-weighted abnormal returns and dashed—value-weighted abnormal returns).

measurably increases the likelihood that an undervalued target is ultimately taken over. Hedge funds' success at effecting a takeover accounts for the high returns to shareholder activism that have been documented in recent work. Events in credit markets in July and August 2007 provide additional support.

One implication of our work is that the scope for hedge-fund activism to have pervasive effects on corporate governance is limited. In our view, hedge funds invest in small, undervalued companies with the ultimate goal of seeing those targets bought out. With the returns highest for targets that are acquired within 18 months of the activist filing, it follows that the activists are less interested in making corporate governance changes that might improve the firm but leave it independent.

An important question, which we do not answer here, is whether the shareholder activism associated with takeovers creates long-term value for acquiring company shareholders. In principle, activists could create value by identifying assets whose value is not being maximized by current management. In this case, the takeover premium represents the present value of having the assets managed more efficiently by another party. Another possibility, however, is that activists are good at identifying firms for which potential acquirers might overpay. A long tradition of papers in corporate finance, starting with Roll (1986) and including Shleifer and Vishny (2003) and Moeller et al. (2005), argues that firms over-pay, on average, for public market acquisitions. In this case, the function of the activist is primarily to market the stock rather than to identify acquirers with true synergies. Given enough data on the future performance of the takeovers in our sample, it should be straightforward to distinguish between these possibilities.

Appendix A: Classification of activist events based on initial demands

Engage management: The activist intends to engage management or to discuss issues with management to increase shareholder value, or makes a general statement that shares are "undervalued" without including any specific plans or proposals. This is the least aggressive form of activism (45.54% of hedge-fund sample and 22.45% of nonhedge-fund sample).

Capital structure: This type of activism relates to a recapitalization, stock or debt issuance, restructuring of debt, dividends, or a stock buyback (10.08% of hedge-fund sample and 6.12% of nonhedge-fund sample).

Corporate governance: This type of activism can include a call to declassify the board, remove a poison pill, elect activist-selected directors, or fire a company officer or board member. The corporate governance classification also applies to activism that targets issues of board or executive compensation, corporate fraud, and lack of transparency (21.94% of the hedge-fund sample and 48.47% of the nonhedge-fund sample).

Business strategy: The activist critiques excess diversification and the level of investment in some business lines or cites poor operating strategy at the target (4.59% of the hedge-fund sample and 6.12% of the nonhedge-fund sample).

Asset sale: The activist calls for the target to sell itself or certain of its assets in order to maximize shareholder value. This classification can also represent an offer by the activist to take over the target (18.11% of the hedge fund sample and 13.27% of the nonhedge-fund sample).

Block merger: The activist blocks a proposed merger, usually because it deems the terms of the deal to be unfavorable to target shareholders. Often, the activist will demand a higher price (5.61% of the hedge-fund sample and 10.20% of the nonhedge-fund sample).

Financing/Bankruptcy: The activist provides financing for a target in bankruptcy or financial distress (1.40% of the hedge-fund sample and 2.04% of the nonhedge-fund sample).

Strategic alternatives: The activist requests that the target pursue various strategic alternatives for the firm, including a spin off of an underperforming division (2.42% of the hedge-fund sample and 5.10% of the nonhedge-fund sample).

Proxy: The activist files under Schedule 14A with the SEC, signaling an intention to solicit proxies from shareholders either to elect its own proposed director(s) or to adopt a shareholder proposal that the activist has submitted or plans on submitting (9.06% of the hedge-fund sample and 3.06% of the nonhedge-fund sample).

References

Bainbridge, S., 2005, "Shareholder Activism and Institutional Investors," Unpublished Working Paper, University of California, Los Angeles.

Bebchuk, L., 2007, "The Myth of Shareholder Franchise," *Virginia Law Review*, 93, 675–732.

Becht, M., J. Franks, C. Mayer and S. Rossi, 2009, "Returns to Shareholder Activism: Evidence from a Clinical Study of the Hermes UK Focus Fund," *Review of Financial Studies*, 22, 3093–3129.

Black, B., 1990, "Shareholder Passivity Reexamined," *Michigan Law Review*, 89, 520–608.

Black, B., 1998, "Shareholder Activism and Corporate Governance in the US," In P. Newman (Ed.), *The New Palgrave Dictionary of Economics and the Law*, Palgrave Macmillan, UK, pp. 459–465.

Brav, A., W. Jiang, F. Partnoy and R. Thomas, 2008, "Hedge Fund Activism, Corporate Governance and Firm Performance," *Journal of Finance*, 63, 1729–1775.

Brunnermeier, M., 2009, "Deciphering the Liquidity and Credit Crunch 2007–2008," *Journal of Economic Perspectives*, 23, 77–100.

Clifford, C., 2007, "Value Creation or Destruction? Hedge Funds as Shareholder Activists," Unpublished Working Paper, Arizona State University.

Cremers, K., V. Nair and K. John, 2007, "Takeovers and the Cross-Section of Returns," *Review of Financial Studies*, 20, 1359–1388.

Daniel, K., M. Grinblatt, S. Titman and R. Wermers, 1997, "Measuring Mutual Fund Performance with Characteristic Based Benchmarks," *Journal of Finance*, 52, 1035–1058.

Fama, E. and K. French, 1993, "Common Risk Factors in the Returns on Stocks and Bonds," *Journal of Financial Economics*, 33, 3–56.

Gillan, S. and L. Starks, 1998, "A Survey of Shareholder Activism: Motivation and Empirical Evidence," *Contemporary Finance Digest*, 2, 10–34.

Gillan, S. and L. Starks, 2000, "Corporate Governance Proposals and Shareholder Activism: The Role of Institutional Investors," *Journal of Financial Economics*, 57, 275–305.

Grossman, S. and O. Hart, 1980, "Takeover Bids, the Free-Rider Problem, and the Theory of the Corporation," *Bell Journal of Economics*, 11, 42–64.

Kahan, M. and E. Rock, 2006, "Hedge Funds in Corporate Governance and Corporate Control," Institute for Law & Economics Research Paper No. 06–16, University of Pennsylvania.

Karpoff, J., 2001, "The Impact of Shareholder Activism on Target Companies: A Survey of Empirical Findings," Unpublished Working Paper, University of Washington.

Karpoff, J., P. Malatesta and R. Walkling, 1996, "Corporate Governance and Shareholder Initiatives: Empirical Evidence," *Journal of Financial Economics*, 42, 365–395.

Khandani, A. and A. Lo, 2007, "What Happened to the Quants in August 2007?" *Journal of Investment Management*, 5, 5–54.

Klein, A. and E. Zur, 2009, "Entrepreneurial Shareholder Activism: Hedge Funds and Other Private Investors," *Journal of Finance*, 64, 187–229.

Mikkelson, W. and R. Ruback, 1985, "An Empirical Analysis of the Interfirm Equity Investment Process," *Journal of Financial Economics*, 14, 523–553.

Moeller, S., F. Schlingemann and R. Stulz, 2005, "Wealth Destruction on a Massive Scale," *Journal of Finance*, 60, 757–782.

Roe, M., 1994, *Strong Managers, Weak Owners: The Political Roots of American Corporate Governance*, Princeton University Press, Princeton, NJ.

Roll, R., 1986, "The Hubris Hypothesis of Corporate Takeovers," *Journal of Business*, 59, 197–216.

Romano, R., 2001, "Less is More: Making Institutional Investor Activism a Valuable Mechanism of Corporate Governance," *Yale Journal on Regulation*, 18, 174–251.

Shleifer, A. and R. Vishny, 1986, "Large Shareholders and Corporate Control," *Journal of Political Economy*, 94, 461–488.

Shleifer, A. and R. Vishny, 2003, "Stock Market Driven Acquisitions," *Journal of Financial Economics*, 70, 295–311.

Wahal, S., 1996, "Public Pension Fund Activism and Firm Performance," *Journal of Financial and Quantitative Analysis*, 31, 1–23.

PART 6

RAISING CASH: DOES DEAL FINANCING MATTER?

Chapter 17

VALUATION EFFECTS OF BANK FINANCING IN ACQUISITIONS[*]

ANU BHARADWAJ

Cornerstone Research, Boston, Massachusetts, USA

ANIL SHIVDASANI[*]

Investment Banking Division, Salomon Smith Barney, New York, New York, USA
Kenan-Flagler Business School, University of North Carolina at Chapel Hill, Chapel Hill,
North Carolina, USA

Contents

[*] We thank Murillo Campello, Urs Peyer, Tod Perry, Bill Schwert, an anonymous referee, and seminar participants at Arizona State University and Indiana University for helpful comments.

This article originally appeared in the *Journal of Financial Economics*, Vol. 67, pp. 113–148 (2003).
Corporate Takeovers, Volume 2
Edited by B. Espen Eckbo
DOI: 10.1016/B978-0-12-381982-6.00018-5

Abstract

In a sample of 115 cash tender offers between 1990 and 1996, banks extend financing in 70% of the tender offers and finance the entire tender offer in half of these takeovers. Bank financing of tender offers is more likely when internal cash reserves are low. Acquisitions that are entirely financed by banks are associated with large and significantly positive acquirer announcement returns. Announcement returns are also positively related to the fraction of the acquisition value financed by bank debt. The benefits of bank financing are most important for both poorly performing acquirers and acquirers facing substantial informational asymmetries. Our results suggest that bank debt performs an important certification and monitoring role for acquirers in tender offers.

Keywords

mergers and acquisitions, bank financing

JEL classification: G21, G34

1. Introduction

The effect of informational asymmetries between firms and external capital market participants has received considerable theoretical and empirical attention. According to received theory, financial intermediaries (and banks in particular) serve as a bridge between firms and external capital markets due to their superior information collection and evaluation capabilities (Campbell and Kracaw, 1980; Diamond, 1984; Leland and Pyle, 1977).

A bank's informational advantage can influence its client firm's investment policy. Consider the case of a firm deciding whether or not to pursue an acquisition that has a positive net present value (NPV). The announcement of the acquisition can be interpreted as management's pursuit of private benefits, such as maximization of firm size or growth, at the expense of shareholder wealth (Jensen, 1986). Without a credible means of communicating the profitability of the acquisition to capital market participants, managers might forgo this acquisition to avoid the decline in stock price associated with the acquisition. In this framework, certification of the acquisition's profitability by an informed investor such as a bank can help overcome the information disparity between the firm and external capital markets, permitting the firm to pursue the value-enhancing investment policy.

The theoretical literature identifies several potential ways in which a bank can influence a borrower's investment policy. In Diamond (1984), banks use their informational advantage to monitor compliance with loan covenants. In the event of default, this monitoring allows banks to renegotiate the loan contract. The prospect of unfavorable revisions in bank loan contingencies and/or interest rates during renegotiations serves as an incentive to avoid poor investment choices. In this framework, bank debt provides an incentive to undertake value-enhancing investment decisions.

Screening is an alternative channel by which banks can influence a client firm's investment policy. In Boyd and Prescott (1986) and Diamond (1991), banks screen out bad investment proposals and fund only the attractive proposals. Therefore, the bank's decision to provide funding conveys a positive signal about project profitability to external capital market participants. Thus, bank screening has a positive certification effect. In related work, Almazan and Suarez (1998) argue that bank debt alleviates conflicts of interests between shareholders and managers over a firm's investment policy. James (1987), Lummer and McConnell (1989), and Billett et al. (1995) show that stock prices respond favorably when firms announce bank loans, which is consistent with both the certification and the monitoring role for banks.

In contrast to these arguments, Rajan (1992) points out that the bank's information advantage can be detrimental to shareholders. He shows that the bank's information monopoly results in a surplus that is appropriable by the bank and that this lowers the firm's incentive to pursue shareholder value-maximizing investments. Evidence of ex post appropriation by banks is reported by Weinstein and Yafeh (1998) who find that Japanese firms with close bank ties face relatively high borrowing costs. Kracaw and Zenner (1998) find that bank loan announcements are associated with significantly negative announcement returns when an officer of a bank is a member of the borrower's board of directors. In such a situation, banks are likely to have greater access to information and influence over the client firm's investment policy.

A bank's interest as a creditor might also diverge from the interests of shareholders. For example, a bank might favor an acquisition that diversifies the firm's operations because it lowers the variance of the firm's cash flows and enhances the value of its debt claim. Similarly, a bank that is concerned about the firm's ability to repay its debt might have incentives to promote acquisitions for firms with relatively unattractive investment opportunities but with stable cash flows. Kroszner and Strahan (2000) present evidence highlighting the importance of conflicts of interests between creditors and shareholders. They show that legal liability arising from conflicts of interests between banks and shareholders serves as a deterrent to banker representation on corporate boards in the United States. According to these arguments, bank financing of acquisitions can be detrimental to shareholder wealth.

This paper investigates the effect of bank financing on a firm's investment decisions using a sample of 115 cash tender offers between 1990 and 1996. Despite the importance of banks as informed intermediaries, there is limited direct evidence on whether and how banks influence firms' investment decisions. Acquisitions provide a natural setting to investigate the effects of banks on firms' investment decisions because details of acquisitions are generally reported in a timely and complete manner. We examine whether bank financing is associated with acquisitions that enhance shareholder wealth or whether banks fund acquisitions that benefit the bank at the expense of shareholder wealth.

Our paper differs from prior studies of acquisitions because we focus on the *source of financing* (as opposed to the method of payment) in tender offers. It is well known that the method of payment for an acquisition has an important influence on acquirer returns, with acquirers earning returns that are close to zero, on average, in cash tender offers and significantly negative returns in stock exchange offers. However, the existing literature does not distinguish between whether tender offers are financed by internally generated funds or by bank borrowings, which is the focus of our paper. Our paper is also related to prior studies that examine bank involvement in corporate control contests. For example, Kracaw and Zenner (1996) study bank involvement in leveraged recapitalizations and the effect on the bank's equityholders. Our analysis differs in that we investigate the effect of bank involvement on the borrowing firms' equityholders.

We investigate the circumstances in which firms choose to obtain bank financing for the tender offer. We find that acquirers seek bank financing for acquisitions primarily when they have lower cash reserves and a large relative transaction size. These findings are consistent with Myers and Majluf (1984) who suggest that informed bank debt can substitute for the availability of financial slack. The acquisitions financed by bank debt appear to be similar, however, to those funded by financial slack. Bank debt is equally likely in diversifying and related acquisitions and banks do not appear to avoid financing acquisitions of high growth targets.

Two-day cumulative abnormal returns (CARs) for acquirers are significantly higher when the acquisition is financed entirely with bank debt. Tender offers financed entirely by bank debt are associated with significantly positive average 2-day CARs of 2.08% and 3-day CARs of 4%. Acquisitions financed entirely with internal funds, in contrast, have statistically insignificant average CARs of -0.32% and 0.54% over 2- and 3-day windows, respectively. The positive CARs for bank-financed acquisitions are in contrast to much of the existing evidence on acquirer returns, and indicate that shareholders view acquisitions financed entirely by banks favorably. In a multivariate framework, we find that the announcement returns for acquirers are positively related to the extent of bank financing obtained for the tender offer.

We explore several explanations for the positive market response to announcements of bank-funded acquisitions. We examine whether the positive CARs arise because the ability to launch a tender offer conveys a positive signal about an acquirer's financial health. We also examine whether the ability to obtain bank financing for an acquisition conveys positive news about the bank's assessment of the firm's prospects. We explore the possibility that the announcement of bank financing conveys information regarding the extent to which the acquirer's equity is overvalued. If our sample firms were expected to finance the acquisition with equity, the decision to use less risky bank debt would be viewed by investors as a positive signal regarding firm value. A fourth possibility that we investigate is that managerial ability drives both the financial structure of the acquisition as well as the market's reaction. This could be the case if managers with high ability make valuable acquisitions and if banks are more comfortable lending to able managers. Finally, we explore whether the market reaction to bank-financed acquisitions reflects the expectation that acquiring managers will be subject to the discipline of bank debt and that this monitoring is expected to result in more profitable acquisitions.

We find that positive CARs in bank-funded offers accrue primarily to firms with poor performance and high information asymmetry. The market's response does not appear to depend on whether the acquisition is financed with an existing bank loan or a new bank commitment. We also find that bank debt contracts contain extensive contractual agreements that place restrictions on managers' future investment choices. However, we do not find evidence that bank debt is detrimental in circumstances when the bank's informational monopoly is expected to be substantial. We argue that the evidence is most consistent with the view that banks actively monitor and certify the quality of acquisitions. Our results do not offer much support for the view that banks distort a firm's investment policies.

A caveat to our interpretation is worth noting. Our sample consists of firms that were successful in obtaining funding for acquisitions. However, if some firms face limited alternatives to bank financing, a bank's refusal to extend credit might cause some firms to forgo the acquisition. In this case, we would not observe the acquisitions that were considered but had to be cancelled due to lack of bank financing. This problem would be most acute for small acquirers that would have limited recourse to alternative financing mechanisms. However, our results show that the CARs for bank-financed acquisitions are more positive for small acquirers. Hence, we suspect that this problem is unlikely to severely confound our interpretation, although we acknowledge the need for caution in generalizing the results.

Our paper adds to evidence from recent studies that link acquirer returns with financing sources. Harford (1999) finds that cash-rich acquirers tend to make value-reducing acquisitions. As we show, such firms are less likely to seek bank financing. Taken together, these findings suggest that substantial financial slack can be costly for shareholders because it insulates them from the monitoring effects of informed inter-mediaries such as banks. Using a sample of Japanese mergers, Kang et al. (2000) find that Japanese firms with close links to a main bank tend to make value-enhancing acquisitions. Neither study directly explores the source of financing of acquisitions. This paper complements existing literature by showing a direct link between the valuation effects and the source of financing for acquisitions.

The paper is organized as follows. Section 2 describes the data. Section 3 discusses the determinants of bank involvement in financing tender offers. Section 4 presents the analysis of acquisition announcement returns. Section 5 concludes.

2. Data

We obtain the sample of cash tender offers between 1990 and 1996 from Securities Data Corporation (SDC). To be included in the sample, we require that: (1) the acquirer is not a utility or financial services company, (2) both the acquirer and target are listed on the NYSE, AMEX, or NASDAQ, (3) daily stock returns for the acquirer for at least 200 days before the announcement date are available on CRSP, and (4) data on the acquirer and the target are available on COMPUSTAT for the fiscal year before the acquisition. A total of 152 cash tender offers satisfy these criteria. We focus on cash tender offers because mergers are predominantly financed with equity while we are interested in identifying distinguishing features of takeovers financed with bank debt.[1]

We use three sources to identify the source of financing in acquisitions, cross-checking the information when data is available from more than one source. SDC provides financing information for some takeovers, but from 1994 to 1996, a more reliable and complete source of information is available: the 14D-1 filings of the acquirer. Regulation S-K of the Securities Act of 1933 and the Securities Exchange Act of 1934 require the acquirer to disclose the sources of the funds needed to complete the transaction. Because the 14D-1 filing is the most comprehensive source of this information, we rely on it whenever it is available. In the majority of cases

---

[1] Twelve tender offers involved some payment in the form of equity and are hence excluded from the sample. Banks are involved in providing partial financing in seven of these tender offers. Inclusion of these observations in the sample yields qualitatively similar results regarding the effects of bank involvement. We also do not observe any of our sample firms switching the method of payment from cash to equity or from equity to cash from the initial announcement to offer completion.

where bank financing is used, the 14D-1 either includes a bank loan commitment letter when a new bank loan is obtained, or details of the credit agreement when an existing bank loan is used. In a few cases, however, the 14D-1 filing states that the acquirer intends to obtain a bank loan for the acquisition. In these cases, we treat the acquisition as bank financed. In all such cases, we are able to verify that a bank loan was actually obtained by examining subsequent amendments to the original 14D-1 filing. An example of such a financing disclosure follows:

Tender Offer by Rockwell International for Reliance Electric shares

(Announcement date: 10/20/94)
Rockwell plans to use funds it has available in its cash accounts and by borrowing under a revolving credit agreement to be negotiated by Rockwell with a group of banks for such capital contribution. Although there are no commitments by such banks at this time, Rockwell believes such credit agreement will be in effect prior to the initial Expiration Date.

(Excerpt from 14D-1 filed by Rockwell International with the SEC on 10/21/94)

An amendment to the 14D-1 confirms that the acquirer obtained loans from certain named banks for the acquisition. In this case, the loan details could also be confirmed from the Dealscan database. Using this information, we categorize this takeover as financed with a combination of internal cash and bank debt.

Although the 14D filings are comprehensive, they are available in only 69 acquisitions in the sample. Therefore when a 14D is unavailable, we search Lexis-Nexis for announcements of financing disclosure, as well as the SDC and Dealscan databases. Using these three sources yields a sample of 115 acquisitions for which we are able to identify the source of financing. An example of such a financing disclosure follows:

Tender Offer by Quaker Oats for Snapple Beverage shares

(Announcement date 11/02/94)
The transaction was financed through a letter of credit provided by NationsBank of NC NA for up to $2.5 billion.
(Text of SDC source of financing data item for this takeover).

Although the 14D-1 was not available to us in this case, we confirm details of the loan from the Dealscan database. This takeover is categorized as financed entirely with bank debt.

For all the 115 tender offers for which we have financing data, we classify whether banks finance the tender offer package entirely, partially or not at all. We define a discrete variable, ONLYBANK, which equals one if the acquisition is financed entirely by bank debt and zero otherwise. We construct an indicator, PARTBANK, which equals one if the acquisition is at least partly financed by bank debt and zero when bank debt is not used.

When bank debt is used, we collect information on whether the bank loan is a new arrangement, an existing loan, or an existing loan revised to accommodate the proposed acquisition. Of the 81 bank loans in the sample, 31 loans are existing agreements, 14 loans represent amendments and/or revisions of existing loans, and 36 are new credit agreements. We define a dummy variable, NEWLOAN, as equal to one if the bank loan is a new or a revised loan and zero otherwise. The dummy variable OLDLOAN is equal to one if the bank loan is an existing loan and is equal to zero otherwise. Both variables are set to zero when bank debt is not used. Our classification scheme treats revised loans as new agreements. In unreported tests, however, we classify these as existing loans and obtain qualitatively similar results throughout.

2.1. Summary of bank involvement

Panel A of Table 1 shows that bank debt is used to finance at least part of the tender offer package in 81 (70%) of the 115 acquisitions. Bank debt represents the only source of financing in 40 (35%) of the tender offers, making such loans the most frequent source of financing. Cash from internal operations is used to finance the entire tender offer in 26 (22%) cases in the sample. Of the 81 takeovers in which at least some bank debt is used, we are able to obtain data on the amount of the bank loan in 67 cases. Panel B of Table 1 shows that the average amount of the bank loan is $1.25 billion, but the median loan amount is much smaller at $350 million. The average ratio of the bank loan amount to the value of the transaction is 7.66, with a median of 1.56. There are two reasons why firms typically borrow much more from banks than is needed solely to finance the acquisition. First, in takeovers for which we have loan-specific data from Dealscan, we find that the bank loans are frequently taken for multiple purposes including the specific takeover, debt repayment, commercial paper backup, and general corporate purposes. Thus, sample firms often combine multiple financing requirements when they borrow from banks. Second, many acquisitions are financed by existing agreements and lines of credit, which are typically much larger than the amount needed to finance the acquisition.

We also construct a continuous variable, BANKPCT, to measure the degree to which the acquisition is financed by bank debt. For acquisitions that are entirely financed by bank debt, BANKPCT equals one, and it equals zero when no bank debt is used. Computing the exact percentage of the transaction financed by banks is, however, complicated because the bank loan amount typically exceeds the transaction value even when banks finance the tender offer only partially. Therefore, for partially bank-financed tender offers, we assume that acquisitions are funded in the same proportion as the firm's ratio of bank debt to internal financial slack. Thus, in partially bank-funded offers we compute BANKPCT as the ratio of bank debt to the sum of bank debt, cash, and marketable securities. Table 1 shows that according to this definition, 59% of the transaction amount is, on average, financed by bank debt.

We compute an alternative measure of the degree of bank loan financing that does not make any assumption of the bank's financing in partially bank-financed offers. This measure, LOANAMT, is defined as the ratio of bank debt amount to the market value of the acquirer's equity. This variable is set to zero when bank debt is not involved in offer financing. Table 1 shows that LOANAMT averages 0.60.

We also collect data on the magnitude of existing bank debt from the 10 K reports in the year prior to the acquisition. We are able to collect this data for 93 of the sample

Table 1

Summary statistics of bank loan involvement

This table shows involvement of banks in financing of 115 successful cash tender offers over the period 1990–1996. The sample of cash tender offers is obtained from the Securities Data Corporation (SDC). The source of financing data is obtained from SDC, 14D-1 filings, and the Dealscan database of the Loan Pricing Corporation.

Panel A

Description	Number of firms	Percentage (%)
Tender offers with any bank financing (PARTBANK = 1)	81	70
Tender offers financed entirely by banks (ONLYBANK = 1)	40	35
Tender offers financed partially by bank debt	41	36
Tender offers financed entirely by internal funds	26	22
Tender offers financed by internal funds and nonbank debt	3	3
Tender offers financed by internal funds and private equity	3	3
Tender offers financed by commercial paper and nonbank debt	2	2
Tender offers financed with new or revised bank loans (NEWLOAN = 1)	50	43

Panel B

Description	Mean	Median
Amount of bank loan (millions)[a]	$1251	$350
Bank loan amount/value of transaction[a]	7.66	1.56
Bank loan amount/acquirer market value of equity[a] (LOANAMT)	0.60	0.43
Proportion of offer financed by bank loan[b] (BANKPCT)	0.59	0.82
Number (percentage) of acquiring firms with existing bank debt[c]	91 (97.85%)	
Amount of existing bank debt for acquiring firms ($ million)[d]	$916.5	$271
Existing bank debt/acquirer market value of equity	0.25	0.14

[a]Bank loan amount data is available in 67 of the 81 bank loans.
[b]For tender offers partially financed by banks, the proportion of offer financed is computed as the ratio of bank loan amount to the sum of the bank loan amount and acquirer's cash and marketable securities.
[c]Existing bank debt data is available for 93 acquiring firms.
[d]Existing bank loan amounts are available for 82 of the 91 acquiring firms with existing bank debt.

firms. Virtually all the firms maintain bank debt in their capital structure prior to the acquisition. Panel B shows that 91 of 93 (97.9%) firms have some bank debt. For 82 of these firms, we can calculate the amount of bank debt and find that the amount is typically sizeable. The average (median) bank debt amount is $916.5 million ($271 million). This represents 25% of the acquirer's equity market value 1 year prior to the acquisition announcement. These statistics are consistent with the patterns on bank debt reported in Houston and James (1996) who note that banks are a major source of financing for US firms.

3. Determinants of the choice of bank financing

We examine the determinants of bank involvement in tender offer financing as a function of acquirer-specific and transaction-specific characteristics. If banks exercise their informational advantage to enhance the value of their debt claim at the expense of shareholder wealth, we expect that bank financing is more likely to be observed in transactions that would be beneficial to creditors. However, if banks use their informational advantage to monitor investment decisions, acquisition characteristics beneficial to shareholders would be expected. We also explore whether the decision to obtain bank financing is related to the availability of internal funds.

3.1. Cash availability and relative size

Myers and Majluf (1984) suggest that firms prefer to use financial slack over external financing for new investments, implying a negative relation between financial slack and the use of bank debt. Because large acquisitions require greater financing for which internal funds can be insufficient, we also expect a positive relationship between the relative size of the acquisition and the use of bank debt.

We measure the financial slack of the acquirer, ACASH, by the ratio of cash plus marketable securities to the book value of total assets of the acquirer. Because normal levels of cash are likely to vary across industries, ACASH is defined in excess of the median ratio for all firms in the same three-digit SIC code. The results are qualitatively similar, however, if we do not adjust ACASH for industry medians. The ratio of the market value of equity of target to the market value of equity of the acquirer, RELSIZE, is used as a measure of the relative size of the target. Here, and in the variable definitions that follow, accounting values are measured as of the fiscal year-end immediately prior to the announcement date.

3.2. Acquirer prior stock price performance

Hadlock and James (1998) argue that firms obtain bank financing when market conditions for raising external financing from public capital markets are unfavorable. They find that the likelihood of bank financing is negatively related to the firm's prior stock price performance. This suggests that acquirers with poor stock price performance prior to the tender offer are more likely to finance the acquisition with bank debt.

The acquirer's 1-year prior stock price return, ARETURN, defined as the percentage change in its stock price from 13 months before to 1 month before the announcement date minus the return on the CRSP value-weighted index over this period, is used to proxy for its past performance.

3.3. Relatedness of the acquisition

Amihud and Lev (1981) argue that managers enter into value-decreasing diversifying acquisitions because they can insure themselves against downturns in their current business. Alternatively, managers doing poorly in managing their current firm might want to try their hand at a new business (Shleifer and Vishny, 1990). In these circumstances, managers could have an incentive to overpay for an unrelated business. If diversifying acquisitions represent negative NPV transactions as suggested by Morck et al. (1990), and if banks have the ability to screen negative NPV projects, we expect an inverse relation between bank involvement and diversifying acquisitions.

An alternative prediction arises from arguments by Lewellen (1971) who suggests that conglomerates can take on higher levels of debt since their cash flow variability is lower, making the firm more attractive to lenders. Shleifer and Vishny (1992) argue that the ability to liquidate assets in those industries that are least afflicted in bad states of the world allows diversified firms to have a higher debt capacity. Thus, banks could prefer lending for diversifying acquisitions because the combined firm could be less likely to default in some states of the world.

We use a measure of acquisition relatedness similar to that used by Morck et al. (1990), based on four-digit SIC codes of the target and acquirer obtained from the Dun and Bradstreet Million Dollar Directory. The indicator variable, RELATED, is defined to be equal to one if any of the target's SIC codes belong to any of the first three of the acquirer's SIC codes, and is equal to zero otherwise.

3.4. Target growth opportunities

Morck et al. (1990) find significantly negative acquirer returns for acquisitions of rapidly growing targets. They argue that in these cases managers pursue maximization of growth rather than firm value, because they want to ensure the continuance of the firm. To the extent that acquisitions of high growth targets are more likely to represent negative NPV transactions, we expect that such acquisitions will be less likely to be financed by bank debt.

To measure the growth opportunities of the target, we define the target's market-to-book ratio as the sum of market value of common equity and book value of total assets less book value of common equity, expressed as a fraction of book value of total assets. Since market-to-book ratios vary across industry, we use TGTMB, the difference between the target's market-to-book ratio and the median market-to-book ratio for all firms in the same three-digit SIC code.

3.5. Acquirer stock price volatility

Hadlock and James (1998) find that the likelihood of bank financing increases with a firm's stock price volatility. They argue that the greater the stock price volatility, the greater is the difficulty in valuing the firm and hence the greater is the likelihood of using a well-informed inside lender. Hence, we expect a positive relationship between the use of bank debt and acquirer stock price volatility. As a measure of acquirer stock price volatility, STDDEV, we use the standard deviation of common stock returns over the period −210 trading days to −60 trading days relative to the initial announcement date.

3.6. Bidder managerial equity ownership

Lewellen et al. (1985) find that announcement returns for acquirers are positively related to the fraction of the acquirer's shares owned by acquirer management and argue that increased equity ownership provides stronger incentives for managers to pursue value-enhancing acquisitions.[2] If positive NPV acquisitions are more likely to be proposed when acquirer managerial ownership is high, and if banks are more likely to ratify positive NPV transactions, we expect a positive association between acquirer managerial ownership and bank involvement in acquisitions. A positive relation between managerial ownership and bank financing can also arise due to risk aversion. May (1995) argues that high ownership makes managers risk averse, making them more likely to engage in diversifying acquisitions. If banks' role as creditors also makes them risk averse, banks might be more likely to support diversifying acquisitions. However, managerial risk aversion can also lead acquirers with high management ownership (MOWN) to seek bank certification for shareholder value-enhancing acquisitions. Zwiebel (1996) develops a model where managers voluntarily choose monitored debt contracts to credibly constrain their own perquisite consumption and future empire building. According to this analysis, high ownership managers employ bank debt to certify the acquisition's profitability to shareholders. The MOWN variable, is the fraction of common stock owned by the acquirer's officers and directors and is obtained from the proxy statement prior to the announcement date.

3.7. Other variables

In addition to the bank involvement variables, and the variables defined in Section 2.1, we use the following control variables in this paper. PREMIUM is defined as the ratio of

---

[2] Evidence on the effect of management ownership and acquirer performance is mixed. Hubbard and Palia (1995) argue that the relation is non-monotonic, while Loderer and Martin (1997) find no relation between management ownership and acquirer returns.

the bid price to the target's stock price 1 month before the announcement. The acquirer's leverage ratio, LEVERAGE, is defined as the total debt of the acquirer scaled by the book value of total assets. Finally, we use ACQMB, the difference between the acquirer's market-to-book ratio and the median market-to-book ratio for all firms in the same three-digit SIC code as a measure of the acquirer's investment opportunities.

Table 2 reports the means and medians of acquisition characteristics for the entire sample of 115 takeovers and for subsamples stratified by the source of financing. Acquisitions involving bank debt are of larger relative magnitude. The ratio of the market value of the target to the market value of the acquirer is 6.3% when no bank debt is used, 16.7% when the deal is partially financed by bank debt, and about 26% when the deal is entirely financed by banks. Bank financing is also more prevalent when firms have relatively low financial slack. The industry-adjusted ratio of cash and marketable securities to assets, ACASH, averages 2.7% when banks are uninvolved, 0.9% when banks are partially involved, and −1.9% when banks finance the entire offer. There is also some evidence that bank commitments are related to the prior performance of the acquirer. Acquirers' prior 1-year market-adjusted stock returns average −9.9% when no bank debt is used, but average −25.3% when banks finance the entire tender offer. These comparisons suggest that firms rely on bank debt in circumstances when internal resources are unlikely to be sufficient to finance the tender offer, a pattern consistent with Myers and Majluf's (1984) pecking order hypothesis. Finally, bank involvement appears to be related to management equity ownership in acquiring firms. Bank financing of offers appears more likely when acquirer managers own a higher fraction of the firm's shares.

A potential explanation for why bank financing and managerial ownership are positively related is that both banks and high ownership managers are risk averse and support diversifying acquisitions. This explanation is not, however, borne out by our data. There is no significant difference in the percentage of related acquisitions between bank-financed tender offers and those financed by internal cash reserves. In the sample, 44% of the takeovers without bank financing are in related industries, while 54% of the partially bank-financed acquisitions are related. The difference is not statistically significant using a χ^2 test. This pattern also holds for tender offers financed entirely by banks, 50% of which are related. These statistics suggest that banks do not selectively finance diversifying acquisitions.

We also explore whether the nature of the acquisition varies systematically with the financing of the offer. Overall, 50% of the acquisitions are in related industries, but there is no noticeable difference between the fraction of related acquisitions in the subsamples of bank and nonbank-financed transactions. Bank-financed acquisitions are more likely to involve multiple bidder contests. However, bank involvement in acquisitions does not appear related to whether the takeover is hostile, or whether the acquirer is a white knight.

We estimate four models to predict the probability that bank financing will be used and the extent of bank financing in tender offers. Column (1) of Table 3 presents estimates from a probit model for the probability that a bank finances a tender offer at

Table 2

Summary statistics of acquisition characteristics

This table shows summary statistics for acquirer and acquisition characteristics for the sample of 115 cash tender offers from 1990 to 1996 and for subsamples where the acquirer uses no bank debt, some bank debt, or only bank debt to finance the acquisition. The sample of cash tender offers is obtained from the Securities Data Corporation (SDC). The source of financing data is obtained from SDC, 14D-1 filings, and the Dealscan database of the Loan Pricing Corporation. The table presents the mean of each characteristic, with the median in parentheses. RELSIZE is defined as the ratio of the market value of equity of the target to the market value of equity of the acquirer. The acquirer's cash and marketable securities to assets ratio (ACASH), the acquirer's market-to-book ratio (ACQMB), the target's market-to-book ratio (TGTMB), and the acquirer's total debt-to-assets ratio (ACQLEV), are adjusted for industry effects by subtracting the median ratio of these variables for firms with the same three-digit SIC code. ARETURN (TRETURN) is defined as the 1-year acquirer (target) stock return immediately prior to the announcement date in excess of the return on the CRSP value-weighted index. MOWN is the fraction of common shares owned by management and is obtained from the latest proxy statement prior to initial announcement. PREMIUM is defined as the initial offer premium scaled by target stock price 1 month before initial announcement. RELATED equals one if any of the target SIC codes is common to the acquirer's first three SIC codes and is zero otherwise. The last four rows summarize indicator variables for whether the takeover was hostile, was a multiple-bidder contest, had a white knight, or included an acquirer who was also the first bidder. All accounting values are measured at fiscal year-end before the initial announcement. The table reports tests of significance of differences for each variable in Columns (3) and (4) with the value of that variable in Column (2). ***, **, and * denote significance at 0.01 and 0.10 levels, respectively, using a t-test for difference in means and a Wilcoxon signed rank test for difference in medians. A χ^2 test is used to test for differences in proportions for the variable RELATED, and the hostile, multiple bidder, white knight, and first bidder indicators.

	Takeovers all (1)	Takeovers no bank debt (2)	Takeovers partially financed with bank debt (3)	Takeovers entirely financed with bank debt (4)
Market value of target equity/market value of acquirer equity	0.168	0.063	0.167***	0.259***
(RELSIZE)	(0.091)	(0.018)	(0.099)***	(0.172)***
Acquirer cash + marketable securities/book value of total assets	0.005	0.027	0.009	−0.019
(ACASH)	(−0.014)	(0.0005)	(−0.002)	(−0.023)***
Acquirer market-to-book ratio	0.166	0.128	−0.024	0.393
(ACQMB)	(0.073)	(0.107)	(−0.023)	(0.086)
Target market-to-book ratio	0.065	0.133	−0.235	0.316
(TGTMB)	(−0.163)	(−0.220)	(−0.259)	(−0.082)
Acquirer total debt/book value of total assets	0.054	0.074	0.058	0.034
(ACQLEV)	(0.047)	(0.064)	(0.042)	(0.025)***
Acquirer 1-year stock return	−0.116	−0.099	0.005	−0.253*
(ARETURN)	(−0.108)	(−0.106)	(−0.073)	(−0.169)
Target 1-year stock return	−0.240	−0.283	−0.192	−0.252
(TRETURN)	(−0.208)	(−0.426)	(−0.212)	(−0.124)
Acquirer managerial ownership	0.108	0.041	0.095***	0.179***
(MOWN)	(0.034)	(0.020)	(0.038)***	(0.070)

(*Continued*)

Table 2 (*Continued*)

	Takeovers all (1)	Takeovers no bank debt (2)	Takeovers partially financed with bank debt (3)	Takeovers entirely financed with bank debt (4)
Tender offer premium	0.471	0.407	0.539[*]	0.456
(PREMIUM)	(0.433)	(0.338)	(0.505)[*]	(0.404)
Relatedness (RELATED): % of	50	44	54	50
takeovers where				
RELATED = 1			$(\chi^2 = 0.68)$	$(\chi^2 = 0.26)$
Hostile takeover indicator: % of	7.83	5.88	4.88	12.50
takeovers where takeover is hostile				
			$(\chi^2 = 0.04)$	$(\chi^2 = 0.94)$
Multiple bidder indicator: % of	7.83	2.94	4.88	15.00[*]
takeovers with multiple bidders				
			$(\chi^2 = 0.18)$	$(\chi^2 = 3.12)$
White knight indicator: % of	1.74	0	0	5.00
takeovers where acquirer is a				
white knight				
				$(\chi^2 = 1.75)$
First bidder indicator: % of take-	92.17	100	95.12	90.00[*]
overs where acquirer is the first				
bidder				
			$(\chi^2 = 1.70)$	$(\chi^2 = 3.59)$

least partially. We find variables intended to proxy for firms' requirements for financing to be important. Specifically, bank financing is more likely to be observed when acquirers' internally generated cash flow is low and the relative size of the transaction is large. Bank debt is also more likely to be observed when managerial equity ownership is high. Transaction-specific characteristics, however, do not appear to have much influence on the use of bank debt. Bank involvement does not appear to depend upon whether the acquisition is of a target in a related industry or whether the target possesses substantial growth prospects. There is also little evidence that banks avoid lending to acquirers that have experienced poor prior performance.

Column (2) reports results from a probit model that estimates the probability that an acquisition is financed entirely with bank debt. Similar results obtain regarding the expected requirement for financing. The probability that the entire offer is bank financed is negatively related to the acquirer's internal cash flow and 1-year stock return, and is positively related to the relative size of the acquisition. Bank financing is also positively related to acquirers' MOWN.[3] This relationship is consistent with the

---

[3] In unreported tests, we also include the square of management ownership to account for the possibility that high levels of ownership make managers more risk averse and increase incentives to pursue diversifying acquisitions that can be costly for shareholders. We are unable, however, to find evidence of nonmonotonicity with this approach.

Table 3

Bidder characteristics and bank financing

This table shows probit estimates of the choice to finance the tender offer with bank debt and tobit estimates of the proportion of bank financing for the sample of 115 cash tender offers from 1990 to 1996. In Column (1), the dependent variable is PARTBANK, which equals one if the acquisition is at least partially financed with bank debt and equals zero otherwise. In Column (2), the dependent variable is ONLYBANK, which equals one when the acquisition is entirely financed by bank debt and equals zero otherwise. In Column (3), the dependent variable is LOANAMT, which equals the amount of the bank loan scaled by the acquirer's market value of equity when the acquisition is financed with at least some bank debt and equals zero when no bank debt is used. In Column (4), the dependent variable is BANKPCT, which equals the bank loan amount scaled by the sum of the bank loan amount and the acquirer's cash + marketable securities when the acquisition is financed partly by bank loan. BANKPCT equals zero when no bank debt is used, and equals one when the tender offer is entirely financed with bank debt. In Column (5), the dependent variable is NEWLOAN, which equals one when the acquisition is financed at least partially with a new or revised bank loan and equals zero when the acquisition is financed at least partially with an existing loan or when no bank debt is used. Independent variables are defined as follows: RELATED equals one when any of the target's SIC codes is common to the acquirer's first three SIC codes, ACASH is the sum of the acquirer's cash and marketable securities scaled by the book value of assets, MOWN is the fraction of common shares owned by the acquirer's management, RELSIZE is the target market value of equity divided by the acquirer market value of equity, ARETURN is the acquirer's 1-year stock return immediately prior to the announcement date in excess of the CRSP value-weighted index, and TGTMB is the target's market-to-book ratio. ACASH, ACQMB, and TGTMB are adjusted for industry effects by subtracting the median ratio of these variables for firms with the same three-digit SIC code. All accounting values are measured at fiscal year-end prior to the announcement date. χ^2 statistics for significance of the estimates are in parentheses.

Variable	Dependent variable PARTBANK (1)	Dependent variable ONLYBANK (2)	Dependent variable BANKPC (3)	Dependent variable LOANAMT (4)	Dependent variable NEWLOAN (5)
Estimation procedure	Probit	Probit	Tobit	Tobit	Probit
Intercept	−0.863*	−1.197***	0.735***	0.158	−1.287***
	(3.60)	(7.48)	(79.11)	(1.96)	(9.92)
RELATED	−0.307	−0.025	−0.040	−0.041	0.265
	(0.81)	(0.006)	(0.44)	(0.30)	(0.88)
ACASH	−3.730***	−3.391***	−0.526**	−0.387	−1.998*
	(9.16)	(7.50)	(5.58)	(1.35)	(3.75)
MOWN	6.510***	3.119***	0.312*	0.079	1.700*
	(6.73)	(11.89)	(3.20)	(0.13)	(3.72)
RELSIZE	6.477***	2.631***	0.111	1.521***	3.725***
	(14.26)	(11.46)	(0.62)	(75.38)	(16.21)
ARETURN	0.163	−1.000**	−0.028	−0.121	0.035
	(0.17)	(5.73)	(0.14)	(1.72)	(0.01)
TGTMB	−0.169	0.077	−0.066	−0.059***	0.013
	(1.26)	(0.46)	(2.78)	(6.07)	(0.01)
STDDEV	21.95	−7.642	−3.880	6.751	11.158
	(1.04)	(0.13)	(1.11)	(1.56)	(0.34)
Log likelihood	47.24	54.84	5.27	27.41	62.40
No. of observations	115	115	105	101	115

***, **, and * indicate that the estimates are significantly different from zero at the 1%, 5%, and 10% levels, respectively.

view that managers owning a high percentage of the firm's equity use bank debt to certify investment decisions. According to Zwiebel (1996), such managers choose to finance their investments with monitored debt to credibly communicate their profitability to investors.

Column (3) presents results from a tobit model that uses BANKPCT, the fraction of the tender offer financed by bank debt, as the dependent variable. As with the previous results, the fraction of the transaction financed by banks decreases with the availability of internal financial slack and increases with managerial ownership. The coefficient on relative size, though positive, is statistically insignificant.

Column (4) shows estimates of a tobit regression of LOANAMT on acquisition and acquirer characteristics. As with the discrete bank involvement variables, the results show that the relative size of the acquisition is an important determinant of the extent of bank financing. In this model, the coefficient on ACASH, while negative, lacks significance at conventional levels.

As discussed earlier, several acquisitions in the sample are financed with existing bank debt, which reduces the need for an acquirer to seek new financing sources. Therefore, in Column (5) we also estimate a probit model that an acquisition is financed by new or revised bank debt (i.e., NEWLOAN = 1). The results for this specification are similar. The likelihood of a new bank loan increases when the firm's cash reserves are low and when the relative size of the transaction is large. In addition, new loans are more likely to be observed when managerial ownership is high.

In unreported tests, we examine whether the probability that an acquisition will be financed by a bank depends upon the amount of existing bank debt. These tests are estimated over a smaller sample of 82 firms for which we have data on the amount of bank loans prior to the acquisition. In all model specifications, we find that the coefficient on the ratio of existing bank debt to acquirer market value is close to zero and statistically insignificant. Also, inclusion of this variable does not materially alter the coefficients on other variables.

Overall, these models demonstrate that variables intended to proxy for the availability of internal funds tend to be important in explaining the extent of bank involvement in tender offers. However, bank financing is not more prevalent for diversifying acquisitions. In addition, the evidence suggests a positive relation between bank involvement and MOWN. A similar positive association between bank loans and managerial ownership is also documented by Mihov (2000) who explores the determinants of new public and private debt financing for a broad sample of firms.

4. Wealth effects of bank loan involvement

4.1. Univariate analysis

We follow the Dodd and Warner (1983) event-study methodology to compute standardized abnormal returns and z-statistics for testing the significance of the CARs.

Market model parameters are estimated using daily returns over the interval -210 trading days to -61 trading days relative to the initial announcement.

Table 4 reports CARs surrounding the initial acquisition announcement over different windows relative to the announcement date, and presents z-statistics to test for statistical significance of CARs. The average CAR for the 2-day window around the initial announcement, CAR$[-1, 0]$, for the full sample of acquirers is $+0.55\%$ and statistically insignificant. This result of small and statistically insignificant acquirer announcement returns in cash tender offers is consistent with evidence reported by earlier studies (Sung, 1993; Travlos, 1987). However, the average CAR for the 3-day window, CAR$[-1, 1]$, is 1.45% and significant at the 1% level.

The wealth effects of bank loan involvement differ substantially when banks finance the entire tender offer. Column (4) of Table 4 reports univariate statistics of CARs for acquisitions that are entirely bank financed and compares these to CARs in Column (2) for acquisitions financed by internal sources. The 2-day CAR averages 2.08% and is statistically significant at the 1% level when the offer is entirely bank financed. In comparison, CARs for offers without any bank involvement average -0.32% and lack statistical significance. The difference in mean CARs between the two subsamples is statistically significant at the 1% level. Offers funded entirely by banks appear to convey a much stronger signal to the market on average than offers that are partially bank financed. Column (3) of Table 4 reports CARs for the subsample of partially bank-financed tender offers. The 2-day CAR for this subgroup averages -0.27% and lacks statistical significance.

A potential concern with a 2-day window is that relevant information regarding the tender offer, the terms, and the target's reaction may not be revealed on the initial announcement date. In particular, the 14D statement, that contains the complete details of the financing arrangement, is sometimes filed a few days after the initial announcement date. For example, in our sample of bank-financed acquisitions, the mean (median) number of days between the initial announcement and the 14D filing is 6.85 (4) days. In many cases, however, investors learn of bank involvement prior to the 14D filings from newspaper reports. Thus, the mean (median) number of days between the initial announcement date and the first revelation of financing details is 3.33 (0) days. Although financing details are usually released in close proximity to the initial announcement, in a few cases, the time lag is 10 or more days. To address the potential impact of nonsynchronous release of financing details, we examine announcement CARs over longer windows. Inspection of CARs computed over longer event windows, however, reveals similar patterns. Over a 3-day window, takeovers financed entirely with bank debt experience an average CAR of 4%, which is significant at the 1% level, while takeovers financed only partly or without bank debt experience statistically insignificant CARs. The difference between 3-day CARs for entirely bank financed and internally financed acquisitions is significant at the 1% level. A similar pattern obtains for 4-, 5-, 7-, and 10-day windows surrounding the initial announcement. Thus, inspection of CARs over alternative windows indicates that investors greet acquisition announcements optimistically when the takeover is

Table 4

Acquirer cumulative abnormal returns

This table shows mean and median cumulative abnormal acquirer returns (CARs) for the sample of 115 cash tender offers from 1990 to 1996, and for subsamples where the acquirer uses no bank debt, some bank debt, or only bank debt to finance the acquisition. The sample of cash tender offers is obtained from the Securities Data Corporation (SDC). The source of financing in these takeovers is obtained from the SDC, 14D-1 filings, and the Dealscan database of the Loan Pricing Corporation. z-statistics for significance of the CARs are in parentheses.

		Takeovers all (1)	Takeovers financed without bank debt (2)	Takeovers financed partially with bank debt (3)	Takeovers financed entirely with bank debt (4)
CAR from day −1 to day 0 (CAR1_0)	Mean	0.55% (0.42)	−0.32% (1.41)	−0.21% (1.16)	2.08% (3.20)***
	Median	−0.04%	−0.06%	−0.34%	0.42%
CAR from day −1 to day +1 (CAR1_1)	Mean	1.45% (2.98)	0.54% (0.70)	−0.27% (1.01)	4.00% (5.43)***
	Median	0.61%	0.56%	−0.06%	2.43%
CAR from day −2 to day +2 (CAR2_2)	Mean	1.52% (2.32)	0.98% (0.87)	−0.27% (0.95)	3.81% (4.09)***
	Median	0.38%	0.24%	−0.50%	1.83%
CAR from day −3 to day +1 (CAR3_1)	Mean	1.38% (1.89)	0.64% (0.58)	−0.51% (1.46)	3.96% (4.15)***
	Median	0.37%	−0.20%	−0.11%	2.70%
CAR from day −3 to day +3 (CAR3_3)	Mean	1.13% (1.10)	0.47% (0.18)	−1.23% (1.95)	4.12% (3.67)**
	Median	0.41%	−0.17%	−1.00%	3.63%
CAR from day −5 to day +5 (CAR5_5)	Mean	1.61% (1.98)	1.65% (1.53)	−0.58% (1.04)	3.83% (2.99)**
	Median	0.67%	1.49%	−0.76%	3.98%

*** and ** indicate estimates that are significantly different from the corresponding estimates in Column (2) at the 1% and 5% levels, respectively.

financed entirely by bank loans. The financing of the entire tender offer package appears to convey a much more credible signal to the market than offers that are partially financed by banks. There appears to be little difference in CARs for offers funded partially with bank debt and those where banks are not involved in the financing. In untabulated tests, we find similar results if we drop firms where details of the bank financing become public information more than 10 days after the initial announcement.

4.2. Multivariate analysis

Since bank involvement is correlated with several acquirer- and transaction-specific characteristics that could be related to announcement returns, we conduct a multivariate analysis of CARs. The primary variable of interest is the extent of bank financing of the tender offer. The regressions control for several other variables including the relative size of the target and the acquirer, the bid premium, the acquirer's market-to-book ratio, the target's market-to-book ratio, the equity ownership by the acquirer's management, financial slack, and leverage.

As shown in Table 3, our sample firms have self-selected among alternative sources of tender offer financing. Therefore, the observed CARs are conditioned upon the choice of financing arrangement by the acquirers. If the factors that determine the choice of financing arrangement are correlated with the factors that determine the acquirer CARs, ordinary least squares estimates will yield biased inferences.

To account for this self-selection, we adopt the self-selectivity model described in Greene (1993). This procedure involves a first-stage estimation of the determinants of bank involvement in tender offers using a probit model. In the second stage, the inverse Mills ratio from the probit model is included as a control variable in the cross-sectional regression of announcement returns. Let the bank involvement probit model be represented as

$$\text{ONLYBANK}_i = \gamma w_i + u_i. \tag{1}$$

Let the multivariate CAR regression be represented as:

$$\text{CAR}(1, -1)_i = \beta_i x_i + \delta \text{ONLYBANK}_i + e_i. \tag{2}$$

If e_i and u_i are correlated, ordinary least squares estimates of the β and δ coefficients will be biased. As shown in Greene (1993), including the inverse mills ratio, λ_I, from the bank involvement probit model in the CAR regression controls for self-selection by alleviating the omitted variable problem, where

$$\hat{\lambda}_i = \frac{\varphi(\hat{\gamma}'w_i)}{\Phi(\hat{\gamma}'w_i)}. \tag{3}$$

When the bank involvement variable in the CAR regressions is measured by ONLY-BANK, the self-selectivity control variable is the inverse Mills's ratio obtained from the probit model reported in Column (1) of Table 3. When the CAR regressions evaluate the effect of partial bank financing (PARTBANK), the fraction of the transaction financed by banks (BANKPCT), or the amount of the bank loan (LOANAMT), the self-selectivity control variable is the inverse Mills ratio obtained from the corresponding model in Table 3.

Column (1) of Table 5 estimates the 3-day CAR[4] as a function of control variables and the indicator variable ONLYBANK. Consistent with the univariate results, the coefficient on this variable is positive and significant at the 1% level, implying that investors greet offers that are funded entirely by bank debt more positively. The point estimate suggests that CARs are 4.5% greater for acquisitions entirely financed by banks than other acquisitions.

To assess the valuation effect of acquisitions that are partially funded by banks, we include in Column (2) the indicator variable, PARTBANK, which equals one if the acquisition is at least partly financed by banks and zero otherwise. The coefficient on this variable is small and lacks statistical significance. In contrast to acquisitions funded entirely by banks, partially bank-financed acquisitions are not associated with higher announcement returns. A possible reason for the difference in investor reactions is that acquisitions funded entirely by banks are seen as a stronger signal than partial bank financing. If the proportion of bank financing is small in partially funded acquisitions, the role of banks might be viewed as being limited in these transactions.

Support for this view is obtained in Column (3) where we use BANKPCT, the fraction of the tender offer financed by bank debt, as the dependent variable in a tobit model. The coefficient on BANKPCT is positive and significant at the 10% level. The point estimate on BANKPCT suggests an economically meaningful relation between the proportion of bank financing and announcement returns. Evaluated at the mean, a 10% increase in the fraction of the offer funded by banks is associated with a 0.34% increase in announcement returns.

The tobit model in Column (4) estimates the announcement return as a function of LOANAMT, the ratio of the amount of the bank loan to the market value of the acquirer's equity. This variable represents another continuous measure of the extent of bank financing. The coefficient on LOANAMT is positive and significant at the 1% level, suggesting that the strength of the signal increases with the degree of bank commitment to the tender offer. This result is consistent with Lummer and McConnell (1989) who find that announcement returns for bank financing agreements are positively related to the size of the loan agreement.

The positive association between bank financing and announcement returns raises an issue regarding the direction of causality. Does bank commitment to the tender offer package constitute a credible signal that leads investors to value the acquisition favorably? Under this scenario, the bank's decision to grant financing conveys a positive signal to investors. Or is it the case that the bank's superior information

---

[4] Use of CARs over a 2-day $(-1, 0)$ window or a 5-day $(-2, +2)$ window as the dependent variable in these regressions yields results similar to those reported.

Table 5

Regressions of 3-day acquirer cumulative abnormal returns

This table shows regressions of acquirer 3-day CAR on bank involvement and other variables for a sample of 115 cash tender offers from 1990 to 1996. Bank financing variables are defined as follows: ONLYBANK equals one when the acquisition is entirely financed with bank debt and equals zero otherwise. PARTBANK equals one when the acquisition is at least partially bank-financed and equals zero otherwise. NEWLOAN equals one when bank debt, if used, is under a new or revised agreement and equals zero if existing bank loan agreements or no bank debt is used. OLDLOAN equals one if bank financing under an existing loan agreement is used and equals zero otherwise. BANKPCT equals the bank loan amount scaled by the sum of the bank loan amount and the acquirer's cash + marketable securities when the acquisition is financed partly by bank loan and equals one when the acquisition is entirely bank financed. LOANAMT equals the bank loan amount scaled by market value of acquirer's equity when the acquisition is financed at least partially with bank debt. Both are set to zero when no bank debt is used. RELATED equals one if any of the target SIC codes is present in any of the acquirer's first three SIC codes and is zero otherwise. PREMIUM is defined as the initial offer premium scaled by target stock price 1 month before initial announcement. Other variables are as defined in the table and in the text. All accounting values are measured at fiscal year-end before the initial announcement. t-Statistics are in parentheses.

	(1)	(2)	(3)	(4)	(5)
Intercept	0.068	0.035	0.032	0.083	0.067
	(0.69)	(0.35)	(0.31)	(0.78)	(0.68)
ONLYBANK	0.045***				
	2.72				
PARTBANK		0.003			
		(0.21)			
NEWLOAN	0.012	0.027	0.009		0.008
	(0.69)	(1.49)	(0.51)		(0.42)
ONLYBANK × NEWLOAN					0.050**
					(2.54)
ONLYBANK × OLDLOAN					0.036
					(1.52)
BANKPCT			0.034*		
			(1.67)		
LOANAMT				0.052**	
				(2.33)	
Relatedness measure (RELATED)	0.015	0.036**	0.048***	0.039**	0.014
	(1.09)	(2.10)	(2.70)	(2.22)	(1.03)
Tender offer premium (PREMIUM)	0.017	0.006	−0.007	−0.003	0.018
	(0.86)	(0.31)	(−0.33)	(−0.15)	(0.92)
Market value of target equity/market value of acquirer equity (RELSIZE)	−0.105	−0.548**	−0.642***	−0.492**	−0.106
	(−1.10)	(−2.36)	(−2.67)	(−2.16)	(−1.11)
Acquirer total debt/book value of total assets (ACQLEV)	0.001	−0.002	0.004	0.023	−0.003
	(0.02)	(−0.05)	(0.10)	(0.51)	(−0.06)
Cash + marketable securities/book value of assets (ACASH)	0.033	0.190	0.279**	0.179	0.032
	(0.33)	(1.50)	(2.05)	(1.39)	(0.31)
Acquirer market to book ratio (ACQMB)	−0.001	0.0004	0.001	0.003	−0.001
	(−0.07)	(0.05)	(0.06)	(0.29)	(−0.12)

(Continued)

Table 5 (*Continued*)

	(1)	(2)	(3)	(4)	(5)
Target market to book ratio (TGTMB)	−0.005	0.010	0.012	0.009	−0.005
	(−0.96)	(1.38)	(1.61)	(1.17)	(−0.98)
Acquirer managerial ownership (MOWN)	−0.077	−0.507	−0.628**	−0.410*	−0.078
	(−0.74)	(−2.15)	(−2.55)	(−1.78)	(−0.75)
Acquirer 1-year prebid stock return	0.009	−0.023	−0.020	−0.004	0.008
	(0.30)	(−1.42)	(−1.20)	(−0.23)	(0.28)
Log of market value of acquirer's equity	−0.008	−0.009	−0.009	−0.008	−0.00
	(−1.37)	(−1.54)	(−1.39)	(−1.31)	(−1.36)
Hostile takeover indicator	−0.017	−0.003	−0.009	−0.008	−0.018
	(−0.70)	(−0.14)	(−0.37)	(−0.35)	(−0.73)
Multiple bidder indicator	0.011	0.033	0.021	−0.009	0.012
	(0.26)	(0.81)	(0.52)	(−0.19)	(0.30)
White knight indicator	−0.041	−0.004	−0.014	−0.015	−0.046
	(−0.71)	(−0.07)	(−0.25)	(−0.27)	(−0.79)
First bidder indicator	0.040	0.062	0.050	0.011	0.042
	(0.80)	(1.22)	(1.01)	(0.20)	(0.82)
Self-selectivity correction	0.031	0.090**	0.107**	0.071*	0.031
	(0.63)	(2.27)	(2.61)	(1.78)	(0.63)
Number of observations	115	115	105	101	115
Adjusted R^2 (%)	5.51	3.39	7.18	10.26	4.78

***, **, and * indicate that the estimates are significantly different from zero at the 1%, 5%, and 10% levels, respectively.

allows it to identify in advance which acquisitions are value-enhancing events and to selectively finance such acquisitions? Under this scenario, the bank's informational advantage simply allows them to "cherry pick" the acquisitions that will have a positive CAR. To understand this issue, we separately examine announcement returns when firms obtain a commitment for a new bank loan and those where an existing bank loan is used to fund the tender offer. If banks choose to lend selectively for acquisitions where their information suggests that the market response will be positive regardless of bank involvement, we expect that this effect will predominate for new bank loans. Cherry picking behavior should be less important for existing bank commitments negotiated prior to the knowledge of an acquisition.

Model (5) includes an interaction between ONLYBANK and NEWLOAN, an indicator that equals one if the bank loan is new or revised (and zero if it is an existing loan). Also included is an additional interaction between ONLYBANK and OLD-LOAN, an indicator that equals one if the acquisition is financed by an existing loan and zero otherwise. Offers funded entirely by a new or revised bank loan have CARs that are 5% higher than other offers, while those funded by existing bank loans have CARs that are 3.6% higher. An *F*-test for the equality of coefficients on the two interaction terms has a *p*-value of 0.61. Therefore, we cannot reject the hypothesis that announcement returns are similar for existing and new bank loans. Thus, our results do not seem to be consistent with the view that banks simply fund acquisitions that would be greeted positively by investors irrespective of bank involvement.

Inspection of the control variables in models (2)-(4) shows that acquirer CARs are higher for related acquisitions, consistent with Morck et al. (1990) and Chevalier (2000), and that acquisitions for large targets and by acquirers with high MOWN are associated with lower CARs. However, in models that include ONLYBANK, the coefficients on relatedness, relative size, and MOWN, become statistically insignificant. This is not surprising, since Table 3 shows that the method of financing is related to acquisition characteristics and MOWN. It is also worth noting that the coefficient on the correction for self-selectivity is positive and statistically significant in three of the five models. This suggests that failure to control for the determinants of bank financing would result in biased coefficient estimates. Among the other control variables included in the analysis, those measuring the nature of the takeover such as hostility, the frequency of multiple bids, and indicators for whether the acquirer is the first bidder or a white knight, are all statistically insignificant.

In summary, the regressions show that acquisitions funded by entirely by bank debt are associated with significantly higher announcement returns and that the market's reaction to acquisitions is positively related to the fraction of the offer financed by bank debt. The positive CARs for acquisitions funded by existing bank loans are informative because they indicate that our results are not simply an artifact of the documented positive announcement effects of bank loan announcements. For existing bank loans, the positive effect of the loan announcement would already be incorporated into the firm's stock price. Hence, the positive returns around the acquisition announcement for these firms would be driven primarily by investors' reaction to the acquisition. Nonetheless, it is still possible that existing bank loan contracts include restrictive covenants that mandate the bank's prior approval of an acquisition. Therefore, a firm's decision to fund an acquisition with an existing loan might convey information regarding the bank's approval of the acquisition. To more closely understand bank involvement in such circumstances, we examine the contractual provisions contained in the bank loan agreements.

4.3. Analysis of bank loan covenants

We obtain details of the bank loans in our sample from the 14D filings. When existing or amended bank loans are used, the 14D filing often contains the complete bank loan agreement. When firms obtain new bank loans, the initial 14D filing contains the bank loan commitment letter that describes the key terms and conditions of the loan. Because the credit agreement is more complete, we use it when the initial filing or a subsequent amendment contains the agreement. We collect complete data from loan commitment letters for 25 new loans and credit agreements for existing bank loans in 15 cases. We report the covenants separately for new and existing loans because the final credit agreement is usually more extensive than the initial commitment letter.

Table 6 shows that bank loans contain extensive covenants and restrictions on investment and financing activities. There are several noteworthy patterns. First, 12

Table 6

Covenants in bank loan agreements

This table shows summary of covenants contained in a sample of 40 bank loan credit agreements and bank loan commitments used to finance cash tender offers from 1990 to 1996. The sample of 115 cash tender offers is obtained from the Securities Data Corporation (SDC). Text of bank loan credit agreements and commitment letters are obtained from 14D-1 filings.

	All bank loans	Existing bank loans	New bank loans
Restrictive covenants			
Structure of tender offer or merger to be satisfactory to bank	12	0	12
No adverse change in business of acquirer	21	2	19
No adverse change in business of target	13	0	13
No adverse change in debt market conditions	17	2	15
Mandatory prepayments of debt required	16	3	13
Restrictions on mergers	31	11	20
Restrictions on capital expenditures	11	1	10
Restrictions on dividends and share repurchases	22	6	16
Restrictions on asset sales	29	11	18
Restrictions on change in lines of business	16	5	11
Interest rate risk management required	2	0	2
Restrictions on prepayment of other debt	10	0	10
Restrictions on incurring additional debt	21	8	13
Restrictions on modifying terms of existing instruments	3	2	1
Limitations on liens	28	10	18
Limitations on operating leases	4	1	3
Conform to schedule for providing information on covenant compliance (information covenants)	20	11	9
Target to rescind poison pill	2	0	2
Financial covenants			
Covenants on leverage ratio	31	10	21
Covenants on interest coverage	21	8	13
Covenants on fixed charge coverage	11	3	8
Covenants on net worth	23	8	15
Covenants on EBITDA	7	3	4
Number of credit agreements	40	15	25

of 25 (48%) commitment letters explicitly require that the structure and terms of the proposed acquisition be satisfactory to the bank. Thus, banks appear to have the option to withdraw support if the terms of the offer are viewed to be detrimental to their interests. Citibank's commitment letter to Williams Co. provides an example of a typical merger covenant:

> The lenders shall be satisfied with the final terms and conditions of the Transaction, including, without limitation, the Tender Offer, and with the proposed terms and conditions of the Merger; the Lenders shall be satisfied with all legal and tax aspects of the Transaction (including, without limitation, the Tender Offer and the Merger); and all documentation relating to the Transaction,

including, without limitation, the Tender Offer, the Merger, the Offer to Purchase, the Merger Agreement, shall in form and substance be satisfactory to the Lenders and the price per share and the number per shares to be acquired shall be as set forth in the Merger Agreement.

Such merger covenants do not appear to be simply boilerplate provisions, but potentially constrain some acquirers. In Northrop's acquisition of Grumman, the commitment letter by Chase Manhattan Bank explicitly addresses this issue:

One of the conditions of funding the Credit Facilities set forth in the Commitment Letter is that a definitive merger agreement, in form and substance satisfactory to the Co-Agents, shall have been entered into by the Borrower and the Target (the "Merger Condition"). We have been discussing with you the basis on which we would agree to remove the Merger Condition.

By this letter we confirm that we would be prepared to commit to finance the Tender Offer without satisfaction of the Merger Condition, subject to a mutually satisfactory agreement with you (i) to pay fees to the Co-Agents in addition to those set forth in the Fee Letter in amounts and at such times as we deem appropriate under the circumstances, (ii) to increase the margins on the loans under the Credit Facilities prior to the merger by an amount which we deem appropriate under the circumstances, and (iii) to limit the length of interest periods under the Credit Facilities prior to completion of the merger.

In addition to covenants requiring bank approval of the tender offer terms, banks also frequently include covenants that allow financing to be withdrawn in the event that unfavorable information on the prospects of the acquirer, the target, or debt market conditions is revealed.

Of particular interest are restrictions on future mergers, which are observed frequently. 20 of 25 commitment letters (80%) and 11 of 15 existing loans (73%) restrict the acquirer's ability to engage in future acquisitions. Such restrictions increase the bank's ability to monitor the firm's investment policy because they force the firm to seek explicit approval for an acquisition. For example, Lear Corp., which financed its acquisition with an existing loan, reports the following contingency in its tender offer:

The Credit Agreement currently prohibits the consummation of the Offer and the Merger. Parent has negotiated with Chemical Bank a form of amendment and consent (the "Credit Agreement Amendment") to the Credit Agreement that would permit the Offer and Merger. The Credit Agreement Amendment will require the written consent of Lenders holding more than 50% of the aggregate outstanding indebtedness under the Credit Agreement, which consent is currently being sought. The consummation of the Offer is conditioned upon, among other things, the execution of the Credit Agreement Amendment by the requisite Banks.

Although most merger covenants either prohibit acquisitions or require explicit bank approval, 10 bank loans in our sample do not impose an outright ban on future acquisitions. In these cases, covenants allow the firm to pursue "permitted acquisitions" that do not require prior approval. Although the definition of permitted acquisitions varies in complexity, two aspects are commonly observed. First, the maximum size of a permitted acquisition is limited either by a predefined amount or by a metric tied to the acquirer's performance. Second, the merger covenant typically defines permitted acquisitions to be those in the same line of business as the acquirer. As an illustration, Clear Channel's credit agreement contains the following definition of permitted acquisitions:

Investments in communication or media related businesses not to exceed, at any time outstanding, an aggregate amount... equal to the sum of (i) 150% of Operating Cash Flow for the immediately preceding four fiscal quarters, plus; (ii) 100% of the first $50,000,000 of Net Cash Proceeds received by the Borrower and its Subsidiaries from the issuance of equity after the Agreement Date, plus; (iii) 50% of the Net Cash Proceeds in excess of $50,000,000 received by the Borrower and its Subsidiaries from the issuance of equity after the Agreement Date, plus; (iv) 50% of Net Cash Proceeds received by the Borrower and its Subsidiaries from the issuance of any subordinated convertible debentures after the Agreement Date.

Overall, the preponderance of merger covenants suggests that the existence of a previously negotiated bank loan does not provide acquirers' management with carte blanche regarding their acquisition strategy. Rather, merger covenants appear to be designed to allow banks the opportunity to evaluate proposed acquisitions and banks' commitment to the offer.

It is also interesting to note that there is no evidence to suggest that banks prefer to encourage diversifying investment policies. In fact, 26 of the 40 loans in the sample prohibit the firm from changing its current line of business or making unrelated acquisitions. For example, Revco's credit agreement with Banque Paribas and Bank of America states:

Revco will not, nor will it permit any of its Subsidiaries to, engage in any business activity other than the ownership and operation of retail drugstores and other such businesses as may be incidental or related thereto or as engaged in by Revco and its Subsidiaries on the Amendment Effective Date.

In addition to mergers, covenants also limit other aspects of investment policy. As expected, frequent among these are restrictions on asset sales and capital expenditures. Loan agreements also employ extensive financial covenants that require minimum leverage, interest coverage, and net worth ratios. In seven cases, covenants on minimum levels of pretax operating income are also observed. A firm's willingness to observe such targets for financial performance might be construed by investors as a positive signal regarding the quality of the proposed acquisition. Similar covenants on asset dispositions, capital expenditures, and financial metrics in bank loans are also documented by Gilson and Warner (2000) who study firms that exchange bank loans for junk bonds.

4.4. Subsample analysis of bank loan involvement

Our final set of tests examines the acquisition CARs for subsamples that are expected to vary in the degree of monitoring intensity, information asymmetry, and bank information monopoly. If banks are involved in certification and monitoring of tender offers, the positive effects of bank involvement should be more pronounced in subsamples where monitoring and certification is expected to be more valuable. However, if banks exploit their informational monopoly, we expect bank involvement to be less beneficial to shareholders when its informational advantage is more pronounced.

We expect that the benefits of monitoring are larger for acquirers that have been performing poorly. Consistent with this view, Morck et al. (1990) and Lang et al.

(1991) find that poorly performing acquirers experience significantly negative announcement CARs. Thus, if banks monitor, the positive relation between bank financing and CARs should be stronger for poorly performing acquirers. To test this, we define HIGHRET as equal to one if the acquirer's stock return over the year prior to the acquisition announcement is above the sample median and as zero otherwise. We define the variable LOWRET as equal to one if the acquirer's 1-year stock return is below the sample median and as equal to zero otherwise. In model (1) of Table 7, we include interaction terms between these variables and ONLYBANK.[5] The positive association between CARs and bank involvement is driven entirely by the subsample of acquirers that are poorly performing. For acquirers with above median stock returns, the association between bank financing and CARs is not significant.

Since bank financing is positively associated with announcement returns primarily for poorly performing acquirers, we revisit the relation between new and existing bank loans in model (2). In this model, we include four interaction terms between bank financing, prior performance, and new or existing loans.[6] Model (2) shows that both new and existing loans are positively associated with acquirer CARs for poorly performing acquirers, but that neither is associated with acquirer returns when acquirers perform well. An F-test reveals that coefficients on the interactions between new and existing loans for poorly performing acquirers that finance entirely with bank debt is not statistically significant. This supports the earlier finding that the market reaction to bank-financed acquisitions does not vary according to whether the bank loan represents a new or revised loan or is an existing agreement.

If bank financing certifies acquisition quality, the certification effect should be most important for firms where there is a substantial amount of informational asymmetry. We use firm size and stock return volatility as measures of information asymmetry. We define the indicator HIGHSIZE as equal to one if the market value of the acquirer's equity exceeds the sample median, and zero otherwise. LOWSIZE is defined as equal to one if the market value of the acquirer's equity is below the sample median and zero otherwise. We also partition the sample according to the volatility of stock return for acquirers in the year prior to the acquisition. The indicator HIGHSTD denotes acquirers whose stock return volatility is above the sample median, and LOWSTD denotes acquirers whose volatility is below the median. We measure stock return volatility over the interval of 60 trading days before to 210 trading days after the acquisition announcement.

Model (3) of Table 7 includes interactions between ONLYBANK and the HIGH-SIZE and LOWSIZE indicators. The effect of bank financing on CARs is positive and

---

[5] For ease of interpretation, we report regressions using interactions between the variables for prior performance and ONLYBANK. In these and subsequent results, our results are qualitatively similar if we interact the prior performance variables with BANKPCT or LOANAMT instead.

[6] The proportion of loans that are new or revised, or existing loans does not vary substantially across the HIGHRET and LOWRET subsamples. New or revised loans comprise 54% of bank-financed acquisitions in the LOWRET sample, and 58% in the HIGHRET sample.

Table 7

Regressions of 3-day acquirer cumulative abnormal returns

This table shows regressions of acquirer 3-day CAR on bank financing for a sample of 115 cash tender offers from 1990 to 1996. Variables are defined as follows: ONLYBANK equals one when the acquisition is entirely financed with bank debt and equals zero otherwise. HIGHRET equals one when the acquirer's prior 1-year stock return is above the sample median and equals zero otherwise. LOWRET equals one when the acquirer's prior 1-year stock return is below the sample median and equals zero otherwise. NEWLOAN equals one when bank debt, if used, is under a new or revised agreement and equals zero if an existing bank loan agreement or no bank debt is used. OLDLOAN equals one if bank financing under an existing loan agreement is used and equals zero otherwise. HIGHSIZE equals one if the acquirer's market value of equity is above the sample median and equals zero otherwise. LOWSIZE equals one if the acquirer's market value of equity is below than the sample median and equals zero otherwise. HIGHSTD equals one if the acquirer's stock return volatility over the prior year is above the sample median and equals zero otherwise. LOWSTD equals one if the acquirer's stock return volatility over the prior year is below the sample median and equals zero otherwise. HIGHMB equals one if the acquirer's market-value-to-book-value of assets is above the sample median and equals zero otherwise. LOWMB equals one if the acquirer's market-value-to-book-value of assets is below the sample median and equals zero otherwise. Other variables are defined in the table and text. All accounting values are measured at fiscal year-end before the initial announcement. *t*-statistics are in parentheses.

	(1)	(2)	(3)	(4)	(5)
Intercept	−0.018	−0.017	−0.018	−0.015	−0.021
	(−1.20)	(−1.16)	(−1.17)	(−1.04)	(−1.38)
ONLYBANK × HIGHRET	0.020				
	(1.02)				
ONLYBANK × LOWRET	0.053***				
	(3.02)				
ONLYBANK × HIGHRET × NEWLOAN		0.030			
		(1.30)			
ONLYBANK × HIGHRET × OLDLOAN		−0.008			
		(−0.22)			
ONLYBANK × LOWRET × NEWLOAN		0.052**			
		(2.58)			
ONLYBANK × LOWRET × OLDLOAN		0.058**			
		(2.13)			
ONLYBANK × HIGHSIZE			0.017		
			(0.88)		
ONLYBANK × LOWSIZE			0.059***		
			(3.31)		
ONLYBANK × HIGHSTD				0.081***	
				(4.77)	
ONLYBANK × LOWSTD				−0.005	
				(−0.29)	
ONLYBANK × HIGHMB					0.032
					(1.67)

(*Continued*)

Table 7 (*Continued*)

	(1)	(2)	(3)	(4)	(5)
ONLYBANK × LOWMB					0.047***
					(2.54)
Relatedness measure (RELATED)	0.021	0.020	0.021	0.017	0.021
	(1.59)	(1.52)	(1.65)*	(1.44)	(1.57)
Tender offer premium (PREMIUM)	0.018	0.017	0.018	0.020	0.019
	(0.95)	(0.91)	(0.97)	(1.13)	(1.01)
Market value of target equity/market value of acquirer equity (RELSIZE)	−0.012	−0.016	−0.053	−0.098	−0.051
	(−0.20)	(−0.26)	(−0.61)	(−1.19)	(−0.63)
Acquirer total debt/book value of total assets (ACQLEV)	−0.003	0.009	0.003	−0.019	0.009
	(−0.06)	(0.20)	(0.06)	(−0.46)	(0.22)
Cash + marketable securities/book value of assets (ACASH)	0.004	−0.002	0.028	0.039	0.029
	(0.06)	(−0.03)	(0.29)	(0.43)	(0.31)
Acquirer market to book ratio (ACQMB)	0.0003	−0.001	−0.0007	−0.003	
	(0.04)	(−0.05)	(−0.09)	(−0.39)	
Target market to book ratio (TGTMB)	−0.004	−0.005	−0.004	−0.008	−0.005
	(−0.83)	(−0.96)	(−0.79)	(−1.70)	(−0.95)
Acquirer managerial ownership (MOWN)	−0.012	0.004	−0.041	−0.097	−0.013
	(−0.17)	(0.06)	(−0.42)	(−1.05)	(−0.14)
Acquirer 1-year prebid stock return			0.003	0.012	0.001
			(0.09)	(0.45)	(0.02)
Self-selectivity correction	0.001	0.003	0.019	0.041	0.021
	(0.02)	(0.09)	(0.40)	(0.91)	(0.45)
Number of observations	115	115	115	115	115
Adjusted R^2	7.10%	6.05%	7.81%	18.73%	5.75%
F-test for equality of interaction coefficients (p-value)	1.94	0.04*	3.72**	17.93***	0.42
	(0.17)	(0.84)	(0.06)	(0.00)	(0.52)

***, **, and * indicate that the estimates are significantly different from zero at the 1%, 5%, and 10% levels, respectively.

significant for small firms. The coefficient estimates indicate that offers by small acquirers that are entirely financed by banks are associated with CARs that are 5.9% higher than other offers. In contrast, bank involvement does not appear to be associated with higher CARs for large acquirers.

Model (4) includes interactions with the acquirer's stock return variability. Entirely bank-financed offers by acquirers with high stock return volatility have CARs that are 8.1% higher than CARs for other acquirers. Bank financing has little discernable influence on acquirer CARs for firms with relatively low stock return variability. These results suggest that bank-financed acquisitions are greeted positively primarily when the informational asymmetry between firms and capital market participants is high.

We test if the effect of bank financing is related to the investment opportunities of the acquirer. In Rajan (1992), bank debt distorts the firm's investment policy because of the bank's informational monopoly. Houston and James (1996) suggest that the bank's informational monopoly will be substantial for firms with a relatively attractive investment opportunity set. Therefore, for these firms, the costs of a distorted investment policy induced by the bank's informational monopoly should be large. We define an indicator, HIGHMB, to denote firms whose market-to-book value of assets is above the sample median, and an indicator, LOWMB, to denote firms whose market-to-book value of assets is below the sample median. Model (5) shows that acquisitions financed by bank debt are associated with positive CARs for LOWMB acquirers. The coefficient on the interaction between bank financing and HIGHMB, while positive, is not significant. An F-test for equality of the interaction terms is not rejected at the 10% level. Thus, these results do not offer support for the view that bank financing is detrimental to shareholder wealth when the bank's informational advantage is large. Instead, these results can be viewed as being consistent with an important certification effect. For firms that are perceived to have attractive investment opportunities, the announcement of an acquisition might be viewed as bad news regarding the firm's investment opportunities. However, the use of bank debt appears to overcome this adverse information revelation effect for these firms.

4.5. Discussion of alternative interpretations

The evidence above shows that announcements of bank-financed acquisitions are good news for investors. This positive effect is most dominant for acquirers that are small, perform poorly prior to the acquisition, or have high stock return volatility. We have interpreted these results as being consistent with a monitoring role for banks. However, the findings are also potentially consistent with different interpretations. In this section, we discuss the evidence that supports or refutes these alternatives.

One explanation for the positive CARs is that investors are pleasantly surprised by a firm's ability to make an acquisition. Particularly for small and poorly performing firms, the ability to launch an acquisition might convey positive news about management's expectation of future profitability. Two findings, however, appear inconsistent with this explanation. First, as shown in Table 5, CARs are not significantly related to either the size of the acquirer or to the acquirer's prior stock return performance. Both acquirer size and performance matter only when interacted with the bank financing indicators, suggesting that if size and performance matter, it is due to their interaction with financing choice. Second, it appears that acquirer size proxies for the degree of information asymmetry. In untabulated tests, we find that including interactions between ONLYBANK and HIGHSIZE and LOWSIZE as well as interactions between ONLYBANK and HIGHSTD and LOWSTD yields a significant coefficient on the interaction with HIGHSTD but not on HIGHSIZE. Therefore, including stock return volatility renders firm size insignificant, suggesting that size proxies for information asymmetry.

Another explanation is that the announcement CARs reflect investors' surprise that the acquisition is not funded by equity. If bank-funded acquisitions were initially expected to be financed by equity, the announcement of bank funding could be viewed as positive news that equity is not being issued. If this is true, we should observe the

CARs should be the most positive when investors viewed an equity issue as most likely. Mikkelson and Partch (1986) and Jung et al. (1996) show that firms tend to issue equity after significant run-ups in stock price. Therefore, well-performing acquirers would be more likely to issue equity, and the decision to use bank debt instead should be more positive news for these firms. However, as shown in Table 7, CARs are higher for poorly performing acquirers that use bank financing, contrary to the predictions of this argument. In unreported tests, we also examine the acquirer's stock return performance over the prior 60-, 90-, and 180-day windows and find no evidence that high prebid performance is associated with higher announcement CARs.

A third possibility is that highly capable managers make more profitable acquisitions, which are viewed favorably by the market. At the same time, banks might be more willing to lend to highly capable managers. Two findings suggest that this is unlikely to be the primary explanation for our results. First, firms run by high ability managers should be valued more highly by investors. This implies that bank-financed acquisitions by highly valued firms should have higher CARs. However, Table 7 shows that the CARs for bank-funded tender offers do not vary according to the acquirer's market-to-book ratio. To the extent that a high market-to-book ratio is indicative of superior management, this result is not consistent with the view that our results are driven by unobserved managerial ability. Further, as discussed in Section 2, the amount of existing bank debt does not vary significantly across firms that have bank-financed and internally financed tender offers, suggesting that banks are equally likely to finance the operations of both groups of firms.

Our results also do not support the interpretation that bank-financed offers have positive CARs because they convey favorable information about the firm's ability to obtain a new bank loan. As discussed in Section 4 and shown in Tables 5 and 7, CARs do not depend upon whether the acquisition is financed by a new loan or by an existing loan agreement.

The results seem most consistent with the interpretation that bank debt financing imposes discipline on acquiring managers and that this leads to improved investment decisions. Supporting this view, we find that bank loan contracts include detailed covenants and restrictions on future investments, particularly acquisitions. Loan contracts often appear to be designed specifically to allow banks the opportunity to review proposed acquisitions. Also consistent with this explanation is the finding that poorly performing firms, which are expected to benefit more from close monitoring, experience significantly larger CARs for bank-financed acquisitions. Our findings are therefore consistent with a monitoring role for banks.

5. Conclusions

The source of financing of tender offers has an important influence on both the characteristics of the acquisition and the market's reaction. We find that tender offers financed entirely with bank debt are viewed positively by investors. Three-day announcement returns for cash tender offers financed entirely by banks average 4% and are statistically significant. In comparison, cash tender offers financed partially by banks or those financed entirely by financial slack are associated with small and statistically insignificant announcement returns. The banks' decision to finance the entire tender offer appears to constitute a strong signal to investors. The announcement returns for bank-financed acquisitions increase with the extent of bank financing, and are more favorable when acquirers are performing poorly, are small firms, and exhibit relatively high stock return variability.

We find evidence consistent with a screening and monitoring role for banks. Bank financing is observed more frequently when acquirers have higher managerial ownership and thereby possess stronger incentives to undertake value-enhancing acquisitions. However, the need for external financing appears to be a first-order determinant of bank financing. Acquirers predicted to have a high need for external financing (such as those with low internally generated funds and those undertaking larger acquisitions) are more likely to employ bank financing. Since bank financing is viewed positively by shareholders, our evidence points to a cost of financial slack that has received little attention. Although financial slack can be useful in circumventing informational frictions associated with external financing identified by Myers and Majluf (1984), it also insulates firms from the screening and monitoring role of informed intermediaries such as banks.

References

Almazan, A. and J. Suarez, 1998, "Why Do Markets React to Bank Loans? A Theory of Managerial Choice Between Public and Private Financing," Unpublished Working Paper, University of Illinios.

Amihud, Y. and B. Lev, 1981, "Risk Reduction as a Managerial Motive for Conglomerate Mergers," *Bell Journal of Economics*, 12, 605–617.

Billett, M. T., M. J. Flannery and J. A. Garfinkel, 1995, "The Effect of Lender Identity on a Borrowing Firm's Equity Return," *Journal of Finance*, 50, 699–718.

Boyd, J. H. and E. Prescott, 1986, "Financial Intermediation and Coalitions," *Journal of Economic Theory*, 38, 211–232.

Campbell, T. S. and W. A. Kracaw, 1980, "Information Production, Market Signaling and the Theory of Financial Intermediation," *Journal of Finance*, 35, 863–882.

Chevalier, J., 2000, "What Do We Know About Cross-Subsidization? Evidence from the Investment Policies of Merging Firms," Unpublished Working Paper, University of Chicago.

Diamond, D., 1984, "Financial Intermediation and Delegated Monitoring," *Review of Economic Studies*, 51, 393–414.

Diamond, D., 1991, Monitoring and Reputation: The Choice Between Bank Loans and Directly Placed Debt," *Journal of Political Economy*, 99, 689–721.

Dodd, P. and J. B. Warner, 1983, "On Corporate Governance: A Study of Proxy Contests," *Journal of Financial Economics*, 11, 401–438.

Gilson, S. C. and J. B. Warner, 2000, "Private Versus Public Debt: Evidence from Firms that Replace Bank Loans with Risky Public Debt," Unpublished Working Paper, Harvard Business School.

Greene, W. H., 1993, *Econometric Analysis*, Macmillan Publishing Company, New York.

Hadlock, C. and C. James, 1998, "Bank Lending and the Menu of Financing Options," Unpublished Working Paper, University of Florida.

Harford, J., 1999, "Corporate Cash Reserves and Acquisitions," *Journal of Finance*, 54, 1969–1997.

Houston, J. and C. James, 1996, "Bank Information Monopolies and the Mix of Private and Public Debt Claims," *Journal of Finance*, 51, 1863–1889.

Hubbard, R. G. and D. Palia, 1995, "Benefits of Control, Managerial Ownership, and the Stock Returns of Acquiring Firms," *RAND Journal of Economics*, 26, 782–792.

James, C., 1987, "Some Evidence on the Uniqueness of Bank Loans," *Journal of Financial Economics*, 19, 217–235.

Jensen, M. C., 1986, "Agency Costs of Free Cash Flow, Corporate Finance and Takeovers," AEA Papers and Proceedings 76.

Jung, K., Y. C. Kim and R. M. Stulz, 1996, "Timing, Investment Opportunities, Managerial Discretion, and the Security Issue Decision," *Journal of Financial Economics*, 42, 159–185.

Kang, J. K., A. Shivdasani and T. Yamada, 2000, "The Effect of Bank Relation on Investment Decisions: Evidence from Japanese Takeover Bids," *Journal of Finance*, 55, 2197–2218.

Kracaw, W. A. and M. Zenner, 1996, "The Wealth Effects of Bank Financing Announcements in Highly Leveraged Transactions," *Journal of Finance*, 51, 1931–1946.

Kracaw, W. A. and M. Zenner, 1998, "Bankers in the Boardroom: Good News or Bad News?" Unpublished Working Paper, University of North Carolina.

Kroszner, R. and P. Strahan, 2000, "Bankers on Boards: Monitoring, Conflicts of Interest, and Lender Liability," *Journal of Financial Economics*, 62, 415–452.

Lang, L., R. M. Stulz and R. A. Walkling, 1991, "A Test of the Free Cash Flow Hypothesis," *Journal of Financial Economics*, 29, 315–335.

Leland, H. and D. Pyle, 1977, "Information Asymmetries, Financial Structure, and Financial Intermediation," *Journal of Finance*, 32, 371–387.

Lewellen, W. G., 1971, "A Pure Financial Rationale for the Conglomerate Merger," *Journal of Finance*, 26, 521–537.

Lewellen, W. G., C. Loderer and A. Rosenfeld, 1985, "Merger Decisions and Executive Stock Ownership in Acquiring Firms," *Journal of Accounting and Economics*, 7, 209–231.

Loderer, C. and K. Martin, 1997, "Executive Stock Ownership and Performance: Tracking Faint Traces," *Journal of Financial Economics*, 45, 223–255.

Lummer, S. L. and J. J. McConnell, 1989, "Further Evidence on the Bank Lending Process and the Capital Market Response to Bank Loan Agreements," *Journal of Financial Economics*, 25, 99–122.

May, D. O., 1995, "Do Managerial Motives Influence Firm Risk Reduction Strategies?" *Journal of Finance*, 50, 1291–1308.

Mihov, V., 2000, "Credit Quality, Information Asymmetry, and the Source of Corporate Debt: Evidence from New Debt Issues," Unpublished Working Paper, Texas Christian University.

Mikkelson, W. and M. Partch, 1986, "Valuation Effects of Security Offerings and the Issuance Process," *Journal of Financial Economics*, 15, 31–60.

Morck, R., A. Shleifer and R. W. Vishny, 1990, "Do Managerial Objectives Drive Bad Acquisitions?" *Journal of Finance*, 45, 31–48.

Myers, S. C. and N. S. Majluf, 1984, "Corporate Financing and Investment Decisions When Firms Have Information that Investors Do Not Have," *Journal of Financial Economics*, 13, 187–221.

Rajan, R., 1992, "Insiders and Outsiders: The Choice Between Informed and Arms' Length Debt," *Journal of Finance*, 47, 1367–1400.

Shleifer, A. and R. W. Vishny, 1990, "Management Entrenchment: The Case of Manager-Specific Investments," *Journal of Financial Economics*, 25, 123–139.

Shleifer, A. and R. W. Vishny, 1992, "Liquidation Values and Debt Capacity: A Market Equilibrium Approach," *Journal of Finance*, 45, 379–396.

Sung, H. M., 1993, "The Effects of Overpayment and Form of Financing on Bidder Returns in Mergers and Tender Offers," *Journal of Financial Research*, 16, 351–365.

Travlos, N. G., 1987, "Corporate Takeover Bids, Methods of Payment and Bidding Firms' Stock Returns," *Journal of Finance*, 42, 943–963.

Weinstein, D. and Y. Yafeh, 1998, "On the Costs of a Bank-Centered Financial System: Evidence from Changing Main Bank Relationships in Japan," *Journal of Finance*, 53, 635–672.

Zwiebel, J., 1996, "Dynamic Capital Structure Under Managerial Entrenchment," *American Economic Review*, 86, 1197–1215.

Chapter 18

FINANCING DECISIONS AND BIDDER GAINS[*]

FREDERIK P. SCHLINGEMANN

Joseph M. Katz Graduate School of Business, University of Pittsburgh, Pittsburgh, Pennsylvania, USA

Contents

[*] The paper benefited greatly from comments by Kathy Kahle, Ken Lehn, Paul Malatesta, Bernadette Minton, Sara Moeller, Jeffry Netter (the editor), Tim Opler, Lee Pinkowitz, Kuldeep Shastri, Deon Strickland, René Stulz, Jim Verbrugge, Rohan Williamson, Ralph Walkling, and from seminar participants at the Financial Management Association meetings, Baruch College, Georgetown University, University of Georgia, McGill University, SUNY-Buffalo, The Ohio State University, University of Delaware, and the University of Pittsburgh, and two anonymous referees. Mehmet Yalin provided excellent research assistance.

This article originally appeared in the *Journal of Corporate Finance*, Vol. 10, pp. 683–701 (2004).
Corporate Takeovers, Volume 2
Edited by B. Espen Eckbo
DOI: 10.1016/B978-0-12-381982-6.00019-7

Abstract

This paper analyzes the relation between bidder gains and the source of *financing* funds available. We document that after controlling for the form of payment, financing decisions during the year before a takeover play an important role in explaining the cross-section of bidder gains. Bidder announcement period abnormal returns are positively and significantly related to the amount of *ex ante* equity financing. This relation is particularly strong for high q firms. We further report a negative and significant relation between bidder gains and free cash flow. This relation is particularly strong for firms classified as having poor investment opportunities. The amount of debt financing before a takeover announcement is not significantly related to bidder gains. Together, we take these findings as supportive of the pecking-order theory of financing and the free cash flow hypothesis.

Keywords

takeovers, financing decisions, managerial discretion, pecking order

JEL classification: G31, G32, G34

1. Introduction

In a world with agency costs and asymmetric information, among other market imperfections, it is well established that the strict Miller and Modigliani (1958) separation of corporate investment and financing decisions no longer holds. In the vast literature on mergers and acquisitions, a number of studies focus specifically on the interaction between financing and investment decisions.[1] In many instances, however, the form of *payment* has been used as a proxy or substitute for the source of *financing*. Yet, even if the takeover is paid for with cash, the actual source of this cash, that is, the actual financing decision, has largely been ignored as an explanatory variable in valuing managerial takeover decisions and establishing the link between financing and investment decisions.

Unfortunately, there is no way to establish a precise correspondence between a dollar raised in time t and a dollar spent on a takeover in time $t + \tau$.[2] However, rather than establishing this exact correspondence, we consider the source of the cash that is available at the time the takeover is announced. In other words, can the source of the firm's cash determine whether the cash used to pay for the takeover can be categorized as costly free cash flow or as valuable financial slack? We specifically analyze the relation between the bidder's financing decisions in the period before the takeover and its subsequent acquisition gains. It is shown that, holding the form of payment constant, knowing the firm's financing decisions before the takeover is a significant factor in explaining the cross-section of bidder returns.

According to the pecking-order theory, a firm's financing choice is determined by its relative costs of raising funds. Generally, equity financing is the most expensive form, both in direct issuance related and adverse selection costs. When a firm raises external financing in the equity market, investors are uncertain about the motive behind the firm's financing decision. For example, an equity issue could be interpreted by the market as a sign of overvaluation (e.g., Myers and Majluf, 1984) or—alternatively—as a sign of a profitable investment opportunity (e.g., Cooney and Kalay, 1993). Consequently, the investment decision helps in resolving the uncertainty associated with motivation behind the firm's prior financing decision. This potentially links bidder gains and prior financing decisions irrespective of the firm's investment opportunities.

---

[1] For theoretical literature on how the form of payment plays a role in takeovers, see, for example, Hansen (1987), Fishman (1989), Eckbo et al. (1990), and Berkovitch and Narayanan (1990). For empirical literature, see, for example, Travlos (1987), Wansley et al. (1983), Franks et al. (1988), Asquith et al. (1987), Amihud et al. (1990), Servaes (1991), and Martin (1996).

[2] Through SEC filling (and through the SDC database), I collect information on the use of funds. The majority (>85%) of firms report the use as "general corporate purposes." Similarly, I collect data on the takeover financing. However, this financing information generally refers to short-term financing arrangements (e.g., bridge financing and issuance of short-term notes) in order to pay for the transaction.

Alternatively, following Stulz (1990), given a poor investment opportunity set, the likelihood for management to invest in negative NPV projects increases in the level of managerial discretion over investment funds. In contrast, firms with a good investment opportunity set are more likely to forego a project for lower levels of managerial discretion. Since the level of managerial discretion depends on the source of financing, a link between financing decisions and bidder gains in cash acquisitions is expected to exist. The qualitative nature of this link depends on the perceived value of the firm's investment opportunities.

The main findings of this study are as follows. We find bidder gains to be positively and significantly related to the amount of cash raised through equity issuance during the fiscal year preceding the takeover announcement. We interpret this as evidence that the takeover announcement serves as a resolution of uncertainty associated with the firm's decision to issue equity. Consistent with the free cash flow hypothesis and the findings of Lang et al. (1991) we do find a negative and significant relation between internally generated free cash flows and bidder gains. We do not find a significant relation between the amount of cash raised from debt financing and bidder gains. This is consistent with the notion that debt could serve a monitoring role as well as a restricting role in managerial discretion depending on the firm's investment opportunities.

When we consider the impact of the firm's growth and investment opportunities, we find the following. Using a measure of Tobin's q to measure investment opportunities, we find that the positive relation between equity flows and bidder gains is particularly pronounced for high q firms. To the extent that our measure of growth opportunities could also proxy for performance and valuation, an equity issue for a high q firm is likely to be perceived as a sign of market timing or overvaluation rather than as a sign of profitable future investment opportunities. The takeover announcement in this scenario serves an even larger role as a resolution of uncertainty for firms, which could explain the strong positive relation between equity financing and bidder gains for high q bidders.

The negative relation between internally generated funds and bidder gains is particularly pronounced for firm with below median investment opportunities. This last result is again consistent with the findings in Lang et al. (1991) and supports the free cash flow hypothesis.

We report little or no support for debt financing playing either a monitoring role or reducing managerial discretion. While the link between debt financing and bidder gains is generally more positive for firms with poor investment opportunities, we do not find a significant difference when we compare this relation to that of firms with good investment opportunities.

The remainder of the paper is organized as follows. Section 2 develops the two main hypotheses that are tested and discusses the related literature. Section 3 presents the sample design, selection criteria, and research methodology. Section 4 presents the results for the univariate and multivariate analysis. Section 5 concludes the paper.

2. Theoretical Background and Hypotheses

2.1. The pecking order of financing choices and bidder gains

Following Myers and Majluf (1984), external financing is generally considered to be more costly, in terms of adverse selection costs and transaction costs, than internal financing. Furthermore, issuing equity is assumed to be more costly than issuing debt. Myers and Majluf (1984) focus on asymmetric information between managers and investors to derive a model, which predicts that firms will never finance their investments with equity and would rather reject a positive NPV project in order to maximize existing shareholders' wealth.[3] The reason for this is that the dilution effect on the existing shareholders' claim on the assets-in-place outweighs the claim on the NPV of the project. Consequently, equity issues are always a signal of overvaluation and hence considered bad news by the market.

Extending the above framework, Cooney and Kalay (1993) develop a model where they allow for negative NPV projects in the firm's investment opportunity set, while maintaining that managers maximize existing shareholder wealth. If a firm chooses equity to finance a project with a relatively high NPV combined with lower valued assets-in-place, then an equity issue is no longer necessarily bad news. Rather, an equity issue could signal a particularly profitable project and hence would generate a potentially positive announcement abnormal return. Consistent with this, McConnell and Muscarella (1985) find evidence of a positive stock price reaction when industrial firms announce an increase in their capital expenditures.[4,5]

Given that firms face positive and negative NPV projects, the stock price reaction associated with a *financing* decision is the net effect of two signals: overvaluation and investment opportunities. Hence, the stock price reaction associated with the ex post *investment* decision reflects both the resolution of the market's uncertainty about the

---

[3] With the possibility of a (risky) debt issue, the decision to issue debt and invest or not to issue and to reject the project will depend on whether the NPV is greater or equal to the capital gain on newly issued debt.

[4] In the absence of negative NPV projects, as in the Myers and Majluf (1984) model, the good news from the announcement of a new project will already be reflected in the preannouncement stock price. Hence, any residual good news from the announcement will be overwhelmed by the bad news of the equity issue.

[5] The empirical evidence is generally supportive of the hypothesis that an equity issue reveals bad news. A number of studies find significant decreases in the share price upon the announcement of a seasoned equity issue (see, e.g., Smith, 1986). These negative returns can be explained using the asymmetric information theory from Myers and Majluf, or using an agency explanation (see, e.g., Stulz, 1990). However, consistent with the Cooney and Kalay model, studies have also documented increases in the share price for announcements of private equity issues (see, e.g., Hertzel and Smith, 1993; Wruck, 1989) and Japanese public issues during the 1980s (see, e.g., Kato and Schallheim, 1993).

firm's ability to materialize the investment opportunity and whether the financing decision was driven by overvaluation.[6]

To illustrate the argument, consider a scenario where (a) managers maximize existing shareholders' value, (b) management and the market are uncertain about availability and timing of a positive NPV project, and (c) the market is uncertain about the motives for a debt or equity issue. For example, assume that financing costs are a percentage of the amount needed to finance a project. Further, assume that the cost of internal cash flow, debt, and equity financing is 1%, 5%, and 10%, respectively, of the initial investment outlay. If a firm determines the NPV of a project before the financing decision has been made, it should consider the financing costs. Take a firm that considers a project for which it needs to raise $1 million. Maximizing shareholder value, the firm will only proceed with the project if it has a present value greater than the financing costs. Hence, the present value has to exceed $10,000, $50,000, or $100,000 in case it has to use internal funds, debt, or equity, respectively. Obviously, firms would always prefer to use internal funds if available, but in case no such funds are available, the financing choice predicts the lower bound present value of the project. Given the uncertainty about the realization of the project after the financing decision has been made, one would expect to see—ceteris paribus—on average a more positive stock price reaction at the takeover announcement when relatively more cash has been raised through equity financing. In case more expensive forms of financing increase the likelihood for realizing a project ex post, the link between financing decisions and stock price reactions at the investment decision might weaken.[7]

2.2. Managerial discretion I: the overinvestment problem

Stulz (1990) theoretically derives the relation between the source of financing and agency costs of managerial discretion over investment funds. Firms with poor investment opportunities benefit from higher leverage because increased capital market discipline and monitoring reduces the overinvestment problem. For firms with good investment opportunities, higher leverage decreases their flexibility and ability to take advantage of value-creating investment opportunities. Debt financing precommits management to pay out free cash flow rather than to waste it when positive NPV investment opportunities are exhausted. To a lesser extent, equity financing serves a

[6] An important observation for the pecking order hypothesis is that, while the expected costs of raising funds are part of the firm's NPV calculation at the time when the financing is selected, these are considered sunk at the time the investment is announced. Hence, the relevant measure to assess the quality of the investment is its incremental value, that is, the discounted expected cash flows from the project.

[7] For example, the information contained in a prospectus at the time of an issue of bonds and stock could reveal something about an upcoming takeover. While unreported, in a logistic specification explaining the likelihood of a takeover bid, the effect of the financing decision was similar among debt, equity, and cash. All three forms of financing are positively associated with the likelihood of a takeover occurring in the year following the financing decision. The logistic model follows the model in Harford (1999) with added variables for the financing decisions.

control function as well. At the time of the equity issue, capital markets have the opportunity to assess the value of the firm's assets in place, its investment opportunities, and its incumbent management. However, an equity issue can also be interpreted as an increase in managerial discretion given that it increases the funds under managerial discretion and reduces the relative amount of debt in the firm's capital structure. Given the underlying assumption that managers derive positive perquisites from investing, overinvestment can be reduced by issuing debt.

This leads to the following testable implications regarding the overinvestment hypotheses and the firm's financing mix. Firms are distinguished by their amounts of free cash flow, equity flow, and debt flow relative to their total financing flows. Firms with poor investment opportunities and relatively high levels of free cash flow in their financing mix are more likely to waste these funds on investment projects with negative net present values. Firms with high levels of debt flow in their financing mix, or firms with relatively high levels of debt in their capital structure, are less likely to engage in overinvestment.[8] Therefore, a larger negative relation is expected between abnormal announcement returns and free cash flow financing, a negative relation for equity financing, and a smaller yet negative relation for debt flows and existing debt in the bidder's capital structure.[9]

2.3. Managerial discretion II: the underinvestment problem

In testing the underinvestment hypothesis, firms with good investment opportunities and high relative levels of free cash flow are more likely to invest in positive NPV investments than firms with high levels of debt in their capital structure or their financing mix.[10] A problem with testing the underinvestment hypothesis is that we cannot observe firms that refrain from a positive NPV investment because of debt constraints. Under the null hypothesis that high q firms will forego more investments with higher levels of debt, observing a takeover for a high q firm with a high level of debt should be less anticipated than for a firm with a low level of debt. Since the announcement return captures the unexpected part of the investors' anticipated gains, we should expect to see a more positive stock price reaction for high q firms with high relative levels of debt financing or leverage, than for high q firms with low levels of debt financing or leverage.

In summary, in testing the over- and underinvestment hypotheses, the expected relation between financing sources and bidder gains is driven by the differences in

---

[8] See Lang et al. (1991) for an extensive discussion on this issue.

[9] These predictions are also consistent with a signaling argument. *Ex post*, equity financing in place at the time of the acquisition announcement is less problematic than debt financing in case the acquisition turns out to be unsuccessful. Debt financing, through its ex post commitment to pay out future cash flows, potentially signals a better takeover to investors than equity financing does.

[10] This results from the assumption made in Stulz (1990) that the perquisites that management derives from investing are increasing in the NPV of the investment.

monitoring and disciplinary roles across debt, equity, and free cash flow financing, and hence depends on the firm's investment opportunities.

2.4. Related literature

The extant literature on corporate investments and takeovers is divided into papers that assume shareholder wealth maximizing behavior by the firm's management, under some constraint, and papers where management is assumed to pursue their own interests. In the first case, suboptimal investment occurs because of factors outside the control of management, like asymmetric information, transaction costs, or taxes (see, e.g., Myers and Majluf, 1984). Alternatively, when managers maximize their own wealth or utility instead of that of the existing shareholders, an agency conflict results in a deadweight loss and reduces shareholder value (see, e.g., Jensen, 1986; Stulz, 1990). Similarly, when agency problems arise between shareholders and bondholders, suboptimal investment decisions and loss in value can result (see, e.g., Myers, 1977; Stulz, 1990). A third possibility exists where suboptimal investment decisions are not driven by self-interested behavior of management, but by irrational behavior like overoptimism (see, e.g., Roll, 1986).

A number of empirical papers have addressed how debt levels and free cash flow affect bidder returns. However, none of the papers incorporates free cash flow, equity flow, and both debt flow and level in a single framework to specifically address the managerial discretion hypothesis and the pecking-order hypothesis.

Lang et al. (1991) test the free cash flow hypothesis by analyzing the bidder abnormal returns around tender offers for low and high q firms with low and high levels of free cash flow. Consistent with the free cash flow hypothesis, they find that the returns for bidders with low investment opportunities and high levels of free cash flow are significantly lower than the returns for high q bidders with high levels of free cash flow. Also, bidders with low investment opportunities and low levels of free cash flow outperform bidders with low investment opportunities and high levels of free cash flow.

Maloney et al. (1993) reported that higher levels of debt in the firm's capital structure are associated with higher abnormal announcement returns. Debt flows and equity flows are not addressed in their paper, nor do they distinguish between good or poor investment opportunities. Maloney et al. (1993) report a negative association between stock payment and bidder announcement returns, confirming earlier evidence in Travlos (1987).

Bruner (1988) and Smith and Kim (1994) find evidence that bidder target combinations of slack-poor and high free cash flow firms generate higher abnormal announcement returns than combinations that both have high levels of free cash flow or are both slack-poor. Bruner (1988) and Smith and Kim (1994) show some evidence of a monitoring role of debt in the bidder's capital structure. Furthermore, Bruner (1988) concludes that bidders are not building up financial slack prior to a takeover, but do have relatively high levels of slack available.

Harford (1999) and Opler et al. (1999) analyze the takeover behavior of cash-rich firms. These papers document that, consistent with Bruner (1988), cash-rich firms are, on average, more likely to become an acquirer. In Harford (1999), the takeovers by cash-rich firms are best explained by Jensen's (1986) free cash flow hypothesis and are, on average, unfavorably received by the market during their announcement and suffer inferior ex post operating performance. Neither Harford (1999) nor Opler et al. (1999) explicitly explores the source of the firm's cash and whether this affects the extent to which cash-rich firms make good or bad investment decisions.

Finally, Jung et al. (1996) and Baker and Wurgler (2002), among others, find that firms with high market values relative to their book values are more likely to issue equity. An investment or takeover announcement subsequent to the equity issue could help clear up the motivation behind the equity issue and thus be welcomed by the market with a positive stock price reaction.

3. Sample Design and Methodology

3.1. Sample and data definitions

The sample is constructed from Securities Data Corporation (SDC) International Merger and Acquisition Database (SDC-IMAD) and contains acquiring firms for the period 1984–1998. The acquiring firms in the sample satisfy the following set of conditions. The transaction is completed and categorized by SDC as a majority takeover transaction, that is, a merger, acquisition of majority interest, or acquisition of all assets. The successful bidder is the bidder making the first bid for the target. The value of the transaction is no smaller than $10 million, the bidder's assets in the fiscal year prior to the announcement date exceed $50 million, and the relative size (RELVAL) of the transaction, measured as the transaction value divided by the bidder's market value of assets, exceeds 1%. Bidders have Standard Industrial Classification (SIC) codes outside the ranges 6000–6999 (Financials) and 4900–4999 (Regulated utilities). To control for the form of payment, only cash transactions are included in the sample. Acquirers must have ordinary shares (CRSP share codes 10 and 11) listed on the AMEX, Nasdaq, or NYSE and exist on both the CRSP and Compustat tapes. Daily security returns and the equally and value-weighted CRSP index are obtained from CRSP.

Table 1 presents the annual distribution of announcement dates of 623 cash takeovers in the final sample grouped by transaction types over the period 1984–1998.

Three sources of cash are considered: internally generated cash flow, the flow of common equity, and flow of total debt. The financing definitions are taken from the Compustat Industrial Annual Expanded file (Primary, Secondary, and Tertiary—Full Coverage and Research files) and the Securities Data Global New Issues database. We apply three methods to define a firm's financing decision.

Table 1

Annual distribution of announcement dates

All data is from SDC International Merger and Acquisitions Database. The form of payment is cash exclusively. Acquirers with SIC codes in the 6000–6999 (financials) and 4900–4999 (regulated utilities) range, ADRs, and any other share listings other than common shares (CRSP codes 10 and 11) are excluded from the sample.

Year	n
1984	6
1985	33
1986	34
1987	44
1988	52
1989	64
1990	35
1991	26
1992	39
1993	42
1994	52
1995	48
1996	57
1997	49
1998	42
Total	623

First, using the cash flow statement, we define internally generated cash flow as operating income before depreciation, minus interest expense on debt, income taxes, and preferred and common dividends (see, e.g., Lehn and Poulsen, 1989). Common stock financing is defined as the difference between the flows of the sale of common and preferred stock and the purchase of common and preferred stock plus the change in the liquidating value of preferred stock. Total debt financing is defined as the change in the sum of short- and long-term debt financing (see, e.g., Hovakimian et al., 2001).

Second, using balance sheet items and following Baker and Wurgler (2002), we define net equity issues as the change in book equity minus the change in balance sheet retained earnings. For internally generated cash flow, we use newly retained earnings, which are defined as the change in retained earnings divided by assets. Net debt issues are defined as the change in assets net of the book value of equity divided by assets.

Third, we compile a sample of equity and debt issues that took place during the fiscal year prior to the takeover announcement from the SDC New Issues Database. We also collect whether sample firms repurchased equity through the open market or executed a self-tender.

Each financing variable is normalized by the firm's book value of assets and measured over the fiscal year prior to the takeover announcement date. Cases where this normalization exceeds one are eliminated. Firms that have not reported a security issue on SDC are assigned zero values for the financing definitions. We calculate the firm's debt-to-equity ratio 2 years prior to the takeover to measure the bidder's capital structure. The results focus on using the Compustat flow numbers, but in some cases, results are reported for the other two measures as well. The results throughout the paper are robust to using either definition.

Finally, following Stulz (1990) and Lang et al. (1989, 1991), bidders are ranked according to their perceived investment opportunity set, as measured by q. Firms are classified as low (high) q based on below (equal or above) sample median values of the firms' average value of q during the 3 years before the takeover announcement.[11]

3.2. Sample description

Table 2 reports summary statistics for the sample. Panel A provides a description of the target and deal characteristics. About 15% of transactions are classified as a tender offer by SDC. Less than 5% of the transactions are classified as hostile by SDC.[12] The target firms in the sample are mostly either subsidiaries or public firms (50.40% and 37.88%, respectively). Almost 9% of the targets in the sample are private firms. More than 40% of the target firms have a two-digit SIC code that is different from the acquirer's SIC code. Finally, 23% of the target firms in the sample are non-US.

Panel B provides some bidder characteristics. The acquirers in the sample are generally larger firms with good investment opportunities, as measured by the 3-year average of q. Transaction values range from 1% (by construction) to more than 40% of the acquirer's market value of assets.

Panel C reports event-study abnormal returns. Three-day $[-1, +1]$ and 11-day $[-5, +5]$ event-study returns surrounding the announcement are calculated using market-adjusted and market-and-risk-adjusted returns. Market-adjusted returns are defined as the difference between the raw return and the CRSP equally weighted index. Market-and-risk-adjusted returns are computed using the market-model residuals estimated over the period beginning 205 days and ending 5 days prior to the announcement. Consistent with cash transactions conveying positive information about its equity value and consistent with prior findings (see, e.g., Schwert, 2000; Travlos, 1987), mean values of the abnormal returns are positive and significant for cash transactions (approximately 1.50%).

Tables 3 and 4 present statistics on the financing definitions. The values in Panel A are based on the financing definitions using the statement of cash flows. The mean and

---

[11] The proxy for q (see Chung and Pruitt, 1994) is calculated as the market value of equity plus the liquidating value of outstanding preferred stock plus current liabilities net of current assets plus the book value of long-term debt divided by the book value of total assets. For robustness, we also use a measure defined as the market value of equity plus total assets minus the book value of equity divided by total assets. All results are qualitatively unchanged when using this q definition.

[12] Schwert (2000) reports that definitions of hostile could differ substantially across databases, and that SDC-identified hostile deals do not result in different bidder announcement period returns than friendly deals.

Table 2

Sample summary statistics

Data on target and deal characteristics is from the SDC database. Return data is from the CRSP database. Accounting data is from Compustat. Deal value is defined as the SDC market value of the deal. Relative size is defined as the deal value relative to the market value of assets of the acquirer. The debt-to-equity and debt-to-assets ratios are measured using book values of equity and debt in year (-2). Tobin's q is calculated as the sum of the market value of equity, the liquidating value of preferred stock, the firm's short-term liabilities net of its short-term assets, and the book value of the firm's long-term debt, divided by the book value of total assets (see Chung and Pruitt, 1994). We report and average value of Tobin's q for the 3-year period prior to the takeover announcement. Market-and-risk-adjusted returns are calculated using alpha and beta estimated over the period from 205 to 5 days before the announcement of the takeover. Both market-and-risk-adjusted and market-adjusted returns use the CRSP equally weighted index as the market portfolio. Statistical significance 1%, 5%, and 10% level is indicated with ***, **, and *, respectively.

Panel A: target and deal characteristics	%				
Tender offer	15.65				
Target opposes deal (hostile)	4.98				
Target is public	37.88				
Target is subsidiary	50.40				
Target is private	8.99				
Target is government-owned	0.80				
Target is joint-ventures	1.93				
Target is in different two-digit SIC	41.09				
Target is non-US	23.11				
Panel B: bidder characteristics	Mean	Median	Min	Max	n
Assets (× $1 million)	3329.82	1187.49	61.54	41,140	620
Sales (× $1 million)	2924.23	995.63	12.35	51,974	620
Deal value (× $1 million)	305.43	110	10.00	9561	620
Relative size	0.37	0.09	0.01	43.11	620
Debt-to-equity	1.23	0.62	0.00	115.99	620
Tobin's q	1.58	1.34	0.43	8.49	569
Panel C: event-study returns (%)	Mean	Median	Min	Max	n
Market-and-risk-adjusted (−1, +1)	1.56***	0.62***	−16.23	49.02	619
Market-adjusted (−1, +1)	1.55***	0.57***	−18.34	47.19	620
Market-and-risk-adjusted (−5, +5)	1.33***	0.77***	−35.57	47.35	617
Market-adjusted (−5, +5)	1.34***	0.48**	−41.82	49.27	619

median value for free cash flow is approximately 10%. The average flow of equity is a little more than 2% of assets, but the median value is close to 0. Debt flows are 28% and 24% at the mean and the median, respectively.

Panel B reports the values from the previous panel on an industry-adjusted basis. Yearly two-digit median values are subtracted from each raw number. On average, bidders experience above normal levels of debt and equity financing in the year before the takeover announcement.

Panel C reports financing variables using a balance sheet identity. The mean and median value for retained earnings is approximately 3%. The mean and median values

Table 3

Financing variables

Free cash flow is operating income before depreciation minus interest expense on debt, income taxes, and preferred and common dividends (see Lehn and Poulsen, 1989). The flow of equity financing is the difference between the flows of the sale of common and preferred, the purchase of common and preferred stock, and the change in the liquidating value of preferred stock (see Hovakimian et al., 2001). Debt financing is the change in the sum of short- and long-term financing, where long-term debt financing is defined as the change in the balance sheet item long-term debt and short-term financing as the change in debt in current liabilities. Industry-adjusted financing flows are calculated as the difference between the unadjusted flow and the yearly two-digit SIC-matched median value. Newly retained earnings are defined as the change in retained earnings from the balance sheet. Net equity issues are defined as the change in book equity minus the change in balance sheet retained earnings. Net debt issues are defined as the change in assets net of the book value of equity. Equity issues are from the SDC database and include all public and private issues of equity. Repurchases include both open-market repurchases and self-tender offers. Debt issues included all SDC listed issues of debt. All financing flows are measured during the fiscal year prior to the takeover announcement (-1) and are normalized by the book value of the firm's assets (ASSETS) and measured in year (-2).

	Mean	Median	Min	Max	n
Panel A: income statement (flow)					
Free cash flow	0.103	0.101	−0.295	0.586	616
Equity flow	0.023	0.001	−0.191	0.790	620
Debt flow	0.282	0.246	0.000	0.989	608
Panel B: industry-adjusted (flow)					
Industry-adjusted free cash flow	0.001	0.000	−0.425	0.485	616
Industry-adjusted equity flow	0.018	−0.001	−0.380	0.786	620
Industry-adjusted debt flow	0.233	0.200	−0.148	0.902	608
Panel C: balance sheet					
Newly retained earnings	0.031	0.030	−0.641	0.786	619
Net equity issues	0.044	0.012	−0.493	0.798	620
Net debt issues	0.137	0.094	−0.558	0.931	618
Panel D: SDC new issues					
Equity issues	0.035	0.000	0.000	0.934	620
Repurchases	0.010	0.000	0.000	0.314	620
Net equity (issues-repurchases)	0.025	0.000	−0.276	0.934	620
Debt issues	0.043	0.000	0.000	0.908	613

of equity financing are 4% and 1%, respectively, of total assets. Net debt issues, defined as the change in equity net of the change in total equity, represent 13% and 9% at the mean and median level, respectively.

Finally, Panel D contains statistics based on data from the SDC database. In the sample of 623 acquisitions, 94 firms have an equity issue reported by SDC, 110 firms report a debt issue, and 81 firms had a share repurchase or self-tender. The mean and median values of SDC-reported equity issues net of share repurchases are very similar to the values found from the Compustat database. The mean and median values for debt issues are substantially lower when measured from the SDC database, reflecting the possibility that many types of debt issues are not filed with the SEC or not reported in the SDC database.

Table 4 reports Pearson correlation coefficients for the different financing variables, grouped under internal, cash equity, and debt financing. The correlation between the balance sheet and statement of cash flow definition of internal financing is 0.511 and statistically significant at the 1% level. The correlation between balance sheet and statement of cash flow definitions of equity financing are much higher at 0.801. The correlation between SDC definitions of equity financing and Compustat definitions is more than 30% and significant at the 1% level. While marginally significant, the correlation between balance sheet and statement of cash flow definitions of debt financing is quite low. Similarly, definitions of debt from the Compustat database and the SDC database have relatively low correlation coefficients.

Table 4

Correlation of financing variables

The following variable abbreviations are used in the table. E, NE, R, and IAE denote, respectively, equity, equity issues minus share repurchases, repurchases, and industry-adjusted equity. C and IAC denote, respectively, internal cash flow and industry-adjusted internal cash flow. D and IAD denote debt and industry-adjusted debt, respectively. Subscripts CF, BS, and SDC refer the source of the data and denote, respectively, the cash flow statement, the balance sheet, and the SDC database. Cash flow statement and balance sheet numbers are from Compustat. The cells denote Pearson correlation coefficients with *p*-values in italics.

Panel A: cash	C_{BS}	IAC_{CF}			
C_{CF}	0.511	0.950			
	0.001	*0.001*			
C_{BS}		0.516			
		0.001			
Panel B: equity	E_{BS}	E_{SDC}	NE_{SDC}	R_{SDC}	IAE_{CF}
E_{CF}	0.801	0.365	0.358	−0.091	0.985
	0.001	*0.001*	*0.001*	*0.023*	*0.001*
E_{BS}		0.320	0.333	−0.013	0.792
		0.001	*0.001*	*0.740*	*0.001*
E_{SDC}			0.962	−0.311	0.361
			0.001	*0.001*	*0.001*
NE_{SDC}				−0.040	0.354
				0.318	*0.001*
R_{SDC}					−0.089
					0.028
Panel C: debt			D_{BS}	D_{SDC}	IAD_{CF}
D_{CF}			0.083	0.140	0.988
			0.040	*0.001*	*0.001*
D_{BS}				0.046	0.071
				0.255	*0.080*
D_{SDC}					0.131
					0.001

4. Results

4.1. Multivariate regression analysis

We use the abnormal announcement period return to proxy for the net present value of the takeover bid from the acquirer's shareholders perspective. The reported regression specifications use the market-model residuals cumulated over the $[-1, +1]$ as the dependent variable, but the results are robust to using the market-adjusted abnormal returns. The main variables of interest in this study are the various definitions of internal, equity, and debt financing. Each specification includes as number of control variables the debt-to-equity ratio measured 2 years prior to the takeover announcement, the relative transaction size, and dummy variables indicating whether the takeover is, respectively, a tender offer, hostile, involves a private target, or involves a non-US target.[13] Year dummies are included in the model, yet not reported. Reported p-values are based on White (1980) heteroscedasticity-consistent standard errors if homoscedasticity is rejected.

4.2. Results

Table 5 presents various specifications of the regression model. In model (1), we confirm the results in Lang et al. (1991) and find that free cash flow is negatively and significantly associated with bidder gains. Consistent with the pecking-order hypothesis, we find in model (2) that funds raised through equity issues are positively and significantly associated with bidder gains. Hence, some of the uncertainty about the firm's intention when it first issued the equity (i.e., exploiting overvaluation or funding investment opportunities) is resolved during the announcement of the takeover. Another interpretation is that investors expect a value-creating takeover if the firm has raised funds through a relatively expensive form of an equity issue. Model (3) shows that funds raised from debt issues are positively yet insignificantly associated with bidder gains. Models (4)-(6) confirm the results using industry-adjusted financing variables. Finally, models (7) and (8) show that the results are robust to including all three financing variables in one regression specification.

The only other variable that is consistently significant is the relative transaction size. Larger transactions will have more impact on the acquirer. The coefficients on each of the dummy variables are insignificant, except for the cross-border dummy variable in models (1) and (4). The negative sign on the cross-border dummy is consistent with Moeller and Schlingemann (2001). The coefficient on the private target dummy is

---

[13] While not reported, we have also run specifications adding a dummy variable for whether the target is within the same two-digit SIC code as the acquirer, the natural logarithm of assets, and a market-to-book value of assets. The coefficient on the related industry dummy is insignificant and does not affect the other coefficients. The coefficient on the size and book-to-market variables are both positive, but insignificant and do not affect the other coefficients.

Table 5

Cross-sectional regression analysis: cash, equity, and debt flows

The dependent variable in the OLS regression is the 3-day market-adjusted return around the announcement of the takeover. See Tables 2 and 3 for data definitions of the independent variables. Statistical significance based on heteroscedasticity-consistent estimates at the 1%, 5%, and 10% level is indicated with ***, **, and *, respectively.

Model	(1)	(2)	(3)	(4)	(5)	(6)	(7)	(8)
Intercept	-0.006	-0.007	-0.017	-0.011	-0.007	-0.015	-0.007	-0.011
	0.823	0.778	0.509	0.668	0.780	0.548	0.768	0.664
Free cash flow	-0.062**						-0.047**	
	0.034						0.041	
Equity flow		0.081***					0.073***	
		0.001					0.004	
Debt flow			0.012				0.002	
			0.346				0.898	
IA free cash flow				-0.061**				-0.052*
				0.040				0.099
IA equity flow					0.073***			0.065***
					0.004			0.009
IA debt flow						0.010		0.000
						0.452		0.976
Debt-to-equity	0.000	0.000	0.000	0.000	0.000	0.000	0.000	0.000
	0.658	0.445	0.634	0.640	0.452	0.602	0.633	0.626
Tender offer dummy	-0.010	-0.009	-0.009	-0.010	-0.008	-0.009	-0.007	-0.007
	0.186	0.248	0.246	0.195	0.264	0.242	0.310	0.326
Relative value	0.009***	0.009***	0.010***	0.009***	0.009***	0.010***	0.009***	0.009***
	0.001	0.001	0.001	0.001	0.001	0.001	0.001	0.001
Hostile dummy	0.008	0.004	0.008	0.007	0.004	0.008	0.007	0.007
	0.302	0.567	0.280	0.332	0.591	0.289	0.345	0.372
Private dummy	-0.001	-0.002	-0.001	-0.001	-0.002	-0.001	-0.002	-0.002
	0.588	0.441	0.702	0.579	0.467	0.714	0.439	0.458
CB dummy	-0.010*	-0.009	-0.009	-0.009*	-0.009	-0.009	-0.008	-0.008
	0.094	0.127	0.139	0.098	0.128	0.132	0.169	0.173
Adj. R^2 (%)	10.76	11.41	10.66	10.72	11.16	10.61	12.36	12.17
n	615	619	607	615	619	607	603	603

negative, but insignificant. This is consistent with the findings in Chang (1998), who shows that bidder returns in stock transactions involving a private target are significantly higher that when a public target is involved, but for cash transactions, no significant effect is reported. Consistent with Schwert (2000), acquirers do not experience different announcement period returns in hostile transactions compared to friendly transactions. Also, the debt-to-equity ratio measured 2 years prior to the takeover announcement is insignificant in each specification.

Table 6 uses the equity issue data from the SDC database. Model (9) shows again that bidder gains are positively and significantly related to the net amount of equity financing taking place during the year before the takeover. The relation is no longer significant when share repurchases are ignored in the total amount of equity financing taking place [see model (10)]. As expected, share repurchases, including self-tenders, and bidder gains are negatively and significantly associated. One interpretation is that a firm repurchasing its own shares has excess cash and poor investment opportunities, and is therefore expected to make poor takeover decisions.

In summary, these results support the notion of the pecking order of financing. Particularly, the positive association between equity financing prior to a takeover announcement and bidder gains is consistent with the takeover announcement being interpreted by the market as a signal for a particularly profitable investment opportunity (see, e.g., Cooney and Kalay, 1993). In other words, the uncertainty surrounding a seasoned equity offering, overvaluation, or signal for a valuable investment opportunity is partially resolved at the announcement of the takeover. Using cash, the firm also avoids the same kind of uncertainty associated with using equity directly to pay for the takeover.

4.3. Investment opportunities

To test the free cash flow hypothesis—or overinvestment hypothesis—the issue of investment and growth opportunities needs to be considered. Specifically, we expect the aforementioned negative relation between free cash flow and bidder gains to be particularly pronounced for low q bidders. To the extent that q could be a measure of overvaluation instead of investment opportunities, high q values could also exacerbate the uncertainty about the motivation behind the equity issue. For example, Baker and Wurgler (2002) find that firms time their equity issues and hence are more likely to issue equity if their average q is high.[14] High q bidders experience in that case a higher degree of uncertainty resolution when they announce a takeover succeeding the equity issue. Hence, under the argument that the takeover resolves this uncertainty, the association between bidder gains and equity financing is expected to be particularly strong for high q bidders. Finally, if debt financing plays a monitoring role for firms with poor investment opportunities and reduces valuable managerial discretion for

---

[14] For other evidence on firms issuing equity when their market values are high relative to their book values, see among others, Asquith and Mullins (1986), Jung et al. (1996), and Hovakimian et al. (2001).

Table 6

Cross-sectional regression analysis: equity issues and share repurchases

The dependent variable in the OLS regression is the 3-day market-adjusted return around the announcement of the takeover. See Tables 2 and 3 for data definitions of the independent variables. Statistical significance based on heteroscedasticity-consistent estimates at the 1%, 5%, and 10% level is indicated with ***, **, and *, respectively.

Model	(9)	(10)	(11)
Intercept	−0.008	−0.008	−0.008
	0.751	0.740	0.739
Net equity issues	0.037**		
	0.032		
Equity issues		0.029	
		0.171	
Share repurchases			−0.146**
			0.042
Debt-to-equity	0.000	0.000	0.000
	0.499	0.477	0.522
Tender offer dummy	−0.009	−0.009	−0.011
	0.213	0.216	0.146
Relative value	0.010***	0.010***	0.009***
	0.001	0.001	0.001
Hostile dummy	0.005	0.005	0.007
	0.462	0.462	0.341
Private dummy	−0.002	−0.002	−0.001
	0.514	0.553	0.668
CB dummy	−0.010	−0.010	−0.010*
	0.103	0.107	0.077
Adj. R^2 (%)	10.39	10.15	10.49
N	615	619	619

firms with good investment opportunities, one would expect bidder gains and debt financing to be positively related for low q firms and negatively for high q firms.

In Table 7, we interact each of the financing variables with a low q and high q dummy variable. Low and high q dummies are based on whether the bidder's 3-year preannouncement average of q is above or below the mean sample value.[15]

In regressions (12)–(14), the financing variables are interacted with, respectively, the low and high q dummy variables. Consistent with the predictions from the free cash flow hypothesis and reports discussed in Lang et al. (1991), we find that the negative association between bidder abnormal returns and free cash flow is particularly

[15] Other cutoffs, like using a 1-year mean, using the median value, or using a value of 1 are used as well, but not reported. The results are robust to these different notions of high versus low q firms. While theoretically, a q of 1 should determine the cutoff, given that we calculate an empirical q here, each cutoff is as arbitrary as picking 1.

Table 7

Cross-sectional regression analysis: growth opportunities

The dependent variable in the OLS regression is the 3-day market-adjusted return around the announcement of the takeover. See Tables 2 and 3 for data definitions of the independent variables. Statistical significance based on heteroscedasticity-consistent estimates at the 1%, 5%, and 10% level is indicated with ***, **, and *, respectively.

Model	(12)	(13)	(14)
Intercept	0.001	−0.009	−0.015
	0.975	0.706	0.552
Free cash flow × low q	−0.083**		
	0.021		
Free cash flow × high q	−0.041		
	0.332		
Equity flow × low q		0.013	
		0.811	
Equity flow × high q		0.100***	
		0.001	
Debt flow × low q			0.021
			0.237
Debt flow × high q			−0.015
			0.786
Debt-to-equity	0.000	0.000	0.000
	0.665	0.463	0.606
Tender offer dummy	−0.009	−0.009	−0.008
	0.205	0.225	0.274
Relative value	0.001***	0.009***	0.010***
	0.001	0.001	0.001
Hostile dummy	0.007	0.005	0.007
	0.329	0.535	0.311
Private target dummy	−0.002	−0.002	−0.001
	0.556	0.518	0.666
Cross-border dummy	−0.009	−0.009	−0.008
	0.113	0.128	0.157
Low q dummy	0.008	0.002	−0.007
	0.407	0.652	0.439
Adj. R^2	10.62	11.43	10.45
N	615	619	607

pronounced for firm with poor investment opportunities. For firms with good invest-ment opportunities, as measured by above average levels of q, the relation between bidder gains and free cash flow is negative but insignificant.

The strong positive and significant relation between equity flows and bidder gains is primarily found for firm with good investment opportunities. Only for high q firms we find a positive and significant coefficient for the equity flow variable. The magnitude of the coefficient for high q bidder is approximately six times larger than the coefficient for low q firms. This is consistent with an equity issue being an incomplete signal of a potentially valuable investment opportunity. The takeover announcement works as a resolution of the uncertainty after the equity issue. While not reported, when the share repurchase variable is interacted with the low and high q dummy, we find that the association between equity flows from share repurchases and bidder gains is negative and significant for high q firms only as well.

The coefficient on the debt flow variable for, respectively, low and high q bidder is positive and negative, yet both are insignificant. Hence, the results provide only marginal support for a monitoring role of debt for low q bidders. Similarly, debt financing does not result in a decrease in valuable managerial discretion for high q bidders.

5. Conclusion

Prior literature has theorized and documented a relation between the form of *payment* and a bidder's abnormal announcement return. When considering pure cash transactions, however, the actual source of the cash available for an investment—the *financing* decision—has largely been ignored as an explanatory variable in valuing managerial takeover decisions. This paper analyzes the relation between the source of the firm's funds available for the acquisition to bidder gains. It is shown that, holding the form of payment constant, prior financing decisions are a significant factor in explaining the cross-section of bidder returns.

The paper addresses two nonmutually exclusive hypotheses that link corporate financing decisions with corporate investment decisions. First, following the pecking-order hypothesis and models by Myers and Majluf (1984) and Cooney and Kalay (1993), firms would issue equity only for particularly profitable investments or not at all given the high adverse selection and other costs associated with equity financing. Market timing theories argue that firms issue equity to take advantage of high current equity values. We argue that the takeover announcement resolves some of the uncertainty on the motivation behind a firm's decision to issue equity. This would predict a positive relation between equity financing and bidder gains. This relation would be especially strong for firms that are expected to have timed the market. Second, the free cash flow or overinvestment hypothesis predicts that managers are more likely to waste cash on unprofitable projects for higher levels of managerial discretion over cash flows. This predicts that particularly for firm with poor investment opportunities, levels of free cash flow and bidder gains are negatively associated.

The main findings of this study are summarized below. Bidder gains are positively and significantly related to the level of equity financing during the fiscal year preceding the takeover announcement. This relation is particularly pronounced for high q bidders. These results support the idea that a takeover announcement serves as a resolution of uncertainty associated with the firm's decision to issue equity. Consistent with the free cash flow hypothesis and the findings of Lang et al. (1991), we find negative and significant relation between internally generated free cash flows and bidder gains for low q bidders, but an insignificant relation for high q bidders. We do not find a significant relation between the amount of cash raised from debt financing and bidder gains. This is consistent with the notion that debt could serve a monitoring role as well as a restricting role in managerial discretion depending on the firm's investment opportunities.

References

Amihud, Y., B. Lev and N. G. Travlos, 1990, "Corporate Control and the Choice of Investment Financing: The Case of Corporate Acquisitions," *Journal of Finance*, 55, 603–616.

Asquith, P. and D. W. Mullins, 1986, "Equity Issues and Offering Dilution," *Journal of Financial Economics*, 15, 61–89.

Asquith, P., R. Bruner and D. W. Mullins, 1987, "Merger Returns and the Form of Financing," Working Paper, Harvard University.

Baker, M. and J. Wurgler, 2002, "Market Timing and Capital Structure," *Journal of Finance*, 57(1), 1–32.

Berkovitch, E. and M. P. Narayanan, 1990, "Competition and the Medium of Exchange in Takeovers," *Review of Financial Studies*, 3, 153–174.

Bruner, R. F., 1988, "The Use of Excess Cash and Debt Capacity as a Motive for Merger," *Journal of Financial and Quantitative Analysis*, 23, 199–219.

Chang, S., 1998, "Takeovers of Privately Held Targets, Methods of Payment, and Bidder Returns," *Journal of Finance*, 53(2), 773–784.

Chung, K. H. and S. W. Pruitt, 1994, "A Simple Approximation of Tobin's q," *Financial Management*, 23, 70–74.

Cooney, J. W. and A. Kalay, 1993, "Positive Information from Equity Issue Announcements," *Journal of Financial Economics*, 33, 149–172.

Eckbo, B. E., R. M. Giammarino and R. L. Heinkel, 1990, "Asymmetric Information and the Medium of Exchange in Takeovers, Theory and Test," *Review of Financial Studies*, 3, 651–675.

Fishman, M. J., 1989, "Preemptive Bidding and the Role of the Medium of Exchange in Acquisitions," *Journal of Finance*, 44, 41–57.

Franks, J. R., R. S. Harris and C. Mayer, 1988, "Means of Payment in Takeovers: Results for the UK and US," In K. H. Wruck (Ed.), *Corporate Takeovers: Causes and Consequences*, NBER University of Chicago Press, Chicago, IL, pp. 221–258.

Hansen, R. G., 1987, "A Theory for the Choice of Exchange Medium in Mergers and Acquisitions," *Journal of Business*, 60, 75–95.

Harford, J., 1999, "Corporate Cash Reserves and Acquisitions," *Journal of Finance*, 54.

Hertzel, M. G. and R. L. Smith, 1993, "Market Discounts and Shareholder Gains for Placing Equity Privately," *Journal of Finance*, 48(2), 459–485.

Hovakimian, A., T. Opler and S. Titman, 2001, "The Debt-Equity Choice," *Journal of Financial and Quantitative Analysis*, 36(1), 1–24.

Jensen, M. C., 1986, "Agency Costs of Free Cash Flow, Corporate Finance, and Takeovers," *American Economic Review*, 76, 323–329.

Jung, K., Y. Kim and R. M. Stulz, 1996, "Timing, Investment Opportunities, Managerial Discretion, and the Security Issue Decision," *Journal of Financial Economics*, 42, 159–185.

Kato, K. and J. Schallheim, 1993, "Private Equity Financings in Japan and Corporate Grouping (Keiretsu)," *Pacific-Basin Finance Journal*, 1(3), 287–307.

Lang, L. H. P., R. M. Stulz and R. A. Walkling, 1989, "Managerial Performance, Tobin's q, and the Gains from Successful Tender Offers," *Journal of Financial Economics*, 24, 137–154.

Lang, L. H. P., R. M. Stulz and R. A. Walkling, 1991, "A Test of the Free Cash Flow Hypothesis: The Case of Bidder Returns," *Journal of Financial Economics*, 29(2), 315–336.

Lehn, K. and A. Poulsen, 1989, "Free Cash Flow and Stockholder Gains in Going Private Transactions," *Journal of Finance*, 44, 771–787.

Maloney, M. T., R. E. McCormick and M. L. Mitchell, 1993, "Managerial Decision Making and Capital Structure," *Journal of Business*, 66, 189–217.

Martin, K. J., 1996, "The Method of Payment in Corporate Acquisitions, Investment Opportunities, and Management Ownership," *Journal of Finance*, 51, 1227–1246.

McConnell, J. J. and C. J. Muscarella, 1985, "Corporate Capital Expenditure Decisions and the Market Value of the Firm," *Journal of Financial Economics*, 14, 399–422.

Miller, M. H. and F. Modigliani, 1958, "The Cost of Capital, Corporation Finance, and the Theory of Investment," *American Economic Review*, 48, 261–297.

Moeller, S. B. and F. P. Schlingemann, 2001, "External Growth of U.S. Corporations: A Comparison Between Cross-Border and Domestic Acquisitions," Working Paper, University of Pittsburgh.

Myers, S. C., 1977, "Determinants of Corporate Borrowing," *Journal of Financial Economics*, 5, 147–175.

Myers, S. C. and N. S. Majluf, 1984, "Corporate Financing and Investment Decisions When Firms Have Information that Investors Do Not Have," *Journal of Financial Economics*, 13, 187–221.

Opler, T. C., L. F. Pinkowitz, R. M. Stulz and R. Williamson, 1999, "The Determinants and Implications of Corporate Holdings of Liquid Assets," *Journal of Financial Economics*, 52, 3–46.

Roll, R., 1986, "The Hubris Hypothesis of Corporate Takeovers," *Journal of Business*, 59, 197–216.

Schwert, G. W., 2000, "Hostility in Takeover: In the Eyes of the Beholder?" *Journal of Finance*, 55(6), 2599–2640.

Servaes, H., 1991, "Tobin's q, Agency Costs and Corporate Control: An Empirical Analysis of Firm-Specific Parameters," *Journal of Finance*, 46, 409–419.

Smith, C. W., 1986, "Investment Banking and the Capital Acquisition Process," *Journal of Financial Economics*, 15, 3–29.

Smith, R. L., J. H. Kim, 1994, "The Combined Effects of Free Cash Flow and Financial Slack on Bidder and Target Returns," *Journal of Business*, 67, 281–310.

Stulz, R. M., 1990, "Managerial Discretion and Optimal Financing Policies," *Journal of Financial Economics*, 26, 3–27.

Travlos, N. G., 1987, "Corporate Takeover Bids, Method of Payment, and Bidding Firm's Stock Returns," *Journal of Finance*, 52, 943–963.

Wansley, J. W., W. R. Lane and H. C. Yang, 1983, "Abnormal Returns to Acquired Firms by Type of Acquisition and Method of Payment," *Financial Management*, 12(3), 16–22.

White, H., 1980, "A Heteroscedasticity-Consistent Covariance Matrix Estimator and a Direct Test for Heteroscedasticity," *Econometrica*, 48, 817–838.

Wruck, K. H., 1989, "Equity Ownership Concentration and Firm Value: Evidence from Private Equity Financings," *Journal of Financial Economics*, 23, 3–28.

Chapter 19

DO FIRMS HAVE LEVERAGE TARGETS? EVIDENCE FROM ACQUISITIONS[*]

JARRAD HARFORD

Foster School of Business, University of Washington, Seattle, Washington, USA

SANDY KLASA

Eller College of Management, University of Arizona, Tucson, Arizona, USA

NATHAN WALCOTT

College of Business, Washington State University, Pullman, Washington, USA

Contents

* We thank two anonymous referees, Tom Bates, Harry DeAngelo, Ed Dyl, Eliezer Fich, Shane Heitzman, Jean Helwege, Kathy Kahle, Jon Karpoff, Adam Kolasinski, Yun Li, Bill Maxwell, Wayne Mikkelson, Micah Officer, Bill Schwert, Mike Stegemoller, Jaime Zender, and seminar participants at Boston College, the Massachusetts Institute of Technology, the Chinese University of Hong Kong, Simon Fraser University, Texas Tech University, Tulane University, the University of Arizona, University of California at Irvine, University of Pittsburgh, Washington State University, and the 2006 Northern Finance Association conference for helpful comments. We also thank Shrikant Jategaonkar for research assistance.

This article originally appeared in the *Journal of Financial Economics*, Vol. 93, pp. 1–14 (2009).
Corporate Takeovers, Volume 2
Edited by B. Espen Eckbo
DOI: 10.1016/B978-0-12-381982-6.00020-3

Abstract

In the context of large acquisitions, we provide evidence on whether firms have target capital structures. We examine how deviations from these targets affect how bidders choose to finance acquisitions and how they adjust their capital structure following the acquisitions. We show that when a bidder's leverage is over its target level, it is less likely to finance the acquisition with debt and more likely to finance the acquisition with equity. Also, we find a positive association between the merger-induced changes in target and actual leverage, and we show that bidders incorporate more than two-thirds of the change to the merged firm's new target leverage. Following debt-financed acquisitions, managers actively move the firm back to its target leverage, reversing more than 75% of the acquisition's leverage effect within 5 years. Overall, our results are consistent with a model of capital structure that includes a target level and adjustment costs.

Keywords

capital structure, leverage targets, mergers and acquisitions, trade-off theory

JEL classifications: G32, G34

1. Introduction

Findings conflict on the extent to which firms have meaningful target capital structures, as hypothesized by the static trade-off theory. We provide evidence on the importance managers place on leverage targets by examining bidders that engage in takeovers with the potential to significantly affect their capital structure. Specifically, we study 1188 takeovers between 1981 and 2000 in which the target firm is at least 20% of the bidder's size. We refer to such acquisitions as large acquisitions. To determine how close a firm is to its target capital structure, we follow Kayhan and Titman (2007) and calculate a firm's leverage deviation each year as the difference between its actual debt ratio and its predicted debt ratio, which is our primary proxy for its unobservable target ratio.

Studying capital structure decisions around large acquisitions allows us to provide unique insights into these decisions. First, it enables us to determine the role of leverage targets in financing decisions that can radically alter a firm's capital structure. Second, analyzing postacquisition changes to a bidder's capital structure after debt-financed large acquisitions allows us to provide evidence on whether bidders actively rebalance their capital structures subsequent to these acquisitions. Fama and French (2005) show that new equity issues for stock-financed mergers are now more frequent than are seasoned equity offerings. Thus, studying the method of financing used for acquisitions broadly sheds light on firms' capital structure decisions.

Static trade-off theory hypothesizes that firms have target debt levels that are reached when firms trade off tax benefits of debt financing against financial distress costs (Modigliani and Miller, 1963), which broadly include default-related agency costs of debt (Jensen and Meckling, 1976; Myers, 1977; Stulz, 1990). Results on the empirical relevance of the concept of target leverage are mixed. For instance, Titman and Wessels (1988), Rajan and Zingales (1995), Graham (1996), and Hovakimian et al. (2001, 2004) show that firm characteristics such as firm size, growth opportunities, liquidation value of assets, and the marginal tax rate are related to debt ratios in ways supporting static trade-off theory. Also, Jalilvand and Harris (1984), Fama and French (2002), and Kayhan and Titman (2007) show that over time capital structure reverts back to target levels. Further, Leary and Roberts (2005) and Flannery and Rangan (2006) find that after accounting for adjustment costs the evidence is consistent with firms actively rebalancing their capital structures. However, a widely documented finding not supportive of traditional static trade-off theory predictions is that a negative association exists between past profitability and current debt ratios.[1] Also, inconsistent

---

[1] The finding of a negative association between profitability and leverage can be explained in the context of the dynamic version of the trade-off model (e.g., Fischer et al., 1989), in which firms allow their leverage ratios to fluctuate if costs of adjusting these ratios are greater than those from having a suboptimal capital structure. Evidence from Almeida and Campello (2007) that, after endogenizing investment decisions, a negative relation could exist between profitability and leverage is consistent with this dynamic trade-off theory explanation.

with static trade-off predictions, but supportive of the pecking order model prediction that firms have a preference for internal over external financing, Shyam-Sunder and Myers (1999) report that variations in external debt financing are mainly driven by the internal financing deficit and not by firm attempts to adjust leverage ratios toward target levels.[2] Finally, Baker and Wurgler (2002) and Welch (2004) provide evidence that changes to a firm's capital structure are mostly the result of its stock returns or cumulative attempts by the firm to time the market.

In this study, we find that, in the planning of large acquisitions, bidders give consideration to their target capital structure. The fraction of a deal that is paid for with cash versus equity is negatively associated with the acquirer's preacquisition leverage deviation. We confirm that most large acquisitions paid for with cash are financed with new debt issues and that the cash component of deals paid for with a mix of cash and equity is also financed with new debt issues. Thus, a bidder is unlikely to pay for a significant amount of a large acquisition with cash and take on more debt when it is already overleveraged.[3]

Further supporting the concept of target leverage, we show that acquirers are more likely to engage in a leverage-increasing acquisition transaction if their target debt ratio also increases as a result of the transaction. In fact, on average acquirers incorporate more than two-thirds of the change to the merged firm's new target leverage through the structure of the acquisition financing.

We complement our analysis of deal payment decisions by examining how the bidding firm adjusts its resulting capital structure in the years following the acquisition. For cash deals we find that, immediately subsequent to the deal, bidders become overleveraged by about eight cents per dollar of assets. However, during each of the 5 years subsequent to these deals this positive leverage deviation is reduced. By the fifth year after cash deals, bidders have lowered their leverage deviation to less than two cents per dollar of assets. Thus, subsequent to important changes to their leverage, firms rebalance their capital structure, consistent with a model of capital structure that allows for costly adjustment.

We also investigate what drives bidders to actively rebalance their capital structure subsequent to cash deals. We find that the more positive a bidder's preacquisition leverage deviation, the more likely it is to reverse the effect of the acquisition on its leverage. This is consistent with our findings suggesting it is suboptimal for bidders with positive leverage deviations to make leverage-increasing cash acquisitions. Further supporting static trade-off theory and the concept of target leverage, we show that the higher a bidder's ex ante bankruptcy risk, the more it reduces its leverage deviation following the acquisition.

---

[2] Frank and Goyal (2003) reexamine this issue and conclude that net equity issues, not net debt issues, closely track the financial deficit, contrary to the predictions of the pecking order theory.

[3] See Bharadwaj and Shivdasani (2003) for additional evidence that most cash offers are debt-financed.

Finally, we investigate a refinement of the predictions of static trade-off theory. The Myers (1977) model demonstrates that the potential for underinvestment makes it more costly for a growth firm to be overleveraged than for a mature firm. He discusses the fact that the problem exists due to costly contracting. We find that the relations discussed earlier are strongest for firms with higher growth opportunities. They pay greater attention than average to their preacquisition leverage deviation and to the combined firm's new target capital structure when financing the acquisition. These findings suggest that it is especially important for firms with larger growth prospects to keep their leverage close to target levels and in particular to avoid positive leverage deviations. Consistent with this proposition, Graham and Harvey (2001) report that chief financial officers of high-growth firms place significant importance on the maintenance of a target debt-to-equity ratio.

In sum, our results concerning financing decisions in large acquisitions imply that firms attempt to minimize deviations between actual and target debt levels. The evidence that during the years subsequent to cash deals, bidders actively move their leverage back toward the target further supports the static trade-off theory prediction that firms have leverage targets. In addition, our results indicate that attempts to reduce contracting costs are important determinants of firms' decisions to maintain a target capital structure.

Our findings also increase the understanding of what determines the method of payment used in takeovers. Despite the inherent connection between the method of payment and the method of financing the acquisition, little evidence exists on the extent to which a firm considers its preacquisition leverage and the potential change in its leverage resulting from the acquisition when deciding which method of payment to use. Our findings suggest that capital structure considerations are an important part of the method of payment decision.

The remainder of the paper is organized as follows. Section 2 develops testable hypotheses. Section 3 discusses methodological issues. Section 4 presents our empirical results. Finally, Section 5 concludes.

2. Hypotheses and testable predictions

An important hypothesis within the static trade-off theory is that firms try to minimize deviations between actual and target debt levels and only tolerate such deviations because it is costly to correct them. We refer to this hypothesis as the target capital structure hypothesis. The empirical analyses in this study are designed to test this hypothesis in the context of large acquisitions that have the potential to significantly affect a bidder's capital structure. A testable prediction of this hypothesis is that a bidder's deviation from its target capital structure impacts how it finances acquisitions and thus the method of payment used for acquisitions. A second testable prediction of this hypothesis is that the potential for an acquisition to change a bidder's target leverage is incorporated in the acquisition financing decision. Finally, a third testable prediction of this hypothesis, is that if an acquisition significantly increases a bidder's leverage deviation, the effect is not permanent. Instead, during the period subsequent to the acquisition, the bidder adjusts its debt level back toward its target level.

Our research design also allows us to test whether the size of a firm's growth opportunity set is related to the firm's attempts to minimize the deviation from its target debt level. In Myers (1977), firms with more growth opportunities suffer from the largest underinvestment problems if their debt level becomes too high. This problem exists because it is too costly to contract around it or renegotiate existing debt contracts as needed. A testable prediction of this contracting costs hypothesis is that the importance of minimizing positive deviations between a firm's actual and target debt level is most pronounced for firms with many growth opportunities.

Finally, prior work shows that the method of payment choice is driven by factors such as growth opportunities (Martin, 1996), agency considerations (Harford, 1999; Jensen, 1986), equity overvaluation (Rhodes-Kropf and Viswanathan, 2004; Shleifer and Vishny, 2003), the need to mitigate information asymmetry about the bidder or target (Eckbo et al., 1990; Fishman, 1989; Hansen, 1987), or strategic considerations in the face of potential competition for the target (Berkovitch and Narayanan, 1990). Our hypotheses will only find support if financing effects are strong enough to have a role in the method of payment choice in spite of these other factors. Our empirical specifications attempt to control for the effects hypothesized in earlier work by including the empirical constructs suggested by this work.

3. Sample and methodology

In this section we discuss our sample. Also, we report how the leverage deviation variable is calculated.

3.1. Sample construction and description

We identify the takeovers in our sample from the Securities Data Corporation (SDC) US Mergers and Acquisitions database. Takeovers are announced and completed between the beginning of 1981 and the end of 2000 (5 years of postacquisition data are needed for our analysis). To be included in our sample, the relative size of the market value of the target's assets to the bidder's assets must be at least 20%. Also, because we need to determine the proportion of deals that are paid for with cash versus equity, we study only deals for which SDC codes the method of payment as being only cash, only equity, or a mix of cash and equity. For deals in which the method of payment is coded as being a mix of cash and equity, we exclude those deals for which we are unable to determine from SDC deal transaction reports the fractions of the payment that are paid with cash and equity. This results in the exclusion of about 45%

Table 1

Method of payment, multiple acquirers, and target public status characteristics

The sample consists of 1188 takeovers that are announced and take place between the beginning of 1981 and the end of 2000 in which the relative size of the target to the bidder is at least 20%.

Deal characteristics	Fraction of sample
Panel A. Method of payment characteristics	
Cash	0.51
Equity	0.32
A mix of cash and equity	0.17
Panel B. Multiple acquirer characteristics	
Fraction of acquisitions made by acquirers making one large acquisition	0.52
Fraction of acquisitions made by acquirers making two large acquisitions	0.25
Fraction of acquisitions made by acquirers making three or more large acquisitions	0.23
Panel C. Target public status characteristics	
Public firm	0.33
Subsidiary of another firm	0.34
Private firm	0.33

of the deals in the mixed deal group (12% of the total sample).[4] Finally, we require that during the year prior to the acquisition we have necessary Compustat and Center for Research in Security Prices (CRSP) data for the acquirer. This leaves us with a sample of 1188 acquisitions.

Panel A in Table 1 shows that the large acquisitions we study are paid for with only cash and only common stock 51% and 32% of the time, respectively. A payment consisting of a mix of equity and cash is used 17% of the time.

Panel B in Table 1 provides information on the number of large acquisitions made by single versus multiple acquirers over our sample period. Prior work such as Schipper and Thompson (1983), Fuller et al. (2002), and Klasa and Stegemoller (2007) shows that many bidders are frequent acquirers who make a series of acquisitions over several years. It is important to understand the frequency with which bidders make large acquisitions when considering the extent to which bidders are likely to rebalance their capital structure toward a target level subsequent to such acquisitions. Panel B shows that 52% of the acquisitions we study are made by bidders who make only one large acquisition over our sample period. Also, this panel shows that 25% of the acquisitions in our sample are made by bidders who make two large acquisitions, while the remaining 23% of acquisitions are made by bidders who make three or more large acquisitions over our 20-year sample period. Finally, Panel C in Table 1 provides information on the public status of the target. The targets are about equally divided among public firms, subsidiaries of another firm, and private firms.

---

[4] For robustness, we include these deals in tests in which we do not need to know the actual breakdown of the acquisition consideration. Our inferences are unchanged.

3.2. Measurement of the leverage deviation

The leverage deviation is defined as the difference between a firm's actual and predicted market leverage in a given year.[5] To calculate a firm's predicted leverage we use the same tobit regression model as in Kayhan and Titman (2007), except that, in contrast to their model in which all variables are measured during the prior year, we consider the effect of future year profitability on leverage.[6] Our analysis also differs from Kayhan and Titman (2007) in that we estimate separate annual regressions to predict leverage instead of estimating a pooled regression model. Due to the length of our sample period, we believe that the use of separate annual regression models is more appropriate for our analysis. For instance, the tax benefits of debt vary over our sample period due to changes in corporate income tax brackets and rates. Also, financial distress costs resulting from debt vary due to time-varying macroeconomic conditions over our sample period.

Below we describe the independent variables appearing in our model of target leverage. These variables regularly appear as determinants of capital structure choice in the literature (e.g., Flannery and Rangan, 2006; Hovakimian et al., 2001, 2004; Rajan and Zingales, 1995). To increase the likelihood that causality runs from the independent variables to debt levels, and not vice versa, all independent variables, except for profitability, are lagged variables.

Future year operating income/total assets: We consider a firm's future year profitability because the classic prediction from the static trade-off theory is that, after trading off tax benefits of debt against financial distress costs, firms with higher expected future profitability hold more debt. If we regress current leverage ratios on lagged profitability, the coefficient on profitability would partly reflect the effect of unexpected profitability on a firm's leverage ratio, which could cause problems in making interpretations of the results of tests that use a bidder's leverage deviation. Measuring expected profitability with a firm's future year profitability allows us to avoid such problems.[7]

According to the dynamic version of the trade-off theory (e.g., Fischer et al., 1989) many firms that are profitable could have low debt levels if for these firms costs of adjusting debt levels exceed those of having a suboptimal capital structure. Likewise, the pecking order model predicts that because firms could have a preference for internal over external capital, more profitable firms tend to have lower debt ratios. Also, as pointed out by Flannery and Rangan (2006), Kayhan and Titman (2007), and

[5] We focus on market leverage instead of book leverage because almost all theoretical predictions related to leverage are made with respect to market leverage. Further, most recent related work such as Hovakimian et al. (2001), Welch (2004), Leary and Roberts (2005), and Flannery and Rangan (2006) focuses on market leverage.

[6] In Appendix, we tabulate the results of our estimation of a model of market leverage.

[7] Nonetheless, we find that our results are robust to using lagged instead of future year operating income/book assets as an independent variable in our model of target leverage.

others, product market concerns could result in a negative association between profitability and leverage. This would occur if higher profitability is an indication of less competition in an industry. If so, then more profitable firms could find it optimal to avoid high debt levels that could constrain them and curtail their ability to effectively respond to competitive threats such as entry into their lines of business and predatory behavior on the part of oligopolistic rivals (Bolton and Scharfstein, 1990; Campello, 2006; Chevalier, 1995; Fudenberg and Tirole, 1986; Phillips, 1995). Consistent with adjustment costs and product market effects being important capital structure considerations, almost all existing empirical evidence shows a negative association between firm profitability and debt levels.

Prior year natural logarithm of sales: Firms with higher sales are expected to be larger firms that hold more debt because they have easier access to external capital and a higher debt capacity resulting from greater firm diversification (geographic, product line, or other) that tends to come with size.

Prior year net property, plant, and equipment/total assets: Firms with more tangible assets can more easily use their assets as collateral for loans. Thus, such firms have a greater debt capacity.

Prior year market-to-book assets: A higher value for market-to-book assets indicates that a firm has larger growth opportunities. Because firms with larger growth opportunity sets are more likely to suffer from underinvestment problems resulting from a high debt load (Myers, 1977), market-to-book assets is expected to be negatively associated with leverage.

Prior year research and development expenses/sales: Firms with higher research and development expenses are expected to have larger growth opportunities and derive a greater proportion of their value from intangibles. Hence, such firms are predicted to hold less debt. Further, firms that are more research and development-intensive are more likely to produce unique or specialized products. Customers, suppliers, and workers of firms that produce such products are likely to suffer the most in the event that a firm goes out of business (Titman, 1984; Titman and Wessels, 1988). Workers and suppliers of such firms are likely to have developed specific skills, while the customers of these firms could find it difficult to obtain alternative servicing of the unique products made by these firms. Thus, the degree to which a firm manufactures specialized or unique products is expected to be negatively associated with a firm's debt level.

Prior year dummy variable for if a firm has no research and development expenses: Many firms have no reported research and development expenses. To differentiate these observations, a dummy variable for these firms is included in the model of target leverage. Its inclusion also creates more flexibility for the form of the R&D effect described above.

Prior year selling expenses/sales: Firms with larger selling expenses are expected to produce more specialized products. Thus, a negative association is predicted between selling expenses and debt levels.

Fama and French (1997) industry dummies: As in Kayhan and Titman (2007), to control for other firm characteristics that could be common to firms in a particular industry we include industry dummies in the model predicting target leverage. These dummy variables correspond to the 48 industries classified by Fama and French (1997).[8]

4. Empirical findings

In this section we first report univariate statistics on bidder and target firm characteristics. Next, we examine the association between the preacquisition leverage deviation and whether a bidder finances a large acquisition with debt or equity. Finally, we investigate how the leverage deviation evolves prior and subsequent to a large acquisition.

4.1. Bidder and target firm characteristics

Table 2 provides median values for selected bidder and target firm characteristics. Panel A shows that the market value of assets of bidders paying with cash is not different from that of bidders paying with equity. However, bidders that pay with a mix of cash and equity tend to be smaller. The higher ratios of market-to-book assets for bidders paying with equity shown in Panel A suggests that such bidders have larger growth prospects, consistent with Martin (1996). Panel A also reports that median cash/total book assets is 0.14 for equity deals, but only 0.06 and 0.08 for cash and mixed deals, respectively. This univariate result is likely due to the correlation between growth prospects and equity financing of acquisitions. High-growth firms tend to hold more cash (see Kim et al., 1998; Mikkelson and Partch, 2003; Opler et al., 1999). The lower cash holdings for bidders who pay for a large acquisition with cash or with a mix of stock and cash suggests that these bidders need to use debt to finance their acquisitions.

Panel A shows that market leverage, defined as total book value of debt scaled by book value of debt plus market value of equity is, 0.23 for cash deals, 0.20 for mixed

---

[8] We examine whether the results of the regression models in the paper are robust to alternative benchmarks for target leverage. First, we consider the effect of the volatility of firm cash flows on a firm's target debt level. We investigate this issue because firms with more uncertain future cash flows could choose to hold less debt, and it is possible that the industry dummy variables included in our model of target leverage do not fully control for the riskiness of future cash flows. We examine whether including the firm-level standard deviation of operating income/total assets over the prior 5 years as an independent variable in our model of target leverage affects our results. Although the use of this variable results in a loss of almost 20% of sample observations, we find that the results of all the regression models in the paper are robust to the inclusion of this additional independent variable to our model of target leverage. We also find that our results are robust to a simple model of benchmark leverage in which the median leverage of the other firms in a firm's industry is used as the firm's target leverage. We calculate this measure using two different definitions for industry. First, we define a firm's industry according to which of the 48 industries classified by Fama and French (1997) the firm belongs to. Next, we define industry using a firm's two-digit Standard Industrial Classification (SIC) code.

Table 2

Bidder and target characteristics

The sample consists of 1188 takeovers that are announced and take place between the beginning of 1981 and the end of 2000 in which the relative size of the target to the bidder is at least 20%. All accounting variables except for net debt issues are measured during the fiscal year prior to the year when a takeover is completed. Market value of assets is book value of liabilities plus market value of equity. CPI is the consumer price index. Market leverage equals long-term debt plus debt in current liabilities scaled by market value of assets. Leverage deviation is actual market leverage minus predicted market leverage from a regression model predicting market leverage. Merger-induced change in the leverage deviation is the change in the leverage deviation from year −1 to 0 around the acquisition, where year 0 is the fiscal year that includes the effective date of the acquisition. Net debt issues are long-term debt issuance minus long-term debt reduction scaled by market value of assets. Relative size of target to bidder is calculated as market value of target assets/market value of bidder assets. There are 243, 85, 131, and 27 observations used to calculate the target firm leverage deviation for all, cash, equity, and mixed deals, respectively. ***, **, and * represent significance at the 1%, 5%, and 10% level, respectively, for two-tailed Wilcoxon rank-sum tests to determine whether distributions differ between cash and equity deals or two-tailed *t*-tests to determine whether mean values differ between cash and equity deals.

Bidder and target firm characteristics	All deals	Cash payment	Equity payment	Mixed payment
Panel A. Median bidder characteristics				
CPI-adjusted market value of assets (millions)	99.71	110.46	131.44	51.46
Market-to-book assets	1.46	1.30***	1.85	1.41
Operating income/book assets	0.13	0.14***	0.11	0.11
Cash/total book assets	0.07	0.06***	0.14	0.08
Market leverage	0.17	0.23***	0.08	0.20
Preacquisition leverage deviation	−0.05	−0.04***	−0.07	−0.03
Merger-induced change in the leverage deviation	0.04	0.12***	−0.01	0.04
Net debt issues	0.05	0.15***	0.00	0.06
Panel B. Median target characteristics				
CPI-adjusted target value (millions)	53.50	55.37	62.32	33.45
Relative size of target to bidder	0.39	0.36***	0.45	0.44
Target firm leverage deviation	−0.04	−0.04	−0.04	0.01

deals, but only 0.08 for equity deals. Given that bidders who pay with equity tend to have larger growth opportunities, it is perhaps not surprising that these bidders are less leveraged. Also, this at least partially reflects an industry effect, where bidders from low leverage industries making horizontal acquisitions are more likely to use equity to fund any investment, including an acquisition.

Panel A also provides information about acquirer firm leverage deviations. The preacquisition year leverage deviation for all deal groups is negative. Specifically, the median leverage deviation is −0.04, −0.07, and −0.03 for cash, equity, and mixed deals, respectively. This evidence suggests most bidders making large acquisitions have unused debt capacity. The median merger-induced change to a firm's leverage deviation, the change in the leverage deviation from year-end −1 to 0, where year 0 is the fiscal year that includes the effective date of the acquisition, is 0.12, −0.01, and

0.04 for cash, equity, and mixed deals, respectively. Also, net debt issues during the acquisition year, defined as long-term debt issuance minus long-term debt reduction scaled by market value of assets, is 0.15, 0.00, and 0.06 for cash, equity, and mixed deals, respectively. Ghosh and Jain (2000) show a general increase in leverage following mergers, which they attribute to increased debt capacity. Here, we find an increase in debt only for deals involving cash as a method of payment.

The leverage deviation and net debt issue statistics establish that large acquisitions paid for with cash are debt financed and result in important increases to a bidder's leverage deviation. They also indicate that large acquisitions that are stock-financed do not markedly affect a bidder's capital structure. As long as the target firm is not significantly overleveraged itself, a stock swap acquisition with the assumption of target firm debt would not make the bidder overleveraged. This is true for the median equity bidder because the acquisition does not increase its financial leverage. The data further show that the cash payment component of mixed payment bids in our sample is likely debt financed. For these deals the median values of the merger-induced change in a firm's leverage deviation and net debt issues fall between those for all equity and all cash deals.[9]

Finally, Panel B in Table 2 provides information on target characteristics. The relative size of the market value of the target's assets to the market value of the bidder's assets is higher for equity than cash deals: 0.45 versus 0.36. For mixed deals this ratio is 0.44. Panel B also reports information on the preacquisition year leverage deviation for 243 targets that are public and have the required Compustat data to calculate this variable. We find that these target firms are slightly underleveraged when only cash or only equity is the method of payment and that they are very close to their predicted leverage when the method of payment is a mix of cash and equity.

4.2. The choice between cash and equity

Table 3 presents the results of multivariate analyses that examine whether the preacquisition leverage deviation can explain financing choices for large acquisitions.[10] The two-sided tobit models in Table 3 explain the fraction of the deal paid for with cash. The dependent variable in these models is truncated at zero and one. Because, as shown in Table 2, debt financing of cash offers or the cash component of mixed deals is the norm, the target capital structure hypothesis predicts that the fraction of the deal paid for with cash is negatively associated with an acquirer's preacquisition leverage deviation.

To control for bidder firm size we include the natural logarithm of consumer price index-adjusted market value of assets. The leverage deviation and actual leverage are

---

[9] For evidence on how issuing equity and debt simultaneously relates to target capital structure in a context other than that for large acquisitions, see Hovakimian et al. (2004).

[10] We acknowledge that a group of bidders likely chooses to not make large acquisitions due to capital structure considerations. Consequently, our research design allows us to make inferences only about the effect of capital structure considerations on large acquisitions that are completed.

Table 3

Explaining the fraction of the deal paid for with cash

The two models are two-sided tobit models explaining the fraction of the deal that is paid for with cash in which the dependent variable is truncated at zero and one. The sample consists of 1188 takeovers that are announced and take place between the beginning of 1981 and the end of 2000 in which the relative size of the target to the bidder is at least 20%. All accounting variables are calculated as of the fiscal year prior to the year when a takeover is completed. Market leverage equals long-term debt plus debt in current liabilities scaled by market value of assets. Leverage deviation is actual market leverage minus predicted market leverage from a regression model predicting market leverage. Market-adjusted 1-year preannouncement bidder return is measured from month -13 to -1 prior to the initial takeover announcement. 12-month change in leading economic indicators is the 12-month change in the index of leading economic indicators from month -13 to -1 prior to the initial takeover announcement. Relative size of target to bidder is calculated as market value of target assets/market value of bidder assets. CPI is the consumer price index. Significance levels for whether estimates are different from zero are in parentheses.

Model	(1)	(2)
Intercept	−0.927 (0.006)	−0.457 (0.200)
Preacquisition year leverage deviation	−3.962 (0.000)	−1.645 (0.124)
Market leverage	5.345 (0.000)	4.200 (0.000)
Market-to-book assets		−0.232 (0.001)
Preacquisition year leverage deviation × market-to-book assets		−1.025 (0.014)
Market-adjusted 1-year preannouncement bidder return	−0.258 (0.000)	−0.229 (0.000)
12-month change in leading economic indicators	−0.022 (0.490)	−0.021 (0.494)
Cash/book assets	−0.278 (0.509)	−0.208 (0.622)
Natural logarithm of CPI-adjusted market value of assets	−0.001 (0.974)	0.029 (0.458)
Relative size of target to bidder	−0.093 (0.182)	−0.092 (0.183)
Target is a private firm dummy	0.725 (0.000)	0.732 (0.000)
Target is a subsidiary dummy	2.205 (0.000)	2.168 (0.000)
Pseudo-R^2	0.162	0.168
Number of observations	1188	1188

positively correlated. To ensure that in our regression models the preacquisition leverage deviation does not proxy for preacquisition actual leverage and to ease interpretation of the leverage deviation variable by explicitly holding the level of debt constant, we control for actual leverage. To control for timing effects whereby bidders would be more likely to pay with equity following an abnormal run-up in their stock price, we include the market-adjusted 1-year preannouncement bidder return. Because prior work suggests that firms are more likely to issue equity when macroeconomic conditions are more favorable and, as a result, asymmetric information problems are lower, we include the change in the index of leading economic indicators during the 12 months prior to an acquisition announcement.[11] We also include cash/

---

[11] We control for the preacquisition change in the index of leading economic indicators instead of the value of the index of leading economic indicators itself because although from month to month the values of this index could increase or decrease, over the long-term horizon the values of the index trend markedly upward.

book assets as an explanatory variable because the pecking order model predicts that, as a result of adverse selection costs, firms prefer to finance their investments with internal slack or debt rather than equity. Thus, this model predicts that firms with higher cash balances are more likely to pay for a large fraction of an acquisition with cash. The relative size of the target to the bidder is used to control for the likelihood that, when a target is larger relative to the bidder, this could increase the bidder's propensity to pay for the target with equity. Finally, we control for the public status of the target as this could influence the method of payment used for the acquisition. Also, more information asymmetry is likely regarding the value of private or subsidiary targets and there is less competition for these targets. Thus, controlling for the public status of the target allows us to partially control for these factors, which can affect the method of payment (see Berkovitch and Narayanan, 1990; Eckbo et al., 1990; Fishman, 1989; Hansen, 1987).

The results for the first model in Table 3 show that the preacquisition year leverage deviation is significantly negatively associated with the fraction of the acquisition paid for with cash.[12] Further, the magnitude of the coefficient on the preacquisition leverage deviation variable indicates that this relation is not only statistically significant, but also economically significant. The coefficient on this variable suggests that a one cent increase in a firm's leverage deviation per dollar of assets reduces the percentage of the deal that is cash-financed by approximately 4% points. Thus, when a firm is already overleveraged it has a lower propensity to pay for a large acquisition with cash or a mix of cash and equity and take on even more debt. This result supports the proposition that firms have leverage targets and that these targets affect financing choices in large acquisitions.

The results for the first model in Table 3 also show significant relations between the fraction of the payment that is cash and several of the other independent variables. As expected, a significant positive relation exists between preacquisition market leverage and the extent to which a large acquisition is paid for with cash. Also, highlighting the importance of controlling for the public status of the target, we find significant positive relations between the fraction of the deal that is paid for with cash and whether a target is a private firm or a subsidiary.

A significant negative relation also exists between the market-adjusted 1-year preannouncement bidder stock return and the fraction of the deal that is paid for with cash. This suggests that market timing could play a role in explaining financing choices for large acquisitions. To further examine the plausibility of a market timing explanation for these financing choices, we reestimate the first model of Table 3 after adding the 12- or 24-month postacquisition equally weighted stock returns of the firms sharing the same two-digit standard industrial classification code as the sample firm (raw or market-adjusted). However, in untabulated results, we find no evidence that

---

[12] The finding of a significant negative coefficient on the preacquisition year leverage deviation variable is robust to including year dummies in the tobit models.

industry stock return performance is worse subsequent to large acquisitions in which a larger fraction of the payment is equity.

Finally, the results for the first model in Table 3 show that a bidder's preacquisition cash/book assets ratio is unrelated to the fraction of the payment that is cash. It is interesting to consider this and the other results in light of the Harford (1999) investigation of acquisitions by cash-rich firms. We study only large acquisitions in which the target is at least 20% of the bidder's size. Even in Harford's sample of cash-rich firms, it would be unusual for a bidder to be able to pay for such an acquisition out of cash reserves. Harford concludes that managers with excess cash at their disposal tend to make value-decreasing acquisitions. He argues that the excess cash reserves free these managers from the discipline of the capital markets during the transaction. In contrast, the managers of the bidder firms we study must access the capital markets. Our results show that, in these cases, the firm's target capital structure is an important consideration. Further, our later results in Tables 5 and 6 establish that, when firms become overlevered as a result of a large acquisition, managers work to quickly relieve this constraint.

The second model in Table 3 provides evidence on whether the negative relation between the preacquisition leverage deviation and the fraction of a large acquisition that is paid for with cash is more pronounced for bidders with larger growth opportunity sets, as it should be according to the contracting costs hypothesis. Specifically, in this model we also include the ratio of market-to-book assets and the interaction of this variable with the preacquisition leverage deviation. Because bidders with greater investment opportunities are more likely to suffer from underinvestment problems as a result of having too high a debt load, they could be more likely to give importance to maintaining target debt levels. Consistent with this proposition, the results for the second model in Table 3 show that the coefficient on the interaction variable is significantly negative.[13] The model in Myers (1977) would predict that this effect should be stronger for overlevered versus underlevered high market-to-book firms. In untabulated tests, we confirm that, while the effect exists for all high market-to-book firms, it is twice as strong for those with a positive leverage deviation.

4.3. Explaining the change in leverage resulting from large acquisitions

Our results so far show that, when deciding whether to finance a large acquisition with debt or equity, managers behave as if they have a target capital structure. In this section, we explain the actual change in leverage resulting from an acquisition to

---

[13] We examine whether the Table 3 evidence that acquirers with positive preacquisition leverage deviations are less likely to finance a large acquisition with debt is robust to estimating the debt versus equity financing decision using a multinomial logit model. Specifically, we use a multinomial logit model that estimates the effect of the preacquisition leverage deviation and the control variables appearing in Table 3 on the decision to pay for a large acquisition only with cash, with a mix of cash and equity, or only with equity. The results of this analysis provide consistent evidence that a positive leverage deviation makes it significantly more likely that a bidder would have a preference to finance a large acquisition with equity rather than debt.

provide further evidence on the existence and importance of a target capital structure. We are particularly interested in the relation between this actual change in leverage and the merger-induced change to the acquiring firm's target leverage. Under the trade-off theory, the method of payment decision incorporates how the merger changes the firm's target level of leverage. Specifically, the more a large acquisition increases an acquirer's target leverage level, the more likely should the acquirer be to finance the acquisition in a manner that increases firm leverage. Consequently, we expect a positive association between the merger-induced changes in actual and target leverage. If the bidding firm were completely unconstrained in structuring the method of payment, then the target capital structure hypothesis would predict a coefficient of one on this variable.[14]

The models in Table 3 test whether bidding management takes its pre-bid leverage deviation into account when structuring the bid. The specifications in Table 4 test whether they look ahead to the target capital structure of the combined firm. It also allows us to further examine the extent to which the preacquisition deviation affects whether a large acquisition is financed in a leverage-increasing way. Finally, it enables us to determine the economic significance, if any, of this deviation on the change in leverage resulting from the acquisition.

Table 4 presents results of models that explain the change in market leverage from year -1 to 0 around large acquisitions, where year 0 is the fiscal year that includes the effective date of the acquisition. The primary explanatory variables of interest in this model are the merger-induced change in the firm's target leverage level and the preacquisition leverage deviation. The former variable is measured as predicted market leverage in year $+1$ subsequent to a large acquisition (from our annual cross-sectional regressions predicting market leverage) minus predicted market leverage in year -1. We use year $+1$ instead of year 0 to calculate the change in predicted market leverage because our model uses a number of firm characteristics in year t to predict leverage in year $t + 1$. Year 0 is the first year-end in which the combined firm characteristics are available. The control variables used in Table 4 models are the same as those that are used in Table 3 models.

The results from the first model in Table 4 show a significant positive association between the merger-induced changes to the acquiring firm's actual and target leverage levels. Thus, managers are more likely to structure a leverage-increasing acquisition

---

[14] The prior literature provides insights into constraints that a bidder could face when structuring the method of payment used for a large acquisition. For instance, Hansen (1987) shows that in situations of two-sided information asymmetry in which both the bidder and target have private information about their value, information problems can be resolved through the use of stock payment. Berkovitch and Narayanan (1990) model how competition for a target affects the method of payment used for takeovers. They find results suggesting that, in cases in which multiple bidders compete for a target, if a bidder increases the fraction of its offer that is cash, this raises the probability the bidder wins the takeover contest. Finally, the literature on how market timing affects the method of payment used in takeovers (e.g., Rhodes-Kropf and Viswanathan, 2004; Shleifer and Vishny, 2003) suggests that, if a bidder's management feels its equity is undervalued by the market, the bidder is reluctant to pay for a large acquisition with stock.

Table 4

Explaining the merger-induced change in market leverage

The two models are ordinary least squares models explaining the change in market leverage from year −1 to 0 around an acquisition, where year 0 is the fiscal year that includes the effective date of the acquisition. The sample consists of 1188 takeovers that are announced and take place between the beginning of 1981 and the end of 2000 in which the relative size of the target to the bidder is at least 20%. All accounting variables are calculated as of the fiscal year prior to the year when a takeover is completed. Market leverage equals long-term debt plus debt in current liabilities scaled by market value of assets. Leverage deviation is actual market leverage minus predicted market leverage from a regression model predicting market leverage. Merger-induced change in target market leverage is the change in predicted market leverage from year −1 to +1 around an acquisition. Market-adjusted 1-year preannouncement bidder return is measured from month −13 to −1 prior to the initial takeover announcement. 12-month change in leading economic indicators is the 12-month change in the index of leading economic indicators from month −13 to −1 prior to the initial takeover announcement. Relative size of target to bidder is calculated as market value of target assets/market value of bidder assets. CPI is the consumer price index. Significance levels in parentheses for whether estimates are different from zero are corrected using the Huber/White/sandwich estimator of variance.

Model	(1)	(2)
Intercept	0.046 (0.061)	0.060 (0.017)
Merger-induced change in target market leverage	0.677 (0.000)	0.648 (0.000)
Preacquisition year leverage deviation	−0.340 (0.000)	−0.255 (0.000)
Market leverage	0.017 (0.735)	−0.030 (0.584)
Market-to-book assets		−0.007 (0.109)
Merger-induced change in target market leverage × market-to-book assets		0.019 (0.038)
Preacquisition year leverage deviation × market-to-book assets		−0.028 (0.000)
Market-adjusted 1-year preannouncement bidder return	−0.024 (0.000)	−0.023 (0.000)
12-month change in leading economic indicators	−0.001 (0.664)	−0.001 (0.675)
Cash/book assets	−0.007 (0.835)	−0.003 (0.929)
Natural logarithm of CPI-adjusted market value of assets	−0.000 (0.925)	0.001 (0.652)
Relative size of target to bidder	0.005 (0.395)	0.005 (0.385)
Target is a private firm dummy	0.007 (0.587)	0.054 (0.640)
Target is a subsidiary dummy	0.054 (0.000)	0.054 (0.000)
R^2-adjusted	0.212	0.216
Number of observations	1030	1030

transaction if their firm's target leverage increases as a result of the acquisition. Further, the magnitude of the coefficient on the merger-induced change in target market leverage variable indicates that, in financing large acquisitions, bidders incorporate more than two-thirds of the change to the merged firm's target leverage. This further supports the hypothesis that managers make efforts to keep their firm's debt close to its target level.

The findings for this model also show the capital structure outcome of the previously documented negative relation between the preacquisition year leverage deviation and the acquisition financing. The effect is economically important. For instance, if the preacquisition year leverage deviation per dollar of assets is ten cents higher, the merger-induced change in market leverage is reduced by approximately 3.4 cents per dollar of assets.

In the second model in Table 4 we test the contracting costs hypothesis by including as additional explanatory variables the acquirer's ratio of market-to-book assets and the interaction of this ratio with the merger-induced change to the acquirer's target leverage and the preacquisition leverage deviation. We find a significant positive coefficient on the first interaction variable and a significant negative coefficient on the second interaction variable. Thus, acquirers with larger growth opportunities incorporate a larger fraction of the merged firm's new target leverage. Also, such acquirers are even less likely to structure a deal for a large acquisition in a leverage-increasing way if they are already overleveraged. These results provide further support to the hypothesis that firms with larger growth prospects place greater importance on minimizing deviations between actual and target debt levels.

4.4. Evolution of leverage deviations and financial deficits around acquisitions

Table 5 presents median statistics on the evolution of leverage deviations and net debt issues over the period from years −5 to +5 around a large acquisition. To make these measures comparable from year to year from the preacquisition year onward, we provide statistics only for takeovers made by bidders who remain on Compustat over the years −1 to +5 around a large acquisition.[15] Panels A and C present results for large acquisitions made by bidders who either make only one such acquisition over our sample period or are making their first large acquisition in our sample period. Because Table 1 shows that almost half of large acquisitions are made by acquirers who make multiple large acquisitions over our sample period we also provide results in Panels B and D of Table 5 for those acquirers who make only one large acquisition over our sample period. This allows us to observe the evolution of leverage deviations during the 5 years after a large acquisition after removing the effect of any subsequent large acquisitions on an acquirer's leverage deviation.

Panel A in Table 5 confirms Table 2's finding that, during the preacquisition year, the majority of sample firms are underleveraged. The leverage deviation for all acquirers, acquirers that pay with cash only, and acquirers that pay with equity only is approximately −7 cents per dollar of assets. For acquirers that pay with cash this contrasts with the findings in Table 2 of −4 cents per dollar of assets for the entire sample of cash bidders. The difference is due to the fact that in this table we require that the bid be the firm's first during the sample period. Comparing the tables, we see that

---

[15] Of the observations that are dropped from the analysis for acquirers paying with cash only, about half are acquired, about a quarter do not have sufficient data to calculate the leverage deviation in at least one of the years, four went bankrupt, and the rest are delisted for not meeting exchange requirements (such as price level and insufficient capital).

Table 5

Median leverage and net debt issues from years −5 to +5

The sample consists of 1188 takeovers that are announced and take place between the beginning of 1981 and the end of 2000 in which the relative size of the target to the bidder is at least 20%. Results are only presented for acquisitions in which the acquiring firm remains in Compustat from years −1 to +5 around the acquisition year, where year 0 is the fiscal year that includes the effective date of the acquisition. Panels A and C provide results for acquisitions made by acquirers that make only one large acquisition over our sample period or for the first large acquisition made by acquirers who make multiple large acquisitions over our sample period. Panels B and D provide results for acquisitions made by acquirers that make only one large acquisition over our sample period. The leverage deviation is actual market leverage minus predicted market leverage from a regression model predicting market leverage. Net debt issues are long-term debt issuance minus long-term debt reduction scaled by market value of assets. *, **, and *** represent significance at the 1%, 5%, and 10% level, respectively, for the signed-ranks test statistic.

					Year relative to acquisition						
	−5	−4	−3	−2	−1	0	1	2	3	4	5
Panel A. Leverage deviation											
All	−0.0376	−0.0681*	−0.0667*	−0.0672*	−0.0686*	−0.0041***	−0.0018***	0.0018*	0.0189*	0.0051*	0.0038*
	298	347	409	472	495	495	495	495	495	495	495
Cash payment	−0.0419	−0.0627	−0.0667*	−0.0638*	−0.0703*	−0.0692*	0.0516*	0.0414*	0.0648*	0.0457*	0.0227*
	176	209	235	257	271	271	271	271	271	271	271
Equity payment	−0.0553	−0.0877*	−0.0690*	−0.0769*	−0.0734*	−0.0760*	−0.0591*	−0.0623*	−0.0510*	−0.0607*	−0.0282***
	73	85	107	137	141	141	141	141	141	141	141
Panel B. Leverage deviation for acquirers that make only one large acquisition											
All	−0.0436	−0.0765*	−0.0694*	−0.0791*	−0.0749*	−0.0063	0.0030**	0.0050*	−0.0029*	−0.0100***	−0.0089***
	207	242	281	323	340	340	340	340	340	340	340
Cash payment	−0.0458	−0.0737**	−0.0757*	−0.0778*	−0.0813*	0.0800*	0.0604*	0.0427*	0.0373*	0.0201*	0.0188*
	114	137	149	161	170	170	170	170	170	170	170
Equity payment	−0.0702	−0.0923*	−0.0683*	−0.0874*	−0.0802*	−0.0778*	−0.0550*	−0.0586*	−0.0468*	−0.0489*	−0.0327**
	61	69	88	110	114	114	114	114	114	114	114

(Continued)

Table 5 (Continued)

	-5	-4	-3	-2	-1	0	1	2	3	4	5
Panel C. Net debt issues											
All	-0.0024***	-0.0008***	-0.0012**	-0.0001	-0.0005	0.0416*	-0.0010	-0.0008	-0.0005	-0.0040*	-0.0023**
	315	367	441	445	442	469	443	447	431	435	422
Cash payment	-0.0062	-0.0010	-0.0034**	-0.0011	-0.0013	0.1390*	-0.0047	-0.0020	-0.0001	-0.0092*	-0.0029***
	183	209	244	248	244	257	241	246	238	243	234
Equity payment	-0.0015***	-0.0019*	-0.0004***	-0.0001	-0.0003	-0.0001	0.0000***	0.0000**	-0.0021**	-0.0018	-0.0012
	78	95	125	122	126	134	127	126	122	121	122
Panel D. Net debt issues for acquirers that make only one large acquisition											
All	0.0026*	-0.0013***	-0.0004	-0.0002	-0.0002	-0.0002	0.0315*	-0.0021	-0.0024**	-0.0050*	-0.0030*
	222	254	299	303	299	320	302	302	292	297	290
Cash payment	-0.0052*	-0.0014	-0.0015	-0.0010	-0.0000	-0.0000	0.1525*	-0.0063	-0.0061***	-0.0044***	-0.0103**
	121	134	151	155	151	151	159	150	152	149	151
Equity payment	-0.0013	-0.0021**	-0.0004	-0.0002	-0.0004	-0.0004	-0.0003	0.0000**	0.0000***	-0.0025**	-0.0035**
	64	76	100	98	100	100	108	102	100	97	98

Year relative to acquisition

cash acquirers were more underlevered before their first acquisition and that some cash acquirers are likely to follow their first cash acquisition with another cash acquisition later.[16]

This panel also shows that at the end of the acquisition year the leverage deviation for all sample firms is close to zero. However, this masks very different acquisition effects for cash and equity bids, which have end-of-acquisition-year leverage deviations of $+7$ cents and -8 cent per dollar of assets, respectively. This is consistent with the Table 2 evidence for the full sample that indicates cash bids, but not equity bids, result in an important increase in the leverage deviation.

Finally, Panel A shows that for cash deals the leverage deviation reverts toward zero during the years following an acquisition. For these deals the leverage deviation decreases to about two cents per dollar of assets by the end of year $+5$. For equity deals the leverage deviation remains negative from years 0 to $+5$ relative to the acquisition but trends upward toward zero from -0.076 to -0.028.

Panel B provides the results for the subsample of large acquirers who make only one large acquisition over our sample period. Inferences made from the results in this panel for equity deals are similar to those made from Panel A. However, by removing any effect of a subsequent large acquisition, we get a clearer picture of what happens to leverage deviations after cash deals. The results are even more supportive of the target capital structure hypothesis. The Panel B results show that, during each of the 5 years subsequent to a large acquisition paid for with cash, the median leverage deviation is lower than it was during the preceding year. Further, the panel shows that this deviation is reduced from eight cents per dollar of assets immediately after the acquisition to slightly less than two cents per dollar of assets at the end of the fifth year subsequent to the acquisition. This indicates that, during the 5 years subsequent to cash deals bidders reverse more than 75% of the effect of the acquisition on their leverage, consistent with the target capital structure hypothesis' prediction that, subsequent to debt-financed large acquisitions, acquirers gradually adjust their leverage levels downward toward the target level.

The median leverage deviation values over the first five years subsequent to large acquisitions paid for with cash reported in Panel B can be used to calculate annual speed of adjustment estimates. Comparing these leverage deviation values with the value at the end of the acquisition year shows that, over the one, two, three, four, and 5 years subsequent to large acquisitions, the annual speeds of adjustment are 24.5%, 23.3%, 17.8%, 18.7%, and 15.3%, respectively. These rates are higher than the rates reported in Fama and French (2002) of 7–10% per year for dividend payers and 15–18% per year for firms that do not pay dividends. However, these rates are lower than the 34% annual rate reported in Flannery and Rangan (2006). Overall, the length of time it takes for firms that make debt-financed large acquisitions to reverse the effect

---

[16] Consistent with this conjecture, we find that, for the full sample of cash acquirers analyzed in Table 2, if we require that a bid is an acquirer's first large acquisition over our sample period the median leverage deviation is approximately -6 cents per dollar of assets.

of the deal on their leverage is consistent with the arguments made in Myers (1984), Fischer et al. (1989), and Roberts (2002) and the empirical evidence presented in Leary and Roberts (2005) and Flannery and Rangan (2006) that firms face adjustment costs when trying to rebalance their capital structures.

DeAngelo and DeAngelo (2007) argue that the value of financial flexibility provided by low leverage is under-appreciated in typical explorations of the trade-off model. The results in Panel B of Table 5 show that underlevered equity acquirers remain so and that their debt levels trend upward only slowly. In comparison, cash acquirers become overlevered and steadily reduce their leverage back down. These findings are broadly consistent with the leverage dynamics predicted in the DeAngelo and DeAngelo (2007) model.

Panels C and D in Table 5 provide information on net debt issues over the period from years -5 to $+5$ around a large acquisition. Net debt issues are defined as in Table 2 as long-term debt issuance minus long-term debt reduction scaled by the market value of assets. We examine the net debt issues statistics to determine whether changes in the leverage deviation over time are related to net debt issues. Because we are principally interested in examining this relation for cash deals, we focus our discussion of this relation there. For cash deals the change in the leverage deviation during the acquisition year and net debt issues are closely related. During this year the leverage deviation for these deals changes from -7 cents per dollar of assets to $+7$ cents per dollar of assets. Most of the increase in the leverage deviation occurs as a result of new debt issues, because during the acquisition year, net debt issues are about 14 cents per dollar of assets.

For acquirers who make only one large acquisition over our sample period, Panel D provides evidence that the decrease in the leverage deviation during the years subsequent to a debt-financed large acquisition is in part a result of firms paying off more debt than they issue over this period. Specifically, we find that, during each of the years from years $+2$ to $+5$ subsequent to a large acquisition paid for with cash, the values for net debt issues are significantly negative and the magnitude of these values are economically important.

4.5. Explaining the postacquisition change in the leverage deviation

Table 6 provides evidence on the determinants of the change in the leverage deviation from year 0 to years $+3$, $+4$, and $+5$ subsequent to the year when a large cash acquisition takes place. The results of this analysis provide insights into what factors lead bidders to actively reverse the effect of a cash acquisition on their leverage. Our Tables 3 and 4 findings show that a bidder above its target leverage is unlikely to pay for a large acquisition with cash and take on even more debt. Consequently, we predict that if such a bidder pays for a large acquisition with cash (perhaps for strategic reasons), it makes an effort to quickly undo the effect of the acquisition on its leverage. We test this prediction in Models 1, 3, and 5 of Table 6 by including as an independent variable the preacquisition leverage deviation. In Models 2, 4, and 6 we replace this variable with the immediate postacquisition

Table 6

Explaining the change in the leverage deviation from years 0 to +3, +4, and +5 subsequent to large acquisitions paid for with cash

The sample consists of 1188 takeovers that are announced and take place between the beginning of 1981 and the end of 2000 in which the relative size of the target to the bidder is at least 20%. The dependent variable in Models 1 and 2, 3 and 4, and 5 and 6 are the changes in the leverage deviation from years 0 to +3, +4, and +5, respectively, subsequent to the acquisition, where year 0 is the fiscal year that includes the effective date of the acquisition. In models 1 and 2, 3 and 4, and 5 and 6 bidders are required to have data on Compustat from years 0 to +3, +4, and +5, respectively, subsequent to the acquisition. Market leverage equals long-term debt plus debt in current liabilities scaled by market value of assets. Leverage deviation is actual market leverage minus predicted market leverage from a regression model predicting market leverage. Unless specified otherwise, all accounting variables are calculated as of the fiscal year prior to the year when a takeover is completed. Bankruptcy risk score is measured as in Graham (1996) and equals (total book assets)/(3.3 times earnings before interest and taxes+sales+1.4 times retained earnings+1.2 times working capital). Bond rating dummy takes a value of one if a firm has a Standard & Poor's credit rating of BBB or better and takes a value of zero otherwise. CPI is the consumer price index. Significance levels in parentheses for whether estimates are different from zero are corrected using the Huber/White/sandwich estimator of variance.

Dependent variable	Leverage deviation Δ from year 0 to +3		Leverage deviation Δ from year 0 to +4		Leverage deviation Δ from year 0 to +5	
Model	(1)	(2)	(3)	(4)	(5)	(6)
Intercept	0.098 (0.017)	0.167 (0.000)	0.116 (0.007)	0.184 (0.000)	0.124 (0.009)	0.209 (0.000)
Preacquisition year leverage deviation	−0.210 (0.050)		−0.303 (0.015)		−0.315 (0.013)	
Preacquisition year market leverage	0.084 (0.356)		0.143 (0.172)		0.168 (0.139)	
End-of-acquisition-year leverage deviation		−0.415 (0.000)		−0.480 (0.000)		−0.544 (0.000)
End-of-acquisition-year market leverage		−0.008 (0.916)		0.050 (0.582)		0.029 (0.761)
Bankruptcy risk score	−0.002 (0.000)	−0.001 (0.001)	−0.002 (0.000)	−0.001 (0.000)	−0.002 (0.000)	−0.001 (0.005)
Bond rating dummy	−0.020 (0.512)	−0.025 (0.405)	−0.008 (0.820)	−0.009 (0.791)	−0.030 (0.408)	0.027 (0.415)
Natural logarithm of CPI-adjusted market value of assets	−0.017 (0.018)	−0.017 (0.005)	−0.024 (0.002)	−0.025 (0.000)	−0.030 (0.000)	−0.030 (0.000)
Postacquisition 3-year, 4-year, or 5-year firm-level stock return	−0.038 (0.000)	−0.036 (0.000)	−0.033 (0.001)	−0.032 (0.001)	−0.025 (0.018)	−0.024 (0.010)
R^2-adjusted	0.104	0.260	0.134	0.275	0.115	0.313
Number of observations	423	423	385	385	350	350

(year 0) leverage deviation. While this latter variable more directly captures the degree of excess leverage that the bidder would like to reverse, it is also subject to the criticism that it could be mechanically related to the dependent variable (post-acquisition change in leverage deviation).

Leary and Roberts (2005) and Flannery and Rangan (2006) provide evidence that, subsequent to shocks to its capital structure, adjustment costs affect a firm's ability to quickly rebalance its capital structure. In our models we include two proxies for adjustment costs used in Leary and Roberts (2005). First, we include a variable measuring the firm's bankruptcy risk. As in Graham (1996) and Leary and Roberts (2005) we use a modified unlevered version of the Altman-Z score based on Mackie-Mason (1990). We construct our variable measuring bankruptcy risk as does Graham (1996). This variable is defined as (total book assets)/(3.3 times earnings before interest and taxes+ sales+1.4 times retained earnings+1.2 times working capital). Our second proxy for adjustment costs is a dummy variable for whether the firm has a Standard & Poor's credit rating that is BBB or higher.

In the Table 6 models we also control for acquirer firm size and for the postacquisition 3-year, 4-year, or 5-year firm-level stock return, because these stock returns affect the change in the leverage deviation from years 0 to +3, +4, or +5 subsequent to a large acquisition. Finally, to explicitly hold the level of preacquisition leverage constant across sample firms, we also control for market leverage in these models.

Consistent with our predictions, the results for Models 1, 3, and 5 in Table 6 show that the higher a bidder's preacquisition leverage deviation, the more the bidder reduces its leverage deviation subsequent to a cash acquisition. Thus, if an already overleveraged bidder pays for a large acquisition with cash, perhaps because the circumstances of the acquisition make this necessary, the bidder is likely to make a concerted effort to reverse the acquisition's effect on its leverage.

These three models further show that the bankruptcy risk measure is significantly negatively related to postacquisition changes in the leverage deviation. Thus, bidders already facing greater bankruptcy risk who then make large debt-financed cash acquisitions are more likely to significantly reduce their leverage after the acquisition. This further supports static trade-off theory predictions that firms have target debt ratios determined by trading off bankruptcy costs against the benefits of debt.

The results for Models 2, 4, and 6 in Table 6 show that the year 0 postacquisition leverage deviation variable is significantly negatively associated with subsequent changes in the leverage deviation. The magnitudes of the coefficients on this variable in the three models are consistent with managers actively rebalancing their capital structures toward target levels following large cash acquisitions. For instance, the coefficient on the postacquisition leverage deviation variable in Model 6 suggests that about 54% of a bidder's postacquisition leverage deviation is reversed 5 years after the deal. Finally, like the Models 1, 3, and 5 results, the Models 2, 4, and 6 results indicate that firms facing higher preacquisition bankruptcy risk reduce their leverage more after large acquisitions paid for with cash.

5. Conclusion

We provide evidence on capital structure targets in the context of 1188 large acquisitions. Such acquisitions can markedly alter a firm's capital structure. Using an unbiased estimate of the bidder's target capital structure, we are able to explore how deviations from that target affect how it chooses to finance an acquisition and how it adjusts its capital structure following the acquisition.

Our evidence suggests that firms have target capital structures and managers try not to move too far from them. A bidder's preacquisition deviation from its target capital structure is directly related to the proportions of equity versus debt-financed cash in the consideration offered. Further, if an acquisition changes a bidder's target debt level, this is incorporated in the acquisition financing decision. Because these are large acquisitions, cash payment significantly increases the leverage of the combined firm, pushing it well above its target leverage on average. Firms respond by reducing their leverage back toward their target level in the years immediately following the acquisition. Within five years of a cash deal, they have reversed more than 75% of the effect of the acquisition financing. The effect of a firm's deviation from its target capital structure on its acquisition financing choice is related to the size of its growth opportunities, supporting the importance of contracting costs. Overall, our evidence is consistent with a model of capital structure that includes a target level and adjustment costs.

Appendix

In Table A.1 we tabulate the results of our estimation of a model of market leverage.

Table A.1

Estimation of a model of market leverage

This table summarizes the results of estimating a tobit model to predict market leverage [total debt/(total debt plus market value of equity)] for a firm. The value of predicted leverage is restricted to lie between zero and 1. The values for predicted leverage used in this study are estimated on a yearly basis using the cross-section of Compustat firms from 1976 to 2005. Industry dummies using the Fama and French (1997) industry definitions are included. This table presents the time series means of the coefficient estimates from the 30 yearly regressions. The significance levels are for a test of the hypothesis that the time series mean is equal to zero, using the time series standard error of the mean estimate for each coefficient.

Model	(1)
(Operating income before depreciation/book assets)$_{t+1}$	−0.121 (0.011)
Ln (sales)$_{t-1}$	0.014 (0.000)
(Property, plant, and equipment/book assets)$_{t-1}$	0.214 (0.000)
Market-to-book ratio of assets$_{t-1}$	−0.024 (0.000)
(Research and development expense/sales)$_{t-1}$	−0.012 (0.234)
Dummy for no research and development expense$_{t-1}$	0.076 (0.000)
(Selling expense/sales)$_{t-1}$	0.001 (0.788)
Number of observations (mean number of firms in yearly regressions)	3994

References

Almeida, H. and M. Campello, 2007, "Financing Frictions and the Substitution Between Internal and External Funds," Unpublished Working Paper, University of Illinois, Urbana-Champaign, IL.

Baker, M. and J. Wurgler, 2002, "Market Timing and Capital Structure," *Journal of Finance*, 57, 1–32.

Berkovitch, E. and M. P. Narayanan, 1990, "Competition and the Medium of Exchange in Takeovers," *Review of Financial Studies*, 3, 153–174.

Bharadwaj, A. and A. Shivdasani, 2003, "Valuation Effects of Bank Financing in Acquisitions," *Journal of Financial Economics*, 67, 113–148.

Bolton, P. and D. S. Scharfstein, 1990, "A Theory of Predation Based on Agency Problems in Financial Contracting," *American Economic Review*, 80, 93–106.

Campello, M., 2006, "Debt Financing: Does It Boost or Hurt Firm Performance in Product Markets?," *Journal of Financial Economics*, 82, 135–172.

Chevalier, J., 1995, "Do LBO Supermarkets Charge More? An Empirical Analysis of the Effects of LBOs on Supermarket Pricing," *Journal of Finance*, 50, 1095–1112.

DeAngelo, H. and L. DeAngelo, 2007, "Capital Structure, Payout Policy, and Financial Flexibility," Unpublished Working Paper, University of Southern California, Los Angeles, CA.

Eckbo, E. E., R. M. Giammarino and R. L. Heinkel, 1990, "Asymmetric Information and the Medium of Exchange in Takeovers: Theory and Evidence," *Review of Financial Studies*, 3, 651–675.

Fama, E. F. and K. R. French, 1997, "Industry Costs of Equity," *Journal of Financial Economics*, 43, 153–193.

Fama, E. F. and K. R. French, 2002, "Testing Trade-Off and Pecking Order Predictions About Dividends and Debt," *Review of Financial Studies*, 15, 1–34.

Fama, E. F. and K. R. French, 2005, "Financing Decisions: Who Issues Stock?," *Journal of Financial Economics*, 76, 549–582.

Fischer, E. O., R. Heinkel and J. Zechner, 1989, "Dynamic Capital Structure Choice: Theory and Tests," *Journal of Finance*, 44, 19–40.

Fishman, M. J., 1989, "Preemptive Bidding and the Role of the Medium of Exchange in Acquisitions," *Journal of Finance*, 44, 41–57.

Flannery, M. J. and K. P. Rangan, 2006, "Partial Adjustment Toward Target Capital Structures," *Journal of Financial Economics*, 79, 469–506.

Frank, M. Z. and V. K. Goyal, 2003, "Testing the Pecking Order Theory of Capital Structure," *Journal of Financial Economics*, 67, 217–248.

Fudenberg, D. and J. Tirole, 1986, "A "Signal-Jamming" Theory of Predation," *RAND Journal of Economics*, 17, 366–376.

Fuller, K., J. Netter and M. Stegemoller, 2002, "What Do Returns to Acquiring Firms Tell Us? Evidence from Firms that Make Many Acquisitions," *Journal of Finance*, 57, 1763–1793.

Ghosh, A. and P. Jain, 2000, "Financial Leverage Changes Associated with Corporate Mergers," *Journal of Corporate Finance*, 6, 377–402.

Graham, J. R., 1996, "Debt and the Marginal Tax Rate," *Journal of Financial Economics*, 41, 41–74.

Graham, J. R. and C. R. Harvey, 2001, "The Theory and Practice of Corporate Finance: Evidence from the Field," *Journal of Financial Economics*, 60, 187–243.

Hansen, R. G., 1987, "A Theory for the Choice of Exchange Medium in Mergers and Acquisitions," *Journal of Business*, 60, 75–95.

Harford, J., 1999, "Corporate Cash Reserves and Acquisitions," *Journal of Finance*, 54, 1969–1997.

Hovakimian, A., T. Opler and S. Titman, 2001, "The Debt-Equity Choice: An Analysis of Issuing Firms," *Journal of Financial and Quantitative Analysis*, 36, 1–24.

Hovakimian, A., G. Hovakimian and H. Tehranian, 2004, "Determinants of Target Capital Structure: The Case of Dual Debt and Equity Issues," *Journal of Financial Economics*, 71, 517–540.

Jalilvand, A. and R. S. Harris, 1984, "Corporate Behavior in Adjusting to Capital Structure and Dividend Targets: An Econometric Study," *Journal of Finance*, 39, 127–145.

Jensen, M. C., 1986, "Agency Costs of Free Cash Flow, Corporate Finance, and Takeovers," *American Economic Review*, 76, 323–329.

Jensen, M. C. and W. H. Meckling, 1976, "Theory of the Firm: Managerial Behavior, Agency Cost, and Ownership Structure," *Journal of Financial Economics*, 3, 305–360.

Kayhan, A. and S. Titman, 2007, "Firms' Histories and Their Capital Structures," *Journal of Financial Economics*, 83, 1–32.

Kim, C., D. C. Mauer and A. E. Sherman, 1998, "The Determinants of Corporate Liquidity: Theory and Evidence," *Journal of Financial and Quantitative Analysis*, 33, 335–359.

Klasa, S. and M. Stegemoller, 2007, "Takeover Activity As a Response to Time-Varying Changes in Investment Opportunity Sets: Evidence from Takeover Sequences," *Financial Management*, 36 (2), 19–43.

Leary, M. T. and M. R. Roberts, 2005, "Do Firms Rebalance Their Capital Structures?," *Journal of Finance*, 60, 2575–2619.

Mackie-Mason, J. K., 1990, "Do Taxes Affect Corporate Financing Decisions?," *Journal of Finance*, 45, 1471–1493.

Martin, K. J., 1996, "The Method of Payment in Corporate Acquisitions, Investment Opportunities, and Management Ownership," *Journal of Finance*, 51, 1227–1246.

Mikkelson, W. H. and M. M. Partch, 2003, "Do Persistent Large Cash Reserves Hinder Performance?," *Journal of Financial and Quantitative Analysis*, 38, 275–294.

Modigliani, F. and M. Miller, 1963, "Corporation Income Taxes and the Cost of Capital: A Correction," *American Economic Review*, 53, 433–443.

Myers, S. C., 1977, "Determinants of Corporate Borrowing," *Journal of Financial Economics*, 5, 147–175.

Myers, S. C., 1984, "The Capital Structure Puzzle," *Journal of Finance*, 39, 575–592.

Opler, T., L. Pinkowitz, R. M. Stulz and R. Williamson, 1999, "The Determinants and Implications of Corporate Cash Holdings," *Journal of Financial Economics*, 52, 3–46.

Phillips, G., 1995, "Increased Debt and Industry Product Markets: An Empirical Analysis," *Journal of Financial Economics*, 37, 189–238.

Rajan, R. G. and L. Zingales, 1995, "What Do We Know About Capital Structure? Some Evidence from International Data," *Journal of Finance*, 50, 1421–1460.

Rhodes-Kropf, M. and S. Viswanathan, 2004, "Market Valuation and Merger Waves," *Journal of Finance*, 59, 2685–2718.

Roberts, M. R., 2002, "The Dynamics of Capital Structure: An Empirical Analysis of a Partially Observable System," Unpublished Working Paper, University of Pennsylvania, Philadelphia, PA.

Schipper, K. and R. Thompson, 1983, "Evidence on the Capitalized Value of Merger Activity for Acquiring Firms,' *Journal of Financial Economics*, 11, 85–119.

Shleifer, A. and R. W. Vishny, 2003, "Stock Market Driven Acquisitions," *Journal of Financial Economics*, 70, 295–311.

Shyam-Sunder, L. and S. C. Myers, 1999, "Testing Static Tradeoff Against Pecking Order Models of Capital Structure," *Journal of Financial Economics*, 51, 219–244.

Stulz, R. M., 1990, "Managerial Discretion and Optimal Financing Policies," *Journal of Financial Economics*, 26, 3–27.

Titman, S., 1984, "The Effect of Capital Structure on a Firm's Liquidation Decision," *Journal of Financial Economics*, 13, 137–151.

Titman, S. and R. Wessels, 1988, "The Determinants of Capital Structure Choice," *Journal of Finance*, 43, 1–18.

Welch, I., 2004, "Capital Structure and Stock Returns," *Journal of Political Economy*, 112, 106–131.

PART 7

HOW DOES TAKEOVER AFFECT CEO AND DIRECTOR COMPENSATION?

Chapter 20

CEO COMPENSATION AND INCENTIVES: EVIDENCE FROM M&A BONUSES[*]

YANIV GRINSTEIN

Johnson Graduate School of Management, Cornell University, Ithaca, New York, USA

PAUL HRIBAR

Johnson Graduate School of Management, Cornell University, Ithaca, New York, USA

Contents

* We gratefully acknowledge the insightful comments and suggestions made by an anonymous referee, Warren Bailey, Lucian Bebchuk, Eli Berkovitch, Ronen Israel, Charles Lee, Roni Michaely, Derek Oler, Oded Sarig, Laura Starks, Bhaskaran Swaminathan, Avi Wohl, Amir Ziv, and seminar participants at Cornell University, IDC, and Tel-Aviv University. We thank Greg Austic for excellent research assistance.

This article originally appeared in the *Journal of Financial Economics*, Vol. 73, pp. 119–143 (2004).

Abstract

We investigate CEO compensation for completing M&A deals. We find that CEOs who have more power to influence board decisions receive significantly larger bonuses. We also find a positive relation between bonus compensation and measures of effort, but not between bonus compensation and deal performance. CEOs with more power also tend to engage in larger deals relative to the size of their own firms, and the market responds more negatively to their acquisition announcements. Our evidence is consistent with the argument that managerial power is the primary driver of M&A bonuses.

Keywords

CEO compensation, mergers and acquisitions

JEL classification: G34, J33

1. Introduction

Anecdotal evidence suggests that some CEOs receive lucrative compensation packages for acquiring other firms. For example, in large recent merger and acquisition (M&A) deals, Exxon, HealthSouth, Bankers' Trust, and Travelers Group paid their CEOs cash bonuses of $5–$14 million dollars for the successful completion of M&A deals.

In spite of these large compensation packages, prior research shows that shareholders of acquiring firms do not typically profit from these deals. For example, Jensen and Ruback (1983) cite studies that find no positive announcement returns to acquiring firms in merger deals. More recently, Moeller et al. (2003) report substantial negative announcement returns and substantial losses to large acquiring firms, especially for acquisitions occurring after 1997. Several studies also show a negative drift in the price of the acquiring firm several years after the acquisition (see, e.g., Agrawal et al., 1992; Jensen and Ruback, 1983; Kohers and Kohers, 2001; Loughran and Vijh, 1997).

The apparent misalignment between compensation and outcomes warrants a closer look at the practice of paying CEOs for M&A deals. In this paper, we provide additional insights with respect to the determinants of M&A compensation by addressing the following questions. First, how common is the practice of providing M&A compensation? Second, to what extent is M&A compensation paid to align CEO incentives with value maximization? Third, to what extent does managerial power affect CEO compensation related to M&A deals? To the extent that M&A compensation packages are associated with self-serving behavior, the costs of these packages can be substantial, as CEOs who acquire other firms because of the rents they can extract from the deals will not necessarily choose value-maximizing deals.

We address these questions by examining compensation related to 327 large M&A deals in the US between 1993 and 1999. We analyze the determinants of the compensation level, and explore how measures of effort, skill, performance, and managerial power explain the cross-sectional variation in the bonus.

We find that 39% of the acquiring firms in our sample cite the completion of the deal as a reason for rewarding their CEOs. In almost all of these cases, the payment is given in the form of a cash bonus. Our cross-sectional analysis suggests that measures of CEO effort and skill in forming the deal explain part of the variation in the level of the M&A bonus—bonuses are larger when the deals are larger, when the deals take longer to complete, and when there are more board meetings during the acquisition year.

Measures of performance, such as the market reaction to the announcement of the deal or the premium paid for the target, do not explain the cross-sectional variation in the compensation. In fact, we find some evidence that such measures are negatively related to the amount of the bonus awarded. In contrast, measures of managerial power add significantly to the explanatory power of the variation in the bonus. For example, within the sample of firms that state that they give M&A bonuses, CEOs on the nominating committee receive, on average, an additional $1.408 million for deal completion. Moreover, CEOs who are also heads of their boards, receive an additional

$1.447 million. We also find that the 2-day announcement period return of firms whose CEOs have the highest power is -3.8%, approximately three times lower than the abnormal return of the rest of the acquiring firms, which suggests that the deals undertaken by CEOs with significant power are received more negatively by the market.

Finally, we find that compensation committee reports typically do not provide much information relating to the reasons behind the payment of M&A bonuses, in spite of SEC requirements that companies report such information. Out of the 125 firms who cite the completion of the deal as a reason for the bonus, only 64 firms (51%) provide more detailed explanation. In those firms, we find that the most frequent motivation for the M&A bonus is the resulting increase in firm size and revenues (36 firms), followed by CEO effort and skill (27 firms). Only 22 firms argue that value enhancement is a reason for the bonus.

The results of our tests indicate that measures of effort and skill explain only a small part of the variation in bonus. Although deal size explains a large part of compensation, it is unclear whether this metric captures only effort and skill. For example, when comparing deal size across CEOs with different managerial power, we find that CEOs with the highest managerial power have the highest size ratio of target to acquirer. This evidence is consistent with previous arguments (e.g., Jensen, 1986) that the propensity to increase size is itself a function of agency. Furthermore, compensation does not appear to increase with deal performance, and, compensation committees rarely consider this dimension when awarding bonuses. Finally, managerial power explains a large part of the variation in compensation.

We interpret our results as consistent with the argument that M&A bonuses are positively related to managerial power: managers who have more board power are likely to get substantially higher bonuses, to engage in larger deals, and to have substantially smaller announcement returns.

This study contributes to the empirical literature that examines the relation between CEO compensation and M&A deals. Denis et al. (1997) and Datta et al. (2001) look at CEO compensation and ownership structures before M&A deals, and show that increased insider ownership and equity-based compensation improve long-run post-acquisition performance. Bliss and Rosen (2001) show that CEO compensation typically increases after bank mergers even if the acquirer's stock price declines. Rose and Shepard (1997) show that diversified firms tend to have higher CEO compensation, although the difference appears to be due to managerial ability. Unlike our study, these studies do not examine the compensation paid to the CEO for completing the deal. In contrast, Hartzel et al. (2001) do examine compensation specifically related to acquisitions; however, they examine the compensation of the CEO of the target firm, rather than that of the acquiring CEO.

Our paper also contributes to the literature that examines the relation between CEO compensation and CEO board power. Hallock (1997) looks at compensation of CEOs of large corporations in 1992 and finds that when there is an interlocking board relation, the CEO receives greater compensation. Core et al. (1999) look at compensation contracts of CEOs of large firms between 1982 and 1984 and find that CEOs that are heads of their boards receive larger compensation. They also find that the reward is larger when a CEO has more influence over the selection of the board members. Cyert et al. (2002) find that CEOs that are heads of their boards receive higher compensation, and that compensation committees with higher equity stakes tend to reduce the nonsalary compensation awarded to the CEO. None of these papers considers incentive compensation related to M&A deals.

The paper proceeds as follows. In Section 2 we provide the hypotheses. In Section 3 we discuss our sample selection and variable measurement. In Section 4 we present the empirical results, including a cross-sectional analysis and a detailed analysis of the compensation committee reports. Section 5 concludes.

2. Hypotheses

In large public corporations, the board of directors is in charge of compensating the CEO. The traditional view is that the board offers the CEO a compensation contract that maximizes shareholder value. The level of compensation depends both on supply and demand in the labor market for CEOs and on the effort level that CEOs exert in managing the firm. Therefore, a CEO whose skills are in short supply or who is required to exert higher effort is paid more for his or her services.

Work by Mirrlees (1974, 1976), Holmstrom (1979), Grossman and Hart (1983), and others all show how to account for the moral hazard problem when designing the compensation contract. In Holmstrom's "hidden action" model, the agent (CEO) is required to perform a series of tasks to maximize the utility of the investors; however, the CEO's tasks are unobservable to the investors and the CEO prefers tasks that do not maximize investors' wealth. In this context, the CEO should receive higher compensation if the tasks require greater skill or if the CEO has to work harder, but since the board does not fully observe the tasks, it should align managerial incentives by tying CEO compensation to observable outcome variables that are correlated with CEOs tasks. Compensation should therefore be based on observable measures of tasks that maximize value, such as market returns or profitability ratios.

In contrast to the above traditional view, a second view, the "managerial power" approach, argues that CEOs have the power to influence board decisions including compensation decisions, and that compensation contracts do not necessarily maximize shareholder wealth. This argument is consistent with empirical evidence about sub-optimal CEO compensation contracts. For example: Blanchard et al. (1994) find that when companies receive a cash windfall, (i.e., cash that has nothing to do with firm performance), they increase the compensation to their CEOs; Yermack (1995) finds that stock options are not awarded optimally; and Yermack (1997) provides evidence consistent with the interpretation that CEOs time their stock option awards just before favorable corporate news.

There are several reasons to believe that CEOs influence board decisions. Shivdasani and Yermack (1999) provide evidence that CEOs have the power to affect the selection of directors. Jensen (1993), Bebchuk et al. (2002), and Bebchuk and Fried (2003) argue that CEOs control the information that the board has about the company because they determine the board meeting agenda and the information given to the board, especially if they are the chairmen of their own boards. These authors also argue that CEOs discourage board members who disagree with them from serving on the board, and that board members often hold a small amount of stock in the company and therefore have little incentives to monitor.

Bebchuk et al. (2002) and Bebchuk and Fried (2003) formally tie managerial power to CEO compensation. They argue that CEOs who have more power will extract more rent in the form of compensation. They also argue that the likelihood of adopting a compensation arrangement that is favorable to executives but suboptimal for share-holders will depend not only on the power that the CEO has, but also on how the arrangement is perceived by shareholders. If the shareholders perceive the arrangement as a blunt expropriation, they are likely to act against it. This argument implies that CEOs that want to maximize rent extraction might try to find justifiable reasons for their compensation. A merger or acquisition could provide such a justification—a manager who acquires another company spends extra time and effort in constructing the deal, and thus the manager can use this task as a justification for additional compensation.

Given these two differing views of managerial compensation, our objective is to examine the extent to which the compensation related to M&A deals is consistent with either the traditional view or with managerial power. Although we recognize that these are not mutually exclusive alternatives, our goal is to learn the extent to which each of these theories is consistent with cross-sectional variation in M&A compensation.

According to the traditional view, there should be a positive correlation across acquiring firms between measures of deal complexity or measures of CEO effort in constructing the deal and the level of deal compensation. Moreover, given the moral hazard problem, we should observe a positive correlation between observable measures of the success of the deal and the level of compensation. Under the managerial power approach, there should be a positive correlation between the level of compensation and the level of managerial power in the firm; managerial skill and performance should play a secondary role in explaining the variability in compensation.

3. Data description and variables

3.1. Data description

We identify mergers or acquisitions in the US between 1993 and 1999 from the SDC database. We choose deals such that the value of the transaction is $1 billion or larger, and the entities involved are public US companies. Our sample is limited to large transactions because they represent economically significant events and are more likely to directly affect managerial compensation. We examine only public companies because of data availability. Deal related information is obtained from the SDC database, financial statement information is obtained from the Compustat database, and returns data are obtained from the CRSP database.

We extract CEO compensation data for every acquiring CEO from the Execucomp database. Execucomp lists CEO compensation since 1993 for every S&P 500, S&P MidCap 400, and S&P SmallCap 600 firms, and for other firms that are not currently included in the indices, but once were. We eliminate any sample firms for which we are unable to obtain compensation information, which results in a sample of 327 M&A deals.

Table 1 presents the summary statistics of our sample. Acquiring firms in our sample are large, averaging $29.5 billion in market capitalization. The median size is around $10 billion and the standard deviation is around $54 billion, which implies that the distribution of firm size in our sample has high variance and is skewed. Acquiring firms in our sample are profitable, with an average book return on assets of 11.7%. Finally, the average market return to the shareholders of the acquiring firm in the year prior to the deal is 25.8%, compared to an average market return of 25.3% on the S&P 500 during that period. This evidence suggests that, on average, the acquiring firms do not perform significantly better than the market in the year prior to the acquisition.

Panel B of Table 1 shows deal characteristics in our sample. The average deal value in our sample is $4.747 billion. The median deal value is $2.212 billion. The large difference between these two metrics suggests that the data is skewed by several particularly large deals.[1] From the day the deal is announced, it takes an average of about 5 months (155 days) to complete it and more than 75% of the firms complete the deal within 6 months.

The market tends to react negatively to the M&A announcement. The 2-day market-adjusted return surrounding deal announcement is -1.5%, with 50% of the firms experiencing a negative announcement effect of more than 1%. The low announcement effect is consistent with earlier research (Jensen and Ruback, 1983; Moeller et al., 2003). However, the large standard deviation suggests that the announcement effect of some of the deals is quite large. Most of the acquiring firms buy companies from the same line of business, (i.e., firms with the same two-digit SIC code). Only 34% of the acquiring firms in our sample buy entities from other industries.

Panel C of Table 1 describes corporate governance characteristics of the acquiring firms. The average number of board members is 13 members, where 30% of the members are "insiders," either employees or former employees of the company, or, directors who declare in the proxy statement that they have a work affiliation with the company (also known as "gray outsiders"). In 73% of the acquiring firms, the CEO is also the chairman of the board. In 25% of the acquiring firms, the CEO is a member of

---

[1] For example, the Exxon-Mobil merger has a deal value of $78.9 billion. Although we explicitly control for size and heteroskedasticity in the regression tests, all findings are robust to excluding the five largest deals from the analysis, each of which are greater than $40 billion.

Table 1

Descriptive statistics of acquiring firms in large M&A deals

The sample includes 327 large M&A deals between the years 1993 and 1999, with a deal value of $1 billion dollars or more, where the acquiring and target firms are publicly traded US companies. The deal data are from the SDC database, the bonus and governance data are from the proxy statements of the acquiring firms and the Execucomp database, and all other financial data are from the Compustat and CRSP databases. *Market Capitalization* is the acquirers' market value of equity a year before the announcement of the deal; *EBITDA* is earnings before interest, taxes, depreciation, and amortization; *ROA* equals *EBITDA* divided by the total book value of assets; *Return* is the stock return of the acquiring firm in the year before the acquisition; *S&P500 Return* is the return on the S&P500 index in the year before the acquisition; *Deal Size* is the dollar value of the deal, as reported by SDC; *Time to Complete* is the number of days between the acquisition announcement and the date of completion; *Adj. Return 2day* is the 2-day market-adjusted return between the day prior and the day after the announcement of the deal; *Diversify* is an indicator variable which equals one if the target firm has a different two-digit SIC code than the acquiring firm, and zero otherwise; *Num Board* is the number of members on the Board of Directors; *Insider Ratio* is the percentage of insiders or gray insiders on the board; *CEO Chair* is an indicator variable which equals one if the CEO is also the chairman of the board; *CEO Nominating* is an indicator variable that equals one if the CEO is on the nominating committee.

	Mean	S.D.	25%	Median	75%
Panel A. Financial characteristics of the acquiring firm					
Market Capitalization	29,596	54,248	4114	10,703	28,088
(premerger; $ millions)					
EBITDA ($ millions)	2420.1	3783.5	561.3	1162.3	2594.0
ROA (%)	11.7	7.6	5.5	10.6	16.7
Return (%)	25.8	66	−6.3	21.9	45.2
S&P500 Return (%)	25.3	9.1	21	28.6	33.4
Panel B. Deal characteristics					
Deal Size ($ millions)	4747.78	8748.95	1408.30	2212.50	4124.82
Time to Complete (# days)	155	117	85	129	182
Adj. Return 2day (%)	−1.5	7.6	−5.6	−1.1	2.5
Diversify (%)	34				
Panel C. Governance characteristics of the acquiring firms					
Num Board	13	4	10	13	15
Insider Ratio (%)	30	19	17	25	40
CEO Chair (%)	73				
CEO Nominating (%)	25				

the nominating committee, the committee that proposes new board members. The governance characteristics in our sample are therefore relatively similar to those of the S&P 500 as reported in previous studies. For example, Shivdasani and Yermack (1999) report that for 1994, an average of 11.4 directors are on the board, 32.5% of CEOs are on the nominating committees, and 83.6% of CEOs head their boards, while Klein (2002) reports that 59% of directors are independent during the years 1992 and 1993.

3.2. CEO compensation related to mergers and acquisitions

For each of the acquiring firms in our sample, we read the proxy statements before and after the deal,[2] which allows us to identify which components of CEO compensation are directly associated with the deal, and to identify governance variables in the acquiring firms. In 129 cases (39%), the compensation committee cites the completion of the deal as a reason for providing compensation. In almost all of these cases, the form of compensation is a cash bonus.[3] Therefore, we focus our analysis on the bonus component.

Table 2 presents summary statistics for the bonuses that CEOs receive after the deal. Out of the 327 acquiring firms, 287 (88%) give an annual bonus after the deal, but only 125 (38%) cite the deal as a reason for the bonus. In seven cases, the compensation committee cites the deal completion as the only reason for the bonus. In 118 cases, the compensation committee cites the deal completion as one of several reasons for the bonus.

When the merger or acquisition is the only cited reason for the bonus, the average deal value is $32.27 billion, and when the deal completion is cited as one of several

Table 2

Stated reasons for CEO bonuses as provided in the compensation committee report

The sample includes 327 large M&A deals between the years 1993 and 1999, with a deal value of $1 billion dollars or more, where the acquiring and target firms are publicly traded US companies. For each deal, we read the discussion of the compensation committee in the annual proxy statement to determine whether the cash bonus is explicitly linked to the merger or acquisition. *Bonus* is the cash bonus paid to the CEO for the year in which the merger is completed, as provided by Execucomp and verified by reading the proxy statement; *Deal Size* is the dollar value of the merger or acquisition, as reported by SDC.

	Bonus ($ thousands)			*Deal size* ($ millions)	
	N	Mean	Median	Mean	Median
Firms not giving cash bonuses	40	0.0	0.0	3648.6	2200.0
Firms giving cash bonuses	287				
M&A is cited as the sole reason for the bonus	7	5501.2	4000.0	32,271.1	21,345.5
M&A is cited as one reason for the bonus	118	2208.0	1500.0	5410.1	2271.9
M&A is not cited as a reason for the bonus	162	1298.6	862.6	3589.9	2054.5

[2] SEC regulation S-K (item 402 executive compensation section K), states that, at the end of every fiscal year, firms must disclose their compensation policies with respect to the manager, and provide a specific discussion describing each measure of the firm performance, whether qualitative or quantitative, on which managerial compensation is based.

[3] In 125 (97%) cases, the committee gave the remuneration in the form of cash bonus. In more than 90% of these cases no other form of compensation was associated with the deal. Results are unaffected by including the value of restricted stock grants related to the merger or acquisition.

reasons for the bonus, the average deal size is \$5.41 billion. The average bonus is \$5.5 million when the deal completion is cited as the only reason for the bonus, compared to \$2.2 million when the deal completion is cited as one of several reasons for the bonus. For the 162 cases in which the deal completion is not cited as a reason for the bonus, both the deals and the bonuses are smaller, averaging \$3.589 billion and \$1.29 million, respectively. Overall, the evidence in Table 2 suggests that the likelihood of the compensation committee stating that they give a bonus for the deal is associated with the size of the deal, and furthermore, that the level of the bonus is related to the size of the deal.

Although compensation committees have to declare the purpose of the bonus, there is a possibility that they engage in ex post labeling, whereby the M&A deal is simply used as a reason for giving a bonus that would have been given regardless of the deal. Since we are interested in bonuses paid explicitly for mergers or acquisitions, our first set of analyses examines whether M&A bonuses actually represent additional compensation to CEOs. We begin by estimating the following regression model using the entire Execucomp sample:

$$
\begin{aligned}
Bonus_{it} = {} & a_0 + a_1 Size_{it} + a_2 ROA_{it} + a_3 ROA\,Growth_{it} + a_4 Return_{it} \\
& + a_5 Sales\,Growth_{it} + a_6 Margin_{it} + a_7 Margin\,Growth_{it} \\
& + a_8 Acquisition\,Dummy_{it} + v_i + \omega_t + \varepsilon_{it}.
\end{aligned}
\tag{1}
$$

The dependent variable in Equation (1) is the bonus that the CEO of firm i receives at the end of year t. The right-hand side consists of performance and control variables: $Size$ is the firm size as measured by the book value of assets; ROA is earnings before interest, depreciation, and amortization, divided by total book assets; $ROA\,Growth$ is the percentage growth in ROA relative to previous year; $Return$ is the stock return of the firm; $Margin$ is the earnings before interest depreciation and amortization divided by sales; $Margin\,Growth$ is the percentage growth in $Margin$ from previous year; and, $Acquisition\,Dummy$ is an indicator variable that equals one if the firm acquired another firm during the year and the deal is worth \$1 billion or more. We also include firm-specific and time-specific fixed effects to control for differences in the average bonus across firms and over time. If firms pay bonuses to their CEOs for acquiring other firms, then the coefficient of $Acquisition\,Dummy$ should be positive and significant. If this were not the case, we might suspect that the declarations of compensation committees do not truly reflect compensation that is related to the acquisition.

The results in Table 3 Column I show that the coefficient of $Acquisition\,Dummy$ is positive and significant. This result suggests that firms pay higher bonuses for acquisitions even after controlling for measures of performance and fixed effects. Consistent with the prior literature, we also find significant effects for $Size$, ROA, and $Return$.

To make sure that we do not capture a substitution effect between bonuses and other forms of compensation, such as salary or options, we rerun our regression and let the dependent variable be bonuses-plus-salary. If there is a substitution effect we should not find a positive relation between bonuses-plus-salary and the acquisition year dummy.

Table 3

Regression of performance, firm size, and M&A activity on CEO compensation

The sample includes all firms in the Execucomp database between 1993 and 1999, that have financial information in the Compustat database. *Acquisition Dummy* is an indicator variable which equals one if the firm was an acquirer in a significant M&A deal (deal value of more than $1 billion) during the year; *Size* is the book value of assets prior to the acquisition; *ROA* is the earnings before interest, taxes, depreciation, and amortization divided by the book value of assets; *ROA Growth* is current *ROA* divided by *ROA* in the previous year; *Return* is the raw return of the stock during the fiscal year; *Sales Growth* is the value of sales divided by sales in the previous year; *Margin* is earnings before interest, taxes, depreciation and amortization divided by sales; *Margin Growth* is the margin in year *t* divided by the margin in the previous year. The regression includes also year-specific and firm-specific fixed effects. The numbers in parentheses are the standard deviation of the coefficient estimates.

	Dependent variable			
	Bonus (I)		Bonus-plus-salary (II)	
	Coefficient	*t*-Statistic	Coefficient	*t*-Statistic
Acquisition Dummy	189.09*	2.30	185.69*	2.22
	(82.34)		(83.61)	
Size	0.0083**	8.03	0.009**	8.56
	(0.001)		(0.001)	
ROA	1138.61**	4.48	1197.90**	4.64
	(254.1)		(258.0)	
ROA Growth	−15.33	−0.65	−21.64	−0.91
	(23.54)		(23.91)	
Return	34.78*	2.20	31.31*	1.96
	(15.78)		(16.0)	
Sales Growth	40.68	1.40	41.74	1.41
	(29.14)		(29.14)	
Margin	−26.05	−0.90	−24.97	−0.85
	(29.04)		(29.49)	
Margin Growth	15.98	0.65	23.00	0.92
	(21.29)		(24.91)	
Adjusted R^2	68.3%		59.7%	
Number of Observations	7334		7334	

**, * significant at the 0.01, 0.05 level (two tailed).

The results in Table 3 Column II show that the coefficient of the *Acquisition Dummy* variable is significant and positive, suggesting no substitution. We also estimate the regression in (1) using only salary, and only other forms of compensation (not shown). In both cases the coefficient of the *Acquisition Dummy* variable is not significantly differ-ent from zero. This result reaffirms the assertion of the compensation committees that they give compensation for the acquisition mainly in the form of bonuses.

To illustrate the acquisition effect on CEO bonus, we plot the bonus-to-base-salary ratio in acquisition and nonacquisition years for our sample of acquiring firms. For each CEO in our sample, we compute the average base salary between 1993 and

1999. Based on that value, we compute the bonus-to-base-salary ratio during the acquisition year and also 2 years before, 1 year before, and 1 year after the acquisition year. We then average the bonus-to-base salary across firms and plot the results in Figure 1.

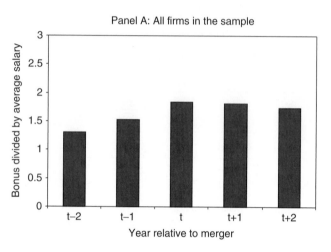

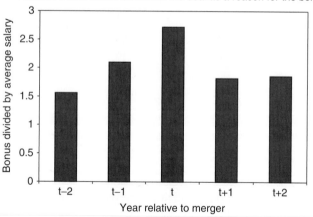

Fig. 1. Magnitude of CEO bonuses as a percentage of their average base salary. For each acquiring firm we identify the bonuses that the CEO receives 2 years before the deal ($t - 2$) to 2 years after the deal ($t + 2$), and we divide the bonuses by the average base salary of that CEO. We then average the bonus-to-base-salary ratio for the firms in the sample and plot the results. Panel (A) shows the results for all 327 firms in the sample. Panel (B) shows the results for the sample of 125 firms whose compensation committees report that they pay the bonus in year t for completing the deal. The sample includes large M&A deals between the years 1993 and 1999, with a deal value of $1 billion dollars or more, where the acquiring and target firms are publicly traded US companies.

Panel A of Figure 1 displays the results for all acquiring firms in our sample. The average bonus is 130% of the base salary 2 years before the deal, 184% of the base salary in the year of the deal, and 174% of the base salary 2 years after the deal. Panel B plots the average bonus ratio for only those firms that declared that they compensated their managers specifically for the deal. The bonus ratio is 156% of the base salary 2 years before the deal, 272% of the base salary in the year of the deal, and 186% in the second year after the deal. The bonus during the year of the deal is significantly higher than the bonus 2 years before or 2 years after the deal, at the 5% level of significance.

To get a sense of how acquisition bonuses change over time, we display in Figure 2 the average bonus paid to the CEOs during the acquisition years for the years 1993 to

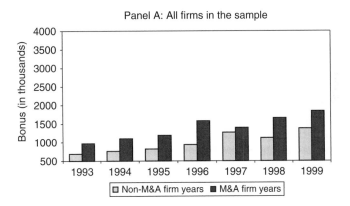

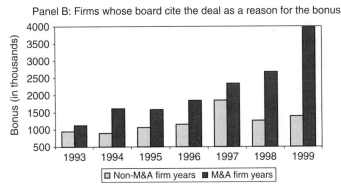

Fig. 2. Average CEO bonus in M&A years versus non-M&A years. This figure shows the average CEO bonus over time for the 327 acquiring firms in the sample. In each year we calculate separately the average bonus of CEOs who acquire in that particular year, and the average bonus of CEOs who do not acquire in that year. Panel (A) shows the average bonus for all the firms in the sample. Panel (B) shows the average bonus for the 125 firms whose compensation committees state that they pay the bonuses for completing the deal. The sample includes large M&A deals between the years 1993 and 1999, with a deal value of $1 billion dollars or more, where the acquiring and target firms are publicly traded US companies.

1999. We also plot the average bonus paid to the firms in our sample in the non-acquisition years. Panel A shows that the average bonus in the acquisition years increases from $1 million in 1993 to $1.8 million in 1999. The average bonus for the nonacquisition years is $0.6 million in 1993 and reaches $1.4 million in 1999. Panel B plots the same statistics, but includes only those firms whose compensation committees state that their CEOs receive bonuses for the deals. The average bonus in the acquisition years for these firms increases from $1.2 million in 1993 to $4 million in 1999. In the nonacquisition years, the average bonus for these firms increases from $1 million in 1993 to $1.8 million in 1999. Both Panels A and B show a trend towards larger bonuses in later years. They also show that when firms acquire, the average bonus is greater than when firms do not acquire. However, the difference is much more pronounced when the compensation committees state that their CEOs receive bonuses for the deals. In summary, the results from Figures 1 and 2 and Table 3 provide us with some assurance that managers receive extra bonus compensation for the M&A deal, and moreover, that boards are not simply engaging in ex post relabeling.

3.3. Measuring effort, skill, performance, and managerial power

In order to examine the determinants of the M&A bonuses, we need to obtain measures of effort, skill, performance, and managerial power. We begin by defining several indirect measures of effort and skill. According to the traditional contracting view, CEOs receive higher M&A bonuses if they are required to exert more effort and if their tasks require more skill. To the extent that the effort in forming and completing the deal is not fully observable, the compensation should rely on indirect measures of effort, such as performance measures.

The first measure we use is the size of the deal, *Deal Size*, defined as the value of the deal and obtained from the SDC database. We expect that larger deals are more complex and thus require more effort and skill on the part of the CEO. We note, however, that larger deal size could also indicate managerial tendency to overinvest (Jensen, 1986) and therefore might also imply that the board does not monitor managerial investment activity properly, and that the CEO has higher board power. The second measure for effort is the time it takes to complete the deal (*Time to Complete*). We define this measure as the log of the difference between the completion date and the announcement date, as provided by SDC. The third measure is a dummy that equals one if the firm acquires a target from a different industry (*Diversify*). We define same-industry acquisition if the two-digit SIC codes of the acquirer and the target are the same. All else equal, we expect an acquisition of a firm from a different industry to require less effort, since there are fewer synergies and integration problems between the target and the acquirer.

We also include a measure of performance, because to the extent that direct measures of effort are unobservable, contracting on performance can help mitigate the moral hazard problem. Our measure of performance is the 2-day abnormal return surrounding the announcement of the merger or acquisition (*Adj. Return 2day*). We use market-adjusted returns, where the S&P500 is used as the relevant market index. This variable is intended to capture the market's assessment of whether the CEO has made a value enhancing acquisition decision.

Our third set of variables captures the amount of managerial power that the CEO possesses. Consistent with Bebchuk et al. (2002) and Bebchuk and Fried (2003), managerial power is defined as the ability of the CEO to influence directors, and thereby affect the compensation decision. We use several variables to approximate the level of managerial power, several of which have been used in the past (e.g., Core et al., 1999; Shivdasani and Yermack, 1999). Our first measure is a dummy variable that equals one if the manager is also the chairman of the board, and zero otherwise (*CEO Chair*). We expect that CEOs who also serve as chairs will be able to exert more influence over the board. Our second measure is a dummy variable that equals one if the CEO is also a member of the nominating committee (*CEO Nominating*). A CEO who is also a member of the nominating committee should be more able to influence the selection of new directors, and directors whose selection was influenced by the CEO might feel compelled to reciprocate with respect to executive compensation (Bebchuk and Fried, 2003; Bebchuk et al., 2002). Our third measure is the ratio of the number of insiders and "gray" directors (those who were once insiders, or that have business relation with the firm) to total directors (*Insider Ratio*), where a higher proportion of insiders would be indicative of greater managerial power. We note, however, that there is mixed evidence on whether higher ratio of outside directors is more effective (see Core et al. (1999) for a review of the literature). Our final measure of managerial power is the number of directors on the board (*Num Board*). We expect larger number of board members to be associated with less effective board and higher managerial power (Jensen, 1993; Yermack, 1996).

4. Empirical results

4.1. Cross-sectional analysis

To investigate the extent to which effort, skill and managerial power explain the level of the bonus, we use the following regression model:

$$
\begin{aligned}
Bonus_i = \alpha_0 &+ \alpha_1 Size_i + \alpha_2 Deal\,Size_i + \alpha_3 Adj.Return\,2day_i \\
&+ \alpha_4 Time\,to\,Complete_i + \alpha_5 Diversify_i + \alpha_6 ROA_i + \alpha_7 Return_i \\
&+ \alpha_8 CEO\,Chair_i + \alpha_9 CEO\,Nominating_i + \alpha_{10} Insider\,Ratio_i \qquad (2) \\
&+ \alpha_{11} Num\,Board_i + \alpha_{12} Heckman_i + [Year\,Dummies] \\
&+ [Industry\,Dummies] + \varepsilon_i.
\end{aligned}
$$

Our dependent variable, *Bonus*, is intended to capture the award paid to the CEO that is associated with the M&A deal. However, because this exact amount is not given in most cases, we use several estimation techniques to isolate the bonus related to the deal (see below). All measures of effort, performance, and managerial power are as defined in the previous section. Our control variables are time and industry fixed effects, to control for the impact of both increasing bonuses over time (see, e.g., Figure 1) and systematic differences in bonuses across industries, and *Size*, which is the book value of the acquirers' assets at the beginning of the acquisition year.

We initially run an ordinary least squares estimation of Equation (2). However, a White test rejects the null of homoskedasticity at the 5% level ($\chi^2 = 34.47$, p-value = 0.024). Further analysis suggests that as the size of the acquirer increases, the absolute value of the error term also increases. Therefore, we normalize all variables by the book value of assets of the acquirer to control for heteroskedasticity. This approach is successful, as we no longer reject the null of homoskedasticity after this adjustment.

Additionally, a potential selection bias exists in this regression because the acquiring firms are not chosen at random from the population of firms. If the omitted variables that determine whether a firm will acquire another firm are correlated with those that determine the bonuses, then a simple regression will have a specification error. To overcome this potential misspecification we use the Heckman (1979) correction. We first run a probit regression over the Execucomp firms to model the probability that a firm will undertake a large acquisition. Our explanatory variables for the probit regression are premerger market to book ratio, cash to assets, debt to assets, ROA, revenue, an indicator variable for new-economy firms, and indicator variables for whether the firm acquired another firm in the previous year or the previous 2 years. We also include year dummies and industry dummies. All variables except ROA are significant at the 5% level.

We use the estimates from the probit regression to construct the *Heckman* variable, which when added to Equation (2), corrects for a potential correlation between the error in the first-stage probit regression and the error term (ε) in Equation (2).

From the compensation committee reports we are able to distinguish firms that pay M&A bonuses from those that do not. However, when the CEO is awarded a bonus both for completing the M&A deal and for performance not related to the deal, the compensation committee often does not isolate that part of the bonus that is associated with the deal. In these cases we need to empirically separate the M&A-related bonus.

We use multiple specifications to isolate the bonus paid for the M&A deal. In the first specification, we assume that whenever the CEO is paid for both performance and the deal, the portion of performance can be reasonably approximated by the CEO's bonus in the year prior to the deal.[4] Therefore, we subtract the previous-year bonus from all bonuses paid for both performance and the deal, and use them as the dependent variable. The bonuses of firms that do not cite the deal as a reason for the bonus are set to zero. We report the results of this procedure in Column I of Table 4.

---

[4] If the firm also acquired in the previous year, we use the bonus from the most recent year in which there was no acquisition.

Table 4

Regression of merger bonus on measures of effort, skill, and managerial power

The sample includes M&A deals between 1993 and 1999 with a deal value of $1 billion dollars or more, where the acquiring and target firms are publicly traded US companies, with nonmissing data for all of the regressors. We categorize the sample into three groups: those that cite the deal as the sole reason for the bonus (group D); those that cite the deal and other nondeal related factors as reasons for the bonus (group DP); and those who do not cite the deal as a reason for the bonus (group P). In models (I) and (II), the dependent variable is the estimated merger bonus, for which we use the entire bonus for group D, normalize the bonus of group DP by subtracting the CEO's prior-year bonus. Model (I) uses the full sample while model (II) uses only groups D and DP. In model (III), the dependent variable is the entire amount of the bonus, and we use regressors to control for the portion of the bonus related to performance. Model (IV) is the same as model (III), except that the dependent variable is the total salary plus bonus. Independent variables are defined as follows: *Size* is the book value of assets prior to the acquisition. *Deal Size* is the dollar value of the deal, as reported by SDC; *Adj. Return 2day* is the 2-day market-adjusted return for the day prior to and the day of the merger announcement; *Time to Complete* is the log of the number of days between the deal announcement and the date of completion; *Diversify* is an indicator variable which equals one if the target firm has a different two-digit SIC code than the acquiring firm; *ROA* is the earnings before interest, taxes, depreciation, and amortization divided by the book value of assets; *Return* is the raw return of the stock during the fiscal year; *CEO Chair* is an indicator variable that equals one if the CEO is also the chairman of the board; *CEO Nominating* is an indicator variable that equals one if the CEO is on the nominating committee; *Insider Ratio* is the percentage of insiders or gray insiders on the Board; *Num Board* is the number of members on the Board of Directors; *Heckman* is the coefficient from the Heckman (1979) correction. The regression also includes 6 year and 11 industry dummies. To eliminate heteroskedasticity, the regression is normalized by the book value of assets.

Variable	(I) Coefficient	t-Statistic	(II) Coefficient	t-Statistic	(III) Coefficient	t-Statistic	(IV) Coefficient	t-Statistic
Size	−0.358	−1.38	−0.207	−1.41	−0.396*	−1.49	−0.437**	−1.64
	(0.259)		(0.147)		(0.265)		(0.266)	
Deal Size	0.271**	4.03	0.322**	3.11	0.213**	2.66	0.212**	2.62
	(0.067)		(0.103)		(0.08)		(0.081)	
Adj. Return 2day	−82.4**	−3.79	25.4	0.68	−51.1*	−2.31	−42.4	−1.90
	(21.8)		(37.5)		(22.1)		(22.3)	
Time to Complete	205.6**	4.19	1425.2**	3.96	188.4**	2.90	203.2**	3.07
	(49)		(360.1)		(64.9)		(66.2)	
Diversify	−845.5** (236.9)	−3.57	−271.2 (421.2)	−0.64	−510.6 (298.1)	−1.71	−512.2 (324.9)	−1.58
ROA	−	-	−	-	1383.2 (1435.5)	0.96	53.2 (1501.7)	0.04

(Continued)

Table 4 (*Continued*)

Variable	(I)		(II)		(III)		(IV)	
	Coefficient	t-Statistic	Coefficient	t-Statistic	Coefficient	t-Statistic	Coefficient	t-Statistic
Return	-	-	-	-	86.2 (54.2)	1.59	82.7 (54.5)	1.52
CEO Chair	578.2* (292.8)	1.98	1447.5** (535.4)	2.70	828.0** (296.7)	2.79	838.0** (308.2)	2.72
CEO Nominating	722.6** (268.4)	2.69	1408.2** (471.6)	2.99	819.6** (260.3)	3.15	889.3** (279.9)	3.18
Insider Ratio	212.1 (140.2)	1.51	178.1 (220.8)	0.81	158.3 (136.1)	1.16	138.0 (136.2)	1.01
Num Board	-332.6** (49.3)	-6.75	-377.4** (91.8)	-4.11	-304.5** (49.1)	-6.21	-295.7** (49.4)	-5.99
Heckman	0.232 (0.128)	1.81	0.090 (0.067)	1.34	0.298* (0.132)	2.26	0.331* (0.132)	2.50
Year Dummies	Included		Included		Included		Included	
Industry Dummies	Included		Included		Included		Included	
Adjusted R^2 (%)	63.6		73.7		63.3		61.5	
Observations	242		122		242		242	

**, * significant at the 0.01, 0.05 level (two tailed).

In the second specification, we account for the portion of the bonus not associated with the deal by considering only those firms whose compensation committees state that they paid the bonus in part because of the deal. This procedure reduces the sample to 122 firms. For these firms, we assume that the bonus is paid only for the deal, and we therefore use the entire bonus amount as the dependent variable. We present the results of this second specification in Column II of Table 4.

In the third specification we use the full sample and the entire amount of the bonus, and also include additional explanatory variables designed to capture nonacquisition-related aspects of firm performance that might explain the bonus. Drawing from our results in Table 3, we include the firm's return on assets (*ROA*), defined as earnings before interest, taxes, depreciation, and amortization divided by book value of assets at the beginning of the year, and the firm's stock return during the acquisition year (*Return*). We then divide the sample into three groups of firms, those that pay a bonus exclusively for the deal (group D), those that pay a bonus both for the deal and for performance not related to the deal (group DP), and those that do not pay a bonus for the deal (group P). The performance variables not associated with the deal are interacted with indicator variables for groups P and DP, because these are the only groups for which the bonus is related to firm performance. The deal-related variables are interacted with indicator variables for groups D and DP, because only these bonuses should be associated with deal characteristics. The variables associated with measures of managerial power are applicable to all firms, and are therefore not interacted with any of the subsamples. We present the results of this specification in Column III of Table 4.[5]

Overall, the results in Table 4 are very similar across all three specifications. The deal size and time-to-complete coefficients are positive and significant in all specifications, suggesting that measures of deal complexity are positively associated with the bonus. The *Deal Size* coefficient varies between 0.213 (Column III) and 0.322 (Column II), and is statistically significant across the three specifications. The *Time to Complete* coefficient varies between 188.4 (Column III) and 1425.23 (Column II), and is statistically significant across the three specifications. The *Diversify* coefficient is significant and negative in the first specification, but insignificant in the second and third specifications. Thus, there is limited evidence suggesting that CEOs of firms that acquire from outside their industry are rewarded differently than CEOs of firms who acquire within the same industry.

Our measure of performance, *Adj. Return 2day*, is in Column I (*t*-statistic −3.79) and Column III, (*t*-statistic −2.31) but not significant in Column II. This result does not support the hypothesis that CEOs are compensated for performance in M&A deals. In fact, the significantly negative relation suggests that the compensation is not paid optimally. Overall, while there appears to be a relation between measures of effort and

---

[5] In model III, the bonus variable is truncated at zero. Therefore, an OLS regression might suffer from misspecification. To check if this is a concern, we reestimate this model using truncated OLS (tobit). All inferences are unchanged using the tobit procedure.

the bonus, there is no evidence that the bonus is related to observable measures of performance, as suggested by moral hazard models.

The governance measures have a significant impact on the bonus. The *CEO Chair* coefficient ranges between 578.2 (Column I) and 1447.5 (Column II), and is statistically significant across the three specifications (*t*-statistics = 1.98, 2.70, 2.79). The *CEO Nominating* coefficient ranges between 722.6 (Column I) and 1408.2 (Column II), and is statistically significant across the three specifications (*t*-statistics = 2.69, 2.99, and 3.15, respectively). The positive sign of these two coefficients suggests that CEOs with greater board influence earn greater bonuses. The *Insider Ratio* coefficient is positive in all three specifications but is not significant at conventional levels. This result is consistent with Core et al. (1999) who do not find a significant relation between the insider ratio and managerial compensation, and might suggest that our measure of insiders is a very noisy proxy for board independence.

Somewhat surprisingly, the *Num Board* coefficient is negative and significant across all three specifications, ranging between -304.5 (Column III) and -377.4 (Column II). This result implies that larger boards pay lower bonuses. On the surface, this result is inconsistent with Yermack's (1996) finding that smaller boards are associated with a higher Tobin Q, and the general notion that smaller boards are more effective.

To better understand our findings with respect to board size, we conduct two supplemental analyses. First, we examine the relation between Tobin's Q and board size in our sample. Consistent with Yermack (1996), we find a negative relation between Tobin's Q and board size. However, closer examination of our sample of firms reveals that about 40% of the firms in our sample that have high Tobin's Q fall into a category of new-economy firms (i.e., firms mainly in the telecommunication and computer industry, which have a higher growth perspective; Murphy, 2003). New-economy firms tend to have smaller boards and larger bonuses. Thus, one difference between our findings and the findings in prior research is that during the period studied here, we have a significantly larger representation of new-economy firms. Thus, high Q in our sample is not only a proxy for the efficiency but also for growth prospects; the larger bonuses in these firms seems to capture an industry effect. We therefore add a new-economy dummy variable to our regressions. This new-economy dummy reduces the magnitude of the negative coefficient of board size, but the coefficient is still significantly negative, which suggests that industry effects explain only part of the result.

Second, we examine the partial correlation between bonus and board size conditional on each of the other explanatory variables, and find that the relation between bonus and board size is only significantly negative conditional on the CEO being on the nominating committee. Therefore, we rerun the regression in Column III separately for those firms that have a CEO on the nominating committee ($n = 64$) and those firms that have a CEO that is not on the nominating committee ($n = 178$). For the latter set of firms, the coefficient on board size is positive, but not significant. For the former set of firms, the coefficient is significantly negative. One interpretation of this finding is that when the CEO is more involved in choosing board members, a smaller board might actually mean that the CEO has more managerial power.

Our last variable, *Heckman*, has a positive coefficient across the three specifications, and is statistically significant in one of them (Column III). The coefficient is an estimate of the product of the standard deviation of the error in Equation (2) and the correlation between the error term in Equation (2) and the error in the first-stage regression. Thus, the sign of the coefficient is determined by the correlation between the two error terms. A significantly positive coefficient therefore means that the error term in Equation (2) is positively correlated with the error term in the first-stage regression. Intuitively, the positive coefficient on the *Heckman* variable suggests that the likelihood of acquiring is positively associated with the bonus paid for the acquisition. This result might also be interpreted as consistent with the managerial power argument, in that CEOs that expect to extract higher bonuses for completing M&A deals are more likely to enter these deals.

To get a sense of the economic significance of our regression results, we examine the magnitude of the statistically significant coefficients in Column III. An increase of one standard deviation in deal size ($8.748 billion) increases the CEO compensation by $1.86 million. An increase in the time to complete the deal by one standard deviation (117 days) from the mean increases the CEO's compensation by $0.106 million. A decrease in abnormal return of 1% is associated with an increase of $51.1 thousand in compensation. A CEO who is also the chair receives on average $828 thousand more than a CEO who is not. A CEO who is on the nominating committee receives on average $819.6 thousand more than a CEO who is not on the nominating committee. An increase of one standard deviation in board size (four members) decreases the bonus by about $1.2 million, and as mentioned above, this is driven by cases where the CEO is also on the nominating committee.

The economic significance of board power becomes even stronger within the sample of firms that state that they give an M&A bonus (Column II). In this specification, a CEO who is also the chair receives on average $1.447 million and a CEO who is on the nominating committee receives on average an additional $1.408 million more. We also get stronger effects in deal size and in the time to complete the deal. An increase of one standard deviation in deal value ($8.748 billion) increases the CEO compensation by $2.816 million. An increase in the time to complete the deal by one standard deviation (117 days) from the mean increases the CEO's compensation by $0.801 million.

Overall, the results indicate that the most economically significant factors that determine the compensation of the CEO appear to be deal size and the measures of power. While deal size might be indicative of greater effort and skill, it might also reflect agency problems associated with "empire building," and in this respect may be related to the managerial power hypothesis. The most direct measure of performance, the 2-day adjusted return, appears to be negatively related to the bonus, which suggests that compensation committees do not consider market reaction to the announcement of the deal as a measure of performance. To the extent that market reaction is indicative of the level of CEO expropriation in the deal, a negative relation between the announcement effect and the bonus is consistent with the managerial power argument.

We also reestimate the regression in Column III, using bonus-plus-salary as the dependent variable. This specification is used to ensure that higher bonuses are not offset by a lower base salary, and that the bonus effect we are capturing does indeed impact the total salary of the CEO. We present the results in Table 4, Column IV. If there is a negative correlation between the bonus and salary, then the results in Column III should not follow in Column IV. Our results indicate that there is no offsetting relation between the two components of compensation.

To get another sense of the effect of managerial power on compensation and other aspects of the deal, we compare summary statistics of the acquiring firms, based on how powerful the manager is in these firms. We first construct an index of managerial power, by taking the sum of the three dichotomous managerial power variables that are significant in Table 4. The three variables included in the index are the indicator variable of whether the CEO is also the chairman of the board, the indicator variable of whether the CEO is on the nominating committee, and the indicator variable of whether the board size is smaller than the median size in our sample. Thus, the managerial power index can range from zero (least managerial power), to three (greatest power). We present the results in Table 5.

Twenty-one acquiring firms have an index of zero, 106 firms have an index of one, 90 firms have an index of two, and 25 firms have an index of three.[6] The deal size of the acquiring firms is largest for the least powerful CEO group, averaging $9.466 billion and it decreases as the CEO becomes more powerful. The most powerful CEO group has an average deal size of $2.743 billion. However, when measuring the size of the deal relative to the size of the acquiring firm, (*Deal to Assets*), the most powerful CEOs engage in larger deals. They acquire companies whose size is on average 36% of their own firms' assets. The least powerful CEOs acquire companies whose size is on average only 23.8% of their own firms' assets. The difference in the average deal size between the two groups is significant at the 5% level (*t*-statistic 1.96). This result suggests that when controlling for acquirer size, deal size is not only correlated with managerial skill but also with managerial power. This result is consistent with the argument that deal size is itself a measure of agency conflicts (Jensen, 1986).

The average bonus levels in the four groups are not statistically different from one another. The average bonus of the most-powerful-CEO group is $1.847 million and the bonus for the least-powerful-CEO group averages $2.118 million. However, the difference in the ratio of bonus to deal size is significant. For the most-powerful-CEO group the ratio is 0.1188%, which is more than twice the ratio of 0.0538% for the least-powerful-CEO group.

The 2-day abnormal return of the deal announcement is negative, on average, in all groups. However, the return is statistically different from zero only in the most-powerful-CEO group. This group also averages the lowest 2-day announcement period

---

[6] For example, an index of 3 implies that the CEO is also the chair, that the CEO serves on the nominating committee, and that the board is below median size.

Table 5

Bonus and deal characteristics based on managerial power variables

The sample includes large M&A deals between 1993 and 1999 with a deal value of $1 billion dollars or more, where the acquiring and target firms are publicly traded US companies. The Managerial Power index is constructed by taking the sum of three dichotomous managerial power indicator variables, and therefore ranges from 0 to 3. The three variables included in the index are whether the CEO is also the chairman (equals one if CEO is chairman, zero otherwise); whether the CEO is on the nominating committee (equals one if CEO is on nominating committee, zero otherwise); and whether the board size is above or below the median board size for the firms in our sample (equals one if board size is lower than median board size, zero otherwise). Thus, firms with a managerial power index of three have a CEO who is also the chairman, who is on the nominating committee, and who is on a relatively small board. Deal Size is the dollar value of the deal, as reported by SDC. Deal to Assets is the value of the deal deflated by the assets of the acquiring firms; Bonus is the annual bonus awarded to the CEO in the year of the merger or acquisition; Bonus to Deal Size is the CEO bonus deflated by the dollar value of the deal; Bonus to Time-to-Complete is the CEO bonus deflated by the time to complete the merger; Adj. Return 2day is the 2-day market-adjusted return for the day prior to and the day of the merger announcement.

| Variable | Statistic | Managerial power index | | | | t-statistic group 3 vs. group 0 | t-statistic group 3 vs. groups 0, 1, 2 |
		0	1	2	3		
Deal Size	Mean	9466.1	6436.7	3607.0	2743.2	2.77	3.35
($ millions)	Median	5309.7	2932.7	1900.0	1657.4		
Deal to Assets	Mean	0.238	0.276	0.271	0.366	1.66	1.96
	Median	0.170	0.190	0.235	0.285		
Bonus	Mean	2118.9	1613.9	1448.5	1847.4	0.37	0.58
($ thousands)	Median	875.0	918.1	875.0	1200.0		
Bonus to Deal Size	Mean	0.538	0.458	0.718	1.188	1.98	2.77
($\times$ 1000)	Median	0.159	0.284	0.361	0.609		
Bonus to Time to Complete	Mean	18.03	12.05	23.64	19.21	0.16	0.34
($ thousands/days)	Median	9.18	6.15	7.52	11.32		
Adj. Return 2day	Mean	-0.0196	-0.0134	-0.0072	-0.0381	1.48	2.14
	Median	-0.0062	-0.0050	-0.0063	-0.0204		
Number of observations		21	106	90	25		

return of -3.8%, which is significantly lower than the return to the other groups (t-statistic $= 2.14$). These results suggest that the market perceives as bad news M&A deals in which the CEO has board power. A CEO with greater power is associated with a larger M&A deal relative to the size of his or her firm, higher cash bonus, and a more negative market perception. The results are consistent with the argument that managerial power enables the extraction of rents by the CEO.

4.2. Robustness

The fact that we get similar results using the three different methodologies suggests that the results are robust across various specifications. Nevertheless, the variables we use to measure effort, skill, and performance might not capture the true managerial input in the deal. We therefore, repeat the regressions using other measures of effort, skill, and performance.[7]

Our first measure is the number of times that the board meets during the acquisition year. This variable might represent the level of complexity and the amount of decision-making associated with the deal. A second measure of effort is the number of advisors who are hired for the acquisition. The larger the number of advisors, presumably the more complex the deal and the more effort required to complete the deal. We also use deal premium as a measure of deal performance, where we define the premium as the target price in the deal, divided by the market value of the target four weeks before the deal. We obtain information on the number of board meetings from the proxy statements, and on the number of advisors and the market premium from SDC.

When we repeat the regression in Equation (2) with the above variables, we find that the coefficients associated with both the number of advisors and the deal premium are not significant. The coefficient associated with the number of board meetings is significant, however, with a coefficient of 67.3. This number suggests that for every additional board meeting, the CEO receives an additional $67.3 thousand. The average number of meetings during the acquisition year is 5.0, and the standard deviation is 3.0, suggesting that an increase in one standard deviation in the number of board meetings is associated with an increase of about $200 thousand in bonus. The coefficients of all other included variables are qualitatively unchanged from the coefficients in the original regressions. Overall, the results of our robustness checks support our original results, namely, that measures of CEO effort and skill have a limited power to explain the cross-sectional variation in the deal bonus, but that measures of performance do not explain cross-sectional variation in the bonus.

---

[7] These variables are not included in our original regression, primarily because they reduce the sample size considerably due to missing data in the SDC database.

4.3. Analysis of the compensation committee report

Our final analysis involves reading the compensation committee report to investigate the reasons cited for the CEO bonus, for cases in which a bonus is given in whole or in part for the merger or acquisition. In 61 cases (49%), the compensation committee does not provide an explicit reason for the bonus, except for mentioning that the CEO completed the deal, or that by executing the deal, the CEO complied with the strategy of the firm. This percentage holds both for firms that pay high bonuses and for firms that pay low bonuses. For the remaining firms, we classify the reasons into seven categories: market reaction; managerial leadership; managerial effort; managerial skill; increasing the size/revenues/growth of the company; recommendation of an independent counselor; and providing opportunities to realize synergies. Compensation committees might cite more than one reason for the bonus. We present the results in Table 6.

Panel A of Table 6 shows that the most frequent justification for the deal bonus (36 cases, or 56.25% of the sample of firms that provide reasons) is an increase in the size, revenue, and growth of the firm. The least frequent reason is independent council (one instance) and market reaction to the deal (four instances). This pattern appears in the sample taken as a whole, as well as when the sample is partitioned by bonus size.

In Panel B, we recategorize the compensation committees comments into three groups, one that relates to effort and skill, one that relates to performance, and one that relates directly to size. In this case, the most frequent reason for compensating the CEO is for increasing firm size, revenues, and growth (56.25%). The second-most frequent reason is managerial effort and skill, and only in 34.3% of the cases is the reason maximizing profits and value.

The results suggest that compensation committees are reluctant to provide information about the CEO bonus. In 49% of the cases, the committees do not justify the bonus beyond the fact that it is paid for completing the deal. In the rest of the cases, the compensation committees appear to be more concerned with paying their CEOs for maximizing firm size and revenues, rather than for maximizing value.

5. Conclusion

Using a sample of 327 large M&A deals between 1993 and 1999, we find that about 39% of the acquiring firms reward their CEOs for the successful completion of a merger or acquisition deal. This compensation is mainly in the form of cash bonuses. Our analysis suggests that CEOs receive higher bonus compensation when the deals are larger. They also receive higher bonuses when they exert more effort in forming the deal. However, except for deal size, we find that measures of effort and skill do not explain a significant amount of the variation in the bonus. We find some evidence that deal size is correlated with more managerial power, since more-powerful CEOs are likely to enter larger deals compared to the size of their own firms. We also find that measures of managerial power explain much of the cross-sectional variation in the bonus.

Table 6

Stated reasons for providing M&A bonuses

The sample consists of 327 M&A deals between 1993 and 1999 that had a deal value in excess of one billion dollars, where the acquirer and target firms were both publicly traded US companies. For each firm that pays M&A bonus, we read the proxy statement to determine the reason for the bonus. Out of the 125 firms who cite the completion of the M&A deal as a reason for the bonus, 64 firms provide detailed justification for the bonus. We classify the reasons into seven categories, and present the number of firms who use these reasons in Panel A. In Panel B we collapse the reasons into three main categories.

	Justification for the bonus						
Bonus size	Market reaction	Leadership	Extra effort	Skill	Increases size/ revenues/ growth	Recommendation of independent counselor	Provides opportunity to realize synergies/ profits
Panel A. Number of firms who justify the deal bonus							
$5 million or greater	0	5	2	0	9	1	2
$1–$5 million	0	4	1	0	16	0	7
Less than $1 million	4	6	6	3	11	0	9
	4	15	9	3	36	1	18

	Justification for the bonus		
Bonus size	CEO effort, skill and leadership	Increases size/ revenues/growth	Market reaction/providing opportunity to realize synergies/profits
Panel B. Number of firms who justify the deal bonus-classification into performance, effort and size			
$5 million or greater	7	9	2
$1–$5 million	5	16	7
Less than $1 million	15	11	13
	27	36	22

Our results suggest that managerial power plays a significant role in determining M&A bonuses. Moreover, the managerial power variables appear to explain much more of the variation in the bonus than measures of effort or performance. These findings are consistent with the argument of Bebchuk et al. (2002) and Bebchuk and Fried (2003), that CEO power is a significant driver of CEO compensation.

We find additional evidence consistent with this argument. When we look at the compensation committee reports, we find that compensation committees seem to hide information relating to why they give M&A bonuses. In about 50% of the cases, they do not provide clear information relating to why they give the deal bonuses. In the rest of the cases, their main arguments for bonuses rely on maximization of firm size rather than on maximization of firm value.

The direct costs of deal bonuses seem small. However, potential indirect costs associated with them could be very large. If CEOs have the power to affect board decisions and if they believe that M&A deals provide opportunities for them to extract rents from the shareholders through salaries and bonuses, CEOs may choose deals that maximize their own wealth rather than shareholder value. We find that M&A deals in which CEOs have more power suffer from a negative abnormal return of -3.8%, which is significantly larger than the abnormal returns observed when CEOs have less power. This large abnormal negative return suggests that the economic losses associated with self-dealing perks can be substantial.

References

Agrawal, A., J. Jaffe and G. Mandelker, 1992, "The Post-Merger Performance of Acquiring Firms: A Re-Examination of an Anomaly," *Journal of Finance*, 47, 1605–1621.

Bebchuk, L. A. and J. M. Fried, 2003, "Executive Compensation as an Agency Problem," *Journal of Economic Perspectives*, 17, 71–92.

Bebchuk, L. A., J. M. Fried and D. I. Walker, 2002, "Managerial Power and Rent Extraction in the Design of Executive Compensation," *The University of Chicago Law Review*, 69, 751–846.

Blanchard, O. J., F. Lopez De Silanes and A. Shleifer, 1994, "What Do Firms Do with Cash Windfalls?" *Journal of Financial Economics*, 36, 337–360.

Bliss, R. T. and R. J. Rosen, 2001, "CEO Compensation and Bank Mergers," *Journal of Financial Economics*, 61, 107–138.

Core, J. E., R. W. Holthausen and D. F. Larcker, 1999, "Corporate Governance, CEO Compensation, and Firm Performance," *Journal of Financial Economics*, 51, 371–406.

Cyert, R., S. Kang and P. Kumar, 2002, "Corporate Governance, Takeovers, and Top-Management Compensation: Theory and Evidence," *Management Science*, 48, 453–469.

Datta, S., M. Iskandar-Datta and K. Raman, 2001, "Executive Compensation and Corporate Diversification Decisions," *Journal of Finance*, 56, 2299–2336.

Denis, D. J., D. K. Denis and A. Sarin, 1997, "Agency Problems, Equity Ownership, and Corporate Diversification," *Journal of Finance*, 52, 135–160.

Grossman, S. and O. Hart, 1983, "An Analysis of the Principal Agent Problem," *Econometrica*, 51, 7–45.

Hallock, K. F., 1997, "Reciprocally Interlocking Boards of Directors and Executive Compensation," *Journal of Financial and Quantitative Analysis*, 32, 331–344.

Hartzel, J., E. Ofek and D. Yermack, 2001, "What's In It for Me? CEOs Whose Firms are Acquired," Unpublished Working Paper, New York University.

Heckman, J., 1979, "Sample Selection Bias as a Specification Error," *Econometrica*, 47, 153–161.

Holmstrom, B., 1979, "Moral Hazard and Observability," *Bell Journal of Economics*, 13, 234–340.

Jensen, M. C., 1986, "Agency Costs of Free Cash Flow, Corporate Finance, and Takeovers," *The American Economic Review*, 76, 323–329.

Jensen, M. C., 1993, "The Modern Industrial Revolution, Exit, and the Failure of Internal Control Systems," *Journal of Finance*, 48, 831–880.

Jensen, M. C. and R. Ruback, 1983, "The Market for Corporate Control: The Scientific Evidence," *Journal of Financial Economics*, 11, 5–50.

Klein, A., 2002, "Audit Committee, Board of Director Characteristics, and Earnings Management," *Journal of Accounting and Economics*, 33, 375–400.

Kohers, N. and T. Kohers, 2001, "Takeovers by Technology Firms: Expectations vs. Reality," *Financial Management*, 30, 35–54.

Loughran, T. and A. M. Vijh, 1997, "Do Long-Term Shareholders Benefit from Corporate Acquisitions?" *Journal of Finance*, 52, 1765–1790.

Mirrlees, J., 1974. "Notes on Welfare Economics, Information, and Uncertainty," In M. Balch, D. McFadden and S. Wu (Eds.), *Essays on Economic Behavior Under Uncertainty*, North-Holland, Amsterdam.

Mirrlees, J., 1976, "The Optimal Structure of Incentives and Authority Within an Organization," *Bell Journal of Economics*, 7, 105–131.

Moeller, S. B., F. P. Schlingemann and R. M. Stulz, 2003. "Do Shareholders of Acquiring Firms Gain from Acquisitions?" Working Paper #2003–4, Ohio State University.

Murphy, K. J., 2003, "Stock-Based Pay in New-Economy Firms," *Journal of Accounting and Economics*, 34, 129–147.

Rose, N. L. and A. Shepard, 1997, "Firm Diversification and CEO Compensation: Managerial Ability or Executive Entrenchment?" *Rand Journal of Economics*, 28, 489–514.

Shivdasani, A. and D. Yermack, 1999, "CEO Involvement in the Selection of New Board Members: An Empirical Analysis," *Journal of Finance*, 54, 1829–1853.

Yermack, D., 1995, "Do Corporations Award CEO Stock Options Effectively?" *Journal of Financial Economics*, 39, 237–269.

Yermack, D., 1996, "Higher Market Valuation of Companies with a Small Board of Directors," *Journal of Financial Economics*, 40, 185–211.

Yermack, D., 1997, "Good Timing: CEO Stock Option Awards and Company News Announcements," *Journal of Finance*, 52, 449–476.

Chapter 21

TAKEOVER BIDS AND TARGET DIRECTORS' INCENTIVES: THE IMPACT OF A BID ON DIRECTORS' WEALTH AND BOARD SEATS[*]

JARRAD HARFORD

School of Business Administration, University of Washington, Seattle, Washington, USA

Contents

* I thank Michael Barclay, John Chalmers, Larry Dann, Wayne Guay, David Haushalter, Wayne Mikkelson, Bob Parrino, Megan Partch, and seminar participants at the University of Oregon, University of Washington, the JFE/Tuck Center for Corporate Governance Conference, and the Second Annual Texas Finance Festival for comments. I also thank Sandy Klasa and Todd Perry for research assistance. This research was completed while I was at the University of Oregon.

This article originally appeared in the *Journal of Financial Economics*, Vol. 69, pp. 51–83 (2003).
Corporate Takeovers, Volume 2
Edited by B. Espen Eckbo
DOI: 10.1016/B978-0-12-381982-6.00022-7

Abstract

I investigate the nature of the incentives that lead outside directors to serve stock-holders' interests. Specifically, I document the effect of a takeover bid on target directors, both in terms of its immediate financial impact and its effect on the number of future board seats held by those target directors. Directors are rarely retained following a completed offer. All target directors hold fewer directorships in the future than a control group, suggesting that the target board seat is difficult to replace. For outside directors, the direct financial impact of a completed merger is predominately negative. This documents a cost to outside directors should they fail as monitors, forcing the external control market to act for them. Future seats are related to prebid performance. Among outside directors of poorly performing firms, those who rebuff an offer face partial settling-up in the directorial labor market, while those who complete the merger do not.

Keywords

mergers and acquisitions, board of directors, director compensation, board seats, settling-up

JEL classification: G34

1. Introduction

When Bank of America merged into Nationsbank, 18 Bank of America directors who were eliminated in the merger received a surprise $300,000 payment with a letter thanking them "for the contributions [they] have made to building this great company." Explaining the highly unusual bonus, a Bank of America official stated that "the purpose also was to thank people who had, after all, voted themselves out of a job by approving the merger" (*Wall Street Journal*, Feb. 10, 1999, B1).

Shareholders depend on the board of directors to represent their interests. While we expect outside directors to align themselves with shareholders, we know little about the incentives driving director diligence in monitoring or the incentives facing these directors as they make major decisions. Walkling and Long (1984) provide some evidence on how the financial impact of the merger on the board affects its response to a bid, and Mikkelson and Partch (1989) show that there is a relation between managerial ownership and completion of a merger. One case in which the board's role is extremely important and its incentives particularly unclear is the case of a takeover bid. The board is charged with receiving and acting on the offer and with ensuring that the interests of shareholders supersede those of the managers. However, the target directors may have personal incentives that conflict with their role as shareholder representatives. If the merger is completed, a director may lose his or her directorship and, through its exposure, future potential directorships.

Thus, the prospect of losing a directorship in a takeover could help motivate directors to be diligent in their role as monitors. However, should a takeover bid actually occur, that same reality potentially causes their incentives to deviate from those of the shareholders they represent. While it is difficult to contract on the handling of a takeover bid and the horizon problem inherent with the end of a firm as a separate entity, settling-up in the directorial labor market can provide proper incentives.

This study has two goals. The first goal is to gain a better understanding of what motivates directors to be diligent in their monitoring role. This is accomplished by documenting how receiving a takeover bid affects a director's wealth and future board seats. The second goal is to examine the ex post settling-up hypothesis in the context of the directorial labor market by asking whether takeover bids and the response of target directors to the bids affect those directors' future directorships. As a result, this study provides some insight into the complex incentives facing the board of directors when considering a merger proposal and directing the target's response.

I start with a sample of 1091 directors from boards of *Fortune 1000* firms receiving takeover bids between 1988 and 1991. The sample directors are compared to cohorts from nontargeted firms, matched on age and number of *Fortune 1000* directorships. I compute the direct financial impact of the merger on both inside and outside directors. Further, the study tracks these directors' abnormal change in directorships in *Fortune 1000* firms and relates them to director characteristics, target firm performance, and measures of how the offer was handled by the directors.

The evidence presented here shows that all directors, and outside directors in particular, are unlikely to be retained on the new board following a successful merger. The target board seat appears to be difficult to replace, because compared to their nontargeted peers, directors in my sample can expect to hold approximately one fewer *Fortune 1000* directorship 2 years following a completed merger. The direct financial impact of the merger for outside directors is predominantly negative. Their token holdings of target equity do not provide enough of a gain to offset the lost stream of income from the board seat. Thus, there is no financial windfall to offset the penalty of the loss of the board seat.

While the specifications used here only partially explain the number of future board seats held by an individual, there is some evidence of a form of ex post settling-up in the directorial labor market and the positive incentives created by such settling-up. These incentives potentially counter the perverse incentive created by the fact that target directors know that, should they accept the offer, they will lose one lucrative and difficult to replace board seat. In particular, if directors of a poorly performing firm successfully block an offer, the outside directors can expect fewer future other direct-orships, on average. However, directors of poorly performing firms who engineer a completed merger transaction for their shareholders do not face fewer other director-ships in the future. A two standard deviation reduction in prebid industry-adjusted operating performance reduces an outside director's future directorships by 0.47 if the takeover bid is terminated. If it is completed, the effect changes to an *increase* of 0.34 directorships. While the directors market does provide some partially offsetting incen-tives, the net incentive, however, is to block the merger because the net impact, including the loss of the target board seat, is still negative.

The results have implications for the understanding of incentives facing boards. Extant empirical research has built the case that independent boards are more likely than insider-dominated boards to act in shareholders' interests. The underlying as-sumption is that outside directors will align themselves with shareholders rather than management. However, these outside directors often have few direct incentives to tie them to shareholders. Except in the case of directors who are also blockholders, directors usually have very low ownership stakes and their compensation is primarily in the form of an annual cash retainer.[1] The findings here demonstrate that outside directors face a loss of directorships should the merger be completed. Thus, there exists a penalty of potentially losing a board seat should an external control event occur. This penalty motivates outside members to be diligent in exercising their internal control authority. However, this very penalty also leaves them with incentives counter to those of shareholders should an external control event actually occur. With the knowledge that these individuals will likely lose at least one lucrative board seat if the merger is

---

[1] Conference Board surveys of director compensation taken during my sample period report that in 1987, only 4% of firms paid their directors either partially or completely in stock and only 9% offered option grants. By 1991, these numbers had grown to 8% and 26%, respectively. Of those with option grant programs, only half made grants in any given year (The Conference Board, 1987-1996).

completed, it is no longer clear why they should be expected to align themselves with target shareholders during a takeover offer. In fact, top executives, with their golden parachutes, may in many cases have incentives that are more closely aligned with shareholders' than other directors do.

Section 2 starts with a motivating background discussion and development of the hypotheses examined here. Section 3 describes the data and presents the univariate analysis of the impact of the merger bid on target directors' retention on the surviving board and their future board seats following the merger. I also calculate the direct financial impact of the merger on both the inside and outside directors of the target firms. Section 4 continues with an examination of the factors influencing whether a target board member is retained following a takeover bid. Finally, evidence on the settling-up hypothesis is examined in a regression setting. Section 5 provides a discussion of the implications of the results and section 6 concludes.

2. Motivation and hypothesis development

Jensen and Meckling (1976) focuses researchers on the agency conflict created by the separation of ownership and control in a public corporation. One event where managers' interests often diverge severely from those of shareholders is in a merger or takeover. Work by Byrd and Hickman (1992) on bidders and by Cotter et al. (1997) on targets suggests that boards dominated by outsiders increase value for their shareholders during an acquisition attempt. Brickley et al. (1994) show that the market reaction to poison pill adoptions is positive for outsider-dominated boards and negative otherwise. Their finding provides additional evidence that investors expect outside directors to choose and exercise defensive mechanisms in shareholders' interests. Further, Rosenstein and Wyatt (1990) report the general finding that the stock price reaction to the addition of an outside director to a board is positive.

While these studies test the hypothesis that investors expect independent boards to align themselves with shareholders, we know little about the incentives facing these directors as they make their decisions. Their contracted compensation is primarily in the form of a cash retainer, which would cease in the event of a successful takeover.[2] Brickley et al. (1999) document that directorships can be very valuable. They report that average annual pay for each directorship is approximately $45,000, and further note that directors can also maintain lucrative consulting arrangements with their companies that, in their sample, ranged from $20,000 per year to $83,333 per month. At least as important for most directors are the nonfinancial rewards, such as influence, networking, and involvement (for retired executives) that would be lost along with the seat. These rewards, while hard to quantify, can have substantial value.

---

[2] Only two firms in my sample recognize this perverse incentive. They have golden parachute plans in place for directors who are not retained following a change in control.

Previous studies have shown that outside directors are expected to act in share-holders' interests in control contests despite the fact that the explicit incentives from their utility would lead them to do otherwise. Consequently, it is important to examine other avenues of incentive alignment. Fama (1980) and Gibbons and Murphy (1992) model the incentives provided by executives' career concerns. Fama suggests a form of ex post settling-up for managers that can be applied to directors as well. In Fama's model, the actions of managers affect their value in the labor market. If managers are terminated for poor performance, then they are unlikely to be hired by another firm, or if they are, it will be in a reduced capacity at a reduced salary.

2.1. The market for directors

There are at least three main factors plausibly at work in the market for directors. First, it can be viewed as a national market in which directors with experience and a reputation for maximizing shareholder value are sought after and receive the most directorships. Second, it could be the case that CEOs control the selection of directors and are looking for passive directors with a reputation for loyalty to management. Finally, personal networking may be an important factor, so that directorships are partly determined by who knows whom. Certainly, all three of these forces character-ize the market for directors. For example, reputation is likely to be important, but networking probably plays a large role in clearing the market. Evidence in the studies cited above suggests that performance-related reputation plays some measurable role in the number of directorships an individual holds. It is important to note that I do not assume any particular mechanism for the market for directors, but instead leave whether performance-related reputational effects impose any settling-up as an empir-ical question. If the market is primarily driven by CEOs looking for lackey-directors or by personal characteristics and networking, then the tests will fail to find support for the settling-up hypothesis. This would be interesting in itself, because unless I have failed to identify and measure performance-related reputational effects, it would imply that such reputation is not an important factor in the allocation of the role of outside monitors in US corporations.

2.2. Hypotheses

This study tests two hypotheses based on its two goals. The first goal is to understand what motivates diligence by outside directors. The first hypothesis, which I will call the *penalty hypothesis*, claims that the effect of a completed merger on a target director is negative. The implication of support for this hypothesis is that the costs borne by outside directors should the external control market need to act for them drive them to vigilantly monitor managers.

Fama and Jensen (1983) emphasize the role of the board of directors in monitoring managers and representing the interests of shareholders and discuss the difficulty involved in providing proper incentives for the board. They hypothesize that directors have incentives to develop reputations as experts in decision control and use their directorships to signal their value as decision experts. Further, Fama and Jensen posit that an outside takeover attempt indicates the breakdown of the internal control mechanism and that directors will see a "substantial devaluation of human capital" as a result (p. 315).

There is some indirect evidence that fear of human capital devaluation is a factor in board effectiveness. First, Weisbach (1988) establishes that boards dominated by outsiders are more likely to take disciplinary actions against a CEO. Second, Mikkelson and Partch (1997) find that CEOs are more likely to be dismissed for poor performance during the active takeover market of the 1980s than during the relatively inactive period in the early 1990s.[3] Notably, the vast majority of these dismissals are not the result of a takeover bid. They conclude that an active takeover market increases the vigilance of the board in monitoring managers. Boards operating in a more active takeover environment know that not only is the unconditional probability of a takeover attempt greater than otherwise, but also it is likely that the probability of a takeover attempt conditional on poor performance is even greater. In order for this increased threat of a takeover attempt to affect the board's vigilance, there must be some penalty paid by directors in the event of a control contest.

Recently, Brown and Maloney (1999) document higher outside director turnover in boards of companies they classify as poorly performing. Their classification is based on Mitchell and Lehn's (1990) definition of bad bidders; that is, firms which make value-decreasing bids and eventually become targets themselves. They show that prior to the value-decreasing bid, there is significantly greater turnover on the sample firms' boards than on boards of control samples. Mitchell and Lehn suggest that it is often easier for outside directors to exit poorly performing firms than to try to effect change. If there is a direct or reputational penalty to staying with a poorly performing firm up to the point where the external control market acts and it receives a takeover bid, then this behavior is rational.

The second hypothesis examined in this study is related to Fama's (1980) *ex post settling-up hypothesis* for managers. While the first hypothesis deals with the consequences to directors of receiving and completing a takeover bid, the second deals with the consequences of thwarting a bid. If the first hypothesis is not rejected, then conditional on receiving a bid, directors have an incentive to keep the target independent. The settling-up hypothesis for directors states that the directorial labor market reacts to such antishareholder actions by reducing target directors' other directorships in the future, penalizing them for putting their own welfare above that of target shareholders.

Extant research provides some support for the supposition that an individual's success in the directorial labor market is tied to reputational capital affected by the performance of firms at which he or she serves as a director or executive. Kaplan and Reishus (1990), Gilson (1990), and Brickley et al. (1999) show that firm performance

---

[3] However, Huson et al. (2001) provide contradictory evidence.

affects directorships. Kaplan and Reishus (1990) demonstrate that the executives of firms that cut their dividends are less likely to receive additional directorships than are other executives. Gilson (1990) establishes that the directors who resign following bankruptcy of a firm hold fewer directorships in the future than do other directors. Brickley et al. (1999) show that a CEO's performance in the final years of service directly affects the CEO's number of postretirement directorships. Thus, the implication of previous work is that for executives, there is a relation between own-firm performance and their success in the directorial labor market. For other directors, an extreme event, such as bankruptcy, has an impact on their future directorships.

2.3. Development of predictions

In this paper, I calculate the abnormal change in the number of board seats a target director holds following a takeover event. The two hypotheses outlined in the previous section generate predictions related to this abnormal change in board seats. The penalty hypothesis states that takeovers are costly for directors and after a completed takeover directors will lose their target board seats and not be able to replace them. The second hypothesis is the settling-up hypothesis. It predicts that even following a cancelled takeover bid, the directorial labor market will impose some degree of settling-up on target directors, reducing their holdings of other directorships. The prediction of the settling-up hypothesis is that directors of a firm that receives a takeover offer, successful or not, will hold fewer future directorships than otherwise.

The settling-up hypothesis can be refined further. Not all takeover attempts are driven by poor management of the target's resources. Therefore, it is likely that the degree to which a takeover offer reflects poorly on the target directors is affected by the prebid performance of the target firm. Consequently, I also test whether prebid performance affects any settling-up in the directorial labor market.

A stronger form of the settling-up hypothesis is related to actions taken by directors conditional on their firm becoming a target. Rather than viewing the existence of the offer as a signal about the directors, one can observe their actions in response to the offer. Thus, the strongest form of the settling-up hypothesis predicts that directors will be judged based on the degree of their resistance, whether they successfully complete the merger, and whether the firm's shares are auctioned.

In summary, the various forms of the settling-up hypothesis produce a series of predictions. In its simplest form, it predicts that directors who reject a takeover bid will hold fewer board seats in the future than will their untargeted peers. When modified to account for performance, it predicts that only directors of poorly performing targets will hold fewer seats in the future. Finally, when modified to account for performance and the outcome of the takeover event, the settling-up hypothesis predicts that the negative impact on future seats will be mitigated if the directors engineer a completed offer for their shareholders. Ancillary predictions are that, at the margin, hostile resistance that staves off an offer will result in fewer, while having an auction for the target's shares will result in more, future board seats.

2.4. Caveats and alternatives

There are several factors that confound the predictions of the settling-up hypothesis. The first is that involvement in a control contest could be a valuable experience that is sought after in the directorial labor market. Thus, directors of targeted firms would be predicted to have more directorships than otherwise, and even more if their experience included a contested or resisted offer. I will refer to this as the *experience hypothesis*.

It is also possible that entrenched CEOs with control over the nomination of directors value intransigence toward bidders. Hermalin and Weisbach (1998) provide a model of bargaining between the board and the CEO over control of the nomination process. If there are enough of these CEOs, then directors who thwart bids should have more future directorships.

3. Data

I start by identifying a sample of takeover targets from 1988 to 1991. The initial sample is drawn from the sample used in Schwert (2000).[4] This is a sample of all NYSE/AMEX listed firms that received an offer for their shares. I narrow this sample to companies that were in the *Fortune 1000* when targeted because directors of such firms are more likely to be holding, or have the potential to hold, additional director-ships. Further, these individuals are likely to be more comparable than a sample drawn from all public boards. I have a final sample of 1091 directors from 91 firms targeted from 1988 to 1991. Information about the directors of a target is obtained from the target's proxy statement current at the time of the offer. Using *Compact Disclosure*, I construct a database of all directors of *Fortune 1000* firms from 1991 to 1994. Consistent with Kaplan and Reishus (1990), I base my tests on *Fortune 1000* direct-orships because they are likely to be more valuable and comparable than a sample of all directorships. From this database, I can track the 1091 target directors' experiences in the directorial labor market.

I classify directors as inside, gray, or outside in a manner consistent with Cotter et al. (1997). Their method is similar to that used in other director research (see, e.g., Byrd and Hickman, 1992). Employees, former employees, or their family members are classified as inside directors. Individuals with actual or potential business ties to the firm are classified as gray. This includes all bankers, lawyers, consultants, and execu-tives of affiliated companies.[5] Finally, all others, including retired executives of other firms, academics, private investors, executives of unaffiliated firms, and others, are classified as outside directors.

Table 1 contains some summary statistics for the sample firms and directors. While 29% of inside directors hold other *Fortune 1000* directorships, 44% of gray and 58% of

---

[4] The data set is available on Schwert's website: http://schwert.ssb.rochester.edu.
[5] Byrd and Hickman (1992) classify these as outsiders if they do not have a *current* business relationship with the firm.

Table 1

Summary statistics for directors and takeover offers

Panel A contains summary statistics for the 1091 directors studied in this paper. The data are drawn from the proxy statement current at the time of the offer. An individual is defined to be a blockholder if he or she controls 5% or more of the stock of the corporation. Statistics for Number of additional directorships and Number of additional *Fortune 1000* directorships are presented for the full sample and for only those directors with additional directorships.

Panel B contains summary statistics for the 91 takeover events of *Fortune 1000* firms occurring from 1988 to 1991. An offer is characterized as hostile if either the *Wall Street Journal* or *Dow Jones News Retrieval* stories characterized the offer as hostile. If more than one bidder emerged then the event is defined to have been an auction. The fraction of events fitting the intersection of the row and column characteristics is given.

Panel A

		All directors	Inside	Gray	Outside
Age	Mean	59.89	$57.02^{g,o}$	61.20^{i}	60.77^{i}
	Median	60	$57^{g,o}$	61^{i}	61^{i}
Fraction of sample		1.00	0.26	0.18	0.56
Years as director	Mean	8.60	9.66^{o}	9.19^{o}	$7.91^{i,g}$
	Median	6	7	7°	$6^{i,g}$
Fraction that are blockholders		0.03	$0.05^{g,o}$	0.01^{i}	0.02^{i}
Fraction with additional directorships		0.71	$0.46^{g,o}$	$0.73^{i,o}$	$0.83^{i,g}$
Fraction with additional *Fortune 1000* directorships		0.48	$0.29^{g,o}$	$0.44^{i,o}$	$0.58^{i,g}$
Number of additional directorships					
Full sample	Mean	1.94	$1.01^{g,o}$	$1.97^{i,g}$	$2.36^{i,g}$
	Median	2	$0^{g,o}$	$2^{i,o}$	$2^{i,g}$
Only directors with additional directorships	Mean	2.74	$2.24^{g,o}$	2.75^{i}	2.86^{i}
	Median	2	$2^{g,o}$	2^{i}	3^{i}
Number of additional *Fortune 1000* directorships					
Full sample	Mean	0.975	$0.45^{g,o}$	$0.83^{i,o}$	$1.26^{i,g}$
	Median	0	$0^{g,o}$	$0^{i,o}$	$1^{i,g}$
Only directors with additional directorships	Mean	2.03	$1.56^{g,o}$	$1.89^{i,o}$	$2.17^{i,g}$
	Median	2	$1^{g,o}$	$2^{i,o}$	$2^{i,g}$

Panel B

	Fraction of events		
	Hostile	Auction	Bid ends in a merger
All events	0.26	0.40	0.67
Bid is characterized as hostile		0.12	0.18
Multiple bidders emerge (auction)			0.28

For the median rows, the superscripts refer to significance levels for the Wilcoxon nonparametric test for differences in distributions.

^{i,g,o}Indicate that the mean is significantly different at the 10% level from the comparable mean for inside, gray, and outside directors, respectively.

^{i,g,o}Indicate that the mean is significantly different at the 5% level from the comparable mean for inside, gray, and outside directors, respectively.

outside directors do. Each of these frequencies is significantly different from the other two. The table also presents statistics on a sample restricted to only those directors who hold additional directorships. For inside directors who hold additional directorships, the mean number of additional directorships is 2.2, significantly smaller than the numbers for gray and outside directors: 2.8 and 2.9. I also present the number of additional *Fortune 1000* directorships held by target directors. For directors who hold additional *Fortune 1000* directorships, the mean numbers held are 1.6 for insiders, 1.9 for gray, and 2.2 for outsiders, each of which is significantly different from the other two. While 5% of inside directors are also blockholders, only 1% of gray and outside directors are. Blockholders are identified from the target proxy statements as holders of at least 5% of the firm's voting equity.

Given the proportion of sample directors holding additional directorships, the directors, particularly outside directors, clearly have a vested interest in their value in the directorial labor market. While 29% of inside directors report additional outside directorships, the proportion of inside directors with an interest in their value in the directorial labor market is most likely higher. Insiders that do not have additional directorships tend to be younger, lower-ranked executives who have not yet achieved positions warranting appointment to the boards of other firms. However, as they advance through their careers, directorships will become increasingly important to them. This future stream of expected directorships will still affect their incentives at the time of the offer.

The second panel of Table 1 contains summary statistics for the takeover events. Twenty-six percent of the bids can be characterized as "hostile." An offer is characterized as hostile if stories in either the *Wall Street Journal* or *Dow Jones News Retrieval* characterized the offer as hostile. This corresponds to the "Host(WSJ)" variable described in Schwert (2000). Offers become hostile if the target board resists the offer, so this variable can alternatively be interpreted as an indicator of board resistance. An auction, defined as multiple bidders for the target, occurred in 40% of the control contests. Overall, two-thirds of the targets were taken over.

4. Empirical tests

4.1. Summary information on target board retention

Table 2 presents summary statistics for characteristics of the target board, surviving board, and retention of prebid directors. Statistics are presented at an aggregate level and also split according to whether the bid was terminated or completed. The first panel of the table, describing target boards prior to the bid, indicates that there is little difference between boards of targets in terminated bids and those in completed bids. The median size of the board for the entire sample is 12, which is the same as the median board size reported by Yermack (1996) for a large sample of US corporations. Twenty-six percent of the target board members are insiders, 20% are gray, and 54%

Table 2

Retention of the target board members

The table presents summary statistics for the characteristics of the target board and the fraction of the target board, and inside, gray, and outside directors separately, that remains on the surviving board. The surviving board is defined as the board of the still-independent target in the event of a terminated bid, or of the new, merged firm following the consummation of a successful bid. Data for postoutcome boards are taken from the first proxy statement following either final termination or completion of the bid.

		All events	Terminated	Merged	*p*-value for difference
Target board size	Mean	11.99	11.90	12.03	0.856
	Median	12	11.5	12	0.822
Insiders	Mean	3.07	2.93	3.13	0.540
	Median	3	3	3	0.424
Fraction of board		0.26	0.26	0.27	0.811
Gray	Mean	2.26	2.37	2.21	0.638
	Median	2	2	2	0.743
Fraction of board		0.20	0.21	0.19	0.523
Outsiders	Mean	6.66	6.60	6.69	0.911
	Median	7	6.5	7	0.705
Fraction of board		0.54	0.53	0.55	0.758
Board size postoutcome	Mean	13.89	12.27	15.10	0.067
	Median	12.50	11	13	0.116
Retention:					
Fraction of board	Mean	0.36	0.85	0.13	0.001
	Median	0.11	0.90	0	0.001
Fraction of insiders	Mean	0.41	0.87	0.19	0.001
	Median	0.33	1.00	0	0.001
Fraction of grays	Mean	0.31	0.73	0.10	0.001
	Median	0.00	1.00	0	0.001
Fraction of outsiders	Mean	0.36	0.87	0.10	0.001
	Median	0.00	1.00	0	0.001
Frequency of:					
CEO is the only survivor		0.04	0	0.07	0.045
Entire board survives		0.10	0.30	0	0.001
New board is enlarged		0.44	0.40	0.48	0.539

are outsiders. While the outside fraction is exactly what Yermack reports, the inside and gray fractions are slightly lower and higher.

The first step in testing the penalty hypothesis is to document how often target board members are retained by the bidder after the bid. The bottom panel of Table 2 presents statistics on the retention of the target board following the outcome of the bid. The data are drawn from the first proxy statement for the combined board or from the first proxy statement for the target following final termination of the bid. The bidder enlarges its board in 44% of the completed mergers, so the postbid board is somewhat bigger in completed mergers. Overall, 36% of the board members are retained, but this average masks two very different retention rates for target boards following terminated and completed bids. Following terminated bids, 85% of the prebid board members remain on the surviving board while only 13% remain following completed mergers. The turnover of 15% of the seats in unsuccessful contests could be due to changes made in response to the bid, regular retirements, or regular turnover of directors. Turnover in response to the bid is what I am studying and turnover due to the latter two reasons should add noise, but not bias to my tests. The entire target slate survives intact in 30% of the terminated bids versus zero cases following completed mergers. In a study of management changes following terminated bids, Denis and Serrano (1996) report a similar result of no changes in ownership or board structure in 42% of their cases.

The fraction of insiders retained on the board in a completed merger is 19% and higher than the 10% retention rates for gray and outside directors. This difference possibly represents either continuation of target management or firm-specific knowledge held by insiders that is valuable to the new board. Consistent with this, the CEO's retention rate (not tabulated) is much higher: 27%. In fact, the CEO is the only survivor from the target board in 7% of the consummated bids and when only the cases where at least one member of the target board is retained are counted, the CEO is the only survivor 20% of the time (not tabulated).

The results presented in Table 2 make it clear that directors, particularly outside directors, should expect to lose their board seat should the takeover be completed. On the other hand, should the takeover be terminated, they enjoy very high retention rates on the still-independent target. The loss of the target board seat is of little consequence if it is easily replaced. In the next section, I examine whether after 2 years the target directors still hold one seat less than their peers.

4.2. Abnormal changes in board seats: univariate results

The next test for the penalty hypothesis comes from examining the number of *Fortune 1000* directorships held by a given director after the control events. I measure the directorships 2 years after the year of the control event. This allows the labor market time to work, avoids any measurement error in the transition year immediately following the event, and accounts for the fact that many firms have staggered elections, leaving directors in my sample with an average of about 1.5 years before they are up for renomination. In Table 3, target directors are stratified by whether the director held additional directorships on other *Fortune 1000* companies at the time of the bid. I will refer to directors whose only *Fortune 1000* directorship was on the target board as single-seat directors. Those with multiple *Fortune 1000* directorships will be called multiple-seat directors. The examination of the single-seat directors will be important because these less-experienced directors provide the cleanest test of the hypotheses. The impact of the takeover event on their career paths will not be muddled or diluted by the effects of other boards on which they serve. Also, to the extent that the experience hypothesis is true, the effect of the event on the overall level of experience

Table 3

Univariate statistics for changes in directorships

Each target director's number of *Fortune 1000* directorships at the time of the takeover bid is compared with the number held 2 years later. The abnormal component of this change is calculated by subtracting the median 2-year change for a cohort of nontarget directors matched on age and starting number of directorships. Two sets of numbers are presented. In the first three columns, the abnormal change, including the effect of the target seat, which is usually lost if the merger is completed, is presented. In the last three columns, the effect of the event on other, nontarget, *Fortune 1000* board seats is isolated. Numbers in bold are significantly different from zero at the 10% level. Numbers in bold italics are significantly different from zero at the 5% level. The number of observations is in brackets.

	Abnormal change, including target seat			Abnormal change, other seats only		
	All events	Terminated	Merged[a]	All events	Terminated	Merged
Inside						
All directors, raw change	*-0.626*	*-0.335*	*-0.761*	0.018	0.006	0.024
	[278]	[88]	[190]	[278]	[88]	[190]
Multiple seats, % change	*-0.260*	-0.083	*-0.369*	-0.069	-0.040	-0.087
	[81]	[31]	[50]	[81]	[31]	[50]
Multiple seats, raw change	*-0.667*	-0.210	*-0.950*	-0.148	-0.081	-0.190
	[81]	[31]	[50]	[81]	[31]	[50]
Single seat, raw change	*-0.609*	*-0.404*	*-0.693*	*0.086*	0.053	**0.100**
	[197]	[57]	[140]	[197]	[57]	[140]
Outside						
All directors, raw change	*-0.731*	*-0.381*	*-0.902*	-0.047	-0.043	-0.049
	[605]	[198]	[407]	[605]	[198]	[407]
Multiple seats, % change	*-0.314*	*-0.170*	*-0.381*	*-0.076*	-0.087	*-0.071*
	[353]	[113]	[240]	[353]	[113]	[240]
Multiple seats, raw change	*-0.983*	*-0.571*	*-1.177*	*-0.292*	*-0.288*	*-0.294*
	[353]	[113]	[240]	[353]	[113]	[240]
Single seat, raw change	*-0.379*	*-0.129*	*-0.506*	*0.296*	*0.282*	*0.302*
	[252]	[85]	[167]	[252]	[85]	[167]

[a]For the columns including the effect of the target board seat, all of the numbers in the merged column are significantly different from their counterparts in the terminated column.

of single-seat directors is likely to be much larger than for multiple-seat directors. For parsimony of presentation and discussion, I will present and discuss only the results for inside and outside directors, dropping the smallest group, gray directors.

To control for a possible downward trend in the number of directorships held by any individual over time, I construct a control group of all *Fortune 1000* directors (excluding those in my sample) in 1991. Using 1991 as the "event" year for the control group, I match the sample directors to control director cohorts with the same age and number of *Fortune 1000* directorships at the time of the event. In the 32 cases where there was not at least one nontarget director for an exact match, the closest match was selected. For each matching cohort, I calculate the median change in the number of *Fortune 1000* directorships held after 2 years, in 1993. The difference between the sample director's change in directorships and his or her matching cohort's change is used in the remainder of the paper. This abnormal change in directorships provides a comparison to otherwise similar directors who were not on a target board.

Table 3 presents two sets of numbers: the first set includes the takeover event's impact on the target board seat and the second set focuses solely on the event's impact on other board seats. As the first set of numbers shows, the overall impact of a takeover bid on target directors is negative, whether the merger is completed or rejected. The effect is clearly and statistically significantly worse if the merger is completed. Following a completed merger, the "all directors, raw change" row shows that both inside and outside directors will hold, on average, up to one less directorship than their peer cohort. This is driven by the low rate of retention for target board members following completed deals (documented in Table 2). It appears that the target seat, once lost through merger, is not easily replaced.

The second set of numbers presents the abnormal change in directorships, not including the target seat. In contrast to the numbers that include the target seat, many of the inside directors' numbers are insignificantly different from zero. The effect for all outside directors as a group is zero as well, but this is the result of two opposite effects. For single-seat directors, particularly outside directors, the effect of the event on other directorships is uniformly positive, regardless of the outcome. They can expect to add, on average, 0.3 additional directorships relative to their single-seat peers. Outside directors who have multiple *Fortune 1000* board seats experience an equal and opposite effect, holding abnormally fewer other board seats regardless of the outcome.

One interpretation of the different net effects for the two groups of directors is that it provides support for both the settling-up and experience hypotheses. Receiving and acting on a takeover bid has two effects for directors: a positive one from the experience that it gives the director and a negative one from the signal about the ability of the board to manage the firm's resources. For inexperienced directors, the marginal impact of the experience effect outweighs the negative signal about their value as decision control experts. However, further untabulated tests indicate that it is more likely that the result occurs because single-seat directors who lose their only seat work very hard to get a new one. First, I examine the change in seats following a completed merger controlling for whether the single-seat director was retained following the merger. There is no increase in other seats for those who are retained. Instead, the entire increase comes from those who are dropped from the board. There is no reason the experience effect should work only for those dropped from the board. Second, I examine single-seat directors who are managers of the target. The only time they receive a new outside seat is when they lose their association with the target firm (after the merger they are dropped from the board *and* lose their job). Again, the evidence supports the explanation that single-seat directors who lose their only seat through merger work extra hard to obtain a new one.

4.3. Direct financial impact of the merger

It is clear that, on average, the majority of directors, and in particular almost all outside directors, face the permanent loss of a board seat if the merger should go through. To complete the picture of the impact of a merger on the target directors, I measure the direct financial impact of the merger. It is possible that the direct financial impact of a completed takeover is enough to alter directors' incentives or to cause them to retire following the takeover. I estimate the direct financial impact of the takeover as follows:

$$
\begin{aligned}
\text{Financial Impact} = &\ (\text{Premium} \times \text{Shares with Financial Interest}) \\
&+ (\text{Premium} \times \text{Shares Underlying Options}) \\
&+ \text{Golden Parachute} - \text{PV(Lost Cash Caompensation)}.
\end{aligned} \tag{1}
$$

Shares with financial interest are shares held by the director, members of his or her immediate family, or trusts benefiting them. Cash compensation can include cash salary and bonus for employees and retainer and meeting fees for outside directors.[6] The loss of cash compensation is calculated as an annuity with a discount rate of 10% and the number of years equal to years until expected retirement age (age 65 for insiders and age 70 for outside directors). For outside directors, the annuity is also calculated using the number of years until his or her board term expires. The first of these annuities is likely to be closer to, but to overestimate, the actual loss. The second one, using only the current term, is almost certain to underestimate the loss. However, as a conservative measure, it is useful for the purposes of demonstrating that outside directors do not receive a large net financial gain to offset any directorial labor market penalties. The golden parachute and loss of current cash compensation are set to zero if the director was retained following the completed takeover.

Table 4 presents some summary statistics for the financial impact variable and its components. The left side of the table shows the compensation components and the financial impact they produce in a merger. The right side summarizes the actual and expected impacts for the events. As the right side of Panel A shows, the median actual financial impact of the event is zero, with at least 35% of the directors experiencing a negative impact. Most of the directors negatively affected by the event are outside directors. The impact of the event on inside directors is predictably large because of their larger shareholdings and large golden parachutes should they be terminated (54% of the managers lose their jobs). However, the last four rows of Panel A document that the direct financial impact of the event on outside directors is small. The median total impact is very close to zero and the median impact from their generally very small equity holdings is only $16,500 (second column).

---

[6] I have collected the regular meeting fees, but I do not have committee membership or committee retainers and meeting fees. Excluding these produces a conservative measure of lost future income for outside directors. Thus, the results in Table 4 would be even more negative if these fees were included.

Table 4

The direct financial impact of the merger on the target directors

Panel A presents summary statistics for all events, whether consummated or terminated. "Shares with financial interest" are only those shares held or underlying options held by the director, his or her immediate family or trusts benefiting them. "Equity-based impact" is the part of the "Financial impact if merged" due to the director's stock and option holdings. For outside directors "Salary" is equal to any annual retainer plus per-meeting fees. The "Salary impact" is calculated as an annuity with a discount rate of 10% and the number of years equal to years until expected retirement (65 for inside and 70 for outside directors) in the "Retire" column. For outside directors, the annuity is also calculated using the number of years until his or her board term expires ("Term up" column). The "Actual financial impact" is defined as the dollar increase in the value of share and option holdings if the merger was completed, plus the value of the director's "Golden parachute" if he or she was actually terminated minus the salary impact if he or she was actually terminated, but is calculated as if the merger went through even for those mergers that were terminated. The "Financial impact if merged" variable is similar to the "Actual financial impact," but is calculated as if the merger went through even for those mergers that were terminated. Bold numbers indicate that the number for inside directors is significantly different from the corresponding number for outside directors.

Panel B compares the variables across terminated and merged events. Bold numbers indicate significant difference between the merged and terminated numbers within director type.

Panel A Directors		% Shares with financial interest	Equity-based impact	Salary impact			Golden[a] parachute	Actual financial impact		Financial impact if merged	
				Salary	Retire	Term up		Retire	Term up	Retire	Term up
Inside and outside	Mean	0.38	1,565,963	202,647	−822,141		1,309,190	712,354	752,472	1,273,311	1,329,769
	Median	0.01	36,559	29,325	−39,050		1,132,888	0	0	−32,884	0
	% > 0	95	92	100	0	0	18	29	37	38	50
	% < 0	0	0	0	100			43	35	60	49
Inside	Mean	**0.83**	**3,752,874**	**581,264**	**−2,517,308**		**1,368,643**	**1,954,835**		**3,130,394**	
	Median	**0.11**	929,913	511,110	−2,055,459		1,163,539	0		**370,744**	
	% > 0	96	94	100	0		54	46		67	
	% < 0	0	0	0	99			26		30	
Outside	Mean	**0.18**	**578,326**	26,935	−134,401	−38,232	**298,500**	150,280	208,546	**446,180**	**527,784**
	Median	**0.00**	**16,500**	24,000	−129,036	−27,727	**115,000**	−3,554	0	**−65,936**	**−4,853**
	% > 0	95	91	100	0	0	1	22	34	46	45
	% < 0	0	0	0	100	100	0	50	39	51	54

(Continued)

Table 1 (*Continued*)

Panel B		% Shares with financial interest: Retire	Equity-based impact	Salary	Salary impact: Term up	Salary impact: Retire	Golden[a] parachute	Financial impact if merged: Term up	Financial impact if merged: Retire
Directors, events									
Inside, terminate	Mean	0.77	51,031,557	645,977	−2,771,802		1,485,026	3,758,515	
	Median	0.41	**582,741**	523,000	−2,113,723		1,017,522	**−25,163**	
	% > 0	95	76	100	0		29	80	
	% < 0	0	0	0	100	0	9		
Inside, merge	Mean	0.86	3,192,650	551,787	−2,402,720		1,338,470	2,872,355	
	Median	0.11	**1,015,327**	482,850	−2,044,465		1,193,300	**543,636**	
	% > 0	96	97	99	0	60	97	0	
	% < 0	0	0	0	99		0	0	
Outside, terminate	Mean	0.10	1,056,924	26,086	−134,708	−36,674	200,000	941,447	1,026,605
	Median		13,343	24,050	−133,897	−25,546	200,000	−69,666	**−11,191**
	% > 0	95	86	100	0	0	2	22	36
	% < 0	0	0	0	100	100	0	78	64
Outside, merge	Mean	0.22	366,007	27,339	−134,257	−38,961	357,600	224,829	304,854
	Median	0.01	17,194	24,000	−128,038	−28,182	30,000	−65,443	**0**
	% > 0	94	94	100	0	0	1	32	49
	% < 0	0	0	0	100	100	0	67	50

[a] Dollar values in the "Golden parachute" column are based only on the subset of individuals covered by a golden parachute.

While Panel A presents statistics based on all events, including terminated events that produced no direct financial impact on some directors, Panel B splits the events according to outcome. The financial impact for terminated events is presented as if the merger had gone through (the average actual financial impact is zero for terminated mergers).[7] Thus, the value that the director could have had from an approved deal can be compared to the value of the deals that were approved. This calculation will provide some insight into whether the expected financial impact for deals that were blocked was significantly different from those that were completed. For inside directors, the median financial impact of the approved mergers ($543,636) is substantially and significantly greater than the potential impact of mergers that were not approved (−$25,163). This difference is driven by larger equity-based gains as the salary and golden parachutes of inside directors did not differ across outcomes. This is consistent with Hartzell et al. (2000) who, in a study of completed mergers, find evidence that CEOs sometimes sacrifice shareholder gains for personal gains. Finally, and notably, the median impact on an outside director from completed deals is negative, falling somewhere between zero and −$65,443. The gains from outside directors' usually token holdings of shares are insufficient to overcome the loss of cash compensation from the lost target board seat.

4.4. Analysis

Tables 2–4 provide some evidence pertaining to the first goal of this paper: the effect of a takeover bid on target directors. The univariate results show that if a firm is targeted for a takeover or merger, its directors pay a penalty. Overall, a board member loses and does not replace about one *Fortune 1000* directorship following the end of the contest. This contributes to and compounds the net negative financial impact that the median director suffers from a completed merger. The evidence overwhelmingly supports the penalty hypothesis. The results indicate the disturbing possibility that target directors know that, should the merger be completed, they will have fewer directorships than if it is blocked, with no offsetting financial gain.

One could imagine an alternative interpretation of the data presented in Table 3. Assume that the mergers that are the most likely to be completed, with or without the board's consent, are the ones in which the target performs particularly badly prior to receiving the bid. Then, it is this bad performance that leads to fewer future directorships for the target board, rather than the merger itself. This interpretation supports the contention in Fama and Jensen (1983) that successful takeovers can be negative signals about target management and directors. The univariate statistics presented in Table 3 do not address this hypothesis. However, later tests will include industry-adjusted

---

[7] In calculating the expected (if merged instead of terminated) cash impact portion of this variable, the average retention rates from Table 2 were used. Thus, outside directors could have expected to keep their board seat (and salary) in 10% of the cases and inside directors could have expected to be retained in 19% of the cases, unless they are CEOs, in which case the retention rate is 27%.

return on assets prior to the bid to address this issue as well as test the form of the settling-up hypothesis modified to account for target performance. Additionally, the strongest form of the settling-up hypothesis predicts that directors' actions during the offer will affect the number of future directorships that they have. The tests in the next section continue the analysis with the inclusion of variables for the characteristics of the directors, actions taken during the takeover contests, and prebid performance.

4.5. Factors affecting the retention of target firm board seats

This section identifies some factors that have the potential to affect whether a target director remains on the board, either of the new merged firm or the still-independent target, following the offer. I then estimate probit specifications to assess the impact of these factors on the likelihood of retention. Following the analysis of retention on the surviving board, the change in the number of nontarget directorships is again analyzed, but in regressions designed to test whether the degree of settling-up varies with actions taken during the offer and the prebid performance of the target firm.

4.5.1. Explaining director retention using director and event characteristics

I estimate a probit for each type of director to assess the ability of director character-istics and aspects of the way the offer evolved to predict whether a particular director will remain on the surviving board. The explanatory variables are separated into three categories: director characteristics, event characteristics, and performance. The dir-ector characteristics include: age,[8] years-as-a-director, and dummy variables for whether the director's term is up, whether he or she is a blockholder, and for the inside specification, whether he or she is the CEO. These are primarily control variables and will not test the settling-up hypothesis. Performance is measured as prebid operating performance relative to the target's industry. The cash flow return on assets [(Operating Income Before Depreciation—Taxes—Changes in Working Cap-ital) divided by beginning of period assets] is averaged over the 4 years prior to the bid and then adjusted by subtracting the corresponding average for all firms in the target's two-digit SIC industry. This method is similar to that used in Brickley et al. (1999), facilitating comparison between the effect of own firm performance on retiring execu-tives documented there and own firm performance on inside and outside directors following a merger event documented here. The event characteristics include dummy variables for whether the target was taken private or acquired by a foreign firm, and for whether the event ended in a merger or termination of the bid. The private or foreign acquirer variable is included to capture any mechanically negative effects on retention

---

[8] Despite the fact that the sample directors are matched to control cohorts based on age and number of directorships, age could still matter. For example, an older, well-known director could recover quickly so that 2 years after the event, he or she looks similar to his or her peers while a younger director could recover more slowly.

of such a takeover. Boards of firms that remain private will be impossible to observe and I was unable to obtain board information for some of the foreign acquirers. Based on similar cases where I could observe the foreign board, in these unobservable cases, the retention variable was coded as zero.

Two other event variables: whether the contest was classified as hostile and whether multiple bidders emerged (an auction), as well as the prebid industry-adjusted operating performance of the target, are interacted with a dummy variable for terminated events in order to allow the effects of these characteristics to vary depending on the outcome of the bid. Table 5 contains definitions and predictions for the event characteristic variables and prebid performance. These variables are intended to test for settling-up through retention and future other directorships by identifying the marginal effect of measures of how the bid was handled and of the prebid performance of the target.

4.5.2. Probit results

Table 6 presents the results of the probits that estimate the probability of retention on the surviving board, computed separately for inside and outside directors. Insiders are less likely to be retained following a hostile deal, probably a result of animosity generated with the bidder. If the target is taken private or acquired by a foreign company, both inside and outside directors are less likely to be retained. The successful merger variable shows that both types of directors are less likely to be retained if the bid is consummated. This demonstrates that the earlier univariate findings of Table 3 are robust to personal and event characteristic controls. Prebid performance has no effect on whether an outside director is retained. However, insiders are more likely to be retained following good performance than bad. This is consistent with the performance-based form of the settling-up hypothesis for target managers and with previous studies on managerial career paths following takeovers (see, e.g., Agrawal and Walkling, 1994; Martin and McConnell, 1991). This suggests that although Table 2 shows very low average retention rates, inside directors of firms with good performance have a stronger chance of being retained on the board following a merger.

Turning to the personal characteristics, age is ineffective in explaining whether an individual is retained on the surviving board. Insiders who are also blockholders are significantly more likely to be retained. This is sensible in that they are unlikely to be unseated in the event of a terminated offer and their cooperation is likely to be necessary to complete a proposed deal. CEOs are more likely to be retained, a reflection of the fact that the target CEO is the only director retained after a number of successful mergers.

Overall, the models do an incomplete job of explaining the retention decision. Additional factors not included here may account for some of the variation in retention. Kini et al. (1995) show that following a takeover, the new board tends to be constructed in a more balanced manner than the target board (e.g., insider-dominated target boards are replaced by boards with more outside seats). In exploring the

Table 5

Variable definitions and predictions

The independent variables for Tables 6 and 7 are defined. Two predicted signs are given in the column labeled "Pred." The first sign is for the effect on retention (Table 6) and the second sign is for the effect on future other board seats (Table 7).

Variable	Definition	Pred.	Relation to board seat retention and future board seats
Hostility	1 if the offer is characterized as hostile by the *WSJ* or *DJNR*, 0 otherwise.	– and +	Should reduce likelihood of retention. However, resistance that still allows a completed deal could characterize hard bargaining in the interests of shareholders and increase other board seats.
Hostility, terminated	1 if the offer is characterized as hostile, but the merger is terminated, 0 otherwise.	+ and –	Marginal effect of termination should counter reduced retention following completed offers. For other directorships, resistance that completely wards off a deal is unlikely to be in the best interests of shareholders (negative effect).
Auction	1 if multiple bidders emerged, 0 otherwise.	? and +	For retention, unclear. For other directorships, if the efforts of the target directors generated the auction, then this is a positive effect. There is also a positive effect from the experience of involvement in an auction.
Auction, terminated	1 if multiple bidders emerged, and the target remained independent, 0 otherwise.	? and –/0	For retention, unclear. For other directorships, failing to consummate a bid following an auction is unlikely to be in the interests of shareholders, but the experience effect may offset it.
Taken private/ acquired by a foreign firm	1 if the target was taken private or acquired by a foreign firm, 0 otherwise.	– and –	Retention is less likely in these cases and there are also potential negative spillover effects from the lower profile of private or foreign board seats.
Successful merger	1 if the merger was complete, 0 if it was terminated	– and +	For retention, the results so far show that a director is much less likely to remain on the surviving board following a completed merger. For future seats, successfully completing a merger is likely to be in shareholders' interests and should be rewarded.
Prebid operating performance	4-year average return on assets (%) prior to the event year, minus the median average ROA from the target's two-digit industry	+ and –/+	Potentially positive effect on both retention and future seats from the good performance of the target. However, for other seats, negotiating a successful acquisition of the firm following poor performance may be rewarded with future seats (negative relation).
Prebid operating performance, terminated	4-year average return on assets (%) prior to the event year, minus the median average ROA from the target's two-digit industry for targets that remained independent, 0 otherwise.	+ and +	Failing to complete a merger following poor performance should have a more negative effect (positive coefficient) than doing so following good performance.

Table 6
Predicting who will remain on the surviving board

The table presents the results of probit models designed to estimate the probability that a director will remain on the surviving board, either of the new merged firm, or of the still-independent target, following a control contest. The model is estimated separately for inside and outside directors. "Hostility" and "Hostility, terminated" take a value of 1 if the offer is characterized as hostile (see Table 1) for all offers and for only terminated offers, respectively, and are 0 otherwise. Similarly, the "Auction" and "Auction, terminated" take a value of 1 if there are multiple bidders regardless of the outcome, and for only offers that were terminated, respectively, and are 0 otherwise. "Taken private/acquired by a foreign firm" and "Successful merger" are self-explanatory dummy variables. "Prebid operating performance" is the industry-adjusted average cash flow return on assets (in %) for the 4 years prior to the bid and is split for terminated and successful offers as with hostility and auction. Marginal effects are presented. *t*-statistics are in parentheses. The pseudo-R^2 is computed as $1 - [(\log$ likelihood of the full model)/(log likelihood of a model including only a constant)].

	Predicted sign	Inside	Outside
Intercept		0.472 (1.524)	**0.519 (2.388)**
Performance			
Prebid operating performance	+	**0.009 (1.715)**	−0.000 (−0.076)
Prebid operating performance, terminated	+	0.001 (0.107)	−0.006 (−0.869)
Event characteristics			
Hostility	−	**−0.312 (−2.470)**	−0.078 (−1.060)
Hostility, terminated	+	0.246 (1.154)	−0.067 (−0.549)
Auction	?	−0.112 (−1.268)	−0.047 (−0.743)
Auction, terminated	?	−0.158 (−0.854)	0.125 (1.061)
Taken private/acquired by a foreign firm	−	**−0.189 (−2.002)**	**−0.305 (−4.315)**
Successful merger	−	**−0.808 (−5.560)**	**−0.719 (−8.680)**
Personal characteristics			
Age		0.002 (0.362)	−0.006 (−0.165)
Years as director		−0.004 (−0.840)	−0.002 (−0.520)
Blockholder	+	**0.324 (1.880)**	−0.174 (−0.995)
CEO	+	**0.167 (2.053)**	
Term is up the following year	−	0.014 (0.181)	−0.004 (−0.077)
Pseudo-R^2		0.389	0.452
Number of observations		277	583

composition of a cross section of boards, Hermalin and Weisbach (1988) find that expertise in particular business lines is a determinant of board membership. This may help explain retention of target board members in diversifying acquisitions.

Aside from providing evidence on the retention decision, the exercise carried out in this section serves as a useful first stage in determining how director and event characteristics affect the change in the number of other *Fortune 1000* directorships held by target directors after a bid. Remaining on the surviving board could have a positive effect on other directorships due to the certification provided by election to the board of the merged firm. Alternatively, it could reduce the director's availability or desire for other directorships. To capture these effects, retention will be included as a regressor to explain the change in other *Fortune 1000* seats held by a target director following a takeover bid. However, retention is endogenous in that it is at least partially a function of the other regressors. In the regressions that follow, the specifications will include only the part of retention that cannot be explained by the other regressors. This reduced form also alters the interpretation of the other coefficients. Since the other regressors partially determine retention, their total effect on future directorships in a regression that includes the raw retention. variable would be their own coefficients plus their indirect effect through the coefficient on retention. Including only unexplained retention avoids this and allows the other coefficients to measure their total impact on the number of other directorships held.

4.6. Changes in other board seats: cross-sectional analysis

This section contains the results and analysis of regressions using the change in other (nontarget) *Fortune 1000* directorships as the dependent variable. The regressions are estimated separately for inside and outside directors. Further, for each director affiliation, two separate groups are analyzed. The first specification analyzes the abnormal change in other *Fortune 1000* directorships for single-seat directors. The second estimates the abnormal percentage change in other *Fortune 1000* directorships for multiple-seat directors.

The specifications contain the same director and event characteristics as the probits in the previous section did. Most of the predicted signs remain the same. Due to possible animosity by the bidder, hostility was predicted to have a negative effect on retention even if the bid resulted in a merger. However, hostility (or resistance) that still results in a successful merger could represent hard-bargaining. Therefore, hostility that results in a merger could have a positive effect on other future directorships held by target directors.

Previous research such as Martin and McConnell (1991) and Agrawal and Walkling (1994) examines turnover of target executives following takeovers. If the takeover forces managers out of the labor market, then any loss of directorships may be attributable to their unemployment, rather than being a separate effect related to the merger. To control for this and to measure any impact the managerial labor market has on the directorial labor market, I include a manager employment variable in the inside director specifications. Using *Standard & Poor's Register of Corporations, Directors, and Executives*, I determine whether each target officer is still employed 2 years following the merger. The variable takes a value of 1 if he or she is employed and is 0 otherwise.

Finally, as discussed above, unexplained retention is included as an explanatory variable. This variable is the error from the appropriate probit specification for probability of retention. If retention is a positive signal to the directorial labor market, its coefficient will be positive. If retention decreases the director's time or desire to seek other board seats, the coefficient will be negative. Further, the endogeneity of retention requires a note of caution for interpreting the coefficients in Table 7.

Table 7

Regression analysis of the change in other *Fortune 1000* directorships

The table presents estimates from regression analyses of the abnormal change in other (not including the target) *Fortune 1000* directorships for single-seat and multiple-seat directors. Abnormal change is the actual change minus the change for a cohort of nontarget directors matched on age and starting number of directorships. Most of the variables are defined in Table 5 and the legend to Table 6. "Unexplained retention" is based on the results of the probit models in Table 6 and adjusts for the endogeneity of the retention decision. Those models attempt to explain whether a director remains on the surviving board, either of the new, merged firm, or of the still-independent target, following the contest. The "Unexplained retention" variable is equal to the error from the probit in Table 6 predicting retention on the surviving board. In the inside director specifications, "Remains employed" is a dummy variable set equal to 1 if the director is still listed as employed, either with the original or merged firm, or with a different firm, in the Register of Corporations, Directors, and Executives 2 years after the end of the takeover event. When a coefficient has a predicted sign from the settling-up hypothesis, it is given in the "Pred. sign" column.

		Inside		Outside		
	Pred. sign	Single	Multiple	Single	Multiple	All
Intercept		**−0.782**	−0.808	**−0.590**	0.645	−0.086
		(−2.508)	(−0.737)	**(−1.911)**	(1.786)	(−0.292)
Performance						
Prebid operating performance	−/+	**−0.010**	**0.042**	**−0.018**	−0.008	**−0.012**
		(−1.853)	**(2.247)**	**(−3.080)**	(−1.459)	**(−2.325)**
Prebid operating performance, terminated	+	0.011	−0.017	**0.030**	**0.028**	**0.019**
		(1.507)	(−0.471)	**(2.027)**	**(2.679)**	**(2.348)**
Event characteristics						
Hostile	+	0.091	−0.318	0.083	−0.139	−0.154
		(0.741)	(−1.173)	(0.643)	(−1.433)	(−1.542)
Hostile, terminated	−	−0.088	0.539	0.124	0.093	**0.310**
		(−0.402)	(1.101)	(0.607)	(0.483)	**(1.753)**
Auction	+	−0.005	−0.474	**0.233**	0.002	0.088
		(−0.054)	(−1.610)	**(2.362)**	(0.017)	(0.984)
Auction, terminated	−/0	0.207	0.453	−0.187	0.129	−0.076
		(0.971)	(0.991)	(−0.877)	(0.693)	(−0.457)
Taken private/acquired by a foreign firm	−	−0.021	0.056	0.051	−0.009	−0.018
		(−0.205)	(0.219)	(0.456)	(−0.098)	(−0.199)
Successful merger	+	0.205	0.124	0.025	**0.210**	0.137
		(1.492)	(0.418)	(0.201)	**(1.715)**	(1.227)
Personal characteristics						
Age		**0.012**	0.007	**0.013**	**−0.015**	−0.001
		(2.061)	(0.375)	**(2.673)**	**(−2.423)**	(−0.281)
Years as director		−0.001	−0.003	−0.008	0.003	0.001
		(−0.226)	(−0.191)	(−1.239)	(0.403)	(0.211)
Unexplained retention		**−0.335**	0.197	0.035	−0.168	−0.128
		(−3.092)	(0.552)	(0.306)	(−1.391)	(−1.232)
Blockholder		**−0.296**	−0.611	−0.060	−0.163	−0.092
		(−1.737)	(−0.655)	(−0.253)	(−0.504)	(−0.444)
CEO		0.144	0.272			0.111
		(1.389)	(1.254)			(0.907)

(Continued)

Table 7 (*Continued*)

	Pred. sign	Inside		Outside		All
		Single	Multiple	Single	Multiple	
Term is up the following year		**0.146**	0.143	0.064	0.029	0.067
		(1.678)	(0.653)	(0.758)	(0.365)	(0.889)
Remains employed		−0.027	0.120			
		(−0.299)	(0.480)			
Number of observations		192	80	237	345	854
Adjusted R^2		0.091	0.000	0.052	0.018	0.003

The predictions given in previous sections and summarized in the column in Table 7 labeled predicted sign are predictions for the structural coefficients. What we observe in Table 7 are the reduced-form coefficients that combine any settling-up effects on future board seats with the effects of retention on future board seats. If losing a board seat (no retention) causes the director to work harder to seek-out new seats, there could be a negative relation between retention and future seats. This can muddle inferences as each coefficient captures its own direct effect on future seats as well as its indirect effect (through its effect on retention). Where necessary, I will discuss the effect on inferences of examining the reduced-form coefficient.

4.6.1. Results

Columns 1 and 2 present the results for the insider regressions. For those with more than one board seat (Column 2), there is some evidence of feedback from firm performance to directorial opportunities; the coefficient on performance is positive and significant. This is consistent with settling-up and with earlier research (e.g., Gilson, 1990; Kaplan and Reishus, 1990) showing a link between performance and board seats. It also fits the argument about executive career concerns and horizons examined in Brickley et al. (1999). They show that firm performance in the 4 years prior to CEO retirement is positively related to the number of directorships he or she holds following retirement, attenuating horizon problems at the end of a career. The evidence here shows the general result that for managers active in the director market, firm performance is positively related to future directorships.

Columns 3 and 4 indicate that outside directors appear to face incentives from potential settling-up. For directors whose only seat is on the target (Column 3), there is an external reward for consummating a merger following poor performance (negative coefficient on the uninteracted performance variable). Directors with multiple board seats (Column 4) partially replace the lost seat from the target (positive coefficient on successful merger). However, I note that this particular reduced-form coefficient does not allow for clear inferences about the structural predictions of the settling-up hypothesis. Directors of poorly performing firms are less likely to be retained, meaning that they are more likely to seek-out new board seats, especially if their only board seat was on the target. This produces an indirect negative relation between performance and future board seats, countering the predicted positive relation from settling-up. Thus, the negative coefficient could reflect a reward for completing the merger following bad performance, or extra effort by the displaced director to find a new seat. Regardless, it is important to note, however, that even if the directors market does provide some positive incentives, it is obvious from the univariate results of Table 3 that, including the target board seat, a completed merger's net effect on total board seats is still negative, meaning that the net incentive for a board member is to spurn the offer.

For all outside board members, regardless of the number of other seats held, the coefficients on the interaction between bid termination and operating performance are positive and significant. The evidence in the previous paragraph was consistent with a reward for directors who complete a merger following poor performance. The evidence from the interactive coefficient is complementary in that it demonstrates a penalty for failing to complete a merger following poor performance. The coefficient indicates that outside directors of poorly performing firms can expect fewer director-ships in the future should they spurn the offer. Thus, while directors can avoid the loss of the target seat by spurning the merger, there is a penalty imposed by the rest of the directors market. The observed reduced-form coefficient is positive and the indirect retention effect is predicted to be negative (and was estimated to be zero in the probits of Table 6), this inference is unaffected by the reduced-form problem discussed above.

The last column of Table 7 presents an overall estimation for all inside and outside target directors. Likely due to combining all types of directors into one specification, the explanatory power of the model is weak. Nonetheless, the operating performance rows continue to provide some support for the settling-up hypothesis. The overall prebid operating performance has a negative coefficient (as it does in two other regressions). Again, this particular coefficient suffers from muddled inferences due to the reduced-form issue. The primary inference comes from the second row, with the positive coefficient on the interaction between terminated bids and operating perform-ance. This inference is unaffected by the reduced-form issue.

The results for the hostility and auction variables show that, in general, specifics of the takeover event have little impact on directors' future holdings of other seats. This is inconsistent with the strongest form of the ex post settling-up hypothesis, which predicted that such event characteristics would have reputational effects in the direct-orial market. For hostility, this is somewhat surprising. Either hostility is not a good indicator of whether the board is acting in shareholders' interests, or the strong form of the settling-up hypothesis lacks explanatory power. In untabulated tests, I find that bidders are more likely to raise their bid when targets react with hostility. However, hostility has no correlation with the whether the bid is completed, either in univariate or multivariate tests. Since hostility appears to produce higher premiums without observably making a completed merger less likely, it appears as if hostility is simply not a good indicator of whether the board is acting in shareholders' interests. This supports Schwert's (2000) conclusion that there is little substance to the hostility distinction in takeovers. Further, for the hostility variables, the indirect effect through retention (positive if hostility makes it more likely that a director will lose his or her seat and seek out another one) is in the same direction as the settling-up effect, so the finding of no relation cannot be due to offsetting effects in the reduced-form coefficient.

One notable result, not directly related to the hypotheses, is the significance of three of the coefficients on age. Despite the exact age matching used in constructing the control sample, age still matters. For example, the single-seat results show that, all else equal, an older director will recover from a takeover event better than a younger director. The result is the opposite for outside directors with multiple board seats. The single-seat director results make sense in that young directors with only one seat may not be well known in business and would be less likely to recover from the loss of their only seat. Older directors may be better known and/or retired executives whose expertise will be valuable. The multiple-seats age result is hard to explain.

4.6.2. Alternative specification: group means

Many of the independent variables in Table 7 regressions are the same for all directors of a target firm. For example, the outside directors specifications include, as four separate observations, four outside directors from the same target firm. For these observations, all of the event-specific independent variables (hostility, auction, taken private or acquired by a foreign firm, successful merger, and prebid performance) will be the same. This lack of independence across observations has the potential to inflate the test statistics on those event-specific variables. I reestimate the specifications using a group means regression to control for this lack of independence. The estimation is described in Kmenta (1971) and is carried out to control for a similar problem in the Tufano and Sevick (1997) study of fee-setting and board structure in the mutual fund industry. Each variable for a particular event is averaged, creating 91 event-specific observations. Doing so results in no loss of efficiency with respect to prebid performance and the event characteristics listed above because they are identical for all directors involved in that event. However, some efficiency is lost by discarding variation in the personal characteristics of the directors (age, years as director, etc.). Thus, there is a tradeoff between reducing cross-observation dependence and loss of efficiency. The results of the grouped means estimation (not tabulated) confirm the robustness of the original findings. Of the event-specific and prebid performance coefficients that were significant in the original specifications, all remain significant. Specifically, this includes the prebid performance variables that show that outside directors of poorly performing targets do have a partial penalty should they block the offer.

Finally, one could be concerned that the financial impact of a completed merger causes some directors to retire from the directorial labor market. Given the results presented in Table 4, overall, it is unlikely that the direct financial impact of the merger provided enough outside directors with a large enough inflow to affect their decision to remain active in the directorial labor market. I have reestimated the regressions from Table 7 including the financial impact variable. Its coefficient is insignificantly different from zero in all specifications and the original inferences are unchanged.

4.6.3. Analyzing resistance

Finally, I estimate a model to determine whether the expected impact of the merger on board members affects how they react to the bid. The models take each of the 91 events as an observation. For control variables, I follow Schwert's (2000) study of hostility. I include return-on-equity, 1-year sales growth, the debt-to-equity and market-to-book ratios, market value of assets, and cash. I industry-adjust the control variables by subtracting the median value for the appropriate two-digit SIC code. For each target, I estimate models similar to those reported in Tables 6 and 7, not including any event variables that could plausibly be influenced by the target board (hostility and auction). For example, for the change in other board seats for multiple-seat directors, the equation is

$$\text{Change in Other Seats}_{\text{multiple-seat director}} = a + b_1 \text{Age}$$
$$+ b_2 \text{Years as Director} + b_3 \text{Blockholder} + b_4 \text{Term is Up} \qquad (2)$$
$$+ b_5 \text{Private / Foreign Bidder} + b_6 \text{Ind} - \text{Adjusted-ROA} + e.$$

Similar models are estimated for retention. These models are estimated over only events ending in a merger and produce coefficient estimates that I use to create predicted postmerger retention and future board seats for each target director. For example, I would use the estimated coefficients from Equation (2) to produce predicted changes in other seats for each multiple-seat director on a particular target. These predictions are averaged over all multiple-seat directors for that target to produce the average predicted change in future board seats for a multiple-seat director on that target should the merger be completed. The same is done for single-seat directors. The CEO is also broken-out separately, given the likelihood that he has the greatest influence on the target's reaction. This approach produces average predicted retention for the board, predicted retention for the CEO individually, predicted future board seats for multiple-seat directors (group average), single-seat directors (group average), and the CEO (individually). Finally, the average if-merged financial impact from Equation (1), computed separately for inside and outside directors is included in the second specification. The results are presented in Table 8.

Two specifications are presented. The first does not include the expected financial impact of the merger on the target directors and the second does. Both specifications show that the more likely it is that the CEO will be retained following the merger, the less likely is the target to resist. The coefficient on predicted future seats for multiple-seat directors shows that the better these directors expect to fare following a completed merger, the less likely they are to resist the merger. The estimations also produce two anomalous results: the coefficients on overall predicted retention and predicted future seats for single-seat

Table 8

Predicting target resistance

The dependent variable is equal to 1 if the event is characterized as hostile by the *Wall Street Journal* or *Dow Jones News Retrieval* and 0 otherwise. Marginal effects from probit estimation are presented. All financial variables are industry-adjusted by subtracting the median value from the appropriate two-digit SIC group. Year 1988-1989 is a dummy variable set equal to 1 if the bid occurred during those years. The "Predicted retention" and change in other seats are computed using coefficients estimated from regressions run only on completed mergers. The specifications for those regressions follow those in Tables 6 and 7, but do not include the auction or hostility variables, over which the board potentially has some influence. The "Financial impact" variables are averages for the inside and outside directors of the "Financial impact if merged" computation shown in Table 4. *t*-statistics are in parentheses.

	Pred. sign	(1)	(2)
Intercept		**−0.355 (−1.736)**	−0.338 (−1.351)
Financial variables			
Return-on-equity		**−0.841 (−2.300)**	**−0.911 (−2.248)**
Sales growth [log(sales$_t$/sales$_{t-1}$)]		0.114 (0.265)	0.215 (0.436)
Debt-to-equity (book)		0.018 (0.471)	0.043 (0.714)
Market-to-book assets		**1.049 (2.966)**	**1.073 (2.923)**
Size (market value of assets)		−0.000 (−0.608)	−0.000 (−0.816)
Cash		**−2.308 (−2.650)**	−2.167 (−2.356)
Year: 1988-1989		−0.154 (−1.118)	−0.224 (−1.350)
Incentive variables			
Predicted retention: CEO	−	**−1.314 (−2.310)**	**−1.485 (−2.292)**
Predicted Δother seats: CEO	−	−0.121 (−0.836)	−0.104 (−0.628)
Predicted retention: other directors	−	**2.112 (1.929)**	**2.215 (1.689)**
Predicted Δother seats: multiple-seat directors	−	**−1.270 (−2.503)**	**−1.447 (−2.486)**
Predicted Δother seats: single-seat directors	−	**1.062 (2.266)**	**1.211 (2.173)**
Predicted financial impact: inside directors	−		0.000 (0.061)
Predicted financial impact: outside directors	−		0.000 (0.377)
No. of observations		91	91
Pseudo-R^2		0.536	0.550

directors are positive. The results for the CEO and multiple-seat directors, the two groups most likely to have the greatest influence on the target's response, are sensible. However, one would expect that the coefficients for the rest of the board would also be negative, or zero. The second specification shows that the financial impact variables have no incremental explanatory power for the target's reaction to the bid.

5. Discussion

The results presented here provide insights into the mechanisms motivating vigilance by directors and the incentives facing them when they are responding to a takeover bid. This study documents that only 10% of target outside directors are typically retained following a completed merger and that the lost seat is not typically replaced.

Consequently, compared to other *Fortune 1000* directors of the same age and with the same number of directorships, they can expect to hold fewer board seats in the future, purely as a result of accepting the bid. Additionally, outside directors' tiny stock holdings provide little to compensate them for the loss of their cash compensation, influence, and connection from the target board seat. In fact, the direct financial impact of the merger is predominantly negative for outside directors. In order to counter these perverse incentives, it is plausible that some form of settling-up take place in the directorial labor market dependent on the actions of the directors during the offer or conditional on the performance of the target. The power of statistical tests to pickup the effects of a takeover event on the future directorships of individuals is low. However, some cautious inferences can be drawn from the results. The results provide some support for previous findings of a link between performance and board seats for inside (manager) directors. However, there is no evidence of settling-up for insiders following terminated offers. For outside directors, the results are consistent with the notion that they are penalized for failing to close a deal following poor performance. This effect from other directorships is actually positive if the deal is completed. Nonetheless, the partial settling-up does not completely offset the loss of their target seat.

Previous research by Walkling and Long (1984) shows that the decision to resist the offer is directly related to the potential wealth loss of officers and directors (as a group) and the top executive (individually) should the offer be completed. The evidence here shows that while those directors can avoid a loss of current wealth by terminating a bid, the directorial labor market will partially settle-up with them by reducing their future wealth from directorships. Poor prebid performance alone does not lead to extra penalties in the directorial labor market. Instead, if they force the termination of a bid, their penalty increases as the prebid performance of their firm declines. An important caveat is that I can only observe the outcome of both the future supply and demand of board seats, so this result is perhaps because directors of poorly performing firms that spurn offers refuse additional directorships in order to concentrate on the target firm. However, whether this cost is self-imposed or imposed by others, it is true that, on average, these directors will hold fewer other directorships should they spurn an offer. Another explanation is that the contest leaves the directors with such a bad experience, that they become disinterested in future directorships. However, this does not explain why 85% of them choose to continue working as a director at the target firm.

6. Conclusion

Prior research (e.g., Weisbach, 1988) shows that outside directors are critical to the internal control function of the board. The results presented here demonstrate that outside directors' incentive to act comes at least partly from the penalty they will pay should the external control market act for them, costing them their seat on the target board. However, the very penalty that drives outside directors' vigilance in internal control matters provides them with incentives counter to those of shareholders should a takeover bid occur. Partially offsetting these perverse incentives is the incentive given to complete a merger following poor performance. This evidence of feedback from the firm's performance to the directorial labor market complements the findings in Kaplan and Reishus (1990), Gilson (1990), and Brickley et al. (1999) of such a feedbak channel in other situations. While Kaplan and Reishus (1990) and Brickley et al. (1999) find a relation between own-firm performance and executives' holdings of other directorships, a relation is found here linking outside directors to the firm's performance as well. Outsider-dominated boards are generally assumed to be the most closely aligned with shareholders' interests. While outside directors' compensation does little to align their incentives with those of shareholders, the potential for their actions to enhance their career paths as directors does more.

Recently, more firms have recognized the incentive problem created by low equity ownership by directors and have increased stock grants to directors. The combination of these large equity incentives and the traditional settling-up should serve to further align directors' incentives with those of their shareholders. Perry (2000) shows that equity-based compensation for independent boards increases the likelihood that a CEO will be fired for poor performance. More research is needed into the causes and effects of changes in direct pecuniary incentives for directors and their interaction with reputational incentives.

References

Agrawal, A. and R. Walkling, 1994, "Executive Careers and Compensation Surrounding Takeover Bids," *Journal of Finance*, 49, 985–1014.

Brickley, J., J. Coles and R. Terry, 1994, "Outside Directors and the Adoption of Poison Pills," *Journal of Financial Economics*, 35, 371–390.

Brickley, J., J. Coles and J. Linck, 1999, "What Happens to CEOs After they Retire? New Evidence on Career Concerns, Horizon Problems, and CEO Incentives," *Journal of Financial Economics*, 52, 341–378.

Brown, W. and M. Maloney, 1999, "Exit, Voice, and the Role of Corporate Directors: Evidence from Acquisition Performance," Unpublished Working Paper, Claremont McKenna College, California.

Byrd, J. and K. Hickman, 1992, "Do Outside Directors Monitor Managers? Evidence from Tender Offers Bids," *Journal of Financial Economics*, 32, 195–222.

Cotter, J., A. Shivdasani and M. Zenner, 1997, "Do Independent Directors Enhance Target Shareholder Wealth During Tender Offers?" *Journal of Financial Economics*, 43, 195–218.

Denis, D. and J. Serrano, 1996, "Active Investors and Management Turnover Following Unsuccessful Control Contests," *Journal of Financial Economics*, 40, 239–266.

Fama, E., 1980, "Agency Problems and the Theory of the Firm," *Journal of Political Economy*, 88, 288–307.

Fama, E. and M. Jensen, 1983, "Separation of Ownership and Control," *Journal of Law and Economics*, 26, 301–325.

Gibbons, R. and K. Murphy, 1992, "Optimal Incentive Contracts in the Presence of Career Concerns: Theory and Evidence," *Journal of Political Economy*, 11, 468–505.

Gilson, S., 1990, "Bankruptcy, Boards, Banks, and Blockholders: Evidence on Changes in Corporate Control When Firms Default," *Journal of Financial Economics*, 27, 355–388.

Hartzell, J., E. Ofek and D. Yermack, 2000, "What's in It For Me? Personal Benefits Obtained by CEOs Whose Firms are Acquired," Unpublished Working Paper. New York University.

Hermalin, B. and M. Weisbach, 1988, "The Determinants of Board Composition," *RAND Journal of Economics*, 19, 589–606.

Hermalin, B. and M. Weisbach, 1998, "Endogenously Chosen Boards of Directors and their Monitoring of the CEO," *The American Economic Review*, 88, 96–118.

Huson, M., R. Parrino and L. Starks, 2001, "Internal Monitoring Mechanisms and CEO Turnover: A Long Term Perspective," *Journal of Finance*, 56, 2265–2297.

Jensen, M. and W. Meckling, 1976, "Theory of the Firm: Managerial Behavior, Agency Costs, and Ownership Structure," *Journal of Financial Economics*, 3, 305–360.

Kaplan, S. and D. Reishus, 1990, "Outside Directorships and Corporate Performance," *Journal of Financial Economics*, 27, 389–410.

Kini, O., W. Kracaw and S. Mian, 1995, "Corporate Takeovers, Firm Performance, and Board Composition," *Journal of Corporate Finance*, 1, 383–412.

Kmenta, J., 1971, *Elements of Econometrics*, McMillan, New York.

Martin, K. and J. McConnell, 1991, "Corporate Performance, Corporate Takeovers, and Management Turnover," *Journal of Finance*, 46, 671–687.

Mikkelson, W. and M. Partch, 1989, "Managers' Voting Rights and Corporate Control," *Journal of Financial Economics*, 25, 263–290.

Mikkelson, W. and M. Partch, 1997, "The Decline of Takeovers and Disciplinary Managerial Turnover," *Journal of Financial Economics*, 44, 205–228.

Mitchell, M. and K. Lehn, 1990, "Do Bad Bidders become Good Targets?" *Journal of Political Economy*, 98, 372–398.

Perry, T., 2000, "Incentive Compensation for Outside Directors and CEO Turnover," Unpublished Working Paper, Arizona State University.

Rosenstein, S. and J. Wyatt, 1990, "Outside Directors, Board Independence, and Shareholder Wealth," *Journal of Financial Economics*, 26, 175–192.

Schwert, G. W., 2000, "Hostility in Takeovers: In the Eyes of the Beholder?," *Journal of Finance*, 55, 2599–2640.

The Conference Board, 1987-1996, *Corporate Directors' Compensation*, The Conference Board, New York.

Tufano, P. and M. Sevick, 1997, "Board Structure and Fee-Setting in the US Mutual Fund Industry," *Journal of Financial Economics*, 46, 321–355.

Walkling, R. and M. Long, 1984, "Agency Theory, Managerial Welfare, and Takeover Bid Resistance," *RAND Journal of Economics*, 15, 54–68.

Weisbach, M., 1988, "Outside Directors and CEO Turnover," *Journal of Financial Economics*, 37, 159–188.

Yermack, D., 1996, "Higher Market Valuation of Companies with a Small Board of Directors," *Journal of Financial Economics*, 40, 185–212.

Chapter 22

MANAGERIAL DISCIPLINE AND CORPORATE RESTRUCTURING FOLLOWING PERFORMANCE DECLINES[*]

DAVID J. DENIS

Krannert Graduate School of Management, Purdue University, West Lafayette, Indiana, USA

TIMOTHY A. KRUSE

School of Business Administration, Loyola University Chicago, Chicago, Illinois, USA

Contents

[*] We are grateful for helpful comments received from Jeff Allen, Jim Brickley, Diane Denis, Jon Garfinkel, David Haushalter, Jack Helmuth, John McConnell, Tom Nohel, Raghu Rau, Anil Shivdasani, Steven Todd, Bharathram Thothadri, Sunil Wahal, Marc Zenner, an anonymous referee, participants at the Arizona Finance Symposium, and finance workshop participants at Loyola University at Chicago, Southern Illinois University, Southern Methodist University, and the University of Illinois. We also thank Sunil Wahal for data on companies targeted by the nine largest pension funds, and Marc Zenner for data on companies targeted by the United Shareholders Association.

This article originally appeared in the *Journal Financial Economics*, Vol. 55, pp. 391–424 (2000).

Abstract

We examine the incidence of disciplinary events that reduce the control of current managers, and corporate restructuring among firms experiencing a large decline in operating performance during an active takeover period (1985–1988) and a less active period (1989–1992). We document a significant decline in the disciplinary events from the active to the less active period that is driven by a significant decline in disciplinary takeovers, those takeovers that result in a top executive change. Following the performance decline, however, there is a substantial amount of corporate restructuring, and a significant improvement in operating performance, during both the active and the less active takeover period. We conclude that, although some managerial disciplinary events are related to overall takeover activity, the decline in takeover activity does not result in fewer performance-enhancing restructurings following performance declines.

Keywords

management turnover, takeovers, restructuring

JEL classification: G32, G34

1. Introduction

Poorly performing managers face disciplinary pressures from both internal and external corporate control mechanisms. An important element of this control process is the threat that if managers deviate from value-maximizing corporate policies, their control will be reduced. Consistent with this view, Jensen and Warner (1988) characterize top executive changes as "a key variable in understanding the forces disciplining managers." In this paper, we focus on the three primary disciplinary events that represent explicit attempts to reduce or eliminate the control of current managers. These events are corporate takeovers, board dismissals, and shareholder activism. Using a sample of firms that experience a sharp decline in industry-adjusted operating performance, we provide evidence on (i) the frequency with which managers experience at least one of the above disciplinary events and (ii) corporate restructuring and changes in operating performance following the performance decline.

Our motivation for pursuing this investigation is threefold. First, although several studies provide evidence on each of these control-reducing disciplinary events individually, none address the more fundamental issue of how frequently managers face some threat to their control when they perform poorly. Second, because the frequency of one of the disciplinary mechanisms, corporate takeovers, fell considerably in the early 1990s, we are interested in whether this decline is associated with a corresponding change in the overall frequency of control-reducing disciplinary events in recent years. Third, because previous studies suggest a strong link between control-reducing disciplinary events and corporate restructuring, we are interested in whether any change in the frequency of disciplinary events over time has changed the manner in which firms address poor performance.

Our sample consists of 350 firms that have total assets greater than $100 million, which achieve measurably high operating performance in 1 year, followed by a marked decline in performance the following year. The sample period, 1985–1992, encompasses an active takeover period (1985–1988) and a less active takeover period (1989–1992), thus allowing us to examine whether managerial discipline and corporate restructuring are linked with activity in the market for corporate control.

We find that a substantial fraction of the sample firms experience control-reducing disciplinary events in the year of and the 3 years following the year of performance decline. In our sample, half of the firms are either the target of corporate takeover activity, are targeted by activist shareholders, or experience nonroutine turnover of the firm's top executive. Nonroutine turnover is defined as any change in the top executive of the firm except those due to death or illness, and those that are classified as normal retirements using the definition of Denis and Denis (1995). Defining disciplinary management turnover as either the nonroutine turnover of the top executive or a change in top executive following a takeover, we find that 36% of the sample firms experience disciplinary turnover in their top executive by the end of the third year following the year of poor performance.

More importantly, we document a significant decline in the frequency of control-reducing disciplinary events from the active to the less active takeover period. During the active takeover period, 57% of the sample firms are either the target of corporate control activity, are targeted by shareholder activists, or experience nonroutine turnover of the firm's top executive, while only 44% of the firms in the inactive period experience one or more of these events. This difference is statistically significant at the 0.01 level. This reduction in disciplinary events corresponds with a significant reduction in the rate of disciplinary managerial turnover, from 42% in the active takeover period to 31% in the inactive period. These effects are driven by a substantial decline in takeover activity. While 42% of the sample firms are targets of takeover activity during the active takeover period, only 17% are takeover targets in the less active period. It is notable that the decline in takeover activity is not offset by an increase in public shareholder activism in the less active takeover period. The fraction of firms experiencing shareholder targeting activities, such as proxy fights for board seats, shareholder resolutions, and other nonproxy targeting events, increases only from 8% in the active takeover period to 12% in the less active period. This difference is statistically insignificant. Consequently, there is a significant net reduction in the incidence of external control market events from the first to the second subperiod. We thus conclude that, among our sample firms, the significant decline in takeover activity in the early 1990s is associated with a significant decline in disciplinary events that reduce the control of current managers.

Because several previous studies suggest that market disciplinary events are an important determinant of corporate restructuring activity,[1] we examine whether the overall decline in disciplinary events from the active to the less active takeover period is associated with a corresponding change in the nature of restructuring activity and other operating changes following poor managerial performance. We find that a large fraction of the sample firms undertake major restructurings following the performance decline. Approximately, two-thirds of the firms either restructure their assets, layoff employees, or initiate major cost-cutting efforts. On average, these restructurings are met with a positive stock price reaction, and are more common among firms experiencing disciplinary events. Nevertheless, there is no significant difference in the frequency of these restructurings across the two subperiods. Moreover, the magnitude of restructuring is similar in the active and less active takeover periods. Among firms that sell assets, the asset sales average 28.2% of the book value of total assets in the first subperiod, and 22.4% in the second subperiod.

We also find that the sample firms exhibit significant improvements in operating performance in the 3 years following the year of performance decline. These operating

---

[1] See, for example, Bhagat et al. (1990), Bhide (1990), and Berger and Ofek (1996) for evidence of restructuring following successful takeovers; Dann and DeAngelo (1988) for evidence on defensive asset restructurings; Del Guercio and Hawkins (1999) for evidence of restructuring following shareholder proposals; and Berger and Ofek (1999) and Denis et al. (1997) for evidence on the influence of external control pressures on corporate refocusing activity.

improvements are economically large, and do not differ significantly between the two subperiods. Moreover, operating improvements are significantly greater among those firms that initiate asset restructurings immediately following the performance decline than in those that do not. We conclude, therefore, that the decline in takeover activity does not result in fewer performance-enhancing restructurings in the less active takeover period.

There have been many previous studies of managerial discipline and corporate restructuring. The three studies most closely related to ours are Morck et al. (1989), Mikkelson and Partch (1997), and Huson et al. (1997). Morck et al. (1989) examine the sensitivity of takeovers and management turnover to alternative measures of firm performance. However, their sample is limited to a cross-section of Fortune 500 firms in 1980. Because they use a relatively small set of poorly performing firms, Morck et al. are unable to examine time-series variation in disciplinary mechanisms. Further, their study omits the examination of corporate restructuring activity. Mikkelson and Partch (1997) and Huson et al. (1997) examine changes in the sensitivity of management turnover, that is not related to takeover activity, to firm performance, comparing an active takeover period to a less active takeover period. Our study differs in two important respects. First, we include a broader set of control-reducing disciplinary events, thereby allowing us to examine whether other control-reducing disciplinary events substitute for a decline in takeovers. Second, we examine corporate restructuring and operating performance following the initial performance decline. This design allows us to draw inferences regarding whether changes in the frequency of explicit disciplinary events have a net effect on the manner in which firms respond to poor performance.

The remainder of the paper is organized as follows. In Section 2, we review related studies of takeovers, shareholder activism, and management turnover. We also discuss the possible effects of a decline in takeover activity on managerial discipline and corporate restructuring. Section 3 describes the sample selection process and reports descriptive statistics. Section 4 reports the incidence of managerial disciplinary events for the full sample and the two subperiods. Section 5 reports the extent of corporate restructuring and operating improvements following the year of poor performance. Section 6 provides a discussion of our results and Section 7 concludes.

2. Managerial discipline in poorly performing firms

Several mechanisms encourage managers to act in the interests of shareholders. These internal and external corporate controls include, but are not limited to, monitoring by the board of directors, by large blockholders, by the takeover market, and by other managers within the firm. In the event of poor performance, an important outcome of this monitoring process is a reduction in managerial autonomy. The most extreme outcome possible is the outright dismissal of the top executive. In this section, we review prior evidence on the three primary methods of reducing current managers' control: board dismissals, takeovers, and shareholder activism. We then discuss the possible effects of a decline in takeovers on (i) the overall frequency of control-reducing disciplinary events, and (ii) the manner in which firms respond to poor performance.

2.1. Prior evidence on board dismissals, takeovers, and shareholder activism

Several studies analyze the effectiveness of internal monitoring mechanisms by examining top management turnover among firms that have not been taken over. Warner et al. (1988) and Weisbach (1988) document an inverse relation between the likelihood of a top management change and prior stock price performance. In addition, Denis and Denis (1995) find that the forced dismissal of a top executive is associated with subsequent improvements in firm performance. These findings suggest that the board of directors serves an important disciplinary role. However, Denis and Denis (1995) and Warner et al. (1988) both question whether the underlying threat of dismissal is large enough to produce meaningful incentives for top executives.

Prior studies also suggest that poor performance increases the likelihood of a firm becoming the target of a takeover attempt. For example, Morck et al. (1989) find that the probability of hostile takeovers is inversely related to firm performance, while Mitchell and Lehn (1990) find that firms making value-decreasing acquisitions are subsequently more likely to become targets themselves. Martin and McConnell (1991) find that the rate of management turnover increases following corporate takeovers, and find that pretakeover performance is significantly worse among those takeover targets that undergo a posttakeover management change. These findings suggest that takeovers play a direct role in disciplining poorly performing managers. Other studies suggest that takeovers play an indirect role as well. Denis and Denis (1995) find that forced resignations of top executives are often due to takeover-related pressures. Denis and Serrano (1996) document a high incidence of management turnover following unsuccessful takeover contests, and find that this turnover is concentrated among poorly performing firms in which outside blockholders acquire equity stakes. These findings suggest that there is some interaction between internal and external corporate control mechanisms.

Finally, several recent studies examine the role of shareholder activists in corporate governance. Consistent with shareholder activists serving an important disciplinary role, these studies, in general, find that the likelihood of shareholder targeting is inversely related to prior firm performance. The net effects of this activism are less clear, however. Studies examining the shareholder wealth and operating performance effects of shareholder targeting have produced mixed evidence.[2] In addition, Karpoff

[2] See, for example, Del Guercio and Hawkins (1999), Karpoff et al. (1996), Opler and Sokobin (1997), Smith (1996), Strickland et al. (1996), and Wahal (1996). Karpoff (1998) provides an excellent survey of the literature on shareholder activism.

(1998, p. 28) reports that "most evidence indicates that firms attracting activist efforts do not experience unusually high rates of CEO turnover."

Although the above studies suggest that the board of directors, the takeover market, and shareholder activists play some role in disciplining poorly performing managers, the joint impact of these disciplinary events remains an open empirical issue. One goal of our study, therefore, is to provide evidence on the following question: Conditional on poor performance, what is the probability of at least one control-reducing disciplinary event taking place? Evidence on this issue represents an important contribution to the debate on whether the threat of a reduction in control provides meaningful incentives to top executives.

2.2. Possible effects of a decline in takeover activity on managerial discipline

The late 1980s were characterized by a dramatic decline in takeover activity. Comment and Schwert (1995) report that the percentage of exchange-listed firms receiving takeover bids declined from 1.5% per month in 1988 to less than 0.5% in 1990 and 1991. Because of the relation between takeover activity and management turnover discussed above, the decline in the takeover market in the early 1990s has led some to suggest that the overall level of managerial discipline has fallen in recent years. Jensen (1993), for example, argues that takeovers are more effective than other forms of market monitoring. According to Jensen, existing regulatory and legal systems are too blunt, product markets are too slow, and internal control mechanisms provide inadequate monitoring. He argues, therefore, that a decline in the takeover market weakens managerial discipline.

Although Jensen's view is plausible, there are other reasonable arguments regarding why the decline in takeover activity would have little impact on managerial discipline. First, a decline in takeover activity is not necessarily evidence of a decline in disciplinary takeovers. The evidence in Mitchell and Mulherin (1996) suggests that external economic shocks, such as deregulation and changes in input costs, account for a large fraction of takeover activity. Consequently, the decline in takeover activity could have resulted from fewer economic shocks, and is therefore unconnected with the level of managerial discipline.

Second, even if disciplinary takeovers have declined, alternative monitoring mechanisms such as active boards and active shareholders can substitute for the takeover market in forcing the replacement of poorly performing managers. Evidence in Kaplan (1994) and Kang and Shivdasani (1997) suggest that such a substitution takes place in Japan, a market historically characterized by a relatively inactive takeover market. These researchers find that blockholders and main banks play an important monitoring role in Japanese firms. Similarly, the emergence of increased activism by large institutional shareholders, such as the California Public Employees Retirement System (CALPERS), can be viewed as a market solution to the decreased monitoring provided by the takeover market in the early 1990s.

Finally, even if control-reducing disciplinary events decline, managers of poorly performing firms can be pressured to undertake necessary restructurings in the absence of management turnover. Pound (1992a,b), for example, describes a political model of corporate governance. Under this model, activist shareholders maintain an ongoing, but private, dialogue with managers and the board of directors, thereby pressuring poorly performing firms to make necessary structural changes without the upheaval of a corporate takeover. Carleton et al. (1998) analyze the negotiations between one financial institution, TIAA-CREF, and the companies it targeted between 1987 and 1996. Their evidence indicates that these negotiations were effective in bringing about desired changes at the targeted companies. Similarly, Del Guercio and Hawkins (1999) find that shareholder proposals are followed by substantial asset sales and restructurings, despite the lack of any unusual top executive turnover. In addition to activist shareholders, other incentive mechanisms can motivate managers to undertake necessary restructurings in the absence of any overt disciplinary threat against the control of current managers. These incentive mechanisms could include direct equity ownership, compensation contracts, and labor market concerns. Labor market concerns refers to the view that managers derive incentives from the knowledge that if they perform poorly, the demand for their services will decline. In an interesting recent study, Brickley et al. (1998) show that these career concerns include not only current managerial opportunities within and outside the manager's company, but also extend to concerns about postretirement board service.

It is therefore an open empirical question whether the recent decline in takeover activity has had a net impact on either the frequency of control-reducing disciplinary events or the manner in which firms respond to performance declines. Our study addresses both of these issues. In a related study, Mikkelson and Partch (1997) examine a random sample of firms and find that, among firms not taken over, the sensitivity of top executive turnover to firm performance is greater in the active takeover period occurring between 1984 and 1989.[3] One explanation for their findings is that the decline in takeover activity in the United States in the early 1990s caused a decrease in disciplinary managerial turnover. Alternatively, however, substitute disciplinary mechanisms, such as shareholder activism, may have replaced takeovers in monitoring managers. Moreover, it is possible that the presence of either these substitute monitoring mechanisms or other incentive mechanisms provided sufficient motivation to managers to undertake value-increasing restructuring actions in the absence of management turnover. By examining the combined disciplinary effects of takeovers, board dismissals, and shareholder activism, our analysis provides further evidence on these issues.

[3] Using a slightly different sampling procedure and empirical approach, Huson et al. (1997) arrive at a different conclusion. They argue that, if anything, internal monitoring mechanisms became more effective in the early 1990s, after the end of the active takeover period.

3. Sample selection and description of data

Our sample selection process attempts to identify a set of firms exhibiting poor managerial performance. Because managerial performance is unobservable, we employ a firm-specific performance measure as a proxy for managerial performance. We recognize that by doing so, our sample will include some firms for which no managerial discipline or corporate restructuring is required. We measure operating performance as the industry-adjusted ratio of earnings before interest, taxes, depreciation, and amortization (EBITDA) to total assets. We select a sample of firms experiencing a substantial decline in operating performance from a year of positive industry-adjusted operating performance to a year of substandard performance. In this way, the sample consists of firms for which there is a clear starting point for their difficulties, as opposed to firms suffering ongoing performance problems. We employ operating performance, as opposed to stock returns, as the performance measure because share prices incorporate the market's expectation of the value of any restructuring or disciplinary activity following the performance decline. In addition, operating performance, unlike net income, is not influenced by special charges. Because we are interested in firms for which the poor performance is isolated to that firm, we adjust the operating performance measure for any market-wide or industry-wide effects.

The sample is constructed as follows. For each firm listed on Compustat's annual, over-the-counter, and research tapes with total assets of at least $100 million, we calculate the ratio of EBITDA to total assets (*Compustat* item # 13 divided by *Compustat* item #6) for each of the fiscal years 1984 through 1992. We impose the $100 million asset size requirement to increase the probability that the firm receives coverage in the *Wall Street Journal* and has available proxy statements. Imposing this requirement may cause us to overstate the role of large institutional investors, which typically target larger firms.[4] We adjust each firm's operating performance by subtracting the median ratio of EBITDA to assets for all other companies having the same three-digit Standard Industrial Classification (SIC) code. Firms are included in the sample if their industry-adjusted operating performance exceeds the overall sample median in 1 year, but is in the bottom quartile of the sample the following year. This process results in an initial sample of 412 observations. After deleting companies for which we are either unable to locate proxy statements or for which there is no *Wall Street Journal* coverage of the firm, we are left with a final sample of 350 observations, representing 339 different firms.

By construction, the sample firms experience a substantial decline in industry-adjusted performance in at least one of the years between 1985 and 1992. We refer to this as the year of poor performance (year 0) and the prior year as the base year (year −1). The distribution of the sample by the calendar year of poor performance is

---

[4] For example, John and Klein (1994) find that the likelihood of the firm's receiving a governance proposal is positively related to the size of the firm. Also, the Council of Institutional Investors draws their annual sample of companies to be targeted from the worst performers in the S&P 500.

fairly uniform, ranging from a low of 34 firms (10% of the sample) in 1987 to 55 firms (16% of the sample) in 1989. In addition, there does not appear to be any substantial industry clustering within the sample. There are 53 different industries, identified using two-digit SIC codes, represented in the sample, and the distribution of two-digit SIC codes within the sample is similar to that of the universe of Compustat firms with total assets greater than $100 million.

Table 1 reports measures of operating performance and stock returns over the 2-year period that includes the base year and the year of poor performance. As depicted in the first column of Panel A, EBITDA as a proportion of total assets averages 0.16 in the base year, and the sample firms outperform the median industry firm by 0.05. In the year of poor performance, operating performance declines substantially to 0.04, and the sample firms now significantly underperform the median industry firm by 0.06. Overall, the data suggest that the sample firms were initially performing well, but suffered an economically large, firm-specific performance shock.

To provide some assurance that we have correctly identified the onset of poor performance, we also examine the operating performance of the sample firms in the 2 years prior to the base year (i.e., years -2 and -3). These results are not reported in a table. We find that the median EBITDA as a proportion of total assets is 0.15 in both years -2 and -3, an amount that is statistically indistinguishable from the median performance level in the base year (year -1). Thus, it appears that the performance in the base year represents the norm, and that the decline in operating performance in year 0 is unusual. We also examine whether the performance decline in year 0 is connected with changes in the firm's top executive. Previous studies provide some evidence that incoming top executives manage earnings such that reported earnings are lower early in their tenure (see, e.g., Murphy and Zimmerman, 1993; Porciau, 1993). In this sample, 37 firms undergo a change in top executive between years -1 and 0. However, the performance declines of these firms are statistically indistinguishable from those of the remainder of the sample firms. Thus, the performance declines that we document in year 0 are not driven by the earnings management decisions of incoming top executives.

Panel A of Table 1 also compares the performance declines of the sample firms experiencing their year of poor performance during the active takeover period (1985–1988) and the less active takeover period (1989–1992). The results indicate that the performance declines in the two subperiods are nearly identical. Thus, it does not appear as if differences in disciplinary actions or corporate restructuring across the two subperiods can be attributed to systematic differences in the magnitude of poor performance.

It is possible that the market becomes aware of performance problems well before these problems become evident in accounting performance measures. If so, our sample selection process will identify the starting point of operating difficulties incorrectly, and we will overstate the speed with which market disciplinary events occur following the performance decline. To examine this issue, Panel B of Table 1 reports adjusted holding period stock returns over the base year and the year of poor performance.

Table 1

Magnitude of the performance decline

Industry-adjusted operating performance and adjusted holding period stock returns for the period surrounding the year of performance decline. The base year is the year prior to the year of performance decline. The sample includes 350 firms with a book value of assets greater than $100 million that are in the top half of industry-adjusted performance in the base year and in the bottom quartile in the year of poor performance. The performance measure that we use is the ratio of earnings before interest, taxes, depreciation, and amortization (EBITDA) to total assets. Industry-adjusted EBITDA is calculated as the difference between the ratio of EBITDA to total assets of the sample firm and the median ratio of EBITDA to total assets for those firms operating in the same three-digit SIC codes. Adjusted holding period stock returns are calculated as the difference between the buy-and-hold return of the sample firm and the buy-and-hold return of a control firm randomly selected from the same market value decile. The sample period is 1985–1992. Significance levels for the test that the means and medians are equal to zero are reported using heteroskedastic *t*-tests and Wilcoxon signed rank tests, respectively. The last two columns report *t*-statistics and *z*-statistics for differences in means and medians, respectively, of each variable across the two subperiods.

	Full sample		1985–1988		1989–1992		Test statistic	
	Mean	Median	Mean	Median	Mean	Median	*t*-Statistic	*z*-Statistic
Panel A: Operating performance								
Performance at end of base year	0.160	0.156	0.165	0.160	0.156	0.155	1.593	1.458
Performance at end of year of poor performance	0.039	0.051	0.042	0.052	0.035	0.050	0.882	1.145
Change in performance	−0.121*	−0.103*	−0.122*	−0.104*	−0.120*	−0.103*	−0.258	0.271
Industry-adjusted performance at end of base year	0.053*	0.041*	0.055*	0.037*	0.052*	0.043*	0.519	−0.574
Industry-adjusted performance at end of year of poor performance	−0.059*	−0.052*	−0.056*	−0.052*	−0.061*	−0.053*	0.716	0.833
Change in industry-adjusted performance	−0.112*	−0.095*	−0.110*	−0.096*	−0.113*	−0.094*	0.774	1.201
Panel B: Adjusted holding period stock returns								
Beginning of base year to end of year of poor performance	−0.360*	−0.286*	−0.368*	−0.336*	−0.352*	−0.244*	−0.173	−0.572
Beginning of base year to end of base year	0.026	0.001	−0.006	−0.031	0.052	0.077	−0.885	−1.335

* indicates significance at the 0.01 level.

Adjusted holding period returns are defined as the buy-and-hold return of the sample firm minus the buy-and-hold return of a control firm randomly selected from the same market value decile as the sample firm as of last day of the fiscal year of the sample firm's poor performance. Test statistics using this method are generally well-specified (Barber and Lyon, 1997). We obtain qualitatively similar results if we compute adjusted holding period returns as the difference between the return of the sample firm and that of the value-weighted index.

The evidence shown in Panel B of Table 1 indicates that the market first becomes aware of the poor performance in the year that operating performance declines. Adjusted holding period stock returns are small and statistically insignificant in the base year, but average a statistically significant decline of 36% in the year of poor performance. Moreover, as was the case with operating performance, there are no significant differences in stock price performance for firms experiencing performance declines in the two subperiods. These findings suggest not only that the performance decline is a surprise to the market, but also that the market considers the decline to be an economically important event.

In Table 2, we report descriptive statistics on several firm characteristics that could be related to the likelihood of managerial discipline. These include the book value of total assets, the ratio of long-term debt to total assets, and several equity ownership and board composition characteristics. Financial data are obtained from Compustat, while ownership and board composition data are obtained from corporate proxy statements. Affiliated blockholders are defined as those that have some connection with the company, such as through an Employee Stock Ownership Plan (ESOP), being a family member of an officer, or a shareholder having substantial business dealings with the sample firm. All other blockholders are labeled as unaffiliated. We follow the convention in the literature of labeling directors as insiders if they are currently employees of the firm, as affiliated outsiders if they have substantial business relations with the firm, are related to insiders, or are former employees, and as independent outsiders if they are neither insiders nor affiliated outsiders.

For the full sample, the firms have average total assets of approximately $800 million at the end of the base year and long-term debt totaling approximately 20% of total assets. The average shareholdings of the officers and directors, as a group, are 20.0%, while the median shareholdings for this group is 11.3%. This level is quite similar to the median 11.6% holdings of officers and directors reported by Mikkelson and Partch (1997) for a randomly selected set of firms listed on the NYSE and Amex exchanges in 1988. On average, stockholders with at least a 5% stake, or blockholders, own 15.5% of the firm's shares. Affiliated blockholders own 6.3% of the firm's shares, while 9.2% are held by unaffiliated blockholders. On average, the board of directors consists of nine members, of which 36% are corporate insiders, 48% are independent outsiders, and 16% are affiliated outsiders. These board composition statistics are comparable to those reported by Denis and Sarin (1999) for a random sample of 583 firms.

The data in Table 2 also indicate that the characteristics of the sample firms are very similar in the two subperiods. There is weak evidence that the equity ownership of

Table 2

Description of the sample

Summary statistics for the sample of 350 companies experiencing performance declines over the period 1985–1992. The sample consists of firms, with a book value of assets greater than $100 million, that are in the top half of industry-adjusted EBITDA/total assets in the base year and in the bottom quartile in the year of poor performance. All reported data are as of the end of the base year. The base year is the year prior to the year of poor performance. Affiliated blockholders are either Employee Stock Ownership Programs (ESOPs) or shareholders having extensive business dealings with the company. All other blockholders are classified as unaffiliated. Inside directors are current or former officers of the company. Affiliated outside directors are family members of officers or directors having substantial business dealings with the company. All other directors are classified as independent outsiders. Dollar values are expressed in millions. The last two columns report heteroskedastic t-statistics and Wilcoxon z-statistics for differences in means and medians, respectively, of each variable across the two subperiods.

	Full sample		1985–1988		1989–1992		Test statistic	
	Mean	Median	Mean	Median	Mean	Median	t-Statistic	z-Statistic
Book value of total assets (millions)	805.27	230.28	802.23	228.24	808.16	233.67	~0.03	~0.71
Long-term debt/total assets	0.22	0.19	0.22	0.20	0.21	0.19	0.29	0.39
Proportion of shares held by officers and directors	0.20	0.11	0.18	0.11	0.22	0.11	~1.77	~0.78
Proportion of shares held by all blockholders	0.16	0.10	0.15	0.09	0.16	0.12	~0.68	~0.99
Proportion of shares held by affiliated blockholders	0.06	0.00	0.05	0.00	0.07	0.00	~1.04	~1.29
Proportion of shares held by unaffiliated blockholders	0.09	0.07	0.09	0.06	0.09	0.07	0.29	~0.63
Number of directors	9.05	9.00	9.69	9.00	8.51	8.00	3.18	3.32
Proportion of the board composed of inside directors	0.36	0.33	0.36	0.33	0.37	0.33	~0.31	0.07
Proportion of the board composed of independent outside directors	0.48	0.46	0.47	0.46	0.49	0.46	~0.84	~0.74
Proportion of the board composed of affiliated outside directors	0.16	0.14	0.17	0.14	0.14	0.13	1.61	1.63

officers and directors is higher in the second subperiod, and weak evidence that the fraction of the board that is composed of affiliated outsiders is lower in the second subperiod. The only characteristic that is significantly different at the 0.05 level in the two subperiods is the number of directors. Consistent with the findings in Huson et al. (1997), firms in the earlier subperiod have significantly larger boards.

4. The incidence of disciplinary events following performance declines

In this section, we report the incidence of control-reducing disciplinary events occurring at the sample firms in the year of and the 3 years following the performance decline. We first examine external control events, such as actual and attempted takeovers, and targeting by shareholder activists and block-holders. We then report the incidence of management turnover, including both those turnovers that follow takeovers and those that do not. Finally, we estimate logit models that test for time-series variation in the incidence of market disciplinary events, while controlling for other factors that might be related to these disciplinary events.

4.1. External control events

Table 3 reports data on the frequency of external control events occurring at the sample firms. We search the Wall Street Journal over the period that includes the year of and the 3 years following the year of poor performance. We record any instance of a sample firm having been taken over, been the subject of takeover rumors, or been the target of a takeover attempt. We report a firm as being the subject of a takeover rumor only if it is not also the target of an attempted or actual takeover during the year in which the rumor occurred. However, if the rumor exists during a year prior to the attempt or takeover, we report both the rumor and the subsequent takeover attempt. Similarly, attempted takeovers are reported only if the sample firm is not taken over during that year. We report the frequency of external control events for the full sample period (1985–1992) and for the subperiods representing the active (1985–1988) and less active (1989–1992) takeover periods. The significance of the difference in event frequencies between the two subperiods is measured using a χ^2 test of equal proportions.

The results in the first four rows of Table 3 indicate that a large fraction of the sample firms become the target of a takeover attempt following the onset of poor performance. During the sample period, 29% of the sample firms are subject to at least one type of takeover activity in the year of and the 3 years subsequent to the year of poor performance. The frequency of takeover events is substantially higher in the first subperiod than in the second subperiod. During the first subperiod, 42% of the firms experience some type of takeover activity, whereas only 17% of the firms experience takeover activity in the second subperiod. The difference between these levels is significant at the 0.01 level. This pattern is repeated when we examine the frequency of actual takeovers, rumors, and attempts. With the exception of rumored takeovers,

Table 3

Corporate control events

The frequency of external corporate control events for the sample of 350 poorly performing firms for years 0 through 3 relative to the year of poor performance. The sample includes firms, with a book value of assets greater than $100 million, that are in the top half of industry-adjusted EBITDA/total assets in the base year and in the bottom quartile in the year of poor performance. Information about takeover activity is taken from the Wall Street Journal. A firm is considered subject to a takeover rumor only if there are no attempted or actual takeovers during the year of the rumor. A firm is considered subject to a takeover attempt only if there are no actual takeovers during the year of the attempt. A firm is considered subject to control activity if it is the subject of a takeover rumor, takeover attempt, or actual takeover at any time from the start of year 0 through the end of year 3. Pension fund targeting is taken from Wahal (1996). Companies targeted by the Council of Institutional Investors are from Opler and Sokobin (1997), Pensions and Investments (Oct. 7, 1994), and the Wall Street Journal. Companies targeted by the United Shareholders Association are from Strickland et al. (1996). The sample period is 1985–1992. The chi-squared statistic tests the hypothesis that the proportion of firms experiencing each event is equal in the two subperiods.

Event	Full sample (n = 350)		1985–1988 (n = 170)		1989–1992 (n = 180)		χ^2
	N	%	N	%	N	%	
Firm is taken over	67	19	49	29	18	10	20.01***
Firm is subject to takeover rumors	25	9	14	3	11	7	2.71*
Firm is subject to takeover attempts	26	9	20	16	6	4	13.37***
Firm is subject to corporate control activity	102	29	72	42	30	17	27.93***
Firm is targeted by pension fund	15	4	3	2	12	7	5.12**
Firm is targeted by United Shareholders Association	9	3	1	1	8	4	5.19**
Firm is targeted by Council of Institutional Investors	4	1	0	0	4	2	3.82**
Firm is targeted by other shareholder	18	5	11	6	7	4	1.20
Firm is targeted by any shareholder activist	35	10	14	8	21	12	1.14
Total firms subjected to takeover activity or shareholder targeting	122	35	76	45	46	26	14.12***

*, **, and *** indicate significance at the 0.10, 0.05, and 0.01 levels, respectively.

the frequencies of these events are significantly greater, at the 0.01 level, in the 1985–1988 subperiod. We thus conclude that the market-wide decline in takeover activity in the late 1980s extends to our sample of poorly performing firms.

To put the frequency of takeover activity in our sample into perspective, we compare the sample takeover rates shown in Table 3 to those reported by Mikkelson and Partch (1997) for a random sample of firms over approximately the same time period. For a random sample of 240 firms selected in 1983, Mikkelson and Partch report that 18.2% were taken over by the end of 1988, an annual takeover rate of approximately 3.6%. For a second set of firms selected in 1989, Mikkelson and Partch report that 7.7% were taken over by the end of 1994, an annual rate of 1.5%. To compare the results for our sample, takeover rates are calculated by dividing the number of firms taken over by the product of number of calendar years in the event window times the number of firms initially in each subsample. Our estimated takeover rate understates the true takeover rate because of the disappearance of firms over time. The annual takeover rate in our sample is 7.3% in the first subperiod and 2.5% in the later subperiod. Thus, our sample firms are targeted for takeover activity at an unusually high frequency, particularly in the earlier subperiod.

As discussed in Section 2, it is possible that monitoring by active shareholders substitutes for takeover activity in the less active takeover period. To examine this possibility, Table 3 also reports the frequency with which the sample firms are targeted by various activist shareholder groups. Data on shareholder targeting is obtained from a variety of sources. Companies targeted by the nine largest activist public pension funds from 1987 through 1993 are from Wahal (1996).[5] Companies targeted by the United Shareholders Association (USA) are from Strickland et al. (1996). A list of the companies targeted by the Council of Institutional Investors (CII) from 1991 through 1993 is provided in the appendix of Opler and Sokobin (1997). Companies targeted by the CII in 1994 and 1995 are from the Oct. 7, 1994 issue of Pensions and Investments (p. 4) and the Oct. 2, 1995 issue of the Wall Street Journal (p. A4), respectively. Companies targeted by other shareholder activists, primarily through proxy fights for board seats and shareholder proposals regarding changes in the structure or management of the firm, are obtained from the Wall Street Journal Index.

Although we find that the incidence of shareholder targeting is greater in the second subperiod, the frequency of these events is relatively low in both the active and the less active takeover period. As reported in rows five through nine of Table 3, 10% of the sample firms are targeted by shareholder activists. This rate is 8% in the first subperiod, and 12% in the second subperiod, a statistically insignificant difference.

In the last row of Table 3, we report the frequency with which the sample firms experience either a takeover event or becoming a target of shareholder activists in the 3 years following the year of poor performance. We find that 35% of the sample firms are the subject of at least one type of external control activity. In addition, we find that the frequency of these control events is substantially higher in the first subperiod, when 45% of the firms experiencing a year of poor performance are the target of at least one control event. In contrast, only 26% of the firms experiencing their year of poor performance between 1989 and 1992 are targeted by outside firms or shareholders. These findings are inconsistent with the view that shareholder activism fully substituted for the decline in the takeover market. Rather, our findings are consistent with a net decline in external control events from the active to the less active takeover period.

---

[5] The pension funds are: California Public Employees Retirement System (Calpers), California State Teachers Retirement System (Calstrs), Colorado Public Employee Retirement System (Colpera), New York City Pension Fund System, Pennsylvania Public School Employee Retirement System (PSERS), State of Wisconsin Investment Board (SWIB), Teachers Insurance and Annuity Association-College Retirement Equities Fund (TIAA-CREF), Florida State Board of Administration (FSBA), New York State Common Retirement System (NYSCR).

4.2. Management turnover

Demonstrating a net decline in external control events is not sufficient to conclude that there has been a decline in managerial discipline. It is possible that managers are disciplined in the absence of any overt external control threat. For example, anecdotal evidence suggests that corporate boards have become more active in disciplining poorly performing managers in recent years. (See, for example, Fortune, January 11, 1993, pp. 34–39.) To provide evidence on the frequency with which managers are disciplined following performance declines, we examine the incidence of top executive turnover among our sample firms. We define the top executive to be the CEO, if there is one, and to be the president, otherwise. Management turnover is defined as any change in the top executive, and is identified by searching corporate proxy statements over the period including the year of and the 3 years following the year of poor performance. In the event of a missing proxy statement, we examine the Standard and Poor's Register of Corporations, Directors, and Executives. Because we are interested in management changes that are due to the performance decline, we exclude those changes that are due to death or illness, and those changes that we classify as normal retirements. Following Denis and Denis (1995) turnovers are classified as normal retirements if the stated reason for the turnover is retirement or normal succession, and the manager is between the ages of 64 and 66. We label the remaining management changes as nonroutine turnovers.

The first row of Table 4 reports the incidence of nonroutine top executive changes among firms not taken over within 3 years following the year of poor performance. Overall, 27% of the sample firms experience a nonroutine change in its top executive at least once from the beginning of the year of poor performance through the end of year 3. Contrary to Mikkelson and Partch (1997), however, we find no evidence that turnover rates differ in the active and inactive takeover periods.

Of course, managers can also be removed from office following the takeover of their firm. As noted earlier, Martin and McConnell (1991) find an unusually high rate of management turnover following corporate takeovers. Accordingly, we investigate the incidence of posttakeover management turnover among those sample firms taken over within 3 years of the year of poor performance. We track the fate of the firm's top executive using the Wall Street Journal and the Directory of Corporate Affiliations, and classify a takeover as disciplinary if it results in a change in the firm's top executive within 2 years following the completion of the takeover. Of the 67 sample firms taken over, we are able to track the top executive's fate in all but one case.

As reported in row 2 of Table 4, 13% of the sample firms experience a disciplinary takeover. This rate is substantially higher during the active takeover period. Of the 47 firms experiencing a disciplinary takeover, 38 experienced their year of poor performance during the first subperiod. This represents 79% of the firms taken over and 22% of all of the firms experiencing poor performance during the earlier period. Conversely, the nine takeovers classified as disciplinary during the second subperiod represent only 50% of the takeovers and 5% of all the firms experiencing poor performance during

Table 4

Management turnover events

The frequency of management turnover events for the sample of 350 poorly performing firms for years 0 through 3 relative to the year of poor performance. The sample includes firms, with a book value of assets greater than $100 million, that are in the top half of industry-adjusted EBITDA/total assets in the base year and in the bottom quartile in the year of poor performance. Nonroutine turnover is defined as the turnover of the top executive except in those cases in which the turnover is classed as a retirement using the definition of Denis and Denis (1995). Turnover is classed as retirement if either (i) the stated reason is retirement or (ii) the stated reason is normal succession and the departing manager is from 64 to 66 years of age. Following Martin and McConnell (1991), a firm is considered to be the subject of a disciplinary takeover if the top manager of the target firm does not retain his or her position following the takeover. The sample period is 1985–1992. The chi-squared statistic tests the hypothesis that the proportion of firms experiencing each event is equal in the two subperiods.

	Full sample ($n = 350$)		1985–1988 ($n = 170$)		1989–1992 ($n = 180$)		
Event	N	%	N	%	N	%	χ^2
Nonroutine turnover of top officer	96	27	44	26	52	29	0.40
Firm is subject to disciplinary takeover	47	13	38	22	9	5	22.65***
Nonroutine turnover of top officer or disciplinary takeover	127	36	71	42	56	31	4.47**
Firm is subject to either corporate control activity or the nonroutine turnover of its top manager	176	50	97	57	79	44	6.07***

*, **, and *** indicate significance at the 0.10, 0.05, and 0.01 levels, respectively.

that period. In other words, not only are there more takeovers in the earlier period, but a higher fraction of the takeovers result in a management change. The net effect is a significant reduction in the incidence of takeover-driven top executive turnover from the first to the second subperiod. The decline in the fraction of takeovers classified as disciplinary is significant at the 0.01 level ($\chi^2 = 5.43$).

The third row of Table 4 combines the incidence of nonroutine top executive turnover with the incidence of disciplinary takeovers to provide a measure of the frequency with which managers are removed from office following the year of poor performance. We find that 36% of the sample firms experience either a disciplinary takeover or the nonroutine turnover of its top manager. Again, the incidence of top executive changes is significantly higher during the active takeover period, affecting 42% of the firms, than in the less active takeover period, affecting 31% of the firms.

Finally, we combine the incidence of external control events, both takeover threats and shareholder activism, with the incidence of nonroutine turnover to provide a measure of how often poorly performing firms experience some type of control-reducing disciplinary event. As reported in row 4 of Table 4, 50% of the sample firms are the target of takeover activity, are targeted by shareholder activists, or experience the nonroutine turnover of its top manager. The percentage of firms experiencing these external and internal control events declines from 57% to 44% from the first to the second subperiod. A χ^2 test of equal proportions is rejected at the 1% level. Overall, therefore, our findings are consistent with a significant decline in the incidence of disciplinary events from the active to the less active takeover period.

4.3. Logistic regressions of disciplinary events

To provide further evidence on time-series variation in disciplinary events, we estimate logit models relating the likelihood of disciplinary events to a set of financial and governance variables. Previous studies have documented that the likelihood of these events is related to firm size, firm performance, industry performance, the firm's debt ratio, whether or not the firm is in financial distress, equity ownership structure, and the composition of the board of directors. To control for the influence of these factors, we include, as independent variables, the logarithm of the firm's total assets at the end of year -1, the change in the firm's unadjusted operating earnings from the end of year -1 to the end of year 0, the change in operating earnings for the median firm in the same three-digit SIC industry, the firm's ratio of total debt to total assets at the end of year -1, the proportion of shares held by officers and directors, the proportion of outsiders on the board of directors, and a binary financial distress variable. The binary distress variable is adopted from Gilson (1989), and equals one if the firm files for Chapter 11 bankruptcy protection, defaults on its debt obligations, restructures or refinances its debt, or makes a debt exchange offer, and zero otherwise. Overall, 17% of the sample firms experience some form of financial distress between the year of poor performance and the end of year 3. The incidence of financial distress is not significantly different between the active and the less active takeover period (19% vs. 16%). Finally, we include a dummy variable that equals one if the firm experienced its year of poor performance during 1989–1992 and zero, otherwise.

The logit results are reported in Table 5. Consistent with prior studies, we find that shareholder targeting is more likely in larger firms, financial distress increases the likelihood of management turnover, and higher managerial ownership decreases the likelihood of a takeover-related event.[6] More importantly, in three of the five logit models we find a significant negative coefficient on the dummy variable denoting the second subperiod. Specifically, the likelihood of a takeover-related event, the likelihood of either nonroutine turnover or a disciplinary takeover, and the likelihood of

---

[6] See Gilson (1989) and Gilson and Vetsuypens (1993) for evidence on management turnover in financially distressed firms, Mikkelson and Partch (1989) and Song and Walkling (1993) for evidence on the relation between equity ownership structure and the likelihood of takeovers, and John and Klein (1994), Karpoff et al. (1996), Smith (1996), and Strickland et al. (1996) for evidence on the relation between firm size and shareholder targeting.

Table 5

Logistic regressions of disciplinary events

Logistic regressions estimating the relation between the probability of disciplinary events and a set of financial and governance variables, as well as a dummy variable equaling one if the year of poor performance occurred during 1989–1992 (*p*-values are in parentheses). A takeover event occurs if the firm is the subject of takeover rumors, is the target of a takeover attempt, or is taken over. Shareholding targeting is any control event initiated by any shareholder activist group. Nonroutine turnover excludes top executive turnover labeled as normal retirements using the classification scheme of Denis and Denis (1995), and those turnovers due to death or illness. Disciplinary takeovers are those cases in which the firm is taken over and the top executive is replaced within 2 years of the takeover. The binary financial distress variable equals one if the firm files for Chapter 11 bankruptcy protection, defaults on its debt obligations, restructures or refinances its debt, or makes a debt exchange offer, and zero otherwise. The sample consists of 350 companies having assets greater than $100 million that are in the top half of industry-adjusted EBITDA/ total assets in the base year and in the bottom quartile in the year of poor performance. The sample period is 1985–1992.

	Takeover event (1)	Shareholder targeting (2)	Nonroutine turnover (3)	Nonroutine turnover or disciplinary takeover (4)	(1), (2), or (3)
Intercept	−6.51 (0.01)	−17.02 (0.00)	−0.57 (0.82)	−2.52 (0.27)	−4.76 (0.04)
Log (total assets)	0.31 (0.02)	0.78 (0.00)	−0.07 (0.60)	0.07 (0.53)	0.25 (0.03)
Change in EBITDA/ total assets from years −1 to 0	−0.81 (0.67)	0.45 (0.89)	−2.46 (0.18)	−1.05 (0.55)	−1.35 (0.45)
Change in industry EBITDA/Assets from years 1 to 0	−2.54 (0.62)	−10.47 (0.18)	2.73 (0.61)	6.77 (0.17)	0.60 (0.90)
Long-term debt/total assets	0.32 (0.72)	−1.07 (0.41)	0.69 (0.41)	0.78 (0.33)	0.29 (0.70)
Dummy equal to 1 if firm encounters financial distress	−0.06 (0.88)	0.29 (0.63)	1.16 (0.00)	0.88 (0.02)	0.34 (0.35)
Fractional equity ownership of officers and directors	−1.63 (0.06)	−3.98 (0.05)	−0.49 (0.50)	−0.87 (0.22)	−1.19 (0.07)
Fraction of board comprised of independent outsiders	0.22 (0.78)	0.18 (0.87)	0.10 (0.90)	0.50 (0.47)	0.04 (0.95)
Dummy equal to 1 if 1989–1992	−1.26 (0.00)	0.60 (0.16)	0.07 (0.81)	−0.56 (0.04)	−0.48 (0.06)
Pseudo R^2	0.11	0.22	0.06	0.06	0.05

any of the disciplinary events (takeover, shareholder targeting, and turnover) are negatively related to the time period dummy variable. In other words, after controlling for other possible determinants of managerial disciplinary events, there is a significant decline in control-reducing disciplinary events in the less active takeover period.

5. Corporate restructuring and changes in operating performance

Our results to this point suggest that poorly performing managers face disciplinary pressure from takeover markets, active shareholders, and corporate boards of directors. However, the incidence of these disciplinary events is significantly lower in the less active takeover period. Because prior studies suggest that corporate restructuring programs often result from external control pressures, a potential implication of these findings is that the reduction in disciplinary pressure reduces the likelihood that firms will undertake value-increasing restructuring actions following performance declines. Alternatively, however, other incentive mechanisms or improvements in internal corporate governance in the later period could induce managers to restructure, generate operating improvements, or both, in the absence of any overt threat to current managers' control. It is also possible that the threat of takeover remains high in the second subperiod, and that the threat is sufficient to induce restructuring. However, it is difficult to believe that the threat of takeover is as high in the second subperiod given the sudden sharp decline in takeovers reported in Comment and Schwert (1995) and our corresponding finding of a significant decline in disciplinary management turnover from the first to the second subperiod.

In this section, we provide evidence on these issues by documenting restructuring actions, the valuation effects of these restructuring events, and changes in operating performance for the sample firms in the year of and the 2 years following their performance decline. Our analysis is hindered by the disappearance of firms that are taken over. Although we attempt to document the restructuring actions of all firms, including those taken over, we acknowledge that we may understate the magnitude of restructuring among firms that have been taken over. Because the incidence of takeovers is substantially higher in the first subperiod, our comparison of restructuring actions and operating changes between the two subperiods must be interpreted with caution. Nevertheless, we can assess whether firms experiencing performance declines in the second subperiod undertake performance-enhancing restructurings. In addition, we later attempt to assess the importance of the bias created by time-series variation in the rate at which firms are taken over.

5.1. Corporate restructuring events following performance declines

We search the Wall Street Journal and Mergers and Acquisitions, published by Mergers and Acquisitions Inc., Washington D.C., for restructuring events over the period from the start of the base year (year -1) through the end of the third year following the year of performance decline (year 3). Similar to Ofek (1993) and Kang and Shivdasani (1997), we report the proportion of firms undertaking asset restructurings, such as divestitures, spin-offs, plant closings, and liquidations, and employee layoff and cost-cutting programs. We compare the frequency of restructuring actions following the performance decline to that in the year prior to the performance decline, and compare the frequency of restructuring actions in the active takeover period with that in the less active takeover period.

The results, reported in Table 6, indicate a substantial amount of corporate restructuring activity among the sample firms, beginning with the onset of poor performance. Asset restructurings are the most common action, with 61% of the firms undertaking some type of asset restructuring between the onset of poor performance and third year following the performance decline. With 34% of the sample firms either initiating a cost-cutting program or laying off employees, a total of 69% of the firms undertake some type of restructuring event within 3 years following the performance decline.

To put these restructuring frequencies into perspective, Table 6 also reports the proportion of sample firms undertaking restructuring actions in the year prior to the year of performance decline. The results indicate that the incidence of restructuring approximately doubles in the year of performance decline (year 0) and the following year (year 1). Restructuring frequencies subsequently decline in years 2 and 3, but still remain slightly above those in the base year, year -1. Thus, the sample firms restructure at an unusually high frequency in the years immediately following the year of performance decline. These findings are consistent with those of Ofek (1993). In addition, our findings for years 0 and 1 are similar to those of Kang and Shivdasani (1997). Although Kang and Shivdasani focus primarily on Japanese firms, they do find that, among 114 US manufacturing firms suffering operating performance declines between 1986 and 1990, 37% sell assets, 32% layoff employees, and 14% initiate cost-cutting programs.

Consistent with prior studies, the frequency of restructuring is greater among those firms experiencing disciplinary events. In results not reported in a table, we find that 76% of the firms that are takeover targets, are targets of shareholder activism, or that experience the nonroutine turnover of the top executive undertake some type of restructuring event in the year of and the 3 years following the performance decline. This rate is significantly greater, at the 0.01 level, than the 63% restructuring frequency among those firms having no disciplinary event. We find similar results if we compare restructuring frequencies in years 1-3 relative to the year of performance decline for those firms experiencing a disciplinary event in years 0 and 1 to those firms having no disciplinary event over this period. Similarly, disciplinary events are associated with a greater magnitude of restructuring. Among firms experiencing a disciplinary event, asset sales average 13.6% of the book value of total assets. For firms with no disciplinary event, asset sales average just 7.1% of the book value of total assets. The difference in asset sales between these groups of firms is significant at the 0.05 level.

To examine whether the decline in disciplinary events from the active to the less active takeover period is associated with a change in the manner in which firms respond to performance declines, Table 6 also reports restructuring frequencies in the two subperiods. The results indicate that the restructuring responses to performance declines are strikingly similar in the two subperiods. Overall, 68% of the firms in the active takeover period initiate restructuring activities between years 0 and 3, while 71% of the firms in the less active takeover period undergo restructuring events. The difference in restructuring frequencies is statistically insignificant using a χ^2

Table 6

Frequency of corporate restructuring actions following performance declines

Proportion of firms undertaking corporate restructuring actions over the period from the year prior to the year of performance decline (year -1) through the third year following the performance decline (year 3). For each restructuring event, the first row reports the percentage of firms in the full sample undertaking the action, while the second and third rows report the restructuring frequencies of firms in the active takeover period and the less active takeover period, respectively. Restructurings include the sale of assets or divisions, the closing or reorganization of a plant or division, spin-offs, liquidations, and the sale of a stake in the firm. The sample consists of 350 companies having assets greater than $100 million that are in the top half of industry-adjusted EBITDA/total assets in the base year and in the bottom quartile in the year of poor performance. The sample period is 1985–992.

Restructuring action	Year −1	Year 0	Year 1	Year 2	Year 3	Years 0 and 1	Years 0-3
Panel A: Asset restructuring							
Sale of asset or division							
Full sample	0.11	0.15	0.17	0.17	0.14	0.28	0.41
1985–1988	0.11	0.19*	0.17	0.18	0.15	0.29	0.41
1989–1992	0.11	0.12	0.18	0.17	0.14	0.27	0.42
Close or reorganize plant or division							
Full sample	0.04	0.13	0.11	0.10	0.06	0.21	0.31
1985–1988	0.05	0.12	0.11	0.11	0.06	0.20	0.31
1989–1992	0.03	0.14	0.11	0.09	0.06	0.22	0.31
Any asset restructuring							
Full sample	0.15	0.27	0.26	0.25	0.20	0.44	0.61
1985–1988	0.15	0.29	0.27	0.25	0.20	0.45	0.59
1989–1992	0.14	0.26	0.26	0.26	0.21	0.43	0.63
Panel B: Employee layoffs and cost cutting							
Layoffs							
Full sample	0.04	0.11	0.12	0.10	0.06	0.20	0.28
1985–1988	0.06	0.11	0.11	0.08	0.06	0.19	0.26
1989–1992	0.03	0.11	0.13	0.12	0.06	0.21	0.31
Cost-cutting efforts							
Full sample	0.03	0.09	0.08	0.09	0.03	0.15	0.21
1985–1988	0.03	0.10	0.05	0.07*	0.05	0.15	0.19
1989–1992	0.03	0.09	0.10	0.10	0.02	0.16	0.23
Any layoff or cost-cutting							
Full sample	0.07	0.05	0.16	0.14	0.08	0.25	0.34
1985–1988	0.07	0.15	0.14	0.11*	0.09	0.25	0.31
1989–1992	0.06	0.14	0.17	0.18	0.07	0.26	0.37
Panel C: All restructuring actions							
Any asset restructuring, layoffs or cost-cutting efforts							
Full sample	0.17	0.33	0.35	0.31	0.25	0.53	0.69
1985–1988	0.18	0.35	0.34	0.29	0.25	0.53	0.68
1989–1992	0.16	0.31	0.36	0.33	0.24	0.52	0.71

* indicates that the proportion of firms undertaking the restructuring action in the active takeover period (1985–1988) is significantly different (at the 0.10 level) from the proportion of firms in the less active takeover period.

test. Similarly, there is no difference in the proportion of firms engaging in asset restructurings, layoffs, or other cost-cutting programs in the two subperiods.

As noted earlier, one concern with our comparisons of restructuring frequencies across subperiods is that we may be missing data for firms that are taken over. To the extent that we understate the incidence of restructuring actions among firms taken over, our subperiod comparisons over years 0–3 are biased because a greater fraction of firms are taken over in the 1985–1988 subperiod. Recall that, of the 350 sample firms, 67 are taken over by the end of year 3. Of these, 49 are from the first subperiod and 18 are from the second subperiod. While it is not possible to completely alleviate this concern, we address this issue in two ways. First, we compare the restructuring frequency of those firms taken over to that of the firms not taken over. We find that 75% of the firms taken over engage in some form of restructuring between years 0 and 3. This rate is higher than the 69% rate documented for the full sample, suggesting that our data sources pick up a high frequency of restructuring even among those firms that are taken over. Second, we compare the frequency of restructuring across the two subperiods under the assumption that every firm taken over engages in some type of restructuring. Under this admittedly strong assumption, we still find no significant difference in restructuring frequencies across the two subperiods. During the active takeover period, 76% of the firms undertake some type of restructuring, while this rate is 73% in the less active takeover period. We thus conclude that our results on the frequency of restructuring are not materially biased by the lack of data for firms that are taken over.

Although restructuring frequencies appear to be similar in the two subperiods, it is possible that the magnitude of the restructurings differ. To examine this possibility, we measure the magnitude of asset restructuring as the total proceeds from asset sales divided by the book value of total assets at the end of year -1. In results not reported in a table, we find that asset sales average 11.4% of total assets in the 1985–1988 subperiod and 9.3% in the 1989–1992 subperiod, an insignificant difference across the two periods. If we examine only those firms that did undertake some asset restructuring between years 0 and 3, asset sales average 28.2% of total assets in the active takeover period, and 22.4% of total assets in the less active takeover period. Median asset sales for firms undertaking asset restructurings are 13.3% of total assets in the active period, and 8.1% in the less active period. Here, the difference in medians is significant at the 0.10 level, but the difference in means is not. Thus, there is little evidence that the scope of restructuring differs between the active and the less active subperiods.

5.2. The valuation impact of restructuring announcements

To assess the valuation impact of the restructuring events, we conduct an event-study analysis of the restructuring announcements. We search the Wall Street Journal and Lexis-Nexis for announcement dates for each asset restructuring, layoff, and cost-cutting event. After excluding events for which there is a confounding announcement on either the day of or the day prior to the restructuring announcement, and those for which there is insufficient stock return data, we are left with 377 announcement dates of restructuring events. Of these, 289 are asset restructurings and 88 are announcements of layoffs or cost-cutting actions.

We measure abnormal returns over the 2-day period, including the day of and the day prior to the announcement, using the market model technique. Market model parameters are estimated over the 250 trading-day period ending 40 days prior to the announcement. Our findings, reported in Table 7, indicate that the restructuring announcements are met with a positive stock price reaction, on average. For the full set of 377 announcements, the average abnormal return over the 2-day announcement period is 0.59%, significant at the 0.10 level. The positive stock price reaction is driven by the subsample of asset sale announcements. Announcement period abnormal returns average 1.75% for asset sales, significant at the 0.01 level and a statistically insignificant −0.39% for cost cutting or layoff announcements. Moreover, we find no difference in average or median stock price reactions across the two subperiods. We thus conclude that the asset restructurings announced in the year of and the 3 years following performance declines are value-enhancing events for the sample firms.

5.3. Changes in operating performance following performance declines

To examine whether the sample firms generate operating improvements following performance declines, Table 8 reports industry-adjusted operating performance over the period from 1 year prior to the performance decline (year −1) through 3 years following the performance decline (year 3). Industry-adjusted operating performance is measured as the ratio of EBITDA to total assets minus the same ratio for the median firm having the same three-digit SIC code.

As noted earlier, industry-adjusted operating performance is significantly positive in year −1, and significantly negative in year 0. More importantly, industry-adjusted operating performance improves substantially in the 3 years following the performance decline. By the end of year 3, the operating performance of the sample firms does not differ from that of the median firm in the industry. Moreover, the results are nearly identical in the two subperiods.

It is possible, however, that the improvement in operating performance simply reflects normal reversion to the mean in operating performance measures.[7] Therefore, to assess the significance of changes in operating performance between years 0 and 3, we follow the procedure described in Barber and Lyon (1996), and compare the change in operating performance for each sample firm to the median change for a set of firms matched by industry and performance in year 0. Our comparison sample includes those firms having the same two-digit SIC code, and whose ratio of EBITDA-to-total assets falls between 90% and 110% of the sample firm as of the end of year 0. We initially attempted to match on the basis of performance and three-digit SIC code. However,

---

[7] See Barber and Lyon (1996) for a discussion of this issue, and Penman (1991) and Fama and French (1995) for evidence that accounting earnings are mean-reverting.

Table 7

The stock price reaction to restructuring announcements

2-day announcement period abnormal returns for the set of 377 announcements of asset restructuring and layoff or cost-cutting events. Announcement dates are obtained from the Wall Street Journal Index and from Lexis/Nexis. Abnormal returns are measured using the market model technique, with parameters estimated over the 250 trading day period ending 40 days prior to each announcement. The test statistics are heteroskedastic t-tests of equal means and Wilcoxon signed-rank tests of equal medians across the two subperiods.

Type of restructuring	Full sample			1985–1988			1989–1992			Test statistic	
	Mean	Median	N	Mean	Median	N	Mean	Median	N	t-Statistic	z-Statistic
All events	0.0059*	0.0025**	377	0.0013	0.0007	195	0.0108**	0.0041**	182	−1.317	−1.131
Asset sales	0.0175***	0.0068***	189	0.0111**	0.0054***	103	0.0251***	0.0108***	86	−1.470	−1.092
Asset reorganizations	−0.0099	−0.0062	70	−0.0126	−0.0080	40	−0.0062	−0.0038	30	−0.374	−0.095
All asset restructurings	0.0088**	0.0036***	289	0.0039	0.0021	159	0.0149*	0.0049***	130	−1.266	−1.293
Layoffs/Cost cutting	−0.0039	−0.0053	88	−0.0103	−0.0039	36	0.0005	−0.0067	52	−0.769	−0.535

***, **, and * denote significance at the 0.01, 0.05, and 0.10 levels, respectively.

Table 8

Industry-adjusted operating performance following performance declines

Mean and median industry-adjusted ratio of EBITDA to total assets for the years −1 to 3 relative to the year of poor performance. Industry-adjusted performance is measured as the difference in operating performance between the sample firm and the median firm in the same three–digit SIC code. The test statistics are heteroskedastic t-tests of equal means and Wilcoxon signed-rank tests of equal medians across the two subperiods.

	Full sample		1985–1988		1989–1992		Test statistic	
	Mean	Median	Mean	Median	Mean	Median	t-Statistic	z-Statistic
Year −1	0.053***	0.040***	0.055***	0.037***	0.051***	0.043***	0.688	−0.486
Year 0	−0.058***	−0.051***	−0.055***	−0.051***	−0.061***	−0.051***	0.802	0.716
Year 1	−0.035***	−0.015***	−0.032***	−0.014***	−0.037***	−0.015***	0.341	0.399
Year 2	−0.016***	0.000	−0.011	0.001	−0.020**	−0.002	0.718	0.861
Year 3	−0.007	0.004	−0.004	0.007	−0.009	0.000	0.475	0.767

*, **, and *** indicate significance at the 0.10, 0.05, and 0.01 levels, respectively.

because we were unable to identify industry matches for a large number of firms, we employed two-digit SIC matches instead.

The results, reported in Table 9, indicate that, following the year of poor performance, operating performance improves significantly for the sample firms. Between years 0 and 3, the median adjusted change in operating performance is 0.032, which represents a 61.5% increase over the ratio of operating income-to-total assets in year 0. The results also indicate that the performance improvements do not differ significantly between the two subperiods. We thus conclude that the increased level of operating performance reported in Table 8 represents an improvement in operating performance over and above that which would be expected due to normal mean reversion of accounting earnings.

To this point, we have established that a large fraction of the sample firms restructure during the year of and the 3 years following a performance decline and that, on average, the sample firms exhibit operating improvements over this period. An interesting remaining question is whether the improved operating performance results in part from the restructuring actions documented in Table 6. To address this issue, we examine the adjusted change in operating performance between years 1 and 3 for those firms that restructure in year 0 with those that do not restructure in year 0. In this way, we examine performance changes over a period following a set of restructuring events. One drawback to this approach, however, is that it ignores those restructurings that take place after year 0, and their potential impacts on performance.

Our results, not reported in a table, suggest that asset restructurings are linked with subsequent operating improvements, but that cost cutting and layoffs are not. Specifically, for those firms with an asset restructuring in year 0, the average adjusted change in operating performance over years 1–3 is 0.026, and the median change is 0.010. The average change is significantly different from zero, and from the statistically insignificant change of −0.009 for those firms with no asset restructuring in year 0. We find no significant adjusted changes in operating performance for either those firms with or without cost cutting or layoff events in year 0.

We note two caveats in interpreting our findings with respect to changes in operating performance. First, as noted previously, we are able to report operating performance only for those firms that remain independent. Because more firms are taken over in the first subperiod, our comparison of operating improvements between subperiods must be interpreted with caution. We examined both the level of industry-adjusted operating profitability in year 0 and the change in industry-adjusted operating profits from years −1 to 0 for evidence that operating profits are systematically different among those firms that are subsequently taken over. We found no significant differences. Second, it is possible that we observe operating improvements partly because the sample firms sell off their least profitable assets. This argument would suggest that the findings reported in Tables 8 and 9 overstate the real improvements in operating performance within the sample firms. Nonetheless, the fact the sample restructurings are met with a positive stock price reaction suggests that, on average, the restructurings are value-enhancing events.

Table 9

Performance-adjusted changes in operating performance following performance declines

Mean and median adjusted changes in operating performance, defined as the change in EBITDA/Assets for the sample firm minus the median change for a set of firms matched by industry and year 0 performance. The comparison sample includes those firms having the same two-digit SIC code and whose ratio of EBITDA to total assets is between 90% and 110% of the sample firm. The test statistics are heteroskedastic t-tests of equal means and Wilcoxon signed-rank tests of equal medians across the two subperiods.

	Full sample			1985–1988			1989–1992			Test statistic	
	Mean	Median	N	Mean	Median	N	Mean	Median	N	t-Statistic	z-Statistic
Change from years 0 to 1	0.015*	0.026***	318	0.013	0.021***	149	0.017	0.029***	169	−0.264	0.816
Change from years 0 to 2	0.030***	0.034***	304	0.028***	0.034***	139	0.032***	0.034***	165	−0.364	−0.010
Change from years 0 to 3	0.028***	0.032***	287	0.025***	0.031***	130	0.031***	0.034***	157	−0.565	−0.479

*, **, and *** indicate significance at the 0.10, 0.05, and 0.01 levels, respectively.

6. Discussion

Our overall findings are broadly consistent with those of Mikkelson and Partch (1997) in that we find that disciplinary events are linked with activity in the takeover market. As noted in Section 2, a decline in the frequency of those disciplinary events that reduce the control of current managers could reduce the incentives of managers to maximize firm value. Under this hypothesis, disciplinary events are an important force in motivating managers to make value-enhancing restructuring decisions. Following a decline in disciplinary events, therefore, one might expect to observe fewer value-enhancing restructurings.

Contrary to this hypothesis, however, we find no difference in either the frequency of restructurings or subsequent operating improvements between the active and the less active takeover period. A possible interpretation of these results is that the disciplinary events that we study are not important in eliciting performance-enhancing restructurings. However, we also find that performance-enhancing restructurings are more likely in firms facing disciplinary events than in those firms with no disciplinary event. This observation raises a puzzle. If restructurings are linked with disciplinary events, and the frequency of disciplinary events declines from the active to the less active takeover period, how is it that firms suffering performance declines restructure with equal frequency in the two subperiods?.

We conjecture that other incentive mechanisms, such as the increased use of stock-based compensation, or other forms of managerial monitoring, such as more active boards of directors and active shareholders, substitute for the takeover market in ensuring that performance-enhancing restructurings take place following substantial declines in operating performance. Our findings suggest that these other control mechanisms are less public and do not involve the replacement of the CEO as often as does the takeover market, but appear to nonetheless generate improvements in performance. This view is consistent with Pound's (1992a,b) political model of corporate governance in which active shareholders maintain ongoing, but mostly private dialogues with managers and the board of directors. Moreover, our findings complement those of Carleton et al. (1998), who find that the private negotiations between one large institutional investor, TIAA-CREF, and a set of targeted companies are remarkably effective in bringing about the changes desired by TIAA-CREF.

Our conjecture is also consistent with Kaplan's (1997) views on why hostile leveraged buyouts (LBOs) and corporate raiders have not reappeared despite the resurgence in takeover activity in the mid-1990s. Kaplan argues that share-holders, boards, and managers have applied the insights learned from LBOs in the 1980s to improve corporate governance practices in US corporations. Our findings fit well with this view in the sense that poorly performing firms in the less active takeover period appear to undertake performance-enhancing restructurings just as frequently as firms in the active takeover period, despite a substantial decline in disciplinary events.

Nevertheless, even if this substitution from takeovers to other incentive and monitoring mechanisms takes place, we cannot conclude from our evidence that takeovers are unimportant as a disciplinary force. It is possible that restructurings following takeovers improve performance to a greater extent than restructurings that take place in the absence of a takeover. Because the firms cease to exist as independent entities, we cannot observe the performance effects of those restructurings that take place following takeovers. Therefore, we cannot fully address this possibility. At a minimum, though, our evidence suggests that the decline in disciplinary events from the first to the second subperiod does not result in fewer performance-enhancing restructurings.

7. Conclusion

We examine the incidence of those disciplinary events that reduce current managers' control, and the extent of corporate restructuring among firms experiencing a substantial decline in industry-adjusted operating performance. We find that approximately one-half of the sample firms are the target of some control-reducing disciplinary event in the year of and the 3 years following the year of poor performance. These disciplinary events include takeover attempts, shareholder activism, and board dismissals. The high frequency of these events suggests that the threat of a control reduction provides meaningful incentives to top executives. In addition, there is a significant decline in the incidence of control-reducing disciplinary events from the active takeover period (1985–1988) to the less active takeover period (1989–1992). This decline suggests that, during the less active takeover period, other monitoring mechanisms do not fully substitute for takeovers in forcing the dismissal of top executives of poorly performing firms. Despite the decline in control-reducing disciplinary events, however, we find evidence of significant increases in corporate restructuring following performance declines in both subperiods. Asset restructuring announcements are more likely in firms experiencing disciplinary events, are met with positive stock price reactions, and are associated with subsequent improvements in operating performance. We thus conclude that the decline in disciplinary events from the active to the less active takeover period does not lead to fewer value-enhancing corporate restructurings. Further studies that provide direct evidence on the process through which boards of directors, active shareholders, and managers interact to produce such changes would represent an important contribution to the corporate governance literature.

References

Barber, B. M. and J. D. Lyon, 1996, "Detecting Abnormal Operating Performance: The Empirical Power and Specification of Test Statistics," *Journal of Financial Economics*, 41, 313–358.

Barber, B. M. and J. D. Lyon, 1997, "Detecting Long Run Abnormal Stock Returns: The Empirical Power and Specification of Test Statistics," *Journal of Financial Economics*, 43, 341–372.

Berger, P. G. and E. Ofek, 1996, "Bustup Takeovers of Value-Destroying Diversified Firms," *Journal of Finance*, 51, 1175–1200.

Berger, P. G. and E. Ofek, 1999, "Causes and Effects of Corporate Refocusing Programs," *Review of Financial Studies*, 2, 311–345.

Bhagat, S., A. Shleifer and R. Vishny, 1990, "Hostile Takeovers in the 1980's: The Return to Corporate Specialization," In *Brookings Papers on Economic Activity: Microeconomics*, pp. 1–84.

Bhide, A., 1990, "Reversing Corporate Diversification," *Journal of Applied Corporate Finance*, 3, 70–81.

Brickley, J. A., J. L. Coles and J. S. Linck, 1998, "What Happens to CEOs After they Retire? New Evidence on Career Concerns, Horizon Problems, and CEO Incentives," *Journal of Financial Economics*, 52, 341–378.

Carleton, W. T., J. N. Nelson and M. S. Weisbach, 1998, "The Influence of Institutions on Corporate Governance Through Private Negotiations: Evidence from TIAA-CREF," *Journal of Finance*, 53, 1335–1362.

Comment, R. and G. W. Schwert, 1995, "Poison or Placebo? Evidence on the Deterrence and Wealth Effects of Modern Antitakeover Measures," *Journal of Financial Economics*, 39, 3–44.

Dann, L. Y. and H. DeAngelo, 1988, "Corporate Financial Policy and Corporate Control: A Study of Defensive Adjustments in Asset and Ownership Structure," *Journal of Financial Economics*, 20, 87–127.

Del Guercio, D. and J. Hawkins, 1999, "The Motivation and Impact of Pension Fund Activism," *Journal of Financial Economics*, 52, 293–340.

Denis, D. J. and D. K. Denis, 1995, "Performance Changes Following Top Management Dismissals," *Journal of Finance*, 50, 1029–1057.

Denis, D. J. and A. Sarin, 1999, "Ownership and Board Structures in Publicly Traded Corporations," *Journal of Financial Economics*, 52, 187–224.

Denis, D. J. and J. M. Serrano, 1996, "Active Investors and Management Turnover Following Unsuccessful Control Contests," *Journal of Financial Economics*, 40, 239–266.

Denis, D. J., D. K. Denis and A. Sarin, 1997, "Agency Problems, Equity Ownership, and Corporate Diversification," *Journal of Finance*, 52, 135–160.

Fama, E. F. and K. French, 1995, "Size and Book-To-Market Factors in Earnings and Returns," *Journal of Finance*, 50, 131–155.

Gilson, S. C., 1989, "Management Turnover and Financial Distress," *Journal of Financial Economics*, 25, 241–262.

Gilson, S. C. and M. R. Vetsuypens, 1993, "CEO Compensation in Financially Distressed Firms: An Empirical Analysis," *Journal of Finance*, 48, 425–458.

Huson, M. R., R. Parrino and L. Starks, 1997, "The Effectiveness of Internal Monitoring Mechanisms: Evidence from CEO Turnover between 1971 and 1994," Unpublished Working Paper, University of Texas.

Jensen, M. C., 1993, "The Modern Industrial Revolution, Exit, and the Failure of Internal Control Systems," *Journal of Finance*, 48, 831–880.

Jensen, M. C. and J. B. Warner, 1988, "The Distribution of Power Among Corporate Managers, Share-holders, and Directors," *Journal of Financial Economics*, 20, 3–24.

John, K. and A. Klein, 1994, "Shareholder Proposals and Corporate Governance," Unpublished Working Paper, New York University.

Kang, J. and A. Shivdasani, 1997, "Corporate Restructuring During Performance Declines in Japan," *Journal of Financial Economics*, 46, 29–66.

Kaplan, S. N., 1994, "Top Executive Rewards and Firm Performance: A Comparison of Japan and the United States," *Journal of Political Economy*, 102, 510–546.

Kaplan, S. N., 1997, "The Evolution of Corporate Governance: We are all Henry Kravis Now," *Journal of Private Equity* (Fall), 7–14.

Karpoff, J., 1998, "The Impact of Shareholder Activism on Target Companies: A Survey of Empirical Findings," Unpublished Working Paper, University of Washington.

Karpoff, J., P. Malatesta and R. Walkling, 1996, "Corporate Governance and Shareholder Initiatives: Empirical Evidence," *Journal of Financial Economics*, 42, 365–395.

Martin, K. J. and J. J. McConnell, 1991, "Corporate Performance, Corporate Takeovers, and Management Turnover," *Journal of Finance*, 46, 671–687.

Mikkelson, W. and M. Partch, 1989, "Managers' Voting Rights and Corporate Control," *Journal of Financial Economics*, 25, 263–290.

Mikkelson, W. and M. Partch, 1997, "The Decline of Takeovers and Disciplinary Managerial Turnover," *Journal of Financial Economics*, 44, 205–228.

Mitchell, M. L. and K. Lehn, 1990, "Do bad Bidders Become Good Targets?" *Journal of Political Economy*, 98, 372–398.

Mitchell, M. L. and J. H. Mulherin, 1996, "The Impact of Industry Shocks on Takeover and Restructuring Activity," *Journal of Financial Economics*, 41, 193–229.

Morck, R., A. Shleifer and R. W. Vishny, 1989, "Alternative Mechanisms for Corporate Control," *American Economic Review*, 79, 842–852.

Murphy, K. J. and J. L. Zimmerman, 1993, "Financial Performance Surrounding CEO Turnover," *Journal of Accounting and Economics*, 16, 273–316.

Ofek, E., 1993, "Capital Structure and Firm Response to Poor Performance," *Journal of Financial Economics*, 34, 3–30.

Opler, T. and J. Sokobin, 1997, "Does Coordinated Institutional Activism Work? An Analysis of the Activities of the Council of Institutional Investors," Unpublished Working Paper, Ohio State University.

Penman, S., 1991, "An Evaluation of Accounting Rate of Return," *Journal of Accounting, Auditing, and Finance*, 6, 233–255.

Porciau, S., 1993, "Earnings Management and Nonroutine Executive Changes," *Journal of Accounting and Economics*, 16, 317–336.

Pound, J., 1992a, "Beyond Takeovers: Politics Comes to Corporate Control," *Harvard Business Review*, 70, 83–93.

Pound, J., 1992b, "Raiders, Targets, and Politics: The History and Future of American Corporate Control," *Journal of Applied Corporate Finance*, 5, 6–18.

Smith, M., 1996, "Shareholder Activism by Institutional Investors: Evidence from CalPERS," *Journal of Finance*, 51, 227–252.

Song, M. H. and R. A. Walkling, 1993, "The Impact of Managerial Ownership on Acquisition Attempts and Target Shareholder Wealth," *Journal of Financial and Quantitative Analysis*, 28, 439–457.

Strickland, D., K. W. Wiles and M. Zenner, 1996, "A Requiem for the USA: Is Small Shareholder Monitoring Effective?" *Journal of Financial Economics*, 40, 319–338.

Wahal, S., 1996, "Pension Fund Activism and Firm Performance" *Journal of Financial and Quantitative Analysis*, 31, 1–23.

Warner, J. B., R. L. Watts and K. H. Wruck, 1988, "Stock Prices and Top Management Changes," *Journal of Financial Economics*, 20, 461–492.

Weisbach, M. S., 1988, "Outside Directors and CEO Turnover," *Journal of Financial Economics*, 20, 431–459.

PART 8

DO CROSS-BORDER MERGERS CAUSE SPILLOVERS
OF GOVERNANCE STANDARDS?

Chapter 23

CROSS-COUNTRY DETERMINANTS OF MERGERS AND ACQUISITIONS[*]

STEFANO ROSSI

London Business School, Regent's Park, London, United Kingdom

PAOLO F. VOLPIN

London Business School, Regent's Park, London, United Kingdom

Contents

* We thank Richard Brealey, Ian Cooper, Antoine Faure-Grimaud, Julian Franks, Denis Gromb, Ernst Maug, Thomas Noe, Antoinette Schoar, Henri Servaes, Oren Sussman, David Webb, an anonymous referee, and participants at the 2004 AFA meetings in San Diego, at the 2003 EFA meetings in Glasgow and at seminars at Humboldt University, London Business School, London School of Economics, Norwegian School of Economics and Business, Norwegian School of Management, and Tilburg University. Paolo F. Volpin acknowledges support from the JP Morgan Chase Research Fellowship at London Business School.

This article originally appeared in the *Journal of Financial Economics*, Vol. 74, pp. 277–304 (2004).
Corporate Takeovers, Volume 2
Edited by B. Espen Eckbo

Abstract

We study the determinants of mergers and acquisitions (M&A) around the world by focusing on differences in laws and regulation across countries. We find that the volume of M&A activity is significantly larger in countries with better accounting standards and stronger shareholder protection. The probability of an all-cash bid decreases with the level of shareholder protection in the acquirer country. In cross-border deals, targets are typically from countries with poorer investor protection than their acquirers' countries, suggesting that cross-border transactions play a governance role by improving the degree of investor protection within target firms.

Keywords

mergers and acquisitions, corporate governance, investor protection

JEL classification: G28, G32, G34

1. Introduction

In a perfect world, corporate assets would be channeled toward their best possible use. Mergers and acquisitions (M&A) help this process by reallocating control over companies. However, frictions such as transaction costs, information asymmetries, and agency conflicts can prevent efficient transfers of control. Recent studies on corporate governance employ measures of the quality of the legal and regulatory environment within a country as proxies for some of these frictions, and show that differences in laws, regulation, and enforcement correlate with the development of capital markets, the ownership structure of firms, and the cost of capital (see, e.g., Bhattacharya and Daouk, 2002; La Porta et al., 1997, 1998).

In this paper we analyze a sample of M&A announced in the 1990s and completed by the end of 2002. Our sample comprises firms in 49 major countries and shows that differences in laws and enforcement explain the intensity and the pattern of M&A around the world. The volume of M&A activity is significantly larger in countries with better accounting standards and stronger shareholder protection. This result holds for several measures of M&A activity, and also when we control for other characteristics of the regulatory environment such as antitrust legislation and takeover laws. Our findings indicate that a more active market for M&A is the outcome of a corporate governance regime with stronger investor protection. We also show that hostile deals are relatively more likely in countries with better shareholder protection. One explanation is that good protection for minority shareholders makes control more contestable by reducing the private benefits of control.

Next, we provide evidence on cross-border M&A. We show that the probability that a given deal is cross-border rather than domestic decreases with the investor protection of the target's country. Even after we control for bilateral trade, relative GNP per capita, and cultural and geographical differences, we find that targets are typically from countries with poorer investor protection compared to their acquirers. This result suggests that cross-border M&A activity is an important channel for effective worldwide convergence in corporate governance standards, as argued by Coffee (1999).

Selling to a foreign firm is a form of contractual convergence similar to the decision to list in countries with better corporate governance and better-developed capital markets. Pagano et al. (2002) and Reese and Weisbach (2002) show that firms from countries with weak legal protection for minority shareholders list abroad more frequently than do firms from other countries. We show that firms in countries with weaker investor protection are often sold to buyers from countries with stronger investor protection.

We also analyze the determinants of the takeover premium and the method of payment in individual transactions. We show that the premium is higher in countries with higher shareholder protection, although this result is driven by deals with US and UK targets. We find that the probability of an all-cash bid decreases with the degree of shareholder protection in the acquirer country, indicating that acquisitions paid with stock require an environment with high shareholder protection.

Our paper belongs to the growing literature exploring cross-country variation in governance structures around the world. Recent studies show that better legal protection of minority shareholders is associated with more developed stock markets (La Porta et al., 1997), higher valuation (La Porta et al., 2002), greater dividend payouts (La Porta et al., 2000b), lower concentration of ownership and control (La Porta et al., 1999), lower private benefits of control (Dyck and Zingales, 2004; Nenova, 2003), lower earnings management (Leuz et al., 2003), lower cash balances (Dittmar et al., 2003), and higher correlation between investment opportunities and actual investments (Wurgler, 2000). Our paper shows that better investor protection is correlated with a more active market for M&A.

We structure the paper as follows. Section 2 describes the data. Section 3 contains the analyses of the determinants of M&A activity. Section 4 discusses the main results. Section 5 concludes.

2. Data

Our sample contains all M&A announced between January 1, 1990 and December 31, 1999, completed as of December 31, 2002, and reported by Securities Data Corporation (SDC) Platinum, a database from Thomson Financial. Because we wish to study transactions clearly motivated by changes in control, we focus on mergers (business combinations in which the number of companies decreases after the transaction) and acquisitions of majority interests (when the acquirer owns less than 50% of the target company's stock before the deal, and more than 50% after the deal). A second reason for this sample selection is that the coverage of transfers of minority stakes (below 50%) is likely to be severely affected by cross-country differences in disclosure requirements. By selecting only transfers of stakes above 50%, we minimize these disclosure biases. However, in interpreting the results, we note that the availability and quality of the data might be better in some countries (such as the United States and United Kingdom) because of broader SDC coverage. A related concern is that the coverage of small countries improves over time. To address this concern, we replicate our analysis on the subsample of deals announced in the second half of the 1990s and find similar results.

The availability of empirical measures of investor protection limits our set to 49 countries. The sample from SDC includes 45,686 deals, 22% of which have a traded company as the target. Excluded deals represent about 6% of the original dataset in number and 1% in value.

The appendix describes the variables we use in this paper and indicates their sources. These variables can be classified into three broad categories corresponding to three different levels of analysis. The first set of variables is at the country level. It includes measures of M&A activity from the target's perspective, as well as broad macroeconomic conditions and proxies for the legal and regulatory environment. We use these variables in our cross-country analysis of the determinants of international

M&A. Our second category of variables measures the flow of M&A activity and cultural differences and similarities between any ordered pairs of acquirer and target countries (there are 49×48 or 2352 ordered pairs). The third set of variables is at the individual deal level and includes data on the premium paid, the value of the deal, and the means of payment. We use these data, together with the country-level variables defined above, in our analysis of the determinants of the premium and the means of payment.

2.1. M&A activity

Tables 1 and 2 show the data on M&A activity sorted by target country. We define volume as the percentage of traded firms that are targets of successful mergers or acquisitions. We interpret this variable as a measure of the ability of an economy to reallocate control over corporate assets. We also use other measures of volume, such as the total number of completed deals divided by population, the value of all completed deals divided by GDP, and the value of completed deals among traded companies divided by stock market capitalization. The qualitative results do not change. As is apparent from Table 1, the market for corporate control plays a different role in different countries. For example, volume is very low in Japan (only 6.4% of Japanese traded companies are targets of a completed deal during the 1990s) and very high in the United States (65.6% of US traded companies are targets in a completed deal). The table also shows some similarities across countries. For example, volume in France, Italy, and the United Kingdom is similar, although their governance regimes are quite different.

Of all M&A, we focus on hostile deals, since they are likely to play an important governance role. We examine the number of attempted hostile takeovers as a percentage of the total number of traded companies. The intuition is that the disciplinary role of hostile takeovers is related to the threat they represent to incumbent managers. In other words, it is likely that attempted (but failed) hostile takeovers play just as important a role in disciplining management as hostile takeovers that are eventually completed.

In all countries, the frequency of hostile takeovers is very small. According to SDC, they are absent in 21 out of 49 countries, and when present they never exceed the 6.44% observed in the United States. Therefore, according to SDC Platinum, hostile takeovers are rare. However, this conclusion could be unwarranted, because our source might fail to record all unsuccessful takeovers. Moreover, in some countries the corporate governance role of hostile takeovers could be performed by hostile stakes, as Jenkinson and Ljungqvist (2001) show for Germany.

We define the cross-border ratio as the percentage of completed deals in which the acquirer is from a different country than the target. In the case of mergers, we follow our data source to distinguish acquirers from targets. For example, in the merger between Daimler and Chrysler, Thomson codifies Daimler as the acquirer and Chrysler as the target.

Table 1

Data on international mergers and acquisitions sorted by target country

Volume is the percentage of traded companies targeted in a completed deal. Hostile takeover is the number of attempted hostile takeovers as a percentage of domestic traded firms. Cross-border ratio is the number of cross-border deals as a percentage of all completed deals.

Country	Volume (%)	Hostile takeover (%)	Cross-border ratio (%)
Argentina	26.80	0.65	53.73
Australia	34.09	4.60	27.16
Austria	38.14	1.03	51.55
Belgium	33.33	0.56	45.14
Brazil	23.08	0.00	52.03
Canada	30.05	2.73	22.66
Chile	10.57	0.42	64.79
Colombia	19.42	0.00	66.67
Denmark	24.03	0.81	38.26
Ecuador	10.53	0.00	68.97
Egypt	1.46	0.00	47.62
Finland	45.45	0.91	22.67
France	56.40	1.68	33.81
Germany	35.51	0.30	26.05
Greece	12.66	0.00	23.13
Hong Kong	33.91	0.41	38.52
India	2.01	0.02	56.02
Indonesia	10.60	0.48	61.03
Ireland	28.90	4.62	52.73
Israel	9.43	0.23	46.94
Italy	56.40	3.04	36.13
Japan	6.43	0.00	13.25
Jordan	0.00	0.00	55.56
Kenya	1.80	0.00	28.57
Malaysia	15.23	0.19	11.27
Mexico	27.51	0.00	51.02
Netherlands	26.49	1.32	43.43
New Zealand	49.82	0.70	46.15
Nigeria	0.61	0.00	58.33
Norway	61.24	5.86	36.76
Pakistan	0.48	0.00	55.56
Peru	12.21	0.00	56.88
Philippines	21.41	0.00	37.97
Portugal	31.37	1.96	40.00
Singapore	34.06	0.40	31.41
South Africa	23.89	0.45	24.65
South Korea	4.81	0.00	53.85
Spain	15.72	0.17	37.55
Sri Lanka	4.83	0.00	42.86
Sweden	62.06	3.74	35.48
Switzerland	38.48	1.43	43.59

(Continued)

Table 1 (*Continued*)

Country	Volume (%)	Hostile takeover (%)	Cross-border ratio (%)
Taiwan	0.89	0.00	49.37
Thailand	17.14	0.00	43.24
Turkey	6.12	0.00	45.45
United Kingdom	53.65	4.39	23.46
United States	65.63	6.44	9.07
Uruguay	7.55	0.00	85.00
Venezuela	14.91	0.00	56.60
Zimbabwe	6.35	0.00	46.15
World average	23.54	1.01	42.82

The number of cross-border M&A is 11,638, corresponding to 25% of the total. Table 1 shows that different countries play different roles in the cross-border M&A market. For instance, 51% of the acquirers in Mexican deals are foreign, compared to only 9.1% in the United States.

To study the cross-country variations in the premiums and means of payment, we use transaction-level data. The premium is the bid price as a percentage of the closing price 4 weeks before the announcement. We characterize the means of payment of an individual deal with a dummy variable that equals 1 if the acquisition is entirely paid in cash, and 0 otherwise. We compute these variables using data available from SDC Platinum. After excluding deals with incomplete information, we have 4007 observations from 35 countries.

As shown in Table 2, the data are highly concentrated: the target is a US firm in 60% of the sample and a UK firm in 15% of the sample. The bid price ranges from 99.6% of the preannouncement price (in Japan) to 227.1% (in Indonesia). In Italy, 88% of the acquisitions of Italian targets are paid entirely in cash. In the United States, only 37% of the deals are paid wholly in cash.

2.2. Investor protection

By reshuffling control over companies, M&A help allocate corporate assets to their best possible use. Investor protection can affect the volume of M&A because it affects the magnitude of frictions and inefficiencies in the target country. As proxies for investor protection, we use several indexes developed by La Porta et al. (1998): an index of the quality of the accounting standards, an index of shareholder protection that combines an index of the quality of law enforcement (rule of law) and an index of the rights that shareholders have with respect to management (antidirector rights), and a dummy variable for common-law countries. These indexes are highly correlated (their pairwise correlations range between 40% and 60%) because they all reflect to some degree the underlying quality of investor protection in a country. However, they measure different institutional characteristics.

Table 2

Summary statistics on the sample of individual deals sorted by target country

Premium is the bid price as a percentage of the closing price of the target 4 weeks before the announcement.
All-cash bid is a dummy variable that equals 1 if the acquisition is entirely paid in cash, and 0 otherwise.

	Premium		All-cash bid		
Country	Mean	S.D.	Mean	S.D.	N observations
Australia	129.5	37.4	0.60	0.49	212
Austria	129.8	25.2	0.83	0.41	6
Belgium	137.2	56.1	0.86	0.38	7
Brazil	110.5	0.0	0.00	0.00	1
Canada	132.9	40.1	0.36	0.48	157
Chile	149.9	24.5	1.00	0.00	3
Denmark	142.2	41.2	0.83	0.41	6
Finland	149.7	53.2	1.00	0.00	7
France	133.4	53.6	0.88	0.32	112
Germany	116.7	35.3	0.77	0.44	13
Greece	165.5	112.8	0.67	0.58	3
Hong Kong	129.8	56.1	0.93	0.25	46
India	178.6	113.2	0.67	0.50	9
Indonesia	222.5	150.1	1.00	0.00	2
Ireland	121.1	22.7	0.78	0.44	9
Israel	220.2	153.2	0.50	0.71	2
Italy	127.7	26.8	0.88	0.33	26
Japan	99.0	41.7	0.36	0.48	73
Malaysia	151.7	76.8	0.91	0.29	23
Mexico	124.5	17.0	1.00	0.00	2
Netherlands	144.7	37.9	0.50	0.52	16
New Zealand	129.2	17.6	0.94	0.25	16
Norway	136.0	37.6	0.76	0.43	37
Philippines	157.7	81.0	0.56	0.53	9
Portugal	149.9	57.1	1.00	0.00	4
Singapore	152.9	79.3	0.85	0.37	39
South Africa	129.5	63.2	0.68	0.48	28
South Korea	145.1	102.7	0.50	0.58	4
Spain	119.8	30.0	0.70	0.48	10
Sweden	141.7	40.6	0.71	0.46	45
Switzerland	111.0	33.3	0.89	0.33	9
Thailand	126.0	79.3	0.92	0.28	13
Turkey	127.5	0.0	1.00	0.00	1
United Kingdom	145.8	41.9	0.64	0.48	614
United States	144.3	42.4	0.37	0.48	2443
Total	141.6	44.7	0.48	0.50	4007

Accounting standards measure the quality of the disclosure of accounting information. The accounting standards quality index is created by the Center for International Financial Analysis and Research and rates the 1990 annual reports of at least three firms in every country on their inclusion or omission of 90 items. Thus, each country obtains a score out of 90, with a higher number indicating more disclosure. This variable affects M&A activity because good disclosure is a necessary condition for identifying potential targets. Accounting standards also reflect corporate governance, because they reduce the scope for expropriation by making corporate accounts more transparent.

Our second measure is an index of shareholder protection that ranges between 0 and 6. It captures the effective rights of minority shareholders with respect to managers and directors and is defined as an antidirector rights index multiplied by a rule of law index and divided by 10. When minority shareholders have fewer rights, they are more likely to be expropriated. As a consequence, the stock market is less developed, and raising external equity, particularly to finance a takeover, is more expensive. At the same time, with low shareholder protection, the private benefits of control are high and the market for corporate control is relatively less effective, because incumbents will try to entrench themselves via ownership concentration and takeover deterrence measures (Bebchuk, 1999).

The common law measure is a dummy variable that equals 1 if the origin of the company law is the English common law, and 0 otherwise. La Porta et al. (1998) argue that legal origin is a broad indicator of investor protection and show that countries with common law as the legal origin better protect minority shareholders than do countries with civil law as the legal origin. Although common law should not directly affect M&A, we include this variable because it is correlated with other proxies of investor protection and is truly exogenous. Hence, it is a good instrument for investor protection.

We note that the number of observations in our empirical analysis varies with the measure of investor protection used, because accounting standards are not available for Ecuador, Indonesia, Ireland, Jordan, Kenya, Pakistan, Sri Lanka, and Zimbabwe.

3. Determinants of M&A activity

We examine five dimensions of M&A: the volume, the incidence of hostile takeovers, the pattern of cross-border deals, the premium, and the method of payment.

3.1. Volume

We start with the relation between the volume of M&A activity and investor protection at the target-country level. Our specification is

$$\text{Volume} = \alpha + \beta X + \gamma \, \text{investor protection} + \varepsilon \tag{1}$$

where the dependent variable, volume, is the percentage of traded firms that are targets of successful mergers or acquisitions. The variables for common law, accounting standards, and shareholder protection are proxies for investor protection. Control factors (X) in all specifications are GDP growth, which proxies for the change in economic conditions, and the logarithm of the 1995 per capita GNP, which proxies for the country's wealth.

Table 3 reports the coefficients of six Tobit models derived from specification (1). We estimate Tobit models because the dependent variable (volume) is bounded between 0 and 100 by construction. Column 1 shows that the frequency of mergers among traded companies is 7.5% higher in common-law countries than in civil-law countries. The results in Column 2 show that accounting standards are positively and

Table 3

Determinants of the volume across countries

The table presents the results of six Tobit models estimated by maximum likelihood for the sample of 49 target countries. The dependent variable is volume, the percentage of traded companies targeted in a completed deal. The independent variables are: common law, a dummy variable that equals 1 if the origin of the company law is the English common law, and 0 otherwise; accounting standards, an index of the quality of accounting disclosure; shareholder protection, a measure of the effective rights of minority shareholders; ownership concentration, the average equity stake owned by the three largest shareholders in the 10 largest nonfinancial domestic firms in 1994; mandatory bid rule, a dummy variable that equals 1 if acquirers are forced to make a tender offer to all shareholders when passing a given ownership threshold, and 0 otherwise; market return, the average annual stock market return in the 1990s; and market dominance, a survey-based measure of product market concentration. The logarithm of GNP per capita and GDP growth are included in all regressions as control variables. Standard errors are shown in parentheses.

	(1)	(2)	(3)	(4)	(5)	(6)
log(GNP per capita)	9.00***	5.61***	6.40***	4.49**	4.75**	8.81***
	(1.24)	(1.94)	(1.48)	(2.04)	(2.02)	(2.05)
GDP growth	−2.42	−2.57*	−2.42**	−3.05**	−3.11**	−2.33
	(1.12)	(1.12)	(1.07)	(1.32)	(1.36)	(1.48)
Common law	7.52* (3.97)					9.06* (5.06)
Accounting standards		0.47**		0.35* (0.20)	0.43**	
		(0.18)			(0.20)	
Shareholder protection			4.27***	2.96 (2.01)	4.65**	
			(1.69)		(2.32)	
Ownership concentration					0.38* (0.20)	
Mandatory bid rule						−0.58
						(4.10)
Market return						0.21 (0.15)
Market dominance						−3.40
						(3.57)
Constant	−48.1***	−43.1***	−31.8***	−30.8*	−58.4***	−38.3**
	(12.0)	(16.5)	(12.5)	(18.1)	(22.1)	(17.7)
Pseudo R^2	0.10	0.08	0.10	0.09	0.09	0.09
N observations	49	41	49	41	39	41

***, **, and * indicate significance at 1%, 5%, and 10% levels, respectively.

significant correlated with volume. A 12-point increase in the accounting standards measure (from the quality of accounting standards in Italy to that in Canada) correlates with a 5% increase in the volume of M&A. Column 3 finds a similar result for shareholder protection. A one-point increase in shareholder protection (e.g., the adoption of voting by mail in a country like Belgium) is associated with 4% more volume. Thus, we find that there are more M&A in countries with better investor protection. We note that a one-point increase in the index of antidirector rights (such as the adoption of voting by mail) translates into a one-point increase in shareholder protection only in a country like Belgium, which also scores 10 in the index of rule of law. In a country like Italy, which scores 8.33 in the index of rule of law, the same change in minority shareholders' rights implies only a 0.833-point increase in shareholder protection.

In Column 4, we estimate a joint regression with accounting standards and shareholder protection and find that only the former is statistically significant. This result suggests that disclosure rules are more relevant for takeovers than are shareholder rights. In Column 5, we add ownership concentration, which is potentially an important explanatory variable. Ownership concentration in a country is the average equity stake owned by the three largest shareholders in the 10 largest nonfinancial domestic firms in 1994, from La Porta et al. (1998). We find that, as in the individual regressions, the coefficients on accounting standards and shareholder protection are positive and significant. The coefficient on ownership concentration is also positive and significant. This finding indicates that, when we control for investor protection, countries with more concentrated ownership have more M&A. This result is consistent with Shleifer and Vishny (1986), who argue that transfers of control are easier in companies with more concentrated ownership structure because they overcome the free-rider problem in takeovers.

The results in Column 5 help explain why shareholder protection is not significant in Column 4. On the one hand, shareholder protection reduces the costs of raising external equity, thereby increasing the volume of mergers. On the other hand, it decreases ownership concentration, which makes friendly transfers of control less likely. By controlling for ownership concentration, we are able to disentangle the two effects.

In Column 6, we evaluate the robustness of the results on investor protection by adding further control variables to capture cross-country differences in the regulatory environment. We show the results only with the common law variable as our proxy for investor protection, although we obtain similar results for accounting standards and shareholder protection. A mandatory bid rule, which we capture with a dummy variable that equals 1 if acquirers are forced to make a tender offer to all shareholders when passing a given ownership threshold and 0 otherwise, might reduce the volume of M&A because it imposes further costs on the potential bidder. The market return, calculated as the average annual stock market return during the 1990s, might affect M&A activity because of valuation waves (Shleifer and Vishny, 2003). However, there are two opposing effects when the stock market is booming. Targets could become too expensive, reducing the volume of deals, but acquirers enjoy low takeover costs because they can pay with more highly valued stock, leading to a high takeover volume.

Market dominance, a measure of product market concentration in 1995 from the 1992 Global Competitiveness Report (published by the World Economic Forum), could reduce the volume because of lower availability of targets.

The results in Column 6 show that common law is still significant and its coefficient is virtually unchanged from Column 1. None of the control variables are statistically significant. Note that the number of observations decreases from 49 to 41 because market return is not available for Taiwan and Uruguay and market dominance is not available for Ecuador, Kenya, Nigeria, Pakistan, Sri Lanka, Uruguay, and Zimbabwe.

3.2. Hostile takeovers

Many financial economists argue that hostile takeovers play an important governance role (e.g., see Franks and Mayer, 1996; Jensen, 1993; Manne, 1965). To analyze cross-country differences in the frequency of hostile takeovers, we estimate

$$\text{Hostile takeover} = \alpha + \beta X + \gamma \text{ investor protection} + \varepsilon, \tag{2}$$

where the hostile takeover variable is the number of attempted hostile takeovers in the 1990s as a percentage of the number of domestic traded companies. Common law, accounting standards, shareholder protection, and ownership concentration are proxies for investor protection, as described in Section 2.2. We include GDP growth and the logarithm of GNP per capita as control factors in all specifications.

The results are presented in Table 4. The first three columns show that common law, accounting standards, and shareholder protection are positively and significantly correlated with hostile takeovers. To interpret these results, note that hostile takeovers require that control be contestable, a feature that is less common in countries with poorer investor protection.

Column 4 shows that shareholder protection dominates accounting standards. A one-point increase in shareholder protection (e.g., the introduction of voting by mail in Belgium) is associated with 0.8 percentage points more hostile takeovers. Shareholder protection makes control more contestable by reducing the private benefits of control.

In Column 5, we add ownership concentration as a control variable. This variable is not significant. It marginally reduces the coefficient on shareholder protection without affecting its statistical significance. This result compares with Table 3, in which ownership concentration is positive and significant. According to Shleifer and Vishny (1986), ownership concentration facilitates only friendly transfers of control, not hostile takeovers. Hence, the insignificant coefficient in Column 5 of Table 4 is not surprising.

To evaluate the robustness of the main result that hostile takeovers are more common in countries with better investor protection, in Column 6 we add some control variables to the specification in Column 1 to capture cross-country differences in the regulatory environment. As in Table 4, we control for mandatory bid rules and market returns. We also incorporate cross-border regulation with a dummy variable that equals 1 if a foreign buyer needs government approval before acquiring control of a domestic firm, and 0 otherwise. Because of cultural differences, deals initiated by foreign

Table 4

Incidence of hostile takeovers

The table presents the results of six Tobit models estimated by maximum likelihood on the sample of 49 target countries. The dependent variable is hostile takeover, or attempted hostile takeovers as a percentage of traded firms. The independent variables are: common law, a dummy variable that equals 1 if the origin of the company law is the English common law, and 0 otherwise; accounting standards, an index of the quality of accounting disclosure; shareholder protection, a measure of the effective rights of minority shareholders; ownership concentration, the average equity stake owned by the three largest shareholders in the 10 largest nonfinancial domestic firms in 1994; cross-border regulation, a dummy variable that equals 1 if foreign buyers need government approval, and 0 otherwise; market return, the average annual stock market return in the 1990s; and mandatory bid rule, a dummy variable that equals 1 if acquirers are forced to make a tender offer to all shareholders when passing a given ownership threshold, and 0 otherwise. The logarithm of GNP per capita and GDP growth are included in all regressions as control variables. Standard errors are shown in parentheses.

	(1)	(2)	(3)	(4)	(5)	(6)
log(GNP per capita)	1.30***	0.93**	0.75***	0.61* (0.32)	0.64**	1.08**
	(0.26)	(0.35)	(0.27)		(0.32)	(0.26)
GDP growth	0.08 (0.19)	0.04 (0.21)	0.06 (0.17)	−0.10	−0.05**	0.09 (0.19)
				(0.18)	(0.19)	
Common law	1.53**					1.57**
	(0.68)					(0.70)
Accounting standards		0.07**		0.02 (0.03)	0.02 (0.03)	
		(0.03)				
Shareholder protection			0.88***	0.84**	0.73**	
			(0.25)	(0.26)	(0.31)	
Ownership concentration					−0.01	
					(0.03)	
Cross-border regulation						−1.80*
						(0.93)
Market return						0.02 (0.02)
Mandatory bid rule						−0.04 (0.59)
Constant	−12.0***	−12.2***	−8.34***	−7.93**	−7.06*	−9.75***
	(2.63)	(3.32)	(2.53)	(3.09)	(3.61)	(2.62)
Pseudo R^2	0.20	0.17	0.24	0.23	0.22	0.23
N observations	49	41	49	41	39	47

***, **, and * indicate significance at 1%, 5%, and 10% levels, respectively.

bidders are more likely to be hostile. Hence, we expect cross-border regulation to reduce the frequency of hostile takeovers.

The results in Column 6 show that common law is significant and that its coefficient is virtually unchanged from Column 1. The frequency of attempted hostile takeovers among traded companies is 1.6% higher in common-law than in civil-law countries. Cross-border regulation is also significant and negative, as predicted. The requirement of government approval for foreign acquisitions reduces the frequency of attempted hostile takeovers by 1.8%. Market returns and mandatory bid rules are not statistically significant.

3.3. Cross-border mergers and acquisitions

La Porta et al. (2000a, p. 23) write that "When a British firm fully acquires a Swedish firm, the possibilities for legal expropriation of investor diminish. Because the controlling shareholders of the Swedish company are compensated in such a friendly deal for the lost private benefits of control, they are more likely to go along. By replacing the wasteful expropriation with publicly shared profits and dividends, such acquisitions enhance efficiency." This statement implies two testable hypotheses that we address in this section: first, the probability that a deal is cross-border rather than domestic is higher in countries with lower investor protection; and second, the acquirers in cross-border deals will come from countries that have higher investor protection than the targets' countries.

3.3.1. Target-country analysis

As before, we adapt specification (1) by changing the dependent variable

$$\text{Cross-border ratio} = \alpha + \beta X + \gamma \text{ investor protection} + \varepsilon, \qquad (3)$$

where the cross-border ratio is the number of cross-border deals as a percentage of all completed deals by target country. Common law, accounting standards, and shareholder protection are our proxies for investor protection. We expect the cross-border ratio to decrease with investor protection. As before, we control for the logarithm of GNP per capita, as a measure of a country's wealth, and GDP growth as a proxy for the change in macroeconomic conditions.

Table 5 reports the coefficients of six Tobit models derived from specification (3). The results confirm our prediction: the probability that a completed deal is cross-border rather than domestic is higher in countries with lower investor protection. The coefficients on common law, accounting standards, and shareholder protection are all negative and significant at the 1% level. In economic terms, the probability that a completed deal is cross-border is 14.5% higher in civil-law than in common-law countries. Raising the accounting standards measure by 12 points (from Italy's to Canada's accounting standards) decreases cross-border deals by 5%. An increase in shareholder protection by one point (e.g., the adoption of voting by mail in Belgium) decreases the cross-border ratio by 4%. Ownership concentration, which we add in Column 5 as a control variable, is not statistically significant.

To evaluate the robustness of the results, in Column 6 we augment the specification in Column 1 with some control variables. We add cross-border regulation because we expect fewer cross-border deals when there are more regulatory requirements. We control for market returns because we expect fewer cross-border deals when the stock market is booming and the target firms' stocks are (potentially) overvalued. At the same time, this variable will not be significant if the acquirer's stock market is also thriving. We include openness, a measure of the cultural attitude towards cross-border deals (from the 1996 Global Competitiveness Report) because such deals are more likely if the

Table 5

Cross-border versus domestic deals

The table presents the results of six Tobit models estimated by maximum likelihood on the sample of 49 target countries. The dependent variable is cross-border ratio, or cross-border deals as a percentage of all completed deals. The independent variables are: common law, a dummy variable that equals 1 if the origin of the company law is the English common law, and 0 otherwise; accounting standards, an index of the quality of accounting disclosure; shareholder protection, a measure of the effective rights of minority shareholders; ownership concentration, the average equity stake owned by the three largest shareholders in the 10 largest nonfinancial domestic firms in 1994; cross-border regulation, a dummy variable that equals 1 if foreign buyers need government approval, and 0 otherwise; market return, the average annual stock market return in the 1990s; and openness, a survey-based measure of the cultural attitude towards cross-border deals. The logarithm of GNP per capita and GDP growth are included in all regressions as control variables. Standard errors are shown in parentheses.

	(1)	(2)	(3)	(4)	(5)	(6)
log(GNP per capita)	−5.32*** (1.20)	−1.99 (1.74)	−1.47 (1.50)	−0.64 (1.79)	−1.21 (1.72)	−4.77*** (1.51)
GDP growth	1.75 (1.08)	0.90 (1.17)	1.44 (1.08)	1.48 (1.15)	1.38 (1.16)	3.48*** (1.19)
Common law	−14.5*** (3.83)					−16.1*** (4.02)
Accounting standards		−0.67*** (0.16)		−0.53*** (0.17)	−0.41** (0.17)	
Shareholder protection			−6.03*** (1.71)	−3.55** (1.76)	−4.14** (1.98)	
Ownership concentration					−0.11 (0.17)	
Cross-border regulation						5.05 (4.36)
Market return						−0.15 (0.13)
Openness						7.77*** (2.84)
Constant	87.7*** (11.7)	96.5*** (14.8)	62.7*** (12.7)	81.7*** (15.9)	85.0*** (18.8)	38.1* (20.0)
Pseudo R^2	0.06	0.07	0.05	0.09	0.08	0.09
N observations	49	41	49	41	39	41

***, **, and * indicate significance at 1%, 5%, and 10% levels, respectively.

country is friendlier to foreigners.[1] Our results show that common law is still significant and that its coefficient is unaffected. Openness is negative and significant, as predicted. The coefficients on market return and cross-border regulation are not significant.

---

[1] Another potential determinant of international mergers and acquisitions is tax competition across countries. For instance, taxes can affect M&A activity if it is easier for domestic firms to take advantage of investment tax credits and accelerated depreciation in the target country than for foreign firms. Moreover, the tax treatment of foreign income differs across countries. However, we do not control for taxes in our study because the complexity of the issue requires a paper on its own.

3.3.2. Ordered-pair analysis

The results in Table 5 indicate that cross-border M&A play a governance role by targeting firms in countries with lower investor protection. To explore this hypothesis, we arrange our dataset to produce a worldwide matrix of (49 × 48) matched pairs. In these pairs, we define each entry, cross-border deals$_{s,b}$, as the number of deals in which the acquirer comes from country b (for buyer) and the target is in country s (for seller), as a percentage of the total number of deals in country s.

With the newly arranged dataset, we can study the pattern of cross-border M&A by simultaneously controlling for the characteristics of target and acquirer countries. The specification is

$$\text{Cross} - \text{border deals}_{s,b} = \beta X_{s,b} + \gamma \, \Delta(\text{investor protection})_{s,b} + \delta_b + \zeta_s + \varepsilon_{s,b}, \quad (4)$$

where the dependent variable is the number of cross-border deals in which the acquirer comes from country b and the target from country $s(b \neq s)$ as a percentage of the total number of deals (cross-border and domestic) in country s. Our hypothesis is that the volume of cross-border M&A activity between country b (the acquirer) and country s (the target) correlates positively with the difference in investor protection between the two countries. The proxies for investor protection are accounting standards and shareholder protection.

We note that our specification also includes fixed effects for target and acquirer countries. These fixed effects control for all cultural and institutional characteristics of the two countries, including the level of investor protection in the individual countries. We control for differences in the logarithm of GNP per capita of the acquirer and target countries as a measure of the relative economic development of the two countries. We also include two dummy variables equal to 1 if the acquirer and target share the same cultural background, that is, if they have the same official language and if they belong to the same geographical area.

Table 6 reports our results. In Columns 1 and 2, we include only one measure of investor protection per regression. We find that the volume of M&A activity between two countries is positively correlated with their difference in investor protection. This result means that acquirers typically come from countries with better accounting standards and stronger shareholder protection than the targets' countries.

In Column 3, we estimate the marginal impact of each variable by estimating a joint regression with the two measures. We find that only the difference in shareholder protection is statistically significant. On average, shareholder protection increases in the target company via the cross-border deal. This finding is consistent with the view that such acquisitions enhance efficiency because the increase in shareholder protection curbs the expropriation of minority shareholders and, therefore, reduces the cost of raising external equity. We also find that richer countries are more likely to be acquirers than targets, and that most cross-border deals happen between countries sharing the same language and geographical area.

Table 6

The governance motive in cross-border M&A

The table presents the results of five OLS regressions for the sample of matched country pairs. The dependent variable is cross-border deals$_{s,b}$, or the number of cross-border deals where the target is from country s and the acquirer is from country $b(s \neq b)$ as a percentage of the total number of deals in country s. The independent variables are the difference between acquirer and target countries' investor protection as measured alternatively by accounting standards, an index of the quality of accounting disclosure, and by shareholder protection, a measure of the effective rights of minority shareholders. We include as control variables the difference between the acquirer's and the target's logarithm of GNP per capita; same language, a dummy variable that equals 1 if the target and acquirer come from countries with the same official language, and 0 otherwise; and same geographical area, a dummy variable that equals 1 if the target and acquirer come from the same geographical area. In Column 4, we add the difference between country b and country s in market return, the average annual stock market return in the 1990s. In Column 5, we add bilateral trade$_{s,b}$, the value of imports by country s from country b as a percentage of total imports by country s. The regressions contain fixed effects both for target and acquirer country (not shown). The standard errors shown in parentheses are adjusted for heteroskedasticity using Huber (1967) and White (1980) corrections.

	(1)	(2)	(3)	(4)	(5)
Δ(Accounting standards)$_{b-s}$	0.02*** (0.01)		0.01 (0.00)		
Δ(Shareholder protection)$_{b-s}$		1.93*** (0.19)	1.89*** (0.21)	1.89*** (0.20)	1.21*** (0.23)
Δ(log(GNP per capita))$_{b-s}$	0.10* (0.05)	0.97*** (0.10)	0.40*** (0.05)	0.95*** (0.10)	0.06 (0.04)
Same language	0.86** (0.36)	0.97*** (0.30)	0.86*** (0.36)	1.02** (0.31)	0.08 (0.22)
Same geographical area	1.30*** (0.14)	1.12*** (0.11)	1.30*** (0.14)	1.13*** (0.12)	0.36*** (0.15)
Δ(Market return)$_{b-s}$				0.00 (0.00)	
Bilateral trade$_{s,b}$					0.67*** (0.10)
Adjusted R^2	0.53	0.50	0.53	0.51	0.67
N observations	1640	2352	1640	2162	1677

***, **, and * indicate significance at 1%, 5%, and 10% levels, respectively.

In Column 4, we add the difference in market return between acquirer and target countries as a control variable. We would expect more deals when the acquirer's stock market is booming relatively to the target's stock market, but we find no such evidence.

A potentially important missing variable in the analysis is the volume of trade between two countries. In fact, companies that export to a given country might engage in M&A activity in that country for reasons that have nothing to do with governance. To control for this alternative explanation, in Column 5 we add bilateral trade to our regression. We define bilateral trade$_{s,b}$ as imports from country b to country s as a percentage of total imports of country s. Bilateral trade is not available for six countries: Belgium, Brazil, Israel, Nigeria, Switzerland, and Zimbabwe. The number of observations in Column 5 changes accordingly. The results for shareholder protection are unchanged. The acquirer typically has stronger shareholder protection than the target. As we expected, bilateral trade is positive and significant, confirming that trade is an important motive for cross-border M&A. Same language and the difference in the logarithm of GNP per capita are no longer significant once bilateral trade is added to the baseline specification.

3.4. Premium

We use the sample of individual transactions to analyze the cross-country determinants of the takeover premium. We estimate the specification

$$\log(\text{premium}) = \alpha + \beta X + \gamma \text{ shareholder protection} + \varepsilon, \tag{5}$$

where premium is the bid price as a percentage of the target's closing price 4 weeks before the announcement of the deal, shareholder protection is measured at the target-country level, and X is a set of control factors. Control variables at the deal level are target size, the logarithm of the target's market capitalization 4 weeks before the announcement, a dummy variable (cross-border) that equals 1 if the deal is cross-border and 0 otherwise; a dummy variable (hostile bid) that equals 1 if the deal is hostile and 0 otherwise; a dummy variable (tender offer) that equals 1 if the deal involves a tender offer and 0 otherwise; and a dummy variable (contested bid) that equals 1 if the number of bidders is larger than 1 and 0 otherwise.

Table 7 shows the results of six regressions based on specification (5). In all regressions, the standard errors shown in parentheses are adjusted for heteroskedasticity, using the Huber (1967) and White (1980) corrections, and for clustering at the country level following Huber (1967). We correct for clustering because observations within a country are likely to be correlated with each other. We also include year and industry (at one-digit SIC-code level) dummies, but we do not report their coefficients.

In Column 1, we find that shareholder protection is positively correlated with the takeover premium. An increase in the level of shareholder protection by one point (e.g., the introduction of voting by mail in Belgium) is associated with a 0.04 increase in the logarithm of the premium, which translates into an average increase of 6% in the premium. Target size is negative and significant, that is, larger deals are associated with lower premiums.

In Column 2, we add the deal-level dummy variables for cross-border, hostile bid, tender offer, and contested bid. The result on shareholder protection does not change and the new controls are all positive, as expected. All but hostile bids are statistically significant. We interpret the finding on tender offers as evidence of the free-rider hypothesis: that is, the bidder in a tender offer needs to pay a higher premium to induce shareholders to tender their shares. This theory would also predict that the premium paid should be higher the more diffuse the target's ownership structure. However, we cannot test this hypothesis directly because we do not have data on ownership structure for individual target companies. Contested bids are associated with a 0.1 increase in the logarithm of the premium, which translates into an average premium increase of 15%, consistent with the view that competition for targets is associated with higher premiums. Cross-border deals are associated with a 0.03 increase in the logarithm of the premium, which translates into an average premium increase of 3%.

Our finding that takeover premiums are higher in countries with higher shareholder protection can be interpreted by noting that the takeover premium measures the gain available to all target shareholders. There are two reasons why the premium might be

Table 7

Determinants of the takeover premium

The table presents the results of six OLS regressions for the sample of individual deals. The dependent variable is the natural logarithm of premium, or the bid price as a percentage of the closing price of the target 4 weeks before the announcement. Independent variables at the country level are shareholder protection, a measure of the effective rights of minority shareholders, and mandatory bid rule, a dummy variable that equals 1 if in 1995 there was a legal requirement to make a tender offer when shareholdings after the acquisition exceed a given ownership threshold, and 0 otherwise. The control variable at the cross-country level is the difference between the acquirer and target countries' shareholder protection. Control variables at the deal level are: target size, the logarithm of the target's market capitalization 4 weeks before the announcement; cross-border, a dummy variable that equals 1 if the deal is cross-border, and 0 otherwise; hostile bid, a dummy variable that equals 1 if the deal is hostile, and 0 otherwise; tender offer, a dummy variable that equals 1 if the deal involves a tender offer, and 0 otherwise; contested bid, a dummy variable that equals 1 if the number of bidders is larger than 1, and 0 otherwise; and bidder M/B, the equity market-to-book ratio of the bidder 4 weeks before the announcement. In all regressions, we also include year and industry (at one-digit SIC-code level) dummies (not shown). In Column 6 we add two dummy variables that identify deals where the target firm is from the United States (US targets) and from the United Kingdom (UK targets), respectively. The standard errors (in parentheses) are adjusted for heteroskedasticity using Huber (1967) and White (1980) corrections and for clustering at country level using the Huber (1967) correction.

	(1)	(2)	(3)	(4)	(5)	(6)
Shareholder	0.04***	0.05***	0.05***	0.07***	0.04***	−0.01 (0.02)
protection	(0.01)	(0.01)	(0.01)	(0.02)	(0.01)	
Target size	−0.01***	−0.01***	−0.01***	−0.02**	−0.02***	−0.02***
	(0.00)	(0.00)	(0.00)	(0.01)	(0.00)	(0.00)
Cross-border		0.03* (0.02)	0.03* (0.02)	0.02 (0.03)	0.03** (0.01)	0.04** (0.02)
Hostile bid		0.04 (0.03)	0.04 (0.03)	0.03 (0.06)	0.04 (0.03)	0.06***
						(0.02)
Tender offer		0.05***	0.05***	0.04 (0.02)	0.07***	0.08***
		(0.01)	(0.01)		(0.01)	(0.01)
Contested bid		0.10** (0.04)	0.10** (0.04)	0.05 (0.05)	0.10** (0.04)	0.11***
						(0.04)
Δ(Shareholder			0.00 (0.01)			
protection)$_{b-s}$						
Bidder M/B				0.01 (0.00)		
Mandatory bid					−0.06**	−0.01 (0.04)
rule					(0.02)	
US targets						0.16** (0.07)
UK targets						0.09***
						(0.03)
R^2	0.03	0.04	0.05	0.08	0.05	0.06
N observations	4007	4007	4007	1005	4007	4007
N countries	35	35	35	27	35	35

***, **, and * indicate significance at 1%, 5%, and 10% levels, respectively.

higher in countries with stronger shareholder protection. First, shareholder protection reduces the cost of capital and therefore increases (potential) competition among bidders and the premium paid by the winning bidder. Second, diffuse ownership is more common in countries with higher shareholder protection. In turn, diffuse owner-ship exacerbates the free-rider problem in takeovers by forcing bidders to pay a higher takeover premium than otherwise (Grossman and Hart, 1980).

A concern with this interpretation is the possibility that the premium measures the private benefits of control. To explore this issue, in Column 3 we add the difference between the acquirer and target countries' shareholder protection as a further control variable. If the premium measures the private benefits of control, we expect to find a negative and significant coefficient on this control variable, as in Dyck and Zingales (2004). The reason is that an acquirer coming from a country with lower shareholder protection is better able to extract private benefits of control than an acquirer coming from a country with stricter rules.

In Column 3, we find that the difference between acquirer and target countries' shareholder protection is not statistically significant. This result indicates that premium is not a proxy for the private benefits of control but for the total premium available to all shareholders. This finding also indicates that acquirers from countries with better shareholder protection do not need to pay more than acquirers from countries with weaker shareholder protection in cross-border deals.

According to Rau and Vermaelen (1998), glamor firms (as measured by high market-to-book ratios, M/B) will tend to overestimate their ability to create synergies in the target and should therefore be willing to pay more than managers of value firms (as measured by low M/B). Therefore, in Column 4, we add the equity M/B of the bidder 4 weeks before the announcement. We obtain this information from Data-stream. As a result of the matching procedure, the number of observations in Column 4 drops to 1005. Contrary to the prediction, our results show that the bidder M/B is not correlated with the premium.

Comment and Schwert (1995) show that takeover laws are an important determinant of the takeover premium. Therefore, in Column 5 we control for differences in takeover laws across countries. The mandatory bid rule variable equals 1 if in 1995 there was a legal requirement to make a tender offer when shareholdings after the acquisition exceed a given ownership threshold, and 0 otherwise. For instance, the mandatory bid variable rule equals 1 in the United Kingdom, where the threshold is 30%, and 0% in the United States, where only a few states have a similar provision. We find a negative and significant coefficient for the mandatory bid rule, perhaps because a mandatory bid rule increases the cost of takeovers and therefore reduces competition among bidders. However, a mandatory bid rule might also increase the premium, because only high-premium takeovers that compensate the bidders for the high take-over costs succeed. To distinguish between the two effects, in an unreported regression we add the interactive term of mandatory bid rule multiplied by target size. The coefficient on this interactive term should measure the impact on the premium that is due to reduced competition, because larger deals are more likely to be deterred. The coefficient on the mandatory bid rule should reflect the fact that low-premium takeovers do not go through. We find that the coefficient on the mandatory bid rule is negative and significant, and that the coefficient on the interactive term is not significant. This result suggests that the mandatory bid rule variable captures an institutional difference across countries.

Because 75% of the deals have a US or UK target, in Column 6 we check the robustness of our findings by using two dummy variables that identify deals with US and UK targets, respectively. The results show that higher premiums are a feature of US and UK targets. The logarithm of the premium is 0.16 higher in the United States and 0.09 higher in the United Kingdom than in the other countries. Note that the mandatory bid rule is no longer significant. This finding suggests that the mandatory bid rule is significant in Column 5 only because it captures the difference between US and UK targets.

3.5. Means of payment

Legal protection of investors may also affect the means of payment used in M&A. In a country with low investor protection, target shareholders are likely to prefer cash over the bidder's equity as the takeover currency, due to the risk of expropriation for being minority shareholders. We therefore expect less equity financing and more cash financing in countries with lower shareholder protection.

We estimate the following regression for the method of payment:

$$\text{Prob(all-cash bid)} = \alpha + \beta X + \gamma \text{ shareholder protection} + \varepsilon. \tag{6}$$

In this regression, which is similar to Equation (3), our control variables are the same as those in Table 6: target size, cross-border, hostile bid, tender offer, contested bid, bidder M/B, and mandatory bid rule. We expect that larger deals are less likely to be paid entirely with cash. Cross-border deals might more often be paid in cash because shareholders dislike receiving foreign stocks as compensation. To entice shareholders to tender, hostile bids, tender offers, and contested bids are likely to be in cash.

Table 8 reports the results of six regressions based on specification (6). In all regressions, the standard errors shown in parentheses are adjusted for heteroskedasticity using Huber (1967) and White (1980) corrections, and for clustering at the country level following Huber (1967). We also include year and industry dummies (at the one-digit SIC-code level), but we do not report their coefficients.

Across all specifications, we find that shareholder protection is negatively correlated with all-cash bids. We note that a one-point increase in the level of shareholder protection is associated with a reduction of between 13% and 18% in the probability of using only cash as the means of payment. Our interpretation of this result is that stocks are a less popular means of payment in countries with lower shareholder protection because stocks entail a higher risk of expropriation.

Among the control variables, target size is negative and significant, and cross-border, hostile bid, and tender offer are positive and significant, as we expected. Contested bids are not associated with more cash as a method of payment. The probability of using only cash as the method of payment is 17% higher in cross-border deals.

Table 8

Means of payment

The table reports estimates of six Probit models for the sample of individual deals. The dependent variable is all-cash bid, or a dummy variable that equals 1 if the acquisition is entirely paid in cash, and 0 otherwise. Independent variables at the country level are shareholder protection, a measure of the effective rights of minority shareholders, and mandatory bid rule, a dummy variable that equals 1 if in 1995 there was a legal requirement to make a tender offer when shareholdings after the acquisition exceed a given ownership threshold, and 0 otherwise. The control variable at the cross-country level is the difference between the acquirer and target countries' shareholder protection. Control variables at the deal level are: target size, the logarithm of the target's market capitalization 4 weeks before the announcement; cross-border, a dummy variable that equals 1 if the deal is cross-border, and 0 otherwise; hostile bid, a dummy variable that equals 1 if the deal is hostile, and 0 otherwise; tender offer, a dummy variable that equals 1 if the deal involves a tender offer, and 0 otherwise; contested bid, a dummy variable that equals 1 if the number of bidders is larger than 1, and 0 otherwise; and bidder M/B, the equity market-to-book ratio of the bidder 4 weeks before the announcement. In all regressions, we also include year and industry (at one-digit SIC-code level) dummies (not shown). In Column 6 we add two dummy variables that identify deals where the target firm is from the United States (US targets) and from the United Kingdom (UK targets), respectively. Displayed coefficients are the change in probability for an infinitesimal change in the independent variables. The standard errors (in parentheses) are adjusted for heteroskedasticity using Huber (1967) and White (1980) corrections and for clustering at country level using the Huber (1967) correction.

	(1)	(2)	(3)	(4)	(5)	(6)
Shareholder protection	−0.18*** (0.03)	−0.13*** (0.03)	−0.14*** (0.03)	−0.08** (0.03)	−0.15*** (0.02)	−0.16*** (0.04)
Target size	−0.06*** (0.01)	−0.07*** (0.02)	−0.07*** (0.02)	−0.02 (0.02)	−0.08*** (0.02)	−0.08*** (0.02)
Cross-border		0.17*** (0.04)	0.14** (0.05)	0.21*** (0.05)	0.14*** (0.04)	0.14*** (0.05)
Hostile bid		0.10*** (0.04)	0.09** (0.04)	0.08 (0.08)	0.10** (0.04)	0.09** (0.04)
Tender offer		0.33*** (0.08)	0.32*** (0.08)	0.36*** (0.11)	0.34*** (0.09)	0.37*** (0.08)
Contested bid		0.04 (0.04)	0.04 (0.04)	0.12* (0.07)	0.05 (0.04)	0.04 (0.04)
Δ(Shareholder protection)$_{b-s}$			−0.06*** (0.01)	−0.01 (0.03)	−0.06*** (0.01)	−0.05*** (0.02)
Bidder M/B				0.00 (0.00)		
Mandatory bid rule					−0.06 (0.08)	
US targets						0.04 (0.10)
UK targets						−0.10 (0.06)
Pseudo R^2	0.11	0.18	0.19	0.20	0.19	0.19
N observations	4007	4007	4007	1005	4007	4007
N countries	35	35	35	27	35	35

***, **, and * indicate significance at 1%, 5%, and 10% levels, respectively.

To deepen the analysis of the means of payment in cross-border deals, in Column 3 we add the difference between acquirer and target countries' shareholder protection as a further control variable. We expect that the use of stocks as a method of payment will be positively correlated with the degree of investor protection in the acquirer country, when acquirer and target countries are different. We find evidence in favor of this prediction because the coefficient on the difference between acquirer and target countries' shareholder protection is negative and significant.

Bidder *M/B* might be correlated with the use of stocks as means of payment because the bidder could try to take advantage of market booms, as argued by Shleifer and Vishny (2003). In Column 4, we add the bidder *M/B*, but we find that its coefficient is not significantly different from zero.

The mandatory bid rule might require the bidder to make a cash offer or an offer with a cash alternative, as in the United Kingdom. If so, mandatory bid rules should be positively correlated with all-cash bids. However, UK bidders often avoid the mandatory tender offer by bidding for 29.9% of the shares, which is just below the 30% threshold for the mandatory tender offer, and then acquiring the remaining shares via a share offer. In this case, mandatory bid rules should not be correlated with all-cash bids. In Column 5, we control for mandatory bid rules, and find that the coefficient is not statistically significant.

In Column 6, we show that our results are not driven by deals involving US and UK firms. The coefficient on shareholder protection is even larger in absolute terms than in Column 1, and equally significant in statistical terms when we include two dummy variables for deals in which the target is a UK or US firm, respectively.

As a further robustness check (not reported), we estimate the specification in Column 2 with weighted least squares, in which the weights are the inverse of the number of observations by country. With this procedure, all countries have the same impact on the final results. The coefficient on shareholder protection is identical to that in Column 2.

One concern is that the control variables used in regressions (5) and (6) (tender offer, hostile bid, and cross-border) are themselves endogenous. As a result, our estimates could be inconsistent. To address this issue, we estimate a recursive system with five equations, one for each endogenous variable: premium, all-cash bid, tender offer, hostile bid, and cross-border. Exogenous variables are target size, bidder *M/B*, shareholder protection, and mandatory bid rule. We do not present the results of these regressions here, because the coefficients on shareholder protection are similar to those in Tables 7 and 8.

4. Discussion

The results presented in Section 3 have implications for the impact of investor protection on M&A activity and the role of cross-border takeovers as a catalyst for convergence in corporate governance regimes. We discuss both implications in the following sections.

4.1. M&A activity and investor protection

Overall, the results in Section 3 characterize M&A activity as correlating with investor-friendly legal environments. We interpret these findings along the lines of La Porta et al. (2000b) and argue that a more active market for M&A is the outcome of a corporate governance regime with stronger investor protection.

With low shareholder protection, there are large private benefits of control (Dyck and Zingales, 2004; Nenova, 2003), and therefore the market for corporate control does not operate freely. Conversely, with high investor protection, there are low private benefits of control, and there is an active market for corporate control. Moreover, better accounting standards increase disclosure, which helps acquirers identify potential targets. Hence, there are more potential targets in countries with better shareholder protection and accounting standards. This view yields two testable predictions: across target countries, both the volume of takeovers and the takeover premium should increase with better shareholder protection and accounting standards.

The results on volume, reported in Table 3, are strongly consistent with this view. The results on the premium, reported in Table 7, are weakly consistent with this view. Table 7 shows that higher shareholder protection in the target company is associated with higher premiums, although US and UK firms drive the results. Our results reject the alternative view that the market for corporate control is a substitute for legal protection of shareholders. According to Manne (1965) and Jensen (1993), if the market for corporate control works efficiently, firms with poor corporate governance become the targets of takeovers from more efficient firms. Extending their argument across countries, the volume of M&A activity and the premium paid should be greater in countries with lower investor protection. These predictions are inconsistent with our findings.

4.2. Convergence in corporate governance

The results in Table 6 relate to the ongoing debate among legal scholars on the possibility of effective worldwide convergence in corporate governance standards. Coffee (1999) argues that differences in corporate governance will persist but with some degree of functional convergence. Hansmann and Kraakman (2001) believe that formal convergence will happen soon. Bebchuk and Roe (1999) question the idea of rapid convergence because political and economic forces will slow down any change. Gilson (2001) argues that convergence will happen through all three channels (formal, contractual, and functional).

Our findings are consistent with the prediction by Coffee (1999) that companies from countries with better protection of investors will end up buying companies from countries with weaker protection. The case for target shareholders to sell out to bidders with higher governance standards is clear. Targets stand to gain from the lower cost of capital associated with higher investor protection. However, it is not obvious why acquirers seek to take over a poorly governed company. The results in Table 7,

Column 3, show that acquirers from countries with better investor protection do not pay higher takeover premiums than acquirers from countries with weaker investor protection. Hence, they share part of the surplus created by improving the corporate governance of the target.

One concern is that they might import the poorer governance of their targets (poor accounting and disclosure practices, board structures, and so on). However, anecdotal evidence of cross-border deals with high press coverage suggests that this is not the case. The targets almost always adopt the governance standards of the acquirers, whether good or bad. In Daimler's acquisition of Chrysler, for instance, the resulting company has adopted a two-tier board structure, as required by German law. Thus, if convergence occurs, it is towards the acquirers' governance standards.

A related issue is that a deal could be motivated by the agency and hubris problems of the acquirer rather than by the desire to improve the governance regime in the target company. If so, the deal might not create value. Assessing this issue requires a study of the performance of the target and acquirer after the acquisition, which we cannot do with our large sample. Instead, we indirectly test this issue. If countries with poorer investor protection (in particular, lower governance standards, as measured by lower shareholder protection) have more severe agency problems, the hypothesis predicts more acquisitions by companies in countries with lower shareholder protection. This is not what we observe. If we sort our data by acquirer country, we find rather the opposite (not reported): more acquisitions by companies in countries with higher shareholder protection.

Our analysis also sheds light on the question as to whether cross-border deals might lead to greater international stock market integration and to a reduction of the home bias in equity investment in target countries. If the foreign bidder pays with stock, target shareholders face the problem of disposing of a new investment domiciled abroad. As a result, they might choose to keep the foreign stocks. In aggregate, these individual decisions would imply a reduction of the home bias in equity investment in target countries. We show in Table 8, Column 3, that target shareholders accept the acquirer's shares more often if the investor protection in the acquirer's country is greater than in the target's country. Hence, the reduction of the home bias puzzle goes together with a convergence in corporate governance regime. In this sense, our findings are consistent with Dahlquist et al. (2003).

5. Conclusion

Using a large sample of deals in 49 major countries, announced in the 1990s and completed by the end of 2002, we find that better investor protection is associated with more M&A, more attempted hostile takeovers, and fewer cross-border deals. We also find that better investor protection is associated with the greater use of stock as a method of payment, and with higher takeover premiums. These results indicate that domestic investor protection is an important determinant of the competitiveness and effectiveness of the market for M&A within a country.

In cross-border deals, we find that acquirers on average have higher investor protection than targets, that is, firms opt out of a weak governance regime via cross-border deals. This result indicates that the international market for corporate control helps generate convergence in corporate governance regimes across countries.

Appendix A: Description of the variables included in our study and their sources

A.1. Country-level variables

Volume	Percentage of domestic traded companies targeted in completed deals in the 1990s. Sources: SDC Platinum, provided by Thomson Financial Securities Data, and the World Development Indicators.
Hostile takeover	Attempted hostile takeovers as a percentage of domestic traded companies. Sources: SDC Platinum and the World Development Indicators.
Cross-border ratio	Number of cross-border deals as target as a percentage of all completed deals. Source: SDC Platinum.
GDP growth	Average annual real growth rate of the gross domestic product in the 1990s. Source: World Development Report.
GNP per capita	Gross national product in 1995 (in US$) divided by the population. Source: World Development Report.
Common law	Equals 1 if the origin of the company law is the English common law and 0 otherwise. Source: La Porta et al. (1998).
Accounting standards	Index created by the Center for International Financial Analysis and Research to rate the quality of 1990 annual reports on their disclosure of accounting information. Source: La Porta et al. (1998).
Rule of law	Assessment of the law and order tradition in the country produced by the risk-rating agency International Country Risk (ICR). Average of the months of April and October of the monthly index between 1982 and 1995. It ranges between 0 and 10. Source: La Porta et al. (1998).
Antidirector rights	The index is formed by adding one when (i) the country allows shareholders to mail their proxy vote to the firm, (ii) shareholders are not required to deposit their shares prior to the general shareholders' meeting, (iii) cumulative voting or proportional representation of minorities in the board of directors is allowed, (iv) an oppressed minorities mechanism is in place, (v) the minimum percentage of share capital that entitles a shareholder to call for an extraordinary shareholders' meeting is less than or equal to 10% (the sample median), or (vi) shareholders have preemptive rights that can be waived only by a shareholders' vote. Source: La Porta et al. (1998).

Shareholder protection	Measure of the effective rights of minority shareholders computed as the product of rule of law and antidirector rights divided by 10. It ranges between 0 and 6.
Ownership concentration	Average equity stake owned by the three largest shareholders in the 10 largest nonfinancial domestic firms in 1994. Source: La Porta et al. (1998).
Cross-border regulation	Equals 1 if in 1995 a foreign buyer needed government approval before acquiring control of a domestic firm and 0 otherwise. Source: Economist Intelligence Unit, Country Surveys.
Market return	Average annual stock market return in 1990s adjusted for inflation with the Consumer Price Index. Source: WorldScope.
Market dominance	Response to survey question: "Market dominance by a few enterprises is rare in key industries (1 = strongly disagree, 6 = strongly agree)." Source: The Global Competitiveness Report, 1996.
Mandatory bid rule	Equals 1 if in 1995 there was a legal requirement to make a tender offer when shareholding after the acquisition exceeds a given ownership threshold and 0 otherwise. Source: Economist Intelligence Unit, Country Surveys.
Openness	Response to survey question: "Foreign investors are free to acquire control of a domestic company (1 = strongly disagree, 6 = strongly agree)." Source: The Global Competitiveness Report, 1996.

A.2. Cross-border variables

Cross-border deals$_{s,b}$	Number of deals in which the target is from country s and the acquirer is from country b, shown as a percentage of the total number of deals with target in country s. Source: SDC Platinum.
Same language	Equals 1 when target and acquirer's countries share the same main language and 0 otherwise. Source: World Atlas 1995.
Same geographical area	Equals 1 when target and acquirer's countries are from the same continent and 0 otherwise. We classify all countries into four areas (Africa, America, Asia, and Europe). Source: World Atlas 1995.
Bilateral trade$_{s,b}$	Value of imports by country s from country b as a percentage of total import by country s. Source: World Bank Trade and Production Database.

A.3. Deal-level variables

Premium	Bid price as a percentage of the closing price of the target 4 weeks before the announcement. Source: SDC Platinum.
All-cash bid	Equals 1 if the acquisition is entirely paid in cash and 0 otherwise. Source: SDC Platinum.
Target size	Logarithm of the market capitalization of the target 4 weeks before the announcement of the deal in US$ million. Source: SDC Platinum.
Tender offer	Equals 1 if the acquisition is done through a tender offer and 0 otherwise. Source: SDC Platinum.
Cross-border	Equals 1 if the target country differs from the acquirer country and 0 otherwise. Source: SDC Platinum.
Hostile bid	Equals 1 if the bid is classified as unsolicited and 0 otherwise. Source: SDC Platinum.
Contested bid	Equals 1 if the number of bidders is larger than 1 and 0 otherwise. Source: SDC Platinum.
Bidder M/B	Equity market-to-book ratio of the bidder computed 4 weeks before the announcement. Source: Datastream.

References

Bebchuk, L., 1999, "A Rent-Protection Theory of Corporate Ownership and Control," NBER Working Paper 7203, National Bureau of Economic Research.

Bebchuk, L. and M. Roe, 1999, "A Theory Of Path Dependence in Corporate Governance and Ownership," *Stanford Law Review*, 52, 127–170.

Bhattacharya, U. and H. Daouk, 2002, "The World Price of Insider Trading," *Journal of Finance*, 57, 75–108.

Coffee, J., 1999, "The Future as History: The Prospects for Global Convergence in Corporate Governance and Its Implications," *Northwestern University Law Review*, 93, 641–708.

Comment, R. and W. Schwert, 1995, "Poison or Placebo? Evidence on the Deterrence and Wealth Effects of Modern Antitakeover Measures," *Journal of Financial Economics*, 39, 3–43.

Dahlquist, M., L. Pinkowitz, R. Stulz and R. Williamson, 2003, "Corporate Governance and the Home Bias," *Journal of Financial and Quantitative Analysis*, 38, 87–110.

Dittmar, A., J. Mahrt-Smith and H. Servaes, 2003, "International Corporate Governance and Corporate Cash Holdings," *Journal of Financial and Quantitative Analysis*, 38, 111–133.

Dyck, A. and L. Zingales, 2004, "Private Benefits of Control: An International Comparison," *Journal of Finance*, 59, 537–600.

Franks, J. and C. Mayer, 1996, "Hostile Takeovers and the Correction of Managerial Failure," *Journal of Financial Economics*, 40, 163–181.

Gilson, R., 2001, "Globalizing Corporate Governance: Convergence of form or Function," *American Journal of Comparative Law*, 49, 329–363.

Grossman, S. and O. Hart, 1980, "Takeover Bids, the Free-Rider Problem and the Theory of the Corporation," *Bell Journal of Economics*, 11, 42–64.

Hansmann, H. and R. Kraakman, 2001, "The End of History for Corporate Law," *Georgetown Law Journal*, 89, 439–468.

Huber, P., 1967, "The Behavior of Maximum Likelihood Estimates Under Non-Standard Conditions," In *Proceedings of the Fifth Berkeley Symposium on Mathematical Statistics and Probability*, Vol. 1, University of California Press, Berkeley, CA, pp. 221–233.

Jenkinson, T. and A. Ljungqvist, 2001, "The Role of Hostile Stakes in German Corporate Governance," *Journal of Corporate Finance*, 7, 397–446.

Jensen, M., 1993, "The Modern Industrial Revolution, Exit, and the Failure of Internal Control Systems," *Journal of Finance*, 48, 831–880.

La Porta, R., F. Lopez-de-Silanes, A. Shleifer and R. Vishny, 1997, "Legal Determinants of External Finance," *Journal of Finance*, 52, 1131–1150.

La Porta, R., F. Lopez-de-Silanes, A. Shleifer and R. Vishny, 1998, "Law and Finance," *Journal of Political Economy*, 101, 678–709.

La Porta, R., F. Lopez-de-Silanes and A. Shleifer, 1999, "Corporate Ownership Around the World," *Journal of Finance*, 54, 471–517.

La Porta, R., F. Lopez-de-Silanes, A. Shleifer and R. Vishny, 2000a, "Investor Protection and Corporate Governance," *Journal of Financial Economics*, 58, 3–27.

La Porta, R., F. Lopez-de-Silanes, A. Shleifer and R. Vishny, 2000b, "Agency Problems and Dividend Policies Around the World," *Journal of Finance*, 55, 1–33.

La Porta, R., F. Lopez-de-Silanes, A. Shleifer and R. Vishny, 2002, "Investor Protection and Corporate Valuation," *Journal of Finance*, 57, 1147–1170.

Leuz, C., D. Nanda and P. Wysocki, 2003, "Earnings Management and Investor Protection," *Journal of Financial Economics*, 69, 505–527.

Manne, H., 1965, "Mergers and the Market for Corporate Control," *Journal of Political Economy*, 75, 110–126.

Nenova, T., 2003, "The Value of Corporate Voting Rights and Control: A Cross-Country Analysis," *Journal of Financial Economics*, 68, 325–351.

Pagano, M., A. Roell and J. Zechner, 2002, "The Geography of Equity Listing: Why do Companies List Abroad?" *Journal of Finance*, 57, 2651–2694.

Rau, R. and T. Vermaelen, 1998, "Glamour, Value and the Post-Acquisition Performance of Acquiring Firms," *Journal of Financial Economics*, 49, 223–253.

Reese, W. and M. Weisbach, 2002, "Protection of Minority Shareholder Interests, Cross-Listing in the United States, and Subsequent Equity Offerings," *Journal of Financial Economics*, 66, 65–104.

Shleifer, A. and R. Vishny, 1986, "Large Shareholders and Corporate Control," *Journal of Political Economy*, 94, 461–488.

Shleifer, A. and R. Vishny, 2003, "Stock Market Driven Acquisitions," *Journal of Financial Economics*, 70, 295–311.

White, H., 1980, "A Heteroskedasticity-Consistent Covariance Matrix Estimator and a Direct Test for Heteroskedasticity," *Econometrica*, 48, 817–838.

Wurgler, J., 2000, "Financial Markets and the Allocation of Capital," *Journal of Financial Economics*, 58, 187–214.

Chapter 24

SPILLOVER OF CORPORATE GOVERNANCE STANDARDS IN CROSS-BORDER MERGERS AND ACQUISITIONS*

MARINA MARTYNOVA

The University of Sheffield Management School, Sheffield, United Kingdom

LUC RENNEBOOG

Tilburg University and European Corporate Governance Institute (ECGI), Tilburg, The Netherlands

Contents

* We thank all the corporate governance regulation experts and lawyers listed in the data appendix for their help. We are grateful for valuable comments from Bernard Black, Arturo Bris, Christos Cabolis, Hans Degryse, Espen Eckbo, Julian Franks, Marc Goergen, Kate Litvak, Dennis Mueller, Steven Ongena, Annette Poulsen, Peter Szilagyi, Hubert Waelrant, Adriaan Willaert, Hannes Wagner, and Chendi Zhang and the participants of seminars at Cambridge University, CUNEF (Madrid), Keele University, New Economic School, Tilburg University, Sheffield University, Standard & Poor's Moscow office, and University of Lille 2. We also acknowledge suggestions from the participants of the Conference on Empirical Legal Studies (New York, 2007), FMA Annual Meeting (Orlando, 2007), EFA Meeting (Ljubljana, 2007), Citicorp's Quantitative Conference (Cannes, 2007), EFMA Meeting (Vienna, 2007), the University of Sheffield—ECGI Symposium on Contractual Corporate Governance (Sheffield, 2007), FinLawMetrics Conference (Milan, 2007), FMA European Meeting (Barcelona, 2007), and Corporate Governance Conference (Cambridge, 2007). The authors gratefully acknowledge support from the European Commission via the "New Modes of Governance"-project (NEWGOV) led by the European University Institute in Florence; contract No. CIT1-CT-2004—506392. Luc Renneboog is also grateful to the Netherlands Organization for Scientific Research for a replacement subsidy of the programme "Shifts in Governance."

This article originally appeared in the *Journal of Corporate Finance*, Vol. 14, pp. 200–223 (2008).
Corporate Takeovers, Volume 2
Edited by B. Espen Eckbo
DOI: 10.1016/B978-0-12-381982-6.00025-2

Abstract

In cross-border acquisitions, the differences between the bidder and target corporate governance (measured by newly constructed indices capturing shareholder, minority shareholder, and creditor protection) have an important impact on the takeover returns. Our country-level corporate governance indices capture the changes in the quality of the national corporate governance regulations over the past 15 years. When the bidder is from a country with a strong shareholder orientation (relative to the target), part of the total synergy value of the takeover may result from the improvement in the governance of the target assets. In full takeovers, the corporate governance regulation of the bidder is imposed on the target (the *positive spillover by law* hypothesis). In partial takeovers, the improvement in the target corporate governance may occur on voluntary basis (the *spillover by control* hypothesis). Our empirical analysis corroborates both spillover effects. In contrast, when the bidder is from a country with poorer shareholder protection, the *negative spillover by law* hypothesis states that the anticipated takeover gains will be lower as the poorer corporate governance regime of the bidder will be imposed on the target. The alternative *bootstrapping hypothesis* argues that poor-governance bidders voluntarily bootstrap to the better-governance regime of the target. We do find support for the bootstrapping effect.

Keywords

takeovers, mergers and acquisitions, cross-border, takeover synergies, corporate governance regulation, contractual convergence, shareholder protection, creditor protection, minority shareholder protection, takeover regulation

JEL classification: G30, G34, G38, G18, G14, G15

1. Introduction

Cross-border merger and acquisition (M&A) activity has increased significantly over the last 15 years (Moeller and Schlingemann, 2005). Expansion through cross-border acquisitions enables companies to exploit differences in tax systems and to capture rents resulting from market inefficiencies, such as national controls over labor and resources markets (Scholes and Wolfson, 1990; Servaes and Zenner, 1994). An additional source of takeover synergy in cross-border M&As may be induced by improvements in the governance of the bidding and target firms as a result of spillovers of corporate governance standards between the two firms.

Wang and Xie (2009) show that both bidder and target firms benefit from corporate governance improvements in domestic US mergers and acquisitions. They use the firm-level shareholder rights indices of Gompers et al. (2003) and show that takeover synergies increase with the differences in the index between the bidder and the target. We hypothesize that the scope for potential improvements in corporate governance is even greater in cross-border M&As as the difference between the bidder and target quality of corporate governance is amplified by the significant variation in national corporate governance standards. Therefore, our main question is: *Do differences in the quality of corporate governance standards between the bidder and target countries explain part of the expected value creation in cross-border takeovers?* In other words, is there a valuation effect of cross-border spillover of corporate governance standards (and more specifically of investor protection)?

Why would we expect such a spillover valuation effect for corporate governance? In international law, a full takeover leads to a change in the nationality of the target firm such that the acquirer's corporate governance regulation will apply to the combined company, in effect replacing the target corporate governance (Bris and Cabolis, 2008). When the bidder is subject to better corporate governance regulation than the target, the acquisition may result in an improvement in corporate governance (e.g., enhanced shareholder orientation) at the target. As improved governance is expected to generate additional value, the abnormal share price returns of both the bidder and target should reflect such value creation. We call this hypothesis the *positive spillover by law hypothesis*. "Positive" refers to the corporate governance improvement for the target as a result of the full takeover by the bidder. In other words, the better the bidder's corporate governance, the higher are the returns to the bidder and target firms from the takeover. Likewise, we define the *negative spillover by law hypothesis:* when the bidder governance standards are below those of the target, the abnormal returns will be lower as the governance standards of the target will now be less strict.

A *negative spillover by law* effect is expected between a bidder in a country with low investor protection and a target in a country with stricter corporate governance regulation, as the induced poor investor protection by the bidder may lessen the quality of corporate governance of the target. This could reduce the value of the target assets in the hands of the bidder. However, there is an alternative hypothesis: bidders can abide by the stricter regulation that the target is subject to. We call this the *bootstrapping hypothesis:* bidders voluntarily bootstrap their corporate governance regulation to a higher level.[1] As such, firms can contract privately on the optimal level of investor protection.[2] If the bidder intends to pursue such bootstrapping to a higher level of corporate governance, its value may actually increase which will be reflected in the bidder share price at the takeover announcement. Bootstrapping may occur in both full and partial acquisitions, but the valuation effect may be stronger in partial takeovers whereby a stake of less than 100% of the voting rights is acquired and the target still remains listed on its national stock exchange.[3] The bootstrapping valuation effect may also be stronger in takeovers with all-equity offers or mixed bids as (some of) the target shareholders will then remain involved with the merged company and may actively resist managerial actions reflecting a reduced shareholder orientation (Starks and Wei, 2005).

International law prescribes that the *positive spillover by law* effect is to take place in a full takeover, which leads to a change in the target firm's nationality. Nonetheless, partial takeovers may also lead to a similar spillover effect, which we call the *spillover by control* hypothesis. Although the target firm is not fully absorbed by the bidder in a partial acquisition, the bidder may still impose its own corporate governance standards on the target, provided that the bidder standards are stricter than the target's. In contrast, if the bidder standards are less strict than the target's, the bidder has to comply (locally) with the target corporate governance law and the listing regulations (in case the target remains listed on a national stock exchange).

The main conclusion from our empirical analysis is that the positive *spillover by law hypothesis* is supported whereas the negative *spillover by law hypothesis* is not. The bidder and target takeover announcement returns are positive when the former's governance standards are stricter than the latter's. This implies that the stricter governance imposed on the target is expected to lead to value creation, possibly to an increased focus on shareholder value and the reduction in managerial private benefits of control. In contrast, when the bidder corporate governance standards are less strict than the target's, neither the bidder nor the target returns are lower. While

[1] One could somehow compare this to the bonding hypothesis: some firms seek a cross-listing on an exchange with stricter investor protection/listing requirements. Cross-listing allows firms to commit credibly to protect the shareholders' interests (see, e.g., Coffee, 1999; Doidge et al., 2006). Such bonding is credible to the market as it involves high costs (complying to different accounting standards, listing regulation, governance standards) and comprises a legal obligation.

[2] A counterexample whereby a firm moves toward less shareholder-orientation is given by Bris and Cabolis (2007): they show that Aventis, the firm arising from the merger of German Hoechst and French Rhone-Poulenc, borrowed from the corporate governance regimes of both firms, resulting in a more protected company than with the French default legal system of investor protection.

[3] In the case of cross-border mergers, a bidder is entitled to subject a foreign-owned subsidiary to its local corporate law, irrespective of the domicile of the subsidiary (Bris and Cabolis, 2008, citing Muchlinski, 1997). When less than 100% of the shares of the target are acquired by the foreign firm, the target firm remains operating under the law of its home country. Furthermore, the extraterritoriality principle in international law states that a state can assert jurisdiction over its nationals abroad. However, the extraterritoriality principle does not apply when a foreign firm acquires 100% of the company's shares.

this evidence goes against the negative spillover by law hypothesis, it does not contradict our *bootstrapping hypothesis*: it seems that poor-governance bidders bootstrap to the better-governance regime of the target, experiencing a share price increase. Importantly, the effect is only valid for partial acquisitions or, in other words, in deals which still involve some of the target shareholders (who did not sell out) and in which the target firm remains listed on the stock exchange in the country of the target.

The *spillover by control hypothesis* holds when the differences between the bidder and target governance regulation have a positive effect on anticipated gains of partial takeovers. The spillover effect from a bidder from a country with stronger shareholder protection to the target explains part of the value creation expected at the announcement of the partial takeover. The potential benefits from the improvement of the target corporate governance are shared by both the bidding and target firms' shareholders: both the bidder and target returns increase. Our results are robust with respect to several model specifications that control for potential endogeneity problems.

Our results also support the view that national corporate governance regulation has a significant impact on the flow of cross-border takeovers. In particular, we find that firms from countries with weak corporate governance regulation are more likely to invest abroad rather than domestically, confirming earlier results by Doidge et al. (2007) and Benos and Weisbach (2004). We also find that bidders are more likely to acquire firms abroad if minority shareholder protection in their home country is strong. This result is in line with the argument by Goergen et al. (2005) that strong protection of minority shareholders makes corporate takeovers costly and hence forces companies to look for potential M&A targets abroad, in countries with weaker (minority) shareholder protection. Strong creditor protection in the home country also has a positive effect on the international takeover activity. This may result from the relation between creditor protection and a firm's access to debt financing (La Porta et al., 1998). Martynova and Renneboog (2007a) show that debt financing is indeed frequently used in cross-border M&As. Therefore, cross-border M&As are more likely to be made by bidders that have access to less expensive debt capital which prevails in countries with strong protection of creditor rights.

Finally, most of our other results on the effect of the relative transaction size, free cash flow, hostility, means of payment, diversification strategies, stock-price run-up, differences in economic development, geographical closeness and language relatedness of the bidder and target, the level of corruption, and other characteristics are in line with the findings in the earlier literature.

This paper contributes to the literature in two ways.

First, we answer the question *how or through which channels cross-border mergers and acquisitions generate value*. Not just purely economic characteristics (of the bid, the target, and the bidder) but also the spillover of corporate governance standards between the bidder and the target explain part of the takeover premiums or the anticipated value (abnormal announcement returns). The impact of national corporate governance standards on the shareholder wealth effect in cross-border M&As has been previously studied in Bris and Cabolis (2008) and Bris et al. 2008, this issue,

Starks and Wei (2005), Kuipers et al. (2003), and Rossi and Volpin (2004). These five studies investigate the valuation effects of corporate governance on M&As from different perspectives and arrive at different results. Our paper is closest to the study by Bris and Cabolis (2008) and Bris et al. (2008, this issue). The authors show that takeover premiums in cross-border deals increase with the difference in shareholder protection and the quality of accounting standards between the bidder and the target. They report that this effect is significant only in M&As when the target changes its nationality (full acquisitions). In contrast, our results reveal that the improvement in the target shareholder protection has a positive effect on takeover synergy irrespective of the type of takeover. Our results thus reveal that governance-related takeover synergies may not only arise from a *spillover by law* effect but also from *spillover by control* and *bootstrapping* effects.

The second contribution is that our analysis is based on new corporate governance indices. Our *country-level indices* are more elaborate than the indices developed by La Porta, Lopez-de-Silanes, Shleifer and Vishny (henceforth LLSV) and employed in the studies mentioned above. With the help of 150 corporate lawyers from 32 European countries, we have created a corporate governance database that comprises the main changes in corporate governance regulation in all European countries over the last 15 years. For each country, we quantify corporate law, stock exchange regulation and corporate practices,[4] and measure their effectiveness in mitigating the conflicts of interest between the various corporate constituencies: management, majority and minority shareholders, and creditors. Our indices reveal that corporate governance regulation has been substantially reformed in virtually every European country since the early 1990s. Therefore, it is important to note that, in contrast to previous studies, all legal indices employed in this paper are time-varying and reflect changes in the legal environment.

There are several reasons why we focus on country regulation (rather than firm-level regulation). First, it is virtually impossible to code the content of corporate charters, to collect the amendments and to gather all major shareholder decisions of AGMs for such a large group of firms. These firms are situated in a heterogeneous group of countries with varying degrees of transparency and disclosure problems. Second, empirical evidence reveals a high correlation between corporate governance at the firm-level and at the country-level. Doidge et al. (2007) analyze the variation in a cross-section of firm-level corporate governance indices and conclude that most of the variation can be explained by country characteristics. They argue that countries matter so much because they influence the costs that firms incur to bond themselves to good governance and the benefits they receive from doing so. The authors also state that firms with concentrated ownership (de facto the vast majority of listed firms in

---

[4] We also capture generally accepted corporate practices in as far as they are stricter than the regulation. For instance, nonvoting shares are legal in the United Kingdom, but are not used by any firm listed on the London Stock Exchange. Therefore, we consider the United Kingdom as a country where the one-share-one-vote is upheld.

Continental Europe) invest less in firm-level governance mechanisms, as the major shareholders monitor their firm's managers more effectively.

The remainder of the paper is organized as follows. Section 2 describes the data sources and sample composition. Section 3 presents the empirical results while Section 4 concludes.

2. Sample description

We select our initial sample of European acquisitions undertaken during the 5th takeover wave (1993–2001) from the Mergers and Acquisitions Database of the Securities Data Company (SDC).[5] The SDC data is filtered down to intra-European cross-border takeovers, whereby both the acquirer and the target are from countries within Continental Europe and the United Kingdom. Our sample also includes deals involving firms from Central and Eastern Europe (including Russia). For reasons of comparison, we also collect information on domestic mergers and acquisitions in Continental Europe and the United Kingdom. We retain only those cross-border and domestic M&As that satisfy the following requirements:

(i) The transaction involves a change in control[6];
(ii) The shares of the bidder or the target firm (or of both) are traded on a Continental European or United Kingdom stock exchange;
(iii) Both parties participating in the M&A transaction are independent corporations[7];
(iv) Neither the bidder nor the target is a financial institution (bank, unit trust, mutual fund or pension fund);
(v) The period between two consecutive bids by the same acquirer is at least 300 trading days[8];
(vi) Financial and accounting data for at least one of the participants of the transaction are available in DataStream or in the Amadeus, Fame or Reach databases.

Our final sample of domestic and cross-border M&A announcements consists of 2419 deals involving firms from 29 European countries. Cross-border M&As represent one-third of the sample (737 deals). Table 1 reports the sample distribution by country of the bidding and target firms. The most active cross-border acquirers are British,

---

[5] The quality of the SDC data is verified by comparing its information on the announcement date, the company's country of origin, the transaction value, payment structure, share of control acquired, bid completion status, and the target's attitude toward the bid with information from the news announcements stored in LexisNexis, the Financial Times, and Factiva. We uncovered inconsistencies in one or more records in 36% of the observations of the SDC database, which we subsequently corrected.

[6] We require either that the transaction leads to a combination of the firms or that the acquirer who held less than 50% of the target's stock prior to the transaction acquires majority control.

[7] The absorption of subsidiaries is not included, nor are divestitures and management buyouts.

[8] The reason for this restriction is that we want to avoid contamination of the windows used to estimate the systematic risk.

Table 1

Sample distribution by country of bidding and target company in domestic and cross-border M&As

The diagonal elements show the number of domestic acquisitions in a particular country. Off-diagonal elements report the number of cross-border bids involving bidding and target companies from the two corresponding countries. $Total \times NUM$ counts the total number of cross-border M&As (excluding domestic deals): $Total \times \%$ shows the percentage of cross-border M&As involving firms from one country in the total number of cross-border M&As. The following country codes are used: AUS, Austria; BEL, Belgium; BUL, Bulgaria; CRO, Croatia; CYP, Cyprus; CZR, Czech Republic; DEN, Denmark; EST, Estonia; FIN, Finland; FRA, France; GER, Germany; GRE, Greece; HUN, Hungary; IRE, Republic of Ireland; ITA, Italy; LAT, Latvia; LIT, Lithuania; LUX, Luxembourg; NL, Netherlands; NOR, Norway; POL, Poland; POR, Portugal; ROM, Romania; RUS, Russia; SLO, Slovenia; ESP, Spain; SWE, Sweden; SWZ, Switzerland; UK, United Kingdom.

| Bidding firms | \multicolumn{29}{Target firms} | | | | | | | | | | | | | | | | | | | | | | | | | | | | Total cross-border | |
	AUS	BEL	BUL	CRO	CYP	CZR	DEN	EST	FIN	FRA	GER	GRE	HUN	IRE	ITA	LAT	LIT	LUX	NL	NOR	POL	POR	ROM	RUS	SLO	ESP	SWE	SWZ	UK	NUM	%
AUS	11	-	-	-	2	-	1	-	-	12	-	2	-	-	1	-	-	1	-	-	4	-	3	1	-	-	-	2	-	31	4.2
BEL	-	23	-	-	1	-	-	-	-	14	4	-	-	-	1	-	-	2	1	1	-	-	-	1	-	-	3	1	3	34	4.6
BUL	-	-	0	-	-	-	-	-	-	-	-	-	-	-	-	-	-	-	-	-	-	-	-	1	-	-	-	-	-	1	0.1
CRO	-	-	-	0	3	-	-	-	-	-	-	-	-	-	-	-	-	-	-	-	-	-	-	-	-	-	-	-	-	1	0.3
CYP	-	-	-	-	9	-	-	-	-	-	-	-	-	-	-	-	-	-	-	-	-	-	-	1	-	-	-	-	1	1	0.1
CZR	-	1	-	-	-	9	-	-	-	-	-	-	-	-	-	-	-	-	1	-	1	-	1	-	-	-	-	-	-	32	4.3
DEN	1	-	-	-	-	-	30	6	3	4	2	-	-	-	3	2	-	1	4	4	1	-	1	-	-	3	3	-	6	32	4.3
EST	-	-	-	-	-	-	1	0	53	-	-	-	-	-	-	-	-	-	-	-	-	-	-	-	-	-	-	-	-	-	-
FIN	1	-	-	-	4	-	4	6	53	3	3	-	-	-	1	1	-	5	2	2	6	1	2	-	-	6	6	1	1	32	4.3
FRA	3	2	-	-	7	-	1	-	1	219	22	1	-	-	13	3	1	7	5	1	6	2	2	1	-	8	3	5	26	110	14.9
GER	9	4	-	-	4	-	1	-	1	10	174	1	1	-	9	-	1	7	7	5	5	2	2	2	-	2	5	10	13	89	12.1
GRE	-	-	-	-	-	-	-	-	-	-	-	-	-	-	-	-	-	-	-	-	-	-	-	-	-	-	-	-	-	-	-
HUN	-	-	-	-	-	-	-	-	1	1	1	-	4	-	-	-	-	-	-	1	-	-	-	-	-	-	-	-	-	5	0.7
IRE	1	-	2	-	2	-	2	-	1	1	-	-	-	11	-	-	-	2	-	-	1	-	1	-	-	1	-	1	19	26	3.5
ITA	-	-	-	-	1	-	-	-	-	7	5	-	-	-	39	-	2	-	-	-	1	1	1	-	-	5	-	-	3	28	3.8
LAT	-	-	-	-	-	-	1	-	1	-	-	-	-	-	-	0	-	-	-	-	-	-	-	-	-	-	-	-	-	1	0.1
LIT	-	-	-	-	-	-	-	-	-	-	-	-	-	-	-	-	1	-	-	-	-	-	-	-	-	-	-	-	-	-	-
LUX	1	-	-	-	1	-	-	-	1	3	3	-	-	1	-	-	-	0	1	-	-	-	-	-	-	1	-	1	1	7	1.0
NL	-	-	-	-	1	-	1	-	7	7	2	-	-	-	2	-	-	2	18	1	3	-	-	1	-	1	-	1	6	27	1.3
NOR	-	-	-	-	3	2	2	2	2	2	4	-	-	-	4	-	-	2	-	58	2	-	2	-	-	-	13	-	4	32	4.3
POL	-	-	-	-	-	-	-	-	-	-	-	-	-	-	-	-	-	-	-	-	22	1	-	-	-	-	-	-	-	-	-
POR	-	-	-	-	-	-	-	-	-	-	-	1	-	-	-	-	-	-	-	-	-	-	-	-	-	1	-	-	-	1	0.1
ROM	-	-	-	-	-	-	-	-	-	-	-	-	-	-	-	-	-	-	-	-	-	-	-	-	-	-	-	-	-	-	-
RUS	1	-	-	-	-	-	-	-	-	-	-	-	-	-	-	-	-	-	-	-	-	-	2	10	-	-	-	-	-	3	0.4
SLO	-	-	-	-	-	-	-	-	-	-	-	-	-	-	-	-	-	-	-	-	-	-	-	-	0	-	-	-	-	-	-
ESP	1	1	-	-	3	-	2	2	5	5	5	2	-	-	2	2	1	1	1	-	3	1	1	1	1	46	1	1	1	9	1.2
SWE	1	1	-	-	6	8	2	16	7	5	5	-	-	-	2	-	1	4	16	4	4	1	1	1	-	-	102	2	2	69	9.4
SWZ	2	-	-	-	1	-	-	-	-	7	6	2	-	-	4	-	-	3	2	2	-	-	-	-	-	2	1	22	8	39	5.3
UK	2	5	-	-	5	4	3	-	3	20	20	3	-	14	8	-	1	18	7	7	5	2	1	1	-	14	12	5	838	159	21.5
NUM	20	14	6	-	25	13	21	13	20	89	90	3	16	14	44	4	6	5	45	37	37	11	11	10	4	33	48	27	94	738	100
%	2.7%	1.9%	0.3%	0.8%	3.4%	1.8%	2.9%	1.8%	2.7%	12.0%	12.2%	0.4%	2.2%	1.9%	6.0%	0.5%	0.8%	0.7%	6.1%	5.0%	5.0%	1.5%	1.5%	1.4%	0.5%	4.5%	6.5%	3.7%	12.7%	100	

German, and French firms, which cumulatively account for 49% of all cross-border M&As. Firms from the United Kingdom, Germany, and France are also most frequently the targets in cross-border acquisitions (37% of all cross-border M&As). Not to be underestimated is the cross-border M&A activity involving Scandinavian firms, which represents 23% and 17% of all cross-border acquirers and targets, respectively.

The domestic M&A activity by the United Kingdom, German, French, and Scandinavian firms substantially exceeds their involvement in cross-border takeovers. In contrast, companies from the Benelux countries, Austria, and Ireland are more frequently involved in cross-border rather than in domestic M&As. Relative to the other major economies in Continental Europe, Southern Europe (Greece, Italy, Portugal, and Spain) has a remarkably low domestic and cross-border takeover activity. In cross-border M&As, Southern European firms are more frequently targets (of German, British, and French bidders) than bidders. Another interesting observation relates to Eastern and Central European countries that have joined the European Union since 2004. Many firms from these new member states are acquired by West-European bidders, predominantly from neighboring countries (Scandinavia, Austria, and Germany). In contrast, the participation of Central European firms as bidders in cross-border acquisitions is small, as is the domestic takeover market in that region.

3. Empirical results

3.1. Variable construction

The next subsections discuss the measurement of four categories of variables: (i) the bidder and target announcement returns (the dependent variables), (ii) corporate governance indices, (iii) measures of corporate governance spillover effects (our key explanatory variables), and (iv) the bidder-, target-, and deal-specific characteristics (our control variables). The definitions of variables and data sources are summarized in Appendix A.

3.1.1. The bidder and target announcement returns

We measure the short-term wealth effects at the takeover announcement using the event study methodology. For each bidding and target firm, we compute the daily abnormal returns realized over the period starting 1 day prior and ending 1 day subsequent to the day of the public takeover announcement.[9] The takeover announcement wealth

---

[9] The event day is either the day of the announcement or the first trading day following the announcement in case the announcement is made on a nontrading day.

effect is the sum of these daily abnormal returns. We also consider longer event windows, such as $[-5, +5]$ and $[-60, +60]$. Daily abnormal returns are the difference between realized and market model benchmark returns. Our market model is based on the MSCI-Europe index and its parameters are estimated over 240 days, starting 300 days prior to the acquisition announcement.[10] To test the significance of the estimated abnormal returns, we use both parametric and nonparametric tests as discussed by Brown and Warner (1985) and Corrado (1989), respectively.

As Panel A of Table 2 shows, the 3 days cumulative average abnormal return (CAAR) is 0.83% and 0.47% for the subsamples of domestic and cross-border bidders, respectively. Both figures are significantly different from zero at the 5% level and the difference in the CAARs between the two subsamples is also statistically significant.[11] This result confirms findings of recent empirical studies that cross-border bidders somewhat underperform their domestic peers (see, e.g., Dennis et al., 2002; Moeller and Schlingemann, 2005). In contrast, targets in cross-border takeovers experience significantly higher returns than targets in domestic bids. For the 3 days window centered on the bid announcement, cross-border target firms accumulate abnormal returns of 12.55% compared to 11.52% for domestic targets. Goergen and Renneboog (2004) document similar differences for large intra-European M&As.

To investigate the influence of the legal environment on the takeover wealth effect, we compare the CAARs for subsamples of bidders (targets) across countries of different legal origins. Countries from the former communist block are classified according to their (staged) accession to the European Union. Panel B of Table 2 reveals the systematic differences in the bidder and target CAARs by legal origin. Whereas bidders of German or Scandinavian legal origin earn significant positive returns in cross-border M&As, their counterparts of English or French legal origin earn more modest or even insignificant returns, and bidders from recent EU Accession countries incur negative returns. For the target firms, we observe that companies of English or Scandinavian legal origin yield the highest announcement returns, which are almost 2.5 times higher than the returns of target companies of French or German legal origin. Remarkably, the CAARs to the target firms from the former communist block countries are not significantly different from zero.

---

[10] Our estimates of the abnormal returns are robust with respect to the geographical scope of the market index (local, European-wide, and worldwide index) and the estimation model of the benchmark returns (the estimated beta adjusted for mean-reversion Blume, 1979, and nonsynchronous trading Dimson, 1979). Changing the market index or the estimation model does not materially change any of the results in the remainder of the paper.

[11] We (conservatively) only report the nonparametric tests. The significance levels of the parametric tests corroborate the nonparametric ones but the former lead to higher levels of significance.

Table 2

Cumulative average abnormal returns (CAARs) to bidding and target firms in cross-border and domestic M&As

Panel A reports the average values of the CARs for bidding and target firms in cross-border and domestic acquisitions conducted in Continental Europe and the United Kingdom. The CAARs are reported in percentages. Panel B reports the CAARs for bidding and target firms in cross-border and domestic acquisitions classified by the legal origin of the bidder and target countries. Abnormal returns are computed as the difference between the realized and market model benchmark returns. For each firm, we calculate daily benchmark returns using MSCI-Europe index returns and the market model parameters are estimated over 240 days starting 300 days prior to the acquisition announcement. The *t-statistics* from the nonparametric test (Corrado, 1989) is reported to assess the significance of the CAARs. *Nobs* stands for the number of observations.

	Cross-border M&As		Domestic M&As		*Diff.* Cross-border-domestic	
	Mean value	t-Statistic [Nobs]	Mean value	t-Statistic [Nobs]	Mean value	t-Statistic
Panel A. Takeover announcement effect						
The bidder CAARs						
[−1, +1]	**0.47****	*2.25 [653]*	**0.83*****	*3.95 [1456]*	**−0.36****	*−2.17*
[−5, +5]	**0.85***	*1.92 [653]*	**0.76*****	*2.56 [1456]*	0.09	*1.15*
[−60, +60]	**−3.63****	*−1.80 [653]*	**−2.49***	*−1.80 [1456]*	**−1.14*****	*−3.40*
The target CAARs						
[−1, +1]	**12.55*****	*5.24 [296]*	**11.52*****	*7.42 [764]*	**1.02*****	*−2.65*
[−5, +5]	**15.61*****	*16.15 [296]*	**12.17*****	*2.60 [764]*	**3.44*****	*−3.54*
[−60, +60]	**26.84*****	*12.04 [296]*	**24.99*****	*10.22 [764]*	**1.85*****	*−3.53*
Panel B. Takeover announcement effect by legal origin						
The bidder CAARs [−1, +1] by legal origin of the bidder country						
English legal origin	0.36	*1.63 [173]*	**0.50*****	*2.69 [744]*	−0.14	*−1.30*
French legal origin	**0.39***	*1.88 [181]*	**0.91****	*2.32 [279]*	**−0.52****	*−2.18*
German legal origin	**0.66****	*2.08 [137]*	**0.59*****	*2.44 [184]*	0.07	*0.61*
Scandinavian legal origin	**0.67****	*2.15 [149]*	**2.29*****	*3.17 [206]*	**−1.62*****	*−3.44*
EU 2004 Accession countries	**−1.25***	*−2.03 [6]*	0.12	*0.56 [35]*	**−1.37*****	*−2.86*
EU 2007 Accession countries, Croatia, and Russia	−1.60	*−0.23 [4]*	−0.51	*−0.15 [8]*	−1.09	*−0.55*

(Continued)

Table 2 (Continued)

	Cross-border M&As		Domestic M&As		Diff. Cross-border-domestic	
	Mean value	t-Statistic [Nobs]	Mean value	t-Statistic [Nobs]	Mean value	t-Statistic
The target CAARs [−1, +1] by legal origin of the target country						
English legal origin	19.42***	7.52 [57]	17.64***	14.00 [306]	1.78****	2.44
French legal origin	7.12***	3.80 [52]	2.82***	3.18 [118]	4.30***	3.19
German legal origin	7.06***	3.46 [33]	4.42***	3.17 [48]	2.64***	2.53
Scandinavian legal origin	17.32***	7.95 [38]	14.77***	7.12 [76]	2.55***	2.72
EU 2004 Accession countries	1.52	1.53 [15]	3.67***	2.74 [11]	−2.15	−1.62
EU 2007 Accession countries, Croatia, and Russia	−0.18	−0.12 [8]	−6.36	−0.78 [5]	6.18***	3.11

***, **, and * stand for statistical significance at the 1%, 5%, and 10% levels, respectively.

3.1.2. Corporate governance standards indices

To measure the quality of corporate governance standards in the bidder and target firms' countries we construct a number of indices.[12] With the help of 150 corporate lawyers from 32 European countries (as reported in Appendix B), we create a corporate governance database comprising the main aspects of and changes in corporate governance regulation in all European countries (including Central and Eastern Europe) since 1990. For each country, we quantify the regulation mitigating the conflicts of interests between the main corporate constituencies: management versus shareholders, majority versus minority shareholders, and creditors versus shareholders. We construct the following three indices (see also Martynova and Renneboog, 2007b). All these indices are rescaled to take values within the [0, 10] interval.

(i) The *shareholder rights* index is based on shareholders' ability to curb managerial opportunistic behavior. The index measures the degree of *shareholder orientation* of a national regulation. The index increases with the number and quality of legal provisions that provide shareholders with effective power to appoint and dismiss the board of directors and to control most of the important corporate decisions on, for instance, equity issues or antitakeover measures. We also take into account the regulatory provisions that ensure that the board of directors acts as an independent body operating on behalf of all shareholders and monitors top management. Provisions that address the quality of information on the management and the frequency of disclosure of accounting information are also considered. A higher index score represents a higher likelihood that management acts in the interest of shareholders and hence reflects better corporate governance standards with respect to shareholder protection.

(ii) The *minority shareholder protection* index hinges on the regulatory provisions that increase the relative power of the minority shareholders in the presence of strong majority shareholders. In a firm with concentrated control, it is possible that the dominant shareholder extracts private benefits of control by influencing managerial decisions for his own benefit (see, e.g., Durnev and Kim, 2005). This may lead to the expropriation of minority shareholders' rights. We quantify the regulatory provisions related to minority shareholder protection (e.g., board representation, minority claims, extraordinary general meetings, blocking minorities), the one-share-one-vote principle (dual class shares, voting caps, break-through rule, equal treatment principle), ownership transparency, and the relative decision

---

[12] These indices overcome some of the limitations of the LLSV indices. First, our indices are based on a broader definition of corporate governance regulation than that used by LLSV. Second, our indices are dynamic: they capture the many regulatory reforms on a yearly basis since 1990. Furthermore, we use functional approach to construct the indices, which differs from the comparative approach employed by La Porta et al. (1998). For a detailed discussion of the limitations and advantages of our indices see Martynova and Renneboog (2007b).

power in case of a takeover threat. A higher index score signifies that minority shareholders' interests are better protected.

The shareholder rights and minority shareholder protection indices are positively correlated because they both reflect to some degree the underlying quality of shareholder protection in a country. However, they are based on different institutional characteristics.

(iii) The *creditors rights* index hinges on the regulatory provisions that allow creditors to force repayment more easily, to take possession of the collateral, or even to gain control over the firm in case of financial distress. In creating this creditor rights index, we closely follow the approach of LLSV and investigate the regulation related to the violation of debt covenants (deviations from the debtor priority ranking in case of bankruptcy), the possibility for debtors to impose restrictions on borrowers (e.g., limitations on filing for reorganization/liquidation), and the creditors rights in financially distressed firms (e.g., automatic stay on assets). The index also captures the difference between creditor-oriented and debtor-oriented bankruptcy codes: we augment the creditor rights index for a country with a pure liquidation code by one, while leaving the index unchanged for a country with a debtor-oriented code.[13] The reason is that a bankruptcy code that facilitates reorganization focuses on corporate survival, usually at the expense of the (more senior) creditors. A higher index score reflects stronger creditor rights, that is, higher corporate governance standards with respect to creditor protection.

The constituents of each index and their coding are given in Appendix C.

It is important to note that a system with strong legal enforcement may substitute for weaker regulation as well-functioning courts can effectively resolve disputes between corporate constituencies (La Porta et al., 1998). Conversely, a law designed to uphold the rights of, for example, minority shareholders may be eroded in case the judiciary does not function effectively. To address these problems, we multiply the above indices by an index capturing the quality of law enforcement. We use the rule of law index developed by the World Bank, which we rescale to take values within the [0, 1] interval. The *rule of law index* measures the extent to which agents have confidence in and abide by the rules of society, which include the effectiveness and predictability of the judiciary and the enforceability of contracts. A higher score of the index signifies that a national judicial system is more effective.

Panel A of Table 3 reports the mean values of the corporate governance indices multiplied by the rule of law index. (Henceforth, when we refer to the corporate governance indices, we refer to the original indices multiplied by the rule of law index).

---

[13] Chapter 11 in the United States and administration in the United Kingdom are the prototype of a debtor-oriented code. In the 1990s, many bankruptcy codes have been reorganized and now frequently include two tracks: a debtor-oriented part and a pure liquidation code. We classify such bankruptcy codes as debtor-oriented.

Table 3

Corporate governance regulation indices

Panel A reports the mean values of the corporate governance indices by legal origin and for every 5th year over the period 1990-2005. All indices are adjusted for the degree of law enforcement by country. N is the number of countries of a specific legal origin. Panel B reports the mean values of the indices for bidder and target countries by domestic and cross-border M&As.

Panel A. Corporate governance indices by legal origin and by year						
	English legal origin	French legal origin	German legal origin	Scandinavian legal origin	EU 2004 Accession	EU 2007 Accession countries, Croatia, and Russia
	$N = 2$	$N = 8$	$N = 3$	$N = 4$	$N = 9$	$N = 4$
Shareholder rights index						
1990	4.79	3.33	2.93	3.34	1.72	1.62
1995	5.21	3.39	3.21	3.55	2.23	1.72
2000	5.91	3.87	4.28	3.97	2.65	2.04
2005	6.13	4.57	4.66	4.18	3.34	2.86
Minority shareholder protection index						
1990	4.25	2.69	3.14	3.21	1.51	0.68
1995	4.58	2.89	3.57	3.38	2.13	1.18
2000	5.20	3.37	4.52	3.60	2.78	1.96
2005	5.05	3.42	4.64	3.63	3.54	2.15
Creditor rights index						
1990	3.40	4.42	5.92	6.67	1.18	1.22
1995	3.40	4.43	5.92	5.33	3.51	2.27
2000	3.51	3.89	4.29	4.07	3.82	2.33
2005	3.41	3.48	4.11	4.03	4.10	2.61

Panel B. Corporate governance indices by the bidder/target country in cross-border and domestic M&As

	Cross-border M&As		Domestic M&As		*Diff.* cross-border-domestic	
	Mean value	*t*-Statistic	Mean value	*t*-Statistic	Mean value	*t*-Statistic
Shareholder rights index						
Bidder country	4.37		5.11		−0.74***	−3.22
Target country	3.74		5.11		−1.37***	−2.84
Diff. bidder-target	**0.63***	*3.16*	-	-	-	-
Minority shareholder protection index						
Bidder country	4.06		4.41		−0.35***	−2.65
Target country	3.74		4.41		−0.67***	−3.11
Diff. bidder-target	**0.32**	*2.31*	-	-	-	-
Creditor rights index						
Bidder country	3.71		3.43		0.28	*1.62*
Target country	3.72		3.43		0.29	*1.61*
Diff. bidder-target	−0.01	−0.04	-	-	-	-
Number Of observation	737		1681			

***, **, and * stand for statistical significance at the 1%, 5%, and 10% levels, respectively.

The indices are reported by legal origin and for every 5th year over the period 1990–2005. The panel shows that in 1995—the reference year of the LLSV indices—our shareholder rights protection index ranks countries in a similar order as it does the LLSV antidirector index. That is, countries of English legal origin have the highest corporate governance standards with respect to shareholder protection. They are followed by the countries of Scandinavian legal origin, and then by the countries of French and German legal origin. The panel also shows that there have been substantial changes in corporate governance standards in virtually every country in Europe over the past 15 years. The changes relate to all three dimensions of corporate governance standards addressed in this paper. However, in 2005, the countries of English legal origin still provide the highest quality of shareholder protection. Over time, shareholder rights and minority shareholder protection have increased throughout Continental Europe and the United Kingdom, whereas creditor protection has been reduced in Western Europe. By 2005, many Continental European countries had improved their legal system and moved closer to the standards set by the English legal system.

Panel B of Table 3 shows the mean values of the corporate governance indices for the countries of bidding and target companies measured in the year of the acquisition. It shows that, in contrast to the targets in cross-border acquisitions, bidding firms are from countries with better legal protection of (minority) shareholders. This pattern is consistent with the evidence by Rossi and Volpin (2004): targets in cross-border acquisitions are typically from countries with poorer standards of shareholder protection than bidders. The difference in creditor rights between the bidder and target countries seems to have no impact on the flow of cross-border M&As.

The correlation matrix in Table 4 shows that the value for the target shareholder rights index is positively correlated with the bidder and target takeover returns. The value of the target minority shareholder protection index is also positively correlated with the target returns but is negatively correlated with the bidder returns. The table also reports the correlations between the indices and the main variables that are used in the regression models below.

3.1.3. Corporate governance spillover effects

We measure the potential corporate governance spillover effect in cross-border mergers and acquisitions in two ways. First, we take the difference between the indices of the bidder and target countries (the differences-approach). This variable captures the scope of the potential improvement (or deterioration) in corporate governance if the target firm were to adopt the standards of the bidder. The quality of corporate governance standards is measured by means of the three indices discussed above; that is, we measure it with respect to the protection of shareholders, minority shareholders, and creditors (while taking into account the quality of the judiciary). Table 4 shows that the shareholder--rights difference is positively correlated with the target takeover returns.

Second, we construct indicator variables capturing the direction of corporate governance spillover effects: from the bidder to the target and vice versa (the indicator-variable

Table 4

Correlation matrix

The p-values testing the difference from zero are given between brackets.

	(Bidder) CAR [−1, +1]	(Target) CAR [−1, +1]	(Bidder) Shareholder rights index	(Bidder) Minority shareholder protection index	(Bidder) Creditor rights index	(Target) Shareholder rights index	(Target) Minority shareholder protection index	(Target) Creditor rights index	Difference bidder-target shareholder rights index	Difference bidder-target Minority shareholder protection index	Difference bidder-target creditor rights index
(Bidder) CAR [−1, +1]	-	0.023 (0.814)	0.035 (0.376)	0.023 (0.763)	0.001 (0.998)	**0.066*** (0.053)	**−0.054*** (0.066)	0.017 (0.653)	−0.008 (0.533)	−0.044 (0.259)	−0.013 (0.744)
(Target) CAR [−1, +1]	0.023 (0.814)	-	0.024 (0.735)	0.058 (0.416)	−0.099 (0.165)	**0.319*** (0.000)	**0.226*** (0.001)	0.056 (0.229)	**0.222*** (0.002)	0.124 (0.185)	−0.076 (0.114)
(Bidder) Q-ratio	−0.031 (0.561)	**−0.166*** (0.072)	**0.146*** (0.005)	**0.110*** (0.035)	−0.047 (0.372)	0.066 (0.209)	0.028 (0.315)	−0.079 (0.129)	0.054 (0.308)	−0.033 (0.531)	0.030 (0.566)
(Bidder) Leverage	0.001 (0.988)	0.084 (0.478)	−0.001 (0.979)	−0.040 (0.439)	**0.178*** (0.032)	0.027 (0.598)	0.057 (0.272)	−0.008 (0.882)	−0.019 (0.707)	−0.072 (0.168)	0.056 (0.283)
(Bidder) Size (log TA)	**−0.222*** (0.009)	0.031 (0.793)	**−0.150*** (0.004)	**−0.132*** (0.011)	−0.001 (0.990)	−0.003 (0.946)	0.008 (0.871)	0.011 (0.827)	**−0.099*** (0.057)	**−0.091*** (0.083)	−0.009 (0.863)
(Bidder) CFlow/TA	−0.063 (0.230)	0.058 (0.218)	0.057 (0.272)	0.081 (0.118)	0.044 (0.401)	0.039 (0.458)	0.055 (0.284)	−0.005 (0.925)	0.012 (0.814)	0.007 (0.900)	0.032 (0.545)
(Target) Q-ratio	**−0.228*** (0.022)	−0.059 (0.474)	0.045 (0.568)	−0.042 (0.595)	0.057 (0.475)	−0.011 (0.892)	−0.016 (0.836)	0.007 (0.932)	0.033 (0.681)	−0.017 (0.829)	0.037 (0.644)

(Target) Leverage	-0.011 (0.914)	0.024 (0.766)	-0.068 (0.380)	-0.096 (0.222)	-0.004 (0.959)	-0.021 (0.794)	-0.127 (0.102)	0.113** (0.047)	-0.023 (0.772)	0.029 (0.711)	-0.077 (0.325)
(Target) CFlow/TA	0.197** (0.045)	0.068 (0.406)	-0.007 (0.928)	-0.032 (0.684)	-0.105 (0.180)	0.045 (0.567)	-0.033 (0.678)	0.121 (0.122)	-0.037 (0.641)	0.003 (0.978)	-0.154 (0.048)
Equity payment	-0.059 (0.254)	-0.215*** (0.005)	-0.110** (0.019)	-0.120** (0.011)	0.028 (0.552)	0.036 (0.447)	0.007 (0.878)	-0.000 (0.999)	-0.096** (0.043)	-0.092* (0.053)	0.018 (0.702)
Public target	-0.035 (0.368)	—	-0.030 (0.413)	-0.019 (0.595)	0.131*** (0.000)	0.254*** (0.000)	0.222*** (0.000)	0.031 (0.406)	-0.193*** (0.000)	-0.188*** (0.000)	0.066* (0.075)
Hostile bid	-0.093* (0.077)	0.189*** (0.008)	-0.032 (0.385)	-0.018 (0.621)	-0.041 (0.266)	0.171*** (0.000)	0.138*** (0.000)	0.046 (0.213)	-0.138*** (0.000)	-0.121*** (0.001)	-0.059 (0.104)
M&A of 100%	0.036 (0.353)	0.337*** (0.000)	0.094*** (0.010)	0.067 (0.067)	-0.006 (0.859)	0.274*** (0.000)	0.219*** (0.000)	0.051 (0.163)	-0.120*** (0.001)	-0.125*** (0.000)	-0.041 (0.267)
Diversification	-0.007 (0.857)	0.100 (0.163)	-0.003 (0.928)	0.008 (0.829)	0.025 (0.495)	0.065* (0.075)	0.054 (0.137)	0.029 (0.432)	-0.046 (0.208)	-0.037 (0.310)	-0.004 (0.914)
Relative size	0.008 (0.878)	-0.083 (0.151)	-0.219*** (0.000)	-0.167*** (0.002)	-0.070 (0.193)	0.132** (0.015)	0.088 (0.104)	0.085 (0.117)	-0.224*** (0.000)	-0.181*** (0.001)	-0.107** (0.049)
(Bidder) Run-up	0.129*** (0.001)	0.141 (0.145)	0.039 (0.311)	0.088** (0.024)	0.053 (0.173)	0.026 (0.499)	0.049 (0.209)	0.004 (0.917)	0.011 (0.789)	0.022 (0.575)	0.032 (0.416)
(Target) Run-up	-0.133 (0.171)	0.137* (0.056)	-0.028 (0.690)	0.052 (0.468)	0.042 (0.557)	0.347*** (0.000)	0.326*** (0.000)	-0.017 (0.813)	-0.272*** (0.000)	-0.202*** (0.004)	0.042 (0.562)

***, **, and * stand for statistical significance at the 1%, 5%, and 10% levels, respectively.

approach). The indicator variable for the spillover of better governance standards from the bidder to the target equals one if the bidder index is above the median and the target index is below the median (the *positive spillover by law/spillover by control effect*), and is zero otherwise. The indicator variable for the spillover of better governance standards from the target to the bidder (the *bootstrapping effect*) equals one if the bidder index is below the median and the target index is above the median, and is zero otherwise. Alternatively, this variable may indicate the spillover of the bidder low governance standards to the target firm (the *negative spillover by law effect*), if its parameter estimate has the inverse sign. Overall, the indicator variables denote whether a bidding company is likely to improve or worsen its own governance and the governance in a target firm. It should be noted that the median value of each index is measured across all countries in a particular year and both the bidder and target indices are compared to the same median.

Table 5 partitions all M&As by the quality of corporate governance standards. It shows that the majority of cross-border bidders are from countries with superior standards of investor protection. More than 76% of all cross-border bidders are from countries with a shareholder rights index above the median (Panel A). This percentage is even higher (about 93%) when we consider minority shareholder protection (Panel B). Panel C shows that the sample is evenly split between bidders from countries with below- and above-median creditor rights. A similar picture arises for target companies: they tend to be from countries with above-median investor protection. These patterns stand in sharp contrast to those documented by Bris and Cabolis (2008) who find that the majority of bidders and targets are from countries with below-median investor protection. This difference may be due to the sample composition. In contrast to Bris and Cabolis (2008), our sample excludes M&As that involve firms from outside Continental Europe and the United Kingdom. Another rationale for the observed differences is that our classification is based on our dynamic corporate governance indices whereas Bris and Cabolis (2008) use the static LLSV indices.

Table 5 shows that bidders from legal systems with below-median investor protection mainly acquire target firms from systems with above-median legal protection (63.46%). Similarly, target firms from legal systems with below average investor protection tend to sell their shares to foreign acquirers coming from systems with superior legal protection (80.71%).

3.1.4. Other determinants of the bidder and target returns

We consider three categories of additional factors that may influence the bidder and target returns: the characteristics of the bidder and target firms, the features of the takeover deal, and the characteristics of the bidder and target countries.

3.1.4.1. Bidder and target characteristics The bidder characteristics that we control for are firm size, Q-ratio, leverage, cash flow, and preannouncement stock-price run-up. The size of the bidder is included as a proxy for managerial hubris (Roll,

Table 5

Sample composition cross-border acquisitions by quality of the bidder and target corporate governance systems for cross-border acquisitions

Frequency denotes the total number of observations falling into a particular category. Percent denotes the percentage of a particular category's observations within the total sample. Row pct stands for the percentage of a particular category's observations in the total number of observations within the same row. Col pct stands for the percentage of a particular category's observations in the total number of observations within the same column.

Frequency Percent Row pct Col pct		Target firms		
		Below median	Above median	Total
Panel A. Shareholder rights index				
Bidding firms	Below median	49	127	176
		6.65%	17.23%	23.88%
		27.84%	72.16%	176
		19.29%	26.29%	
	Above median	205	356	561
		27.82%	48.30%	76.12%
		36.54%	63.46%	
		80.71%	73.71%	
	Total	254	483	737
		34.46%	65.54%	100.0%
Panel B. Minority shareholder protection index				
Bidding firms	Below median	16	33	49
		2.17%	4.48%	6.65%
		32.65%	67.35%	
		11.85%	5.48%	
	Above median	119	569	688
		16.15%	77.20%	93.35%
		17.30%	82.70%	
		88.15%	94.52%	
	Total	135	602	737
		18.32%	81.68%	100.0%
Panel C. Creditor rights index				
Bidding firms	Below median	154	193	347
		20.90%	26.19%	47.08%
		44.38%	55.62%	
		44.90%	48.98%	
	Above median	189	201	390
		25.64%	27.27%	52.92%
		48.46%	51.54%	
		55.10%	52.02%	
	Total	343	394	737
		46.54%	53.46%	100.0%

1986), as larger acquirers tend to overpay in takeovers (Moeller et al., 2004). Therefore, the bidder returns are expected to decrease with firm size. The bidder Q-ratio is a proxy for the firm's growth potential and quality of internal corporate governance. Lang et al. (1989) and Servaes (1991) document higher returns for bidders with higher Q-ratios. In contrast, Moeller et al. (2004) find a negative relationship between bidder returns and Q-ratio for their sample of M&As from the 1990s. Therefore, the expected effect of the bidder Q-ratio on returns is ambiguous. We also include cash flow and leverage to control for acquisitions driven by free cash flow motives (Jensen, 1986). Bidders with high cash flow and low leverage are more likely to make value-destroying acquisitions. Finally, we include the bidder preannouncement stock-price run-up to control for the bidder's prior stock performance.

The target characteristics that we include as control variables are leverage and cash flow, as a bidder is likely to pay higher premiums for targets with lower leverage and higher cash flows. For the analysis of (public) target CARs, we also include the target Q-ratio and preannouncement stock-price run-up to control for its growth opportunities and prior stock performance, respectively.

3.1.4.2. Deal characteristics Both the theoretical and empirical M&A literature have shown that the following transaction attributes affect the bidder and target takeover returns: the form of and the attitude toward the bid (opposed bids, unopposed tender offers, friendly M&As), the legal status of the target firm (listed vs. privately held), the industry relatedness of the bidding and target firms (a focus vs. diversification strategy of the bidder), the type of acquisition (full vs. partial acquisition), the means of payment (all-cash, all-equity, mixed offer), and the relative deal size.[14] It is argued that the market interprets all these pieces of information as a signal of the quality of the bidding and target firms and of the potential value creation in the takeover, which triggers share price adjustments. Therefore, to capture the effect of this signal we also control for the above deal characteristics in our models.

3.2. Controlling for the selection bias

We recognize that a decision to participate in a cross-border acquisition is an endogenous choice made by the bidding and target firms and these endogeneity issues may affect the conclusions of our analysis. In particular, Rossi and Volpin (2004) find that bidders and targets from countries with high shareholder protection are more likely to be involved in domestic rather than cross-border M&As. Therefore, we expect that a cross-border acquisition involving a bidder or a target from a country with high shareholder protection will occur only if the takeover synergies are sufficiently high to overcome all additional costs arising from integrating with a foreign firm.[15] This

---

[14] For an overview of the evidence on the wealth effect of M&As and its determinants, see Jensen and Ruback (1983), Jarrell et al. (1988), Agrawal and Jaffe (2000), Bruner (2004), and Martynova and Renneboog (2008).

implies a positive relationship between the bidder and target shareholder protection indices and the announcement stock returns.

Therefore, to control for the sample-selection bias, we employ Heckman (1976, 1979) procedure. By applying a Probit analysis to the sample of all European bidding firms involved in domestic and cross-border acquisitions, we estimate the probability that a firm will undertake a cross-border rather than a domestic acquisition. The resulting parameters are used to compute Heckman's λ (inverse Mill's ratio) for each bidding firm in our sample. We subsequently include Heckman's λ as an additional regressor into the regressions on the bidder returns. Similarly, we estimate the probability that a target firm is involved in a cross-border rather than domestic acquisition by computing Heckman's λ and including it into the target returns' regressions. Although the bidder and target selection equations seem very similar, they refer to different flows of foreign direct investments. The bidder equations estimate the determinants of the investment outflow from the country, whereas the target equations estimate the determinants of the investment inflow to the country.

The explanatory variables of the two selection equations (presented in Table 6) are based on previous studies on the determinants of foreign direct investments and international financial integration (see, e.g., Claessens and Schmukler, 2007; Pagano et al., 2002; Sarkissian and Schill, 2004). First, we include the characteristics of the bidding/target firms (size, leverage, cash flow, and Q-ratio) and the nonnegotiated features of the intended takeover (public/private target, industry focus/diversification, the period within the takeover wave). Second, we also include macro variables such as GDP growth, income per capita, and the level of corruption in the bidder/target country. We expect bidding firms to initiate M&As abroad (rather than domestically) when their home countries offer a poor investment environment, which is proxied by low economic growth and high levels of corruption. An underdeveloped M&A market resulting from various obstacles such as takeover-unfriendly regulation may be another reason that motivates firms to acquire foreign targets. Therefore, we also include a proxy variable for the scope of domestic M&A activity in the country. Finally, the impact of the regulatory environment on the decision to acquire abroad is captured by our corporate governance indices.

The estimates of the selection equations of the bidding and target firms reveal interesting results with respect to the impact of the regulatory environment on the flow of cross-border M&A activity (Table 6). In particular, a bidding firm is more likely to make a cross-border acquisition if it is from a country with low standards of shareholder rights. The result supports the view that firms from countries with weak corporate governance regulation are more likely to invest abroad rather than domestically (Benos and Weisbach, 2004; Doidge et al., 2007). We also find that bidders are more likely to acquire firms abroad if minority shareholder protection in their home country is strong. This result is in line with Goergen et al. (2005) who argue that strong protection of minority shareholders

---

[15] For the discussion of additional costs associated with cross-border takeovers see, for example, Dennis et al., (2002) and Moeller and Schlingemann (2005).

Table 6

Heckman sample selection equations for bidding and target firms in cross-border M&As

This table shows the selection equations of sample selection models for the bidding and target firms. The selection equations model the probability that a bidder (target) firm participates in a cross-border (rather than domestic) acquisition. The depended variable equals one if the bidder (target) firm participates in a cross-border takeover, and zero if in a domestic takeover. The definitions of the included variables are given in Appendix A.

	Probability of a BIDDING company acquiring a foreign firm (vs. domestic firm)		Probability of a TARGET company being acquired by a foreign firm (vs. a domestic firm)	
	Coefficient	Pr > Chi-square	Coefficient	Pr > Chi-square
Corporate governance regulation in the firm country				
Shareholder rights index	**−0.3123*****	0.000	**−0.2149***	0.092
Minority shareholder protection index	**0.3945*****	0.009	−0.1311	0.596
Creditor rights index	**0.2804*****	0.000	**0.2962*****	0.000
Firm characteristics				
Q-ratio	**0.0229****	0.022	0.0398	0.174
Leverage	−0.2117	0.590	−0.4936	0.346
Size (log TA)	**0.2159*****	0.000	**0.1949*****	0.000
Cash flow/TA	0.5508	0.362	0.2502	0.770
Deal characteristics				
Public target	**−0.4561****	0.032	-	
Same industry	0.0438	0.720	−0.0274	0.875
1997–1999	0.2326	0.114	**0.5145****	0.019
2000–2001	**0.2987****	0.049	**0.5936****	0.011
Characteristics of the firm's country				
Anticorruption index	−0.1045	0.418	**0.3511*****	0.007
Log GNP per capita	−0.3639	0.522	0.2862	0.284
GDP growth	**−0.1593***	0.078	**0.2707****	0.012
# Domestic acquisitions/ # listed firms 1 year prior	−0.0267	0.218	−0.0400	0.560
Intercept	**−2.9004*****	0.000	**−2.1785*****	0.003
Number of obs.	2271		760	
Pseudo-R^2	21.15%		27.08%	

***, **, and * stand for statistical significance at the 1%, 5%, and 10% levels, respectively.

makes corporate takeovers very costly and hence forces companies to look for potential M&A targets in countries with weaker minority shareholder protection. Strong creditor protection in the home country also has a positive effect on the international acquisition activity. This may follow from the positive relationship between creditor protection and a firm's access to debt financing (LaPorta et al., 1998). Martynova and Renneboog (2007a) show that debt financing is frequently used in cross-border M&As. Therefore, cross-border M&As are more likely to be made by bidders who have access to inexpensive debt capital which prevails in countries with strong creditor rights.

Unsurprisingly, the selection equation for the target firms shows that a target is more likely to sell its shares to a foreign bidder if the standards of shareholder protection in the target country are low and the standards of creditor protection are high.

3.3. Regression results

3.3.1. The bidder returns

3.3.1.1. The impact of corporate governance regulation on the bidder returns We start our analysis with the bidder returns regressions that include the bidder and target corporate governance indices in levels, while controlling for the fact that making a cross-border acquisition is an endogenous decision (selection bias problem). Model 1 of Table 7 shows that the effect of the bidder and target national governance standards on the bidder returns is insignificant. The coefficients remain insignificant in Model 2 after controlling for growth potential, leverage, share price run-up, means of payment and many other characteristics of the deal, the target, the bidder and the countries of the bidder and target. We also fail to find any significant coefficients when we reestimate this model including one of the corporate governance indices at the time (see Models 4-6). Overall, the evidence suggests that, apart from its impact on the decision to acquire a firm abroad (see Section 3.2), corporate governance regulation has no significant effect on the takeover returns to the bidding firm's shareholders.

Most of our results with respect to the control variables are consistent with previous empirical findings (see, e.g., Bris and Cabolis, 2008; Moeller et al., 2004; Starks and Wei, 2005). Specifically, we observe that (i) the bidder size has a significantly negative effect on the bidder returns suggesting that large bidders are more likely to make poor takeover decisions; (ii) the bidder Q-ratio has no significant effect on the bidder returns; (iii) the proxies for free cash flow—the bidder cash flow and leverage—have the expected (but insignificant) impact on the bidder returns (respectively, a negative and positive effect) which indicates that there is little evidence that cross-border acquisitions occur as a result of empire building; (iv) the bidder returns are significantly lower for hostile takeovers suggesting that the bidder shareholder fear overbidding in case of opposition by the target firm; (v) the returns are also lower for acquisitions involving equity payments (signaling overvaluation of the bidder shares), for public targets, for diversifying mergers (leading to a diversification discount), and for full takeovers; (vi) the bidder preannouncement stock-price run-up has a significantly positive effect on the bidder announcement returns; (vii) the bidder returns are also higher when the bidder and target countries are neighbors or belong to the same language group, as both may enhance transparency or induce trust[16]; (viii) the differences in economic development between the bidder and target countries is not correl-

---

[16] This result is interesting as it suggests that acquisitions of companies belonging to similar cultures lead to a higher value creation. The evidence is in spirit of Guiso et al. (2006, 2007) who show that international transactions are more common between firms from countries that display a higher level of cultural similarities.

Table 7

The impact of corporate governance *regulation* on the bidder CARs in cross-border M&As

This table reports the results of the OLS regression of the bidder CARs for the sample of cross-border takeovers. The dependent variable is the bidder CARs [−1, +1]. Variable definitions are given in Appendix A. Seven different specifications are estimated. A Heckman sample selection correction is applied to control for potential biases due to the bidder's endogenous choice of participating in a cross-border (rather than domestic) takeover. For each variable we list the coefficient and the heteroskedasticity-consistent p-value.

	(1)	(2)	(3)	(4)	(5)	(6)	(7)
Corporate governance regulation effect							
(Bidder) Shareholder rights index	0.0017 (0.329)	0.0020 (0.248)	0.0027 (0.253)	0.0029 (0.156)			
(Bidder) Minority shareholder protection index	0.0043 (0.389)	0.0026 (0.771)	0.0022 (0.810)		0.0020 (0.753)		
(Bidder) Creditor rights index	0.0005 (0.726)	0.0012 (0.680)				0.0006 (0.830)	
(Target) Shareholder rights index	0.0021 (0.415)	0.0015 (0.511)	0.0018 (0.618)	0.0011 (0.314)			
(Target) Minority shareholder protection index	−0.0013 (0.357)	−0.0032 (0.229)	−0.0034 (0.216)		−0.0030 (0.118)		
(Target) Creditor rights index	0.0004 (0.796)	0.0014 (0.551)				0.0019 (0.408)	
Bidder and target firms' characteristics							
(Bidder) Q-ratio		−0.0003 (0.689)	−0.0002 (0.753)	−0.0002 (0.745)	−0.0003 (0.664)	−0.0004 (0.552)	−0.0013 (0.323)
(Bidder) Leverage		0.0044 (0.869)	0.0038 (0.883)	0.0029 (0.910)	0.0012 (0.963)	0.0024 (0.928)	0.0028 (0.568)
(Bidder) Size (log TA)		−0.0012** (0.031)	−0.0012*** (0.034)	−0.0012** (0.019)	−0.0009* (0.005)	−0.0009** (0.029)	−0.0018*** (0.006)
(Bidder) Cash flow/TA		−0.0508 (0.326)	−0.0522 (0.309)	−0.0511 (0.318)	−0.0533 (0.299)	−0.0525 (0.306)	−0.0153 (0.780)
(Target) Leverage		−0.0303 (0.702)	−0.0355 (0.653)	−0.0117 (0.883)	−0.0162 (0.839)	−0.0021 (0.979)	−0.0730 (0.127)
(Target) Cash flow/TA		0.0805 (0.569)	0.0724 (0.399)	0.0866 (0.251)	0.0911 (0.241)	0.0945 (0.336)	0.0582 (0.647)
Deal characteristics							
Equity payment		−0.0140 (0.268)	−0.0148 (0.239)	−0.0150 (0.232)	−0.0153 (0.223)	−0.0144 (0.253)	−0.0163 (0.122)

	(1)	(2)	(3)	(4)	(5)	(6)	(7)
Public target		−0.0077 (0.459)	−0.0065 (0.521)	−0.0069 (0.491)	−0.0055 (0.585)	−0.0043 (0.663)	0.0034 (0.924)
Hostile bid		**−0.0302** (0.021)	**−0.0311** (0.015)	**−0.0314*** (0.010)	**−0.0291** (0.029)	**−0.0269*** (0.062)	**−0.0419*** (0.006)
M&A of 100%		−0.0013 (0.892)	−0.0009 (0.918)	−0.0012 (0.897)	0.0003 (0.970)	0.0012 (0.895)	0.0016 (0.556)
Diversification		−0.0013 (0.886)	−0.0012 (0.894)	−0.0009 (0.916)	0.0002 (0.977)	0.0006 (0.945)	0.0007 (0.935)
Relative size		0.0238 (0.277)	0.0232 (0.287)	0.0240 (0.267)	0.0246 (0.257)	0.0242 (0.263)	0.0242 (0.262)
(Bidder) Run-up		**0.0352*** (0.009)	**0.0361*** (0.007)	**0.0360*** (0.006)	**0.0358*** (0.007)	**0.0354*** (0.007)	**0.0360*** (0.006)
Bidder and target country characteristics							
Same language group		**0.0010*** (0.064)	**0.0012** (0.031)	**0.0011** (0.036)	**0.0012** (0.048)	0.0008 (0.107)	**0.0026** (0.012)
Common border		**0.0017** (0.015)	**0.0021** (0.020)	**0.0022** (0.032)	**0.0024*** (0.018)	**0.0014*** (0.071)	**0.0043** (0.017)
(Bidder) log GNP per capita		0.0046 (0.316)	0.0038 (0.415)	0.0036 (0.422)	0.0038 (0.385)	0.0043 (0.368)	0.0175 (0.211)
Difference (Bidder-target) log GNP per capita		0.0020 (0.532)	0.0012 (0.701)	0.0013 (0.655)	0.0012 (0.629)	0.0024 (0.828)	0.0034 (0.502)
(Target) Anticorruption index		0.0003 (0.788)	0.0002 (0.872)	0.0004 (0.667)	0.0004 (0.654)	0.0002 (0.988)	0.0008 (0.428)
Intercept	−0.0147 (0.426)	−0.0190 (0.554)	−0.0088 (0.750)	−0.0104 (0.635)	−0.0029 (0.917)	−0.0063 (0.679)	0.0023 (0.753)
Heckman λ (inverse Mill's ratios)	**−0.0034*** (0.002)	**−0.0032*** (0.005)	**−0.0032*** (0.004)	**−0.0033*** (0.002)	**−0.0032*** (0.005)	**−0.0034*** (0.004)	**−0.0033*** (0.003)
Number of obs.	641	641	641	641	641	641	641
Adjusted-R^2 (%)	3.40	5.33	4.67	5.55	4.91	4.85	4.80

*, **, and *** stand for statistical significance at the 1%, 5%, and 10% levels, respectively.

ated to the bidder returns; and (ix) the level of corruption in the target country has an insignificant effect on the bidder returns.

All estimated models reveal that Heckman's λ is significant confirming that ignoring the selection bias may induce estimation problems. To rule out any further possibility that our results are driven by the endogeneity of the control variables, we also reestimate Model 7 excluding the corporate governance indices. Our results are upheld.

3.3.1.2. The impact of corporate governance spillover effects on the bidder returns

Whereas Table 7 concentrates on the impact of corporate governance *regulation* on the bidder returns in cross-border acquisitions, we now switch to the question whether potential corporate governance *spillover* is reflected in the bidder returns. We do not report the parameter estimates of the control variables in Table 8, as they are similar to those reported in Table 7. As in previous sections, we correct the models of Table 8 for sample-selection biases. We now primarily focus on the potential improvement (or deterioration) of bidder and target firms corporate governance standards as a result of the takeover and its effect on the bidder returns.

In Panel A of Table 8, we measure the scope for potential corporate governance spillover by the differences between the bidder and target corporate governance indices. In line with Bris and Cabolis (2008), the parameter coefficient shows that the shareholder-rights difference has a positive, albeit insignificant, effect on the bidder CARs. A significantly positive coefficient would be consistent with the *spillover by law hypothesis* which states that the improvement in the corporate governance of the target firm via the transfer of the bidder governance standards is a source of synergistic gains in corporate takeovers.

The insignificance of the coefficients may be due to the fact that not only bidding companies from countries with superior corporate governance standards may benefit from cross-border M&As but also bidders from countries with low investor protection. These may bootstrap their corporate governance standards to a higher level, namely that of the target firm. To disentangle the different directions of the spillover effect, we apply an indicator-variable approach. Panel B of Table 8 reports the results of the regressions that include an indicator-variable capturing M&As involving a bidder with corporate governance standards above the median and a target with standards below the median. We also include an indicator variable that captures the opposite case: a bidder with low standards and a target with high investor protection. While the first variable is a proxy for the improvement of the target firms' corporate governance (the *positive spillover by law and the spillover by control hypotheses*), the second variable is a proxy for the improvement of the bidder corporate governance (the *bootstrapping effect*) or for the dilution of the governance of the target if the bidder imposes its lower standards (the *negative spillover by law hypothesis*).

The regression results from Models 1–4 (Panel B) show that the coefficient on the indicator-variable capturing the improvement in the target shareholder rights is positive

Table 8

The impact of the corporate governance *spillover effects* on the bidder CARs in cross-border M&As

This table reports the results of the OLS regression of the bidder CARs for the sample of cross-border takeovers. The dependent variable is the bidder CARs [−1, +1]. Variable definitions are given in Appendix A. Six different model specifications are estimated. A Heckman sample selection correction is applied to control for potential biases due to the bidder endogenous choice of participating in a cross-border (rather than domestic) takeover. We do not report the parameter estimates of the control variables, as they are similar to those reported in Table 7. The indicator "Yes" denotes that a particular control variable is included in the regression and "No" that it is not. Panel A reports the regression estimates of the *differences*-approach while Panel B reports the estimates of the indicator-variable approach. For each variable we list the coefficient and the heteroskedasticity-consistent *p*-value. The number of observations in each regression is 641.

Panel A. Differences-approach	(1)	(2)	(3)	(4)	(5)	(6)
Corporate governance regulation effect						
(Bidder) Shareholder rights index	0.0012 (0.478)	0.0047 (0.242)	0.0055 (0.145)	0.0042 (0.231)		
(Bidder) Minority shareholder protection index	0.0006 (0.368)	0.0019 (0.934)	0.0019 (0.852)		0.0020 (0.753)	
(Bidder) Creditor rights index	0.0001 (0.672)	0.0026 (0.504)				0.0025 (0.512)
Corporate governance spillover effect						
Diff. (Bidder-target) Shareholder rights index	0.0005 (0.725)	0.0007 (0.777)	0.0001 (0.943)	0.0001 (0.914)		
Diff. (Bidder-target) Minority shareholder protection index	0.0013 (0.757)	0.0035 (0.618)	0.0041 (0.555)		0.0040 (0.381)	
Diff. (Bidder-target) Creditor rights index	−0.0004 (0.796)	−0.0014 (0.551)				−0.0019 (0.409)
Characteristics of the bidder and target, the M&A deal, and the bidder and target countries	No	Yes	Yes	Yes	Yes	Yes
Intercept	Yes	Yes	Yes	Yes	Yes	Yes
Heckman λ (inverse Mill's ratio)	Yes	Yes	Yes	Yes	Yes	Yes
Adjusted-R^2 (%)	1.68	4.82	4.67	4.55	3.91	3.85

(Continued)

Table 8 (*Continued*)

Panel B. Indicator-variable approach	(1)	(2)	(3)	(4)	(5)	(6)
Corporate governance regulation effect						
(Bidder) Shareholder rights index	0.0001 (0.782)	0.0014 (0.557)	0.0009 (0.652)	0.0013 (0.649)		
(Bidder) Minority shareholder protection index	0.0046 (0.395)	0.0022 (0.815)	0.0014 (0.879)		0.0016 (0.783)	
(Bidder) Creditor rights index	0.0020 (0.341)	0.0025 (0.478)				0.0017 (0.624)
Positive spillover by law/spillover by control hypotheses (spillover form bidder to target)						
(Target) Shareholder rights improvement	**0.0173***** (0.009)	**0.0166***** (0.008)	**0.0153***** (0.008)	**0.0148*****		
(Target) Minority shareholder protection improvement	−0.0014 (0.832)	0.0088 (0.384)	0.0086 (0.389)		0.0055 (0.566)	
(Target) Creditor rights improvement	−0.0075 (0.344)	0.0014 (0.912)				−0.0017 (0.886)
Bootstrapping hypothesis (spillover from target to bidder)						
(Bidder) Shareholder rights improvement	**0.0115**** (0.036)	0.0041 (0.218)	0.0042 (0.272)	0.0024 (0.589)		
(Bidder) Minority shareholder protection improvement	−0.0001 (0.990)	0.0050 (0.720)	0.0036 (0.792)		0.0071 (0.591)	
(Bidder) Creditor rights improvement	−0.0013 (0.864)	0.0068 (0.588)				0.0058 (0.642)
Characteristics of the bidder and target, the M&A deal, and the bidder and target countries	No	Yes	Yes	Yes	Yes	Yes
Intercept	Yes	Yes	Yes	Yes	Yes	Yes
Heckman λ (inverse Mill's ratio)	Yes	Yes	Yes	Yes	Yes	Yes
Adjusted-R^2 (%)	2.13	5.87	4.65	5.71	4.54	4.17

***, **, and * stand for statistical significance at 1%, 5%, and 10% levels, respectively.

and statistically significant (at the 1% level). This is consistent with the *positive spillover by law* (and *spillover by control*) predictions that acquisitions of firms with poor shareholder orientation by firms with a strong shareholder orientation generate abnormal returns for the bidder through the imposition of better corporate governance on the target.

Model 1 also shows that the bidder returns are positive and significant when the target has a stronger shareholder orientation than the bidder. The fact that the bidder shareholders react positively to this type of deal is congruent with the fact that the bidding firm may adopt a higher level of shareholder orientation on a voluntary basis.[17] This increased shareholder orientation is then anticipated by the bidder shareholders, as reflected in the announcement returns. However, the significance of this *bootstrapping* effect disappears after taking into account the characteristics of the target, the bidder, the deal and countries of the bidder and target.

3.3.2. The target returns

3.3.2.1. The impact of corporate governance regulation on the target returns   We first focus on whether corporate governance standards in the bidder and target countries have a significant effect on the target returns (after controlling for the sample-selection bias described in Section 3.2). Table 9 shows that the target returns strongly increase with the quality of shareholder protection in the target country. The coefficient on the target shareholder rights index is positive and statistically significant in all model specifications. The evidence suggests that target companies from countries with better shareholder protection are able to extract higher premiums from the bidding firms, which is also consistent with Rossi and Volpin (2004) but not with Bris and Cabolis (2008).

When we focus on minority shareholder protection by excluding shareholder and creditor protection indices (Model 5), minority shareholder protection in the target country is still positively associated with the target returns. This implies that powerful minority shareholders are able to extract an additional premium in the deal. Still, this finding is not corroborated when other different measures of investor protection are included in the model.

The degree of shareholder orientation in the bidder country has a positive effect on the target returns but only in Model 1 of Table 9. This lack of a consistent significant impact of the bidder shareholder protection on the target returns is also documented by Rossi and Volpin (2004). They conclude that bidders from countries with better shareholder protection do not pay more for cross-border M&As than bidders from other countries. Overall, our evidence suggests that the corporate governance regime in the target (but not the bidder) country positively affects the target shareholders returns.

---

[17] This result does not support the negative *spillover by law hypothesis* as under this hypothesis we would expect negative or at best insignificant bidder returns.

Table 9

The impact of corporate governance *regulation* on the target CARs in cross-border M&As

This table reports the results of the OLS regression of the target CARs for the sample of cross-border takeovers. The dependent variable is the target CARs $[-1, +1]$. Variable definitions are given in Appendix A. Seven different model specifications are estimated. A Heckman sample selection correction is applied to control for potential biases due to the target endogenous choice of participating in a cross-border (rather than domestic) takeover. For each variable we show the heteroskedasticity-consistent p-value.

	(1)	(2)	(3)	(4)	(5)	(6)	(7)
Corporate governance regulation effect							
(Bidder) Shareholder rights index	**0.0169*** (0.087)	0.0069 (0.324)	0.0029 (0.434)	0.0026 (0.659)			
(Bidder) Minority shareholder protection index	0.0070 (0.733)	0.0254 (0.193)	0.0240 (0.542)		0.0119 (0.569)		
(Bidder) Creditor rights index	−0.0090 (0.202)	−0.0103 (0.354)				−0.0107 (0.332)	
(Target) Shareholder rights index	**0.0442*** (0.003)	**0.0478** (0.015)	**0.0508*** (0.008)	**0.0505*** (0.001)			
(Target) Minority shareholder protection index	0.0075 (0.771)	0.0015 (0.576)	0.0002 (0.596)		**0.0557*** (0.005)		
(Target) Creditor rights index	0.0013 (0.890)	0.0016 (0.891)				0.0010 (0.930)	
Bidder and target firms' characteristics							
(Bidder) Q-ratio		−0.0130 (0.212)	−0.0131 (0.196)	−0.0128 (0.198)	−0.0122 (0.232)	−0.0109 (0.322)	−0.0111 (0.296)
(Bidder) Leverage		0.0655 (0.777)	0.0437 (0.844)	0.0041 (0.984)	−0.0674 (0.754)	0.0903 (0.686)	0.0847 (0.697)
(Bidder) Size (log TA)		−0.0041 (0.759)	−0.0036 (0.785)	−0.0029 (0.822)	−0.0021 (0.874)	−0.0036 (0.798)	−0.0035 (0.802)
(Bidder) Cash flow/TA		−0.2838 (0.343)	−0.3063 (0.289)	−0.3223 (0.237)	−0.3135 (0.279)	−0.2952 (0.323)	−0.2973 (0.307)
(Target) Leverage		−0.0169 (0.856)	−0.0018 (0.984)	0.0190 (0.832)	0.0429 (0.643)	−0.0034 (0.971)	0.0174 (0.851)
(Target) Cash flow/TA		0.1026 (0.559)	0.1377 (0.431)	0.1522 (0.377)	0.1969 (0.266)	0.1214 (0.502)	0.1681 (0.350)
(Target) Q-ratio		−0.0018 (0.393)	−0.0018 (0.382)	−0.0016 (0.457)	−0.0015 (0.489)	−0.0015 (0.499)	−0.0015 (0.481)

(Continued)

Table 9 (Continued)

	(1)	(2)	(3)	(4)	(5)	(6)	(7)
Deal characteristics							
Equity payment		−**0.0929*** (0.078)	−**0.0938*** (0.069)	−**0.0942*** (0.065)	−**0.0989*** (0.054)	−**0.1054*** (0.039)	−**0.1067**** (0.033)
Hostile bid		0.0892 (0.149)	**0.1012*** (0.093)	**0.1021*** (0.086)	**0.0996*** (0.099)	0.0895 (0.142)	**0.1021*** (0.086)
M&A of 100%		**0.1408**** (0.015)	**0.1430**** (0.011)	**0.1452***** (0.009)	**0.1545***** (0.005)	**0.1648***** (0.001)	**0.1682***** (0.001)
Diversification		0.0832 (0.264)	0.0864 (0.253)	0.0862 (0.250)	0.0864 (0.253)	0.0806 (0.170)	0.0841 (0.257)
Relative size		−0.0932 (0.221)	−0.0929 (0.219)	−0.0878 (0.234)	−0.0904 (0.227)	−0.0996 (0.175)	−0.0989 (0.174)
(Target) Run-up		−0.1043 (0.177)	−0.1166 (0.123)	−0.1160 (0.120)	−0.1082 (0.150)	−0.0791 (0.263)	−0.0894 (0.197)
Bidder and target country characteristics							
Same language		0.0117 (0.342)	0.0094 (0.760)	0.0076 (0.563)	0.0084 (0.702)	0.0009 (0.987)	0.0214 (0.426)
Common border		−0.0056 (0.572)	−0.0038 (0.718)	−0.0043 (0.745)	−0.0045 (0.711)	−0.0066 (0.424)	−0.0020 (0.756)
(Target) log GNP per capita		−0.0018 (0.342)	−0.0016 (0.486)	−0.0021 (0.505)	−0.0018 (0.280)	−0.0012 (0.798)	−0.0036 (0.222)
Difference (Bidder-target) log GNP per capita		0.0108 (0.308)	0.0112 (0.276)	0.0118 (0.268)	0.0118 (0.243)	0.0102 (0.405)	0.0215 (0.155)
(Target) Anticorruption index		**0.0033*** (0.082)	**0.0042*** (0.078)	**0.0040*** (0.064)	**0.0044*** (0.057)	**0.0025*** (0.128)	**0.0058*** (0.018)
Intercept	−0.1060 (0.307)	−0.0392 (0.855)	−0.0795 (0.675)	−0.1311 (0.267)	−0.1030 (0.569)	0.1026 (0.189)	0.0619 (0.201)
Heckman λ (inverse Mill's ratios)	**0.0027***** (0.000)	**0.0018***** (0.000)	**0.0018***** (0.000)	**0.0017***** (0.000)	**0.0018***** (0.000)	**0.0022***** (0.000)	**0.0031***** (0.000)
Number of obs.	296	296	296	296	296	296	296
Adjusted-R^2 (%)	10.21	14.97	15.03	13.76	13.36	8.11	9.15

***, **, and * stand for statistical significance at 1%, 5%, and 10% levels, respectively.

As to the control variables, most of our findings are in line with those of other empirical studies on cross-border M&As (see, e.g., Dewenter, 1995; Harris and Ravenscraft, 1991). In particular, we observe that target returns are significantly higher in hostile takeovers and in full takeovers, and are significantly lower when equity is used as a means of payment and when corruption in the target country is high.

3.3.2.2. The impact of corporate governance spillover effects on the target returns
Whereas Table 9 examines the impact of the national *regulation* on the target returns, we now analyze in Table 10 the impact of corporate governance *spillover*. Panel A of Table 10 reports that the target returns increase with the scope of potential shareholder protection spillover as measured by the differences between the bidder and target shareholder rights indices. When a bidding firm is from a country with higher shareholder protection than the target, the bidder (better) corporate governance standard will be imposed—by law in case of a full acquisition—on the target firm (the *positive spillover by law effect*) which leads to significantly higher target announcement returns. Similarly, in case of a partial acquisition, the bidder firm may voluntarily impose its better shareholder protection standards on the target (the *spillover by control effect*) which leads to higher target shareholder returns. This implies that part of the synergies in cross-border acquisitions result from corporate governance improvements at the target. As the target shareholders anticipate this, they are able to claim part of the expected value improvement given that they are sellers in a strong bargaining position.

Moreover, when we differentiate between the cases where the bidder is subject to stronger (weaker) shareholder protection than the target (Panel B of Table 10), we find further confirmation of our result. Target returns increase when there is a positive spillover effect from the bidder to the target, that is, when the bidder is from a country with a stronger shareholder orientation. These results yield support to our *positive spillover by law* and *spillover by control hypotheses*. Interestingly, the evidence does not support the *negative spillover by law hypothesis*: in takeovers by bidders from countries with poorer standards, the target returns are not significantly lower.

3.4. Additional analyses

3.4.1. Does a change in the target nationality matter?

Bris and Cabolis (2008) emphasize that target companies benefit from corporate governance spillovers only when the bidder acquires 100% of the target firm's shares, that is, when the target firm de facto changes its nationality (*spillover by law hypothesis*). In case of a full acquisition, the target firm becomes a part of the bidding firm and hence will have to comply with the corporate governance regulation in the bidder country. To further test this hypothesis, we split our sample into full and partial acquisitions and we reestimate the models from Tables 8 and 10. Table 11 shows that, irrespective of the type

Table 10

The impact of the corporate governance *spillover effect* on the target CARs in cross-border M&As

This table reports the results of the OLS regression of the target CARs for the sample of cross-border takeovers. The dependent variable is the target CARs [−1, +1]. Variable definitions are given in Appendix A. Six different model specifications are estimated. A Heckman sample selection correction is applied to control for potential biases due to the target endogenous choice of participating in a cross-border (rather than domestic) takeover. We do not report the parameter estimates of the control variables, as they are similar to the ones reported in Table 9. The indicator "Yes" denotes that a particular control variable is included in the regression and "No" that it is not. Panel A reports the regression estimates of a *differences*-approach while Panel B reports the estimates of an *indicator*-variable approach. Variable definitions are given in Appendix A. For each variable we show the heteroskedasticity-consistent *p*-value. The number of observations in each regression is 296.

Panel A. Differences-approach	(1)	(2)	(3)	(4)	(5)	(6)
Corporate governance regulation effect						
(Target) Shareholder rights index	**0.0612*** (0.007)	**0.0435** (0.020)	**0.0463** (0.013)	**0.0309** (0.018)		
(Target) Minority shareholder protection index	0.0146 (0.632)	0.0261 (0.515)	0.0292 (0.445)		**0.0402** (0.025)	
(Target) Creditor rights index	0.0041 (0.701)	0.0018 (0.883)				0.0005 (0.968)
Corporate governance spillover effect						
Diff. (Bidder-target) Shareholder rights index	**0.0169** (0.017)	**0.0189*** (0.007)	**0.0168*** (0.002)	**0.0113*** (0.007)		
Diff. (Bidder-target) Minority shareholder protection index	0.0070 (0.733)	0.0159 (0.529)	0.0096 (0.670)		0.0016 (0.928)	
Diff. (Bidder-target) Creditor rights index	−0.0089 (0.202)	−0.0095 (0.224)				−0.0092 (0.228)
Characteristics of the bidder and target, the M&A deal, and the bidder and target countries	No	Yes	Yes	Yes	Yes	Yes
Intercept	Yes	Yes	Yes	Yes	Yes	Yes
Heckman λ (inverse Mill's ratio)	Yes	Yes	Yes	Yes	Yes	Yes

	(1)	(2)	(3)	(4)	(5)	(6)
Adjusted-R^2 (%)	10.18	14.83	14.75	14.08	13.70%	10.02%
Panel B. Indicator-variable approach						
Corporate governance regulation effect						
(Target) Shareholder rights index	**0.0501***** (0.003)	**0.0295**** (0.022)	**0.0245**** (0.030)	**0.0144**** (0.032)	**0.0246**** (0.029)	
(Target) Minority shareholder protection index	0.0076 (0.794)	0.0231 (0.573)	0.0142 (0.716)			
(Target) Creditor rights index	0.0117 (0.247)	0.0026 (0.824)				0.0041 (0.700)
Positive spillover by law/spillover by control hypotheses (spillover form bidder to target)						
(Target) Shareholder rights improvement	**0.0107***** (0.007)	**0.0111***** (0.004)	**0.0177***** (0.000)	**0.0229***** (0.004)		
(Target) Minority shareholder protection improvement	0.0301 (0.415)	0.0264 (0.508)	0.0248 (0.539)		0.0256 (0.519)	
(Target) Creditor rights improvement	0.0673 (0.889)	0.0729 (0.105)				0.0597 (0.171)
Bootstrapping hypothesis (spillover from target to bidder)						
(Bidder) Shareholder rights improvement	−0.0171 (0.605)	−0.0069 (0.854)	−0.0125 (0.741)	−0.0125 (0.733)		
(Bidder) Minority shareholder protection improvement	0.0183 (0.584)	0.0109 (0.774)	0.0110 (0.774)		−0.0086 (0.816)	
(Bidder) Creditor rights improvement	0.0941 (0.953)	0.1104 (0.850)				0.1043 (0.101)
Characteristics of the bidder and target, the M&A deal, and the bidder and target countries	No	Yes	Yes	Yes	Yes	Yes
Intercept	Yes	Yes	Yes	Yes	Yes	Yes
Heckman λ (inverse Mill's ratio)	Yes	Yes	Yes	Yes	Yes	Yes
Adjusted-R^2 (%)	11.71	15.31	15.53	14.77	12.99	10.48

***, **, and * stand for statistical significance at 1%, 5%, and 10% levels, respectively.

Table 11

The impact of corporate governance *spillover* on the bidder CARs in full and partial acquisitions

This table reports the results of the OLS regression of the bidder CARs for the samples of full and partial cross-border takeovers. The dependent variable is the bidder CARs $[-1, +1]$. Variable definitions are given in Appendix A. Four different model specifications are estimated. A Heckman sample selection correction is applied to control for potential biases due to the bidder endogenous choice of participating in a cross-border (rather than domestic) takeover. We do not report the parameter estimates of the control variables, as they are similar to the ones reported in Table 7. The indicator "Yes" denotes that a particular control variable is included in the regression and "No" that it is not. For each variable we show the heteroskedasticity-consistent p-value.

	M&A of 100% (full acquisitions)				M&A of less than 100% (partial acquisitions)			
	(1)	(2)	(3)	(4)	(1)	(2)	(3)	(4)
Corporate governance regulation effect								
(Bidder) Shareholder protection index	−0.0005	−0.0006	0.0004		0.0030	0.0017	0.0000	
	(0.986)	(0.734)	(0.942)		(0.422)	(0.518)	(0.995)	
(Bidder) Minority shareholder protection index	0.0009	0.0011		0.0019	0.0029	0.0036		0.0036
	(0.413)	(0.450)		(0.819)	(0.559)	(0.624)		(0.741)
(Bidder) Creditor protection index	0.0000	0.0003			0.0034	0.0022		
	(0.987)	(0.529)			(0.125)	(0.527)		
Positive spillover by law/spillover by control hypotheses (spillover form bidder to target)								
(Target) Shareholder rights improvement	0.0134*	0.0178**	0.0170**		0.0130*	0.0137**	0.0140*	
	(0.081)	(0.029)	(0.022)		(0.065)	(0.037)	(0.074)	
(Target) Minority shareholder protection improvement	0.0059	0.0132		0.0097	−0.0064	0.0032		−0.0035
	(0.639)	(0.378)		(0.487)	(0.428)	(0.728)		(0.968)
(Target) Creditor rights improvement	−0.0128	−0.0056			−0.0034	−0.0014		
	(0.380)	(0.752)			(0.681)	(0.904)		
Bootstrapping hypothesis (spillover from target to bidder)								
(Bidder) Shareholder rights improvement	0.0128**	0.0122	0.0107		0.0217**	0.0290**	0.0285**	
	(0.041)	(0.206)	(0.267)		(0.014)	(0.041)	(0.028)	
(Bidder) Minority shareholder protection improvement	0.0006	0.0041		0.0049	−0.0022	0.0013		0.0076
	(0.968)	(0.829)		(0.786)	(0.788)	(0.927)		(0.556)

(Bidder) Creditor rights improvement	−0.0011	0.0032			0.0062	0.0034		
	(0.447)	(0.860)			(0.438)	(0.769)		
Characteristics of the bidder and target, the M&A deal, and the bidder and target countries	No	Yes	Yes	Yes	No	Yes	Yes	Yes
Intercept	Yes	Yes	Yes	Yes	Yes	Yes	Yes	Yes
Heckman λ (inverse Mill's ratio)	Yes	Yes	Yes	Yes	Yes	Yes	Yes	Yes
Number of observations	292	292	292	292	356	356	356	356
Adjusted-R^2 (%)	2.05	4.05	4.07	3.27	3.47	4.29	5.42	3.59

***, **, and * stand for statistical significance at 1%, 5%, and 10% levels, respectively.

of the takeover (full or partial), bidding firms from countries with above-median shareholder protection experience significantly higher returns when they acquire target firms from countries with below-median shareholder protection. The evidence supports the *spillover by control hypothesis*: a well-governed bidding firm improves the governance at the target firm in which it holds a majority stake such that the target firm's assets are used more efficiently and create more shareholder value.

Table 11 also unveils another interesting result: bidder returns are also higher in a partial acquisition involving a bidder from a country with below-median shareholder protection and a target from a country with above-median shareholder protection. We interpret the positive coefficients as evidence consistent with the *bootstrapping hypothesis*: poorly governed firms acquire well-governed firms to credibly bootstrap themselves to better corporate governance standards. They bootstrap the quality of their corporate governance standards by (voluntary) adhering to the higher shareholder protection of the target firm. Given that the nationality of the target firm does not change, and that part of the equity of the target firm is still held by its (old) shareholders, the bidder may feel pressurized by the target minority shareholders or voluntary decide to emulate the high corporate standards in the country of the target firm. This is reflected in the bidder returns.

We also perform the analysis of the target returns for the subsamples of full and partial acquisitions in Table 12. We observe that partitioning our sample does not materially change our original results as the *positive spillover by law hypothesis* (full acquisitions) and the *spillover by control hypothesis* (partial acquisitions) are upheld. Thus, the target returns increase with the scope of the potential corporate-governance improvement irrespective of the degree of control change (full vs. partial takeovers): acquisitions by bidders with stronger shareholder protection create more value than other types of acquisitions irrespective of the takeover type (full or partial).

3.4.2. The bidder returns and the decision to participate in a takeover

In Section 3.2, we have discussed the potential endogeneity problem associated with the bidder and target decision to participate in cross-border M&As and have corrected for this by using Heckman's λ. While Heckman's λ allows us to control for the differences in cross-border and domestic acquisitions, this still ignores the fact that firms involved in a takeover (be it a domestic or cross-border one) may be different from firms that stayed clear of the takeover process. Factors such as financial constraints, growth opportunities, and share price performance (most of which are likely to be associated with corporate governance regulation) are likely to be important determinants of the bidder decision (not) to participate in a takeover. In other words, we may observe fewer takeovers by bidders from countries with weak corporate governance regulation (in terms of both (minority) shareholder and creditor protection). To control for this potential bias, we estimate yet another Heckman's λ. Applying a Probit analysis on the sample of all European public firms (with data available in

Table 12

The impact of corporate governance *spillover* on the target CARs in full and partial acquisitions

This table reports the results of the OLS regression of the target CARs for the samples of full and partial cross-border takeovers. The dependent variable is the target CARs $[-1, +1]$. Variable definitions are given in Appendix A. Four different model specifications are estimated. A Heckman sample selection correction is applied to control for potential biases due to the target endogenous choice of participating in a cross-border (rather than domestic) takeover. We do not report the parameter estimates of the control variables, as they are similar to the ones reported in Table 9. The indicator "Yes" denotes that a particular control variable is included in the regression and "No" that it is not. For each variable we show the heteroskedasticity-consistent *p*-value.

	M&A of 100% (full acquisitions)				M&A of less than 100% (partial acquisitions)			
	(1)	(2)	(3)	(4)	(1)	(2)	(3)	(4)
Corporate governance regulation effect								
(Bidder) Shareholder protection index	0.0439** (0.021)	0.0261* (0.073)	0.0377** (0.036)		0.0376 (0.035)	0.0239 (0.050)	0.0400 (0.022)	
(Bidder) Minority shareholder protection index		0.0159 (0.818)		0.0115** (0.042)	0.0174 (0.398)	-0.0039 (0.926)		0.0204 (0.075)
(Bidder) Creditor protection index	0.0084 (0.567)	-0.0014 (0.928)			0.0098 (0.342)	0.0100 (0.484)		
Positive spillover by law/spillover by control hypotheses (spillover form bidder to target)								
(Target) Shareholder rights improvement	0.0356*** (0.001)	0.0198** (0.045)	0.0173** (0.029)		0.0266** (0.043)	0.0194** (0.048)	0.0226** (0.034)	
(Target) Minority shareholder protection improvement	0.0333 (0.290)	0.0516 (0.314)		-0.0235 (0.715)	-0.0019 (0.952)	-0.0111 (0.768)		-0.0329 (0.448)
(Target) Creditor rights improvement	0.0962 (0.097)	0.0929 (0.122)			0.0179 (0.657)	-0.0308 (0.587)		
Bootstrapping hypothesis (spillover from target to bidder)								
(Bidder) Shareholder rights improvement	-0.0059 (0.896)	-0.0141 (0.765)	-0.0072 (0.878)		-0.0284 (0.427)	-0.0272 (0.658)	-0.0214 (0.673)	
(Bidder) Minority shareholder protection improvement	0.0143 (0.757)	0.0037 (0.938)		-0.0049 (0.917)	0.0259 (0.465)	0.0250 (0.672)		-0.0207 (0.674)

(Continued)

Table 12 (*Continued*)

	M&A of 100% (full acquisitions)				M&A of less than 100% (partial acquisitions)			
	(1)	(2)	(3)	(4)	(1)	(2)	(3)	(4)
(Bidder) Creditor rights improvement	0.0432 (0.356)	0.0454 (0.408)			0.0037 (0.919)	−0.0466 (0.409)		
Characteristics of the bidder and target, the M&A deal, and the bidder and target countries	No	Yes	Yes	Yes	No	Yes	Yes	Yes
Intercept	Yes	Yes	Yes	Yes	Yes	Yes	Yes	Yes
Heckman λ (inverse Mill's ratio)	Yes	Yes	Yes	Yes	Yes	Yes	Yes	Yes
Number of observations	121	121	121	121	72	72	72	72
Adjusted-R^2 (%)	12.13	19.05	18.34	17.14	13.73	18.92	20.14	20.50

***, **, and * stand for statistical significance at 1%, 5%, and 10% levels, respectively.

Amadeus and DataStream), we estimate the probability that a firm will undertake an acquisition.[18]

We perform two tests of the significance of this censoring problem. First, in the regression analysis of the bidder returns, we include the new Heckman's λ instead of the Heckman's λ estimated based on the equation that predicts a cross-border bidder. We find that the null hypothesis that the new Heckman's λ is insignificant cannot be rejected. This suggests that this type of sample-selection bias is not a significant problem in our sample and hence is not likely to cloud our estimation procedure. Second, we also reestimate our regressions by including both the initial (cross-border takeover) Heckman's λ and the new one (related to the general M&A decision). We find that whereas the former is still significant, the new Heckman's λ remains insignificant.

3.4.3. Means of payment effect of the offer

Starks and Wei (2005) hypothesize that the means of payment has a significant impact on the premiums paid in cross-border acquisitions. The argument is the following: when target shareholders accept equity in an all-equity or mixed offer, they remain involved in the merged firm and will demand additional compensation when the bidding firm is from a country with low shareholder protection. Thus, they require a higher premium to make up for the increased risk exposure due to the poor governance standards of the bidder (and hence the merged firm if the bidder does not voluntarily bootstrap its governance standards). Thus, the takeover premium should be decreasing in the corporate governance quality of the bidding firm. Although our analyses include a variable capturing the means of payment, we reestimate our models for subsamples of all-equity payment/mixed offers, and of all-cash offers. Unlike Starks and Wei (2005), we find that our results regarding the spillover by law and the bootstrapping hypotheses do not depend on the means of payment.

3.4.4. Further sensitivity tests

Our results are also robust to the following alternative specifications: (i) we measure abnormal returns over alternative event windows such as $[-5, +5]$ and $[-60, +60]$; (ii) we employ industry-adjusted characteristics of bidding and target firms such as Q-ratio, leverage, size, and cash flow; (iii) we control for both bidder and target collateral (the fixed assets) as a proxy for financial takeover synergies and access to debt financing; (iv) we include year and industry fixed effects; (v) we control for the bidder toehold in the target company accumulated prior to the initial takeover bid; and (vi) we control for the stock market "bubble" period (1998–1999).

---

[18] The regression results are not reported but available from the authors upon request.

4. Conclusion

We demonstrate that differences between the bidder and target corporate governance standards have an important impact on the returns from cross-border mergers and acquisitions. To proxy for the quality of corporate governance in the countries of the target and the bidder, we have developed with the help of 150 lawyers in 32 countries time-varying corporate governance indices capturing the changes in corporate governance regulation over the past 15 years. The indices cover three dimensions of corporate governance: shareholder rights, minority shareholder rights, and creditor rights, while also embedding the efficiency of the judicial systems.

In a full takeover, the corporate governance standards of the bidder may be imposed on the target. When the bidder is from a country with stronger shareholder orientation, part of the total synergy value of the takeover may result from the fact that the stronger shareholder focus of the acquirer may generate additional returns due to better management of the target assets. We call this the *positive spillover by law hypothesis*. Given that this future value creation can be anticipated at the takeover announcement, the abnormal returns will reflect this potential. We expect that both the bidder and target firms share the returns from improved corporate governance (improved shareholder rights protection) and that their relative bargaining power determines how these returns are shared. Our empirical analysis corroborates the *positive spillover by law hypothesis*: the better the bidder corporate governance standards, the higher are the bidder and target takeover announcement returns.

While the *positive spillover by law effect* applies to full takeovers, we define the *spillover by control hypothesis* for partial takeovers (whereby a bidder acquires majority control but buys less than 100% of the voting rights). In partial takeovers, the bidder may impose its governance standards which may yield positive returns if it is from a country that protects shareholder rights better than the target. The bidder may voluntary opt to apply such standards or may be pressurized by the minority shareholders of the target firm. Our results confirm the *spillover by control hypothesis*: both the bidder and target returns are higher in a partial acquisition if the bidder is subject to stronger shareholder rights protection than the target.

In full takeovers where the bidder is from a country that protects shareholders less well than the target country, the *negative spillover by law hypothesis* states that the target and bidder anticipated gains will be lower given that the poorer corporate governance regime will be imposed on the target. The alternative *bootstrapping hypothesis* is that poor-governance bidders voluntarily bootstrap to the better-governance regime of the target, which yields a share price increase. Our evidence supports the *bootstrapping hypothesis*: the bidder abnormal returns are higher when a bidder with weaker shareholder orientation acquires a target with better standards. Importantly, the effect is only valid for partial acquisitions or, in other words, for deals which still involve some of the target shareholders (who did not sell out) and for which the target firm remains listed on the stock exchange in the country of the target. The results are robust with respect to several model specifications that control for potential endogeneity problems. We conclude that an improvement in corporate governance at the target firm is an important source of gains in cross-border M&As.

Overall, our results suggest that cross-border takeovers between bidders and targets with dissimilar corporate governance standards can generates synergies which are partially related to corporate governance improvements (especially, those consisting of increases in shareholder rights).

Appendix A: Variable definition

Variable	Definition
# Domestic acquisitions/# listed firms 1 year prior	Number of domestic acquisitions in the bidder/target country during the year prior to the deal announcement divided by the number of listed firms registered in this country. Source: computed from SDC, DataStream
(Bidder) Creditor rights improvement	Indicator equals one if the bidder creditor rights index is below the median index and the target index is above the median, zero otherwise. Source: Martynova and Renneboog (2007b) and Appendix B/C
(Bidder) Minority shareholder protection improvement	Indicator equals one if the bidder minority shareholder protection index is below the median index and the target index is above the median, zero otherwise. Source: Martynova and Renneboog (2007b) and Appendix B/C
(Bidder) Shareholder rights improvement	Indicator equals one if the bidder shareholder rights index is below the median index and the target index is above the median, zero otherwise. Source: Martynova and Renneboog (2007b) and Appendix B/C
(Target) Creditor rights improvement	Indicator equals one if the bidder creditor rights index is above the median index and the target index is below the median, zero otherwise. Source: Martynova and Renneboog (2007b) and Appendix B/C
(Target) Minority shareholder protection improvement	Indicator equals one if the bidder minority shareholder protection index is above the median index and the target index is below the median, zero otherwise. Source: Martynova and Renneboog (2007b) and Appendix B/C
(Target) Shareholder rights improvement	Indicator equals one if the bidder shareholder rights index is above the median index and the target index is below the median, zero otherwise. Source: Martynova and Renneboog (2007b) and Appendix B/C
1997–1999	Indicator equals one if the bid was initiated in the period between January 1, 1997 and December 31, 1999 (the climax of the 5th takeover wave); and equals zero otherwise
2000–2001	Indicator equals one if the bid was initiated in the period between January 1, 2000 and December 31, 2001 (the decline of the 5th takeover wave); and equals zero otherwise
Anticorruption index	The extent to which one can exercise public power for private gain. It quantifies indicators ranging from the frequency of "additional payments to get things done" to the effects of corruption on the business environment. The index ranges between 0 and 5, with higher values corresponding to the lower level of corruption. Source: The World Bank (http://www.worldbank.org/wbi/governance/)

(Continued)

Appendix A (*Continued*)

Variable	Definition
CFlow/TA	Ratio of total cash flow (including cash flow from operating, financial, and investment activities) to total assets, at the year-end prior to the deal announcement. Source: based on SDC and Amadeus/Fame/Reach and DataStream
Common border	Indicator equals one if the bidder and target are from countries that have a common border, and equals zero otherwise
Creditor rights index	The value of the Creditor rights index (defined in Appendix C) multiplied by the Rule of Law index. Source: Martynova and Renneboog (2007b) and Appendix B/C
Diff. (Bidder-target) creditor rights index	Variable equals the difference between the bidder and the target Creditor rights indices. Source: Martynova and Renneboog (2007b) and Appendix B/C
Diff. (Bidder-target) minority shareholder protection index	The difference between the bidder and the target Minority shareholder protection indices. Source: Martynova and Renneboog (2007b) and Appendix B/C
Diff. (Bidder-target) shareholder rights index	The difference between the bidder and the target Shareholder rights indices. Source: Martynova and Renneboog (2007b) and Appendix B/C
Diversification	Indicator equals one if the bidder and target operate in different industries (their primary two-digit SIC codes are not equal), and equals zero otherwise. Source: based on SDC and Amadeus/Fame/Reach
Equity payment	Indicator equals one if the acquisition is fully paid with equity, and equals zero otherwise. Source: based on SDC, LexisNexis, Factiva, and Financial Times
Hostile bid	Indicator equals one if the initial takeover offer is met by a negative reaction by the management of the target firm or if a competing bid is made. Source: based on SDC, LexisNexis, Factiva, and Financial Times
Leverage	Ratio of total (long-term and short-term) debt to total assets at the year-end prior to the deal announcement. Source: based on Amadeus/Fame/Reach and DataStream
M&A of 100%	Indicator equals one if the bidder fully acquires the target and hence holds 100% of the share capital after the completion of the deal, and equals zero otherwise. Source: based on SDC, LexisNexis, Factiva, and Financial Times
Minority shareholder protection index	Variable that takes the value of the Minority shareholder protection index (defined in Appendix C) multiplied by the Rule of Law index. Source: Martynova and Renneboog (2007b) and Appendix B/C
Public target	Indicator equals one if the target firm was a stand-alone firm listed on a European stock exchange at the moment of the bid announcement, and is zero otherwise. Source: based on SDC and Amadeus/Fame/Reach
Q-ratio	Ratio of market value of equity (ordinary and preferred) plus book value of total (long-term and short-term) debt over the sum of book value of equity and book value of total debt. The market value of equity is taken 60 days prior to deal announcement, book value of equity and debt are at year-end prior to deal announcement. Source: based on Amadeus/Fame/Reach and DataStream

(*Continued*)

Appendix A (*Continued*)

Variable	Definition
Relative size	The ratio of the transaction value over the sum of the transaction value plus the bidder market value of equity and book value of total (long-term and short-term) debt. If the transaction value is undisclosed, we use the book value of the target firm's assets 1 year prior to the bid multiplied by the percentage of share capital acquired. Source: based on SDC, LexisNexis, Factiva, and Financial Times and Amadeus/Fame/ Reach and DataStream
Rule of law index	The Rule of Law index measures the extent to which agents have confidence in and abide by the rules of society; these also include the effectiveness and predictability of the judiciary and the enforceability of contracts. The index ranges between 0 and 5, with higher values corresponding to the better quality of law enforcement. Source: The World Bank (http://www.worldbank.org/wbi/governance/)
Run-up	Cumulative abnormal returns (CARs) of the bidder/target over the window $[-60, -2]$ preceding the day of the deal announcement. Abnormal returns are computed with the market model adjusted for thin-trading and reversion to the mean. The market model's parameters are estimated over the period of 300–60 days before the M&A announcement; the market index is the MSCI Europe index. Source: based on DataStream
Same industry	Indicator equals one if the bidder and target operate in same industries (their primary two-digit SIC codes are the same), and equals zero otherwise. Source: based on SDC and Amadeus/Fame/Reach
Same language group	Indicator equals one if at least one official language of the target country belongs the same language group (Romance languages, Germanic (excluding English), Slavic, English) as that of the one of the official languages of the bidder country, and equals zero otherwise. Source: based on SDC
Shareholder rights index	The value of the Shareholder rights index (defined in Appendix C) multiplied by the Rule of Law index. Source: Martynova and Renneboog (2007b) and Appendix B/C
Size (log TA)	Logarithm of the firm's total assets at the year-end prior to deal announcement. Source: DataStream and Amadeus/Fame/Reach

Appendix B: The names of the legal experts who contributed to the corporate governance database

Austria: Prof. Susanne Kalls (University of Klagenfurt), Prof. Christian Nowotny and Mr. Stefan Fida (Vienna University of Economics and Business Administration);

Belgium: Prof. Eddy Wymeersch (University of Ghent, Chairman of the Commission for Finance, Banking and Assurance), Prof. Christoph Van der Elst (University of Ghent);

Bulgaria: Dr. Plamen Tchipev (Institute of Economics, Bulgarian Academy of Sciences), Ms. Tania Bouzeva (ALIENA Consult Ltd., Sofia), Dr. Ivaylo Nikolov (Centre for Economic Development, Sofia);

Croatia: Dr. Domagoj Racic and Mr. Josip Stajfer (The Institute of Economics, Zagreb), Mr. Andrej Galogaža (Zagreb Stock Exchange), Prof. Drago Čengić (IVO PILAR Institute of Social Sciences), Prof. Edita Culinovic-Herc (University of Rijeka);

Cyprus: Mr. Marios Clerides (Chairman) and Ms. Christiana Vovidou (Cyprus Securities and Exchange Commission);

Czech Republic: Prof. Lubos Tichy, Mr. Martin Abraham, and Mr. Rostislav Pekar (Squire, Sanders & Dempsey, Cousellors at Law), Dr. Petr Kotáb and Prof. Milan Bakes (Charles University of Prague), Dr. Stanislav Myslil (Čermák Hořejš Myslil a spol, Lawyers and Patent Attorneys), Dr. Jan Bárta (Institute of State and Law, The Academy of Science of Czech Republic), Ms. Jana Klirova (Corporate Governance Consulting, Prague);

Denmark: Prof. Jesper Lau Hansen and Prof. Ulrik Rammeskow Bang-Pedersen (University of Copenhagen);

Estonia: Prof. Andres Vutt (University of Tartu), Mr. Toomas Luhaaar, Mr. Peeter Lepik, and Ms Katri Paas (Law Office of Lepik & Luhaäär);

Finland: Prof. Matti J. Sillanpää (Turku School of Economics and Business Administration), Mr. Ingalill Aspholm (Rahoitustarkastus/ Financial Supervision Authority), Ms Ari-Pekka Saanio (Borenius & Kemppinen, Attorneys at Law, Helsinki), Ms Johan Aalto (Hannes Snellman, Attorneys at Law; Helsinki);

France: Prof. Alain Couret (Université Paris I-Panthéon-Sorbonne), Ms. Joëlle Simon (MEDEF-French Business Confederation), Prof. Benoit Le Bars (MC Université de Cergy-Pontoise), Prof. Alain Pietrancosta (Universities of Tours and Paris I-Panthéon-Sorbonne), Prof. Viviane de Beaufort (ESSEC-MBA), Prof. Gerard Charreaux (Université de Bourgogne Pôle d'économie et de gestion);

Germany:
Prof. Peter O. Muelbert (University of Mainz), Prof. Klaus Hopt and Dr. Alexander Hellgardt (Max Planck Institute for Foreign Private and Private International Law), Prof. Theodor Baums and Mr. Tobias Pohl (Johann Wolfgang Goethe University, Frankfurt/Main);

Greece:
Prof. Loukas Spanos (Centre of Financial Studies, University of Athens); Dr. Harilaos Mertzanis (Hellenic Capital Market Commission), Prof. Georgios D. Sotiropoulos (University of Athens);

Hungary:
Dr. Tamás Sándor (Sándor Bihary Szegedi Szent-Ivány Advocats), Dr. Andras Szecskay and Dr. Orsolya Görgényi (Szecskay Law Firm-Moquet Borde & Associés), Prof. Adam Boóc and Prof. Anna Halustyik (Corvinus University of Budapest);

Iceland:
Mr. Gunnar Sturluson and Mr. Olafur Arinbjorn Sigurdsson (LOGOS legal services), Dr. Aalsteinn E. Jónasson (Straumur Investment Bank and Reykjavik University), Mr. David Sch. Thorssteinsson (Iceland Chamber of Commerce);

Ireland Republic:
Dr. Blanaid Clarke (University College Dublin), Ms. Kelley Smith (Irish Law Library, Barrister);

Italy:
Prof. Guido Ferrarini and Mr. Andrea Zanoni (University of Genoa), Dr. Magda Bianco and Dr. Alessio Pacces (Banca d'Italia), Prof. Luca Enriques (Università di Bologna);

Latvia:
Prof. Kalvis Torgans and Dr. Pauls Karnups (University of Latvia), Mr. Uldis Cerps (Riga Stock Exchange);

Lithuania:
Mr. Virgilijus Poderys (Chairman) and Ms. Egle Surpliene (The Securities Commission of Lithuania), Mr. Rolandas Valiūnas, Dr. Jaunius Gumbis, and Dr. Dovilėė Burgienė (Lideika, Petrauskas, Valiūnas ir partneriai), Dr. Paulius Cerka (Vytautas Magnus University), Mr. Tomas Bagdanskis (Tomas Bagdanskis, Attorney at Law);

Luxembourg:
Mr. Jacques Loesch (Linklaters Loesch Law Firm), Mr. Daniel Dax (Luxembourg Stock Exchange);

Netherlands:
Prof. Jaap Winter (De Brauw Blackstone Westbroek, High Level Group of Company Law Experts European Commission Office (Chairman), University of Amsterdam), Mr. Marcel van de Vorst and Mr. Gijs van Leeuwen (Norton Rose Advocaten & Solicitors), Mr. Johan Kleyn and Dr. Barbara Bier (Allen & Overy LLP), Dr. Pieter Ariens Kappers (Boekel De Nerée), Prof. A.F. Verdam (Vrije Universiteit Amsterdam), Prof. Mr. C. A. Schwarz (Maastricht University);

Norway:
Prof. Kristin Normann Aarum (Oslo University), Prof. Tore Brathen (University of Tromsø), Prof. Jan Andersson (University of Bergen);

Poland: Prof. Stanisław Sołtysiński and Dr. Andrzej W. Kawecki (The law firm of Sołtysiński Kawecki & Szlezak), Mr. Igor Bakowski (Gotshal & Manges, Chajec, Don-Siemion & Żyto Sp.k.), Dr. Piotr Tamowicz, Mr. Maciej Dzierżanowski, and Mr. Michał Przybyłowski (The Gdańsk Institute for Market Economics), Ms. Anna Miernika-Szulc (Warsaw Stock Exchange);

Portugal: Mr. Victor Mendes (CMVM-Comissão do Mercado de Valores Mobiliários), Mr. Carlos Ferreira Alves (CEMPRE, Faculdade de Economia, Universidade do Porto), Prof. Manuel Pereira Barrocas (Barrocas Sarmento Rocha-Sociedade de Advogados), Dr. Jorge de Brito Pereira (PLMJ—A.M. Pereira, Sragga Leal, Oliveira Martins, J dice e Associados—Sociedade de Advogados), Dr. Manuel Costa Salema, Dr. Carlos Aguiar, and Mr. Pedro Pinto (Law firm Carlos Aguiar P Pinto & Associados), Mr. Antonio Alfaia de Carvalho (Lebre Sá Carvalho & Associados);

Romania: Mr. Gelu Goran (Salans, Bucharest office), Dr. Sorin David (Law firm David & Baias SCPA), Ms. Adriana I. Gaspar (Nestor Nestor Diculescu Kingston Petersen, Attorneys & Counselors), Mr. Catalin Baiculescu and Dr. Horatiu Dumitru (Musat & Associates, Attorneys at Law), Ms. Catalina Grigorescu (Haarmann Hemmelrath Law Firm);

Slovak
Republic: Dr. Jozef Makuch (Chairman) and Dr. Stanislav Škurla (Financial Market Authority, Slovak Republic), Dr. Frantisek Okruhlica (Slovak Governance Institute);

Slovenia: Prof. Janez Prasnikar and Dr. Aleksandra Gregoric (University of Ljubljana), Prof. Miha Juhart, Mr. Klemen Podobnik, and Ms. Ana Vlahek (Securities Market Agency);

Spain: Prof. Candido Paz-Ares (Universidad Autonoma de Madrid), Prof. Marisa Aparicio (Universidad Autonoma de Madrid and Universidad Pontificia Comillas de Madrid), Prof. Guillermo Guerra (Universidad Rey Juan Carlos);

Sweden: Prof. Per Samuelsson and Prof. Gerard Muller (School of Economics and Management at Lund University), Prof. Rolf Dotevall (Göteborg University), Dr. Catarina af Sandeberg, and Prof. Annina Persson (Stockholm University), Prof. Björn Kristiansson (Linklaters Sweden);

Switzerland: Dr. Urs P. Gnos (Walder Wyss & Partners), Prof. Gerard Hertig (Swiss Federal Institute of Technology-ETH Zurich), Dr. Michel Haymann (Haymann & Baldi), Prof. Wolfgang Drobetz (University of Basel-WWZ), Prof. Karl Hofstetter (Universität Zürich), Prof. Peter Nobel and Mr. Marcel Würmli (Universität St. Gallen);

United Kingdom: Prof. Antony Dnes (Bournemouth University), Prof. Dan Prentice and Ms. Jenny Payne (Oxford University), Prof. Brian R Cheffins, Mr. Richard Charles Nolan, and Mr. John Armour (University of Cambridge), Prof. Paul Davies (London School of Economics), Mr. Gerard N. Cranley, Ms. Holly Gregory, and Ms. Ira Millstein (Weil, Gotshal & Manges), Ms. Eva Lomnicka (University of London);

Appendix C: Design of corporate governance standards indices

The table shows how specific regulations are quantified to construct three corporate governance standards indices: the shareholder rights index, the minority shareholders protection index, and the creditor rights index. Some regulatory aspects are incorporated in several indices.

1. ***The shareholder rights index*** reflects the shareholders' ability to mitigate managerial opportunistic behavior. The index is constructed by combining the following four subindices:

1.1. The appointment rights subindex is based on the rules to appoint and replace executive and nonexecutive directors. It measures the degree of alignment of the interests of management and shareholders. The regulatory provisions are quantified as follows:

- Employee representation: 0 if required, 2 if not.
- Nomination to the board by shareholders: 2 if required, 0 if not.
- Tenure on the board: 0 if more than 4 years, 1 if 4 years, 2 if less than 4 years
- Cross-shareholdings:
  - Cross-shareholdings between 2 independent companies: 1 if regulated, 0 if not.
  - Maximum shareholding of a subsidiary in its parent company: 1 if regulated, 0 if not
- Election rules:
  - Proxy voting by mail: 2 if allowed, 0 if not
  - Requirement to Deposit/Register shares prior to a general meeting:
    - ⇨ Bearer shares: 0 if deposit is required, 1 if only registration of shares is required, 2 if none is required
    - ⇨ Nominal shares: 0 if deposit is required, 2 if deposit requirement is forbidden.

1.2 The decision rights subindex captures the shareholders' ability to mitigate managerial discretion. The decision rights index cover regulatory provisions that mandate direct shareholder decision-making. The regulatory provisions are quantified as follows:

- Shareholders approval of antitakeover measures: 2 if required, 0 if not.
- Shareholders approval of preemption rights: 2 if required, 0 if not.

- Percentage needed to call for extraordinary meeting: 0 if no rule or more than 20%, 1 if 20% or less but more than 5%, 2 if 5% and less.
- Voting caps: 0 if allowed, 2 if not.

1.3 *The trusteeship subindex* measures the efficiency of the board of directors in monitoring the actions of CEOs. The following regulatory provisions are quantified as follows:

- Board independence:
  - o 2 if CEO cannot be the chairman of the board of directors (in 1-tier board structure), 0 otherwise
  - o 2 if the overlap between management and supervisory board is forbidden (in 2-tier board structure), 0 otherwise
- Employee representation: 0 if required, 2 if not.
- Separate board of auditors: 1 if required, 0 otherwise.

1.4 *The transparency subindex* is based on the quality of information about company, its ownership structure, and management available to investors

- Requirement to disclose managerial compensation: 0 if not required, 1 if required on aggregate basis, 2 if required on individual basis.
- Requirement to disclose any transactions between management and company: 2 if required, 0 if not
- Frequency of financial reports: 0 if once per year, 1 if twice per year, 2 if more than twice per year
- Comply or explain rule: 1 if the requirement is present, 0 otherwise.

The higher each index, the better is the protection of the shareholders.

2. **The minority shareholders protection index** is based on the regulatory provisions aimed at increasing the relative power of the minority shareholders in a context of strong majority shareholders. The index is constructed by combining the following 4 subindices:

2.1. *Minority shareholders appointment rights subindex* is based on the appointment rights that can be used to protect minority shareholders. These include rights to reserve seats on the board of directors for minority shareholders or to limit voting power of large shareholders. The regulatory provisions are quantified as follows:

- Minority representation on the board: 2 if required, 0 otherwise.
- Voting caps limiting power of large shareholders: 1 if voting caps are allowed, 0 if not.
- One-share-one-vote rule: 0 if both multiple voting rights and nonvoting shares are allowed; 1 if one of the two is allowed; 2 if none is allowed.

2.2. Minority shareholders decision rights subindex captures the ability of minority shareholders to affect fundamental corporate transactions that require a shareholder vote. The regulatory provisions are quantified as follows:

- Supermajority requirement for approval of major company's decisions: 0 if 50% or less; 1 if more than 50% but less than 75%; 2 if 75% or more
- Percentage needed to call for extraordinary meeting: 0 if the rule is not present or required percentage is 20% or more; 1 if the required percentage is between 20 and 5%; 2 if the percentage is 5% or less.

2.3. The minority shareholders trusteeship rights subindex indicates the extent to which the board of directors serves as a trustee for minority shareholder, that is, the directors are independent from the firm's controlling shareholders. The regulatory provisions are quantified as follows:

- Nomination to the board by shareholders: 2 if shareholders voting to elect nonexecutive directors is not required (2-tier boards); 0 if required or 1-tier board
- Board independence: 2 if CEO cannot be the chairman of the board of directors (in 1-tier board structure) or if the overlap between management and supervisory board is forbidden (in 2-tier board structure), 0 otherwise.

2.4. The minority shareholders affiliation rights subindex groups the remaining regulatory provisions aimed at protecting minority shareholders: the principle of equal treatment (or shared returns) and rights for entry and exit on fair terms. The regulatory provisions are quantified as follows:

- Equal treatment rule: 2 if required, 0 if not,
- Mandatory disclosure of large ownership stakes: 0 if disclosure is not required or the minimum percent is 25% or more; 1 if 10% or more (less than 25%); 2 if 5% or more (less than 10%); 3 if less than 5%.
- Mandatory bid rule: 0 if not required; 1 if 50% or control; 2 if between 50 and 30%; 3 if 30% or less.
- Sell-out rule: The squeeze-out rule is used as a proxy for the sell-out rule, (assumption: sell-out is always in place if squeeze-out is adopted, with the same terms as squeeze-out): 0 if no squeeze-out; 1 if squeeze-out at 95% or more; 2 if squeeze-out at 90% or less.
- Minority claim: 0 if no; 1 if 10% or more; 2 if 5% or more; 3 if less than 5%.
- Break-through rule: 1 if required; 0 if not.

The higher each index, the better is the protection of the minority shareholders.

*3. **The creditor rights index*** is based on regulatory provisions that allow creditors to force repayment more easily, take possession of collateral, or gain control over firm in financial distress. The regulatory provisions are quantified as follows:

- Debtor-oriented versus creditor-oriented code: 1 if no reorganization option (liquidation only); 0 if reorganization + liquidation option;
- Automatic stay on the assets: 1 if no automatic stay is obliged in reorganization (if debt-orient code) or liquidation procedure (if liquidation code); 0 otherwise;
- Secured creditors are ranked first: 1 if secured creditors are ranked first in the liquidation procedure; 0 if government and employees are ranked first;
- Creditor approval of bankruptcy: 1 if creditor approval is required to initiate reorganization procedure (if debtor-oriented code) or liquidation procedure (if liquidation code); 0 otherwise;
- Appointment of official to manage reorganization/liquidation procedure: 1 if it is required by law in a reorganization procedure (if debtor-oriented code) or a liquidation procedure (if liquidation code); 0 otherwise.

The higher the index, the better is the protection of the creditors.

References

Agrawal, A. and J. Jaffe, 2000, "The Post-Merger Performance Puzzle," In: A. Gregory and C. Cooper (Eds.), *Advances in Mergers and Acquisitions*, vol. 1, JAI Press, Amsterdam, pp. 7–41.

Benos, E. and M. Weisbach, 2004, "Private Benefits and Cross-Listings in the United States," *Emerging Markets Review*, 5 (2), 217–240.

Blume, M., 1979, "Betas and Their Regression Tendencies: Some Further Evidence," *Journal of Finance*, 34, 265–267.

Bris, A. and C. Cabolis, 2007, "Corporate Governance Convergence Through Cross-Border Mergers: The Case of Aventis," In G. Gregoriou and L. Renneboog (Eds.), *Corporate Governance and Regulatory Impact on Mergers and Acquisitions: Research and Analysis on Activity Worldwide Since 1990*, Elsevier, Massachusetts, pp. 71–101.

Bris, A. and C. Cabolis, 2008, "The Value of Investor Protection: Firm Evidence from Cross-Border Mergers," *Review of Financial Studies*, 21 (2), 605–648.

Bris, A., N. Brisley and C. Cabolis, 2008, "Adopting Better Corporate Governance: Evidence from Cross-Border Mergers," *Journal of Corporate Finance*, 14, 224–240, (this issue).

Brown, S. J. and J. B. Warner, 1985, "Using Daily Stock Returns: The Case of Event Studies," *Journal of Financial Economics*, 14 (1), 3–31.

Bruner, R. F., 2004, "Does M&A Pay?" In R. F. Bruner. *Applied Merges and Acquisitions*, Chapter 3, Wiley Finance, New Jersey, pp. 30–86.

Claessens, S. and S. Schmukler, 2007, "International Financial Integration Through Equity Markets: Which Firms from Which Countries Go Global?" *Journal of International Money and Finance*, 26 (5), 788–813.

Coffee, J., 1999, "The Future as History: The Prospects for Global Convergence in Corporate Governance and Its Implications," *Northwestern University Law Review*, 93, 641–708.

Corrado, C. J., 1989, "A Nonparametric Test for Abnormal Security-Price Performance in Event Studies," *Journal of Financial Economics*, 23 (2), 385–395.

Dennis, D. J., D. K. Dennis and K. Yost, 2002, "Global Diversification, Industrial Diversification, and Firm Value," *Journal of Finance*, 57 (5), 1951–1979.

Dewenter, K., 1995, "Does the Market React Differently to Domestic and Foreign Takeover Announcements? Evidence from the US Chemical and Retail Industries," *Journal of Financial Economics*, 37, 421–441.

Dimson, E., 1979, "Risk Measurement When Shares are Subject to Infrequent Trading," *Journal of Financial Economics*, 7, 197–226.

Doidge, C., A. Karolyi, K. Lins, D. Miller and R. Stulz, 2006, "Private Benefits of Control, Ownership, and the Cross-Listing Decision," ECGI–Finance Working Paper No. 77/2005.

Doidge, C., A. Karolyi and R. Stulz, 2007, "Why Do Countries Matter So Much for Corporate Governance?" *Journal of Financial Economics*, 86 (1), 1–39.

Durnev, A. and H. Kim, 2005, "To Steal or Not to Steal: Firm Attributes, Legal Environment, and Valuation," *Journal of Finance*, 60, 1461–1493.

Goergen, M. and L. Renneboog, 2004, "Shareholder Wealth Effects of European Domestic and Cross-Border Takeover Bids," *European Financial Management*, 10 (1), 9–45.

Goergen, M., M. Martynova and L. Renneboog, 2005, "Corporate Governance Convergence: Evidence from Takeover Regulation Reforms," *Oxford Review of Economic Policy*, 21 (2), 243–268.

Gompers, P., J. Ishii and A. Metrick, 2003, "Corporate Governance and Equity Prices," *Quarterly Journal of Economics*, 118 (1), 107–155.

Guiso, L., P. Sapienza and L. Zingales, 2006, "Does Culture Affect Economic Outcomes?" *Journal of Economic Perspective*, 20 (2), 23–48.

Guiso, L., P. Sapienza and L. Zingales, 2007, "Cultural Biases in Economic Exchange," Mimeo.

Harris, R. and D. Ravenscraft, 1991, "The Role of Acquisitions in Foreign Direct Investment: Evidence from the US Stock Market," *Journal of Finance*, 46 (3), 825–844.

Heckman, J., 1976, "The Common Structure of Statistical Models of Truncation, Sample Selection, and Limited Dependent Variables and a Sample Estimator for Such Models," *Annals of Economic and Social Measurement*, 5 (4), 475.

Heckman, J., 1979, "Sample Selection Bias as a Specification Error," *Econometrica*, 47 (1), 153–162.

Jarrell, G., J. Brickley and J. Netter, 1988, "The Market for Corporate Control: The Empirical Evidence Since 1980," *Journal of Economic Perspectives*, 2, 49–68.

Jensen, M., 1986, "Agency Costs of Free Cash Flow, Corporate Finance, and Takeovers," *American Economic Review*, 76 (2), 323–329.

Jensen, M. and R. Ruback, 1983, "The Market for Corporate Control: The Scientific Evidence," *Journal of Financial Economics*, 11, 5–50.

Kuipers, D., D. Miller and A. Patel, 2003, "The Legal Environment and Corporate Valuation: Evidence from Cross-Border Takeovers," Texas Tech University Working Paper.

La Porta, R., F. Lopez-de-Silanes, A. Shleifer and R. Vishny, 1998, "Law and Finance," *Journal of Political Economy*, 106, 1113–1155.

Lang, L., R. Stulz and R. Walkling, 1989, "Managerial Performance, Tobin's Q and the Gains from Successful Tender Offers," *Journal of Financial Economics*, 24 (1), 137–154.

Martynova, M. and L. Renneboog, 2007a, "What Determines Sources of Transaction Financing in Corporate Takeovers: Costs of Capital, Agency Costs, or Means of Payment?" Mimeo.

Martynova, M. and L. Renneboog, 2007b, "A Corporate Governance Index: Convergence and Diversity of National Corporate Governance Regulations," Mimeo.

Martynova, M. and L. Renneboog, 2008, "A Century of Corporate Takeovers: What Have We Learned and Where Do We Stand?" *Journal of Banking and Finance*, 32, 2148–2177.

Moeller, S. and F. Schlingemann, 2005, "Global Diversification and Bidder Gains: A Comparison Between Cross-Border and Domestic Acquisitions," *Journal of Banking and Finance*, 29, 533–564.

Moeller, S., F. Schlingemann and R. Stulz, 2004, "Firm Size and the Gains from Acquisitions," *Journal of Financial Economics*, 73, 201–228.

Muchlinski, P., 1997, *Multinational Enterprises and the Law*, Blackwell Publishers, Oxford.

Pagano, M., A. Roell and J. Zechner, 2002, "The Geography of Equity Listing: Why Do Companies List Abroad?" *Journal of Finance*, 57 (6), 2651–2694.

Roll, R., 1986, "The Hubris Hypothesis of Corporate Takeovers," *Journal of Business*, 59, 197–216.

Rossi, S. and P. Volpin, 2004, "Cross-Country Determinants of Mergers and Acquisitions," *Journal of Financial Economics*, 74 (2), 277–304.

Sarkissian, S. and M. Schill, 2004, "The Overseas Listing Decision: New Evidence of Proximity Prefer-
    ence," *Review of Financial Studies*, 17 (3), 769–809.

Scholes, M. and M. Wolfson, 1990, "The Effects of Changes in Tax Laws on Corporate Reorganization
    Activity," *Journal of Business*, 63, 141–164.

Servaes, H., 1991, "Tobin's Q and the Gains from Takeovers," *Journal of Finance*, 46 (1), 409–419.

Servaes, H. and M. Zenner, 1994, "Taxes and the Returns to Foreign Acquisitions in the United States,"
    Financial Management, 42–56.

Starks, and Wei, 2005, "Cross-Border Mergers and Differences in Corporate Governance," Working Paper,
    University of Texas.

Wang, C. and F. Xie, 2009, "Corporate Governance Transfer and Synergistic Gains from Mergers and
    Acquisitions," *Review of Financial Studies*, forthcoming (in press).

Chapter 25

ADOPTING BETTER CORPORATE GOVERNANCE: EVIDENCE FROM CROSS-BORDER MERGERS[*]

ARTURO BRIS

IMD, European Corporate Governance Institute, Lausanne, Switzerland
Yale International Center for Finance, New Haven, Connecticut, USA

NEIL BRISLEY

Richard Ivey School of Business, University of Western Ontario, London, Ontario, Canada

CHRISTOS CABOLIS

Yale International Center for Finance, New Haven, Connecticut, USA
ALBA Graduate Business School, Vouliagmeni, Greece

Contents

* We are grateful for the helpful comments received from Marc Goergen and Luc Renneboog (the editors), an anonymous referee, Judy Chevalier, Ted Frech, Will Goetzmann, Yrjö Koskinen, Clement Krouse, Catherine Labio, Florencio López de Silanes, Toni Whited, and seminar participants at the University of Alberta, McGill University, Universitat Pompeu Fabra, Universidad Carlos III, and the 2002 Annual Conference on Financial Economics and Accounting at the University of Maryland, Universidad Carlos III, the 2002 Annual Conference on Financial Economics and Accounting at the University of Maryland, the 2007 Conference on Contractual Corporate Governance at the Sheffeld University, and the 2007 Annual Conference of the Hellenic Finance and Accounting Association. We thank Vanessa Janowski for excellent research assistance. Brisley acknowledges support from a Social Sciences and Humanities Research Council of Canada standard research grant.

This article originally appeared in the *Journal of Corporate Finance*, Vol. 14, pp. 224–240 (2008).
Corporate Takeovers, Volume 2
Edited by B. Espen Eckbo
Copyright © 2008 Elsevier B.V. All rights reserved.
DOI: 10.1016/B978-0-12-381982-6.00026-4

Abstract

Cross-border mergers allow firms to alter the level of protection they provide to their investors, because target firms usually import the corporate governance system of the acquiring company by law. Therefore, cross-border mergers provide a natural experiment to analyze the effects of changes in corporate governance on firm value, and on an industry as a whole. We construct measures of the change in investor protection induced by cross-border mergers in a sample of 7330 "national industry years" (spanning 39 industries in 41 countries in the period 1990–2001. We find that the Tobin's Q of an industry—including its unmerged firms—*increases* when firms within that industry are acquired by foreign firms coming from countries with better shareholder protection and better accounting standards. We present evidence that the transfer of corporate governance practices through cross-border mergers is Pareto improving. Firms that can adopt better practices willingly do so, and the market assigns more value to better protection.

Keywords

corporate governance, market regulation, cross-border acquisitions

JEL classification: F3, F4, G3

I think that for active investors like us, corporate governance is built into the analytic process of assessing deals and will figure ultimately in the decision as to whether or not premiums have to be paid for a company. I think this is a global investor issue. When global investors look at deals, particularly cross-border deals, they will often factor corporate governance issues into the equation, and these may have a practical effect on price and value.

Peter Clapman, Former Senior Vice-president and Chief Counsel Investments, TIAA-CREF (from Alexander, 2000)

1. Introduction

The political economy approach to corporate governance has documented the importance of legal rules in determining corporate finance and corporate governance decisions. Legal rules—this approach argues—determine the extent to which countries differ in the degree of investor protection and, in turn, the impact of such differences on the size of capital markets, as well as firms' value, distribution policies, ownership structures, and financial choices.[1] This articles extends the existing literature by evaluating the effects on industry value of adopting better corporate governance practices induced by cross-border mergers.

Our study is based on the observation that in a cross-border merger, the target firm usually adopts the accounting standards, disclosure practices, and governance structures of the acquiring firm.[2] This implies that, even when there is no formal change of the domestic legal system, firms in a country can adopt different levels of investor protection, depending on the firms they merge with. Bris and Cabolis (2008) have shown that stronger shareholder protection and accounting standards in the acquirer's country result in a higher merger premium. Martynova and Renneboog (2008, this issue) find similar results in an analysis of announcement returns to cross-border mergers. These results are in line with other papers in the literature that find a high correlation between transparency and accountability improvements and higher stock returns. Gompers et al. (2003) and Cremers and Nair (2005) study the US market and determine that improvement of investor protection is associated with higher returns, while Bergman and Nicolaievsky (2007) examine the effect of strengthening investor protection in Mexico with similar results.

A natural question that follows is the effect on the industry as a whole of an increase in the governance quality of an individual firm. There are at least two ways in which the industry may be positively affected. First, there can be a *spillover* effect as firms in an industry recognize that an input of production—corporate governance—is used

---

[1] Legal rules have been shown to determine: corporate valuation (Himmelberg et al., 2002; La Porta et al., 2002); firms' financing choices (Demirgüç-Kunt and Maksimovic, 1998, 1999); capital allocation (Beck and Levine, 2002; Claessens and Laeven, 2003; Wurgler, 2000); market efficiency (Mørck et al., 2000); and even the severity of currency crises (Johnson et al., 2000).

[2] Nothing precludes the acquiring firm from adopting some corporate governance provisions of the target firm. For a case study on the cross-border merger that resulted in Aventis, see Bris and Cabolis (2007).

more efficiently by the target firm and so strengthen their own governance levels as a response. Doidge et al. (2007), for instance, show that even after controlling for country characteristics, firms do not differ much in their corporate governance levels, at least in developing countries. This may be interpreted as an attempt by industry participants to maintain similar governance structures. Second, as Bris and Brisley (2007) show, corporate governance reform by a single firm in the industry can increase profits even for firms that do not reform. The reason is that, in a nonperfectly competitive setting with less than stringent corporate governance, all firms tend to overproduce. Corporate governance reform induces the reforming firm to produce less, leaving room for competitors to increase their production further and increase their profits. Overall, the profits of the entire industry benefit from a single firm improving its corporate governance.

It is conceivable that an industry could be negatively affected by an increase in the governance quality of an individual firm. For example, if the firm that reforms its corporate governance is the dominant firm in the industry, the increase in the profits of this firm might be insufficient to offset the losses caused to the industry followers, resulting in an overall decrease in industry value. Prohibitively high costs associated with the renegotiation of contracts related to corporate governance could contribute to this effect. Bergman and Nicolaievsky (2007) show that public companies in Mexico do not improve corporate governance standards beyond what is required by the law.

Ultimately, the industry-level effect of a strengthening of investor protection in a target firm is an empirical question. We measure the average change in investor protection in a given industry and country by considering all the cross-border mergers that take place in any given year. We then relate these changes in investor protection to a measure of value—the median Tobin's Q of the firms in the industry—in order to examine whether the industry realizes an increase in the average return due to the strengthening of investor protection.

There are several advantages to working with industry-level data. First, our panel of industry-country-year observations allows us to control for country-specific events, such as changes in regulation, trends in the market for corporate control, and taxation. Second, it expands the scope of our research to the whole industry, instead of focusing merely on its merging firms. Third, because the target firm in a cross-border merger effectively adopts the nationality of the acquiring firm, a firm-level analysis would not identify any benefits of improved investor protection to the country where the target is located. Finally, and consistent with our hypotheses, corporate governance change mechanisms such as institutional ownership and external monitoring are instrumental in transmitting the benefits of improved corporate governance from merged firms to unmerged firms. A sample restricted to merging firms would be biased towards those in countries where the direct effect of the takeover market is a dominant corporate governance mechanism and would miss altogether the indirect positive externality effect that we document here. By studying all industries in all countries with available data, we address each of these issues.

Our sample includes more than 15,000 cross-border acquisitions in the period 1990–2001, corresponding to firms in 39 industries and 41 countries. We construct industry-wide corporate governance indices by calculating the value-weighted averages of the corporate governance quality indices in La Porta et al. (1998). When a cross-border merger takes place in a given industry, the corporate governance indices of the industry may change since the target firm adopts the governance system of the acquirer. We use two indicators of corporate governance quality: shareholder protection and accounting standards.

We estimate panel regressions with Tobin's Q of the corresponding industry as the endogenous variable. We control for industry, year and country effects. Additionally, we control for concentration and the merger activity in the industry and country under consideration. The key explanatory variables are the two indicators of corporate governance change that we construct. We find that when firms in a given industry are acquired by firms from countries with stronger shareholder protection practices, there is a significant increase in the value of that industry, as measured by the industry's Tobin's Q. Similarly, importing better accounting standards creates value for the target industry. This is consistent with corporate governance reform in one firm having a positive effect on other industry participants. We test whether the value increase is related to the degree of competition in the industry, measured by the Herfindahl index, and find a positive but insignificant relationship. Ultimately, we conclude that our results are consistent both with both the *spillover effects* and *industry competition* hypotheses.

As a robustness test, we check whether our results are due to the value of governance being greater in industries where there is greater need to raise external capital. We interact cross-border merger-related governance improvements with an indicator of external financial needs (Almeida and Wolfenzon, 2005). Contrary to this hypothesis, we find that the relationship between governance improvements and industry Tobin's Q is weaker when financial constraints are stronger.

Overall, we find strong evidence that the change in corporate governance practices through cross-border mergers is Pareto improving. Industries targeted by foreign firms from stronger corporate governance countries do benefit from an increased market valuation. Interestingly, industries containing firms that are targeted by acquirers from a weaker corporate governance country do *not* seem to be negatively affected. Consistent with the quote at the beginning of this paper, we do not find evidence that corporate governance is a *motive* for cross-border acquisitions, rather corporate governance considerations significantly determine the valuation effects of cross-border mergers, even at the industry level. Our results are robust to using alternative measures of governance quality, such as the modified LLSV index of Pagano and Volpin (2005), and the World Bank Rule of Law Index, both of which are time-varying.

Our results are consistent with the literature on intraindustry valuation effects of mergers (Akhigbe and Martin, 2000; Eckbo, 1982, 1985). Measuring the pure valuation effects of cross-border mergers is *not* our objective. Instead, we control for the pure valuation effects and study the impact on the median firm in an industry of changes in corporate governance induced by cross-border mergers. Our paer is also related to La Porta et al. (2002) and Gompers et al. (2003) which, relying on country-level data and firm-specific corporate governance characteristics respectively, identify a positive relationship between corporate governance quality and value. Both papers provide cross-sectional results, indeed Gompers et al. (2003) argue that it is not possible to identify any causal relationship between governance and value in their setting. We extend this literature by using a panel data sample. The majority of the corporate governance literature provides cross-sectional results on the relationship between investor protection and corporate finance variables in a given year. Unfortunately, whether one is arguing in favor of or against legal change, such static evidence is not particularly helpful. Indeed, one cannot conclude that improvements in investor protection within a country have positive effects, unless there is localized evidence (Glaeser et al., 2001, on the Poland-Czech Republic difference), or new indicators are constructed (as in Pistor, 2006, for transition economies, and Hyytinen et al., 2003, for Finland). Ours is the first attempt to document the effect of changes in corporate governance by using a large sample of countries, from four different legal origins and including both developed and emerging markets, all spanning a period of 12 years.

Rossi and Volpin (2004) use cross-sectional data and find that the majority of targets in cross-border acquisitions come from countries with poor investor protection, whereas the majority of acquirers come from more investor-friendly regimes. Our paper complements theirs, and asks whether changes in corporate governance are priced by the market. Finally, our rich dataset allows us to extend the results of Daines (2001), who provides cross-sectional evidence that the market assigns a higher value to the assets of firms incorporated in Delaware.

The study of mergers has provided a vast empirical literature which focuses on the effects of integration on the values of both the acquiring and the target firm. However, Andrade et al. (2001) point out that the empirical literature has had little to say on the more fundamental question surrounding merger activity: how—and not whether—mergers create or destroy value. Our work posits the transfer of corporate governance practice as a conduit through which mergers can improve value.

The paper is organized as follows. Section 2 presents the alternative hypotheses provided by the literature. Section 3 describes the data and its sources. Section 4 outlines the construction of industry-level corporate governance indices from the original merger sample. Section 5 analyzes the relationship between industry value and corporate governance. In Section 6 we perform robustness tests, and Section 7 concludes.

2. Testable hypotheses

There are three alternative hypotheses that explain the relationship between corporate governance improvements at the individual firm level, and the overall value of the industry. These arguments rely on the assumption that corporate governance improvements have a positive effect on the value of the reforming firm. There is ample empirical evidence supporting this statement (Bris and Cabolis, 2008; Gompers et al., 2003; La Porta et al., 1998; Martynova and Renneboog, 2008, this issue). The three alternative hypotheses differ in the way corporate governance improvements in one firm impact the way the other industry participants behave. In the subsequent sections we proceed to test them.

2.1. Market control hypothesis

If the firm that reforms its corporate governance is the dominant firm in the industry, the increase in the profits of this firm might be insufficient to offset the losses caused to the industry followers, resulting in an overall decrease in industry value. In this case the industry will be negatively affected by an increase in the governance quality of an individual firm. Prohibitively high costs associated with the renegotiation of contracts related to corporate governance could contribute to this effect and Bergman and Nicolaievsky (2007) show that public companies in Mexico do not improve corporate governance standards beyond what is required by the law. The market control hypothesis can explain a negative relationship between corporate governance improvements induced by cross-border mergers, and industry value.

2.2. Spillover effects hypothesis

Corporate governance can be considered as an additional input in production. A corporate governance reforming firm utilizes this input more efficiently, and so can increases profits and can allow this firm to charge lower prices. Competition then forces other industry participants to imitate, or face being driven out of the market. The spillover effects hypothesis predicts a positive relationship between corporate governance improvements and industry value and does not presume or rely upon any particular industry structure.

2.3. Industry competition hypothesis

This hypothesis is formulated in Bris and Brisley (2007). In their model of an industry with less-than-perfect investor protection, firms competing in quantities produce more than in a perfect corporate governance (profit maximizing) setting. If a subset of firms in the industry improve their corporate governance standards (e.g., by means of cross-border mergers), then these target firms have less incentive to expropriate shareholders, leading them to reduce output. Paradoxically, restricting output by the target firms leaves more room for the unmerged firms to expand output and produce even more than before. The net effect is a decrease in output for the industry and hence an increase in prices. Higher prices and lower costs for target firms, albeit on reduced volumes, increase their profits. Higher prices and higher output for unreformed firms increase their profits. Overall, this simple model provides a competitive argument for why corporate governance improvement through cross-border mergers is beneficial for a whole industry. Competition acts as a complement to corporate governance at the industry level. If one firm in an industry improves corporate governance, the resulting increase in efficiency leads to an increase in the value of the firm. The improved governance provides a positive externality to other industry participants—by reducing production, the better-governed firm leaves more room for profits to the industry incumbents. The model shows that increases in industry value do not necessarily rely on competing firms being implicitly forced to reform. Instead, good governance forces the target firm to become a more efficient competitor, and allows unreformed firms to capture a larger market share. The value of all firms increases and so does the total industry value. The industry competition hypothesis predicts a positive relationship between corporate governance and industry value.

3. Data

3.1. Industry data

We use all available firms in CRSP, Compustat and Datastream to construct annual series of industry-specific variables within each country for the years 1990–2001. We classify firms within each of the 39 industrial groups defined in Datastream.[3] Initially, firms in the United States are classified by their two-digit SICs. Since there is no mechanical correspondence between Datastream industries and SIC codes, we handmatch two-digit SIC codes with their corresponding four-digit Datastream Industrial Classification Codes. For each industry within a country we calculate the annual Tobin's Q. Datastream calculates the book value of assets *net* of intangible assets, so Tobin's Q calculated from Compustat and Datastream are not exactly comparable. Moreover, some of the resulting book equity values from Datastream are negative. To overcome the distorting effect of the negative values, we calculate the annual industry Tobin's Q by inverting the median of the inverted firm-specific Tobin's Q.[4] Additionally, in the econometric analysis, we use country-random effects, and time-invariant, country-specific controls.

Individual Tobin's Q for US firms are calculated as the market value of the firm's assets divided by its book value (Gompers et al., 2003; Kaplan and Zingales, 1997). The market value of the assets is computed as the book value of the assets plus the market value of common stock, minus the book value of common stock and deferred taxes. For non-US firms, the market value of the firm is calculated as the market value of equity plus the book value of the firm's liabilities. The latter is computed by

---

[3] Datastream Industrial classifications exist at six levels. Level four comprises 39 sectors based on the FTSE Actuaries System.

[4] Shin and Stulz (1998) and Gertner et al. (2002) also calculate industry Tobin's Q using the median Q of the firms within each industry.

subtracting the book value of equity (Datastream company account item # 307) from the book value of total assets (Datastream item # 392). In each year, we calculate individual Tobin's Q for firms that remain listed at December 31. We also include in our industry measures of Tobin's Q, those acquired target firms that are delisted during the year. We record the most recent information available for those firms—stock price data in the month prior to delisting, and accounting data for the year of delisting. Because delisting happens after the acquisition announcement, the market value of the target firms already incorporates the effect of the takeover premium on stock prices.

We are able to calculate industry Tobin's Q for 7233 industry-country-years from 39 industries from 41 different countries, across a period of 12 years. We consider only the countries for which we have merger data and corporate governance indices, as described in the following section.

3.2. Merger and acquisitions data

The base mergers sample includes all the cross-border acquisitions of public companies available in Securities Data Corporation, from January 1, 1990, through December 31, 2001. We only consider completed transactions, and we exclude from the initial sample LBOs, spin-offs, recapitalizations, self-tender and exchange offers, repurchases, acquisitions of minority stakes, and privatizations. Because corporate governance changes are legally effective only when 100% of the shares of the target get acquired (Bris and Cabolis, 2008), our sample includes only this type of transaction. We also exclude deals that involve firms from countries without corporate governance data available in La Porta et al. (1998) and also countries defined by them as being of socialist legal origin. This leaves us with 16,772 cross-border acquisitions of targets from 41 different countries.

For each acquisition we obtain the industry classification and country of bidder and target, the dollar value of the transaction, and the date of announcement of the deal.[5] We have data on the dollar value of the transaction for a reduced sample of 7597 acquisitions. Throughout the paper, we report results for the full 16,772 samples, unless data on the dollar value of the deal is necessary, in which case we report results for the reduced sample.

We group acquisitions within an industry depending on the industry classification of the target, as outlined above. We calculate the number of listed firms in a given

---

[5] The dollar value of the transaction is the total value of consideration paid by the acquirer, excluding fees and expenses. It includes the amount paid for all common stock, common stock equivalents, preferred stock, debt, options, assets, warrants, and stake purchases made within 6 months of the announcement date of the transaction. Assumed liabilities are included in the value if they are publicly disclosed. Preferred stock is included only if it is being acquired as part of a 100% acquisition. If a portion of the consideration paid by the acquirer is common stock, the stock is valued by using the closing price on the last full trading day before the announcement of the terms of the stock swap. If the exchange ratio of shares offered changes, the stock is valued based on its closing price on the last full trading date before the date of the exchange ratio change.

industry, country, and year, from CRSP (US firms) and Datastream (non-US firms). This allows us to construct the following measures of merger intensity:

$$AV_{jit} = \frac{VA_{jit}}{MC_{jit}}, \tag{1}$$

$$AN_{jit} = \frac{NA_{jit}}{NC_{jit}}. \tag{2}$$

VA_{jit} denotes the *dollar* value of all completed cross-border acquisitions *of* firms from industry j, in country i and in year t. MC_{jit} denotes the dollar denominated market capitalization of industry j in country i and in year t. Similarly, NA_{jit} is the *number* of completed cross-border acquisitions and NC_{jit} is the number of listed companies in industry j in country i and in year t. Thus AV_{jit} is a measure of the relative acquisition *value* and can be interpreted as the percentage of a domestic industry's market capitalization that is bought by foreigners in a given year. Similarly, AN_{jit} represents the *percentage* of the publicly listed companies in an industry that are acquired by foreigners in a given year.[6]

In Table 1 we report the aggregate AV_{jit} (cross-border $ value) and AN_{jit} (cross-border number) by geographic region and report also their 'all merger' (i.e., cross-border *and* domestic) analogues. We distinguish between European Eurozone countries, and European non-Eurozone countries. In the period 1990–1994, there are significant differences across regions. The number and value of cross-border mergers of firms in North America, Oceania, and Western Europe is relatively high, compared to Africa, Central and South America, and Asia. Overall there is a significant increase in the merger volume during the second half of the 1990s. In North America for instance, 0.45% of the market capitalization was acquired by foreign corporations between 1990 and 1994; the ratio increased to 1.43% during the years 1995–2001. The volume of cross-border mergers in Central and South America increases 14 times.

4. Corporate governance indices

In this section we describe our calculation of industry-specific corporate governance indices. Our starting point is the country-specific indices of shareholder rights and accounting standards from La Porta et al. (1998). As Bris and Cabolis (2008) discuss,

---

[6] Datastream does not provide information on *all* the firms listed in a given industry. In this respect, the merger ratios we calculate are an approximation. Using data from IFC manuals, we have also estimated (but do not report) our regressions using the market capitalization of all firms in the country, and the number of all listed firms in the country, as denominators in the corresponding ratios of merger activity. There is no qualitative change in the results. Moreover, the total number of firms (in a country) that we obtain from Datastream, and the total market capitalization of the country, do not differ much from their IFC equivalents after 1985. We report results based on industry because their interpretation is more appropriate.

Table 1

Merger activity around the world

This table provides measures of Merger Intensity by geographical region and time period. We measure the dollar Value of Acquisitions relative to the Total Market Capitalization, and the Number of Acquisitions relative to the Number of Listed Firms. Value of Acquisition is calculated as the amount paid for all common stock, common stock equivalents, preferred stock, debt, options, assets, warrants, and stake purchases made within 6 months of the announcement date of the transaction excluding fees and expenses. Liabilities are included if their value has been publicly disclosed. The common stock used as payment in an acquisition is valued at the closing price of the last full trading day before the announcement of the stock swap's terms. In the case of a change in the exchange ratio of shares offered, the stock is valued according to the closing price of the last full trading date. The number of listed firms is the number of firms with available stock price information in Datastream. The sample includes all the completed acquisitions of 100% interest in a public company available in the Securities Data Corporation, from January 1, 1990 to December 31, 2001. The sample does not include LBOs, spin-offs, recapitalizations, self-tender and exchange offers, repurchases, minority stake purchases, acquisitions of remaining interest, and privatizations.

| | 1990–1994 | | | | 1995–2001 | | | |
| | All mergers | | Cross-border | | All mergers | | Cross-border | |
	$ Value (%)	Number (%)	$ Value (%)	Number (%)	$ Value (%)	Number (%)	$ Value (%)	Number (%)
Africa	0.60	3.27	0.27	0.86	2.07	9.98	0.55	2.39
Asia	0.37	1.46	0.03	0.48	1.02	3.43	0.15	0.93
North America	2.63	17.92	0.45	2.25	7.42	35.12	1.43	5.12
Oceania	2.24	12.98	1.05	5.55	3.17	24.05	1.48	7.55
Central and South America	0.04	3.92	0.02	2.94	0.84	8.71	0.69	6.47
Western Europe— Eurozone	1.81	15.55	0.69	5.04	3.97	15.87	2.08	6.09
Western Europe— No Euro	1.49	5.65	0.96	3.25	2.14	6.77	0.76	4.72
All countries	1.19	12.25	0.27	2.58	4.47	17.82	1.26	4.24

these indices describe the initial corporate governance environment of target and acquirer in a cross-border merger and hence can be used to describe the potential for change in environment caused by an acquisition. The shareholder protection index is the product of shareholder rights multiplied by the efficiency of the judicial system index.

4.1. Corporate governance quality

Every acquisition in our sample is characterized by the shareholder protection index and accounting standards index for the country of the acquiring firm, and those for the country of the target firm. The simple differences between the corresponding indices of the two countries provide an indication of the *corporate governance quality transfer* that results from the cross-border merger. To illustrate, suppose that a UK firm acquires a Greek firm. Since the shareholder protection index in Greece is 14, and the shareholder protection index in the United Kingdom is 50, the acquisition serves as a potential way of transferring corporate governance practices from the United Kingdom to Greece, or vice versa.

The La Porta et al. (1998) indices have different ranges, and so it is difficult to draw comparisons in absolute terms. Therefore, we classify countries into two groups for each index, depending on whether the corporate governance indicator for a country is above or below the median. We assign a value of 1 to the corresponding index when the country has an index above the median, zero otherwise. Since the median shareholder protection index is 20, we assign to Greece an index of shareholder protection of 0, and we assign to the United Kingdom an index of shareholder protection of 1. When a UK firm acquires a Greek firm we measure the corporate governance transfer from the United Kingdom to Greece as the difference between the shareholder protection indices in the two countries: $1 - 0 = 1$. This convention yields three types of cross-border mergers with respect to corporate governance transfer index: *corporate-governance-improving* acquisitions (difference index equals 1), *corporate-governance-preserving* acquisitions (difference index equals 0), and *corporate-governance-worsening* acquisitions (difference index equals -1).

In an earlier version of this paper we used the absolute difference between the corporate governance indices of the acquiring and target firms. Qualitatively, our results were not different from the ones presented here. By adopting the current classification between two categories, we reduce the impact of a potential errors-in-variables problem in the La Porta et al. (1998) indices.

Table 2 shows the corporate governance quality transfer for the cross-border acquisitions in our sample. We report the percentages of cross-border mergers that are corporate governance worsening, preserving, and improving, from the point of view of the target firm. Our results contrast with Rossi and Volpin (2004), who report that the corporate governance quality of acquirers in cross-border mergers is significantly higher than the quality of targets. In the period 1995–2001, we find slightly more cross-border transactions involving a below-median shareholder protection acquirer buying an above-median target (18.13% of the cases) than the reverse (16.93%).

The next step is to average the indicators across firms in an industry, country and year. To separate the effect of the acquisitions on acquiring and target firms, we first consider, for every industry, only those acquisitions where firms in the industry are target firms. We then calculate weighted averages, weighting by the dollar value of the acquisition. In the case of no cross-border merger activity within a particular industry and year, we set the corresponding difference index to zero.

Weighting by the dollar value of the merger has one important advantage. The difference in corporate governance quality between the acquiring and target firms for a given industry will tend to zero as the number of cross-border mergers tends to zero. Therefore, our indices reflect the volume of cross-border mergers in a given industry, as well as the differential quality of the firms involved in the acquisition in terms of

Table 2

Cross-border mergers and corporate governance quality transfer

This table classifies the corporate governance quality transfer for each cross-border merger in our sample. We obtain the corporate governance index for the country of nationality of both the acquiror and target from La Porta et al. (1998). We classify each country into one of two categories: "Above the median" and "Below the median" for each of the four indices. An acquisition is classified as "Corporate Governance Worsening" if the acquirer's corresponding index is below the median while the target's is above the median; "Corporate Governance Improving" if the acquirer's corresponding index is above the median while the target's is below the median; and "Corporate Governance preserving" otherwise. The table reports the number as well as the percentage of the cross-border mergers which are Corporate Governance Worsening, Preserving and Improving for each index and subperiod. The sample includes all the completed acquisitions of 100% interest in a public company available in the Securities Data Corporation, from January 1, 1990 to December 31, 2001. The sample does not include LBOs, spin-offs, recapitalizations, self-tender and exchange offers, repurchases, minority stake purchases, acquisitions of remaining interest, and privatizations.

		1990–1994			1995–2001		
		Worsening	Preserving	Improving	Worsening	Preserving	Improving
Shareholder protection	Number of acquisitions	449	2124	602	1523	5454	1422
	Percent	14.14	66.90	18.96	18.13	64.94	16.93
Accounting standards	Number of acquisitions	370	2232	573	1310	5557	1532
	Percent	11.65	70.30	18.05	15.60	66.60	18.24

corporate governance practices. However, because we only weight those cross-border mergers where the levels of shareholder protection in the acquirer and the target differ, we are effectively using as a natural control sample both the subsample of mergers where the levels of shareholder protection in the acquirer and the target are the same, and the subsample of firms that do not get involved in acquisition activity.

5. The value of corporate governance: industry-level evidence

In this section we analyze the relationship between industry value, measured by the Tobin's Q, and the merger-specific corporate governance indicators.

5.1. Shareholder protection and industry value

Let q_{jit} be the natural logarithm of the Tobin's Q in industry j, country i, and year t, calculated as described in Section 3.1. For any set of corporate governance variables G_{jit}—be it the index corresponding to either the target or the acquiring firms, or the difference between them, or both—we estimate the following regression:

$$q_{jit+1} = D_{jt} + \delta AV_{jit} + \theta H_{jit} + \beta G_{jit} + \varepsilon_{jit} \qquad (3)$$

We use a panel of 7233 industry-country-year observations. D_{jt} is a vector of (39 $\times$ 12) industry-year fixed-effects, which captures any specific event affecting industry j in year t. We estimate the model with country-year random effects, which allow us to isolate idiosyncratic events such as the prediction by Pagano and Volpin (2005) that the frequency of mergers and acquisitions is negatively correlated with employment protection. Similarly, the presence or absence of merger laws affects the number of mergers. In countries and periods without a merger law, SDC reports a limited number of acquisitions. The reason is that, absent such laws, there are no notification requirements for the acquirer, and so mergers can take place without public knowledge. Finally, in some countries, acquisitions are an important means of effecting change in control, while in others they play a minor role.[7] These type of effects will be captured by our random effects.

The value of the industry is also determined by three industry-country-year specific characteristics. We first control for the dollar volume of cross-border mergers, AV_{jit}, as calculated in Equation (1). In other words, we separate the corporate governance characteristics of the acquiring firms from the merger volume in a particular industry. We also control for the time-varying Herfindahl index of the industry, H_{jit}, calculated using the dollar value of the sales in every firm in the industry, with available data from Datastream. Eckbo (1985) fails to find evidence of a positive relationship between industry concentration and the benefits to rivals of merging firms, that industrial organization models such as Stigler (1964) would predict.

Dual-listing of securities in the United States is often claimed to be a means for foreign issuers to commit to better governance (e.g., Coffee, 1999). There is some evidence that the announcement of an American Depositary Receipt (ADR) has a positive and significant effect (Miller, 1999), which becomes larger for firms from countries with weaker shareholder protection (Lins et al., 2001). These results would seem to indicate that convergence to a better corporate governance is possible through a cross-listing, and that it creates firm value. To measure the importance of cross-listings as an alternative way to import improved corporate governance, for each industry and country we identify the firms listed on a US exchange, either through a direct listing or an ADR, and compute the percent of listed firms each year. We use this fraction as an explanatory variable in the regression. Our hypothesis is that industries will be more valuable the more firms list abroad.

Our specification offers two additional advantages. Unlike La Porta et al. (2002), who have to estimate a random effect model because of the time invariance of the corporate governance measures, we specify the more natural industry-year fixed-effect model. In addition, because of the availability of time-varying industry data, our results are interpretable in a time-series setting. That is, the vector of coefficients β indicates to

---

[7] In countries with concentrated ownership-all except the US, Canada, and the UK-control changes are often not by public acquisition. See Dyck and Zingales (2004) and Bris et al. (2007), for an analysis of takeover laws and their effect on merger activity.

what extent a change in the corporate governance indices in industry j, country i, from time $t - 1$ to t, determine the change in the Tobin's Q of the industry in the next period.

5.1.1. Results

Table 3 reports the result of the estimation when the dependent variable is the Tobin's Q of the industry of the target firms. The independent variables in the estimation are the corresponding corporate governance indicators for the average acquirer in that industry, the average of the corporate governance index differences between the

Table 3

Tobin's Q and corporate governance quality of target firms

This table presents regressions of Tobin's Q (in logs) by industry, country, and year, on corporate governance indices. Each acquisition is characterized by the corporate governance characteristics of the acquiring and target firms. We consider the indices of shareholder protection and accounting standards, from La Porta et al. (1998). We classify countries either as "Above the median" or "Below the median" for each index. Each country index equals 1 if it is "Above the median", and zero otherwise. Each characteristic index difference is calculated for each acquisition as the corporate governance index of the acquirer, minus that of the target. We then calculate the weighted average of the indices by industry, country and year, where each observation is weighted by the dollar value of the acquisition. The sample covers 1990–2001 and includes 39 industries in 41 countries. Standard errors are adjusted for heteroskedasticity. All regressions are estimated with industry-year fixed-effects, and country-random effects. Absolute value of z-statistics in brackets.

	(I)	(II)	(III)
Constant	0.366** [2.05]	0.365** [2.04]	0.365** [2.04]
Industry Herfindahl index	0.003 [0.22]	−0.01 [0.88]	−0.011 [0.96]
Percent of firms in industry with ADR or cross-listing	0.088* [1.76]	0.112** [2.24]	0.112** [2.22]
Total value of cross-border M&A/market capitalization industry	−0.008 [0.20]	0.042 [1.04]	0.033 [0.82]
Number of firms in industry/100	−7.1 [0.52]	15.246 [1.15]	16.035 [1.21]
Shareholder protection index—acquirer country	0.053* [1.93]		
Shareholder protection index—target country	−0.023 [0.66]		
Accounting standards—acquirer country	−0.03 [0.99]		
Accounting standards—target country	0.070* [1.91]		
Difference in shareholder protection (acquirer minus target)		0.005 [0.22]	
Difference in accounting standards (acquirer minus target)			−0.023 [1.01]
Observations	6909	6909	6909
Number of countries	41	41	41
R^2 within	0.24	0.24	0.24
R^2 between	0.38	0.32	0.32
R^2 total	0.22	0.22	0.22

*, **, and *** significant at 10%, 5%, and 1% levels, respectively.

acquirer and the target, and a decomposition of these variables between positive and negative values. We also control for the shareholder protection and the accounting standards of the target firm's country.

Our results show that shareholder protection improving cross-border mergers increase industry value. We find that the Tobin's Q of the target industry is higher the better the protection provided in the country of origin of acquiring firms.

The Tobin's Q of the target industry is higher the larger the difference in protection between the acquiring and the target firms. However, this result is not statistically significant. We obtain similar results for accounting standards. Therefore, it seems in principle that changes in corporate governance induced by cross-border mergers bring about a valuation effect in the industries involved, consistent with the firm-specific results presented by Bris and Cabolis (2008). There is a positive and significant effect of cross-listings. In model I, a 10% increase in the number of cross-listed firms in the industry, increases Tobin's Q by about 1%. This result is statistically significant at the 10% probability level.

6. Improvements and deteriorations in corporate governance

In this section we differentiate cross-border mergers based on the relative corporate governance indices of the acquirer and the target. Specifically, we decompose the industry corporate governance indices into positive and negative values. A positive value means that the average corporate governance quality of the target industry improves as a result of cross-border mergers. Similarly, a negative value means that the average acquirer comes from a country with a lower value of the corresponding index.

In Table 4 we present the results of our panel estimation. In contrast to Table 3, we now find significant effects of corporate governance changes. In particular, when we consider only the industries where the difference in shareholder protection between the acquirer and the target is positive, the estimated coefficient is 0.046, significant at the 10% level. The economic significance of such an effect can be substantial. To illustrate, consider the Telecommunications industry in South Korea. South Korea has a shareholder protection index of 10.7, a value below the median. Suppose that 20% of the firms in that industry were acquired in 1998 by Spanish firms. Spain has a shareholder protection index of 25, a value that is above the median. Therefore, the shareholder protection index of the Telecommunications industry in 1998 in South Korea increases by 0.2 points, and, from the regression in Table 4, the Tobin's Q of the industry would increase by 0.9%. Note that this result is independent of the quality of the firms involved and depends only on the relative qualities of corporate governance in the home countries of acquiring and target firms.

We also find that adopting better accounting standards significantly increases industry value. In model II, the coefficient of the "Accounting Standards Difference if >0" is 0.059, significant at the 10% level. In economic terms, the coefficient means that

Table 4

Tobin's Q and corporate governance quality of target firms: improvements and deteriorations in corporate governance

This table presents regressions of Tobin's Q (in logs) by industry, country, and year, on corporate governance indices. Each acquisition is characterized by the corporate governance characteristics of the acquiring and target firms. We consider the indices of shareholder protection and accounting standards from La Porta et al. (1998). We classify countries either as "Above the median" or "Below the median" for each of the four indices. Each index equals 1 if it is "Above the median", and zero otherwise. The index difference is calculated for each acquisition as the index of the acquirer, minus that of the target. We then calculate the weighted average of the indices by industry, country and year, where each observation is weighted by the dollar value of the acquisition. The sample extends between 1990 and 2001 and includes 39 industries in 41 countries. Standard errors are adjusted for heteroskedasticity. All regressions are estimated with industry × year fixed-effects, and country-random effects. Absolute value of z-statistics in brackets

	(I)	(II)
Constant	0.365** [2.04]	0.365** [2.04]
Industry Herfindahl index	−0.01 [0.81]	−0.012 [0.97]
Percent of firms in industry with ADR or cross-listing	0.110** [2.19]	0.108** [2.15]
Total value of cross-border M&A/market capitalization industry	0.026 [0.62]	0.002 [0.04]
Number of firms in industry/100	15.001 [1.13]	15.95 [1.20]
Difference in shareholder protection if >0	0.046* [1.81]	
Difference in shareholder protection if <0	−0.017 [0.65]	
Difference in accounting standards if >0		0.059* [1.76]
Difference in accounting standards if <0		−0.079*** [2.58]
Observations	6909	6909
Number of countries	41	41
R^2 within	0.24	0.24
R^2 between	0.31	0.34
R^2 total	0.22	0.22

*, **, and *** significant at 10%, 5%, and 1% levels, respectively.

increasing the domestic industry accounting standards by 0.2 (acquisition of 20% of the firms in the industry by firms coming from better governance environments) leads to an increase in Tobin's Q of 1.2%.

The valuation effects of changes in shareholder protection are not symmetric. That is, while we find that increases in the level of shareholder protection increase the value of the industry in which the target firm operates, it is not true that reductions in the level of protection harm target industries.

With respect to accounting standards however, we do find a highly significant impact of reduction in accounting standards on industry valuation. In fact, when 20% of the industry value is acquired by firms coming from countries with weaker accounting standards, the Tobin's Q of the industry actually increases by 1.6%. We show in the next section that this result is driven by a nonlinear relationship between accounting standard changes and Tobin's Q.

6.1. Results by OECD membership

We now consider which countries benefit most from improvements in corporate governance induced by cross-border mergers. We classify the country of origin of the target firms by OECD membership, a proxy for economic development which does not depend on subjective classification such as groupings based on GDP per capita.

In our sample, we have 21 OECD members,[8] and 20 non-OECD members.[9] For the non-OECD members, we find a positive statistically insignificant effect of improvements of shareholder protection, and a negative significant effect of deteriorations in shareholder protection. The latter result implies that, when 20% of the value of the industry in a non-OECD country is acquired by firms coming from countries with lower levels of shareholder protection, the industry's Q drops by 3.5%. Conversely, we find a positive significant valuation effect of deteriorations in accounting standards, for non-OECD members. In economic terms, when 20% of an industry in a non-OECD country is acquired by firms coming from countries with below-median accounting standards, the Tobin's Q of the industry increases by 16.4%. In a (nonreported) regression with individual countries we find that this result is caused by acquisitions in Ireland (Table 5).

6.2. Industry concentration and corporate governance

The valuation effect that we identify in the previous sections derives from a spillover to the whole industry of the benefits of improving corporate governance in a single firm. One reason for such an effect is that unmerged firms tend to imitate the improved corporate governance of target firms and benefit from doing so. Alternatively, competitive effects also predict that, without being forced to improve their governance, unmerged firms would nevertheless enjoy the benefits of the cross-border merger because it would allow them to increase their output. Therefore, spillover effects depend ultimately on competitive forces. We do not have an empirical test for the imitation hypothesis, other than a case-by-case examination of corporate governance reforms. However, we can analyze the effect of the competitive structure of the industry on the valuation effects of international mergers.

For each industry-country-year in our sample, we proxy competition with the Herfindahl index. In Table 6 we reestimate our panel regressions using an interactive term between industry concentration and corporate governance. Irrespective of which proxy for concentration we use, the sign of the interaction is positive (a negative coefficient when there are governance deteriorations is evidence of a positive effect), but results are not statistically significant. This result is consistent with the *industry*

---

[8] Australia, Austria, Belgium, Canada, Denmark, France, Germany, Greece, Italy, Japan, Netherlands, New Zealand, Norway, Portugal, South Korea, Spain, Sweden, Switzerland, Turkey, USA, and the UK.

[9] Argentina, Brazil, Chile, Colombia, Egypt, Hong Kong, India, Indonesia, Ireland, Israel, Malaysia, Pakistan, Peru, Philippines, Singapore, South Africa, Taiwan, Thailand, Venezuela, and Zimbabwe.

Table 5

Tobin's Q and corporate governance quality of target firms: OECD vs. non-OECD countries

This table presents regressions of Tobin's Q (in logs) by industry, country, and year, on corporate governance indices. Each acquisition is characterized by the corporate governance characteristics of the acquiring and target firms. We consider the indices of shareholder protection and accounting standards from La Porta et al. (1998). We classify countries either as "Above the median" or "Below the median" for each of the four indices. Each index equals 1 if it is "Above the median", and zero otherwise. The index difference is calculated for each acquisition as the index of the acquirer, minus that of the target. We then calculate the weighted average of the indices by industry, country and year, where each observation is weighted by the dollar value of the acquisition. The sample extends between 1990 and 2001 and includes 39 industries in 41 countries. Standard errors are adjusted for heteroskedasticity. All regressions are estimated with industry × year fixed-effects, and country-random effects. Absolute value of z-statistics in brackets.

	Non-OECD countries		OECD countries	
	(I)	(II)	(III)	(IV)
Constant	−0.379 [0.76]	−0.361 [0.72]	0.362** [2.45]	0.362** [2.45]
Industry Herfindahl index	−0.097*** [3.47]	−0.099*** [3.56]	0.023* [1.87]	0.022* [1.80]
Percent of firms in industry with ADR or cross-listing	0.189** [1.96]	0.131 [1.33]	0.096* [1.74]	0.099* [1.80]
Total value of cross-border M&A/market capitalization industry	0.094 [0.62]	−0.032 [0.21]	−0.047 [1.26]	−0.05 [1.33]
Number of firms in industry/100	2.52*** [2.69]	2.62*** [2.80]	1.579 [0.14]	1.73 [0.15]
Difference in shareholder protection if >0	−0.02 [0.19]		0.039 [1.10]	
Difference in shareholder protection if <0	0.175* [1.88]		0.023 [0.98]	
Difference in Accounting Standards if >0		0.024 [0.19]		0.047 [1.38]
Difference in accounting standards if <0		−0.166* [1.83]		−0.037 [1.28]
Observations	2294	2294	4615	4615
Number of countries	20	20	21	21
R^2 within	0.35	0.34	0.34	0.34
R^2 between	0.77	0.79	0.06	0.06
R^2 total	0.35	0.35	0.31	0.31

*, **, and *** significant at 10%, 5%, and 1% levels, respectively.

Table 6

Tobin's Q and corporate governance quality of target firms: impact of industry concentration

This table presents regressions of Tobin's Q (in logs) by industry, country, and year, on corporate governance indices. Each acquisition is characterized by the corporate governance characteristics of the acquiring and target firms. We consider the indices of shareholder protection and accounting standards, from La Porta et al. (1998). We classify countries either as "Above the median" or "Below the median" for each of the four indices. Each index equals 1 if it is "Above the median", and zero otherwise. The index difference is calculated for each acquisition as the index of the acquirer, minus that of the target. We then calculate the weighted average of the indices by industry, country and year, where each observation is weighted by the dollar value of the acquisition. The sample extends between 1990 and 2001 and includes 39 industries in 41 countries. Standard errors are adjusted for heteroskedasticity. All regressions are estimated with industry × year fixed-effects, and country-random effects. Absolute value of z-statistics in brackets.

	(I)	(II)	(III)	(IV)
Constant	0.365** [2.04]	0.366** [2.04]	0.365** [2.04]	0.365** [2.04]
Industry Herfindahl index	−0.01 [0.79]	−0.014 [1.15]	−0.011 [0.90]	−0.01 [0.87]
Percent of firms in industry with ADR or cross-listing	0.111** [2.21]	0.108*** [2.14]	0.112*** [2.24]	0.112*** [2.24]
Total value of cross-border M&A/market capitalization industry	0.045 [1.10]	0.021 [0.51]	0.042 [1.05]	0.037 [0.94]
Number of firms in industry/100	15.373 [1.16]	15.471 [1.17]	14.338 [1.05]	15.377 [1.13]
Herfindahl index × increase in shareholder protection	0.029 [0.33]			
Herfindahl index × decrease in shareholder protection	0.032 [0.67]			
Herfindahl index × increase in accounting standards		0.095 [1.04]		
Herfindahl index × decrease in accounting standards		−0.06 [1.33]		
Number of firms × increase in shareholder protection			23.852 [0.30]	
Number of firms × decrease in shareholder protection			79.042 [0.42]	
Number of firms × increase in accounting standards				3.675 [0.04]
Number of firms × decrease in accounting standards				−160.553 [0.68]
Observations	6909	6909	6909	6909
Number of countries	41	41	41	41
R^2 within	0.24	0.24	0.24	0.24
R^2 between	0.32	0.33	0.32	0.32
R^2 total	0.22	0.22	0.22	0.22

*, **, and *** significant at 10%, 5%, and 1% levels, respectively.

competition hypothesis which predicts that cross-border mergers always result in increases in profitability irrespective of the number of firms that are acquired. However, we cannot make a conclusive statement on the transmission mechanism between corporate governance improvements at the single-firm level, and overall industry valuation effects.

6.3. Possible nonlinearities

As in the previous section, the effects of industry concentration suggest a nonlinearity in the relationship between corporate governance improvements and valuation effects. If 90% of the market capitalization of an industry is acquired by foreign companies that bring a much better level of corporate governance, the direct effect on industry value will be large. Similarly for industries not exposed to foreign entrants, where only one of the firms is acquired by a foreigner, the spillover effects can be sizeable as well. However, for intermediate acquisition volumes, the market concentration effect partly offsets the benefits of improving the average corporate governance in the industry.

We test this hypothesis by computing the square value of the corporate governance indices that we use in the previous analyses, and we report the results in Table 7. Once we control for nonlinearities, the relationship between improvements in shareholder protection and accounting standards, and Tobin's Q is positive and statistically significant. The magnitude of the effect of shareholder protection and accounting standards is very similar.

The effect of accounting standard deteriorations reported in Table 3 (which results in an increase in Tobin's Q) is due to a nonlinear relationship between accounting standard changes and Tobin's Q. Model I shows a significant concavity, which suggests there exists a level of accounting standards for which further deterioration has no effect on the industry's Tobin's Q.

6.4. Results by industry

Finally, we provide results by industry, exploiting the cross-sectional variation in our sample. In Table 8 we report the estimated coefficients in regressions similar to Table 4, by industry group. The positive valuation effect of improvements in shareholder protection is most evident in a few industries—Construction & Materials, Healthcare Equipment & Services, Pharmaceuticals and Biotechnology, and Steel. Common to these industries is the need for significant up-front investment in capital goods or in R&D and we conjecture that such circumstances make most important the shareholders' ability to hold management accountable for its actions. Likewise, the positive valuation effects of improvements in accounting standards are driven by: Construction & Materials, Media, Mobile Telecommunications, Tobacco, Travel & Leisure. Construction is an industry notoriously linked with side-payments and we conjecture that improved accounting standards may play a significant role in limiting this and other black market practices. Similarly, accounting standards may be particu-

Table 7

Tobin's Q and corporate governance quality of target firms: nonlinearities

This table presents regressions of Tobin's Q (in logs) by industry, country, and year, on corporate governance indices. Each acquisition is characterized by the corporate governance characteristics of the acquiring and target firms. We consider the indices of shareholder protection and accounting standards, from La Porta et al. (1998). We classify countries either as "Above the median" or "Below the median" for each of the four indices. Each index equals 1 if it is "Above the median", and zero otherwise. The index difference is calculated for each acquisition as the index of the acquirer, minus that of the target. We then calculate the weighted average of the indices by industry, country and year, where each observation is weighted by the dollar value of the acquisition. The sample extends between 1990 and 2001 and includes 39 industries in 41 countries. Standard errors are adjusted for heteroskedasticity. All regressions are estimated with industry × year fixed-effects, and country-random effects. Absolute value of z-statistics in brackets.

		(I)	(II)
Constant	0.365** [2.04]	0.365** [2.04]	0.365** [2.04]
Industry Herfindahl index	−0.012 [1.04]	−0.009 [0.75]	−0.011 [0.93]
Percent of firms in industry with ADR or cross-listing	0.108** [2.15]	0.108** [2.15]	0.107** [2.12]
Total value of cross-border M&A/market capitalization industry	0.01 [0.25]	0.022 [0.53]	0 [0.01]
Number of firms in industry/100	15.718 [1.18]	13.226 [0.99]	14.615 [1.10]
Difference in shareholder protection acquirers minus targets	0.044* [1.82]		
Difference in shareholder protection—squared	−0.013 [0.40]		
Difference in accounting standards acquirers minus targets	0.027 [0.85]		
Difference in accounting standards—squared	0.075** [2.27]		
Difference in shareholder protection if >0		0.441** [1.97]	
Difference in shareholder protection if >0—squared		−0.217 [1.21]	
Difference in shareholder protection if <0		−0.256 [1.09]	
Difference in shareholder protection if <0—squared		−0.244 [1.01]	
Difference in accounting standards if >0			0.223* [1.79]
Difference in accounting standards if >0—squared			−0.183 [0.97]
Difference in accounting standards if <0			−0.183 [0.63]
Difference in accounting standards if <0—squared			−0.106 [0.36]
Observations	6909	6909	6909
Number of countries	38	41	41
R^2 within	0.24	0.24	0.24
R^2 between	0.35	0.32	0.34
R^2 total	0.22	0.22	0.22

*, **, and *** significant at 10%, 5%, and 1% levels, respectively.

Table 8

Tobin's Q and corporate governance quality of target firms: results by industry

This table presents regressions of Tobin's Q (in logs) by industry, country, and year, on corporate governance indices. Each acquisition is characterized by the corporate governance characteristics of the acquiring and target firms. We consider the indices of shareholder protection and accounting standards, from La Porta et al. (1998). We classify countries either as "Above the median" or "Below the median" for each of the four indices. Each index equals 1 if it is "Above the median", and zero otherwise. The index difference is calculated for each acquisition as the index of the acquirer, minus that of the target. We then calculate the weighted average of the indices by industry, country and year, where each observation is weighted by the dollar value of the acquisition. The sample extends between 1990 and 2001 and includes 39 industries in 41 countries. Standard errors are adjusted for heteroskedasticity. All regressions are estimated with industry × year fixed-effects, and country-random effects.

	Difference in shareholder protection if >0	Difference in shareholder protection if <0	Difference in accounting standards if >0	Difference in accounting standards if <0
Automobile & parts	0.003 (0.9943)	-0.074 (0.9271)	-0.009 (0.9871)	-0.167 (0.8610)
Beverages	0.022 (0.9613)	-0.154 (0.8453)	0.202 (0.2435)	-0.170 (0.8207)
Construction & materials	0.246** (0.0111)	-0.091 (0.9000)	0.265** (0.0000)	-0.158 (0.8669)
Diversified industrials	-0.055 (0.9323)	-0.353 (0.7112)	-0.157 (0.8427)	0.691*** (0.0000)
Electricity gas, water	-0.131 (0.8692)	-0.337 (0.7353)	-0.085 (0.9152)	-0.256 (0.7951)
Electronic & electrical equipment	-0.080 (0.9147)	(0.003) (0.9952)	0.004 (0.9935)	0.209*** (0.0000)
Engineering	-0.083 (0.8958)	-0.120 (0.8965)	-0.057 (0.9280)	-0.152 (0.8702)
Food & drug retailers	0.002 (0.9973)	-0.231 (0.7955)	-0.127 (0.8607)	0.016 (0.9743)
Food producers	-0.274 (0.7391)	-0.071 (0.9170)	-0.672 (0.3708)	-0.020 (0.9713)
Forestry & paper	0.128 (0.1395)	-0.012 (0.9819)	0.080 (0.6879)	-0.022 (0.9673)
Household goods	0.114 (0.5426)	-0.051 (0.9456)	0.114 (0.5488)	-0.076 (0.9262)
Healthcare equipment & services	2.706*** (0.0000)		-0.033 (0.9537)	-0.241 (0.8043)
Information technology	-0.191 (0.8152)	0.038 (0.9206)	0.120 (0.6362)	-0.025 (0.9645)
Leisure goods	0.032 (0.9398)	-0.067 (0.9220)		
Media	0.216 (0.1501)	-0.173 (0.8397)	0.259*** (0.0092)	-0.603 (0.5469)
Mining	0.140 (0.7335)	-0.098 (0.8721)	0.050 (0.9133)	0.228 (0.4865)
Oil & gas producers	-0.038 (0.9515)	-0.126 (0.8823)	0.031 (0.9355)	0.136 (0.3801)
Personal goods	-0.150 (0.8441)		0.174 (0.6811)	

*, **, and *** significant at 10%, 5%, and 1% levels, respectively.

larly important in industries such as Media and Leisure where the finished product is intangible and of potentially subjective value. Interestingly, even though the coefficient of "Difference in Accounting Standards if <0" is negative and significant for the whole sample, it is positive and significant for only two industries—Diversified Industrials, and Electronic & Electrical Equipment. The task of generating and testing rigorous hypotheses on these cross-industry effects we leave to future research.

7. Robustness issues

7.1. Alternative measures of corporate governance quality

Our study relies on the corporate governance indices developed in La Porta et al. (1998) and inevitably is subject to identified weaknesses of those indices. For example, the Daimler-Chrysler merger led to the new company being domiciled in Germany, requiring the company to implement a two-tier board structure, yet La Porta et al. (1998) report that the index of shareholder protection in Germany is lower than the one in the United States The index-based conclusion that the merger was corporate governance quality reducing for Chrysler could be questioned in this case. Another reasonable concern is that the LLSV index are time-invariant and computed from 1998 only, while our dataset spans the period 1990–2001. We therefore use two alternative indices of governance quality.

First, we employ the adjusted LLSV index constructed by Pagano and Volpin (2005) (The "PV index"), using questionnaires.[10] Second, we consider the World Bank Indicator of Rule of Law. This index is one of the World Bank Worldwide Governance Indicators (WGI), available for 212 countries and territories over the period 1996–2006. As we use an earlier period, we extrapolate the 1996 indices back to 1990. Additionally, because the World Bank data does not cover all years between 1996 and 2001, we assume for each year without data the value of the index from the previous year. In this way we construct a somewhat time-varying index of corporate governance quality that takes into account dynamic regulatory reform.[11] It measures the extent to which agents have confidence in and abide by the rules of society, and in particular the quality of contract enforcement, the police, and the courts, as well as the likelihood of crime and violence.

We construct similar measures to the differences described in Section 4. For the PV Index we classify countries into two groups for which the value of the index is above $(+1)$ or below (-1) the median. We then weight the $+1/-1$ differences by the dollar value of the acquisition, and standardize by the market capitalization of the industry. For the Rule of Law Index we compute, for each industry, a weighted average of the

---

[10] For details on the construction of the index, see http://www.e-aer.org/data/sept05_data_snyder.zip.

[11] The correlation matrix in the Appendix shows that this measure is positively and significantly correlated with the LLSV indices.

differences in the index between the acquirer and the target countries, where the weight is the dollar value of the acquisition. We standardize the difference by the market capitalization of the industry.

The advantage of our approach is that the two indices are time-varying. However, they are both based on purely legal variables that ignore the role of enforcement. The Rule of Law Index is based on the quality of the written law alone, and the PV Index is based on the LLSV Antidirector Rights Index, which is a summary of the legal provisions related to shareholder protection. In some countries there is a great difference between what merger regulations say and what the common practice is.

We report results in Table 9. We confirm our previous results and show a positive relationship between governance quality and industry's Tobin's Q. Model IV also shows that governance deteriorations are significantly related to reductions in industry value.

7.2. Alternative explanations: the role of financial constraints

The previous sections show that cross-border mergers result in an increase in industry value, and that such an increase is larger the better the governance of the acquiring firm, relative to the target industry. We find support for the hypothesis that there are spillover effects in corporate governance reform that benefit other firms in the same industry.

An alternative explanation could be that cross-border mergers are an efficient way for firms in an industry to reduce their financial dependence on external sources of capital. If the availability of capital is limited in a country, having one firm being acquired by a foreign firm with available capital could make the target firm more valuable. Additionally, it could free up capital to be used by domestic, nontarget firms which would also enjoy positive valuation effects.

We test this hypothesis by collecting data on firm's financial dependence. Unfortunately, the standard measure in the literature, based on Rajan and Zingales' (1998) US study, provides a measure of financial dependence only for manufacturing firms. In our paper, it can be used in only four of the 39 industries we consider. The Rajan and Zingales (1998) approach has been extended to all industries using regression analysis. The methodology consists of estimating financial dependence as a linear combination of firm characteristics. However, one of these characteristics is Tobin's Q, which is the endogenous variable in our regressions.

Almeida and Wolfenzon (2005) construct a country-specific measure of financial dependence, based on Rajan and Zingales (1998). For each country in their sample they compute the percentage of output produced by manufacturing industries. Then they calculate the weighted average of the Rajan and Zingales (1998) industry measures. The advantage of the Almeida and Wolfenzon (2005) EFN Index is that it proxies financial dependence for all industries. It has the disadvantage that it is not industry-specific.

In Table 10 we interact measures of governance improvement with the EFN Index of financial dependence. If our results were caused by more dependent firms benefiting more from cross-border mergers, then the interaction would have a positive coefficient.

Table 9

Tobin's Q and corporate governance quality of target firms: alternative measures of corporate governance

This table presents regressions of Tobin's Q (in logs) by industry, country, and year, on corporate governance indices. We use two alternative indices of corporate governance quality. The "PV Shareholder Protection Index" is the modified LLSV index from Pagano and Volpin (2005). For details on the construction of the index, see http://www.e-aer.org/data/sept05_data_snyder.zip. The "World Bank Rule of Law Index" measures the extent to which agents have confidence in and abide by the rules of society, and in particular the quality of contract enforcement, the police, and the courts, as well as the likelihood of crime and violence. Both indices are time-varying. The sample extends between 1990 and 2001 and includes 39 industries in 41 countries. Standard errors are adjusted for heteroskedasticity. All regressions are estimated with industry × year fixed-effects, and country-random effects. Absolute value of z-statistics in brackets.

	(I)	(II)	(III)	(IV)
Constant	0.365** [2.04]	0.365** [2.04]	0.365** [2.04]	0.365** [2.04]
Industry Herfindahl index	−0.01 [0.87]	−0.01 [0.86]	−0.01 [0.88]	−0.011 [0.90]
Percent of firms in industry with ADR or cross-listing	0.112** [2.23]	0.112** [2.23]	0.113** [2.26]	0.120** [2.38]
Total value of cross-border M&A/market capitalization	0.04 [1.01]	0.04 [1.01]	0.037 [0.92]	0.039 [0.98]
Number of firms in industry/100	15.486 [1.17]	15.481 [1.17]	15.45 [1.17]	15.978 [1.21]
Difference in WB Rule of Law	0.13* [1.67]			
Difference in WB rule of law if difference >0		0.012 [0.55]		
Difference in WB rule of law if difference <0		0.015 [0.38]		
Difference in PV shareholder protection			0.32* [1.74]	
Difference in PV shareholder protection if difference >0				0.002 [0.72]
Difference in PV shareholder protection if difference <0				0.964** [2.09]
Observations	6909	6909	6909	6909
Number of country	41	41	41	41
R^2 within	0.24	0.24	0.24	0.24
R^2 between	0.31	0.31	0.32	0.31
R^2 total	0.22	0.22	0.22	0.22

*, **, and *** significant at 10%, 5%, and 1% levels, respectively.

Table 10

Tobin's Q and corporate governance quality of target firms: external financial dependence

This table presents regressions of Tobin's Q (in logs) by industry, country, and year, on corporate governance indices. The EFN index is the index of External Financial Needs in the Manufacturing sector constructed by Almeida and Wolfenzon (2005). This index is computed as a weighted average of the industry-level measures of external finance dependence taken from Rajan and Zingales (1998). The weights are the industrial shares in total manufacturing output. Data is from UNIDO, Industrial Statistics Database. The sample extends between 1990 and 2001 and includes 39 industries in 41 countries. Standard errors are adjusted for heteroskedasticity. All regressions are estimated with industry $\times$ year fixed-effects, and country-random effects. Absolute value of z-statistics in brackets.

	(I)	(II)
Constant	0.366** [2.04]	0.366** [2.04]
Industry Herfindahl index	−0.009 [0.69]	−0.01 [0.77]
Percent of firms in industry with ADR or cross-listing	0.121** [2.21]	0.110** [2.01]
Total value of cross-border M&A/market capitalization industry	0.038 [0.83]	0.007 [0.16]
Number of firms in industry/100	7.002 [0.52]	9.224 [0.68]
Difference in shareholder protection if >0	0.241 [1.18]	
EFN Index $\times$ difference in shareholder protection if >0	−0.661 [0.99]	
Difference in shareholder protection if <0	−0.494*** [2.93]	
EFN Index $\times$ difference in shareholder protection if <0	1.578*** [2.81]	
Difference in accounting standards if >0		0.541* [1.88]
EFN index $\times$ difference in accounting standards if >0		−1.631* [1.73]
Difference in accounting standards if <0		−0.154 [0.84]
EFN index $\times$ difference in accounting standards if <0		0.269 [0.43]
Observations	5739	5739
Number of country	31	31
R^2 within	0.24	0.24
R^2 between	0.39	0.40
R^2 total	0.23	0.23

*, **, and *** significant at 10%, 5%, and 1% levels, respectively.

We find the opposite: in model I, the interaction between EFN Index and Negative Difference in Shareholder Protection has a positive coefficient, which suggests a negative effect. In model II, the interaction between EFN Index and Positive Difference in Accounting Standards displays a negative coefficient as well. Overall, we do not find evidence of a role for financial constraints, at least based on the proxies that we have available.

8. Interpretation of the results

This paper presents evidence that firm-specific improvements in corporate governance induced by cross-border mergers improve the corporate governance of the whole industry and that this is positively valued by the market. In general, target firms in a weaker corporate governance environment relative to the acquiring firms, adopt the better practices because of a change in the country of incorporation of the firm. The converse is not true: when the target firm is bought by a firm from a less protective country, the market valuation of the target firm's industry does not decrease.

The quality of the accounting standards in the firms involved in a cross-border merger matter. In principle, a transfer of nationality of the target firm implies a change in the accounting standards, by default. In Section 5.1.1 we find some weak evidence that importing good accounting standards increases the Tobin's Q of the target industry. We have noted that opting into a particular standard during merger negotiations is fairly easy, and the merging parties may even choose accounting standards that are different from the ones in either the acquirer's or the target's country—the most common choice being either US GAAP or I.A.S. Hence, it is not surprising that the evidence we find regarding accounting standards is not conclusive.

We claim that changes in corporate governance have an impact on the whole industry of the target firm. We acknowledge the potential problems of dealing with industries rather than with firms directly. Initially, if the governance of one firm improves as a consequence of the cross-border acquisition, it is plausible that rival firms in the same industry suffer a loss in value as they lose out to the better governed merged firm as it attracts investors. The average industry value could then decrease as a consequence of the merger. Our results are not consistent with this explanation. Akhigbe and Martin (2000) do find evidence in favor of value reductions: they show that domestic competitors of cross-border acquisition targets in the US experience a significant increase in stock price upon the announcement of the merger.[12] This suggests that the merger is value-reducing for the target firm. And these mergers are, at most, corporate governance preserving transactions, because acquirers come from less—or equally—protective regimes.

Whatever the transmission mechanism is, we concentrate on industry-wide effects rather than firm-specific effects. Our analysis of the country-wide benefits of cross-border mergers enables us to draw implications for public policy. In fact, our results at the industry level show that cross-border mergers are Pareto improving. We do not find evidence that the value of an industry reduces as the result of a corporate-governance-improving acquisition. Quite the opposite, there is strong evidence that the *whole industry* benefits from the corporate governance improvements affecting some firms in an industry. We argue that when some firms improve corporate governance, competitors are also induced to improve to avoid being dominated themselves.

---

[12] The effects of corporate events of rival firms have been studied extensively: for stock repurchases, Hertzel (1991); for bankruptcy announcements, Lang and Stulz (1992); for dividend announcements, Laux et al. (1998); for corporate capital investment, Chen et al. (2002); for mergers and acquisitions, Eckbo (1985), among others.

9. Conclusion

This paper presents evidence showing that improvements in corporate governance are positively valued by the market. We consider the changes in corporate governance induced by cross-border mergers. For each of 39 industries in 41 different countries over the period 1990–2001, we construct measures of the corporate governance quality of the industry considering the cross-border mergers *by* and *of* firms in that industry. Two corporate governance indicators are considered: shareholder protection and accounting standards. In the absence of cross-border mergers we assign no change in corporate governance quality at the firm level. For each cross-border acquisition, we calculate the difference in corporate governance measured by each indicator, between the countries of the acquiring and targeted firms. We weight these differences by dollar value of the acquisition and aggregate across industries, countries, and years. We then investigate the relationship between corporate governance quality changes and Tobin's Q at the industry level.

Our main result is that acquisitions of firms in weaker shareholder protection countries by firms in stronger protective regimes significantly increase the Tobin's Q of the target industry. This result is robust to country, year, and industry characteristics. However, targets acquired by firms from worse corporate governance environments do not lose value.

Our results do not suggest that corporate governance is a motive for cross-border acquisitions and we have no evidence that acquirers necessarily target firms from worse corporate governance countries. Quite the contrary, our study finds that acquiring firms do not gain or lose value by merging with firms that provide weaker protection to investors and poorer accounting standards. Why these mergers happen remains an unanswered question beyond the scope of this paper.[13]

Another area for future research is the study of the specific characteristics of cross-border mergers that affect industry value. In this paper, we control for the value of the cross-border acquisitions affecting a particular industry, and show that this variable has a positive valuation effect for the target industry. Exploring the factors behind these costs and benefits, and documenting the differences between domestic and cross-border mergers, merits further attention.

---

[13] As Alexander (2000) indicates, there can be several reasons why firms undertake cross-border mergers: intensive consolidation or preempting restructuring, battle for scale driven by structural pressures, response to technological changes, increases in scale to market, the need to advertise globally, exhaustion of the domestic merger route, and the opportunity to gain a foothold in new markets.

Appendix A: Table A: Correlations among the variables

The following table shows the correlation matrix of the variables used in the paper. We provide indices for Shareholder Protection and Accounting Standards for each cross-border merger in our sample. We obtain the corporate governance index for the country of nationality of both the acquirer and target from La Porta et al. (1998). We classify each country into one of two categories: "Above the median" (value 1) and "Below the median" (value 0) for each of the indices. We then compute the difference between the acquirer's and the target's indices, and average across industries and countries, where each acquisition is weighted by the dollar value of the transaction. The "PV Shareholder Protection Index" is the modified LLSV index from Pagano and Volpin (2005). For details on the construction of the index, see http://www.e-aer.org/data/sept05_data_snyder.zip. The "World Bank Rule of Law Index" measures the extent to which agents have confidence in and abide by the rules of society, and in particular the quality of contract enforcement, the police, and the courts, as well as the likelihood of crime and violence. Both indices are time-varying. The sample includes all the completed acquisitions of 100% interest in a public company available in the Securities Data Corporation, from January 1, 1990 to December 31, 2001. The sample does not include LBOs, spin-offs, recapitalizations, self-tender and exchange offers, repurchases, minority stake purchases, acquisitions of remaining interest, and privatizations.

	Tobin's Q	$ Value of cross-border mergers/ industry market capitalization	Shareholder protection difference, acquirer minus target	Accounting standards difference, acquirer minus target	Difference in WB rule of law
$ Value of cross-border mergers/ industry market capitalization	0.023**				
Shareholder protection difference, acquirer minus target	−0.013	−0.195***			
Accounting standards—difference acquirer minus target	−0.005	−0.213***	0.548***		
Difference in WB rule of law	−0.003	−0.079***	0.038***	0.055***	
Difference in PV shareholder protection	0.021	0.090***	0.047***	0.044***	0.0004

*, **, and *** indicates significant at the 10%, 5%, and 1% levels, respectively.

References

Akhigbe, A. and A. D. Martin, 2000, "Information-Signalling and Competitive Effects of Foreign Acquisitions in the U.S," *Journal of Banking and Finance*, 24, 1307–1321.

Alexander, L., 2000, "Corporate Governance and Cross-Border Mergers," Conference Board Research Report 1273–00-RR.

Almeida, H. and D. Wolfenzon, 2005, "The Effect of External Finance on the Equilibrium Allocation of Capital," *Journal of Financial Economics*, 75, 133–164.

Andrade, G., M. Mitchell and E. Stafford, 2001, "New Evidence and Perspective on Mergers," *Journal of Economic Perspectives*, 15, 103–120.

Beck, T. and R. Levine, 2002, "Industry Growth and Capital Allocation: Does having a Market- Or Bank-Based System Matter?" *Journal of Financial Economics*, 64, 147–180.

Bergman, N. and D. Nicolaievsky, 2007, "Investor Protection and the Coasian View," *Journal of Financial Economics*, 84, 738–771.

Bris, A. and N. Brisley, 2007, "A Theory of Optimal Expropriation, Mergers, and Industry Competition," Working Paper.

Bris, A. and C. Cabolis, 2007, "Corporate Governance Convergence Through Cross-Border Mergers: The Case of Aventis," In G. N. Gregoriou and L. Renneboog (Eds.), *International Mergers and Acquisitions Activity Since 1990: Quantitative Analysis of Recent Research*, Elsevier, USA.

Bris, A. and C. Cabolis, 2008, "The Value of Investor Protection: Firm Evidence from Cross-Border Mergers," *Review of Financial Studies*, 21, 605–648.

Bris, A., C. Cabolis and V. Janowski, 2007, "The Effect of Merger Laws on Merger Activity: International Evidence," In G. N. Gregoriou and L. Renneboog (Eds.), *International Mergers and Acquisitions Activity Since 1990: Quantitative Analysis of Recent Research*, Elsevier, USA.

Chen, S.-S., L.-C. Ho and Y.-C. Shih, 2002, "Intra-Industry Effects of Corporate Capital Investments," Working Paper.

Claessens, S. and L. Laeven, 2003, "Financial Development, Property Rights, and Growth," *Journal of Finance*, 58, 2401–2436.

Coffee, J. C., 1999, "The Future As History: The Prospects for Global Convergence in Corporate Governance and its Implications," The Center for Law and Economic Studies, Columbia University School of Law. Working Paper No. 144.

Cremers, K. M. and V. Nair, 2005, "Governance Mechanisms and Equity Prices," *Journal of Finance*, 60, 2859–2894.

Daines, R., 2001, "Does Delaware Law Improve Firm Value?" *Journal of Financial Economics*, 62, 525–558.

Demirgüç-Kunt, A. and V. Maksimovic, 1998, "Law, Finance and Firm Growth," *Journal of Finance*, 53, 2107–2137.

Demirgüç-Kunt, A. and V. Maksimovic, 1999, "Institutions, Financial Markets and Firm Debt Maturity," *Journal of Financial Economics*, 54, 295–336.

Doidge, C., G. A. Karolyi and R. M. Stulz, 2007, "Why Do Countries Matter So Much for Corporate Governance?" *Journal of Financial Economics*, 86, 1–39.

Dyck, A. and L. Zingales, 2004, "Private Benefits of Control: An International Comparison," *Journal of Finance*, 59, 537–600.

Eckbo, B. E., 1982, "Horizontal Mergers, Collusion, and Stockholder Wealth," *Journal of Financial Economics*, 11, 241–273.

Eckbo, B. E., 1985, "Mergers and the Market Concentration Doctrine: Evidence from the Capital Market," *Journal of Business*, 58, 325–349.

Gertner, R., E. Powers and D. Scharfstein, 2002, "Learning About Internal Capital Markets from Corporate Spinoffs," *The Journal of Finance*, 57, 2479–2506.

Glaeser, E., S. Johnson and A. Shleifer, 2001, "Coase Versus the Coasians," *The Quarterly Journal of Economics*, 116, 853–899.

Gompers, P. A., J. L. Ishi and A. Metrick, 2003, "Corporate Governance and Equity Prices," *Quarterly Journal of Economics*, 118, 107–155.

Hertzel, M. G., 1991, "The Effects of Stock Repurchases on Rival Firms," *The Journal of Finance*, 46, 707–716.

Himmelberg, C., R. G. Hubbard and I. Love, 2002, "Investor Protection, Ownership, and the Cost of Capital," World Bank Working Paper Series No. 2834, Washington, DC.

Hyytinen, A., I. Kuosa and T. Takalo, 2003, "Law or Finance? Evidence from Finland," *European Journal of Law and Economics*, 16, 59–89.

Johnson, S., P. Boone, A. Breach and E. Friedman, 2000, "Corporate Governance in the Asian Financial Crisis," *Journal of Financial Economics*, 58, 141–186.

Kaplan, S. N. and L. Zingales, 1997, "Do Investment-Cash Flow Sensitivities Provide Useful Measures of Financing Constraints?" *Quarterly Journal of Economics* 112, 169–216.

La Porta, R., F. Lopez-de-Silanes, A. Shleifer and R. Vishny, 1998, "Law and Finance," *Journal of Political Economy*, 106, 1113–1147.

La Porta, R., F. Lopez-de-Silanes, A. Shleifer and R. Vishny, 2002, "Investor Protection and Corporate Valuation," *The Journal of Finance*, 57, 1147–1170.

Lang, L. and R. Stulz, 1992, "Contagion and Competitive Intra-Industry Effects of Bankruptcy Announcements," *Journal of Financial Economics*, 32, 45–60.

Laux, P. A., L. Starks and P. Yoon, 1998, "The Relative Importance of Competition and Contagion in Intra-Industry Information Transfers: An Investigation of Dividend Announcements," *Financial Management*, 27, 5–16.

Lins, K. V., D. Strickland and M. Zenner, 2001, "Do Non-U.S. Firms Issue Equity on U.S. Exchanges to Relax Capital Constraints?" *The Journal of Financial and Quantitative Analysis*, 40(2005), 109–133.

Martynova, M. and L. Renneboog, 2008, "Spillover of Corporate Governance Standards As a Takeover Synergy in Cross-Border Mergers and Acquisitions," *Journal of Corporate Finance*, 14 (this issue), 200–223, doi:10.1016/j.jcorpfin.2008.03.004.

Miller, D., 1999, "The Market Reaction to International Cross Listing: Evidence from Depositary Receipts," *Journal of Financial Economics*, 51, 103–123.

Mørck, R., B. Yeung and W. Yu, 2000, "The Information Content of Stock Markets: Why Do Emerging Markets have Synchronous Price Movements?" *Journal of Financial Economics*, 58, 215–260.

Pagano, M. and P. Volpin, 2005, "The Political Economy of Corporate Governance," *American Economic Review*, 95, 1005–1030.

Pistor, K., 2006, "Patterns of Legal Change: Shareholder and Creditor Rights in Transition Economies," In M. B. Fox and M. A. Heller (Eds.), *Corporate Governance Lessons from Transition Economy Reforms*, Princeton University Press, USA.

Rajan, R. and L. Zingales, 1998, "Financial Dependence and Growth," *American Economic Review*, 88, 559–573.

Rossi, S. and P. Volpin, 2004, "Cross-Country Determinants of Mergers and Acquisitions," *Journal of Financial Economics*, 74, 277–304.

Shin, H. and R. Stulz, 1998, "Are Internal Capital Markets Efficient?," *Quarterly Journal of Economics*, 113, 531–552.

Stigler, G. J., 1964, "A Theory of Oligopoly," *The Journal of Political Economy*, 72, 44–61.

Wurgler, J., 2000, "Financial markets and the allocation of capital," Journal of Financial Economics 58, 187–214.

PART 9

WANNA BET? MARKET EFFICIENCY AND RETURNS TO MERGER ARBITRAGE

Chapter 26

DETERMINANTS AND IMPLICATIONS OF ARBITRAGE HOLDINGS IN ACQUISITIONS*

JIM HSIEH

School of Management, George Mason University, Fairfax, Virginia, USA

RALPH A. WALKLING

Faculty of Finance, Fisher College of Business, Ohio State University, Columbus, Ohio, USA

Contents

* The authors thank Natasha Burns, Tim Burch, Stephen Cosslett, Jean Helwege, David Hirshleifer, Jan Jindra, Kathy Kahle, Jon Karpoff, Semi Kedia, Mike Lemmon, Jun Qian, Rene Stulz, Steve Sun, James Travis, Russ Wermers, Karen Wruck, an anonymous referee, and participants in the finance workshops at the University of Arizona, Dartmouth College, The University of Delaware, Drexel University, George Mason University, The University of Manitoba, Queen's University (Canada), Southern Illinois University, Southern Methodist University, Ohio State University, the University of Wisconsin-Milwaukee, and the 2003 FMA Annual Meetings for valuable discussions and comments. All remaining errors are our own.

This article originally appeared in the *Journal of Financial Economics*, Vol. 77, pp. 605–648 (2005)
Corporate Takeovers, Volume 2
Edited by B. Espen Eckbo
DOI: 10.1016/B978-0-12-381982-6.00027-6

Abstract

We find evidence of passive and active roles for arbitrageurs in the acquisition process.
Using a simultaneous-equation framework to recognize endogeneity, we analyze 608
acquisition bids over the 1992–1999 period. Our results indicate that the change in
arbitrage holdings is greater in successful offers. However, changes in arbitrage
holdings are also related to the probability of success, bid premia, and arbitrage
returns. In addition, the change in arbitrage holdings is positively associated with
both revision returns and the occurrence of subsequent bids. Overall, we find that
merger arbitrageurs play an important role in the market for corporate control.

Keywords

mergers, arbitrage, market for corporate control

JEL classification: G34, G14, D82

1. Introduction

Nearly 15 years after the era of Ivan Boesky, the role of arbitrageurs in the acquisition process is receiving renewed attention in the financial literature. Existing empirical studies report significant and substantial positive arbitrage returns (see, e.g., Baker and Savasoglu, 2002; Dukes et al., 1992; Jindra and Walkling, 2004; Karolyi and Shannon, 1999; Mitchell and Pulvino, 2001). However, the role of arbitrageurs in the acquisition process remains unclear. Larcker and Lys (1987) suggest a passive role for arbitrageurs, arguing that superior ability to predict offer outcomes leads to their abnormal returns.

Recent theoretical work by Cornelli and Li (2002) and Gomes (2001) suggests an active role for arbitrageurs. Cornelli and Li develop an information-based model in which the information advantage that an arbitrageur possesses arises from his or her own holdings, and these holdings influence offer outcomes and deal characteristics. Gomes shows that arbitrageurs are capable of attaining hold-out power by accumulating large blocks of target shares. This potential threat forces bidders to offer higher takeover premia ex ante. Thus, while the existing empirical literature demonstrates positive abnormal returns to arbitrage, the theoretical studies suggest testable hypotheses concerning the active involvement of arbitrageurs in the takeover process. In particular, Cornelli and Li and Gomes suggest that the change in arbitrage holdings is positively related to both the probability of deal success and the level of bid premia.

The primary objective of our research is to examine the role of arbitrageurs in the takeover process, testing empirical implications of Larcker and Lys, Cornelli and Li, and Gomes while controlling for the inherent endogeneity of key acquisition characteristics. We also investigate the factors that motivate arbitrage trading during acquisitions and the relation between arbitrage holdings and key takeover variables such as bid premia and arbitrage returns. As one example, a higher level of holdings can facilitate a takeover and provide greater arbitrage returns. Alternatively, increased competition among arbitrageurs could reduce returns. In the model of Cornelli and Li, arbitrageurs' profits initially increase when more arbitrageurs decide to participate. However, at some point, profits decline with increased competition among arbitrageurs.

Our methodology relies on an empirically based definition of arbitrageurs similar to that of Baker and Savasoglu (2002): Arbitrageurs are defined as those institutions that regularly increase their holdings of firms targeted for acquisition. Analyzing 608 offers over the 1992 to 1999 period, we find empirical evidence of an endogenous link among the changes in arbitrage holdings, bid premia, arbitrage returns, and offer outcomes. Arbitrage holdings increase in offers that are likely to be successful, even after controlling for the market's assessment of offer success. This is consistent with the work of Larcker and Lys (1987). At the same time, the change in arbitrage holdings is positively correlated with the probability of bid success, bid premia, and arbitrage returns. Thus, our results are consistent with both passive and active roles played by arbitrageurs. To the best of our knowledge, this is the first evidence to test the active influence of arbitrageurs and contrast the passive versus active arbitrage models.

Furthermore, we find that after controlling for deal attributes, arbitrageurs purchase fewer shares in large deals. However, the change in arbitrage holdings is not materially different in multiple-bidder cases or across categories of target management attitude. We also find a positive relation between initial changes in holdings and revision returns. Deals with a greater increase in arbitrage holdings over the first quarter of an acquisition are more likely to be revised. Additional findings indicate that if the initial deal is cancelled, the possibility of the target firm receiving a subsequent bid within 1 year is significantly correlated with the change in arbitrage holdings. The last two results are consistent with active arbitrage theories.

The remainder of the paper is organized as follows. Section 2 discusses related literature. Section 3 details the sample selection procedure and describes the basic characteristics of the sample. Section 3 also describes the empirical identification and distribution of arbitrageurs. Section 4 analyzes the determinants of the change in arbitrage holdings. Recognizing the endogeneity issue, we present a multivariate analysis in Section 4 that investigates four variables of interest in a simultaneous-equations framework. Section 5 presents robustness checks and extensions. Section 6 concludes.

2. Background and testable implications

2.1. Arbitrage returns

Merger arbitrageurs purchase a target company's stock in the hope of profiting from the deal. If the deal succeeds, arbitrageurs profit from the difference between the purchase price and the final selling price. In stock-swap deals, the purchase of target shares is often accompanied by shorting the acquirer's stock simultaneously.[1] Empirical studies on arbitrage returns report positive (and generally large) excess returns. Dukes et al. (1992) and Jindra and Walkling (2004) document annualized returns to arbitrageurs of 117% and 46.5%, respectively, for samples of cash tender offers. Baker and Savasoglu (2002) report an average annualized risk-adjusted return of 9.6% for a sample of cash and stock deals from 1981 to 1996. Using a portfolio of 37 mergers in Canada in 1997, Karolyi and Shannon (1999) document a 26% annualized return. In contrast, Mitchell and Pulvino (2001) find that merger arbitrage generates a 4% annualized excess return after taking into account transactions costs and controlling for different returns in hot and cold markets.

---

[1] This process is called merger (or risk) arbitrage. By definition, classic arbitrage refers to a simultaneous transaction in two separate markets without incurring risks. Two differences are noticed in risk arbitrage. First, the transactions of buying and tendering are not simultaneous as in the traditional arbitrage process. Arbitrageurs typically buy the target shares, wait until the effective date of the deal, and then tender the shares to the bidder. Second, takeover transactions could be cancelled; thus, their profit is not secure. If this happens, the target prices may drop and arbitrageurs may suffer large losses.

2.2. *Active versus passive roles of arbitrageurs*

The explanation for these abnormal returns to arbitrageurs can be categorized by the roles they play in the acquisition process. *Passive arbitrageurs* do not influence acquisition outcomes or terms. In contrast, *active arbitrageurs* do influence acquisition terms and outcomes. In the paragraphs below we expand our discussion of these roles and explain their empirical implications.

There are two roles the passive arbitrageur could play in the acquisition process. In the first passive role, arbitrageurs are naïve investors, investing in deals that the market expects to succeed. These include friendly deals, deals with high bidder toeholds, and deals with low first-quarter spreads. Spread is defined as the percentage difference between offer price and market price, so that a low value implies a high expectation of offer success. Arbitrageurs subsequently increase their holdings if the probability of success improves. Thus, for multiple-quarter deals that are ultimately successful, we would observe a gradual increase in arbitrage holdings over time. We would also find a correlation between observable indicators of expected success (the change in the spread from one quarter to the next) and the change in arbitrage holdings.[2] In this explanation, arbitrageurs do not utilize superior predictive abilities to select profitable acquisitions but they earn positive returns simply as a matter of "the limits to arbitrage" (Shleifer and Vishny, 1997). Arbitrageurs are passive in the sense that their accumulation of holdings do not influence offer outcomes or bid characteristics.[3] With the exception of Larcker and Lys (1987), the returns described as arbitrage returns by previous research are generated using strategies available to all investors. In this sense, all of these results are consistent with this first passive role of arbitrageurs.

Motivation for employing a purely passive investment behavior is apparent in the well-documented research that such a strategy earns abnormal returns. However, it seems likely that arbitrageurs are more selective in their investments, concentrating on deals where the expected benefits of success (i.e., earning the spread and any revision returns) outweigh the costs of investment (including possible losses). Thus, arbitrageurs would be more likely to participate in deals in which their assessment indicates a greater probability of success than that implied by the spread. This is the approach of Larcker and Lys (1987). Under their explanation, arbitrageurs earn abnormal returns because of their superior ability to predict offer outcomes. Note that this is also a passive role since arbitrageurs do not influence the terms or outcomes of a deal. Using a sample of 94 SEC 13D filings from 1977 to 1983, Larcker and Lys show that the deals in which arbitrageurs invest have higher success rates than the expected probability of success implied in the market. As a result, arbitrageurs generate average

---

[2] Of course, to the extent that the market knows the level of arbitrage trading and believes it has an impact on offer outcomes, this would also be reflected in the spread. We will discuss this in more detail in our multivariate analysis.

[3] We thank the referee for suggesting this alternative.

excess returns of 5.3% on their portfolio positions from the transaction date to the resolution date.

In our work, a finding that the change in arbitrage holdings is higher in deals that are successful, while controlling for the (contemporaneously measured) spread, would be consistent with this second passive role. Also consistent with this role would be a finding that arbitrageurs invest more in deals that have higher returns. In an efficient market, the spread is compensation for the expected risks of the deal. Arbitrageurs increasing their holdings in deals that yield higher returns must (on average) be placing their bets wisely.

Active arbitrageurs influence the terms and outcomes of acquisitions. Ex ante, bidders increase premia in anticipation of arbitrage holdings. Other implications of active arbitrageurs include high correlations among the changes in arbitrage holdings, bid success, and bid revision while controlling for the inherent endogeneity.

An active role for arbitrageurs is modeled in two recent theoretical studies by Cornelli and Li (2002) and Gomes (2001). In these models, arbitrage holdings (and the anticipation of arbitrage holdings) influence the terms and outcome of an offer. Participation from arbitrageurs can influence the takeover process *irrespective of* their ability to predict takeover outcomes.

Unlike small shareholders or noise traders, arbitrageurs tend to accumulate blocks of target shares after an acquisition announcement and sell their shares to the bidder at resolution of the offer. As a result, their presence helps overcome the free-rider problem described by Grossman and Hart (1980), and facilitates the takeover process. In Cornelli and Li (2002), arbitrageurs possess an information advantage from knowing their own position and are capable of paying a higher price to persuade small shareholders to sell their shares to the arbitrageurs. The process of purchasing target shares continues as long as arbitrage profit is positive. In equilibrium, the size of arbitrage holdings and the purchase price are determined endogenously. The model further predicts that the increased presence of arbitrageurs is positively related to both the probability of offer success and a higher takeover premium.

In the context of freeze-out tender offers, Gomes (2001) develops a dynamic model in which arbitrageurs accumulate large blocks of target shares by trading with noise traders (e.g., current shareholders) as in Kyle and Vila (1991). After a majority of shareholders approve a tender offer, the remaining shareholders are required to tender their shares at the bid price even if they did not vote for the offer. Thus, they are *frozen out* of the takeover process. Because of the hold-out power derived from accumulated shares, arbitrageurs and other block shareholders can purposely delay their tenders until the bidder offers a higher premium. Bidders that anticipate increased arbitrage activity offer higher bid premia ex ante. Ex post, the increased price markup will also attract greater arbitrage holdings after deal announcements.

To some extent, arbitrageurs in Gomes' model (2001) are more active than in Cornelli and Li's (2002). It is difficult, however, to distinguish between these theories empirically. Both theories imply that ex ante, bidders are more likely to increase premia if they take into account the potential influence of arbitrageurs in the takeover process. Ex post, both theories suggest a positive relation between arbitrage holdings, the probability of success, and bid premia. However, an implication of the "more active" role of arbitrageurs is a significant relation between the change in arbitrage holdings, deal revisions, and the probability of subsequent takeover of failed deals.

The active and passive explanations for the abnormal returns to arbitrageurs are not mutually exclusive. It is possible, and indeed likely, that arbitrageurs play different roles in the acquisition process. To the best of our knowledge, however, this paper provides the first empirical test of the active arbitrageur hypothesis. At the same time, it updates the important work of Larcker and Lys (1987).

2.3. Testing the active versus passive theories: the importance of endogeneity

More formally, we test the hypotheses of arbitrage trading in the following model:

$$\Delta holdings_j = \gamma_0 + \gamma_1 \, Premium_j + \gamma_2 \, Success_j + \sum_{i=3,k} \gamma_i X_{ij} + \varepsilon_j, \tag{1}$$

$$Premium_j = \alpha_0 + \alpha_1 \Delta \, holdings_j + \sum_{i=2,k} \alpha_i X_{ij} + e_j, \tag{2}$$

$$Success_j = \beta_0 + \beta_1 \Delta \, holdings_j + \sum_{i=2,k} \beta_i X_{ij} + \kappa_j, \tag{3}$$

where $\Delta holdings_j$ is the change in holdings for all arbitrageurs; $Premium_j$ is the premium in jth acquisition; $Success_j$ is a binary variable relating to the actual outcome of an offer j (Equation (1)) or the arbitrageur's expected probability of success for the jth acquisition (Equation (3)); and X_{ij} is a vector of control variables. We will use the phase "the change in arbitrage holdings" and Δholdings (or $\Delta Q1$Hold) synonymously throughout the paper, for ease of exposition. Intercepts are α_0, β_0, and γ_0 while ε, e, and κ are the error terms in each equation.

The first passive arbitrage argument implies that $\gamma_2 = 0$. This argument does not rely on the superior predictive powers of arbitrageurs to determine their investments, but instead suggests that they utilize the same publicly available indicators of success as average traders. These indicators include target managerial attitude (hostile or friendly), the size of the bid premium, and the size of the speculation spread (the percentage difference between the offered price and the postannouncement market price). The passive arbitrage argument of Larcker and Lys (1987), on the other hand, asserts that arbitrageurs utilize their superior abilities to predict offer outcomes. Thus, the change in arbitrage holdings is positively related to the expected probability of success: $\gamma_2 > 0$.

In contrast, the active arbitrageur models suggested by Cornelli and Li (2002) and Gomes (2001) imply $\alpha_1 > 0$ and $\beta_1 > 0$. That is, deal attributes are actually correlated with the participation of arbitrageurs. Here, bid premia and offer success are both related to the change in arbitrage holdings. In sum, Equation (1) is a test of the two passive hypotheses while Equations (2) and (3) are tests of the active hypothesis.

There are two important points to note from this discussion. First, as we have discussed, the passive hypothesis of Larcker and Lys and the active hypothesis of Cornelli and Li and Gomes are by no means mutually exclusive. Both could exist simultaneously in practice. Arbitrageurs could have the ability to predict deal outcomes and/or exert influence in the takeover process. Second, the models and the theoretical literature outlined above emphasize the simultaneous, endogenous nature of many key aspects in the process. The theoretical literature also argues that toeholds and arbitrage returns are endogenous in addition to the three dependent variables above (premia, Δholdings, and acquisition outcomes). Correspondingly, we perform endogeneity tests among these variables and then further expand our system of estimation to include returns. Since ordinary least squares (OLS) estimates ignore the endogeneity problem and produce biased coefficients, we perform extensive sensitivity tests to examine and mitigate the problem. Our research design recognizes the possibility of endogeneity, testing and controlling for it empirically with the appropriate methodology. Nevertheless, our conclusions are similar using OLS or more sophisticated approaches.

3. Sample description and preliminaries

3.1. Sample of acquisition bids

Our initial sample of acquisitions is taken from the Securities Data Corporation (SDC) Mergers and Acquisitions database for the period 1992–1999. Specific trading strategies used by arbitrageurs are inherently linked to form of payment. Thus, we are careful to incorporate three different methods of payment: cash, stock, and collar offers. The collar offer is a new, relatively unexplored innovation in form of payment that combines elements of stock and cash offers (i.e., contingent and fixed payouts) utilizing option-like features. Fuller (2003) and Officer (2002) provide additional details and note important differences among these three methods of payment. SDC began recording merger agreements with collars in 1992. Although collar offers are relatively unknown before the 1990s, we find that they comprise more than 20% of our sample. To avoid sample selection bias by including years before these data were recorded, we begin our analysis in 1992.

To be included in our initial sample, an acquisition must meet four criteria. (1) Both target and bidding firms must be covered on CRSP for at least 100 days before the deal announcement and have stock prices available to calculate arbitrage returns. (2) The transaction is pure cash, pure stock, or pure stock with collar terms. Mixed forms of payment (e.g., convertible preferred, convertible notes, etc.) are excluded because it is impossible to determine the appropriate hedge ratios for hybrid securities unless their market values are known. Mitchell and Pulvino (2001) examine the robustness of omitting deals with mixed forms, concluding that their results are not affected by this exclusion. (3) The acquirer owns less than 50% of the target stock before the announcement and is seeking control of the target company. (4) One firm is clearly identified as the target. Thus, 32 mergers of equals are excluded from the sample. We further exclude 13 cases classified by SDC as divestitures, restructurings, and bankruptcy takeovers.

Our selection criteria produce a sample of 680 offers. Seventy-two of these deals are deleted when we match with our sample of arbitrageurs. (Further details are described in the next section.) The first five columns of Panel A in Table 1 show the distribution of the sample by year and by the form of payment. The total number of deals ranges from 39 in 1992 to 120 in 1998, increasing steadily over the sample period, except for 1999. The decline in this last year is due to our requirement that all deals be resolved by the end of 1999. We then are able to track subsequent acquisition activity for at least 2 years following failed bids.

Stock offers account for more than half of the sample while cash and collar offers comprise 19% and 23%, respectively. However, it does not appear that the proportion of each method of payment varies significantly over time. One exception is that collar offers represent about 41% of the sample in 1993 (i.e., 16 of 39 offers). Collar offers are close to the average of 23% in other years. The overall pattern is consistent with those in Fuller (2003) and Officer (2002) who examine collar offers but not arbitrage. Andrade et al. (2001) also document the popularity of stock deals during the 1990s; they do not explicitly separate collar offers from their stock sample.

Data on announcement dates, agreement dates, withdrawal dates, deal values, and target manager's attitude are collected from SDC. However, SDC usually does not reveal a detailed description of collar offers or classify them as fixed-exchange-rate (FX) or fixed-value (FV) offers. This classification is important in estimating arbitrage returns. The payoff in collar offers typically varies as a function of the bidder's stock price at the end of the offer. In the FV offer, the amount of payment is fixed within specified boundary prices. In the FX offer, the exchange ratio is fixed within these boundaries. See Appendix A for the detailed estimation of arbitrage returns. We collect detailed transaction terms on collar offers and double check original data accuracy using Lexis/Nexis Business News (Mergers and Acquisitions) or the SEC Edgar Database. Before providing additional descriptive statistics on our sample of acquisitions, we turn to the identification of arbitrageurs.

3.2. Identification of arbitrageurs

Since no database of arbitrageurs is currently available, the identity of arbitrageurs is, of necessity, an empirical one. Our procedure, similar in spirit to that of Baker and Savasoglu (2002), is designed to recognize institutions *actively involved in the purchase of shares during acquisitions*. Following Baker and Savasoglu, our procedure starts with the SEC 13F filings of institutional ownership recorded by Spectrum over the period from 1992 to 1999. The Spectrum Database provides information about quarterly holdings of financial institutions with investment discretion over $100 million in equity securities. These institutions are required to disclose all common stock positions greater than $200,000 or 10,000 shares.

Table 1

Distribution of acquisitions, arbitrage holdings and arbitrageurs, 01/1992 to 12/1999

The table reports the distribution of our sample of mergers and summary statistics of identified arbitrageurs. The sample sources are Securities Data Corporation (SDC), Lexis/Nexis, and SEC Edgar filings. In order to be included in the sample, the deals must be for at least $10 million with both the acquiring and the target firms listed in the CRSP database and at least 100 daily returns available to estimate the market model. "Collar" offers are 100% stock offers with a collar provision identified by SDC. The identification of arbitrageurs and the change of arbitrage holdings in each deal are derived as follows. First, we calculate the net change of institutional ownership in the target firm from the quarter immediately before to the quarter immediately after a takeover announcement. Second, to be identified as a risk arbitrageur, the institution needs to have positive net changes in holdings for more than 60% of deals in which they are involved and participate in at least six deals in our sample. Finally, we calculate the change of holdings in all of our sample deals for the identified arbitrageurs. The net change of holdings is calculated by summing all holdings in the quarter ending before the deal resolution and subtracting the reported holdings the quarter before the deal announcement. Panel A presents the time-series distribution of mergers, Δholdings, and number of arbitrageurs during our sample period. Panel B presents a summary of identified arbitrageurs according to the types of asset managers. The five different types are classified by Spectrum. Panel C reports sample statistics of the number of arbitrageurs and the estimated arbitrage holdings in each deal. Level of arbitrage holdings is calculated as arbitrage holdings divided by the target firm's total shares outstanding. Change of arbitrage holdings is the change from the quarter before deal announcement either to the quarter after announcement ($\Delta Q1$Hold) or to the quarter right before the deal is closed (Δholdings).

Panel A. Distribution of sample and change in arbitrage holdings by year

Year	Number of deals	By form of payment			N_{arbs}		Δholdings	
		Cash	Stock	Collar	Mean	Median	Mean (%)	Median (%)
1992	39	9	21	9	6.2	5.0	2.69	1.23
1993	39	7	16	16	8.3	5.0	3.09	1.96
1994	73	11	38	24	8.1	5.0	3.17	1.59
1995	83	15	49	19	9.2	5.0	5.13	2.75
1996	79	23	46	10	9.3	6.0	4.65	2.12
1997	109	13	72	24	10.2	8.0	6.86	4.91
1998	120	18	78	24	12.6	7.0	4.33	2.14
1999	66	17	33	16	8.7	4.0	2.70	0.96
Total	608	113	353	142				
(percentage)	(100%)	(18.6%)	(58.1%)	(23.4%)				

Panel B. Summary of identified arbitrageurs

Type of asset managers	Number of arbitrageurs	Percentage (%)	Mean (median) number of deals	The range of number of deals
1. Banks	10	8.9	88.2 (26.5)	(7, 380)
2. Insurance companies	5	4.5	48.6 (45.0)	(26, 88)
3. Investment companies and their managers	5	4.5	24.0 (20.0)	(16, 44)
4. Independent investment advisors	74	66.1	53.4 (32.5)	(7, 354)

(Continued)

Table 1 (*Continued*)

Type of asset managers	Number of arbitrageurs	Percentage (%)	Mean (median) number of deals	The range of number of deals
5. Others	18	16.1	36.6 (25.5)	(9, 188)
	112	100.0	52.3 (29.5)	(7, 380)

Panel C. Summary statistics of change in holdings per deal in the full sample (N = 608 deals)

	Mean	Min	Q1	S.D.	Median	Q3	Max
Number of arbitrageurs (N_{arbs})	9.63	0.00	2.00	10.92	6.00	13.00	63.00
Level of holdings (holdings) (%)	15.6	0.0	4.6	14.3	11.2	23.3	72.5
Change in holdings (Δholdings) (%)	4.4	−4.1	0.3	5.9	2.4	6.7	51.9
Level of holdings (first quarter only) (%)	15.4	0.0	4.6	13.9	11.1	23.1	72.8
Change in holdings (first quarter only) (%)	4.2	−4.1	0.3	5.5	2.2	6.3	37.9

There are four limitations of using the Spectrum Database to identify arbitrageurs. First, institutions are not required to disclose holdings below the threshold of $200,000 or 10,000 shares. This introduces a downward bias in the measure of total arbitrage holdings in each deal. An alternative source is SEC 13D filings as in Larcker and Lys (1987). However, only 20 of 135 collar offers during the period of 1992–1996 are found in the Insider's Chronicle which reports 13D filings each week. The second limitation is that institutions are only required to report their holdings in an aggregate level. The arbitrage position of one department of a firm could be cancelled out by the selling position of a separate department, negating the need to report.

Third, since institutions only report their holdings on a quarterly basis, information about arbitrage holdings between the latest reporting date and the final resolution date is unattainable. As a result, it is assumed that arbitrageurs' positions at quarters' ends closest to (but before) the resolution are indicative of their positions until the deal resolution. Finally, Section 13(f)(3) of the Securities Exchange Act stipulates that institutions, excluding business trusts and investment companies, can be exempted from the 13F filing requirements. This is the so-called "confidential treatment" (CT) rule.[4] In general, to support its CT application, an institution must provide sufficient evidence that disclosure of its security holdings would harm the institution's competitive position or would simply reveal its investment strategy. CT is usually applicable only for a limited period of time (e.g., within 1 year) but is available to a merger-arbitrage position through the end of the quarterly period in which an acquisition is

---

[4] More detailed information can be found at http://www.sec.gov/divisions/investment/13ffaq.htm.

resolved. It is particularly attractive to arbitrageurs who do not want to disclose their holdings. The rules of CT will lower our estimate of arbitrage holdings. To the extent that these limitations reduce the precision of our estimates of arbitrage holdings, they bias against our finding significant results.

Existing hedge fund database(s) such as Tremont Advisory Shareholders Services (TASS) and Hedge Fund Research, Inc. (HFR) are not suitable for this study. Unlike mutual funds, hedge funds are not required to disclose their asset holdings to the SEC. Reporting to TASS and HFR is purely voluntary for hedge fund companies. Even more important, neither database provides the detailed holdings necessary for this research. Nonetheless, it is interesting to check the overlap of our sample institutions derived from Spectrum (procedures described later) and those in either database. To do this, we use the TASS database which covers 2400 hedge funds during the period of January 1994 to December 1999. We find that more than 49% of our sample institutions are also covered in TASS. As will be described in the next section, we identify 112 institutions from Spectrum as merger arbitrageurs. Forty-seven of them are also in TASS. However, many of our sample institutions are easily be identified as arbitrageurs and yet are not in TASS. For example, we identify Long-Term Capital Management (LTCM) as an arbitrageur based on our selection procedure but it is not covered in TASS. We will return to an extensive analysis of the robustness of our sample selection procedure just before the conclusion. In general, our results are not sensitive to this issue.

3.3. Filter rules to identify arbitrage holdings

To specifically identify those institutions actively involved in purchasing shares around acquisitions, we use the methodology illustrated in Figure. 1. First, the change of institutional ownership in a target firm is calculated from the quarter immediately before to the quarter immediately after a takeover announcement.[5] Seventy-two deals are deleted from our sample of 680 deals because they do not cross two quarters. Second, we require that a risk arbitrageur have a positive change in holdings for at least six deals and in more than 60% of all deals in which they have holdings. Institutions meeting these criteria are classified as arbitrageurs. These cutoff points are arbitrary. To ensure the results are insensitive to these choices, we report robustness checks later in the paper. Overall, these choices do not alter our main conclusions.

Third, changes in holdings in *all* of the sample deals are calculated for all of the identified arbitrageurs. Changes in holdings for each deal are measured from the quarter ending just before the announcement date to the quarter ending just before the deal resolution date. (In a later section we discuss the stability of these changes across multiple-quarter offers.) In practice, arbitrageurs typically tender their shares to

---

[5] While we expect arbitrageurs to be net buyers in most cases, some arbitrageurs with established positions in a target could analyze the characteristics of a deal and decide to sell.

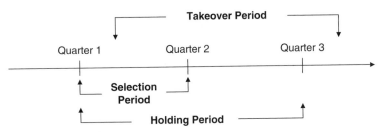

Fig. 1. An illustration of identifying arbitrageurs. Example: Suppose a takeover is announced between quarter one and quarter two, and the case is resolved (successful or withdrawn) after quarter three. To identify arbitrageurs, we compute the change of holdings in the target firm from quarter one to quarter two, which is the first reporting quarter after the announcement. We require that arbitrageurs are net buyers in six or more deals (i.e., the net change of holdings is positive), and that they are "frequent buyers" as well. Thus, for an institution in the Spectrum database to be an arbitrageur, it needs to have a positive change in holdings for at least six deals and in more than 60% of all deals in which they are involved. We then measure the change in arbitrage holdings from the quarter ending just before the announcement to the quarter ending just before the case is resolved. In this example, those quarters are quarter one quarter three, respectively.

the bidder at the completion of an acquisition. Even if this were not the case, we could not follow holdings through the quarter after an acquisition since most of the target firms disappear, eliminating the need for reporting by the institutions. Finally, the total change of holdings per deal is aggregated by summing all changes in holdings for that deal across all arbitrageurs. This aggregate change in holdings is normalized by total target shares outstanding. To illustrate: Suppose a target firm has 100,000 shares outstanding. If half (56) of our arbitrageurs increase their holdings by 100 shares each from the quarter before an acquisition announcement to the quarter before its resolution, the change in holdings by arbitrageurs would be 5600 shares, or 5.6%.

There are more than 2000 institutions reported in Spectrum during our sample period. Our procedure classifies 112 institutions as arbitrageurs. Spectrum divides institutional investors into five categories: banks, insurance companies, investment companies and their managers, independent investment advisors, and other institutions. In 1998, Spectrum reassigned the types of institutions. We find that many institutions are reassigned from types 3 or 4 to type 5 ("others"). In order for the types to be consistent over time, we use the originally assigned types for existing institutions throughout the sample period.

Panel B of Table 1 reveals the number of selected arbitrageurs in each institutional category. As expected, independent investment advisors account for 66.1% of the sample. This group includes large investment banks and brokerage firms as well as hedge funds. Interestingly, 16.1% of the sample consists of "other" institutions; these include the largest pension funds, foundations, and university endowments. As discussed in Moore (1999), pension funds used to be net sellers of target companies' stocks once the transactions were announced. Since the late 1980s, pension funds have hired arbitrageurs to make investment decisions on securities subject to acquisitions.

Intuitively, we might expect that most arbitrageurs fall into the category of independent investment advisors. Our results, however, reveal that several types of institutions have started to show interest in the business of merger arbitrage. In fact, the growing nature of multibusiness groups in many institutions has made it more difficult to classify them by just one type. For example, since the 1980s, banks (type 1) and investment companies (type 3) have begun to establish arbitrage departments which were generally managed in the capital markets area of the firms (Moore, 1999). Since regulation and the nature of business provide different incentives for each type of institution, we also examine whether our results vary across different types of institutions.

In Table 1, the right two columns of Panel B present the mean, median, and range in the number of deals for each type of arbitrageur. Summary statistics over all 112 arbitrageurs are shown in the last row of Panel B. A typical arbitrageur participates in 30 deals during our sample period, with the mean number of deals being 52. The least active arbitrageur invests in seven deals; the most active invests in 380 deals.[6] Considering the categories of asset managers, investment companies took part in the fewest acquisitions (mean of 24), while banks and independent investment advisors took part in the most (88 and 53, respectively). The range of the number of deals for banks shows the most variation, spanning the entire range from 7 to 380 deals. The number of deals for insurance and investment companies is more concentrated—the range is only from 26 to 88 and 16 to 44, respectively.

3.4. Sample distribution of number of arbitrageurs and their change in holdings (Δholdings and ΔQ1Hold)

Panel C of Table 1 displays the distribution of both levels and changes in arbitrage holdings per deal. On average, there are about 10 arbitrageurs per deal with average arbitrage holdings increasing by 4.4% of shares outstanding. Although our average holdings are rather conservative due to the stringent screening procedure and the fact that the changes in holdings are an aggregate measure, subsequent analyses reveal that even a modest Δholdings impacts returns and premia. In addition, note that we measure the change of holdings until the last quarter before the deal is resolved. If arbitrageurs unload their stocks before the resolution date in deals spanning several quarters, the change could be negative even though their holdings are positive across the first two quarters. Thus, our measured change in holdings may be lower than the initial change in holdings. We explore this issue in our sensitivity tests. Although our calculated Δholdings may underestimate the actual figure, we do not expect our measure to be systematically biased. In fact, it may cause our results to be more conservative.

---

[6] Note that the first selection rule we use to choose arbitrageurs requires a positive change in holdings in at least six deals. However, even if arbitrageurs pass this rule, they must still satisfy the second criteria. That is why the minimum number of deals an arbitrageur invested in is 7.

Of course, arbitrageurs can purchase fewer target shares at an early stage and then increase their holdings later if the probability of success increases. To examine this, we report the level of and change in holdings across the first quarter of the acquisition. Panel C reveals that the average level of holdings is higher when it is measured throughout the whole process, but the Δholdings is similar when it is estimated either across the first quarter or across the whole process. The mean (median) change in holdings across the entire acquisition period is 4.4% (2.4%); across only the first quarter, the mean (median) change in holdings is 4.2% (2.2%). In tests not shown of multiple-quarter deals, we find that the largest increase in holdings occurs over the first two quarters. Since many deals are initiated near the end of the quarter, continued purchasing in the second quarter is not surprising. The change in arbitrage holdings declines substantially afterward. In subsequent multivariate analysis, we test our model using both measures of change in holdings. Our results are not sensitive to these different measures of holdings.

Other basic statistics reveal that both Δholdings and the number of arbitrageurs vary greatly across the sample. The maximum number of arbitrageurs per deal is 63. The maximum change in holdings is an increase of more than 51% of shares outstanding while the minimum is a reduction of 4.1%. In a subsequent section, we also reveal that Δholdings varies significantly with different deal characteristics.

The last four columns of Panel A of Table 1 reveal the time-series distribution of the number of arbitrageurs and the mean and median change in holdings. Note that the number of deals increases over our sample period. Interestingly, the average number of arbitrageurs per deal also increases, rising from 6.2 in 1992 to 12.6 in 1998 with a low of 8.7 in 1999. The average change of holdings ranges from 2.7% of shares outstanding in 1992 to a peak level of 6.9% in 1997, with a lower 4.3% in 1998 and 2.7% in 1999. The fact that the number of deals grows over time with a higher average increase in arbitrage holdings in each deal indicates that more arbitrageurs became active in accumulating a greater number of target shares as our sample period progressed.

We further examine the changes in holdings by year and by type of asset manager. The results (available upon request) indicate that independent investment advisors (type 4) have the highest Δholdings and the greatest number of arbitrageurs, and that those figures are generally stable over the years of our sample. On the other hand, there is an upward trend in banks (type 1) and pension fund management (type 5). Insurance companies (type 2) and investment companies (type 3) have the lowest holdings among the five different types of asset managers. Overall, independent investment advisors dominate the business of merger arbitrage; however, other financial institutions are showing increased interest in arbitrage.

3.5. Acquisition characteristics and the change in arbitrage holdings

Table 2 describes some of the salient characteristics of our sample and how they differ across deals associated with smaller and larger changes in arbitrage holdings. Panel A examines variables more closely aligned with theories of passive arbitrage, while

Table 2

Summary statistics of deal characteristics for the full sample and by change in arbitrage holdings

The table reports deal characteristics for the full sample and by change in holdings. Toehold is the percentage of target shares held by the bidder prior to the announcement. First-quarter spread is calculated as (offer price $-P^T)/P^T$, where P^T is the target firm's stock price on the last day of the announcement quarter. Final-quarter spread is measured until the last day of the last quarter before the deal is consummated. Attitude, measured as the percentage of friendly deals in each group, is based on whether target management resisted or was faced with an unsolicited offer as determined by SDC. Success is a dummy variable equal to one if the target is successfully acquired. Runup is the cumulative abnormal return to the target firm's stock for trading days $(-54, -1)$ before the first bid. Markup is calculated as (final offer price $- P^T_{-1})/P^T_{-1}$, where P^T_{-1} is the target firm's stock price 1 day before the announcement. Takeover premium is calculated as stock price runup plus markup. Annualized return is calculated as (unannualized returns) $\times$ 365/(deal duration). See the text for calculations of unannualized buy-and-hold returns. Thirty-day return is calculated by accumulating daily returns until the earliest of resolution date or the 30th business day after announcement, then normalizing by multiplying 30/(deal duration) if the deal duration is less than 30 days. Revision return is calculated as (final offer price $-$ initial offer price)/P^T_{-1}. Transaction value is the total market value of consideration in millions, excluding fees and expenses. Deal duration is measured as the length of time between the first formal announcement of the takeover and the announced resolution of the deal. We test the difference between the whole sample and the subgroups in means and medians using the two-sided t-test and the Wilcoxon rank sum test.

	All (1)	Split of median of Δholdings		
		<Median (2)	≥Median (3)	Difference (2)–(3)
	Mean [median]	Mean [median]	Mean [median]	Mean [median]
Panel A. Variables associated with theories of passive arbitrage				
1. Toehold	0.86% [0.00%]	0.93% [0.00%]	0.80% [0.00%]	0.12% [0.00%]
2a. First-quarter spread	10.49% [7.27%]	14.06% [9.24%]	6.91% [5.38%]	7.15% [3.86%]***
2b. Final-quarter spread	9.28% [4.56%]	13.63% [7.57%]	4.93% [2.60%]	8.70% [4.97%]***
3. Attitude (% Friendly)	97.37%	96.71%	98.03%	−1.30%
4. Deal status (success rate)	90.95%	88.49%	93.42%	−4.90%**
Panel B. Variables associated with theories of active arbitrage				
5. Runup	8.70%[7.88%]	7.14%[6.99%]	10.27%[8.95%]	−3.10% [−1.96%]
6. Markup	28.53%	29.16%	27.90%	1.26% [−4.16%]
	[23.20%]	[21.02%]	[25.18%]	
7. Premium	37.23%	36.30%	38.17%	−1.90% [−1.49%]
	[33.25%]	[32.77%]	[34.26%]	
Panel C. Other deal-specific variables				
8a. Annualized return	49.84%	39.83%	59.85%	−20.00% [−1.99%]*
	[18.55%]	[17.46%]	[19.45%]	
8b. Thirty-day return	5.34% [1.57%]	2.89% [1.08%]	7.80% [1.97%]	−4.90% [−0.89%]***
9. Revision return	0.23% [0.00%]	0.02% [0.00%]	0.44% [0.00%]	−0.40% [0.00%]
10. Value of transaction ($MM)	886.17 [161.6]	770.78 [91.30]	1001.56 [308.85]	−230.80 [−217.55]
11. Duration	154.16 [129.0]	152.23 [125.5]	156.10 [130.0]	−3.87 [−4.50]

***, **, and * indicate significance at the 1%, 5%, and 10% levels, respectively.

Panel B examines variables more closely aligned with active arbitrage. Panel C contains other deal-specific variables. Note that the variables in Panels A and B are likely to be related. Moreover, some variables, such as offer success, are related to both passive and active theories of arbitrage. Passive arbitrageurs are expected to invest in deals with a higher probability of success; active arbitrageurs are expected to influence the probability of success. Our main purpose in this section is to present the characteristics of our sample. A multivariate analysis, controlling for any inherent endogeneity, is presented in a subsequent section.

Column 1 of Table 2 provides the mean and median values for sample characteristics while the remaining columns contrast these values across subsamples of deals associated with small and large changes in arbitrage holdings, respectively. The final column displays the level and significance of differences between the subsamples.

As shown in Panel A, we find that most targets are successfully acquired (91%), most deals are friendly (97%), and the average toehold is quite small (0.9%). Most bidders do not own target shares before the acquisitions. These deal characteristics are typical of the literature for this period. We next calculate two different measures of arbitrage spread: First-quarter spread is calculated as (offer price $- P^{T}$)/P^{T}, where P^{T} is the target firm's stock price on the last day of the announcement quarter, and final-quarter spread is measured on the last day of the last quarter before the deal is consummated. The mean and median first-quarter spreads are 10.5% and 7.3%, respectively. Since the vast majority of offers are successful, it is not surprising to find that the mean and median final-quarter spreads have narrowed to 9.3% and 4.6%, respectively.[7]

Following Schwert (1996, 2000), we calculate price runup and markup; the sum of these two items is the bid premium. Price runup is the cumulative abnormal return to the target firm's stock from trading days -54 to -1 before the first bid. Price markup is calculated as (final offer price $- P^{T}_{-1}$)/P^{T}_{-1}, where P^{T}_{-1} is the target price 1 day before the announcement. Means and medians for these variables are shown in the first column of Panel B. Price runup averages 8.7%, just a bit higher than the median of 7.9%. The markup has a mean and median of 28.5% and 23.2%, respectively. The average premium is 37%, slightly higher than the median of 33%.

Panel C describes other deal-specific variables. These include measures of return, the value of the transaction, and deal duration. Baker and Savasoglu (2002) and Mitchell and Pulvino (2001) provide interesting analyses of returns in cash and stock portfolios. We follow their lead in modeling different arbitrage strategies with respect to the form of payment. In a cash deal i, an arbitrageur simply purchases the target stock and holds the position until deal consummation. For a stock swap or a collar

---

[7] We also calculate the spread on the day after the acquisition announcement as in Jindra and Walkling (2004). The magnitude of this spread is similar to the first-quarter spread defined in Table 2. However, we use first-quarter spread and final-quarter spread (as shown in Table 2) in our multivariate analysis since these variables are aligned chronologically with our estimates of change in arbitrage holdings. Our results are robust to different measurements of spread.

transaction, arbitrageurs typically take a long position in the target stock and hedge their position by shorting δ shares of the acquirer's stock. Here δ is the exchange rate of the offer. (Appendix A provides a more detailed description of these procedures.) We find that the mean and median annualized returns (from day 1 through offer resolution) are 50% and 19%, respectively. Thirty-day returns average 5% with a median of about 1.6%.[8] Revision returns are calculated as the change from the initial offer price to the final offer price normalized by the target price on day 1. The mean revision return is 0.23% while the median is 0%. Fewer than 13% of sample deals are revised (79 out of 608). The mean value of the acquisition bid is $886 million. The median ($162 million) is substantially lower. The mean duration of an offer is 154 days, about 5 months; the median duration is nearly a month shorter (129 days).

The last three columns of Table 2 contrast variable characteristics across deals with high and low changes in arbitrage holdings. Passive arbitrageurs are expected to invest more heavily in deals associated with a higher probability of success. The results of Panel A are generally consistent with this. Deals with the greatest change in arbitrage holdings have lower spreads and are more likely to be successful. Smaller spreads indicate greater market adjustment towards the bid price and lower uncertainty surrounding the deal. Mean and median spreads are 6.9% and 5.4% in deals with the highest change in arbitrage holdings. These figures are significantly smaller than the 14.1% mean and 9.2% median noted in deals with the smallest change in arbitrage holdings. As mentioned above, spread and deal success are also associated with theories of active arbitrage. Thus, it is difficult to distinguish the passive versus active theories from the univariate results presented here. We discuss this issue in more detail in our multivariate analysis.

To the extent that the level of arbitrage activity is known at the end of the quarter, we would expect it to be reflected in the determination of the spread. However, this information is still uncertain at the end of the quarter. Cornelli and Li (2002) utilize this fact, noting that arbitrageurs have an informational advantage from knowledge of their own holdings. Also in Panel A, we find that while the deals with higher changes in holdings are more likely to be friendly, the difference across the groups is insignificant. We do not find a significant difference in toeholds between deals with high and low accumulations of arbitrage holdings.

---

[8] Deals differ in their duration. To put returns on a comparable basis across offers, we annualize arbitrage return. Three alternatives for annualization are actual duration, median-duration return, and 30-day return. We are concerned that actual duration may distort annualized returns. A high return earned on short duration offers produce extreme values when annualized. These extreme annualized returns are not available to arbitrageurs unless they can repeatedly duplicate such offers. As two alternatives, we calculate median-duration return by accumulating daily return until day 129 (median duration in our sample) and the 30-day return accumulating until the earliest of resolution date or the 30th business day after announcement. Multivariate results using these different definitions of returns are qualitatively similar.

In Panel B, we examine variables discussed in the theories of active arbitrage. Active arbitrageurs influence both offer outcome and the size of the bid premium. We have already examined the univariate relation between offer success and arbitrage holdings. While we find that runup is higher in the deals with greater arbitrage holdings, the differences in runup, markup, and premium are not significantly different from each other across categories of holdings.

In Panel C we note significant differences across small and large Δholdings in mean or median levels of annualized returns and 30-day returns. For example, 30-day returns average 7.8% in deals with the largest change in arbitrage holdings. This is significantly larger than the 2.9% for deals with the smallest change in arbitrage holdings. The returns earned here are available to any investor purchasing the day after the announcement of the acquisition. The fact that Δholdings is greater in deals with larger annualized and 30-day returns is consistent with the returns reported here being lower bounds for returns to arbitrageurs. The positive relation between Δholdings and arbitrage returns is consistent with both the passive arbitrage hypothesis of Larcker and Lys (1987) and the active arbitrage theories modeled in Cornelli and Li (2002) and Gomes (2001). Panel C also reveals a univariate finding of a greater increase in arbitrage holdings in larger deals; this result will be reversed when we control for other deal characteristics in our multivariate analysis.

3.6. Deal characteristics categorized by number of arbitrageurs and their holdings

Table 2 illustrated the level of characteristics across deals with low and high changes in arbitrage holdings. Table 3 inverts this analysis, examining the number of arbitrageurs and the change in arbitrage holdings for deals categorized across the variables of our sample. Categorical variables are naturally split by their attributes; some continuous variables are also naturally split by their attributes (e.g., the existence or absence of toeholds and whether spreads are positive or negative). Other continuous variables are split into groups above and below the median. Our previous caution about endogeneity continues to apply throughout this table.

Panel A displays results for variables associated with passive arbitrage. We classify spreads into positive and negative groups. Although the spread is positive in most cases, Jindra and Walkling (2004) find that over 23% of the spreads are negative in their sample of cash tender offers. Our sample covers a later time period and also includes stock and collar offers. Overall, we find that 23% of first-quarter spreads are negative and 28% of final-quarter spreads are negative. A negative spread means that the postannouncement price exceeds the offered bid price; Jindra and Walkling (2004) associate this with a greater probability of deal revision. In the current sample, both the mean and median number of arbitrageurs and the mean and median change in the level of arbitrage holdings are significantly greater in the negative spread cases. This is true for both the first- and final-quarter spreads.

Table 3

Sample distribution of arbitrage holdings by deal characteristics and method of payment

Panels A–C show the estimated number of arbitrageurs and their change in holdings, Δholdings categorized by deal characteristics. Panel D presents the estimated number of arbitrageurs and their change in holdings categorized by methods of payment: cash, stock, and collar. The data source is the Spectrum Database, which provides the quarterly holdings of financial institutions with more than $100 million in securities under management. The identification of arbitrageurs and the change of arbitrage holdings in each deal are derived as follows. First, we calculate the change of institutional ownership in the target firm from the quarter immediately before to the quarter immediately after a takeover announcement. Second, to be identified as a risk arbitrageur, the institution needs to have positive changes in holdings for more than 60% of the deals in which they are involved and participate in at least six deals in our sample. Finally, we calculate the change of holdings in all of our sample deals for the identified arbitrageurs. The change of holdings is calculated by summing all holdings in the quarter ending before the deal resolution and subtracting the reported holdings the quarter before the deal announcement. See Table 2 for variable definitions. The right four columns of all panels test the difference in means and medians between two groups. The p-values under mean, as reported in parentheses, are associated with t-statistics using a two-sided t-test of no difference in mean between two groups. Figures under the median are p-values associated with the Wilcoxon rank sum test of no difference in medians between two groups.

		Below group median [<median]		Above group median [≥median]		Test of differences	
		Mean	Median	Mean	Median	Mean	Median
Panel A. Variables associated with theories of passive arbitrage							
1. Toehold		No (N = 575)		Yes (N = 33)			
	N_{arbs}	9.60	6.00	10.30	7.00	−0.71	−1.00
	Δholdings (%)	4.47	2.44	3.78	2.32	0.69	0.12
2a. First-quarter spread		Negative (N = 138)		Nonnegative (N = 470)			
	N_{arbs}	12.83	9.00	8.70	5.00	4.13***	4.00***
	Δholdings (%)	5.56	3.68	4.10	2.12	1.46**	1.56***
2b. Final-quarter spread		Negative (N = 169)		Nonnegative (N = 439)			
	N_{arbs}	13.25	9.00	8.24	5.00	5.01***	4.00***
	Δholdings (%)	6.10	3.72	3.79	1.89	2.31***	1.83***
3. Attitude		Hostile (N = 16)		Friendly (N = 592)			
	N_{arbs}	13.88	9.50	9.52	6.00	4.35	3.50*
	Δholdings (%)	5.21	1.03	4.41	2.45	0.80	−1.42
4. Deal status		Withdrawn (N = 55)		Success (N = 553)			
	N_{arbs}	9.25	7.00	9.67	6.00	−0.42	1.00
	Δholdings (%)	2.67	1.16	4.61	2.61	−1.94***	−1.46**

Panel B. Variables associated with theories of active arbitrage

5. Runup	N_{arbs}	10.18	6.00	9.08	5.00	1.10	1.00
	Δholdings (%)	3.92	2.12	4.95	2.79	−1.02**	−0.68
6. Markup	N_{arbs}	9.72	5.00	9.55	6.00	0.18	−1.00
	Δholdings (%)	3.77	1.81	5.11	2.82	−1.34***	−1.01**
7. Premium	N_{arbs}	10.27	7.00	8.97	5.50	1.30	1.50
	Δholdings (%)	3.81	2.27	5.08	2.63	−1.27***	−0.36*

Panel C. Other deal-specific variables

8a. Annualized return	N_{arbs}	10.54	6.00	8.74	6.00	1.80**	0.00
	Δholdings (%)	4.28	2.28	4.59	2.72	−0.31	−0.44
8b. Thirty-day return	N_{arbs}	9.22	5.00	10.05	7.00	−0.83	−2.00**
	Δholdings (%)	4.03	1.92	4.83	2.82	−0.80*	−0.90*
9. Value of transaction	N_{arbs}	3.45	3.00	15.90	13.00	−12.46***	−10.00***
	Δholdings (%)	2.64	0.80	6.25	4.61	−3.61***	−3.82***
10. Duration	N_{arbs}	8.94	6.00	10.18	6.00	−1.24	0.00
	Δholdings (%)	4.10	2.02	4.69	2.65	−0.59	−0.63

Panel D. Distribution of arbitrage holdings categorized by method of payment

		Mean	Median	Test of difference between selected subsamples		
					Mean	Median
Cash (N = 142)	N_{arbs}	7.58	5.00	Cash/stock	−2.64***	−1.00**
	Holding (%)	4.11	1.75		0.07	−0.38
Stock (N = 353)	N_{arbs}	10.23	6.00	Cash/collar	−2.21*	−1.00
	Holding (%)	4.04	2.13		−1.56**	−2.54***
Collar (N = 113)	N_{arbs}	9.80	6.00	Stock/collar	0.43	0.00
	Holding (%)	5.67	4.29		−1.63***	−2.16***

***, **, and * indicate significance at the 1%, 5%, and 10% levels, respectively.

Successful deals are associated with a greater increase in holdings. In successful deals, the mean and median levels of holdings are 4.6% and 2.6%, respectively; comparable values for withdrawn deals are 2.7% and 1.1%. This result is consistent with both the passive and active arbitrage theories. The number of arbitrageurs, however, does not significantly differ across deal outcomes. The results also suggest that target management's reaction to the bid and the existence of bidder toeholds do not affect the number of arbitrageurs or the change of their holdings. An exception is that the number of arbitrageurs is significantly greater in hostile deals.

Panel B contains results for variables associated with theories of active arbitrage. The average change in arbitrage holdings is significantly smaller in deals with a lower level of price runup. Mean and median changes in holdings are also significantly smaller in deals with lower levels of markup and premium.

Panel C contains results for other deal-specific variables. Our univariate results do not indicate a significant relation between the change in holdings and annualized returns. However, unless a particular type of deal can be constantly replicated (an unlikely assumption), annualized returns will be unrepresentative of the returns available to arbitrageurs. We do note that the mean and median levels of Δholdings are significantly smaller in the deals earning lower than median 30-day returns in comparison to deals above the median. The mean and median number of arbitrageurs for large transactions is 15.9 and 13.0, respectively. This is significantly greater than the corresponding numbers for the small firms (3.5 and 3.0). The mean and median increase in arbitrage holdings is also significantly greater for large deals in comparison to smaller deals. As we have noted, however, the univariate results with regard to Δholdings and deal size will be reversed in our multivariate analysis. Finally, the change in arbitrage holdings and the number of arbitrageurs are insignificantly different across samples of short and long deal durations. This is consistent with the notion (and results we will present later) that arbitrageurs tend to retain their positions until the deal is resolved.

Panel D of Table 3 displays the relation between Δholdings and the method of payment offered to target firms' shareholders. Analyzing these characteristics is important since arbitrage strategies are known to differ by form of payment. In addition, Travlos (1987) and Huang and Walkling (1987) show how form of payment affects bidder and target returns. The second and third columns show the means and medians of the number of arbitrageurs and Δholdings while the two columns at the far right test for significant differences in Δholdings among payment methods. Arbitrageurs have the highest mean and median Δholdings in collar deals (5.7%, 4.3%) and the lowest in stock or cash deals. Stock and cash deals have mean (median) Δholdings of 4.0% (2.1%) and 4.1% (1.8%), respectively. The difference between the change in holdings for cash and stock offers is insignificant. Collar offers, however, are associated with significantly greater Δholdings than either stock or cash offers. The average number of arbitrageurs shows a different ordering, being highest in stock offers (10.2 arbitrageurs per deal) and lowest in cash offers (7.6 arbitrageurs per deal). The median number of arbitrageurs per deal is six in stock and collar offers and five in cash offers.

4. Simultaneous estimation of premium, Δholdings, probability of success, and returns

4.1. Description of the empirical model

The main objective of this research is to examine arbitrage activity as it relates to the passive and active arbitrageur hypotheses suggested in the literature. The main implications of the active and passive theories are indicated in Equations (1)–(3). The first passive model implies that the change in arbitrage holdings will be unrelated to arbitrage returns and the probability of deal success; arbitrageurs earn the same returns as naïve investors without utilizing superior ability to predict deal success. The passive argument of Larcker and Lys (1987) suggests the opposite, with arbitrageurs adjusting their holdings accordingly. On the other hand, the active arbitrageur hypothesis of Cornelli and Li (2002) and Gomes (2001) suggests that deal attributes are materially affected by arbitrage activity. Thus, Δholdings would be significant in explaining the probability of bid success, arbitrage returns, and the level of bid premia.

As mentioned previously, the theoretical models indicate that many takeover variables are endogenously determined. These include Δholdings, bid premia, and arbitrage returns. For example, Gomes' (2001) model implies that bidders are willing to increase bid premia to mitigate the potential hold-out problem. At the same time, arbitrageurs are also more likely to increase their holdings when the premia are high. Cornelli and Li (2002) suggest that there is a positive relation between Δholdings and returns.[9] We recognize this potential endogeneity in our analysis, testing for its existence and controlling for its effects through the use of appropriate instruments with two-stage least squares (2SLS). At the same time, we note that our main conclusions are unaltered if we use a simpler technique (OLS) or a more elaborate one (three-stage least squares).[10]

However, rather than rely solely on the theory, we test for endogeneity empirically. Our results, shown in Appendix B, indicate that Δholdings, bid premia, and arbitrage returns are endogenous while toeholds are more likely to be exogenous. If variables are endogenous, estimates from ordinary least squares will be biased and inconsistent, in which case it is necessary to estimate coefficients within a system of simultaneous equations. Consequently, we estimate a system of equations by regressing these

---

[9] Several theoretical models related to toeholds indicate that premia and toeholds could be jointly determined (see, e.g., Bulow et al., 1999; Hirshleifer and Titman, 1990). Our endogeneity test, however, indicates that toeholds are more likely to be exogenous. Nevertheless, including toeholds in our system of estimation does not change our conclusions.

[10] Greene (1997) documents that the choice between 2SLS and 3SLS is unclear. More efficient estimates could be provided by 3SLS, but it is prone to any specification error in the structure of the model (3SLS results are available upon request). With one minor exception, OLS results are similar to those with simultaneous equations. The exception occurs in the regression explaining arbitrage return: The coefficient for premium becomes insignificant in the OLS regression (p-value = 0.12). Otherwise, results are similar. Because the theory emphasizes endogeneity, we focus on 2SLS results in our discussions.

endogenous variables on each other as well as appropriate control variables suggested in the literature. In earlier versions of this paper, we include in each equation only control variables recognized in the literature as related to the dependent variable. Although this approach is legitimate for single-equation regressions, recent studies (e.g., Coles et al., 2003) suggest inclusion of all control variables in each equation. Our results are similar using either approach.

The regressions reported in our tables and in our text discussion use 30-day returns. Our main conclusions remain if we use annualized returns or returns based on the median duration of offers, 129 days. Additional control variables not previously discussed include a measure of abnormal volume following the offer and three binary variables to recognize the existence of multiple bids, defensive strategies and tender offers, respectively. Abnormal postannouncement volume is defined as $AV_i = (1/T) \sum_{t=+1}^{\min[50, \text{delisting}-1]} V_{it} - (1/73) \sum_{t=-126}^{t=-54} V_{it}$, normalized by total shares outstanding. The latter two variables are known ex ante. The system is estimated using 2SLS with at least one instrument in each equation. The requirement for the instrument is that it should be closely correlated with the corresponding dependent variable but not with other dependent variables. We use price runup as the instrument for bid premium, number of arbitrageurs and deal size for change in holdings, and lockup for returns.[11]

One of our important control variables is the spread. At each point at which it is measured, it captures the prevailing market wisdom about the outcome of the offer. We wish to test whether the change in arbitrage holdings contains additional information about offer outcomes while controlling for the spread. In order for spread to function as a control, however, it must be measured contemporaneously or simultaneously with the change in arbitrage holdings. Otherwise, the change in holdings will adjust to information not contained in the spread, imparting a "look ahead" bias in our analysis.

4.2. Multivariate analysis

Table 4 shows the results from the estimated equations. In Panel A, the change in arbitrage holdings is measured from the quarter before deal announcement to the quarter after announcement ($\Delta Q1$Hold). In Panel B, the change in arbitrage holdings is estimated until the quarter before deal consummation (Δholdings). In each Panel we use a measure of spread estimated contemporaneously with the change in holdings. Thus, in Panel A, spread is measured at the end of the first quarter, the same time at which the change in holdings is measured. In Panel B, spread and the change in

---

[11] Although we have used the instrumental approach to mitigate the potential causal effects, we are careful not to assert strong causality. Even the best efforts to find appropriate instruments will be imperfect. For instance, an (expected) successful deal could attract both larger positions and a greater number of arbitrageurs. If this is the case, then the number of arbitrageurs becomes less suitable as an instrument.

Table 4

Simultaneous-equation estimation of cross-sectional models for the takeover premium, arbitrage holdings, and returns

The table presents the results from the simultaneous-equation estimation of the relations among the takeover premium, arbitrage holdings, and annualized returns. The systems are estimated using two-stage least squares (2SLS). The variable "$\Delta Q1\text{Hold}$" refers to the aggregate change of arbitrage holdings from the quarter before deal announcement to the quarter after the announcement while "$\Delta\text{holdings}$" is the aggregate change of arbitrage holdings from the quarter-end before the announcement to the quarter-end preceding its resolution. N_{arb} is the number of arbitrageurs in each deal. Return is calculated by accumulating daily returns until the earliest of resolution date or the 30th business day after announcement, normalizing by multiplying 30/(deal duration). See the text for calculations of daily returns. First-quarter spread is calculated as (offer price $- P^{\text{T}})/P^{\text{T}}$, where P^{T} is the target firm's stock price on the last day of the announcement quarter. Final-quarter spread is similarly measured on the last day of the last quarter before the deal is consummated. We match the initial spread with $\Delta Q1\text{Hold}$ and the final spread with $\Delta\text{holdings}$ in our regressions. Revision return is calculated as (final offer price $-$ initial offer price)$/P^{\text{T}}_{-1}$. Friendly is a dummy variable with a value of 1 for friendly deals and 0 otherwise based on whether the target firm resisted or faced an unsolicited offer as determined by SDC. Toehold is the percentage of target shares held by the bidder prior to the announcement. Runup is the cumulative abnormal returns to the target firm's stock for trading days $(-54, -1)$ before the first bid. Markup is calculated as (final offer price $- P^{\text{T}}_{-1})/P^{\text{T}}_{-1}$, where P^{T}_{-1} is the target firm's stock price 1 day before the announcement. Premium is the target's price runup plus markup. Deal duration is measured as the length of time between the first formal announcement of the takeover and the announced resolution of the deal. Success is a dummy variable with a value of 1 for successful deals. Collar (Stock) is a dummy variable with a value of 1 for the collar (stock) deals. Multiple bidders is a dummy variable with a value of 1 if multiple-bid contest. Defense is a dummy variable with a value of 1 for deals in which the target firm has adopted defensive tactics as reported in SDC. Tender is a dummy variable with a value of 1 if the bid is a tender offer. Abnormal volume is defined as

$$\text{AV}_i = (1/T) \sum_{t=+1}^{\min[50,\,\text{delisting}-1]} V_{it} - (1/73) \sum_{t=-126}^{t=-54} V_{it}.$$

Deal value, in millions, is the total market value of consideration, excluding fees and expenses. The variable "days" is measured as the length of time between the last reporting date in Spectrum before deal announcement and the first formal announcement of the takeover. Arbitrage capital is estimated by aggregating the values of all deals for the institutions identified as arbitrageurs for each quarter in the sample. Heteroskedasticity-consistent covariance is applied in the estimation procedure. The p-values are reported in parentheses. Endogeneity tests for the regressors in this table are shown in the appendix, Table 9.

	Panel A: 2SLS $- \Delta Q1\text{Hold}$			Panel B: 2SLS $- \Delta\text{holdings}$		
	Premium	$\Delta Q1\text{Hold}$	Return	Premium	$\Delta\text{holdings}$	Return
Constant	0.438	0.057	0.253	0.415	0.031	0.027
	(0.059)	(0.078)	(0.112)	(0.082)	(0.374)	(0.093)
Premium		0.018	0.045		0.018	0.046
		(0.000)	(0.044)		(0.000)	(0.037)
$\Delta Q1\text{Hold}$ or	0.375		0.600	0.318		0.726
$\Delta\text{holdings}$	(0.120)		(0.086)	(0.168)		(0.010)
$(\Delta Q1\text{Hold})^2$ or			-0.728			-1.214
$(\Delta\text{holdings})^2$			(0.637)			(0.226)

(Continued)

Table 4 (*Continued*)

	Panel A: 2SLS − ΔQ1Hold			Panel B: 2SLS − Δholdings		
	Premium	ΔQ1Hold	Return	Premium	Δholdings	Return
Return	0.318	0.015		0.324	0.018	
	(0.000)	(0.060)		(0.000)	(0.044)	
Runup	0.903			0.896		
	(0.000)			(0.000)		
$\log(1 + N_{\mathrm{arb}})$		0.043			0.045	
		(0.000)			(0.000)	
log(Deal value)		−0.012			−0.012	
		(0.000)			(0.000)	
Lockup			0.033			0.032
			(0.101)			(0.103)
Toehold	−0.003	0.000	−0.002	−0.003	0.000	−0.002
	(0.224)	(0.678)	(0.277)	(0.289)	(0.472)	(0.291)
Collar	0.019	0.020	−0.060	0.032	0.018	−0.061
	(0.702)	(0.004)	(0.081)	(0.528)	(0.013)	(0.075)
Stock	−0.036	0.006	−0.025	−0.025	0.004	−0.025
	(0.416)	(0.367)	(0.409)	(0.583)	(0.521)	(0.418)
Revision returns	0.671	0.019	0.101	1.066	0.004	0.097
	(0.000)	(0.428)	(0.398)	(0.000)	(0.873)	(0.416)
First- or final-quarter spread	0.652	−0.024	0.001	0.506	−0.031	0.002
	(0.000)	(0.011)	(0.976)	(0.000)	(0.001)	(0.965)
Success	0.077	0.011	0.009	0.085	0.014	0.006
	(0.118)	(0.106)	(0.802)	(0.095)	(0.050)	(0.867)
Multiple bidders	−0.057	0.002	0.014	−0.061	−0.004	0.014
	(0.422)	(0.799)	(0.783)	(0.403)	(0.705)	(0.774)
Friendly	−0.122	−0.004	0.002	−0.136	−0.005	0.002
	(0.174)	(0.748)	(0.972)	(0.141)	(0.711)	(0.970)
Defense	0.038	0.034	0.149	−0.028	0.036	0.149
	(0.794)	(0.082)	(0.134)	(0.853)	(0.093)	(0.133)
Tender	0.034	0.005	−0.008	0.048	0.002	−0.008
	(0.568)	(0.523)	(0.841)	(0.431)	(0.814)	(0.845)
log(Duration)	−0.012	−0.006	−0.024	0.000	−0.004	−0.025
	(0.638)	(0.093)	(0.161)	(0.990)	(0.306)	(0.135)
Abnormal volume	0.020	0.003	0.010	0.018	0.003	0.009
	(0.001)	(0.002)	(0.022)	(0.004)	(0.003)	(0.025)
log(Days)	0.001	−0.006	−0.003	0.003	−0.004	−0.004
	(0.925)	(0.007)	(0.764)	(0.856)	(0.074)	(0.729)
log(Arbitrage capital)	−0.012	−0.001	−0.010	−0.014	0.000	−0.011
	(0.436)	(0.634)	(0.327)	(0.363)	(0.938)	(0.303)
Year dummies	Yes	Yes	Yes	Yes	Yes	Yes
Adjusted R^2	0.475	0.464	0.039	0.475	0.445	0.042

holdings are measured at the end of the last quarter before the deal concludes. Overall, the results in Table 4 support the case that arbitrageurs establish their positions early; results are similar across both measurements.

We divide our discussion of Table 4 into three parts: Results concerning control variables previously analyzed in the literature, results for our endogenous variables of interest, and results related to determinants of arbitrage holdings and returns. Endogenous variables are shown in the shaded areas; instrumental and other control variables are shown in nonshaded areas.

In general, results for the control variables are consistent with the literature. For example, deals with a higher runup also provide higher premia. Moreover, neither toeholds nor target management attitude show a strong correlation with premia. We also find that offers with higher spreads and revision returns are associated with higher premia.

More importantly, the results of Table 4 provide support for both the passive and active explanations for positive abnormal returns to arbitrageurs. Three variables in the regression explaining Δholdings can be considered proxies for the probability of success: spread, friendly, and success itself. Spread and friendly are pure ex ante proxies for success that are readily observable by all investors, not just those with superior ability. The significance of these variables in the equations is consistent with both passive-arbitrageur arguments. The major difference between the purely passive role of arbitrageurs and the passive arbitrage theory of Larcker and Lys (1987) is that in Larcker and Lys, arbitrageurs are superior at forecasting offer success and increase their holdings correspondingly. Success can be considered a "perfect foresight" proxy for success. Both $\Delta Q1$Hold and Δholdings are significantly smaller in high spread offers (i.e., those in which the market anticipates a smaller probability of success). This is consistent with the passive role of arbitrageurs. $\Delta Q1$Hold and Δholdings are significantly larger in successful offers. This is consistent with the Larker and Lys assertion that arbitrageurs have superior predictive ability. Our results indicate that Δholdings is insignificantly related to target managerial attitude. Overall, the evidence from Table 4 is consistent with arbitrageurs having superior ability to predict deal outcomes. The results of the regressions are also consistent with the active arbitrage theories of Cornelli and Li (2002) and Gomes (2001) since they reveal significant endogenous relations among Δholdings, bid premia, and returns.

We also explore the dynamic tension between the degree of arbitrage activity and the level of arbitrage returns: A higher level of holdings can facilitate the takeover and provide greater arbitrage returns. Alternatively, increased competition among arbitrageurs could reduce their returns. We test whether there is a curvilinear relation between Δholdings and returns by adding the square of Δholdings to the return equation. This variable is motivated by Cornelli and Li's model in which increased arbitrage presence is associated with decreased marginal returns caused by competition. While the sign of the coefficient of $(\Delta holdings)^2$ is consistent with the Cornelli and Li conjecture, the effect is statistically insignificant.

Apart from the primary variables of interest, the coefficients of several control factors also shed light on the determinants of Δholdings and returns. Interestingly, we find that arbitrageurs do not increase holdings in multiple-bidder deals. One plausible explanation is in line with the argument of limited arbitrage by Shleifer and Vishny (1997). Arbitrageurs desire to hedge their long positions in target shares but face increased capital constraints in the case of multiple bidders. That is, capital constraints are exacerbated by the quick arrival of competition. Betton and Eckbo (2000), for example, document that rival bids on average arrive within 15 days. We also find that after controlling for other deal characteristics, the changes in holdings are lower in larger deals. This might be because of the capital constraints as mentioned above. Another possibility is that arbitrageurs restrict the maximum amount of capital they invest in each deal.

Changes in arbitrage holdings are significantly higher in collar offers while the changes in stock deals are comparable to those in cash offers. Target management attitude, on the other hand, is not associated with $\Delta Q1$Hold or Δholdings. This is consistent with arbitrageurs believing that target management resistance at the beginning of the process is simply a bargaining strategy (Schwert, 2000). The insignificant result from target management attitude does not support the pure passive arbitrage theory that arbitrageurs are simply naïve investors without predictive abilities. We also find that there is no significant relation between Δholdings and deal duration. Since we measure Δholdings from the quarter end before the acquisition announcement until the first quarter after announcement ($\Delta Q1$Hold) or through the quarter before the resolution (Δholdings), this result implies that arbitrageurs do not try to unload their positions at an early stage of the takeover process. All results are also robust to the inclusion of year dummies to control for time effects.

The third equation of Table 4 estimates the relation between arbitrage returns and deal characteristics. We find that collar offers are associated with lower arbitrage returns. Interestingly, arbitrage returns are not affected by target managerial attitude or competition among bidders. Finally, there exists a positive contemporaneous relation between arbitrage returns and abnormal postannouncement volume in the stock of target companies. To the extent that this measure is correlated with stock liquidity, the results are consistent with higher returns earned in more liquid stocks in which it is easier for arbitrageurs to disguise their trading.

4.3. Is the probability of offer success correlated with the change in arbitrage holdings?

Larcker and Lys (1987), Cornelli and Li (2002), and Gomes (2001) all suggest a positive relation between the involvement of arbitrageurs and the probability of offer success. The implied alternative hypothesis to these three studies is that arbitrageurs are noise traders whose participation does not affect the market for corporate control. Under this scenario, bidders can ignore the presence of arbitrageurs when they determine deal characteristics.

A direct way to test these hypotheses is to include an equation relating Δholdings to bid success in the system estimated in Table 4. Indeed, Table 9 in the appendix reveals that the probability of deal success is endogenously determined with other variables of interest, especially in conjunction with Δholdings. It is important to recognize this endogeneity. To check for robustness, we actually use two different econometric models to test whether the change in holdings is related to deal success: The systems approach and a separate logistic analysis.

Our first approach treats deal success as a fourth linear equation in the system that we have previously estimated. Again, we include at least one instrument in each equation and other control variables in all equations. In particular, we use the target managerial attitude as an instrument for deal success. Note that although the target managerial attitude is exogenous with our main variables of interest, it still has potential limitations as an instrument. Specifically, a perfect instrument for deal success is a variable correlated with success but unknown at the time of the change in holdings.

Ideally, the probability of success should be estimated as a nonlinear probability model (e.g., probit or logit). However, it is technically infeasible to incorporate logit or probit into the system of equations because the probability of deal success is a discrete variable while the other four dependent variables in the system are continuous. Although the applied linear system has some shortcomings, the obtained estimates are consistent. The system of equations estimated in Panel A of Table 5 produces results suggested by the active arbitrageur hypothesis: The probability of success is positively related to Δholdings. In addition, our previous results still hold after including the probability of bid success into our system of estimation.

The second approach to test whether the change in holdings is related to deal success follows the procedure in Maddala (1983, p. 244). We first estimate a model to predict "expected" changes in holdings by regressing Δholdings against other explanatory variables excluding "Success," which is the perfect foresight proxy for the probability of success. One requirement for those independent variables is that they should be highly correlated with Δholdings but not with offer success. Specifically, we include the following variables to estimate the expected Δholdings: $\log(1 + N_{arb})$, log(deal value), abnormal volume, premium, collar, stock, tender, and return. The first two are instrumental variables while the others are controls. All these variables have significant correlations with Δholdings but have low correlations with the probability of success.

This first-stage procedure yields "fitted" and "error" components of Δholdings in each deal. If the probability of success has a significant effect on Δholdings, it will exist in the error component of the first equation. Since we would like to isolate the effect of the probability of success away from Δholdings in the second-stage regression, we include the fitted value as a regressor in logistic models explaining the probability of deal success. The coefficient of Δholdings directly tests its impact on the probability of deal success.

The four columns in Panel B present the results from the logistic regressions. Regression (I) uses Δholdings itself as an explanatory variable while the fitted value is used in regressions (II)–(IV). The results still hold and most importantly, the relation between the probability of deal success and Δholdings remains significant. This result

Table 5

Simultaneous-equation estimation of cross-sectional models for the takeover premium, the arbitrage holdings, probability of deal success, and returns, 01/1992 to 12/1999

The table presents the results from the simultaneous-equations estimation of the relations among bidder's toehold, takeover premium, probability of deal success, arbitrage holdings, and annualized returns. The systems are estimated using two-stage least squares (2SLS) and two-stage logistic regressions. To facilitate estimation and obtain more consistent results, 2SLS estimates the probability of deal success as a linear model. The variable "Δholdings" is used in model I of the logistic regressions. Following the suggestion in Maddala (1983, p. 244) to correct for the endogeneity problem, models II, III, and IV include the fitted holdings as a regressor. The fitted holding is estimated by regressing holdings against other explanatory variables, except the probability of deal success, and then calculating the expected holding for each deal. Lockup is a dummy variable with a value of 1 if the bidder obtains a lockup option from the target. See Table 4 for other variable definitions. Heteroskedasticity-consistent covariance is used in the estimation procedure. The p-values are reported in parentheses. Endogeneity tests for the regressors in this table are shown in the appendix, Table 9.

	Panel A: 2SLS				Panel B: Logistic regressions (dependent variable: success = 1; 0, else)			
	Premium	Success	Δholdings	Return	(I)	(II)	(III)	(IV)
Constant	0.318 (0.166)	0.003 (0.983)	0.031 (0.361)	0.267 (0.081)	-4.809 (0.220)	-3.984 (0.002)	-4.855 (0.136)	-9.622 (0.019)
Premium			0.017 (0.000)	0.046 (0.036)				
Success	0.057 (0.228)		0.014 (0.043)	0.006 (0.851)				
Δholdings	0.317 (0.170)	0.421 (0.020)		0.743 (0.009)	14.630 (0.001)			
$(\Delta$holdings$)^2$				-1.261 (0.209)				
Return	0.324 (0.000)							
(fitted) Δholdings						28.378 (0.007)	31.170 (0.007)	88.395 (0.000)
Runup	0.894 (0.000)		0.018 (0.041)					
Friendly		0.679 (0.000)			6.423 (0.040)	5.193 (0.000)	4.993 (0.001)	7.982 (0.006)
log(1 + N_{arb})			0.045 (0.000)					
log(Deal value)			-0.012 (0.000)					
Lockup		0.038 (0.105)	0.000 (0.733)	0.033 (0.098)	0.654 (0.202)	0.792 (0.084)	0.569 (0.238)	0.502 (0.306)
Toehold	-0.003 (0.355)	0.004 (0.049)	0.000 (0.268)	-0.002 (0.268)	0.151 (0.058)	0.160 (0.001)	0.153 (0.012)	0.201 (0.024)

	(1)	(2)	(3)	(4)	(5)	(6)	(7)	(8)
Collar	0.023 (0.637)	−0.019 (0.638)	0.018 (0.013)	−0.061 (0.070)	−0.605 (0.540)			−2.492 (0.018)
Stock	−0.033 (0.459)	−0.032 (0.384)	0.004 (0.585)	−0.025 (0.414)	−1.023 (0.269)			−1.749 (0.041)
Revision returns	1.096 (0.000)	0.134 (0.336)	−0.003 (0.904)	0.101 (0.396)	2.205 (0.129)			−0.210 (0.893)
First- or final-spread	0.505 (0.000)	−0.136 (0.009)	−0.031 (0.001)	0.003 (0.952)	−1.819 (0.111)	−1.487 (0.206)		1.807 (0.275)
Multiple bidders	−0.058 (0.424)	−0.378 (0.000)	−0.005 (0.623)	0.015 (0.762)	−3.492 (0.000)	−3.140 (0.000)		−3.976 (0.000)
Defense	0.041 (0.775)	0.093 (0.435)	0.039 (0.057)	0.148 (0.118)	−0.089 (0.973)			2.397 (0.444)
Tender	0.043 (0.473)	0.062 (0.202)	0.001 (0.865)	−0.008 (0.848)	0.915 (0.351)			0.040 (0.964)
log(Duration)	0.000 (0.985)	0.058 (0.004)	−0.004 (0.234)	−0.025 (0.141)	0.764 (0.117)		0.665 (0.149)	0.578 (0.260)
Abnormal volume	0.018 (0.005)	−0.005 (0.328)	0.003 (0.002)	0.009 (0.026)	−0.088 (0.157)			−0.447 (0.001)
log(Days)	0.003 (0.850)	−0.027 (0.028)	−0.004 (0.073)	−0.004 (0.734)	−0.694 (0.073)		−0.459 (0.165)	−0.308 (0.432)
log(Arbitrage capital)	−0.015 (0.357)	0.008 (0.300)	0.000 (0.891)	−0.011 (0.303)	0.071 (0.580)			0.138 (0.305)
Year dummies	Yes	Yes	Yes	Yes	Yes			
Adjusted R^2	0.444	0.267	0.454	0.045	0.325	0.188	0.289	0.343

is robust to a different estimate of holdings ($\Delta Q1$Hold) measured across only the first quarter of deal announcement.

Consistent with Schwert (2000) and Walkling (1985), managerial resistance is significantly related to the probability of success with either the analysis of Panels A or B. In addition, both techniques of estimation indicate that higher toeholds increase the probability of deal success, a result consistent with Betton and Eckbo (2000).

In general, the results of Tables 4 and 5 provide strong empirical support for both the passive arbitrage model of Larcker and Lys (1987) and the active arbitrage models of Cornelli and Li (2002) and Gomes (2001). The change in holdings is significantly related to offer success as implied by Larcker and Lys. The change in holdings is also significantly related to the spread between offered bid price and the market price. However, the probability of success, arbitrage returns, and bid premia are all significantly related to Δholdings as implied by Cornelli and Li and Gomes.

4.4. Regression analysis of the change in arbitrage holdings and revision returns

Is arbitrage activity related to deal revision? If a deal is terminated, can arbitrageurs predict or influence the possibility that the target firm receives subsequent bid(s) in the near future? If the answers to these questions are affirmative, it strengthens the argument that arbitrageurs have a significant active impact on takeovers.

Table 6 presents a multivariate analysis by regressing revision returns against changes in arbitrage holdings and associated control variables. To minimize the causality issue between the changes in holdings and revision returns, our tests are performed by only using the initial change in holdings ($\Delta Q1$Hold) from the quarter immediately before to the quarter immediately after the announcement. We also modify our second measure of the change in holdings (Δholdings) for deals lasting more than two quarters by deleting arbitrage holdings accumulated after the deal is revised. The results indicate that both measures of the change in holdings are strongly related to revision returns. When arbitrageurs increase their initial holdings, deals are more likely to be revised. The relation is statistically and economically significant. For example, the first regression indicates that when arbitrage holdings increase one standard deviation (5.9%), revision returns increase about 0.77%.

It is also possible, however, that arbitrageurs tend to choose deals with characteristics associated with the revision returns. (For example, recall that the average number of arbitrageurs was greater in deals with negative spreads.) To recognize this type of effect, we include spread, target management attitude, and bidder's initial toehold as control variables in regressions III–V. In regressions VI and VII, we also include control variables for multiple bidders, tender offers, existence of defensive tactics, and form of payment. The only significant control variable is the dummy variable for multiple bidders. As expected, offers with multiple bidders are more likely to have further positive revisions.

Table 6

Regressions explaining revision returns

The dependent variable is the revision return calculated as (final offer price − initial offer price)/P^T_{+1}, where P^T_{+1} is the target firm's stock price 1 day after the announcement. First-quarter spread is calculated as (offer price − P^T)/P^T, where P^T is the target firm's stock price on the last day of the announcement quarter. Final-quarter spread is similarly measured on the last day of the last quarter before the deal is consummated. We match the initial spread with $\Delta Q1$Hold and the final spread with Δholdings in our regressions. "$\Delta Q1$Hold" is the aggregate change of arbitrage holdings in each deal from the quarter before announcement to the quarter after announcement. The change is then normalized by the target firm's share outstanding. Δholdings is the aggregate change of arbitrage holdings in each deal from the quarter before announcement until the quarter end before the deal is revised. Following the suggestion in Maddala (1983, p. 244) to correct for the endogeneity problem, we also include the fitted $\Delta Q1$Hold as a regressor. The fitted change in holdings is estimated by regressing $\Delta Q1$Hold against other explanatory variables, except the revision return, and then calculating the expected $\Delta Q1$Hold for each deal. Friendly is a dummy variable with a value of 1 for friendly deals and 0 otherwise, it is based on whether the target firm resisted or faced an unsolicited offer as determined by SDC. Toehold is the percentage of target shares held by the bidder prior to the announcement. Runup is the cumulative abnormal returns to the target firm's stock for trading days (−54, −1) before the first bid. Collar (Stock) is a dummy variable with a value of 1 for the collar (stock) deals. Multiple bidders is a dummy variable with a value of 1 if it is a multiple-bid contest. Defense is a dummy variable with a value of 1 for deals in which the target firm has adopted defensive tactics as reported in SDC. Tender is a dummy variable with a value of 1 if the bid is a tender offer. Heteroskedasticity-consistent covariance is used in the estimation procedure. The p-values are reported in parentheses.

	(I)	(II)	(III)	(IV)	(V)	(VI)	(VII)	(VIII)
Constant	−0.003	−0.002	−0.003	−0.002	−0.006	0.037	0.038	0.037
	(0.366)	(0.541)	(0.507)	(0.659)	(0.226)	(0.283)	(0.277)	(0.283)
$\Delta Q1$Hold	0.139		0.130			0.098		
	(0.013)		(0.018)			(0.064)		
Δholdings (*before revision*)		0.105		0.097			0.078	
		(0.044)		(0.048)			(0.092)	
$\Delta Q1$Hold (*fitted*)					0.180			0.098
					(0.013)			(0.149)
Toehold			0.003	0.003	0.003	0.002	0.002	0.002
			(0.135)	(0.135)	(0.140)	(0.142)	(0.142)	(0.147)
Runup			0.011	0.012	0.014	0.018	0.018	0.020
			(0.355)	(0.332)	(0.252)	(0.128)	(0.124)	(0.096)
First- or final-quarter spread			−0.030	−0.031	−0.030	−0.032	−0.033	−0.033
			(0.282)	(0.262)	(0.270)	(0.227)	(0.216)	(0.205)
Friendly						−0.049	−0.049	−0.049
						(0.123)	(0.121)	(0.119)
Multiple bidders						0.090	0.092	0.090
						(0.008)	(0.007)	(0.008)
Tender						0.003	0.003	0.004
						(0.764)	(0.719)	(0.694)
Defense						−0.007	−0.007	−0.007
						(0.758)	(0.782)	(0.769)
Collar						0.006	0.007	0.007
						(0.491)	(0.459)	(0.469)
Stock						0.006	0.006	0.007
						(0.487)	(0.462)	(0.446)
Adjusted R^2	0.008	0.005	0.036	0.034	0.033	0.094	0.091	0.093

As shown in regression III, the positive relation between $\Delta Q1\text{Hold}$ and revision returns remains significant with a p-value of 0.02. Similar results are obtained using fitted values of $\Delta Q1\text{Hold}$ (as in regression V). Similar results (available upon request) are also obtained in sensitivity tests using: (a) a logistic regression with the dependent variable set equal to one for revised-up offers; and (b) the simultaneous estimation of revision returns and $\Delta Q1\text{Hold}$ in a 2SLS estimation. In specification (b) we use toehold as the instrument for the equation of revision returns and both the number of arbitrageurs and deal size as instruments for $\Delta Q1\text{Hold}$. As before, revision returns are significantly, positively related to $\Delta Q1\text{Hold}$.

4.5. The relation between the change in arbitrage holdings in withdrawn offers and subsequent bids

In the previous section we find that the magnitude of revision returns is significantly related to the change in arbitrage holdings. Nevertheless, some acquisition bids inevitably fail. In this section we examine whether Δholdings in failed offers is linked to the probability of subsequent offers.

For 55 failed deals during the period of 1992–1999, we first exclude seven multiple-bidder cases in which the target firms are acquired by other bidders during the initial takeover period. For the remaining 48 deals we search the SDC database and Lexis-Nexis to determine whether there are new bids by the end of 2001. Panel A of Table 7 shows that 14 firms receive new takeover attempts within 1 year, six firms after 1 year but within 2 years, and eight firms after 2 years. We do not find information in SDC or Lexis-Nexis related to the remaining 20 firms.

Panel B of Table 7 compares Δholdings and the number of arbitrageurs in deals receiving subsequent bids with those in other deals. Target firms are more likely to receive new bids when the increase of arbitrage holdings remains high. On average, Δholdings are a significant 1.9% higher in firms receiving new bids than those in other firms. The cumulative frequency distribution of Δholdings (summarized by the minimum through the maximum holdings) is consistently higher in deals that attract new bids.

Panel C provides a similar analysis comparing firms receiving new bids within 1 year to the rest of the sample. The results are even stronger. The average (median) difference in Δholdings between firms with new bids and those without is 3.4% (1.7%). Both differences are significant at the 5% level.

We next perform a logistic analysis of the same issue, setting the dependent variable equal to 1 if the target receives another bid within 1 year, and 0 if it does not. Table 8 reports logistic results using five different specifications. The first and second regressions show that the probability of receiving another bid increases significantly with the number of arbitrageurs or with Δholdings. The coefficient of the number of arbitrageurs becomes insignificant after both variables are included. Regressions (IV) and (V) include several control variables related to the original bids. The coefficient of Δholdings remains significant in both regressions. Further, we find that if the original deals had

Table 7

The relation between subsequent bids for failed tender offers and arbitrage holdings

This table reports the incidence of target firms that receive subsequent bids after the announcement of deal failure. Panel A presents the distribution of failed deals according to the date at which they received new takeover attempts. Panel B compares arbitrage holdings in deals in which the target firms receive subsequent bids by the end of 2001 and deals without any subsequent attempts during the same period. Panel C compares arbitrage holdings in cases in which the target does and does not receive subsequent bids within 1 year after the announcement of deal failure. Δholdings is the aggregate change of holdings in each deal normalized by target firm's shares outstanding. N_{arb} is the number of arbitrageurs in each deal. The procedure of selecting arbitrageurs is described in the text and Table 2.

Panel A. The distribution of failed deals

	Number of firms	Percentage (%)
Firms receiving multiple bids and acquired	7	12.7
Firms receiving subsequent bids		
<1 year	14	25.5
1–2 years	6	10.9
>2 years	8	14.5
Other firms	20	36.4
Total	55	100.0

Panel B. Comparison of Δholdings in deals receiving subsequent bids by the end of 2001 ($N = 28$) versus holdings in other deals ($N = 20$)

	Min	Q1	Mean	S.D.	Median	Q3	Max
Number of arbitrageurs							
Deals with new bids	0.0	3.0	10.0	12.2	7.0	13.5	61.0
Deals have no new bids	0.0	2.0	7.9	6.2	5.5	12.5	20.0
Difference	0.0	1.0	2.1	5.9	1.5	1.0	41.0
Δholdings in each deal							
Deals with new bids (%)	−0.79	0.19	3.25	4.18	1.79	4.82	12.97
Deals have no new bids (%)	−0.68	0.11	1.31	2.00	0.44	1.53	7.16
Difference (%)	−0.11	0.08	1.94**	2.18	1.35*	3.29	5.82

Panel C. Comparison of Δholdings in deals receiving subsequent bids within 1 year ($N = 14$) versus holdings in other deals ($N = 34$)

	Min	Q1	Mean	S.D.	Median	Q3	Max
Number of arbitrageurs							
Deals with new bids	2.0	5.0	15.1	15.2	13.0	18.0	61.0
Deals have no new bids	0.0	2.0	6.7	5.7	5.0	10.0	20.0
Difference	2.0	3.0	8.4*	9.5	8.0**	8.0	41.0
Δholdings in each deal							
Deals with new bids (%)	−0.79	0.49	4.83	5.18	2.37	9.80	12.97
Deals have no new bids (%)	−0.68	0.13	1.46	1.99	0.70	2.66	7.16
Difference (%)	−0.11	0.36	3.37**	3.18	1.67**	7.15	5.82

***, **, and * indicate significance at the 1%, 5%, and 10% levels, respectively.

Table 8

Logistic regressions of the probability of target firms receiving subsequent bids within 1 year of failed takeovers

This table shows logistic estimations of the probability of target firms receiving subsequent bids within 1 year after the initial deals failed. The dependent variable equals one if the target firm receives a new takeover attempt and zero if the firm does not receive a subsequent bid within a year. Δholdings is the aggregate change of arbitrage holdings in each deal normalized by target firm's shares outstanding. N_{arb} is the number of arbitrageurs in each deal. The procedure of selecting arbitrageurs is described in the text and Table 2. Friendly is a dummy variable with a value of 1 for friendly deals and 0 otherwise based on whether the target firm resisted or received an unsolicited offer as determined by SDC. Collar (Stock) is a dummy variable with a value of 1 for collar (stock) deals. Runup is the cumulative abnormal returns to the target firm's stock for trading days $(-54, -1)$ before the first bid. Markup is calculated as (final offer price $- P_{-1}^T)/P_{-1}^T$, where P_{-1}^T is the target firm's stock price 1 day before the announcement. Premium is target's price runup plus markup. Multiple bidders is a dummy variable with a value of 1 if the original deal was a multiple-bid contest. Heteroskedasticity-consistent covariance is used in the estimation procedure. The p-values are reported in parentheses.

	(I)	(II)	(III)	(IV)	(V)
Constant	−2.886 (0.005)	−1.647 (0.001)	−2.710 (0.013)	−4.243 (0.006)	−4.000 (0.009)
$\log(1 + N_{arb})$	0.961 (0.023)		0.587 (0.205)	0.479 (0.368)	0.502 (0.355)
Δholdings		27.344 (0.002)	21.260 (0.022)	24.826 (0.034)	23.624 (0.044)
Premium				0.344 (0.775)	0.149 (0.906)
Collar				0.314 (0.762)	
Stock					−0.569 (0.535)
Multiple bidders				2.611 (0.006)	2.746 (0.002)
Friendly				1.505 (0.080)	1.778 (0.048)
Log likelihood	−25.94	−24.64	−23.83	−20.59	−20.49
P-value for the model	0.014	0.003	0.006	0.010	0.009
McFadden R^2	0.105	0.150	0.178	0.289	0.293

multiple bidders or if target management was friendly, the target firms are more likely to receive another bid in the future. The results in this section suggest that both the number of arbitrageurs and Δholdings are associated with higher revision returns. After initial acquisitions are terminated, their holdings are positively correlated with the possibility that new bids will eventually emerge in those deals.

5. Additional robustness checks and extensions

We have already reported several robustness checks in the preceding text. These include the use of different econometric specifications (OLS, 2SLS, and 3SLS), and the use of 30-day arbitrage returns, 129-day returns (the median duration), and annualized returns. In this section we report robustness checks with regard to the identification of arbitrageurs, financial firms, momentum traders, and the various types of institutions identified as arbitrageurs.

5.1. Identification of arbitrageurs

The series of tests presented in previous sections are contingent upon the empirical procedure for selecting arbitrageurs. In this section, we perform four sensitivity checks with regard to the identification of arbitrageurs; all four tests produce conclusions similar to our original results.

Recall that to be identified as a merger arbitrageur, an institution needs to have a positive change in holdings in at least six deals and in more than 60% of all deals in which they are involved. Our first robustness check is to verify whether our main results are sensitive to these two cutoff points. To be specific, we modify the first cutoff so as to be a positive change in holdings in 11 deals or 16 deals. The increment of 10 (from our original 6–16) is about one standard deviation of the number of deals involved in our sample. In our second test we alter the criteria for the number of deals in which institutions have a positive change in holdings, increasing it to 70% and 80% of the deals in which they are involved. These first two screening rules produce four new sets of arbitrageurs with more stringent selection criteria. We then reestimate our results. While several coefficients become less significant, the relation among the four endogenous variables of interest (premia, success, Δholdings, and returns) remains significant beyond the 5% level. We conclude that adopting more stringent filter rules does not materially affect our main results.[12]

Third, we reestimate our results using the change in holdings from the top six arbitrageurs and the top 10 arbitrageurs only, rather than all of our identified arbitrageurs. Six is the median number of arbitrageurs in each deal and 10 is the average number. Arguably, these top arbitrageurs are more active and purchase more shares during acquisitions. Thus, this reestimation also serves as a further test of the active arbitrageur hypothesis. The models of Cornelli and Li and Gomes imply that sizable changes in holdings will drive the results. Arbitrageurs accumulating smaller positions after the announcement would not be as influential as those accumulating larger positions. Nevertheless, correlations between our original measure of Δholdings and these two variations all exceed 0.95. Our multivariate results are robust to these alternate definitions.

Fourth, we reestimate our results using only those arbitrageurs from our sample that are found in the TASS Hedge Fund Database. The correlation of Δholdings between this database and our original measure is very high (0.99). Correspondingly, our results are similar.

5.2. Are our results driven by financial firms?

Financial firms account for about 30% of our sample (183 out of 608). Several studies (see, e.g., Officer, 2002) have also documented the popularity of mergers and acquisitions in the

---

[12] Results of any of these tests are available upon request.

financial industry during the 1990s. However, financial mergers exhibit systematically different motivations and characteristics from nonfinancial counterparts. Arbitrageurs may use different decision criteria to determine whether to participate in financial mergers. To investigate if this is the case, we separate the sample into financial and nonfinancial mergers, classifying the deal as a financial merger if either the bidder's or the target's two-digit CRSP SIC code is between 60 and 69.

In general, there seems to be little systematic difference between the two subsamples with regard to our analysis—the interrelations among endogenous variables are quite similar. One exception is the weak relation between Δholdings and takeover premia in the financial sample. Also, several control variables are insignificant as determinants of Δholdings in financial firms. For example, while the method of payment and target management attitude explain holdings in the subsample of nonfinancial firms, they are insignificant for financial companies. This is probably due to the lack of variation in these variables in the subsample of financial mergers. We find that financial mergers tend to use either stock or collars as the method of payment. They also tend to be friendly. In our sample of 183 financial mergers, only 26 deals use cash as the method of payment and only two deals are classified as hostile takeovers.

5.3. Are our results driven by momentum trading?

It is well documented that some institutions, especially mutual funds, are "momentum investors," buying past-winning stocks (see, e.g., Grinblatt et al., 1995; Lakonishok et al., 1992). In contrast, Gompers and Metrick (2001) provide evidence that "large" institutions are not momentum investors. Wermers (1999) and Nofsinger and Sias (1999) show that stock price momentum is positively correlated with institutional herding behavior. Badrinath and Wahal (2002) show that institutions act as momentum investors when they initiate the purchase of stocks but act as contrarian investors when they unload their positions.

Momentum traders purchase shares when the price is increasing regardless of any corporate news about acquisitions. Arbitrageurs, on the other hand, usually do not accumulate the target company's stock before the deal is announced; by this definition, they are not momentum investors. However, due to the fact that the target stock could experience price runups, we may simply be choosing institutions that are also momentum or positive-feedback investors. Although we cannot completely rule out this possibility, it seems unlikely that the institutional investors we identify have acted independent of important news about corporate acquisitions. Further tests confirm this conjecture.

First, we analyze our group of arbitrageurs versus the remainder of the institutions identified in Spectrum. It has been suggested that arbitrageurs in general do not purchase target shares before the deal is formally announced. We find some support for this argument. Fewer than 45% of identified arbitrageurs in our sample report holdings of target shares before announcements. The corresponding percentage for nonarbitrageurs (the remaining institutions) is more than 63%. The difference is significant at the 1% level. Thus, it is consistent with the notion that arbitrageurs usually do not hold target shares beforehand.

Second, we compare the trading activities between arbitrageurs and nonarbitrageurs during the takeover process. In particular, we are interested in the question: How long would arbitrageurs maintain their positions after they purchase target shares? If nonarbitrageurs own target shares after a deal is announced, we expect many of them to reduce their holdings before the deal is resolved. In contrast, we expect arbitrageurs to hold on to their positions for a longer period to realize the return. To test this possibility, we calculate the percentage of arbitrageurs and nonarbitrageurs who have positive holdings in the announcement quarter and who do not sell their shares until the quarter just before the resolution date. The results show that more than 33% of nonarbitrageurs lower their positions, compared to only 6% of our arbitrageurs: once our arbitrageurs decide to take part in mergers, they retain most of their holdings over the whole process.

Finally, even though the above tests do not suggest that our identified arbitrageurs are simply momentum investors, we control for the momentum effect in the regressions presented in Tables 5 and 6 by including two variables, the target price runups and the logarithm of the number of days between the last reporting quarter before the takeovers and the deal announcement date (log(Days)). If the momentum effect exists in our sample, we should observe a positive relation between price runup and holdings as well as log(Days) and holdings. The coefficient of runup is insignificant while the coefficient of log(Days) is negative and significant. Taken together, the evidence suggests that the institutions we select do exhibit the merger-arbitrage behavior we desire and that they are distinct from other regular institutions.

5.4. Do the results vary across different types of institutions?

Our results suggest that independent investment advisors are the dominant category of arbitrageurs. Two other facts support this finding. If hedge fund companies file their holdings, they mostly fall into this category. Also, merger arbitrage accounts for a large portion of the business these firms conduct. Thus, independent investment advisors tend to be more active in accumulating target shares, thereby pushing deals to completion, and they have a greater incentive to function as active blockholders.

On the other hand, other types of institutions might be more passive with regard to active participation in acquisitions, functioning, in effect, as free riders. There are several reasons to suspect this. One possibility is that the capital they invest is not as large as that of other institutions and thus their potential influence on deals is not strong enough for them to actively participate. It is also possible that some institutions are constrained by prudent-man laws and regulations. Various types of institutions have different levels of exposure to fiduciary liability. As a result, some institutions might try to avoid a huge loss on one deal by trading less. They could also tend to act passively to avoid adverse publicity. Del Guercio (1996) asserts that bank managers are the most likely to be constrained by prudent-man laws while mutual fund managers are the least likely to be constrained. Using data derived from the CDA Spectrum database, she focuses her analysis on three types of institutions: banks, mutual funds, and pension funds.

From a regulatory point of view, we might expect individual investment advisers (type 4) to be the least constrained by regulatory burdens followed by mutual fund companies and their managers (type 3) (although they are not allowed to short-sell securities). These two types of institutions are only regulated by the SEC. Banks (type 1) and pension funds (in type 5) are explicitly governed by the prudent-man laws. Pension funds, in particular, are regulated by the Employees Retirement Income Security Act (ERISA). Similarly, insurance companies have a maximum equity limitation of 15% in their portfolios. Given different levels of regulatory constraints across institutional investors, we examine whether different types of institutions behave differently during the takeover process.

When we reestimate our results for each of the five different types of institutions identified in Table 1, we find that independent investment advisors (type 4) are the active players in mergers and acquisitions. Their holdings of target stocks are positively associated with deal success rates and bid premia. Banks and others (mostly pension funds) are the next-most active. Although our main results hold in these two subsamples, the relation between Δholdings and premia is not significant in either subsample. The subsamples of insurance and investment companies (type 2 and 3) have the weakest relations among five endogenous variables, perhaps because of their differential exposure to legal liability.

6. Conclusions

Despite the increased prominence of merger-arbitrage activity since the 1980s, much remains unknown about the process and impact of an arbitrageurs' decision to participate in the takeover market. The empirical literature documents positive abnormal returns in takeover portfolios. This study provides the first test of the active theory of arbitrage activity and updates earlier research relating to the passive theory of arbitrage returns. The purely passive argument asserts that arbitrageurs act as naïve investors with no ability to predict deal outcomes; arbitrageurs do not influence deal attributes or outcomes. Under this argument, the change in arbitrage holdings will be significantly related to ex ante measures of deal success observable in the market (such as target management attitude), but insignificantly related to a perfect foresight model of success (actual deal outcome) and arbitrage returns. On the other hand, Larcker and Lys (1987) suggest another passive arbitrage explanation: Arbitrageurs have superior ability to predict takeover outcomes. Here, the change in holdings is indicative of superior skill in predicting offer outcomes. Implications of this superior skill include a significant relation among arbitrage holdings, returns, and the probability of deal success while controlling for the contemporaneously measured spread.

More recently, Cornelli and Li (2002) and Gomes (2001) develop active arbitrageur models, suggesting that the involvement of arbitrageurs effectively influences bid premia, arbitrage returns, and the probability of bid success. The results of our research provide support for both the passive and active arbitrage hypotheses. Our evidence is consistent with arbitrageurs possessing superior ability to predict offer success; moreover, the presence of arbitrageurs is strongly associated with different terms and outcomes of the offer. To the best of our knowledge, this is the first evidence testing the active influence of arbitrageurs and contrasting the passive versus active arbitrage models.

We control for the endogeneity of arbitrage holdings by explicitly accounting for the joint impact of four key acquisition variables (offer premium, probability of success, arbitrage returns, and the change in arbitrage holdings) as well as other control variables recognized in the literature. Using a sample of 608 offers over the 1992–1999 period, we find that in addition to the ability to anticipate deal success rates, the probability of deal success and takeover premia are also positively related to the increase in arbitrage holdings. In addition, the change in arbitrage holdings is also shown to be an important determinant of deal success, bid premia, and arbitrage returns. These results are consistent with both passive and active arbitrage theories.

We also investigate the factors driving arbitrageurs to get involved in acquisitions. Arbitrageurs purchase more target shares in collar offers than in cash or stock offers. In our multivariate analysis, the change in holdings is lower in larger deals. Interestingly, the decision of arbitrageurs to participate in acquisitions does not appear to be affected by target management hostility or the existence of multiple bidders.

Finally, we find that the changes in holdings during the announcement quarters are positively associated with revision returns. In cases in which the initial acquisitions fail, changes in arbitrage holdings are also positively correlated with target firms receiving subsequent bids within the next year. These last two findings are consistent with an active role of arbitrageurs in the takeover process.

Appendix A: Estimation of arbitrage returns

In a cash deal i, an arbitrageur simply purchases the target stock and holds the position until deal consummation. The first source of arbitrage profit is the difference between the price at which the target company trades after the deal announcement and the cash price finally offered by an acquirer or the stock price prevailing in the market immediately after failed offers. The second source of profit comes from any dividend received on the target stock before the deal was completed. Besides these two sources of profit, the transaction also requires arbitrageurs to pay a financing cost known as the broker call rate. We assume that arbitrageurs borrow at the risk-free rate. Therefore, the return for a cash deal i on day t has the form:

$$r_{it} = \frac{P_{it}^{T} + D_{it}^{T}}{P_{it-1}^{T}} - 1 - r_{ft}, \qquad (A.1)$$

where P_t^{T} and D_t^{T} are the target firm's price and dividend payment at time t, respectively, and r_{ft} is the risk-free rate at time t.

For a stock-swap or a collar transaction, arbitrageurs typically take a long position in the target stock and hedge their position by shorting δ shares of the acquirer's stock, where δ is the exchange rate of the offer. Thus, in comparison to the cash offer above, a stock/collar offer return also includes the proceeds from a short position in the acquirer's stock. We also assume arbitrageurs earn the risk-free rate from the proceeds of their short position. The associated costs are the borrowing cost (the risk-free rate by assumption) and the return and payment of the dividend from the short position. Therefore, the return for a stock/collar deal i on day t has the form:

$$r_{it} = \frac{P_{it}^{T} + D_{it}^{T}}{P_{it-1}^{T}} - 1 - r_{ft} - \left(\frac{P_{it}^{A} + D_{it}^{A}}{P_{it-1}^{A}} - 1 - r_{ft} \right) \delta \frac{P_{it-1}^{A}}{P_{it-1}^{T}}, \qquad (A.2)$$

where P_t^{A} and D_t^{A} are the acquiring firm's price and dividend payment at time t, respectively. (In the case of unsuccessful offers, P_t^{A} is the price prevailing in the market immediately after its termination.) For a FX stock/collar deal, arbitrageurs' short positions are determined immediately after the takeover announcement. For a FV stock/collar deal, the exchange rate δ varies across time until the end of the valuation period. Ideally, an arbitrageur's short position also varies with δ such that a perfectly hedged net position is reached. In reality, it is generally not possible to reach this goal due to transaction costs. Thus, it is assumed that the arbitrageur determines the exchange ratio by the formula: δ = (acquirer's offer price)/(acquirer's stock price 1 day after announcement), and that their position is held until deal resolution (defined below). If the deal is revised, we assume arbitrageurs rebalance their positions, and the new exchange ratio is applied in the return formula.

Daily returns are calculated from the day after the announcement to the resolution day. The return is not calculated on any shares arbitrageurs accumulate prior to the deal announcement. This assumption is not unreasonable. Larcker and Lys (1987) report in their sample that in only three cases did arbitrageurs take positions prior to the takeover announcement. In fact, arbitrageurs usually start to assemble as much information as possible about the deal after a transaction is announced. They do not try to predict the occurrence of the events before the announcement (Moore, 1999). For successful deals, the resolution day is the day on which the target company's stock is delisted from CRSP. For unsuccessful deals, the resolution day is the day after deal failure is publicly announced. To be conservative, we use the return on the day after the deal cancellation is publicly announced as the last date to calculate holding-period returns. Thus, we assume that arbitrageurs clear their positions 1 day after the deal is cancelled.

Arbitrage returns are calculated as follows. First, daily returns are compounded from the day after announcement to the resolution day. The computed deal return serves as a proxy for arbitrageurs' buy-and-hold return in that deal. One potential problem in buy-and-hold returns is that offers have different periods of time. Thirty-day returns are calculated from the day after the announcement until 30 business days later. To calculate annualized returns, we multiply the buy-and-hold returns by 365/(offer duration).

Appendix B: Endogeneity tests

Table 9 shows the results from the exogeneity tests regarding toeholds, bid premia, the change in arbitrage holdings, and arbitrage returns. An exogeneity test checks whether a regressor assumed to be exogenous in the system is in fact endogenous. Greene (1997, p. 763) and Spencer and Berk (1981) provide detailed descriptions of the procedure. As one example, we are interested in whether arbitrage return is exogenous in the equation in which the premium is the dependent variable. This corresponds to the second equation in our system. The null hypothesis is that the arbitrage return (the regressor in this equation) is exogenous. The F-statistic (60.317) in Table 9 indicates the rejection of the null hypothesis at the 1% level. Therefore, arbitrage return is more likely to be endogenous in the equation for the premium.

Overall, the tests in the top section of Table 9 indicate that toehold is more likely to be an exogenous variable. The other three variables, on the other hand, appear to be endogenous. Several coefficients indicate the rejection of the null hypothesis that those three variables are exogenous at the 1% level. For example, when we estimate the takeover premia and the returns, the endogeneity issue arises. When we estimate Δholdings, both the premium and the return are very likely to be endogenous as well. Since these variables are continuous, simultaneous-equations models provide a convenient and effective approach to control for the endogeneity bias.

In Table 9, we add another important variable, probability of deal success, into the system and repeat the exogeneity test. In this table, we only report the F-statistic and its p-value related to the probability of success. The top panel shows that the probability of success is more likely to be determined endogenously with three other variables of interest.

Table 9

Endogeneity tests of bidder's toehold, takeover premium, arbitrage holdings, and returns

Panel A reports the F-statistic from the exogeneity tests of three endogenous variables in the system of simultaneous equations. Panel B reports the F-statistic from the exogeneity tests of four endogenous variables. Under the null hypothesis, each variable is exogenously determined. The systems in Tables 4 and 5 are estimated using two-stage least squares and three-stage least squares (not reported). Δholdings is the aggregate change of holdings in each deal normalized by target firm's shares outstanding. N_{arb} is the number of arbitrageurs in each deal. Return is annualized buy-and-hold returns, calculated as (unannualized returns) $\times$ 365/(deal duration). Toehold is the percentage of target shares held by the bidder prior to the announcement. Premium is target's price runup plus markup. Runup is the cumulative abnormal return to the target firm's stock for trading days $(-54, -1)$ before the first bid. Markup is calculated as (final offer price $- P_{-1}^{T})/P_{-1}^{T}$, where P_{-1}^{T} is the target firm's stock price 1 day before the announcement. Success is dummy variable with a value of 1 for successful deals. The p-values are reported in parentheses.

Panel A. F-statistic (p-value) from the exogeneity test of four regressors

	Dependent variables in simultaneous equations (in Table 4)		
Endogenous variables as regressors	Premium	Δholdings	Return
Toehold	2.396 (0.122)	0.925 (0.337)	1.228 (0.268)
Premium		9.633 (0.002)	4.170 (0.041)
Δholdings	6.420 (0.013)		7.761 (0.005)
Return	60.317 (0.000)	6.990 (0.008)	

Panel B. F-statistic (p-value) from the exogeneity test of five regressors

	Dependent variables in simultaneous equations (in Table 5)			
Endogenous variables as regressors	Premium	Success	Δholdings	Return
Toehold		5.362 (0.021)		
Premium				
Success			9.508 (0.002)	0.134 (0.714)
Δholdings		4.733 (0.030)		
Return				

References

Andrade, G., M. Mitchell and E. Stafford, 2001, "New Evidence and Perspectives on Mergers," *Journal of Economic Perspectives*, 103–120.

Badrinath, S. and S. Wahal, 2002, "Momentum Trading by Institutions," *Journal of Finance*, 57, 2449–2478.

Baker, M. and S. Savasoglu, 2002, "Limited Arbitrage in Mergers and Acquisitions," *Journal of Financial Economics*, 64, 91–116.

Betton, S. and B. Eckbo, 2000, "Toeholds, Bid-Jumps and Expected Payoffs in Takeovers," *Review of Financial Studies*, 13, 841–882.

Bulow, J., M. Huang and P. Klemperer, 1999, "Toeholds and Takeovers," *Journal of Political Economy*, 107, 427–454.

Coles, J., M. Lemmon and J. Meschke, 2003, "Structural Models and Endogeneity in Corporate Finance: The Link Between Managerial Ownership and Corporate Performance," Unpublished Working Paper, Arizona State University and University of Utah.

Cornelli, F. and D. Li, 2002, "Risk Arbitrage in Takeovers," *Review of Financial Studies*, 15, 837–868.

Del Guercio, D., 1996, "The Distorting Effect of the Prudent-Man Laws on Institutional Equity Investments," *Journal of Financial Economics*, 40, 31–62.

Dukes, W., C. Frohlich and C. Ma, 1992, "Risk Arbitrage in Tender Offers," *Journal of Portfolio Management*, 18, 47–55.

Fuller, K., 2003, "Why Some Firms Use Collar Offers in Mergers," *The Financial Review*, 38, 127–150.

Gomes, A., 2001, "Takeovers, Freezeouts, and Risk Arbitrage," Unpublished Working Paper, University of Pennsylvania.

Gompers, P. and A. Metrick, 2001, "Institutional Investors and Equity Prices," *The Quarterly Journal of Economics*, 116, 229–259.

Greene, W., 1997, *Econometric Analysis*, third ed, Prentice-Hall, Englewood Cliffs, NJ.

Grinblatt, M., S. Titman and R. Wermers, 1995, "Momentum Investment Strategies, Portfolio Performance, And Herding: A Study of Mutual Fund Behavior," *American Economic Review*, 85, 1088–1105.

Grossman, S. and O. Hart, 1980, "Takeover Bids, the Free Rider Problem and the Theory of the Corporation," *Bell Journal of Economics*, 11, 42–64.

Hirshleifer, D. and S. Titman, 1990, "Share Tendering Strategies and the Success of Hostile Takeover Bids," *Journal of Political Economy*, 98, 295–324.

Huang, Y. and R. Walkling, 1987, "Target Abnormal Returns Associated with Acquisition Announcements: Payment, Acquisition Form, and Managerial Resistance," *Journal of Financial Economics*, 19, 329–349.

Jindra, J. and R. Walkling, 2004, "Speculation Spreads and the Market Pricing of Proposed Acquisitions," *Journal of Corporate Finance*, 10, 495–526.

Karolyi, G. and J. Shannon, 1999, "Where's the Risk in Risk Arbitrage?" *Canadian Investment Review*.

Kyle, A. and J. Vila, 1991, "Noise Trading and Takeovers," *RAND Journal of Economics*, 22, 54–71.

Lakonishok, J., A. Shleifer and R. Vishny, 1992, "The Impact of Institutional Trading on Stock Prices," *Journal of Financial Economics*, 32, 23–43.

Larcker, D. and T. Lys, 1987, "An Empirical Analysis of the Incentives to Engage in Costly Information Acquisition," *Journal of Financial Economics*, 18, 111–126.

Maddala, G., 1983, *Limited Dependent and Qualitative Variables in Econometrics*, Cambridge University Press, New York.

Mitchell, M. and T. Pulvino, 2001, "Characteristics of Risk in Risk Arbitrage," *Journal of Finance*, 56, 2135–2175.

Moore, K., 1999, *Risk Arbitrage*, Wiley, New York.

Nofsinger, J. and R. Sias, 1999, "Herding and Feedback Trading by Institutional and Individual Investors," *Journal of Finance*, 54, 2263–2295.

Officer, M., 2002, "Collar Bids in Mergers and Acquisitions," Unpublished Working Paper, University of Southern California.

Schwert, G., 1996, "Markup Pricing in Mergers and Acquisitions," *Journal of Financial Economics*, 41, 153–192.

Schwert, G., 2000, "Hostility in Takeovers: In the Eyes of the Beholder?" *Journal of Finance*, 55, 2599–2640.

Shleifer, A. and R. Vishny, 1997, "The Limits of Arbitrage," *Journal of Finance*, 52, 35–55.

Spencer, D. and K. Berk, 1981, "A Limited Information Specification Test," *Econometrica*, 49, 1079–1085.

Travlos, N., 1987, "Corporate Takeover Bids, Methods of Payment, and Bidding Firms' Stock Returns," *Journal of Finance*, 42, 943–963.

Walkling, R., 1985, "Predicting Tender Offer Success: A Logistic Analysis," *Journal of Financial and Quantitative Analysis*, 20, 461–478.

Wermers, R., 1999, "Mutual Fund Herding and the Impact on Stock Prices," *Journal of Finance*, 54, 581–622.

Chapter 27

LIMITED ARBITRAGE IN MERGERS AND ACQUISITIONS*

MALCOLM BAKER

Graduate School of Business Administration, Harvard University, Boston, Massachusetts, USA

SERKAN SAVAŞOGLU

Morgan Stanley, New York, USA

Contents

* The authors would like to thank Paul Gompers, Scott Mayfield, Andrew Metrick, Mark Mitchell, Todd Pulvino, Rick Ruback, Jeremy Stein, Jeff Wurgler, an anonymous referee, seminar participants at Charles River Associates, Harvard University, Harvard Business School, Koc University, and the European Financial Management Association 2000 Conference, and especially André Perold and Andrei Shleifer for helpful comments. This study has been supported by the Division of Research of the Harvard Graduate School of Business Administration.

This article originally appeared in the *Journal of Financial Economics*, Vol. 64, pp. 91–115 (2002).
Corporate Takeovers, Volume 2
Edited by B. Espen Eckbo
DOI: 10.1016/B978-0-12-381982-6.00028-8

Abstract

A diversified portfolio of risk arbitrage positions produces an abnormal return of 0.6–0.9% per month over the period from 1981 to 1996. We trace these profits to practical limits on risk arbitrage. In our model of risk arbitrage, arbitrageurs' risk-bearing capacity is constrained by deal completion risk and the size of the position they hold. Consistent with this model, we document that the returns to risk arbitrage increase in an ex ante measure of completion risk and target size. We also examine the influence of the general supply of arbitrage capital, measured by the total equity holdings of arbitrageurs, on arbitrage profits.

Keywords

arbitrage, mergers and acquisitions, market efficiency

JEL classification: G14, G23, G34

1. Introduction

This paper examines the market pricing of merger and acquisition offers. Professional risk arbitrageurs claim to profit by providing insurance to selling shareholders in the following way.[1] After a merger or acquisition is announced, investors in the target firm face completion risk. Some shareholders may wish to insure this risk by selling their shares. In an efficient capital market, the price of the target and acquirer will fully and immediately reflect the terms of the merger. In reality, shareholders sell to a limited number of capital-constrained investors and financial institutions specializing in risk arbitrage. As a result of this selling pressure, the price of the target firm can fall below its efficient market price. This market inefficiency—what Shleifer and Vishny (1997) call the limits of arbitrage—leaves abnormal profits.

We construct risk arbitrage positions for 1901 cash and stock merger and acquisition offers over the period from 1981 to 1996. Each is designed to provide a fixed payoff if the deal is successfully completed according to its original terms. We develop a simple model of limited arbitrage where selling pressure, imperfect substitutes, and a small number of arbitrageurs combine to create an abnormal return to risk arbitrage positions. The model predicts that the expected return is increasing in completion risk and selling pressure and decreasing in risk arbitrage capital.

Our analysis of the cross section of returns points to limited arbitrage. First, excess returns are increasing in completion risk, which rises when the probability of success moves toward 0.5 and when the difference in payoffs between success and failure increases. To estimate the probability of success, we use predictions from a regression of merger outcome on acquirer attitude. As in Walkling (1985) and Schwert (2000), for example, we find that acquirer attitude is the best single predictor of merger success. As a proxy for the difference in payoffs, we use the takeover premium scaled by the value of the target firm after announcement. Second, excess returns are increasing in target size following the merger announcement, which can proxy for the dollar value of selling pressure by target shareholders.

Third, we examine the influence of the general supply of arbitrage capital, measured by the total equity holdings of arbitrageurs, on arbitrage profits. We identify risk arbitrageurs with data on institutional holdings. Risk arbitrage involves taking a long position in a target following a merger announcement. By our classification, arbitrageurs are institutions that frequently move from zero to positive holdings in the target firms. We define risk arbitrage capital as the aggregate quarterly equity holdings of

---

[1] For example, Boesky (1985) claims that the arbitrageur "provides liquidity to the marketplace. He is typically buying from those who do not want to bear the risk of waiting to see if the deal will go through." In addition to providing insurance, arbitrageurs play an active role in the takeover process as large shareholders (Gomes, 2000; Cornelli and Li, 2002; Singh, 1998) and play an information gathering role (Larcker and Lys, 1987). Our focus is on the returns available for a marginal arbitrageur, not an active or privately informed investor. Howard and Perold (1998) and Perold (1999) provide case studies and additional detail on risk arbitrage.

these arbitrageurs. Consistent with limited arbitrage, when this measure of capital falls, subsequent returns rise. However, this third cross-sectional result is not as strong statistically as the first two.

Before undertaking the cross-section analysis, we analyze the returns to risk arbitrage. The existing literature suggests that target firm shares earn very high returns. Lakonishok and Vermaelen (1990) evaluate repurchase offers, and Larcker and Lys (1987), Dukes et al. (1992), and Karolyi and Shannon (1999) analyze cash tender offers. All find abnormal profits. We corroborate these past studies with the new approach of measuring the abnormal return to a risk arbitrage portfolio. This helps us evaluate the systematic risk and the economic and statistical significance of the returns in a way that previous research has not.[2] A merger or acquisition is included in the portfolio beginning 2 days after announcement and ending with the withdrawal or successful completion of the deal. While we use a different approach and a much larger sample of cash and stock offers, our results are broadly consistent with the existing literature. Risk arbitrage beats its capital asset pricing model and Fama-French three-factor benchmarks. However, the economic significance of the abnormal returns, while high at 0.6–0.9% per month, are not as dramatic as those reported in earlier studies of event returns. In one specification, the intercept is not statistically significant at the 10% level.

The rest of the paper is organized as follows. Section 2 reviews the theory of limited arbitrage and develops a price pressure model in the context of mergers and acquisitions. Section 3 describes the data from Securities Data Company (SDC). Section 4 shows that a risk arbitrage portfolio earns abnormal profits. Section 5 evaluates the cross-section implications of limited arbitrage. Section 6 concludes.

2. Limited arbitrage in the context of mergers and acquisitions

A textbook arbitrage opportunity arises when two identical assets sell for different prices. By selling the expensive asset and buying the cheap asset, an arbitrageur earns positive profits with no capital and no risk. Real-world risk arbitrage differs in two respects. First, instead of identical assets, a merger offer creates two similar assets. For example, after a stock merger offer, there are two ways to buy the acquiring firm's shares: with a direct purchase and with an indirect purchase. The indirect purchase involves buying the target firm's shares and waiting for the deal to go through, at which

---

[2] Mitchell and Pulvino (2001), in a contemporaneous and independently written paper, use the same portfolio approach in measuring the abnormal returns to risk arbitrage. Their data produce a slightly higher gross return of about 1% per month over the period from 1963 to 1999. Mitchell and Pulvino also evaluate a practical risk arbitrage portfolio, which limits the dollar level and percentage investment in any single deal and, as a result, contains a substantial amount of cash. This cash reduces the magnitude of the abnormal return by about two-thirds without materially changing its statistical significance. We consider risk aversion implicitly in our cross-sectional analysis, rather than explicitly reducing the exposure of the portfolio to idiosyncratic risks.

point the target shares are exchanged for acquirer shares. These two approaches have identical payoffs if the merger offer is completed according to its original terms. A risk arbitrageur faces fundamental risk because the deal can fail or be revised. Second, real-world risk arbitrage requires capital. The proceeds of selling the expensive asset cannot be used to buy the cheap asset. The lender typically requires 102% of the short position as collateral (e.g., see Perold and Singh, 1995).

Textbook arbitrage prevents identical assets from selling at different prices. Real-world risk arbitrage will also eliminate the possibility that two similar assets can have systematically and dramatically different average returns under two scenarios. First, in the classic analysis of Friedman (1953) and Fama (1965), a very large number of small arbitrageurs are effectively risk neutral when they take only a small position in an idiosyncratic gamble. In the mergers and acquisitions context, however, this sort of arbitrage is not likely to be feasible. The idea of an individual investing a very small part of her wealth—without financial intermediation—into a diversified portfolio of target firms seems implausible. Even small fixed transaction costs related to implementing a dynamic risk arbitrage strategy convert to large percentage costs when divided by a marginal component of an individual investor's wealth.

Second, when the mispriced security has a perfect and correctly priced substitute, even a small number of arbitrageurs will force price to fundamental value.[3] Only stocks with perfect substitutes, because they can be arbitraged without risk, are not affected by selling pressure. A stock without perfect substitutes can have a downward sloping demand curve (Scholes, 1972; Shleifer, 1986). Wurgler and Zhuravskaya (2002) show that the impact of demand by index funds on a stock included in the S&P 500 depends on its substitutes. In mergers and acquisitions, the idiosyncratic risk of deal completion cannot typically be hedged. This gives the first empirical prediction:

Prediction 1. The returns to risk arbitrage depend on selling pressure and completion risk.

The second empirical prediction relates to financial intermediation, which can improve the effectiveness of arbitrage. If a relatively small number of hedge funds and proprietary trading groups could raise capital from a large number of small investors, we are back to the convincing arguments of Friedman and Fama. However,

---

[3] Even when there are perfect substitutes, arbitrage may fail if arbitrageurs have short horizons or if transaction costs and institutional constraints limit short selling. In De Long et al. (1990), noise trader risk can lead price to diverge from fundamental value within the arbitrageur's horizon. For example, the shares of Royal Dutch and Shell, although perfect substitutes, often diverge significantly in part because there is no identifiable date at which the two prices will converge (Froot and Dabora, 1999). In mergers and acquisitions, the horizon is comparatively short. Nonetheless, the effect of pure noise trader risk may play some role. For example, in stock deals, a short position in the acquirer could be liquidated beyond the arbitrageur's control at a time when prices diverge from fundamental value. In addition, Lamont and Thaler (2001) document that costly short selling causes persistent violations of the law of one price in tech stock carve-outs. D'Avolio (2001) and Geczy et al. (2002) examine short selling costs in larger samples.

Shleifer and Vishny (1997) and Shleifer (2000) argue that agency and information costs limit the amount of capital that arbitrageurs can raise. Furthermore, Merton and Perold (1993) and Froot and Stein (1998) show that capital-constrained financial institutions can have a limited appetite for taking idiosyncratic and unhedgeable risks.[4] As Stein (1999) argues, capital constraints depend on two conditions. The first is that there are "flow" costs to adding new capital, which can arise from adverse selection. The second is that there are "stock" costs to holding excess cash balances, which can arise from taxes and agency problems. Flow and stock costs are particularly problematic in risk arbitrage, because the volume of mergers and acquisitions varies dramatically across time. The end result is that a finite number of arbitrageurs with limited capital are prepared to provide liquidity to selling shareholders. This gives the second empirical prediction:

Prediction 2. The returns to risk arbitrage depend on arbitrageurs' capital.

Some risk arbitrageurs are also active investors, directly influencing the takeover process and outcome. First, some purchase shares prior to announcement, speculating on the possibility of a merger offer. Singh (1998) examines toeholds in takeover bidding, but the focus is on bidders rather than arbitrageurs. Bidders with a toehold bid more aggressively than those without. Gomes (2000) examines freezeouts, where the bidder can by force acquire residual shares not tendered. In this case, by accumulating shares prior to announcement, arbitrageurs can force the bidder into paying a high takeover premium. In contrast to these papers, we examine arbitrage profits after the announcement of the merger. Second, the existence of arbitrageurs can help with the Grossman and Hart (1980) free-rider problem. In Cornelli and Li (2002), risk arbitrageurs make abnormal profits because they have an informational advantage: They know the size of their own position. The size of their position affects the probability that the merger will go through. This theoretical work does not predict abnormal profits on the average deal or systematic relations between deal characteristics and subsequent returns. By contrast, the focus of this paper is on the returns of a marginal arbitrageur. The model and the empirical analysis below are not an attempt to shed light on the active role that arbitrageurs play in the takeover process as large shareholders in the target firm.

2.1. A model of limited arbitrage in mergers and acquisitions

In reality, the possibility of revisions and competing bidders means that a merger offer has an infinite number of outcomes. However, in our stylized model, there are only two outcomes. A merger offer succeeds with probability π, and the target shareholders receive $1 + p$. The offer fails with probability $(1 - \pi)$, and the target is worth 1.

---

[4] In a particularly clean test of the hypothesis that idiosyncratic risk can command a risk premium, Green and Rydqvist (1997) show that Swedish lottery bonds command a higher return.

We calculate the price of the target shares in three scenarios. In each case, we assume that a set of target shareholders does not want to bear completion risk and instead sells a total of X shares, where X is exogenous.[5]

In the first case, there are a large number of small investors with no transaction costs who are willing to absorb these shares. Because they each must take only a small position in the idiosyncratic gamble, they require no compensation for risk, and the price following a takeover offer is equal to the expected payoff of a target share:

$$P_T = 1 + \pi p. \tag{1}$$

In the second case, these investors face transaction costs. These costs include fixed and proportional costs of implementing a risk arbitrage strategy. Fixed costs cannot be divided across a large number of small investors, but must be separately incurred by each trader. For this reason, the total transaction cost c can be large relative to the small investor's position:

$$P_T = 1 + \pi p - c. \tag{2}$$

In the third and final case that we evaluate, a limited number A of arbitrageurs with no transaction costs compete with small investors to provide insurance. We assume that the arbitrageurs are mean-variance utility maximizers with a coefficient of absolute risk aversion γ. Because there are only a small number of arbitrageurs, they must bear completion risk. To sell X shares of the target, the selling shareholders must offer the arbitrageurs a risk premium, even for idiosyncratic risk:

$$P_T = 1 + \pi p - \frac{X}{A} \gamma \pi (1 - \pi) p^2. \tag{3}$$

The second term represents the reduction in price required to compensate the limited number of arbitrageurs A for the idiosyncratic risk that they bear. The expected excess return is r/P_T where $r \equiv (X/A) \gamma \pi (1 - \pi) p^2$. If r is smaller than the individual investor's transaction costs c, price will be determined by Equation (3). If not, the nonarbitrageur is the marginal investor, and price will be determined by transaction costs alone as in Equation (2). Whether Equation (2) or Equation (3) holds is an empirical question. If Equation (2) holds, variation in transaction costs can explain the cross section of returns. If Equation (3) holds, risk arbitrage returns are increasing in selling pressure X, the takeover premium p, and the arbitrageurs' risk aversion γ. Returns are decreasing in the number of arbitrageurs A, and related to the ex ante probability of successful completion π in a nonlinear way. In sum, Equation (3) provides a somewhat more formal motivation for Predictions 1 and 2 and a precise notion of completion risk based on the takeover premium and the probability of success.

---

[5] A model that endogenizes the amount sold X is available from the authors upon request. For a more general model of the effects of arbitrageurs' wealth, see Kyle and Xiong (2000).

Unlike Jindra and Walkling (2001), we focus on explaining the cross section of returns, rather than the cross section of initial spreads—the difference between the offer price and the postannouncement trading price. This allows us to separate out the impact of the probability of success and the takeover premium that arises because of limited arbitrage in Equation (3) from the direct impact in Equation (1).

Our model leaves out many risks faced by real-world arbitrageurs. These include the possibility that the original deal terms will be revised, that a new offer will emerge, that the deal will take longer to complete than anticipated, and, in the case of stock deals, the costs of short selling. First, in the empirical analysis, we measure the frequency of revisions and try to gauge their economic importance. Second, competing offers lower risk for the arbitrageur. If one deal fails, the other might succeed. To examine this possibility, we consider a portfolio of only initial offers and a portfolio that contains all offers. Third, we capture holding costs by deducting the risk-free rate from the arbitrage portfolio in the time series and deducting the risk-free rate and a measure of systematic risk from the dependent variable in the cross section. The possibilities of delayed completion and a short position that is involuntarily liquidated are largely idiosyncratic risks that, like completion risk, would be priced in a more general version of Equation (3), but not in Equation (2). Without a good empirical proxy for the ex ante probability of delay, we are forced to omit this risk from the empirical model.

3. Data

We start with all merger and acquisition offers recorded by SDC between 1981 and 1996. 1978 is the first year in the SDC mergers database. But, prior to 1981, SDC does not provide full coverage of mergers and acquisitions. From this large sample, we restrict our attention to the 4135 announced merger and tender offers where both the target firm and the acquirer firm are public companies and the target firm is listed by the Center for Research on Security Prices (CRSP).[6] Figure 1 and the first column of Table 1 show the number of mergers in each year between 1981 and 1996.

[6] The sample excludes deals in the SDC mergers database classified as leveraged buyouts, spin-offs, recapitalizations, self-tenders, exchange offers, repurchases, minority stake purchases, acquisitions of remaining interests, and privatizations. It also excludes rumors and acquirers seeking an unspecified target or targets seeking an unspecified buyer. Despite these exclusions, the sample includes a small number of offers for less than 100% of the shares outstanding. For successful deals, SDC records the percentage of the shares outstanding acquired in the transaction. For unsuccessful deals, SDC often reports the percentage sought. In the final sample, we have data on the percentage acquired or sought for 1552 firms. Where we have data, the average percent acquired (we use percentage sought when the percentage acquired is missing) is 94%. For 89% of the deals, the percentage acquired or sought was for 90% or more of the shares outstanding.

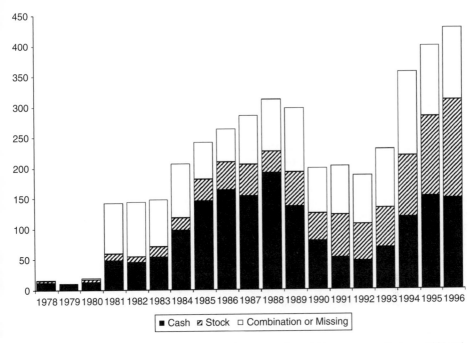

Fig. 1. Mergers and acquisitions, 1981–1996. Annual mergers and acquisitions announced between 1981 and 1996 and recorded by *Securities Data Company* (SDC). The sample contains only deals where the target firm was listed by the *Center for Research on Security Prices* (CRSP) and the acquirer firm was a public company. We use the SDC description of the consideration to identify deals that are pure cash offers or pure stock offers.

3.1. Coding the data

For each deal, SDC provides us with a brief summary of the offer, the announcement date, and the effective or withdrawal date. We classify these offers as pure cash deals, pure stock deals, or as a mixture of cash and stock. In a pure cash deal, the consideration does not depend on the level of the acquirer's share price. For example, Union Pacific's bid of $25 for each share of Southern Pacific Rail on August 2, 1995, is a cash deal. A cash deal, by our classification, need not be paid for in cash. For example, Johnson & Johnson's bid of $109 in common stock for each share of Cordis on October 19, 1995, is also a cash deal. In a pure stock deal, the consideration varies one for one with the level of the acquirer's share price. For example, Frontier offered to buy each share of ALC Communications for two of its own shares on April 10, 1995. We exclude deals where the consideration is part cash and part stock or has option-like features. Many recent deals include "collars" where the offer is fixed in terms of the acquiring firms' shares over some prespecified range. The collar ensures that the takeover price is above some minimum level but does not exceed some maximum level in dollar terms. In the initial sample, SDC reports that 167 offers, or 4% of the sample, included a collar. These deals are excluded from our final sample.

Table 1

Mergers and acquisitions, 1981–1996

Provided here is a comparison of the number of mergers and acquisitions in the SDC database and in the final sample. The first three columns show annual mergers and acquisitions announced between 1981 and 1996 and recorded by SDC. The sample contains only deals where the target firm was listed in the CRSP database and the acquirer firm was a public company. We use the SDC description of the consideration to identify deals that are pure cash offers or pure stock offers. Of the total sample of 4135 mergers and acquisitions, 1485 deals combined stock and cash or had insufficient information. The second three columns show the subset of pure stock offers and pure cash offers used in the analysis. The remaining sample is reduced from 2650 to 1901 for several reasons. In 681 cases, there was insufficient CRSP data. In some of these cases, the target firm was delisted prior to the announcement date, typically because of bankruptcy. Frequently, there was insufficient data on the acquiring firm in a stock deal. And, in some cases, the SDC target name or acquirer name in the case of stock deals did not match the CRSP company name. In 36 cases, we performed additional research using Lexis-Nexis that lead to the exclusion of the deal, because the announcement was not a merger or acquisition offer. Finally, in 32 cases, the SDC consideration was more than double the postannouncement value of the target.

	Complete SDC data			Sample		
Announcement year	All	Pure cash	Pure stock	All	Pure cash	Pure stock
1981	134	50	12	36	29	7
1982	141	44	10	34	30	4
1983	145	53	16	52	39	13
1984	208	96	22	88	75	13
1985	245	145	37	128	108	20
1986	267	162	45	152	128	24
1987	287	153	51	159	125	34
1988	327	198	38	187	162	25
1989	303	136	57	147	111	36
1990	207	78	45	85	58	27
1991	209	52	70	76	37	39
1992	194	48	60	71	37	34
1993	240	69	67	88	50	38
1994	375	122	105	163	101	62
1995	410	156	134	207	123	84
1996	443	155	164	228	122	106
Total	4135	1717	933	1901	1335	566

In many cases, we make additional assumptions to calculate risk arbitrage returns. First, in the early 1980s, SDC describes the type of deal, cash, or stock, but not the amount. For these deals, we use the SDC offer price to infer the amount of cash or the number of shares offered. Second, we use Lexis-Nexis to find missing completion and withdrawal dates. Third, when either the target or the acquirer (in the case of a stock deal) underwent a stock split, we adjusted the offer accordingly. We use the CRSP event database to identify stock splits.

3.2. Sample selection

Our final sample consists of 1901 merger offers. The second three columns of Table 1 show the 1335 pure cash offers and 566 pure stock offers used in the analysis. Of the total sample of 4135 mergers and acquisitions, 1485 deals combined stock and cash or had insufficient information. The remaining sample is reduced from 2650 to 1901 for several reasons. In 681 cases, there was insufficient CRSP data. In some of these cases, the target firm was delisted prior to the announcement date, typically because of bankruptcy. Frequently, there was insufficient data on the acquiring firm in a stock deal. And, in some cases, the SDC target name or acquirer name in the case of stock deals did not match the CRSP company name. In 36 cases, we performed additional research using Lexis-Nexis that lead to the exclusion of the deal, because the announcement was not a merger or acquisition offer. Finally, in 32 cases, the SDC consideration was more than double the CRSP postannouncement value of the target, suggesting a mismatched company or an SDC error. We exclude these deals. Including these deals increases the average monthly return to the value-weighted risk arbitrage portfolio by 0.1% per month, from 1.5% to 1.6%.

Figure 1 and Table 1 show our sample of pure cash and pure stock deals. There are two identifiable periods of relatively higher merger activity in the late 1980s and the middle 1990s. Also apparent is the increasing prevalence of stock deals. Before 1990, 19% of the deals were stock deals. After 1990, over 44% were stock deals.

The 1901 offers in our final sample were for 1556 target firms. The remaining 345 offers represent competing bids. As a result, we perform the analysis in two ways. In the first, we treat all offers identically, whether or not there is another outstanding. As a result, the risk arbitrage portfolio contains multiple bets on completion for a particular firm when there are multiple offers. In the second, we discard follow-on offers, where a follow-on offer is defined using the full sample of 4135 deals recorded by SDC. As a result, this second risk arbitrage portfolio never contains more than one bet on completion for a particular firm.

4. The returns to risk arbitrage

In this section we evaluate the performance of a risk arbitrage portfolio. As a benchmark we use both the CAPM and the Fama-French three-factor model (Fama and French, 1996). The portfolio of 1901 risk arbitrage positions earned abnormal returns of 0.6–0.9% per month over the period from 1981 through 1996. This result is robust for value and equal-weighted returns, though the statistical significance is stronger for equal-weighted returns.

4.1. Calculating portfolio returns

A merger or acquisition is included in the portfolio beginning 2 days after announcement. This is to exclude explicitly the large abnormal returns that are associated with takeover announcements (see, e.g., Jensen and Ruback, 1983). The merger or acquisition is removed from the portfolio when completed or withdrawn.

Each day we calculate the return for all active deals. The arbitrage position for each active deal is designed to provide a fixed-dollar payoff if the deal is a success and an uncertain payoff if the deal fails. For a cash deal, constructing this position is simple. The offer itself is fixed, so an investment in the target firm provides a fixed payoff conditional on completion. The return for a cash deal i on day t is the return on the target firm T from CRSP:

$$r_{it} = r_{Tit}.$$
(4)

Constructing the arbitrage position for stock deals is more complicated. The offer is a fixed amount δ of the acquirer's shares. To provide a fixed payoff conditional success, each share of the target firm must be balanced by a short position in δ of the acquirer's shares. The daily return for stock deals then has three pieces: the return on the target, the return from a short position in acquirer shares, and the risk-free return on the short sale proceeds. Our assumption is that arbitrageurs do not have access to the short sale proceeds. In practice, they often receive less than the risk-free rate and face the additional risk that the lender recalls the short position prior to the completion of the merger. Each target share requires an initial investment equal to the target price P_T. The arbitrageur receives the dollar return on the target stock $r_T P_T$ and pays out the return in excess of the risk-free rate $(r_A - r_f)$ times the acquirer price P_A for δ shares.[7] Dividing the sum of these two amounts by the initial investment gives the return for stock deal i on day t:

$$r_{it} = r_{Tit} - (r_{Ait} - r_{ft})\, \delta \frac{P_{Ait-1}}{P_{Tit-1}}.$$
(5)

It is important to note that both deals require the same up front investment of P_T. In the case of a cash deal, this is straightforward. In the case of a stock deal, an investment is required because arbitrageurs do not have access to the short sale proceeds.

We then average the returns across all active deals to get a daily portfolio return. To check for robustness, we evaluate six portfolios: both value-weighted and equal-weighted combinations of all deals, of cash deals only, and of stock deals only. Compounding the daily average returns across each month gives us 192 monthly portfolio returns beginning in January 1981 and ending with December 1996:[8]

$$R = \prod \left[1 + \sum_{i=active} w_{it} r_{it} \right] - 1.$$
(6)

Table 2 reports the mean, standard deviation and Sharpe ratio for the monthly arbitrage portfolio returns. The first three columns in Panel A show returns where the weight w is

---

[7] The risk-free rate is from Ibbotson Associates (1999).

[8] There are 5 months where there are no deals in the stock portfolio.

Table 2

Monthly portfolio returns, 1981–1996

Provided here are monthly compound arbitrage portfolio returns. Value-weighted (VW) and equal-weighted (EW) portfolio returns for pure cash offers c and pure stock offers s are calculated as follows:

$$r_{cit} = r_{Tit}, \quad r_{sit} = r_{Tit} - (r_{Ait} - r_f)\delta \frac{P_{Ait-1}}{P_{Tit-1}}, \quad \text{and} \quad R = \prod \left[1 + \sum_{i=active} w_{it} r_{it} \right] - 1.$$

Active deals i and the number of acquirer shares offered δ are from SDC. The daily acquirer firm returns r_A, acquirer firm stock prices P_A, target firm returns r_T, and target firm stock prices P_T are from CRSP. The daily Treasury bill return r_f is calculated from Ibbotson Associates (1999). Panel A shows arbitrage portfolio returns. Panel B shows market returns for comparison. In the first three columns, daily returns are weighted by the target firm market value from CRSP and compounded to monthly returns. In the second three columns, the daily returns are weighted equally across deals. Each set of three columns shows the mean, standard deviation, and Sharpe ratio for the monthly portfolio returns.

	Value-weighted			Equal-weighted		
Portfolio	Mean (%)	S.D. (%)	Sharpe ratio	Mean (%)	S.D. (%)	Sharpe ratio
Panel A: Arbitrage portfolios, all offers						
All deals	1.54	4.25	0.23	1.55	2.54	0.39
Cash deals	1.62	4.84	0.22	1.48	3.13	0.29
Stock deals	1.67	4.42	0.25	1.97	4.81	0.29
Panel B: Arbitrage portfolios, first offers						
All deals	1.63	3.49	0.30	1.51	2.72	0.35
Cash deals	1.76	4.32	0.28	1.40	3.30	0.25
Stock deals	1.40	4.62	0.18	1.95	5.03	0.27
Panel C: Market returns						
Market	1.21	4.16	0.15	1.41	5.08	0.17
T-bills	0.57	0.24		0.57	0.24	

the CRSP target firm market value scaled by the total target firm market value for all deals in the portfolio. The mean value-weighted return is 1.5% per month. The second three columns in Panel A show returns where the weight w is the inverse of the number of deals in the portfolio. The mean equal-weighted return is 1.6% per month. Panel B shows the returns for only first offers. This eliminates the possibility that the arbitrage portfolio contains more than one position in a single target company. Also, a follow-on offer has a different risk profile for an arbitrageur. If one deal fails, the other still can succeed, limiting downside risk. However, the returns are broadly similar, with some higher and some lower than the full sample returns. Panel C shows that the average monthly market return is 1.2% on the CRSP value-weighted market portfolio and 1.4% on the CRSP equal-weighted market portfolio. In a simple comparison, the merger arbitrage portfolio beats these market returns. In Panels A and B, we also report returns on portfolios of pure cash and pure stock deals. The merger arbitrage portfolios beat the market in all cases but one.

We also compare Sharpe ratios, the excess return over Treasury bills per unit of standard deviation. The Sharpe ratio for the value-weighted arbitrage portfolio is 0.23 (annualized 0.80), or the mean return of 1.5% less the return on Treasury bills of 0.6% divided by the standard deviation of 4.3%. The Sharpe ratio for the equal-weighted arbitrage portfolio is 0.39 (annualized 1.35). Both exceed their market benchmarks of 0.15 (annualized 0.52) and 0.17 (annualized 0.59).

None of the analysis thus far has considered systematic risk. If the arbitrage portfolios had more systematic risk than the market as a whole, the high returns would not be surprising. However, even before benchmarking the returns, we would expect merger arbitrage to have *less* not more systematic risk than the market: The 1901 merger offers failed less than 22.7% of the time. When we take into account competing offers, the target firm remained independent a year later for only 16.3% of the offers. So, with rational expectations, about 83.7% of the portfolio had only the risk associated with possibility of revisions and competing offers.

4.2. Benchmarking portfolio returns

Abnormal returns must be defined relative to some benchmark model. In Table 3, we test the portfolio returns against the CAPM by regressing the monthly excess arbitrage portfolio return against the excess market return. We also use the Fama-French three-factor model, adding the size (*SMB*) and book-to-market (*HML*) factors to the regression. In each case, we check whether the intercept is positive and statistically significant.

Panel A of Table 3 shows results for the full sample, and Panel B shows results for first offers only. When all deals are included in the portfolio, the point estimate is 0.8% per month for both value-weighted returns and equal-weighted returns. When only first offers are included, the value-weighted results are slightly higher at 0.9%. The Fama-French factors explain some of this abnormal return. The loadings on the size and value factors are positive and reduce the intercept by 0.1%, to 0.6% for the full sample, and 0.7% for first offers. The intercepts are all statistically significant at the 10% level, with one exception. The value-weighted Fama-French three-factor intercept has a p-value of 0.11. The equal-weighted results are all significant at least at the 2% level.

We do not separate out the returns for cash and stock deals in Table 3. The portfolio of only stock deals has no deals at all for 5 months between 1981 and 1996, and in the first half of the sample often contains fewer than five deals. When we do separate out the two sets of returns, we do not find a statistically significant difference between the intercept for all deals and the intercept for cash deals alone.

To put these returns in perspective, we compare our results to another pricing anomaly. Ritter (1991) and Loughran and Ritter (1995) focus on the abnormal returns

Table 3

Market model and Fama-French three-factor portfolio regressions, 1981–1996

This table provides OLS regressions of the monthly excess arbitrage portfolio returns on the monthly excess market return and the Fama-French size and book-to-market factors, where

$$R_t - R_f = a + b(R_{Mt} - R_f) + sSMB_t + hHML_t + \varepsilon_t.$$

In the first two rows of each panel, the daily returns are weighted by the target firm market value from CRSP and compounded to monthly returns. In the second two rows of each panel, the daily returns are weighted equally across deals. Panel B limits the sample to first offers for a target firm. Fama and French provided the monthly risk-free rate, the excess market return, SMB, and HML. Heteroskedasticity robust p-values are shown in parentheses.

			Intercept		$R_{Mt} - R_f$		SMB		HML	
	N	R^2	a	p-value	b	p-value	s	p-value	h	p-value
Panel A: All offers										
Value-weighted										
Market model	192	0.09	0.78	(0.02)	0.30	(0.03)				
Fama-French three-factor	192	0.12	0.59	(0.11)	0.37	(0.01)	0.26	(0.05)	0.32	(0.01)
Equal-weighted										
Market model	192	0.13	0.84	(0.00)	0.22	(0.00)				
Fama-French three-factor	192	0.18	0.74	(0.00)	0.25	(0.00)	0.22	(0.01)	0.18	(0.03)
Panel B: First offers										
Value-weighted										
Market model	192	0.15	0.86	(0.00)	0.32	(0.04)				
Fama-French three-factor	192	0.20	0.72	(0.02)	0.37	(0.02)	0.31	(0.04)	0.25	(0.07)
Equal-weighted										
Market model	192	0.12	0.80	(0.00)	0.22	(0.00)				
Fama-French three-factor	192	0.16	0.73	(0.00)	0.24	(0.00)	0.23	(0.01)	0.15	(0.11)

of firms issuing new equity, either through initial public offerings (IPOs) or seasoned equity offerings (SEOs). Brav and Gompers (1997) employ an identical portfolio approach to IPO firms over a similar time period, beginning in 1972 and ending in 1992. The IPO portfolio underperforms its benchmarks by approximately 0.5% per month. The abnormal returns in merger arbitrage are at least as large.

Direct transaction costs reduce these abnormal returns. However, the impact is small for this time period. When we follow Mitchell and Pulvino (2001) and include a transaction cost of $0.05 per share for the period between 1981 and 1990 and $0.04 for the period after 1990, the intercepts fall by less than 0.1%.

4.3. Revisions and portfolio returns

We try to gauge the economic importance of revisions in two ways. First, we tabulate revisions from SDC. SDC mentions revisions in the description of the consideration.

The descriptions offer more detail in recent years. So, we focus on the last 5 years of our sample. Of the 624 deals recorded by SDC between 1992 and 1996 that end up in our final sample, only 82%, or 13%, are listed as revised or amended one or more times. Of the total number of revisions, 16 are downward revisions. Second, we recalculate the monthly portfolio returns. This recalculation restricts the price of the target below the original consideration to either a fixed-dollar ceiling or, in the case of stock deals, a ceiling in terms of the acquirer's stock price. Put another way, we replace the price of the target with the consideration, whenever the price of the target is higher. Of course, using this price series reduces the raw and abnormal returns. The raw return for the full sample is 1.0% per month for value-weighted returns, and 1.1% per month for equal-weighted returns.

Our aim in analyzing revisions is to gauge the accuracy of the stylized model of limited arbitrage, which has only two outcomes, success and failure. Real-world arbitrageurs face a number of other risks, including the possibility that the deal will be revised or a competing offer will emerge. While we do not precisely quantify the relative importance of these additional risks, these two analyses provide some guidance. 2.6% of the deals are revised downward, 10.6% are revised upward, and the remaining 86.8% fit the model in an ex post sense. Downward revisions represent risk. However, a downward revision, even a substantial outcome, is a better outcome for an arbitrageur than outright withdrawal. The second analysis shows that upward revisions and competing offers explain about a third of the abnormal return. Capping the target stock price reduces the abnormal return by 0.5% per month for value-weighted returns. To sum up, revisions are not a trivial risk, but the majority of merger and acquisitions are not revised. So, the primary concern for risk arbitrageurs is typically whether or not the deal will be completed according to its original terms or withdrawn.

5. The cross section of merger arbitrage returns: testing for limited arbitrage

In this section, we use event returns to test the cross-section predictions of limited arbitrage. First, we describe a measure of systematic risk for cash and stock deals that is a function of the ex ante probability of success. Second, we describe the calculation of event returns. And third, we describe the empirical proxies and the cross-section results.

5.1. Benchmarking event returns

An event return r has three components: the probability of success π, the return conditional on success r_s, and the return conditional on withdrawal r_w. This model of returns,

$$r = \pi r_s + (1 - \pi)r_w, \tag{7}$$

which matches our stylized model of limited arbitrage, does not directly take into account the possibility of renegotiated terms, competing bids, and delays. In this simplified decomposition, outcomes other than the completion of the original deal are implicitly lumped into the return conditional on withdrawal r_w. In other words, withdrawal can be a favorable outcome. Conditional on success, there is no risk, systematic or otherwise. In the case of a cash deal, r_s is known in advance. In a stock deal, when the acquirer offers δ shares for each target share, the arbitrage position is long a single target share and short δ of the acquirer. If the deal goes through, the two positions exactly cancel, and again r_s is risk free.

The chance of failure gives rise to risk. When a cash deal fails, the arbitrageur is left with a share of target stock, which has uncertain value. For the average target, this component has market risk. When a stock deal fails, the arbitrageur has an unhedged position long the target and short the acquirer. For the average deal, this is approximately market neutral.

As a benchmark for event returns, we use a probability weighted average of the required return conditional on success and the required return conditional on failure.[9] For stock deals, the benchmark is simply the risk-free rate r_f. If the deal succeeds, the arbitrageur receives a fixed profit, if the deal fails, the position is market neutral. For cash deals, the chance of failure leads to systematic risk:

$$r_f + (1 - \pi)(r_M - r_f). \tag{8}$$

This benchmark requires a risk-free return r_f and a market return r_M, each over the event window, and a measure of the ex ante probability of success π. The event window begins 2 days after the announcement of the merger and ends with completion or withdrawal. We use the risk-free rate from Ibbotson Associates (1999), and the value-weighted market return from CRSP.

To estimate π, we use predictions from an in sample regression of the merger outcome on the acquirer attitude. Whether the acquirer attitude is classified as hostile by SDC is the best single predictor of merger success in our sample of mergers. Target and acquirer firm size also have some explanatory power in a probit regression of merger outcome on deal characteristics. However, the impact is smaller than the attitude indicator variable. Walkling (1985) concludes that managerial resistance is a "decisive deterrent to offer success." This is also consistent with Schwert (2000), who finds that moving from a hostility index of 0 to 1 reduces the success rate by 45%. The probit regression predictions of merger outcome on acquirer attitude are simply the sample averages. Only 38% of the 201 hostile deals succeed. Some of these target firms are ultimately taken over by other acquirers within 1 year of the hostile offer, raising the probability that a hostile offer leads to an eventual acquisition up to 65%.

---

[9] The formula is more complicated if the probability of failure itself has systematic risk. But, we find that the number of failed deals in each month both as a fraction of active deals and completed deals does not have a statistically significant correlation with contemporaneous and lagged market returns. In other words, deals typically fail for idiosyncratic reasons, such as regulatory hurdles and takeover defenses.

Of the remaining nonhostile deals, 82% succeed and 86% are ultimately acquired in the broader definition of success. The merger outcome regressions are described in the Appendix.

5.2. Event returns

We calculate event returns from a buy and hold strategy in each deal. A cash deal event return,

$$r_c = \prod_{t=2}^{T}(1 + r_{Tt}) - 1,$$

(9)

is the return on a single target share from 2 days after announcement through completion or withdrawal $T - 2$ days later.

An example illustrates the excess return calculation for cash deals. On September 9, 1993, Viacom Inc. made a friendly cash bid for Paramount Communications. The deal closed successfully on July 7, 1994. During the period 2 days after announcement until completion, Paramount shares had a return of 23.4%. The Treasury bill and market returns were 2.6% and −1.6%, respectively. The benchmark return of 1.9% is the sum of the risk-free return and an ex ante probability of failure of 0.16 times the excess return of the market. The excess event return is 21.5% (23.4% minus 1.9%).

As before, the event return for a stock deal has three pieces: the return on a single target share, the return from a short position in δ acquirer shares, and the risk-free return on the short sale proceeds. The buy and hold return, computed from the announcement date to completion or withdrawal $T - 2$ days later on this portfolio, is

$$r_s = \prod_{t=2}^{T}\left[1 + r_{Tt} - (r_{At} - r_f)\,\delta\frac{P_{At-1}}{P_{Tt-1}}\right] - 1.$$

(10)

Another example illustrates the excess return calculation for stock deals. On July 19, 1995, Banc One Corporation made a friendly bid for Premier Corporation by offering 0.6 shares of its own for each Premier share. The deal closed successfully on January 2, 1996. During the time period beginning 2 trading days after announcement and ending approximately 6 months later, an arbitrage position long one Premier share and short 0.6 Banc One shares returned 8.7%. Returns for Treasury bills and the market were 2.5% and 12.7%, respectively. The excess return is 6.2% (8.7% minus the Treasury bill return of 2.5%) since the arbitrage position is market neutral.

5.3. Determinants of the cross section of returns

If arbitrageurs are the marginal investors and the assumptions of our stylized model of limited arbitrage hold, their risk aversion leads to a discount on the target of $(X/A)\gamma$ $\pi(1 - \pi)p^2$. By contrast, in a transaction cost theory, the discount compensates arbitrageurs for their transaction costs c. We use the cross section of returns in an attempt to identify the characteristics of the marginal investor. In particular, we consider three predictions of limited arbitrage. The first prediction is that returns are increasing in idiosyncratic risk. Idiosyncratic risk increases as the ex ante probability of successful completion falls toward 0.5 and $\pi(1 - \pi)$ rises. It also increases with the takeover premium p. The empirical test of this prediction does not distinguish between the limited arbitrage and transaction cost theories, but positive coefficients are consistent with the limited arbitrage explanation. The second prediction is that returns are increasing in the number of shares sold X after announcement. Unlike limited arbitrage, transaction costs predict that mergers involving larger target firms have lower required returns. Finally, we consider the prediction that arbitrage capital A reduces returns.

To measure the probability of success π, we take the same approach as in the benchmarking section, using fitted values from the regression of merger outcome on acquirer attitude described in the Appendix.

To measure the takeover premium p, we subtract the target share price 20 days prior to the takeover announcement from the offer price. We also rerun the regressions subtracting the target price 30 and 60 days prior to the announcement of the merger. The coefficient on the takeover premium is unaffected. We censor this premium at zero and scale it by the target share price 2 days after announcement, which is the required investment in a risk arbitrage position. This is meant to capture the difference between the return if the takeover offer is withdrawn (the price following withdrawal divided by the postannouncement price) and the return if the takeover offer succeeds according to the original terms (the offer price divided by the postannouncement price). All that is required is that a larger takeover premium increases proportionally with the difference between success and expected failure payoffs. It is not necessary that the target fall all the way back to its preoffer share price.

To measure the number of shares sold X after the announcement of a merger, we use target firm size. Ideally, we would like to measure the total dollar value of seller-initiated trades. Unfortunately, this information is not available. So, we use target firm size as a proxy. If the propensity to sell shares following a merger announcement is independent of firm size, then firm size will increase the dollar value of seller-initiated volume. We measure firm size as the log of target market value, the number of shares outstanding times price 2 days after announcement, converted into 1996 dollars using the consumer price index from Ibbotson Associates (1999).

To measure arbitrage capital, our approach is to identify arbitrageurs using 13F filings of institutional ownership recorded by Spectrum.[10] These data are available

---

[10] Larcker and Lys (1987) use an alternative definition of arbitrageurs. They collect data on 13D filings where the stated purpose was described as "arbitrage or other business activities" or "to participate in a potential merger or tender offer." A large majority of these filings either preceded or followed an initial announcement of a corporate reorganization. Our approach can be distinguished in two ways. First, we identify a broader range of arbitrageurs and investors providing liquidity to target shareholders. A 13D filing is required only when an investor exceeds an ownership limit of 5% of the outstanding shares. Second, we are able to use the same data source on institutional ownership to produce a time series of capital available for arbitrage.

back to 1981, covering our full sample period. For each merger where data are available, we measure institutional ownership for the target company for the quarter end immediately before and immediately after announcement. These data are summarized in Table 4. The institutions are divided into five categories: banks, insurance companies, investment companies including mutual funds, independent investment advisors, and all others. The first panel shows ownership as a percentage of shares outstanding, and the second panel shows ownership as a percentage of total institutional shares. Institutional ownership falls following the announcement of a merger or acquisition. However, some of the reduction in Table 4 can occur prior to announcement if, for example, the acquirer accumulates shares to gain a toehold. The fall in ownership is most pronounced for banks, insurance companies, and investment companies. The share of institutional ownership for independent investment advisors rises by about 5%. This group includes some known arbitrageurs, such as Farallon Capital Management (Howard and Perold, 1998) and Long-Term Capital Management (Perold, 1999).

Table 4

Institutional ownership

This table shows institutional ownership before and after a takeover announcement. The first column shows ownership for the quarter ending prior to announcement, the second column shows ownership for the quarter ending after announcement, and the third column reports the difference between the first two. Panel A shows ownership as a fraction of shares outstanding for five types of asset managers. Panel B shows ownership as a fraction of total institutional ownership.

Group	Quarter before announcement	Quarter after announcement	Change as a percent of initial holdings
Panel A: Percent of shares outstanding			
Banks	5.52	4.25	−23.01
Insurance companies	2.07	1.52	−26.57
Investment companies	3.04	2.29	−24.67
Independent investment advisors	13.15	11.07	−15.82
All others	1.74	1.40	−19.54
All institutions	25.52	20.53	−19.55
Panel B: Percent of institutional ownership			
Banks	25.28	24.14	−4.50
Insurance companies	6.82	6.15	−9.83
Investment companies	9.90	8.81	−11.02
Independent investment advisors	52.99	55.88	5.46
All others	5.01	5.01	0.14
All institutions	100.00	100.00	0.00

We define an institution as an arbitrageur if its holdings go from zero to positive in at least 20 mergers in the 1981 through 1996 sample period.[11] The screen picks up known arbitrageurs and other institutions that are evidently willing to provide some form of deal completion insurance. We aggregate the nonmerger-related equity holdings of this set of institutions for each quarter from 1981 through 1996 and label this arbitrage capital. Spectrum does not provide information on nonequity sources of capital. As a result, the measure is a noisy proxy for arbitrage capital.

We scale each independent variable by its standard deviation. As a result, each coefficient is comparable in the sense that it measures the change in average return per standard deviation move in the independent variable.

5.4. Regression results

We present the regression results in Table 5. Because the deal lengths vary, we focus on the first 30-day excess return.[12] The first column of Table 5 shows the predicted sign for the limited arbitrage variables. Our theoretical predictions pertain to expected returns. The realized 1-month excess return is equal to the expected return plus an error. This noise lowers the model fit and increases the standard errors of our estimates. Also, returns are overlapping in time and thus are not independent. To address this problem, we cluster the residuals by announcement month. Rogers (1993) describes the estimation of robust standard errors that relaxes the assumption of independence across groups.

In the first column, the takeover premium p/P and the transformed probability of success $\pi(1 - \pi)$ enter with the expected positive sign. The probability term and the takeover premium term are significant at the 5% level. Importantly, the standard errors are corrected for heteroskedasticity. The uncorrected errors are sometimes less than half as large. The coefficients suggest that a one standard deviation change in the transformed probability of success leads to a 1.1% increase in average returns and a

---

[11] The top 10 independent investment advisors by our measure are: Schroder & Co. (349 deals), Beacon Capital Management (312), Furman Selz (227), Fleming Capital (169), Sheer Asset Management (168), Soros Fund Management (163), Morgan Stanley Dean Witter (152), Arnhold & A Bleichroeder (148), Kellner Dileo (144), and Farallon Capital Management (143). Of the 1901 deals, we have Spectrum data for 1874.

[12] We use a relatively short horizon for the cross-sectional analysis for two reasons. First, many deals take considerably longer to be completed. The median time to completion or withdrawal for our sample is 120 days. Yet, some deals are withdrawn in less than 30 days. Ideally, we would like our dependent variable to be measured over the same horizon for all deals. Only 6% of the sample offers are completed or withdrawn within 30 days. Meanwhile, over 20% of the sample offers are completed or withdrawn within 60 days. Second, benchmarking returns over a longer horizon is challenging (Barber and Lyon, 1997; Lyon et al., 1999). We also rerun the cross-section results for 2-month returns. The coefficients and statistical significance of the probability of success term, firm size, and arbitrage capital rise in the 2-month regressions. The coefficient on the takeover premium falls slightly. A table is available from the authors upon request.

Table 5

Estimating the model of returns

This tables shows OLS regressions of 1-month excess event returns on measures of idiosyncratic risk, target firm size, and arbitrage capital. Idiosyncratic risk is a function of the probability of success π and the takeover premium p. As an estimate of π, we use fitted values from a regression of merger outcome on acquirer attitude. The takeover premium, p, is equal to the offer price minus the price 20 days before the takeover announcement date. P is the target price 2 days after. All prices are from CRSP. Log market equity is the log target equity measured in 1996 dollars. Arbitrage capital is described in the text. All independent variables are standardized to have zero mean and unit variance. The residuals are clustered by month. Heteroskedasticity robust p-values are shown in parentheses.

	Prediction	All offers				First offers			
		(1)	(2)	(3)	(4)	(1)	(2)	(3)	(4)
Probability of	+	1.13	0.96	0.96	0.85	1.13	0.98	0.97	0.83
success $\pi(1 - \pi)$		(0.00)	(0.01)	(0.01)	(0.02)	(0.01)	(0.02)	(0.02)	(0.05)
Takeover premium	+	1.64	1.72	1.77	1.81	1.72	1.79	1.84	1.90
$[p/P]$		(0.00)	(0.00)	(0.00)	(0.00)	(0.00)	(0.00)	(0.00)	(0.00)
Log market equity	+		0.77	0.79	0.82		0.67	0.70	0.75
($1996)			(0.00)	(0.00)	(0.00)		(0.01)	(0.01)	(0.01)
Past arbitrage	−			−0.48				−0.61	
return (%)				(0.19)				(0.15)	
Change in	−				−0.52				−0.45
capital (%)					(0.08)				(0.20)
Stock deal	?	−0.64	−0.77	−0.88	−0.77	−0.75	−0.92	−1.05	−0.95
		(0.21)	(0.13)	(0.08)	(0.12)	(0.16)	(0.09)	(0.05)	(0.07)
R^2		0.04	0.05	0.06	0.06	0.05	0.05	0.06	0.06
N		1901	1901	1889	1874	1556	1556	1544	1534

one standard deviation change in the takeover premium leads to a 1.6% increase in average returns. We conclude that excess returns are increasing in completion risk.

In all the regressions, we include an indicator variable for stock deals. The coefficient is negative and sometimes significant at the 10% level. This provides some evidence against transaction costs as the primary determinant of returns. On the one hand, stock deals are taxed differently from cash deals. In a stock transaction, target shareholders need not realize a capital gain and can have less incentive to sell following the announcement of a merger or acquisition, leading to lower arbitrage returns. On the other hand, transaction costs predict higher returns for stock deals because entering into a risk arbitrage position for a stock deal requires two transactions instead of one. The arbitrageur incurs direct costs for both the long and short positions and often does not receive full interest on the short sale proceeds.

In next column, we add a proxy for seller-initiated volume. Firm size has two possible effects. First, holding risk and arbitrage capital constant, a larger firm and a larger dollar amount sold leads to higher returns. However, arbitrageurs also focus on larger companies where more information is available and transaction costs are lower.

This could reduce returns. The first column shows that target firm size enters with a positive coefficient, and is significant at the 1% level. A one standard deviation change in firm size leads to a 0.8% increase in average returns. This result suggests that limited arbitrage effects dominate transaction costs.

Another test of the limited arbitrage model is to examine the influence of arbitrage capital on returns. Froot and O'Connell (1999) find evidence of capital constraints in catastrophe reinsurance. Following a catastrophe that depletes the capital of reinsurers, prices for insurance rise. More interestingly, the effect works across markets. For example, a hurricane increases the price of earthquake insurance. This supports limited capital, rather than a higher probability of a subsequent earthquake, as the cause of higher insurance prices. In this spirit, we would like to measure changes in capital available for risk arbitrage across time.

In the third column, we add the arbitrage portfolio return in the two calendar quarters prior to the merger announcement to the basic model. This first measure of capital enters negatively and has a *p*-value of 0.19. A one standard deviation reduction in past returns leads to an increase in average 1-month returns of 0.5%. The second column shows the change in arbitrage capital based on the Spectrum data. Again, the coefficient is negative and is now significant at the 10% level. A one standard deviation reduction in this measure of capital also leads to an increase in average 1-month returns of 0.5%.

We also run but do not report regressions using past returns on distressed securities hedge funds from the MAR Hedge Fund database. The same money managers often focus on both risk arbitrage and distressed securities. Although there is no obvious direct economic link between the returns on target firms and the returns on bankrupt firms, there can be an indirect connection through limited arbitrage. Unfortunately, these data are only available from 1990. As a result, we lose a little over half of the sample. The coefficient on the distressed securities return is negative, but it has a *p*-value greater than 0.3.

The second set of four columns in Table 5 repeat the analysis using only first offers. The results are broadly similar, though the measure of arbitrage capital derived from institutional holdings is no longer statistically significant.

To sum up, we find evidence in favor of a model of limited arbitrage as an explanation for the abnormal returns to risk arbitrage. Excess returns are increasing in target firm size, two measures of idiosyncratic risk, the takeover premium and the transformed probability of success, and decreasing in a measure of arbitrage capital.

6. Conclusions

Past research suggests that merger arbitrage produces very high returns. This paper addresses *why* these returns are not arbitraged away. Unlike in previous empirical studies of limited arbitrage (e.g., Pontiff, 1996), we focus on the merger and acquisition market, a large and economically important component of the stock market. And, unlike earlier studies of merger arbitrage, we develop a model and test the cross-section implications of a limited number of arbitrageurs. We find evidence that supports a model where undiversified investors sell to avoid completion risk. Arbitrageurs, limited in capital and number, require a premium for bearing this risk. Consistent with limited arbitrage, a cross-section analysis reveals that idiosyncratic risk and firm size are determinants of expected returns. Our results on arbitrage capital are also consistent with limited arbitrage. A proxy for changes in arbitrage capital is negatively related to future risk arbitrage returns. When capital falls, subsequent returns rise.

This paper also provides quantitative evidence about the limits of arbitrage. The average risk-adjusted return on a risk arbitrage portfolio is about 0.6–0.9% per month. This portfolio beat the market outright by 0.3% per month. If fairly precise information on merger terms is not fully absorbed in prices, arbitrage may fail to guarantee market efficiency elsewhere. Put in terms of Scholes (1972), the target firm has an almost perfect substitute in merger arbitrage, that is, perfect conditional on the completion of the original offer and a completion rate of over 83%. When stocks do not have good substitutes, mispricing could be more severe.

Appendix: Predicting merger success

Table 6 shows the determinants of merger outcome. The dependent variable is defined in two ways. In the first two columns, success is equal to one if the merger offer succeeds. In the second two columns, success is equal to one if the merger offer succeeds or the firm is taken over by any acquirer within 1 year of the offer. In the first column, the only independent variable is a categorical variable equal to one if the deal is classified as hostile by SDC. This measure of acquirer attitude explains 8% of the variation in outcomes and is significant at the 1% level.

The second column adds other deal characteristics. First, target and acquirer firm size are the log of target and acquirer equity market value after the announcement of the merger, converted to 1996 dollars using the consumer price index from Ibbotson Associates (1999). Larger firms may have an easier time acquiring smaller firms. Second, we include a categorical variable equal to one if the target and acquirer are in the same two-digit SIC code. Horizontal mergers may face regulatory hurdles. Third, the takeover premium is the difference between the target share price 20 days prior to the takeover announcement and the offer price scaled by the target share price 2 days after announcement. A higher premium may increase the odds of target shareholder approval. Fourth, stock is equal to one if the consideration is in acquirer shares. The means of payment may also influence the attractiveness of the deal. For example, Travlos (1987), Huang and Walkling (1987), and Eckbo and Langhor (1989) find the means of payment affect bidder and target announcement returns.[13] Target and

---

[13] Managerial ownership is another influence on takeover completion. For example, Mikkelson and Partch (1989) and Song and Walkling (1993) find that managerial ownership influences the probability of completion. Unfortunately, we do not have ownership data for our sample of target firms.

Table 6

Predicting merger outcome

This table shows probit regressions of merger outcome on acquirer attitude and other deal characteristics. Offer completed is equal to one if the particular merger or acquisition offer is completed successfully. Target acquired is equal to one if any merger or acquisition offer for the target is completed successfully. Hostile is equal to one if SDC characterizes the deal as such. The other deal characteristics are the log target equity measured in 1996 dollars, the log acquirer equity measured in 1996 dollars, whether the target and acquirer are in the same industry, and the takeover premium. The takeover premium is equal to the offer price minus the price 20 days before the takeover announcement date scaled by the target price 2 days after. All prices are from CRSP. Stock deal is equal to one if the consideration is in acquirer stock. Heteroskedasticity robust p-values are shown in parentheses.

	Offer completed (success = 1)		Target acquired (success = 1)	
	(1)	(2)	(3)	(4)
Acquirer attitude				
Hostile	−0.44 (0.00)	−0.38 (0.00)	−0.21 (0.00)	−0.20 (0.00)
Other deal characteristics				
Target log market equity ($1996)		−0.04 (0.00)		−0.02 (0.17)
Acquirer log market equity ($1996)		0.10 (0.00)		0.08 (0.00)
Target and acquirer in same industry		−0.01 (0.60)		−0.02 (0.35)
Takeover premium [p/P]		0.00 (0.80)		0.01 (0.47)
Stock deal		0.03 (0.12)		0.00 (0.97)
R^2	0.08	0.11	0.03	0.07
N	1901	1670	1901	1670

acquirer firm size are statistically significant, but the four variables together increase the R^2 by less than 3%.

The second set of two columns uses a broader measure of success. The results are similar, though the explanatory power falls and only the acquirer attitude and acquirer size are statistically significant. Because acquirer firm size is not universally available, we use fitted values from the regression in the third column to measure the ex ante probability of a successful outcome in the main analyses.

References

Barber, B. and J. Lyon, 1997, "Detecting Long-Run Abnormal Stock Returns: The Empirical Power and Specification of Test Statistics," *Journal of Financial Economics*, 43, 341–372.

Boesky, I., 1985, *Merger Mania*, Holt, Rinehart, and Winston, New York.

Brav, A. and P. A. Gompers, 1997, "Myth or Reality? The Long-Run Underperformance of Initial Public Offerings: Evidence from Venture and Nonventure Capital-Backed Companies," *Journal of Finance*, 52, 1791–1821.

Cornelli, F. and D. Li, 2002, "Risk Arbitrage in Takeovers," *Review of Financial Studies*, 15, 837–868.

D'Avolio, G., 2001, "The Market for Borrowing Stock," Unpublished Working Paper, Harvard University.

De Long, J. B., A. Shleifer, L. H. Summers and R. J. Waldmann, 1990, "Noise Trader Risk in Financial Markets," *Journal of Political Economy*, 98, 703–738.

Dukes, W. P., C. J. Frohlich and C. K. Ma, 1992, "Risk Arbitrage in Tender Offers," *Journal of Portfolio Management*, 18, 47–55.

Eckbo, E. B. and H. Langhor, 1989, "Information Disclosure, Method of Payment, and Takeover Premiums: Public and Private Tender Offers in France," *Journal of Financial Economics*, 24, 363–403.

Fama, E. F., 1965, "The Behavior of Stock Market Prices," *Journal of Business*, 38, 35–105.

Fama, E. F. and K. French, 1996, "Multifactor Explanations of Asset Pricing Anomalies," *Journal of Finance*, 51, 55–84.

Friedman, M., 1953, "The Case for Flexible Exchange Rates," In: M. Friedman (Ed.), *Essays in Positive Economics*, Chicago University Press, Chicago, pp. 157–203.

Froot, K. and E. Dabora, 1999, "How are Stock Prices Affected by the Location of Trade?" *Journal of Financial Economics*, 53, 189–216.

Froot, K. and P. O'Connell, 1999, "The Pricing of U.S. Catastrophe Reinsurance," In: K. Froot (Ed.), *The Financing of Catastrophe Insurance*, MIT Press, Cambridge, pp. 195–227.

Froot, K. and J. Stein, 1998, "Risk Management, Capital Budgeting, and Capital Structure Policy for Financial Institutions: An Integrated Approach," *Journal of Financial Economics*, 47, 55–82.

Geczy, C., D. Musto and A. Reed, 2002, "Stocks are Special Too: An Analysis of the Equity Lending Market," *Journal of Financial Economics*, 15, 241–269.

Gomes, A., 2000, "Takeovers, Freezeouts, and Risk Arbitrage," Unpublished Working Paper, University of Pennsylvania.

Green, R. C. and K. Rydqvist, 1997, "The Valuations of Nonsystematic Risks and the Pricing of Swedish Lottery Bonds," *Review of Financial Studies*, 10, 447–480.

Grossman, S. and O. Hart, 1980, "Takeover Bids, the Free Rider Problem, and the Theory of the Corporation," *Bell Journal of Economics and Management Science*, 11, 42–64.

Howard, R. and A. Perold, 1998, "Farallon Capital: Risk Arbitrage," Harvard Business School Case N9-299-020.

Huang, Y. and R. A. Walkling, 1987, "Target Abnormal Returns Associated with Acquisition Announcements: Payment, Acquisition Form, and Managerial Resistance," *Journal of Financial Economics*, 19, 329–349.

Ibbotson Associates, 1999, *Stocks, Bonds, Bills, and Inflation*, Ibbotson Associates, Chicago.

Jensen, M. and R. S. Ruback, 1983, "The Market for Corporate Control: The Scientific Evidence," *Journal of Financial Economics*, 11, 5–50.

Jindra, J. and R. A. Walkling, 2001, "Speculation Spreads and the Market Pricing of Proposed Acquisitions," Unpublished Working Paper, Ohio State University.

Karolyi, A. and J. Shannon, 1999, "Where's the Risk in Risk Arbitrage?" *Canadian Investment Review*, 12, 12–18.

Kyle, A. S. and W. Xiong, 2000, "Contagion as a Wealth Effect," Unpublished Working Paper, Duke University.

Lakonishok, J. and T. Vermaelen, 1990, "Anomalous Price Behavior Around Repurchase Tender Offers," *Journal of Finance*, 45, 455–477.

Lamont, O. and R. Thaler, 2001, "Can the Market Add and Subtract? Mispricing in Tech-Stock Carve-Outs," Unpublished Working Paper, University of Chicago.

Larcker, D. and T. Lys, 1987, "An Empirical Analysis of the Incentives to Engage in Costly Information Acquisition," *Journal of Financial Economics*, 18, 111–126.

Loughran, T. and J. Ritter, 1995, "The New Issues Puzzle," *Journal of Finance*, 50, 23–51.

Lyon, J., B. Barber and C. Tsai, 1999, "Improved Methods for Tests of Long-Run Abnormal Stock Returns," *Journal of Finance*, 54, 165–201.

Merton, R. and A. Perold, 1993, "The Theory of Risk Capital in Financial Firms," *Journal of Applied Corporate Finance*, 5, 16–32.

Mikkelson, W. H. and M. Partch, 1989, "Managers' Voting Rights and Corporate Control," *Journal of Financial Economics*, 25, 263–290.

Mitchell, M. and T. Pulvino, 2001, "Characteristics of Risk in Risk Arbitrage," *Journal of Finance*, 56, 2135–2176.

Perold, A., 1999, "Long-Term Capital Management," L.P. Harvard Business School Case N9-200-007.

Perold, A. and K. Singh, 1995, "The Boston Company: Securities Lending," Harvard Business School Case 9-294-024.

Pontiff, J., 1996, "Costly Arbitrage: Evidence from Closed-End Funds," *The Quarterly Journal of Economics*, 111, 1135–1151.

Ritter, J., 1991, "The Long-Run Performance of Initial Public Offerings," *Journal of Finance*, 42, 365–394.

Rogers, W. H., 1993, "Regression Standard Errors in Clustered Samples," *Stata Technical Bulletin*, 13, 19–23.

Scholes, M., 1972, "The Market for Securities: Substitution Versus Price Pressure and Effects of Information on Share Prices," *Journal of Business*, 45, 179–211.

Schwert, G. W., 2000, Hostility in Takeovers: In the Eye of the Beholder," *Journal of Finance*, 55, 2599–2640.

Shleifer, A., 1986, "Do Demand Curves for Stocks Slope Down?" *Journal of Finance*, 41, 579–590.

Shleifer, A., 2000, *Inefficient Markets*, Oxford University Press, Oxford.

Shleifer, A. and R. W. Vishny, 1997, "The Limits of Arbitrage," *Journal of Finance*, 52, 35–55.

Singh, R., 1998, "Takeover Bidding with Toeholds: The Case of the Owners Curse," *Review of Financial Studies*, 11, 679–704.

Song, M. H. and R. A. Walkling, 1993, "The Impact of Managerial Ownership on Acquisition Attempts and Target Shareholder Wealth," *Journal of Financial and Quantitative Analysis*, 28, 439–457.

Stein, J., 1999, "Comment on the Pricing of U.S. Catastrophe Reinsurance," In: K. Froot (Ed.), *The Financing of Catastrophe Insurance*, MIT Press, Cambridge, pp. 227–231.

Travlos, N. G., 1987, "Corporate Takeover Bids, Methods of Payment, and Bidding Firms' Stock Returns," *Journal of Finance*, 42, 943–963.

Walkling, R. A., 1985, "Predicting Tender Offer Success: A Logistic Analysis," *Journal of Financial and Quantitative Analysis*, 20, 461–478.

Wurgler, J. and K. Zhuravskaya, 2002, "Does Arbitrage Flatten Demand Curves for Stocks?" *Journal of Business*, 75, 583–608.

AUTHOR INDEX

SUBJECT INDEX